THE NEW NEGRO

A History in Documents, 1887–1937

Edited by MARTHA H. PATTERSON and HENRY LOUIS GATES, JR.

Princeton University Press

Princeton and Oxford

Published by Princeton University Press
41 William Street, Princeton, New Jersey 08540
99 Banbury Road, Oxford OX2 6JX

press.princeton.edu

GPSR Authorized Representative: Easy Access System Europe - Mustamäe tee 50, 10621 Tallinn, Estonia, gpsr.requests@easproject.com

Library of Congress Control Number: 2024952161

ISBN 9780691268583
ISBN (pbk.) 9780691268590
ISBN (e-book) 9780691268606

British Library Cataloging-in-Publication Data is available

Editorial: Anne Savarese, James Collier, Emma Wagh
Production Editorial: Elizabeth Byrd
Jacket: Karl Spurzem
Production: Erin Suydam
Publicity: Kate Hensley (US), Carmen Jimenez (UK)
Copyeditor: Brian Bendlin

Jacket/Cover Credit: Freelon, Alan R. *The New Negro*, 1921. Print originally published in the May 1921 issue of *Carolina Magazine*. Published by the Dialectic and Philanthropic Literary Societies of the University of North Carolina. Courtesy of the North Carolina Digital Heritage Center.

This book has been composed in Minion Pro and Roc Grotesk

Printed in the United States of America

10 9 8 7 6 5 4 3 2 1

To Bill, Mark, and Walter,
with love
and
to Jeffrey Conrad Stewart

Contents

IV   RED SUMMERS AND BLACK RADICALISMS, 1917–1921   229

VII   **THE DEPRESSION, THE NEW DEAL, AND ETHIOPIA, 1933–1937   495**

APPENDIX: LOOKING BACKWARD, LOOKING FORWARD, 1938–1950   523

Illustrations

Preface

The Black Floating Signifier: "The New Negro"

"The New Negro" is one of the oldest, longest serving, and most fascinating concepts in the history of African American culture. Expansive and elastic, capable of morphing and absorbing new content as circumstances demand, contested and fraught, it assumes an astonishingly broad array of ideological guises, some diametrically opposed to others. The New Negro functions as a trope of declaration, proclamation, conjuration, and desperation, a figure of speech reflecting deep anguish and despair, a cry of the disheartened for salvation, for renewal, for equal rights.

While most of us first encounter the "New Negro" as the title of the seminal anthology that Alain Locke published in 1925, at the height of the Harlem Renaissance, we find the origin of the term—so closely associated by scholars and students alike with the multihued cacophony of the Jazz Age—actually goes back to 1887, set firmly in the wake of the rollback to Reconstruction, in the first decade of what the historian Rayford W. Logan called "the nadir" in the history of race relations in the United States.[1]

The figure of the New Negro channels despair into audacity, attempting to dream a new social identity into being simply through a rhetorical act. The New Negro is born in the service of the goal widely shared by intellectuals and artists over the span of the fifty years covered in this volume: to regain the rights enjoyed by Black people during Reconstruction and dramatically stripped away after what W. E. B. Du Bois so famously called "a brief moment in the sun."[2] As this anthology attests, the concept was nothing if not capacious. Ultimately, it is perhaps one of the most *American* of African American cultural practices, in the long and grand tradition of American claims of "newness."

Stuart Hall has perceptively noted that the concept of "race" is a "floating signifier" in Western philosophical discourse.[3] It can also be said that the "New Negro" was perhaps *the* key floating signifier throughout the first half century of its myriad repetitions and revisions in African American discourse. Its extraordinary utility is attested to by both its longevity and the exceptionally broad and rich array of the social, political, and aesthetic positions embraced by those who deployed it.

Despite its wide usage over a remarkably long period of time, the New Negro remains one of the least analyzed concepts in the history of the African American artistic tradition. Locke's collection of essays was meant to testify to the existence of a vibrant new cultural movement—a "renaissance"—still unfolding, one marked by sublimely stunning achievements in literature, primarily, but also in art. The anthology was a larger version of a special issue of *Survey Graphic* magazine that Locke had edited in March 1925 under the arresting title "Harlem: Mecca of The

New Negro." But by the time he published the expanded book version, the center of gravity of the artistic *movement* whose existence he celebrated—Harlem, the Black Mecca—had given way in importance to the actors creating the movement, the "New Negroes" themselves. And thus "The New Negro Renaissance" was born, a name that would yield to "The Harlem Renaissance" as early as 1929.[4]

The term had long been widely attributed to Locke himself—a reasonable assumption, since Locke did not cite usages of the term before 1925. But today we know that the figure of the New Negro had been put to a wide variety of uses by the time Locke cleverly employed it as his title and in his text: indeed, it had been in use for at least thirty-eight years prior to Locke's proclamation. We know this thanks to a round of research that I've engaged in for almost four decades now, first in "The Trope of the New Negro," published in *Representations* in 1998; then in the reader I coedited with Gene Andrew Jarrett in 2007, *The New Negro: Readings on Race, Representation, and African American Culture, 1892–1938*; in my 2024 book *The Black Box: Writing the Race*; and now in this expanded publication that resulted from the extraordinarily detailed research of my colleague and coeditor, Martha H. Patterson, who discovered the term's very first usage, in 1887, and so many of the other examples of its employment by Black intellectuals in the fifty-year period covered in this book.

We can safely assume that Locke, a voracious consumer of Black publications in the first quarter of the twentieth century, would have seen the phrase used by his own contemporaries, including William Pickens in *The New Negro* (1916), A. Philip Randolph in the pages of his socialist magazine, the *Messenger*, and—more extensively than anyone else in the history of its usage—Marcus Garvey in the pages of his weekly newspaper, *Negro World*. We cannot say what motivated Locke to title the movement he was heralding with this term without reference to what had come before. What we do know, however, is that, until recently, scholars of the Harlem Renaissance and of Locke's life and works have not looked at the ways in which earlier uses of the phrase informed his own articulation of it, an articulation that we now understand was his extension and redefinition of an already existing tradition, not his invention of something new. Since the phrase had been circulating virtually continuously in so many different guises in Black culture for so very long, Locke's choice to use it to put a name on the movement he was announcing was ingenious, since it would resonate almost unconsciously at so many levels with African Americans.

Jeffrey C. Stewart takes steps toward exploring this in his multiple award–winning biography, *The New Negro: The Life of Alain Locke* (2018), in which he makes the case that Locke used the term as a palimpsest, with its previous manifestations operating like traces: "By appropriating the term, Locke sought to evoke all of these prior references but to add a new one—the idea of the New Negro was a generational awakening in the city, especially in Harlem, where the streams of the uneducated and educated of the race came out of a sense of *opportunity*, not flight from oppression."[5] I look at Locke's borrowing not as additive but rather in the opposite way, as emptying the term of the figure's contents in order to fill it with a bold new meaning: that the race—at least, the "vanguard" of the race, its intellectual and artistic elite, a tiny subsection of Du Bois's "Talented Tenth"—would, counterintuitively, be liberated from its post-Reconstruction trials and tribulations through the creation of great art and literature, an entirely *new* version of the New Negro, surfacing in the middle of the second decade of the Great Migration and at the height of the Jazz Age, just under forty years after it was first coined.

Even Locke's exceptionally daring reiteration of the term would soon succumb to other usages, including Locke's own redefinitions of an even "Newer" Negro. This gets to the point of this anthology: hundreds of writers over the fifty years (1887–1937) covered herein would treat the phrase as an empty vessel, filling it with their own content, like new wine in a very old and well-used bottle, making no reference to any previous vintages at all. Sometimes, such as in the half dozen years leading up to Locke's annexation of the figure, competing uses of "the New Negro" were set in dueling matches in the journalistic organs of ideological opponents, such as Marcus Garvey and A. Philip Randolph, with not even a mention that someone else had defined the New Negro differently, creating a sometimes riotously humorous chain of signifiers over the history of the term's meaning. To put it in another way, if "New Negro" were an entry in *The Oxford English Dictionary*, its etymological history would include at least twelve senses, the number of discrete manifestations that Martha H. Patterson identifies in the introduction to this book, ranging from race consciousness and racial uplift to socialist and Black nationalist revolution.

What are we to make of this fascinating chapter in African American intellectual history? It is important to return to its beginnings. The New Negro was born in the most challenging—and frightening—period since the abolition of slavery, four years after the US Supreme Court had voided the liberal and forward-looking Civil Rights Act of 1875, thereby declaring with ultimate finality the end of Reconstruction. This was a time of great despair in the African American community, especially among the elite, educated, middle and upper middle classes. How to fight back? How to regain the race's footing on the path to full and equal citizenship, in the face of the diabolical campaign launched by the Lost Cause Movement, whose origin can be traced directly to Henry Grady's "New South" speech in 1886, which generated the Black version of the trope of newness just a year later? In an act of desperation and a bit of conjuration, this is how and when the "New Negro" was born, in an attempt to find a way around the mountain of racist stereotypes being drawn upon to justify the deprivation of Black civil rights, the disenfranchisement of Black men, and the formalization of Jim Crow segregation, all leading to the onset of a period of "second-class citizenship" that would last for many decades to come—far longer, I think, than any of the first New Negroes could have imagined.

At its most problematic, the claim of the existence of a Negro who is, somehow, "new" is a claim that inevitably concedes, regardless of the intention of the writer, that at least some of the unfortunately demeaning aspersions being cast on the "nature" of African Americans bore some truth to them. Hence, this unfortunate line of thinking went, the need to proclaim the existence of *another* kind of Negro, one sui generis, who has suddenly, miraculously arisen, phoenix-like, out of the ashes of the remnants of Reconstruction, just as George Henry White predicted in his farewell speech in the House of Representatives in 1901. At its best, however—at its most innovative and imaginative—the trope is a testament to the wide variety of arrows in the African American's quiver, a rhetorical weapon that intellectuals and activists employed in their resolute, tenacious attempt to fashion a trope that would counter, and ideally erase, the horrifically demeaning images that racists had crafted in a relentless effort to restore the hallmarks of slavery, by another name.

—Henry Louis Gates, Jr.

Acknowledgments

I have been working on this project since my 2018–19 McKendree University sabbatical, so my debts of gratitude could well be a manuscript in themselves. I could not have assembled this collection without the help of institutions, scholars, librarians, students, colleagues, curators, and friends worldwide, and especially without the scholarship of Henry Louis Gates, Jr. and Gene Jarrett, whose 2007 *New Negro* reader inspired this collection.

Librarians from around the globe graciously helped me gather material. Renee Jones and other librarians of the Rare Books & Manuscripts collection at the St. Louis Public Library offered database tips and access to the *St. Louis Argus* as well as the fascinating St. Louis magazine *Reedy's Mirror*. Harvard University librarians Emily Bell and Susan Gilroy answered numerous email requests, helping me track down obscure references and camera-ready images. Reference librarians Helen McGettrick and Matt Rutherford from the Newberry Library in Chicago provided crucial biographical information about Black Chicago writers. Research service specialist Caitlyn Rahschulte of Berea College Special Collections and Archives offered key details about Rev. W. E. C. Wright. Evan Washechek, the manager of Information and Reference Services, and Ronda Cornelius at the Kansas City Public Library kindly helped me access the *Kansas City Star*. Jeremy Smith at the University of Massachusetts–Amherst archive of the Robert S. Cox Special Collections and the University Archives Research Center responded quickly and kindly to queries regarding a Du Bois manuscript. Grace Bichler, reproductions coordinator at the Division of Rare and Manuscript Collections at Cornell University, helped me find the yearbook photograph of James Bertram Clarke (aka José Clarana / Jaime Clarana Gil). Diona E. Layden, special collections librarian at the John Hope and Aurelia E. Franklin Library at Fisk University, offered very helpful research assistance on Charles S. Johnson. Laurids Nielsen and Martin Sejer Danielsen of the Danish National Archives at the Royal Danish Library helped me track down photographs of David Hamilton Jackson. Bright Kojo Botwe, the director of Needmet International in Accra, Ghana, sent me numerous photographs of Joseph Ephraim Casely Hayford. Librarians at the Vivian G. Harsh Research Collection of the Carter G. Woodson Regional Library of the Chicago Public Library, the Beinecke Rare Book and Manuscript Library at Yale University, and the Schomburg Center for Research in Black Culture, New York Public Library, offered help with images, permissions, and access to crucial sources.

Museum exhibits around the country also provided inspiration and images. I particularly want to thank the Northwest African American Museum for its exhibit on Horace Cayton Sr. and the *Seattle Republican*, and Jena P. Jones at the Kenan Research Center at the Atlanta History Center for their assistance with photographs from the Cotton States and International Exposition. Diana Edkins of Art Resource helped me secure permissions to reprint a photograph by James Van Der Zee. Steven Kramer, the registrar of the Columbia Museum of Art in South Carolina, gave us permission to publish the powerful photograph we include by Richard Samuel Roberts. Paul R. Spitzzeri, director at the Workman and Temple Family Homestead Museum, offered crucial information about Charles Summer Blodgett and helped me obtain the highest-resolution photograph of him and his crew of painters.

Teaching McKendree's English senior literature seminar, American survey, and African American literature courses enabled me to read this work anew through the eyes of my students. I am grateful for my students' insightful questions, research ideas, and class discussions.

A handful of exceptional students performed many hours of work on the manuscript as copyeditors, researchers, and proofreaders: Elizabeth Bocock, Christian Davidson, Landree Erwin, Alivia Garcia, Sophie Jeffery, Jake Kingsley, Averee McNear, and Tessie Naumovich, your steadfast efforts and attention to detail made this manuscript better. I am especially indebted to Jake for his tireless work researching and drafting footnotes, seeking permissions, compressing image files, transcribing essays, and proofreading.

My colleagues and friends in the Department of English at McKendree—Brenda Boudreau, Nichole DeWall, and Jenny Mueller—offered weekly encouragement, advice, and inspiration. Amid tight budgets, my division chairs Kevin Zanelotti and Nancy Ypma supported my research, and I am very grateful. McKendree librarians Jen Funk and Debbie Houk provided critical resources, and McKendree's Faculty Colloquium series offered me wonderful opportunities to present my arguments about the New Negro's long history.

Scholars at other institutions provided invaluable help with sources. I want to thank especially Brooks Hefner of James Madison University and Gary Edward Holcomb of Ohio University for directing us to one of Claude McKay's fabulous letters they had collected and which we then included. George Hutchinson kindly directed me to an unpublished speech by Charles S. Johnson. Suraj Yengde's expertise in caste helped me better understand an early W. E. B. Du Bois reference to it. Vanessa Hays's research enabled me to find more information about John N. Abbey. Shawn Christian's thoughtful reading of my work on the New Negro before the Renaissance helped me uncover lesser-known writers and consider how their work reshapes our understanding of the New Negro movement. I am very grateful to my new friend Marc Blanc, whose fascinating work on Oscar Micheaux and Sutton Griggs inspired me to include their work in this volume. Emily Lutenski very graciously helped us envision the New Negro's experience in Los Angeles. Thank you, Lenny Cassuto, for connecting me with scholars who enriched my work and for your always sage advice!

Jenny Mueller, with support from Harvard University's Hutchins Center for African & African American Research, summarized articles, edited the manuscript, and developed a style guide to help this project come to fruition. She also provided guidance to my student editors at crucial stages in the process.

Two National Endowment for the Humanities (NEH) Summer Institutes were enormously helpful in providing theoretical frameworks, interdisciplinary connections, archival suggestions, and access to research archives. Mark Noonan's exceptional NEH Summer Institute, "City of Print: New York and the Periodical Press" (2020), helped me develop the guiding framework for my research in periodical studies. Susan Manning and Liesl Olson's fantastic NEH Summer Institute, "Making Modernism: Literature, Dance, and Visual Culture in Chicago, 1893–1955" (2022), helped me think especially about the New Negro in the context of performance, especially in the under-researched Midwest. I would like to thank participant Theresa Leininger-Miller for her help locating Augusta Savage's New Negro sculpture.

I could not have completed this project without essential research funding. McKendree University offered me a sabbatical for the 2018–19 academic year that allowed me to complete the work for this project and my monograph. A Sheila Biddle Ford Foundation Fellowship during the 2020–21 academic year at Harvard's Hutchins Center for African & African American Research provided me invaluable time and resources to finish these two projects. Although the coronavirus-19 pandemic compelled our meetings to be virtual, the reading group I formed with other Hutchins Fellows—Darius Bost, Eve Dunbar, Belinda Edmondson, William Pruitt, Jesse Shipley, and Justin Steil—offered invaluable feedback and indispensable support. Thank you all!

A New York Public Library Short-Term Research Fellowship in the summer of 2021 enabled me to dig into the wonderfully rich archival resources of the Schomburg Center for Research in Black Culture. Research support from a Hutchins Family Fellowship in the spring of 2025 has helped me continue the New Negro story.

Thank you to the editors of *PMLA* for their feedback on my essay about the two lost Du Bois articles in their "Little-Known Documents" section; your comments strengthened my analysis.

The Hutchins Center provided crucial research time, archival access, and support that helped generate a far richer anthology reaching across national and linguistic boundaries. Abby Wolf graciously helped me navigate the project by securing translation and transcription services. Julie Wolf's editorial work—made all the more difficult by my continual additions of material—was exemplary. Kevin Burke, Amy Gosdanian, Rob Heinrich, Krishnakali Lewis, and Tom Wolejko—all part of the fantastic team at the Hutchins Center—helped in myriad ways to move this project forward. Rob graciously directed me to key sources early on. Steven J. Niven generously proofread our author biographies. Marial Iglesias Utset provided research advice and helped us locate Afro-Cuban sources.

Princeton University Press has provided exceptional stewardship of this essay collection. Thank you, Anne Savarese, for your excellent editorial suggestions, and to your entire staff for their astute editorial eye.

Dear friends Genny Beemyn, Debra Blake, Jamie Bossart, Sue Everson, John Greenfield, Anett Jessup, Kathy Knox, Jennifer and Karl Knutsen, Shelly Lemons, Stacy Sorenson, and Carol Wallace provided encouragement, asked questions, offered advice, and sustained me through their friendship. Carol, thank you for helping me decipher some of the Spanish articles and for being the most supportive friend anyone could ever imagine. Kathy, thank you for transcribing articles at a crucial juncture, for always listening, and for being the best neighbor imaginable. Brenda and Jenny, our texting trio is a gift that daily gives support, laughter, and great reads. I love you guys—thanks for always being there!

I could not have finished this book without the love and support of my family: John and Colleen Patterson, Cheryl and Craig Peerenboom, my nephews, and niece, my extended family on both coasts, and my in-laws, Bill Thomas Sr., Jenny Thomas, Dan Sjogren, and Sarah Thomas. Thank you for always asking about how it was going even when this project took so long to complete.

My sons, Mark and Walter Thomas-Patterson, accomplished researchers and writers themselves, read and commented on drafts, shared my excitement when I found something important, cooked family meals with their dad, cheered me on, and made me laugh. Mark and Walter, I so appreciate your support, and I am profoundly grateful and honored to be your mom. And, yes, Walter, searching newspaper databases may well be my version of playing video games.

My husband of twenty-six years, Bill Thomas, an accomplished historian of World War I government suppression, read and commented on multiple drafts, accompanied me to museums and archives, listened to my enthusiasm about discoveries, helped me figure out what to include, and supported this project at every stage through his steadfast love, kindness, vast knowledge, and astute editorial eye. I dedicate this book to my sons and to Bill, who is my partner in life.

Martha H. Patterson

I would like to thank Kevin Burke, Robert Heinrich, Julie Wolf, Amy Gosdanian, Phoebe Braithwaite, Fred Shapiro, Jennifer Heinmiller, and, as always, my wife, Dr. Marial Iglesias Utset.

Henry Louis Gates, Jr.

THE NEW
NEGRO

Introduction

by Martha H. Patterson

On December 22, 1886, at the eighty-first annual celebration of the New England Society, sat three renowned white Americans symbolic of a nation divided. Generals William Tecumseh Sherman, famous for leading the Union Army's devastatingly effective 1864 March to the Sea campaign, and John Schofield would be guest speakers along with the first Southerner ever asked to address the Society, *Atlanta Constitution* editor Henry W. Grady.

Grady was visibly nervous. More than two hundred of the most powerful industrialists and cultural figures of the day had arrived at New York's Delmonico's restaurant, its banquet hall draped in American flags, to hear some of the nation's most distinguished men reflect on whether an illustrious Puritan past could reunite a country riven by the Civil War and the bitter resentment white Southerners sustained against Reconstruction.[1]

After rousing remarks from the society president and from the presiding clergyman, the chairman introduced General Sherman, who, in recounting a conversation he had with a Georgian planter during his Savannah campaign, reminded his audience that Georgia was one of the original thirteen colonies, that Northern states wrote bonds that paid for slaves, and joked that, because of the Confederacy's hasty secession, they "will never get paid for these niggers."

With the audience laughing and primed for approval, Grady delivered his "New South" address. The fusing of the Southern "Cavalier" and the Northern "Puritan," Grady declared, had forged great Americans like Abraham Lincoln. After a jesting aside to General Sherman—"considered an able man in our parts though . . . kind of a careless man about fire"—Grady defined the New South as a phoenix risen "from the ashes left to us in 1864." Created anew as a "perfect democracy," the New South, according to Grady, offered a peaceable kingdom of white plantation owners and Black workers, an implicit stark contrast to the labor strife fomenting the Haymarket Square bombing in Chicago just a few months earlier: "No section shows a more prosperous laboring population than the negroes of the South, none in fuller sympathy with our employing and land-owning class. He shares our school fund, has the fullest protection of our laws and the friendship of our people. . . . The relations of the Southern people with the negro are close and cordial."[2] As Grady described them, formerly enslaved African Americans had been loyal retainers during the war and remained "humble," as well as "simple and sincere," relying on the guidance of Southern white people who, he claimed, knew best how to govern them.

Grady's speech concluded, the band played "Way Down South in Dixie," the crowd cheered, and the dominant vision of the South after Reconstruction crystallized in the American consciousness. Newspaper reports around the country celebrated the speech. The *St. Louis Post-Dispatch* declared Grady a "National Santa Claus," having given the country the Christmas gift of sectional reconciliation, while the *Chicago Daily Tribune* called his address "brilliant and eloquent . . . as earnest and sincere as it was manly." The *Cincinnati Enquirer* announced that Grady's speech helped "prove beyond question that the war is over." The *New York Herald* went so far as to suggest that Grady be the vice presidential running mate for Grover Cleveland in his 1888 reelection campaign.[3]

Yet a few white journalists and most of the Black press denounced Grady's calculated New South pastoral propaganda, which omitted the growing assault on Black civil rights by the so-called Redeemers abetted by the US Supreme Court. Southern white Democrats and white supremacists saw themselves as "redeeming" the South by using propaganda, trickery, and violence to reverse the gains made by African Americans during Reconstruction and to remove Republicans from power. In 1883, the US Supreme Court, for its part, had struck down the Civil Rights Act of 1875. Nonetheless, Black and white editors alike saw the extent to which the power of Grady's New South moniker and the charisma of the "new," was taking hold.[4] To discard Grady's rhetoric of transformation wholesale risked leaving African Americans out of narratives of national progress, consigning the tremendous gains made by Black people during Reconstruction to the Redeemers, like Grady, who sought to reverse them.

Almost immediately following Grady's speech, journalists hailed as "New Negroes" those Black Americans who claimed economic, educational, or political power. Rather than a postwar South, it was postemancipation African Americans who represented the true phoenix, the genuinely "new." Having suffered generations of enslavement and Reconstruction's rollback, they had managed to seize whatever opportunities for advancement they could, deploying the figure of the New Negro to signal their resistance to the unfolding ruthlessness of a Jim Crow system that Grady and his fellow Redeemers helped to orchestrate.[5]

Inspired by Henry Louis Gates, Jr. and Gene Andrew Jarrett's *The New Negro: Readings on Race, Representation, and African American Culture, 1892–1938* (2007), *The New Negro: A History in Documents, 1887–1937* offers readers a dramatically expanded collection of African American, Afro–Latin American, and African texts, some quite obscure, tracing the origins of the New Negro trope and seven of its major versions until 1937.[6] That year marked the signing of a collective bargaining agreement between the Pullman Company and the Brotherhood of Sleeping Car Porters and Maids, the first African American union to be recognized by a major US company; the decisive shift of African Americans away from the party of Lincoln and to the Democratic Party; and the bloody conclusion of fascist Italy's merciless war on Ethiopia.[7]

Different variations of the New Negro figure largely emerged out of what Black intellectuals saw as moments of transformative possibility for a people theoretically, but not in practice, protected by the Fourteenth and Fifteenth Amendments, enduring assaults on their humanity even as they fought for respect. For Black writers and activists during this period, the transitional moment might be a groundbreaking address, political appointment, election victory, or publication; wartime military service; an especially horrific outburst of white supremacist violence; a decision to rally on behalf of civil rights, socialist, nationalist, internationalist, Pan-African, and/or anticolonial movements; a dramatic shift in social mores or economic opportunities; or the dawning of a local, national, or transnational Black network that offered collective hope. Within that moment, New Negro proponents responded by adopting sometimes contradictory ideologies: social Darwinism, Christianity, eugenics, New Thought, capitalism, consumerism, accommodationism, separatism, integration, feminism, antifeminism, imperialism, decolonization, socialism, communism, Black nationalism, fascism, and antifascism.[8] Although the trope reinforced a Black/white binary and elided the often complex multiracial identities of those under its capacious umbrella, the New Negro was versatile enough to serve the needs of those holding vastly different artistic, social, political, and cultural allegiances.

Given the systemic and cumulative disadvantages faced by Black periodical publishers, publicizing the New Negro would be a formidable task requiring extraordinary initiative. Well before 1887, the monopoly-controlled telegraph industry had risen to become the dominant means of rapidly transmitting not only news events but also the white supremacist ideology that shaped how readers understood those events.[9] In response, proponents of the New Negro used the Black press, distributed in part by Pullman porters over vast rail networks, to deliver a crucial rebuttal when Jim Crow strictures and violence increasingly blocked political participation in the South.[10] When in 1919 Claude Barnett launched his alternative to the Associated Press (AP), the Associated Negro Press, "news-hungry" Black papers "virtually stood in line" to sign up. By the end of its first year, eighty out of approximately 350 Black papers had joined.[11]

Indeed, with the rapid increase in Black literacy during and after Reconstruction, Black newspapers strove to meet the needs of an ever-expanding reading audience eager for news and opinions from a Black perspective. From 1880 to 1890, 504 African American newspapers were started. During the period from 1895 to 1915, 1,219 African American newspapers were founded, with a peak in 1902, coinciding with a pinnacle of Jim Crow white mob violence, when 101 Black newspapers were launched.[12] By 1921, wrote American sociologist Frederick Detweiler, "every Negro who can read does read a race paper."[13]

Because Latin American governments encouraged, if not insisted on, a "deracialized consciousness" and pressured Black citizens to de-emphasize racial difference in the public sphere, significantly fewer Afro–Latin American papers arose during the same period. Usually they comprised no more than four pages and relied almost exclusively on a Black urban audience whose wages and literacy rates were higher than in the countryside. They rarely sold enough copies or garnered enough advertising to make them profitable;[14] almost all Afro–Latin American papers lost money, and only a tiny fraction continued publishing beyond four or five years.[15] Nevertheless, as Paulina Laura Alberto, George Reid Andres, and Jesse Hoffnung-Garskof note, the Afro–Latin American press served a vital political and social function. By the 1920s these Black newspapers were denouncing structural racism, class oppression, and colonial rule as they covered Black community events left unaddressed by the white Latin American press and unified Black citizens by emphasizing an Afro-diasporic consciousness.[16]

Like the Afro–Latin American press, the Black African press under colonialism was also almost always desperately underfunded. Incorporating less news reporting (especially early in this period) than its American counterparts, the Black African press built political communities through editorials, content reprinted from other papers, travel essays, poetry, and reflections from correspondents. As Derek Peterson and Emma Hunter write, however, even as the Black African press generally, but not exclusively, sought to inspire nationalist sentiment against colonial rule, some African journalists saw their mission as inspiring a Pan-African consciousness beyond national boundaries. Regardless, Black African editors usually had to be attuned to colonial authorities, and thus the Black African press was "never free."[17] After World War I, the South African and West African presses grew exponentially, but in South Africa the white press exerted increased control over Black newspapers as it sought to curb the power of the African National Congress, founded in 1912. Even though the readership measured by literacy rates may appear comparatively small—in 1921, roughly 10 percent of Black South Africans were literate—out-loud reading events likely extended the reach of newspaper content considerably. The English-language press in West Africa, meanwhile, was primarily controlled by African descendants of Black Americans who had emigrated to Liberia and freed Sierra Leoneans and saw its audience as an educated elite.[18]

As this discourse mobilized, unified, and inspired Black people around the globe, it also divided, casting some—especially educated young Black men and women—as racial representatives but relegating most others as seemingly outside the modern or respectable spheres. Even as a number of New Negro writers we include pitched a wider New Negro tent as they challenged the "politics of respectability"—what Evelyn Higginbotham describes as the belief that "'respectable' behavior in public would earn . . . [African Americans] a measure of esteem from white America"—others did not.[19] As my coeditor, Henry Louis Gates, Jr., has argued, the figure implied "a cause-and-effect relation": the idea that if Black people could fashion new, self-empowered modern selves, they would defy the vicious, dehumanizing Old Negro stereotypes of Sambos, coons, brutes, mammies, and Jezebels.[20] That logic left those who did not appear to fit the modern image vulnerable, stuck within a paradigm that required by its very name demonstrable evidence of change.

Our guiding principle in compiling this anthology was to include only nonfiction articles (and a few pieces of autobiographical fiction) in which the concept of the New Negro, or some variation of the "new," appears. Overall, we sought to include those voices that represented the full geographic, social, aesthetic, and political diversity of the trope, with only some regard to whether the authors were or are well known. We see then the textual recovery in this volume, in the words of Brigitte Fielder, "not [only as] hunts for missing treasure but a research practice[e] that must reimagine criteria for textual valuation as preconditions for recovery work."[21] At the same time, we had to be mindful that many Black women writers eschewed any explicit use of the New Negro Woman trope because the Black counterpart of the New (white) Woman, associated with sexual freedom and other traditional gender-role transgressions, triggered the Jezebel stereotype. To compensate, we have included a number of pieces by Black women employing broader "new" rhetoric responding to changing Black women's roles. In total, the anthology reveals at least twelve variations of the New Negro characterized by historical period, a particular Black leader, or a new social movement: 1) the rise of Jim Crow, 2) the age of Washington, 3) the New Negro Woman, 4) the age of Du Bois, 5) the post–World War I Black Left, 6) the age of Garvey, 7) Alain Locke's New Negro, 8) the "jazz-mad" flapper, 9) the New Negro Alliance, 10) the New Deal New Negro, 11) the antifascist New Negro, and 12) the fascist New Negro.

Deploying the trope of the New Negro was a considered, important decision, and, despite its capaciousness and flux, not all famous, talented, or successful Black people would have been considered New Negroes. Although it is tempting to call a boxing legend such as Jack Johnson or a blues icon such as Bessie Smith a New Negro, respectability's tenacious hold on the trope precluded them from receiving such an accolade. Athleticism needed the imprimatur of education, so college athletes could wear the mantle. "Hot and dirty" jazz needed an unassailable reputation, along with extraordinary talent. Langston Hughes's "bad new Negroes" certainly embraced the "sad, raggy tune[s]" and the "whirling cabaret," yet only those jazz and blues performers who had garnered the artistic bona fides along with educational, oratorical, or respectability credentials were bestowed the title. "The great colored baritone" and two-time all-American athlete Paul Robeson graduated from Columbia Law School; the actress of "sterling character," Florence Mills, earned the adulation of the prince of Wales; "father of the blues" W. C. Handy published *Blues: An Anthology* (1926), illustrated by the celebrity Harlem Renaissance caricaturist Miguel Covarrubias. While not an exclusive list, these poetic and musical figures, and in the case of Robeson, this renowned college athlete, stage actor, and Black activist had garnered enough respectability to represent the race as New Negroes.[22]

Just as Black people traveled across continents, countries, and regions for a better life, the New Negro concept was on the move through wire transmission, word of mouth, the mail and rail services, films, phonograph records, and radio broadcasts.[23] Original content and reprints of American New Negro articles, both informally and through syndication, appeared in newspapers around the nation and the globe, offering a fascinating window into what content editors considered culturally relevant enough to claim. For leaders of the Négritude movement, the New Negro became "le nègre nouveau"; for the Afro-Cuban Gustavo Urrutia, the figure was the "Nuevo Negro."[24] We have sought to include those voices—regardless of whether they were well known—who represented the full geographic, social, aesthetic, and political diversity of the trope.

By including documents from the Black diaspora, we seek to tell a complex Afro-Atlantic story often forged by direct personal initiatives. Marcus Garvey, with substantial leadership assistance from his wives Amy Ashwood Garvey and later Amy Jacques Garvey, proved exceptionally adept at spreading his Pan-African Black nationalist version of the New Negro to workers' rights movements in Central America and East, Southern, and West Africa.[25] From 1929 to 1940, Paulette Nardal and her sisters Andrée and Jeanne (Jane) hosted Aimé Césaire, Langston Hughes, Etienne Léro, Alain Locke, Claude McKay, and Léopold Senghor in their Clamart salon southwest of Paris.[26] In March 1930 Langston Hughes, during his second visit to Cuba, enjoyed dinner in Havana with Urrutia and the leading poet of the Afrocubanismo movement, Nicolás Guillén.[27]

We also have included many New Negro images, not simply to augment the text but as interpretative documents themselves. These include illustrations from newspapers, magazines, and books; photographs from exhibits meant to dispel racist stereotypes; photographs of authors whose dress or demeanor suggests New Negro assertion; and photographs taken by Black and white artists to reflect New Negro ideals. We also include selections from white supremacist media outlets that sought to portray the New Negro as ridiculous, menacing, or criminal.

I. The New South and the New Negro, 1885–1894

Even before Henry Grady's address, the eminent African American Episcopal minister Alexander Crummell, in "The Need of New Ideas and New Aims for a New Era," heralded the "new" as a turn away from the trauma of enslavement. In his 1885 commencement address at the historically Black Storer College in Harpers Ferry, West Virginia, whose graduates would have been among the first generation to have no direct memory of slavery, Crummell enjoined his audience to meet the "urgent needs of the present" and the "fast-crowding and momentous interests of the future" rather than "dwell[ing] morbidly and absorbingly upon the servile past." For Crummell, speaking to his audience of future race leaders, the "new" would elevate the Black family, improve the status of Black laborers, and lead a "*moral* revolution."[28]

Yet Crummell's audience faced the prospect of seeking opportunities amid what Eric Foner has called the "twilight zone" after Reconstruction yet before the full implementation of Jim Crow.[29] By 1885, white supremacist Southern Democrats had put in place or tacitly condoned a slew of measures aimed at denying Black Americans their civil rights. In 1883 the US Supreme Court declared the 1875 Civil Rights Act unconstitutional. Even those Black passengers who had paid first-class railroad fares were forced into the crude and dirty accommodations of the smoking car; white land and shop owners had locked most rural Black Americans into perpetual debt due to a predatory credit lien system; Black women had almost no protection from the sexual predation of white men; Black voting rights were increasingly under attack through intimidation, violence, or deceit; white vigilantes increasingly lynched Black people with impunity as a means of social control through terrorism; Southern white journalists, in concert with business and political interests, increasingly worked to justify systemic anti-Black racism; and, by the end of the 1880s, at least ten thousand African American men had been forced into working as virtual slave laborers in the South through the convict lease system.[30] The supposed "new crime" of Black men raping white women became, according to Joel Williamson, "the subject of intense observation" in the late 1880s, roughly coterminous with Black writers' first use of the trope of the New Negro in 1887.[31]

Within this context, the New Negro we see in the documents of this section reflect real progress that African Americans made as they fought against Reconstruction's complete rollback. On January 6, 1887, the white-owned *Independent*, a weekly New York newspaper, published a six-part series, "What Educated Colored People in the South Report concerning Their Material Condition."[32] After the first installment, the white-owned *Hartford Daily Courant* published a summary of the *Independent*'s findings in an article titled "The New Negro in the New South." Despite "very low wages" and an exploitive "store-credit system" that functioned as a "clog to progress, a millstone around the negro's neck," the *Courant* observed, African Americans were advancing. In Richmond County, North Carolina, the article reports, "they are fast accumulating property" and buying homes. Even though "few own farms of any considerable size," noted an interviewee from Arkansas, "a new spirit seems to have come over them in the last few years, and they are looking toward the ownership of larger farms."[33]

The following month, the Black-edited *Washington Bee* republished an article from the Black *St. Louis Advance* that defined the New Negro as one who emerged in tandem with the New South, had been born after slavery, had gained higher education, and sought to "soften the asperities of race antagonism" through direct political involvement.[34]

In other words, despite a sectional reconciliation forged on the conviction of a shared commitment to white supremacy—what David Blight calls "a soul-killing hydra worse than slavery itself"—the New Negro represented hope.[35] The New Negro, explained the *Washington Bee*, "is coming forth in platoons of ten thousand deep from the colleges and schools of the Nation, with reverence for the past, but with all his energies bent on the prospect of the future."[36] While the *Courant*'s article may or may not be the first published usage of "New Negro"—too many gaps in the historical record remain—the New Negro as a "social media campaign" was born.[37]

In the Black press, "New Negro" quickly became shorthand for Black men claiming race consciousness, education, and political power on behalf of full civil rights. The African American journalist and civil rights spokesman John Edward Bruce, who adopted the evocative pen name Bruce Grit [John Edward Bruce], deployed the New Negro in 1888 for the *New York Age* when he urged the Republican National Committee to hire the lawyer and former US ambassador to Liberia John H. Smythe as a campaign orator.[38] The Black-owned Kansas *Times-Observer* meanwhile hailed the "new Negro voter" who could not be bought: he was one "whose education and acquaintance with our political systems renders him a restless and an almost unknown factor in the political arena."[39] In Virginia, the "Fighting Negro Editor" of the *Richmond Planet*, John W. Mitchell Jr., took such a courageous stance against racial injustice and white mob violence that the Indianapolis *Freeman* called him "a man, who, conscious of his own strength of Manhood Dares to Hurl the Thunderbolts of Truth Into the Ranks of the Wicked—Injustice a Target for his Unerring Arrow."[40]

A staunch Republican, Mitchell epitomized the New Negro as an erudite defender of the race who exposed racist capitalist exploitation, the hypocrisy of white supremacy, and the ruthless tactics white Democrats used to ensure domination. In his December 20, 1890, editorial in response to the local white supremacist L***, Mitchell recalled the savagery of white mobs who had recently lynched a man: "their sensitive stomachs [*sic*] possibly prevented them from proceeding with the act of mastication."[41] Mitchell, having himself been threatened with lynching for his reporting, ended his editorial by extolling the many accomplishments in business, education, and politics of the New Negro while evoking a not-too-distant time past when Virginians made meaningful cross-racial alliances over economic and education issues.[42]

Black women claimed the imagery of the "New Negro" to organize for greater respect, racial uplift, and a political voice. In *A Voice from the South* (1892), Anna Julia Cooper, who had lived with Alexander Crummell in Washington, DC, as a boarder just a few years prior, saw the Woman's Christian Temperance Union, the first mass organization of women committed to social, and, by extension, political reform, as perhaps the most powerful example of this "new era" and a "woman's place in it."[43] Cooper insisted that this "new era" required Black women's affective influence "to bring a heart power into this money getting, dollar-worshipping civilization . . . to stand for God and Home and Native Land *versus gain and greed and grasping selfishness*."[44] That same year she helped to launch the Colored Women's League, whose primary mission was to improve the lives of Black women, children, and the city's poor. The following year she joined the prominent Chicago club-woman and speaker Fannie Barrier Williams, who had joined the fight for Black representation at Chicago's Columbian Exposition, to speak at the World's Congress of Representative Women held at the exposition. Decrying stereotypes of Black female immorality, Williams celebrated the "new ideals of womanhood" in which a "new generation" of Black women claimed the privileges of "grace and delicacy" so long enjoyed by affluent white women.[45] Although initially committed to Frederick Douglass's vision of "egalitarian protest ideology," after Douglass's death in 1895, Williams, like so many others, lauded the accommodationist philosophy of the era's most prominent and well-funded Black industrial educational leader, Booker T. Washington.[46]

II. The Booker T. Washington Era, 1895–1903

On a bright, warm afternoon in Atlanta in September 1895, thousands of Americans—among them regional dignitaries, Civil War veterans, Black people in carriages, and reporters from the nation's major newspapers—came to witness the spectacular opening ceremonies of what would be the grandest testament thus far to the New South: the Cotton States and International Exposition. As one of a series of speakers introduced by the state's Reconstruction-era, Republican former governor Rufus B. Bullock, Booker T. Washington, the founder and president of the Tuskegee Normal and Industrial Institute in Alabama, alone gained national attention, captivating his audience with his promise of a loyal Black workforce that "cast down [its] bucket" and accepted segregation as the only reasonable course.[47] Two days later, in a letter to the *New York World*, Washington reiterated his deference to white leadership, insisting if the Negro would "cast his lot materially, civilly and morally with the South . . . cultivate the closest friendship with the Southern white man; [and] that when he can . . . vote for and with the Southern white man . . . there will be soon not only a new South but a new negro."[48] Less than two weeks later, Chicago's *Daily Inter Ocean* heralded Washington's "practical plans for harmonizing all race differences," providing the New South its basis for prosperity and embodying the era's "new negro."[49]

Given the South's increasingly brutal Jim Crow practices, Washington's public accommodationist stance may have been the only pragmatic choice. By the mid-1890s, the Jim Crow system, designed to terrorize, subjugate, and control, had reached its apogee. White mobs murdered more than seven hundred mostly male African Americans from 1890 to 1900, often in ghastly spectacles of ritualized torture. Southern states disenfranchised Black voters, with Mississippi adopting a new state constitution in 1890 that instituted a poll tax and literacy test as a voting requirement; other states followed suit. State and local governments, particularly in the South, passed a torrent of laws segregating transportation and public facilities, with the 1896 Supreme Court decision upholding segregation, *Plessy v. Ferguson*, greenlighting the process. Throughout the country, Black people were usually relegated to the most menial labor and denied opportunities for advancement. Enduring the seemingly overwhelming obstacles of systemic racial and gender oppression and the ever-present threat of sexual violence, Black women faced an even more treacherous path.[50]

Working in the South, where the majority of African Americans still lived, Margaret Murray Washington urged clubwomen, and particularly white clubwomen, to refocus their efforts where she felt the need was most dire—in the South. Although Washington delivered her address "Individual Work for Moral Elevation" at the First National Conference of Colored Women of America in Boston almost two months before her husband's famous Atlanta Exposition speech in September 1895, it was not until October, during the ongoing exposition, that the Boston philanthropic monthly *Lend a Hand* printed and renamed the address "The New Negro Woman" for a predominantly Northern white progressive audience.

With its new title, Margaret Murray Washington's speech offered an implicit critique of what had become a dominant stereotype of (white) New Womanhood—selfishness. Although both white and Black New Woman advocates maintained that their "newness" benefited "the race," the dominant press frequently criticized (white) New Women's demands as at odds with their biological imperative to be mothers. In this view, campaigning for suffrage; pursuing higher education; and advocating for dress reform, sexual freedom, and artistic expression made women mannish, barren, or degenerate. Margaret Murray Washington, by contrast, positioned the dominant version of the New Negro Woman as selfless, committed to helping her less fortunate Southern Black sisters: "It is the lifting up as we climb which means growth to the race."[51] Transforming the New Woman trope to invoke older (white) "true women's" ideals of domesticity, piety, and purity and applying them to Black women, especially in the club movement, Washington combated the degendering that Black women suffered during enslavement.[52] At the same time, she shifted the New Woman's working location from the urban North to the rural South, where thousands of Black women, she maintained in a letter to the white reformer Ednah Dow Littlehale Cheney, "live a living death." Beginning in the home, this New Negro Woman instilled Christian faith and morality, the "responsibility of motherhood," cooking, cleaning, tidiness, "neatness of dress," and "wholesome habits."[53] Only after such work "helping our women," Washington argued, would "there be fewer thrusts at the immorality of the race," fewer lynchings, and the eventual interracial acknowledgment of the "brotherhood of man and the fatherhood of God."[54]

At the same time, the ubiquitous popularized version of the (white) New Woman as Charles Dana Gibson's statuesque Gibson Girl presented a challenge to Black women. As the Gibson Girl luxuriated in her own beauty, drained her father's finances, juggled eager suitors, and engaged in the latest athletic sensation of golf, she represented a new feminine power at once appealing and dangerous for Black women to adopt. The prevailing racist and sexist stereotypes of Black women as Jezebels and viragos, coupled with the patriarchal imperatives of racial uplift, meant that the New Negro Woman's illustrators often drew her as having the Gibson Girl's stylishness but the modesty and deference of the "true woman." In other words, while adopting a Gibson Girl look—Margaret Murray Washington was, in fact, compared to a Gibson Girl by a white settlement house leader— the New Negro Woman eschewed the Gibson Girl narrative.[55] Committed to service rather than solipsism, "sacrifice" rather than self-indulgence, separate spheres rather than social mixing, and sisterly loyalty rather than cutthroat competition, the New Negro Woman sought to shift from the *I* of the Gibson Girl icon to the *we* of interracial sisterhood.[56] As white periodicals of the period portrayed New Negro Women as garish parodies of white Gibson Girls, Black writers and artists depicted them as reserved and accomplished Gibson Girl types.[57] Not until 1916 would a Black-owned magazine feature a female golfer on the cover as a sign of Black women's modernity.

Other Black women eschewed the trope entirely as irrelevant or counterproductive given systemic discrimination. The Black-owned *Leavenworth* (KS) *Herald* reprinted and endorsed an article by the white-owned *Tacoma* (WA) *Herald*, claiming that the "new woman" was so tied to middle-class privilege that it was inconceivable to apply it to African American women: "Being less independent than the young women who have and relish the opportunity to support themselves by money-making, the colored girl has no prospect in life except in matrimony. She . . . never gets a chance to know the significance of the term, 'the new woman.'" Pauline E. Hopkins appears to have eschewed the term because of its primary association with woman's suffrage. In 1900, she cautioned not only against the corrupting effects of the "political arena" but also about the increased power the vote would give to southern white women: "If we are not the 'moral lepers' that the white women of Georgia accuse us of being, then we ought to hesitate before we affiliate too happily in any project that will give them greater power than they now possess to crush the weak and helpless."[58]

Perhaps because of her close ties to Booker T. Washington, Fannie Barrier Williams, by contrast, envisioned the New Negro Woman as the "happy refutation of the idle insinuations and common skepticism as to the womanly worth and promise of the whole race of women."[59] As historian Brittney C. Cooper writes, Williams, like Anna Julia Cooper before her, went "beyond respectability," powerfully "linking the fleshy precarity of Black life to the forward-looking possibilities of progressive social discourse." To combat what Brittney Cooper calls Black women's "civic unknowability," Williams deployed the New Negro Woman trope to center the Black women's club movement in a whole host of progressive causes crucial to the race: promoting early childhood education, ensuring employment opportunities for women, and protesting the convict lease system.[60]

All the clamor about a New Woman only accelerated fascination with the New Negro, which a twenty-seven-year-old W. E. B. Du Bois proclaimed needed guiding principles. In December 1895, in a now lost issue of the *New York Age*, Du Bois published his "Creed for the 'New Negro.'" At this point in his career, Du Bois, who was teaching at Wilberforce University, had not yet publicly voiced objections to Booker T. Washington's worldview and, in fact, had congratulated Washington on his "phenomenal success at Atlanta—it was a word fitly spoken."[61]

In its emphasis on moral purity, self-reliance, and "industrial training," as well as its accedence to social segregation, Du Bois's "Creed" reads like something Washington would endorse. Yet Du Bois, even this early in his career, distinguishes his position from Washington's. In addition to industrial education, Du Bois emphasizes the need for "the cultivation of our best intellectual ability." He calls for the "founding of a university of the negro" (which he would later describe as the unique curriculum based on each "race-soul").[62] In urging the "preservation of our best race characteristics and products" as expressed in Black music and folklore, he celebrates Black culture in itself rather than as measured by white achievement. Finally, Du Bois expresses a commitment to judicious political involvement that Washington, in Alabama, had publicly renounced. The order of Du Bois's "Creed"—especially the fact that the "strictest moral purity'" must be observed before the affirmation of Black culture—suggested the hazards of celebrating Black culture and higher education when most Southern white people associated Black men with criminality and Black women with sexual immorality.[63]

Yet at this point in his career, Du Bois had neither the stature nor inclination to take on Washington, whose vision dominated the Black press. In 1902, Washington D.C.'s *Colored American* newspaper, with its banner prominently featuring the US capitol and various tools of learning, hailed Professor James B. Dudley as the president of the Agricultural and Mechanical College in Greensboro, North Carolina, and one of a series of New Negro "Men of the Hour." Born enslaved, trained as a carpenter, and committed to "every kind of education," Dudley embodied the Washington ideals of "thrift and economy," "racial harmony," and "sectional development." Despite the 1898 Wilmington, North Carolina, massacre and coup d'état, when white supremacists overthrew a democratically elected Fusionist government of Black and white leaders, burned the offices of the city's Black newspaper, and killed dozens of Black citizens (what the *Colored American* called the "unfortunate occurrences in Wilmington"), Dudley represented a commitment to public service and self-improvement that promised the cooperation of "white and black" as "full-fledged citizens" in the "New South."[64]

By 1900, in fact, Washington's influence was so great that even white publishers capitalized on it to sell copy. In what Washington would call an "outrage[ou]s fraud," the white American Publishing House president John Emmett MacBrady designed the book *A New Negro for a New Century*

(1900) to appear as if Washington had edited it, even though Washington contributed only one chapter, and that was ghostwritten by T. Thomas Fortune.[65] Known later for his marketing of beauty products to Black consumers, MacBrady arranged the book to showcase the celebrity power of Washington as the consummate New Negro.[66] Just five years after Booker T. Washington's "Atlanta Compromise" speech had launched him into national fame, MacBrady would use Washington's image to sell a more vigorous ideal of Christian New Negro manhood, one that highlighted to a primarily Black audience the contributions of prominent Black servicemen and newspaper editors.

While Washington's contribution, "Afro-American Education," describes the "marvelous work" of colleges educating Black Americans after slavery, and Fannie Barrier Williams's contribution, "The Club Movement among Colored Women of America,"[67] focuses on the racial uplift mission of the Black women's club movement, the heart of the book, as advertised on the title page, celebrates the "Superb Heroism and Daring Deeds of the Negro Soldier." In fact, seven of the anthology's eighteen chapters focus on Black military service, especially in US imperialist ventures, which Washington had publicly expressed ambivalence toward two years earlier.[68] Despite the fact that the US conquest and annexation of the Philippines, Puerto Rico, and Guam had its foundation in a conviction of white American racial superiority and that, as George P. Marks III writes, "the cardinal emphasis in the Black press" was on the hypocrisy of a war to liberate Black Cubans in the Spanish-American War while not protecting Black Americans in the South, the collection celebrated the Spanish-American War and Black soldiers serving in it.[69]

The New Negro that emerges in the book hews to a line of racial uplift rooted in white bourgeois values—thrift, hard work, patriarchy, valor, Christianity, and patriotic imperialism—while also revealing its fault lines and contradictions. Evoking what historian Darlene Clark Hine termed a "culture of dissemblance"—Black women feigning candor while keeping their true feelings hidden—and later described by Kevin K. Gaines as both a Black means of survival and "part of the majority American culture's silence, evasion, or outright distortion on matters of race," the anthology reflects the incentive by both Black writers and white editors to present a carefully guarded New Negro.[70] The New Negro in MacBrady's collection points out white prejudice but does not mention the South's "Red Record" of lynching and its terroristic function within the systemic brutality of Jim Crow. This New Negro may demonstrate bravery in battle but must acknowledge and appease the psychological needs of white people for dominance and heroism; he may be a man in fellowship with other similarly accomplished men, but not in avowed partnership with Black women; and he may show evidence of exceptional "race progress" but, within the social Darwinist context of what historian Marlon Ross calls the "race of the races," must promote a pseudoscientific taxonomy that positions him above the supposed "wild Indians."[71]

Any assertion of "race progress" in MacBrady's volume, however, was up against syndicated white supremacist views that US imperialism only risked expanding the so-called Negro problem. J. M. Scanland's bitterly racist "Special New Orleans Letter, 'Some Reasons Why the Mixed Population of Porto [sic] Rico and the Philippines Should Not Be Granted Citizenship'" (1900), argues that the US acquisition of nations with "mixed populations" presented a deeply vexing problem. According to Scanland, Negroes of any nationality, whether they were "new niggers" or not, were incapable of self-government.[72]

Whether the New Negro should strive to prove his mettle in service to his nation or shun such service because of Jim Crow would spur one Western Black writer to propose a radically different solution: colonization, led by a New Negro, of a portion of the United States. In 1899, the Baptist educator, pastor, novelist, newspaper founder, and editor Sutton E. Griggs, who grew up in Texas, self-published the fictional *Imperium in Imperio* (1899). Appearing one year after the Spanish-American War, Griggs's *Imperium* offers a New Negro remarkable for his commitment to direct action protest, the militancy of his response to imperialist conquest and Jim Crow atrocities, and his embrace of emigration as a means of redress.[73] The New Negro protagonist, Belmont Piedmont, whose views mirror those of Griggs himself, describes the African American as a colonized person, "an unprotected foreigner in his own home."[74] Within the safety of the New Negro's clandestine imperium—a Black nation within the US nation—a fierce debate ensues. Despite the objections of the more temperate Piedmont, the New Negro antagonist, Bernard Belgrave, resolves to wrest control of the domestic imperialist project, launching an armed reconquest of land already long occupied by peoples also suffering colonization—Native Americans and Latinos: "We will demand the surrender of Texas and Louisiana to the Imperium. Texas, we will retain. Louisiana, we will cede to our foreign allies in return for their aid. Thus will the Negro have an empire of his own, fertile in soil, capable of sustaining a population of fifty million people."[75] Even as Griggs clearly shows the influence of Du Bois's and Washington's conceptions of the New Negro in his commitment to racial uplift, women's chastity, and voluntary social segregation, he comes closer to proposing a Black nationalist perspective than either race leader. Griggs's New Negro novel finally issues an ultimatum: either the US returns to what Griggs sees as its fundamental Christian and democratic ideals or it risks a mass exodus of Black labor and violent secession. *Imperium* emphasizes both the irony and the potential catastrophic repercussions of a nation committed to imperialist missions abroad while failing to acknowledge how its internal conquest of Black people has undermined its national security.

Griggs was not alone in seeing the West as a more democratic geographical space, less consumed by the all-encompassing systemic brutality of Jim Crow and thus the best home for the New Negro.[76] Echoing the spirit of the post-Reconstruction Exodusters, when tens of thousands of Black people left the South to homestead in Kansas, Colorado, and Oklahoma, some Western Black newspapers maintained that the New Negro spirit could best be forged on lands west of the Mississippi.[77] In 1895, the *Leavenworth Herald*, edited by Blanche Ketene Bruce, nephew of Blanche Kelso Bruce, the first African American to serve a full term in the US Senate (from 1875 to 1881), maintained that "the West is noted for its free ideas, liberality of thought, and especially for the magnificent chances presented for young Afro-Americans to make ladies and gentlemen of themselves."[78] In 1906, Horace Cayton Sr.'s Black weekly, the *Seattle Republican*, expressed a similar sentiment, declaring, "The solution of the so-called 'race problem,' in the United States, is the scattering of the blacks, like the whites, to every nook and corner of the country; yea, even to every nook and corner of the South and Central American republics. . . . Now, Mr. New Negro, go thou and do likewise."[79]

Yet, while Griggs elides any common cause with Native Americans or Hispanics, literary scholar Emily Lutenski charts a New Negro emerging from a multiethnic West and borderlands where Mexican Americans, Native Americans, and Asian Americans often lived and worked alongside African Americans.[80] Indeed, although the New Negro trope emphasizes a Black/white binary, in particularly racially and ethnically diverse cities such as Los Angeles in the early twentieth century, the New Negro appears, as Lutenski argues, "at the nexus of the borderlands and the Pacific world."[81] Coupled with this multiracial nexus, as Douglas Flamming writes, Black Americans "found in Los Angeles . . . an oddly half-free environment" where "the rules of the game and the hierarchies of power seemed always in flux."[82] In 1924, the Black-owned Los Angeles *California Eagle* extolled the Black contractor and businessman Charles S. Blodgett as one who embodied the "very practical decision of the New Negro . . . [who] by his unselfish devotion for his people . . . has lighted the path of progress for greater things than have ever been dreamed of before." In the extraordinary photo of Blodgett in Los Angeles from 1909 that we include here, he kneels in a dark suit in front of his painting crew—likely ethnically diverse—to document a moment where Los Angeles' own version of Jim Crow seems to have, at least partially, slipped.[83]

Proponents of the New Negro, especially in the early 1900s, used the medium of photography to offer evidentiary proof of the existence of the New Negro. With its sixty-one photographs including Black servicemen, journalists, educators, and women's club movement leaders, Mac-Brady's anthology served as a visual testament to race progress in much the same way as W. E. B. Du Bois's 363 photographs, two-thirds of which were portraits of Black middle-class southerners, for his American Negro Exhibit at the 1900 Paris Exhibition. Du Bois's collection of photographs—assembled while he served as professor of sociology at Atlanta University and designed to show "what the negro really is in the South,"—offered seemingly irrefutable evidence of Black accomplishment, dignity, and humanity. As Shawn Michelle Smith notes, the photographs Du Bois curated offered a "counterarchive that challenges a long legacy of racist taxonomy, intervening in turn-of-the-century 'race science' by offering competing visual evidence."[84] It wasn't enough to describe the New Negro in words; one had to use a mimetic, modern technological medium to corroborate the New Negro's emergence—all the more remarkable in former slave states.

Regardless, the onslaught of anti-Black racist propaganda both justifying and spurring Jim Crow discrimination, exploitation, and violence only accelerated. In what must have seemed bitterly ironic to Booker T. Washington after his "Atlanta Compromise" concessions and his assurances to his largely white audience that Blacks were the "most patient, faithful, law-abiding, and unresentful people that the world has seen," white Southerners unleashed not only a torrent of discriminatory laws and mob acts of terrorism directed against African Americans but also a deluge of anti-Black racist imagery to rationalize that brutal treatment.[85] As historian Rayford Logan writes, throughout the country Americans were bombarded with images of, "lazy, improvident, child-like, irresponsible, chicken-stealing, crap-shooting, policy-playing, razor-toting, immoral and criminal" Black people. As their status in American society degenerated, they became even more vulnerable to such attacks.[86]

Increasingly nostalgic for the plantation "darkey" and fearful of any Black assertion of rights, Southern white people created an alternate narrative of the New Negro. In their version, according to Rev. S. A. Steel of Nashville, Tennessee, slavery had been a benign institution that "civilized" barbaric slaves, a "mild and humane system of bondage, almost misnamed slavery." Reconstruction was a tragic folly that had created a "new negro" (the pejorative use of the trope is rarely capitalized) who, free from all restraint, acted on his singular urge (since sexual passions predominated in his race) for "social equality," a drive manifesting itself as an overwhelming lust for white women. Untethered to slavery's Christian influence and corrupted by Northern opportunities, this "new negro" had devolved into a rapist deserving of incarceration and lynching.[87]

For such prominent white Southern writers as Thomas Nelson Page, even Booker T. Washington as the representative New Negro could not be trusted. Despite his assurances that "in all things that are purely social we can be as separate as the five fingers," in accepting President Theodore Roosevelt's invitation to the White House in 1901, Washington proved, according to Page, that "the most passionate aspiration of the new negro was for the bugbear of 'social equality.'" Page followed a familiar pattern of white supremacist rhetoric of the time: despite the shallow appearances of change, the New Negro was hopelessly stuck in ineradicable racial barbarism. Roosevelt's invitation and Washington's acceptance had emboldened the New Negro's sense of race consciousness: "The new negro when he gets an education . . . becomes the 'Afro-American'" (and, consequently, becomes even more desirous of "social equality"). The more the New Negro identifies as Afro-American, Page suggests, the more he reverts to his primitive "dark continent" self, making it only a matter of time before he adopts "sword and torch" to overthrow the white power structure and claim his real prize, white Southern womanhood.[88] In 1904, *Life* magazine depicted Washington as an ape in a cartoon titled, "Life's Presidential Impossibilities." No need to fear, *Life* assured its white readers; the idea of a Black president was laughable.[89]

III. The W. E. B. Du Bois Era, 1903–1916

From June 1903 to January 1904, the esteemed *Harper's Weekly* devoted a series of articles to the "new negro crime" of Black men's alleged sexual assault of white women. Newspapers around the country reprinted it. The first article in the series maintains that Mississippi's redrawn 1890 constitution disenfranchising Black voters prevented such assaults. Although "it is generally acknowledged . . . that the new negro at the South is less industrious, less thrifty, less trustworthy, and less self-controlled than was his father or his grandfather," it was the right to vote that was the primary cause of his savage criminality. Americans, then, "may have cause to bless the refusal of the United States Supreme Court to enforce the Fifteenth Amendment" in the South and its protection of voting rights.[90] The second article in the series blames Reconstruction, as well as the Fourteenth and Fifteenth Amendments, as political developments all "favorable to amalgamation"— that is, interracial sex.[91]

In the final article in the series, the *Harper's* editorialist insists that "the average negro does not believe in the chastity of women," leading the Black man not merely to misunderstand the concept of rape but to "condone" it. Since his "sexual desire [has] always been a controlling force," with the "new teaching of social and political equality" it has become a "desire for the white woman." The author wonders if Thomas Nelson Page's proposed solution, the hiring of Black lawmen to patrol their own race, would be effectual or if, as Page fears, the "racial instincts" of "Black criminals" have "roots so deep . . . [that] . . . nothing can eradicate them."[92] And with that premise, any means of social control—be it through the justice system or the mob—can be justified. The New Negro in the white press had become overwritten as the Black male rapist.

For Southern social observers such as Eleanor Tayleur, writing for New York's *Outlook* in January 1904, the New Negro Woman had been wrenched into newness by the violence of the Civil War and the folly of Reconstruction and now appeared as a "Frankenstein product of civilization," ruled by her appetites and indifferent to whether they defied the bounds of marriage or law. For Tayleur the New Negro Woman was both a fright and an object of pity because with the "brain of a child and the passions of a woman," she absurdly imitated white women's dress but not their refined behavior. Characterized by "social and moral decadence," the New Negro Woman stood "forsaken and deserted" at "the garden of free-loveism" crying out for rescue.[93]

As the Jim Crow caste system and the vicious anti-Black propaganda sustaining it increasingly became embedded into virtually every sector of American life, and especially in the South, Washington's public silence on Jim Crow discrimination and violence provoked rebellion among a number of Black leaders. Most famously, in 1903 W. E. B. Du Bois published his critique of Washington and celebration of a Black aesthetic, *The Souls of Black Folk*. Writing from the perspectives of two worlds—the Black and white, "within and without the Veil"—Du Bois reflected on Black Americans longing to "attain self-conscious manhood."[94] Now it was the Southerner, Washington, who embodied the Old Negro, the "old attitude of adjustment and submission . . . a silent submission to civic inferiority such as is bound to sap the manhood of any race in the long run," while Du Bois's increasingly vocal civil rights protest constituted the new. For Du Bois, "so thoroughly did [Washington] learn the speech and thought of triumphant commercialism, and the ideals of material prosperity" that he had given up on the idea of "true manhood," which lay in political power, civil rights, and higher education. It was Washington's feminine "submission," his spirit of "kindliness and reconciliation," all designed "to sell" a debased form of Black manhood, that constituted a "civic death" for Black men. For Du Bois, that "true manhood" was more likely to be found in the North and required exercising the franchise.[95]

Two years later, in July 1905, Du Bois collaborated with other Black intellectuals, including *Voice of the Negro* editors John Wesley Edward Bowen and Jesse Max Barber and *Guardian* editor

William Monroe Trotter, to launch the Niagara Movement, a precursor to the National Association for the Advancement of Colored People (NAACP). In what must have seemed to Washington an audacious affront, the delegates promoted their ambitious platform committed to "full manhood" rights: the right to vote (for "with the right to vote goes everything"); equal access to all public facilities, including all means of transportation and education ("we want our children trained as intelligent human beings should be"); freedom of speech and assembly, and equal protection under the law (for "we are more often arrested, convicted, and mobbed"). Washington immediately tried to quell the attack on his own New Negro vision, but despite his best efforts, the civil rights organization had swelled its ranks to 150 members by the end of 1905.[96]

Yet, even before the founding of the Niagara Movement, some Black writers, even in the New South's iconic city of Atlanta, challenged Washington's status as the nation's preeminent New Negro. In March 1905, as a young Black art professor writing for the Atlanta-based *Voice of the Negro*, John H. Adams Jr. passed the New Negro torch from Booker T. Washington, the Virginia native who had been born into slavery, to W. E. B. Du Bois, the Massachusetts native born after the ratification of the Thirteenth Amendment. In a biographical sketch of the thirty-seven-year-old civil rights leader, Adams maintained that "our ancestors'" stories of enslavement—the "lash of the overseer, the midnight escape, the patrollers . . . the all night tramp through a black, muddy swamp"—only elicited anger. What the nation needed now was the "cool resolute and determinate" leadership of Du Bois, who, having graduated from Fisk and Harvard Universities and studied at the University of Berlin, represented "the strongest evidence of the capabilities and possibilities of his people." Adams's drawing of Du Bois in profile, his head bent in thought and occupying two-thirds of the page, epitomized his "intellectual strength."[97]

Even before inaugurating Du Bois's reign as the *new* New Negro, Adams proclaimed himself as the era's New Negro artist of record, drawing for the first time in the trope's history multiple renditions of whom he saw as the era's New Negro Women and Men. His New Negro Woman, once "fettered with the chains of caste" but now imbued with the "dignified countenance" of "college training," exuded a beauty infused with meaning. Despite "Negro restrictive laws . . . and prejudices," her "intellectual graces" and "moral stamina," associated with "true womanhood," shone. As such, she inspired men to be worthy of her and to rally to her defense. The caption for Adams's "Eva," who sits with her arms folded atop a desk, her gaze cast ahead in reflection, reads: "This is a death-knell to the dude and the well-dressed run-around." Among the seven portraits in Adams's essay, his last, and the only one in full-length, is "Gussie," who stands arms akimbo, with corseted waist, upswept hair, and the Anglo-American features of the Gibson Girl. Yet unlike the sexually "dangerous" Gibson Girl, the statuesque "Gussie" is "a performer on the violin and the piano, a sweet singer, a writer . . . and home making girl."[98]

Adams's essay on the New Negro Man in October 1904 begins with a photograph of Adams himself—an artist whom, the caption reads, "the Atlanta Constitution pronounces . . . nothing short of a genius . . . [who] may some day startle the world with his paintings"—and ends with a full page portrait of the *Voice of the Negro* managing editor reading a book: "Mr. Barber is a very close student of current, economic and sociological questions." As if anticipating his own article on Du Bois the following year, Adams declared that the New Negro Man had learned to read the "ugly circumstances that surrounds him" through the lens of the "Veil" so "touchingly" rendered in *The Souls of Black Folk*.[99]

In the years immediately preceding World War I, Black journalists overall employed less New Negro rhetoric, but when they did, it reflected both growing race consciousness due to segregation and Jim Crow violence and increasing anxiety about competition with immigrants—who, despite a rising pitch of nativist sentiment, seemed more quickly to reap the systemic advantages of whiteness. For Rev. S. Laing Williams of Chicago, a friend and ally of Booker T. Washington, the New

Negro had already proved his loyalty to the nation through service in every American military operation, campaigns essential to American sovereignty and westward expansion, and yet he was still deemed inferior to newly arrived Asian and European immigrants. The New Negro, according to Williams, was simply a man who "asks and fights for a chance."[100]

For the Afro-Caribbean / Brazilian journalist and educator José Clarana, the New Negro's best hope lay in becoming a kind of cultural chameleon, adopting the characteristics of immigrant groups unfettered by the chains of Jim Crow. Clarana himself was a master of international self-reinvention. Born James Bertram Clarke in the British West Indies, he wrote under that name as a student at Cornell University, then adopted the Clarana pseudonym while teaching Spanish in the Brooklyn public schools; he then moved to Brazil in 1916 and returned to New York in 1919, where he adopted the pseudonym Jaime Clarana Gil.[101] Writing for the NAACP's *Crisis* magazine in 1913, the polyglot Clarana—fluent in Spanish, Portuguese, French, English, and Italian—urged readers to integrate themselves among the new immigrants: "The new Negro who wants to be faithful to himself as well as others must adapt himself to the character of his new neighbors—the Italian in the South, the cosmopolitan immigrant everywhere in the North. . . . He can best do this by going to school with them, using the same books they use, thinking the same thoughts they think." Alluding to legacies of slavery, Jim Crow, internalized racism, and the hardening of housing segregation as Black people moved north, as well as the rapidity through which recent European immigrants were gaining the privileges of whiteness, Clarana contended that the New Negro's greatest hope lay in leveraging the social adjustments waves of new immigrants necessitate: "Where the humanizing influence of this contact is denied to them, colored youth may still insist on equality of opportunity for the broadest and fullest education that their white fellows receive."[102]

In 1915, almost a year after the outbreak of World War I in Europe, Black Harvard graduate and educator Leslie Pinckney Hill insisted that rather than abandoning Christian and democratic ideals, compromised by the hypocrisy of anti-Black racism, the New Negro must eschew violence—"all the blood-letting of Europe and Asia is teaching him this lesson anew in the thunder of howitzers"—to claim "moral and spiritual victories." As he rises to the occasion, the New Negro offers to the world a "new spiritual type" of moral honor even as endemic white bigotry threatens to unleash "a new colossal conflict."[103]

That same year, just as the migration of Southern Blacks to Northern cities accelerated, the racist New Negro narrative's national dissemination reached a pinnacle. Based on the best-selling 1905 Thomas Dixon novel, *The Clansman*, which had been adapted into a hugely successful play of the same name, D. W. Griffith's 1915 blockbuster film *The Birth of a Nation* not only celebrated the birth of the Ku Klux Klan but contributed to the Klan's spectacular revival. According to one Black newspaper, the drama represented the New Negro not as he was, "intelligent, aggressive, manly, [and] independent," but, in the spirit of demagoguery, as "having an unquenchable longing to join himself in marriage to his white contemporary."[104] Within the juggernaut of early twentieth-century white supremacist media, virtually all civil rights roads led to interracial sexual union between white women and Black men.

A year later, William Pickens seized on World War I as the crucible for Black civil rights in his book *The New Negro: His Political, Civil and Mental Status and Related Essays.* The son of former slaves and one of the founding members of the NAACP, Pickens maintained that the New Negro was still loyal to the nation but that Jim Crow discrimination and brutality had severely tested that loyalty. Calling for a "new abolitionism" to fight Jim Crow, Pickens presciently envisioned the dramatic reform of society that would follow the Great War with a New Negro figure arising in its midst.[105]

For a nation that faced the possibility of entering World War I, the treatment of the Negro under Jim Crow, Pickens argued, weakened its ability to fight. By disclaiming a hyphenated name for the race, Pickens concluded his book by assuring his readers of the Negro's loyalty: "There is no hyphen in the short word *Negro*; he is every inch American; he is not even Afro-American." And as an American, the New Negro, "the patient, unquestioning . . . proud young man," is "resolved to fight, and live or die, on the side of God and the Eternal Verities."[106]

IV. Red Summers and Black Radicalisms, 1917–1921

World War I and its immediate aftermath proved to be a crucible, but perhaps not in the way Pickens had envisioned. In July 1917, white mobs in East St. Louis, Illinois, killed, by one estimate, well over a hundred African Americans, and seven thousand terrorized Black residents fled across the Mississippi River to St. Louis. In response Marcus Garvey declared, "The . . . massacre of Monday 2nd, will go down in history as one of the bloodiest outrages against mankind for which any class of people could be held guilty."[107] If the East St. Louis Riot lit the fire forging the eighth version of the New Negro, World War I, the Russian Revolution, and the Red Summer of 1919 completed the casting process. At least twenty-six major race riots erupted in American cities in the summer of 1919, while the Tulsa race massacre of 1921 marked perhaps the "single worst incident of racial violence in American history." All the riots involved white mobs attacking Black individuals or an entire Black community for transgressing caste boundaries in acts of white racial terrorism often directly or indirectly assisted by law enforcement. Fueled by job and housing competition among veterans returning from the war, Blacks coming North as part of the Great Migration, Black veterans' demands for civil rights following the war, and the white press's race-baiting crime coverage, these riots occurred in the South and the North, the East and the West, and in urban areas and small towns.[108]

The seemingly egalitarian promise of the 1917 Russian Revolution, which many on the left viewed as a triumph of progress toward economic equality; the violence of the long Red Summer, and the widespread postwar labor unrest catalyzed a New Negro determined to fight back. In the words of Afro-Caribbean socialist Hubert Harrison, this New Negro demanded "equal justice before the law" or else "'an eye for an eye, a tooth for a tooth,' and sometimes two eyes or a half dozen teeth for one.'"[109] Deployed to recruit members into actual movements, this New Negro repeatedly appeared in print and in speeches. Connoting the revolutionary potential of the socialist, labor, or communist movements, as well as the "new" collective empowerment of their adherents, many of whom were Caribbean immigrants unaccustomed to what historian Winston James calls the "crude kick-'em-in-the-teeth discipline of Jim Crow," this New Negro assailed the brutality of racial capitalism while rejecting more moderate civil rights organizations.[110]

Born in St. Croix in the Danish West Indies, Hubert Harrison arrived in the United States in 1900 and, with his brilliant intellectual and oratorial gifts, quickly became known as the "father of Harlem radicalism." After breaking with the Socialist Party in 1914, he adopted a "race first" program and in 1916 started speaking about a "New Negro manhood movement." In 1917, two days after the East St. Louis pogrom, frustrated by what he perceived as the NAACP's obsequiousness to white allies, Harrison founded the Liberty League and the league's organ, the short-lived but successful *The Voice: A Newspaper for the New Negro*, which urged violent resistance to the white mobs. "The first Negro journal of the new dispensation," the *Voice* almost immediately attracted a sizable Black audience, reaching a peak circulation of eleven thousand; the US Justice Department began monitoring the publication. After the Red Summer of 1919, Harrison began editing the monthly *New Negro* (formerly the *Clarion*), self-described as "an organ of the international consciousness of the darker races—especially of the Negro race," which would epitomize the newly militant New Negro. Far more than their more mainstream counterparts, Harrison's Black radical publications, like others that followed, would repeatedly deploy the trope of the New Negro to recruit members. In January 1920, as Garvey's Universal Negro Improvement Association (UNIA) movement grew increasingly successful, Harrison accepted the position of associate editor of its newspaper, the *Negro World*.[111]

Shortly after migrating from the South to Harlem, Chandler Owen and A. Philip Randolph joined the Socialist Party and in 1917 launched the *Messenger*, which they proclaimed offered readers "the only magazine of scientific radicalism in the world published by Negroes!" Even before founding the Brotherhood of Sleeping Car Porters and Maids in 1925 and making the *Messenger* the union's official organ, Randolph used the idea of the New Negro repeatedly as a call to action.[112] Undeterred by Pullman Company intimidation, spying, and paternalism, the New Negro represented a leader "in this monster drive for economic freedom. He stands out as a liberator, a conqueror, one without fear," willing to stand up to the "enormous capital of the Pullman Company" to organize for a living wage and more humane working conditions. In 1928 Eugene Gordon encapsulated the *Messenger*'s mission as "birth[ing] . . . the so-called new Negro," a "youth who . . . dared to state . . . a desire for complete social equality; an admiration for the Bolshevistic experiment in Russia; and contempt for all Negroes who were less radical than the writers themselves were."[113] New Negro Women in the pages of the *Messenger*, accordingly, would "stand up and fight as the political, economic and social equals of their white sisters."[114]

Indeed, the *Messenger* cast out the previous era's New Negroes as old and unable to address the crisis of the Red Summer. In the September 1919 issue, the *Messenger* included a half-page satirical political cartoon, "Following the Advice of the 'Old Crowd' Negroes," that featured Du Bois, Robert Russa Moton (the successor to Booker T. Washington at the Tuskegee Institute after Washington died in 1915), and Emmett Jay Scott, secretary to Moton and a close adviser of Washington. On the left side of the cartoon, a white man in military uniform leads a jeering, torch-carrying mob, and wields a club to attack an already bloodied Black woman who struggles to raise herself from the ground. Another bloodied Black victim sits propped up at the base of the Statue of Liberty. On the night of July 18, 1919, in Washington, DC, over one hundred white servicemen, a "mob in uniform," wielded pipes, clubs, rocks in handkerchiefs, and pistols to attack Black people they saw on the street. The Black historian Carter G. Woodson, in fact, fled the mob on foot.[115] In the cartoon, three august "Old Negroes" propose accommodationist responses to the violence. A seated Du Bois implores, "CLOSE RANKS LET US FORGET OUR GRIEVANCES," a reference to his famous *Crisis* editorial the previous year urging Black readers to support World War I. Beside him, with hands clasped, stands Moton, who urges, "BE MODEST AND UNASSUMING!" Scott, reaching back to Moton, says, "WHEN THEY SMITE THEE ON ONE CHEEK—TURN THE OTHER." On the next page, another cartoon, "The 'New Crowd Negro' Making America Safe for Himself," features a clearly younger New Negro veteran in a speeding roadster—labeled "THE NEW NEGRO," equipped with guns firing in the front and sides, and displaying a banner commemorating infamous 1919 sites of race riots, "Longview, Texas, Washington, D.C., Chicago, ILL.—?" As he fires at the fleeing white mob, a fallen member of which is in uniform, he declares, "SINCE THE GOVERNMENT WONT STOP MOB VIOLENCE ILL TAKE A HAND." In the clouds of smoke appears the caption "GIVING THE 'HUN' A DOSE OF HIS OWN MEDICINE." Running just above the cartoon, the editors quote Woodrow Wilson's April 1918 Great War rallying cry against Germany: "FORCE, FORCE TO THE UTMOST—FORCE WITHOUT STINT OR LIMIT!" Clearly, socialism, for Randolph, offered New Negroes the organizational fighting power Black people needed to fend off the most symbolically treacherous of all white mob attacks—those by US military servicemen in uniform.

As circulation of the socialist *Messenger* grew—reaching a peak in 1919 of twenty-six thousand, with a readership, according to the editors, that was two-thirds Black and one-third white—so did the US Justice Department's fears of its influence.[116] What made it especially threatening in the eyes of federal officials was the supposed radicalism of the New Negro themes it espoused: calls for armed self-defense against white rioters, demands for social equality and legalizing interracial marriage, and support for the Industrial Workers of the World, as well as for Bolshevism. Calling the *Messenger* "the most able and the most dangerous of all Negro publications," Attorney General A. Mitchell Palmer declared that "no amount of mere quotation could serve as a full estimate" of the magazine's "evil scope" and initiated a crusade against it.[117] J. Edgar Hoover, head of the US Bureau of Investigation's new Radical Division, ramped up the campaign, adding what would become a communist-leaning *Crusader* as well as the Marcus Garvey movement as special targets. Under such government pressure, the *Crusader* ceased publication in 1922; the *Messenger* divested itself of most of its radical content by 1924, and Garvey's newspaper, the *Negro World*, by then had largely retreated from socialism.[118]

Prompted by his opposition to World War I, the Nevis-born journalist Cyril Briggs, called a man "of great physical and moral courage" by the Black communist leader Harry Haywood, founded the short-lived *Crusader* in 1918, a month after Garvey's *Negro World* appeared.[119] Although Briggs would continue to support the Universal Negro Improvement Association (UNIA) in his magazine until their bitter falling out in the early 1920s, as the *Crusader* became more avowedly procommunist—in a 1919 editorial Briggs declared, "If to fight for one's rights is to be Bolshevists, then we are Bolshevists"—they increasingly diverged politically. Formed during the brutal Red Summer of 1919 and under intense US government surveillance, Briggs launched his African Blood Brotherhood (ABB) as a secret society committed to self-defense, revolutionary Black socialism, and Black nationalism where "race-first" New Negroes were "willing to suffer martyrdom for the Cause." Although never reaching beyond roughly three thousand members, it attracted many significant Black leaders in leftist causes—including Hubert Harrison and Claude McKay, as well as Grace Campbell, likely the first Black woman to join the Communist and Socialist Parties. By 1921, Briggs and most of the leadership of the ABB had joined the Communist Party, and in 1923, the ABB was absorbed into the organization.[120]

No other Black political leader, however, used the trope more often as a rallying cry than Marcus Garvey. When Garvey launched the UNIA in Jamaica in 1914, he envisioned it as a nonpolitical organization based on the principles of fraternal cooperation, self-improvement, and Booker T. Washington–style industrial education. Yet, after Garvey arrived in New York two years later, and then, in the aftermath of the East St. Louis pogrom, the first of what would become a series of white mob rampages over the next five years, the brilliant orator and organizer soon insisted that the "new spirit of the new Negro does not seek industrial opportunity" but a "political voice."[121] For the first three years of Garvey's career in the United States, that voice was avowedly socialist. Eventually, however, and under tremendous pressure from Bureau of Investigation agents, Garvey would disassociate his movement from any political party affiliation.[122] In almost every issue of his weekly UNIA newspaper, the *Negro World*, Garvey hailed New Negroes as those who committed themselves to intellectual development, economic self-reliance, Black nationalism, the UNIA's back-to-Africa vision, and his Black Star Line steamship corporation. Through the pages of the *Negro World*, with sections later printed in French and Spanish, Garvey and his staff spread his vision to tens of thousands of dues-paying members and millions of worldwide followers, who, in turn, adapted his philosophy to meet the particular needs of their respective communities.[123]

Indeed, more than any other newspaper or periodical in the twenties, the *Negro World* explicitly hailed readers as New Negroes (by one count, the trope appears in the newspaper at least 665 times from 1921 to 1933), idolized Garvey as the supreme New Negro, and spread the UNIA's message around the globe.[124] For Joseph Raphael Ralph Casimir of the small Caribbean island of Dominica, the UNIA's New Negro fought for higher wages, better education, and lower rates of exchange. In a 1920 letter to the editor of the *Dominica Guardian*, Casimir declared, "Away with Crown Colony Rule, the time has come for the Negro to take a share in the Government of the country.

He is tired of being oppressed." Garvey's Black Star Line, meanwhile, not only promised safer passage than the native canoes relied on by most Afro-Dominicans but also transportation free of the discrimination so often endured on white-owned ships—"the cry everywhere is 'When will a Black Star Liner come to Dominica!'"[125] For Clements Musa Kadalie, founder in 1919 of the first major South African trade union, the Industrial and Commercial Workers' Union, and a year later its organ *The Black Man: A Journal Propagating the Interests of Workers throughout the African Continent*, the New Negro represented the Pan-African, transnational struggle for workers' rights, which included the "immediate return of our brothers and sisters from the land of banishment to the land of their progenitors" to prevent a "White South Africa."[126]

Yet even after Garvey's conviction for mail fraud in 1923, incarceration in 1925, and deportation in 1927, all while Alain Locke's cultural New Negro took center stage among the Black and sympathetic white elite, Garvey's legacy continued, in large part because his second wife, Amy Jacques Garvey, took charge of the movement. In fact, both his first wife, Amy Ashwood Garvey, and his second played crucial leadership roles in the UNIA and the *Negro World* and forged feminist elements within the movement's patriarchal guiding principles. For Amy Jacques Garvey, the New Negro Woman emerged as part of a global movement of increasingly emancipated women who embodied the UNIA's tenets and cultivated their minds while still publicly deferential to patriarchal norms, "wield[ing] the proper influence over" their husbands and ensuring their home's domestic purity and commitment to race motherhood. From February 1924 to June 1927, Jacques Garvey not only served as associate editor for the *Negro World* but also edited the paper's women's page, "Our Women and What They Think," which she had launched, and where her vision of New Negro Womanhood took shape.[127]

For Chicago UNIA member Eunice Lewis, writing in 1924, the New Negro Woman's "pure womanhood" and ability to "conquer the beastly side of man" meant that her influence should extend beyond the home; she desired "to work on par with men in the office as well as on the platform." The same year, UNIA organizer Saydee Parham meanwhile extolled the New Negro Woman as "at last rising to a pinnacle of power and glory so great . . . that she has actually become the central figure of all modern civilization."[128]

V. The New Negro Renaissance: Part One, 1922–1926

The next two sections of the anthology—The New Negro Renaissance, Parts One and Two—take their dates from James Weldon Johnson's prefaces to the first and second editions of his *Book of American Negro Poetry*, published in 1922 and 1931, respectively, and the publication of Sterling A. Brown's book of poetry *Southern Road* in 1932. In 1922 Johnson had called the production of "great literature and art" essential to the fight against racism, while simultaneously denouncing the use of dialect in Black poetry as "mere mutilation of English spelling and pronunciation," possessing but two stops, "humor and pathos." After declaring in 1931 that "the passing of traditional dialect as poetry is almost complete," Johnson would do an about-face just a year later in his 1932 preface to Brown's *Southern Road*, heralding Brown's poetic diction as the "common, racy, living speech of the Negro in certain phases of *real* life" and, as such, a "distinctive contribution to American poetry."[129] Just two years later, in Nancy Cunard's *Negro: An Anthology*, clearly a signifying riff on Alain Locke's *The New Negro*, Locke himself celebrated Brown as the "New Negro folk-poet" whose work ushered in a "new era in Negro folk expression."[130] The Harlem Renaissance was over.

While Cunard's anthology includes nine writers whom Locke had included in *The New Negro*, it has a decidedly more insistent political thrust—Cunard writes in her foreword that "Langston Hughes is the revolutionary voice of liberation"—auguring the social realism that would predominate in the 1930s.[131] Whereas Locke had advocated social change through artistic achievement per se, Cunard advocated more explicit direct political engagement. As Henry Louis Gates, Jr. concludes, "Even a casual reading of its pages makes clear that a new discursive period in African American literary history had begun."[132]

The New Negro Renaissance evolved, in fact, via a series of literary events marking not only its emergence but also its ideological and gendered divisions. When the University of Chicago–trained sociologist and *Opportunity* magazine editor Charles S. Johnson organized a banquet on March 24, 1924, at New York City's integrated Civic Club in downtown Manhattan, ostensibly to celebrate the publication of Jessie Fauset's 1924 novel *There Is Confusion*, he envisioned an event where the white and mostly male literary establishment would applaud and publish the New Negro literary artists in their midst. As master of ceremonies, however, Alain Locke, with Charles Johnson's approval, deftly turned attention away from the almost forty-two-year-old Fauset and what he saw as her "old" emphasis on the Black elite to younger voices more in keeping with his modernist vision. At the end of the evening, *Survey Graphic* editor Paul Kellogg invited Charles Johnson to devote an entire issue of the magazine to the evening's theme. Johnson then asked Locke to edit what would become the famous March 1925 issue, which excluded Fauset's work.[133] A decade later, Fauset, who had played a pivotal role in the movement as literary editor of the *Crisis* from 1919 to 1926, still winced at Locke's *Opportunity* dinner slight and the wresting of power it signified. In a letter to the now New Negro icon, she recalled the "consummate cleverness with which you that night as toastmaster strove to keep speech and comment away from the person for whom the occasion was meant."[134] Although Fauset had been among the first to publish some of the most important writers of the Harlem Renaissance—namely Jean Toomer and Langston Hughes—Alain Locke and Charles S. Johnson's *Opportunity* would now take the lead.[135]

On a warm Tuesday evening in August 1925, at more than a two-hour walk from the Civic Club but just fifteen minutes away from Garvey's Liberty Hall, A. Philip Randolph hosted what New York City's *Amsterdam News* called the "greatest labor mass meeting ever held" in the grand auditorium of the Imperial Lodge of the Elks. Almost five hundred porters, as well as a contingent of Pullman Company spies, assembled to hear the charismatic Randolph detail the "wrongs, insults and indignities inflicted upon the porters." George Schuyler followed, offering "clever quips and jokes at the expense of the Pullman Company [that brought] gales of laughter." Despite Pullman Company threats and intimidation, Randolph's New Negroes signed the union application form in droves and that night officially organized the Brotherhood of Sleeping Car Porters and Maids. For years afterward, in advertisements, cartoons and articles, Randolph recruited prospective members by portraying the Pullman Company bloated with profits and angling to dissuade prospective New Negroes from joining what the *Pittsburgh Courier* saw as among "the best traditions of militant labor unionism." Under Randolph's leadership, in 1937 the Brotherhood became the first Black labor union officially recognized by a major US corporation.[136]

Four months after Randolph rallied labor activists in Harlem, Harvard-trained philosopher and "midwife" to the Harlem Renaissance Alain Locke published his signature opus, *The New Negro: An Interpretation*, a revision and expansion of his groundbreaking March 1925 special issue of the *Survey Graphic*, ushering in the most iconic variation of the figure. While Randolph and Locke both celebrated the New Negro to signal a change in consciousness, Locke rooted his panegyric to Black creative genius, cosmopolitanism, and culture rooted in an Afrocentric folk tradition.[137]

Featuring bold Africanist designs by Aaron Douglas, European modernist illustrations by Winold Reiss, and a jazzy but cautious assemblage of many of the most acclaimed "younger generation" of New Negro writers evoking the cosmopolitan "great race-welding" that is Harlem, Locke's anthology defiantly positioned the New Negro as culturally modern but careful to avoid offense. It includes few references to lynching, no references to A. Philip Randolph or the *Messenger*, scattered references almost exclusively disparaging to Marcus Garvey, and, while a number of the writers Locke included were gay or bisexual, no explicitly queer content. Ignoring earlier versions of the trope, Locke staked his claim in his introductory essay that the New Negro channeled all the positive energy of newness—the "new psychology," "new spirit," "new democracy," "his new internationalism," and despite Jim Crow, "a significant and satisfying new phase of group development, and with it a spiritual Coming of Age."[138]

Even as Locke briefly praised Garvey for making Pan-Africanism central to his movement, he clearly saw Garvey's messianic theatricality as one of the "quixotic radicalisms" to be "cured" by his New Negro's call for "argosies of cultural exchange and enlightenment" sharing the best of Black American art, literature, and music. While Garvey provoked outrage among the Black literary elite by his commitment to "race purity" and segregation—going so far as to meet the Klan's grand wizard, Edward Young Clarke, in 1922—Locke's New Negro sought to prove Black openness to a "new social understanding . . . tearing down the "'spite-wall' that the intellectuals built over the 'color-line.'"[139]

In the bitterest of ironies, in the same month that Locke published his anthology, over thirty thousand Ku Klux Klan members marched down Pennsylvania Avenue in Washington, DC, robed but unmasked in the August 1925 heat, in what the *Washington Post* reported as "one of the greatest demonstrations this city has ever known."[140] Locke hardly needed such a visceral reminder that he had launched the New Negro amid the Klanification of America. Every week a sea of anti-Black Old Negro stereotypes sold tens of thousands of books, tickets, newspapers, and magazines. Indeed, even as Locke's famous *Survey Graphic* issue presented its iconic cover of a realistic image of a Black male face poised not to please but in thought, marking a turning point in New Negro image making, the back cover of the same issue, Adam McKible points out, offered the Old Negro to perhaps an equally eager audience. An advertisement for R. Emmet Kennedy's *Black Cameos*, with a silhouette of the uncle stereotype, promised readers the "true spirit of the Negro as he is still to be found away from the sophistication of town life."[141]

The white and Black press around the globe celebrated Locke's achievement, which helped to build the race consciousness at the core of the Négritude anticolonial literary movement. Writing in the Parisian newspaper *La dépêche africaine* in early 1928, the Martinican writer Jeanne (Jane) Nardal described Locke's anthology as a "pioneer" in building the "race spirit" of Black internationalism: "that peculiar effect of the colonization: that of linking together, of unifying in a racial solidarity."[142] She would later write to Locke requesting permission to translate his collection into French, and he readily agreed.[143]

VI. The New Negro Renaissance: Part Two, 1927–1932

The younger generation of American Black writers, however, chafed at Locke's strictures against content that risked perpetuating anti-Black stereotypes or could be perceived as indecent or radical. Langston Hughes's "Bad New Negroes" were at once more likely to offend, avant-garde, leftist, and, in Bruce Nugent's case, flamboyantly gay. Unlike Locke's *New Negro*, Wallace Thurman's first and only issue of the magazine *Fire!!* (1926)—"the soul an inward flush of fire . . . flesh on fire—on fire in the furnace of life blazing"—eschewed uplift narratives. Instead, it unabashedly offered readers Nugent's explicit homoerotic love scenes, Wallace Thurman's depictions of prostitution, Zora Neale Hurston's "dirty secret" of colorism, and Langston Hughes's bitter, despondent elevator operator. In Thurman's concluding essay, he defends perhaps the most inflammatory of any New Negro Jazz Age novel, the white author Carl Van Vechten's bombshell *Nigger Heaven* (1926), whose title alone ensured its condemnation in almost every corner of the Black press. Even though Locke's anthology would become the center of the New Negro Renaissance literary canon, the writing and ethos of these "Bad New Negroes" reflected the sexual and political edginess of a restless Black avant-garde.

By 1926, the flapper version of the New Negro Woman dominated the Black press—almost every issue of the nationally circulating *Pittsburgh Courier* featured some version of the flapper on its front page—but, still, most Black women writers eschewed New Negro Woman rhetoric. Instead, for civil rights activist Sadie T. M. Alexander, the New Negro Woman was the emancipated woman. For the civil rights activist, suffragist, and writer Alice Dunbar Nelson, she was a whirling dervish, whose transgressions evoked masculine excess: "All over this jazz-mad, radio-crazed hysteric nation," she had claimed "masculine prerogatives . . . governors who are in danger of impeachment, . . . bandits, bank robbers, embezzlers, female Ponzis, high flyers in finance." For Juanita Ellsworth, a graduate of the University of Southern California and founder of the Sigma Delta Theta chapter on that campus, she was the "woman of the West." Writing in 1929 for the short-lived Black-owned Los Angeles magazine *Flash*, Ellsworth notes that Western women enjoy significantly more freedom—even the freedom to keep their names after marriage—than their sisters elsewhere: "Freedom of speech, dress, manners, customs, and business opportunities. . . . If a woman chooses to wear knickers or trousers or mannish suits and vests, collars and ties, tuxedoes or Stetson hats, unless her fair sisters raise an objection, none is forthcoming."[144]

At least one Black newspaper, however, the *Philadelphia Tribune*, questioned whether Locke's New Negro was perhaps too cultured, a "knight at the tea table" who had gone "flabby" thinking only of "layer cake" and "pink teas." During the first Red Scare, "pink teas" connoted "weak" followers of Bolshevism who, because they "supposedly lacked the courage to become full "Reds," were therefore "sissy Bolshevists." The reading man, in turn, as historian Marlon Bryan Ross notes, "inadvertently amplifies the sissy-boy's gender deviance." The misogyny and red baiting of the "pink teas" satire was further compounded by the feminization of the Old Negro Uncle Tom racist stereotype, enshrined in academic circles when the "father" of sociology, Robert Ezra Park, declared that the "genial, sunny" Negro was "the lady among the races."[145]

The cartoon accompanying the article "Pink Teas" in the *Philadelphia Tribune* shows a light-skinned mustached dandy seated with a cigarette holder and teacup and surrounded by bobbed-hair women. His chair is labeled "THE NEW NEGRO ('SELF-STYLED')," and the cartoon's larger caption reads "He Had Better Go to Work." As the *Tribune*'s jest invoked the era's pervasive homophobia—a charge particularly ironic given that, as Henry Louis Gates, Jr. writes, "the Harlem Renaissance was surely as gay as it was black"—it also reveals anxiety that Locke's New Negro had strayed too far from the "hard practical things of life"—"business enterprises and political achievement."[146] Even before the *Philadelphia Tribune*'s cartoon, in fact, Alice Dunbar Nelson had expressed similar sentiment. In 1926 she questioned whether Locke's young urban New Negroes demonstrated the necessary grit and cautioned that the spirit of the New Negro existed not only in the "youthful poets and artists in the metropolis" who "age rather young" but perhaps more powerfully in elderly Black Southern farmers who, with "the indomitable will that conquers time," had gone to school to learn to read and write.[147]

In works directed at an interracial or predominantly white audience, some writers insisted that in tandem with the New Negro, a New White was striving for an antiracist consciousness. For the white pacifist and socialist Devere Allen, when the "new white" has achieved "victory over ignorance, superstition, greed, and fear," the fingers of his hand, instead of a symbol of voluntary segregation in Booker T. Washington's Atlanta Exposition address, "fall very naturally together" in fellowship with those of his brother, the New Negro.[148] For the Afro-Cuban journalist and public leader Gustavo Urrutia, the New White, like the New Negro, is not fooled by romantic notions of a supposedly raceless, equitable Cuban nation but instead acknowledges how Negroes have been "cheated out of their economic and social rights, left to starve to death, and dissolved in surrounding whiteness." Together with the New Negro, Urrutia's New White works on behalf of a "new liberating crusade for social and economic justice for all the inhabitants of our country."[149]

After the stock market crashed in October 1929 and the Great Depression took hold, Black people around the nation bore the brunt of the era's economic collapse. By 1930, 25 percent of the Harlem population was unemployed. "Last hired" and "first fired," African American residents in Harlem saw their median income in 1932 plunge to 43.6 percent of what it had been before the crash, while racial segregation continued to drive up already disproportionately high housing costs. As white men increasingly claimed semiskilled or unskilled jobs formerly held by African American men, Black men scrambled for whatever work they could get. As the Depression wore on, the desperation for work only worsened. As the National Urban League's industrial relations director T. Arnold Hill observed, "At no time in the history of the Negro since slavery has his economic and social outlook seemed so discouraging."[150]

In December 1930, Ella Jo Baker and George Schuyler launched the Young Negroes' Co-operative League, which was dedicated to establishing a network of credit unions, wholesale cooperative housing ventures, and stores. Castigating the older generation of race leaders for promoting a disastrous "bourgeois ideology," Schuyler's 1932 organizational pamphlet, *Appeal to Young Negroes*, repeatedly denounced the failures of "old Negroes" and urged younger ones to claim their rightful "economic power" and join the "ultra democratic" and gender-egalitarian Co-operative League.[151]

VII. The Depression, the New Deal, and Ethiopia, 1932–1937

Although Baker and Schuyler's Co-operative League was short-lived—officially ending in 1933, the same year the newly elected president of the United States, Democrat Franklin Delano Roosevelt, launched the New Deal—it reflected another revolution in New Negro ideology. Even before the New Deal, Black voters were growing increasingly frustrated with Republican president Herbert Hoover's inability to alleviate Black suffering during the Depression. Writing for the *Crisis* in 1935, Ella Baker and Marvel Cooke recounted how female Black domestic workers were driven by poverty to sell their labor to unscrupulous "Mrs. Simon Legree" in the "Bronx slave market": "Under a rigid watch she is permitted to scrub floors on her bended knees, to hang precariously from window sills cleaning window after window, or to strain and sweat over heavy blankets, spreads, and furniture covers." If she was fortunate, she might be "rewarded" a dollar for her day's toil.[152] Despite Zora Neale Hurston's 1937 masterpiece, *Their Eyes Were Watching God*, and African American women's prominent activist roles during the 1930s—most notably those of Ella Baker, Mary McLeod Bethune, and Black nationalist Mittie Maude Lena Gordon—by the early 1930s, when the effects of the Depression hit hardest, New Woman and New Negro Woman rhetoric subsided. Given the dire financial situation, the flapper's devil-may-care jazz-age pleasures had lost at least some of their vogue.

Roosevelt's New Deal programs accelerated the shift to the Democratic Party, which Robert Vann, editor of one of the nation's leading Black newspapers, the *Pittsburgh Courier*, famously summarized: "I see millions of Negroes turning the picture of Abraham Lincoln to the wall."[153] Notwithstanding endemic discrimination in most New Deal agencies, the Public Works Administration, under the leadership of Harold L. Ickes, was considered a success; for many Black Americans, its abbreviation, PWA, stood for "Poppa's working again."[154] And even though Mississippi had one of the worst records of employing Black people in New Deal programs, Clister L. Johnson, the supreme lecturer of Yazoo, Mississippi's fraternal organization the Afro-American Sons and Daughters, declared, "The New Deal has given the New Negro a better chance to develop than any other administration." In the presidential election of 1936, the vast majority of African Americans voted for the Democratic Party, the first time a Democratic presidential candidate had won a majority of the Black vote.[155]

Concomitant with this Black Democratic shift and embrace of New Deal work programs, Black writers increasingly depicted the New Negro as a grassroots, direct action organizer. In 1933, when the white-owned Hamburger Grill in Washington, DC, fired its three Black employees and hired three white people to replace them, recent college graduate John Davis organized a boycott. Together with Belford V. Lawson Jr. and M. Franklin Thorne, they formed the New Negro Alliance, which fought for employment equity and higher wages, eventually winning a Supreme Court victory against the Sanitary Grocery Company in 1938 that affirmed their right to picket the grocery chain for refusing to hire Black workers. Only their more militant strategy of picketing, boycotting ("Don't Buy Where You Can't Work"), and pursuing court victories promised change.[156]

Meanwhile, for the Afro-Cuban intellectual and civic leader Gustavo Urrutia, socialism offered the best hope for greater economic opportunity for all Cubans, regardless of race. According to Urrutia, the New Negro had discovered that "even genuine liberal democracy would not be able to guarantee collective economic and social justice, because it is essentially individualistic and plutocratic. He has pointed himself toward the promotion of some form of socialism . . . compatible with our own character and our international relations." Although he was not a Marxist, Urrutia promoted socialism, in the words of Anne Marie Guarnera, "as the 'natural' choice for those who have come to recognize their subaltern status within Cuban society."[157]

When on October 3, 1935, the Italian National Fascist Party dictator Benito Mussolini invaded Ethiopia, one of only two independent African nations, Black people around the world—and especially in the United States, where Ethiopia held special religious, political, and historical significance—suffered yet another blow. As Italian planes bombed villages and dropped poison gas, and as Ethiopian emperor Haile Selassie appealed in vain to the League of Nations for assistance, African Americans rallied to Ethiopia's defense, raising money, lobbying, protesting, and training to aid in battle. Given its abiding principle of "Africa for the Africans," Garvey's UNIA stood at the forefront of campaigns to fortify Ethiopia's defense.[158]

In May 1936, when Ethiopia's defeat seemed all but assured and after news reached Black US residents that Italy had conducted mass executions of Ethiopian patriots, hundreds of African Americans attacked Italian-owned Harlem businesses.[159] In the midst of this fervor, George Schuyler published two serialized New Negro novels in what had become the most popular Black newspaper in the United States, the *Pittsburgh Courier*, that seemed directly at odds not only with his own previous condemnations of fascism but with leading antifascist Black intellectual sentiment.[160] Writing for the *Courier* in August 1935, Schuyler declared that there was virtually no "difference between Fascist Germany or Fascist Italy and 'Communist' Russia. All three are ruthless dictatorships. All three brutally suppress all minorities. . . . All three are gigantic Ku Klux Klans triumphant." Black socialist Frank Crosswaith agreed. The New Negro, he wrote in 1936, must fight the "march of Fascism, Hitlerism and other foes of civilized progress."[161]

Yet, like his nemesis Marcus Garvey, Schuyler would, at least publicly, depict a New Negro as what Mark Christian Thompson calls a "generic fascist": one who celebrates nationalism to unite a disenfranchised populace, charismatic authoritarian leadership, militarized mass mobilization, and violence and masculinity as domination.[162] Even though in a private letter Schuyler called his writings "The Black Internationale: Story of Black Genius against the World" (November 1936–July 1937) and "Black Empire: An Imaginative Story of a Great New Civilization in Modern Africa" (October 1937–April 1938) "hokum and hack of the purest vein," he later endorsed the New Negro vision within them.[163] In the serials, Schuyler's New Negro dictator and leader of the Black Internationale, Dr. Belsidus, launches a "world-wide Negro revolutionary organization" to forge a "Great New Civilization in Modern Africa," a "new religion . . . for suppressed colored people," an "amazing new clinic and diet kitchen," a "new electric steel plant," "new stratosphere planes," and a "new kind of [biological] warfare." Early in the series, Belsidus declares, "Christians, Communists, Fascists and

Nazis were at first called crazy. Success made them sane." Dr. Belsidus enjoins his recruit, "We must be hard. We must be cruel. We must be unrelenting, neither giving nor asking quarter, until either we or the white race is definitely subjugated or even exterminated." Eventually the brilliant Belsidus deploys biological and chemical weapons to kill thousands of Europeans.[164]

Readers loved the serials, with some asking if they could join the Black Internationale, and Schuyler seized the moment. Writing for the *Crisis* in August 1938, Schuyler defined the newest New Negro as one who "believes that to combat this White International of oppression a Black Internationale of liberation is necessary. . . . No longer ignorant, terrorized or lacking confidence, he waits, and schemes and plans. He is the Damoclean sword dangling over the white world."[165]

*   *   *

Appeals to the New Negro did not end in 1938—the trope would be repeatedly invoked until 1969, when the rise of the Black Power movement resulted in the jettisoning of "Negro" into the dustbin of all that was outdated and tainted by Jim Crow—but the New Black Man quickly took its place. When in October 1995 Minister Louis Farrakhan led tens of thousands of what he called New Black Men to Washington, DC, in the Million Man March, he lay claim to a myth-making "newness" that he knew would resonate.

As flags of "new" Black perspectives in the ongoing fight against systemic discrimination and state-sanctioned anti-Black violence, often validated and propelled by prominent voices in the media and online, the New Negro / Black Man still demands a response. In a consumerist age where the "new" is invariably used to sell products, this trope repudiates, warns, and rallies as it calls on audiences to critically remember the past and summon the resolve to build a better future.[166] Even as proponents of the New Negro commanded a hearing and offered hope for a more just society, the many versions and long history of the trope—more varied and deployed far longer than any other modern "new" trope I know of—suggest not only profound resilience—mantras of courage and unity—but also, in response to Fascist Italy's brutal invasion of Ethiopia, a longing for lethal retribution.

As readers of our collection map their own interpretations of the trope, seeing echoes of previous versions in supposed new renditions and charting the figure's changes through time and across distance, we hope they will read the anthology's notes and author biographies to help better envision the people who authored these texts and the specificity of the historical moments from which they arose. The Black writers in this volume (and some of the white ones), to borrow Ta'Nehesi Coates's words, know all too well that the West is a "house [that] is haunted, that there is blood in the bricks and ghosts in the attic."[167] Our bitterly divided present reminds us that this house, too, often garish in its wealth and brutal in its power, hails us all repeatedly with the promise of a greater future, free of an inconvenient past and its history of plunder.

PART I

THE NEW SOUTH AND THE NEW NEGRO, 1885–1894

Alexander Crummell

"The Need of New Ideas and New Aims for a New Era"

Address to the graduating class of Storer College, Harpers Ferry, West Virginia, 1885[1]

Address.

I TAKE it for granted that the young men and women who close their pupilage here to-day are thinking not only of their own personal life desires, but, also, of the destinies of the people with whom they are connected. In such a place as this, full of the most thrilling memories in the history of our race, it seems impossible that any of you could possibly pass over such thoughts. The very hills here seem breezy with the memories and the purposes of old John Brown. And so tragic and so august are those memories and purposes, so vivid, too, is the imagination of man, that there is danger not only that the youthful, but even the elder, mind should be carried back with constant and absorbing interest, especially in those memories and purposes.

But let me remind you here that, while indeed we do live in two worlds, the world of the past and the world of the future, DUTY lies in the future. It is in life as it is on the street: the sentinel DUTY, like the policeman, is ever bidding man "Pass on!" We can, indeed, get inspiration and instruction in the *yesterdays* of existence, but we cannot healthily live in them. We can send back sorrows and repentances to the past. We can, by the magic touch of Fancy, summon the tragedies and commedies [*sic*] of by-gone days; but the sense of obligation, the ideas of responsibility, all pertain to the time to come. It is on this account that I beg to call your attention to-day, to—"THE NEED OF NEW IDEAS AND NEW AIMS FOR A NEW ERA."

The subject divides itself in two heads:—
1st. The *need* suggested, and 2nd, the *aims for a new era*, which shall meet the need.

I choose this topic because it seems to me that there is an irresistible tendency in the Negro mind in this land to dwell morbidly and absorbingly upon the servile past. The urgent needs of the present, the fast-crowding and momentous interests of the future appear to be forgotten. Duty for to-day, hope for the morrow, are ideas which seem oblivious to even leading minds among us. I fear there is a general incapacity to reach forward to a position and the acquisitions which are in advance of our times. Enter the schools, and the theme which too generally occupies the youthful mind is some painful memory of servitude. Listen to the voices of the pulpit, and how large a portion of its utterances are pitched in the same doleful strain! Send a man to Congress, and observe how seldom possible it is for him to speak upon any other topic than slavery. We are fashioning our life too much after the conduct of the children of Israel. Long after the exodus from bondage, long after the destruction of Pharaoh and his host, they kept turning back, in memory of the longings, after Egypt, when they should have kept both eye and aspiration bent toward the land of promise and of freedom.

Now I know, my brethren, that all this is natural to man. God gave us judgment, fancy and memory, and we cannot free ourselves from the inherence of these or of any other faculty of our being. But the great poet tells us that "man is a being who looks before and after." There is a capacity in human nature for prescience. We were made to live in the future as well as in the past. The qualities both of hope and imagination carry us to the regions which lie beyond us. But both hope and imagination are qualities which seem dismissed from the common mind among us; and many of our leaders of thought seem to settle down in the dismal swamps of dark and distressful memory.

And nothing can be more hurtful for any people than such a habit as this. For to dwell upon repulsive things, to hang upon that which is dark, direful, and saddening, tends, first of all, to morbidity and degeneracy. Accustom this race to constant reminiscence of its degradation and its sorrow, bring before your own minds or the minds of the rising generation, as a perpetual study and contemplation, the facts of servitude and inferiority, and its mind will, of necessity, be ever

> Sickled o'er with the pale caste of thought;

And there will be a constant tendency to

> Nurse the dreadful appetite of death!

And next to this comes the intellectual narrowness which results from a narrow groove of thought. For there are few things which tend so much to dwarf a people as the constant dwelling upon personal sorrows and interests, whether they be real or imaginary. We have illustrations of this fact both at home and abroad. The Southern people of this nation have given as evident signs of genius and talent as the people of the North.

If we go back to Colonial times, if we revert to the early history of the nation, we see in them, as conspicuous evidence of intellectual power, in law, in capability of government, in jurisprudence, in theology, in poetry, and in art, as among their more northern brethren. But for nigh three generations they gave themselves up to morbid and fanatical anxieties upon the subject of slavery. To that one single subject they gave the whole bent and sharpness of their intellect. And history records the direful result. For nigh sixty years have "laws and letters, art and learning," died away; and we can hardly discover the traces of any conspicuous genius or originality among them. So, too, the people of Ireland. For a century and more they have been indulging in the expensive luxury of sedition and revolution. As a portion of the great Celtic people of Europe, they are an historic race, alike in character and in genius. They are mercurial, poetic and martial, and in some of the lands of their heritage they have shown large powers for governmental control. But in Ireland, sterility has been a conspicuous feature of their intellectual life. The mind of the whole nation has been dwarfed and shriveled by morbid concen-

tration upon an intense and frenzied sense of political wrong, and an equally intense and frenzied purpose of retaliation. And commerce, industry, and manufactures, letters and culture, have died away from them. And while, indeed, shrieking constantly for freedom, their idea of freedom has become such an impracticable and contemptuous thing it has challenged the sneer of the poet, who terms it

> The school-boy heat,
> The blind hysterics of the Celt.

If men *will* put themselves in narrow and straightened grooves, if they will morbidly divorce themselves from large ideas and noble convictions, they are sure to bring distress, pettiness, and misery into their being; for the mind of man was made for things grand, exalted, and majestic.

For 200 years the misfortune of the black race has been the confinement of its mind in the pent-up prison of human bondage. The morbid, absorbing and abiding recollection of that condition—what is it but the continuance of that same condition, in memory and dark imagination? Dwell upon, reproduce, hold on to it with all its incidents, make its history the sum and acme of thought, and then, of a surety, you put up a bar to progress, and eventually produce that unique and fossilated state which is called "arrested development." For it is impossible for a people to progress in the conditions of civilization whose thought and interest are swallowed up in morbid memories, or narrowed to the groove of a single idea or purpose. I am asked, perchance, would you have us as a people forget that we have been an oppressed race? I reply, that God gave us memory, and it is impossible to forget the slavery of our race. The memory of this fact may ofttimes serve as a stimulant to high endeavor. It may act, by contrast, as a suggestive of the best behests of freedom. We are *forced*, not seldom, to revert to our former servile state in defense of the race, against the unreasoning traducers who, not unfrequently, impute to us a *natural* inferiority, which is simply the result of that former servile state. What I would fain have you guard against is not the memory of slavery, but the constant *recollection* of it, as the commanding thought of a new people, who should be marching on to the broadest freedom of thought in a new and glorious present, and a still more magnificent future. You will notice here that there is a broad distinction between memory and recollection. Memory, you will observe, is a passive act of the mind. It is the necessary and unavoidable entrance, storage and recurrence of facts and ideas to the understanding and the consciousness.

Recollection, however, is the actual seeking of the facts, is the painstaking endeavor of the mind to bring them back again to consciousness. The natural recurrence of the idea or the fact of slavery is that which cannot be faulted. What I object to is the unnecessary recollection of it. This pernicious habit I protest against as most injurious and degrading. As slavery was a degrading thing, the constant recalling of it to the mind serves, by the law of association, to degradation. Words are vital things. They are always generative of life or death. They cannot enter the soul as passive and inoperative things. Archbishop Trench, referring to the brutal poverty of the language of the savage, says—"There is nothing that so effectually tends to keep him in the depth to which he has fallen. You cannot impart to any man more than the words which he understands either now contain, or can be made, intelligibly to him, to contain. Language is as truly on one side *the limit and restraint of thought*, as on the other side that which feeds and unfolds it."[2] My desire is that we should escape "the limit and restraint" of both the *word* and the *thought* of slavery. As a people, we have had an exodus from it. We have been permitted by a gracious Providence to enter the new and exalted pathways of freedom. The thought, the routine, the usages, and calculations of that old system are dead things; absolutely alien from the conditions in which life presents itself to us in our disenthralled and uplifted state. We have new conditions of life and new relations in society. The great facts of family, of civil life, of the Church, of the State, meet us at every turn; not lightly and as ephemeral things, but as permanent and abiding realities; as organic institutions, to be transmitted, in our blood to live, to the latest generations. From these relations spring majestic duties which come upon us

With a weight—
Heavy as death, and deep almost as life.

These changed circumstances bring to us an immense budget of new thoughts, new ideas, new projects, new purposes, new ambitions, of which our fathers never thought. We have hardly space in our brains for the old conditions of life. God "has called into existence a new world," to use the language of CANNING, "to redress the balance of the old."

We have need, therefore, of new adjustments in life. The law of fitness comes up before us just now with tremendous power, and we are called upon, as a people, to change the currents of life, and to shift them into new and broader channels.

Says an old poet:—

The noble soul by age grows lustier,
Her appetite and her digestion mend;
We cannot hope to feed and pamper her
With women's milk and pap unto the end!
Provide you manlier diet!

I have thus attempted to show the need "of new ideas, new aims and new ambitions for the new era" on which we have entered.

2. And now, in the second place, allow me to make the attempt to suggest some of these new ideas which I think should be entertained by us.

Before passing to them, let me say that it is hardly possible to ignore one or two of the especial ambitions which now-a-days command wide attention in certain classes among us, and in which I fear we are making great mistakes. I do lament the political ambitions which seem the craze of very many young minds among us. Not, indeed, because I expect the continuance of that caste in politics, which is the extension of that social caste which is the disgrace of American society; but because I dislike always to witness a useless expenditure of forces. For, for a long time, the political ambitions of colored men are sure to end in emptiness. And, if so, men will waste energies and powers which might be expended profitably in other directions. I expect, I desire, and when the fitting time arrives, it will be ours then to demand *all* the prerogatives and *all* the emoluments which belong to American citizenship, according to our fitness and our ability; and without let or hindrance, because of race or former condition. At the same time, I must remind you here that no new people leap suddenly and spontaneously into Senatorial chairs or Cabinet positions. So narrow have been the limitations of our culture, so brief, too, the period of our opportunity, that it is impossible, if even we had the highest genius, that we should mount the high rounds of the ladder of judicial or statesmanlike capacity. There is no such thing possible as intuitive apprehension of state-craft or the extemporaneous solution of the intricate problems of law. The road by which a people reach grand administrative ability is a long road, now full of deep ruts, and now formidable with its steep acclivities, jagged and rugged in all its pathways, and everywhere obstructed with thorns and briers.

The only means by which its formidable difficulties may be overcome are time, and arduous labor, and rugged endurance, and the quiet apprenticeship in humble duties, and patient waiting, and the clear demonstration of undoubted capacities. All these I am certain the black man of this country can eventually present as racial qualities. But it is well to remember that they are not the product of a day; that they cannot be made to spring up, gourd-like, in a night season. And hence, you will take no offense if I venture to say that you can leave, for a *little while* at least, all idea of being President of the United States, or even of being sent as Minister to the Court of St. James.

Equally skeptical am I as to the manifest desire which I see in many quarters for addiction to aesthetical culture as a special vocation of the race in this country. It is an aptitude, I acknowledge, constitutional to the race, and it cannot be ignored. After two hundred years'

residence in the higher latitudes, we are still a tropical race; and the warmth of the central regions constantly discovers itself in voice and love of harmonies, both those which appeal to the eye by color, and those which affect the sensibilities through the ear. Such an aboriginal quality is not to be disregarded, and I do not disregard it. All I desire to say is that there is something higher in life than inclination, however indigenous it may be. Taste and elegance, albeit natural cravings, are always secondary to the things absolute and necessary.

There are circumstances constantly occurring wherein we are bound to ignore the strongest bent of nature and yield to the manifest currents of Providence. There are, moreover, primal duties in life, to which all other things must give way. Art and culture must yield to these needs. It is not necessary that we should debase our natural qualities. But style and beauty are secondary to duty and moral responsibility. Men cannot live on flowers. Society cannot be built up upon the strength which comes from rose-water. While I have the firmest conviction that the black race in this country will, eventually, take rank among the very highest in the several spheres of art, I am equally convinced that the great demand of *this* day is for the homely industries among us; that a premature addiction to it will be morally disastrous, that, as a people, we should be careful to avoid a useless expenditure of our strength and our resources.

What, then, are the special needs of this race? What are the grand necessities which call for the earliest recognition and solicitude?

We find our answer to these queries in the discovery of the deadliest breaches made in the character of our people. We all recognize the evident harm we have suffered in the times of servitude; and hence arises the duty of seeking reparation for them. But to this end we must single out the sorest calamities and the deadliest wounds these injuries have left behind.

Now I do not ignore the intellectual evils which have fallen upon us. Neither am I indifferent to the political disasters we are still suffering. But when I take a general survey of our race in the United States I cannot avoid the conclusion,

1st. That there are evils which lie deeper than intellectual neglect or political injury; and 2nd, that to pass over the deeper maladies which destroy a man or a people, to attend to evils less virulent in their effects, shows the greatest unwisdom. "That the soul should be without knowledge is not good;" but wide attention *is* given to the schooling and instruction of the black population of the land; and there need be no fear that the race can relapse into its former ignorance and benightedness. And next, with regard to political rights,—they are grand prerogatives, and to be highly prized. But do not forget that manhood has been reached even under great civil deprivations. Even in the times of the Caesars, St. Paul could exhort men in "the city of God"—"Quit ye like men, be strong!"[3] And the first Christians, under greater disabilities than ours, were the grandest of their kind.

The *three* special points of weakness in our race at this time are, I apprehend:—

1. THE STATUS OF THE FAMILY.
2. THE CONDITIONS OF LABOR.
3. THE ELEMENT OF MORALS.

It is my firm conviction that it is our duty to address ourselves more earnestly to the duties involved in these considerations than to any and all other considerations.

1st. THE STATUS OF THE FAMILY.

I shall not pause to detail the calamities which slavery has entailed upon our race in the domain of the family. Every one knows how it has pulled down every pillar and shattered every priceless fabric. But now we have begun the life of freedom, we should attempt the repair of this, the noblest of all the structures of human life. For the basis of all human progress and of all civilization is the family. Despoil the idea of family, assail rudely its elements, its framework and its essential principles, and nothing but degeneration and barbarism can come to any people. Just here, then, we have got to begin the work of reconstruction and up-building. Nothing, next to religion, can compare with the work

which is to be done in this sphere. Placed beside this, all our political anxieties are but a triviality. For if you will think but for a moment all that is included in this word *family*, you will see at once that it is the root idea of all civility, of all the humanities, of all organized society. For, in this single word are included all the loves, the cares, the sympathies, the solicitudes of parents and wives and husbands; all the active industries, the prudent economies and the painful self-sacrifices of households; all the sweet memories, the gentle refinement, the pure speech and the godly anxieties of womanhood; all the endurance, the courage and the hardy toil of men; all the business capacity and the thrifty pertinacity of trades and artisanship and mechanism; and all the moral and physical contributions of multitudinous habitations to the formation of towns and communities and cities, for the formation of states, commonwealth, churches and empires. All these have their roots in the family. Alas! how widely have these traits and qualities been lost to our race in this land! How numerous are the households where they have never been known or recognized! How deficient in manifold quarters, even now, a clear conception of the grandeur of the idea of family! And yet this is the beginning of every people's true life. See where the forerunner of the Christian system aimed to plant the germs of the rising faith of Jesus—"And he shall turn the heart of the fathers to the children, and the heart of the children to the fathers."[4] For the beginning of all organized society is the family! The school, the college, the professions, suffrage, civil office, are all valuable things; but what are they compared to the FAMILY?

Here, then, where we have suffered the greatest of our disasters, is a world-wide field for thought and interest, for intellectual anxieties and the most intelligent effort.

2nd. THE CONDITIONS OF LABOR.

Turn to another and, in its material aspects, a kindred subject. I refer to the *industrial conditions* of the black race in this nation. No topic is exciting more interest and anxiety than the labor question. Almost an angry contest is going on upon the relations of capital to labor. Into this topic all the other kindred questions of wages, hours of labor, co-operation, distribution of wealth, all are dragged in, canvassed, philosophized upon in behalf of the labor element of the country. All the activity of the keenest intellects is employed in this regard; but *all*, I may say exclusively, for the *white* labor of this great nation.

And yet here is the fact, that this white labor is organized labor, it is intelligent labor, it is skilled labor, it is protected labor, protected in a majority of the States by legislative enactments. It is labor nourished, guarded, shielded, rooted in national institutions, propped up by the suffrage of the laboring population, and needs no extraordinary succors. And yet here is the fact, that this immense system of labor, with all its intelligence and its safeguards, is dissatisfied, querulous and complaining; and everywhere, and especially in the great centres of industry, agonistic and belligerent, because it is fretting under a deep sense of inequality, wrong, and injustice. But, my friends, just look at the *black* labor of this country, and consider its sad conditions, its disorganized and rude characteristics, its almost servile status, its insecure and defenseless abjectness. . . .

Now, if I do not make the very greatest of mistakes, *this* is the marked peculiarity of the black labor of this country. I am not unmindful of the fact that the black man *is* a laborer. I repel the imputation that the race, as a class, is lazy and slothful. I know, too, that, to a partial extent, the black man, in the Southern States, *is* a craftsman, especially in the cities. I am speaking now of aggregates. I am looking at the race in the mass; and I affirm that the sad peculiarity of our labor in this country is that our labor is rude, untutored, and debased. Let any man examine the diverse crafts of labor in the multitudinous businesses in which men are employed; the almost numberless trades; the heterogeneous callings and the multiform manufactures, which go to make up the industrial civilization of this vast nation; and then see the scores, nay, hundreds, of these careers from which the black man is purposely and inexora-

bly excluded; and *then* you will take in the fact, that the black labor of this land is, of necessity, crude, unskilled, and disorganized labor. And remember here that I am speaking of no less than two millions of men, and women and children; for, to a large extent, black women and children are the laborers of the South, and still work in field and factory.

Join to this the thought of its sad conditions, its servile status and its defenseless abjectness. Here is the fact that tens of thousands of men and women of our race are toiling, have been toiling for years, for men who never think of paying them the worth and value of their toil,—men who systematically "keep back the hire of the laborer by fraud"; men who skillfully and ingeniously, at the close of every year, bring their ignorant laborers into debt to themselves; men who purposely close the portals of all hope, and "shut the gates of mercy" upon the victims of their fraud, and so drive hundreds and thousands of our people into theft and reckless indifference, and many thousands more into despair and premature graves!

Here, then, is a great problem which is to be settled before this race can make the advance of a single step. Without the solution of this enormous question, neither individual nor family life can secure their proper conditions in this land. *Who* are the men who shall undertake the settlement of this momentous question? How are they to bring about the settlement of it? I answer, first of all, that the rising intelligence of this race, the educated, thinking, scholarly men, who come out of the schools trained and equipped by reading and culture; they are the men who are to handle this great subject. Who else can be expected to attempt it? Do you think that men of other races will encourage *our* cultivated men to parade themselves as mere carpet knights upon the stage of politics, or, in the saloons of aestheticism, and they, themselves, assume the added duty of the moral and material restoration of our race? Wherever has philanthropy shown itself thus over-officious and superserviceable? Never in the history of man has it either assumed superfluous cares or indulged a people in irresponsible diversions. The philanthropists of the times expect every people to bear somewhat the burdens of their own restoration and upbuilding; and rightly so. And *next*, as to the other question—How this problem of labor is to be settled? I reply, in all candor, that I am unable to answer so intricate a question. But this I do say, (1) that you have get to bring to the settlement of it all the brain-power, all the penetration, all the historical reading and all the generous devotedness of heart that you can command; and (2) that in the endeavor to settle this question that you are not to make the mistake, *i.e.*, that it is *external* forces which are chiefly to be brought to bear upon this enormity. No people can be lifted up by others to grand civility. The elevation of a people, their thorough civilization, comes chiefly from *internal* qualities. If there is no receptive and living quality *in* them which can be evoked for their elevation, then they must die! The emancipation of the black race in this land from the injustice and grinding tyranny of their labor servitude is to be effected mainly by the development of such personal qualities, such thrift, energy and manliness, as shall, in the first place, raise them above the dependence and the penury of their present vassalage, and next, shall bring forth such manliness and dignity in the race as may command the respect of their oppressors.

To bring about these results we need intelligent men and women, so filled with philanthropy that they will go down to the humblest conditions of their race, and carry to their lowly huts and cabins all the resources of science, all the suggestions of domestic, social and political economies, all the appliances of school, and industries, in order to raise and elevate the most abject and needy race on American soil. If the scholarly and enlightened colored men and women care not to devote themselves to these lowly but noble duties, to these humble but sacred conditions, what is the use of their schooling and enlightenment? Why, in the course of Providence, have they had their large advantages and their superior opportunities?

3. I bring to your notice one other requirement of the black race in this country, and that

is *the need of a higher plane of morality*. I make no excuse for introducing so delicate and, perchance, so offensive a topic—a topic which necessarily implies a state of serious moral defectiveness. But if the system of slavery did not do us harm in every segment and section of our being, why have we for generations complained of it? And if it *did* do us moral as well as intellectual harm, why, when attempting by education to rectify the injury to the mental nature, should we neglect the reparation of the *moral* condition of the race? We have suffered, my brethren, in the whole domain of morals. We *are* still suffering as a people in this regard. Take the sanctity of marriage, the facility of divorce, the chastity of woman, the shame, modesty and bashfulness of girlhood, the abhorrence of illegitimacy; and there is no people in this land who, in these regards, have received such deadly thrusts as this race of ours. And these qualities are the grandest qualities of all superior people. You know, as well as I do, how these qualities are insisted upon in Holy Scripture, and there is no need of my referring to it. . . .

This moral elevation should be the highest ambition of our people. *They* make the greatest mistakes who tell you that money is the master need of our race. *They* equally err who would fain fasten your attention upon the acknowledged political difficulties which confront us in the lawless sections of the land. I acknowledge both of these grievances. But the one grand result of all my historic readings has brought to me this single and distinct conviction, that

> "By the soul only the nations
> shall be free."

If I do not greatly err, I have made it evident to-day that a mighty revolution is demanded in our race in this country. The whole status of our condition is to be transformed and elevated. The change which is demanded is a vaster deeper one than that of emancipation. *That* was a change of state or condition, valuable and important indeed, but affecting mainly the *outer* conditions of this people. And that is all a civil status can do, how beneficent soever it may be. But outward condition does not necessarily touch the springs of life. That requires other, nobler, more spiritual agencies. How true are the words of Coleridge:—

> I may not hope from outward things to win
> The passion and the life, whose fountains are within.

What we need is a grand *moral* revolution which shall touch and vivify the inner life of a people, which shall give them dissatisfaction with ignoble motives and sensual desires, which shall bring them to a resurrection from inferior ideas and lowly ambitions; which shall shed illumination through all the chambers of their souls, which shall lift them up to lofty aspirations, which shall put them in the race for manly moral superiority.

A revolution of this kind is not a gift which can be handed over by one people, and placed as a new deposit, in the constitution of another. Nor is it an acquisition to be gained by storm, by excitement or frantic and convulsive agitation, political, religious or other.

The revolution I speak of is one which must find its primal elements in qualities, latent though they be, which reside *in* the people who need this revolution, and which can be drawn out of them, and thus secure form and reality.

The basis of this revolution must be character. *That* is the rock on which this whole race in America is to be built up. Our leaders and teachers are to address themselves to this main and master endeavor, viz., to free them from false ideas and injurious habits, to persuade them to the adoption of correct principles, to lift them up to superior modes of living, and so bring forth, as permanent factors in their life, the qualities of thrift, order, acquisitiveness, virtue and manliness.

And who are the agents to bring about this grand change in this race?

Remember, just here, that all effectual revolutions in a people must be racial in their characteristics. You can't take the essential qualities of one people and transfuse them into the blood of another people, and make them indigenous to them. The primal qualities of a family, a clan, a nation, a race are heritable qualities. They abide in their constitution. They are absolute and congenital things. They remain, notwithstanding the conditions and the changes of rudeness, slavery, civilization and enlightenment. The attempt to eliminate them will only serve to make a people factitious and unmanly. It is law of moral elevation that you must allow the constant abidance of the essential elements of a people's character.

And, therefore, when I put the query—*Who* are to be the agents to raise and elevate this people to a higher plane of being? the answer will at once flash upon your intelligence. It is to be affected by the scholars and philanthropists which come forth in these days from the schools. *They* are to be the scholars; for to transform, stimulate and uplift a people is a work of intelligence; it is a work which demands the clear induction of historic facts and their applications to new circumstances,—a work which will require the most skillful resources and the wise practicality of superior men.

But these reformers must not be mere scholars. The intellect is to be used, but mainly as the vehicle of mind and spiritual aims. And hence, these men must needs to be both scholars and philanthropists; the intellect rightly discerning the conditions, and the gracious and godly heart stimulating to the performance of the noblest duties for a people.

Allow me, in conclusion, to express the hope that, mingled with the sweet melodies of poetry, the inspiring voices of eloquence and the mystic tones of science, you will have an open ear to hear the voice of God, which is the call of duty. And may he who holds the hearts of all men give you the spirit to forget yourselves, and live for the good of man and the glory of God. Such a field and opportunity is graciously opened to you in the conditions and needs of our common race in this country. May you and I be equal to them!

Anonymous

"The Negro on the Negro"

Independent, January 6, 1887[5]

What Educated Colored People in the South Report Concerning Their Material Condition.

In the great mass of literature about the colored race in the United States, it is remarkable how little there is that is the colored man's own production. Half a dozen of the foremost men of the race have written books, chiefly on the historical side of the subject, many more than half a dozen have spoken prominently both historically and practically, as politicians, as teachers, and as preachers. But these have been the exceptional men of the race. Nowhere has there been presented anything that may fairly be called colored public opinion about the colored people's condition and outlook. Students of the subject have missed the opinion of the average educated Negro on the Negro.

To supply this, THE *INDEPENDENT* caused an investigation to be made. During the past summer a circular was sent to two hundred representative intelligent colored men and women in all the Southern states "to ascertain the prevailing opinion and feelings of the colored people themselves about the relation of the races and the outlook of the colored race." The following inquiries were made, and answers were requested from both men and women:

I. *Material Prosperity.*—Are the colored people fast accumulating property? What proportion of the families of your acquaintance own their own homes? As regards business transactions, the hiring of laborers, the payment of wages, the credit system, what changes, if any, do the colored people of your community desire?

II. *The Races and the Laws.*—Are there any laws in your state more oppressive to one race than to the other? Is the law administered different to the two races?

III. *Race Feeling, Schools, and Churches.*—What unfairness, if any, is shown to the colored people because of their color? Do the colored people prefer separate to mixed schools and churches?

IV. *Civil Rights.*—What social customs, if any, are objectionable or oppressive to the colored people?

V. *Greatest Hindrance and Most Pressing Duty.*—What is the greatest single hindrance to the race's advancement? And what is its most pressing duty, under present conditions?

VI. *The Mingling of Races.*—Are there more children of mixed blood born now than in slavery? Do present tendencies point to the ultimate general commingling of the races?

Answers have been received to these inquiries from teachers (male and female), preachers, lawyers, editors and merchants, in Virginia, North Carolina, Georgia, Florida, Alabama, Mississippi, Louisiana, Tennessee, and Arkansas. Answers to each of these groups of inquiries, which present all shades of opinion expressed in them all, will be presented in the order named. Following are such replies to the first group, concerning the Material Prosperity of the Negro and the Negro's view of it.

The Accumulation of Property.

The colored people are getting property rapidly, and they surpass the "poor whites" as accumulators of property. The reason is, the wives of the whites do not work, while the colored women work more than the men, and they know how to save. Many of them support their whole families. I know of several cases where colored men, aided by their wives, have bought and paid for good homes, raising large families at the same time.—*Virginia. . . .*

There has been quite satisfactory advancement made in this regard. Between twenty and twenty-five per cent. of the colored families in Southeast Virginia own their homes.—*Virginia.*

In towns and cities about one-tenth of the colored people own homes; but throughout the country not more than one in a hundred.—*Eastern North Carolina.*

The colored people are fast accumulating property, real and personal. About forty per cent. of my acquaintances own their little homes. There is yet some feeling among the whites against selling a colored man land; for when he once acquires it, he never sells it.—*Richmond County, N.C.*

They are not accumulating anything very fast. Not more than six per cent. of my acquaintances own their homes. Perhaps this is too low an estimate, generally, but not too low within the range of my acquaintance.—*Guilford County, N.C. . . .*

They are doing well in accumulating little properties, and some are awaking to the importance of undertaking joint-stock enterprises. Half the families I know own their homes.—*Atlanta, Ga.*

The accumulation of property is rapid. Perhaps two-thirds of the families of my acquaintance own their homes.—*Atlanta, Ga.*

Rapidly. Three-fourths of the families I know own houses.—*Jacksonville, Fla.*

The Negroes are anxious to acquire property, and they make many sacrifices to procure homes. Often they are poor huts in the unhealthy parts of the town, but they are the best they can do. Their families are too large and their wages too small to buy handsome property. Sixty per cent. of those I know own homes, and half these other property besides. In this state the colored people pay taxes on $10,000,000 of real estate. In the country land is the last thing offered for sale to a Negro; and yet a large number own farming land.—*Augusta, Ga.*

As many as 90 per cent. of the families I know own their little homes.—*Montgomery, Ala.*

Three-fifths of my acquaintances are property owners.—*Greenville, Miss.*

Few accumulate at all. One in ten own real estate. There is great room for improvement in the way of frugality.—*Madison Co., Miss.*

Our people are rapidly gaining as property holders. They are industrious and would accumulate faster if they had a fair chance. As they become educated, they economize. At least two-thirds of the best people of the race here own their homes, and some own other property; still the mass of our people are very poor.—*Meridian, Miss. . . .*

About one-third of my acquaintances are property holders. The colored people own much property in the towns. As yet few own farms of any considerable size; but a new spirit seems to have come over them in the last few years, and they are looking toward the ownership of larger farms.—*Arkansas.*

These answers show uniformly an ambition and an effort to become holders of property, and every correspondent reports progress. The estimates given of the proportion of families that own their own homes are so wide apart that they give no very accurate idea, and the proportion varies very greatly in different communities. Yet these estimates show an average of prosperity that is remarkable, and they report the continued existence of the prejudice in some communities of the whites against selling land to the blacks.

Wages and the Credit System.

Average wages in Georgia are about 75 cents a day. Laborers in the country receive the greater part of their pay in the shape of groceries, the employer usually having a store of his own and supplying his laborers from his friend's store. Thus the labor usually pays for ninety day's credit from 25 to 33 1/3 per cent interest. The only change that the colored man desires is as much pay, and pay in the same way, as a white man receives for similar work.—*Teacher, at Atlanta, Ga.*

It is a notorious fact that of two laborers, one white and the other colored, possessing equal efficiency, the white laborer will receive higher compensation. Common laborers receive from 60 to 75 cents a day; mechanics about $1.50.—*Atlanta, Ga.*

Our people often ignorantly sign contracts they cannot keep. Many of them know nothing about interest or partial payments, and they often imagine that they are cheated when they are not. The credit system is abused by both races. There are some designing white men who live by imposing on Negroes in business transactions; but they are not numerous. Wages for men range from 50 cents to $1 a day, or from $10 to $30 a month; but very few get $30; for women from 25 to 50 cents a day, or $4 to $8 a month.—*Augusta, Ga.*

In business transactions the colored people are generally at a disadvantage. The average wages of laborers is about $100 a year; but, owing to the obnoxious system of credit, in nine cases out of ten, not a dollar of the hundred dollars passes through the hands of the laborer. Payment in currency is earnestly desired.—*Richmond, Va.*

In the towns in the valley of Virginia, many colored men keep stores, and most of them do well. A colored man at Staunton has a large second-hand store, and his stock is worth $3,000. All classes patronize him. White contractors will not as a rule employ skilled mechanics of color, nor do the colored people themselves hire them. The credit system is not in vogue here, and the colored people are paid in cash for their labor. Common laborers receive about $1.50 a day; women $8 a month. Most of the Negroes who live in the valley of Virginia in *ante bellum* times have gone North, and their places have been taken (more than taken, so to speak) by plantation Negroes from Eastern Virginia.—*Staunton, Va.* . . .

In all business transactions the colored people are fairly treated, except in those sections where the credit system exists. In these sections the colored people are systematically swindled, and by false charges and overcharges are constantly brought in debt to the landlords and storekeepers. The credit system, however, does not exist to any considerable extent in this state. Laborers receive an average of about $1 a day.—*Jacksonville, Fla.*

Some of the colored laborers are so hired as not to give them more than four or five months' work in the year. Some are paid in scrip and orders which, keeps them dependent. We want cash payments and longer working time.—*Washington, N.C.*

Fifty cents a day for unskilled labor; more for skilled. No special change desired.—*Greensboro, N.C.* . . .

The colored people desire equal pay for equal work. They dislike very much to see labor, inferior to their own, in many cases, command better pay. They average about $1 a day.—*Montgomery, Ala.*

There is here a uniform price per day for laborers, white or colored; for field-hands 75 cents a day, without provisions, 60 cents with them; for cutting wood, 75 cents a cord. Wages are increased during October, November and December from 75 cents to $1 or $1.50 for eighteen hours' work.—*Terrebonne Parish, La.*

Wages, $2.50 to $12 a month. We desire a change in the mortgage and lien and garnishee laws, and the law which practically compels men with their wives and children to stay on the large and unhealthy plantations, and to vote for their employers. We would rather not have any credit system at all, for the ignorance and poverty of the Negroes are taken advantage of by the whites, and we are forced to work for very low wages, and to take our pay in store supplies at very high prices for necessaries.—*Meridian, Miss.*

The colored people wish to be treated as other men, but they do not enjoy the discrimination by which white laborers are paid more than they are for the same work. Their average wages here are about ten dollars a month.—*Greenville, Miss.*

Colored people here are almost excluded from business, except as servants or tools. There are, of course, exceptions. The price of labor is fixed by the employer, and is about thirty-five or forty cents a day.—*Madison County, Miss.*

Plainly the credit system and the fashion of payment in "supplies" must yield to a cash system before the race which is the chief laboring race in the South can get a fair chance to become independent.

Anonymous
"The New Negro in the New South"

Hartford Courant, January 8, 1887[6]

Last summer a circular letter was mailed by the editors of the New York *Independent* to two hundred of the most intelligent colored men and women in the southern states, asking first-hand information as to the actual condition of their sort of folks down there,—materially, socially and morally. The object was, as the editors explain, to "ascertain the prevailing opinion and feelings of the colored people themselves about the relation of the races and the outlook of the colored race." Answers have been received from teachers, preachers, lawyers, editors and merchants in Virginia, North Carolina, Georgia, Florida, Alabama, Mississippi, Louisiana, Arkansas and Tennessee; and in this week's *Independent* the editors give us in condensed form what their correspondents have to say on the first point in the inquiry,—"the material prosperity of the negro, and the negro's view of it." We condense the condensation. . . .

Several of the *Independent's* correspondents complain that white men are paid more than black men for the same work, and those of them who write from localities where the store-credit system prevails are emphatic in condemning it as fruitful in injustice, a clog to progress, a millstone around the negro's neck. On this point the Meridian correspondent speaks the mind of all. "We would rather not have any credit system at all," he writes, "for the ignorance and poverty of the negroes are taken advantage of by the whites, and we are forced to work for very low wages, and to take our pay in store-supplies at very high prices for necessaries."

At a number of places in the New South the more ambitious and energetic negroes are pushing their way into mercantile business, and are making money in it, too. There is only one intimation of this very interesting fact, however, in the *Independent's* letters. "In the towns in the valley of Virginia," writes a Staunton informant, "many colored men keep stores, and most of them do well. A colored man in Staunton has a large second-hand store, and his stock is worth $3,000. All classes patronize him. There will be a good many more of these colored retail tradesman down there fifteen or twenty years hence, unless all signs fail."

Anonymous

"Ingalls Denounced. The Colored Press Demands Justice and Fair Play. Let Everybody Read This."

Washington Bee, February 19, 1887[7]

—St. Louis, (Mo.) Advance:[8]

The President, in his message to the Senate beseeching the confirmation of Matthews,[9] says: "That he desires in this way to tender just recognition and good faith towards our colored fellow-citizens." That August body, at least the 26 republicans who assented to the Ingalls letter, reply that the Senate was not aware of the question of "just recognition and good faith towards our colored fellow citizens" was involved in the question; that the classification of color was abolished by the New Amendment and is "No longer properly to be recognized in dealing with public affairs."

No, these Senators were not aware, of the fact that the just recognition of the rights and merits of our colored fellow citizens has entered largely into the discussions and legislation of Congress, including the Senate this last half century. They are not "aware" that Senator Hoar asks them to consider his bill appropriating $100,000 for a colored Soldier's Monument, because the classification of color must not be recognized in dealing with public affairs. These sublime Senators in the sublimity of their indifference, are not "aware?" that hundreds of thousands of colored soldiers fought in the Union Army and were designated by the Senate itself as "U.S. colored infantry." Ingalls, Chace and Hoar were not "aware?" that these soldiers were colored men and that four regiments still remain in the army officially known as colored troops.

Senator Sherman introduced a bill in comport with the President's message, to re-imburse the depositors of the Freedman's Bank, but the Supernal Republican Senators were not "aware?" that freedmen are colored people, for they have not been officially informed. Senator Dawes gets a bill through the Senate that "persons of African descent," citizens of the Cherokee nation, shall have their share of $300,000 out of which they were defrauded, and yet these oblivious Solons were not "aware?" that "persons of African descent" were colored people. Philip Josep of Alabama gets his bill before the Senate for a large appropriation for the Colored World's Fair to be held at Birmingham in September, and Philip is "of that color which is common to his race of the deepest dye" but forsooth, Mr. Ingalls and his color-blind colleagues are not "aware?" that this man is a Negro and this fair is an exclusive colored people's enterprise.

Chief Justice Taney was aware that Dred Scott was a black man; Chief Justice Waite was aware that it was a question of color in the case where the Supreme Court decided that the laws of Alabama, punishing intermarriage of races were constitutional; and Senator Ingalls, Sherman and others have descended so far into the depth of intellectual oblivion that they are not aware that black laws still exist in the statutes of Kansas and Ohio.

"The Senate has no official information," says those solons who sign Ingalls' letter, "other than that in the message of the President, whether Matthews is white or black." Is there, for conscience sake, is there any higher information, known to the Senate, than that contained in the Message of the President of the United States? What "other" official information do these innocent and unsophisticated Senators require? Shall Moses rise from the dead, shall an angel proclaim from the heights of heaven? The clouds break at last and we discover that these Senators do know something. They know without being officially informed that Frederick Douglass is a colored man, and "they cannot forbear to apprise the President" that he is the most distinguished representative of the colored race, not only in this country, but in the world," and further that J. C. Matthews is "an unknown and obscure partisan."

Here is an official document issued with the high seal of the American Senate, by Senators whose business should be legislation and not laudation or defamation that establishes a censureship of character upon the merits and demerits of the individual Negro citizen. Has it come to this that we are to be officially informed, by the August Senate, that this Negro is great and that other Negro is an obscure partisan, that in Douglass resides the Negro race, and when he dies the race dies in him and with him? In this, the United States Senate becomes the supreme architect and arbiter of the destiny of each individual Negro, and, Senator Ingalls will hereafter inform us which Negro is great and which obscure.

But they cap the climax when they say, that Matthews, "had never been a slave and therefore represents the enfranchised race only by the accident of color." It is the same accident that afflicts these senators and gives them the opportunity to misrepresent the people by such samples of demagoguery.

This statement is seditious, it smacks a little of the "horrors of San Domingo," when the blacks were arrayed against the mulattoes, and it further takes us back to the old slave times when the slave Negro was taught to despise the free Negro. Here is the insinuation of caste among the Negroes. The slave born are to be favored, the free born are to be despised. It means to dissociate the educated and illiterate Negro, to play upon the prejudice of the unfortunate, to instil the false idea that there is merit in the bare fact of being born a slave.

There were 500,000 free Negroes before the war and natural increase since that time has, at least, added 4,000,000 free born Negroes to our population; one half of the 4,00,000 [*sic*] ex-slaves have died, and the remainder must inevitably pass away, thus leaving the free born Negro population vastly preponderating in numbers. If according to the edict of these senators the representative character of a Negro must be based upon the fact of his having or not having been a slave Matthews belongs to the most numerous class and becomes therefore the most representative character, as between himself and Fred Douglass.

It is too late, we have a new south and a new Negro and the new Negro is coming forth in platoons of ten thousand deep from the colleges and schools of the Nation, with reverence for the past, but with all his energies bent on the prospect of the future. You cannot explain to this post-bellum product, why white republicans "Shake hands over the bloody Chasm," welcome into National Citizenship and confirm for the highest places men who boast of their record to destroy the Nation, and, at the same time these republicans, try to crush the Negro who by his political action tries to soften the asperities of race antagonisms which so much oppress his people. This letter ostensibly for the President is simply meant for the Negro, and the young and vigorous element of that race will not be entrapped by the fulsome blandishments which it bestows even upon the venerable head of Douglass.

Bruce Grit [John Edward Bruce]
"National Capital Topics. Discrimination in the Pension Office."

New York Age, July 28, 1888

John H. Smythe, Esq.,[10] who is certainly a representative colored man, should not be overlooked by the National Committee when it goes out hunting for effective campaign orators. There is no better public speaker, white or black, in or out of Washington, than John H. Smythe. He is a prosperous attorney and real estate man, and he is not looking for a job. He is a true blue and loyal Republican and would not refuse to respond to the call of his party by serving it in any way in his power. The National Republican Committee would honor itself by honoring modest John H. Smythe in the manner indicated. He is a forcible and eloquent speaker and a scholarly gentleman, and I hope to be among those who will listen to him, during the progress of the coming exciting campaign. He represents the new Negro in all that that term implies, and his knowledge of the history of his race and his country is comprehensive and thorough. Twice honored by his party as its representative to a foreign government, he acquitted himself in a manner to merit its confidence in his ability and integrity. The Republican managers can hardly afford to ignore the really useful and valuable men of either race, in this campaign. Certainly, I should hate to know that Mr. Smythe had not been remembered by them.

T. Thomas Fortune
"The Afro-American Agitator"

New York Age, December 21, 1889

"The Afro-American Agitator" is a brand new thing under the sun. He has sprung full-fledged from the head of Jove in so short a time that the country has hardly had time to recognize the new arrival.

Where did he come from?
What does he look like?
What is his mission?

He came into existence two years ago, when the idea of the Afro-American League was flashed over the wires of the Associated Press Association, reaching to the utmost parts of the Nation,—marking the death-knell of the shuffling, cringing creature in black who for two centuries and a half had given the right of way to white men, and proclaiming in no uncertain voice that a new man in black, a freeman every inch, standing erect and undoubted, an American from head to foot, had taken the place of the miserable creature dead.

What does he look like? *He looks like a man!* He bears no resemblance to a slave, or a coward, or an ignoramus.

What is his mission? His mission is to force the concession to him of absolute justice under State and Federal Constitutions.

The Afro-American Agitator has come to stay until his work, like that of the famous Abolitionists, has been crowned with success in every corner of the Republic.

It remained for Mr. Henry W. Grady of the Atlanta *Constitution*,—whose magnetic eloquence, whose varied learning and whose intense loyalty to the South, the white South, provoke my profoundest admiration,—it remained for Mr. Grady to take notice in a public manner of the new man, "the Afro-American Agitator," who has come upon the scene as noiselessly as a tiger treads the velvet carpet of the umbrageous forest palaces of nature.

At a banquet given by the Boston Merchants' Association, at Boston, on Thursday evening of last week, at which ex-President Cleveland also spoke, Mr. Grady said, in the course of his brilliant oration on "The Race Problem":

> We give to the world this year a crop or 7,500,000 bales of cotton, worth $450,000,000, and its cash equivalent in grains, grasses and fruit. This enormous crop could not have come from the hands of sullen and discontented labor. It comes from peaceful fields, in which laughter and gossip rise above the hum of industry, and contentment runs with the singing plow. It is claimed that this ignorant labor is defrauded of its just hire. I present the tax books of Georgia, which show that the Negro, twenty-five years ago a slave, has in Georgia alone $10,000,000 of assessed property worth twice that much. Does not that record honor him, and vindicate his neighbors? What people penniless, literate, has done so well? *For every Afro-American agitator, stirring the strife in which alone he prospers,* I can show you a thousand Negroes, happy in their cabin homes, tilling their own land by day, and at night taking from the lips of their children the helpful message their State sends them from the schoolhouse door. And the schoolhouse itself bears testimony. In Georgia, we added last year $250,000 to the school fund, making a total of more than $1,000,000—and this in the face of prejudice not yet conquered, of the fact that the whites are assessed for $368,000,000, the blacks for $10,000,000, and yet 49 per cent of the beneficiaries are black children—and in the

doubt of many wise men if education helps, or can help our problem.

It is a charming picture that Mr. Grady presents. It allures and beguiles me. But in the same breath that be anathematizes the "Afro-American Agitator" he gives one potent reason for his existence, in the claim that while the Afro-American is the source from which $450,000,000 of wealth is added to the State he is still a pensioner on the whites and is practically educated out of their bounty! The claim is preposterous and ludicrous on its face. Instead of being a credit to the Georgians that the Afro-American has managed to acquire property to the value of $20,000,000 since the war, while producing annually $450,000,000 of solid wealth, it is highly discreditable, and really destroys the beautiful picture Mr. Grady has drawn of contented laborers, happy in their lot, adequately compensated for their toil, and protected in all their rights by the strong arm of the law impartially, blindly administered.

Two hundred Afro-Americans recently gathered in Mr. Grady's own city of Atlanta. They represented every county in the State. They were men of character, intelligence, force and property. What called them together? To denounce the wage system of Georgia. To denounce the reign of mob and lynch law violence. To denounce the insolence and cowardice of individual white men in their conduct towards black men. To denounce the suppression of the ballot in Georgia. To denounce the existence of taxation without representation. To denounce the one-sided administration of justice in which Afro-Americans are made the victims. To denounce the universal denial of civil rights of Afro-Americans in Georgia.

In short, the 200 "Afro-American Agitators" who met in Atlanta on the 12th of November last answered in advance the speech delivered by Mr. Grady in Boston on the 12th of December.

Mr. Grady says further:

> Now, Mr. President, can it be seriously maintained that we are terrorizing the

people from whose willing hands comes every year $1,000,000,000 of farm crops? Or have robbed a people, who in twenty-five years from unrewarded slavery have amassed in one State $20,000,000 of property? Or that we intend to oppress the people that we are arming every day? Or deceive them, when we are educating them to the utmost limit of our ability? Or outlaw them when we work side by side with them?

Verily, verily, the "Afro-American Agitator" is a misfit creature, according to this showing; but 200 of him met in Atlanta on the 12th of November and pronounced against the position of Mr. Grady, and in any court on earth the testimony of 200 men will be accepted as against that of one man.

But all the extraordinary eulogium of Afro-Americans indulged in by Mr. Grady, all the more strange considering the source of it, vanishes into mist and dissolves into cloud vapor before the following climax in Mr. Grady's speech:

> You may pass force bills, but they will not avail. You may surrender your own liberties to federal election law, you may submit, in fear of a necessity that does not exist, that the very form of this Government may be changed—this old State which holds in its charter the boast that it "is a free and independent commonwealth" may deliver its election machinery into the hands of the government it helped to create—but never, sir, will a single State of this Union, North or South, be delivered again to the control of an ignorant and inferior race. If the Negro had not been enfranchised, the South would have been divided and the Republic united. His enfranchisement—against which I enter no protest—holds the South united and compact.

Here, then, after all the oratorical taffy leading up to it, we have the plain, unvarnished truth, spoken with brutal force and bluntness.

Here, then, is the reason for his coming and the argument of his staying of the "Afro-American Agitator." It is not a question of "ignorant and inferior race" control and domination. No one expects that; no one desires it; no one is contending for it. But the "Afro-American Agitator" expects that his rights under the Constitution as amended shall be conceded to him, not grudgingly and in part but freely and in whole; he expects, not that he shall have delivered to him and that he shall control any State in the Union, but that he shall have a fair and equal share in the administration of the State, not as an Afro-American, but as a co-equal citizen under the Constitution; he expects that the "united and compact South," of which he is an indivisible part, shall become as disunited and uncompact in its political opinion and conduct as the electorate of Massachusetts, for instance; and he hurls back in Mr. Grady's teeth as a vile slander the charge that he is an "inferior race."

I give Mr. Grady credit for the pleasant and truthful and even eulogistic things he says of the Afro-American, his progress in wealth and in education, in thrift and economy; but after all he has said on this head, I maintain, and I leave it to the Nation to decide if Mr. Grady himself has not stated causes of sufficient moment to justify the birth of the "Afro-American Agitator," whom, properly enough, he has been the first to recognize as he steps forth to the contention for absolute justice under the Constitution.

The issues are squarely joined.

"The Afro-American Agitator" has come to stay, and the Afro-American Leagne [*sic*] is the fortress of his strength.

T. Thomas Fortune.

John Mitchell Jr.

"What the Negroes Owe Us"

Richmond Planet, December 20, 1890

A WRITER TO THE Dispatch of the 14th inst, [issue] over the nom de plume of "L***" discourses on "What the Negroes Owe Us." Here are his words;

> To the Editor of the Dispatch;

> "Bloodshed must follow the unlawful practices of the Democratic party in Virginia. A free people will not much longer tolerate it."

> The above is copied from the Richmond PLANET of November 8th.

> Langston has also talked of "hogs heads of blood."

All this furnishes much food for thought. Not that we fear any danger from the "bloodshed" threatened, but when two of the most prominent and perhaps the best educated Negroes in Virginia are guilty of such expressions as those above quoted, it is well calculated to convince us that the millions of dollars taken out of the pockets of the southern white people by taxation for the purpose of educating that race to make them better citizens have been worse than thrown away, because it is being clearly demonstrated every day that the more education these people have the worse citizens they become.

The author of those sentiments has certainly been studying the obsolete doctrine of the Bourbons of the old school and in the 19th Century—the era of science, art and literature, announces that education serves to make worse citizens of his fellow-man, that it serves to deteriorate rather than elevate his brothers; for if the principles of Christianity are to be accepted, ADAM and EVE were our common parents, and this assertion is further substantiated by the announcement that He made of one blood all nations, and peoples. Education unfits any people for slavery and serfdom.

The declaration made to the fact that continued oppression or tyranny must end in bloodshed are testified to by history and proven by experience.

It is only by the equal poise of justice that revolutions are averted, and peace maintained.

While we thank the people of the South in general, and those in Virginia in particular for the educational advantages accorded, we must enter our protest against the likening of the Negro to paupers—abject objects of educational charity by the grace of the white tax-payers of the South, who if they are like the croaking writer have unwillingly contributed their means for that purpose.

He seems to be oblivious of the fact that the South has always been the seat of aristocratic indolence, made possible by the Negro's industry. He seems to forget that the very education which makes it possible for him to write such articles against an inoffensive people was obtained by the money accumulated from the black man's labor.

He does not remember now that it was a practice to sell a Negro in order to obtain the necessary funds to defray the college expenses of the young "marster" should the cash in hand not be sufficient to supply the immediate demands.

He is unwilling to understand the prindiple [*sic*] that labor is the basis of all wealth.

The cry before the war that "Cotton is king" should have been the Negro is king, since he was the necessary factor in its production, and accordingly had his hand on the lever that created the financial prosperity of the Southland.

The writer witnesses the abject servility of the Negro passing away under the subtle, but powerful influences of education. He sees in the look on the countenance, the erect carriage, the disposition to penetrate into the fields of science, a sign that the Negro of twenty years ago is passing away forever. In fact he is looking on a new Negro, the Negro of the past no longer. He listens to statements and reads of oratory as announced by the Negro, and when he thinks of the fact that but a few years back no man of that race would have dared to have exercised such a privilege, which he regards as the sole right of white men, he stops his ears to enlightening instruction, closes his eyes on the material progress and yells like one mad that education has made these people worse citizens. He says:

> The average Negro hates us and will continue to hate us no matter what we do for him. We have civilized, Christianized, and educated him; but that which if not the most prominent is certainly one of the most commendable traits of the white man's character is totally wanting in his—gratitude.

His assertion relative to the Negroes' hatred of white men is erroneous. We hate your manner and method in dealing with us, and this refers only to men of your stripe. Of the liberal minded white men in the South (and there are thousands) we have nothing ill to say.

When you say, you have civilized, Christianized and educated us, you must remember the conditions under which this was accomplished. The civilization and Christianization of us came by association. In that condition we could better answer your purposes. The education of us came by force.

The engrafting of the 13th, 14th and 15th Amendments to the Constitution of the United States alone caused the education of the Negro since under their provisions, which you and every one else stand sworn to support, you could not establish a white free school without establishing a Negro one. And notwithstanding this, there was a strong element who stood in favor of abolishing the free school system for both races in order that they might see the blacks continue to grow up in ignorance. It was openly charged that our Senator JOHN W. DANIEL

was in favor of such a proposition, and the said change caused his defeat by a combination of these same Negroes and the poor white men of Virginia whose interests were being mutually sacrificed in order to satisfy the prejudices of the rich who were able to educate their children in the best colleges of the land.

When he charges ingratitude on the part of the Negro, he has but to read the eloquent words of the later HENRY W. GRADY on the fidelity of the Negro during the late war and the tribute he pays to his black mammy who led him "smiling into sleep." No, no, Mr. L*** charge everything else but ingratitude. In the same issue of the Dispatch, your words are refuted by "One who loves and esteems his former slaves" as he tells the story of Mammy JUDY BAGBY, and thousands of white men can testify to similar occurrences.

History furnishes no record of any greater devotion of slaves to their oppressors. He says:

> The history of the world mentions no instance in which the African race has ever been taught civilization successfully except in a condition of slavery, and these Negro editors, professors and politicians who want our "blood" now would have been eating each other with their cousins in the wilds of Africa had not their ancestors been brought to this country and sold into slavery. I want Mr. Langston, Mr. John Mitchell, Jr., and all their admirers to put that in their pipes and smoke it.

You seem to forget, sir, all of the truths of history. You should remember that the Britains from whom you claim to have descended, were first enslaved and then civilized. They were more than five centuries (500 years) passing from heathenism to civilization.

Can you expect the African race to be any greater than your ancestors? or to accomplish in forty, even fifty years what they did in the time stated? And yet sir, there are Negroes in Africa, who have never submitted to slavery, who have never "bended the supple hinges of the knee" to the white man and from present indications, never will.

All of the tribes of Africa are not man-eaters. In this respect, they are a trifle beyond the civilized white men of the South, who only a few weeks ago roasted a Colored man while he lived.

Their sensitive stomachs possibly prevented them from proceeding with the act of the mastication of that lone Negro, but we are assured of the fact that they were angry enough with him so to do.

It may be said however of the Africans that they never stole savings banks, robbed helpless widows and orphans, murdered innocent men with shotguns and bludgeons, whipped defenseless women and children until blood spurted and professed to believe in the Lord Jesus Christ when their actions demonstrated that they were in league with the Devil. They never severed men's heads, arms and legs from their bodies placed them in trunks, and shipped them to other parts of the country.

They never tied men by their necks and swung them over a log fire while they slowly boiled and their heart rending mourns rent the air. . . .

The Negro is progressing. He has lawyers, doctors, historians, congressmen, senators, authors, scientists, inventors, college presidents, professors, editors, electricians, machinists, Doctors of Divinity, druggists, real estate agents, merchants, bank presidents, bank directors, and cashiers in his midst. He has become a land owner and a tax-payer. He is advancing along all of the avenues the white man has traversed. He has attained honor in the best colleges in the country, Harvard, Cornell, Philips Exeter have placed him at the head of the list—a place he had won. Oppression spurs him on to greater efforts. He is buying every hog-path and investing in every piece of real estate it is possible for him to obtain. He is striving to own the earth, and there by establish a firm foundation upon which to aspire to greater things. For two hundred and fifty years he has been studying the precepts of Christianity and endeavoring to master the principles of Christ as taught by the white man.

Already we have seen it announced and expect some day to testify to the fact that a Negro translation of the Holy Bible by and for the Negro has been made. Then the black man will have seen for himself. In these laudable undertakings which are especially valuable to us on account of the engrafting indelibly in our bosoms the principles of self reliance, we will be cordially assisted by the liberal minded white men of every section, and long after the Bourbons of this writer's stripe have crossed the river, the Negro will be living under his own vine and fig tree with none to molest him or make him afraid.

The doom of Bourbonism is at hand. The wall of this lone writer sounds shrill upon the air, dies away and he and his notes are forgotten.

The era of liberal ideas and the observances of great principles of political economy is making itself felt and to the southern oligarchy as represented by L*** we may well exclaim in the words of HOMER:

> Yet come it will, the day decreed by fates:
> (How my heart trembles, while my tongue
>   relates)
> The day when thou, imperial Troy, must
>   bend,
> And see thy warriors fall, thy glories end.

Anonymous
"Pointers: Colored Voters Need Fixing"

Times-Observer, September 4, 1891[11]

There is an unusual amount of restlessness apparent among Afro-American voters at present, and the discontent grows rather than diminishes. The recent meeting at Cincinnati, O., while of a local nature, has a general significance. In Pennsylvania there is a growing dissatisfaction. In Ohio it amounts to almost a declaration of "we owe allegiance to no party." In Indiana the same sign of discontent appears, while from all over the country there are evident signs of apathy. A prominent politician, who has the reputation of being an effectual organizer, said the other day: "The colored voter needs fixing." We have calmly studied the situation, asked for, received and sifted the opinions of leading colored men throughout the country, and the conclusion reached is, they do "need fixing." A few dollars distributed on election day, a deluge of fulsome praise or fawning flattery sandwiched with guileful promises will not answer now to do the "fixing."

Political promises are deceptive, and none have learned this better than the average colored voter. Deeds and acts that are equitable and just are the only "fixing" that will prove effectual at this time. There is a change in the race kaleidoscope caused by the shaking of the hand of education and progress.

New and brighter figures are seen. New men. Young men, active, aggressive and vigorous, who are alive to the interests of the race.

They have shook off the timerity [*sic*] born and nurtured in slavery's existence. Young men who have no such word as fear in their lexicon are in the van today, hence it is absolutely necessary that the "fixing" must contain the requisite ingredient—equity. . . .

The above clearly defines the present political position of the race. The new Negro has appeared on the stage. The white political "fixer" has been so busy fishing the Irish and Dutch that he has failed to note the presence of the young blood, whose education and acquaintance with our political systems renders him a restless and an almost unknown factor in the political arena. The Negro will stand by the Republicans only so long as they are properly treated. He recognizes the fact that a white man's a white man from the lakes to the gulf.

Anna Julia Cooper
"The Status of Woman in America"

In *A Voice from the South*, 1892

JUST four hundred years ago an obscure dreamer and castle builder, prosaically poor and ridiculously insistent on the reality of his dreams, was enabled through the devotion of a noble woman to give to civilization a magnificent continent.

What the lofty purpose of Spain's pure-minded queen had brought to the birth, the untiring devotion of pioneer women nourished and developed. The dangers of wild beasts and of wilder men, the mysteries of unknown wastes and unexplored forests, the horrors of pestilence and famine, of exposure and loneliness, during all those years of discovery and settlement, were braved without a murmur by women who had been most delicately constituted and most tenderly nurtured.

And when the times of physical hardship and danger were past, when the work of clearing and opening up was over and the struggle for accumulation began, again woman's inspiration and help were needed and still was she loyally at hand. A Mary Lyon, demanding and making possible equal advantages of education for women as for men, and, in the face of discouragement and incredulity, bequeathing to women the opportunities of Holyoke.

A Dorothea Dix, insisting on the humane and rational treatment of the insane and bringing about a reform in the lunatic asylums of the country, making a great step forward in the tender regard for the weak by the strong throughout the world.

A Helen Hunt Jackson, convicting the nation of a century of dishonor in regard to the Indian.

A Lucretia Mott, gentle Quaker spirit, with sweet insistence, preaching the abolition of slavery and the institution, in its stead, of the brotherhood of man; her life and words breathing out in tender melody the injunction:

> Have love. Not love alone for one
> But man as man thy brother call;
> And scatter, like the circling sun,
> Thy charities *on all*.

And at the most trying time of what we have called the Accumulative Period, when internecine war, originated through man's love of gain and his determination to subordinate national interests and black men's rights alike to considerations of personal profit and loss, was drenching our country with its own best blood, who shall recount the name and fame of the women on both sides the senseless strife,—those uncomplaining souls with a great heart ache of their own, rigid features and pallid cheek their ever effective flag of truce, on the battle field, in the camp, in the hospital, binding up wounds, recording dying whispers for absent loved ones, with tearful eyes pointing to man's last refuge, giving the last earthly hand clasp and performing the last friendly office for strangers whom a great common sorrow had made kin, while they knew that somewhere—somewhere a husband, a brother, a father, a son, was being tended by stranger hands—or mayhap those familiar eyes were even then being closed forever by just such another ministering angel of mercy and love.

But why mention names? Time would fail to tell of the noble army of women who shine like beacon lights in the otherwise sordid wilderness of this accumulative period—prison reformers and tenement cleansers, quiet unnoted workers in hospitals and homes, among imbeciles, among outcasts—the sweetening, purifying antidotes for the poisons of man's acquisitiveness,—mollifying and soothing with the tenderness of compassion and love the wounds and bruises caused by his overreaching and avarice.

The desire for quick returns and large profits tempts capital ofttimes into unsanitary, well nigh inhuman investments,—tenement tinder boxes, stifling, stunting, sickening alleys and pestiferous slums; regular rents, no waiting, large percentages,—rich coffers coined out of the life-blood of human bodies and souls. Men and women herded together like cattle, breathing in malaria and typhus from an atmosphere seething with moral as well as physical impurity, revelling in vice as their native habitat and then, to drown the whisperings of their higher consciousness and effectually to hush the yearnings and accusations within, flying to narcotics and opiates—rum, tobacco, opium, binding hand and foot, body and soul, till the proper image of God is transformed into a fit associate for demons,—a besotted, enervated, idiotic wreck, or else a monster of wickedness terrible and destructive.

These are some of the legitimate products of the unmitigated tendencies of the wealth-producing period. But, thank Heaven, side by side with the cold, mathematical, selfishly calculating, so-called practical and unsentimental instinct of the business man, there comes the sympathetic warmth and sunshine of good women, like the sweet and sweetening breezes of spring, cleansing, purifying, soothing, inspiring, lifting the drunkard from the gutter, the outcast from the pit. Who can estimate the influence of these "daughters of the king," these lend-a-hand forces, in counteracting the selfishness of an acquisitive age?

To-day America counts her millionaires by the thousand; questions of tariff and questions of currency are the most vital ones agitating the public mind. In this period, when material prosperity and well earned ease and luxury are assured facts from a national standpoint, woman's work and woman's influence are needed as never before; needed to bring a heart power into this money getting, dollar-worshipping civilization; needed to bring a moral force into the utilitarian motives and interests of the time; needed to stand for God and Home and Native Land *versus gain and greed and grasping selfishness.*

There can be no doubt that this fourth centenary of America's discovery which we celebrate at Chicago, strikes the keynote of another important transition in the history of this nation; and the prominence of woman in the management of its celebration is a fitting tribute to the part she is destined to play among the forces of the future. This is the first congressional recognition of woman in this country, and this Board of Lady Managers constitute the first women legally appointed by any government to act in a national capacity. This of itself marks the dawn of a new day.

Now the periods of discovery, of settlement, of developing resources and accumulating wealth have passed in rapid succession. Wealth in the nation as in the individual brings leisure, repose, reflection. The struggle with nature is over, the struggle with ideas begins. We stand then, it seems to me, in this last decade of the nineteenth century, just in the portals of a new and untried movement on a higher plain and in a grander strain than any the past has called forth. It does not require a prophet's eye to divine its trend and image its possibilities from the forces we see already at work around us; nor is it hard to guess what must be the status of woman's work under the new regime.

In the pioneer days her role was that of a camp-follower, an additional something to fight for and be burdened with, only repaying the anxiety and labor she called forth by her own incomparable gifts of sympathy and appreciative love; unable herself ordinarily to contend with the bear and the Indian, or to take active part in clearing the wilderness and constructing the home.

In the second or wealth producing period her work is abreast of man's, complementing and supplementing, counteracting excessive tendencies, and mollifying over rigorous proclivities.

In the era now about to dawn, her sentiments must strike the keynote and give the dominant tone. And this because of the nature of her contribution to the world.

Her kingdom is not over physical forces. Not by might, nor by power can she prevail. Her position must ever be inferior where strength of muscle creates leadership. If she follows the instincts of her nature, however, she must always stand for the conservation of those deeper moral forces which make for the happiness of homes and the righteousness of the country. In a reign of moral ideas she is easily queen.

There is to my mind no grander and surer prophecy of the new era and of woman's place in it, than the work already begun in the waning years of the nineteenth century by the W. C. T. U. [Woman's Christian Temperance Union] in America, an organization which has even now reached not only national but international importance, and seems destined to permeate and purify the whole civilized world. It is the living embodiment of woman's activities and woman's ideas, and its extent and strength rightly prefigure her increasing power as a moral factor.

The colored woman of to-day occupies, one may say, a unique position in this country. In a period of itself transitional and unsettled, her status seems one of the least ascertainable and definitive of all the forces which make for our civilization. She is confronted by both a woman question and a race problem, and is as yet an unknown or an unacknowledged factor in both. While the women of the white race can with calm assurance enter upon the work they feel by nature appointed to do, while their men give loyal support and appreciative countenance to their efforts, recognizing in most avenues of usefulness the propriety and the need of woman's distinctive co-operation, the colored woman too often finds herself hampered and shamed by a less liberal sentiment and a more conservative attitude on the part of those for whose opinion she cares most. That this is not universally true I am glad to admit. There are to be found both intensely conservative white men and exceedingly liberal colored men. But as far as my experience goes the average man of our race is less frequently ready to admit the actual need among the sturdier forces of the world for woman's help or influence. That great social and economic questions await her interference, that she could throw any light on problems of national import, that her intermeddling could improve the management of school systems, or elevate the tone of public institutions, or humanize and sanctify the far reaching influence of prisons and reformatories and improve the treatment of lunatics and imbeciles,—that she has a word worth hearing on mooted questions in political economy, that she could contribute a suggestion on the relations of labor and capital, or offer a thought on honest money and honorable trade, I fear the majority of "Americans of the colored variety" are not yet prepared to concede. It may be that they do not yet see these questions in their right perspective, being absorbed in the immediate needs of their own political complications. A good deal depends on where we put the emphasis in this world; and our men are not perhaps to blame if they see everything colored by the light of those agitations in the midst of which they live and move and have their being. The part they have had to play in American history during the last twenty-five or thirty years has tended rather to exaggerate the importance of mere political advantage, as well as to set a fictitious valuation on those able to secure such advantage. It is the astute politician, the manager who can gain preferment for himself and his favorites, the demagogue known to stand in with the powers at the White House and consulted on the bestowal

of government plums, whom we set in high places and denominate great. It is they who receive the hosannas of the multitude and are regarded as leaders of the people. The thinker and the doer, the man who solves the problem by enriching his country with an invention worth thousands or by a thought inestimable and precious is given neither bread nor a stone. He is too often left to die in obscurity and neglect even if spared in his life the bitterness of fanatical jealousies and detraction.

And yet politics, and surely American politics, is hardly a school for great minds. Sharpening rather than deepening, it develops the faculty of taking advantage of present emergencies rather than the insight to distinguish between the true and the false, the lasting and the ephemeral advantage. Highly cultivated selfishness rather than consecrated benevolence is its passport to success. Its votaries are never seers. At best they are but manipulators—often only jugglers. It is conducive neither to profound statesmanship nor to the higher type of manhood. Altruism is its *mauvais succes* and naturally enough it is indifferent to any factor which cannot be worked into its own immediate aims and purposes. As woman's influence as a political element is as yet nil in most of the commonwealths of our republic, it is not surprising that with those who place the emphasis on mere political capital she may yet seem almost a nonentity so far as it concerns the solution of great national or even racial perplexities.

There are those, however, who value the calm elevation of the thoughtful spectator who stands aloof from the heated scramble; and, above the turmoil and din of corruption and selfishness, can listen to the teachings of eternal truth and righteousness. There are even those who feel that the black man's unjust and unlawful exclusion temporarily from participation in the elective franchise in certain states is after all but a lesson "in the desert" fitted to develop in him insight and discrimination against the day of his own appointed time. One needs occasionally to stand aside from the hum and rush of human interests and passions to hear the voices of God. And it not unfrequently happens that the All-loving gives a great push to certain souls to thrust them out, as it were, from the distracting current for awhile to promote their discipline and growth, or to enrich them by communion and reflection. And similarly it may be woman's privilege from her peculiar coigne of vantage as a quiet observer, to whisper just the needed suggestion or the almost forgotten truth. The colored woman, then, should not be ignored because her bark is resting in the silent waters of the sheltered cove. She is watching the movements of the contestants none the less and is all the better qualified, perhaps, to weigh and judge and advise because not herself in the excitement of the race. Her voice, too, has always been heard in clear, unfaltering tones, ringing the changes on those deeper interests which make for permanent good. She is always sound and orthodox on questions affecting the well-being of her race. You do not find the colored woman selling her birthright for a mess of pottage. Nay, even after reason has retired from the contest, she has been known to cling blindly with the instinct of a turtle dove to those principles and policies which to her mind promise hope and safety for children yet unborn. It is notorious that ignorant black women in the South have actually left their husbands' homes and repudiated their support for what was understood by the wife to be race disloyalty, or "voting away," as she expresses it, the privileges of herself and little ones.

It is largely our women in the South to-day who keep the black men solid in the Republican party. The latter as they increase in intelligence and power of discrimination would be more apt to divide on local issues at any rate. They begin to see that the Grand Old Party regards the Negro's cause as an outgrown issue, and on Southern soil at least finds a too intimate acquaintanceship with him a somewhat unsavory recommendation. Then, too, their political wits have been sharpened to appreciate the fact that it is good policy to cultivate one's neighbors and not depend too much on a distant friend to fight one's home battles. But the black woman can never forget—however lukewarm the party may to-day appear—that it was a Republican president who struck the manacles from her own wrists and gave the possibilities of manhood to her helpless little ones; and to her mind a Democratic Negro is a traitor and a time-server. Talk as much as you like of venality and manipulation in the South, there are not many men, I can tell you, who would dare face a wife quivering in every fiber with the consciousness that her husband is a coward who could be paid to desert her deepest and dearest interests.

Not unfelt, then, if unproclaimed has been the work and influence of the colored women of America. Our list of chieftains in the service, though not long, is not inferior in strength and excellence, I dare believe, to any similar list which this country can produce.

Among the pioneers, Frances Watkins Harper could sing with prophetic exaltation in the darkest days, when as yet there was not a rift in the clouds overhanging her people:

> Yes, Ethiopia shall stretch
> Her bleeding hands abroad;
> Her cry of agony shall reach the burning
>   throne of God.
> Redeemed from dust and freed from
>   chains
> Her sons shall lift their eyes,
> From cloud-capt hills and verdant plains
> Shall shouts of triumph rise.

Among preachers of righteousness, an unanswerable silencer of cavilers and objectors, was Sojourner Truth, that unique and rugged genius who seemed carved out without hand or chisel from the solid mountain mass; and in pleasing contrast, Amanda Smith, sweetest of natural singers and pleaders in dulcet tones for the things of God and of His Christ.

Sarah Woodson Early and Martha Briggs, planting and watering in the school room, and giving off front their matchless and irresistible personality an impetus and inspiration which can never die so long as there lives and breathes a remote descendant of their disciples and friends.

Charlotte Fortin Grimké, the gentle spirit whose verses and life link her so beautifully with

America's great Quaker poet and loving reformer.

Hallie Quinn Brown, charming reader, earnest effective lecturer and devoted worker of unflagging zeal and unquestioned power.

Fannie Jackson Coppin, the teacher and organizer, pre-eminent among women of whatever country or race in constructive and executive force.

These women represent all shades of belief and as many departments of activity; but they have one thing in common—their sympathy with the oppressed race in America and the consecration of their several talents in whatever line to the work of its deliverance and development.

Fifty years ago woman's activity according to orthodox definitions was on a pretty clearly cut "sphere," including primarily the kitchen and the nursery, and rescued from the barrenness of prison bars by the womanly mania for adorning every discoverable bit of china or canvass with forlorn looking cranes balanced idiotically on one foot. The woman of to-day finds herself in the presence of responsibilities which ramify through the profoundest and most varied interests of her country and race. Not one of the issues of this plodding, toiling, sinning, repenting, falling, aspiring humanity can afford to shut her out, or can deny the reality of her influence. No plan for renovating society, no scheme for purifying politics, no reform in church or in state, no moral, social, or economic question, no movement upward or downward in the human plane is lost on her. A man once said when told his house was afire: "Go tell my wife; I never meddle with household affairs." But no woman can possibly put herself or her sex outside any of the interests that affect humanity. All departments in the new era are to be hers, in the sense that her interests are in all and through all; and it is incumbent on her to keep intelligently and sympathetically *en rapport* with all the great movements of her time, that she may know on which side to throw the weight of her influence. She stands now at the gateway of this new era of American civilization. In her hands must be moulded the

strength, the wit, the statesmanship, the morality, all the psychic force, the social and economic intercourse of that era. To be alive at such an epoch is a privilege, to be a woman then is sublime.

In this last decade of our century, changes of such moment are in progress, such new and alluring vistas are opening out before us, such original and radical suggestions for the adjustment of labor and capital, of government and the governed, of the family, the church and the state, that to be a possible factor though an infinitesimal in such a movement is pregnant with hope and weighty with responsibility. To be a woman in such an age carries with it a privilege and an opportunity never implied before. But to be a woman of the Negro race in America, and to be able to grasp the deep significance of the possibilities of the crisis, is to have a heritage, it seems to me, unique in the ages. In the first place, the race is young and full of the elasticity and hopefulness of youth. All its achievements are before it. It does not look on the masterly triumphs of nineteenth century civilization with that *blasé*, world-weary look which characterizes the old washed out and worn out races which have already, so to speak, seen their best days.

Said a European writer recently: "Except the Sclavonic, the Negro is the only original and distinctive genius which has yet to come to growth—and the feeling is to cherish and develop it."

Everything to this race is new and strange and inspiring. There is a quickening of its pulses and a glowing of its self-consciousness. Aha, I can rival that! I can aspire to that! I can honor my name and vindicate my race! Something like this, it strikes me, is the enthusiasm which stirs the genius of young Africa in America; and the memory of past oppression and the fact of present attempted repression only serve to gather momentum for its irrepressible powers. Then again, a race in such a stage of growth is peculiarly sensitive to impressions. Not the photographer's sensitized plate is more delicately impressionable to outer influences than is this high strung people here on the threshold of a career.

What a responsibility then to have the sole management of the primal lights and shadows! Such is the colored woman's office. She must stamp weal or woe on the coming history of this people. May she see her opportunity and vindicate her high prerogative.

Rev. W. E. C. Wright
"The New Negro"

Advance, November 2, 1893[12]

By Rev. E. C. Wright. District Secretary, Cleveland, Ohio.

The American negro of thirty years ago was the product of African paganism and American slavery that called itself Christian. Two widely different pictures of the negro of that period are to be found in the descriptions and allusions of writers both of that time and of the present day. In apologies for slavery, whether direct or indirect, the negro appears as docile and happy, loyal to his master and to his master's family, kind in disposition, of a warm religious nature, and so trustworthy that his very vices leaned to virtue's side. Such idyllic pictures of the negroes as the best laboring population in the world are to be found abundantly in the literature of the past and present generation, and in wayside conversations of to-day.

On the other hand, in criticism of the legislatures of the reconstruction period, and in excuses made for separate railway coaches, separate schools and churches, and the exclusion of negroes from all offices and from the ballot-box, the negro appears as ignorant, depraved, given over to all the vices, and incapable of cultivation in mind or in morals.

A judicial estimate of what the millions of the freedmen were when just emancipated, must no doubt retain enough features from the last characterization, to show that if slavery was in any sense a missionary instrumentality it was not efficient for producing the highest Christian civilization. It did not develop in the slave thrift, foresight and self-reliance to make him more and more fit for successful freedom. It did not graft firmly upon the religiosity of his nature the virtues of honesty, truthfulness and chastity.

When we add the fact of universal illiteracy on the part of the freedmen at the close of the war, it is evident that their condition called for something slavery had not given them. There was crying need of some new form of missionary work other than the "peculiar institution." It was necessary not only for their own sake, but for the welfare of the whole South and the entire nation. The situation demanded not the development of a better slave nor the production of a serf, but the transformation of a vast population trained as slaves into a population with the character, habits and virtues of freemen. The nation could not prosper with these millions continuing as they were. The problem for statesman, philanthropist, Christian, was no less than to make a new negro.

The American Missionary Association was one of the most important agencies that grappled with this problem. It rightly regarded the school-house as the starting point for the great transformation. The change must come in response to intelligent appeal. In developing individual intelligence and character, the school-house can build into society all the elements of Christian civilization. For the school-house has to do with health and skill and thrift and morals and religion.

Thirty years have brought many changes to the South. The greatest of them all is to be found in the results already attained by Christian education in making a new negro. In putting forward this claim and some of the evidence in its support, I shall deal but slightly with statistics, and confine myself largely to testimony from personal observation.

In the matter of physical stamina and health, Christian education cannot claim that it has up to the present time improved on the old negro, when the whole mass is taken into view. The death-rate among the colored population in such Southern cities as published record, is nearly double that of the white population. It is undoubtedly much larger than it was among the slaves. This high death-rate is not surprising in view of their poverty and ignorance and, moreover, is partly to be explained by the high birth rate among the same population. For in all cities nearly half the deaths are of little children. The higher rate than in slave times shows that we have not yet carried education far enough with the negro population to secure as good care of themselves and their children as the old masters took of them when each had a high market value. Every missionary school gives instruction in hygiene and sanitation. The new negro in this sphere of the physical life is to be seen in the trained colored teachers and the growing company of thoroughly educated colored physicians. The number of both these classes must be increased, and they will lift the millions to a new physical level.

In the intellectual sphere, the new negro is unmistakably prominent. We marvel at the literature which has sprung up in the white South since the war. This brilliant constellation of writers now glowing in the Southern sky, is not so indicative of a new era for the South and the nation as are the gatherings of the state associations of colored teachers. I have attended that of Alabama where were some four hundred present, of whom the president said the larger part owed their education at first or second hand to the American Missionary Association. They were principals and teachers of city and village schools, shaping the colored youth of their respective communities. They were presidents and professors in colleges and normal schools, training the teachers of the majority of the children of that state which has a larger colored

than white population. Whether old enough to have been born in slavery or only the children of slaves, these earnest, capable, and many of them highly educated, teachers were the new negro in sharp contrast with the absolutely illiterate slave population of less than a generation before.

New negroes worthy of all honor are the multitudes of our pupils and pupils of our pupils who are pushing out into the remoter public school districts of the Black Belt. They are at once examples and apostles of a new era, for they are missionaries of a better life to the rural millions of the South. I have seen them at their work and found them not only good teachers in the school-house, but also a spiritual power in the churches and practical examples of thrift and nobly ambitions in their communities.

Quite as important as lists of taxable property is the new spirit of self-reliance and independence beginning to show itself among many of the negroes who are still poor. It would be an impressive sign of the new industrial South if we could gather in one assembly the white iron masters of Alabama whose skill and energy have in twenty years brought that state from zero in the production of pig iron to a position next to Pennsylvania and Ohio. I affirm in all truth and soberness that far more significant to one that looks deep into the sources of civilization, was the gathering I saw of some hundreds of hard-handed negro cotton planters in the black belt met to discuss their condition, prospects, and means of improvement. Some of this company had not much book learning, and others were teachers for a part of the year. All had felt the influence of the missionary movement of Christian education. They lived, most of them, in cabins without glass windows, and many of them in the one-roomed cabin. Few of them owned land. Year by year their cotton crops were mortgaged for food while they tilled the fields. But there was in them the spirit of freemen. They raised no clamor for government aid. They indulged in no chimerical visions of reaching the millennium by wholesale emigration. All day long they exhorted one another to more intelligent farming, more unremitting industry, greater economy, and the purchase of land. They urged that the pulpits be purged of immoral preachers. They applauded loudly the exhortation to talk religion less and live it more. Such spirt and purpose among the laborers is the best of all auguries of industrial improvement.

The graduates and former pupils of our missionary schools are to be found everywhere in the South among the foremost leaders of every upward movement. The steady and rapid development of industrial training in our schools makes them important factors in diversifying and developing the industries of the South. The amount and character of Biblical study in our schools of all grades is a powerful instrumentality for changing the old time religion of emotion into a religion that concerns the intelligence and the conduct as well as the feelings. We are making a new negro.

When criticisms of our work call attention to millions of negroes who are still ignor an [sic] and degraded, we are only incited to press our work the more vigorously, till the lowest are lifted. When we are told that many partially and some highly educated negroes are in Southern penitentiaries, we remember that our Northern prisons hold some white graduates of colleges, and are moved not to educate less, but to increase the moral and religious elements in education.

A Georgia critic complained in the *Forum* for October that education is leading the negro away from "his feeling of dependence" and causing him to cease showing "proper respect to the white people," and says "a little education is all the negro needs," and that he "will have to be disfranchised" and have "a separate code enacted that will fit him." This leads one to wonder whether the Anglo-Saxon race in the South has lost its capacity of adjustment to new conditions. Many even of the educated men of that race seem to have learned nothing on this subject in thirty years. They still have no suggestion to make for the negro, but to suppress him. They still write in the spirit of Chancellor Harper's ante-bellum memoir on slavery, in which he maintained that the aspirations of a freeman

unfit a laborer for his situation, and asked triumphantly, "Would you do a benefit to the horse or the ox by giving him a cultivated understanding of fine feelings?"

The almost universal prevalence of such a sentiment among the old masters thirty years ago, unfitted them for the new training of the negro. The persistence of the sentiment keeps most Southern whites of to-day unfit to deal with negro education. The tradition that the negro must be kept in his place by white authority, is so fixed in the average white mind in the South, that it is impossible for him to work along the line of letting the negro, as well as every other human being, find his place by natural selections, as Providence gives him capacity and opportunity. Even Judge Gundy says a social law forbids white people to teach negroes. Bill Arp in the *Forum* would not give one of the seven million negroes the higher education, nor let one of them enter a profession.

In Judge Gundy's very liberal address on negro education at the Southern Teachers' Association in Atlanta a year ago, he urged better schools for negroes and giving them all the education for which they have desire and capacity, but said that they should be taught in school that they are inferior to the white race. It is worthy of notice, however, that while this sentence appeared in the Atlanta *Journal's* report of the address at the time, it was left out when the address was given to the nation a few weeks later in the *Journal of Politics*. The original utterance in the most liberal address recently heard from any Southern man, shows the persistence of the influence of slavery on the master race.

I have heard the superintendent of education of a great Southern state address the colored teachers assembled in their state association and put the chief emphasis of his address of an hour's length on assuring these teachers that the Southern whites are much better friends of negro than the Northerners are, and on warning these teachers against "social equality," whatever that may mean. As if the work of the chief school official of a state were to prevent somebody from getting somewhere or trying to get somewhere, instead of doing everything possible to increase the capacity of every child in the commonwealth to achieve good results for the commonwealth and honorable rewards for himself.

Too much of the white South that expresses itself is still in the attitude of repressing the old negro instead of reorganizing the new negro and helping him upward. If half the pains were taken to find out what the best negroes are doing and saying and thinking, that is taken to hunt down a negro suspected of crime, the mind of the white South would be rapidly changed on the whole subject of the treatment and the prospect of the negro. Such change in the Southern white mind would be of incalculable service in accelerating the change in the negro. There are open-eyed southerners who recognize the enormous progress made by the negro in a generation. We who are in the work know the appalling needs still unmet, but we are not appalled, for we see the improvement to be so great that we regard the time as not remote historically when the negro shall be so completely made new to become wholly an element of strength and hope in the nation's life and the world's evangelization.

~~~~~~

Fannie Barrier Williams

"The Intellectual Progress of the Colored Women of the United States since the Emancipation Proclamation"

In *The World's Congress of Representative Women*, edited by May Wright Sewall, 1894[13]

CONGRESS OF REPRESENTATIVE WOMEN.

THE INTELLECTUAL PROGRESS OF THE COLORED WOMEN OF THE UNITED STATES SINCE THE EMANCIPATION PROCLAMATION—AN ADDRESS BY FANNIE BARRIER WILLIAMS OF ILLINOIS.

Less than thirty years ago the term progress as applied to colored women of African descent in the United States would have been an anomaly. The recognition of that term to-day as appropriate is a fact full of interesting significance. That the discussion of progressive womanhood in this great assemblage of the representative women of the world is considered incomplete without some account of the colored women's status is a most noteworthy evidence that we have not failed to impress ourselves on the higher side of American life.

Less is known of our women than of any other class of Americans.

No other organization of far-reaching influence for their special advancement, no conventions of women to take note of their progress, and no special literature reciting the incidents, the events, and all things interesting and instructive concerning them are to be found among the agencies directing their career. There has been no special interest in their peculiar condition as native-born American women. Their power to affect the social life of America, either for good or for ill, has excited not even a speculative interest.

Though there is much that is sorrowful, much that is wonderfully heroic, and much that is romantic in a peculiar way in their history, none of it has as yet been told as evidence of what is possible for these women. How few of the happy, prosperous, and eager living Americans can appreciate what it all means to be suddenly changed from irresponsible bondage to the responsibility of freedom and citizenship!

The distress of it all can never be told, and the pain of it all can never be felt except by the victims, and by those saintly women of the white race who for thirty years have been consecrated to the uplifting of a whole race of women from a long-enforced degradation.

The American people have always been impatient of ignorance and poverty. They believe with Emerson that "America is another word for opportunity," and for that reason success is a virtue and poverty and ignorance are inexcusable. This may account for the fact that our women have excited no general sympathy in the struggle to emancipate themselves from the demoralization of slavery. This new life of freedom, with its far-reaching responsibilities, had to be learned by these children of darkness mostly without a guide, a teacher, or a friend. In the mean vocabulary of slavery there was no definition of any of the virtues of life. The meaning of such precious terms as marriage, wife, family, and home could not be learned in a school-house. The blue-back speller, the arithmetic, and the copy-book contain no magical cures for inherited inaptitudes for moralities. Yet it must ever be counted as one of the most wonderful things in human history how promptly and eagerly these suddenly liberated women tried to lay hold upon all that there is in human excellence. There is a touching pathos in the eagerness of these millions of new home-makers to taste the blessedness of intelligent womanhood. The path of progress in the picture is enlarged so as to bring to view these trustful and zealous students of freedom and civilization striving to overtake and keep pace with women whose emancipation has been a slow and painful process for a thousand years. The longing to be something better than they were when freedom found them has been the most notable characteristic in the development of these women. This constant striving for equality has given an upward direction to all the activities of colored women.

Freedom at once widened their vision beyond the mean cabin life of their bondage. Their native gentleness, good cheer, and hopefulness made them susceptible to those teachings that make for intelligence and righteousness. Sullenness of disposition, hatefulness, and revenge against the master class because of two centu-ries of ill-treatment are not in the nature of our women.

But a better view of what our women are doing and what their present status is may be had by noticing some lines of progress that are easily verifiable.

First it should be noticed that separate facts and figures relative to colored women are not easily obtainable. Among the white women of the country independence, progressive intelligence, and definite interests have done so much that nearly every fact and item illustrative of their progress and status is classified and easily accessible. Our women, on the contrary, have had no advantage of interests peculiar and distinct and separable from those of men that have yet excited public attention and kindly recognition.

In their religious life, however, our women show a progressiveness parallel in every important particular to that of white women in all Christian churches. It has always been a circumstance of the highest satisfaction to the missionary efforts of the Christian church that the colored people are so susceptible to a religion that marks the highest point of blessedness in human history.

Instead of finding witchcraft, sensual fetiches, and the coarse superstitions of savagery possessing our women, Christianity found them with hearts singularly tender, sympathetic, and fit for the reception of the doctrines. Their superstitions were not deeply ingrained, but were of the same sort and nature that characterized the devotees of the Christian faith everywhere.

While there has been but little progress toward the growing rationalism in the Christian creeds, there has been a marked advance toward a greater refinement of conception, good taste, and the proprieties. It is our young women coming out of the schools and academies that have been insisting upon a more godly and cultivated ministry. It is the young women of a new generation and new inspirations that are making tramps of the ministers who once dominated the colored church, and whose intelligence and piety were mostly in their lungs. In this new and growing religious life the colored people have laid hold of those sweeter influences of the King's Daughters, of the Christian Endeavor and Helping Hand societies, which are doing much to elevate the tone of worship and to magnify all that there is blessed in religion.

Another evidence of growing intelligence is a sense of religious discrimination among our women. Like the nineteenth century woman generally, our women find congeniality in all the creeds, from the Catholic creed to the no-creed of Emerson. There is a constant increase of this interesting variety in the religious life of our women.

Closely allied to this religious development is their progress in the work of education in schools and colleges. For thirty years education has been the magic word among the colored people of this country. That their greatest need was education in its broadest sense was understood by these people more strongly than it could be taught to them. It is the unvarying testimony of every teacher in the South that the mental development of the colored women as well as men has been little less than phenomenal. In twenty-five years, and under conditions discouraging in the extreme, thousands of our women have been educated as teachers. They have adapted themselves to the work of mentally lifting a whole race of people so eagerly and readily that they afford an apt illustration of the power of self-help. Not only have these women become good teachers in less than twenty-five years, but many of them are the prize teachers in the mixed schools of nearly every Northern city.

These women have also so fired the hearts of the race for education that colleges, normal schools, industrial schools, and universities have been reared by a generous public to meet the requirements of these eager students of intelligent citizenship. As American women generally are fighting against the nineteenth century narrowness that still keeps women out of the higher institutions of learning, so our women are eagerly demanding the best of education open to their race. They continually verify what President Rankin of Howard University recently said, "Any theory of educating the Afro-American that does not throw open the golden gates of the highest culture will fail on the ethical and spiritual side."

It is thus seen that our women have the same spirit and mettle that characterize the best of American women. Everywhere they are following in the tracks of those women who are swiftest in the race for higher knowledge.

To-day they feel strong enough to ask for but one thing, and that is the same opportunity for the acquisition of all kinds of knowledge that may be accorded to other women. This granted, in the next generation these progressive women will be found successfully occupying every field where the highest intelligence alone is admissible. In less than another generation American literature, American art, and American music will be enriched by productions having new and peculiar features of interest and excellence.

The exceptional career of our women will yet stamp itself indelibly upon the thought of this country.

American literature needs for its greater variety and its deeper soundings that which will be written into it out of the hearts of these self-emancipating women.

The great problems of social reform that are now so engaging the highest intelligence of American women will soon need for their solution the reinforcement of that new intelligence which our women are developing. In short, our women are ambitious to be contributors to all the great moral and intellectual forces that make for the greater weal of our common country.

If this hope seems too extravagant to those of you who know these women only in their humbler capacities, I would remind you that all that we hope for and will certainly achieve in authorship and practical intelligence is more than prophesied by what has already been done, and more that can be done, by hundreds of Afro-American women whose talents are now being expanded in the struggle against race resistance.

The power of organized womanhood is one of the most interesting studies of modern sociology. Formerly women knew so little of each other mentally, their common interests were so sentimental and gossipy, and their knowledge of all the larger affairs of human society was so meager that organization among them, in the modern sense, was impossible. Now their liberal intelligence, their contact in all the great interests of education, and their increasing influence for good in all the great reformatory movements of the age has created in them a greater respect for each other, and furnished the elements of organization for large and splendid purposes. The highest ascendancy of woman's development has been reached when they have become mentally strong enough to find bonds of association interwoven with sympathy, loyalty, and mutual trustfulness. To-day union is the watchword of woman's onward march.

If it be a fact that this spirit of organization among women generally is the distinguishing mark of the nineteenth century woman, dare we ask if the colored women of the United States have made any progress in this respect?

For peculiar and painful reasons the great lessons of fraternity and altruism are hard for the colored women to learn. Emancipation found the colored Americans of the South with no sentiments of association. It will be admitted that race misfortune could scarcely go further when the terms fraternity, friendship, and unity had no meaning for its men and women.

If within thirty years they have begun to recognize the blessed significance of these vital terms of human society, confidence in their social development should be strengthened. In this important work of bringing the race together to know itself and to unite in work for a common destiny, the women have taken a leading part.

Benevolence is the essence of most of the colored women's organizations. The humane side of their natures has been cultivated to recognize the duties they owe to the sick, the indigent and ill-fortuned. No church, school, or charitable institution for the special use of colored people has been allowed to languish or fail when the associated efforts of the women could save it.

It is highly significant and interesting to note that these women, whose hearts have been wrung by all kinds of sorrow, are abundantly manifesting those gracious qualities of heart that characterize women of the best type. These kinder sentiments arising from mutual interests that are lifting our women into purer and tenderer relationship to each other, and are making the meager joys and larger griefs of our conditions known to each other, have been a larger part of their education.

The hearts of Afro-American women are too warm and too large for race hatred. Long suffering has so chastened them that they are developing a special sense of sympathy for all who suffer and fail of justice. All the associated interests of church, temperance, and social reform in which American women are winning distinction can be wonderfully advanced when our women shall be welcomed as co-workers, and estimated solely by what they are worth to the moral elevation of all the people.

I regret the necessity of speaking to the question of the moral progress of our women, because the morality of our home life has been commented upon so disparagingly and meanly that we are placed in the unfortunate position of being defenders of our name.

It is proper to state, with as much emphasis as possible, that all questions relative to the moral progress of the colored women of America are impertinent and unjustly suggestive when they relate to the thousands of colored women in the North who were free from the vicious influences of slavery. They are also meanly suggestive as regards thousands of our women in the South whose force of character enabled them to escape the slavery taints of immorality. The question of the moral progress of colored women in the United States has force and meaning in this discussion only so far as it tells the story of how the once-enslaved women have been struggling for twenty-five years to emancipate themselves from the demoralization of their enslavement.

While I duly appreciate the offensiveness of all references to American slavery, it is unavoidable to charge to that system every moral imperfection that mars the character of the colored American. The whole life and power of slavery depended upon an enforced degradation of everything human in the slaves. The slave code recognized only animal distinctions between the sexes, and ruthlessly ignored those ordinary separations that belong to the social state.

It is a great wonder that two centuries of such demoralization did not work a complete extinction of all the moral instincts. But the recuperative power of these women to regain their moral instincts and to establish a respectable relationship to American womanhood is among the earlier evidences of their moral ability to rise above their conditions. In spite of a cursed heredity that bound them to the lowest social level, in spite of everything that is unfortunate and unfavorable, these women have continually shown an increasing degree of teachableness as to the meaning of woman's relationship to man.

Out of this social purification and moral uplift have come a chivalric sentiment and regard from the young men of the race that give to the young women a new sense of protection. I do not wish to disturb the serenity of this conference by suggesting why this protection is needed and the kind of men against whom it is needed.

It is sufficient for us to know that the daughters of women who thirty years ago were not allowed to be modest, not allowed to follow the instincts of moral rectitude, who could cry for protection to no living man, have so elevated the moral tone of their social life that new and purer standards of personal worth have been created, and new ideals of womanhood, instinct with grace and delicacy, are everywhere recognized and emulated.

This moral regeneration of a whole race of women is no idle sentiment—it is a serious business; and everywhere there is witnessed a feverish anxiety to be free from the mean suspicions that have so long underestimated the character strength of our women.

These women are not satisfied with the unmistakable fact that moral progress has been made, but they are fervently impatient and stirred by a sense of outrage under the vile imputations of a diseased public opinion.

Loves that are free from the dross of coarseness, affections that are unsullied, and a proper sense of all the sanctities of human intercourse felt by thousands of these women all over the land plead for the recognition of their fitness to be judged, not by the standards of slavery, but by the higher standards of freedom and of twenty-five years of education, culture, and moral contact.

The moral aptitudes of our women are just as strong and just as weak as those of any other American women with like advantages of intelligence and environment.

It may now perhaps be fittingly asked, What mean all these evidences of mental, social, and moral progress of a class of American women of whom you know so little? Certainly you can not be indifferent to the growing needs and importance of women who are demonstrating their intelligence and capacity for the highest privileges of freedom.

The most important thing to be noted is the fact that the colored people of America have reached a distinctly new era in their career so quickly that the American mind has scarcely had time to recognize the fact, and adjust itself to the new requirements of the people in all things that pertain to citizenship.

Thirty years ago public opinion recognized no differences in the colored race. To our great misfortune public opinion has changed but slightly. History is full of examples of the great injustice resulting from the perversity of public opinion, and its tardiness in recognizing new conditions.

It seems to daze the understanding of the ordinary citizen that there are thousands of men and women everywhere among us who in twenty-five years have progressed as far away from the non-progressive peasants of the "black belt" of the South as the highest social life in New England is above the lowest levels of American civilization.

This general failure of the American people to know the new generation of colored people, and to recognize this important change in them, is the cause of more injustice to our women than can well be estimated. Further progress is everywhere seriously hindered by this ignoring of their improvement.

Our exclusion from the benefits of the fair play sentiment of the country is little less than a crime against the ambitions and aspirations of a whole race of women. The American people are but repeating the common folly of history in thus attempting to repress the yearnings of progressive humanity.

In the item of employment colored women bear a distressing burden of mean and unreasonable discrimination. A Southern teacher of thirty years' experience in the South writes that "one million possibilities of good through black womanhood all depend upon an opportunity to make a living."

It is almost literally true that, except teaching in colored schools and menial work, colored women can find no employment in this free America. They are the only women in the country for whom real ability, virtue, and special talents count for nothing when they become applicants for respectable employment. Taught everywhere in ethics and social economy that merit always wins, colored women carefully prepare themselves for all kinds of occupation only to meet with stern refusal, rebuff, and disappointment. One of countless instances will show how the best as well as the meanest of American society are responsible for the special injustice to our women.

Not long ago I presented the case of a bright young woman to a well-known bank president of Chicago, who was in need of a thoroughly competent stenographer and typewriter. The president was fully satisfied with the young woman as exceptionally qualified for the position, and manifested much pleasure in commending her to the directors for appointment, and at the same time disclaimed that there could be any opposition on account of the slight tinge of African blood that identified her as a colored woman. Yet, when the matter was brought before the directors for action, these mighty men of money and business, these men whose prom-

inence in all the great interests of the city would seem to lift them above all narrowness and foolishness, scented the African taint, and at once bravely came to the rescue of the bank and of society by dashing the hopes of this capable yet helpless young woman. No other question but that of color determined the action of these men, many of whom are probably foremost members of the humane society and heavy contributors to foreign missions and church extension work.

This question of employment for the trained talents of our women is a most serious one. Refusal of such employment because of color belies every maxim of justice and fair play. Such refusal takes the blessed meaning out of all the teachings of our civilization, and sadly confuses our conceptions of what is just, humane, and moral.

Can the people of this country afford to single out the women of a whole race of people as objects of their special contempt? Do these women not belong to a race that has never faltered in its support of the country's flag in every war since Attucks fell in Boston's streets?

Are they not the daughters of men who have always been true as steel against treason to everything fundamental and splendid in the republic? In short, are these women not as thoroughly American in all circumstances of citizenship as the best citizens of our country?

If it be so, are we not justified in a feeling of desperation against that peculiar form of Americanism that shows respect for our women as servants and contempt for them when they become women of culture? We have never been taught to understand why the unwritten law of chivalry, protection, and fair play that are everywhere the conservators of women's welfare must exclude every woman of a dark complexion.

We believe that the world always needs the influence of every good and capable woman, and this rule recognizes no exceptions based on complexion. In their complaint against hindrances to their employment colored women ask for no special favors.

They are even willing to bring to every position fifty per cent more of ability than is required of any other class of women. They plead for opportunities untrammeled by prejudice. They plead for the right of the individual to be judged, not by tradition and race estimate, but by the present evidences of individual worth. We believe this country is large enough and the opportunities for all kinds of success are great enough to afford our women a fair chance to earn a respectable living, and to win every prize within the reach of their capabilities.

Another, and perhaps more serious, hindrance to our women is that nightmare known as "social equality." The term equality is the most inspiring word in the vocabulary of citizenship. It expresses the leveling quality in all the splendid possibilities of American life. It is this idea of equality that has made room in this country for all kinds and conditions of men, and made personal merit the supreme requisite for all kinds of achievement.

When the colored people became citizens, and found it written deep in the organic law of the land that they too had the right to life, liberty, and the pursuit of happiness, they were at once suspected of wishing to interpret this maxim of equality as meaning social equality.

Everywhere the public mind has been filled with constant alarm lest in some way our women shall approach the social sphere of the dominant race in this country. Men and women, wise and perfectly sane in all things else, become instantly unwise and foolish at the remotest suggestion of social contact with colored men and women. At every turn in our lives we meet this fear, and are humiliated by its aggressiveness and meanness. If we seek the sanctities of religion, the enlightenment of the university, the honors of politics, and the natural recreations of our common country, the social equality alarm is instantly given, and our aspirations are insulted. "Beware of social equality with the colored American" is thus written on all places, sacred or profane, in this blessed land of liberty. The most discouraging and demoralizing effect of this false sentiment concerning us is that it utterly ignores individual merit and discredits the sensibilities of intelligent womanhood. The sorrows and heartaches of a whole race of women seem to be matters of no concern to the people who so dread the social possibilities of these colored women.

On the other hand, our women have been wonderfully indifferent and unconcerned about the matter. The dread inspired by the growing intelligence of colored women has interested us almost to the point of amusement. It has given to colored women a new sense of importance to witness how easily their emancipation and steady advancement is disturbing all classes of American people. It may not be a discouraging circumstance that colored women can command some sort of attention, even though they be misunderstood. We believe in the law of reaction, and it is reasonably certain that the forces of intelligence and character being developed in our women will yet change mistrustfulness into confidence and contempt into sympathy and respect. It will soon appear to those who are not hopelessly monomaniacs on the subject that the colored people are in no way responsible for the social equality nonsense. We shall yet be credited with knowing better than our enemies that social equality can neither be enforced by law nor prevented by oppression. Though not philosophers, we long since learned that equality before the law, equality in the best sense of that term under our institutions, is totally different from social equality.

We know, without being exceptional students of history, that the social relationship of the two races will be adjusted equitably in spite of all fear and injustice, and that there is a social gravitation in human affairs that eventually overwhelms and crushes into nothingness all resistance based on prejudice and selfishness.

Our chief concern in this false social sentiment is that it attempts to hinder our further progress toward the higher spheres of womanhood. On account of it, young colored women of ambition and means are compelled in many instances to leave the country for training and education in the salons and studios of Europe. On many of the railroads of this country women of refinement and culture are driven like cattle into human cattle-cars lest the occupying of an individual seat paid for in a first-class car may result in social equality. This social quarantine on all means of travel in certain parts of the country is guarded and enforced more rigidly against us than the quarantine regulations against cholera.

Without further particularizing as to how this social question opposes our advancement, it may be stated that the contentions of colored women are in kind like those of other American women for greater freedom of development. Liberty to be all that we can be, without artificial hindrances, is a thing no less precious to us than to women generally.

We come before this assemblage of women feeling confident that our progress has been along high levels and rooted deeply in the essentials of intelligent humanity. We are so essentially American in speech, in instincts, in sentiments and destiny that the things that interest you equally interest us.

We believe that social evils are dangerously contagious. The fixed policy of persecution and injustice against a class of women who are weak and defenseless will be necessarily hurtful to the cause of all women. Colored women are becoming more and more a part of the social forces that must help to determine the questions that so concern women generally. In this Congress we ask to be known and recognized for what we are worth. If it be the high purpose of these deliberations to lessen the resistance to woman's progress, you can not fail to be interested in our struggles against the many oppositions that harass us.

Women who are tender enough in heart to be active in humane societies, to be foremost in all charitable activities, who are loving enough to unite Christian womanhood everywhere against the sin of intemperance, ought to be instantly concerned in the plea of colored women for justice and humane treatment. Women of the dominant race can not afford to be responsible for the wrongs we suffer, since those who do injustice can not escape a certain penalty.

But there is no wish to overstate the obstacles to colored women or to picture their status as hopeless. There is no disposition to take our place in this Congress as faultfinders or suppliants for mercy. As women of a common country, with common interests, and a destiny that will certainly bring us closer to each other, we come to this altar with our contribution of hopefulness as well as with our complaints.

When you learn that womanhood everywhere among us is blossoming out into greater fullness of everything that is sweet, beautiful, and good in a woman; when you learn that the bitterness of our experience as citizen-women has not hardened our finer feelings of love and pity for our enemies; when you learn that fierce opposition to the widening spheres of our employment has not abated the aspirations of our women to enter successfully into all the professions and arts open only to intelligence, and that everywhere in the wake of enlightened womanhood our women are seen and felt for the good they diffuse, this Congress will at once see the fullness of our fellowship, and help us to avert the arrows of prejudice that pierce the soul because of the color of our bodies.

If the love of humanity more than the love of races and sex shall pulsate throughout all the grand results that shall issue to the world from this parliament of women, women of African descent in the United States will for the first time begin to feel the sweet release from the blighting thrall of prejudice.

The colored women, as well as all women, will realize that the inalienable right to life, liberty, and the pursuit of happiness is a maxim that will become more blessed in its significance when the hand of woman shall take it from its sepulture in books and make it the gospel of every-day life and the unerring guide in the relations of all men, women, and children.

PART II

THE BOOKER T. WASHINGTON ERA, 1895–1903

Anonymous
"A Race Problem to Solve"

Leavenworth Herald, July 20, 1895[1]

The question cannot fail to be interesting to the men and women who are interested in the well being of all the people. That a whole race of women should be so obscured by the peculiar sentiments of American life as to suggest an inquiry of this sort ought to excite some degree of interest in all fair-minded people.

The question, what becomes of colored girls or young women? certainly cannot be answered by searching for them in any of the great places of business where girls and women of other races are so extensively employed. From a recent bulletin of the census bureau showing the occupations of the American people, it appears that within the past few years American women have successfully and extensively invaded all but two of the 221 occupations. In some of these occupations, the increase of female employes [*sic*] has been 26 per cent.

In this great expansion of the opportunities for American women to become self-supporting, it is a startling fact that colored women are the only women not benefited. Indeed, they are the only women in this land of equality for whom virtues and ability count for nothing in seeking employment. The persistence of American prejudice against the American Negro is nowhere better illustrated than in this relentless exclusion of colored women from any of the expanding chances for women to compete with men in earning a living.

What a novelty it would be to see a colored girl acting as saleswoman in any of the stores of Chicago! What a sensation it would be to see colored young women at work in the thousands of factories and other places where now women of foreign tongue and doubtful patriotism enjoy a monopoly of the right to earn a living! Even the powers that fatten on the "sweat shop," I suppose, would draw the color line in horror over the prospect of cleanly American women of Af-

rican blood asking the privilege of sweating for a penny. Even such kind of work as laundrying and domestic service, for which young colored women were supposed to be perculiarly fitted, now affords but slight employment to women of dark complexions. It cannot be urged that this fanatic sort of discrimination is due to a lack of qualification. Thousands of these young people are trained in the same schools and have the same educational advantages as their more fortunate schoolmates. It has certainly not been proved by experience that colored girls have less aptitude for the various kinds of employment in which other girls find such an abundance and variety of work.

But it is a fact that those who employ labor or skill or intelligence are either afraid of the experiment of "mixing the races," or else they refuse point blank because of their natural antipathy to the Negro race.

A striking instance of this kind occurred recently in Chicago, in the case of a young colored woman who had worked for nearly three years in a composing room, as a compositor, without being known as a colored woman. She was rated high because of her efficiency, and was in every way one of the most desirable of the force. Through the accident of an unfortunate inquiry made by a darker relative of the young woman her identity became known to the manager and she was summarily discharged. This is not an aggravated case. Such being the difficulty of obtaining employment of any kind, the question, what becomes of this class of girls? is all the more interesting.

It is true that in spite of this unfavorable sentiment to their employment, some of these young women succeed by force of good fortune and daring in getting good positions as stenographers, bookkeepers and clerks. Many of them secure positions in the South, and occasionally in the North, as schoolteachers. Others follow music, hairdressing, elocution and dressmaking. This, of course, does not account for the thousands who are hopelessly shut out from a chance to earn a living.

In following up this question in search of these unemployed young women, some curious facts are developed. In the first place, early marriages seem to be one of the means of escape from enforced idleness. Being less independent than the young women who have and relish the opportunity to support themselves by money-making, the colored girl has no prospect in life except in matrimony. She, unfortunately, never gets a chance to know the significance of the term, "the new woman." This may seem to be a very satisfactory way to dispose of these dark sisters of the republic, but the results of such marriages are by no means certain. Unfortunately for thousands of intelligent young colored women, they must not only marry earlier than other young women, but they are forced in very many cases to marry men who are not equal to them in intelligence, refinement and culture. The public schools and other institutions of learning have done more for the girlhood than the boyhood of the race. Like the boys of other races, colored boys are compelled to leave school much earlier than the girls, and accept employment that seldom offers any hope of advancement or tendency to a higher development. On account of this uneven condition of things the average intelligence of young colored women is much higher than that of the young men. It is an ordinary thing to see women of decided superiority of mind and heart married to men miserably inferior to them in all important respects. The reverse of all this is generally true with young women who happen to have a white complexion. It is always easy for them to be mated to men strong in the elements of superior-mindedness and nobility of heart.

Below the cuticle there is a persistent likeness in human nature. The refined and cultivated woman of whatever complexion who expects by marriage to elevate an inferior husband to her level of intelligence is more apt to experience bitter heart-breaking than success. The average man, white or black, is altogether too foolishly perverse and proud in his ignorance to brook instruction from his superior wife, even if such instruction or superiority may be asserted in terms of tenderness and love. For these reasons it is to be feared that the inequalities of the enforced early marriages of the educated colored women are not always blissful. As a general rule in all marriages of this sort, the finer sense and superior intellect of the wife are overmastered by the coarse instinct and vulgar weaknesses of the ignorant husband.

There is, to me, something awful in the suggestion of what becomes of the young colored woman who can find neither work nor suitable husband. It is difficult to understand how those who are responsible for the condition of this class of women can feel comfortable and Heavenward. If those who are responsible for the social laws that purposely imperil many to protect the false sentiment of others feel perfectly happy, Heaven preserve their species as a warning to coming generations!

In the meantime we can only hope that the day may speedily come when the gospel love of humanity shall make ridiculous all race antipathies, and the terms strong and weak between people of different tongues and complexions will suggest duties rather than oppressions. These are the only conditions under which men and women of all races can realize the high possibilities of their destiny.

—Tacoma Ledger.

Booker T. Washington
"To the Editor of the *New York World*"

New York World, September 19, 1895[2]

Atlanta, Ga. Sept. 19.

To the Editor of The *World:*

My present feeling is that yesterday was the brightest, most hopeful day in the history of the negro race. It was the day for which Garrison and Douglass and [Henry] Grady worked and prayed. It has been my privilege to address audiences in all parts of the North and West. It has remained for the South, and here in the heart of the South, where Sherman and Hood fought, and where lived Toombs and Brown and Stephens, and our beloved Grady, to give my words the most hearty and overwhelming reception in the history of my public speaking. I had no dream that any colored man thirty years after slavery could be received and treated in Atlanta with such distinction and honor.

As I sat on the platform, with the flower and culture and beauty of the South on either side, and in front of me black men who were slaves, and near them ex-Confederate soldiers, who only a little while ago were the masters of these slaves and on this very ground fought to keep enslaved these black men, and as I saw these Southern men and these black men and beautiful and cultured Southern women wave their hats and handkerchiefs and clap their hands and shout in approval of what I said, I seemed to have been carried away in a vision, and it was hard for me to realize as I spoke that it was not all a beautiful dream, but an actual scene, right here in the heart of the South.

A Year of Jubilee for the Negro.

I care nothing for the personal commendation. It is the race that I speak for. This is the year of jubilee of the negro. It is the beginning of an era. The heart of the South is open to-day to the negro as it has never been before. The greatest problem is now with the negro himself. Will he throw aside his vagaries and enter in and reap the harvest that is right about him. It is an equality of industrial opportunity that the negro should seek, rather than spend time over questions of social equality, which has no existence among any people.

As I have received during the last few hours the hearty handshake of hundreds of Southern men and women, and as they have spoken in my ear the "God bless you" and the "I am with you," I can see and feel that we are on the threshold of a new life. The South is the negro's home. Here he is surrounded by them that know him and by those whom he knows. Here the black man and the white man work in the same field and on the same house and at the same bench.

Let us as a race throw aside complaints and useless criticism and enter with hand and mind as we have never done before the industrial field. No one will scorn the negro that has a half million dollars to lend. As a race we must decide within the next ten years whether we are going to hold the place we now have in the industrial world or whether we are going to give it up to foreigners. To hold our place we have no time to spend in fretting and fussing over non-essentials.

Casts His Lot with the South.

The hand as well as the head of every black boy and girl in the South should be trained to useful occupation. We want to make ourselves so skillful that we will be indispensable. No one cares much for a man with empty hand, pocket and head no matter what his color is.

Beginning from to-day let the negro register an oath in heaven that from henceforth he will cast his lot materially, civilly and morally with the South; that he will cultivate the closest friendship with the Southern white man; that when he can he will vote for and with the Southern white man; that he will praise his good deeds, and that he will in a dignified and sensible manner tell the white man of his wrongs to the negro. And I am more convinced to-day than ever that if this course is followed there will be soon not only a new South but a new negro.

Though we are not yet where we want to be, yet, thank God, we are not where we used to be.

Booker T. Washington

L. W. B.

"Is He a New Negro?"

Daily Inter Ocean, October 2, 1895[3]

Booker T. Washington at The Cotton States Exposition.

The Negro Building

A Great Exhibit of Negro Skill and Industry.

Bishop Turner Says There Is No New Negro, but a New White Man.

Atlanta. Ga., Sept. 28.—Staff Correspondence.— "We have a new woman and a new negro in the South, and you will find them both in this Cotton States Exposition." So said a brilliant Southern woman, one of the social leaders of Atlanta, to me. She spoke only of what have been the greatest subjects of talk since the exposition opened. The new woman and the new negro are in evidence here, and they are attracting universal attention. I propose to take up both these subjects, and shall reverse the order of their consideration—not because I would put the new negro ahead of the new woman, but because the opening address of Booker T. Washington, of Tuskegee, Ala., was the sensation of that great day in Atlanta. Mr. Washington opened the eyes of the white people of the South. They heard his address in amazement. They applauded him as a new Moses of his people. They talked about it and about him. The papers wrote about both speaker and speech. Booker T. Washington is still the subject of more talk than any other man who figured in the exercises at the formal opening of the Cotton States Exposition. The Atlanta papers received requests from all over the country for copies of Mr. Washington's address. I was in the Atlanta Journal office when a Californian came in and asked for the paper containing that address. "I understand that it was a great speech for a negro." "A great speech for a man," said the editor. "One of the greatest speeches I ever heard from any man, black or white." This is the sample of the comment. Southern men refer to this speech and the negro exhibit as evidences of an awakening of the race. It seems to me, however, that it would be more appropriate to speak of the awakening of the white race to the real merit of the earnest effort, the work accomplished, and the possibilities of the colored people.

*   *   *

Booker T. Washington may be a new type of a negro to most white men; but he is not a new discovery. His work is not new. He has been working on the lines laid down in his exposition address for fifteen years, and he has accomplished a great deal in that time. Five years ago The Inter Ocean told the story of Washington and his work. It has made both well known in the Northwest—so well known that Mr. Washington was invited to Chicago to take a conspicuous part in the labor congress at the World's Fair. When I first visited the Tuskegee Normal and Industrial Institute, five years ago, I began my first letter to The Inter Ocean with this paragraph:

> What are the colored people doing for themselves in the South? Many Northern people ask this question every year, and they hear different answers to the question, but these do not encourage. They hear only of what is being done for the colored people by good missionaries. I came to the Black Belt of Alabama with that impression. I had heard only of that kind of work, and of colored politicians; but I found that there was another and a more hopeful work here. In telling the story of that work, I can answer the question, "What are the colored people doing for themselves?" Just in the suburbs of an old-time aristocratic Southern town there is a group of a dozen buildings, large and small, brick and frame, covering the highest ground in Macon County. These buildings are the most conspicuous in the landscape. They dwarf the grand old houses of the planters, which still stand as monuments to a past that was looked upon as glorious. They are the most modern in architecture that are to be found in the whole county. They are known as the Tuskegee Normal School for Colored People, and every one of them was designed by colored skill and built by colored labor. Colored men made the drawings, colored men made the working plans, colored men cut the timber and sawed the lumber, colored men made the brick, colored men laid these brick, fashioned the timbers, and colored men alone are represented in the construction of these most modern buildings in the Black Belt; but the work of colored creation does not stop there. Grouped around among these school buildings and colleges are shops, where colored boys are making wagons to sell to the white merchants of Tuskegee; harness, buggies, house, office, and church furniture, for white people to buy; boots and shoes, clothing, bed mattresses, and, in fact, carrying on, in a small way, almost every industry known in the South. These colored boys and girls are not learning to handle tools in toy shops, to waste material in becoming familiar with them. They are making their own tools in many instances, and in every school shop they are turning out goods ready for the market which the whites are glad to buy, and acknowledge that they do so because they cannot do better elsewhere.

*   *   *

The story of Washington and his practical work was then told in these columns and it has been told again and again, but when the man appeared on the platform at the opening of the Cotton States Exposition and delivered his address, saying what he had said many times before and giving utterance to ideas he had already worked out most successfully in a practical way, he was a revelation to the great majority of the people who heard him, and he was heralded as the new negro. But the awakening was on the part of the white men, not the negro. Booker T. Washington has been awake and working and talking for fifteen years, but the white people of the South have not heard him until he was here given an audience as the first negro to be placed on an official programme in the South to stand beside a white man and speak for his race with the same freedom. The white people heard him and awoke to the realization that there was a new negro in the South, a negro who had as much promise in him as the white man, a negro who had a plan to solve the race troubles.

When it came to the selection of the negro for this address Mr. I. Garland Penn, the chief of the negro commission, wrote to negroes in all parts of the country for suggestions as to the man. Langston and Bruce and others were named and a few named Booker T. Washington. Mr. Penn knew Washington and his work and proposed his name. He told the committee on ceremonies about the work at Tuskegee, and the selection was made. Mr. Washington was invited to deliver the address. He did it, and talk with the people who were present at the opening of the exposition and you will get the impression that there was but one speech, and but one speaker there—Booker T. Washington, the new negro.

*   *   *

The negro building and the negro exhibit at the fair are not new. They are the product of negro skill and industry and largely the product of just such industrial training as Booker T. Washington has been giving his pupils at Tuskegee, and advocating for negro youth all over the South. Commissioner Garland Penn, who has charge of the negro building, says that it was not because the race desired to draw the line that they demanded separate representation at the World's Fair, but because in the mass the colored people can in no wise equal the dominant race, but they do measure up very well when their past and present environments are considered. They presented their request for separate exhibit to the directors of the Cotton States Exposition and it was granted. The colored people offered to erect their own exposition building, but the exposition company would not allow them to do what was not asked of others. It paid for this building as for others. But it let the contract for the building [go] to negroes and they employed negro workmen, so that the negro building stands as an example of negro skill and work.

This building is in the southeastern corner of the park at the main entrance from the railway terminal station. It covers 25,000 square feet. It is 276 feet long by 112 feet wide. It has a central tower and four corner pavilions, and the pediment over the main entrance is decorated with relief work, representing the past and the present conditions of the negro. The one side of the pediment represents the slave mammy, with the one-room log cabin, the rake, and the basket in 1865. On the other side is the face of Frederick Douglass, a true representative of the growth and intelligence of the colored man. Near the relief of Douglass are the comfortable residence, the stone church, and symbols of the race's progress in science, art, and literature, all

representative of the new negro in 1895. The well-fed mule and the plow occupy the center of the grouping, representing the negro's property and industry. There is no building at the fair which attracts more attention than this one built by negroes and for the exhibition of the products of negro labor.

*   *   *

The largest exhibits in the building are from schools and colleges, but there are many individual exhibits and one of them is a painting marked "30 equals 453." It was painted by a negro, Mr. Freeman, of Washington, and it represents two boys at work at a blackboard. One is a white boy and the other is a colored boy. They both have the same figures before them and are subtracting 30 from 453. The colored boy has put down the result and has a look of triumph on his face. The white boy has a puzzled expression as he looks at the result and still sees the statement that "30 equals 453." But the result is the colored boy by his side, who represents thirty years emancipation for his race, while the white boy represents 453 years of emancipation for his race. The two races stand equal before the law and in their work here at the exposition, as the two boys stand equal in their work at the blackboard. It is not a striking picture, except in the story it tells, but it is well executed and it attracts much attention from whites and blacks for the conception and the story told. In the central square under the dome of the building there is quite a large collection of pictures and several pieces of statuary. Most of the work is from the Amateur Art Club, of Washington. Mr. Freeman has portraits of Douglass, Bruce, and Langston, and several other figure pieces which are very creditable. Mr. W. C. Hill, of Washington, has several pieces of statuary that are very good, one of them called "The Stubborn Shoe," representing a little girl trying to put on her shoe with her toes stuck into the heel of the shoe and puzzling her brain how to get it on. Another represents the negro with chains broken, but not free. The same society has a large collection of crayons, photo-

Interior photograph of the Negro Building at the Cotton States and International Exposition, Atlanta, September 1895. The sculpture in the foreground is W. C. Hill's *A Negro with Chains Broken but Not Off*. Courtesy of the Fred L. Howe 1895 Cotton States and International Exposition Photographs Collection, Kenan Research Center, Atlanta History Center.

graphs of colored churches and schools and hospitals in Washington and some exquisite art needlework.

In the art collection there are also three pictures by Mr. H. O. Tanner, the son of Bishop Tanner, of the African M. E. Church. Mr. Tanner is a talented and finely educated young negro, and is now studying art in Paris. One of his pictures in the last Salon received honorable mention this year. There is also a marble bust of Charles Sumner, by Edmona Lewis, the colored sculptor, who has her studio now in Italy.

*   *   *

Two of the largest and best exhibits of industrial work are from the Tuskegee Normal and Industrial Institute and Hampton Normal and Agri-cultural Institute. Tuskegee is known as the child of Hampton, because Booker T. Washington had his training at Hampton, and was recommended as president of the Tuskegee Institute by General Samuel C. Armstrong, the founder of Hampton. But Tuskegee's exhibit in the negro building is almost, if not quite, equal to that from Hampton, and both show what industrial training has done for the negro.

In the Tuskegee exhibit there are large cases containing the work of the sewing, dressmaking, and millinery departments, the tailor shop, the harness and shoe shops, desks, chairs, and tables from the furniture shop, a handsome carriage, a light buggy, a phaeton, and a farm wagon from the carriage shop, a steam engine built by the boys in the ironworking department, tools made in the same shop, a dairy exhibit, farm products, fruits, some trade before they are allowed to graduate. The work is not amateurish, but equal in finish to that put upon the market by manufacturers of these products.

In the Hampton Institute exhibit there are similar examples of students' work, some of it of a more pretentious character than that from Tuskegee. There is a handsome revolving bookcase, a richly-carved sideboard, a mantel, and a hall tree of exceptionally fine workmanship, and any of these pieces will compare favorably with any furniture exhibit to be found in the exposition. There are carriages, buggies, phaetons, and wagons from the Hampton shops, a large drill press and a half-power engine to run it. These were both made for use in the shops by the students who work there. Hampton also shows some fine ornamental iron work in banquet and large standard lamps, to show that there are artists in iron as well as artists in bronze, marble, and clay, some fine samples of book printing and binding from the printing department, and a large exhibit of various kinds of work to show how complete is the great industrial school established by General Armstrong, who had charge of the freedmen at that point at the close of the war, and started a school to teach colored youths how to earn their own living by systematic work from trained hands and developed intellects.

* * *

There are many other school exhibits from the Knoxville College, Clark University, at Atlanta; the Georgia State Industrial College, at Savannah; the State Normal College, at Montgomery, Ala.; the State Normal and Industrial School, Normal, Ala.; the Gammon Theological Seminary, at Atlanta; the Atlanta Baptist Seminary; the Central Tennessee College, at Nashville; the Fisk University, at Nashville; the Atlanta University, the Spellman Female Seminary, at Atlanta; the Schofield Normal and Industrial Institute, at Aiken, S. C., and a number of other educational and industrial institutions for negroes. The colored people of Chicago have an exhibit of various kinds of work, and there are many individual exhibits of art, mechanical; and agricultural work. There are a number of patents by colored men, some fine tile mantels from a colored manufacturer at Atlanta; a large drug exhibit from the pioneer negro druggists in the South, fancy needle work, collections of fine fruits and grains, and enough excellent work of great variety to demonstrate the capabilities and development of the negro in every department of labor. The negro building has in its exhibits more variety than any other building at the exposition, because it shows the work of the race in all departments.

There is one small corner of the negro building which represents the other extreme of the race. It is marked "Uncivilized Africa," and is an exhibit of some of the natural resources and some of the crude manufactures of the west coast of Africa. Bishop Turner, who has been for years urging the negroes to emigrate to Liberia, brought this exhibit home with him when he returned from Africa, a few weeks ago. He says that it does not represent civilized Africa, but the uncivilized natives, the heathen of that country. He has a collection of their swords, knives, and spears, which, he says, were hammered out of iron ore found there so rich that the natives use it without any knowledge of smelting; samples of the woods that grow on the west coast of the Dark Continent; palm and cocoanut oils, made by the natives; samples of leather and cloth, made by the heathen; and many other curious specimens of African products. Over this exhibit the Bishop has strung a line of delicately woven birds' nests, which are shaped like the long-handled gourd. They are the nests of the weaver bird, and they are as carefully woven as a bit of wicker work. The long arm is attached to the limb of a tree, and through it the bird passes to the large and bulb-like nest in the bottom. There is one article in the Bishop's collection which is not heathen. It is a beautiful silk quilt of the same pattern as that made by a Liberian woman and presented to Queen Victoria. She duplicated the work for Bishop Turner. It is a delicate and intricate piece of patch work, and represents the African coffee tree in bloom.

*   *   *

Bishop Turner has little patience with those who talk about the new negro. He strolled through the negro building with me, but saw little that was new in the workmanship that was evidenced by the exhibits.

"There is nothing new in all this fine work," said he. "The negroes always did the finest kind of work in the South. The slaves were skilled carpenters and wheelwrights and blacksmiths. They did all the work in the old days of slavery. They were not mere drudges without skill. They built the grand old mansions of the planters. They made the carriages and wagons and buggies used by their masters; they did the iron work, as well as the wood work. They made much of the furniture, and were skilled cabinetmakers. In fact, the slaves did all of the work in the South then; and there were skilled mechanics and carpenters among them—more than we now have, perhaps. In that respect, we have a very old-fashioned negro exhibit here. The men who owned slaves gave the best testimony to their skill and intelligence as workmen when they had their own carpenters, blacksmiths, wheelwrights, and cabinet-makers among their slaves, and trusted them to build all the houses, manufacture most of the comforts which surrounded the Southern home. The women could do as fine sewing then as now, and they were the skilled cooks, famous for their dishes. No, this work is not the evidence of a new negro. It is the skill of the same old negro who was in slavery. The only thing new about it is the freedom of the negro to learn what trade he pleases and work out his own salvation in his own way. I am as proud of this exhibit as any one, but I have no patience with the talk about the new negro as a workman. Why, that was the reason he was kept in slavery so long. He was too valuable to be set free."

"Do you still think the negroes should emigrate to Africa?"

"Yes; several million of them. They can be spared from this country, and they can do much better in Africa. They will become the leaders and the civilizers of that continent.

The stalwart old negro Bishop strolled out of the negro building with me, and we turned our steps to the Midway. In front of the Dahomey Village there was a big-nosed white man urging the visitors to not miss seeing the wild cannibals from the west coast of Africa. The old Bishop stopped and heard the stereotyped speech, and remarked that here must be the "new negro." Then he walked up to the showman and said:

"Why do you white men pursue the negro to Africa with your lying? You have for years lied about the negro in this country, and now, when you are being found out, you are lying about the negro at home on his native heath."

The showman stopped, startled for a moment, while the crowd gathered about. Then he asked, "What do you know about it?" and began again on his speech. But the Bishop was not to be ignored.

"I know all about it, sir," he replied. "I am a negro, and I live in Africa a good part of the time. There are not, and never have been, any cannibals on the west coast of Africa. You are simply repeating some of the lies told by white men who went to Africa and had to lie about the country to magnify their own efforts and pose as heroes of great courage and endurance. The natives of the west coast of Africa may be heathens and uncivilized, but they are more peaceable and gentle than many of you civilized and enlightened white men here in America; and these wild negro cannibals you have here, cavorting around like apes and baboons, never saw Africa. They are lazy, good-for-nothing negroes from New York, or some other town, where they have been taught to jump about like monkeys and yell like hyenas, while you tell these people that they are talking in their native tongue. Stop your lying about the negro!"

The crowd shouted, the showman looked stupefied, and the Bishop walked on down the Midway, telling me that there was no new negro. He was simply the same old negro showing his capacity as he was given opportunity by the new white man: and I am not sure that he is wrong. Booker T. Washington and Bishop Turner are not so far apart, except on the question as to where the negro is to work out his own salvation. Washington insists that by applying the industry and capacity that made the negro valuable in slavery to the new condition of freedom the negro can do the work and become independent here in America. Bishop Turner wants the negro to go to Africa and apply these new conditions in a new country.

General Armstrong said to me, just before he died:

"This man Washington is worthy of the name he bears. He will live to be known as the Washington of his race."

The speech of Washington has awakened the white men of the South to the realization that there has been a change. The new building, with its exhibits of the work of negroes, offers its testimony to the truth of Booker T. Washington's teachings.

L. W. B.

J. W. E. Bowen

"An Appeal to the King: The Address Delivered on Negro Day in the Atlanta Exposition," October 21, 1895

Mr. President, Ladies and Gentlemen:

As a representative of the American Negro, I venture to address a modest statement and to appeal to the king. We realize that, although the king is invisible, his personality is tangible. He occupies a front seat in the halls of legislation; he dictates the political policy of the nation; his nod of approval is more significant than the mythological rod of Jupiter, while his disapproving nod spreads fear and consternation far and wide amid the ranks of his subjects. He determines what statutes shall be enacted, and should his subjects in a mad freak enact any statute contrary to his wishes he annuls them immediately and relegates the reckless and vituline political Titans to the limbo of political forgetfulness. He sits in high chair in the police, the criminal, the equity, and appellate and supreme courts of the states and of the nation and interprets the law. He then prescribes to the police, the sheriff, the constable, the mayor, the governor and president how these interpretations shall be carried out. The great body of his laws is unwritten, but they are executed with scrupulous exactness in the minutest detail. He

sets the pace in the drawing room; the swing of his baton describes the movement of the foot, the hum of the music and the color, quality and style of the dress.

Recent Social Changes

The whirligig of time is merciless and providential—merciless to the indolent and reckless, but providential to the faithful and honorable. The poetic truth that "there is a divinity that shapes our lives, rough hew them as we may," may be rewritten in the prosaic facts of today as found in the experience of individuals as well as in that of peoples and of nations. The changes are so rapid and radical in human society, flitting before our gaze like the fast-unfolding views of a huge panorama, or like dissolving and charming lines in the Kaleidoscope, that we can scarcely get more than an outline or rightly esteem their far-reaching effects. The eye grows weary and the brain is overpowered in contemplating these monotonous and astounding changes. And yet we have but come to the outskirts of a mighty and

John Wesley Edward Bowen, 1880s.

harmless cataclysm in society when the present inequalities and misadjustments will be remedied and human society become so based that there shall be equality of opportunity for every human being. In actual illustration the Greeks are at our doors. We are too near the recent civil and fratricidal strife to appreciate this fact, whereby a new people was born in a day; a people that to all practical appearance, as well as by antecedents, were no people at all. And even more marvelous is that other incomparable fact standing alone in its gracious magnanimity and in the silence of its untarnished splendor is the revolution in the moral and social sentiment toward the Negro on the part of his former master. This fact alone is a sufficient and an unwitting confirmation of the existence of an undertow of righteousness in human society; and moreover it is a reason-

able guarantee that ultimately all the world will brothers become.

Our eyes have seen strange sights and our ears have heard strange sounds. When Booker T. Washington delivered his unmatched speech from this platform, a distinguished citizen of Georgia, the successor to one of her proudest sons, said: "That man's speech is the beginning of a moral revolution in America." That utterance is proof in itself that the revolution has already come, and it only remains for time to crystallize its various phases and essentials into the component elements of civilization.

The erection and equipment of the Negro building; the Negro's place of usefulness and honor, in this most notable of southern expositions; and the general satisfaction expressed with his accomplishments are all additional marks of unperceived but positive changes in society. And once again the Negro wishes to put himself on record in the most positive, hearty, and unequivocal terms, without the least tinge of Jesuitical sophistry, that he loves the land of his nativity and is ready, as of yore, to pour out his heart's best blood for the institutions of that land. The sad and sweet memory of his historic sorrows saturate this atmosphere and every foot of ground in Southern soil is made holy because it embalms the sacred dust of his faithful sires. The memory of our deeds is still a fragrant and faithful theme. I appeal to the bronzed lips of your orator on Marietta street, who stands supremely alone in painting the devotion of my sable and ignorant sires. Hear him in his speech before the Merchants' Association of Boston in their annual banquet, December 1889: "I see a slave scuffling through the smoke, winding his black arms around the fallen form, reckless of the hurtling death, bending his trusty face to catch the words that tremble on his stricken lips, so wrestling meantime with agony that he would lay down his life for his master's stead. I see him by the weary bedside ministering with uncomplaining patience, praying with all of his humble heart that God would lift his master up until death comes in mercy and in honor to still the soldier's life. I see him by the open grave, mute, motionless, uncovered suffering for the death of him who in life fought against his freedom. I see him when the mound is heaped and the great drama of his life is closed, turn away with downcast eyes and uncertain step, start out in the new and uncertain fields, faltering, struggling, but moving on until his shambling figure is lost in the light of this better and brighter day. And from the grave comes a voice saying: 'Follow him! Put your arms about him in his need, even as he puts his arm about me. Be his friends as he was mind.'"

Our ears have become familiar with the so-called race problem, which has been popularly interpreted to mean the Negro race problem. A truer and larger conception of the subject would speak of the human race problem, instead of the narrower Negro race problem. This great problem assumes different names in different parts

of the world. We have nihilism in Russia, socialism in Germany, communism in France, socialism and the submerged tenth in England, while in the United States it is as multiform in its elements as the nation is composite in its blood and physiognomy. In California it is the problem of the Chinese, in the great middle west it is the Scandinavian and other foreign struggles; in the north, central and eastern states it is the Irish and Italian problem, while overreaching all of these is the problem of the battle for bread, and in the south it is the Negro problem. It is, therefore, no sign of breadth of vision to declare that there is only one great problem in the United States and that one part is the Negro problem. These problems will require centuries of persistent effort that they may be solved upon the ethical and equitable basis of the New Testament teachings. In dealing with all of these principles of equality and of brotherhood should obtain.

Three Feet Make a Yard

It is a basal and sociological truth that, other things being equal, like treatment and like opportunities produce like results, the breadth and quality of which will depend upon native power and inherent ability. What is the condition for the development of the noblest type among men? There can be but one answer to this question, namely, equality of opportunity. The largest struggle of human society is to attain this concrete reality of civil justice. Under it, each will produce according to his ability for the good of mankind, and that good will not be a passive uniformity cast into the stereotyped mold of racial capacity, but will be complex in its essentials and divinely human in its cast.

The Negro has learned that three feet make a yard in mathematics, and he believes that they make a yard in politics, economics, and ethics; in Europe, Asia, and Africa; among whites and among blacks. It is noteworthy that inside of one generation the Negro should learn such valuable lessons. And in consequence of which he has begun the study of himself and is seeking to locate himself as a factor among men. The

Negro has a definite sphere to fill in history, and although his day is a day of small beginning, the present results are prophetic of large victories in the future. His educational life has just begun and his teachers, without bias, say that he will some day fill the world with his name. This belief to the contrary notwithstanding, the old question still lives and with vital pertinacity challenges the soberest thought of statesmen, namely: Has the Negro any place in American life? If so, what is that place to be? But the most encouraging feature about this question is the fact that the Negro himself has addressed his best thought to its answer. A certain school of political economists assume to lay down as a maxim to govern the formation and development of a nation this theory: Without amalgamation of blood, there can be no national life to those not amalgamated. This is as crude a notion as the ancient theory of the flatness of the earth. The present progress of mankind in every clime is its best refutation. Nevertheless in spite of the fact that the noble Sinbad is almost ridden to death by this Old Man of the Sea, it must be observed that America is the only country that is at work upon this problem. England and Europe have not had the courage nor disposition, if they had the wisdom, so much as to read the problem through once. But the American people have the disposition and the audacity not only to read it through, but to begin its wise solution upon the broad basis of humanity, and please God, the Negro will have sense enough to stay and contribute to its correct solution until this nation shall become in truth homogenous in sentiment though heterogeneous in blood.

The United States is the sphere of nationality and not of raciality; blood makes a race, but sentiment a nation; and the chief corner stone of the nation is the first statement in the original charter of the proud republic: "We hold these truths to be self-evident: that all men are created equal; that they are endowed by their Creator with certain inalienable rights; that among these are life, liberty, and the pursuit of happiness." The question of the equality of the races as familiarly understood and as commonly interpreted is a threadbare and musty saying and is groundless in reason and in the concrete facts of today.

There is no such thing as perfect equality of individuals or races. This is a figment clung to by minds that are woefully deficient in rudimentary training or are still wrapped in the swaddling bands of medieval infancy. The true or native equality of men as stated by the great Jefferson in the fundamental charter of the republic, and as rationally and biblically interpreted in biology, philosophy, reason, Scripture, and common sense, is that all men are natively and equally endowed with the essentials of humanity and of divinity. And because of this, all should be permitted to develop their endowments for the good of society within the limits of unprejudiced legislation. Such an interpretation and process of development must lead to the largest good for the largest number.

The Negro's Place in History

With regard to the Negro's place in American life, it was formerly stated that he was only fit for servitude; that the best part of him was his faithful muscle; that even today and forevermore he must remain a serf or a hewer of wood and a drawer of water to the vast revolving machinery of civilization; he must be the ignorant workman and the unassimilated pariah of American society. It is to his credit that in his early days he had brawn; that it drove the ax that rang through the forest of the old Dominion and the plow that upturned the sod of Louisiana and Mississippi for the cane and cotton, while his voice endowed their leaves with a tongue never before heard. With his powerful might, he scattered the silver grain in the Carolinas, and the golden grain in Maryland and Georgia, and disemboweled the mountains of Tennessee of their ancient black treasury, and from his earliest days in this country unto a very recent day, his sweat was almost the only oil for the machinery of Southern industry and his arm the driving wheel of its trade. And when we shall be removed from the struggles of recent times in the social and political world to the centuries beyond, in which the prejudices engendered in the participants of the strife shall be known only through the cold type of history, then under the unblurred eye and the cold and unsympathetic logic of the patient historian, the period of the servitude of the Negro will shine forth with a luster unapproachable in American history.

When it is asserted that he must be a worker, all sensible Negroes answer yea and amen? A worker in clay wrenching from nature her hidden stores; a worker in wood, iron, brass, steel, and glass turning the world into an habitation fit for the Gods; a worker in the subtle elements of nature in obedience to the original command to subdue and conquer it; a worker in the realm of mind contributing to the thought-products of mankind, thereby vindicating for himself a birthright to the citizenship of the republic of thought; a statesman in church and in state; a publicist and a political economist; in short, he must be a man among men, not so much a Black man but a MAN though black. And for the attainment of the possibilities of his rich, unexplored African nature of docility and tractability of enthusiasm and perseverance, with his burning African fervor, there must be measured to him as well as to the white man three feet to make a yard. Such an equality of opportunity not only establishes an equality of responsibility, but must be reached before human society shall prosper under the normal laws of true development. The Negro does not shrink or ask to be exempted from the working of the latter half of this statement, namely, equality of responsibility; but simply prays to the American sentiment, who is the king, for equality of opportunity in all matters that affect the welfare of the state. In all matters relating to the security of the homes of the people and the institutions of the republic, we say to the king that the story of our past fealty is the best answer we can make touching upon our future devotion and interest. It is on record for us, written by one of the greatest of democratic presidents, Andrew Jackson, that we may be actuated by lofty purposes, as seen in the noble defense made by the Negro soldiers of the city of New Orleans in the second British war. It is on record for us that in all of the social upheavals between capital and labor, the Negro has never been found with firebrand in hand. We point with pride to our loving and lucid history that we are humane as well as human.

A Plea for the Higher Education of the Negro

Before asking, now what is the Negro's place in American civilization?, a larger question comes into notice that affects all men, namely, what is the place of any branch or family of the human race in the sum total of humanity? The man who attempts to answer this question will risk his wit. The Negro's place will be what he makes for himself, just as the place of every people is what that people makes for itself, and he will be no exception to the rule. The method whereby he shall make that place is under consideration. One class contends that he must make it by staying in the three "R's" and they are specially at pains in ridiculing the higher education of the Negro, even for leaders in church or state. Yea, he must learn the three "R's"; he must master the king's English and then he must plume his pinions of thought for a flight with Copernicus, Keppler, and Herschel; he must sharpen his logic for a walk with Plato, Immanuel Kant, and Herbert Spencer; he must clarify his vision for investigations with Virchow, Huxley, and Gray; he must be able to deal in the abstruse questions of law as do Gladstone, Judge Story, and Judge Speer; he must fortify himself to divine rightly the Word as do Cannon Farrar, Bishop Foster, Bishop Haygood, Dr. John Hall, and Dr. H. L. Wayland. In short, the education of the Negro must be on a par with the education of the white man. It must begin in the kindergarten, as that of the white child, and end in the University, as that of the white man. Anything short of this thorough preparation for all of the stages of life for the Negro would be unfair to a large part of humanity. We ask that nothing be done that would spoil his nature or emasculate his personality, but let everything be done that would fit him to fill every situation in life that man may fill, from the blacksmith and hod carrier to the statesman and philosopher. And if such preparation require a knowledge of the old blue-black spelling book or of Aristotle's logic; a knowledge of the plow or the trip hammer or of the spade or of the driving wheel; or of simple addition or integral calculus; or the first reader of Kant's "Critique," simple justice and common sense require that he be acquainted with whatever shall fit him to fill his station in life. Does this mean that the Negro be turned into a white man? Is he to be so educated that he will cease to be what God meant that he should be? Nay! Verily, for any education that makes a people dissatisfied with their racial personality is a farce and a reproach.

Protect Every Woman

Gentlemen of the South, and of the North, may I speak for myself. If so, "Hear me for my cause and be silent that ye may hear." You are the representatives of the noblest civilization that ever leaped from the brain of man. In the earliest days of Puritan discipline in this country, and even in England, your fathers were giants in the land, and in many parts their sons are worthy successors. Your indomitable courage and resistless power have won for you victories upon battlefields that reduce the victories of Xerxes and Alexander to the achievements of novices. Your triumphs in the world of mind, in science, philosophy, history, and ethics, are unparalleled in history. Your ethical and political conceptions have honeycombed the world, and although your record is stained with spots unworthy of your training and privileges, still like the sun, though spotted, it is glorious. Your conception of the sacredness of the family relation and the value of personal chastity and of the paramount necessity for the protection of womanly virtues is the crown and glory of your splendid history. We cannot but bow to you for these magnificent achievements. As a representative of the thinking people of my race I take off my hat to the white man of this country, North and South, when he swears by all that liveth that the sanctity of his home and the pu-

rity of his family shall be maintained inviolate at every hazard. Our noblest nature affirms this. *We too* have come to learn that the purity of woman means the purity of the family and the purity of the family the purity of the race and nation, and whosoever insults that purity is an enemy to society and in league with hell. And when it is said that we have no conception of the value of purity or the sacredness of the marriage relation, we simply ask that the sins of the vicious be not charged to the whole race. We confess with shamed face that our notions of these relations, on the whole, are not what they should have been. With this confession it ought to be stated that our training on the whole has not been what it should have been. But the race is making a heroic effort to expel from its system all the virus of degrading sin and thus far we have made progress. We pray thee to deal gentle with thy servants in this respect, seeing that we are struggling to make our race a race of purity, sobriety, and Christian power. We do not ask that the criminal escape, but we plead that he receive the full measure of punishment according to law. We ask that justice—sure unbiased, and remorseless—be meted out to all criminals, black and white, who violate the purity of any woman, white or black, South or North, and we here would join hands with you around our common altar and swear allegiance to those principles to aid you in finding and punishing the criminals wherever found. Thus the education that the Negro needs is the education that the white man needs to make him honorable, virtuous and industrious, and to fit him to fill his place, whatever it may be.

A Tribute to Northern Philanthropists

We have come today to present to you and to the country a few products of our brain and skill wrought out under adverse and trying circumstances. We present them humbly and modestly, not as complete products, but as the earnest of our undeveloped power and the prophecy of our possible future. We record with grateful recognition the magnanimity of our Southern friends in this opportunity given us to come before the country in a new light. This act in itself is a clear indication of future developments. By observation it will be seen that the exhibits from the schools among the American Negro are by far in excess of that of a promiscuous character, and this is as it should be, for the largest life of the Negro since emancipation has been a school life. These results are due to our philanthropic friends. The Negro would be unworthy of the confidence of his Southern white friends and prove himself a sordid ingrate did he not hold in grateful memory the unstinted deeds of his philanthropic Northern friends. When the smoking throat of the angry gun ceased to belch forth death and destruction, and when the shotted cannon ceased in its carnage of death and the thunders were "hushed on the moor," suddenly there leaped upon the stage of action a people crude, rude, ignorant, superstitious, with only a few marks of divinity left, but enough to be identified as human. Then it was that the messengers of love came into our bleeding and sorely distressed South, and with a patience and cheerful generosity that would make the angels hush their heavenly harps to watch and admire, they began their tedious, discouraging, and seemingly fruitless, but self-imposed, task to teach the Negro the elements of civilized life in a state of freedom. The philanthropists in the North of every church and of no church poured out their millions for the work. Their monuments and those of the workers are in every Southern state in brick and mortar, the lighthouses of civilization, the fortresses of American patriotism, and the institutes of religion. Their names are legion, but among them stand out prominently John F. Slater, Daniel Hand, Alexander Meharray, Clinton B. Fisk, Mr. Fayerweather, Elijah H. Gammon, William F. Stewart, and others. And moreover the sacred dust of some of those heroes and heroines lies sleeping in Southern soil. On yonder hill, beneath the classic shade of Atlanta University, is laid in perpetual peace the remains of the late Dr. Ware, whose very life is a constant source of inspiration to all who knew him, and there is an atmosphere of holy awe that surrounds the solitary grave. The monument of those heroic laborers

and generous givers is in more than brick and stone. It is in flesh and blood, in the multitudes of broadly educated and scholarly and cultured men and women who are working out a magnificent destiny in the South, in the leaders of the race, in the pulpit, at the bar, in the medical profession, in the school room, in the workshop, at the bench, and in every trade and calling, to bless mankind and advance civilization. Their work has begun to show what the possibilities of the Negro mind are. And ever true to our proverbial and African instinct and the warm blood that circulates in our veins, we place upon the brow of these, our noble friends, the garland of our heart's divinest gratitude.

The New Negro

These simple results that may be seen in the Negro building are from a people just thirty years in freedom. They represent many spheres of labor and enterprise and show what may be accomplished under a more perfect system of life and labor. They show, moreover, that the Negro has been an apt and faithful student of his teachers in the mechanism of his skill as well as in the intellectual product of his brain. Thirty years, freedom is scarcely enough to take the first steps in the arts of peace. It required centuries for the Anglo-Saxon to reach his present commanding position. The Negro's present days of infancy and of small beginnings are no criterion to measure his future by. The depths from which he has come and the obstacles surrounding him must be remembered when expressing judgment of him; and when superficial writers on the other side of the water, as well as on this side, declare that the Negro can never assimilate to a high civilization or approach the present attainments of the Anglo-Saxon, they discover an immaturity of thought worthy of the schoolboy's effort. This proves that the social problems of any country are to be learned only by long years of contact and of unprejudiced study. A railroad observation in sociology may make fascinating reading, but it lacks the elements of endurance and accuracy and cannot command the respectful notice of more than novelistic readers for one decade. To understand the rapid strides that the Negro has taken one must know the pit from which he was dug, and the rock from which he was hewn. The cold facts of his present standing press out in bold relief with the distinctness of a mosaic and declare that there is a wealth unmeasured in that hidden mine. The first step has been taken and if the South and North will measure to him an equality of opportunity, there will come as the result splendid achievements for society. He longs to have a full chance; he longs to do nobly.

Finally, oh king! a new Negro has come upon the stage of action. As you enter the main entrance of the Negro building, you will observe the statue of a Negro with broken manacles upon his wrists. This statue was born in the fruitful brain of a Negro, Mr. Hill of Washington. His frame is muscular and powerful; his eye is fixed upon his broken but hanging chain; his brow is knit in deep thought. This is the new Negro. What is he doing? He is thinking! And by power of thought, he will think off those chains and have both hands free to help you build this country and make a grand destiny of himself. In generous affection for our native soil, in fealty to our institutions, and in a universal love for all men, his spirit is that of his fathers made over. Being to the manor-born, he cannot be alienated in sentiment and patriotic devotion to the institution of the South and the whole country. It must be remembered, however, that this Negro has had born in him the consciousness of a racial personality under the blaze of a new civilization. With this new birth of the soul, he longs for an opportunity to grow into the proportions of a new and diviner manhood that shall take its place in the ranks of one common humanity. This Negro, when educated in all of the disciplines of civilization and thoroughly trained in the arts of civil and moral life, cannot fail to be an invaluable help to our American life. It is his deepest desire to rise and work manfully, and he is willing to bide his time until the American white man shall have that element conquer in him which always conquers, namely, the love of fair play. Having been so generously treated by our Southern friends in this exposition, we shall go forth to prove to them that, in the development of the South and in the protection of our institutions, we are at heart one with them. And in the classic words of Edmund Burke before his constituents in Bristol, England, we pray: "Applaud us when we run; console us when we fall; cheer us when we recover; but let us pass on, for God's sake, let us pass on."

Rev. S. A. Steel
"The Modern Negro"

Southwestern Christian Advocate, November 28, 1895[4]
By Rev. S. A. Steel, D.D., Editor of "The Epworth Era," Organ of the M. E. Church South.

I am fully convinced that the Methodist Episcopal Church South ought to take hold of this question of Negro evangelization. The experiment of the North has failed. It has broken down completely. Its fine theories about the Negro are blown to the winds by the actual results of thirty years of freedom. The South received the Negro from Africa as a barbarian of the lowest type, and by its mild and humane system of bondage, almost misnamed slavery, it converted him in a generation into an industrious, useful, contented and happy race, devoted in their attachments and faithful in their services to the white people they called their masters. The North set them free, enfranchised them with the ballot, preached the doctrines of equality to them; and, in a single generation, has succeeded pretty nearly in undoing all that had been done for them. A few schools here and there are educating a few hundred, but the level of the race is slowly sinking. The Negro is to-day far below what he was in 1860, in all that constitutes moral character. Take this single crime of rape as an illustration. In 1860 a lady might have walked, unattended, without fear of harm, from the Atlantic to the Mississippi. Every man, white or black, was bred to that chivalrous regard for woman, that almost reverential sentiment of esteem for the female sex, that pledged him to her defense against every evil agency. So thoroughly had Christianity done its work in the hearts of the simple Africans that their masters left their homes, their wives and daughters under their protection while they went far away to war; and not a life was lost, not a house was burned, not a woman touched in all the chaos of that time. Thirty years have passed under the Northern system of instruction, and to-day there is not a country district in the South where it is safe for a lady, unattended, to go out of sight of her home. The modern Negro is a failure. Our Northern friends—and many of them read the *Era*—will not like this; but it is the good Lord's truth, and the sooner we all face it, the better for all parties concerned. . . .

This problem can't be solved by the Boston Monday Lecture Course, or the philanthropic visionaries, who know about as much of the Southern darkey as I do of the aborigines of the moon. Under their policy he is drifting to inevitable destruction. What modern philosophers call the "social efficiency of the race" is far below the point where he can successfully compete with the dominant white race, and it is steadily sinking lower. *Hic, haec, hoc*, will be the ruin of the African. . . .

I want to see Southern Methodism grapple with this great problem with an energy and earnestness and intelligence that will clear its conscience of all responsibility for the further degeneration of the Negro. I give the North credit for the best intentions, and admire the generosity that has prompted their efforts, and the heroic self-sacrifice of many earnest men and women who have faced obloquy and toil to elevate the Negro. But they have proceeded on a wrong theory, and the deplorable lynchings that disgrace our civilization are the fruit of their mistaken policy. That old race, born and reared in slavery, is almost gone. Now and then a venerable old man, with the high bred politeness he learned as a slave, takes off his hat and salutes you as "Marster"; or an old auntie, with a kerchief around her head, "curtsies" as once she did in stately halls; but such touching courtesies are fast becoming a memory. The old darkies are nearly all gone to their long home; and, as far as we have able to ascertain, not one of all who have been lynched in the South belonged to this old panel. We are dealing now with the "new Negro," the product of freedom; and he is about as worthless, good-for-nothing a specimen of the *genus homo* as can be found in creation. Politeness he does not know, morals he has not; insolent, lustful, and trifling, he is a candidate for 'the pen,' or, like too many of his race, finds himself caught in the cyclone of a mob, and dangling, bullet ridden and mutilated, from a limb. Nobody would put him back in bondage—too glad to be free ourselves. But there are plenty of people who, unless we can improve him, would put him where the mythical McGinty is said to have gone—at the bottom of the sea. We must do something to make a better man of him, or his doom is sealed. Let us try the Gospel.

W. E. B. Du Bois
"A Creed for the 'New Negro'"

Iowa State Bystander, December 13, 1895[5]

In the year of God, 1896, let the new negro turn to a new creed, which though not perfect, not satisfactory to all, yet is broad and practicable:

1. The strictest moral purity of family life.
2. The cultivation of our best intellectual ability, in part through the best existing universities, in part through the founding of a university of the negro.
3. The careful preservation of our best race characteristics and products; as negro music, and negro folk-lore.
4. Industrial training and cooperation, and the formation of habits of steady, honest, manual toil, saving of earnings and providence, in order that the race may become self-supporting, and may aid in the development of Africa.
5. Social separation from all people who for any reason do not desire our company, until such time as they shall voluntarily remove all barriers.
6. Political activity confined solely to the placing of such men in office, as will competently and honestly administer the government.

W. E. B. Du Bois
"A Negro on Etiquet of Caste"

Iowa State Bystander, December 13, 1895

We await breathlessly the gifted author of an Etiquet of Caste, and more especially his fifth and sixth chapters, where he leaves the elite, and stoops to common clay—to the ostracized and socially unbidden. We all know, down to the minutest detail, just what the divine circle of society's leaders must do, under all circumstances and accidents; how they must bow at a drawing room, how they must lace their shoes, how [they] must dress for a ball, and how they must butter their bread. But if democracy means anything (and great America has conclusively proved that it does not mean the absence of a smart set) it means that there are numberless other sets and circles, who heed for their own use a code of guiding good form.

Take ourselves for instance: How shall a negro conducted [*sic*] himself when, by accident, he finds himself among persons who do not like his company? How much of assertiveness and how much of modesty, how much of firmness and how much of compliance ought a negro gentleman to exhibit there? Or again, a black man and his wife, in a strange city enter a restaurant for lunch; the guests stare and bridle; the proprietor says politely, but firmly: "We do not accommodate colored people here!" What would the gentleman's book of etiquet [*sic*] say was good form here?

Indeed, this half-mocking inquiry has really its serious side. We are all the time finding ourselves in situations, arising from our peculiar social position in America which demand a careful, consistent line of manly conduct—a studied niceness of distinction which shall preserve our self respect on the one side, and avoid unmerited and unnecessary offense on the other.

Mrs. Booker T. Washington
"The New Negro Woman"

Lend a Hand 15 (1895)[6]

Paper read at the Conference of Colored Women held in Boston, August, 1895. [Note in original]

Our world is made up of nations. The nations are made up of races, which, in their turn, are formed of classes or clans. There are, in each of these, the masses who, in their immensity, ought to not only attract the greatest attention in the way of criticism, but ought to receive the most through and systematic care from the rest of the world.

It is to the masses of negro women that I wish to call your attention for a few minutes. We certainly have no time to be idle in reference to these sisters of ours, for sisters they surely are. Not many days ago I was talking with a Northern white lady who told me this story: She said that, sitting beside a colored woman in a street car, she turned and said to her, "I am greatly interested in your people. I have for a number of years taught in the South," when all to the surprise of this good woman, the younger one turned, and, with a contemptuous sneer said: "Oh, we don't have anything to do with those folks down there; they are none of us." The North, the South, the East, the West, must be one united whole in this great uplifting of our women—there can be no separation of interests, and the sooner each of us recognizes this fact, the sooner will the work be accomplished.

I repeat, we cannot be slow. We are the children of parents who were not the architects of their destiny, and perhaps we should not to-day be censured for having handed down to us a womanhood not equalling in strength that of our Caucasian sisters. But in the years that are to come we will be held responsible if the manhood, the womanhood, of the race is not higher, nobler, and stronger than it is to-day. In the words of Dr. Hale, let us "Look up and not down; look out and not in; look forward and not back, and lend a hand" to this mass of women who, in their helplessness, appeal to us, their older sisters—if not older in years, certainly in advantages and the things which go to make life happier and more hopeful. Women of all races had a friend in George Eliot, and it is she who says to us:

> For they, the royal-hearted women are,
> Who nobly love the noble,
> Yet have grace
> For needy suffering lives in lowliest place;
> Carrying a choicer sunlight in their smile,
> The heavenliest ray that pitieth the vile.
> Though I were happy, throned beside the
>   king,
> I should be tender to each little thing.
> With hurt-warm breast that had no
>   speech to tell
> Its inward pangs; and I would sooth it
>   well with tender touch,
> And with a low, soft moan for company.

We are a race of servants, not in the low sense of this word, but in the highest and purest sense, and, in our serving, let us keep these beautiful lines of the servant of all women as our guide.

In the struggle for money, for power, for intellectual attainment, for growth of any sort, there is always, and must always be, a starting-point. Thus it is with the struggle to uplift the negro woman there is a starting-point, and this I believe to be the home. The two words, home and woman, are so closely connected that I could not, even if I desired, separate one from the other.

Someone has said, "No race can rise above its women." This is just as true as the fact that no river can rise above its source; are we not the source of the home life, and if our influence upon this life is not good, how can the home be better? History will bear us out in all we say in reference to woman and home. Our own Emerson says, "A sufficient measure of civilization is the influence of good women." Plato, the Athenian philosopher, when he stood at the height of his intellectual attainments, gave to the ancient and modern world his great "Republic," which he had thought it worth the while to write to show to the world his regard for woman in the home. He held that women are a very important factor in the human race, and that, holding out to her the help she so much needed, she will raise the standard of home, and thus from the home will come stronger men to execute the nation's plan.

In every race there are many societies, and these societies are higher or lower as the case may be. But, for convenience, I shall divide the negro race of women into two classes, viz., that class which has had opportunity to improve and develop themselves mentally, physically, morally, spiritually, and financially, and that class who, because of the lack of these advantages, because of their unblamed-for ignorance, who, because of the cruelty of the master for more than two centuries—the master who, thirty years ago, turned his slave mothers away without giving them a single idea of the beauty of home life, a single idea of the responsibility of womanhood, wifehood, or citizenship—are our inferiors. This latter class is overwhelming in its numbers, mighty in its strength if only these numbers and this strength can be lifted up, can be inspired, taught and sustained. Is there no bond between these two classes of the same race? Yes, there is a tie which no attempt on our part can sever.

I sometimes fear that we are too slow in doing for others because we are, as we think, doing well. Individuals here and there among our men and women are climbing the ladder in almost all of the avenues of life, but this is not race progress; it is the lifting up as we climb which means growth to the race.

Thirty years ago the negro slaves were declared free. The most helpless members of the race at that time, as now, were its women. During all the black days of slavery they had come and gone only as commanded by the man and the woman who called themselves master and mistress.

The negro woman had been given in marriage as the whim of the master's family saw fit; she had been sold from her husband as the master's financial interests demanded, with no more pity than was exhibited at the selling of a hog. Was it possible that she should know or think very strongly of the cultivation of the sacredness of the marital relations which are at the very root of the home? Was there anything in these lessons to inspire morality, or even a respect for it? And yet these same people, with all their boasted chivalry for their own women, are ever ready to thrust the sword at this race of which these poor women, their own pupils, are members. In this time of the master and slave, it was not the mother who taught the responsibility of motherhood. The children came, and as soon as possible the mother went to the field or elsewhere to work, and the children were left practically alone. There was no time to bathe the babies, even once a day. There was no time to dress the children, to comb their hair, to see that they were getting clean, wholesome habits in order to become clean, wholesome men and women. It was not the slave mother who said how her children should be dressed, whether they should wear shoes or go bare-footed, and thus have inculcated within themselves respect for personal appearance and decency of dress. It was not the chattel-mother who said the baby was sick enough to need medical aid. These things and more in reference to the children were decided by the master and mistress. Was there anything in a lesson like this to teach responsibility of motherhood? Was there a single thing in a lesson like this to bring about the sanctity of family life? Was there anything in a life like this to establish confidence between mother and daughter, father and son, which is absolutely necessary in the home, in a truly happy family life?

In the awful days gone by, the word "home," the word "woman" was a mockery, so far as we are concerned; in fact, there was no home, there was no manhood. All were chattel, bought, used, and sold at the master's will.

The log cabin of one room, with perhaps no hole to let in sunlight and air, holding the household goods, cooking utensils, furnishing room for cooking, sleeping, eating, and living, was a substitute for home. Could anything good and healthy come out of this? Was it at all probable that these mothers could hand down to their daughters and sons correct ideas of home-making, pure ideas of family life? Was it at all probable that there should have come from homes like these women strong to fight disease, strong to fight the tempter who stands in the South as a sentinel by day and by night? Was there anything in this sort of living to instil purity of thought, and purity of action?

The women of this class are to-day needing our aid, needing our sympathy. We will answer as Cain answered the Master, "Am I my brother's keeper?" Surely we are the keepers of these women, and will answer, "Here am I; use me."

Let us not suppose that although more than thirty years have gone by, there is a very great change in the condition of the masses of the women of whom I speak. Turned loose with no knowledge of these things, she has groped the way but slowly. In the country districts of the Southern states in which slaves were held, a condition of affairs exists to-day that would touch the heart of any woman. Look for a moment into a log cabin in Alabama. There is only one room, 12×10, with a little hole in the side for a window, which in winter time is kept tightly closed. In this hut live father and mother, and in here their eight or ten children are born and reared and die. I draw the curtain. I could show you other pictures more pathetic in their hopelessness, but I refrain.

Lessons in making home neat and attractive; lessons in making family life stronger, sweeter, and purer by personal efforts of the woman; lessons in tidiness of appearance among women; lessons of clean and pure habits of everyday life in the home, and thus bringing to the women self-respect and getting for them the respect of others; how to keep the girls near the mother, and many other kindred subjects, need to be given to the class of women to-day.

In the village of Tuskegee, in the state of Alabama, a little more than a year ago, a few of us women undertook this kind of work for this class of women. To us it was not a very inviting work, but we could not rid ourselves of the recognition of the bond which linked us to these women. We knew that as they were lifted up, so might we rise. We meet the women in a hall in the central part of the town on Saturday afternoon, when they usually flock to the town from the neighboring plantations and country districts and congregate on the street corners to gossip and eat peanuts. Our meetings are very informal, and hence, I believe, very helpful; for the women would not come if the meetings were not informal. During the past few months we have talked in a simple way on home-getting, home-making, cultivating confidence between the parent and the child, how to protect our girls, plain and simple dress for the children, kinds of food best for the home, and many like subjects tending to better them along all lines. We have had emphasized the respect that comes to a woman because of her neatness of dress, and upon the disrespect that comes to her by reason of her love for gaudy and extravagant dress. We have tried to get our women to substitute the neat calico dress of to-day for the slave homespun of the past. We have tried to teach them the self-respect which comes from wearing shoes instead of going bare-footed as the master taught them; the lack of self-respect and the physical injury incident to wrapping the hair. These are only a few of the crude things which these women will do. They have been taught these lessons by people who have had hundreds of years of advantages and experience, and they would naturally be loth to give up these habits. But we do not feel discouraged.

In addition to the work we are trying to do for the women, we have also each week a meeting for young girls, to whom we give lessons in simple sewing, in house-cleaning, in street and church manners, and in every line which goes to make young womanhood purer and nobler. Much of the social purity literature is given out to these girls, and here and there a seed is being sown which will bring forth a better wifehood and motherhood.

We only want women who will, everywhere that is needed, take up this cause of the large class of negro women who have not had the same opportunity which you and I have had. Are we not all of one race? Are not the interests of this class our interests? There is a hearty response in the efforts of the women to rise and shake off the terrible habits which, for two hundred and fifty years, were being fastened upon them. It is not rapid work, but I believe that it is sure work. I believe that in this kind of work is the salvation of the negro women, and all will agree with me that just in proportion as the women rise will the race rise. Work for these masses and you work for the race.

But this lamentable condition of affairs is not confined to any particular section of our country; but is it not true that right here, under the shadow of the Cradle of Liberty, as it were, and where a "man's a man for a' that and a' that," there are to be found parallel cases? In picturing to you the condition of affairs at the South, and pleading for my Southern sisters, I do not wish to withdraw your interest in and for the needy ones nearer home, but my heart goes out with great longing in the interest of the Southern negro woman who is what she is because of force of circumstances, and not because of a lack of desire to be otherwise.

Let us all rise, shine and push right along in the work of helping our women in the South, in the North, everywhere that it is needed—and it is needed everywhere; let us rise with our money, though it be little; let us rise with our voices even though they be weak, with our hands even though they be feeble, and do this all-important work. Then only will there be fewer thrusts at the immorality of the race; there will be less lynchings of negro men and women; then only will the white man who hates everything that is black, and the black man who despises everything white, recognize in the broadest and truest sense the brotherhood of man and the fatherhood of God, and more readily accept that doctrine that of one blood hath he made the nations of the earth.

Booker T. Washington

"Our New Citizen"

Address delivered to the Hamilton Club, Chicago, January 31, 1896[7]

From whence came our new citizen? Who is he? And what is his mission? It is interesting to note that the Negro is the only citizen of this country who came here by special invitation and by reason of special provision. The Caucasian came here against the protest of the leading citizens of this country in 1492. We were so important to the prosperity of this country that special vessels were sent to convey us hither.

Shall we be less important in the future than in the past? The Negroes are one eighth of your population. Our race is larger than the population of the Argentine Republic, larger than Chile, larger than Peru and Venezuela combined—nearly as large as Mexico.

Whether the call has come for us to clear the forests of your country, to make your cotton, rice, and sugar cane, build houses or railroads, or to shoulder arms in defense of our country, have we not answered that call? When the call has come to educate our children, to teach them thrift, habits of industry, have we not filled every school that has been opened for us? When with others there have been labor wars, strikes, and destruction of property, have we not set the world an example in each one quietly attending to his own business? When, even here in the North, the shop, the factory, the trades have closed against us, have we not patiently, faithfully gone on taking advantage of our disadvantages, and through it all have we not continued to rise, to increase in numbers and prosperity? If in the past we have thus proven our right to your respect and confidence, shall it be less so in the future? If in proportion as we contribute, by the exercise of the higher virtues, by the product of brain and skilled hand, to the common prosperity of our country, shall we not receive all the privileges of any other citizen, whether born out of this country or under the Stars and Stripes?

You of the great and prosperous North still owe a serious and uncompleted duty to your less fortunate brothers of the white race South who suffered and are still suffering the consequences of American slavery. What was the task you asked them to perform? Returning to their destitute homes after years of war, to face blasted hopes, devastation, a shattered industrial system, you asked them to add to their burdens that of preparing in education, politics, and economics, in a few short years, for citizenship four or five millions of former slaves. That the South, staggering under the burden, made blunders, that in some measure there has been disappointment, no one need be surprised.

And yet, taking it all in all, we may, I think, safely challenge history to find a case where two races, but yesterday master and slave, today citizen and citizen, have made such marvelous progress in the adjustment of themselves to new conditions, where each has traveled so fast in the divine science of forgetting and forgiving; and yet do not misunderstand me that all is done or there are not serious wrongs yet to be blotted out.

In making these observations I do not, I cannot, forget as an humble representative of my race the vacant seat, the empty sleeve, the lives offered up on Southern battlefields, that we might have a united country and that our flag should shelter none save freemen, nor do I forget the millions of dollars that have gone into the South from the hands of philanthropic individuals and religious organizations.

Nor are we of the black race leaving the work alone to your race in the North or your race in the South—mark what this new citizen is doing. Go with me tonight to the Tuskegee Institute in the Black Belt of Alabama, in an old slave plantation where a few years ago my people were bought and sold, and I will show you an industrial village, which is an example of others, with nearly eight hundred young men and women working with head and hand by night and by day, preparing themselves, in literature, in science, in agriculture, in dairying, in fruit-growing, in stock-raising, in brick-making, in brick masonry, in woodwork, in ironwork, in tinwork, in leatherwork, in cloth, in cooking, in laundrying, in printing, in household science—in the duties of Christian citizenship—preparing themselves that they may prepare thousands of others of our race that they may contribute their full quota of virtue, of thrift and intelligence to the prosperity of our beloved country. It is said that we will be hewers of wood and drawers of water, but we shall be more, we shall turn the wood into houses, into machinery, into implements of commerce and civilization. We shall turn the water into steam, into electricity, into dairy and agricultural products, into food and raiment—and thus wind our life about yours, thus knit our civil and commercial interests into yours in a way that shall make us all realize anew that "of one blood hath God made all men to dwell and prosper on the face of the earth."

But when all this is said, I repeat, gentlemen of the club, that you of this generation owe to the South, not less than to yourselves, an unfulfilled duty. Surely, surely, if the Negro, with all that is behind him, can forget the past, you ought to rise above him in this regard. When the South is poor you are poor, when the South commits crime you commit crime, when the South prospers you prosper. There is no power that can separate our destiny. Let us ascend in this matter above color or race or party or sectionalism into the region of duty of man to man, American to American, Christian to Christian. If the Negro who has been oppressed, ostracized, denied rights in a Christian land, can help you, North and South, to rise, can be the medium of your rising to these sublime heights of unselfishness and self-forgetfulness, who may say that the Negro, this new citizen, will not see in it a recompense for all that he has suffered and will have performed a mission that will be placed beside that of the lowly Nazarine?

Let the Negro, the North, and the South do their duty with a new spirit and a new determi-
nation during this, the dawning of a new century, and at the end of fifty years a picture will be painted—what is it? A race dragged from its native land in chains, three hundred years of slavery, years of fratricidal war, thousands of lives laid down, freedom for the slave, reconstruction, blunders, bitterness between North and South. The South staggers under the burden; the North forgets the past and comes to the rescue; the Negro, in the midst, teaching North and South patience, forbearance, long-suffering, obedience to law, developing in intellect, character and property, skill and habits of industry. The North and South, joining hands with the Negro, take him whom they have wronged, help him, encourage him, stimulate him in self-help, give him the rights of man, and, in lifting up the Negro, lift themselves up into that atmosphere where there is a new North, a new South—a new citizen—a new republic.

—January 31, 1896.

Anonymous
"Domestic Evolution"

Daily Picayune, May 3, 1896[8]
The Old Chloe and Mammy of Antebellum Times.
The Ornamental New Colored Woman of To-day.

With the passing away of a single generation of old negroes, now, alas, nearing the end of the journey of life, one of the most picturesque features of the south will be lost. Already the sight of a neat, respectful, respectable old colored aunty, with a gay bandana tignon on her head, is growing rare. She has been superseded by the "cullud lady," who parades the street in cheap and gaudy finery, and who scorns to demean herself by being polite to any white person, or doing any work.

For there is a new colored woman, as well as a new white woman. If the new white woman is an anomaly in the world, who is neither man
nor woman, neither fish, flesh, fowl or good red herring, the new colored woman is the Frankenstein of civilization. She is a misfit in creation, who has borrowed all the vices and faults of her model and added to them frills that are peculiarly her own. The new white woman has to get over the traditions of centuries of virtue and respectability before she acquires the courage of her theories; but the new colored woman is foot loose and fancy free to do as she pleases.

And the first article in her confession of faith is a deep and abiding determination not to work. Sometimes this is temporarily shaken by hunger, or a desire to purchase some gaudy finery to wear to the forthcoming ball of the "Amalgamated Sons and Daughters of Rest," and she will condescend for a short time to preside in your kitchen, or languidly make your beds. But she does it under protest. She has no pride in her work; no desire to do it well. The least work for the most money is the legend she inscribes on her banner, and she mentally registers a vow to leave you the first time you are indiscreet enough to invite company, and to come up missing, as an Irishman might say, the first cold morning.

The Aunt Dinahs, ample of girth, clad in clean cottonnade, who went about in a sort of charmed atmosphere of savory smells that made the very mouth water with anticipatory delight, belonged to the old generation. They boasted that they laid a heavy hand on the seasoning in compounding the delicacies for which they were famous,[9] and at dinner would poke an anxious head through the dining-room door to hear the compliments bestowed upon their art. In their kitchens hungry children know surreptitious dainties were to be had for the teasing; that wonderful ducks and chickens were fashioned out of biscuit dough, and that the perpetual grumbling of the high priestess of the pots and pans meant nothing more than that the roast and the gumbo lay heavy on her mind. Here and there such a figure still lingers in a kitchen, but she is growing too old to work, and her mistress thinks with horror of the time when Dinah will be gone and the new colored woman reign in her stead. Then, indeed, will dyspepsia and confusion worse confounded stalk through the house. For the new colored woman does not burden her mind with the insignificant details that go to make good cooking. She dashes a lot of things together, and if they turn out all right, well and good; if not, also well. All she is concerned is in drawing her wages, and carrying back and forth the basket that is the commissary department of a tribe of hungry and idle friends.

Time was when every housekeeper pointed with pride to her neat housemaid in a blue calico so stiffly starched it rattled like the best taffeta. With what precision did she draw your

mosquito bar! with what sympathy did she press on you the hot bread at breakfast! She, too, might answer to the auctioneer's cry of "Going, going, gone!" Now a frowsy girl in a dirty lace-trimmed party waist condescends to wait at table, or make beds, or answer the door bell, when she feels like it. It is said that an intelligent Chinese servant can insult his master in several thousand ways, so deftly that the master remains in ignorance of it. The new colored woman employs no such finesse. She goes right to the point, and makes the distinction of invariably speaking of her race as "ladies and gentlemen," and yours as "men and women." When you are told that there is a woman downstairs you know that it is probably some friend noted for her aristocratic lineage, her culture, wealth and position, while the maid's announcement that a lady wants to see you sends you to the back door to interview the charwoman.

The new colored woman has one desire that ranks above all others, one fixed ambition, and that is to be a school teacher. There must be in the south several hundred thousand young negro women who have announced their determination to follow this career. They are in the process of being educated. Year after year they go to school, with so far as the outsider can see no direct results except an added insolence and laziness. Of course, here and there one probably gets a fair education, but the most never get beyond the superior elegance of saying "have came," and scorning the humble and admiring mother who takes in washing to support her daughter in idleness. If all the young women who are expecting to make a living by teaching carry out their intention, the government will have to subsidize every little kinky-headed coon and farm him out, for there won't be more than one scholar a piece. Sometimes indeed Mary Jane, now Mary Jane no longer, but Miss Birdie or Lilly or Daisy, gets a diploma from her seminary and comes home to astonish the community of St. Kinkleville with her airs and graces. No school coming in search of her distinguished talents, she scorns the humble occupation of a house maid or cook, and lives—God knows how.

The marriage tie is seldom the tie that binds with her, and she is so far advanced that she practically illustrates the matrimonial theories advanced by Mr. Thomas Hardy and Grant Allen in their recent fiction. She has no shame and no remorse. In the peculiar theory of life and morality held by the new colored woman, anything is better and more respectable than to make a living by work.

The older generation of negro women who were brought up before the war had the advantage of close association with gentle and refined ladies. Essentially imitative as the colored race is, they copied the manners and the graces of the people they served, and many an old black mammy has the manners of a grande dame, many an old uncle the courtly grace of a Chesterfield. The young negroes have had no such opportunities, and would not have used them if they had. They have chosen to imitate the worst class of whites, and it is, as if one saw a vulgar picture ineffably seasoned by being reproduced in glaring colors that emphasized in every unlovely detail. They believe liberty is a license, and do not know that reverence and respect are attributes that adorn the highest station.

One of the saddest features of this passing away of the old fashioned negroes is the loss of that negro mammy. In every southern home she was a figure unique in the peculiar love and tenderness that surrounded her. In her strong arms every white baby was first laid, with the certainty that nothing amiss could befall it there. On her broad breast childish sorrows sobbed themselves out, and broken baby hearts were mended by the magic of mammy's touch. Her hands guided the first faltering step, her tongue first opened the doors of romance and marvels; her voice, deep, soft, mellow, and sweet as the voice of love, croned [sic] the lullabies that lie on the threshold of hush-a-by-land. The passing years but strengthened the ties that bound the black mammy and her white children. It was her province to watch over their growth, and her "mind you manners" was a stern admonition no well bred southern child dared disregard. She packed the trunk of the boy about to start to college, she inspected the suitors who came awooing, and passed judgment, often as shrewd as unconventional, upon them, she pinned the veil over the face of the bride, and gave sage advice on the best way to manage husbands to her "baby" about to embark on the uncertain sea of matrimony. In every event of life, joy and sorrow, mammy's faithful heart beat like the echo of her white folks.

Did sickness come, what hand so tender on the aching brow, what watching so unwearied as mammy's? Who so wise in the knowledge of herbs and simples? What broth had ever such a flavor as that made by her skillful hand? And when death kissed the eyelids down it was mammy's loving hand that did the last sad offices for the dead and robed them for their burial. She folded lilies in the pulseless hands, and she and her mistress, white mother and black mammy, who had both known the passion and the pain of motherhood, who had both lost the child that had lain upon their breasts, walked hand in hand behind the tiny coffin to the little graveyard in the corner of the garden. Afterwards, when the sweet ground myrtle had hidden the mound with living green, it was mammy who would go in the quiet dusks of summer evenings and bring her mistress away from that hallowed spot.

Truth, loyalty, devotion, knightly qualities, were stamped in every line of mammy's fine old face, and made it beautiful. Sometimes misfortune befell her white people, but mammy's love never faltered. The war came and set her free. Mammy staid on. She scorned new people and would not leave her own. Shrined in the unwritten history of a thousand southern homes, is the story of the faithful devotion of some old negro woman who remained and served for love the people too poor to pay her wages. Sometimes she turned to account her talent for cooking or nursing, and with the money thus made she educated the children of her former mistress, and gave them a start in life. If anything could justify slavery it was this mutual love and tenderness that existed between the black mammys and their white "chillen."

So few, so few are the white children now who are privileged to know the spoiling and correction and chiding of a black mammy, who listen to the tales of "Brer Rabbit" and the "Tar Baby" from the inspired lips that embroider the tale to suit the occasion, who miss the delicious terror of having their souls scared out of them by tales of witches and "hants." Unfortunate little people, who know nothing of a colored nurse except somebody who jerks the little arms out of the socket and stands the baby perambulator in the glaring sun, while she examines the millinery in a shop window, or flirts with a "cullud gentleman" in tan shoes and hand-me-down clothes, who, too, has embraced the profession of loafing for a livelihood.

Soon the last bandana headdress will be gone from the streets. The merchants will have no more call to display guinea blue calico, for imitation French millinery will crown every colored woman's head, and ragged finery clothe her body. Dinah no longer will wheel the baby carriage. She has taken a step forward or backwards in the process of evolution. The house is unswept, the food uncooked, the husky pickaninny sprawls unheeded across the cabin door, for the new colored woman has gotten a bicycle, and is making a spin up the avenue, instead of spinning at home. But we who knew what it was to be rocked to sleep in the loving arms of a black mammy, look back sorrowfully, and mourn the vanished grace of a day that is dead, and regret the evolution that is bringing to the front the colored new woman.

Fannie Barrier Williams
"The Colored Woman of To-day"

Godey's Magazine, July 1897[10]

Some Notable Types of the Present Generation in America

There is something very interesting and wonderfully hopeful in the development of the woman side of the colored race in this country, yet no women amongst us are so little known as the thousands of bright, alert, cultured, and gracious colored women of to-day.

A little over a century ago colored women had no social status, and indeed only thirty years ago the term "womanhood" was not large enough in this Christian republic to include any woman of African descent. No one knew her, no one was interested in her. Her birthright was supposed to be all the social evils that had been the dismal heritage of her race for two centuries. This is still the popular verdict to an astounding degree in all parts of our country. A national habit is not easily cured, and the habit of the American people, who indiscriminately place all colored women on the lowest social levels in this country, has tended to obscure from view and popular favor some of the most interesting women in the land.

But in spite of these prejudicial hindrances and a lack of confidence the young colored women of this generation are emerging from obscurity in many interesting ways that will happily surprise those who have never known them by their womanly qualities and graceful accomplishments. Such women seem to have no relationship to the slavery conditions of the yesterday of history. In a surprisingly brief period of time they have been completely lifted out of the past by the Americanism which transforms and molds into higher forms all who come under the spell of American free institutions.

It should also be noted that the thousands of cultured and delightfully useful women of the colored race who are worth knowing and who are prepared to co-operate with white women in all good efforts, are simply up-to-date new women in the best sense of that much-abused term. If there be one virtue that is conspicuous in the characters of these women it is the passion to be useful and active in everything that befits high-minded and cultivated women.

It can also be said that they stand for something higher than mere social aims. Society there is, and much of it, but there is in all the graces and accomplishments that make good society something better than mere exchange of courtesies and formalities.

That they appreciate the value of culture and intelligence is shown in the ever-increasing number of young women who are graduates of those universities and professional institutions whose doors are open wide enough to include all women, regardless of color. Not a few of them are found in the institutions and studios of Europe, pursuing special courses of all kinds. There are few professions or callings to which women of special intelligence are eligible into which colored young women are not winning their way in spite of the paganish prejudice that would restrict their ambitions. In fact, to know these women of a new race, aspiring, buoyant, and achieving, gives one a happy sense of interest in them and what they typify.

The group of women whose faces are here given aptly illustrate all that has been said. They are merely representative and not difficult to duplicate hundreds of times. If the "new woman" has appeared in the colored race, these young women are fair types of that class. They have all won their independence in the world of effort, competition, and achievement.

That there are intellectual and gracious young women, like Dr. Harriet Rice and Dr. Ida Gray Nelson, of Chicago, with diplomas from Wellesley and Ann Arbor, respectively, pursuing the professions of medicine and dentistry successfully, are facts scarcely believed by those who still insist upon the hopeless inferiority of the Negro race.

Miss Ida Platt, also of Chicago, is a rather unique personality, because of her mental versatility. Either as lawyer, linguist, musician, or stenographer, she is exceptionally qualified to follow law, music, or stenography as a profession.

The employment of Miss Josephine Bartlett in one of the largest business houses in Chicago, where only the best intelligence in her profession as stenographer is tolerated, is interesting chiefly from the fact that it is next to impossible for colored young women to obtain such employment in this free America. In nothing is the color-line so relentlessly drawn as it is against the employment of accomplished young colored women in the higher grades of occupations.

School-teaching has afforded the best field for young colored women. That profession has laid requisition upon the very best women of the race, and they in return have elevated the profession by a great variety of accomplishments. It is easy to find these young women capable of teaching everything that comes within the curriculum of the best American institutions. Miss Helene Abbott, of the St. Louis schools, is an interesting type of the young women who bring to the colored schools of the country everything that is best in modern pedagogy. Her specialty is kindergarten work, and she is the efficient assistant of Mrs. Haide Campbell, who is herself a woman of rare social accomplishments, and who has done more than any other colored woman in the country to develop the kindergarten system in public schools. These two progressive women have charge of a model kindergarten school at the Tennessee Exposition.

Miss Alice Ruth Moore and Miss Emma Rose Williams are fair types of the New Orleans Creoles, who are classed among the colored people. Whatever is best and distinctive in the Creole life of Louisiana is reflected in these young women. Their French is as musical and their personality quite as charming and attractive as the best Creole types, around which have clustered so much delightful romance and poetry. Miss Williams is one of the prized teachers in the public schools of New Orleans. Miss Moore is now pursuing a special course of study in Boston. She is a little woman of many accomplishments. She is not only a bright and racy newspaper correspondent, but has published a book of delightful sketches and charming bits of poetry. Miss Mitchell is teacher of Latin and higher English in the St. Louis High School, and is a graduate of Oberlin College.

The Provident Hospital and Training-School for Nurses in Chicago is the first institution in the country to open up a new field of employment for young colored women. It has graduated several classes, and they have met with remarkable success. Miss Belle Garnett is one of the most promising graduates of the institution. For some time she was assistant superintendent of the training-school. Aside from her profession, she is a young woman whose rare qualities of character make her typical of the highest ideals of womanhood in the colored race.

Perhaps in no other city are there so many accomplished and efficient colored women as in Washington, D.C. The public schools and the Government departments give employment to a large number. The higher social life among the colored people of Washington is a most grati-fying study and reveals much that is best in the race. Art-clubs, Shakespeare circles, folk-lore societies, and other organizations aiming at mental and social refinements and culture are a distinguishing feature of Washington life. With the last two years this spirit of organization among the women has broadened out into clubs and leagues, with the stronger purposes of affecting helpfully the social condition of the more unfortunate of the colored race. A federation of clubs has been formed having a truly national character.

Enough has been said, perhaps, to show that colored women are proving themselves in every way to be women of spirit and progressiveness. They are fully alive to their responsibilities and have already advanced far beyond their opportunities. The types here shown are merely representative of a large class of women who are a beautiful fulfilment of the prophecy that out of the social disorders of a bondaged race there shall arise a womanhood strong, spirited, and chaste in all the things that make for social uplifting and refinement.

Sutton E. Griggs

Imperium in Imperio: A Study of the Negro Race Problem, 1899

[This speech, by the New Negro protagonist Belmont Piedmont, occurs near the end of Griggs's speculative novel in a debate with the more radical New Negro antagonist, Bernard Belgrave, president of the clandestine Black shadow government, the Imperium in Imperio, of Waco, Texas. After the sinking of the USS *Maine* and the looming Spanish-American War, coupled with the white mob's murder of Imperium member and South Carolina postmaster Felix A. Cook (part of a long list of atrocities against Black people, whom the US government re-fuses to protect),[11] the Imperium faces a crisis. Its members must either volunteer to fight for the United States against the Spanish and help the Cubans—"in a large measure Negroes"—or fight against the United States given the nation's brutal hypocrisy. Bernard calls for an armed revolution against the United States and the establishment of a separate Black nation in Texas, with Louisiana as a gift to the Imperium's foreign allies. Belmont, a likely stand-in for Griggs himself, offers the following alternative resolution.[12]]

Politics.

"The South has defrauded us out of the ballot and she must restore it. But in judging her crime let us take an impartial view of its occasion. The ballot is supposed to be an expression of opinion. It is a means employed to record men's ideas. It is not designed as a vehicle of prejudice or gratitude, but of thought, opinion. When the Negro was first given the ballot he used it to convey expression of love and gratitude to the North, while it bore to the South a message of hate and revenge. No Negro, on pain of being ostracised or probably murdered, was allowed to exercise the ballot in any other way than that just mentioned. They voted in a mass, according to the dictates of love and hate.

"The ballot was never designed for such a purpose. The white man snatched the ballot from the Negro. His only crime was, in not snatching it from him also, for he was voting on the same principle. Neither race was thinking. They were both simply feeling, and ballots are not meant to convey feelings.

"But happily that day has passed and both races are thinking and are better prepared to vote. But the white man is still holding on to the stolen ballot box and he must surrender it. If we can secure possession of that right again, we shall use it to correct the many grievous wrongs under which we suffer. That is the one point on which all of our efforts are focused. Here is the storm center. Let us carry this point and our flag will soon have all of our rights inscribed thereon. The struggle is on, and my beloved Congress, let me urge one thing upon you. Leave out revenge as one of the things at which to aim.

"In His Holy Word our most high God has said: 'Vengeance is mine.' Great as is this Imperium, let it not mount God's throne and attempt by violence to rob Him of his prerogatives. In this battle, we want Him on our side and let us war as becometh men who fear and reverence Him. Hitherto, we have seen vengeance terrible in his hands.

"While we, the oppressed, stayed upon the plantation in peace, our oppressors were upon the field of battle engaged in mortal combat; and it was the blood of our oppressor, not our own, that was paid as the price of our freedom. And that same God is alive to-day; and let us trust Him for vengeance, and if we pray let our prayer be for mercy on those who have wronged us, for direful shall be their woes.

"And now, I have a substitute proposition. Fellow Comrades, I am not for internecine war. O! Eternal God, lend unto these, my Comrades, the departed spirit of Dante, faithful artist of the horrors of hell, for we feel that he alone can paint the shudder-making, soul-sickening scenes that follow in the wake of fast moving internecine war.

"Now, hear my solution of the race problem. The Anglo-Saxon does not yet know that we have caught the fire of liberty. He does not yet know that we have learned what a glorious thing it is to die for a principle, and especially when that principle is liberty. He does not yet know how the genius of his institutions has taken hold of our very souls. In the days of our enslavement we did not seem to him to be much disturbed about physical freedom. During the whole period of our enslavement we made only two slight insurrections.

"When at last the war came to set us free we stayed in the field and fed the men who were reddening the soil with their blood in a deadly struggle to keep us in bondage forever. We remained at home and defended the helpless wives and children of men, who if they had been at home would have counted it no crime to have ignored all our family ties and scattered husbands and wives, mothers and children as ruthlessly as the autumn winds do the falling leaves.

"The Anglo-Saxon has seen the eyes of the Negro following the American eagle in its glorious flight. The eagle has alighted on some mountain top and the poor Negro has been seen climbing up the rugged mountain side, eager to caress the eagle. When he has attempted to do this, the eagle has clawed at his eyes and dug his beak into his heart and has flown away in disdain; and yet, so majestic was its flight that the Negro, with tears in his eyes, and blood dripping from his heart has smiled and shouted: 'God save the eagle.'

"These things have caused us to be misunderstood. We know that our patient submission in slavery was due to our consciousness of weakness; we know that our silence and inaction during the civil war was due to a belief that God was speaking for us and fighting our battle; we know that our devotion to the flag will not survive one moment after our hope is dead; but we must not be content with knowing these things ourselves. We must change the conception which the Anglo-Saxon has formed of our character. We should let him know that patience has a limit; that strength brings confidence; that faith in God will demand the exercise of our own right arm; that hope and despair are each equipped with swords, the latter more dreadful than the former. Before we make a forward move, let us pull the veil from before the eyes of the Anglo-Saxon that he may see the New Negro standing before him humbly, but firmly demanding every right granted him by his maker and wrested from him by man.

"If, however, the revelation of our character and the full knowledge of our determined attitude does not procure our rights, my proposition, which I am about to submit, will still offer a solution.

Resolutions.

"1. Be it *Resolved*: That we no longer conceal from the Anglo-Saxon the fact that the Imperium exists, so that he may see that the love of liberty in our bosoms is strong enough to draw us together into this compact government. He will also see that each individual Negro does not stand by himself, but is a link in a great chain that must not be broken with impunity.

"2. *Resolved*: That we earnestly strive to convince the Anglo-Saxon that we are now thoroughly wedded to the doctrine of Patrick Henry: 'Give me liberty or give me death,' Let us teach the Anglo-Saxon that we have arrived at the stage of development as a people, where we prefer to die in honor rather than live in disgrace.

"3. *Resolved*: That we spend four years in endeavors to impress the Anglo-Saxon that he has a New Negro on his hands and must surrender what belongs to him. In case we fail by these means to secure our rights and privileges we shall all, at once, abandon our several homes in the various other states and emigrate in a body to the State of Texas, broad in domain, rich in soil and salubrious in climate. Having an unquestioned majority of votes we shall secure possession of the State government.

"4. *Resolved*: That when once lawfully in control of that great state we shall, every man, die in his shoes before we shall allow vicious frauds or unlawful force to pursue us there and rob us of our acknowledged right.

"5. *Resolved*: That we sojourn in the state of Texas, working out our destiny as a separate and distinct race in the United States of America.

"Such is the proposition which I present. It is primarily pacific: yet it is firm and unyielding. It courts a peaceable adjustment, yet it does not shirk war, if war is forced.

"But in concluding, let me emphasize that my aim, my hope, my labors, my fervent prayer to God is for a peaceable adjustment of all our differences upon the high plane of the equality of man. Our beloved President, in his message to this Congress, made a serious mistake when he stated that there were only two weapons to be used in accomplishing revolutions. He named the sword (and spear) and ballot. There is a weapon mightier than either of these. I speak of the pen. If denied the use of the ballot let us devote our attention to that mightier weapon, the pen.

"Other races which have obtained their freedom erect monuments over bloody spots where they slew their fellow men. May God favor us to obtain our freedom without having to dot our land with these relics of barbaric ages.

"The Negro is the latest comer upon the scene of modern civilization. It would be the crowning glory of even this marvelous age; it would be the grandest contribution ever made to the cause of human civilization; it would be a worthy theme for the songs of the Holy Angels, if every Negro, away from the land of his nativity, can by means of the pen, force an acknowledgment of equality from the proud lips of the fierce, all conquering Anglo-Saxon, thus eclipsing the record of all other races of men, who without exception have had to wade through blood to achieve their freedom.

"Amid all the dense gloom that surrounds us, this transcendent thought now and then finds its way to my heart and warms it like a glorious Sun. Center your minds, beloved Congress, on this sublime hope, and God may grant it to you. But be prepared, if he deems us unfit for so great a boon, to buckle on our swords and go forth to win our freedom with the sword just as has been done by all other nations of men.

"My speech is made, my proposition is before you. I have done my duty.

Your destiny is in your own hands."

Belton's speech had, like dynamite, blasted away all opposition. He was in thorough mastery of the situation. The waves of the sea were now calm, the fierce winds had abated, there was a great rift in the dark clouds. The ship of state was sailing placidly on the bosom of the erstwhile troubled sea, and Belton was at the helm.

His propositions were adopted in their entirety without one dissenting voice.

When the members left the Congress hall that evening they breathed freely, feeling that the great race problem was, at last, about to be definitely settled.

But, alas! how far wrong they were!

As Belton was leaving the chamber Bernard approached him and put his hands fondly on his shoulders.

Bernard's curly hair was disordered and a strange fire gleamed in his eye. He said: "Come over to the mansion to-night. I wish much to see you. Come about nine P.M."

Belton agreed to go.

John N. Abbey
"Dr. Abbey on the Negro: Comparison of the New and Old Negro"

Star of Zion, July 26, 1900[13]

"Toting Your Own Tote."

[Rev. John N. Abbey, D. D., one of the most intelligent Negro ministers in the city of Memphis, Tenn., delivered a lecture last night at Clinton A. M. E. Zion church to a large audience of his race. "Toting Your Own Tote" was the rather unique title of this discourse. He takes the position that the new Negro has contributed very little toward the material advancement of the race.]

"I am convinced, from evidences in sight, that the Negro has made some progress on all lines; but I am fully of the opinion that there are strong grounds upon which to base an argument for his inactivity as a great factor in the moral, intellectual, industrial and commercial world," said the speaker. "Our advancement is retarded largely on business lines, on account of lack of confidence, the shifting of responsibilities and proper training.

"There are two distinct classes of the Negro race in America—the old and the new Negro. The first class may be described as the antebellum Negro. He lived before the interstate war. He lived at the time of the issuing of the proclamation of emancipation by Lincoln. He lives to-day. He is the greatest figure known to the historian. As a representative of this first class he is in touch with three generations and stands in relation to three periods. He marks an important point in the history of the nation before the war, in the days of master and slave. He lived amid the shot, shell, smoke and fire back in the 60s; he heard the anunciation [*sic*] of the declaration of freedom; he witnessed the end of slavery, the fall of the Confederacy. He has witnessed the passing away of the midst of darkness, superstition and ignorance, journeyed into a new revelation of things, admitted to the ballot box, voted for and by the side of his master, and was inducted into the school room. He has lived to establish institutions of learning all through our Southland, representing all grades of professions. He is the recognized leader in the establishment of churches and perpetuation of Christian denominations.

"The Negro of the class first is the rockbed of our moral superstructure, the arch of our intellectual period, and the capstone of our industrial monument. He stands in proximity with the generations of the present, past and future. Having learned without books, in the school of hard experiences, and having pushed his way to the front, it can be well said of him that he has 'toted his own tote.' He is the only real, substantial character of the race, representing 95 per cent of the business carried on by us. He represents the farmers, the industries, the ballot and the money. Notwithstanding his efforts to build up a substantial national character among the races of our great republic, and to put his people in a position creditable to any nationality, he has reached the point of despair on account of existing conditions.

"This second class to which I have alluded, claim birth this side of the civil war. They represent a new dispensation, a new day and a new generation. They represent also the age of research and reform. This class, mark you, is the Negro which we are now to consider, while the first class represent the old Negro. This new Negro is a student of some of the best schools of this country, a graduate, a teacher, doctor, lawyer, preacher, bicyclist, gossiper, gambler, and a loafer. Of course, you understand that there are exceptional cases, but I am addressing myself to the masses. This new Negro of whom I am speaking has been and is given advantages that his father never dreamed of, and yet he is worthless and shiftless. He is an embodiment of humanity; all clothes, ribbons and flowers and a befitting representative of pride and poverty. He is a shadow without a substance; an existence without an object; and an object without an aim. He can play well his part around the barber shops and saloons; he is enabled to make a creditable showing in the church social and theatrical circles. He is simply a dark spot in the Negro firmament. In fact, to say the truth, he has no future. Futures are based upon actions of the present and are governed by laws of action and reaction; and when there are no real acts upon the part of the actor the play is a failure and the audience is dismissed without having obtained any real benefit.

"I wish to assert here with emphasis that there is a condition confronting us which must be met. How shall we meet it, and what is to be done with this new Negro of class second? Will the old Negro give him up or will he hold on to him and strive further to help him make for himself a substantial existence in the future?

"There is no comparison between the new women of this class and the old women of the former. The first class represents a type of industry, economy, morality and Christianity. The new woman of class two represents idleness, fashion, vanity, gossip, fast living and churchianity; the former is a real exhibition of the old-time Christian stepping in the footprints of the Master, singing today amid the ecstasy of the new songs and new method of worship: 'Give me the old time religion; it's good enough for me.' I am ashamed of the new Negro woman. She is all flowers and dress and as vain as a peacock. She is on a strain year in and year out for dress without a home, and without a tangible income. She dresses beyond her means and parades through the streets of our cities and towns as a specimen of humanity in clothes on exhibition. She is a curse college or institution of learning; she is history and a stumbling block to our progress. If she is a graduate of some college or institution of learning she is without a literary turn of mind. She is above work. She is a stranger to the domestic system, is anxious to marry and will never make a wife, because she is not in possession of any of the essential qualities or elements that constitute and form the basis of a real help meet.

"You ask, then, is she not a reader of books? Well, yes; she is a reader of trashy literature of the third-class novel grade. Her library consists of the very meanest publications in the catalogue of printed matter. She has not learned as yet to give attention to study and research of our best literature. She will spend hour after hour reading 5 and 10-cent novels, from which no real benefit can accrue. The new Negro woman is a mere cipher in the race's great problem. I advise her to come down from her perch, lay aside her bicycle and bloomers, put away forever trashy books, walk and work with the people of her race, and stand in touch with those whose superior advantages cover centuries before her. I advise her to cultivate a taste for domestic work; learn to read the best books and periodicals; to enter into her study; make books, write articles, and take instruction that will be helpful to the race."

Dallas, (Tex.) Item.

John E. MacBrady

"Introduction"

In *A New Negro for a New Century*, 1900

Introduction

This book has been rightly named "A New Negro for a New Century." The Negro of today is in every phase of life far advanced over the Negro of 30 years ago. In the following pages the progressive life of the Afro-American people has been written in the light of achievements that will be surprising to people who are ignorant of the enlarging life of these remarkable people.

In the succeeding pages, both History and Reminiscence of the Afro-American have been collected in attractive form. The stories given have been gathered from the lips of the heroes themselves. Stories, which once woven into the text-books of the Nation, will obtain for the brave contemporaries of our own times places in history along with those of our heroic forefathers. To these reminiscences gathered fresh from the field, the colored pupil and historian of this new Century must turn for their narrative.

Sectionalism, which threatened the disruption of the Union in 1861, has been banished forever. The cries of an enthralled and afflicted people have been answered and humanity has been redeemed.

The numberless histories of the Spanish-American War that have been published and which all have given national praise to the white soldiers, the patriotism, the valor and bravery of the colored soldiers has scarcely, if ever, been mentioned. I hope that these chapters will be accepted as an authentic statement of the thrilling experiences and daring acts of the brave black men, both regulars and volunteers, who faced the perilous exploits of war with indomitable courage and have made what ought to be an imperishable impress upon the whole country, teaching a lesson in patriotism, which speaks volumes for the stability of our struggling race.

The stand that our colored soldiers took throughout the war is discussed pro and con in the following pages. All the colored regiments and officers that were sent to Cuba, as well as the regiments and officers which were afterwards sent to the Philippine Islands, are carefully and correctly listed herein.

The section on Education is especially apt at a time when the American people have begun to speculate as to the value of the last 30 years of education among the colored people. As on all questions relative to the race problem, Prof. Booker T. Washington is especially original and helpful in giving the right point of view in estimating the value of the education already given to the Negro and the kind of education most needed. The race is fortunate in having so masterful a man to present these subjects with a thoroughness and authority of an Historian.

Mr. Wood's chapters reciting the achievements of the Negro from the days of reconstruction are full of interest and happy surprises.

The club movement among the colored women of the country, written by Mrs. Fannie Barrier Williams, the well-known club woman and newspaper correspondent, will be found to be one of the most interesting parts of the book. Nothing in the whole book represents so distinctively the new life of this progressive race as the ambitions, the social energy, and achievements of colored women in the organized efforts for social betterment.

This is the first attempt to publish in permanent form a history of the progressive life of the colored women of America, with the names and locations of all the clubs belonging to the National Association. These clubs are composed of some of the best women in the country and their location will prove of inestimable value to women traveling unprotected or as strangers in any part of the country. We have been frequently requested to furnish just such a helpful directory of women's clubs.

The photographs contained in this book make a most pleasing gallery of intelligent and progressive men, and strong, intellectual and charming women.

J. E. MacB.

Booker T. Washington
"Afro American Education"

In *A New Negro for a New Century*, 1900

That the age of prophecy, like that of chivalry, has passed away was never more signally shown than in the utter breaking down of all the predictions that followed the Afro-American people out of the house of bondage into the home, the church, and the school-house of freedom. It was confidently predicted by his enemies that he was incapable of mastering the common rudiments of education, and the idea that he could master the higher education was laughed out of court. When the war came to a close in 1865 a large portion of the American people regarded the Afro-American people "as less than man, yet more than brute." They had no faith in the possibility of his mental or moral regeneration.

And yet, in those early days when the race was enslaved, there appeared among them men of great piety and learning, who devoted themselves, where they were allowed to do so, to the education of such of their fellows as were classed as "free negroes." Such pioneers in the

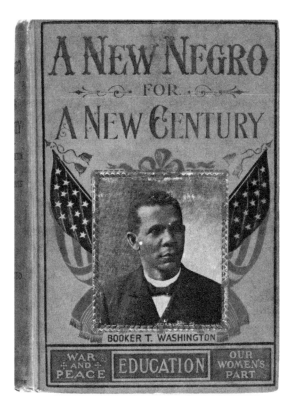

Cover of *A New Negro for a New Century* (Chicago: American Publishing House, 1900).

work of education were Rev. Daniel Alexander Payne of South Carolina, Rev. J. W. Hood of North Carolina, Rev. John Peterson of New York, and George B. Vashin of Missouri—men who illustrated in their lives and work those higher virtues of capacity, industry, devotion to race, which were to have such a splendid army of emulators in the after years and under more favoring conditions.

No sufficient tribute has ever been paid to General O. O. Howard, who laid the foundation of the Afro-American educational work while he had charge of the important work of the Freedmen's Bureau. It is meet that General Samuel Chapman Armstrong, the founder of the Hampton Normal and Agricultural Institute, should pay him such a tribute. General Armstrong said:

General Howard and the Freedmen's Bureau did for the ex-slaves, from 1865 to 1870, a marvelous work, for which due credit has not been given; among other things, giving to their education an impulse and a foundation, by granting three and a half millions of dollars for schoolhouses, salaries, etc., promoting the education of about a million colored children. The principal negro education institutions of to-day, then starting, were liberally aided, at a time of vital need. Hampton received over $50,000 through General Howard for building and improvements.

But it is not alone in the money expended by General Howard as the representative of the Government in the direction indicated by General Armstrong are we indebted to this great soldier and philanthropist; out of his private purse he founded Howard University at the capital of the nation and endowed it with a princely domain, which must to-day be worth $5,000,000 in the open market. It was through no fault of General Howard's that this endowment was scattered to the winds.

General Armstrong was also one of the pioneers in this educational work, having been placed by General Howard, Commissioner of the Freedmen's Bureau, in charge of ten counties in Eastern Virginia, with headquarters at Hampton, the great "contraband" camp, "to manage negro affairs and to adjust, if possible, the relations of the races." How the Hampton work, one of the best and strongest, was planted, is best told in the language of General Armstrong himself:

> On relieving my predecessor, Captain C. B. Wilder, of Boston, at the Hampton headquarters, I found an active, excellent educational work going on under the American Missionary Association of New York, which, in 1862, had opened, in the vicinity, the first school for freedmen in the South, in charge of an ex-slave, Mrs. Mary Peake. Over 1,500 children were gathering daily; some in old hospital barracks—for here was Camp Hamilton, the base hospital of the Army of the James, where, during the war, thousands of sick and wounded soldiers had been cared for, and where now over 6,000 lie buried in a beautiful national cemetery. The largest class was in the "Butler School" building, since replaced by the "John G. Whittier schoolhouse."
>
> Close at hand the pioneer settlers of America and the first slaves landed on this continent; here Powhatan reigned; here the Indian child was baptized; here freedom was first given the slave by General Butler's "contraband" order; in sight of this shore the battle of the Merrimac and Monitor saved the Union and revolutionized naval warfare; here General Grant based the operations of his final campaign.
>
> I soon felt the fitness of this historic and strategic spot for a permanent and great educational work. The suggestion was cordially received by the American Missionary Association, which authorized the purchase, in June, 1867, of "Little Scotland," an estate of 125 acres (since increased to 190), on Hampton River, looking out over Hampton Roads. Not expecting to have charge, but only to help, I was surprised one day by a letter from Secretary E. P. Smith of the A. M. A., stating that the man selected for the place had declined, and asking me if I could take it. I replied "Yes." Till then my own future had been blind; it had only been clear that there was a work to do for the ex-slaves, and where and how it should be done.
>
> A day-dream of the Hampton school nearly as it is had come to me during the war a few times; once in camp during the siege of Richmond, and once one beautiful evening on the Gulf of Mexico, while on the wheelhouse of the transport steamship Illinois en route for Texas with the Twenty-fifth Army (Negro) Corps, for frontier duty on the Rio Grande River, whither it had been ordered, under General Sheridan, to watch and if necessary defeat Maximilian in his attempted conquest of Mexico.
>
> The thing to be done was clear: To train selected Negro youth who should go out at once and teach and lead their people, first by example, by getting land and homes; to give them not a dollar that they could not earn for themselves; to teach respect for labor; to replace stupid drudgery with skilled hands; and, to these ends, to build up an industrial system, for the sake not only of self-support and intelligent labor, but also for the sake of character. And it seemed equally clear that the people of the country would support a wise work for the freedmen. I think so still.
>
> They have done it. From the small seed planted at Hampton, and as an outgrowth of the work of the Freedmen's Bureau, schools of elementary and higher education rapidly sprang up in every state. The enthusiasm with which these schools were filled, not only by the young, but by the adults, astonished not only the people

of the North, but those of the South. Many who watched the phenomenon, and who had their doubts about the capacity of the Afro-American people to receive mental discipline and to continue in well doing, said that when the novelty should wear off those schoolhouses would be emptied of their eager disciples. But they were not. Each succeeding year has seen the grand army of schoolchildren grow larger and larger and more earnest in enthusiasm; and the numerous academies, seminaries, institutes, and colleges have been and are overcrowded.

In the early stages of the work there were very few Afro-Americans competent to teach and there were no funds to carry on the work, as the common school system in the Southern states had not been inaugurated; it was to come later, after the work of foundation-laying had been done under the inspiration of the Freedmen's Bureau and the organized missionary associations of the North. But where were the teachers to come from? Unfortunately, I think, as events have demonstrated, the whites were indisposed to undertake this necessary work, and were in many instances hostile to those who did do it. There are few brighter pages in the missionary history of the world than that which records the readiness and willingness with which the white men and women of the Northern states went into the South, into its large cities and its waste places, and labored year in and year out, to lay the foundation of the Afro-American's religious and educational character, and the unparalleled financial support which was given them, and is continued to this day, by the philanthropic people of the North. It is estimated that in the maintenance of the educational work among the Afro-American people of the South the philanthropists of the North, directly and through organized associations like the American Missionary Association and the Peabody Fund, have expended annually an average of one million dollars since 1867, making a grand total of $32,000,000. Fully a hundred colleges, institutes, and the like have been established and maintained, and are to-day doing a marvelous work. A majority of these schools have white management, but all of them are represented in their faculties by their graduates. A great many of them are managed in all their departments by Afro-Americans.

As has been said, these schools of higher learning are maintained, for the most part, by the organized charities and individual philanthropists of the North. There are two funds set apart for this work, besides the Peabody Fund, of which the whites receive a large share—the John F. Slater Fund and the Hand Fund, of a million dollars each, the income of which is applied to helping these Afro-American schools.

Mention should be made here of the fact that Hon. Jonathan C. Gibbs, one of the first Afro-American graduates of Dartmouth College, was one of the state superintendents of education of Florida in the Reconstruction era, and died while holding that position. His son, Hon. Thomas V. Gibbs, died in 1898, after having done much as its secretary and treasurer, in connection with President T. DeS. Tucker, to place the State Normal and Agricultural College, at Tallahassee on a prosperous foundation.

With the inauguration of the public school system in the Southern states the voluntary schools were gradually absorbed and their Northern teachers displaced by those they had prepared. The extent and importance of their work may be judged by the fact that when they entered the field in 1866–67 there were comparatively few Afro-American teachers in the South, whereas to-day there are no fewer than 25,000 employed in the public schools. Baltimore, I believe, is the only Southern city in which white teachers are now employed in these schools. Any unbiased person must admit that this is not only a creditable but a remarkable showing, one alike creditable to the race and to those who lavished upon it time and money to effect it.

Most of the Southern states maintain normal and agricultural schools for the education of Afro-American youths. Alabama not only does this, but makes a generous appropriation for the work of the Tuskegee Normal and Industrial Institute. Prof. Richard R. Wright, president of the State Normal College, at College, Ga., is perhaps the best known of the presidents of these State institutions. The one in North Carolina, presided over by James B. Dudley, at Greensboro, also has a good reputation. In South Carolina, ex-congressman Thomas E. Miller has charge of the State School at Orangeburgh. A very excellent work is being done by Prof. S. G. Atkins, at the Slater Academy, at Winston, N.C., one of the few schools of its kind in the South supported in large part by the native whites.

The African Methodist Episcopal and the African Methodist Episcopal Zion Churches maintain a large number of schools. The main school of the former is located at Wilberforce, Ohio, with S. T. Mitchell as president. Prof. W. S. Scarborough, who has written a Greek grammar and many treaties on Greek subjects, is connected with the school—Wilberforce University. The main school of the latter is located at Salisbury, N.C., W. H. Goler being president. The school was built up in its earlier stages by Rev. Joseph C. Price, who had the reputation in his lifetime of being one of the most eloquent men in the Republic. The Baptist denomination also maintains a large number of schools.

Among the schools of higher learning which have an assured standing may be mentioned Lincoln University, in Chester County, Pa.; Howard University, Washington, D.C.; Shaw University, Raleigh, N.C.; Claflin University, Orangeburgh, S.C.; Atlanta and Clark Universities, Morris Brown College, Gammon

Theological Seminary and Spelman Seminary, all of Atlanta; Fisk, Roger Williams, and Central Tennessee Colleges at Nashville, Tenn.; Knoxville College, Knoxville, Tenn.; Berea College, where both races are educated, at Berea, Ky.

Among the normal and industrial schools Hampton Institute and its offspring, the Tuskegee Institute, at Tuskegee, Ala., head[s] the list; the Calhoun School, at Calhoun, Ala.; the Mt. Meigs School, at Mt. Meigs, Ala.; the Gloucester School, at Gloucester, Va., with the state industrial schools in most of the Southern states.

The educational work in the Southern states is accomplishing wonders in the moral and intellectual uplift of the people, which has already been felt in the life of the South, and must be felt in larger measure in the years to come. There has been a marked tendency of late years to make the education conform more to the industrial lines laid by General Armstrong. This is a healthy sign, as the more practical education is the better, especially as the tendency of modern industrialism is more and more towards specialization in all departments of learning and activity of whatever sort; and this is said without intending in the least to depreciate or underrate what is regarded as the higher education. All education is good, but assuredly that is the best which enables a man to fit in most readily with the conditions of life in which he finds himself.

Fannie Barrier Williams

"The Club Movement among Colored Women in America"

In *A New Negro for a New Century*, 1900

Afro-American women of the United States have never had the benefit of a discriminating judgment concerning their worth as women made up of the good and bad of human nature. What they have been made to be and not what they are, seldom enters into the best or worst opinion concerning them.

In studying the status of Afro-American women as revealed in their club organizations, it ought to be borne in mind that such social differentiations as "women's interests, children's interests, and men's interests" that are so finely worked out in the social development of the more favored races are but recent recognitions in the progressive life of the negro race. Such specializing had no economic value in slavery days, and the degrading habit of regarding the negro race as an unclassified people has not yet wholly faded into a memory.

The negro as an "alien" race, as a "problem," as an "industrial factor," as "ex-slaves," as "ignorant" etc., are well known and instantly recognized; but colored women as mothers, as homemakers, as the center and source of the social life of the race have received little or no attention. These women have been left to grope their way unassisted toward a realization of those domestic virtues, moral impulses and standards of family and social life that are the badges of race respectability. They have had no special teachers to instruct them. No conventions of distinguished women of the more favored race have met to consider their peculiar needs. There has been no fixed public opinion to which they could appeal; no protection against the libelous attacks upon their characters, and no chivalry generous enough to guarantee their safety against man's inhumanity to woman. Certain it is that colored women have been the least known, and the most ill-favored class of women in this country.

Thirty-five years ago they were unsocialized, unclassed and unrecognized as either maids or matrons. They were simply women whose character and personality excited no interest. If within thirty-five years they have become sufficiently important to be studied apart from the general race problem and have come to be recognized as an integral part of the general womanhood of American civilization, that fact is a gratifying evidence of real progress.

In considering the social advancement of these women, it is important to keep in mind the point from which progress began, and the fact that they have been mainly self-taught in all those precious things that make for social order, purity and character. They have gradually become conscious of the fact that progress includes a great deal more than what is generally meant by the terms culture, education and contact.

The club movement among colored women reaches into the sub-social condition of the entire race. Among white women clubs mean the forward movement of the best women in the interest of the best womanhood. Among colored women the club is the effort of the few competent in behalf of the many incompetent; that is to say that the club is only one of many means for the social uplift of a race. Among white women the club is the onward movement of the already uplifted.

The consciousness of being fully free has not yet come to the great masses of the colored women in this country. The emancipation of the mind and spirit of the race could not be accomplished by legislation. More time, more patience, more suffering and more charity are still needed to complete the work of emancipation.

The training which first enabled colored women to organize and successfully carry on club work was originally obtained in church work. These churches have been and still are the great preparatory schools in which the primary lessons of social order, mutual trustfulness and united effort have been taught. The churches have been sustained, enlarged and beautified principally through the organized efforts of their women members. The meaning of unity of effort for the common good, the development of social sympathies grew into woman's consciousness through the privileges of church work.

Still another school of preparation for colored women has been their secret societies. "The ritual of these secret societies is not without a certain social value." They demand a higher order of intelligence than is required for church membership. Care for the sick, provisions for the decent burial of the indigent dead, the care for orphans and the enlarging sense of sisterhood all contributed to the development of the very conditions of heart that qualify women for the more inclusive work of those social reforms that are the aim of women's clubs. The churches and secret societies have helped to make colored women acquainted with the general social condition of the race and the possibilities of social improvement.

With this training the more intelligent women of the race could not fail to follow the example and be inspired by the larger club movement of the white women. The need of social reconstruction became more and more apparent as they studied the results of women's organizations. Better homes, better schools, better protection for girls of scant home training, better sanitary conditions, better opportunities for competent young women to gain employment, and the need of being better known to the American people appealed to the conscience of progressive colored women from many communities.

The clubs and leagues organized among colored women have all been more or less in direct response to these appeals. Seriousness of purpose has thus been the main characteristic of all these organizations. While the National Federation of Woman's Clubs has served as a guide and inspiration to colored women, the club movement among them is something deeper than a mere imitation of white women. It is nothing less than the organized anxiety of women who have become intelligent enough to recognize their own low social condition and strong enough to initiate the forces of reform.

The club movement as a race influence among the colored women of the country may be fittingly said to date from July, 1895, when the first national conference of colored women was held in Boston, Mass. Prior to this time there were a number of strong clubs in some of the larger cities of the country, but they were not affiliated and the larger idea of effecting the social regeneration of the race was scarcely conceived of.

Among the earlier clubs the Woman's League of Washington, D.C., was organized in 1892, and the Woman's Era Club of Boston, organized in January, 1893, were and are still the most thorough and influential organizations of the kind in the country.

The kind of work carried on by the Washington League since its organization is best indicated by its standing committees, as follows:

Committee on Education.
Committee on Industries.
Committee on Mending and Sewing.
Committee on Free Class Instruction.
Committee on Day Nursery.
Committee on Building Fund.

These various activities include sewing schools, kindergartens, well-conducted night schools, and mother's meetings, all of which have been developed and made a prominent part of the educational and social forces of the colored people of the capital. The league has made itself the recognized champion of every cause in which colored women and children have any special interests in the District of Columbia.

The league is also especially strong in the personnel of its membership, being made up largely of teachers; many of whom are recognized as among the most cultured and influential women of the negro race in this country.

Mrs. Helen Cook, of Washington, was the first president elected by the league, and still holds that position. Mrs. Cook belongs to one of the oldest and best-established colored families in the country. She has had all the advantages of culture, contact and experience to make her an ideal leader of the leading woman's organization of the colored race.

The Woman's League claims to have originated the idea of a national organization of colored women's clubs. In its annual report for 1895 there occurs the following language:

> The idea of national organization has been embodied in Woman's League of Washington from its formation. It existed fully developed in the minds of the original members even before they united themselves into an association which has national union for its central thought, its inspiring motive, its avowed purpose—its very reason for being.

Having assumed a national character by gaining the affiliations of such clubs as the Kansas City League, the Denver League, and associations in Virginia, South Carolina and

Pennsylvania, the Washington League was admitted into the membership of the National Council of Women of the United States.

The league is very tenacious of its name and claim as the originators of the idea of nationalizing the colored women's clubs of America, but its claim has always been challenged with more or less spirit by some of the clubs composing the National Association.

The New Era Club of Boston was organized in the month of February, 1893. The desire of the cultures and public-spirited colored women of that city to do something in the way of promoting a more favorable public opinion in behalf of the negro race was the immediate incentive to this organization. The club began its work of agitation by collecting data and issuing leaflets and tracts containing well-edited matter in reference to Afro-American progress. Its most conspicuous work has been the publication of the Women's Era, the first newspaper ever published by colored women in this country. This paper gained a wide circulation and did more than any other single agency to nationalize the club idea among the colored women of the country. The New Era Club has sustained its reputation as the most representative organization of colored people in New England. It has taken the initiative in many reforms and helpful movements that have had a wide influence on race development. This club has been especially useful and influential in all local affairs that in any way affect the colored people. Deserving young men and women struggling to obtain an education, and defenseless young women in distress have always been able to find substantial assistance in the New Era Club.

This Boston organization embraces a membership of about one hundred women, many of whom are prominent in the ranks of New England's strongest women.

Mrs. Josephine St. Pierre Ruffin has been the president of the Era Club all the time since its organization. She is an active member in many of the influential women's organizations in Massachusetts. She is a woman of rare force of character, mental alertness and of generous impulses. She has played a leading part in every movement that has tended to the emancipation of colored women from the thraldom of past conditions. Her husband, the late Judge Ruffin, held the first position of a judicial character ever held by a colored man in New England.

These two clubs, located respectively in Washington and Boston, were worthy beginnings of the many local efforts that were destined to grow and spread until there should be such a thing in the United States as a national uprising of the colored women of the country pledged to the serious work of a social reconstruction of the negro race.

But these two clubs were not the only examples of the colored woman's capacity for organization. The following clubs were thoroughly organized and actively engaged in the work of reform contemporaneously with the clubs of Boston and Washington:

The Harper Woman's Club of Jefferson City, Mo., was formed in 1890 and had established a training school for instruction in sewing; a temperance department and mothers' meetings were also carried on. The Loyal Union of Brooklyn and New York was organized in December, 1892. It had a membership of seventy-five women and was engaged largely in agitating for better schools and better opportunities for young women seeking honorable employment; the I. B. W. Club of Chicago, Ill., organized in 1893; the Woman's Club of Omaha, Neb., organized February, 1895; the Belle Phoebe League of Pittsburg, Pa., organized November, 1894; the Woman's League of Denver; the Phillis Wheatley Club of New Orleans; the Sojourner Club of Providence, R.I., and the Woman's Mutual Improvement Club of Knoxville, Tenn., organized in 1894.

It will thus be seen that from 1890 to 1895 the character of Afro-American womanhood began to assert itself in definite purposes and efforts in club work. Many of these clubs came into being all unconscious of the influences of the larger club movement among white women. The incentive in most cases was quite simple and direct. How to help and protect some defenseless and tempted young woman; how to aid some poor boy to complete a much-coveted education; how to lengthen the short school term in some impoverished school district; how to instruct and interest deficient mothers in the difficulties of child training are some of the motives that led to formation of the great majority of these clubs. These were the first out-reachings of sympathy and fellowship felt by women whose lives had been narrowed by the petty concerns of the struggle for existence and removed by human cruelty from all the harmonies of freedom, love and aspirations.

Many of these organizations so humble in their beginnings and meager in membership clearly needed behind them the force and favor of some larger sanction to save them from timidity and pettiness of effort. Many of them clearly needed the inspirations, the wider vision and supporting strength that come from a national unity. The club in Mississippi could have a better understanding of its own possibilities by feeling the kinship of the club in New England or Chicago, and the womanhood sympathy of these northern clubs must remain narrow and inefficient if isolated in interest from the self-emancipating struggles of southern clubs.

As already noted some of the more progressive clubs had already conceived the idea of a National organization. The Woman's Era journal of Boston began to agitate the matter in the summer of 1894, and requested the clubs to express themselves through its columns on the question of holding a National convention. Colored women everywhere were quick to see the possible benefits to be derived from a National conference of representative women. It was everywhere believed that such a convention, conducted with decorum, and along the lines of serious purpose might help in a decided manner to change public opinion concerning the character and worth of colored women. This agitation had the effect of committing most of the clubs to the proposal for a call in the summer of 1895. While public-spirited Afro-American women everywhere were thus aroused to this larger vision in plans for race amelioration, there occurred an incident of aggravation that swept away all timidity and doubt as to the necessity of a National conference. Some obscure editor in a Missouri town sought to gain notoriety by publishing a libelous article in which

the colored women of the country were described as having no sense of virtue and altogether without character. The article in question was in the form of an open letter addressed to Miss Florence Belgarnie of England, who had manifested a kindly interest in behalf of the American negro as a result of Miss Ida B. Wells' agitation. This letter is too foul for reprint, but the effect of its publication stirred the intelligent colored women of America as nothing else had ever done. The letter, in spite of its wanton meanness, was not without some value in showing to what extent the sensitiveness of colored women had grown. Twenty years prior to this time a similar publication would scarcely have been noticed, beyond the small circles of the few who could read, and were public-spirited. In 1895 this open and vulgar attack on the character of a whole race of women was instantly and vehemently resented, in every possible way, by a whole race of women conscious of being slandered. Mass meetings were held in every part of the country to denounce the editor and refute the charges.

The calling of a National convention of colored women was hastened by this coarse assault upon their character. The Woman's Era Club of Boston took the initiative in concentrating the widespread anxiety to do something large and effective, by calling a National conference of representative colored women. The conference was appointed to meet in Berkeley Hall, Boston, for a three days' session, July 29, 30 and 31, 1895. . . .

The terms good and bad, bright and dull, plain and beautiful are now as applicable to colored women as to women of other races. There has been created such a thing as public faith in the sustained virtue and social standards of the women who have spoken and acted so well in these representative organizations. The National body has also been felt in giving a new importance and a larger relationship to the purposes and activities of local clubs throughout the country. Colored women everywhere in this club work began to feel themselves included in a wider and better world than their immediate neighborhood. Women who have always lived and breathed the air of ample freedom and whose range of vision has been world-wide, will scarcely know what it means for women whose lives have been confined and dependent to feel the first consciousness of a relationship to the great social forces that include whole nationalities in the sweep of their influences. To feel that you are something better than a slave, or a descendent of an ex-slave, to feel that you are a unit in the womanhood of a great nation and a great civilization, is the beginning of self-respect and the respect of your race. The National Association of Colored Women's Clubs has certainly meant all this and much more to the women of the ransomed race in the United States.

The National association has also been useful to an important extent in creating what may be called a race public opinion. When the local clubs of the many States became nationalized, it became possible to reach the whole people with questions and interests that concerned the whole race. For example, when the National association interested itself in studying such problems as the Convict Lease System of the Southern States, or the necessity of kindergartens, or the evils of the one-room cabin, it was possible to unite and interest the intelligent forces of the entire race. On these and other questions it has become possible to get the cooperation of the colored people in Mississippi and Minnesota and of New York and Florida. Such co-operation is new and belongs to the new order of things brought about by nationalized efforts.

Through the united voice of the representative colored women of the country the interests of race are heard by the American women with more effect than they were in other days. There is certainly more power to demand respect and righteous treatment since it has become possible to organize the best forces of all the race for such demands.

The influence of the National association has been especially felt in the rapid increase of women's clubs throughout the country, and especially in the South. There are now about three hundred of such clubs in the United States. There is an average membership of about sixty women to each club. Some have an enrollment of over two hundred women and there are but few with less than twenty-five. Wherever there is a nucleus of intelligent colored women there will be found a woman's club. The following is only a partial list of the clubs composing the National association. . . .

There are of course hundreds of clubs that are not yet members of the National association, but these outside clubs have all been brought into being by the influence of the National body, and have received their inspiration and direction from the same source.

A study of the plans and purposes of these clubs reveals an interesting similarity. They show that the wants, needs, limitations and aspirations of the Afro-American are about the same everywhere—North, South, East and West.

If the question be asked: "What do these clubs do; what do they stand for in their respective communities, and what have they actually accomplished? [a] satisfactory answer will be found by studying them a little at short range.

The first thing to be noted is that these club women are students of their own social condition, and the clubs themselves are schools in which are taught and learned, more or less thoroughly, the near lessons of life and living. All these clubs have a program for study. In some of the more ambitious clubs literature, music and art are studied more or less seriously, but in all of them race problems and sociological questions directly related to the condition of the negro race in America are the principle subjects for study and discussion.

Many of the clubs, in their programs for study, plan to invite from time to time prominent men and women to address them on questions of vital interest. In this way club members not only become wide awake and interested in questions of importance to themselves and their community, but men and women who help to make and shape public opinion have an opportunity to see and know the better side of the colored race.

Race prejudice yields more readily to this interchange of service and helpfulness than to any other force in the relationship of races.

The lessons learned in these women's organizations of the country all have a direct bearing on the social conditions of the negro race. They are such lessons that are not taught in the schools or preached from the pulpits. Home-making has been new business to the great majority of the women whom the women's clubs aim to reach and influence. For this reason the principal object of club studies is to teach that homes are something better and dearer than rooms, furniture, comforts and food. How to make the homes of the race the shrines of all the domestic virtues rather than a mere shelter, is the important thing that colored women are trying to learn and teach through their club organizations.

Take for example one club in Chicago, known as the "Colored Women's Conference," and it will be found that its aims and efforts are typical of the best purposes of club life among colored women. The special activities and aims of this particular club are the establishment of kindergartens, mothers' meetings, sewing schools for girls, day nurseries, employment bureau; promoting the cause of education by establishing a direct line of interest between the teacher and the home life of every child; friendly visiting and protection to friendless and homeless girls; and a penny savings bank as a practical lesson in frugality and economy. The special thing to be noted in this program is that colored women are not afraid to set for themselves hard and serious tasks and to make whatever sacrifices necessary to realize their high purposes.

A lack of kindergarten teachers more than a lack of money has retarded the work of establishing kindergartens, especially in the South, where they are specially needed. The progressive woman feels that an increased number of kindergartens would have a determining influence in shaping and moulding the character of thousands of colored children whose home lives are scant and meager.

The success of the kindergarten work in St. Louis, Mo., under the direction of Mrs. Haydee Campbell and her able assistant, Miss Helene Abbott, is a happy justification of the wisdom and anxiety of the colored club women to extend these schools wherever it is possible to do so.

The mothers' meetings established in connection with almost every club have probably had a more direct and beneficial influence on the everyday problems of motherhood and home-making than any other activity. Meetings of this sort have been the chief feature of the women's clubs organized by the Tuskegee teachers among the women of the hard plantation life, within reach of the Tuskegee Institute. Thousands of these women in the rural life of the South continue to live under the shadow of bondaged conditions. There has come to them scarcely a ray of light as to a better way of how to live for themselves and their offspring.

It is to the credit of the high usefulness of the colored club woman that she has taken the initiative in doing something to reach and help a class of women who have lived isolated from all the regenerating and uplifting influences of freedom and education. It is the first touch of sympathy that has connected the progressive colored woman with her neglected and unprogressive sister.

In this connection especial word ought to be said in behalf of these clubs as agencies of rescue and protection to the many unprotected and defenseless colored girls to be found in every large city. No race of young women in this country have so little done for them as the young colored woman. She is unknown, she is not believed in, and in respect to favors that direct and uplift, she is an alien, and unheeded. They have been literally shut out from the love, favor and protection that chivalry and a common pride have built up around the personality and the character of the young women of almost every other race. The colored women's clubs have had heart enough and intelligence enough to recognize their opportunity and duty toward their own young women, and in numerous instances have been the very salvation of unfortunate colored girls.

An interesting example of the usefulness of these clubs in this rescue work was recently shown by the success of the Colored Woman's Conference, above mentioned, in saving a girl, friendless, and a victim of unfortunate circumstances, from the stain of the penitentiary by pledging to take her in charge and to save her to herself and society by placing her under good and redeeming influences.

These women's clubs have never failed to champion the cause of every worthy applicant for advice and assistance. They have made the cause of the neglected young colored woman one of commanding interest, and are interesting in her behalf every possible means of education, and are endeavoring to create for her a kindlier feeling and a better degree of respect, and to improve her standing among young women generally. The clubs have entered upon this department of their work with great heartiness and have enlisted in behalf of young women new influences of helpfulness and encouragement. Colored girls with poor homes and no homes are many. Thousands of them are the poor, weak and misguided daughters of ill-starred mothers. To reach out for and save them from a bitter fate; to lift them into a higher sphere of hopefulness and opportunity is a task altogether worthy of the best efforts of club women.

What has been said of the earnestness and practical aim of colored women's clubs in behalf of kindergartens for the children and salvation for the girls may also be said of the practical way in which they have established and sustained sewing schools, mending schools and friendly visitations in behalf of neighborhood respectability and decency, and of their various committees that visit reformatory institutions and jails in search of opportunities to be useful. Numerous and interesting instances might be given to show to what extent these women are realizing their desire to be useful in the social regeneration of their race.

This chapter on the club movement among colored women would be incomplete without some notice of the leaders of the movement. Nothing that these club women have done or aimed to do is more interesting than themselves. What a variety of accomplishments, talents, successes and ambitions have been brought into view and notice by these hitherto obscure women of a ransomed race! Educated? Yes, besides the thousands of educated in the common schools, hundreds of them have been trained in the best colleges and universities in the country, and some of them have spent several years in the noted schools of Europe.

The women thus trained and educated are busily pursuing every kind of avocation not prohibited by American prejudices. As educators, fully twenty thousand of them are at work in the schools, colleges and universities of the country, and some of them teach everything required to be taught from the kindergarten to the university. Among these educators and leaders of Afro-American womanhood are to be found linguists, mathematicians, musicians, artists, authors, newspaper writers, lecturers and reform agitators, with varying degrees of excellence and success. There are women in the professions of law, medicine, dentistry, preaching, trained nursing, managers of successful business enterprises, and women of small independent fortunes made and saved within the past twenty-five years.

There are women plain, beautiful, charming, bright conversationalists, fluent, resourceful in ideas, forceful in execution, and women of all sorts of temperament and idiosyncrasies and force and delicacy of character.

All this of course is simply amazing to people trained in the habit of rating colored women too low and knowing only the menial type. To such people she is a revelation.

The woman thus portrayed is the real new woman in American life. This woman, as if by magic, has succeeded in lifting herself as completely from the stain and meanness of slavery as if a century had elapsed since the day of emancipation. This new woman, with the club behind her and the club service in her heart and mind, has come to the front in an opportune time. She is needed to change the old idea of things implanted in the minds of the white race and there sustained and hardened into a national habit by the debasing influence of slavery estimates. This woman is needed as an educator of public opinion. She is a happy refutation of the idle insinuations and common skepticism as to the womanly worth and promise of the whole race of women. She has come to enrich American life with finer sympathies, and to enlarge the boundary of fraternity and the democracy of love among American women. She has come to join her talents, her virtues, her intelligence, her sacrifices and her love in the work of redeeming the unredeemed from stagnation, from cheapness and from narrowness.

Quite as important as all this she has come to bring new hope and fresh assurances to the

Portrait of Mrs. Booker T. Washington, from *A New Negro for a New Century* (Chicago: American Publishing House, 1900).

hapless young women of her own race. Life is not a failure. All avenues are not closed. Womanly worth of whatever race or complexion is appreciated. Love, sympathy, opportunity and helpfulness are within the reach of those who can deserve them. The world is still yearning for pure hearts, willing hands, and bright minds. This and much more is the message brought by this new woman to the hearts of thousands discouraged and hopeless young colored women.

It is a real message of courage, a real inspiration that has touched more sides of the Afro-American race than any other message or thing since the dawn of freedom.

This is not exaggeration or fancy. Demonstration of it can be seen, heard and felt in the widespread renewal of hope and effort among the present generation of young Afro-American women.

These young women, thus aroused to courage, to hope and self-assertion toward better things, can find inspiring examples of success and achievements in the women of their own race. They have begun to feel something of the exaltation of race pride and race ideals. They have been brought face to face with standards of living that are high and ennobling, and have been made conscious of the severe penalties of social misdoings.

Around them has been created a sentiment of care, pride, protection and chivalry that is every day deepening and widening the distinctions between right and wrong in woman's relationship to man, child and society.

The glow of optimism has coursed so easily through this chapter concerning the work done and attempted by colored women that the importance of it all may seem somewhat exaggerated.

It, perhaps, should be confessed that in spite of the actual good already realized, the club movement is more of a prophecy than a thing accomplished. Colored women organized have succeeded in touching the heart of the race, and for the first time the thrill of unity has been felt. They have set in motion moral forces that are beginning to socialize interests that have been kept apart by ignorance and the spirit of dependence.

They have begun to make the virtues as well as the wants of the colored women known to the American people. They are striving to put a new social value on themselves. Yet their work has just begun. It takes more than five or ten years to effect the social uplift of a whole race of people.

The club movement is well purposed. There is in it a strong faith, an enthusiasm born of love and sympathy, and an ever-increasing intelligence in the ways and means of affecting noble results. It is not a fad. It is not an imitation. It is not a passing sentiment. It is not an expedient, or an experiment. It is rather the force of a new intelligence against the old ignorance. The struggle of an enlightened conscience against the whole brood of social miseries born out of the stress and pain of a hated past.

J. M. Scanland

"Negroes as Voters"

Paxton Daily Record, April 25, 1900[14]

As a Race They are Indifferent to Governmental Affairs.

Some Reasons Why the Mixed Population of Porto [*sic*] Rico and the Philippines Should Not Be Granted Citizenship.

[Special New Orleans Letter.]

TRAVELERS in the southern states, especially along the gulf coast, are impressed with the indifference of the great mass of the negroes in governmental affairs. This may serve as an illustration for the mixed population in the West Indian islands and the Philippines. In our new possession of Porto Rico, which some of our people wish to erect into a territory, negroes predominate, and there is also a large population of mixed blood. These are as incapable of self-government as are the full-blooded negroes. This is the spot where African slavery was introduced in the new world by the Spaniards, and from this island and Cuba it spread to the gulf states. The negroes brought from the African coast, from whence they were kidnaped, their barbarisms and superstitions and their incapacity for self-government. There they lived in tribes, warred upon each other, and the more powerful sold their neighbors into bondage. For centuries the experiment of self-government was tried in Africa, and that country has steadily deteriorated in population, morals and in tribal governments.

The experiment of self-government, or rather negro government, was tried in the late rebellious states of the south after the conclusion of the civil war. True, they had corrupt white men for leaders, and every state was plundered. But the negroes were in the majority, and the white "carpet-baggers" would have been powerless had the negroes not been easy to corrupt. Will it not be the same in Porto Rico and in the Philippines?

While the negroes of the south had been born and reared in slavery they knew what freedom was by comparing their burdensome lives to those of their masters who lived in ease upon their labor. Yet, when the opportunity came, the negro did not appreciate it, and went in for plunder. After 35 years of freedom he is scarcely more qualified for self-government than when liberated at the close of the war. By nature he is indifferent to government, and cares not who governs, so long as he is undisturbed in his "happy-go-lucky" manner of living. While the slave generation was not expected to make much progress in education, or in ideas of self-government, much was expected of the newer generation, especially by the "theorists" who believed that the negro was capable of self-government. Though the negroes have had the advantage of public schools for more than a third of a century, the advance of the generation born in the south since the war has been very slow. There are a few exceptional cases where a negro has risen above the average mass of his people, but in most of these cases the white blood predominated, and to this fact his rise is mainly attributable. It is the same in Porto Rico, in Cuba and the Philippines. The south may be taken as an illustration of the incapability of these islands for self-government. The negroes of the south have not demonstrated their fitness for self-government. They are little better educated than were their slave parents. The children of the second generation show the same indifference to education, and so may other generations, perhaps. It is thus demonstrated that the intellect of the plantation negro is not capable of being enlightened to the intellectual standpoint of average citizenship, or that he is interested in the science of government. My observations, recently, in Mississippi, Louisiana, Alabama, Tennessee and Virginia failed to denote any material progress of the darky from his former condition. This applies to the former slave and "the new nigger," as the later generation is styled. He still grovels in the superstitions of his remote ancestors and firmly believes in witches and witchcraft.

The schools and churches, with which they are well supplied, have not removed these delusions from his cloud brain, imported from Africa and the West Indies. The "intelligent" voter and citizen, who determines the rights of others and construes the law to his own dark way of thinking, still believes that the placing of a frog under the doorstep of an enemy will cause the death of that person when he has crossed the threshold. He goes to the polls to exercise his rights in our scheme of government, carrying in his pocket the left hind foot of a rabbit killed in a graveyard at midnight at full moon. This not only brings to him good luck generally, but protects him from personal danger. As an evidence of their little faith in themselves they prefer, as a rule, to be tried by white juries. Their superstitions are so numerous that the white people give very little attention to them, and on the more important cases the negro is generally "excused" from jury service. There are not many people in this age of learning who would feel safe in being tried by a "jury of peers" composed of negroes who believe in the rabbit-foot and frog theories, and who frequently hold close communion with "ghosts."

The razor is the darky's favorite weapon— it is a greater talisman than the rabbit's foot, and more effective. All carry razors, both men and women, and to all places—the polls, the jury box, the dance and the church. Three-fourths of the crimes committed in any southern community, on an average, are due to negroes, while they contribute little or nothing towards the expenses of local government. Their natural ignorance is the principal cause of so many "misunderstandings." Another is the frequent use of very bad whisky.

The Saturday night dance is a fruitful source of disturbances. On these nights "razors are in the air," but the festivities are not marred by the carving of a few, unless it is to the death, when the "function" suddenly comes to a period. They do not obey the usual injunction: "Lebe yer razzer at de do," regarding it as a mere form. Neither is it etiquette to search one for weapons—that would bring on an engagement. The same habit prevails at weddings. It is not always that disturbances occur, but when they do the "razzer" cuts an important figure. The courts seem to be powerless to stop the practice of carrying such weapons. From the fact that all negroes carry them, there are few informers among them. Those who do, however, give such information become subjects for carving by the aggrieved ones, and the rabbit's foot is of no protection.

The marriage and divorce system, or rather the lack of the latter, is a strange custom in negro life. They imitate white people in their marriages, even as to style, but their "divorce"

system is an improvement upon the Oklahoma quick and easy style. While they are willing to pay two dollars for a license, they rarely sue for divorce. Not that they care so much for the publicity as the expense. They just quit—and that ends it. In a very short time both find other affinities. Prosecution seldom follows these informal divorces and "common law" marriages. They are so numerous that the people do not care to burden the local governments with the expense. The minister's fee is usually one dollar, seldom more, notwithstanding his placarded hint "De Lawd Lubs de Cheerful Giber." Strictly construed, it means that that minister wants a raise from the usual fee.

While the negro has made little or no progress in education and in governmental affairs, he is "getting along" in other directions. He is mastering the mysteries of that great and popular game "poker." Some of them are adept in the art of "holding out" big cards and "good hands." The methods adopted by the darky adepts are primitive, but perhaps as effective as holding cards up the sleeve, or secreting them in the "patent vest" device used by white gamblers. In a "gemmen's game," it is in bad form for a darky to remove his shoes from his feet. This is considered as prima facie evidence of an intent to "skin" his friend.

The darky also keeps pace with his white brother in the cigarette habit, and he begins about as early as the other youth, but it is not believed that he lives as long under it.

The negro "progresses" in our voices, but does not seem capable of advancing intellectually. Before he can do so, his superstitions must be removed. How long this will require may be estimated from his slow progress during the past 35 years. The same reasoning may apply to our Porto Rican neighbors, who are asking for self-government.

J. M. Scanland

Four African American women seated on the steps of a building at Atlanta University, 1899 or 1900. Photo by Thomas E. Askew. Collected by W. E. B. Du Bois for the American Negro Exhibit at the Paris Exposition Universelle in 1900. Courtesy of the Library of Congress.

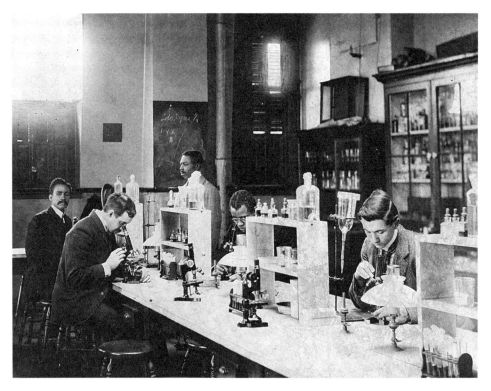

Class in bacteriology laboratory, ca. 1900, Howard University.
Collected by W.E.B. Du Bois for the "American Negro Exhibit" at the Paris Exposition Universelle in 1900. Courtesy of the Library of Congress.

George H. White

"Defense of the Negro Race—Charges Answered: Speech of Hon. George H. White, of North Carolina, in the House of Representatives, January 29, 1901"

Sow the seed of a tarnished name—
You sow the seed of eternal shame.

It is needless to ask what the harvest will be.

The House being in the Committee of the Whole on the state of the Union, and having under consideration the bill (H.R. 13801) making appropriations for the Department of Agriculture for the fiscal year ending June 30, 1902—

Mr. White said: . . .

I would like to advance the statement that the musty records of 1868, filed away in the archives of Southern capitols, as to what the negro was thirty-two years ago, is not a proper standard by which the negro living on the threshold of the twentieth century should be measured. Since that time we have reduced the illiteracy of the race at least 45 per cent. We have written and published near 500 books. We have nearly 300 newspapers, 3 of which are dailies. We have now in practice over 2,000 lawyers and a corresponding number of doctors. We have accumulated over $12,000,000 worth of school property and about $40,000,000 worth of church property. We have about 140,000 farms and homes, value at in the neighborhood of $750,000,000, and personal property valued at about $170,000,000. We have raised about $11,000,000 for educational purposes, and the property per capita for every colored man, woman, and child in the United States is estimated at $75.

We are operating successfully several banks, commercial enterprises among our people in the Southland, including 1 silk mill and 1 cotton factory. We have 32,000 teachers in the schools of the country; we have built, with the aid of our friends, about 20,000 churches, and support 7 colleges, 17 academies, 50 high schools, 5 law schools, 5 medical schools, and 25 theological seminaries. We have over 600,000 acres of land in the South alone. The cotton produced, mainly by black labor, has increased from 4,669,770 bales in 1860 to 11,235,000 in 1899. All this we have done under the most adverse circumstances. We have done it in the face of lynching, burning at the stake, with the humiliation of "Jim Crow" cars, the disfranchisement of our male citizens, slander and degradation of our women, with the factories closed against us, no negro permitted to be conductor on the railway cars, whether run through the streets of our cities or across the prairies of our great country, no negro permitted to run as engineer on a locomotive, most of the mines closed against us. Labor unions—carpenters, painters, brick masons, machinists, hackmen, and those supplying nearly every conceivable avocation for livelihood have banded themselves together to better their condition, but, with few exceptions, the black face has been left out. The negroes are seldom employed in our mercantile stores. At this we do not wonder. Some day we hope to have them employed in our own stores. With all these odds against us, we are forging our way ahead, slowly, perhaps, but surely. You may tie us and then taunt us for a lack of bravery, but one day we will break the bonds. You may use our labor for two and a half centuries and then taunt us for our poverty, but let me remind you we will not always remain poor. You may withhold even the knowledge of how to read God's word and learn the way from earth to glory and then taunt us for our ignorance, but we would remind you that there is plenty of room at the top, and we are climbing.

After enforced debauchery, with the many kindred horrors incident to slavery, it comes with ill grace from the perpetrators of these deeds to hold up the shortcomings of some of our race to ridicule and scorn.

"The new man, the slave who has grown out of the ashes of thirty-five years ago, is inducted into the political and social system, cast into the arena of manhood, where he constitutes a new element and becomes a competitor for all its emoluments. He is put upon trial to test his ability to be counted worthy of freedom, worthy of the elective franchise; and after thirty-five years of struggling against almost insurmountable odds, under conditions but little removed from slavery itself, he asks a fair and just judgment, not of those whose prejudice has endeavored to forestall, to frustrate his every forward movement, rather those who have lent a helping hand, that he might demonstrate the truth of 'the fatherhood of God and the brotherhood of man.'"

Mr. Chairman, permit me to digress for a few moments for the purpose of calling the attention of the House to two bills which I regard as important, introduced by me in the early part of the first session of this Congress. The first was to give the United States control and entire jurisdiction over all cases of lynching and death by mob violence. During the last session of this Congress I took occasion to address myself in detail to this particular measure, but with all my efforts the bill still sweetly sleeps in the room of the committee to which it was referred. The necessity of legislation along this line is daily being demonstrated. The arena of the lyncher no longer is confined to Southern climes, but is stretching its hydra head over all parts of the Union.

> Sow the seed of a tarnished name—
> You sow the seed of eternal shame.

It is needless to ask what the harvest will be. You may dodge this question now; you may defer it to a more seasonable day; you may, as the gentleman from Maine, Mr. LITTLEFIELD, puts it—

> Waddle in and waddle out,
> Until the mind was left in doubt,
> Whether the snake that made the track
> Was going south or coming back.

This evil peculiar to America, yes, to the United States, must be met somehow, some day.

The other bill to which I wish to call attention is one introduced by me to appropriate $1,000,000 to reimburse depositors of the late Freedman's Savings and Trust Company.

A bill making appropriation for a similar purpose passed the Senate in the first session of the Fiftieth Congress. It was recommended by President Cleveland, and was urged by the Comptroller of the Currency, Mr. Trenholm, in 1886. I can not press home to your minds this matter more strongly than by reproducing the report of the Committee on Banking and Currency, made by Mr. Wilkins on the Senate bill above referred to. . . .

May I hope that the Committee on Banking and Currency who has charge of this measure will yet see its way clear to do tardy justice, long deferred, to this much wronged and unsuspecting people. If individual sections of the country, individual political parties can afford to commit deeds of wrong against us, certainly a great nation like ours will see to it that a people so loyal to its flag as the black man has shown himself in every war from the birth of the Union to this day, will not permit this obligation to go longer uncanceled.

Now, Mr. Chairman, before concluding my remarks I want to submit a brief recipe for the solution of the so-called American negro problem. He asks no special favors, but simply demands that he be given the same chance for existence, for earning a livelihood, for raising himself in the scales of manhood and womanhood that are accorded to kindred nationalities. Treat him as a man; go into his home and learn of his social conditions; learn of his cares, his troubles, and his hopes for the future; gain his confidence; open the doors of industry to him; let the word "negro," "colored," and "black" be stricken from all the organizations enumerated in the federation of labor.

Help him to overcome his weaknesses, punish the crime-committing class by the courts of the land, measure the standard of the race by its best material, cease to mold prejudicial and unjust public sentiment against him, and my word for it, he will learn to support, hold up the hands of, and join in with that political party, that institution, whether secular or religious, in every community where he lives, which is destined to do the greatest good for the greatest number. Obliterate race hatred, party prejudice, and help us to achieve nobler ends, greater results, and become more satisfactory citizens to our brother in white.

This, Mr. Chairman, is perhaps the negroes' temporary farewell to the American Congress; but let me say, Phoenix-like he will rise up some day and come again. These parting words are in behalf of an outraged, heart-broken, bruised, and bleeding, but God-fearing people, faithful, industrious, loyal people—rising people, full of potential force.

Mr. Chairman, in the trial of Lord Bacon, when the court disturbed the counsel for the defendant, Sir Walter Raleigh raised himself up to his full height and, addressing the court, said:

> Sir, I am pleading for the life of a human being.

The only apology that I have to make for the earnestness with which I have spoken is that I am pleading for the life, the liberty, the future happiness, and manhood suffrage for one-eighth of the entire population of the United States. [*Loud applause.*]

N. C. Bruce
"An Appeal from the New to the New"

Biblical Recorder, the Organ of the North Carolina Baptists, February 26, 1902[15]

N. C. Bruce, Prof., Dean of the College Department, Shaw University, Speaks to the Young White Man on Behalf of the Young Negro. "An Appeal from the New to the New."

You were kind enough some two-years ago to publish the first appeal of the kind that this purposes to be and to strongly endorse it at the same time. But Methodists from Trinity College, Episcopalians and young people from other faiths have apparently responded quite as much as those who read the Recorder and to whom the appeal was especially made. It has rejoiced, encouraged and added new life to the endeavors of Durham colored people, for instance, to have been visited by bands of Trinity students and encouraged and afterwards to see in the Southern Workman, published by Hampton Institute, true and favorable reports of their home-life, the variety of advancements, differences and the like found among Durham Negroes and written by their own young white men, who had actually seen inside of hundreds of the homes of colored people of Durham.

Just here it gives joy for us to say that even within the past few weeks Shaw University students and Negro Baptist Sunday Schools and

other meetings have been visited and spoken to not only by the truly great older men like Mr. J. T. Pullen, Dr. R. T. Vann, Mr. N. B. Broughton, Mr. J. E. Ray, Dr. Skinner, Dr. Marshall and other such deeply spiritual followers of the Christ, but a few younger men like Rev. Mr. Hubbard, Rev. A. A. Butler, Mr. T. Neil Johnson, Lawyer R. N. Simms and Mrs. Weathers, have looked in upon our young people, have spoken to them and pointed out the more excellent way with power and kindly interest, charity and faith, which works by love. We do hope and pray that more of such help be speedily given.

What the New Negro Needs.

The Need, the time and those who can are here. Why not now, while so many of ours are at your doors, in your back yards, on the streets and in your towns so close by? And such needs! How ours are allowed to grope in the darkness, to be duped and be deceived and to be fed with that which chokes and maketh not alive! Negroes need alms least of any race; nor do they need pity and grace and mercy and money half so much as they need something else, which a combination of circumstances has in the past kept from them. We are told that before the Civil War our fathers' masters felt it a bounden duty to see to it that our fathers, their servants, have a faithful, true and correct foreman during the week and a true preacher on the Sabbath: that these masters, themselves, often read and preached the Bible to groups of slaves, so anxious were they that their Negroes should hear the pure truth and to have all help and receive protection both as to their person, their good name and their moral character. This is believed and gloried in. We have nothing to do with the view point of that day and of that system. The fact that help of a certain sort was needed by Negroes for those antebellum times and that help was not withheld by white Christians, young masters and their wives, is what God smiled upon and the world applauded. Help is needed now from the sons of those same masters to the sons and daughters of those same slaves.

Conditions have changed, to the great advantage certainly of the whites, if not of both and, before God, assistance ought not be withheld. Here are young Negroes by the thousands making early fires, attending the babies, cooking, driving, waiting, butlering, dairying, plowing, sowing, reaping, digging, ditching, felling, picking, quarrying, renting, eating, drinking, dying, mainly for the sake of ease, leisure and profit to the white owners, employers and rulers. Young Negroes, docile, impressible, full of laugh even in pains, hunger and cold, believers in white people. How easy it would be to see to these getting Christ's Truth and Justice presented to these and accorded these. The time, too, is now, while they are young and here, when political and party passion has for a season spent its force and done its worst or best; when peace reigns and a revival in universal education and universal Christhood is preached. Never before has the time been more auspicious. Then, too, white people are so capable,

so prepared by thousands of years of training and the lavish outlay of money now on [their] higher and superior education [illegible] States and the Nation, and their pulpits. Their extra preparation for doing missionary work among Negroes at their door lies in their opportunity for knowing Negroes, if they don't know them already.

Obstacles More Imaginary Than Real.

Many, nearly all heretofore like those people at the Bible wedding have pleaded apparently good excuses for not helping us more with the Gospel. Some have said, "Negroes are free now and so heady, self-opinioned and full of repulsive habits that we will wait till they get more meek and humble." Others say, "We shall be misunderstood both by our own and by the Negroes themselves, and more harm, therefore, than good will be done." While still others say, "Teaching Negroes salvation and right living is a waste of time and effort, certainly while so many of our own white race are in need." A few might be found who sincerely believe that it is casting pearls before swine. All of these hindrances do not nor need one of them really hinder the young of the white Christians from doing what they can easily do for young Negroes in the way of compelling them to better lives and to Christ. The New Testament is so full of directions and guidance for Christians who are enlightened that they need not make a mistake in leading the poor, weak and vile to Christ. It has not bred any social evils nor has it ever yet lowered a person in the social scale to save a sin-sick soul.

This help ought to come from young white men for the New Negro. He ought not be allowed to sicken, become steeped in crime and to die for the want of it. Neither ought Christians from far away North and West be burdened with the right teaching, leading and righteous living of Negroes. Our own opposition should not even drive these away from helping us, these who are young and right among us or we among them. It is incumbent upon all thoughtful, enlightened Negroes to pray and live so that our own young white Christians will come among us and work and see to it that they help us to help our own out of

darkness, ignorance and crime into the very light of life. Will young white neighboring Christians come and help Negroes to Christ? Will they? Won't they?

Albreta Moore Smith

"Women's Development in Business"

Colored American Magazine, March 1, 1902[16]

That there is nothing new under the sun is an assertion that was made by King Solomon thousands of years ago and accepted by many men of all ages to be true. Many philosophers also maintain that we are progressing in a circle—are reverting back to the ways and customs of centuries ago.

From the view-point of the creation of new material, the science of geology teaches us that King Solomon never uttered a more self-evident truth; and whether what the philosophers say is true or not, if history has correctly recorded the facts of past events, we know that many of our civilized nations could profit by much of what the ancients did.

In the world of business many improvements have been wrought upon old methods, but all of them are not new. To the minds of many there is a "new" woman, but in actuality she does not exist. Theories have been put forth to prove that she is new, but the only satisfactory evidence or conclusion agreed upon is that she is simply progressing, her natural tendencies not having changed one iota.

Ever since the days of Cleopatra, who, skilled in music and conversant in arts, was acknowledged to possess superior intellectual talents, women have been aggressive and their capabilities recognitory.

Early in the seventeenth century there arose a class of women who won great celebrity by a display of knowledge upon subjects other than "How babies cut teeth." Prominent amongst them were Madame de Maintenon and

Hannah More, two of the greatest women writers and educators of any age.

From that time until the present many women have assiduously sought the blessings of higher education, and a more accurate knowledge of all that pertains to business. They have surmounted many obstacles, and in this, the dawn of the 20th century, many links have been forged by them in the chain of "progress." There is nothing surprising in this statement, however, for the spirit of advancement is a legacy that has been handed down to them by the many brave women, who in the face of persecution and opposition, gave their lives and talents to the cause.

"As a nation grows its people are destined to feel the influence and its enlightened development." For thirty years the influence of progress has been so strong and benign upon the American nation that it was as impossible for women to remain in obscurity as it was for men to refrain from progressing.

The talk of American women being "new" is arrant nonsense, for they have been developing their latent talents, lo! these many years, and were only waiting until the world was ready for their reception. The practical business woman is the sole produce of America. In no other country does she enjoy the same privileges, liberty, independence and freedom of person as she does here.

If she be true to her calling she does not abuse these privileges—to the contrary—with all the knowledge gained from a free and unconventional education she takes her place in society as a faithful friend, in the business world as a judicious counsellor and in the home as a loving wife and queen. She is as womanly and gentle as was her grandmother; contact with the business world does not wear off the fineness which men so much admire in women if this quality be inherent.

Woman's entrance into the business world and her ratification along all lines where she has the slightest chance for intellectual improvement has aroused strong prejudice against her advancement. It will take years of education, agitation and discussion to win her enemies over to the side of justice and truth.

The American business man possesses indomitable courage and business daring, in fact, all the essential qualities which go to make a successful business career. He is far ahead of the men of other nations in commerce and trade. He stops at nothing short of success. Why, then, so many of them are persistent in their endeavors to withhold all knowledge of business from their ambitious wives and daughters is one of the great puzzles of our national life. That opposition would arise from many indolent women was to be expected for woman's deadliest enemy is woman.

The taking away the right of franchise, the only means whereby the Negro can best assert his rights as a citizen and a man in many of the Southern states does not discourage the aspiring youth any more so than the barring of many doors of commerce and trade weakens the purpose and intentions of the energetic business woman.

It is generally conceded that woman is man's equal, intellectually, and is only in need of a broader education and greater opportunities to constitute her a dangerous competitor to him. This virtue has won, and will continue to win an enviable place for woman in the world of letters and trade.

Fair-minded business women do not ask for equal rights in a political sense, but they do ask that they be given an equal showing with man, with the same freedom to use accessible facilities as those which are accorded business men. It is hardly fair for man to declare that

woman is not his equal, and is incapable of attaining the business heights he has reached and enjoys, while systematically withholding from her the very means by which he reached his giddy station in the commercial world.

Ruskin truthfully summarizes this question when he says, "We are foolish in claiming the superiority of our sex to the other, in truth, each has what the other has not; one completes the other, and they are in nothing alike. The happiness of one depends upon each asking and receiving from each what the other only can give. We are no better or worse, higher or lower, because the loftiest ideals of humanity demands that each shall be perfect in its kind and not be hindered in its best work." This quotation is applicable to all art, science and trade where the question is one of ability and general fitness.

As women become more generally educated along all lines, their thoughts will become expanded, their energies increased and their homes conducted upon a higher plane intellectually, physically, morally and spiritually.

Why impede the progress of progressive women when they are heartily welcomed in all works of the home and church? If they are efficient co-workers in matters of reform they surely are able assistants in the business world and all other work which tends to promote progress to humanity at home and abroad.

The thirst and striving after business knowledge which many women display is good if not accompanied by the restlessness so characteristic of the American business man. Many leisure women, as well as business women, have been caught up in this electrical tide, and are fast drifting away from their true mission in life. No matter what a woman's work or aim might be she can never shake off entirely the responsibilities of the home, for they are joined by inalienable ties. The one link which brings her closer to God than any other power, the blessings of wifehood and motherhood, will not allow her to forget.

The business world is a field of labor and enlightenment, to which women hasten with high ambitions and great expectations, the home is the haven of rest to which she flees with exalted thoughts and tired brain, only too willing to receive the love, peace and quietude which daily awaits her within its sacred walls.

But why deviate from our subject? We just write of woman as she is seen in the cold, work-a-day world and not as the regal queen of the hearth and home.

We encourage women to go into business, but not to the extent that there will be a general exodus, for all women are no more fitted to explore the mysteries of the business world any more so than all men are capable of becoming president of the United States.

To those who have inclinations for the work we would say, you must examine yourself carefully,—physically and intellectually—by the sharpest criticism imaginable before entering the arena, for you have chosen no small task. To be successful your life must be one of self-devotion and self-sacrifice. Many disappointments will appear, mighty obstacles will obstruct your way and only a strong determination to succeed or die in the attempt will remunerate you for your struggles.

Never be discouraged, for the thousands of women in positions of trust today is evidence of the fact that there is a growing demand for the work of competent women in all branches of business. There is no room for mediocrity; competency alone will stand the test of time.

At no time of our country's history have so many women been thrown upon their own resources as now. They have entered every accessible avenue of work. Many from sheer necessity, others from the knowledge to be gained by contact with business people.

There is need of woman's work and much good in it, but there can be seen a growing evil. Many employers in their greed for gold are making women "hewers of wood and drawers of water." The strength of many young women is being wasted by laborious work in sweat-shops, factories and stores. Women bread-earners should be given work in keeping with their strength. Woman's labor, they say, is cheap, but the price given in exchange by the workers will be felt by coming generations.

In many branches of the professional, commercial and industrial world women receive smaller wages than men, regardless of ability. This is unfair, for there should be no alignment drawn between the work of a competent woman and that of a capable man. Women should receive the highest price paid for their work and give in exchange the best knowledge they possess.

The necessity of becoming proficient in trades, as well as professions is fast taking possessions of Negro girls and women. This is one of the most gratifying results of higher education. All over the country our girls are seeking diplomas in these studies of their own volition.

Much of this awakening is doubtless due to the assiduous labors of Prof. B. T. Washington, who is leading thousands of Negro youths to that kind of an education which creates a demand for their services. Let our women continue to stimulate their dormant talents along these lines for their sphere of general usefulness is being supplanted by the well-trained, skilled white artisan. Look well to your laurels of old, dear sisters.

One of the main solutions of this much-talked-of race problem lies in the proper training of every Negro child in some profession, trade or economic science. When we as a race prove our own worth and strength of purpose along these lines, then and then only will we be recognized as a power in the business world. We need more competent business men and women and less aimless ornaments, for such obstructions are detrimental to the progress of any race of people.

That the Negro is winning the recognition he so justly deserves is being demonstrated daily all over this country. An excellent proof of this statement is the National Negro Business League, which, only fifteen months old, is doing more in enlightening the world of the actual progress and status of our people than any other force.

It is by such movements as this that the actual progress and moral strength of the Negro should be measured. His standard should be gauged by the energetic and aspiring element of the race, and not by the criminals in the jails, paupers in the poor-houses and idle vagrants to be seen loitering around the street corners and dram shops. This recognition is accorded other nations and should be given the Negro as well. The sins and weaknesses of other races are generally hidden from public gaze when the question is one of honesty, sobriety and morality, but those of the Negro are forever laid bare before the illuminable rays of the searchlight of public opinion.

Should this be his treatment when one thinks of the many eminent ministers, missionaries, doctors, lawyers, scholars, merchants, philanthropists and scientists who have won an international, as well as national reputation, by dint of their hard labors? Was not the Negro exhibit at the Paris Exposition a proud testimonial of this fact? Out of an unwholesome, immoral condition have arisen these grand beacon lights of the race. They should be encouraged, rather than discouraged, for the wonderful moral, mental and spiritual improvement made within the past thirty-five years.

What is true of Negro men is true of Negro women. The progress of one effects the other, each lifts as it climbs. The sooner our men see the wisdom of entering into all branches of business, the better it will be for the women who are qualified for the work, but cannot secure employment. We must first help ourselves before condemning other races for not assisting us along this line. We must work, hope and pray. A rich reward awaits those who have patience to endure until the end. John Lord has well said that "Extraordinary genius cannot forever remain hidden or forgotten. Sooner or later some one will bring forth the knowledge to light." As this rule knows no race, no class and no creed it is applicable to every one of you who yearn to earn a living and help swell the army of those who are developing praiseworthy business ability.

J. J. L.
"Crisis to Virginia Farmer"

Richmond Dispatch, November 7, 1902[17]

To the Editor of the Dispatch:

Virginia is far in the rear in progress. Her roads are highways of the colonial days, patched up by ignorance and reluctant toll. Such are our clumsy methods. The gravest question is farm labor.

The training to habits of industry by the system of lifetime contract to service converted the negro from a barbarian and vagabond into a bread winner and best agricultural "hand." The dissolution of this system of industrial training giving "freedom" to the semi-barbarian, has, in a third of a century, destroyed habits of a hundred years, relegating the negro to the idleness of his native Africa.

At any railway depot there are twenty to thirty young negroes from 16 to 20, at train time, sitting in the autumn sun, chattering or nodding. The offer of employment is scorned—where do they get the rations? In numbers of cases their food is taken from the white man's kitchen. Or the father or mother, trained to labor under slavery, continue to work, in their old age, for these lazy scamps. Within the last twenty years, stealing has become the only exertion of many a "new negro." If he passes by a farm house, a bridle, hoe or axe is carried off. The Legislature taxes the farmer's guard dog so as to give the negro free access to the orchard, crib, hen roost, garden. What's the remedy?

The Colored American

A NATIONAL NEGRO NEWSPAPER

VOL. XI, NO. 14.   WASHINGTON, D. C., JULY 19, 1902.   PRICE, FIVE CENTS

LIFE HIS TEXT-BOOK.

PRESIDENT DUDLEY TEACHES SOUND PHILOSOPHY.

That Education Is Best Which Takes Common Sense as Its Basis—A Career That Combines Literary Lore with Business Acumen—Accurate in Measuring Resources.

The educators who are laying firm and deep the foundation of racial glory in the Southland are those who see clearly the conditions about them, who think quick of remedies for existing ills, and act promptly along an intelligently-planned course. They do not fritter away valuable energy by attempting the impossible. They measure their strength and their weaknesses; they consult their environment and its opportunities and decide to proceed with the principles laid down in physics—that the greatest amount of power can be adduced from a given momentum by reducing frictional forces to a minimum, consistent with the motive power. Human nature is a people's opportunities only when studied from its own unskillful chemist. The master who is able to profit by experience comes to a nicety the kinetic force of the element with which he must deal; he learns the resisting quality of raw force residing within himself and his followers. The resultant of this fact, whether the problem be educational, religious or commercial, will set the value of the projector or the project in the community. The law of nature knows no color or creed, and like causes followed by like conditions will produce identical results.

These everyday principles lay at the base of education of the Negro in the Southland, and the successful treatment of the lines of progress depends upon the caliber of the men and women actually engaged in the work. A distinguished representative of that happily numerous class of instructors who are devoted to the subject of education and unselfish advancement of the Negro in his newer science is Prof. James B. Dudley. The scene of his splendid activity is the Greensboro Agricultural and Mechanical College at Greensboro, a school which stands as prominently for the highest and best in the educational study, character and success in its results as does its honored head for the true, character and is the model elements that go to make up a successful Christian gentleman.

He teaches not only from text-books and the paths of a prepared curriculum, but places before his pupils the great book of Life and essays from its invisible treasure trove the jewels that point men to the sacrifice of the trust committed to them in a scene of no mean city;" the duty to man; the uselessness of strife that does not ultimately lead to peace; the value of industry, and how to get on

in the world; the beauty of universal brotherhood; and finally, that education is of no avail if it does not bring common sense and keen perception to bear upon the trials that must be met and conquered. The story of Professor Dudley's life furnishes a cheering example for the youth of today. His success is a text-book in itself, and ought to suggest strongly to his pupils that if he could rise to eminence over a rocky road, how much more secure is their future, with environments far more favorable.

James Benson Dudley was born a slave in Wilmington, N. C., November 3, 1859. He was the son of John Bishon and Annie (Hatch) Dudley. His father, a skilled mechanic, was emancipated and given permission to go to the free states, but declined the offer, preferring to remain with his slave wife and son. The son was first sent to private tutors and then to the public schools of his native city, and later to the Institute for Colored Youth at Philadelphia, Pa., and Shaw University, Raleigh, N. C.

His vacations during his school life were spent in learning carpenter's trade. His first labors as an educator were in the counties of Onslow, Duplin and Sampson, where, because of his superior advantages and acknowledged ability, he held a kind of monopoly, passing at the close of one school to another and then another. He taught in the public schools of his own County, and was principal of Peabody graded school of Wilmington, N. C., from 1883 to 1896. He became president of the Agricultural and Mechanical College for the colored race at Greensboro, N. C., in 1896, and has since held this post, giving utmost satisfaction to all concerned.

The degree of A. M. was conferred upon Prof. Dudley in 1898 by Livingston College. He was state organizer for the Chatauqua, and editor of the Wilmington Chronicle, and because of his brilliant editorials and other productions of unquestioned merit, became easily one of the literary leaders of the

Continued on fourth page.

MEN OF THE HOUR.

PROF. JAMES B. DUDLEY,

President A. and M College, Greensboro, N. C. A Practical Educator Who Is Developing a New Negro for a New South.

THE TRUE REFORMERS.

LEAD THE VAN IN THE NEGRO BUSINESS WORLD.

Marvelous Rise of a Useful Order—Grand Master W. L. Taylor a Worthy Heir to Mantle of Founder Browne—A Magnificent Object Lesson in Industry, Thrift and Economy.

Once a noted financier in Wall street told a British banker that if every Negro business concern in this country were bundled together and dropped into the ocean, there would scarcely be a ripple upon the surface of the commercial sea to mark the event. This was twenty-odd years ago. He could not from his narrow point of view foresee the leavening effect that the schools, colleges and churches would have upon the race just out of bondage. He could not measure the imitative tendency of the discerning Negro, nor did he imagine how far we would realize the necessity for copying the intelligence, enterprise and thrift of our Caucasian contemporaries and how well we could resist the temptations to adopt their vices. He had never heard of William W. Browne, a colored man whose rare organizing genius found concrete expression in 1881 in the formation of a society that should not only "take care of the sick and bury the dead"—as others had been doing for years—but which would enhance the race's opportunities along material lines. This was the GRAND UNITED ORDER OF TRUE REFORMERS.

And its birthplace was Richmond, Va., where its National Headquarters are still located, and from which central trunk the branches and blossoms spread out to every section of the United States.

At the death of Rev. W. W. Browne, in 1897, the order had firmly entrenched itself in the confidence of the people, and its membership was more than 40,000—an organized army of men and women, resolute and enthusiastic in building up the race by the sensible and practical plan of saving money, investing it judiciously, buying real estate and conducting enterprises that will bring rich financial returns to both the race and to the individual.

When Providence ordains the removal of a valuable man from the scene of his activity he never fails to produce an equally strong force to take up the work where the predecessor left off. It frequently happens that a man of certain masterful characteristics is best fitted for the task of laying broad and deep foundations, which when thoroughly settled complete his earthly mission. Another follows him who has within him a peculiar magnetic force and physical energy that combines in one body the rigid pioneer organizer, and the

Continued on ninth page.

Masthead and illustration for "Men of the Hour," *The Colored American* (Washington, DC), July 19, 1902.

This writer in visiting another Southern State found no bunches of loafers either at depots or in villages. The reason was soon discovered. The Legislature contained men of common sense. A law was enacted that every idler must give account of himself. If he had no regular means of living he went to the gang that mended the roads and streets. If he contracted to work on a farm, he must stay till the crop was harvested, on which he had a lien for his labor. He must work, but his pay was guaranteed to him. If he "flew the contract," he went to the road gang. The cotton must not be left unpicked in the patches by unreliable "hands." The upshot was that farmers had steady laborers. Loafing or stealing were discouraged. The schooling in idleness, the temptation "to take things," the degradation of the negro, his retrogression to

Foster Morse Follett, "Life's Presidential Impossibilities II: A Dark Horse from Alabama," cartoon, *Life*, April 21, 1904. The cartoon depicts an apelike Booker T. Washington, and the caption suggests that the idea of a Black president is laughable.

the primitive ways of his savage ancestors (the fault of the destruction of a patriarchal system of utilizing and training a race that never rose, like its neighbors. Carthaginian, Egyptian, to civilization), this descent to the devil and dirt was arrested.

Shall a Virginia Legislature waste days on petty politics, when such an imperative and practical problem clamors for attention and can be solved by adopting a law, tested by another State, which will do us more good than all the piddling on a code till the crack of doom? Virginia, now relieved of the negro votes, must select citizens of practical sense, with a stake in the community, familiar with the urgent needs of the hour, for the Legislature. What a

curse has been politics to this old State! We must have useful schemes to improve the condition of the people. Let every farmer write to his "member," demanding this "labor law" to rid the land of thieves, idlers, scoundrels. The present deplorable situation in Virginia is chargeable to the neglect, perhaps ignorance, of legislators.

The limit of endurances has been reached. Stir up your representative in Richmond by urgent letters. Let him attempt improvements or get out and give place to energy.

J. J. L.

PART III

THE W. E. B. DU BOIS ERA, 1903–1916

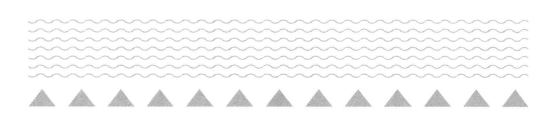

W. E. B. Du Bois
"Of Mr. Booker T. Washington and Others"

In *The Souls of Black Folk*, 1903

> From birth till death enslaved; in word, in
>   deed, unmanned!
> . . . .
> Hereditary bondsmen! Know ye not
> Who would be free themselves must
>   strike the blow?
>
> BYRON.

Easily the most striking thing in the history of the American Negro since 1876 is the ascendancy of Mr. Booker T. Washington. It began at the time when war memories and ideals were rapidly passing; a day of astonishing commercial development was dawning; a sense of doubt and hesitation overtook the freedmen's sons,— then it was that his leading began. Mr. Washington came, with a simple definite programme, at the psychological moment when the nation was a little ashamed of having bestowed so much sentiment on Negroes, and was concentrating its energies on Dollars. His programme of industrial education, conciliation of the South, and submission and silence as to civil and political rights, was not wholly original; the Free Negroes from 1830 up to war-time had striven to build industrial schools, and the American Missionary Association had from the first taught various trades; and Price and others had sought a way of honorable alliance with the best of the Southerners. But Mr. Washington first indissolubly linked these things; he put enthusiasm, unlimited energy, and perfect faith into this programme, and changed it from a by-path into a veritable Way of Life. And the tale of the methods by which he did this is a fascinating study of human life.

It startled the nation to hear a Negro advocating such a programme after many decades of bitter complaint; it startled and won the applause of the South, it interested and won the admiration of the North; and after a confused murmur of protest, it silenced if it did not convert the Negroes themselves.

To gain the sympathy and coöperation of the various elements comprising the white South was Mr. Washington's first task; and this, at the time Tuskegee was founded, seemed, for a black man, well-nigh impossible. And yet ten years later it was done in the word spoken at Atlanta: "In all things purely social we can be as separate as the five fingers, and yet one as the hand in all things essential to mutual progress." This "Atlanta Compromise" is by all odds the most notable thing in Mr. Washington's career. The South interpreted it in different ways: the radicals received it as a complete surrender of the demand for civil and political equality; the conservatives, as a generously conceived, working basis for mutual understanding. So both approved it, and today its author is certainly the most distinguished Southerner since Jefferson Davis, and the one with the largest personal following.

Next to this achievement comes Mr. Washington's work in gaining place and consideration in the North. Others less shrewd and tactful had formerly essayed to sit on these two stools and had fallen between them; but as Mr. Washington knew the heart of the South from birth and training, so by singular insight he intuitively grasped the spirit of the age which was dominating the North. And so thoroughly did he learn the speech and thought of triumphant commercialism, and the ideals of material prosperity, that the picture of a lone black boy poring over a French grammar amid the weeds and dirt of a neglected home soon seemed to him the acme of absurdities. One wonders what Socrates and St. Francis of Assisi would say to this.

And yet this very singleness of vision and thorough oneness with his age is a mark of the successful man. It is as though Nature must needs make men narrow in order to give them force. So Mr. Washington's cult has gained unquestioning followers, his work has wonderfully prospered, his friends are legion, and his enemies are confounded. To-day he stands as the one recognized spokesman of his ten million fellows, and one of the most notable figures in a nation of seventy millions. One hesitates, therefore, to criticise a life which, beginning with so little, has done so much. And yet the time is come when one may speak in all sincerity and utter courtesy of the mistakes and shortcomings of Mr. Washington's career, as well as of his triumphs, without being thought captious or envious, and without forgetting that it is easier to do ill than well in the world.

The criticism that has hitherto met Mr. Washington has not always been of this broad character. In the South especially has he had to walk warily to avoid the harshest judgments,—and naturally so, for he is dealing with the one subject of deepest sensitiveness to that section. Twice—once when at the Chicago celebration of the Spanish-American War he alluded to the color-prejudice that is "eating away the vitals of the South," and once when he dined with President Roosevelt—has the resulting Southern criticism been violent enough to threaten seriously his popularity. In the North the feeling has several times forced itself into words, that Mr. Washington's counsels of submission overlooked certain elements of true manhood, and that his educational programme was unnecessarily narrow. Usually, however, such criticism has not found open expression, although, too, the spiritual sons of the Abolitionists have not been prepared to acknowledge that the schools founded before Tuskegee, by men of broad ideals and self-sacrificing spirit, were wholly failures or worthy of ridicule. While, then, criticism has not failed to follow Mr. Washington, yet the prevailing public opinion of the land has been but too willing to deliver the solution of a wearisome problem into his hands, and say, "If that is all you and your race ask, take it."

Among his own people, however, Mr. Washington has encountered the strongest and most lasting opposition, amounting at times to bitterness, and even to-day continuing strong and insistent even though largely silenced in outward expression by the public opinion of the nation. Some of this opposition is, of course, mere envy; the disappointment of displaced demagogues and the spite of narrow minds. But aside from this, there is among educated and thoughtful colored men in all parts of the land a feeling of deep regret, sorrow, and apprehension at the wide currency and ascendancy which some of Mr. Washington's theories have gained. These same men admire his sincerity of purpose, and are willing to forgive much to honest endeavor which is doing something worth the doing. They coöperate [*sic*] with Mr. Washington as far as they conscientiously can; and, indeed, it is no ordinary tribute to this man's tact and power that, steering as he must between so many diverse interests and opinions, he so largely retains the respect of all.

But the hushing of the criticism of honest opponents is a dangerous thing. It leads some of the best of the critics to unfortunate silence and paralysis of effort, and others to burst into speech so passionately and intemperately as to lose listeners. Honest and earnest criticism from those whose interests are most nearly touched,—criticism of writers by readers, of government by those governed, of leaders by those led,—this is the soul of democracy and the safeguard of modern society. If the best of the American Negroes receive by outer pressure a leader whom they had not recognized before, manifestly there is here a certain palpable gain. Yet there is also irreparable loss,—a loss of that peculiarly valuable education which a group receives when by search and criticism it finds and commissions its own leaders. The way in which this is done is at once the most elementary and the nicest problem of social growth. History is but the record of such group-leadership; and yet how infinitely changeful is its type and character! And of all types and kinds, what can be more instructive than the leadership of a group with a group?— that curious double movement where real progress may be negative and actual advance be relative retrogression. All this is the social student's inspiration and despair.

Now in the past the American Negro has had instructive experience in the choosing of group leaders, founding thus a peculiar dynasty which in the light of present conditions is worth while studying. When sticks and stones and beasts form the sole environment of a people, their attitude is largely one of determined opposition to and conquest of natural forces. But when to earth and brute is added an environment of men and ideas, then the attitude of the imprisoned group may take three main forms,—a feeling of revolt and revenge; an attempt to adjust all thought and action to the will of the greater group; or, finally, a determined effort at self-realization and self-development despite environing opinion. The influence of all of these attitudes at various times can be traced in the history of the American Negro, and in the evolution of his successive leaders.

Before 1750, while the fire of African freedom still burned in the veins of the slaves, there was in all leadership or attempted leadership but the one motive of revolt and revenge,—typified in the terrible Maroons, the Danish blacks, and Cato of Stono, and veiling all the Americas in fear of insurrection. The liberalizing tendencies of the latter half of the eighteenth century brought, along with kindlier relations between black and white, thoughts of ultimate adjustment and assimilation. Such aspiration was especially voiced in the earnest songs of Phyllis, in the martyrdom of Attucks, the fighting of Salem and Poor, the intellectual accomplishments of Banneker and Derham, and the political demands of the Cuffes.

Stern financial and social stress after the war cooled much of the previous humanitarian ardor. The disappointment and impatience of the Negroes at the persistence of slavery and serfdom voiced itself in two movements. The slaves in the South, aroused undoubtedly by vague rumors of the Haytian [*sic*] revolt, made three fierce attempts at insurrection,—in 1800 under Gabriel in Virginia, in 1822 under Vesey in Carolina, and in 1881 again in Virginia under the terrible Nat Turner. In the Free States, on the other hand, a new and curious attempt at self-development was made. In Philadelphia and New York color-prescription led to a withdrawal of Negro communicants from white churches and the formation of a peculiar socio-religious institution among the Negroes known as the African Church,—an organization still living and controlling in its various branches over a million of men.

Walker's wild appeal against the trend of the times showed how the world was changing after the coming of the cotton-gin. By 1830 slavery seemed hopelessly fastened on the South, and the slaves thoroughly cowed into submission. The free Negroes of the North, inspired by the mulatto immigrants from the West Indies, began to change the basis of their demands; they recognized the slavery of slaves, but insisted that they themselves were freemen, and sought assimilation and amalgamation with the nation on the same terms with other men. Thus, Forten and Purvis of Philadelphia, Shad of Wilmington, Du Bois of New Haven, Barbadoes of Boston, and others, strove singly and together as men, they said, not as slaves; as "people of color," not as "Negroes." The trend of the times, however, refused them recognition save in individual and exceptional cases, considered them as one with all the despised blacks, and they soon found themselves striving to keep even the rights they formerly had of voting and working and moving as freemen. Schemes of migration and colonization arose among them; but these they refused to entertain, and they eventually turned to the Abolition movement as a final refuge.

Here, led by Remond, Nell, Wells-Brown, and Douglass, a new period of self-assertion and self-development dawned. To be sure, ultimate freedom and assimilation was the ideal before the leaders, but the assertion of the manhood rights of the Negro by himself was the main reliance, and John Brown's raid was the extreme of its logic. After the war and emancipation, the great form of Frederick Douglass, the greatest of American Negro leaders, still led the host. Self-assertion, especially in political lines, was the main programme, and behind Douglass came Elliot, Bruce, and Langston, and the Reconstruction politicians, and, less conspicuous but of greater social significance Alexander Crummell and Bishop Daniel Payne.

Then came the Revolution of 1876, the suppression of the Negro votes, the changing and shifting of ideals, and the seeking of new lights in the great night. Douglass, in his old age, still bravely stood for the ideals of his early manhood,—ultimate assimilation *through* self-assertion, and on no other terms. For a time Price arose as a new leader, destined, it seemed, not to give up, but to re-state the old ideals in a form less repugnant to the white South. But he passed away in his prime. Then came the new leader. Nearly all the former ones had become leaders by the silent suffrage of their fellows, had sought to lead their own people alone, and were usually, save Douglass, little known outside their race. But Booker T. Washington arose as essentially the leader not of one race but of two,—a compromiser between the South, the North, and the Negro. Naturally the Negroes resented, at first bitterly, signs of compromise which surrendered their civil and political rights, even though this was to be exchanged for larger chances of economic development. The rich and dominating North, however, was not only weary of the race problem, but was investing largely in Southern enterprises, and welcomed any method of peaceful cooperation. Thus, by national opinion, the Negroes began to recognize Mr. Washington's leadership; and the voice of criticism was hushed.

Mr. Washington represents in Negro thought the old attitude of adjustment and submission; but adjustment at such a peculiar time as to make his programme unique. This is an age of unusual economic development, and Mr. Washington's programme naturally takes an economic cast, becoming a gospel of Work and Money to such an extent as apparently almost completely to overshadow the higher aims of life. Moreover, this is an age when the more advanced races are coming in closer contact with the less developed races, and the race-feeling is therefore intensified; and Mr. Washington's programme practically accepts the alleged inferiority of the Negro races. Again, in our own land, the reaction from the sentiment of war time has given impetus to race-prejudice against Negroes, and Mr. Washington withdraws many of the high demands of Negroes as men and American citizens. In other periods of intensified prejudice all the Negro's tendency to self-assertion has been called forth; at this period a policy of submission is advocated. In the history of nearly all other races and peoples the doctrine preached at such crises has been that manly self-respect is worth more than lands and houses, and that a people who voluntarily surrender such respect, or cease striving for it, are not worth civilizing.

In answer to this, it has been claimed that the Negro can, survive only through submission. Mr. Washington distinctly asks that black people give up, at least for the present, three things,—

First, political power,
Second, insistence on civil rights,
Third, higher education of Negro youth,—

and concentrate all their energies on industrial education, the accumulation of wealth, and the conciliation of the South. This policy has been courageously and insistently advocated for over fifteen years, and has been triumphant for perhaps ten years. As a result of this tender of the palm-branch, what has been the return? In these years there have occurred:

1. The disfranchisement of the Negro.
2. The legal creation of a distinct status of civil inferiority for the Negro.
3. The steady withdrawal of aid from institutions for the higher training of the Negro.

These movements are not, to be sure, direct results of Mr. Washington's teachings; but his propaganda has, without a shadow of doubt, helped their speedier accomplishment. The question then comes: Is it possible, and probable, that nine millions of men can make effective progress in economic lines if they are deprived of political rights, made a servile caste, and allowed only the most meagre chance for developing their exceptional men? If history and reason give any distinct answer to these questions, it is an emphatic *No*. And Mr. Washington thus faces the triple paradox of his career:

1. He is striving nobly to make Negro artisans business men and property-

owners; but it is utterly impossible, under modern competitive methods, for workingmen and property-owners to defend their rights and exist without the right of suffrage.

2. He insists on thrift and self-respect, but at the same time counsels a silent submission to civic inferiority such as is bound to sap the manhood of any race in the long run.

3. He advocates common-school and industrial training, and depreciates institutions of higher learning; but neither the Negro common-schools, nor Tuskegee itself, could remain open a day were it not for teachers trained in Negro colleges, or trained by their graduates.

This triple paradox in Mr. Washington's position is the object of criticism by two classes of colored Americans. One class is spiritually descended from Toussaint the Savior, through Gabriel, Vesey, and Turner, and they represent the attitude of revolt and revenge; they hate the white South blindly and distrust the white race generally, and so far as they agree on definite action, think that the Negro's only hope lies in emigration beyond the borders of the United States. And yet, by the irony of fate, nothing has more effectually made this programme seem hopeless than the recent course of the United States toward weaker and darker peoples in the West Indies, Hawaii, and the Philippines,—for where in the world may we go and be safe from lying and brute force?

The other class of Negroes who cannot agree with Mr. Washington has hitherto said little aloud. They deprecate the sight of scattered counsels, of internal disagreement; and especially they dislike making their just criticism of a useful and earnest man an excuse for a general discharge of venom from small-minded opponents. Nevertheless, the questions involved are so fundamental and serious that it is difficult to see how men like the Grimkes, Kelly Miller, J. W. E. Bowen, and other representatives of this group, can much longer be silent. Such men feel in conscience bound to ask of this nation three things:

1. The right to vote.
2. Civic equality.
3. The education of youth according to ability.

They acknowledge Mr. Washington's invaluable service in counselling patience and courtesy in such demands; they do not ask that ignorant black men vote when ignorant whites are debarred, or that any reasonable restrictions in the suffrage should not be applied; they know that the low social level of the mass of the race is responsible for much discrimination against it, but they also know, and the nation knows, that relentless color-prejudice is more often a cause than a result of the Negro's degradation; they seek the abatement of this relic of barbarism, and not its systematic encouragement and pampering by all agencies of social power from the Associated Press to the Church of Christ. They advocate, with Mr. Washington, a broad system of Negro common schools supplemented by thorough industrial training; but they are surprised that a man of Mr. Washington's insight cannot see that no such educational system ever has rested or can rest on any other basis than that of the well-equipped college and university, and they insist that there is a demand for a few such institutions throughout the South to train the best of the Negro youth as teachers, professional men, and leaders.

This group of men honor Mr. Washington for his attitude of conciliation toward the white South; they accept the "Atlanta Compromise" in its broadest interpretation; they recognize, with him, many signs of promise, many men of high purpose and fair judgment, in this section; they know that no easy task has been laid upon a region already tottering under heavy burdens. But, nevertheless, they insist that the way to truth and right lies in straightforward honesty, not in indiscriminate flattery; in praising those of the South who do well and criticising uncompromisingly those who do ill; in taking advantage of the opportunities at hand and urging their fellows to do the same, but at the same time in remembering that only a firm adherence to their higher ideals and aspirations will ever keep those ideals within the realm of possibility.

They do not expect that the free right to vote, to enjoy civic rights, and to be educated, will come in a moment; they do not expect to see the bias and prejudices of years disappear at the blast of a trumpet; but they are absolutely certain that the way for a people to gain their reasonable rights is not by voluntarily throwing them away and insisting that they do not want them; that the way for a people to gain respect is not by continually belittling and ridiculing themselves; that, on the contrary, Negroes must insist continually, in season and out of season, that voting is necessary to modern manhood, that color discrimination is barbarism, and that black boys need education as well as white boys.

In failing thus to state plainly and unequivocally the legitimate demands of their people, even at the cost of opposing an honored leader, the thinking classes of American Negroes would shirk a heavy responsibility,—a responsibility to themselves, a responsibility to the struggling masses, a responsibility to the darker races of men whose future depends so largely on this American experiment, but especially a responsibility to this nation,—this common Fatherland. It is wrong to encourage a man or a people in evil-doing; it is wrong to aid and abet a national crime simply because it is unpopular not to do so. The growing spirit of kindliness and reconciliation between the North and South after the frightful differences of a generation ago ought to be a source of deep congratulation to all, and especially to those whose mistreatment caused the war; but if that reconciliation is to be marked by the industrial slavery and civic death of those same black men, with permanent legislation into a position of inferiority, then those black men, if they are really men, are called upon by every consideration of patriotism and loyalty to oppose such a course by all civilized methods, even though such opposition involves disagreement with Mr. Booker T. Washington. We have no right to sit silently by while the inevitable seeds are sown for a harvest of disaster to our children, black and white.

First, it is the duty of black men to judge the South discriminatingly. The present generation of Southerners are not responsible for the past, and they should not be blindly hated or blamed for it. Furthermore, to no class is the indiscriminate endorsement of the recent course of the South toward Negroes more nauseating than to the best thought of the South. The South is not "solid"; it is a land in the ferment of social change, wherein forces of all kinds are fighting for supremacy; and to praise the ill the South is to-day perpetrating is just as wrong as to condemn the good. Discriminating and broad-minded criticism is what the South needs,—needs it for the sake of her own white sons and daughters, and for the insurance of robust, healthy mental and moral development.

To-day even the attitude of the Southern whites toward the blacks is not, as so many assume, in all cases the same; the ignorant Southerner hates the Negro, the workingmen fear his competition, the moneymakers wish to use him as a laborer, some of the educated see a menace in his upward development, while others—usually the sons of the masters—wish to help him to rise. National opinion has enabled this last class to maintain the Negro common schools, and to protect the Negro partially in property, life, and limb. Through the pressure of the money-makers, the Negro is in danger of being reduced to semi-slavery, especially in the country districts; the workingmen, and those of the educated who fear the Negro, have united to disfranchise him, and some have urged his deportation; while the passions of the ignorant are easily aroused to lynch and abuse any black man. To praise this intricate whirl of thought and prejudice is nonsense; to inveigh indiscriminately against "the South" is unjust; but to use the same breath in praising Governor Aycock, exposing Senator Morgan, arguing with Mr. Thomas Nelson Page, and denouncing Senator Ben Tillman, is not only sane, but the imperative duty of thinking black men.

It would be unjust to Mr. Washington not to acknowledge that in several instances he has opposed movements in the South which were unjust to the Negro; he sent memorials to the Louisiana and Alabama constitutional conventions, he has spoken against lynching, and in other ways has openly or silently set his influence against sinister schemes and unfortunate happenings. Notwithstanding this, it is equally true to assert that on the whole the distinct impression left by Mr. Washington's propaganda is, first, that the South is justified in its present attitude toward the Negro because of the Negro's degradation; secondly, that the prime cause of the Negro's failure to rise more quickly is his wrong education in the past; and, thirdly, that his future rise depends primarily on his own efforts. Each of these propositions is a dangerous half-truth. The supplementary truths must never be lost sight of: first, slavery and race-prejudice are potent if not sufficient causes of the Negro's position; second, industrial and common-school training were necessarily slow in planting because they had to await the black teachers trained by higher institutions,—it being extremely doubtful if any essentially different development was possible, and certainly a Tuskegee was unthinkable before 1880; and, third, while it is a great truth to say that the Negro must strive and strive mightily to help himself, it is equally true that unless his striving be not simply seconded, but rather aroused and encouraged, by the initiative of the richer and wiser environing group, he cannot hope for great success.

In his failure to realize and impress this last point, Mr. Washington is especially to be criticized. His doctrine has tended to make the whites, North and South, shift the burden of the Negro problem to the Negro's shoulders and stand aside as critical and rather pessimistic spectators; when in fact the burden belongs to the nation, and the hands of none of us are clean if we bend not our energies to righting these great wrongs.

The South ought to be led, by candid and honest criticism, to assert her better self and do her full duty to the race she has cruelly wronged and is still wronging. The North—her co-partner in guilt—cannot salve her conscience by plastering it with gold. We cannot settle this problem by diplomacy and suaveness, by "policy" alone. If worse come to worst, can the moral fibre of this country survive the slow throttling and murder of nine millions of men?

The black men of America have a duty to perform, a duty stern and delicate,—a forward movement to oppose a part of the work of their greatest leader. So far as Mr. Washington preaches Thrift, Patience, and Industrial Training for the masses, we must hold up his hands and strive with him, rejoicing in his honors and glorying in the strength of this Joshua called of God and of man to lead the headless host. But so far as Mr. Washington apologizes for injustice, North or South, does not rightly value the privilege and duty of voting, belittles the emasculating effects of caste distinctions, and opposes the higher training and ambition of our brighter minds,—so far as he, the South, or the Nation, does this,—we must unceasingly and firmly oppose them. By every civilized and peaceful method we must strive for the rights which the world accords to men, clinging unwaveringly to those great words which the sons of the Fathers would fain forget: "We hold these truths to be self-evident: That all men are created equal; that they are endowed by their Creator with certain unalienable rights; that among these are life, liberty, and the pursuit of happiness."

W. H. A. Moore
"The New Negro Literary Movement"
AME Church Review 21 (1904)

The New Negro Literary Movement is not the note of a reawakening, it is a halting, stammering voice touched with sadness and the pathos of yearning. Unlike the Celtic revival it is not a potent influence in the literature of to-day; neither is it the spirit of an endeavor to recover the song that is lost or the motive of an aspiration to reclaim the soul-love that is dead. Somehow it can not be measured by the standard of great achievement; and yet it possesses an air of distinction and speaks in the language of promise. It is the culminating expression of a heart growth the most strange and attractive in American life. To most of us it is as oddly unfamiliar as though it breathed and spoke in the jungles of its forbears. True, we have stopped in the busy ways and listened to a voice, as we thought without a soul, with bated breath and delighted ear and wondered why. But in the sum-total of our notion of things worth while this voice—seeking in its own tender, strangely accentuated way to give light and love and song to the soul of democracy—finds no place. No soul lost in the world's wild sway of shadow and anguish ever shed gentler tears; no heart touched with the play and gold of light ever laughed so joyously. From Phyllis Wheatley to Paul Dunbar has been one long day of sun, cloud and—pain. In the contemplation of what I am pleased to call "The New Negro Literary Movement," it might be well to consider from whence it came, what it promises, and whither is it tending. One chilly spring morning in the last half of the eighteenth century Boston Common was alive with an eager, surging throng absorbed in the buying of a shivering group of Africans. Near the end of the sale a comely, black girl is brought to the block and after a period of indifferent bidding is sold to a Mrs. Wheatley. At the moment there came to the moving impulse of American life the soul-faith of the Negro with its fidelity of heart and its virgin love for the motive of democracy. There is no need to attempt to find a high place in the range of the American branch of English Literature for the work of this savage. There is smaller need to point out how completely and how sanely she mastered the expression of her time. But as the first effort of the alien-African spirit to fill a place in the life-motive of the alien-democratic spirit of the north temperate zone, what she has bequeathed to us is unique, significant and, mayhap, permanent. In the disclosure of the aim and spirit of American democracy the voice of this child of

the Benighted Strand speaks with astonishing clearness. She possesses the accent of its every hope, she evinces every desire of its pulsing singleness of purpose. In another quieter, subtler way it presents to us that different yearning that somehow is not yet accustomed to the cold, grey skies of the north and the blatant, noisy swirl of her peculiar notion of intercourse and civilization. What if the great weight of mass, magnitude and physical agencies should fail us at the critical moment? Is power all? May not sweetness of temper bring us more? Phyllis Wheatley sings in the sweetness of temper and from this distance her song seems oddly out of harmony with the stress and harshness of the endeavor to put our beloved Republic on its feet. This may appear "mighty like" straining a point to endeavor to set apart the poetry of this African girl as the beginning of [the] Negro literary movement. But it is so close to the truth of things that there is no other way out of the dilemma. There is a difference, not instinctive but temperamental, between the Caucasian and the African. There has never been a lack of sympathy between the kinds, it is the unlikeness of temperaments, which we mistake for inherent differences, that makes the trouble. If we take this unlikeness of temperaments seriously it accounts, very materially, for the distinctness of outline in which the "Race Problem" insistently menaces the peace and quiet of American life. We can not escape from it and we do not try to escape from it. In the question of this Negro literary movement it does not matter that as yet it evidences no strikingly original features. To get at the bottom of its significance we must go deeper than its method of expression before we will find the truth, beauty and color of its purpose. It has made an almost frantic effort to shape itself in the likeness of its environment. The form and method of its utterance is modelled on the lines of the undefiled standards of the highest English literary expression. A first hand reason why its position is not pronounced and its influence stands for little else than naught. That group of ante-bellum writers and speakers among whom the most prominent were Frederick Douglass, Alexander

Crummell, Charles L. Reason, John Vashon and Francis [*sic*] Ellen Watkins, suffer with the single exception of Douglass, the fate of obscurity born in this womb of unnaturalness. Here and there we catch the spirit of the fervor and fragrance of the tropics, but when we reach out for its substance it eludes us and presents in its stead a train of unsatisfying longing and disappointed seeking. Yet, notwithstanding this absence of original, virile achievement, there is a decided charm in determining the outline of its course through the maze and tangle of the Republic's activities and the perplexing trend of its thought and hope. Let us consider for a brief while its most apparent characteristics. We look in vain for the great or promising novel and for the distinctive and enduring poem. This voice speaks in the main, with the accent of controversy. Its language is the essence of elegance, refinement, courage, but it does not convince. Many times the music has gone out of the voice and its pleading and debating becomes the hoarse utterance of baffled protest. Aweary of the unequal contest it finally turns to an inquiry of itself. At first the freedman could not comprehend the teachings of his own preachers. He turned the unwilling ear of skepticism to the story and was not sure that he stood in the presence of Truth. A not unnatural attitude. Most of us forget that truth, whether found in the life of the jungle or in the gilded halls of civilization's boulevards, is different, true, absolute. Different in its manifestations of habit, true in its fidelity to virtue, absolute in its relation to the stronger faith, the better love, the higher life. And so we find Frederick Douglass denounced, Cordelia Ray ignored and Fanny Jackson chained to the desk of a commonplace public school room by their own kith and kind. But no single force or combination of forces could hinder the birth of the child. The new literary movement came to the Negro race when the war of social and industrial economics was being bitterly and unrelentingly waged. It did not, it could not flourish. But it grew sturdily, persistently, if not with an acute sense of proportion and a delicately adjusted notion of the motive of beauty and the originality of purpose. During the post-bellum period it was still, in the main, controversial in scope and character, with the difference that it was in a perceptible measure concerned with beauty and beauty's general manifestations of form and harmonies. In December, 1892, there was organized at Wilmington, North Carolina, a society of Negro authors. Bishop Benjamin W. Arnett was elected the president and I. Garland Penn was chosen as the secretary. Both are authors of considerable note among their people. As I remember them now Anna J. Cooper, the author of "A Voice of a Black Woman"; John C. Dancy, the editor of the *A.M.E. Zion Church Quarterly*; Mrs. Francis Ellen Watkins-Harper, poet and novelist, and some lesser names I can not bring to mind at this moment, were members of the society. It was a distinct departure, as distinct as it was short lived. Mrs. Cooper struck the note of the society's purpose when she declared in the course of her address to the meeting that, "We must begin to give the character of beauty and power to the literary utterance of the race." It was not long after this meeting that Paul Dunbar was discovered by William Dean Howells. Dunbar sings a song of alluring attractiveness and has been hailed as not only a large figure in the literary life of his race, but he has been greeted as an associate in the bigger world of American letters. Since we have grown away from the glamor of this remarkable young Negro's first successes we are not quite sure where we will place him in the new Negro literary movement. He is so apt and attractive that our admiration for his unquestioned cleverness stuns the judgment and makes one uncertain what to do. I think we may take his "When Malindy Sings" and put it in the company of America's great lyrics. I am not so sure of the enduring life of the large bulk of his work in verse and story. His stories certainly present no imposing picture of any phase of Negro or American life; and yet I would be ungrateful indeed if I did not feel thankful for what this splendid type of his race has contributed of value to the literary output of the American Negro. Charles W. Chesnutt is another of the large figures in this literary movement. As a minor short story and novel writer his work commands high respect and displays the firmest hand and the clearest vision of any of the present-day story writers of Negro blood. Perhaps the largest figure in the new Negro literary movement is William E. Burghardt-DuBois. His "Souls of Black Folk" is the one book written by a Negro which has arrested the attention of the entire American people. There is an old Arabic song which says:

> One saith that love is filled with sweet-
> ness. . . . Nay,
> I who am wise have never found it so!
> Love is to suffer, day on endless day,
> And see fresh blood from new wounds
> gush and flow.

The "Souls of Black Folks" [*sic*] tells the story of the Negro's love that suffers. It is the lay-ing bare of the "new wounds gush and flow." It is the attitude of the new Negro toward the new life. No one can afford to ignore the presence of the new Negro any more than he can consistently ignore the presence of the new life. Each is here to stamp the impress on the onward impulse of modern democracy. Each demands its own works, its own laws, its own worship. In this book of Prof. DuBois' we hear the first demand and get the first clear outline of the final purpose of the new Negro literary movement. We can not tell what it will bring us of good or evil. But when we come to a willing recognition of the existence of a potent, if alien influence which is at work giving a new character and import to the literary expression of the entire race, we are going a long way in the direction of reaching a true understanding of the highest precept and purpose of the final democracy.

~~~~~~

Anonymous

"Some Fresh Suggestions about the New Negro Crime"

Harper's Weekly, January 23, 1904[1]

On January 10 Dr. Felix Adler discussed the negro question at Carnegie Hall in New York City. He sensibly said that the North, while it cannot evade its share of responsibility for the difficulties presented, ought not to assume any airs of superiority over the South, but, on the contrary, should recognize that the South, by long experience, is peculiarly qualified to solve, or at least attempt a solution of, the problem. We have no doubt that Dr. Adler and the many thousands of Northerners who concur in his views will read with interest an article on the cause and prevention of the lynching of negroes, contributed to the January number of the *North American Review*. Before and since the civil war, the author of the article, Mr. Thomas Nelson Page, a native of Virginia, has been an eye-witness and a student of the relations between the whites and the blacks. He lends the weight of his name to the assertion, supported by innumerable authorities, that the assault of white women by colored men may fairly be described as the "new" negro crime. In conjunction with many other careful students of Southern history, he avers that during the whole period of slavery the crime did not exist. Even during the civil war, when all able-bodied white men were away in the army, the negroes were loyal guardians of the white women and children. On isolated plantations and in lonely neighborhoods, white women at that period were as secure as in the streets of Boston or New York. Neither were many examples of the crime here contemplated observed for a good many years after emancipation. The particular crime to which we refer did not become frequent at the South until the old paternal relation which had survived even the strain of reconstruction passed away with the departure of the old generation of negroes from the stage. There was no extensive outbreak of the new negro crime until the teaching that accompanied the attempt to impose carpet-bag government had borne its fruit in the new generation of negroes. The substance of the teaching was that the negro was the equal of the white, that the white was his enemy, and that the black must assert his equality. The growth of the idea was gradual in the negro's mind, but, when it became widely and deeply rooted, its effect was shown in many ravishings of white women by negroes, sometimes in the presence of the victim's family. Mr. Page points out that conditions in the South render the commission of the crime peculiarly easy. The white population is thin, the forests are extensive, the officers of the law are distant and difficult to reach. Above all, the negro population, as a whole, seems inclined to condone the fact of mere assault. Touching this point, the author testifies that the average negro does not believe in the chastity of women. Such a belief could not be evolved from his acquaintance with the female members of his race. He cannot accept the credibility of an assault being committed against the will of the victim. Such a state of facts is beyond his comprehension. On the other hand, his sexual desire, which always was a controlling force with him has become, since the new teaching of political and social equality, a desire for the white woman. This assertion is confirmed by William Hannibal Thomas, himself a colored man, in the interesting work entitled *The American Negro.*

It is obvious, however, that the negro had the same animal instincts under the slavery régime that he exhibits now. Neither is it deniable that the punishment which follows the crime is no more certain, terrible, and swift to-day than it would have been in slavery times. To what, then, must be attributed the alarming increase of the horrible brutality? By Mr. Page the emergence of the new negro crime is attributed to two things—first, as we have seen, to racial antagonism and to the talk of social equality that inflames the negro, unregulated and undisciplined; but, secondly and mainly, to the absence of a strong restraining opinion among the negroes of any class, however enlightened and law-abiding. It is manifestly important to note

what a specially qualified observer like Mr. Thomas Nelson Page has to say upon the latter point. He tells us that a close examination of the examples of rape and lynching, and of the ensuing public discussion thereon, has led him to the painful conviction that most of the leaders of the negro race have rarely, by act or word, evinced a right appreciation of the crime of ravishing and murdering women. Their denunciation has been levelled almost exclusively at the crime of lynching. Underlying most of their protests against that supersession of the law is the suggestion that the victim of the mob is a martyr. Mr. Page avers that, so far as his own observation has gone, the records of negro meetings will show, for one righteous outcry against the violation of women, much furious reprobation of the attacks of mobs upon the criminals. As to any serious and determined effort to stamp out the atrocious crime that is blackening the whole colored race to-day, and arousing against them the deadly and, possibly, undying enmity of their white neighbors, he has been able to find scarcely a trace of such a thing, except in the utterances of a few individuals like Booker Washington, who always speaks for the right, of Hannibal Thomas, and of Bishop Turner. A crusade against lynching of negroes has been preached as far as England, but no crusade has yet been heard of against the ravishing and tearing to pieces of white women and children. In a word, so far as Mr. Page's observation goes—and whose is wiser—the sympathy of negro orators and preachers, and of the whole negro race, is generally exhibited for the object of mob violence, and not for his victim.

Mr. Page does not touch upon the fact—we believe it to be a fact—that, since colored men were practically excluded from the exercise of the franchise in Mississippi, there has been no instance of the new negro crime in that State. Evidently he does not believe that the crime can be exterminated by statute or by any exterior pressure, but thinks that it can only be gradually eliminated by the inward regeneration of the colored race itself. He holds that, until the negroes shall create amongst themselves a sound public opinion—such as existed before the civil war—which, instead of fostering and condoning, shall reprobate and sternly repress, the crime of assaulting white women and white children, the new negro crime will never be extirpated; and that, until this crime is stopped, the crime of lynching will never be suppressed. Never will lynching be done away with while the sympathy of the whites is with the lynchers; no more will the ravishing of white women be done away with while the sympathy of the negroes, more or less veiled, is with the ravisher. When the negroes, as a race, shall stop applying all their energies to harboring and shielding negro criminals, no matter what their crime may be, so long as it is against the whites; when the negroes as a race shall distinguish, sharply and sternly, between the law-abiding negro and the colored law-breaker—a long and effective step toward the extinction of the fundamental cause of lynching will have been taken. It is Mr. Page's belief that the arrest and prompt handing over to the law of negroes by negroes for assaults on white women would do more to break up ravishing and to restore amicable relations between the two races than all the harangues of all the politicians, all the resolutions of all the conventions, and, we presume that he means us to add, all the discriminating laws of all the Southern legislatures. Should the negroes, he says, sturdily and faithfully set themselves to prevent the raping of white women by members of their race, the crime would be stamped out. Should the whites, on their part, set themselves against lynching, that defiance of the law would cease. The remedy, then, he thinks, is plain. Let the negroes, he says, take charge of the crime of ravishing, and put it firmly away from them; let the whites take charge of the crime of lynching, and renounce it with equal firmness.

Is Mr. Page's suggestion Utopian? He is by no means prepared to assert its practicability. He submits, however, that the method of dealing with the new negro crime which he advocates is worth trying, and that from foreign countries a little evidence may be gathered in favor of its feasibility. Is it not possible, he asks, that, in every American community which contains a large colored element, negroes might be appointed officers of the law for the express purpose of controlling law-breakers of their own race? Attention is directed to the fact that in the Mediterranean and in the East the English manage such matters pretty well under similar, if not equally complicated and delicate, conditions. On the island of Malta, for example, where the population is composed of different nationalities, between whom a good deal of jealousy exists, there are several divisions of police, to each of which is assigned the charge of one of the three elements of which the insular population is composed. In Hong-kong [sic], also, where the situation presents an even more complicated problem, there are several kinds of police—English, Chinese and Hindoo. The first alone have comprehensive powers; the two other classes of officers are authorized to arrest members of the races to which they respectively belong. Mr. Page suggests that, similarly, negro officials might be clothed with powers sufficiently large to enable them to keep order among their own people, while for the efficient exercise of such powers they would be held accountable. It seems that the recent vagrant laws of Georgia represent an effort in this direction.

To what conclusion are we driven if Mr. Page's suggestion be pronounced impracticable; if, in other words, it be impossible to entrust the suppression of the new negro crime to colored men themselves? We should, then, as Mr. Page admits, be driven to the conviction that the ravishings of white women by negroes and the resultant murders of black criminals by mobs, have their roots so deep in racial instincts that nothing can eradicate them, except a desperate resort to the supreme arbitrament of force.

Eleanor Tayleur

"The Negro Woman: I—Social and Moral Decadence"

Outlook, January 30, 1904[2]

The most anomalous and portentous figure in America to-day is the negro woman. Little account has been taken of her in the discussion of the race problem, yet if the key to that dark riddle is ever found, hers must be the hand that first discovers it.

It is an axiom that no people can rise higher than their source. The measure of its womanhood is the measure of the potentialities of a race. If this be virtuous, clean of mind and body, filled with high ideals and noble aspirations, all things are possible to its sons. If, on the contrary, it be unchaste, diseased physically and morally, with groveling and material desires, the race is doomed, for death and decadence have set their seal upon it. Women mold the character of a people. It is eternally true that the hand that rocks the cradle rules the world. In the great crises of life the thing that determines the action of the great majority of men is not the code of ethics of their mature years, or the system of philosophy that they have reasoned out. It is the teaching that they imbibed at their mother's knee—it is the memory of old prayers they lisped in childhood, old songs and stories, a mother's kiss, a mother's tears that have crystalized into character, and that at the crucial moment decides their action for right or wrong, and whether they shall go forward or backward. Before a mother's influence political decrees are as empty and powerless as sounding brass and tinkling cymbals, and even the education of books and schools falls back impotent and defeated. At the last it is the woman who bears the race who determines its destiny.

It is this that gives a somber interest to the negro woman, for she is the pivot upon which the great race question turns. It is her hand that rocks the cradle in which the little pickaninny sleeps; it is she who sweeps the cabin floor, and makes it a home that is clean and bright or else an abode of disease; it is she who bequeaths to the child that is bone of her bone and flesh of her flesh, soundness of body and soul or else the tendencies that make it a moral and physical leper; it is her hand that sets the little feet about her knee on the road which they are to travel in life. All that the white woman is to the white race, the negro woman is to the black. Her influence is just as potent, and she is the dominant factor that must be reckoned with in every effort to help the negro.

In the Northern cities there are many, and in the South a few, negro women who in intelligence, nobility of character, and refinement would challenge comparison with any women in the world. These are exceptions, and it is not proposed to consider them here, but the great dark, helpless, hopeless mass of the women of their race as they are found leading their lawless and purposeless lives in the cane and cotton field, or herded together in the streets of the cities.

As she exists in the South to-day the negro woman is the Frankenstein product of civilization, a being created out of conditions of sectional hate and revenge, and set in motion by wild experimentalists who knew not what they did; and within the length and breadth of Christendom there is no other figure so forlorn and pathetic as she. Doubly cursed by her color and her sex, on her has fallen alike the heaviest burden of the negro and of womanhood. Shut out by her blood from the privileges of the white woman and by her sex from the opportunities of the negro man, she is the victim of every injustice of society, and she revenges herself upon it by striking at the very foundations of the political and social structure. She has always been a hapless sacrifice to the lust of man, and retribution has made her a Nemesis who has forged the thunderbolts of the race question for the white man, who stands a sinister figure behind the black man, forever dragging him downward.

No women in the world ever went through such a radical change as has taken place among the negro women since the Civil War. For them emancipation meant the severing of every association, habit, and custom of their lives, and the inauguration of a new heaven and a new earth; and the negro woman of to-day, in character and thought, in aspiration and ideal, is no more like that negro woman of ante-bellum days than if a thousand generations, instead of one or two, rolled between them. History records no change of the women of a whole race so rapid and so radical; and the sadly significant feature of this change is that it has been for the worse and not for the better.

Many explanations may be offered to account for the decadence of the negro woman. First and foremost is the abolition of the home; for woman's highest virtues, whatever her color or her race, are garden flowers that flourish best about her doorstep, and lacking this congenial soil they wither and die. Whatever the burdens and wrongs of slavery, and they were great and many, it at least gave the negro woman a home in which she was sure of food and warmth and privacy; and when within the four walls of her cabin, or her quarters in the city mansion, she was as truly and completely mistress of her home as the chatelaine of her castle. So much was the slave's unquestioned right; but now, when the negro must pay rent for the roof that shelters him, whole herds of them crowd together in a single room, like rabbits in a warren, without regard to age or sex or consanguinity. Under such conditions all privacy, or even decency, is impossible.

In the country the cabin may still be seen with the gourd vine trained above the door, with its beds covered with gay patchwork, with its floors scrubbed until they shine with glistening whiteness, and these homes furnish the great percentage of the respectable, thrifty, and industrious men and women of the negro race. In the cities the majority of negro women have no homes, but a room which they oftener than not share with strangers. The beds are unmade, the dishes unwashed, the floor unswept. Here children are born to be thrust out into the street as soon as possible to get them out of the way, and thus the mother and the child are deprived of the home influence that is one of the strongest powers for good in the world.

Another reason for the decadence of the negro woman is that she no longer has the uplift of close personal association with white women. Before the war the negro woman was brought into intimate contact with the refined and educated women of the dominant race. Essentially imitative as negroes are, they copied the manners and the morals of the mistress they served. Many a black woman was a grande dame who would have graced a court and imbued with as high and lofty a sense of loyalty and fealty as any knight; and among the most cherished recollections of the old South are the memories of these women, between whom and their owners existed a bond of affection that only death could sever.

No such conditions prevail to-day, save in the rare instances when a family is fortunate enough to attach to itself some negress whose ideals and traditions were formed in the days of slavery, when, as foster-sister to some white child, or handmaiden to some white woman, she imbibed the preceipts [*sic*] of honor and honesty and duty that must alike guide both races. The modern negro woman has no such object-lesson in morality or morals or modesty, and she wants none. She hates the white woman with a hatred born of hopeless envy, and her most exquisite pleasure is in insulting her with childlike brutality. She does this in a thousand little puerile ways—by rudely jostling her in a crowd, by pushing her off the sidewalk, and—favorite method of all—by invariably speaking of her own race as "ladies and gentlemen" and the white as "men and women." Thus the announcement by your maid that a lady wishes to speak to you sends you down the back stairs to interview a dusky charwoman, while, when you are told that there is a strange woman downstairs, you prepare to receive your friend of a most aristocratic lineage and exquisite refinement. When the black woman imitates the

The Fat Lady on the Hill: MISTER WIMPLE DECLINES TO FINISH DE GAME WIF YOU. DAT LAST DRIVE OB YOURS HAB KNOCKED OUT ALL HIS FRONT TEEF, AND HE FEARS HE HAB SWALLOWED DE BALL.

Edward W. Kemble, "The Fat Lady on the Hill," cartoon, *Life*, July 13, 1899. Courtesy of the Newberry Library, Chicago.

white, she only imitates what is worst in her. She copies her extravagance in tawdry finery that is a grotesque exaggeration of fashion, she copies her independence in utter abandon of all restraints, she copies her vices and adds to them frills of her own, and it is as if one saw a vulgar picture ineffably coarsened by being reproduced in hideous and glaring colors that emphasized every unlovely detail.

Before the war the negro women also had the uplifting influence of honest work. They were taught the various branches of domestic labor, and had the pride in their work that comes from skillful craftsmanship. But the Aunt Dinahs, ample of girth, clad in clean cottonade, who boasted that they laid a heavy hand on the seasoning when they compounded dainties, and who at dinner would poke an anxious head through the doorway to hear the compliments bestowed upon their art, are almost as extinct as the dodo.[3] Gone, too, are the neat housemaids in guinea-blue calicoes, starched until they rattled like the best taffeta, who felt a personal pride in keeping the mahogany shining like a mirror, and whose ministrations were benedictions, so filled were they with loving care and solicitude. Gone, also, are the old black mammies on whose broad breasts childish sorrows sobbed themselves to sleep and broken baby hearts were mended.

In their places is an ignorant creature in dirty finery, the first article of whose faith is a settled determination not to work. For the time being this has been shaken by hunger or a desire to buy a sleazy silk dress, and she condescends to preside in your kitchen or make your beds, but she does it under protest. She has no pride in her occupation, or desire to do it well. She does not burden her mind with the insignificant details that go to make good cooking. She dashes a lot of things together, and if they turn out all right, well and good. If not, also well and good. All that she is interested in is in drawing her wages, and carrying back and forth the basket that is the commissary department of a horde of idle and shiftless friends.

In the particular code of ethics that governs the new negro woman any way of obtaining a livelihood is more honorable and respectable than working for it. The colored Mrs. Grundy does not frown on the demi-mondaine, nor does the conviction of theft call forth any social ostracism. Nor is this surprising. It was to have been expected that a childish race, suddenly freed from slavery, would mistake liberty for license, and that the men and women whose own backs had been bowed with toil should wish to save their children from the burdens they had borne. More than that, the masters and mistresses they idealized did not work with their hands, and so the distorted belief prevails among the negroes that the first step toward being a lady or a gentleman is to be idle. In this the young of both sexes are encouraged by their parents; and nothing could be more grotesquely sad than the feeble old black mothers who are bending over washtubs and cooking-stoves earning the money to support strapping sons and daughters, while they boast proudly that their children never did a lick of work!

So far, education has done but little for the great mass of negro women. Here and there a girl achieves the common-school education, and in rare instances one even develops the ability to take a college course; but these latter cases are as unusual as genius is among the whites. Negroes are avid of schooling, and it is nothing uncommon to see a girl go to school, session after session, for eight or ten years, without achieving anything more than the ability to read and write like a child in the second grade, while the superior elegance of saying "have came," and scorning the humble and admiring mother who goes out scrubbing to support her, entitles her to a diploma. It may be that this tentative education, whose uplifting influence is unseen and unfelt as yet, is the little leaven that will eventually leaven the whole lump and raise the entire race to a higher level; but as yet the only visible result has been to teach the girl a scorn of the work she is fitted to do, and to implant in her breast an insatiable ambition to be a school-teacher—an ambition that must be futile unless the supply of scholars can be miraculously increased, or the Government subsidizes every kinky-headed little coon and farms him out among the several million negro girls in the South who are looking forward to the glorious career of being schoolma'ams. Never was the truth of the old adage that a little learning is a dangerous thing so fully illustrated as by these imperfectly educated women; yet it is this half-awakened intelligence, struggling with problems that is too ignorant to understand, misreading both the past and the present, drawing false meanings from history and philosophy, that is one of the menaces of our time.

Important, however, as is the relation of the negro woman to the white race, it is not so important as her relations to her own. Among her own people her position is one peculiar among the women of the world, and it is one full of cruel injustice and bitter suffering. No other woman among civilized people is so little protected, so little cherished, and evokes so little chivalry from the men of her race. All the hardships that other women endure she bears, and more. She loves, but no sense of loyalty, no convention of faithfulness, binds her lover to her. She may marry, but with no certainty of the tie being permanent. She bears children, but with oftener than not no husband's sympathy to cheer her, no husband's hand to even provide the food and clothing. When she toils, it is only too frequently to have her meager wage taken from her by a drunken brute.

There are, of course, negro men who are admirable husbands, but among the vast majority of them the responsibility of the marriage relationship as white people understand it does not exist. The wedding ceremony and the divorce decree are held in light esteem as ornaments that one may have, but that there are not necessities by any means and the average negro man manifests absolutely no sense of obligation about providing for his wife and children. That burden falls upon the woman. His wage, if he works, is generally spent upon his own pleasures and vices. On every Saturday afternoon through the South pathetic groups of these defrauded wives may be witnessed, waiting humbly with their empty baskets on the outskirts of the cotton-gin, or factory, or sawmill where their husbands work, trying to wheedle a little of their week's salary out of their lords and mas-

ters to feed the hungry mouths at home. Often the man does not work at all, but lives in a paradise of ease and luxury on the dainties his wife purloins from the pantry of the white people for whom she cooks. No other race in the world shows such a number of men supported by women as does the negro race. The answer to the question, how the vast idle male negro population in the South lives without work, finds its answer in the basket that the cooks invariably carry back and forth between their home and the kitchen in which they are employed.

As a general thing, the negro woman is of a tropical temperament, and loves madly and passionately. When roused to jealousy, she is a furious demon who not infrequently kills her rival or the lover who forsakes her. Often her love is as brief as it is stormy, but there are innumerable cases where she displays a dog-like devotion, and follows, year after year, the footsteps of the man who beats her, and mistreats her, and is faithless to her, and sometimes even brings another wife to live under the very roof-tree that her own hard toil supports. For her children she has a fierce passion of maternity that seems to be purely animal, and that seldom goes beyond their childhood. When they are little, she indulges them blindly when she is in good humor, and beats them cruelly when she is angry; and once past their childhood her affection for them appears to be exhausted. She exhibits none of the brooding mother-love and anxiety which the white woman sends after her children as long as they live. Infanticide is not regarded as a crime among negroes, but it is so appallingly common that if the statistics could be obtained on this subject they would send a shudder through the world. The story of many negro midwives, who are veritable female Herods, is not a thing to be told.

The negro woman also occupies a unique position in this, that of all women she is the one who personally best illustrates the fallacy of the theory of free love and the abolition of all the conventions and laws that hedge about matrimony. She is literally "the woman who did" of Mr. Richard Grant White's dream. All that the most advanced theorists who rail at the bondage of marriage advocate she does, and under ideal conditions. There is no public opinion to be defied, no society to turn the cold shoulder upon her. She loses no caste changing husbands as the whim seizes her, and no odium is attached to the possession of what she graphically and picturesquely described as a "bandanna family"—meaning thereby one in which each child is a different color.

Yet, with all these advantages of freedom in securing a soul mate, and, if she makes a mistake in selecting the first time, in being able to seek an affinity to the third and fourth and hundredth time if she pleases, the negro woman is the most unanswerable refutation that the imagination could devise to those who believe that love should never be fettered. A forlorn and warning figure, forsaken and deserted, with her own burdens a hundredfold heavier because no man is bound to help her bear them, crushed under the weight of a motherhood that no fatherhood lightens, the negro woman stands at the gate of the garden of free-loveism, and cries out that it is a false paradise—that all of its fruit are apples of Sodom, and that nowhere else is a woman's sorrow so inescapable, and her lot so bitter, as in that mockery of freedom.

Such is the negro woman of to-day, the most unfortunate and sinned against creature in all the world, the victim of heredity, of social conditions, of environment, the very sport and plaything of destiny, yet holding in her hands the fate of a race. There is some-

thing almost sardonically humorous in the thought of this woman, with the brain of a child and the passions of a woman, steeped in centuries of ignorance and savagery, and wrapped about with immemorial vices, playing with the die of fate.

Yet there she sits, unthinking, unknowing, with no desire save of the senses, no ambitions, no aspirations, and the most momentous problem of our day is how to rouse this lethargic giantess to a sense of her responsibilities. In the home of all the real progress of a people must begin. You cannot raise a race above its motherhood. Until that is done, until the childhood of the little negro girl is safeguarded, until the negro woman is inspired with ideals of virtue, until the mother teaches the child at her knee the precepts of right and honest living, there can be no real uplift for the negro race, and no solving of the race problem.

The mission of the white woman of this country is to the black woman. If ever there was a God given and appointed task set to the womanhood of any people, it is to the women of America to take these lowly sisters by the hand and lift them out of the pit into which they have fallen. Humanity pleads for it, Christianity prays for it, the very salvation of the country demands it, for be assured unless we succor these Hagars who have been thrust out into the desert of their own ignorance and superstition and sin, they will raise up Ishmaels whose hands shall be against our sons forever.

William Ferris

"A Historical and Psychological Account of the Genesis and Development of the Negro's Religion"

AME Church Review 20, no. 4 (1904)

Is There Anything that Psychologically Differentiates the Negro from Other Races?

Every time the Negro minister is referred to before a white congregation, immediately a

broad grin spreads over their countenance and they call to mind the darkey preacher often referred to, who looked apprehensively at the sun and said, "De grass am gittin' weedy, de sun am gittin' hot, dis man's gittin' old and feeble; guess dis darkey am called to preach." When you speak of the Negro's religion, this audience will immediately call to mind another Negro, also often referred to, who pays his respects to the chicken coop on his way home from the prayer meeting. The Negro's religion is not taken seriously, and yet despite the superstitions, the incongruities and inconsistencies manifested in the Negro's religion, there is a deep vein of serious religion in the Negro's nature.

I will admit that the Negro race is not as practical and hard-headed as the Anglo-Saxon race, but neither had the Greeks and Romans of long ago, nor have the Germans, French, Italians, Russians or Spaniards of to-day that phlegmatic temperament that can coolly and calmly view every subject. But the Negro is as imaginative, versatile, plastic and imitative a race as the Greeks. He has a poetic imagination. Even the illiterate Negro has fastidious notions as to dress. The Negro has remarkable ability in adjusting himself to a varied and changing environment. That is why he thrives under changed surroundings, where other races perish.

The Negro race is the greatest race of natural talkers that ever appeared upon the stage of history. It is pre-eminently endowed with the gift of gab. It has its oratory on tap. All you have to do is to turn the faucet and a copious stream of oratory will gush forth. On election days, in the large cities of the North and East, every street corner is a rostrum, every barber shop a forum and every bar room a free lecture platform. We think then of that brilliant epoch in Greek history, the days of Pericles, when the Athenian orators made the market place ring with their eloquence, when the Peripatetic philosophers discoursed of high things in the grove of the Academy and Socrates held his divine conversations in the streets of Athens. The Greeks were a race of talkers. But they could not compare with the Negro race. I know you will think of that fair moment in Grecian history, when, as DeWitt Clinton declared, "The herb women could criticize the phraseology of Demosthenes and pronounce judgment upon the

works of Phidias and Apelles." I know you will recall how Pericles, Aeschines and Demosthenes held the Athenian multitude spell-bound under the magic wand of their matchless eloquence. But reflect that in the cotton and corn fields of the South, our sugar and rice plantations and in the turpentine camps, there are untutored Negro preachers from whose lips issue forth eloquence that, though rude, is noble.

I know you will say that the Negro is prone to emotional excitement. But the only difference between the Negro camp meetings and the camp meetings of the poor whites is that you can hear the whites singing and shouting two miles away, while you can hear the colored singing and shouting three miles away. The rites at the Delphic Oracle, the Bacchanalian Festivals in Greece and Rome and the miracles at Lourdes exhibit as much excitement and intoxication and frenzy as do those recent converts who go crazy and let themselves go when they picture themselves wearing white robes and golden slippers, and treading upon a sea of glass, surrounded by jasper and sapphire walls.

Then again, the Negro race has an innate ear for harmony, an instinctive love of music. The aspiration and longing and sorrow and cravings of the Negro burst into expression through the jubilee songs and plantation melodies. Besides the soothing and plaintive melodies of these songs the Gospel Hymns of Moody and Sankey sound like sounding brass and a tinkling cymbal. These songs touch and move everyone because they come up out of the elemental depths of the Negro's nature. The Negro race is richer, then, in emotional endowment than any other race in the world.

It has an aspiring nature, for immediately after his emancipation the Negro began to aspire after the highest things in the American civilization. He tried to absorb the most complex political psychology ever evolved from the brain of man. The Reconstruction politicians even aspired to using Dresden china cuspidors. . . .

The savage saw the sun rise and then set. He saw the stars shine in the firmament. He saw the trees and grains and grasses and fruits and flowers grow. He saw the frost and rain spoil his crops. He saw the cyclone sweep everything before it. He saw the rivers rise and surge and rage. He trembled at the thunder and lightning. He saw sickness and disease and death take away his fellows. He felt the rheumatism steal in upon him and was driven by the necessity of human thought to account for it. What more natural than that he, in seeking causes for the beneficent and baleful operations of nature should ascribe them to good and evil spirits with a conscious, sentient and volitional life that was akin to his own. From the time when primeval man looked up to the stars and at the world around him and peopled nature with spirits akin to his own, up to the present time this has ever remained the process by which religion has germinated and unfolded in the mind of man. The wild African, the ancestors of the Aryan race on the hills of Northern Asia, and the poetical Greeks, all saw nature throbbing and pulsating with animate life.

Now if nature was believed to be peopled with good and evil spirits, where will these spirits exist. Primitive man had not reached that stage of advanced thought where he could conceive of disembodied spirits, neither could he believe that the objects of nature that he saw moving and growing were inanimate. He believed that all the physical objects and all the animals were impelled by some spirit. What more natural, then, than that he should believe that the unseen and invisible spirits that lived and moved in things and animals should be the spirits who benefited or harmed them?

It is significant in this respect that animus is the Greek or Latin for spirit, and this is the step from nature worship to Fetichism. "A Fetich," in the words of one scholar, "is not an idol and is not properly a symbol, but is looked upon as the actual and visible dwelling place of a preternatural power." In Fetichism, then, the object is not worshipped or prized highly, because it itself has power to benefit or harm a man, but because it is the abode and habitat of some invisible spirit or unseen power.

"Every object," says Petschel, "that attracts the glance of the savage, who espies a ghost in every corner, may become in his eyes the abode of a deity." Sticks, stones, household utensils, ornaments, plants, trees, snakes and animals were thus looked upon and regarded as Fetiches.

Oscar Peschel, on page 77 of his "Races of Man," says, "All true Negroes adhere either to a rude animal and fetich worship or to Islam."

Now these seem to be rather sweeping statements, but if the hearer will but turn over the pages of Ratzel's History of Mankind, by far the most exhaustive and comprehensive account of the darker races, their customs, institutions and religions, he will receive numerous instances which verify these statements of Peschel.

Fetichism is now common in Central Africa, among the Kaffirs, in Dahomey and among the degraded tribes of Senegal and Congo. At one time or another Fetichism has been common among the Red Indians, the Mexicans, the Germans, the Saxons, the Brahmins, the Hindoos and other tribes. When the Fetich was a household utensil, it was punished, or beaten or broken if misfortune befall its owners, or it did not grant his wish. Says Peschel again, "Before every great enterprise, the Negro of Guinea, if no old and tried fetich is at hand, selects a new one; whatever his eye falls upon as he leaves his house, be it a dog, a cat, or any other creature, he takes as his deity and offers sacrifices to it on the spot. If the enterprise succeeds, the credit of the fetich is increased; if it fails, the fetich returns to its former position." African Fetichism is not different then, from the Fetichism that is found among other peoples and has been found in other ages.

It is but a step, then, from African Fetichism to African Shamanism. If nature was looked upon and regarded as peopled with invisible spirits, who bring not only beneficent results, but also misfortune, calamities, sickness, disease and death upon men; if in the religion of ancestor worship, the departed spirits of ancestors must be propitiated when angry, what more natural than that the primitive savage should seek for some means of counteracting the baleful operations of these evil spirits. In this way, priests or magicians, such as the African Shaman or Indian medicine man, grew up.

The Shaman, by his magic and peculiar medicines, is supposed to be able to cure sickness and disease, prolong life, ward off death, counteract the effect of witchcraft and come into direct communication with evil powers and the spirits of departed ancestors, thus receiving supernatural knowledge.

Says Petchel, "Of all nations the South African Bantus suffer most from this mental malady of Shamanism. Whenever a death occurs, inquiries are made of the Mzango or local Shaman as to its author. . . . When the seer indicates a suspected person, a trial by ordeal takes place, etc." Thus in African Shamanism, no man is regarded as dying from a natural cause; but from the malice of some wizard or some person who sought its evil powers.

African Shamanism is not only the religion of the South African and Bantu Negro, the Australians, Papuans and the Kaffirs, but is the religion of some Siberian tribes of primitive North Asiatic and Central Asiatic tribes, of the Brazilian Piand and of the North American Indians. It is something, that is not peculiar to the Negro *per se*.

Now this native African with tropical and luxuriant imagination, a passionate, sensuous, voluptuous and emotional temperament and nature religion; taking the form of a crude and superstitious Fetichism, was suddenly imported to an alien country as a slave. His condition here has been graphically portrayed by Dr. W. E. B. Du Bois. He says, "Endowed with a rich tropical imagination and a keen delicate appreciation of nature, the transplanted African lived in a world animate with gods, devils, elves and witches, full of strange influences of good to be implored, of evil to be propitiated. Slavery then was to him the dark triumph of evil over him. All the hateful powers of the under world were striving against him and a spirit of revolt and revenge filled his heart. He called up all the resources of heathen sin to aid,—exorcism and witchcraft, the mysterious Obi worship, with its barbarous rites, spells and blood sacrifice even,

now and then, of human victims. Weird midnight orgies and mystic conjurations were invoked, the witch woman and the voodoo priest became the centers of Negro group life and that vein of vague superstition which characterizes the unlettered Negro even to-day was deepened and strengthened."

But this is where I differ from Prof. Du Bois: the conjure woman and voodoo priest were not creations of the American Negroes in their slave life; they were rather modifications of the African Shaman or Medicine Man, who was at the same time judge, physician, priest, magician and wizard. What more natural than that the Negro in his new environment and new sorrows and trials should turn for comfort and solace to his old healer, the African Shaman.

To-day, even in some sections of the Bahama islands and the South, no man or woman is supposed to die of a natural disease, if consumption or typhoid fever takes him off. If rheumatism or paralysis afflicts him some enemy is supposed to work a charm and the conjure man or woman is consulted and sought after.

What Was There in the Environment of the American Negro Which Caused His Religious Development to Take the Form It Did?

We have seen how the native African, following that primal instinct which is common to every primitive race, was led in seeking a cause for every effect to believe in the existence of unseen forces and invisible powers who could help or injure him. We have seen how he worshipped the various objects in nature, or animals in which these supernatural spirits were supposed to reside. We have seen how next he had recourse to the Shamans who were magicians or priests supposed to have the power to ward off the witchcraft of evil-minded persons and the mischievous designs of wizards and departed spirits. We have seen, too, how Negro Voodism, Gopherism and Conjurism is a direct evolution from African Shamanism. And the medicine men and conjure women who were familiar figures on Southern plantations were lineal descendants of the African Shamans.

Prof. W. E. Burghardt Du Bois, the eminent sociologist, in his article upon the religion of the American Negro in the New World for March or June, 1901, gives a graphic and eloquent picture of the transformation of the family and clan life of the newly imported slaves. He there says, "He (the slave) was brought from a definite social environment, the polygamous clan life under the leadership of the chief and the potent influence of the priest. The first rude change in this life was the slave ship and the West Indian sugarfields. The plantation organization replaced the clan, and the tribe and the white master replaced the chief, with his thirst for greater and more despotic powers. Forced and long-continued toil became the rule of life, the old ties of blood relationship and kinship disappeared, and instead of the family appeared a new polygamy and polyandry, which, in some cases, almost reached promiscuity. It was a terrific social revolution, and yet some traces were retained of the former group life, and the chief remaining institution was the priest or medicine man. He early appeared on the plantation and found his function as the healer of the sick, the interpreter of the unknown, the comforter of the sorrowing, the supernatural avenger of wrong and the one who rudely, but picturesquely, expressed the longing, disappointment and resentment of a stolen and oppressed people."

Before we proceed, it will be well for us to make a resume of the ground already covered. We have shown that the genetic method of explaining things by the principle of growth by and through development, the comparative method of showing how all religions necessarily appeal to some fundamental element in human nature is entirely forgotten and lost sight of when we study the Negro's religion, when in reality the Negro's religion is not outside of the stream of the general religious development of mankind. His religion is not, as commonly supposed, a phenomenon that is separate and apart from the historical development of the human race. In his religion, as in the white

man's religion, we see but stages in the evolution of human thought. The colored man is gradually shuffling off his old superstitions and absorbing from his environment materials for further growth. The presentation of a religion whose heaven and hell gave his imagination room to play, the presentation of a God and Saviour who awakened his religious aspiration and satisfied the cravings of his spirit, the songs of Christendom that appealed to his sense of music, the depression of slavery that caused him to lean upon an unseen friend for comfort was what caused the transported African to embrace Christianity.

The depression of slavery caused him to rest his hopes of happiness in heaven. His utter helplessness caused him to lean upon an unseen friend for comfort. And the aspiration and longing and sorrow and cravings of the Negro burst into expression through the jubilee songs and plantation melodies. The emancipation hope may be likened to the Jewish hope of the coming of a Messiah. And the relation between sexual and religious excitement is illustrated in the emotional excitement of the Negro in the ecstasies of the religious fervour.

The consequent effect of the change in the Negro's soul life that was produced by his emancipation upon his religion must be noted. The influence of the American Missionary Association, the Freedman's Aid and Southern Education Society, Wilberforce University, the Presbyterian and Episcopalian churches in giving the Negro an educated ministry, raised the ethical standard of his religion. The general diffusion of intelligence among the masses broadened their faith. But the irreligious tendencies in the new Negro must be noted. The sportive and epicurean tendencies of the young Negro is the reflex manifestation of the irreligion of the present day. The rise of the Gospel of industrialism, of the "Get Cash Gospel," has caused men to forget that man has higher aspiration than feeding his belly; that eating and drinking and sleeping do not circumscribe and limit man's activity. The educated Negro sometimes belongs to church for policy's sake and forgets that religion is the life of God in the soul of man. What is needed is a faith that will suit the intellectual and ethical demands of the twentieth century, a higher gospel than get food, shelter and clothing, get bread and nothing but bread.

There was often a divorce between religion and ethics in the ante-bellum days, and even now the Negro has not sufficiently shaken off the influences of slavery, which disrupted family ties, and has not completely assimilated the civilization and religion of a race that differs in history and tradition from his own. But the day is breaking; the Negro will never completely lose his rich emotional endowment, but his rich emotional life will be a life directed by intelligence and controlled by the will.

Wm. H. Ferris.

Thomas Nelson Page
"The Lynching of Negroes: Its Causes and Prevention"
North American Review 178 (1904)[4]

IN dealing with this question the writer wishes to be understood as speaking not of the respectable and law-abiding element among the negroes, who unfortunately are so often confounded with the body of the race from which come most of the malefactors. To say that negroes furnish most of the ravishers is not to say that all negroes are rapists.

The crime of lynching in this country has, at one time or another, become so frequent that it has aroused the interest of the whole people, and has even arrested the attention of people in other countries. It has usually been caused by the boldness with which crime was committed by lawbreakers, and the inefficiency of the law in dealing with them through its regular forms. Such, for instance, were the acts of the Vigilantes in California in the old days, and such have been the acts of the Vigilantes in other sections of the country at times. In these cases, there has always been a form of trial, which, however hasty, was conclusive on the essential points, of the commission of the crime, the identification of the prisoner, the sentence of "Judge Lynch"—that is, of the mob—and the orderly execution of that sentence. And, in such cases, most persons cognizant of all the conditions and circumstances have found some justification for this "wild justice."

Lynching, however, has never before been so common, nor has it existed over so extended a region as of late years in the South. And it has aroused more feeling outside of that section than was aroused formerly by the work of the Vigilantes. This feeling has undoubtedly been due mainly to the belief, that the lynching has been directed almost exclusively against the negroes; though a part has, perhaps, come from the supposition that the laws were entirely effective, and that, consequently, the lynching of negroes has been the result of irrational hostility or of wanton cruelty. Thus, the matter is, to some extent, complicated by a latent idea that it has a political complexion.

This is the chief ground of complaint in the utterances of the negroes themselves and also of a considerable part of the outside press. And, indeed, for a good while, the lynching of negroes appeared to be confined to the South, though lynching of whites was by no means the monopoly of that section, as may be recalled by those familiar with the history of Indiana and some of the other Northwestern States.

Of late, however, several revolting instances of lynching of negroes in its most dreadful form, burning at the stake, have occurred in regions where hitherto such forms of barbarous punishment have been unknown; and the time appears to be ripe for some efficient concert of action, to eradicate what is recognized by cool heads as a serious menace to our civilization.

In discussing the means to put an end to this barbarity, the first essential is that the matter shall be clearly and thoroughly understood.

The ignorance shown by much of the discussion that has grown out of these lynchings would appear to justify plain speaking.

All thoughtful men know that respect for law is the basic principle of civilization, and are agreed as to the evil of any over-riding of the law. All reasonable men know that the over-riding of law readily creates a spirit of lawlessness, under which progress is retarded and civilization suffers and dwindles. This is as clearly recognized at the South as at the North. To overcome this conviction and stir up rational men to a pitch where the law is trampled under foot, the officers of the law are attacked, and their prisoner taken from them and executed, there must be some imperative cause.

And yet the record of such over-riding of law in the past has been a terrible one.

The Chicago *Tribune* has for some time been collecting statistics on the subject of lynching, and the following table taken from that paper, showing the number of lynchings for a series of years, is assumed to be fairly accurate:

```
1885.................................184
1886.................................138
1887.................................122
1888.................................142
1889.................................176
1890.................................127
1891.................................192
1892.................................235
1893.................................200
1894.................................190
1895.................................171
1896.................................131
1897.................................166
1898.................................127
1899.................................107
1900.................................115
1901.................................135
1902..................................96
1908 (to Sept. 14, eight and a half months) . . 76
```

Total lynchings.		Whites.	Negroes.	In the South.	In the North.
1900	115	8	107	107	8
1901	135	26	107	121	14
1902	96	9	86	87	9
1903 (to Sept. 14)	76	13	63	66	10

Causes Assigned.				
	1900.	1901.*	1902.**	1903.
Murder	39	39	37	32
Rape	18	19	19	8
Attempted rape	13	9	11	5
Race prejudice	10	9	2	3
Assaulting white	6	—	3	3
Threats to kill	5	—	1	—
Burglary	4	1	—	—
Attempt to murder	4	9	4	6
Informing	2	—	—	—
Robbery	2 "Theft"	12	1	—
Complicity and murder	2	6	3	5

Note.—The lynchings in the various States and Territories in 1900 were as follows:

Alabama	8
Arkansas	6
California	0
Colorado	3
Connecticut	0
Delaware	0
Florida	9
Georgia	16
Idaho	0
Illinois	0
Indiana	3
Iowa	0
Kansas	2
Kentucky	1
Louisiana	20
Maine	0
Maryland	1
Massachusetts	0
Michigan	0
Minnesota	0
Mississippi	20
Missouri	2
Montana	0
Nebraska	0
New Jersey	0
New Hampshire	0
New York	0
Nevada	0
North Carolina	3
North Dakota	0
Ohio	0
Oregon	0
Pennsylvania	0
Rhode Island	0
South Carolina	2
South Dakota	0
Tennessee	7
Texas	4
Vermont	0
Virginia	6
West Virginia	2
Wisconsin	0
Washington	0
Wyoming	0

Arizona	0
District of Columbia	0
New Mexico	0
Utah	0
Indian Territory	0
Oklahoma	0
Alaska	0

*In 1901 one Indian and one Chinaman lynched.
**In 1902 one Indian lynched.

From these tables certain facts may be deduced. The first is that, in the year of which an analysis is given (1900), over nine-tenths of the lynchings occurred in the South, where only about one-third of the population of the country were, but where nine-tenths of the negroes were; secondly, that, of these lynchings, about nine-tenths were of negroes and one-third were in the three States where the negroes are most numerous; thirdly, that, while the lynchings appear to be diminishing at the South, the ratio, at least, is increasing at the North.

It further appears that, though lynching began as a punishment for assault on white women, it has extended until less than one-fourth of the instances are for this crime, while over three fourths of them are for murder, attempts at murder, or some less heinous offence. This may be accounted for, in part, by the fact that the murders in the South partake somewhat of the nature of race-conflicts.

Over 2,700 lynchings in eighteen years are enough to stagger the mind. Either we are relapsing into barbarism, or there is some terrific cause for our reversion to the methods of mediævalism, and our laws are inefficient to meet it. The only gleam of light is that, of late years, the number appears to have diminished.

To get at the remedy, we must first get at the cause.

Time was when the crime of assault was unknown throughout the South. During the whole period of slavery, it did not exist, nor did it exist to any considerable extent for some years after Emancipation. During the War, the men were away in the army, and the negroes were the loyal guardians of the women and children. On isolated plantations and in lonely neighbor-hoods, women were as secure as in the streets of Boston or New York.

Then came the period and process of Reconstruction, with its teachings. Among these was the teaching that the negro was the equal of the white, that the white was his enemy, and that he must assert his equality. The growth of the idea was a gradual one in the negro's mind. This was followed by a number of cases where members of the negro militia ravished white women; in some instances in the presence of their families.[6]

The result of the hostility between the Southern whites and Government at that time was to throw the former upon their own acts for their defense or revenge, with a consequent training in lawless punishment of acts which should have been punished by law. And here lynching had its evil origin.

It was suggested some time ago, in a thoughtful paper read by Professor Wilcox, that a condition something like this had its rise in France during the religious wars.

The first instance of rape, outside of these attacks by armed negroes, and of consequent lynching, that attracted the attention of the country was a case which occurred in Mississippi, where the teaching of equality and of violence found one of its most fruitful fields. A negro dragged a woman down into the woods and, tying her, kept her bound there a prisoner for several days, when he butchered her. He was caught and was lynched.

With the resumption of local power by the whites came the temporary and partial ending of the crimes of assault and of lynching.

As the old relation, which had survived even the strain of Reconstruction, dwindled with the passing of the old generation from the stage, and the "New Issue" with the new teaching took its place, the crime broke out again with renewed violence. The idea of equality began to percolate more extensively among the negroes. In evidence of it is the fact that since the assaults began again they have been chiefly directed against the plainer order of people, instances of attacks on women of the

upper class, though not unknown, being of rare occurrence.[7]

Conditions in the South render the commission of this crime peculiarly easy. The white population is sparse, the forests are extensive, the officers of the law distant and difficult to reach but, above all, the negro population has appeared inclined to condone the fact of mere assault.

Twenty-five years ago, women went unaccompanied and unafraid throughout the South, as they still go throughout the North. To-day, no white woman, or girl, or female child, goes alone out of sight of the house except on necessity; and no man leaves his wife alone in his house, if he can help it. Cases have occurred of assault and murder in broad day, within sight and sound of the victim's home. Indeed, an instance occurred not a great while ago in the District of Columbia, within a hundred yards of a fashionable drive, when, about three o'clock of a bright June day, a young girl was attacked within sight and sound of her house, and when she screamed her throat was cut. So near to her home was the spot that her mother and an officer, hearing her cries, reached her before life was extinct.

For a time, the ordinary course of the law was, in the main, relied on to meet the trouble; but it was found that, notwithstanding the inevitable infliction of the death penalty, several evils resulted therefrom. The chief one was that the ravishing of women, instead of diminishing, steadily increased. The criminal, under the ministrations of his preachers, usually professed to have "gotten religion," and from the shadow of the gallows called on his friends to follow him to glory. So that the punishment lost to these emotional people much of its deterrent force, especially where the real sympathy of the race was mainly with the criminal rather than with his victim. Another evil was the dreadful necessity of calling on the innocent victim, who, if she survived, as she rarely did, was already bowed to the earth by shame, to relate in public the story of the assault—an ordeal which was worse than death. Yet another was the delay in the execution of the law. With these, however, was one other which, perhaps, did more than all the rest together to wrest the trial and punishment from the Courts and carry them out by mob violence.

This was the unnamable brutality with which the causing crime was, in nearly every case, attended. The death of the victim of the ravisher was generally the least of the attendant horrors. In Texas, in Mississippi, in Georgia, in Kentucky, in Colorado, as later in Delaware, the facts in the case were so unspeakable that they have never been put in print. They could not be put in print. It is these unnamable horrors which have outraged the minds of those who live in regions where they have occurred, and where they may at any time occur again, and, upsetting reason, have swept from their bearings cool men and changed them into madmen, drunk with the lust of revenge.

Not unnaturally, such barbarity as burning at the stake has shocked the sense of the rest of the country, and, indeed, of the world. But it is well for the rest of the country, and for the world, to know that it has also shocked the sense of the South, and, in their calmer moments, even the sense of those men who, in their frenzy, have been guilty of it. Only, a deeper shock than even this is at the bottom of their ferocious rage—the shock which comes from the ravishing and butchery of their women and children.

It is not necessary to be an apologist for barbarity because one states with bluntness the cause. The stem underlying principle of the people who commit these barbarities is one that has its root deep in the basic passions of humanity; the determination to put an end to the ravishing of their women by an inferior race, no matter what the consequence.

For a time, a speedy execution by hanging was the only mode of retribution resorted to by the lynchers; then, when this failed of its purpose, a more savage method was essayed, born of a savage fury at the failure of the first, and a stern resolve to strike a deeper terror into those whom the other method had failed to awe.

The following may serve as an illustration. Ten or twelve years ago, the writer lectured one afternoon in the early spring in a town in the cotton-belt of Texas—one of the prettiest towns in the Southwest. The lecture was delivered in the Court-house. The writer was introduced by a gentleman who had been a member of the Confederate Cabinet and a Senator of the United States, and the audience was composed of refined and cultured people, representing, perhaps, every State from Maine to Texas. Two days later, the papers contained the account of the burning at the stake in this town of a negro. He had picked up a little girl of five or six years of age on the street where she was playing in front of her home, and carried her off, telling her that her mother had sent him for her; and when she cried, he had soothed her with candy which, with deliberate prevision, he had bought for the purpose. When she was found, she was unrecognizable. With her little body broken and mangled, he had cut her throat and thrown her into a ditch.

A strong effort was made to save him for the law, but without avail: the people had reverted to the primal law of vengeance. Farmers came from fifty miles to see that vengeance was exacted. They had resolved to strike terror into the breasts of all, so that such a crime could never occur again. This was, perhaps, the second or third instance of burning in the country.

Of late, lynching at the stake has spread beyond the region where it has such reason for existence as may be given by the conditions that prevail in the South. Three frightful instances by burning have occurred recently in Northern States, in communities where some of these conditions were partly wanting. The horror of the main fact of lynching was increased, in two of the cases, by a concerted attack on a large element of the negro population which was wholly innocent. Even the unoffending negroes were driven from their homes, a consequence which has never followed in the South, where it might seem there was more occasion for it.

It thus appears that the original crime, and also the consequent one in its most brutal form, are not confined to the South, and, possibly, are only more frequent there because of the greater number of negroes in that section. The deep racial instincts are not limited by geographical bounds.

These last-mentioned lynchings were so ferocious, and so unwarranted by any such necessity, real or fancied, as may be thought to exist at the South by reason of the frequency of assault and the absence of a strong police force, that they not unnaturally called forth almost universal condemnation. The President felt it proper to write an open letter, commending the action of the Governor of Indiana on the proper and efficient exercise of his authority to uphold the law and restore order in his State. But who has ever thought it necessary to commend the Governors of the Southern States under similar circumstances? The militia of some of the Southern States are almost veterans, so frequently have they been called on to protect wretches whose crimes stank in the nostrils of all decent men. The Governor of Virginia boasted, a few years ago, that no lynching should take place during his incumbency, and he nearly made good his boast; though, to do so, he had to call out at one time or another almost the entire force of the State.

Editorials in some of the Eastern papers note with astonishment recent instances where law-officers in the South have protected their prisoners or eluded a mob. The writers of these editorials know so little of the South that one is scarcely surprised at their ignorance. But men are hanged by law for this crime of assault every few months in some State in the South. A few years ago, Sheriff Smith, of Birmingham, protected a murderer at the cost of many lives; a little later, Mayor Prout, of Roanoke, defended a negro ravisher and murderer, and, though the mob finally succeeded in their aim, six men were killed by the guards before the jail was carried. These are only two of the many instances in which brave and faithful officers have, at the risk of their lives, defended their charges against that most terrible of all assailants—a determined mob.[8]

For a time, the assaults by negroes were confined to young women who were caught alone in solitary and secluded places. The company even of a child was sufficient to protect

them. Then the ravishers grew bolder, and attacks followed on women when they were in company. And then, not content with this, the ravishers began to attack women in their own homes. Sundry instances of this have occurred within the last few years. As an illustration, may be cited the notorious case of Samuel Hose, who, after making a bet with a negro preacher that he could have access to a white woman, went into a farmer's house while the family, father, mother and child, were at supper; brained the man with his axe; threw the child into a corner with a violence which knocked it senseless, and ravished the wife and mother with unnamable horrors, butchered her and bore away with him the indisputable proof of having won his wager. He was caught and was burnt.

Another instance, only less appalling, occurred two years ago in Lynchburg, Virginia, where the colored janitor of a white female school, who had been brought up and promoted by the Superintendent of Schools, and was regarded as a shining example of what education might accomplish with his race, entered the house of a respectable man one morning, after the husband, who was a foreman in a factory, had gone to his work; ravished the wife, and, then putting his knee on her breast, coolly cut her throat as he might have done a calf's. There was no attempt at lynching; but the Governor, resolved to preserve the good name of the commonwealth, felt it necessary to order out two regiments of soldiers, in which course he was sustained by the entire sentiment of the State.

These cases were neither worse nor better than many of those which have occurred in the South in the last twenty years, and in that period hundreds of women and a number of children have been ravished and slain.

Now, how is this crime of assault to be stopped? For stopped it must be, and stopped it will be, whatever the cost. One proposition is that separation of the races, complete separation, is the only remedy. The theory appears Utopian. Colonization has been the dream of certain philanthropists for a hundred years. And, meantime, the negroes have increased from less than a million to nine millions. They will never be deported; not because we have not the money, for an amount equal to that spent in pensions during three years would pay the expenses of such deportation, and an amount equal to that paid in six years would set them up in a new country. But the negroes have rights; many of them are estimable citizens; and even the body of them, when well regulated, are valuable laborers. It might, therefore, as well be assumed that this plan will never be carried out, unless the occasion becomes so imperative that all other rights give way to the supreme right of necessity.

It is plain, then, that we must deal with the matter in a more practicable manner, accepting conditions as they are, and applying to them legal methods which will be effective. Lynching does not end ravishing, and that is the prime necessity. Most right thinking men are agreed as to this. Indeed, lynching, through lacking the supreme principle of law, the deliberateness from which is supposed to come the certainty of identification, fails utterly to meet the necessity of the case even as a deterrent. Not only have assaults occurred again and again in the same neighborhood where lynching has followed such crime; but, a few years ago, it was publicly stated that a negro who had just witnessed a lynching for this crime actually committed an assault on his way home. However this may be, lynching as a remedy is a ghastly failure; and its brutalizing effect on the community is incalculable.

The charge that is often made, that the innocent are sometimes lynched, has little foundation. The rage of a mob is not directed against the innocent, but against the guilty; and its fury would not be satisfied with any other sacrifice than the death of the real criminal. Nor does the criminal merit any consideration, however terrible the punishment. The real injury is to the perpetrators of the crime of destroying the law, and to the community in which the law is slain.

It is pretty generally conceded that the "law's delay" is partly responsible for the "wild justice" of mob vengeance, and this has undoubtedly been the cause of many mobs. But it is far from certain if any change in the methods of administration of law will effect the stopping of lynching; while to remedy this evil we may bring about a greater peril. Trial by jury is the bed-rock of our liberties, and the inherent principle of such trial is its deliberateness. It has been said that the whole purpose of the Constitution of Great Britain is that twelve men may sit in the jury-box. The methods of the law may well be reformed; but any movement should be jealously scanned which touches the chief barrier of all liberty. The first step, then, would appear to be the establishment of a system securing a reasonably prompt trial and speedy execution by law, rather than a wholesale revolution of the existing system.

Many expedients have been suggested; some of the most drastic by Northern men. One of them proposed, not long since, that to meet the mob-spirit, a trial somewhat in the nature of a drumhead court-martial might be established by law, by which the accused may be tried and, if found guilty, executed immediately. Others have proposed as a remedy emasculation by law; while a Justice of the Supreme Court has recently given the weight of his personal opinion in favor of prompt trial and the abolishment of appeals in such cases. Even the terrible suggestion has been made that burning at the stake might be legalized!

These suggestions testify how grave the matter is considered to be by those who make them.

But none of these, unless it be the one relating to emasculation, is more than an expedient. The trouble lies deeper. The crime of lynching is not likely to cease until the crime of ravishing and murdering women and children is less frequent than it has been of late. And this crime, which is well-nigh wholly confined to the negro race, will not greatly diminish until the negroes themselves take it in hand and stamp it out.

From recent developments, it may be properly inferred that the absence of this crime during the period of Slavery was due more to the feeling among the negroes themselves than to any repressive measures on the part of the whites. The negro had the same animal instincts in Slavery that he exhibits now; the punishment that follows the crime now is as certain, as terrible, and as swift as it could have been then. So, to what is due the alarming increase of this terrible brutality?

To the writer it appears plain that it is due to two things: first, to racial antagonism and to the talk of social equality, from which it first sprang, that inflames the ignorant negro, who has grown up unregulated and undisciplined; and, secondly, to the absence of a strong restraining public opinion among the negroes of any class, which alone can extirpate the crime. In the first place, the negro does not generally believe in the virtue of women. It is beyond his experience. He does not generally believe in the existence of actual assault. It is beyond his comprehension. In the next place, his passion, always his controlling force, is now, since the new teaching, for the white woman.[9]

That there are many negroes who are law-abiding and whose influence is for good, no one who knows the worthy members of the race, those who represent the better element, will deny. But while there are, of course, notable exceptions, they are not often of the "New Issue," nor even generally among the prominent leaders: those who publish papers and control conventions.

As the crime of rape had its baleful origin in the teaching of equality and the placing of power in the ignorant negroes' hands, so its perpetration and increase have undoubtedly been due in large part to the same teaching. The intelligent negro may understand what social equality truly means; but to the ignorant and brutal young negro, it signifies but one thing: the opportunity to enjoy, equally with white men, the privilege of cohabiting with white women. This the whites of the South understand; and if it were understood abroad, it would serve to explain some things which have not been understood hitherto. It will explain; in part, the universal and furious hostility of the South to even the least suggestion of social equality.

A close following of the instances of rape and lynching, and the public discussion consequent thereon, has led the writer to the painful realization that even the leaders of the negro race—at least, those who are prominent enough to hold conventions and write papers on the subject—have rarely, by act or word, shown a true appreciation of the enormity of the crime of ravishing and murdering women. Their discussion and denunciation have been almost invariably and exclusively devoted to the crime of lynching. Underlying most of their protests is the suggestion, that the victim of the mob is innocent and a martyr. Now and then, there is a mild generalization on the evil of lawbreaking and the violation of women; but, for one stern word of protest against violating women and cutting their throats, the records of negro meetings will show many against the attack of the mob on the criminal. And, as to any serious and determined effort to take hold of and stamp out the crime that is blackening the entire negro race to-day, and arousing against them the fatal and possibly the undying enmity of the stronger race, there is, with the exception of the utterances of a few score individuals like Booker Washington, who always speaks for the right, Hannibal Thomas and Bishop Turner, hardly a trace of such a thing. A crusade has been preached against lynching, even as far as England; but none has been thought of against the ravishing and tearing to pieces of white women and children.

Happily, there is an element of sound-minded, law-abiding negroes, representative of the old negro, who without parade stand for good order, and do what they can to repress lawlessness among their people. But for this class and the kindly relations which are preserved between them and the whites, the situation in the South would long since have become unbearable. These, however, are not generally among the leaders, and, unfortunately, their influence is not sufficiently extended to counteract the evil influences which are at work with such fatal results.

One who reads the utterances of negro orators and preachers on the subject of lynching, and who knows the negro race, cannot doubt that, at bottom, their sympathy is generally with the "victim" of the mob, and not with his victim.

Until the negroes shall create among themselves a sound public opinion which, instead of fostering, shall reprobate and sternly repress the crime of assaulting women and children, the crime will never be extirpated, and until this crime is stopped the crime of lynching will never be extirpated. Lynching will never be done away with while the sympathy of the whites is with the lynchers, and no more will ravishing be done away with while the sympathy of the negroes is with the ravisher. When the negroes shall stop applying all their energies to harboring and defending negroes, no matter what their crime so it be against the whites, and shall distinguish between the law-abiding negro and the law-breaker, a long step will have been taken.

Should the negroes sturdily and faithfully set themselves to prevent the crime of rape by members of that race, it could be stamped out. Should the whites set themselves against lynching, lynching would be stopped. The remedy then is plain. Let the negroes take charge of the crime of ravishing and firmly put it away from them, and let the whites take charge of the crime of lynching and put it away from them. It is time that the races should address themselves to the task; for it is with nations as with individual men; whatsoever they sow that shall they also reap.

It is the writer's belief that the arrest and the prompt handing over to the law of negroes by negroes, for assault on white women, would do more to break up ravishing, and to restore amicable relations between the two races, than all the resolutions of all the Conventions and all the harangues of all the politicians.

It has been tried in various States to put an end to lynching by making the county in which the lynching occurs liable in damages for the crime. It is a good theory; and, if it has not worked well, it is because of the difficulty of executing the provision. Could some plan be devised to array each race against the crime to which it is prone, both rape and lynching might be diminished, if not wholly prevented.

The practical application of such a principle is difficult, but, perhaps, it is not impossible. It is possible that in every community negroes might be appointed officers of the law, to look exclusively after lawbreakers of their own race. The English in the East manage such matters well, under equally complicated and delicate conditions. For example, in the Island of Malta, where the population are of different classes among whom a certain jealousy exists, there are several classes of police: the naval police, the military police, and the civil or municipal police. To each of these is assigned more especially the charge of one of the three classes of whom the population of the Island is composed. Again, in Hong Kong, where the situation is even more delicate, there are several classes of police: the English, the Chinese, and the Indian police. Only the first are empowered to make general arrests; the others have powers relating exclusively to the good order of the races to which they belong, though they may in all cases be called in to assist the English police.

Somewhat in the same way, the negroes might be given within their province powers sufficiently full to enable them to keep order among their people, and they might on the other hand be held to a certain accountability for such good order. It might even be required that every person should be listed and steadily kept track of, as is done in Germany at present. The recent vagrant laws of Georgia, where there are more negroes than in the entire North, are an attempt in this direction.

In the same way, the white officials charged with the good order of the county or town might be given enlarged powers of summoning posses, and might be held to a high accountability. For example, *ipso facto* forfeiture of the official bond and removal from office, with perpetual disability to hold any office again, might be provided as a penalty for permitting any persons to be taken out of their hands.

Few ravishings by negroes would occur if the more influential members of the race were held accountable for the good order of their race in every community; and few lynchings would occur, at least after the prisoners were in the hands of the officers of the law, if those officers, by the mere fact of relinquishing their prisoners should be disqualified from ever holding office again. These suggestions may be as Utopian as others which have been made; but if they cannot be carried out, it is because the ravishings by negroes and the murders by mobs have their roots so deep in racial instincts that nothing can eradicate them, and in such case the ultimate issue will be a resort to the final rest of might, which in the last analysis underlies everything.

Thomas Nelson Page.

Mary Church Terrell
"Lynching from a Negro's Point of View"

North American Review 178 (1904)[10]

By Mary Church Terrell, Honorary President of the National Association of Colored Women.

Before 1904 was three months old, thirty-one negroes had been lynched. Of this number, fifteen were murdered within one week in Arkansas, and one was shot to death in Springfield, Ohio, by a mob composed of men who did not take the trouble to wear masks. Hanging, shooting and burning black men, women and children in the United States have become so common that such occurrences create but little sensation and evoke but slight comment now. Those who are jealous of their country's fair name feel keenly the necessity of extirpating this lawlessness, which is so widespread and has taken such deep root. But means of prevention can never be devised, until the cause of lynching is more generally understood.

The reasons why the whole subject is deeply and seriously involved in error are obvious. Those who live in the section where nine-tenths of the lynchings occur do not dare to tell the truth, even if they perceive it. When men know that the death-knell of their aspirations and hopes will be sounded as soon as they express views to which the majority in their immediate vicinage are opposed, they either suppress their views or trim them to fit the popular mind. Only martyrs are brave and bold enough to defy the public will, and the manufacturer of martyrs in the negro's behalf is not very brisk just now.

Those who do not live in the section where most of the lynchings occur borrow their views from their brothers who do, and so the errors are continually repeated and inevitably perpetuated.

In the discussion of this subject, four mistakes are commonly made.

In the first place, it is a great mistake to suppose that rape is the real cause of lynching in the South. Beginning with the Ku-Klux Klan, the negro has been constantly subjected to some form of organized violence ever since he became free. It is easy to prove that rape is simply the pretext and not the cause of lynching. Statistics show that, out of every hundred negroes who are lynched, from seventy-five to eighty-five are not even accused of this crime, and many who are accused of it are innocent. And, yet, men who admit the accuracy of these figures gravely tell the country that lynching can never be suppressed, until negroes cease to commit a crime with which less than one-fourth of those murdered by mobs are charged.

The prevailing belief that negroes are not tortured by mobs unless they are charged with the "usual" crime, does not tally with the facts. The savagery which attended the lynching of a man and his wife the first week in March of the present year was probably never exceeded in this country or anywhere else in the civilized world. A white planter was murdered at Dodds-ville, Miss., and a negro was charged with the crime. The negro fled, and his wife, who was known to be innocent, fled with him to escape the fate which she knew awaited her, if she re-mained. The two negroes were pursued and captured, and the following account of the trag-edy by an eye-witness appeared in the "Evening Post," a Democratic daily of Vicksburg, Miss.

When the two negroes were captured, they were tied to trees, and while the funeral pyres were being prepared they were forced to suffer the most fiendish tortures. The blacks were forced to hold out their hands while one finger at a time was chopped off. The fingers were distributed as souvenirs. The ears of the murderers were cut off. Hol-bert was beaten severely, his skull was fractured, and one of his eyes, knocked out with a stick, hung by a shred form the socket. Neither the man nor the woman begged for mercy, nor made a groan or plea. When the executioner came forward to lop off fingers, Holbert extended his hand without being asked. The most excru-ciating form of punishment consisted in the use of a large corkscrew in the hands of some of the mob. This instrument was bored into the flesh of the man and the woman, in the arms, legs and body, and then pulled out, the spirals tearing out big pieces of raw, quivering flesh every time it was withdrawn. Even this devilish torture did not make the poor brutes cry out. When finally they were thrown on the fire and allowed to be burned to death, this came as a relief to the maimed and suffer-ing victims.

The North frequently sympathizes with the Southern mob, because it has been led to believe the negro's diabolical assaults upon white women are the chief cause of lynching. In spite of the facts, distinguished representatives from the South are still insisting, in Congress and elsewhere, that "whenever negroes, cease com-mitting the crime of rape, the lynchings and burnings will cease with it." But since three-fourths of the negroes who have met a violent death at the hands of Southern mobs have not been accused of this crime, it is evident that, in-stead of being the "usual" crime, rape is the most unusual of all the crimes for which ne-groes are shot, hanged and burned.

Although Southern men of prominence still insist that "this crime is more responsible for mob violence than all other crimes com-bined," it is gratifying to observe that a few of them, at least, are beginning to feel ashamed to pervert the facts. During the past few years, several Southern gentlemen, of unquestioned ability and integrity, have publicly exposed the falsity of this plea. Two years ago, in a masterful article on the race problem, Profes-sor Andrew Sledd, at that time an instructor in a Southern college, admitted that only a small number of the negroes who are lynched are even accused of assaulting white women. Said he:

On the contrary, a frank consideration of all the facts, with no other desire than to find the truth, the whole truth and nothing but the truth, however contrary to our wishes and humiliating to our section the truth may be, will show that by far the most of our Southern lynchings are carried through in *sheer, unqualified and increasing brutality*.

But a heavy penalty was paid by this man who dared to make such a frank and fearless statement of facts. He was forced to resign his position as professor, and lost prestige in his section in various ways. In the summer of 1903, Bishop Candler of Georgia made a strong pro-test against lynching, and called attention to the fact that, out of 128 negroes who had been done to death in 1901, only 16 were even accused of rape.

In the second place, it is a mistake to sup-pose that the negro's desire for social equality sustains any relation whatsoever to the crime of rape. According to the testimony of eye-witnesses, as well as the reports of Southern newspapers, the negroes who are known to have been guilty of assault have, as a rule, been ignorant, repulsive in appearance and as near the brute creation as it is possible for a human being to be. It is safe to assert that, among the negroes who have been guilty of ravishing white women, not one had been taught that he was the equal of white people or had ever heard of social equality. And if by chance he had heard of it, he had no clearer conception of its meaning than he had of the principle of the binomial theorem. In conversing with a large number of ignorant negroes, the writer has never found one who seemed to have any idea of what social equality means, or who expressed a desire to put this theory into practice when it was explained to him.

Negroes who have been educated in Northern institutions of learning with white men and women, and who for that reason might have learned the meaning of social equality and have acquired a taste for the same, neither assault white women nor commit other crimes, as a rule. A careful review of the facts will show that negroes who have the "convention habit" developed to a high degree, or who are able to earn their living by editing newspapers, do not belong to the criminal class, although such negroes are always held up by Southern Gentlemen as objects of ridicule, contempt and scorn. Strange as it may appear, illiterate negroes, who are the only ones contributing largely to the criminal class, are coddled and caressed by the South. To the educated, cultivated members of the race, they are held up as bright and shining examples of what a really good negro should be. The dictionary is searched in vain by Southern gentlemen and gentlewomen for words sufficiently ornate and strong to express their admiration for a dear old "mammy" or a faithful old "uncle," who can neither read nor write, and who assure their white friends they would not, if they could.

On the other hand, no language is sufficiently caustic, bitter and severe, to express the disgust, hatred and scorn which Southern gentlemen feel for what is called the "New Issue," which, being interpreted, means, negroes who aspire to knowledge and culture, and who have acquired a taste for the highest and best things

in life. At the door of this "New Issue," the sins and shortcomings of the whole race are laid. This "New Issue" is beyond hope of redemption, we are told, because somebody, nobody knows who, has taught it to believe in social equality, something, nobody knows what. The alleged fear of social equality has always been used by the South to explain its unchristian treatment of the negro and to excuse its many crimes. How many crimes have been committed, and how many falsehoods have been uttered, in the name of social equality by the South! Of all these, the greatest is the determination to lay lynching at its door. In the North, which is the only section that accords the negro the scrap of social equality enjoyed by him in the United States, he is rarely accused of rape. The only form of social equality ever attempted between the two races, and practised to any considerable extent, is that which was originated by the white masters of slave women, and which has been perpetuated by them and their descendants even unto the present day. Of whatever other crime we may accuse the big, black burly brute, who is so familiar a figure in the reports of rape and lynching-bees sent out by the Southern press, surely we cannot truthfully charge him with an attempt to introduce social equality into this republican form of government, or to foist it upon a democratic land. There is no more connection between social equality and lynching to-day than there was between social equality and slavery before the war, or than there is between social equality and the convict-lease system, or any other form of oppression to which the negro has uniformly been subjected in the South.

The third error on the subject of lynching consists of the widely circulated statement that the moral sensibilities of the best negroes in the United States are so stunted and dull, and the standard of morality among even the leaders of the race is so low, that they do not appreciate the enormity and heinousness of rape. Those who claim to know the negro best and to be his best friends declare, that he usually sympathizes with the black victim of mob violence rather than with the white victim of the black fiend's lust, even when he does not go so far as to condone the crime of rape. Only those who are densely ignorant of the standards and sentiments of the best negroes, or who wish wilfully to misrepresent and maliciously to slander a race already resting under burdens greater than it can bear, would accuse its thousands of reputable men and women of sympathizing with rapists, either black or white, or of condoning their crime. The negro preachers and teachers who have had the advantage of education and moral training, together with others occupying positions of honor and trust, are continually expressing their horror of this one particular crime, and exhorting all whom they can reach by voice or pen to do everything in their power to wash the ugly stain of rape from the race's good name. And whenever the slightest pity for the victim of mob violence is expressed by a negro who represents the intelligence and decency of his race, it is invariably because there is a reasonable doubt of his innocence, rather than because there is condonation of the alleged crime.

Everybody who is well informed on the subject of lynching knows that many a negro who has been accused of assault or murder, or other violation of the law, and has been tortured to death by a mob, has afterward been proved innocent of the crime with which he was charged. So great is the thirst for the negro's blood in the South, that but a single breath of suspicion is sufficient to kindle into an all-consuming flame the embers of hatred every smouldering in the breasts of the fiends who compose a typical mob. When once such a bloodthirsty company starts on a negro's trail, and the right one cannot be found, the first available specimen is sacrificed to their rage, no matter whether he is guilty or not.

A white man who died near Charleston, South Carolina, in March of the present year, confessed on his death-bed that he had murdered his wife, although three negroes were lynched for this crime at Ravenel, South Carolina, in May, 1902. This murder was one of the most brutal ever committed in the State, and the horrible tortures to which the three innocent negroes were subjected indicated plainly that the mob intended the punishment to fit the crime. In August, 1901, three negroes, a mother, her daughter and her son, were lynched in Carrollton, Miss., because it was rumored that they had heard of a murder before it was committed, and had not reported it. A negro was accused of murdering a woman, and was lynched in Shreveport, Louisiana, in April, 1902, who was afterward proved innocent. The woman who was lynched in Mississippi this year was not even accused of a crime. The charge of murder had not been proved against her husband, and, as the white man who was murdered had engaged in an altercation with him, it is quite likely that, if the negro had been tried in a court of law, it would have been shown to be a case of justifiable homicide. And so other cases might easily be cited to prove that the charge that innocent negroes are sometimes lynched is by no means without foundation. It is not strange, therefore, that even reputable, law-abiding negroes should protest against the tortures and cruelties inflicted by mobs which wreak vengeance upon the guilty and innocent and upon the just and unjust of their race alike. It is to the credit and not to the shame of the negro that he tries to uphold the sacred majesty of the law, which is so often trailed in the dust and trampled under foot by white mobs.

In the fourth place, it is well to remember, in discussing the subject of lynching, that it is not always possible to ascertain the facts from the accounts in the newspapers. The facts are often suppressed, intentionally or unintentionally, or distorted by the press. The case of Sam Hose, to which reference has so often been made, is a good illustration of the unreliability of the press in reporting the lynching of negroes. Sam Hose, a negro, murdered Alfred Cranford, a white man, in a dispute over wages which the white employer refused to pay the colored workman. It was decided to make an example of a negro who dared to kill a white man. A well-known, influential newspaper immediately offered a reward of $500 for the capture of Sam Hose. This same newspaper predicted a lynching, and stated that, though several modes of punishment had been suggested, it was the consensus of opinion that the negro should be burned at the stake and tortured before being burned. A rumor was started, and circulated far and wide by the press, that Sam Hose had assaulted the wife of Alfred Cranford, after the latter had been killed. One of the best detectives in Chicago was sent to Atlanta to investigate the affair. After securing all the information it was possible to obtain from black and white alike, and carefully weighing the evidence, this white detective declared it would have been a physical impossibility for the negro to assault the murdered man's wife, and expressed it as his opinion that the charge of assault was an invention intended to make the burning a certainty.

The Sunday on which Sam Hose was burned was converted into a holiday. Special trains were made up to take the Christian people of Atlanta to the scene of the burning, a short distance from the city. After the first train moved out with every inch of available space inside and out filled to overflowing, a second had to be made up, so as to accommodate those who had just come from church. After Sam Hose had been tortured and burned to death, the great concourse of Christians who had witnessed the tragedy scraped for hours among his ashes in the hope of finding a sufficient number of his bones to take to their friends as souvenirs. The charge has been made that Sam Hose boasted to another negro that he intended to assault Alfred Cranford's wife. It would be difficult for anybody who understands conditions in the South to believe that a sane negro would announce his purpose to violate a white woman there, then deliberately enter her husband's house, while all the family were present, to carry out his threat.

Two years ago a riot occurred in Atlanta, Georgia, in which four white policemen were killed and several wounded by a colored man named Richardson, who was himself finally burned to death. Through the press the public was informed that the negro was a desperado. As a matter of fact, Richardson was a merchant, well to do and law-abiding. The head and front

of his offending was that he dared to reprimand an ex-policeman for living in open adultery with a colored woman. When it was learned that this negro had been so impudent to a white man, the sheriff led out a posse, consisting of the city police, to arrest Richardson. Seeing the large number of officers surrounding his house, and knowing what would be his fate, if caught, the negro determined to sell his life dear, and he did. With the exception of the Macon "Telegraph," but few white newspapers ever gave the real cause of the riot, and so Richardson has gone down to history as a black desperado, who shot to death four officers of the law and wounded as many more. Several years ago, near New Orleans, a negro was at work in a cornfield. In working through the corn he made considerable noise, which frightened a young white woman, who happened to be passing by. She ran to the nearest house, and reported that a negro had jumped at her. A large crowd of white men immediately shouldered guns and seized the negro, who had no idea what it meant. When told why he was taken, the negro protested that he had not even seen the girl whom he was accused of frightening, but his protest was of no avail and he was hanged to the nearest tree. The press informed the country that this negro was lynched for attempted rape. Instance after instance might be cited to prove that facts bearing upon lynching, as well as upon other phases of the race problem, are often garbled—without intention, perhaps—by the press.

What, then, is the cause of lynching? At the last analysis, it will be discovered that there are just two causes of lynching. In the first place, it is due to race hatred, the hatred of a stronger people toward a weaker who were once held as slaves. In the second place, it is due to the lawlessness so prevalent in the section where nine-tenths of the lynchings occur. View the question of lynching from any point of view one may, and it is evident that it is just as impossible for the negroes of this country to prevent mob violence by any attitude of mind which they may assume, or any course of conduct which they may pursue, as it is for a straw dam to stop Niagara's flow. Upon the same spirit of intolerance and of hatred the crime of lynching must be fastened as that which called into being the Ku-Klux Klan, and which has prompted more recent exhibitions of hostility toward the negro, such as the disfranchisement acts, the Jim Crow Car Laws, and the new slavery called "peonage," together with other acts of oppression which make the negro's lot so hard.

Lynching is the aftermath of slavery. The white men who shoot negroes to death and flay them alive, and the white women who apply flaming torches to their oil-soaked bodies today, are the sons and daughters of women who had but little, if any, compassion on the race when it was enslaved. The men who lynch negroes to-day are, as a rule, the children of women who sat by their firesides happy and proud in the possession and affection of their own children, while they looked with unpitying eye and adamantine heart upon the anguish of slave mothers whose children had been sold away, when not overtaken by a sadder fate. If it be contended, as it often is, that negroes are rarely lynched by the descendants of former slaveholders, it will be difficult to prove the point. According to the reports of lynchings sent out by the Southern press itself, mobs are generally composed of the "best citizens" of a place, who quietly disperse to their homes as soon as they are certain that the negro is good and dead. The newspaper who predicted that Sam Hose would be lynched, which offered a reward for his capture and which suggested burning at the stake, was neither owned nor edited by the poor whites. But if it be conceded that the descendants of slaveholders do not shoot and burn negroes, lynching must still be regarded as the legitimate offspring of slavery. If the children of the poor whites of the South are the chief aggressors in the lynching-bees of that section, it is because their ancestors were brutalized by their slaveholding environment. In discussing the lynching of negroes at the present time, the heredity and the environment, past and present, of the white mobs are not taken sufficiently into account. It is as impossible to comprehend the cause of the ferocity and barbarity which attend the average lynching-bee without taking into account the brutalizing effect of slavery upon the people of the section where most of the lynchings occur, as it is to investigate the essence and nature of fire without considering the gases which cause the flame to ignite. It is too much to expect, perhaps, that the children of women who for generations looked upon the hardships and the degradation of their sisters of a darker hue with few if any protests, should have mercy and compassion upon the children of that oppressed race now. But what a tremendous influence for law and order, and what a mighty foe to mob violence Southern white women might be, if they would arise in the purity and power of their womanhood to implore their fathers, husbands and sons no longer to stain their hands with the black man's blood!

While the men of the South were off fighting to keep the negro in bondage, their mothers, wives and daughters were entrusted to the black man's care. How faithfully and loyally he kept his sacred trust the records of history attest! Not a white woman was violated throughout the entire war. Can the white women of the South forget how black men bore themselves throughout that trying time? Surely it is not too much to ask that the daughters of mothers who were shielded from harm by the black man's constancy and care should requite their former protectors, by at least asking that, when the children of the latter are accused of crime, they should be treated like human beings and not like wild animals to be butchered and shot.

If there were one particularly heinous crime for which an infuriated people took vengeance upon the negro, or if there were a genuine fear that a guilty negro might escape the penalty of the law in the South, then it might be possible to explain the cause of lynching on some other hypothesis than that of race hatred. It has already been shown that the first supposition has no foundation in fact. It is easy to prove that the second is false. Even those who condone lynching do not pretend to fear the delay or the uncertainty of the law, when a guilty negro is concerned. With the courts of law entirely in the hands of the white man, with judge and jury belonging to the superior race, a guilty negro could no more extricate himself from the meshes of the law in the South than he could slide from the devil-fish's embrace or slip from the anaconda's coils. Miscarriage of justice in the South is possible only when white men transgress the law.

In addition to lynching, the South is continually furnishing proof of its determination to wreak terrible vengeance upon the negro. The recent shocking revelations of the extent to which the actual enslavement of negroes has been carried under the peonage system of Alabama and Mississippi, and the unspeakable cruelties to which men, women and children are alike subjected, all bear witness to this fact. In January of the present year, a government detective found six negro children ranging in age from six to sixteen years working on a Georgia plantation in bare feet, scantily clad in rags, although the ground was covered with snow. The owner of the plantation is one of the wealthiest men in northeast Georgia, and is said to have made his fortune by holding negroes in slavery. When he was tried it was shown that the white planter had killed the father of the six children a few years before, but was acquitted of the murder, as almost invariably happens, when a white man takes a negro's life. After the death of their father, the children were treated with incredible cruelty. They were often chained in a room without fire and were beaten until the blood steamed from their backs, when they were unable to do their stint of work. The planter was placed under $5,000 bail, but it is doubtful whether he will ever pay the penalty of his crime. Like the children just mentioned hundreds of negroes are to-day groaning under a bondage more crushing and more cruel than that abolished forty years ago.

This same spirit manifests itself in a variety of ways. Efforts are constantly making to curtail the educational opportunities of colored children. Already one State has enacted a law by which colored children in the public schools are prohibited from receiving instruction higher than the sixth grade, and other States will,

doubtless, soon follow this lead. It is a well-known fact that a Governor recently elected in one of the Southern States owes his popularity and his votes to his open and avowed opposition to the education of negroes. Instance after instance might be cited to prove that the hostility toward the negro in the South is bitter and pronounced, and that lynching is but a manifestation of this spirit of vengeance and intolerance in its ugliest and most brutal form.

To the widespread lawlessness among the white people of the South lynching is also due. In commenting upon the blood-guiltiness of South Carolina, the Nashville "American" declared some time ago that, if the killings in the other States had been in the same ratio to population as in South Carolina, a larger number of people would have been murdered in the United States during 1902 than fell on the American side in the Spanish and Philippine wars.

Whenever Southern white people discuss lynching, they are prone to slander the whole negro race. Not long ago, a Southern writer of great repute declared without qualification or reservation that "the crime of rape is well-nigh wholly confined to the negro race," and insisted that "negroes furnish most of the ravishers." These assertions are as unjust to the negro as they are unfounded in fact. According to statistics recently published, only one colored male in 100,000 over five years of age was accused of assault upon a white woman in the South in 1902, whereas one male out of every 20,000 over five years of age was charged with rape in Chicago during the same year. If these figures prove anything at all, they show that the men and boys in Chicago are many times more addicted to rape than are the negroes in the South. Already in the present year two white men have been arrested in the national capital for attempted assault upon little children. One was convicted and sentenced to six years in the penitentiary. The crime of which the other was accused was of the most infamous character. A short account of the trial of the convicted man appeared in the Washington dailies, as any other criminal suit would have been reported; but if a colored man had committed the same crime, the newspapers from one end of the United States to the other would have published it broadcast. Editorials upon the total depravity and the hopeless immorality of the negro would have been written, based upon this particular case as a text. With such facts to prove the falsity of the charge that "the crime of rape is well-nigh wholly confined to the negro race," it is amazing that any writer of repute should affix his signature to such a slander.

But even if the negro's morals were as loose and as lax as some claim them to be, and if his belief in the virtue of women were as slight as we are told, the South has nobody to blame but itself. The only object lesson in virtue and morality which the negro received for 250 years came through the medium of slavery, and that peculiar institution was not calculated to set his standards of correct living very high. Men do not gather grapes of thorns nor figs of thistles. Throughout their entire period of bondage colored women were debauched by their masters. From the day they were liberated to the present time, prepossessing young colored girls have been considered the rightful prey of white gentlemen in the South, and they have been protected neither by public sentiment nor by law. In the South, the negro's home is not considered sacred by the superior race. White men are neither punished for invading it, nor lynched for violating colored women and girls. In discussing this phase of the race problem last year, one of the most godly and eloquent ministers in the Methodist Episcopal Church (white) expressed himself as follows: "The negro's teachers have been white. It is from the white man the negro has learned to lie and steal. If you wish to know who taught the negro licentiousness, you have only to look into the faces of thousands of mulatto people and get your answer." When one thinks how the negro was degraded in slavery, which discouraged, when it did not positively forbid, marriage between slaves, and considers the bad example set them by white masters, upon whom the negroes looked as scarcely lower than the angels, the freedman's self-control seems almost like a miracle of modern times. In demanding so much of the negro, the

South places itself in the anomalous position of insisting that the conduct of the inferior race shall be better, and its standards higher, than those of the people who claim to be superior.

The recent lynching in Springfield, Ohio, and in other cities of the North, show how rapidly this lawlessness is spreading throughout the United States. If the number of Americans who participate in this wild and diabolical carnival of blood does not diminish, nothing can prevent this country from becoming a byword and a reproach throughout the civilized world. When Secretary Hay appealed to Roumania in behalf of the Jews, there were many sarcastic comments made by the press of that country and of other foreign lands about the inhuman treatment of the negro in the United States. In November, 1903, a manifesto signed by delegates from all over the world was issued at Brussels, Belgium, by the International Socialist Bureau, protesting against the lynching of negroes in the United States.

It is a source of deep regret and sorrow to many good Christians in this country that the church puts forth so few and such feeble protests against lynching. As the attitude of many ministers on the question of slavery greatly discouraged the abolitionists before the war, so silence in the pulpit concerning the lynching of negroes to-day plunges many of the persecuted race into deep gloom and dark despair. Thousands of dollars are raised by our churches every year to send missionaries to Christianize the heathen in foreign lands, and this is proper and right. But in addition to this foreign missionary work, would it not be well for our churches to inaugurate a crusade against the barbarism at home, which converts hundreds of white women and children into savages every year, while it crushes the spirit, blights the hearth and breaks the heart of hundreds of defenseless blacks? Not only do ministers fail, as a rule, to protest strongly against the hanging and burning of negroes, but some actually condone the crime without incurring the displeasure of their congregations or invoking the censure of the church. Although the church court which tried the preacher in Wilmington, Delaware, accused of inciting his community to riot and lynching by means of an incendiary sermon, found him guilty of "unministerial and unchristian conduct," of advocating mob murder and of thereby breaking down the public respect for the law, yet it simply admonished him to be "more careful in the future" and inflicted no punishment at all. Such indifference to lynching on the part of the church recalls the experience of Abraham Lincoln, who refused to join church in Springfield, Illinois, because only three out of twenty-two ministers in the whole city stood with him in his effort to free the slave. But, however unfortunate may have been the attitude of some of the churches on the question of slavery before the war, from the moment the shackles fell from the black man's limbs to the present day, the American Church has been most kind and generous in its treatment of the backward and struggling race. Nothing but ignorance or malice could prompt one to disparage the efforts put forth by the churches in the negro's behalf. But, in the face of so much lawlessness today, surely there is a rôle [*sic*] for the Church Militant to play. When one reflects upon the large number of negroes who are yearly hurled into eternity, unshriven by priest and untried by law, one cannot help realizing that as a nation we have fallen upon grave times, indeed. Surely, it is time for the ministers in their pulpits and the Christians in their pews to fall upon their knees and pray for deliverance from this rising tide of barbarism which threatens to deluge the whole land.

How can lynching be extirpated in the United States? There are just two ways in which this can be accomplished. In the first place, lynching can never be suppressed in the South, until the masses of ignorant white people in that section are educated and lifted to a higher moral plane. It is difficult for one who has not seen these people to comprehend the density of their ignorance and the depth of their degradation. A well-known white author who lives in the South describes them as follows:

Wholly ignorant, absolutely without culture, apparently without even the capacity to appreciate the nicer feelings or higher sense, yet conceited on account of their white skin which they constantly dishonor, they make, when aroused, as wild and brutal a mob as ever disgraced the face of the earth.

In lamenting the mental backwardness of the white people of the South, the Atlanta "Constitution" expressed itself as follows two years ago: "We have as many illiterate white men over the age of twenty-one years in the South to-day as there were fifty-two years ago, when the census of 1850 was taken." Over against these statistics stands the record of the negro, who has reduced his illiteracy 44.5 per cent in forty years. The hostility which has always existed between the poor whites and the negroes of the South has been greatly intensified in these latter days, by the material and intellectual advancement of the negro. The wrath of a Spanish bull, before whose maddened eyes a red flag is flaunted, is but a feeble attempt at temper compared with the seething, boiling rage of the average white man in the South who beholds a well-educated negro dressed in fine or becoming clothes. In the second place, lynching cannot be suppressed in the South until all classes of white people who dwell there, those of high as well as middle and low degree, respect the rights of other human beings, no matter what may be the color of their skin, become merciful and just enough to cease their persecution of a weaker race and learn a holy reverence for the law.

It is not because American people are cruel, as a whole, or indifferent on general principles to the suffering of the wronged or oppressed, that outrages against the negro are permitted to occur and go unpunished, but because many are ignorant of the extent to which they are carried, while others despair of eradicating them. The South has so industriously, persistently and eloquently preached the inferiority of the negro, that the North has apparently been converted to this view—the thousands of negroes of sterling qualities, moral worth and lofty patriotism to the contrary notwithstanding. The South has insisted so continuously and belligerently that it is the negro's best friend, that it understands him better than other people on the face of the earth and that it will brook interference from nobody in its method of dealing with him, that the North has been persuaded or intimidated into bowing to this decree.

Then, too, there seems to be a decline of the great convictions in which this government was conceived and into which it was born. Until there is a renaissance of popular belief in the principles of liberty and equality upon which this government was founded, lynching, the Convict Lease System, the Disfranchisement Acts, the Jim Crow Car Laws, unjust discriminations in the professions and trades and simi-

lar atrocities will continue to dishearten and degrade the negro, and stain the fair name of the United States. For there can be no doubt that the greatest obstacle in the way of extirpating lynching is the general attitude of the public mind toward this unspeakable crime. The whole country seems tired of hearing about the black man's woes. The wrongs of the Irish, of the Armenians, of the Roumanian and Russian Jews, of the exiles of Russia and of every other oppressed people upon the face of the globe, can arouse the sympathy and fire the indignation of the American public, while they seem to be all but indifferent to the murderous assaults upon the negroes in the South.

John Henry Adams Jr.

"Rough Sketches: A Study of the Features of the New Negro Woman"

Voice of the Negro, August 1904[11]

One day while standing in the centre of the business section of Atlanta, there approached me a bright eyed, full-minded youth of some nine years of respectable rearing. Both of us looked with eyes and soul upon the passing mixed panorama of men and women and children, and horses, and vehicles, and up to the modern ten and fourteen stories of stone, brick and steel structures out of whose windows, here and there, poked curious heads peering tamely upon the seeming confusion below. I saw an uncommon life picture pass slowly through the gang-way of humming electric cars, and rattling drays and of shifting humanity. Alford Emerson Clark, my innocent companion saw it also; and the throng of hurrying black and white folks paused in contemptible curiosity as the rubber-tired wheels of the open carriage rolled silently along the Peachtree thorough-fare. In the carriage sat two ladies, one white, one colored, engaged in a happy, spirited conversation all the

while unconscious, of the Southern social monster which argues the inferiority of the Negro to the white folk.

Two opposing worlds riding happily, peacefully, aye, lovingly together in the worst of Negro hating cities. Is it real? Is it natural? Is it right? What a healthy breath passed over me; and I smiled and went on with my jolly companion to the outer South end of the city.

The picture continued to press upon young Alford's mind, and with the peculiar vigor of youth, he had stopped to quander [*sic*] over the outward aspect of the situation. Said he, "which one is the better looking, the colored lady or the white?" Expressing my inability to decide pending a closer scrutiny of the two, I asked which did he think is the better in appearance. "The colored woman of course," he replied, as though he were greatly surprised at my not having a reason to say the same thing. Asking him for his reason, Alford looking me straight in the face said, "why the other woman is white." White? Well, what has that to do with a woman's real physical charm, either adding to or detracting from her? thought I to myself. To the black man a white face means little or nothing. To the white man it means his tradition, his civilization, his bond and recognition in the present age, and his safe guard in the future. Alford saw beneath the first skin surface down to the last layer of race greatness,—the preserving and honoring of race identity and distinction. He saw in that colored woman that which he could not see in the white woman so long as "white" in America stands for hope and black for despair.

The white woman's beauty was real, pure, substantial, but it came to thoughtful Alfred with no meaning. The black woman's beauty was real, pure, substantial, but it came with a life, a soul, which had touched his and which he not only understood but which inspired him to love.

I looked into his rich brown eyes, into his sun-lit smiling face and caught the gilded thread wire that, from his heart, followed the trail of Negro womanhood into all the ends of the earth. I fixed tight hand on it. I felt the fast beating of over nine million human hearts, as but the beating of one woman's heart when all hope seems lost, as they struggle with an inspiration which has too many times found its bed in the bosom of American prejudice. Still holding on to the gilded wire and placing my head close against his throbbing breast, there was something within, with the silence of maddened power which seemed to say: Ye gods of the earth! this woman—mine, whom you have fettered with the chains of caste, whom you have branded with the red iron of infamy, whom you have degraded with the finger of your own lustful body, shall be free. God made it fast and eternal. This beauty which you have used to tame your generations shall be yours no more, and this person that has served your rawest purposes shall not enter again into your halls.

Some day however these Negro restrictive laws, these phantasms and prejudices shall be beat and bent and tuned to the music of a more perfect civilization in which men shall love to do honor to all women for the sake of their sacred mission and meaning in the shaping of human destiny. There is an inseparable linking between mother and mother, be one white and one black; and the final triumph of civilization shall be when womanhood is a unit in all things for good and when manhood is a common factor in her defense.

We present the colored woman today as she impresses herself in the world as a growing factor for good and in her beauty, intelligence and character for better social recognition. Here she is in characteristic pose, full of vigor, tender in affection, sweet in emotion, and strong in every attribution of mind and soul.

Look upon her, ye worlds! and, since there is none better, swear by her. If there is none purer, none nobler, which have stamped preeminence in the very countenance of man, woman and child, cast your glittering swords, and sheaths, and armor, at her untarnished feet and pledge the very life that you enjoy to the defense of her life. Look upon her, ye nations! Measure her by all the standards of human perfection. Weigh her upon the scales that were employed in the weighing of queens, and noblemen's wives and daughters. And, if, after the test has been exhausted in the finding her real merits, she is found to have not only the physical beauty, not only the intellectual graces but also the moral stamina, the purity of heart, the loftiness of purpose and the sober consciousness of true womanhood the same as her white or red or olive sisters, then let all men whose blood finds eternal unity in the brotherhood of America's proscribed, whose traditions reach back into two-hundred and fifty years of mean slavery, and worse—of enforced ignorance:—I say, let all men, even they that be not us, who love woman for woman's sake fling their full lives to the uncertain wind when her honor is at stake.

linking between mother and mother, be one white and one black; and the final triumph of civilization shall be when womanhood is a unit in all things for good and when manhood is a common factor in her defence.

We present the colored woman today as she impresses herself in the world as a growing factor for good and in her beauty, intelligence and character for better social recognition. Here she is in characteristic pose, full of vigor, tender in affection, sweet

We want more men who have the proper sense of appreciation of deserving women and who are deserving themselves. This is a death-knell to the dude and the well-dressed run-around. You ought to write a book on that, Eva.

life. Look upon her, ye nations! Measure her by all the standards of human perfection. Weigh her upon the scales

Here one catches a glimpse of rare beauty. But it is not buried there alone, Eva.

in emotion, and strong in every attribution of mind and soul.

Look upon her, ye worlds! and, since there is none better, swear by her. If there is none purer, none nobler, which have stamped pre-eminence in the very countenance of man, woman and child, cast your glittering swords, and sheaths, and armor, at her untarnished feet and pledge the very life that you enjoy to the defense of her

In this admirable face rises a happy response to the lofty impulses of her poetic soul. In the language of art this is Lacolia.

A page from John Henry Adams Jr., "Rough Sketches: The New Negro Woman," *Voice of the Negro*, August 1904.

John Henry Adams Jr.
"Rough Sketches: The New Negro Man"

Voice of the Negro, October 1904

To find the new Negro man, one must take the narrow, rugged winding path as it leads from the humble one room log cabin, through the corn fields and cotton field, pass the country school shanty on to the quiet village in the dale. There, the broader pathway leads from the rough frame cottage, through the smoky, dismal quarters of hirelings; pass the shopping district to the humble academy over on the hill; then take right angles down by the Sunday meeting house to the signal railway station. Tell the conductor you want to get off at Atlanta. Arriving there, take the electric car for any one of the Negro institutions of higher learning, thence to the Negro modern home locality on the broad and sunny avenue, where on either side the playing of innocent colored children, dressed in white laundried jackets and dresses, out upon the green lawns amid blossoming flowers, reveals the meaning of progress peculiar to the black folk. Stop there long enough to realize the gravity and force of the character whose real self you are yet to know as he toils earnestly for place and power in the world, and as he clings to the higher self assdrtion [*sic*] of the man with a soul.

Now venture on. Here is the real new Negro man. Tall, erect, commanding, with a face as strong and expressive as Angelo's Moses and yet every whit as pleasing and handsome as Rubens's favorite model. There is that penetrative eye about which Charles Lamb wrote with such deep admiration, that broad forehead and firm chin. On the floor and the tables of his office lie the works of a ready craftsman, a master mechanic. Scattered harmonously [*sic*] on the walls, hang framed specimens of well designed office buildings and expensive residences, and over on his desk are filed a dozen or more bids, which at one time or another had made vain competition seem as but a cotton thread hanging to his coat sleeve. Such is the new Negro man, and he who finds the real man in the hope of deriving all the benefits to be got by acquaintance and contact does not run upon him by mere chance, but must go over the paths by some kind of biograph, until he gets a reasonable understanding of what it actually costs of human effort to be a man and at the same time a Negro.

Again, to find the new Negro man, you must equip yourself for the tedious study rising out of his singular environment. You must be prepared to comprehend the awkward and oftimes ugly circumstances, which surround him in his very inception, before he knew what he was, and long before he knows of the "Veil" of which Mr. Du Bois speaks so touchingly in his "Souls of Black Folk."

Here, drawn near the bosom of his good black mother, whose face is lighted with joy and hope and anxiety that only a mother feels, is the bouncing, laughing, little creature whose future days are as dark as his skin and whose very life is as uncertain as an approaching storm. Look into his face and then into the mother's face. Observe that interlacing of love and prospect and adventure as it weavens about the two, the life long singleness of heartbeats and sorrows and sufferings. What promise does that devoted mother foresee in that black infant face? Listen to the musings of that mother: "Where will twenty, forty, sixty years find this 'jewel' spending the love and sacrifice which my heart gives freely, fully, wholly to it?"

The boys grows, develops, enters school, begins the routine of office boy, learns companionship, discerns a little of the outer world, begins a study of the greater inner world—himself discovers his likes and dislike, goes pleasure seeking, and now he has reached his fifteenth year, the beginning of the critical period of a boy's life. Now his mind gets a breath of the intense vigor of his body. Something, he knows not what, moves mad with passion and fire through his veins. The boy's quiet is replaced by amazing wonder at the beauty and significiance [*sic*] of the objects beyond the mist and haze of his understanding. Question after question come and go unanswered. These are the harrows of his age.

At sixteen, seventeen, on to his twentieth year, the young man contends with temptations such as only the Negro boy meets. The opportunity to work, but a work and an employer whose sole aims are to keep him working at his beginning point; the opportunity to idle, with but the chaingang as the highest form of recompense; the pleasure of friends, who are as vagabond as the days are long; the modern dive with all its gilded hallucination, doors wide open, tables strewn with gobblers and beer growlers, and the breath of lounging, half-drunken women that contaminate the very atmosphere; the billiard room filled with old and hardened gamblers; and lastly, but of as grave disaster as either of the already named clamps of degradation, is the regular "hang-out corner," the temptation of the new young Negro.

Steadily, persistently, earnestly the young man clings to his aspiration to be a man. His college books, his Bible lessons, his mother's ringing words of love-truth, his pastor's soul inspiring sermons, and the passing lectures and educative entertainment, all instruct him as to the best uses of his time, as to the ultimate meaning of his life, and the real mission of man in this wilderness of love and labor.

The young man stands at last an achiever, and speaks the parting college words from the flower-dressed platform of his dear Alma Mater to the hundreds of admiring friends, who gather to place their benediction of success upon his brow. Nearest his feet sits that failing form of woman, upon whose heart the rich words of her son fall like drops of refreshing rain, after the burning rays of years of anticipation had crisped and withered the beauty and splendor of her face and body. Thrilled to the highest note, with tears streaming silently down her furrowed checks, her soul whispers in perfect ecstasy, "Thank God.—my son!—my son!"

This is not the end, rather the commencement of methodic, painstaking, fundamental living. The desire of success has been greatly enlarged in the black man's soul. A half-dozen years and that black man has woven himself into the industrial fibre of his locality, has gone where there seemed to be no water and brought forth the sparkling flow to which his people may go and quench their longing thirst. And he has set the standard of man in his community not upon a man's ability to think or work, be that ever so vital, but rather upon the purpose and end of the man's thinking or working.

This is the new Negro man as followed from the cradle through boyhood and college days on to the larger life, where men are known according as they do less theorizing and more actual, practical work; according as they turn their vast learning and wealth into simple, kindly helps to the poor, distressed and suffering; and in proportion as they make the play and music and revelry of the high head, the common enjoyment of all.

The new Negro man is facing a brighter sun than ever his father knew, in spite of the dark prophecies and hopeless [*sic*] pessimism which greet him on every side. The Negro father, on the one hand, irresponsibly hedged in with ignorance too dense to admit of much foresight, sees nothing for the son but a perpetuation of his own social, political, and material advancement to the abnormal state of affairs now existing, but goes more often far contrary to what he really thinks is the best and right in the long run in the preparation of his son for life's work in the hope of at least meeting present exigencies.

On the other hand, most of the newspapers and the evil men behind them, paint the new Negro out of the pigments of senseless antipathy, call him a brute and, fixing suspicion on him, seek to revert the cast of manhood into cowardly, cringing and wilful [*sic*] serfdom. Here then, is no encouragement. What of the new Negro man's future? The future is the man's, and he is relying on the strong arm of merit which providence has developed so as to cope with all human means and needs.

THE "NEGRO" IN JOURNALISM.

The above sketch shows Editor Jesse Max Barber in his characteristic attitude while engaged in study in what he calls his "Sanctum Sanctorum." Mr. Barber is a very close student of current, economic and sociological questions, as his narrations of current events in "Our Monthly Review" will show.

"The 'Negro' in Journalism," in John Henry Adams Jr., "Rough Sketches: The New Negro Man," *Voice of the Negro*, October 1904.

The new Negro man as represented in the accompanying sketches sees nothing but vital principles to sustain him in his struggle for place and power, and, like Socrates, would prefer the hemlock, or its equivalent, to all the vain pleasures outside of death than give over a single unit of right. He will do this not for his own sake merely, but for the sake of humanity, even the sake of the human who would decry principle to raise temporarily himself. The present fight is a fight for manhood—not man. Man dies. Manhood lives forever.

"I can die!" says that brave young man in Attick's review. "I can die for principle.—die loving and kissing my enemy."

This is the new Negro man's day. Let him be found always studying, thinking, working, for the social hour, when dancing and merrymaking are to enter, has not come. Gird up your loins, young man, and hurry.

John Henry Adams Jr.
"Rough Sketches: William Edward Burghardt Du Bois, Ph.D."

Voice of the Negro, March 1905

There are no hair-raising incidents running through the career of William E. Burghardt Du-Bois. It reads like the calm, steady, positive approach of a great *will* to do and live. His life is full of interest—not the sensational kind, but the kind that best serves as stimulus to the New Negro.

The drudgery of slavery, the slave market, the lash of the overseer, the midnight escape, the patrollers, the recapture, the blood-curdling reprimand, the second escape, the all night tramp through a black, muddy swamp, cold, hungry, naked, penniless, friendless: these were awful, hellish experiences, but they are of the past—dead. Let that history pass. The repetition of our ancestors' life stories only makes us mad and unfits us for the cool, resolute and determinate course by which only we can achieve the high mark set before us. Examples of opportunity taken and wisely used are what latter day young men need, and this is what Dr. DuBois' career is brimful of. This is one of the many reasons why his life is worth telling, if such is possible.

The effort to relate the desperate upward struggle of the man who has everything in his favor is hard. But where at first is seen a condition which in itself makes the whole of life painful, distressing, doubly burdensome, how, after the man has achieved, may we reckon justly with the man's innate power and give the world the full benefit of the inspiring object lessons accruing therefrom?

The right purpose of biography is to lead, to teach, to inspire men; is to give hope to the faint heart, promise to the young and undeveloped character, strength to the weak and easily beset ambition, and good-cheer to the weary soul upon which has poured a continuous stream of bitter disappointment; and more, biography is a beacon light to the shipwrecked, the sinking, the almost lost: is a thunder voice speaking through the trumpet of example to the heedless prodigal, dissipater, gambler, murderer, suicide; is the nerve center by which this entire human family is moved with increased vigor and quickened step nearer and nearer to the realm of the infinitely good and beautiful.

Show me a boy that is full of purpose, whether that purpose shows itself in his successfully robbing a bird nest, or in his standing at the head of his spelling class, and I will give you the cue to every great man and event since Adam. Purpose is the one great prerequisite to achievement. Circumstances might make possible a way to noble fame, heredity might pour in her fine blood and breeding and power, opportunity might be lavish in accruements and gracious in ripening and pruning occasion, but nothing—not one of these—can assure a man of enduring honor and power unless beneath the crossties of his ambition are firm and fast the ballast rocks of purpose. This is what no man can give to another. It cannot be inherited. You must find something to do; must find a wrong to righten, an evil to destroy, a caste and a class distinction to abolish, a name and an honor to reestablish, stolen rights and denied privileges to regain, persecutions and injustices to disclose and bitterly denounce. You must discover above all that a personal morality to improve, a personal ignorance to enlighten, a personal poverty to enrich, a personal character to develop and dignify, and a personal soul to Christianize and cleanse from all hate and malice, and all selfishness and prejudice. This finding of a large and glorious work to perform is in itself the true and appointed mother of Purpose.

Who can say that William E. Burghardt DuBois has not found a work to do, and that the very finding of that work has not stamped him of great and enduring purpose?

February 23, 1868, in the neighborhood of Great Barrington, Mass., Alfred and Mary (Burghardt) DuBois looked for the first time into the large brown eyes and upon the well rounded form of their baby and only son. At this birth dawned the new hope of the loving and handsome young couple. Alfred was a very ambitious and studious young man, and Mary Burghardt came of a family resident in Massachusetts two hundred years. She was of African and Dutch descent and of a dark brown complexion. Her grandfather fought in the Revolution and her uncle was one of the first American missionaries to Africa. Alfred's father was one of the founders of St. Luke's Episcopal Church, New Haven, Conn. His family was of African, West Indian and French Huguenot descent. With the strength, endurance, bravery

and courage of the African; with the serious temper and unforgetful mind, loyalty and steadfastness of the Dutch; and with the sweet temperament, forethought, jest, and in the time of war, warlikeness of the French, the DuBois of today represents the poise, the sweet nature, and the force of character out of which rise all true and enduring service.

Young DuBois entered the public schools of his native city at the age of five, and from the start showed an aptitude that at once secured for him the closest attention of his teachers. In his sixteenth year he graduated from the high school, and a year later entered the Fisk University, graduating at the age of twenty. Not satisfied at that training, DuBois at once entered Harvard, graduating two years later from a class of 281 members. He was one of the six commencement speakers of his class.

Finding a need of broader research, Mr. DuBois went abroad and pursued his studies at the University of Berlin. On his return he became a professor at Wilberforce University. On May 12, 1896, he was married to Miss Nina Gomer, a beautiful and accomplished young woman of Cedar Rapids, Iowa. He was for some time fellow in Sociology at Harvard; late assistant in Sociology, University of Pennsylvania; President American Negro Academy. He is author of "The Suppression of the Slave Trade;" "The Philadelphia Negro"; "The Souls of Black Folk." Now Professor of Economics and History, Atlanta University.

Thirty-seven years in the making of one of the strongest characters in America; thirty-seven years in the lifting of an infant race out of the chaos of ignorance, superstition and poverty to the mental, moral, physical and social radiance of our day. This is the progress, the substantial progress, made by a black man who is the strongest evidence of the capabilities and possibilities of his people.

In appearance DuBois is clean and neat. In height he is a little below the average, and weighs about one hundred and forty-five pounds. His body is symmetrical and well developed. A look into his face betrays the deep import of his cul-

"Head Picture of the Du Bois of Today at His Desk," in John Henry Adams Jr., "Rough Sketches: William Edward Burghardt Du Bois, Ph.D.," *Voice of the Negro*, March 1905.

tivated mind. The face is oval, tapering toward the chin, and the richness of its brown color, together with the evenness of his features makes him rather handsome and attractive. His modesty and unassumptive tone press themselves upon the most casual observer, and when he has to come to the front, he comes with that positive manly address which is a mark of good breeding and race culture. There is never a time when one may not approach him if that some one has something to say or do, but Mr. DuBois shows little patience with the fellow who simply wants to be around and make himself *sociable*. Mr. DuBois is a busy man, a thinking man, and whether he is sitting quietly looking through the forestry from his office window, or taking his afternoon walk or ride, or tied down to his desk dictating to his secretary he is following up and working out some *new thought*, some race problem, some sociological investigation. And, as busy a man as he is, there is never a moment during the day that his soul cannot respond to the peculiar humor and awkward expressions of the green boys and girls and people generally with whom he is often surrounded. His gentle nature makes him enjoy to the fullest the sunny-side or jest and amusement. In his home one may ofttimes, "in season and out of season," hear the baby voice of Yolande calling—"Papa!" to which the affectionate father replies—"Come baby!" and, in delight the beautiful child totters to her father's knees where after a brief interval of loving embraces the child returns to mamma to repeat what papa said.

Mrs. DuBois is a domestician. Nothing interests her more than the duties of the home, that is because in her own words: "No one can do for you what you see is needed to be done and do it effactually as you can. The home should always be a reflection of the ideas and tastes of the housewife, and no one can carry out her ideas for her. Servants are never housekeepers, but assistance to housekeepers." From this anyone can see the force of her personality and originality. Mrs. DuBois is of medium height, of excellent form and pleasing carriage. I did hear some ladies say she is a beautiful woman. When women make such an acknowledgement of one of their sex (jealous as they are) we men do not have to pass any further judgment. It is so.

No man is without faults. No man can steer himself clear of mistakes. No man can please everybody any more than he can have the personal acquaintance with everybody. The man's work and influence as well as the man himself are necessarily limited to a particular sphere and class. All within his sphere are touched directly by him and know and feel his power. They that are without see only the passing shadow of the man and are incapable of either commenting or passing judgment upon him and his worth. Men are generally so narrow as to see only their personal predilections. "If you bow down to me you are *it* otherwise *no*." Church denomination and even "sectional" prejudices have gone so far in shaping the attitude of one man toward another that no matter to what eminence a man may rise, he is not accorded brotherly respect and fellowship unless he bends his knees to these denominational and sectional gods.

Dr. DuBois is a man as other men and wishes to claim no higher distinction. He delights in open and fair criticism and indulges very freely in the *sport*. But he does not and will not bow down to gods. The work that he has outlined before him is large and great, and instead of courting the favor of men, white or black, Dr. DuBois is following his work to its happy end. What more do you ask of a man than that he do his work? Does not his reward depend upon that? When he was told that he is considered as one hard to approach DuBois said: "Why who thinks that thinks wrong. I am no harder to approach than the man who wants to approach me. If two men have a reason for wanting to know each other it is as easy for the one as the other to become acquainted." Why the idea of such an opinion of a man. Only those who have not shaken his cordial hand, who have not sought the sunny side of his life and stood in the full radiance of it can say that Dr. William Edward Burghardt DuBois is not a man of great intellectual strength and vigor, and excelling in those manly attributes which insure the support of enduring friendship and which will ultimately bring to him lasting honor and fame.

Anonymous
"The Passing Throng"

Seattle Republican, September 18, 1906[12]

The following excerpt is taken from an eastern exchadge [*sic*]:

Bishop Smith, of the African Methodist Episcopal church, who has just returned to his home in Detroit, Michigan, from Haiti, says that, "Haiti and not Africa is the place for Colored Americans. Twenty thousand could be assimilated there at once." Bishop Smith is considering the question of agitating the emigration of Colored people from the Southern states to Haiti.

There are equally as good opportunities for the Negro all over the South and Central American countries, and he would do well to emigrate thither and thereby relieve the South of these United States of its congested Negro population. It is impossible to build up a Negro race distinct from the Anglo-Saxon race in the United States, and so long as there is a "black belt" in the United States just so long will there be fatal clashes between the whites and the blacks. The solution of the so-called "race problem," in the United States, is the scattering of the blacks, like the whites, to every nook and corner of the country; yea, even to every nook and corner of the South and Central American republics. If the South was relieved of half or more of its Negro population their places would soon be filled with European emigrants, and in a comparatively short time both the Negroes and the South would be the better for that change. Already Negroes have occasionally wandered to the South and Central American republics, and in most cases they have done exceedingly well. Now, Mr. New Negro, go thou and do likewise.

Anonymous
"Worm Will Turn"

Cleveland Gazette, November 3, 1906[13]

In the face of such provocation as the outrage at Atlanta, the Negro may not always remain non-resistant. We are hearing much from the south of the "uppishness" of the new generation of Negroes. The older Negroes, it is said, are docile, and the white race have no difficulty in getting along with them; but the new Negro is aggressive and resentful. God help the white community where that is a fact, and which allows its mobs to kill with impunity unresisting Negroes. For the "uppishness" of the new Negro means that human nature in the Negro is asserting itself, and that the time is approaching when the upturned faces after a "race war" will not all be black. White men cannot forever mob and slay the people of another race, however docile that race may seem to be, without in time being mobbed and slain in turn.

—Chicago Public.

Anonymous

"A Lesson from 'The Clansman'"

Sedalia Weekly Conservator, January 21, 1907[14]

Thursday evening, we witnessed "The Clansman" at the New Sedalia Theatre. While we found the drama full to the brim of sentiment that engenders race hate in the hearts of uncultured and fire eating elements of both races, yet, we did not see all that we anticipated. As we observed the effect the production had on its audience, which was 95 or 98 per cent white, we could see and fear danger from the radicals on both sides.

"The Clansman" may represent the feelings and sentiment of a large element of the white race but it certainly misrepresents the cultured Negro of today in any section of our land, and, especially in the South. It presents a weak argument, when it features the intelligent, industrious, aggressive, manly, independent and New Negro as having an unquenchable longing to join himself in marriage to his white contemporary. Demagogues, white and black may flaunt the banner of Social Equality before the thoughtless in both races, for the purpose of using them for political or other service. Many of both races may follow this delusion either to oppose its realization or to enjoy its imagined bliss. But the sensible, brave and conscientiously patriotic will consider it at its face value which is practically a myth.

Social equality is not a creature of legislation. It is derived from and by affinities of mutual attraction from the hearts of individuals concerned. Hence, so long as race antipathy exists between the Negro and the American white man, social equality and social intermingling is an utter impossibility. Kingdoms and empires have in the past stipulated marriages. Republics never have and never will. The above propositions are philosophic truths well authenticated by common sense and historical facts.

People of sober judgement are not worrying themselves about propositions that are absolutely personal and individual in their "sphere of influence."

Negroes and the entire American people are being brought face to face with conditions today as never before since the early Sixties. As a nation, America can not much longer administer her laws under a dual standard, one for white men and another for black men. And at the same time claim both as citizens under our expanding constitution. Negro-haters, demagogues, firebrands, cowards and the selfish bigots may misrepresent the Negro's motive in his contention for his political and God given rights but the day is not far distant when the facts will be clearly seen. The Negro's traducers have deluded the unthinking white man for a generation with the "social equality" bogey. They shout from house top, throughout the valleys and upon the plains that the Negro by seeking his political rights is also eager to sit at the white man's table, marry the white man's daughter and subvert the white man's government. Look at the argument presented! Study the conditions as they are! Just think of it! Ten millions of Negroes whom the white man calls ignorant, shiftless and unattractive are going to within the next two or three generations destroy the racial identity, subvert the governmental machinery, transform the social fabric, revolutionize the political organisms and demoralize, denationalize and annihilate seventy millions of the white race—the race that boasts of its 1500 years of culture and supremacy. Looking the matter squarely and honestly in the face, does not the contentions set forth by "The Clansman," The Carmacks, The Vaudamans [*sic*; Vardamans] and all of that gallant array of Southern voodoos, who see things at night, appear so comical that to the enlightened they are colossal examples of ridiculousness. They either have

The front page of the *New York Age*, March 14, 1907, shows a cartoon with the title, "Social Equality Is It? Well, Who Created 3,000,000 'Afro-Americans' and Denied Them Fathers by Law?" ["Are we ready to make of the American people a negroid nation? This is the aspiration of the Negro—not of the old-time Negro, perhaps, for he was well brought up; but of the new Negro the 'Afro-American.' Whatever social equality may signify to the white, to the ignorant Negro, and apparently to many who are not ignorant, it means one thing; the right to stand on the same footing with a white woman as that on which a white man stands with her. It means this and nothing but this."—Thomas Nelson Page, in *McClure's Magazine* for March.

COMMON LAW WIFE—"But, Mistah W'ite Man, ain't them 'ere yo chilluns?"

MR. WHITE MAN (confused)—Stammers.

THE CHILDREN—"Yes, indeed; he's our pa! We knows it."

very little confidence in their valor or believe the American people to be a vast aggregation of fools.

America's New Negro does not seek social or marital equality with the whites. He does and will continue to contend for his rights under the constitution. He brands as a malicious slander any allegations from any source by any body that he is anxious, even remotely, to merge his identity with any race. He asks other races to refrain from emptying their illegitimate blood into his veins.

Ray Stannard Baker

"Following the Color Line: The Clash of the Races in a Southern City"

American Magazine, May 1907[15]

I arrived in Atlanta, Georgia, on the first day of last November. The riot, which I described a month ago, had taken place about six weeks before, and the city was still in the throes of self-examination and reconstruction. Public attention had been peculiarly riveted upon the facts of race relationships not only in Atlanta but throughout the South, and all manner of remedies and solutions were under sharp discussion. If I had traveled the country over, I could not have found a more favorable time or place to begin following the color line. . . .

. . . the Negro in the South is both the labor problem and the servant question: he is pre-eminently the political issue, and his place, socially, is of daily and hourly discussion. A Negro minister I met told me a story of a boy who went as a sort of butler's assistant in the home of a prominent family in Atlanta. His people were naturally curious about what went on in the white man's house. One day they asked him:

"What do they talk about when they're eating?"

The boy thought a moment; then he said:

"Mostly they discusses us culled folks." . . .

. . . not long afterwards. I was lunching with several fine Southern men, and they talked, as usual, with the greatest freedom in the full hearing of the Negro waiters. Somehow, I could not help watching to see if the Negroes took any notice of what was said. I wondered if they were sensitive. Finally, I put the question to one of my friends:

"Oh," he said, "we never mind them; they don't care."

One of the waiters instantly spoke up:

"No, don't mind me; I'm only a block of wood." . . .

I commented that evening to some Southern people I met, on the impression, almost of jollity, given by the Negro workers I had seen in the streets. One of the older ladies made what seemed to me a very significant remark:

"They don't sing as they used to," she said. "You should have known the old darkies of the plantation. Every year, it seems to me, they have been losing more and more of their carefree good humor. I sometimes feel that I don't know them any more. Since the riot they have grown so glum and serious that I'm free to say I'm scared of them!" . . .

Passing the post office, I saw several mail-carriers coming out, some white, some black, talking and laughing, with no evidence, at first, of the existence of any color line. Interested to see what the real condition was, I went in and made inquiries. A most interesting and significant condition developed. I found that the postmaster, who is a wise man, sent Negro carriers up Peachtree and other fashionable streets, occupied by wealthy white people, while white carriers were assigned to beats in the mill districts and other parts of town inhabited by the poorer classes of white people.

"You see," said my informant, "the Peachtree people know how to treat Negroes. They really prefer a Negro carrier to a white one; it's natural for them to have a Negro doing such service. But if we sent Negro carriers down into the mill district they might get their heads knocked off."

Then he made a philosophical observation:

"If we had only the best class of white folks down here and the industrious Negroes there wouldn't be any trouble."

The Jim Crow Car

One of the points in which I was especially interested was the "Jim Crow" regulations, that is, the system of separation of the races in street cars and railroad trains. . . .

No other one point of race contact is so much and so bitterly discussed among the Negroes as the Jim Crow car. I don't know how many Negroes replied to my question: "What is the chief cause of friction down here?" with a complaint of their treatment on street cars and in railroad trains.

Why the Negro Objects to the Jim Crow Car

Fundamentally, of course, they object to any separation which gives them inferior accommodations. This point of view—and I am trying to set down every point of view, both colored and white, exactly as I find it, is expressed in many ways.

"We pay first class fare," said one of the leading Negroes in Atlanta, "exactly as the white man does, but we don't get first class service. We don't know when we may be dislodged from our seats to make a place for a white man who has paid no more than we have. I say it isn't fair."

In answer to this complaint the white man says: "The Negro is inferior, he must be made to keep his place. Give him a chance and he assumes social equality, and that will lead to an effort at intermarriage and amalgamation of the races. The Anglo-Saxon will never stand for that." . . .

Conditions on the railroad trains, while not resulting so often in personal encounters, are also the cause of constant irritation. . . . Well-to-do Negroes who can afford to travel, also complain that they are not permitted to engage sleeping-car berths. Booker T. Washington usually takes a compartment where he is entirely cut off from the white passengers. Some other Negroes do the same thing, although they are often refused even this expensive privilege. Railroad officials with whom I talked, and it is important to hear what they say, said that it was not only a question of public opinion—which was absolutely opposed to any intermingling of the races in the cars—but that Negro travel in most places was small compared with white travel, that the ordinary Negro was unclean and careless, and that it was impracticable to furnish them the same accommodations, even though it did come

hard on a few educated Negroes. They said that when there was a delegation of Negroes, enough to fill an entire sleeping car, they could always get accommodations. All of which gives a glimpse of the enormous difficulties accompanying the separation of the races in the South. . . .

One curious and enlightening example of the infinite ramifications of the color line was given me by Mr. Logan, secretary of the Atlanta Associated Charities, which is supported by voluntary contributions. One day, after the riot, a subscriber called Mr. Logan on the telephone and said:

"Do you help Negroes in your society?"

"Why, yes, occasionally," said Mr. Logan.

"What do you do that for?"

"A Negro gets hungry and cold like anybody else," answered Mr. Logan.

"Well, you can strike my name from your subscription list. I won't give any of my money to a society that helps Negroes."

Psychology of the South

Now, this sounds rather brutal, but behind it lies the peculiar psychology of the South. . . .

The Negro who makes his appeal on the basis of this old relationship finds no more indulgent or generous friend than the Southern white man, indulgent to the point of excusing thievery and other petty offenses, but the moment he assumes or demands any other relationship or stands up as an independent citizen, the white men—at least some white men—turn upon him with the fiercest hostility. . . . It was not necessarily cruelty to a cold or hungry Negro that inspired the demand of the irate subscriber, but the feeling that the associated charities helped Negroes and whites on the same basis, as men; that, therefore, it encouraged "social equality," and that therefore it was to be stopped. . . .

The New Racial Consciousness among Negroes

One of the natural and inevitable results of the effort of the white man to set the Negro off, as a race, by himself, is to awaken in him a new consciousness—a sort of racial consciousness. It drives the Negroes together for defense and offence. Many able Negroes, some largely of white blood, become of necessity leaders of their own people. And one of their chief efforts consists in urging Negroes to work together and stand together. In this they are only developing the instinct of defense against the white man which has always been latent in the race. . . .

The Negro has long been defensively secretive. Slavery made him that. In the past, the instinct was passive and defensive; but with growing education and intelligent leadership it is rapidly becoming conscious, self-directive and offensive. And right there, it seems to me, though I speak yet from limited observations, lies the great cause of the increased strain in the South.

Let me illustrate. In the People's Tabernacle in Atlanta, where thousands of Negroes meet every Sunday, I saw this sign, in huge letters:

> For Photographs, Go to
> Auburn Photo Gallery,
> Operated by Colored Men.

The old-fashioned darkey preferred to go to the white man for everything; he didn't trust his own people; the new Negro, with growing race consciousness, and feeling that the white man is against him, urges his friends to patronize Negro doctors and dentists, and to trade with Negro storekeepers. The extent to which this movement has gone was one of the most surprising things that I, as an unfamiliar Northerner, found in Atlanta. In other words, the struggle of the races is becoming more and more rapidly economic.

Story of a Negro Shoe-Store

One day, walking in Broad Street, I passed a Negro shoe-store. I did not know that there was such a thing in the country. I went in to make inquiries. It was neat, well kept and evidently prosperous. I found that it was owned by a stock company, organized and controlled wholly by Negroes; the manager was a brisk young mulatto named Harper, a graduate of Atlanta University. I found him dictating to a Negro girl

stenographer. There were two reasons, he said, why the store had been opened; one was because the promoters thought it a good business opportunity, and the other was because many Negroes of the better class felt that they did not get fair treatment at white stores. At some places—not all, he said—when a Negro woman went to buy a pair of shoes, the clerk would hand them to her without offering to help her try them on; and a Negro was always kept waiting until all the white people in the store had been served. Since the new business was opened, he said, it had attracted much of the Negro trade; all the leaders advising their people to patronize him. I was much interested to find out how this young man looked upon the race question. His first answer struck me forcibly, for it was the universal and typical answer of the business man the world over, whether white, yellow or black:

"All I want," he said, "is to be protected and let alone, so that I can build up this business."

"What do you mean by protection?" I asked.

"Well, justice between the races. That doesn't mean social equality. We have a society of our own, and that is all we want. If we can have justice in the courts, and fair protection, we can learn to compete with the white stores and get along all right."

Such an enterprise as this indicates the new, economic separation between the races. . . .

Greatest Difficulties Met by Negro Business Men

I asked [one businessman] what was the greatest difficulty he had to meet. He said it was the credit system; the fact that many Negroes have not learned financial responsibility. . . .

Of course only a comparatively few Negroes are able to get ahead in business. They must depend almost exclusively on the trade of their own race, and they must meet the highly organized competition of white men. But it is certainly significant that even a few—all I have met so far are mulattoes, some very white—are able to make progress along these unfamiliar lines. Most Southern men I met had little or no idea of the remarkable extent of this advancement among the better class of Negroes. Here is a strange thing. I don't know how many Southern men have prefaced their talks with me with words something like this:

"You can't expect to know the Negro after a short visit. You must live down here like we do. Now, I know the Negroes like a book. I was brought up with them. I know what they'll do and what they won't do. I have had Negroes in my house all my life."

But curiously enough I found that these men rarely knew anything about the better class of Negroes—those who were in business, or in independent occupations, those who owned their own homes. They *did* come into contact with the servant Negro, the field hand, the common laborer, who make up, of course, the great mass of the race. On the other hand, the best class of Negroes did not know the higher class of white people, and based their suspicion and hatred upon the acts of the poorer sort of whites with whom they naturally came into contact. The best elements of the two races are as far apart as though they lived in different continents; and that is one of the chief causes of the growing danger of the Southern situation. . . .

Many Southerners look back wistfully to the faithful, simple, ignorant, obedient, cheerful, old plantation darkey and deplore his disappearance. They want the New South, but the old darkey. That darkey is disappearing forever along feudalism and the old-time exclusively agricultural life.

A New Negro is not less inevitable than a new white man and a New South. And the New Negro, as my clever friend says, doesn't laugh as much as the old one. It is grim business he is in, this being free, this new, fierce struggle in the open competitive field for the daily loaf. Many go down to vagrancy and crime in that struggle; a few will rise. The more rapid the progress (with the trained white man setting the pace), the more frightful the mortality.

S. Laing Williams
"The New Negro"

Alexander's Magazine, November 1908[16]

An Address Delivered by Hon. S. Laing Williams at the Morning Service, Held at All Souls Church in the Abraham Lincoln Centre, Chicago, Sunday, July 26, 1908.

The rise of a man from a low estate to a high estate, from dependence to independence, from ignorance to intelligence and self-sufficiency, is always interesting, always important and always more or less disturbing. The immediate problem of this man is to get himself known, respected and believed in. He may be worthy, he may be aspiring, he may be competent for high service, but he is mistrusted and even hated because he is aspiring. It is a tremendously difficult thing for this new applicant for citizenship to gain the good will and confidence of a whole nation of people who are in undisputed power and control.

The difficulty is enhanced when this new man comes in the visage of Othello and in the condition of dependence.

The new man merely asks for standing room, yet he is crowded back. He asks to be heard and is silenced. He asks to be trusted and he is denied. He pleads to be tested by his intelligence and his honor as a man, and he is scorned. In short, he "asks for bread and is given a stone." His presence is a menace, his proffered service is ignored. Indeed, all the higher laws of God and man are set aside when this new man comes with his undisputed credentials of worth and sufficiency. Yet this new man, conscious of his worth, persists in his quest for recognition. He knows that what is right must eventually prevail.

No country can afford to deny the right of any man to be respected. Men of character and force are the chief assets of a nation. The greatest nations are those that have the highest uses for their best men. While this is true, yet the passion for keeping some men down is everywhere in evidence. This is so because the fixed opinion of men and things is hard to change. Give a man a bad name and it will pass current in spite of his innocence and his virtues.

In this great country of ours we freely judge and misjudge men according to our feelings. The worth of a man is not always a shield of protection against bad opinions of him. Whether we are liked or disliked, trusted or mistrusted, often depends upon such superficial things as race, color, intelligence, ignorance, poverty or wealth. The most unyielding of all separating causes between man and man is race prejudice. Race prejudice needs no definition. The sting of it, the mean force of it, and the cruelty of it are a part of our common experience. No race of men has been entirely free from opposition due to race prejudice, and the Negro race in America is conspicuously no exception to the rule.

For over two hundred years the force of race prejudice in this country has overridden justice, morality and religion in keeping our people below the level of men of white complexion. By a strange perversity of human nature our very uprising in intelligence, moral worth and economic efficiency has been regarded as a menace to American civilization.

There is nothing to be gained by reopening this dark chapter in our nation's history. If we have suffered many things because of our worthy aspirations to deserve well of the American people, the American people have also suffered by violating the laws of God and man in their effort to establish two standards of righteousness, one black and one white. There are some things about which there can be no compromise. A righteous man is neither white nor black. He is simply a righteous man. To hate him because he is either white or black is wicked; to mistrust him is folly; to be afraid of him is cowardly. Somewhere and at some time or place in this great world of human beings such a man is needed and will find his place. It is sometimes said that the Negro race in America is on trial and it might be as fittingly added that the jury is packed and the verdict made up even before the evidence is heard. Hence the burden of our plea always is: hear the evidence. The evidence is more interesting than the possible verdict.

Some great things have been going on in this country of ours during the past forty years. Much of it is unseen, unknown and not believed, but is more or less distinctly felt in the social and economic life of the American people.

As a result of it all we have in this country today what may be fittingly called a "new Negro," and the race problem may be defined as the failure of the American people to recognize and know this new Negro. So hard and uncompromising has been the separation between the races that this new and well-equipped man of the hour has had no chance to reveal himself to those who still have in their minds types of the cotton field and log cabin Negro of fifty years ago. It seems to be human nature to dislike people we don't know. The Negro people of this country have moved on and up at such a wonderful pace that their splendid worth has dazed the American people.

It is not too much to say that the average American knows more about the Japanese and Chinese, who are separated from them by almost impassable barriers of differences, than he does about the race that for over two hundred years has been helping to build up a great nation. It is a long and weary distance from Jamestown to Tuskegee, and the pathway is strewn with suffering and sadness, yet the journey has been made and all we ask of the American people is to turn around and at least recognize the size of our burden.

The New Negro is not a fictitious man. He is not a child of fortune—a man without a history—without an expanding soul and without a destiny. There have been two emancipations of the Negro race. The one was physical and was consummated in 1865, the other has been a continuous emancipation from slavish heritages of conditions and instincts, to a persistence and extent that few Americans can understand. The drastic and uncompromising laws of separations have made it impossible for the people in whose midst we live and move to feel the extent of this second emancipation. No recitals of mere facts and figures can tell the whole story of this wonderful self-emancipation. The test of a race's worth is the kind of men it is capable of producing. An Indian Chief is merely stronger but not ethically better than the rest of his tribe. There are no distinguished Esquimaux. They are all on the low level of an ice-enduring existence. Out of such races no civilization develops, but its people are held everlastingly to the primal instincts of animalism.

The significant and compelling thing about the Negro race is that it has always shown a capacity for the highest and best things in our national life. As an illustration some facts and figures are significant. Emerson says somewhere that "it is inhuman not to believe in education, since amelioration is the law of life." Education has been the controlling passion of the Negro race. Within forty years they have overcome quite sixty per cent of their illiteracy. Thousands of young colored men and women have won academic degrees in many of the best colleges and universities of America and Europe. The Negro that most Americans picture as mendicant, shiftless and unenterprising, now pays taxes on over $300,000,000 worth of real estate. This race that is so greatly feared as a menace to Anglo-Saxon social morality has been busy since 1865 building churches, schools, colleges, hospitals, homes for the aged, some thirty banks, and taking a conspicuous part in all those movements that indicate an increase in civic virtue and individual morality. In other words, the man who forty-five years ago was a chattel has become in some instances a lawyer, a physician, a theologian, an artist, a poet, a journalist, a banker, a diplomat, a linguist, a soldier unafraid, an ardent patriot and a man who dares to have courage in the midst of discouragements. Who can afford not to respect men of this kind? Surely there must be some real

1900
"The colored man that saves his money and buys a brick house will be universally respected by his white neighbors."

1910
"New and dangerous species of Negro criminal lately discovered in Baltimore. He will be segregated in order to avoid lynching."

Two illustrations, "1900" and "1910," by John Henry Adams Jr., *Crisis*, February 1911.

soul, something heroic, in the man who can thus honorably give an account of himself. The chattel of the cotton field has become a gentleman in spirt and in fact. He is a self-made man and challenges the respect of all mankind. He asks to be respected for what he is and stands for in his new status and not for what the American people meanly think he is.

This new man has been wonderfully tested and has borne himself with heroic patience. He is a man of distinctly American spirit, in language, in religion, in democratic instincts, in enterprise, in his ethical impulses and patriotism, the most ardent of Americans, ready at all times to fight or work for our national security. He lives in the present, in spite of the people who think of him and treat him as a backward race.

Civilization has been defined as "the power of good men." Is this aphorism large enough to include men and women of African descent? Within two generations at least, five Negro men have added to the glory of American annals: Frederick Douglass, the orator; Booker T. Washington, the educator; Dunbar, the poet; DuBois, the sociologist; Tanner, the artist; Kelly Miller, the teacher, and Frank J. Grimke, the preacher. A race that can produce a group of men such as these in a single generation cannot be forever written down as a race without an interesting future.

This new Negro is an optimist in spite of the wrongs that he endures. Formerly he complained without hope; now he hopes without complaint. The American who cannot see and appreciate this new man is himself blind and need not be feared. No race that has the power to redeem itself can be kept in an inferior position. When you can pity the man who wantonly hates you, you have achieved the mastery over him and his tribe.

The race problem of today, in spite of the people who think, feel and act as if it were the same as it was in 1860, is a new problem and may be defined: What shall be the status of this educated, high-spirited, ambitious and deserving man of the Negro race or this new Negro? He knocks and knocks persistently at the door of opportunity. Shall it be opened? Justice and fair play say, yes; race prejudice, in the spirit of

1860, says no. The American Negro has become well accustomed to the American "No." In a sort of triumphant spirit, the noble Frederick Douglass used to say, when beset on all sides by evil forces in the dark days of the '60's: "I sometimes forget the color of my skin and remember that I am a man; I sometimes forget that I am hated of men and remember that I am loved of God." And so these black men of today, in spite of the recurrent fury of race prejudice, keep their faith in God and the growing spirit of tolerance of all mankind. Bad laws may be written and enforced to prevent a good man from being an uncontested citizen, but we feel strong in the fact that before man made us citizens, great nature made us men, and the man behind the citizen is more important than a man-made citizen. Let us be tested by what we deserve and the problem is solved. Let us not make the mistake of believing it is possible to compel any class of freemen in this Republic "to keep his place." A man's place in this country should be wherever he himself can make it.

Every colored man or woman in this country who has come into prominence because of his or her worth has done so in defiance of all the evil forces that for two hundred years have insisted that this is a "white man's country." The Negro people have performed a great service by proving that you cannot found a great civilization on complexion alone. It is scarcely worthy a great nation of people to be afraid and become hysterical for fear of losing their social exclusiveness. While this new Negro is struggling upward through cruel repression to become a God-fearing and man-loving citizen of the world of mankind, our white friends are continuously haunted by the unworthy bugbear of "social equality." This new Negro asks for nothing that he dares not deserve and it is inhuman to expect him to be satisfied with less. If the right to vote, if the right to pay taxes, if the right to defend our position as American citizens and deserve the good opinion of the Lincolns and the Sumners of the past make for social equality, the fault must be theirs who feel so insecure in their social status. Certainly the tide of progress of one race of people must not be kept back until some other race can make itself socially impregnable. In the name of this social equality mania more sins have been committed by our white friends than can be expiated in a century of good will. To the new Negro this social equality terror is both amusing and exasperating. His character, his culture, his good sense and fine manners are an offense and a menace to people who are so sure of their unapproachable superiority. Certainly there must be something fundamentally wrong with the man or woman who becomes meanly afraid because I can read and appreciate Emerson and Herbert Spencer, and can be stirred by an ambition to serve well my county. Ah, my friends, there is a wrong in all this that goes to the heart of our national honor. It discounts our religion, it cheapens our patriotism and casts a shadow of falsehood over our pretended national greatness.

Some forty years ago the people of this country became so alarmed over the multitude of freedmen at the close of the Civil War that they established a Freedmen's Bureau to aid the freedmen in their transition from slavery to freedom. That was a great service and was inspired by true love of humanity. The ignorant, uncivilized and empty-handed man of 1865 has become a man of culture, a man of force and a man of independence. We shall have to look to this new man to complete the great work of reconstruction. In other words, the new Negro people have a race problem on their hands which is both interesting and far-reaching in its consequences, and that is to teach white Americans how possible it is to be both just and respectable towards this expanding race of ours without their loss of anything worth having.

We must save the American people from the debilitating effects of the fears they have that our increase of intelligence and independence mean their own loss of social prestige. Let me enjoy all the rights I deserve—who will suffer? To this end let us be confident as to these things:

(1) The rise of the Negro people in intelligence, in social efficiency, in self-pride, in the power to add its share toward the wealth and social uplift of the nation must not be hindered or prevented by race prejudice.

(2) Injustice, race hatred, discriminations in the matter of fundamental rights will never solve the race problem.

(3) The fear of social equality has become a national fetish. It is a fear that was born in the dark days of slavery out of a guilty conscience, and is today fostered and nourished by people who have not yet been touched by the expanding thought of this new era of national growth.

(4) In the conflict between race prejudice and the Negro's advancement I am satisfied that whatever is fundamentally right will finally triumph.

(5) A state built on the foolish fear of social equality will remain where it began, and will make no history worth reading.

This new Negro only asks and fights for a chance. He sees about him men from all Europe and Asia. Every shop, factory, office and honor is open to this man from across the sea. The descendants of the man who fought under Jackson at New Orleans, with Perry on Lake Erie, who triumphantly died at Fort Wagner, who helped Custer in the West to make room for the Norwegians and Swedes, who planted out conquering flag at El Caney, are asked to step aside and be satisfied to blacken the shoes of these newcomers.

The new Negro who sees and feels all this is asked to be patient—simply to wait and watch. And so he has watched and waited patiently, heroically and confidently. But he now begins to feel that his heroic patience has invited contempt rather than praise. This new Negro, unlike his grandfather, is sensitive to wrongs, writhes under injustice and is fretful under discriminations copied from South Carolina and Alabama.

This country of ours is a country teeming with opportunities. The man of thorough education, the man of technical training, the inventor, the man skilled in law, medicine, diplomacy and statesmanship can find here his opportunity. This new Negro that I have been talking about is here and ready for all kinds of service. His worth is admitted; why not give him a chance? By everything we pretend to be in this country, in religion, in morals, democracy and spirit of fair play, the ambitions of this well equipped man should be honored and he be given the chance he deserves. There are never too many fit men to do the high services of a great and ever expanding nation.

Here, then, is our new race problem that has been brought to the nation by this new and ambitious Negro.

What shall be done for or with this new man with a black face? Here in America we have a wide-open civilization. We are made up of all kinds and conditions of people, and we are alike ambitions to do the low and high services of the nation and to be rewarded according to our worth.

The new Negro today offers himself as a fit man for everything that comes within the range of superior intelligence and worthy ambition. Shall he be encouraged, or shall he be turned away hopeless and discouraged? Can this nation, with its limitless opportunities, afford to fix a limitation to the ambitions of any of its people?

Thanks to the progress of humane sentiment in this country, this new man who asks the question can help to answer it. There was a time when all the questions asked as to what should be the status of the Negro were asked and answered by the same man. Thanks to the growth of intelligence and the manhood spirit of the race, no question concerning us is completely answered without our participation in the answer. This shows progress.

This new Negro is an aggressive man, and he will be increasingly heard, and deserves to be increasingly respected. This new Negro may be impatient, as he has a right to be, but he is not altogether discouraged. He is strong in the faith that he is right and fit, and what is right will some day be the unchallenged law of conduct everywhere.

The race problem of today is not one of social equality, but rather one of recognized moral and mental equality—of the right to aspire, of the right to realize what one deserves, of the right to serve our common country in times of peace as well as in times of war. There never can be too many good men and good women in the world, come they from whatever country or race.

The United States is a nation of great problems, and the nation cannot afford to make it impossible for some men to serve the nation in their solution. In spite of unworthy fears of some Americans concerning the new Negro of today and tomorrow, the unfolding of new opportunities for men of brawn, brain and courage will need us. This new Negro will be wanted. In this growing nation of ours there is to be a new political economy to meet the new conditions of our ever expanding nation. A new social ethics that will enable all men to respect each other without fear or loss of social prestige. A new spirit of politics that shall make public office a public trust. A new spirit of brotherhood when it will be more honorable for men to be just to each other than to be socially equal, and a new awakening of all the higher senses of man in his duty to man. Such a consummation is devoutly to be wished. But none of this "vision splendid" can be realized until our interest in mankind shall be greater than our interest in some men.

Today we are fettered by the spirit of the tribe and those who claim to be most free are most fettered. It is not the things we own and the power we have and misuse that makes our nation truly great. Why cannot we afford to be just and patient to a race that daily grows in independence and power of self-hood? Who cannot respect a man of worth, even though he be brown or black? Who cannot afford to be just and have faith that what is just will hurt no man? All of us are ready to say yes to these questions, yet we all painfully know that it is easier to live below our ideals. The man who compels me to pay a first class fare for worse than a second class accommodation in a "Jim Crow" car from Chicago to Tuskegee is often a churchman who gives liberal alms to the poor and needy. The man who thinks most of Thomas Jefferson because he stood for the great idea of equality is apt to be the man who is most violent in insisting that this is "a white man's country." The man who thinks he is a Christian and who pretends to conform his life to the Golden Rule of the Bible is too often the man who practices the iron rule of injustice.

The new Negro knows all this and feels this and yet he is a man of faith and courage. Though held down he continues to look up and in all honorable ways struggles for his rights. He submits heroically to the things he cannot overcome. Opposition has made him heroic, and his love of justice has made him optimistic. His ambition is to deserve what he claims, and his high privilege is to pity the man who merely stands in the way of progress.

This new Negro is approaching an era of great things. Tremendous are the problems of tomorrow. In the larger world of higher politics, in the new ideals of a higher citizenship, in the social atmosphere of the new ethics of fellowship and in a more exalted religious sense, this new man of our republic will be needed and will find his place, and will be honored for what he is and can do for the world of mankind.

Nannie Burroughs

"Report to the Eighth Annual Session of the Woman's Convention, Auxiliary to the National Baptist Convention"

In *National Baptist Convention, Journal of the Eighth Annual Assembly of the Woman's Convention Held in the First Baptist Church of Lexington, Kentucky, Sept. 16–21, 1908, 1909*

Minutes.
Eighth Annual Report of the Corresponding Secretary

Madam President, Co-laborers and Friends:

> *Beneath earth's starry arch*
> *Nothing rests, nor is still;*
> *But all things hold their march*
> *As if by one Great Will.*

Nature knows no pause—time controls her course. "Move one, move all—press forward," is her great command. That indefinable thing that we call time, travels so fast that the past is gone and the present becomes the past even while we attempt to define it, and like the flash of the lightning, at once exists, and expires. Even now, we are moving, and the very place in which we stand is but the vestibule to glorious mansions, into which a moving crowd forever presses.

You have reached Lexington in the great old Commonwealth of Kentucky; you are in the State that gave to the world the immortal Lincoln. You stand under the shadow of the monument of Henry Clay, the Unionist, who plead with his countrymen to be spared the anguish of souls should they not hear the voice of reason and council, but decide to secede from the Union.

You are in the State where there is less antagonism between races than any other State in the South. You may read of the assassination of Governors, feuds of mountaineers, the destructive work of night riders; but in Kentucky you will find many wide-visioned, liberal-minded lovers of justice and defenders of human rights, of the "Augustus Wilson and Henry Watterson Brand."

Lexington is one of the most progressive cities of its size you have ever visited. You will find the best white citizens interested in all that makes for our uplift, and though the horrifying picture of the Russellville outrage is painted in blood before you,[17] you hear on the other hand the voice of the press expressing the sentiments of two-thirds of the people against this atrocious crime.

This is the Eighth Annual Session of the Woman's Convention, Auxiliary to the National Baptist Convention. In submitting the report of the Executive Board and Corresponding Secretary for the past year, we turn with grateful hearts to the God who has led us through dangers, seen and unseen. We have moved forward under the protecting shadow of the August Presence. We have been encompassed with God; the angel of his presence has gone before us. Seas of discouragement have dried up, and mountains of obstacles have melted to plains, and in the midst of our fiercest conflicts, we have seen with the eye of faith, the invisible hosts of God encamped around us, to deliver us. We can say to-day, in stronger language than ever before, the work of the Lord is advancing. The final triumph of the Gospel is as sure as the promise of God. More than all the generations on whose dust we tread, can we today take up the prophecy.

> Jesus shall reign where'er the sun
> Doth his successive journeys run.

This is the century of missions, such as has never been seen before. The age of world-wide missions has begun, and the figure of Jesus Christ appears upon the world's horizon, in bold belief, and the entire world will be lighted up by the radiance of His countenance. His word is read and studied by more people to-day than at any time since the leaves of the Tree of Life have been coming forth from the press. "These words have the charm of antiquity, with the freshness of yesterday; the simplicity of a child with the wisdom of God; the softness of kisses from the lips of love, and the force of the lightning rendering the tower. His parables are like groups of matchless statuary; His prayers like an organ peal floating round the world and down the ages, echoed by the mountain peaks and plains into rich and varied melody, in which all devout hearts find their noblest feelings at once expressed, sustained, refined. His truths are self-evidencing. They fall into the soul as seed into the ground, to rest and germinate. He speaks, and all nature and life become vocal with theology." Fortunate for us if we have been

with him, and have learned of Him, and will travel with him on his march through the ages, and around the world.

Our Corresponding Secretary has traveled as much this year as possible. The office work must be carefully supervised, and she has given considerable attention to the preparation of tracts and other literature that would help us in our work. We have at this meeting, a One-Act Drama, written by her, that we consider one of the most unique, semi-humorous productions we have ever read. It has been a very difficult matter to leaders in missionary societies, to get up an interesting evening's program. Slabtown Convention will prove a blessing to those who want something humorous, and at the same time, really helpful.[18]

The business of the Convention has grown to such proportions as to demand the closest attention, and it taxes one's physical and mental power to keep the business end of your work going. We have received twice as many letters this year as last. Our correspondence has been just double. The work has been exceedingly heavy, and yet our correspondents will testify that their letters have received prompt attention. We do not allow any letters to go unanswered, and every order, however large or small, receives immediate attention.

Whatever has been accomplished this year, much credit is due to the good friends throughout the country, and in the cities and towns visited by the Secretary and the missionaries. We have been most cordially received, and the work has been most substantially remembered. The Secretary spent over a month in Texas last fall, and she was given a hearty reception by churches, organizations and citizens. No words can express our gratitude to the leaders of both conventions in Texas, through whose influence the people turned out en masse to every meeting held in the State. You have but to look at our report to see that they were most liberal in their contributions. Texas leads the roll this year.

Our Secretary spent two weeks in New Jersey, in the interest of the Capetown Home. The good women, the State Foreign Mission Board, and the Ministers' Union united in making these meetings a success. Jersey Baptists conduct an annual Foreign Mission Campaign, and bring to the State specialists on this work. There is an educational and spiritual awakening throughout the state that is destined to put New Jersey far ahead of her sister states. The people need information, before they can be truly awakened. Missionary campaigns that are truly educational and deeply spiritual will arouse the most slothful. The far-seeing leaders are even now planning for a greater campaign next year.

All of the institutes have been largely attended, and we believe much good has been accomplished. A number of special meetings in the interest of the Training School have been held in various states. The last, and the one of which a single church gave the largest amount, was with the Ebenezer Church at Pittsburg. Six churches, three conventions and three individuals have thus far given the required one hundred dollars for Memorial Windows in the National Training School. In all of the meetings, the people seemed more anxious than ever to take Higher Ground, and attempt great things for God and expect great things of God. We firmly believe that institutions of this kind are constantly tending to gravitate. Like your clock, they must be occasionally cleansed, wound up, and set to true time. These annual conclaves are for that purpose. Without this annual touching up, some of us would be too dustworn for service; others would run completely down.

The coming year is going to bring to our denomination a marvelous awakening. Would that you could be with us in some of these blessed meetings, where from the least to the greatest seems to come the question, "What can I do?" Our women are just beginning to feel that they can do something, and there is an army of them down in the bottoms that you have never seen, and never will see until you walk the streets of the New Jerusalem, who are beginning to sing,

> I'm to the Highlands bound,
> I'm seeking higher ground;
> I can't remain in all the plain,
> I'm to the Highlands bound.

We have conducted institutes, missionary study classes, held meetings for women, young girls and children, as well as public mass meetings. It is impossible to mention every place visited. You will see from our financial report, that churches and individuals have given all the way from two cents to one hundred dollars. We would like to make special mention of all the friends in all the churches, but suffice it to say that we have gone east and west, north and south, women, ministers and people have opened wide their homes, churches and purses, and there is on every hand evidence of increasing interest in the work of this Convention.

The women throughout this country are waking up. The ordinary, everyday, purehearted women who have not lifted their souls to vanity, nor sworn deceitfully, are lining up. Even now we hear the tramp of the advance guard.

Marvel not at the success of the Lord's work. The common people of whom God has made more than of the other kind, are shouting the tidings of salvation as they dig the trenches and throw up the breastwork for battle and the children of Amalek will be routed and the giant sons of Anak driven back, and Satan's strongholds shall tumble before a blow is struck. God is going to line up the common people, and sweep the earth for the work so rapidly that with him one day is as a thousand years. You may not feel it; you may not hear it; but put your ear to the ground: the chariot of God is coming. True, there are stones in the way, and professed disciples drag on as dead weights, but this chariot has a divine motor, and like the stone cut out of the mountains without hands, it will crush beneath it all the avarice, secular spirit, worldly schemes, ignorance and practical indifference. We have been asking for over two thousand years that the Kingdom of this world might become the Kingdom of our Lord, and of his Christ. If we have not been in earnest, God is getting in a hurry.

"Every conceivable motive, therefore, urges us to undertake the last great crusade against the powers of darkness. The command of our ascended Lord, the voice of an enlightened conscience, the impulse of the new nature, the leading of the providential pillar, the working of transforming grace, the grandeur of the opportunity and the peril of delay—all these converge like rays in one burning focus, urging us onward and forward to the outposts of civilization and the limits of human habitation with the word of life. Let the trumpet signal be heard all along the lines! God has already sounded his signal, and, like that peal at Sinai, it is long and loud. The last precept and promise of our Lord, which have inspired all true service and sacrifice, echo with new voice and emphasis, louder and clearer, in the face of new openings and new victories. Blessed is he who, like Paul, is immediately obedient unto the heavenly vision."

J. Rosamond Johnson
"Why They Call American Music Ragtime"

Colored American Magazine, January 1, 1909

I have been asked "why do they call American music ragtime?"

To answer this question, musically, I must place what is commonly known as "ragtime" in the class of music where it belongs, i.e., syncopation. Since there is no record or definition in the dictionaries of music of "ragtime" we must then consider the appellation "ragtime" simply a slang name for that peculiarly, distinctive, syncopated rythm [sic] originated by the American Negro. And not until it reaches that higher development, only to be accomplished by scholarly musicians, will it be called "ragtime," such as the Spanish syncopated rhythm is called the "Bolero."

We all know that the Spanish used their peculiar rhythm of syncopation many years as dance music before it was designated in musical literature as the "bolero." The original Spanish "bolero" was a sensuous dance which was extremely popular among the Spanish peasants and tabooed by the Castillian aristocracy, among whom were those whose censorship governed what Spanish music should be. But the wonderful popularity of the "bolero" movement and the unique fascination of the dance which accompanied it overruled this Castillian censorship and influenced the entire music of Spain. Thereby, we have all the music of Spain, direct or indirect expressions of the emotions of the Spanish peasant people. So, like-wise, with American music, as it is known here and the world over, it is the direct expressions of the American peasant, the Negro.

The happy expressions of the Negro's emotions in music have been dubbed "ragtime," while his more serious musical expressions have been called "plantation" and "jubilee" songs, and these two styles of his expression in music are all that I can see that is distinctively American music. It is the only music that the musical centers of the world and great musicians of the world recognize as American music.

When such men as Dvorak, Safanoff, McDowell, Chadwick and Damrosch realize the real worth of Negro melody we need not consider the opinions of Finck, Farwell, Loomis and others of less note, who claim that there is no distinctive character in the original melodies of the Negro. Finck, Farwell and Loomis claim that the Indian music is the only American music to base American individuality on, but I can see no ground for their argument, as the Indian has given us no melodies to equal those of "Steal Away to Jesus" and "Go Down Moses." The latter Dvorak said is as great as the motif in Siegfried.

The Indian is a morbid race, and morbid people are not musical. The younger generation of educated and civilized Indians have produced no composers who have expressed their emotions, as true to their own life, to reach the popular or classic ear of the world, as have been expressed by the Negro (and the Indian has been in the hands of American civilization many years before the Negro). You will find no such melodies among the modern Indian music to equal in popularity "Big Indian Chief," "Navajo," "Big Red Shawl," etc. I know that neither of these songs were written by Indians, for Cole and Johnson are responsible for two of them, and the other was written by a white man. These songs typify Indian life lyrically, but not musically, for the movement and melody are Negro in character except for an occasional tom-tom accompaniment. Had they been set to the broken rythm [sic] of two beats in one measure, five in the next and so on, with the discordant harmonies known as Indian music, they would never have caught the ear of the American people. And if there is to be such a thing as American music it must be a music that the American people enjoy.

Why is it that the American loves to hear the sound of "Dixie"? Analyze the melody and you will find it a typical Negro tune. As to the setting of an Indian subject in the classic form such as oratorio, you will find that S. Coleridge-Taylor's setting of Longfellow's "Hiawatha" is the best of them all.[19] And, by the way, for those who don't know it, S. Coleridge-Taylor is a Negro notwithstanding the fact that he was born in London, England. And is the rival of the great European oratorio composer, Sir Elgar.

In analyzing this peculiar American syncopation we can easily see why it has been called "ragtime." The origin of "ragtime" began with the old darkey patting his foot, and strumming on the banjo, while the pickannies [sic] clapped their hands at the same time.

Example: Clapping of hands, strumming on banjo, patting of foot. [SCORE ILLUSTRATION][20]

And this you will find if placed as an accompaniment to any melody, be it Hungarian, German, Italian or any other, you will find that it will change the entire atmosphere, and the listener will say "Oh, that's ragtime," just as they

would if you made the accompaniment in "bolero" style [SCORE ILLUSTRATION] listener would then say: "Oh, that's Spanish music. For instance, take the last movement (the Rondo) to Beethoven's "Pathetique sonata," and instead of playing the broken arpeggios, play the accompaniment [SCORE ILLUSTRATION] or [SCORE ILLUSTRATION] and your listener will say "ragtime"; likewise they would say "that's Spanish form" [if] the accompaniment is put in the "bolero" movement.

As to the future possibilities of what is known as "ragtime" or Negro melody, we may hope for great American music to spring from its influence. For as Paderewski says in the November Century "... When lively, they dance.... The music of the Negro has been used simply because he has a natural sense for music, in which the Indians are lacking.... Mendelssohn's use of the minor mode may be connected with the Jewish tendency to complaint, to querulousness, which is in turn due to the trials and vicissitudes the race has suffered."

Then, there is a greatness in Negro melody because the sad, minor and dissonant harmonies of the plantation songs were created by the emotions of the suffering slaves.

Whenever *art* is great, there is always some tragic or sad motive connected with it. There is no joy without ever having had sorrow. We all agree that the slaves of America knew what grief was, and their emotions were expressed in their songs of "Jesus," some from the fear of their masters and others from the hope they had for deliverance.

After slavery we find the Negro singing his happy minstrel songs, giving expressions of his joy. I will admit that some of these songs were written by white men, but when we remember that some of the *best* of them, such as "Golden Slippers," "Carve Dat Possum," "In De Ebenin' By De Moonlight," were written by Sam Lucas and Jim Bland, both Negroes, we have the right to claim them as being the outcome of a happy sense of emotions prompted by the fact of being free men. And so on from stage to stage through the "Razor-Blade," "Black Gal of Mine" type of song to present emotions of the Negro of to-day, who gives us such songs as "Bamboo Tree," "Congo Love Song," "Owl and the Moon," by Cole and Johnson; "Island of Bye and Bye," by Rogers and Williams; "Mandy Lou," by Will Marion Cook, and the excellent setting of "Ethiopia," by Harry T. Burleigh, due to the conditions of the new Negro's ambitions and training.

If music is the art of expressing emotions, then the Negro has certainly given to us his conditions expressed in song. And what is folklore but the expressions of a peasant people in song. And this is proof that there is a school of music in that peculiar rythm [sic] of syncopation originating from the patting of the foot, the clapping of the hand and the strumming on the banjo by the old plantation darkey, which has passed through the same stages of improvement by new emotions of the new Negro of to-day just as he has improved in every other way. We know that the Negro is capable of doing things now that were impossible for him to do forty years ago. I am one among the many other Negroes who can write my own music and arrange it for voice and orchestra. And this is due to my good fortune of being able to study at the New England Conservatory of Music in Boston.

In the days of slavery I would have known nothing of the science of music, and some white man like Foster might have written down my expressions in music just as I have done for many white song writers of today, who were unable to write music for themselves. And yet the same spirit of melody can haunt me now, as it did the slave in his plantation songs.

Sometime ago I read in the "Literary Digest" a statement from Mr. Booker T. Washington, saying that "the Negro folk-song is the only distinctively American music." To this Mr. Henry T. Finck took exception, and claimed that "Old Folks at Home," or better known as "Swanee River," was written by Stephen Foster, a white man, and for that reason it is a white man's melody and has no character of Negro melody in it. According to Mr. Finck's argument Mr. Foster (whom I consider was a great song writer of his day) was a bad song writer, because

it is quite necessary for a song writer to apply the character and atmosphere of the text in the musical setting of a song, and this is exactly what Mr. Foster did in "Swanee River," and that is why it has lived these many years the world over.

Mr. Finck in his article admits that Mr. Foster attended Negro camp meetings and lived on the plantations. Yes, and the truth of it is that Mr. Foster did this for the purpose of placing himself in the direct atmosphere of the Negro style of melody. Sir Arthur Sullivan was a white man, but no one can deny that the "Mikado" is not influenced by Japanese character of music. I am a Negro, but that does not prevent my writing a German, French or Italian melody. One of my teachers in harmony and composition was all German, and couldn't speak English.

This ought to serve to give somewhat of a German influence to my compositions. And after having studied compositions for piano by the greatest composers along with the best grand operas for fifteen years, why should I be unable to blend such treatment of the classic with the underdeveloped music of my race? Some day some great composer (who knows perhaps he may be some *brave* white man) will take up the work where Dvorak left off and give to the world of music just what the American music-lover is clamoring for. The popular ear both white and black likes the "ragtime" song, and just so soon as this peculiar American syncopation is developed into a classic form will the censors of music find a place for "ragtime" in the history of music. Perhaps they may call it con "Raggioso."

It is just as hard for the American people to recognize Negro music as the distinctive music in America as it was for the Russians to realize that the Japanese could fight. Had our wonderful Mr. McDowell followed the advice of the great Dvorak and given much attention to the Negro folk-song, his works would have reached the hearts of the American people with greater force. His "From an Indian Lodge" is purely a Negro melody only for the tom-tom accompaniment. As I have said before, accompaniment changes the color of any melody.

If composers want themes for American symphony, or American grand opera, let them study the sad strains of the Negro plantation songs and they will find food and inspiration for great works. As Paderewski says: "All great music is mostly done in the minor mode." If the baby laughs to-day we soon forget it until he laughs again, but if the baby dies to-day we never forget, for it has struck the chord of the heart. Just so with lively music; we think of it while we hear it, and enjoy it as we do the pleasing things of life. But when we hear the minor strains in music we call up the sad memories we never can forget. Therefore, dissonant chords are used to express the tragedies of life, which are far more impressive than our moments of pleasure which we so soon forget.

"Negro music," "American syncopation," "ragtime" or "Raggioso," just whatever you choose to call it, is here, and it is here to stay, for it has already caught the ear of the people the world over. As the Toledo Blade, of November 14th, in reviewing Cole and Johnson's "Red Moon" production, says: "When the Negro first made his appearance on the stage as a musical comedy entertainer, the public looked askance at him. They could see nothing in the Ethiopians' contribution to American melody but 'ragtime' and the cheap, syncopated music of the dance halls, but the black man has surprised them. If he has done anything at all in the past few years it has been to raise the tone of the popular price offerings. And he is climbing higher every year. Where he will stop time alone can tell.

"Perhaps it will be at grand opera. Anyhow he seems to be headed that way."

Benjamin J. Davis

"Man May Evade His Duty, but He Cannot Escape the Penalty of Responsibility"

Atlanta Independent,[21] November 6, 1909

Our civilization is a white man's creation, and there is no question but the white man is not only the strong and wealthy race but that he is all-powerful and superior. It is equally true that his superiority and advancement in art, letters, wealth and character make him largely responsible for the development and usefulness of his less fortunate brother, the negro. Holy Writ has ordained that the strong shall bear the infirmities of the weak, and the white man can not escape the penalty which must inevitably overtake him for his failure to afford his black brother the best opportunity consistent with his growth to improve his time and talent.

The Negro is the weaker factor in our national life, and will not be able to survive the rigor of a white man's civilization, if the white man does not hold out to him his example and encouragement. The only thing that makes the American white man look little in the eyes of the world is, his miserly dealings with his black neighbor and brother. The American white man is great in everything except his willingness to stoop down and lift up his Negro neighbor.

The theoretical, superficial and political Negro is passing, and a new moral, industrial and economic Black factor is appearing under the leadership and enthusiasm of Booker T. Washington. And all the constructive Negro needs to fit himself constructively into his immediate environs in the community where he lives, is the co-operation and encouragement of his white neighbors. Not along social and political lines, but along industrial and economic undertakings. The Booker Washington Negro wants an equal opportunity to buy land, own a farm, in the shop and to educate his children, his social and political increment will take care of themselves when they get ripe.

The new Negro is not hankering after political emolument or social equality, but ample and adequate opportunities and facilities to educate his children; for an equal chance in the fields, at the trades and every other industry. We do not object to any advantage or opportunity our white neighbors now enjoy, we only appeal to them to increase our opportunities and chances to improve our condition and help ourselves.

It ought to be the delight and religion of a strong and powerful race to lift up a less fortunate one. If the white man has any Christ in his soul he can not always escape his plain duty. Our neighbors do not seem to understand that greatness is what greatness does in real service for humanity. A religion is of a peculiar character that will send a book nine thousand miles to a heathen Chinese and will refuse a black waif at its door the opportunity to read and improve his time and talent.

The Independent does not object to our white neighbors having the Carnegie Library, or the branch library on the north side. In the bigness of our soul, we sincerely wish that our white neighbors had a branch library for the edification of the people in every ward. The only thing we object to, is the lack of preparation for the Negro folk of the city. Now, our neighbors can not long profess the religion of Christ if they do not grow more liberal with their black neighbors. We can not understand a religion that will allow so selfish a sin to run loose unbridled. We can not understand how our white neighbors, admittedly superior in everything that constitutes greatness, can walk into the public treasury and appropriate public funds for the benefit of themselves and children, and deny their Negro neighbors the same benefits. Strength of racial character does not need any advantage of the weaker. Greatness does not need to possess itself of any advantage of littleness. The white man had as well look this situation squarely in the face and shoulder his responsibility. His duty is plain and he can not

always successfully evade it and escape the penalty of his criminal negligence. It is little less than criminal for the white men and women of the South, who are charged with the administration of public affairs to allow half of the people to grow up at their doors in ignorance and immorality. It is the duty of the white man to afford the Negro every opportunity to improve his condition, morally, economically and intellectually. The white man can not, in the light of his religion, deny the Negro any economic or industrial opportunity he avails himself; he can not, in the strength of his racial superiority, deny the Negro any moral, intellectual, or political opportunity he affords himself. If he provides ample and adequate school opportunities and facilities for his child he must, as a matter of fairness and common every-day honesty, make the same provisions for every child in the community. If the authorities provide libraries and other public utilities for white children they must, in the same spirit, prepare for every child in the municipality or prove their unfitness to administer public affairs. Our white neighbors have no more schools and equipment for moral and intellectual improvement than the progress of the age demands, but the things we complain about are the utter lack of facilities for Negroes. Libraries for the whites and nothing for Negroes does not look like the spirit of a republican form of government. Five thousand children walking the streets of Atlanta without the opportunity to go to school looks more like barbarism in Africa than it does like the proud proverbial Atlanta spirit. Our neighbors have got to help us, and they had as well address themselves to their task. The sooner they pick up the cudgel, the lighter will be their burden. God did not endow the proud Caucasian with all his wealth, moral and intellectual equipment to be dissipated in selfishness, but for real service to God and humanity. The white man must either spend himself in honest endeavor to alleviate the human ills at his door, or he will rust out in sin and selfishness. Nations and races as proud and powerful as the American white man have fallen because of their oppression to their less fortunate fellowmen.

Our neighbors may for a time successfully evade their plain, Christian duty to neighbors, and their neighbors' children, but they can not always escape the penalty of their disobedience. The best test of racial strength is the treatment accorded by a superior people to a weaker one. The Negro is deserving and the white man owes it to him to help him into the most useful citizenship. If the white man does not help the Negro up the Negro will pull him down in spite of himself. Our neighbors can not rise permanently any higher than they lift us. Self-preservation demands that the white man take care of his Negro ward with a view of constructing him into a helpful citizenship.

José Clarana

"The Schooling of the Negro"

Crisis, July 13, 1913[22]

Sooner or later, often and again, every colored man of intelligence and some colored men of no intelligence must face the question, "Which do you think is the better way of elevating your people—industrial or higher education?" Not infrequently this query takes the form, "Which of the two leaders of your race do you follow?" Assuming that one of two men can have absolute control over the destiny of ten millions of people who must in all places and under all circumstances blindly and unthinkingly regulate their conduct according to the supposed will of this demigod, the white solver of the Negro problem has been in the habit of formulating an answer to his own proposition in the following typical opinion of a sophomore debater in a Northern university, who had lived some time in Alabama.

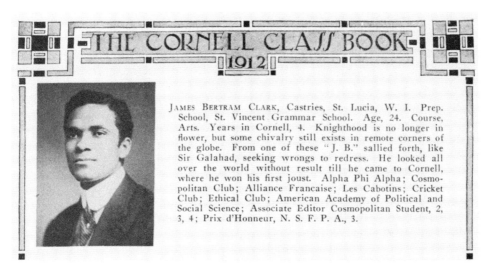

Yearbook portrait of James Bertram Clarke (aka José Clarana / Jaime Clarana Gil) from the *Cornell Class Book 1912*. Courtesy of the Burt Green Wilder Papers, Division of Rare and Manuscript Collections, Cornell University.

The Negroes are an inferior race, but though they can never equal the achievements of the white man, they ought to be trained to be useful members of society and to be self-dependent. The only way by which this end can be accomplished is by giving industrial education to the masses. It is true that a few individuals have displayed great mental capacity, but experience has shown that it is unwise to give to these men opportunities to cultivate their talents, for as soon as a Negro becomes highly educated he wants to marry a white woman. For this reason I am for educating the whole people industrially instead of wasting time and money in trying to give to the few privileges which they are bound to abuse. Of the two Negroes whose opinion is worth considering, the former position is held by Booker T. Washington, the latter by Du Bois. Washington is therefore the only real leader of his race.

I do not believe in allowing Negroes to attend schools with white people in the North, for they are not allowed in the South. I once heard Booker T. Washington say that he did not want colored men to go to Yale and I suppose he would say the same thing of this university. Negro teachers should be trained for the Negro industrial schools, but this work should be done at normal schools in the South, where the masses of the race will always be.

Fortunately the wisdom of this young fool readily became apparent to his fellow sophomores when the junior who had given rise to the color query chose to answer it in his own way by asking the questioner to name any co-ed who has expressed a willingness to marry a highly educated Negro, with or without his having particularly "wanted" to marry her; to reconcile the statement that the "only real leader" of the Negroes did not want his people to attend Northern schools with the fact that this same man had sent his own children to the best schools that would admit them and was at that moment searching these universities for colored

graduates to teach the pupils of his school for colored people; to explain, finally, where the Negro teachers in the Negro normal schools, who would be the ultimate teachers in the Negro industrial schools, would get their training if not in the universities, North and South, which offer the broadest training to students who have had the fullest and most thorough preparation in high schools and colleges, North and South.

It is thus evident on the slightest investigation that "industrial" education for Negroes is inseparably dependent upon "higher" education and that, far from neglecting the latter for the supposed advantage of the former, both processes must go on at the same place and time if either is to succeed.

In America there can be no arbitrary selection of Negroes for high, higher or highest education and of Negroes for "lower" or industrial education, for in America there is no such selection of white people. The caste and class system of European educational methods has never been reproduced among white Americans, and there is no reason to suppose that it would be advantageous among Negro Americans. In Alabama, as in New York, all children should have equal educational opportunities at the public expense. When once these opportunities are secured, those Negro children who have the capacity and ambition to rise above their fellows will do so, just as white children have done and are doing. Deny these opportunities to Negro children anywhere, and you defeat your purpose of uplifting the race by robbing it of its potential agents of self-dependence. No colored man who has the interest of his people at heart and can see far enough into its future could say otherwise.

The young sophomore was unable to state when or where he had heard a colored teacher say that colored men should not go to Yale. He had probably confused a statement of the dean of Yale College to the effect that that institution tolerated rather than encouraged Negroes. Had the debate taken place two years later the sophomore might have learned that one young man who declined to take a hint from the dean of

Yale to the effect that his room was preferable to his company, stayed and got probably the first fellowship in economics ever conferred upon a Negro at that university. Surely no optimist of the future of the American Negro would seek to prevent a colored man from obtaining in Connecticut educational advantages which he may not have yet, and perhaps not soon, in his native Kentucky, or in Tennessee, or in Alabama.

It cannot be denied, however, that the most prominent and the most influential Negro has, I doubt not unintentionally, given to sophomores, deans and other white people in and out of college an untenably biased attitude toward the educational needs of his people by reiterating, in one way or another, the notion that certain excellent forms of mental training were not good for his people—an assumption that readily finds causation in the fact that this man has made his own remarkably successful career without having had such training. But this does not prove that he has not felt the lack of such training in the years when he was best able to absorb it; that he could not have been a more prominent, more influential, more successful man if his youthful schooling had not been confined almost solely to the grim struggle for existence of an orphan of slavery. Above all, it does not give him the right to say that other Negro children should not have privileges and opportunities which he himself has not enjoyed.

No colored educator has a more promising future of the humblest beginning that the young man who, on receiving from the University of Iowa the degree of Bachelor of Philosophy—a degree which suggests familiarity with Greek roots rather than with potato sprouts—set out for Mississippi and established a school beneath a cedar tree, with a dilapidated barn for change of scenery when shade was turned to sunlight. Speaking of him the other day, a German cab driver said to a white classmate of the young Negro: "I knew Jones when he was night clerk in the O'Reilly Hotel at Iowa City, working his way through the State University. He used to put in most of his spare time studying, and whenever I was hanging around for the night trains he would practice his German on me. He was a 'live one' all right. I always knew that colored boy would show up somewhere." When this young man "shows up" in Europe on his quest of the man farthest down he will hardly need the services of a German-speaking secretary and companion.

The teaching of languages to Negroes has, I think, been the especial object of adverse criticism by the colored educator who receives the readiest hearing from white people. As to time and place, I am in as much of a quandary as was the sophomore, but I have a vague remembrance of an animadversion of Dr. Booker T. Washington upon a colored boy whom he saw sitting under a tree poring over a French grammar. This was industry with a vengeance, especially if the sun was hot. It was useful conversation of time and of bodily energy. But the apostle of industrial education thought the lad ought to have been picking cotton or husking corn.

I have, on the other hand, a very definite recollection of the young woman who came to a Northern university to fit herself for teaching at Tuskegee, the institution which had sent her out to teach in the small rural schools for Negroes in the South. She had the courage, and the courage presupposed the intelligence to do the work of this university. But prospective teachers of Tuskegee who wish to study even in an agricultural college are required to have a good knowledge not only of English, but of some modern foreign language as well. The young lady had the English, because she had not lived in a rural community in Alabama, but she did not have the French and could not acquire it in the time at her disposal and with the work that she was doing to support herself. She had never seen a French word in its Latin form. She had heard much of potato roots, but had never had anything to do with a Greek root. At 22 she could not change her way of thinking and speaking as readily as she might have at 12. Her chemistry and physics were of the same stamp as her French, for these subjects are studied in Northern colleges mostly from books or from classroom demonstrations, and not from out-door "object" lessons, with the emphasis on the object rather than on the lesson. The university authorities admired this young woman's pluck and, partly from a spirit of chivalry, they stretched her entrance units enough to let her attend the classes for just one term. Then they "busted" her. And this brave little soul returned to her home, rueing bitterly the day she had set out for far-away Alabama thinking that indus-try, usefulness to one's self and to others, capac-ity for adaptation to circumstances, were qual-ities which could be acquired only in some school labeled "industrial."

The acceptance of the dollar ideal of schol-arship by colored people who prefer to have a "leader" think for them rather than to use their own minds is not a very encouraging aspect of the future of the American Negro. In Greater New York, with a colored population of more than 90,000, only seven young men are to re-ceive diplomas from the high schools this year. The reason assigned by the hundreds who have failed to use the opportunities so fully and freely given to them is not far to seek: "There is noth-ing for us to do with a good education. We could only use it among our own people and they are in the South. We do not want to go down South, so we quit school and work for enough to keep body and soul together. [T]hough we can al-ways find a little change for dancing and a little time for the street corners. Ain' nothin' we can git out o' school. Ain' no money in books."

The problem of finding employment for an educated colored man is undeniably difficult, but it is becoming less and less difficult propor-tionately with the increase of educated colored men. The greater breadth of vision insures keener and quicker perception of opportunities. The possession of a good education is more often an incentive rather than a detriment to in-dustry and respect for labor. The difference be-tween the waiter, the bricklayer, the coachman who knows Greek and algebra and the one who does not is that the one who knows must get a chance to do something else if he will only try hard enough, whereas the one who does not know anything else but waiting can never ex-

pect to do something to which he has not been trained to adapt himself. As a matter of fact, col-ored men hold positions in New York and other Northern cities that they could never oc-cupy in the South because they are not white, and their own people have no such places to offer. These men have the courage and the pa-tience to seek their positions, and their courage rests on the knowledge that they have the abil-ity to fill the positions which they seek.

But why expect to see a green or yellow-back to every book you open? In education the Negro must "cast down his bucket" where he is, but he need not stop casting and hauling if he cannot draw a load of gold every time. Not all commodities are equally readily exchangeable for money. Cotton and corn and cane will sell almost anywhere and at any time, because their value, like their cost, is comparatively less than that of Greek, French or German, for which the market is not always apparent, though always real and enduring. You can grow cotton at any time without having gone to any school, pro-vided only you have the sense, the interest and the experience to do it. Sam McCall, an illiter-ate ex-slave, 75 years old, grew eight bales of cotton on an acre of land that would not have produced one-eighth of a bale when he got it. The experts of the United States Department of Agriculture have never done likewise; no other farmer, white or Negro, has ever approached this achievement.

But Sam McCall, at 75, could hardly make much headway with an English copy book or a French grammar, for although Cato began to study Greek at 80, he was already acquainted with Roman letters. Without the study and the schooling no amount of sense and interest will open to you the treasures of other people's mind and thought as expressed in their language; no amount of patient hope and longing will give you that contact with other people which is the basis of all civilization and without which human beings speedily degenerate to the level of the Bleasites of South Carolina, who dismem-bered a dead Negro in order to get and take away souvenirs of a lynching party that had reached their man too late.

It is this broadening, civilizing, humanizing aspect of the so-called "higher" education that makes it so essentially and so practically valuable to Negroes and to whites alike. A young sailor on a United States warship is sent to ship's prison for five days' solitary confinement on bread and water for wanting to read when his work is done and for telling a white petty officer not to call him Rastus. While he is supposed to be brooding over the consequences of a Negro's "insolence" to a white man, he strengthens the foundation of a knowledge of Italian from a grammar book which he has had smuggled in to him. Some months later, when the ship is at an Italian port, the same Negro boy has the satisfaction of seeing himself appealed to by every other man on the ship, the captain and the brutal petty officer included, to act as interpreter. He gets no dollars and scant thanks from them, but though dollars enough have since come in to pay several times over the cost of that Italian grammar, the greatest factor in the subsequent career of this young man can be traced to the wholesome use of those five days on bread and water, and not the least important part of this career has been the winning of the friendship of Italians, dead and living.

Again, a Negro enters a candy store in New York and, before the proprietor comes to him, his eye is attracted by a Greek daily paper lying on the counter. When the proprietor does come he wants the Negro to read aloud something from the paper. The colored man who reads Greek, ancient or modern, is not the one who was struck on the head with a bottle by a Hellenic restaurateur.

The Shaw Settlement House in Boston very wisely provides instruction in French as well as in cooking and waiting. The colored waiter who knows French is far less likely to have a dispute with a Parisian chef than the servitor whose only recommendation to the good graces of a white man is his dark skin and his half-understood speech. More than this, the Negro who reads the letters of Toussaint l'Ouverture and the novels of Dumas in the original will see for himself that Theodore Parker, the Boston abolitionist, was wrong in saying that a colored man could at best be only a good waiter. The Negro who reads in Spanish the poems of Plácido, the novels and speeches of Morua Delgado, of Gualberto Gómez and of other representative colored men of Cuba, cannot fail to receive new inspiration and new confidence in the power of black blood to redeem itself, without as well as within the United States.

These observations may not prove anything, but they have an important bearing on the Negro problem. Those who look out for the future of the American Negro cannot fail to see that the component elements of white America are changing and have rapidly changed since the Civil War. The faithful old Negro was more or less thoroughly "understood" by his aristocratic master, his red-shirt neighbor and rival, and his philanthropic liberator. But the new Negro who wants to be faithful to himself as well as to others must adapt himself to the character of his new neighbors—the Italian in the South, the cosmopolitan immigrant everywhere in the North. The Negro's best hope for a place in the new America lies in learning to understand the new Americans. He can best do this by going to school with them, using the same books they use, thinking the same thoughts they think. Where the humanizing influence of this contact is denied to them, colored youth may still insist on equality of opportunity for the broadest and fullest education that their white fellows receive. "Cast down your buckets where you are" is the gospel to Negro boys and girls of school age. If there be no well of knowledge in sight, then go where you can find one, or insist that your elders make you one. Do not stop to assay the haul, but cast a bucket now and always and everywhere for high, higher, highest education, for without this you could have no industrial education—you could have no education at all.

Leslie Pinckney Hill

"Negro Ideals: Their Effect and Their Embarrassments"

Journal of Race Development 6, no. 1 (1915)[23]

By Leslie Pinckney Hill, A.M., Principal of Cheyney Training School for Teachers, Cheyney, Penn.

Ideals Determine Racial or National Destiny

Conscious ideals determine the destiny of nations. The Greeks sought elasticity and symmetry of body and mind. To this end the state directed all its conscious training. To this same end tended the influence of the Greek's environment. Hence in Hellas the world's highest aesthetic and philosophical development. The Roman sought grandeur, organization, military glory. Hence the unconquerable armies of Julius Caesar, and the wonders of the Augustine era. Germany has taught its youth for nearly a century the arts of war. Authority has insisted that every citizen should doff his cap to the military officer. The mighty energies of her people have been centered in the production of armament. The result is such a miracle of overweening military efficiency that the rest of the civilized world is called upon to check its progress. The aim of conscious Chinese training has been for centuries a perfect memorizing of the precepts of Confucius and Mencius. Chinese adolescents have been saturated in the needs, principles and practices of their forbears. The result in China has been unparalleled stagnation, and the formation of a "cake of custom" which all the force of western civilization can hardly break. In our own land there is everywhere apparent a striving for material success. Zealous enjoyment of the outward things of life and "making money" are characteristics. The result in our nation is the submergence of the scholar, the poet, the saint, the artist, the philosopher, and the ascendency of the great magnate, the captain of industry, the millionaire.

The Inadequacy of Racial and Nation Ideals

But although a people's conscious training and environment make it possible fairly to determine the quality of a people's spiritual, political and industrial order, it is not possible by these tokens to say whether any race group will endure. There has thus far been no nation whose ideal has been sufficient for its cumulative needs. Thus far there has been no ideal that adequately squared with practical conduct on a wide racial or national scale. Whether in Egypt or Persia, the far East or the nearer West, the characteristic ideal of every people thus far has been wanting in some essential. The love of the beautiful has failed. Worship of military might and glory has been sterile of good. By this program men have reaped little more than interracial and inter-national hatred. Even Jehovah's wars have always aborted. All of Europe has at times been astir with a mighty religious enthusiasm, but this enthusiasm has not brought enduring peace. The perfect sanctity of St. Francis himself was not sufficient. Europe has at other times worshipped the lure of flesh and blood. No one will forget the day when a woman from the streets of Paris was lifted to the holy place in Notre Dame as a symbol of reason. Not all the blood of the disastrous French Revolution has yet been able to make amends for this travesty. So each ideal in turn has appeared and disappeared through the centuries. Magnificence, organization, beauty, material power, have all left something to be desired. No nation has been able permanently to stand. We can speak with authority of the future of no human group.

Europe as Example

The present European war, for instance, is making over again the map of Europe. Races will be inter-fused, which heretofore were widely separated. The ends of the world have met in the blood-stream of battle; boundary lines have been effaced, and racial and national animosities have been both relieved and deepened. Here is the world's latest shifting, re-casting and abandonment on a gigantic scale of race and national ideals, here also the unparalleled exhibition of their inadequacy. The conflagration in Europe brings to mind anew one of Francis Galton's pessimistic conclusions. "We find ourselves," he says, "face to face with two indisputable facts which everywhere force themselves on the attention and compel consideration. The one is that the whole of the living world moves steadily and continuously towards the evolution of races that are progressively more and more adapted to their complicated mutual needs and to their external circumstances. The other is that the process of evolution on this earth, so far as we can judge, has been carried on neither with intelligence nor ruth." Clearly, that which has neither intelligence nor ruth is governed by no law of logic, and lends itself to no prevision.

The Peculiar General Plight of the Negro

In this world view, then, it is impossible for an enlightened mind to be dogmatic as to the complete sanity and lasting efficacy of any program or ideal having for its aim the enduring development of any group of people like the Negroes in the United States. It is hazardous to prophesy what the future is to bring forth for a people so peculiarly circumstanced. The Japanese have proved how difficult it is for an upward-striving race to set up for itself an ideal that will embrace the enduring elements of civilization, and at the same time escape the weaknesses and pitfalls of the races and the nations that have not endured. The condition of the civilized Negro in America is complicated by the fact that he does not occupy a separate territory in which he may

freely develop according to his innate or acquired genius, but is inextricably involved in the conflicting ideals, sentiments, opinions, customs and practices of the environing white race. He is also well nigh hopelessly embarrassed by the deliberate organized efforts of the numerically superior white group in the midst of which he lives to fasten upon him in varied forms the stamp of inferiority.

Christianity and the Negro

The Negro is still further baffled by the instability and chameleon-like character of those ideals which have been offered to him by those from whom he has learned the arts of life. Christianity magnifies the importance of humility, teaches the brotherhood of man and the fatherhood of God, and brings to the world the convincing Gospel of love as the solvent of human problems. The colored man, however, fails to see in his relations with his white neighbor any faithful practice either of the fatherhood of God or the brotherhood of man. The humility which is in him a native trait has been exploited for material profit. Putnam Weale in "The Conflict of Color" has been frank enough to warn all white civilization that it will do well to continue its preaching of the gospel of humility to the prolific colored races of man. If once these innumerable peoples were indued with some militant faith like Mohammedanism there might come upon the world such a race conflice [sic] as would pall the horror of Europe. The Negro in America, then, finds a wide divergence between the teachings of Christianity and its actual practices. The church of God, with all its professions of peace and righteousness, shuts its doors deliberately in the black man's face. Those whom it most needs to serve are those whom it deliberately avoids. If it serves, it renders that service in isolation, and in the spirit of condescension. In 1915 a Negro who should enter a white church of God anywhere in the South— barring the Catholic, Christian Science, and Bahai Communions—with the idea of worshipping at ease and with confidence by the side of his white brother would be considered a disturber of the public peace. Of what worldly value, then, to the black man is Christ?

Democracy and the Negro

His case is not simplified when he ponders Democracy. He is living in a land where man was to be freed from the trammels of caste and unreasoned prejudice. Here oppressed men sought "freedom's largest home." Here were to be no metes or bounds to advancement, other than what might lie in lack of ability, energy or spirit. America was dedicated to the proposition that all men are, as human souls, equal and endowed by the Creator with the inalienable rights of life, liberty and the pursuit of happiness. But each one of these great principles the Negro finds prostituted as soon as they are applied to him. He is not permitted really to be a citizen. His liberty of movement, residence and enjoyment is curtailed by all the devices of Jim-Crowism. He is shut out from the ballot; he is forced to reside in segregated areas; he is denied the ordinary public conveniences and utilities; he is unprotected by law; and he is, finally, of such small account in the public view that he can be lynched with impunity. This unbridled licentiousness of race prejudice lays the axe to the root of the tree of Democracy. Nobody has ever found any reasonable defense of these traducements of the republican spirit; but the great majority of the black man's neighbors endorse them. What, then, to the black man does Democracy mean?

Education and the Negro

Education itself offers him, as yet, no certain guarantees. The present pathetic condition and influence of the average southern public Negro school is notorious. It needs no description here. A reprint from the report of the Commissioner of Education for the year ended June 30, 1912, on this subject, can be had by addressing the Department of the Interior. Other fuller studies now in progress are to be reported in the near future. Everywhere throughout the southland the Negro private secondary school is at-

tempting, against desperate odds, what it is the confessed duty of the State to accomplish.

The Southern States do not even pretend to accord to the colored youth any adequate or just opportunity in the public schools for self-realization. For twenty-five or thirty years white public opinion has enthusiastically embraced industrial education for the Negro as a race. But this endorsement has been slow in taking material form. In 1915 there is only one Hampton and one Tuskegee where there should be a hundred. All men know how great the need is of industrial training for any people, white or black, especially in a materialistic era like our own. But no one really supposes that industrial education, even when liberally provided, is to be any solvent of the Negro's problems. No one can minimize the importance of industrial experience for the Negroes by stating its limitations. It will solve no race issue. Only the intellectually indolent can think it will. Only the blind can believe it. In spite of all our industrial propaganda throughout the land, the blunt fact today, more apparent and, in important respects, more discouraging than it was twenty-five years ago, is that there is a strong general, increasing tendency to exclude Negroes everywhere from skilled industrial pursuits. The labor unions are practically solid in their opposition to the admission of colored men. Nobody expects, in these days, to see anywhere in the land a Negro railroad conductor or motorman, engineer or pilot. In the northland any considerable group of Negro carpenters, masons, apprentices or skilled artisans of any kind in any of the great industrial establishments would create a public sensation. Employment for the colored man in the North is progressively narrowing down to menial public and domestic service. Efficiency and desert do not avail. A colored man who seeks an opening in skilled, dignified employment is met with the frank statement that the white force will "walk out" if he is admitted. Industrial education, as far as we can judge, has accomplished little or nothing in diminishing the evils of prejudice.

It is equally true that intellectual education has done no more to heal these hurts. A strong tendency has set in to exclude Negroes, however ambitious or qualified, from most of the higher technical and collegiate institutions. In numerous ways—sometimes by frank statement, sometimes by unmistakable suggestions—the American Negro is given to understand that he is not welcome in the holy places dedicated to truth. In 1915 it is, for example, practically impossible for a colored man or woman to live at Princeton University, Vassar, or even at Bryn Mawr College. Few denials of Democracy and Christianity could be more heart-rending. When seminaries of pure learning draw the color line, what defense can black folks expect in the grosser avenues and activities of life. What, then, is the essential value of education of any description to the Negro at that crucial point where the path of his progress crosses the way of the white man?

The Problems of the Twentieth Century Negro

The clear, bare question presented to the young Negro of the twentieth century is, then, not whether the white man's Democracy and Christianity with respect to him have failed, but what his own attitude towards that failure shall be. What is to be his conscious ideal, his mind-picture of the development possible, under these embarrassed circumstances, to him? What definite program is he to project for himself?

These questions will no longer be answered by dispirited or gentle Negroes of the "mammy" type. Those pure and loyal souls could be cozened, deceived and abused without complaint. Because of their innocent impotency and their unqualified acceptance of the inferior social place, because they never even dreamed of rising above that station, the public flag is still set at half-mast when one of these worthies passes. The fidelity of the Negro slave to a sincerely appreciative master was often indeed a noble and beautiful thing; but, let it be understood, this type of Negro is to be no more in this land. The race problems of the future are to be confronted by Negroes who have known nothing of the slave regime, who have education, who believe

in the unconquerable power of truth, who hate all the forms of bigotry and double dealing, who have learned to think and aspire, and who test their efficiency and success in life by no other than the highest social standards. They have been taught pride, and self-respect. They have an increasing will to rise. They chafe under anything less than a man's chance. Above all things, they are determined to spare neither their voices nor their energies in Zion until they have achieved full, untrammeled American citizenship, or gone down in the midst of a glorious warfare for it.

Fundamental Convictions

This new Negro, in forming his ideal, is sure of two things taught by all the experience of the civilized world. He knows that the law of God and man alike, and all of nature, are with him in two fundamental convictions. The first is that there can be no peace among races or nations without righteousness and justice. The second is, that loyalty to truth alone can make men free. The new Negro knows that as long as injustice and unrighteousness are practiced against him on every hand, there can be neither race adjustment nor lasting national peace. As long as the fundamental truth as to his human nature and human worth is denied, as long as he is regarded by law and custom as an outcast from the brotherhood of man, there can be no effective coöperation [sic] between the races. The palliatives of politics and the cunning sophistries of opportunists may be triumphant for awhile, but these at last must break down, exactly as they have all broken down in Europe, and the whole battle for Christianity and Democracy fought over again. He knows that he must erect for himself some definite goal, must build for himself some clear mind-picture of his future, which will be based squarely upon these immovable convictions, and that he must have intellectual and moral strength to follow this ideal in good and evil report. He feels that there rests upon him now, in the providence of God, nothing less than the drastic responsibility of leading Christianity and

Democracy back to their ancient professions. Finally, he is convinced that his cause is no longer to be supported by vicarious champions. The days of Garrison, Sumner, John Brown, Julia Ward Howe and Thomas Wentworth Higginson are gone, just as the days of the beloved "mammy" are gone. In the future the American Negro must work out more largely his own salvation—in wholesome coöperation with white neighbors, if he can, but single-handed, if he must. "Personal liberty," says one of his severest critics, "has, in most cases, been attained by the mass of men in a community after a severe struggle. Where it has been self-developed it is almost secure; if it has been a gift from others, the inner qualities needed to maintain it are far less likely to exist." Colored men in positions of influence and leadership are pondering this truth now as never before.

Race Ideals

The young Negro knows, moreover, that in framing a program for his future conduct he must steadily remember that physical force is non-availing. All the blood-letting of Europe and Asia is teaching him this lesson anew in the thunder of howitzers. His victories, in so far as they are substantial and lasting, must be invariably moral and spiritual victories. A sturdy self-control must be the first signal conquest. He must cultivate for himself and his children an uncompromising attitude with regard to the respect which he must insist that all men shall accord his integrity and humanity. He must refuse to accept the stamp of inferiority. He must have no ease until the ravages of segregation, discrimination and ignorance are checked. Yet in all of this he must exalt the principles of peace. He must speak truth without wavering, and yet with all true humility and courtesy. He must fight with all his might the good fight against isolation, and yet not stir up race animosities. He must rid himself of obsequiousness, servility of all sorts and of insincerity. Still he must assiduously cultivate the friendship of his white neighbor. In short, the young Negro

of the twentieth century in America is called, by the extraordinary circumstances of his position, to a plane of idealistic moral conduct which must, in the nature of things, be superior to the behavior of the great masses of white men. He must not only be the apostle of peace; he must bring back to our world belief in the essential worth of human nature and faith in God. If he rises to this, the American Negro may give to the world a new spiritual type, and to civilization an enduring spiritual contribution.

Now in a large view, it is just this spiritual ideal, here roughly outlined, this lofty ideal of peaceful race adjustment on a moral and spiritual basis, that the intelligent Negro minister, teacher, business man and family head are holding up for the younger generation of Negroes in these first decades of the twentieth century. I myself know nothing of slavery, but my father was a slave, and my mother, though always "free," knew at first-hand the iniquities of that disastrous system which it required the civil war to destroy. In all the thirty-five years of my life I have never heard spoken by either of my parents one word of hatred towards white people. The fear of God, belief in the ultimate triumph of righteousness, faith in the future, industry, self-control, and the moral law were ever upon their lips. Nor have I in all my life heard any Negro teacher or preacher counsel sedition or hatred or retaliation. Every representative Negro leader and spokesman known to me in the past, or known to me now, has counseled peace, coöperation, industry, self-reliance, self-control, tactful self-assertion, education, faith in man and belief in God. There has perhaps in reality been more idealism among American Negroes than among any other ethnic group in the whole population. The Negro is compelled to be an idealist.

The Fruit of These Ideals

In a great world view, two important questions with reference to such a people remain. The first is what fruit have these conscious ideals borne? Can we see natural results flowing from them as definitely as we can in retrospect from the ideals of the races that lived in Greece or Italy or Mesopotamia centuries ago?

Fortunately, the last census furnishes invaluable special statistics on Negroes in the United States. . . .

These statistics are, of course, finally conclusive of nothing. They serve, however, to show that the Negroes in America are, in spite of severe educational disabilities, social and political ostracism, lack of organization and adequate race consciousness, poverty, ignorance, disease and crime, a virile, advancing body. What the race may accomplish in the future, if opportunity can be provided and the gyves of sheer prejudice broken, seems, in this view, to be clear. This race even now exhibits, by statistics, a power of production and reproduction and a large spiritual quality that will stand favorable comparison with any similar mass contribution made by Greek or Roman to the highest culture of the past. The Negro, in short, appears by all the facts we have in hand to be a national asset, not a national burden, and to be capable of unlimited progress.

The Great Obstacle

But the final question is this: Will the white man of the future admit in spirit and in practice that the Negro must be given the fullest freedom and opportunity to continue his development? Here is the acid test. It is the white man's stubborn refusal to grant that full freedom and opportunity that constitutes the great obstacle now to the progress not only of nearly 10,000,000 human souls, but more fundamentally to the progress of Christianity and Democracy for all men. Because there is neither reason nor moral principle in the white man's present attitude towards the colored races of man the world over, it is impossible at times to see in the future anything other than a new colossal conflict. That attitude must voluntarily yield or be broken. . . .

What of the Future?

The future for the Negro, as well as for the white man in this country, is shrouded in uncertainty. If the dark man's ideals continue to be what they have been in the past, and what they are now, his race, as far as human calculation can venture, promises unlimited and widely varied advancement. But on every hand this progress is balked and embarrassed by the white man's unconscionable denial to the Negro of Christian and Democratic treatment. The issue which this denial has already sharpened, and the increased race friction which is sure to follow the progress of education among colored people forbode nothing good. Looking back over the disasters of civilizations long since perished the enlightened Negro discerns in the nation-wide triumph of prejudice over principle all the seeds of that racial and national dissolution which has made of the world thus far a stage for unending tragedies. Only righteousness exalteth a nation; only the truth can make men free; social equilibrium is impossible where the brotherhood of man is repudiated; and morality never long survives the rejection of God. The Negro believes in Christianity and Democracy. He has measurably shaped his conscious ideals according to those supreme standards. Nothing seems now more certain than that the highest development of the Negro and the peace and security of American institutions must rest upon the degree in which the white race in America can in practice, as well as in theory, adopt the same criteria.

~~~~~~

Oscar Micheaux

"Chapter Eight: Henry Hugh Hodder"

In *The Forged Note: A Romance of the Darker Races*, book 1 (1915)[24]

Weeks had passed, and a touch of spring time was in the Dixie air. Sidney Wyeth's canvass was now assisted by another, while from over the country he had secured, here and there, an agent to sell the book. He found desk space in an office on the second floor, hired a stenographer, and filled the country with circular letters. Perhaps fifty or more replies were received, a few with a money order and requests for further information.

Although most of the letters were sent to preachers and teachers throughout the south, two-thirds of the replies came from the north. From Boston, New York, Chicago, and centers where literature is obtainable from the libraries which are open to Negroes, more letters by far came, than from the south where such is not always available. And out of these, a few agents were secured. But it seemed almost an impossibility to interest those at the south in a subject of literature.

One day, there came a letter from a small town in Florida that amused Wyeth. It was from the secretary of the board of trade. In reply to the circular inquiry, requesting the names of the Negro preachers in that city, it ran thus:

> MY DEAR SIR: Replying to your favor of recent date relative to the names of Negro preachers of this city. In regard to this, I am compelled to say, that I cannot fully enlighten you, for this reason: Everything with trousers appears to be a preacher, or, any one who can spell "ligon."
>
> My gardener is a preacher, although he finds my work more remunerative, apparently; but you could, however, write to him, and he would, I feel sure, give you the desired information.

When Sidney appraised Tompkins of his failure to get the cooperation of southern preachers, in his exploit, he was advised that the preachers were working that "side of the street."

*   *   *

We cannot appreciatively continue this story, without including a character that is very conspicuous in Negro enterprise. That is the undertaker. He is always in evidence. Mortality among Negroes exceeds, by far, that among whites. This is due to conditions that we will not dwell upon, since they will develop during the course of the story; but in Attalia, there was one undertaker who was particularly successful. He had the reputation of burying more Negroes than any man in the world. He had a son, a ne'er-do-well, to say the least, and they called him "Spoon."

Sidney, who at this time shared a room with Thurman, became acquainted with "Spoon" one Sunday night. It was at a "tiger," of which, as we now know, there were plenty.

Spoon had a reputation in local colored circles, as well as his father; but Spoon's reputation was not enviable. He was booziogically inclined, and reputed by those who knew him, to be able to consume more liquor than any other ordinary society man. Moreover, Spoon was "some" sport, too; could play the piano, in ragtime tune, and could also "ball the jack." He would lean back upon the stool, play the latest rag, as no other could, and at the end, cry: "Give me some more of that 'Sparrow Gin'!"

Wyeth and Spoon became close friends following their first meeting, and Sunday nights, they would roam until one or two in the morning. Spoon knew where every "tiger" in town was; and, moreover, he proved it.

Thurman, although two and fifty, was no "poke"; but was a sport too. His began early Sunday morning. One Sunday morn, as they lay abed, after the light of the world had come back and claimed its own, Thurman called to Sidney where the other lay reposing in the pages of a "best seller." "Say, kid! how 'bout a little toddy this mawnin'?"

"I'm there," came the reply.

"Good!" exclaimed Thurman. "Guess, tho' I'll haf to go after it, 's see you lost in a book all time. Gee! Looks lak you'd lose your mind a-readin' so much." No comment. "Guess that's why you got all these nigga's a-argun' 'roun' heah though; cause you read and they don't. M-m; yeh, yeh; that makes a diff'nce. M-m."

"Wull, reckon' ah'll haf t' git in muh breeches and crawl ou' and git dat stuff t' make it wid. M-m. Old Mis' 'roun' the conah 'll be glad t' git dis twenty cents dis mawnin'. M-m. Wull, kid, be back t'rectly."

He was, sooner than expected. He didn't get outside. He peeped out. What met his gaze would send any southern rheumatic Negro back.

It was snow.

"Jesus Chr-i-s-t!" he exclaimed, returning hastily from the hallway. "Hell has sho turned on dis' mawnin out dare. K-whew! 'f the's anything in this world I hates, it's snow."

Sidney stopped reading long enough for a good laugh, as Thurman skinned off his trousers and clambered back into bed.

"Aw, shucks, Thur, this is a morning for toddies."

"A mawnin' fo' Hell, yes, hu! hu! Wow!"

After a spell, he peeped from beneath the coverlets. "Say! since ah come t' think uv't, we c'n have dem toddies wid-out get'n froze out in doin' it."

"How's that?' asked the other.

"I'll get dat liquah from John."

"And who is John?"

"John? Wull, did'n' you git 'quainted wi'im when I brung you heah? John's the man we room with. He sells liquah."

*   *   *

"Say Spoon," said Sidney one day, "I'm going to cut the tiger kitin' out."

"Aw, gwan, kid, what you talkin' 'bout?"

"I'm going to church in the mornings, and in the evenings, I hope to find a place that will be more in keeping with respectable people," announced Sidney.

"Come on, let's go up here to old lady Macks, and get some of that 'Sparrow Gin,'" Spoon suggested, temptingly.

"To prove that I am not likely to keep my resolution."

"You've none to keep as I can particular see. I have never seen you drink anything stronger than beer when you've been with me. You seem to go along with me, to see me and the others act a fool. Sometimes you impress me as being a strange person. . . . I wonder. Now I wonder. . . ."

"Where is a church that would be likely to appeal to you and myself?"

"Up on Herald Street is one that I think will appeal to *you*. You're serious. Me—I'm quite unfit for any; but I'll take you up there, and sit through one of Hodder's sermons if you care to go. My people are members of that church, and it is a progressive one."

"We will attend services there—Sunday morning."

Wyeth became a regular visitor.

The following Sunday, the pastor appraised the congregation of the fact, that on the following Sunday, they would have with them the Reverend W. Jacobs, the energetic young man who was doing such great work for the training of wayward children. And this takes our story into a matter of grave human interest.

Coincident with better educational facilities, and the more careful training of the children, time had brought a change that was slowly but surely being felt by these black people in the south. It has already been stated, that the Baptist church required little literary training in order to preach; but, in this church, it is quite different, and no man would be tolerated as a minister, who had not a great amount of theological, as well as literary training.

Henry Hugh Hodder was a man, not only prepared in the lines of theology and literature, but was fully supplied with practical knowledge as well. He had, at the time Sidney Wyeth became acquainted with him, gathered to his church, a majority of Attalia's best black people. His popularity was, moreover, on the increase, and his church was filled regularly with a class of people who listened, studied and applied to their welfare, what he said each Sunday in the pulpit.

His church stood on a corner to the edge of the black belt, and near a fashionable white neighborhood. And it had, at the time it was constructed, caused considerable agitation. When Sidney and Spoon came to the door, prayer was being offered, and when it was over, they entered, taking seats near the door.

It was a nicely ventilated church, with large colored windows, arranged to allow air to pass in without coming directly upon the congregation. At the front, a small rostrum rose to the level of the rear, and contained, in addition to the altar, only four chairs. Sidney was told afterwards, that, due to a practice always followed in other churches, particularly the Baptist, of allowing journeymen preachers to put themselves before the congregation uninvited, Hodder had removed the chairs in order to discourage such practice.

Apparently he had succeeded, for, on the Sundays that followed, Sidney saw only those who were invited, facing the congregation.

Directly over the rostrum hung a small balcony, which contained the choir and a pipe organ. Following a song, the pastor came forward. He was a tall man, with width in proportion, perhaps two hundred and twenty pounds. Not unlike the average Negro of today, he was brown-skinned. His hair, a curly mass of blackness, was brushed back from a high forehead. His voice, as he opened the sermon, was deep and resonant. And for his text that day, he took "Does It Pay!"

Not since Sidney Wyeth had attended church and heard sermons, had he been so stirred by a discourse! Back into the ancient times; to the history of Judea and Caesar, he took the listener, and then subtly applied it to the life of today. Never had he heard one whose eloquence could so blend with everyday issues, and cause them to react as moral uplift. For he knew the black man's need. Pen cannot describe its effect upon Sidney Wyeth. It seemed, as the words of the pastor came to him, revealing a thousand moral truths, which he had felt, but could not express, that he had come from afar for a great thing, that sermon. It lifted him out of the chaos of the present, and brought him to appreciate what life, and the duty of existence really meant.

Having, in a sense, drifted away from the pious training he had received as a youth, Sidney Wyeth was suddenly jerked back to the past, and enjoyed the experience. On account of his progressive ideas, he had been accused, by some of his people, since his return to live among them, of being an unbeliever. He was often told that he was not a Christian; they meant, of course, that he was not a member of a church, which, to most colored people, is equivalent to disbelief. Sidney Wyeth saw the life, the instance of Christ as a moral lesson.

When the sermon closed, Wyeth had one desire, and fulfilled it, and that was to shake Henry Hugh Hodder's hand; moreover, to tell him, in the only way he knew how, what the sermon had been to him.

He did so, and was received very simply.

As he approached the rostrum, at the foot of which stood the pastor, shaking hands with many others who had come forward in the meantime, he was like one walking on air. He recalled the many sermons preached to satisfy the emotion of an ignorant mass, and which, in hundreds of instances, went wide of the mark, causing a large portion of the congregation to rise in their seats, and give utterance to emotional discordance, the same being often forgotten by the morrow.

Hodder was not only as he was just described, but he proved to Sidney Wyeth to be a practical, informed, and observing man as well. When he had received the card, he inquired of the country from whence Sidney came, and related briefly the notices he had followed, regarding its opening a few years previous.

At that moment, a large man, almost white—that is, he was white, although a colored man—was introduced to him as Mr. Herman.

The Largest and Finest Barber Shop in the World

Interior View of Shop (66 Peachtree St. and N. Broad St.) Street to Street

25 CHAIRS
20 BATHS

The Finest and Largest
BARBER SHOP
In the World

A. F. HERNDON
Proprietor of
HERNDON'S
BARBER SHOPS

Interior View of Shop at 7 North Broad Street

Interior View of Shop at 100 North Pryor Street

HERNDON'S BARBER SHOPS

ANYONE who can "pull" a razor without cutting a person's throat can OPEN a barber shop. It is the man who "knows how" to CONDUCT a barber shop that keeps his place open. Herndon's Barber Shops in Atlanta have stood this test.

The conduct of a barber shop is a matter of cleanliness and workmanship.

Unless tools are kept clean and sharp the trade ends. Herndon's shops are conducted on strictly sanitary lines. Every barber changes his white linen suit daily. Every barber sterilizes his hands four times a day in a medicinal solution. Every towel, razor, comb, brush and shaving brush is sterilized before and after using.

Compounds, calculated to kill any possible germ, are used in washing the floors in Herndon's Barber Shops. Porters are required to clean all brass and mirrors twice daily.

These are the reasons why Herndon's Barber Shops are known the country over as the finest establishments of their kind in the universe.

HERNDON'S BARBER SHOPS

66 Peachtree Street   7 North Broad Street   100 North Pryor Street

Advertisement for "The Largest and Finest Barbershop in the World," featuring Alonzo Herndon, *Atlanta Constitution*, May 12, 1914.

He proved to be the proprietor of the large barber shop on Plum Street, which had caught Sidney's attention the day he came. After Mr. Herman's introduction, he met many others prominent in Negro circles, including the president and cashier of the local Negro bank. And thus it came that Sidney Wyeth met these, the new Negro, and the leaders of a new dispensation.

Two hours after the services had closed, he passed a big church on Audubon Avenue; a church of the "old style religion" and, which most Negroes still like. It was then after two o'clock. Morning service was still in order—no, the sermon had closed, but collection hadn't. Out of curiosity, he entered. The pastor had, during this period, concentrated his arts on the collection table. He was just relating the instance of people who put their dollar over one eye, so closely, that it was liable to freeze to the eye and bring about utter blindness. "So now," he roared, brandishing his arms in a rally call, "*We jes' need a few dollahs mo' to make the collection fo'ty-fo'. I'll put in a quata', who'll do the rest,*" whereupon the choir gave forth a mighty tune, that filled the church with a strain which made some feel like dancing.

The following Tuesday, an editorial appeared in one of the leading dailies, concerning the sermon and the instance of Henry Hugh Hodder. It dwelt at some length on his work for the evolution of his people, and concluded by praying that (among the black population) great would be the day when such men and such sermons were an established order.

Sidney, now in an office to himself, read it to a man next door. Whereupon the other said:

"Oh, that is nothing unusual. They often speak of him and his work in the editorial columns. Which might account for his having such a fine church." . . .

Wyeth was silent, apparently at a loss what to say. The silence had reached a point which was becoming strained, when another, who happened to be in the office, relieved it by spitting out sneeringly:

"White fo'kes 'll give any nigga plenty money, when he says what they want him too." He was a deacon in the big church referred to. This was not investigated.

Wyeth called him a liar then and there.

William Pickens

"The New Negro"

In *The New Negro: His Political, Civil and Mental Status, and Related Essays*, 1916

What I aspired to be,
And was not, comforts me:
A brute I might have been, but would not
  sink i' the scale.

—From Browning's "Rabbi Ben Ezra."

The "new Negro" is not really new: he is the same Negro under new conditions and subjected to new demands. Those who regret the passing of the "old Negro" and picture the "new" as something very different, must remember that there is no sharp line of demarcation between the old and the new in any growing organism like a germ, a plant or a race. The present generation of Negroes have received their chief heritage from the former and, in that, they are neither better nor worse, higher nor lower than the previous generation. But the present Negro is differently circumstanced and must be measured by different standards. He has not less fidelity to duty than had the old Negro: the present Negro soldier is just as true to his uniform, his flag and his country as was the old Negro slave to his master's family. He is not more indolent: certainly the present Negro does a great deal more of voluntary work than did the Negro slave. He is not as much more criminal than the old Negro as his criminal *record* would seem to indicate: the present Negro gets into jail for offenses and charges for which the slave received thirty-nine *unrecorded* lashes. Besides, a repressive attitude toward a man in freedom subjects him to worse temptations than a bond-slave is subjected to. Furthermore and quite as important as anything else, there has been some change of attitude in the white people among whom the Negro lives: there is less acquaintanceship,—less sympathy and toleration than formerly.

The average white man of the present generation who sees the Negro daily, perhaps knows less of the Negro than did the similarly situated white man of any previous generation since the black race came to America. This lack of knowledge has a fearful influence on the judgment: it is both history and psychology that where knowledge is wanting, imagination steps in. What naive explanations men once gave of natural phenomena, what odd shapes they ascribed to the earth, and what erroneous proportions and fanciful relations they imagined among the heavenly bodies. The most serious handicap to the creation of a wholesome public opinion on matters affecting the Negro, is the ignorance of the better class of white people concerning the better class of colored people who live in their community. They often know the other classes: the servants through their kitchens and the criminals through the newspapers. In a large Southern city lived the most experienced Negro banker in the United States, with his bank, for twenty-five or thirty years; but, excepting the few bankers and others with whom he came into business contact, practically the whole group of intelligent white people in that city were ignorant of the fact that this Negro existed. In another Southern town of seven thousand people, half white and half colored, an elderly, cultured, Christian white woman, who had lived there all her life, did not know that the Negroes were not given a public school building by her municipality, and had

supposed that a primary school for Negroes which had been maintained by a missionary society for thirty or forty years, was the Negro public school. From an old Maryland community a young Negro went out, got an education in some of the best schools, took a course in theology at Yale, and then returned to that community to pastor a church. He worked with great energy, aroused his people to build a fine new church, and awakened so much enthusiasm in the colored masses that finally some inklings of his success trickled in behind the ivied walls of an old mansion where lived two wealthy white ladies of the "good old days," when the Negro was so much better than he is now, as they could well testify from the superb character of the "black mammy," now dead and gone, but who had been for many years an indispensable part of their household conveniences. Hearing of the fine new building, for the first time in their lives they decided to attend the dedication of a Negro church. On learning the name and antecedents of the young pastor they found him to be the son of their bemoaned "black mammy,"—him whom they supposed had long since gone to the dogs, whither their daily newspapers were saying all the young and aspiring Negroes were bound. The mother had been a "member" of their family, but the son had struggled against poverty and prejudice, had got his education and done his work without any encouragement from them, without even so much as their confidence or their knowledge. How can a people so hedged about by tradition and handicapped by prejudice "know the Negro" as he now is, even though they be good people and knew him as he once was?

Not only does this ignorance of the Negro prevent many white people from sympathizing with his condition and struggles, but it does a mischief more positive than that: it prepares them to believe any charge of crime or viciousness or depravity which may be brought against the race. They will not analyze the evidence. If it is said that in proportion to their population there are four or five times as many blacks as whites in a Southern penitentiary, men will conclude at once, without thought or investigation, that such is the ratio of the criminality of the Negro and the white man. They overlook the multitude of other differences which may account for this difference in criminal statistics: the poverty, the ignorance, the homelessness and helplessness, and the very sort of prejudice which they themselves are substituting for thought. The ease with which a Negro can be lynched in the South should make them know how much more easily he can get into the penitentiary. Another thing that largely accounts for the Negro's superior numbers among the prisoners: most Southern states allow the discretion of the court a very wide latitude as to the number of years for which the condemned is to be sentenced. The law is often like this: a fine of so many dollars, or ten years in prison, or both. The Negro usually gets the limit, perhaps "both." To make an extreme but simplifying case, suppose one Negro and one white man commit a certain crime every year; if the white criminal is either fined or given only one year in prison, while the colored criminal is given ten years, in the tenth year when the visitor goes to that prison he will find nine or ten Negroes there for a certain crime, but only one white man. The easy-going investigator might conclude that the Negro is ten times as criminal in that respect as is the white man, while as a matter of fact both races would have committed exactly the same number of crimes. The long-term sentences of Negroes cause them to *accumulate* in prison. There are much more scientific ways of explaining the Negro's situation in this country than by reference to an unprovable something like innate depravity.

One of the greatest handicaps under which the new Negro lives is the handicap of the lack of acquaintanceship between him and his white neighbor. Under the former order, when practically all Negroes were either slaves or servants, every Negro had the acquaintance of some white man; as a race he was better known, better understood, and was therefore the object of less suspicion on the part of the white community. But under the present order there are many Negroes who are independent, in occu-

pation or in fortune, doing business for themselves, rendering professional service to their own race or living independently at home. These Negroes, unknown to the white mass, are the objects of its special suspicions and distrust, for they are "something new under the sun." When riots breakout, this unknown Negro, well-to-do and equally well-behaved, the one who ought to be safest, is the one most liable to attack by the mob. This is because ignorance and prejudice have made the very things which pass for virtues in white men, seem like vices in the Negro; pride, ambition, self-respect, unsatisfaction with the lower positions of life, and the desire to live in a beautiful house and to keep his wife and children at home and out of "service." There can be no sympathy where there is no knowledge, and the Negro of this class, being rather a stranger to his white neighbors, is regarded as a bad example to those humbler and more helpless Negroes who are servants. This is not so in every case, but this is the rule, and the rule is the thing. And we are not talking hearsay but speaking out of the experiences of our lifetime.

If prejudice could only reason, it would dispel itself. If it could think, its thoughts might run like this: If it be true that the Negro is innately low and criminal in his instincts, then the Negro must be the same in all places,—but the Negroes of other countries do not bear this reputation; those of Brazil and the rest of South America, of Central America, of the West Indies and of Mexico, are not distinguished as criminals. There are great numbers of Negroes in parts of these countries, and being in many of them unrestricted as to the position to which they may aspire in society and state, they would have a better chance to demonstrate any essential inferiority in those lands than in the United States. The truth is, that if the Negro be inferior, in the United States he has never yet had a chance to prove his inferiority. But prejudice does not investigate or reason.—What we are trying to do in this essay, concerning the new Negro, is to tell what *is*, and not what *ought to be*, though the latter would make a more pleasing story than the former.

Another thing which gets the better of our normal psychology and causes us to believe almost any wild report about the Negro, is the free and superior advertising given Negro crime above that accorded to any other form of Negro achievement. Booker Washington used to tell with great amusement how he entered a little town and spoke to a large gathering, making as good a speech as he was capable of. The next morning he picked up the town paper, expecting to see himself and the meeting given considerable and prominent space, but found only an inch or so of recognition on the last page. He had made a successful speech, but the whole front page was given to a Negro who at the same time had made an *unsuccessful* attempt to snatch a woman's purse. An unsophisticated outsider, reading that paper, would have concluded that the constructive work which such Negroes as Booker Washington are doing, is of small consequence as compared with the failing efforts of a Negro criminal. Again, when a white person commits a crime, the papers say simply that a burglar was caught, a man shot a woman, or a highwayman has been sentenced,—not *white* burglar, not *white* man and woman, and not *white* highwayman. In the case of colored people, however, it is reported as *Negro* thief, *Negro,* loafer, *black* brute, *Negress.* This forms in us an association of ideas: *black* and *Negro* are made to suggest *crime.* The one term calls up the other in the public mind; they are tied together by as definite a law as the law of gravitation. If the word *white* were written with every Caucasian criminal, it would be as bad for the word *white,*—or worse. We might say that we also give the Negro credit for his good deeds by attaching the word *black* or *colored.* But do we, with the same emphasis and persistence with which we link him with his bad deeds? Booker T. Washington was given an inch on the last page, and the Negro purse-snatcher was given the whole of the front page. I know a black Negro who did well in a Northern University, and I have his picture from some newspapers wherein they deliberately lightened his complexion, straightened his hair, peaked his nose and labeled him thus as a mulatto. And often we refuse to mention the racial identity at all when the Negro's deed is good. While we write, every newspaper in the United States is mentioning the good work of the Tenth Cavalry in Mexico, but very few of the dailies take time to say that the Tenth Cavalry is a regiment of black men. When the Negro soldiers were discharged for shooting up Brownsville, Tex., not a newspaper in the whole Republic failed to mention the race to which they belonged. Suppose we pursued the same policy with respect to the red-heads among us: whenever a black-haired, brown-haired or gray-haired person committed a crime, we should say simply that a man or woman did this or that, but when the hair was red, should say red-headed burglar, red-headed embezzler, red-headed murderer, red-headed rapist,—very soon the red-haired would be marked as criminals among us and we should be prejudiced at the very sight of them.

It is an interesting inquiry as to how the Negro stands to-day as a patriot. In that regard he is still one of the soundest classes in America, but he does not stand to-day where he used to stand. He still loves America, his native land,—it is the only country he has or knows anything about,—but he is more prone to-day to identify "the country" with the powers who happen, for the time being, to have control thereof. One hears expressions from individual Negroes now which were not to be heard twenty years ago: that the United States needs humiliation; that it would "help the Negro if any foreign power should humble this country"; that the Negro has "nothing to fight for" in the United States, and "nothing to defend"; that he (the individual who may be speaking) "would not volunteer"; that it would be "inconsistent for the Negro to fight the Japanese, who have done nothing to him, and in behalf of American white people"; that no foreign conqueror could possibly "make conditions any worse for the Negro here"; and many other expressions which show that the Negro is beginning to look for deliverance from abroad rather than at home. This is a small and at present impotent beginning, but it is foreboding. And it is too bad that some American newspapers and congressmen are seconding these thoughts of the Negro by proclaiming a "white man's country" and a "white man's war," and by obstructing the enlistment of patriotic colored people in the army and navy. How different is the present Negro spirit from that of 1898 when his youth, wherever admitted, rose as one man to meet the Spaniard; from many of his Southern schools the whole male student body who could qualify as soldiers went into the camps. That is not because the Negro was not mistreated or oppressed at that time, but because he still looked upon "Uncle Sam" as being some personality separate and apart from the oppressor. He then regarded the oppressor as a merely local character; but he looked up to the great Nation with hope and confidence, as the embodiment of rigid justice and high ideals. He thought that the spirit of the Emancipator and of the defenders of the Union still ruled in the highest councils of the land, and he swore by "Uncle Sam." He hoped, too, to better his local conditions by this opportunity to show his patriotism at San Juan Hill and in the Philippines. But since that time one or two weak Republican administrations and a very hostile Democratic term have made him identify his former ideal of the nation with the oppressor himself. This impression has been deepened especially by lynchings, segregation and discrimination in the North, from which he once expected ultimate justice. We fear that the extent and importance of this new feeling is not generally understood by white people. The foundation of preparedness should be laid in the mind and the heart. As we write, the newspapers are full of comments on the fact that a little black boy of Des Moines, Iowa, refused under threats to salute the American flag, on the ground that it meant nothing to him and his. Some are advocating punishment for this lad as the remedy. That reminds us of the "remedy" offered by the little boy who, when he was frankly told by the little girl that she did *not love* him, replied, as he sailed into her with his fists: "When I get through beatin' the stuffin' out o' you, I bet you'll love me!" He was adopting the method which would not only fail to change indifference into love but would finally arouse

hatred and hostility. The Negro will not fail to love the flag and be its staunchest defender, if it means to him a reasonable measure of protection for life, liberty and property and civil and political rights. If these things are denied him, no amount of preaching or cussing or killing will make him love America. He could be compelled for the time being to employ the weapons of the weak,—pretense and cunning.

But the colored soldier and the masses of the race are still loyal. There is no hyphen in the short word *Negro*; he is every inch American; he is not even Afro-American. One Negro regiment beat all records by not having a single desertion in twelve months. Nobody has any doubt as to what the Negro soldiers are doing in Mexico now; that they can be relied on implicitly to carry out orders and serve the interests of the American people. During our strained relations with various European nations there have been frequent expressions of doubt as to the loyalty of many elements of our population, but never one word of doubt as to the Negro's loyalty has parted the lips of even his fondest enemies. He is loyal and is understood to be loyal, but a continuous adverse pressure will finally break even the strongest bar,—or bend it.

At present the Negro would stand fast and firm by America against any European state; but on the other hand when the Negro goes into any European state he finds himself better treated and freer from insult than in any state of the American Union. How long will his loyalty last under that test? The Negro abroad in any of the other really civilized countries of the world, is practically never insulted or treated as an inferior unless he runs into a party of his own white fellow-citizens from the United States. There are Americans, of course, to whom this inconsistent attitude toward one of the most loyal classes of all our citizenry is a shame and a distaste.

Naturally it proves disagreeable, at first, for many American white people to turn from the old to the new Negro: from the patient, unquestioning, devoted semi-slave to the self-conscious, aspiring, proud young man. It always shocks our psychology to have our old and accustomed ideals contradicted. The changes from tallow candles to oil lamps, to gas lights and to electric bulbs must have been unpleasant experiences for many of the older members of the community. The older folk did not want to put pipe organs and other musical instruments into the church service. It is a plain matter of psychology: the old ideal was being smashed by something new, which is disagreeable even when the something new is something better. Nearly all concede that there are good Negroes, but they are very slow to revise their ideals as to what constitutes a "good" Negro. To some it means the old "uncles" and "aunties" or the present usable servants. It is difficult for them to conceive of an independent, self-respecting, self-directing Negro as good. There is a great motion-picture film, the chief fault of which, aside from its perversions of common history, is the fact that it attempts to teach that the Negro is good only as a slave or servant, and that every intelligent and aspiring Negro in society, law or state, is bad and criminal. This hoary prejudice is our great stumbling block: it causes intolerance and opposition to the rising and aspiring but perfectly human and normal younger Negroes. There are white people, apparently fair minded, who probably wish the Negro well, and who can stand or sit and talk for a long time with a dirty, ignorant and comical Negro, but who could not have five minutes of patience with one that is clean, intelligent and self-respecting. I heard a Negro say that it mystified him how white people would hire as servants in their homes, or nurses for their children Negro men and girls whom he would not permit to touch his children. In the other direction, too, the thing often runs to the ridiculous: a young Negro was to be ousted by his white associates from a certain position; they admitted that his morals were sound, that his education and general qualifications were all right, that his logic was good and his arguments irrefutable,—but, they explained, when he talks on some phases of the race question he sometimes *clinches his teeth*! They evidently preferred that when he talked of the great injustices he would *not* do what Horace says the speaker

should always do (show the feeling himself which he would arouse in others), but that he would rather show his teeth in the conciliatory, apologetic grin of the old-fashioned Negro.

The greatest risk that the strong have to run is the risk of their morals and ideals. The white people of America are in a position to be greatly tempted to regard the Negro only in the light of his usefulness to them,—only as a utility, and not as a personality to pursue his own ends and fulfil his own destiny. This little drop of selfishness is likely to vitiate a great many efforts "on behalf of the American Negro." The Negro is beginning to insist, however, that he must be regarded first as a man and only incidentally as a usable article. For example, the Negro really believes in all kinds of education, and especially in those forms of training which will best fit the masses to become independent workers and of the greatest service to themselves and others. But that little drop of gall has caused many of those who are trying to educate him, to view their mission exclusively from the selfish-utilitarian standpoint. These enthusiasts have themselves put the Negro on the defensive as to his right to pursue other forms of culture. And that is why many of his best friends and the ablest thinkers of his own race have insisted and do insist that the race needs *not only* farm-hands, domestic servants, carpenters and other industrial workers, but also business men, doctors, lawyers and well educated preachers. The white people who desire that the Negro be a separate race in America, often fail to see that this very separateness would make it more imperative that the race develop all occupations and professions and advance along all lines. I heard a white speaker, at a great missionary meeting held "on behalf of Negro education," say: We want the Negroes to produce farmers and other industrial workers,—we already have plenty of lawyers, doctors, historians and poets. His "we" could not really include the Negro, about whom he was supposed to be speaking, for the Negro has very few lawyers, doctors, historians and poets,—and the white historian and poet will not really write the Negro's history nor sing his songs.

The new Negro is a sober, sensible creature, conscious of his environment, knowing that not all is right, but trying hard to become adjusted to this civilization in which he finds himself by no will or choice of his own. He is not the shallow, vain, showy creature which he is sometimes advertised to be. He still hopes that the unreasonable opposition to his forward and upward progress will relent. But, at any rate, he is resolved to fight, and live or die, on the side of God and the Eternal Verities.

> For thence,—a paradox
> Which comforts while it mocks,—
> Shall life succeed in that it seems to fail.

Anonymous
"The Negro in Fiction"

Evening Post, June 5, 1916[25]

The complaint is frequent that contemporary literature discriminates against one race or another; that its treatment of it is inadequate or tends to caricature. Ever since Hans Breitmann, the German-American has fancied himself sinned against. The Irishman feels that his countrymen in fiction are too much like those in vaudeville, and the Jew has complained that stage, comic paper, short story, and novel conspire against him. As a rule, the injustice done is but partial, and only the less substantial forms of literature participate in it. A better-founded charge is brought in the *Dial*, by Mr. Benjamin Brawley, against contemporary writers on the negro. The development of the negro and the shifting race question, as he points out, constitute a theme such as is seldom offered the literary artist. Character study, varied incident, and philosophy of the deepest sort are latent in it. Yet, he asserts, writers remain "content to embalm old types and work over outworn ideas," and the new negro, neither a comic savage nor tragic child, but a manly and serious character, is unattempted. A study of the best magazine stories of negro life in the last decade supports his argument.

Of a dozen stories in the *Century*, the *Atlantic*, *Harper's*, *Everybody's*, and so on, his summary makes it plain that none really fulfils the conditions he names, and but one or two are modern and serious studies at all. One deals, for example, with the courtship by which a negro blacksmith of forty wins the heart of a capricious girl, his doggedness carrying him through ludicrous mistakes. Another is concerned with the custom of having on negro plantations a negro "governor" whose duty it is to settle disputes, and with the choice of the negro logically in line after a contest of wits with one loud-mouthed Sambo. Two or three others are of the bright comedy bred by Uncle Remus's success as of a negro jockey robbed in Louisville by negroes who send him to Chicago, and the use of his superstitious instincts to win more money at the race there than he had ever seen before. A story by Grace McGowan Cooke of the friendship of two white and black boys is criticised because the relationship is on too low a plane; the black boy "is very much like a dog following his master." Margaret Deland has written a story which lacks more breadth to be significant of a white youth's love for a girl who has a bare shade of negro blood. Most of the others belong to the class that regards the negro as an animal or minor, never a man. Mr. Brawley quotes one opening, "An old darkey sat drowsing on the stoop. There was something ape-like about his long arms, his flat, wide-nostriled nose, and the mat of gray wool which crept his forehead to within two inches of his eyebrows." In the majority sincerity is plainly lacking. Picturesqueness is the whole. The negro seems unpicturesque if he is intelligent, earnest, educated, upright, to many writers he is not picturesque if the more laughable or primitive qualities even of the backward negro are not accentuated.

The accusation would clearly hold that the modern writer lags behind him of thirty years since in both the truthfulness and power of his handling of the negro. Mr. Brawley, indeed, asserts that the negro has never been done justice. But a generation ago, before the change had set in, it was legitimate to draw the negro in his older aspect. A charming aspect several authors made of it. Cable's best books, "Old Creole Days" and "The Grandissimes," dealt with New Orleans before the war: and no one denies they treat fairly the mulatto population of a restricted locality during a restricted period. Joel Chandler Harris was under the necessity of finding a childlike teller for his primitive folk stories, and no reader is deceived by the simple but wise and kind Uncle Remus. His "Mingo and Other Sketches" and "Free Joe" are in different vein, and while the humor and pathos are overdone, they do not malign the negro of days following the war. For the negroes of Mark Twain, from the slaves of "Pudd'nhead Wilson" to the Uncle Dan'l of his and Warner's "The Gilded Age," whose first sight of a steamboat is classic farce, there is less to be said. But Mark Twain never really pretended to describe the negro. Thomas Nelson Page was content to draw again the old patriarchal life of negro and master in "Red Rock" and "In Ole Virginia," when he might have treated this bustling day and generation; and Ruth McEnery Stuart evidently went back many years in "The Golden Wedding" and other stories. But the result was in each case excellent. The real fault is with the present-day writers who describe the negro of 1916 as if he were the negro of 1870 or 1885.

Our authors are properly cautious of approaching sociological topics; but it is not a sociological novel of the negro that is wanted. It is fictional treatment of the South that will allot due representation to the new element in the race: to the progressive and striving element that gives such promise of growing from a small minority to a majority. By all right standards, there is as much interest, color, and variety in this new negro as in the types that have been presented again and again; in the negro farmer or teacher as in the old body-servant or "mammy." It is the race as a whole that ought to be treated, in all the stages of its advancement from old-time conditions.

THE HALF-CENTURY MAGAZINE

OCTOBER, 1916

10 Cents a Copy

The
Half-
Century
Magazine
Publishing
Company

Chicago,
Illinois

75 Cents a Year

A female golfer appears on the cover of *Half-Century Magazine*, October 1916.
Courtesy of the Vivian G. Harsh Research Collection, Chicago Public Library.

PART IV

RED SUMMERS AND BLACK RADICALISMS, 1917–1921

Fenton Johnson
"The Editor's Blue Pencil"

Champion Magazine, January 1917[1]

The closing year has been for the Negro a year rich with the fullness of events. The black man has gained remarkably in the respect of the world round him, largely through that lovable temperament that has been his weapon since the dawn of history.

The American Negro astonished his public by displaying at Carrizal the most remarkable heroism since the charge of the Light Brigade. The hearts of the North and the South melted toward those who laid down their lives in the interest of their fairer brother and an administration noted for its hostility to colored races. The martyrdom of Carrizal was the happiest stroke in the calendar of Negro achievement. The hour of racial reconciliation was brought nearer, the glory of man's brotherhood shone on that Mexican field as bright as the halo of a Christian saint.

Industrially, the Negro was granted a new leader in Robert Russa Moton, who was elected to succeed the late Booker T. Washington at Tuskegee Institute. The first six months of Dr. Moton's leadership have not been marked by anything startling; so far he has shown himself to be a very conservative man, perhaps more so than his illustrious predecessor. Dr. Moton finds himself face to face with a new problem, the Negro hegira, and is handling it in the true Washington fashion.

To 1916 is due the credit of this new Negro problem. The more radical publicists of the darker race attribute it to the abuses of race prejudice and yellow sheets, representing unbridled journalism hurl insults at the entire South and picture the North as a Mecca for the oppressed black man. The conservatives tell us to remain in the South; the radicals advise us to flee from the wrath that is at hand and bask in the sunshine of economic competition and high prices that we will find in the North. The cause of the hegira, as we have expressed hitherto, is due not to oppression, but to economic conditions rising out of the great war. It will not be abated for some time and is a benefit to both races.

In the world of achievement, 1916 can boast of the success of Charles Young in obtaining through sheer merit the rank of Lieutenant Colonel in the regular United States army. Fred Pollard's brilliant defeat of Harvard University on the football gridiron gave the world another startling demonstration of the Negro's athletic superiority. In literature, the American Negro advanced no new star, though occasionally we heard something from the established writers. In commercial life the National Negro Business League showed that the black man is gaining ground. The number of banks has increased and there are fewer failures than there were ten years ago.

The most astonishing feature of the year is the social growth of the Negro. The National Association for the Advancement of Colored People has developed into the most useful agency for the repression of racial wrongs that America can boast. It is not a group of unscrupulous agitators but of earnest men and women striving to make their country a better and a greater America. Side by side with these soldiers of uplift are the members of the National Negro Urban League, who during this year have been sowing their seed in almost every hamlet in the Union. The social welfare of this race depends upon the support the world gives this great league in its endeavor to make better the lives of those who dwell on the other side.

Yes, the year Nineteen Hundred and Sixteen has been a year of inestimable value to the Negro race in America.

Pippa

"The New Negro Is Here: Negro Socialists Are Helping to Solve Race Problem in New Way"

New York Call, November 4, 1918[2]

Theodore Dreiser in his story, "Nigger Jeff," has voiced a great argument in favor of one of the planks in the Socialist party platform, the abolition of lynching by federal law.

The American novelist tells of this "Nigger Jeff," who is lynched by an infuriated mob in the Middle West and then strung up in the moonlight.

A piece of fiction, but it has had its birth in recent events in the South and the Middle West, where Negroes were lynched and burned by white men.

Solve Old Problem.

Just what the Socialist party of the world has done for the solution of the Negro question is summed up in the leaflet issued by the Negro candidates in this city of the Socialist party; George Frazier Miller, candidate for Congress from the 21st district; A. Philip Randolph, running for Assembly from the 19th district, and Chandler Owen, candidate in the 21st district.

In part, the leaflet says:

It will be remembered that the Socialist party was the only party in the United States which condemned the East St. Louis lynching of Negroes.

The Socialist party has been just and fair to colored people in every country in the world. In 1912, in the Reichstag, the German Socialists voted unanimously to put a halt to the abuse of the African women by the German junkers, autocrats and bourbons. The justice and fair play which men of color receive in France is due very largely to the extensive power of the Socialists and Diagne, the Negro Socialist Representative, just elected to the French Chamber of Dep-

uties. In Oklahoma the Socialists called a referendum and defeated the grandfather clauses which disfranchised Negroes.

In the United States the reactionaries hate the Socialists, and they are abused and maligned. The same was true of Garrison and Phillips and Lovejoy. Garrison was dragged through the streets of Boston. Sumner was struck down in Congress, Phillips was libeled and slandered. All who live off cheap Negro labor will be opposed to Socialism, just as all slaveholders were opposed to the Abolitionists. Slave owners stole Negro labor by paying nothing for chattel slavery, whereas capitalists are paying for only part of what you earn now. In working to secure better food, clothing and shelter; more education and recreation for children; for comfort and pleasure for the oppressed people which they rightly earn, the Socialist party will not meet with the approval of the plutocratic bosses.

Why? Because the Socialist party demands that the workingman should get the full product of his labor.

The new Negro in Harlem, as the Socialist Negro is known, is waging an earnest campaign by means of the spoken and written word from the headquarters at 2305 Seventh avenue. Where—once the Republican banner waved on the avenue between 135th and 136th streets the Socialist banner with the names of the Negro Socialist candidates on it is a more than satisfactory substitute now.

A Negro Socialist speaker usually addresses his people in a low musical voice, having recourse more often to the descriptive and expositive form of speech than the one liberally sprinkled with the oratorical expressions. What seems unique with the Negro Socialist speaker is the fact that he always leaves his audience in possession of a new fact about Socialism; his is a lecture on a political theory, besides being a lively, interesting heart-to-heart talk with the audience individually.

Expose Treachery.

Negro women, such as Helen Holman and Emily Jones, the Socialist organizers, are in the fight, too, to acquaint their brothers and sisters with the treachery of the Republican and Democratic parties, which shear the Negro of his economic rights.

"Will you vote for the Democratic party to strengthen the forces of which Senators John Sharp Williams of Mississippi and Vardaman of Mississippi, are members?" they ask. "Vardaman opposed woman suffrage because it would give to the Negro woman of the South the right to vote. When you vote for Tammany Hall, you are voting for mob law, lynch law, disfranchise- ment of Negroes, peonage, the jim-crow car and all forms of race discrimination."

How does the average Negro citizen act or react to the Socialist philosophy as voiced by the Socialist speakers? At one meeting, in a little church in Harlem, of the Negro men and women, the answer was supplied. The mobile faces of the Negroes appeared to express every emotion which they were experiencing. To the pleasantries and humorous truths that Judge Panken presented, they smiled and then burst into natural child-like laughter. They were enjoying themselves. At the next moment, when one of their own race reminded them of the jim-crow system still used on the cars, and their empty vote in the South, they were silent, not morosely so, but with the sort of silence that bodes ill for those who heap such indignities on the Negro.

The new Negro is here—and there will be many more of them to enrich the Socialist movement in the United States.

W. H. Mixon

"A Great Day for the New Negro and the New South, All Daily White Papers Give Very Prominent and Clever Mention in Their Columns"

Voice of the People, January 4, 1919[3]

[Dr. w. h. mixon, d. d., Presiding Elder of the A. M. E. Church, and one of the leaders of the Negro, known and read of throughout the civilized world. He was the orator of the day for the Negro Civic League, Dr. Freeman, president. His able address is found elsewhere in these columns and one organization alone has already engaged 200 extra copies for that membership. He swayed the great audience on Emancipation Day, and caused judges of the law to stand up in the open and to declare that his equals on the oratorical platform are few. Dr. Mixon is strong in his church and race and is identified with most of the secret organizations.]

The Great Emancipation Address Delivered in St. Paul A. M. E. Church by Rev. W. H. Mixon, D. D. P. E.

Birmingham, Ala., Jan. 1, 1919.

Mr. President, Fellow Countrymen and Fellow Citizens:

I am charmed above measure to see this great concourse of free people today. We have the honor of witnessing and participating in the Jubilee and closing of the greatest international conflict known in history. This brings me to consider a subject I have styled:

The Giants of Nations.

Yesterday we stood at the grave of 1918; today we stand at the cradle of 1919. We have great reasons for rejoicing. Without multiplying words we shall claim your attention on the subject, "Giants of Nations."

I shall not deal with the Bible giants like Ishbibenob whose brass spear weighed 300 shekels or [12-1/2] pounds. In antediluvian world, there were giants, mighty men. The sons of Anax were giants. King Og of Bashan was a giant. He was 12 feet high, 6 feet broad, a mighty man. His bed was made of iron. It was nine cubits in length and four cubits in breadth.

The ancients believed the first inhabitants of the earth to be produced from the ground because of their statue and enormous size; they were known as giants.

I want that you walk with me today with the giants of intellect. The giants of mind rather than the physical giants. King Alfred said, "There is nothing in the world great but man, and nothing in man great but mind."

Adam and Eve[,] the father and mother of the human family, lived in Eden or Paradise. Because of disobedience, they were ejected, driven out of their habitation. Men lived in the antediluvian as well as the postdiluvian world. The ship called Ark rescued or saved by special dispensation of Providence, eight persons[:] Noah, his wife, three sons and their wives. The first nations were formed in Shinar near the borders of the Euphrates, south of Mount Ararat. This became the center of the population of the universe. The descendants of Shem distributed themselves over the country near the Euphrates. The descendants of Japhetta settled in Greece, and thus laid the foundation of several European nations. The descendants of Ham took a westerly direction and went into Africa. They settled in Egypt and laid the foundation of a great nation, a great race.

Nimrod the mighty hunter built the great city of Babylon. In the year 1775 Ashur built the city of Nineveh. Athens, Rome and other great cities were built by master minds, gigantic intellects. Abraham founded the Hebrew nation.

In sacred and profane history, victorious accomplishments and achievements have been gained by master minds. Who would dispute the giant intellect of Cicero, Caesar, Demosthenes, Socrates, Plato and Pompey? Who would dispute the military tactics of Alexander, Napoleon, Charlemagne, Hannibal and Toussaint L'Overture?

We have watched the current of thought advanced by Newton, Archimedes, Galileo, Benjamin Franklin and Thomas Edison. The student is inspired by the brilliant mind of Shakespeare, Milton, Hawthorne, Holmes, Longfellow, Tennyson, Dante and our own Paul Laurence Dunbar.

The sweeping eloquence of a Talmage, Beecher, Spurgeon, Hall, Ward and Abraham Grant has lifted nations and caused them to look and live. Beside dealing with the giants of nations, we may deal with a giant race. The Negro was brought here not by his own volition, but as a cargo of freight in 1619. He was kept in abject slavery for 244 years. January 1, 1863, Abraham Lincoln issued the Emancipation Proclamation which was a death blow to slavery. Well might we make this a day of jollification. Men desired to see the things we see today, but died without the sight. More than four million slaves were set free. They were without culture, scholarship and money. A green race, a raw race, a race without a family record: indeed, without a name, depending upon others to think and act for them. A race without the knowledge of an Almanac, Calendar, or numbers. The personal records and important events were dated from rain, storms, floods, planting and gathering time, when the stars fell, the dark day, wars and the time they moved from one plantation to another. In those days of gloom, doubt and fear were born gigantic minds. A few like Frederick Douglass, Henry Highland Garner, Henry McNeal Turner, Daniel Alexander Payne, Frances E. W. Harper, Phillis Wheatly,

Fannie Jackson Coppin. Today our leaders are numberless. Leadership is recognized. No agencies today can keep the Negro race down or keep him back. Seal him up in a dungeon, his mind will break out. A few brief years have passed since we left the auction block where mothers, fathers, sisters and brothers were sold to the highest bidder as a commodity. In after years that auctioned brother and sister met and were united in wedlock without knowing that relationship existed between them. Slavery was degrading, a curse and abomination. John Wesley said: "Slavery was the sum of all villainy."

Proud America.

America is the proudest nation of the world. It is our home. We are citizens of this commonwealth. Blackstone says: "The strongest claim to citizenship is birthplace." The stars and stripes are ours. This is our birthplace, this is our native soil. It is our duty as well as a Divine privilege to claim an equal place among the American citizens. The Negro is identified with the American interests. We are property owners, tax payers, builders of churches and schools, dealers in stocks and bonds. Our habits are commercial, industrial, educational, religious and social. America has been an open door for immigrants. It has a wide territory wherein the genius of man may be developed. The color of my race has been a badge for criticism and proscription. Character, intellect, wealth, culture and refinement should be the equalizer of races and nations.

Prejudice.

Prejudice is an element of hate. It is out of place when it lodges in the breast of the human family. The Golden Rule should be, "You For Me and I For You." Prejudice blights the hope of a race, damages the prospects of a nation and crucifies the ambition of manhood. It overlooks the fact that under a black skin is a lofty mind. This race with which I am highly identified has had to wade the deep waters of prejudice, swim the rivers of criticism and climb the mountains of op-

position. But because of our giant Intellects, we have been considered and called upon to help dethrone autocracy and enthrone universal Democracy.

Soldiers.

Ancient and modern time will prove the valor of the Negro soldier. He has been a soldier from the earliest times. He served in the Egyptian army long before the Christian era. The run-away slaves fought in Trinidad, British Guiana and St. Domingo. The unmixed Negro in Hayti rose to the full dignity of a modern soldier. It is said that the martial spirit is born on the Negro. He can well be classed with Napoleon, Cromwell, Washington and Pershing. The rejected soldiers of color fought in the Revolutionary war. Crispus Attucks was first to christen the earth with human blood for human liberty. But when the dense smoke cleared away and the fiery balls ceased to rain, the black soldier found himself shackled and chained by the demon of slavery. He fought in the second war with Great Britain, and at the close found himself a slave. Thirty-six thousand eight hundred and forty-seven Negro soldiers sacrificed their precious lives in the war of the "Sixties." At the close of that great struggle he was found a free man, a citizen.

The Negro soldier has a history. Trace him at Bunker Hill, Ft. Wagner, Ft. Pillow and [the] battle of New Orleans. Do you remember? Can you forget the battle of San Juan Hill?

When it was necessary to protect the American citizenry and trade in the recent conflict, the Negro volunteered his service, and when drafted, none went more willingly and readily to the battle field than the black man. The words of Patrick Henry inspired him to greater heights. Listen! "Give Me Liberty or Give Me Death."

Watchman.

Watchman, what of the night? What will the Negro soldier find at the close of this war? What will be the result when the white soldier and black soldier return to this country? While the war last we met as brothers and citizens. We rode in the same automobiles, spoke from the same platform, bought Liberty Bonds from the same windows, conserved food, labor, and time alike, endorsed every measure suggested by the Government. Now that the war is over, are we needed in the council of consideration as a race? Will that friendly hand of fellowship remain the same? Will the giants of this nation give the Negro his franchise as a reward for obeying when obedience was hard? Will the railroad system and electric car authorities remove the boards of proscriptions or lengthen the space for Negro traffic? Why charge a helpless race a first class fare and give them second, third and no class accommodation? Is it just? Is it right? Will it stand? We answer: "No, no! ten thousand times no!" The days of Reconstruction are here. New conditions are arising. The things that satisfied the fathers will not satisfy the sons. This is a Reconstruction period with individuals, families, races and nations. President Woodrow Wilson is a giant. He handles the nations like play things. It was said of William E. Gladstone, he can take his seat any where and call the world to order. President Wilson has planned a league of nations and I trust a league of races. At the Peace Table in Versailles he will be more than the space he occupies. Today we have a Government of all the people, by all the people and for all the people. That is universal Democracy. All wars are cruel. Yet the colored man has received out of this war more than he put into it. Some of the soldiers will return home hale and hardy, others will be maimed for life with the loss of one or both eyes, an empty sleeve and an absent leg. It is to be regretted that the Government is discontinuing the schools for military training. I believe the training should go on so that the nation will be prepared for any emergency. Notwithstanding the war has closed, I believe the wage earner should still receive due consideration for his labor.

Distribution.

God is distributing the Negro all over the world. At first, they were in a few countries. Today they are in South America and the Brit-

ish Islands where white and black are treated alike. In Central, South and North America they are coalescing.

The colored man can be depended upon. In the hours of danger he protected the White House. As giants of the race, Major R. R. Moten and Dr. DuBois have been selected to represent the Negroes across the sea.

Think of Ralph Tyler being sent as a newspaper representative to France.

During the National Strife, Four-Minute Men and Women of this race have been heard on every mountain, in every valley, village, town, hamlet and city. Their voices have been heard in every pulpit, school room, theater, shop, mine, mill, the open air and on the platform.

Progress.

The strength of intellect promoted Mr. Emmet J. Scott to the position of Assistant Secretary of War. The race has advanced. In the last election. J. V. Coleman, H. J. Capehart and T. G. Mutter were elected to the Lower House of West Virginia State Legislature. William Riley of St. Louis, Mo., to the Lower House of the State Legislature. A. E. Johnson as an Assemblyman in New York.

Preparedness.

Our race must prepare to meet the new conditions, (1) by honesty; (2) by industry; (3) by frugality; (4) they must have confidence in themselves and their leaders; (5) they must know the value of a dollar, be economical; (6) buy, build and beautify homes; (7) live out of home products; (8) educate your children; (9) encourage race unity and race enterprise by patronizing each other in business; (10) observe the laws of sanitation; put cleanliness next to Godliness; (11) work every day in the week; average 100 per cent in your daily occupation; (12) don't spend your money before you make it.

The time has come for the Negro to set up his kingdom. Stop wandering from nowhere to nowhere, but from nowhere to somewhere.

England and her Gladstone, Germany her Bismarck, France her Carnot, America her Blaine, but the Negro race her Booker T. Washington. These were men with gigantic minds. They eclipsed any and every leader in their day and generation.

Suffrage.

The demands of the age and reconstruction will settle the knotty problems and difficult measures of Woman Suffrage. The day is at hand when the mothers, sisters, wives and daughters must be given a greater latitude. In every instance where they have been privileged by legislative, judicial or executive authority, they have proven serviceable and efficient.

Education.

I call upon the men to make your wives your partners. As you advance, see that they advance. Wherever they have been considered in business, office, banks, schools or even the pulpit they have been the equal and many times the superior to men.

I call upon the parents to see to your children being educated.

Let the teacher take ignorance by the throat and choke it to death.

Let the ministers in the pulpit drive the shining steel of education through the head of ignorance.

Mob Violence.

As civilians, we call upon the giant minds and rulers in proud America to protect us from mob violence and lynch laws. I firmly believe that there are governors like our own Governor Henderson, sheriffs and deputies as well as some of our white friends who have and will exercise every means to protect the human life and see that the supposed guilty party has a fair and impartial trial. Every man is innocent until he is proven guilty. When they are forced to leave this world for the unknown by the rope route or by the report of guns, they have no chance for vindication. Stop mob violence. You make and execute the laws. We do not make them.

When an angry mob of one hundred or more shoot, cut, burn and flay one helpless being, it engenders hatred and ill will between the races. The Negro's suffering for better protection has caused them to change quarters. The cooler brains have tried to keep them in the South, but their efforts have proven fruitless. They continue to go. Our friends can help settle this unsettled condition and stop this unrest.

The greatest advantages for the Negro are in the South. His friends are here. Some of the best white friends in the world are here.

The question of social equality has staggered this nation. I want the friends to know that we lay no claim to social equality with other races. It is not our desire, nor our purpose, and not our plan to impose ourselves socially upon other people. We are not cringing. We are not begging. We only urge a fair chance in life. We need more friends like Ex Governor Emmett O'Neal.

Unity.

This nation will testify that we have been loyal and patriotic. While the peace conference is going on where the different nations will confer with each other, I call upon the colored race to plan well and let's have a National Conference of Negroes. Let us hold conventions, debate subjects, pass resolutions and memorialize state legislature, congress and the United States senate for better protection of our race.

We have many friends who sympathize with us in our weakness. They are willing to lend a helping hand, but we must prove ourselves worthy of their confidence.

Men, women and children who are able to accomplish something will always be in demand. A woman is a better cook if she is educated. A servant is a better servant if he is educated. The farmer is a better farmer if he is educated.

Take these great shipbuilding plants, foundries, furnaces, steel corporations, factories, the authorities need prepared persons. Service and efficiency are in demand.

Confidence.

One of the greatest drawbacks of the race is the lack of confidence in each other. I call upon the colored people of Birmingham to put your monies together and re-organize a bank.

Time.

I want to urge my people to study, learn and know the value of time. Waste of time, non confidence and not seeing 100 cents in a dollar have thrown the race back 50 years.

"On time" should be our motto.

In the days of Henry VIII, the messenger bore this kind of message: "Haste, post haste, haste for thy life."

Caesar delayed reading a letter. It cost him his life.

Colonel Rable, a Hessian commander, was playing cards when a messenger brought a letter, stating that Washington was crossing the Delaware. He did not read it in time. The game was over. That delay cost him his honor, liberty and life.

Napoleon laid great stress on the Supreme moment or "nick of time."

The African association wanted to send Ledgard, a traveler, to Africa. When he was asked "When he would be ready to go," he said: "Tomorrow." When they asked John Jervis or Earl Vincent when he could join the ship, he replied, "Directly."

It is said doing a deed is like sowing a seed, if not done at just the right time, it will be forever out of season.

Hyde Park–Kenwood Property Owners' Association
"The New Negro"

Property Owners' Journal, March 1919[4]

Negroes are boasting, individually and through the colored press, that the old order of things for the Negro is changing and that a new condition is about to begin. As a result of the boastful attitude, the Negro is filled with bold ideas, the realization of which means the overturning of their older views and conditions of life. The Negro is unwilling to resume his status of other years; he is exalting himself with idiotic ideas on social equality. Only a few days ago Attorney General Palmer informed the Senate of the nation of the Negroes' boldest and most impudent ambition, sex equality.

From the Negro viewpoint sex equality, according to Mr. Palmer, is not seen as the equality of men and women; it is the assertion by the Negro of a right to marry any person whom he chooses, regardless of color. The dangerous portion of their outrageous idea does not consist in the accident that some black or white occasionally may forget the dignity of their race and intermarry. That has happened before; doubtless it will recur many times. Where the trouble lies is in the fact that the Department of Justice has observed an organized tendency on the part of Negroes to regard themselves in such a light as to permit their idea to become a universal ambition of the Negro race.

As a corollary to their ambition on sex equality, it is not strange that they are attempting to force their presence as neighbors on the whites. The effrontery and impudence that nurses a desire on the part of the Negro to choose a white as a marriage mate certainly will not result in making the Negro a desirable neighbor. That fact alone is enough to determine the property owners of this district to declare to the Negroes that they must stay out. As neighbors they have nothing to offer. "They lived for uncounted centuries in Africa on their own resources, and never so much as improved the make-up of an arrow, coined a new word, or crept an inch nearer to a spiritual religion," and it is a certainty that their tenure of those unfortunate buildings now occupied by them will not be improved by a single nail if it [is] left to the Negro to provide and drive the nail.

Keep the Negro in his place, amongst his people, and he is healthy and loyal. Remove him, or allow "his newly discovered importance to remove him from his proper environment and the Negro becomes a nuisance." He develops into an overbearing, inflated, irascible individual, overburdening his brain to such an extent about social equality that he becomes dangerous to all with whom he comes in contact; he constitutes a nuisance of which the neighborhood is anxious to rid itself. If the new Negro desires to display his newly acquired veneer of impudence where it will be appreciated we advise that they parade it in their own district. Their presence here is intolerable.

As stated before, every colored man who moves into Hyde Park knows that he is damaging his white neighbor's property.

Therefore, he is making war on the white man.

Consequently, he is not entitled to any consideration and forfeits his right to be employed by the white man.

If employers should adopt a rule of refusing to employ Negroes who reside in Hyde Park to the damage of the white man's property it would soon show good results.

Anonymous

"The Ku Klux Are Riding Again!"

Crisis, March 1919

Back to life and very active after forty years! This is the thrilling story that one hears today in various parts of the South. The old Klan with its white-robed citizens going out to maintain the supremacy of the white race, as depicted by Thomas Dixon and his satellite, D. W. Griffith, has again come to life. Read this article printed in a daily in Montgomery, Ala.:

"Ku Klux Klansmen Suggest Silent Parade!"

The city of Montgomery was visited last night by a Ku Klux Klan that bore all the earmarks of the ancient honorable order that placed white supremacy back in the saddle after a reign of terror for several years by Negroes and scalawags.

About one hundred white-robed figures silently paraded through the town and, as the paper specially mentioned, went into that section where the Negroes lived. The Klan, according to the paper from which we quote, is the only authorized organization of its kind in existence, having a charter from the state and the governor.

Montgomery is not the only city in Alabama in which demonstrations of the Ku Klux Klan have been made; Mobile, Birmingham, Troy, and some smaller towns have seen it and there are indications of a revival of the Klan in Texas, Oklahoma, Louisiana, Mississippi Georgia, Florida and South Carolina.

In Tennessee it is being revived under a new name, the Columbian Union. The Chattanooga *Times* of December 12 made this statement on the subject:

"Organizer of Ku Klux Gets Busy Locally."

The spirit of the Ku Klux Klan seems embodied in this Columbian Union, a new secret order originally chartered in Nashville, which is

Film still from D. W. Griffith's *The Birth of a Nation*, released February 18, 1915.

being organized in Chattanooga by Arthur Mills, Majestic Viceroy. The purposes of the order are mysteriously surrounded with the traditions of the past, and are among the most unusual of any secret organization yet attempted. That the organizers anticipate racial troubles following the demobilization of the soldiers is indicated in the literature of the order, and Mr. Mills is outspoken in the belief that some such organization is necessary, especially in the South, when the Negro troops are mustered out and returned to their homes.

Allegiance to the United States, the support of the president and the suppression of enemy propaganda, are among the strict requirements of the order.

Prominent among the members of the Columbian Union are many important officials in state and city governments and influential business men. Mr. Mills declares that the Union will be the greatest society ever organized in the South and will be the most important factor in getting the government completely in the hands of the white race and making permanent white supremacy.

What purpose is back of the revival of this Klan?

Ostensibly it is revived for reasons of patriotism, to apprehend all slackers in the purchase of Liberty Bonds and Thrift Stamps. But for that purpose such an organization should have been alert long ago. On the contrary, the Ku Klux are first reported to us this autumn and the Columbian Union is a very recent secret order. Apprehending slackers North, South, East and West, has been the great stay-at-home sport of the war, but the Ku Klux, as their name implies, gave little time to this task, as compared with the other set before it, the keeping of the Negro in his place—the place of a submissive worker of an inferior race.

Why then should dominant whites have found this task especially needful today? The reason is obvious: The Negro with daily stride is taking his place as an equal of the white man. This has happened in two ways, in labor and in war.

Since the European war opened, the South has been suffering from a shortage of working men and women. From five hundred thousand to one million, five hundred thousand Negroes, as variously estimated, have in the last four years left the South. They have gone North to seek greater economic opportunity, education for their children, safety from lynch law. They have also gone as soldiers into the service of the United States. This has given the remaining Negroes better positions than formerly, the chance to bargain for work, to demand a decent wage, to rise in the world. It is amusingly illustrated by the story of a white woman in a southern town who was unable to secure the services of a washer-woman. Seeing a Negro woman sitting on her porch, idle for a moment, the white woman approached her and said that she wanted some one to do her washing. "Do you?" the colored woman answered placidly, "Why so do I." A law was passed in one southern town (it may have been this one) forbidding any colored woman's working for another colored woman. Prosperity and a degree of leisure on the part of the wife and mother have formerly been unusual among the colored working women of the South and the Klan feels they do not keep the Negro in a properly subordinate "place."

If the Ku Klux Klan feels it has a task in keeping the worker in his place, how much more difficult it will find its job of reducing to subserviency the returning soldier. What will the black private and officer do when he gets back home? That is a question frequently asked in the South and there is some anxiety to be detected in the questioning. The matter was honestly, if not tactfully, put by the mayor of a small Georgia town on addressing a group of Negro draftees about to depart for Camp Gordon. Ac-

cording to one of his auditors he spoke in the following manner:

> You boys are going out to fight for your country and for democracy and that is a very fine thing, but there is one idea some of you have been expressing and I want you to get it out of your minds. Don't think that after the war you are going to change things. I want to tell you here today that this isn't so, and you want to remember that our white boys are going over to France and learning how to fight, and that we here at home are preparing for you when you come back. Don't get any new fangled ideas about democracy.

The mayor was indiscreet enough to voice his personal opinion and the Ku Klux riding white-robed through the streets of Montgomery are a sign of applause to his utterance.

What were the Ku Klux, anyway? Dixon and Griffith to the contrary, they were not noble white citizens, but the precursors of the mobs that today burn and torture colored men and women criminals, or suspected criminals, or relatives of persons suspected of crime. We have ample evidence of this. In 1871 the complaints against the Ku Klux Klan in the South were so numerous that the Federal government instituted an investigation. It gathered testimony from all classes that fills many closely printed volumes. The crimes thus chronicled read extraordinarily like lynchings today. The Klan enters a Negro cabin and, enraged at not finding the father and older sons whom it seeks, drags the youngest boy out of the house and shoots him to death. The mother it hangs. An old colored man is shot at and wounded and then beaten to death. An aged Methodist minister, a white man this time, is dragged from his house hanged for a few moments for sport, cut down, beaten and then left with the admonition to leave the country within fifteen days. Whipping, bloodshed, raping of colored girls by white men, destruction of Negro property, a little library in a Negro cabin thrown into the fire with the stern command that no book be found again in that house—this is the real Ku Klux that an element in the South today proposes to emulate. It may have originated with a better group who desired simply to overawe the black man, but it soon degenerated into an organized mob actuated by the cruel, murderous impulses of the lynching mob today.

However, despite the advertisement given this new Klan in various places, there seems little danger that it will succeed. The best element in the South is outspoken in its denunciation of such tactics. The Department of Labor at Washington has as Director of Negro Economics, Dr. George E. Haynes, who has been working for months to bring about better relations between white employers of Negro labor and their employees. Law and Order Leagues have sprung up, notably the one in Nashville which gives as its platform the desire:

> To create and arouse a more active public sentiment in the young and old in favor of enforcement of law and to combat the evils of lawlessness. To hold public meetings, prepare and distribute literature, provide lectures, and to urge the pulpit, press and schools to stress the necessity for the suppression of crime and the maintenance of law and order, to the end that mob violence and at least the more serious crimes shall be condemned by public sentiment and certainly punished by the established processes of the law.

Leading southern papers, among them the Chattanooga *Daily Times*, have written

against this revival of old-time terrorism. Let them take to heart the pronouncement against lynching in the address to the country on July 26. President Wilson then called upon the "Governors of all the states, the law officers of every community and above all the men and women of every community in the United States, all who revere America and wish to keep her name without stain or reproach, to co-operate, not passively merely but actively and watchfully, to make an end of this disgraceful evil. It cannot live where the community does not countenance it." No Ku Klux Klan can endure where this pronouncement of our great executive is taken to heart.

And lastly, the Ku Klux will not succeed because they have a new Negro to threaten and terrify. When the white-robed figures went through the woods and the back places of the South shortly after the Civil War, they found a recently emancipated people, unlettered for the most part, without organization. Today the "Majestic Viceroys," or whatever they may call themselves, will fail to terrify men who have trained at camp, who have stood sentinel in the French forests, who have met and battled with a magnificently trained and relentless foe. And they will not be able to terrify those who have followed the exploits of their men at the front. It is a new Negro who inhabits the South today, especially it is a new Negro youth—a youth that will not be cowed by silly superstition or fear.

W. E. B. Du Bois
"Returning Soldiers"

Crisis, May 1919

My Mission

I went to Paris because today the destinies of mankind center there. Make no mistake as to this, my readers.

Podunk may easily persuade itself that only Podunk matters and that nothing is going on in New York. The South Sea Islander may live ignorant and careless of London. Some Americans may think that Europe does not count, and a few Negroes may argue vociferously that the Negro problem is a domestic matter, to be settled in Richmond and New Orleans.

But all these careless thinkers are wrong. The destinies of mankind for a hundred years to come are being settled today in a small room of the *Hotel Crillon* by four unobtrusive gentlemen who glance out speculatively now and then to Cleopatra's Needle on the Place de la Concorde.

You need not believe this if you do not want to. They do not care what you believe. They have the POWER. They are settling the world's problems and you can believe what you choose as long as they control the ARMIES and NAVIES, the world supply of CAPITAL and the PRESS.

Other folks of the world who think, believe and act;—THIRTY-TWO NATIONS, PEOPLES and RACES, have permanent headquarters in Paris. Not simply England, Italy and the Great Powers are there, but all the little nations; not sim-

ply little nations; but little groups who want to be nations, like the Letts and Finns, the Armenians and Jugo-Slavs, Irish and Ukrainians. Not only groups, but races have come—Jews, Indians, Arabs, and All-Asia. Great churches, like the Greek Orthodox and the Roman Catholic, are watching on the ground. Great organizations, like the American Peace Society, the League to Enforce Peace, the American Federation of Labor, the Woman's Suffrage Association and a hundred others are represented in Paris today.

In fine, not a single great, serious movement or idea in Government, Politics, Philanthropy or Industry in the civilized world has omitted to send and keep in Paris its Eyes and Ears and Fingers! And yet some American Negroes, actually asked WHY I went to help represent the Negro world in Africa and America and the Islands of the Sea.

But why did I not explain my reasons and mission before going? Because I am not a fool.

James Van Der Zee, *Soldiers on Parade, Lenox Avenue near 134th Street, Harlem 1919*. Courtesy of the Studio Museum of Harlem Archives, Donna Van Der Zee Photographic Collection. Image © The Metropolitan Museum of Art; Image source Art Resource, NY.

Because I knew perfectly well that any movement to bring the attention of the world to the Negro problem at this crisis would be stopped the moment the Great Powers heard of it. When, therefore, I was suddenly informed of a chance to go to France as a newspaper correspondent, I did not talk—I went.

What did I do when I got there? First, there were certain things that I did NOT do. I did not hold an anti-lynching meeting on the Boulevard des Italiens. I would to God I could have, but I knew that France is still under martial law,—*that no meeting can be held today in France, anywhere or at any time, without the consent of the Government; no newspaper can publish a line without the consent of the Censor and no individual can stay in France unless the French consent.*

But it did not follow that because I could not do everything I could do nothing. I first went to the American Peace Commission and said frankly and openly: "I want to call a Pan-African Congress in Paris." The Captain to whom I spoke smiled and shook his head. "Impossible," he said, and added: "The French Government would not permit it." "Then," said I innocently: "It's up to me to get French consent!" "It is!" he answered, and he looked relieved.

With the American Secret Service at my heels I then turned to the French Government. There are six colored deputies in the French Parliament and one is an under-secretary in the War Department. "Of course, we can have a Pan-African Congress," he said—"I'll see Clemenceau." He saw Clemenceau, and there was a week's pause. Clemenceau saw Pichon, and there was another pause. Meantime, our State Department chuckled and announced that there would be no Congress and refused Negroes passports. England followed suit and refused to allow the Secretary of the Aborigines Protection Society even to visit Paris, while the South African natives were not allowed to sail.

But there are six Negroes in the French House and Clemenceau needs their votes. There were 280,000 black African troops in the war before whom France stands with uncovered head. The net result was that Clemenceau,

Prime Minister of France, gave us permission to hold the Pan-African Congress in Paris.

What could a Pan-African Congress do? It could not agitate the Negro problem in any particular country, except in so far as that problem could be plausibly shown to be part of the problem of the future of Africa. The problem of the future of Africa was a difficult and delicate question before the Peace conference—so difficult and so delicate that the Conference was disposed to welcome advice and co-operation.

If the Negroes of the world could have maintained in Paris during the entire sitting of the Peace Conference a central headquarters with experts, clerks and helpers, they could have settled the future of Africa at a cost of less than $10,000.

As it was the Congress cost $750. Yet with this meagre sum a Congress of fifty-eight delegates, representing sixteen different Negro groups, was assembled. This Congress passed resolutions which the entire press of the world has approved, despite the fact that these resolutions had two paragraphs of tremendous significance to us:

> *Wherever persons of African descent are civilized and able to meet the tests of surrounding culture, they shall be accorded the same rights as their fellow citizens; they shall not be denied on account of race or color a voice in their own Government, justice before the courts and economic and social equality according to ability and desert.*

> *Whenever it is proven that African natives are not receiving just treatment at the hands of any State or that any state deliberately excludes its civilized citizens or subjects of Negro descent from its body politic and cultural, it shall be the duty of the League of Nations to bring the matter to the attention of the civilized world.*

Precisely the same principles are being demanded today by the Jews and the Japanese. And despite the enormous, significance of these demands, Colonel House of the American Peace Commission received me and assured me that he wished these resolutions presented to the Peace Conference. Lloyd George wrote me that he would give our demands "his careful consideration." The French Premier offered to arrange an audience for the President and Secretary of the Conference. Portugal and Belgium, great colonial powers, offered complete co-operation.

The League for the Rights of Man, which freed Dreyfus, appointed a special commission to hear not only of the African, but the facts as to the American Negro problem.

We got, in fact, the ear of the civilized world and if it had been possible to stay longer and organize more thoroughly and spread the truth,—what might not have been accomplished?

As it was, we have organized the "Pan-African Congress" as a permanent body, with M. Diagne as president and myself as secretary, and we plan an international quarterly BLACK REVIEW to be issued in English, French and possibly in Spanish and Portuguese.

The world-fight for black rights is on! . . .

Returning Soldiers

We are returning from war! *THE CRISIS* and tens of thousands of black men were drafted into a great struggle. For bleeding France and what she means and has meant and will mean to us and humanity and against the threat of German race arrogance, we fought gladly and to the last drop of blood; for America and her highest ideals, we fought in far-off hope; for the dominant Southern oligarchy entrenched in Washington, we fought in bitter resignation. For the America that represents and gloats in lynching, disfranchisement, caste, brutality and devilish insult—for this, in the hateful upturning and mixing of things, we were forced by vindictive fate to fight, also.

But today we return! We return from the slavery of uniform which the world's madness demanded us to don to the freedom of civil garb. We stand again to look America squarely in the face and call a spade a spade. We sing: This country of ours, despite all its better souls have done and dreamed, is yet a shameful land.

It *lynches*.

And lynching is barbarism of a degree of contemptible nastiness unparalleled in human history. Yet for fifty years we have lynched two Negroes a week, and we have kept this up right through the war.

It *disfranchises* its own citizens.

Disfranchisement is the deliberate theft and robbery of the only protection of poor against rich and black against white. The land that disfranchises its citizens and calls itself a democracy lies and knows it lies.

It encourages *ignorance*.

It has never really tried to educate the Negro. A dominant minority does not want Negroes educated. It wants servants, dogs, whores and monkeys. And when this land allows a reactionary group by its stolen political power to force as many black folk into these categories as it possibly can, it cries in contemptible hypocrisy: "They threaten us with degeneracy; they cannot be educated."

It *steals* from us.

It organizes industry to cheat us. It cheats us out of our land; it cheats us out of our labor. It confiscates our savings. It reduces our wages. It raises our rent. It steals our profit. It taxes us without representation. It keeps us consistently and universally poor, and then feeds us on charity and derides our poverty.

It *insults* us.

It has organized a nation-wide and latterly a world-wide propaganda of deliberate and continuous insult and defamation of black blood wherever found. It decrees that it shall not be possible in travel nor residence, work nor play, education nor instruction for a black man to exist without tacit or open acknowledgment of his inferiority to the dirtiest white dog. And it looks upon any attempt to question or even discuss this dogma as arrogance, unwarranted assumption, and treason.

This is the country to which we Soldiers of Democracy return. This is the fatherland for which we fought! But it is *our* fatherland. It was right for us to fight. The faults of *our* country are *our* faults. Under similar circumstances, we would fight again. But by the God of Heaven, we are cowards and jackasses if now that that war is over, we do not marshal every ounce of our brain and brawn to fight a sterner, longer, more unbending battle against the forces of hell in our own land.

We *return.*
We *return from fighting.*
We *return fighting.*

Make way for Democracy! We saved it in France, and by the Great Jehovah, we will save it in the United States of America, or know the reason why.

Anonymous
"Mothers of Men and Women of Mark"

Half-Century Magazine, May 1919[5]

In Commemoration of Mothers' Day, May 12th

Wear a red carnation for the living and white for the dead

An Appreciation of Mothers

This issue of the magazine expresses our love for our mothers. Mothers occupy in our hearts the greatest of reverence. Rightly does our appreciation of our mothers reach deeper in our nature than for any other blood relation. The Colored mother's road since she first set her shackled foot on American soil has bee[n] anything except one strewn with roses. From across the fence of time we still hear the echoing voice of her slave song filled with pathos, energy, hope. Hardships beset her from all sides. Children arrived at a rate that mothers of today little dream of as possible. Often all her children were torn from her by the blood curdling institution of the auction block. Often she would stray away to the rice swamps and die of chills and hunger rather than see the last of her blood "sold way down South."

The message of the North star buoyed up these slave mothers' hope above the crushing blows of the slave driver's whip. The day of freedom burst upon the horizon, for the weight of these mothers' prayers could not be refused by heaven any longer. Turned like canary birds into a strange world, the mothers came into the world of freedom without strong wings and with large broods to feed. They soon learned the way of the world, and today the race rises to a status of manhood as the product of loyal, persistent, noble minded womanhood.

Our little homage in this dedication we give with hearts full of devotion. Out of their centuries of sacrifice and hard labor in the cotton fields, and from rough labor in general, arises a new stock of Negro manhood and womanhood. The off-spring have chiseled their way into almost every avenue of America life—in industry, the professions, the arts. The new Negro has proven his worth by his fulfilling our mothers' prayers for the life of free souls and deep love.

A. Philip Randolph

"Who's Who: A New Crowd—A New Negro"

Messenger, May–June 1919[6]

Throughout the world among all peoples and classes, the clock of social progress is striking the high noon of the Old Crowd. And why?

The reason lies in the inability of the old crowd to adapt itself to the changed conditions, to recognize and accept the consequences of the sudden, rapid and violent social changes that are shaking the world. In wild desperation, consternation and despair, the proud scions of regal pomp and authority, the prophets and high priests of the old order, view the steady and menacing rise of the great working class. Yes, the Old Crowd is passing, and with it, its false, corrupt and wicked institutions of oppression and cruelty; its ancient prejudices and beliefs and its pious, hypocritical and venerated idols.

It's all like a dream! In Russia, one-hundred and eighty million of peasants and workmen—disinherited, writhing under the ruthless heel of the Czar for over three hundred years, awoke and revolted and drove their hateful oppressors from power. Here a New Crowd arose—the Bolsheviki, and expropriated their expropriators. They fashioned and established a new social machinery, the Soviet—to express the growing class consciousness of teaming millions, disillusioned and disenchanted. They also chose new leaders—Lenin and Trotsky—to invent and adopt scientific methods of social control; to marshal, organize and direct the revolutionary forces in constructive channels to build a New Russia.

The "iron battalions of the proletariat" are shaking age-long and historic thrones of Europe. The Hohenzollerns of Europe no longer hold mastery over the destinies of the German people. The Kaiser, once proud, irresponsible and powerful; wielding his sceptre in the name of the "divine right of kings," has fallen, his throne has crumbled and he now sulks in ignominy and shame—expelled from his native land, a man without a country. And Nietzsche, Treitschke, Bismarck, and Bernhardi, his philosophic mentors are scrapped, discredited, and discarded, while the shadow of Marx looms in the distance. The revolution in Germany is still unfinished. The Eberts and Scheidemanns rule for the nonce; but a New Crowd is rising. The hand of the Sparticans must raise a New Germany out of the ashes of the old.

Already, Karolyi of the old regime of Hungary, abdicates to Bela Kun, who wirelessed greetings to the Russian Federated Socialist Soviet Republic. Meanwhile the triple alliance consisting of the National Union of Railwaymen, the National Transport Workers' Federation and the Miners' Federation, threaten to paralyze England with a general strike. The imminence of industrial disaster hangs like a pall over the Lloyd George government. The shop stewards' committee or the rank and file in the works, challenge the sincerity and methods of the old pure and simple union leaders. British labor would build a New England. The Sein Feiners are the New Crowd in Ireland fighting for self-determination. France and Italy, too, bid soon to pass from the control of scheming and intriguing diplomats into the hands of a New Crowd. Even Egypt, raped for decades prostrate under the juggernaut of financial imperialism, rises in revolution to expel a foreign foe.

And the natural question arises: What does it all mean to the Negro?

First it means that he, too, must scrap the Old Crowd. For not only is the Old Crowd useless, but like the vermiform appendix, it is decidedly injurious, it prevents all real progress.

Before it is possible for the Negro to prosecute successfully a formidable offense for justice and fair play, he must tear down his false leaders, just as the people of Europe are tearing down their false leaders. Of course, some of the Old Crowd mean well. But what matter is [it] though poison be administered to the sick intentionally or out of ignorance. The result is the same—death. And our indictment of the Old Crowd is that: it lacks the knowledge of methods for the attainment of ends which is desires to achieve. For instance the Old Crowd never counsels the Negro to organize and strike against low wages and long hours. It cannot see the advisability of the Negro, who is the most exploited of the American workers, supporting a workingman's political party.

The Old Crowd enjoins the Negro to be conservative, when he has nothing to conserve. Neither his life nor his property receives the protection of the government which conscripts his life to "make the world safe for democracy." The conservative in all lands are the wealthy and the ruling class. The Negro is in dire poverty and he is no part of the ruling class.

But the question naturally arises: who is the Old Crowd?

In the Negro schools and colleges the most typical reactionaries are Kelly Miller, Moton and William Pickens. In the press Du Bois, James Weldon Johnson, Fred R. Moore, T. Thomas Fortune, Roscoe Conkling Simmons and George Harris are compromising the case of the Negro. In politics Chas. W. Anderson, W. H. Lewis, Ralph Tyler, Emmet Scott, George E. Haynes, and the entire old line palliating, me-to-boss gang of Negro Republican politicians, are hopelessly ignorant and distressingly unwitting of their way.

In the church the old crowd still preaches that "the meek will inherit the earth," "if the enemy strikes you on one side of the face, turn the other," and "you may take all this world but give me Jesus." "Dry Bones," "The Three Hebrew Children in the Fiery Furnace" and "Jonah in the Belly of the Whale," constitute the subjects of the Old Crowd, for black men and women who are overworked and under-paid, lynched, jim-crowed and disfranchised—a people who are yet languishing in the dungeons of ignorance and superstition. Such then is the Old Crowd. And this is not strange to the student of history, economics, and sociology.

A man will not oppose his benefactor. The Old Crowd of Negro leaders has been and is subsidized by the Old Crowd of White Americans—a group which viciously opposes every demand made by organized labor for an opportunity to live a better life. Now, if the Old Crowd of white people opposes every demand of white labor for economic justice, how can the Negro expect to get that which is denied the white working class? And it is well nigh that economic justice is at the basis of social and political equality.

For instance, there is no organization of national prominence which ostensibly is working in the interest of the Negro which is not dominated by the Old Crowd of white people. And they are controlled by the white people because they receive their funds—their revenue—from it. It is, of course, a matter of common knowledge that Du Bois does not determine the policy of the National Association for the Advancement of Colored People; nor does Kinckle Jones or George E. Haynes control the National Urban League. The organizations are not responsible to Negroes because Negroes do not maintain them.

This brings us to the question as to who shall assume the reins of leadership when the Old Crowd falls.

As among all other peoples, the New Crowd must be composed of young men who are educated, radical and fearless. Young Negro radicals must control the press, church, schools, politics and labor. The condition for joining the New Crowd are: equality, radicalism and sincerity. The New Crowd views with much expectancy the revolutions ushering in a New World. The New Crowd is uncompromising. Its tactics are not defensive, but offensive. It would not send notes after a Negro is lynched. It would not appeal to white leaders. It would appeal to the plain working people everywhere. The New Crowd sees that the war came, that the Negro fought, bled and died; that the war has ended, and he is not yet free.

"Following the Advice of the 'Old Crowd' Negroes," cartoon, *Messenger*, September 1919.

The New Crowd would have no armistice with lynch-law; no truce with jim-crowism, and disfranchisement; no peace until the Negro receives complete social, economic and political justice. To this end the New Crowd would form an alliance with white radicals such as the I.W.W., the Socialists and the Non-Partisan League, to build a new society—a society of equals, without class, race, caste or religious distinctions.

Anonymous

"Changes in Psychology"

Crisis, August 1919[7]

The United States, says the Chicago, Ill., *Tribune*, has a new type of black man to deal with. This type is developing a strong social consciousness out of which arise questionings and resentments. The paper continues:

The new type works hard, grows steadily prosperous, and simultaneously with the realization of the worth of its labor, is irked by patronage, by those jokes about the razor, which some of us still think are droll,

"The 'New Crowd Negro' Making America Safe for Himself," cartoon, *Messenger*, September 1919.

and by that lofty petting which some of us still believe colored men from 17 to 70 must like. They do not.

All this new Negro psychology and new Negro consciousness is as surely a fact and a factor in the local situation as is the increasing number of Negroes in our midst. It cannot be left out of the problem if the problem is to be approached rationally and humanely. It may seem like writing all around the subject and not getting into it to harp on this theme of growing social consciousness of the Negroes as a race and the growing sense of his personal dignity

manifested by the Negro as an individual—a sense not the less real because it often manifests itself in surliness and rudeness.

For several decades the enfranchised Negro sought patronage and liked it. Then he came to distrust and resent it. And now the clear-headed representatives of the race take it with equanimity and as it is meant—take it kindly when it is meant kindly, but they don't like it the better for that.

The returning colored soldiers are a big factor in, and big contributors to, this new Negro consciousness. They return with heads up, with a more acute sense of the hard conditions to which they were born, and with a fresh determination, since they rightly enough have been made much of, to make something of themselves. They have been under discipline and the effect of discipline is dual. It both tames and makes a man, and it has done both for thousands of these once irresponsible lads.

Dr. Cary says that many of them have told him that they tire and sicken of the banquets and dances given them upon their return and that they seek "something lasting, something worth while."

The phrase epitomizes the new aspiration of the new Negro.

"Something lasting, something worth while."

Hubert Harrison

"As the Currents Flow"

New Negro 3, no. 7 (1919)

During the past fortnight great events have taken place. The race battles in Washington and Chicago, although tragical, are nevertheless to be recorded as brilliant events in the history of the Negro race in America. It is most gratifying for us to note that the New Negro spirit is a fait accompli. It has found an abode in the hearts of all the truly liberty-loving and progressive Negroes. It has been too long the practice of the Southern Negro victims to beg and plead for mercy at the hands of a sordid mob. We have often wondered why these men, at the first sign of trouble, do not arm themselves preparatory for self-defense. If they are to die at the hands of a "legalized" mob, then it is up to them to sell their lives as dearly as possible. The white man must be made to take his own medicine so that he may learn to appreciate its disagreeable and disgusting flavor.

The white press of this country has noted that the Negro American has entered a new epoch in the history of his country. The baneful effects of the lessons forced upon him during his period as a chattel slave is wearing off. The New Negro—unlike the Negro of the "old conservative crowd" who is ever willing to compromise everything that is held dear to his race in order to obtain for himself a miserable pittance and some sympathy from his former master— is identifying himself with every progressive and radical movement; he is uncompromising and non-partisan, as the *New York World* stated in an editorial a part of which we reproduce here:

> There are enough points of friction between the races without introducing party. The Negro owes nothing to any party. He has been abandoned by all of them, most notably by the Republicans, who in 1877 TRADED HIS RIGHTS AT THE SOUTH TO PERFECT THE TITLE OF A STOLEN PRESIDENCY. Colored men assuming to lead their people should know this by this time that the political and incidentally the legal privileges conferred upon them can never be enjoyed so long as they are the mere chattels of a party.

The New Negro is Negro first, Negro last, and Negro always. He needs not the white man's sympathy; all he is asking for is equal justice before the law and equal opportunity in the battle of life. He needs and asks for no special privileges that are not granted to the other races; he is not a weakling. He has proven his physical strength as well as his intellectual equality which enables him to live both as a savage among savages and as the most cultured and civilized being among those who profess to have reached that stage of life.

That stuff about "he who humbleth himself shall be exalted" is being left untouched by him in the book in which it is written, so that the Anglo-Saxon and other allied mixtures, may use it to their hearts' content and gratification. Then there is that other stuff about turning the left cheek to the assailant after the right cheek has been smitten. There can be no stronger proof of the positive rejection of this unmanly teaching than the exposition of the New Negro spirit during the recent royal racial battles in Washington—the most cultured and civilized city in the world—and Chicago.

"An eye for an eye, a tooth for a tooth," and sometimes two eyes or a half dozen teeth for one is the aim of the New Negro. Since life is sweet, our first object is to preserve life. If any one is to be killed let it be the other fellow as self-preservation is the first law of nature. Render good for evil? Bah! it is not practical amongst christianized hypocrites,

and furthermore, that is the kind of argument the fellow who does the evil first puts forward. Why? Because he fears retaliation. That is what the conservative and reactionary white press has discovered, and much space is now dedicated to its discussion. But while editorials are written, many of which we have reproduced in this issue, singing the praises of the Negro, the news and reports concerning him which occupy the front page, are, in the majority of cases, biased, discreditable, and heartrending.

Who is foolish enough to assume that with 239,000 colored men in uniform from the Southern States alone, as against 370,000 white men, the blacks whose manhood and patriotism were thus recognized and tested are forever to be flogged, lynched, burned at the stake, and chased into concealment whenever Caucasian desperadoes are moved to engage in these infamous pastimes?

It is a dreadful thing to see a man of ideals and principles desert them and reveal his traitorous soul to public scorn and contempt, in order that he may serve a master.

Joseph Bibb
"The Black Man's Barrier"

Chicago Whip, September 27, 1919

THE PATH of the Black man is not padded with roses. Instead it is bestrewn with thorns, thistles and quick sands. The obstacles that loom up as alpine barriers are multitudinous. The Black sojourner has stumbled, tottered and has even fallen to his knees, but ever anon, he has trodded and he is still trodding up to the heights delectable. HIS CROSS HE BEARS WITH PHILOSOPHICAL OPTIMISM, REALIZING NO CROSS, NO CROWN.

OVER AND ABOVE this philosophical optimism there has been created a systematic attempt by the American Black man to lay aside

every weight and to run the race as a strong man should. The progressive, advancing Negro is stripping himself of ignorance, superstition, religious fanaticism, color consciousness, conservatism and unwarranted credulity. The American Black man is also beginning a scientific eradication of the barriers in his pathway. Hannibal was the first man to cross the Alps, others had tried in vain, centuries afterward Napoleon the Great, tunneled through the Alps, thence the classic platitude "Hannibal Crossed the Alps, but Napoleon Overturned Them," THERE HAVE BEEN GREAT GROUPS IN OUR RACE

WHO HAVE BY SHEER NERVE AND INDOMITABLE WILL POWER CROSSED THE BARRIERS, BUT BEHIND THEM THERE STILL LAGS THE APATHETIC AND WEAK MEMBERS THAT STILL STRUGGLE AND FALL. IT THEREFORE BEHOOVES US TO EITHER TUNNEL THE BARRIERS OR TO CUT THEM OUT OF OUR WAY.

This paper advocates permanent elimination and eradication of all evils and deterrent forces. Expediency and innate limitations will not permit us to attack all evils at once. We will however, begin our militant campaign on these restraining forces and stumbling blocks. THERE MUST BE A CRUSADE ON OFFENDING EVILS IN CHRONOLOGICAL ORDER AND IN CONSONANCE WITH THEIR GRAVITY AND WEIGHT.

The predominant barrier in the pathway of the American Black man is the "old school type of Negro." The half-cocked individual, who discourages the young men, who disparages their every constructive effort, who reaches his conclusions on the affairs of life through emotion and impulse rather than logical reasoning and intelligent appraisal of comparative human values.

THESE OLD FOGGYS HAVE SAPPED THE VITALITY OF INTELLIGENT ORGANIZATION. They have put cogs in the wheels of racial stability. They have used the heritable tendency and trait of the slave to snoop around and seize the ideas, propaganda and methods of the young Negroes and slip around and tell some white man that "such and such" an individual is to be scrutinized. These old-fashioned recalcitrants have sneered and riled the efforts of the younger men and bellowed such criticisms and cynicisms that THEY HAVE MADE RACIAL COHESION A JOKE AND INTELLIGENT CO-OPERATION A FARCE.

The most cruel blow of all is that these scheming, planning and plotting "Merchants of Venice" have taken every asset that the young men produced and capitalized it without giving them equitable consideration. THEY HAVE TEMPTED YOUNG MEN WITH POLLUTED FINANCIAL BAIT AND STEERED THEM FROM DOING

CONSTRUCTIVE WORK AND REAL SERVICE. These old school individuals who have no information on the world's work, these Uncle Toms who reason by old, old sayings and wornout proverbs, refuse to patronize young professional men, who distrust everybody and even steal from themselves, are prooving [sic] the whole race in the unsanitary environment in which they revel and bask.

THE FOSSILIZED TYPES that must be cut off are those who believe that the Negro must stay in a Negroe's [sic] place. Who believe that the Negro race is inherently inferior. Who believe that education turns Negroes into fools. Who believe everything that the white man prints. Who believe that the white man's conclusion is the verdict reached by highest tribunal under the sun. Who believe in the old order of things.

They do not believe that the Negro is worthy of his hire; they do not believe in the survival of the fit, but in the survival of the slick. They believe in getting money and have no regard for methods. THEY DO NOT BELIEVE IN ANY CORPORATE BUSINESS, UNLESS THEY HAVE THE CONTROLLING STOCK. They do not believe in public meetings unless their ignoble faces can be seen on the platforms. They believe in extolling their own virtues from the house tops. They believe in getting all the graft they can in all the ways they can. They believe in putting the young Negro down and keeping him down. The late Booker T. Washington, strangely out of a mediocre mind, gave birth to one good anecdote; that of the crabs in the basket that pulled back every venturous brother who tried to climb out. He, also, related the story of the frog in the buttermilk who kept on kicking until the milk was churned into butter and Mister Frog walked away on the golden buttery substance. These old fossils and foggies must be churned out of existence. The time is ripe. THE NEW NEGRO WILL DO THE KICKING, BUT THE WHOLE RACE WILL REAP THE FRUITION. Away with these backward individuals that checkmate the future of our Race. "If thy right arm offend thee, cut it off."

W. A. Domingo
"If We Must Die"

Messenger, September 1919

America won the war that was alleged to be fought for the purpose of making the world safe for democracy, but in the light of recent happenings in Washington, the Capital city, and Chicago, it would seem as though the United States is not a part of the world. In order to win the war President Wilson employed "force, unstinted force," and those who expect to bring any similar desirable termination to a just cause can do no less than follow the splendid example set them by the reputed spokesman of humanity. That the lesson did not take long to penetrate the minds of Negroes is demonstrated by the change that has taken place in their demeanor and tactics. No longer are Negroes willing to be shot down or hunted from place to place like wild beasts; no longer will they flee from their homes and leave their property to the tender mercies of the howling and cowardly mob. They have changed, and now they intend to give men's account of themselves. If death is to be their portion, New Negroes are determined to make their dying a costly investment for all concerned. If they must die they are determined that they shall not travel through the valley of the shadow of death alone, but that some of their oppressors shall be their companions.

This new spirit is but a reflex of the great war, and it is largely due to the insistent and vigorous agitation carried on by younger men of the race. The demand is uncompromisingly made for either liberty or death, and since death is likely to be a two-edged sword it will be to the advantage of those in a position to do so to give the race its long-denied liberty.

The new spirit animating Negroes is not confined to the United States, where it is most acutely manifested, but is simmering beneath the surface in every country where the race is oppressed. The Washington and Chicago outbreaks should be regarded as symptoms of a great pandemic, and the Negroes as courageous surgeons who performed the necessary though painful operation. That the remedy is efficacious is beyond question. It has brought results, for as a consequence the eyes of the entire world are focused upon the racial situation in the United States. The world knows now that the New Negroes are determined to observe the primal law of self-preservation whenever civil laws break down; to assist the authorities to preserve order and prevent themselves and families from being murdered in cold blood. Surely, no one can sincerely object to this new and laudable determination. Justification for this course is not lacking, for it is the white man's own Bible that says "Those who live by the sword shall perish by the sword," and since white men believe in force, Negroes who have mimicked them for nearly three centuries must copy them in that respect. Since fire must be fought with hell fire, and diamond alone can cut diamond, Negroes realize that force alone is an effective medium to counteract force. Counter irritants are useful in curing diseases, and Negroes are being driven by their white fellow citizens to investigate the curative values inherent in mass action, revolvers and other lethal devices when applied to social diseases.

The New Negro has arrived with stiffened back bone, dauntless manhood, defiant eye, steady hand and a will of iron. His creed is admirably summed up in the poem of Claude McKay, the black Jamaican poet, who is carving out for himself a niche in the Hall of Fame:

IF WE MUST DIE

If we must die, let it not be like hogs
Hunted and penned in an inglorious spot,
While round us bark the mad and hungry dogs,
Making their mock at our accursed lot.

If we must die, oh, let us nobly die,
So that our precious blood may not be
    shed
In vain; then even the monsters we defy
Shall be constrained to honor us, though
    dead!
Oh, kinsmen! We must meet the common
    foe;
Though far outnumbered, let us still be
    brave.

And for their thousand blows deal one
    death-blow!
What though before us lies the open
    grave?
Like men we'll face the murderous,
    cowardly pack,
Pressed to the wall, dying, but—fighting
    back!

W. A. D.

Hubert Harrison
"The White War and the Colored Races"

New Negro 4, no. 2 (1919)

[The following article was written last year while the Great War still raged. It was written for a certain well-known radical magazine; but was found to be "too radical" for publication at that time. It is given now to the Negro public partly because the underlying explanation which it offers of the root-cause of the war has not yet received treatment even among socialistic radicals, and partly because recent events in China, India, Africa and the United States have proved the accuracy of its forecasts.]

The 19th Christian Century saw the international expansion of capitalism—the economic system of the white peoples of Western Europe and America—and its establishment by force and fraud over the lands of the colored races, black and brown and yellow. The opening years of the 20th Century present us with the sorry spectacle of these same white nations cutting each other's throats to determine which of them shall enjoy the property which has been acquired. For this is the real sum and substance of the original "war aims" of the belligerents; although in conformity with Christian cunning, this is one which is never frankly avowed. Instead, we are fed with the information that they are fighting for "Kultur," and "on behalf of small

nationalities." Let us look carefully at this camouflage.

In the first place, we in America need not leave our own land to seek reasons for suspecting the sincerity of democratic professions. While we are waging war to establish democracy three-thousand miles away, millions of Negroes are disfranchised in our own land by the "cracker" democracy of the southern states which is more intent upon making slaves of their black countrymen than upon freeing the French and Belgians from the similar brutalities of the German Junkers. The horrible holocaust of East St. Louis was possible only in three modern states—Russia of the Romanoffs, Turkey and the United States—and it ill becomes any one of them to point a critical finger at the others.

But East St. Louis was simply the climax of a long series of butcheries perpetrated on defenseless Negroes which has made the murder rate of Christian America higher than that of heathen Africa and of every other civilized land. And, although our government can order the execution of thirteen Negro soldiers for resenting the wholesale insults to the uniform of the United States and defending their lives from

Unidentified portrait by Richard Samuel Roberts, 1920s. Courtesy of the Columbia Museum of Art, Gift of Gerald E. Roberts, Beverly Roberts, Cornelius C. Roberts and Wilhelmina R. Wynn.

civilian aggressors, not one of the murderers of black men, women and children has been executed or even ferreted out. Nor has our war Congress seen fit as yet to make lynching a federal crime. What wonder that the Negro masses are insisting that before they can be expected to enthuse over the vague formula of making the world "safe for democracy" they must receive some assurance that their corner of the world—the South—shall first be made "safe for democracy"! Who knows but that perhaps the situation and treatment of the American Negro by our own government and people may have kept the Central Powers from believing that we meant to fight for democracy in Europe, and caused them to persist in a course which has driven us into this war in which we must spend billions of treasure and rivers of blood.

It should seem, then, that "democracy," like "Kultur," is more valuable as a battle-cry than as real belief to be practiced by those who profess it. And the plea of "small nationalities" is estopped by three facts: Ireland, Greece, and Egypt, whose Khedive, Abbas Hilmi, was tumbled off his throne for failing to enthuse over the claims of "civilization" as expounded by Lord Grey.

But this is merely disproof. The average American citizen needs some positive proof of the assertion that this war is being waged to determine who shall dictate the destinies of the darker peoples and enjoy the usufruct of their labor and their lands. For the average American citizen is blandly ignorant of the major facts of history and has to be told. For his benefit I present the following statement from Sir Harry Johnston, in "The Sphere" of London. Sir Harry Johnston is the foremost English authority of Africa and is in a position to know something of imperial aims.

> Rightly governed, I venture to predict that Africa will, *if we are victorious, repay us and all our allies the cost of our struggle with Germany and Austria*. The war, deny it who may, was really fought over African questions. The Germans wished, as the chief gain of victory, to wrest rich Morocco from

French control, to take the French Congo from France, and the Portuguese Congo from Portugal, to secure from Belgium the richest and most extensive tract of alluvial goldfield as yet discovered. This is an auriferous region which, properly developed, will, when the war is over, repay the hardest-hit of our allies (France) all that she has lost from the German devastation of her home lands. The mineral wealth of trans-Zambezian Africa—freed forever, we will hope, from the German menace—is gigantic: only slightly exploited so far. Wealth is hidden amid the seemingly unprofitable deserts of the Sahara, Nubia, Somaliland and Namaqua. Africa, I predict, will eventually show itself to be the most richly endowed of all the continents in valuable vegetable and mineral substances.

There is the sum and substance of what Schopenhauer would have called "the sufficient reason" for this war. No word of "democracy" there, but instead the easy assumption that, as a matter of course, the lands of black Africa belong to white Europe and must be apportioned on the good old principle:

> the simple plan,
> That he shall take who has the power,
> And he must keep who can.

It is the same economic motive that has been back of every modern war since the merchant and trading classes secured control of the powers of the modern state from the battle of Plassey to the present world-war. This is the natural and inevitable effect of the capitalist system of what (for want of a worse name) we call "Christendom." For that system is based upon the wage relationship between those who own and those who operate the gigantic forces of land and machinery. Under this system no capitalist employs a worker for two dollars a day unless that worker creates more than two dollars worth of wealth for him. Only out of this surplus can profits come. If ten million workers should thus create one-hundred-million dollars worth of wealth each day and get twenty or fifty millions in wages, it is obvious that they can expend only what they have received, and that, therefore, every nation whose industrial system is organized on a capitalist basis must produce a mass of surplus products over and above, not the needs, but the purchasing power of the nation's producers. Before these products can return to their owners as profits they must be sold somewhere. Hence the need for foreign markets, for fields of exploitation and "spheres of influence" in "undeveloped" countries whose virgin resources are exploited in their turn after the capitalist fashion. But, since every industrial nation is seeking the same outlet for its products, clashes are inevitable and in these clashes beaks and claws—armies and navies—must come into play. Hence beaks and claws must be provided beforehand against the day of conflict, and hence the exploitation of white men in Europe and America becomes the reason for the exploitation of black and brown and yellow men in Africa and Asia. And, therefore, it is hypocritical and absurd to pretend that the capitalist nations can ever intend to abolish wars. For, as long as black men are exploited by white men in Africa, so long must white men cut each other's throats over that exploitation. And thus, the selfish and ignorant white workers' destiny is determined by the hundreds of millions of those whom he calls "niggers." "The strong too often think that they have a mortgage upon the weak; but in the domain of morals it is the other way."

But economic motives have always their social side; and this exploitation of the lands and labor of colored folk expresses itself in the social theory of white domination: the theory that the worst human stocks of Montmartre, Seven Dials and the Bowery are superior to the best human stocks of Rajputana or Khartum. And when these colored folks who make up the overwhelming majority of this world, demand decent treatment for themselves, the proponents of this theory accuse them of seeking social equality. For white folk to insist upon the right to manage their own ancestral lands, free from the domination of tyrants, domestic and foreign, is variously described as democracy

and self-determination. For Negroes, Egyptians and Hindus to seek the same thing is impudence. What wonder, then, that the white man's rule is felt by them to rest upon a seething volcano whose slumbering fires are made up of the hundreds of millions of Chinese, Japanese, Hindus, and Africans! Truly has it been said that "the problem of the 20th Century is the problem of the Color Line." And wars are not likely to end; in fact, they are likely to be wider and more terrible—so long as this theory of white domination seeks to hold down the majority of the world's people under the iron heel of racial repression.

Of course, no sane person will deny that the white race is, at present, the superior race of the world. I use the word "superior" in no cloudy, metaphysical sense, but simply to mean that they are on top and their will goes,—at present. Consider that fact as the pivotal fact of the war. Then, in the light of it, consider what is happening in Europe to-day. The white race is superior—its will goes—because it has invented and amassed greater means for the subjugation of nature and of man than any other race. It is the top dog by virtue of its soldiers, guns, ships, money, resources and brains. Yet there in Europe it is deliberately burning up, consuming and destroying these very soldiers, guns, ships, money, resources and brains, the very things upon which its supremacy rests. When this war is over, it will be less able to enforce its sovereign will upon the darker races of the world. Does any one believe that it will be as easy to hold down Egypt and India and Persia after the war as it was before? Hardly.

Not only will the white race be depleted in numbers, but its quality, physical and mental, will be considerably lowered for a time. This is inevitable. War destroys first the strongest and bravest, the best stocks, the young men who were to father the next generation. The next generation must, consequently, be fathered by the weaker stocks of the race. And thus, in physical stamina and in brain-power, they will be less equal to the task of holding down the darker millions of the world than their fathers were. This was the thought back of Mr. Hearst's objection to our entering the war. He wanted the United States to stand as the white race's reserve of man-power when Europe had been bled white.

But what will be the effect of all this upon that colored majority whose preponderant existence our newspapers ignore? In the first place, it will feel the lifting of the pressure as the iron hand of "discipline" is relaxed. And it will expand, when that pressure is removed, to the point where it will first ask, then demand, and finally secure, the right of self-determination. It will insist that, not only the white world, but the whole world, be made "safe for democracy." This will mean a self-governing Egypt, a self-governing India, and independent African states as large as Germany and France—and larger. And, as a result, there will come a shifting of the basis of international politics and business and of international control. This is the living thought that comes to me from the newspapers and books that have been written and published by colored men in Africa and Asia during the past three years. It is what I have heard from their own lips as I have talked with them. And, yet, of this thought which is inflaming the international underworld, not a word appears in the parochial press of America, which seems to think that if it can keep its own Negroes down to servile lip-service, it need not face the world-wide problem of the "Conflict of Color," as Mr. Putnam-Weale calls it.

But that the more intelligent portions of the white world are becoming distressingly conscious of it, is evident from the first great manifesto of the Russian Bolsheviki last year when they asked about Britain's subject peoples.

And the British workingmen have evidently done some thinking in their turn. In their latest declarations they seem to see the ultimate necessity of compelling their own aristocrats to forego such imperial aspirations as that of Sir Harry Johnston, and of extending the principle of self-determination even to the black people of Central Africa. But eyes which have for centuries been behind the blinkers of Race Prejudice cannot but blink and water when compelled to face the full sunlight. And Britain's workers insist that "No one will maintain that the Africans are fit for self-government." But no one has yet asked the Africans anything about it. And on the same principle (of excluding the opinion of those who are most vitally concerned) Britain's ruling class may tell them that "No one maintains that the laboring classes of Britain are fit for self-government." But their half-hearted demand that an international committee shall take over the British, German, French and Portuguese possessions in Africa and manage them as independent nationalities (?) until they can "go it alone," would suggest that their eyesight is improving.

To sum it all up, the war in Europe is the result of the desire of the white governments of Europe to exploit for their own benefit the lands and labor of the darker races, and, as the war continues, it must decrease the white man's stock of ability to do this successfully against the wishes of the inhabitants of those lands. This will result in their freedom from thralldom and the extension of political, social, and industrial democracy to the twelve-hundred-million black and brown and yellow peoples of the world. This, I take it, is what President Wilson had in mind when he wished to make the world "safe for democracy." But, whether I am mistaken or not, it is the idea which dominates to-day the thought of those darker millions.

Cyril Briggs
"The Old Negro Goes: Let Him Go in Peace"

Crusader, October 1919[8]

The old Negro and his futile methods must go. After fifty years of him and his methods the Race still suffers from lynching, disfranchisement, jim-crowism, segregation and a hundred other ills. His abject crawling and pleading have availed the Cause nothing. He has sold his life and his people for vapid promises tinged with traitor gold. His race is done. Let him go.

The New Negro now takes the helm. It is now OUR future at stake. Not his. His future is in the grave. And if the New Negro, imbibing the spirit of Liberty, is willing to suffer martyrdom for the Cause, then certainly the very least that the Old Negro can do is to stay in the background for his remaining years of life or to die a natural death without in his death struggles attempting to hamper those who take new means to effect ends which the Old Leaders throughout fifty years were not able to effect.

Can the Old Leaders deny that there is more wholesome respect for the Negro following the race riots in Washington, Chicago, Knoxville and other places than there was before those riots and when there were only lynchings and burnings of scared Negroes and none of the fear in the white man's heart that comes from the New Negro fighting back? They cannot deny it, so let them go their way. The future is the New Negro's. It should have come to us safeguarded. But the Old Leaders have failed ignobly. Ours now is the task of safeguarding that future and of giving it to our children secured for all time. For us the future and all the great tasks that lie ahead. For the Old Leaders *Requiescat en Pace!*

Anonymous
"Reconstruction: Prominent Men of Both Races Discuss a Program for the Improvement of Race Relations"

Black Dispatch, October 10, 1919[9]

Rev. Baird Says, Apply Kindness to All Our Acts

Governor Robertson presided. He plainly stated that the purpose of the call is to promote a more friendly relationship between the two races. "All of us know," said the Governor, "that the Negro is mistreated, and it is up to us to work out some plan that will mean for him a larger measure of justice." A round table discussion of the subject was had and without a single exception every one stated that he was in favor of the idea of Governor Robertson and entered heartily into the program. Gen. T. D. Turner said that he had fought in the Confederate army and had been a southerner from birth, but he said that he was glad to have lived long enough to have changed some of the ideas that he once had. The Reverend Phil C. Baird said that the solution of all of our difficulties was the application of kindness to all of our actions.

Editor Roscoe Dunjee spoke extendedly and said in part:

> Your Excellency and Gentlemen: We of the black race court this opportunity here

today. This is the moment that we have longed and yearned for. This is the moment for which we have prayed; the time when you would set down in the open forum and have, with us, discourse to reason.

Charles Lamb said "I cannot hate a man I know." In this life that is about all there is to the solution of any human difficulty, "KNOWING MEN," and if you white men who sit here today understood what the longing, yearning and objective of the black man were, if you really knew what he wanted out of life, you could not oppose him, for the objective, the purpose, the longing and the yearning of the Black man is identical and the same as yours. Now how could you oppose a man in hoping to reap the same harvest from the field of life as you, if you operate upon the plains of justice and fairness.

The cornerstone upon which rests all of our difficulties is YOUR UNWILLINGNESS TO RECOGNIZE THE NEGRO AS A MAN. Now the Negro is a man, and a free man. I might say to make clearer my point that you have now with you a NEW NEGRO. I do not mean the new Negro that you have had described to you. You have had what was a termed a NEW NEGRO described to you. You have had what was termed a NEW NEGRO described to you as an insolent, arrogant individual, a creature who would not assimilate himself properly into organized forms of government. I mean this, that out of the education that you have permitted us to get and which we have acquired out of our own efforts also, there has developed a different creature than the inert clod that you one knew as a slave. IN YOUR FAILURE TO RECOGNIZE JUST THIS ONE FACT RESTS ALL OF THE DIFFICULTY.

All there is to any man is his spirit, and when you educate a man, when his vision becomes enlarged, when his soul and spirit begins to ramble out into the realm of imagination and new thought, when that happens THAT MAN is on the road to Freedom, and this is the status of the mind of the NEW NEGRO that I desire that you know better.

This New Negro, who stands today released in spirit, finds himself, in America and in this state, physically bound and shackled by LAWS AND CUSTOMS THAT WERE MADE FOR SLAVES, and all of the unrest, all of the turbulence and all of the violence that now is charged to my people, IS THE BATTLE OF FREE MEN, POUNDING UPON WALLS THAT SURROUND THEM AND THAT WERE MADE FOR SLAVES.

You see, it is impossible to regulate anything for a free man that was made for a slave. The only thing that can be done is to irradicate and do away with some of the forms of government that we now have. Fortunate indeed it was for America that she rid herself of slaves; unfortunate it is that we have failed to do away with the laws that were made for those former slaves.

I am alarmed at the idea that some of the people of this country have as to the cause of the unrest among us. Some say, if I read correctly your newspapers, that there are I. W. W. [Industrial Workers of the World] agitators among us. Others say that it is Bolshevik or anarchistic influences that seek to draw us into their radical division. This is an improper conclusion. The Negro has arrived at the place where he now finds himself through his own processes of reasoning. For example, it does not take an I. W. W. to clinch the argument that the majority of the Negroes in the United States cannot vote. It does not take an anarchist to ride with us on the railroad for us to know that when we pay three cents per mile that we do not get what you get by paying the same and identical amount. It does not take a Bolshevist to inform us that freedom of movement is restricted to us and that, under the guise of law a separate status as citizens is designed for the black man.

I think you ought to know how the black man talks and feels at times when he knows that you are nowhere about, and I want to tell you, if you were to creep up tonight to a place where there are 10,000 Negroes gathered, you would find no division on this one point. I know that they all would say, "WE HAVE NO CONFIDENCE IN WHITE POLICEMEN." I speak of a general proposition. In particular instances we have had police protection and I think I would be unfair to the moment and would not properly interpret the feeling of the Negroes of this city, were I not to compliment Mayor Walton and Chief Smith for the manly and courageous position they have taken here in Oklahoma City in this recent disturbance of the past week. These officials have done their duty and every black man and woman in Oklahoma City has felt a large measure of safety because of their attitude.

But how can the Negro forget Houston, East St. Louis, Memphis, Washington, Chicago or Knoxville. In every one of these cities there was a total and complete breaking down of the police authority; in every one of these cities THE POLICE JOINED HANDS WITH THE MOB IN THE MASSACRE OF MY PEOPLE. How would you feel and HOW DO YOU THINK WE WOULD FEEL TO LAY DOWN TO SLEEP WITH OUR MOTHERS, WIVES AND SISTERS GUARDED WITH SUCH ALLEGED POLICE PROTECTION? Why a man who works out in my office took a post course in Chicago University this summer. He was in Chicago at the time of the riots. He says that a white policeman who patrolled the beat on the street where he lived, went home in the afternoon and changed his uniform for civilian clothing and returned at night at the head of a mob. Now we are not mistaken in our idea that he led the mob, for the reason that HE WAS ONE OF THOSE WHO LAY DEAD IN THE STREETS THE NEXT MORNING. Oh, I wish it were possible for you to just stretch yourself over far enough to drop into our shoes and feel the way we must and do feel, laboring under such conditions.

If you were to listen to that same group of Negroes talk when they are alone, let there be one hundred or one hundred thousand, they would with me accord all say, WE HAVE NO CONFIDENCE IN THE WHITE MAN'S COURT. I think you ought to know this, for it is with what men think that we have to deal. They would say in such a meeting that they know before they get into the court what the verdict will be. If their cause is the cause of a black man against a white man they will say that they know that a verdict would be rendered in favor of the white man.

Now what is the psychology in this situation. How does the black mans' [sic] mind operate under such conditions. If a Negro commits an offence he is apt to think like this. "I cannot turn myself over to the police. FOR IT IS THE MOB; neither can I afford to turn myself over to the court, for it will lynch me of justice["] and he reaches this final conclusion that there are two avenues open to him. EITHER SUCCESSFULLY HIDE OR FIGHT AND DIE. How would you feel and how do you think that the Negro feels laboring under such conditions.

None of my race is dreaming of what you so often term "SOCIAL EQUALITY." Really I feel that we get this term mixed with the idea of social intermingling. Equality among men and races is an evolutional process that develops on the inner side of the man or race and cannot be fixed by law or by what you think or by what I think. No Negro is hunting for the society of the white man. Why, we are the lesser influence in this civilization; we belong to the submerged class, and yet we know that you cannot come into our homes to mingle with us unless we want you to. How then, would it be possible for us to force our society and ourselves upon you, the dominant class, when you know there is no provision in law or custom for you to get into ours, the least protected society?

What we want is "SOCIAL JUSTICE." We want to feel a larger security in our homes from the hand of the mob. We want the free, untrammeled right at the ballot box. We want justice in the courts and the right, under the law, to do anything that other citizens of this government may do. . . .

No intelligent Negro leader is inciting his people to aggression and strife, but you do not know of how we have to labor so that the masses of our race can grasp the vision that we have; we who lead can turn and look backwards to know that there is a long, long trail a-winding from the days when we black folk were down low in the scale of humanity. Right here in America we have watched the conscience of America as it has mounted the ladder of human fairness to the plain where we now are. We are dissatisfied and yet we know that though our enemies are striking harder at our liberty and our lives, they are also fewer than ever before. The masses are not planning to attack you or anybody. There is only this determination, to protect ourselves. This is the forum that we need—a place where men of both races can have discourse to reason. . . .

Marcus Garvey
"The New Negro and the U.N.I.A."

Negro World, November 1, 1919
Newport News, Va., Oct. 25, 1919

Stirring Speech Delivered by Hon. Marcus Garvey in the South

Mr. President, Officers and Members of the Newport News Division of the Universal Negro Improvement Association—Indeed, it is a pleasure to be with you. From the first time I visited your city I became impressed with your earnestness. Ever since I came here and went away, an impression, an indelible impression, was made on me relative to your earnestness in the great onward and upward movement engineered under the leadership of the Universal Negro Improvement Association.

Since I visited you last the Universal Negro Improvement Association has grown financially and otherwise, numerically, to the extent that tonight, this very hour, the Universal Negro Improvement Association is regarded as the strongest Negro movement in the world. [*Cheers.*] We have been able to force entry into every civilized country where Negroes live, and tonight the colors that you and I are wearing in Newport News are being worn by Negroes all over the world.

U.N.I.A.: Serious Movement

As I have told you in many addresses before, the Universal Negro Improvement Association is a very serious movement. We are for serious business. We are out for the capturing of liberty and democracy. [*Cheers.*] Liberty is not yet captured, therefore we are still fighting. We are in a very great war, a great conflict, and we will never get liberty, we will never capture democracy, until we, like all the other peoples who have won liberty and democracy, shed our sacred blood. This liberty, this democracy, for which we Negroes of the world are hoping, is a thing that has caused blood as a sacrifice by every people who possess it today.

The Defeat of Germany

The white man of America who possesses his liberty and his democracy won it through the sacrifice of those thousands of soldiers who fought and fell under the leadership of George Washington. The French people, who are enjoying their liberty and their democracy today, are enjoying it because thousands of Frenchmen fought, bled, and died to make France safe. That America, England, and France have had peace with the world and with themselves is simply through the fact that they have defeated Germany and won for themselves liberty and democracy.

Liberty and Democracy Are Expensive

Therefore, you will realize that liberty and democracy are very expensive things, and you have to give life for it. And if we Negroes think we can get all these things without the shedding of blood for them we are making a dreadful mistake. You are not going to get anything unless you organize to fight for it. There are some things you can fight for constitutionally, such as your political rights, your civic rights, but to get liberty you have to shed some blood for it. And that is what the Universal Negro Improvement Association is preparing your minds for—to shed some blood so as to make your race a free and independent race. That blood we are not going to shed in Newport News, that blood we are not going to shed in America, because America will not be big enough to hold the Negro when the Negro gets ready. But that blood we are preparing to shed one day on the African battlefield, because it is the determination of the New Negro to re-possess himself of that country that God gave his forefathers. Africa is the richest continent in the world; it is the country that has given civilization to mankind and has made the white man what he is.

What the White Man Owes the Negro

After the white man is through abusing the Negro, when he gets back his sober senses, he will realize that he owes all that he possesses today to the Negro. The Negro gave him science and art and literature and everything that is dear to him today, and the white man has kept them for thousands of years, and he has taken advantage of the world. He has even gone out of his way to reduce the African that gave him his civilization and kept him as a slave for two hundred and fifty years. But we feel that the time has come when we must take hold of that civilization that we once held. The hour has struck for the Negro to be once more a power in the world, and not all the white men in the world will be able to hold the Negro from becoming a power in the next century. Not even the powers of hell will be able-to [*sic*] stop the Negro in his onward and upward movement. With Jesus as our standard bearer the Negro will march to victory.

The Negro Rules

There will be no democracy in the world until the Negro rules. We have given the white man a chance for thousands of years to show his feelings towards his fellow men. And what has he done up to this twentieth century? He has murdered man; he has massacred man; he has deprived man of his rights even as God gave to man. The white man has shown himself an unfit subject to rule. Therefore he has to step off the stage of action. I believe it is Shakespeare who said:

> The Quality of mercy is not strained,
>
> It droppeth like the gentle rain from
>   heaven
> Upon the place beneath;
> It is twice blessed;
>
> It blesseth him that gives and him that
>   takes.

Has the white man any mercy? Not before the black man returns to power will there be any mercy in the world. The Negro has been the savior of all that has been good for mankind.

But the future portends great things. It portends a leadership of Negroes that will draw man nearer to his God, because in the Negroes' rule there will be mercy, love, and charity to all.

Marcus Garvey in a car, New York City, 1922. Courtesy of Getty Images.

Man Created for a Purpose

I want you colored men and women in Newport News to realize that you form a great part in this creation, for God has created you for a purpose; that purpose you have to keep in view; that purpose you must live. God said through the Psalmist that Ethiopia shall stretch forth her hands unto him and that princes shall come out of Ethiopia. I believe fervently that the hour has come for Ethiopia to stretch forth her hands unto God, and as we are stretching forth our hands unto God in New York, in Pennsylvania, in the West Indies, in Central America, and in Africa and throughout the world I trust that you in Newport News are stretching forth your hands unto God.

Endless Chain of Negroes

There is an endless chain of Negroes all over the world, and wherever Negroes are to be found this day they are suffering from the brutality of the white man, and because Negroes are suffering all over the world we feel that the time has come for the four hundred millions of us scattered all over the world to link up our sentiment for one common purpose—to obtain liberty and democracy.

Africa Must Be Restored

I want you to understand that you have an association that is one of the greatest movements in the world. The New Negro, backed by the Universal Negro Improvement Association, is determined to restore Africa to the world, and you scattered children of Africa in Newport News, you children of Ethiopia, I want you to understand that the call is now made to you. What are you going to do? Are you going to remain to yourselves in Newport News and die? Or are you going to link up your strength, morally and financially, with the other Negroes of the world and let us all fight one battle unto victory? If you are prepared to do the latter, the battle is nearly won, because we of the Universal Negro Improvement Association in-

tend within the next twelve months to roll up a sentiment in the United States of America that will be backed up by fifteen million black folks, so that when in the future you touch one Negro in Newport News you shall have touched fifteen million Negroes of the country. And within the next twenty-four months we intend to roll up an organization of nearly four hundred million people, so that when you touch any Negro in Newport News you touch four hundred million Negroes all over the world at the same time.

Liberty or Death

It falls to the province of every black man and every black woman to be a member of the Universal Negro Improvement Association, because there is but one purpose before us, which is the purpose of liberty—that liberty that Patrick Henry spoke about in the legislature of Virginia over one hundred and forty years ago. We new Negroes of America declare that we desire liberty or we will take death. [*Cheers.*] They called us out but a few months ago to fight three thousand miles away in Europe to save civilization, to give liberty and democracy to the other peoples of the world. And we fought so splendidly, and after we died, after we gave up our blood, and some of us survived and returned to our respective countries, in America, in the West Indies, in Central America, and in Africa, they told us, as they told us in the past, that this country is the white man's country. What is it but menial opportunities for you where you live in contact with white men? Because they have told us that in America, because they have told us that in France, because they have told us under the government of Great Britain that our opportunities are limited when we come in contact with white men, we say the war is not over yet. The war must go on; only that the war is not going on in France and Flanders, but the war will go on in the African plains, there to decide once and for all in the very near future whether black men are to be serfs and slaves or black men are to be free men.

Black Men Are Going to Be Free

We have decreed that black men are going to be free as white men are free or yellow men are free. We have declared that if there is to be a British Empire, if there is to be a German Empire, if there is to be a Japanese Empire, if there is to be a French Republic, and if there is to be an American Republic, then there must be a black republic of Africa. [*Cheers.*]

The White Man Hid the Book from the Negro

The New Negro has given up the idea of white leadership. The white man cannot lead the Negro any longer any more. He was able through our ignorance to lead us for over three hundred years since he took us from Africa, but the New Negro has learned enough now. When the white man took the black man from Africa he took him under a camouflage. He said to the Queen of England that he was taking the black man from Africa for the purpose of civilizing and Christianizing him. But that was not his purpose. The white man's purpose for taking the Negro from his native land was to make a slave of him, to have free labor. Some of us were brought to the Southern States of this country, some of our brothers and sisters were taken to Central America and others were taken to the West Indian Islands, and we labored under the bonds of slavery for 250 years. The white man never schooled us for the 250 years. He hid the book from us, even the very Bible, and never taught the Negro anything.

The Negro Made a Rush for the Book

But God moves in a mysterious way, and he brought about Lincoln and Victoria, and he said, "You must let those people free," and they did let us free. As soon as we were freed we made a rush to get the book, and we did get the book. We got the Bible first, and we began to sing songs and give praise to God, and that is why the Negro shouts so much in church. But after he was through with the first he got hold of the school book and went from his A B C to Z, and what has happened in fifty years? There is not a white man so educated that you cannot find a Negro to equal him. None in France, none in England, none in America to beat the Negro educationally, and because we stand equal with him we say no longer shall the white man lead us, but we shall lead ourselves.

The Negro and the Gun and Powder

If we had not a complete training in knowledge before 1914 in that we only knew the book and were only able to read and write, they of themselves gave us training and placed two million of us in the army and gave us gun and powder and taught us how to use them. That completed the education of the Negro. Therefore, tonight the Negro stands complete in education. He knows how to read his book, he knows how to figure out, and he knows how to use the sword and the gun. And because he can do these things so splendidly, he is determined that he shall carve the way for himself to true liberty and democracy which the white man denied him after he was called out to shed his blood on the battlefields of France and Flanders.

The Black Star Line Steamship Corporation

I did not come down to Newport News to talk to you merely from a sentimental standpoint. I have come to talk to you from a sentimental and business standpoint. We cannot live on sentiment. We have to live on the material production of the world. I am here representing the Black Star Line Steamship Corporation of the world. The purpose of the Black Star Line Steamship Corporation is to float a line of steamships to run between America, Canada, the West Indies, South and Central America, and Africa, carrying freight and passengers, thus linking up the sentiment and wealth of the four hundred million Negroes of the world. Every day I spend away from New York means a financial loss of $5,000 a day; but I have sacrificed all that to come and speak to you in

Newport News, because you in Newport News have a history in connection with the Black Star Line.

First Stock Sold

I want to say to you that on the 31st of this month the S.S. *Frederick Douglass* will sail out of New York harbor, the property of the Black Star Line—the property of the Negro peoples of the world. I also want you to understand that the first stock that was sold in the Black Star Line was sold in the Dixie Theatre in Newport News. [*Cheers.*] The first five hundred dollars that we sold was sold in Newport News. Therefore, you gave the real start to the Black Star Line, and as you started the Black Star Line we want you to finish the Black Star Line.

So that is why I took the chance of leaving New York to speak to you in Newport News. I telegraphed your President a few days ago and asked him up to a conference to let him see what New York is doing to come back and tell you. The Negroes are alive in New York and they are alive in Philadelphia also. New York is supplying its quota to the Black Star Line and so is Philadelphia. I have taken the chance to come to Newport News to find out if you are going to supply your quota towards the Black Star Line. I want you to understand that opportunity is now knocking at your door. You know that opportunity knocks but once at every man's door. The Black Star Line is the biggest industrial and commercial undertaking of the Negro of the Twentieth Century. The Black Star Line opens up the industrial and commercial avenues that were heretofore closed to Negroes.

The Negro Must Protect Himself

Every ship, every house, every store the white man builds, he has his gun and powder to protect them. The white man has surrounded himself with all the protection necessary to protect his property. The Japanese government protects the yellow man, and the English, German, French, and American governments protect the white man, and the Negro has absolutely no

Universal Negro Improvement Association parade, corner of 135th Street and Lenox Avenue in Harlem, 1920. Courtesy of the Photographs and Prints Division, Schomburg Center for Research in Black Culture, The New York Public Library, Astor, Lenox and Tilden Foundations.

protection. And that is why they lynch and burn us with impunity all over the world, and they will continue to do so until the Negro starts out to protect himself. The Negro cannot protect himself by living alone—he must organize. When you offend one white man in America, you offend ninety millions of white men. When you offend one Negro, the other Negroes are unconcerned because we are not organized. Not until you can offer protection to your race as the white man offers protection to his race, will you be a free and independent people in the world.

Archibald H. Grimké
"The Shame of America, or the Negro's Case against the Republic"

Speech, 1919[10]

The author of the Declaration of Independence said once that he trembled for his country when he remembered that God was just. And he did well to do so. But while he was about it he might have quaked a little for himself. For he was certainly guilty of the same crime against humanity, which had aroused in his philosophic and patriotic mind such lively sensations of anxiety and alarm in respect to the Nation. Said Jefferson on paper: "We hold these truths to be self-evident, that all men are created equal; that they are endowed by their Creator with certain unalienable rights; that among these are life, liberty and the pursuit of happiness," while on his plantation he was holding some men as slaves, and continued to hold them as such for fifty years thereafter, and died at the end of a long and brilliant life, a Virginia slaveholder. And yet Thomas Jefferson was sincere, or fancied that he was, when he uttered those sublime sentiments about the rights of man, and when he declared that he trembled for his country when he remembered that God was just. This inconsistency between the man's magnificence in profession and his smallness in practice, between the grandeur of what he promised and the meanness of what he performed, taken in conjunction with his cool unconsciousness of the discrepancy, is essentially and emphatically an American trait, a national idiosyncrasy. For it has appeared during the last one hundred and forty-four years with singular boldness and continuity in the social, political, and religious life of the American people and their leaders. I do not recall in all history such another example of a nation appearing so well in its written words regarding human rights, and so badly when it comes to translating those fine words into corresponding action, as this Republic has uniformly exhibited from its foundation, wherever the Negro has been concerned.

Look at its conduct in the War of the Revolution, which it began with the high sounding sentiments of the Declaration of Independence. . . .

Thus it happened that black men fought in that war shoulder to shoulder with white men for American Independence. In every colony from Massachusetts to Georgia, they were found faithful among the faithless, and brave as the bravest during those long and bitter years, fighting and dying with incomparable devotion and valor, by the side of Warren at Bunker Hill, and of Pulaski at Savannah. . . .

What was his guerdon? In the hour of their triumph did the patriot fathers call to mind such supreme service to reward it? In the freedom which they had won by the aid of their enslaved countrymen, did they bethink them of lightening the yoke of those miserable men? History answers, no! Truth answers, no! The descendants of those black heroes answer, no!

What then? What did such bright, such blazing beacons of liberty, the Washingtons, Hamiltons, Madisons and Franklins, the Rufus Kings, Roger Shermans, and Robert Morrises? They founded the Republic on slavery, rested one end of its stately arch on the prostrate neck of the Negro. They constructed a national Constitution which safeguarded the property of man in man, introducing into it for that purpose its three fifths slave representation provision, its fugitive slave clause, and an agreement by which the African slave trade was legalized for nineteen years after the adoption of that instrument. That was the reward which the founders of the Republic meted out with one accord to a race which had shed freely its blood to make that Republic a reality among the nations of the earth. Instead of loosening and lifting his heavy yoke of oppression, they strengthened and tightened it afresh on the loyal and long suffering neck of the Negro. Notwithstanding this shameful fact, the founders of the Republic were either so coolly unconscious of its moral enormity or else so indifferent to the amazing contradiction between what they said and what they did, as to write over the gateway of the new Constitution this sonorous preamble: "We, the people of the United States, in order to form a more perfect union, establish justice, insure domestic tranquility, provide for the common defense, promote the general welfare, and secure the blessings of liberty to ourselves and our posterity, do ordain and establish this Constitution for the United States of America."

"We the people!" From the standpoint of the Negro, what grim irony; "establish justice"! What exquisitely cruel mockery; "to insure domestic tranquility"! What height and breadth and depth of political duplicity; "to provide for the common defense"! What cunning paltering with words in a double sense; "to promote the general welfare"! What studied ignoring of an ugly fact; "and secure the blessings of liberty to ourselves and posterity"! What masterly abuse of noble words to mask an equivocal meaning, to throw over a great national transgression an air of virtue, so subtle and illusive as to deceive the framers themselves into believing in their own sincerity. You may ransack the libraries of the world, and turn over all the documents of recorded time to match that Preamble of the Constitution as a piece of consummate political dissimulation and mental reservation, as an example of how men juggle deliberately and successfully with their moral sense, how they raise above themselves huge fabrics of falsehood, and go willingly to live and die in a make believe world of lies. The muse of history, dipping her iron pen in the generous blood of the Negro, has written large across the page of that Preamble, and the face of the Declaration of Independence, the words, "sham, hypocrisy."

It is the rage now to sing the praises of the fathers of the Republic as a generation of singularly liberty loving men. They were so, indeed, if judged by their fine words alone. But they were, in reality, by no means superior to their sons in this respect, if we judge them by their acts, which somehow speak louder, more convincingly to us than their words, albeit those words proceed out of the Declaration of Independence, and the Preamble of the Constitution. If the children's teeth today are set on edge on the Negro question, it is because the fathers ate the sour grapes of race wrong, ate those miserable grapes during their whole life, and, dying, transmitted their taste for oppression, as a bitter inheritance to their children, and children's children, for God knows how many black years to come. . . .

History repeats itself. In America, on the Negro question, it has been a series of shameful repetitions of itself. The Negro's history in the first war with England was repeated exactly in the second. In this conflict no more loyal and daring hearts bled and broke for the country than were those of its colored soldiers and sailors. On land and water in that war the Negro died as he fought, among the most faithful and heroic defenders of the American cause. . . .

Jackson's black troops proved themselves in the actions of Mobile Bay and New Orleans entitled to every mouthful of the ringing applause which Old Hickory gave them without stint. They got fair enough words as long as the enemy was in sight and his navy covered the waters of the country. But as soon as the peril had passed those fear words were succeeded by the foulest ingratitude. On every hand Colorphobia reared its cursed head, and struck its cruel fangs into those brave breasts which had just received the swords and the bullets of a foreign foe. They were legislated against everywhere, proscribed by atrocious laws everywhere. They had given the nation in its dire need, blood and life, and measureless love, and had received as reward black codes, an unrelenting race prejudice, and bondage bitterer than death.

Strange irony of fate which reserved to Andrew Jackson, whose mouth overflowed with praise in 1814 for his black soldiers and with fair promises of what he intended to do for them. Strange irony of fate, I say, which reserved to that man, as President in 1836, the elevation of Roger B. Taney to the Chief Justiceship of the United States, of Taney, the infamous slave Judge who wrote the Dred Scott Decision, which argued that black men had no rights in America which white men were bound to respect. . . .

As in Egypt more than three thousand years ago, the Eternal spoke to the master race at divers times and with divers signs, saying, "let my people go," so he spoke to the master race in this land through divers omens and events, saying likewise, "let my people go." Those with ears to hear might have heard that divine voice in the Hartford Convention and the causes which led to its call; in the successive sectional conflicts over Missouri, the Tariff, and Texas; in the storm winds of the Mexican war, as in the wild uproar which followed the annexation of new national territory at its close; in the political rage and explosions of 1850 and 1854, and in the fierce patter of blood drops over Kansas. They might have surely heard that commanding voice from the anointed lips of holy men and prophets, from the mouths of Garrison and Summer, and Phillips, and Douglass, from the sacred gallows where John Brown heard and repeated it while his soul went marching on from city to city, and State to State, over mountain and river, across a continent, and from the Lakes to the Gulf with rising accent saying, "let my people go." Alas! the nation hearkened not to the voice of justice, but continued to harden its heart, until thunder like that voice broke in the deep boom of Civil War. . . .

Need I repeat in this presence the old, grand story, how in numbers nearly two hundred thousand strong our colored boys in blue, left their blood and their bones in every State from Virginia to Louisiana? How, like heroes, they fought and died for the Union at Port Hudson, and Fort Wagner, and Petersburg, and Honey Hill, and Olustee, and Milliken's Bend? How in winter and summer, in cold and heat, in valley and on hilltop, on horse and on foot, over rivers and swamps, through woods and brakes, they rushed to meet the foe? How leaving behind them fields strown thick with their dead and wounded, they mounted the blazing sides of grim fortresses, climbing on great deeds and self sacrifices through storms of shot and shell, to death and a place among the stars?

No, no, it is not required of me on this occasion to read afresh that glorious record. Sufficient then this: The Northern army, reinforced by the strength which it drew from that of the Negro, broke in time the back of the Rebellion, and saved the Union, so that in 1865 the flag of the nation floated again over an undivided country, and the Republic, strong and great beneath that flag, launched anew to meet the years, and to reach her fair ideals of liberty and equality which were flashing like beacon lights upon her way.

Amid widespread rejoicing on the return of peace and the restoration of the Union, the Negro rejoiced among the gladdest, for his slave fitters were broken, he was no longer a chattel. He imagined in his simple heart, in his ignorance and poverty, that he had not only won freedom, but the lasting affection and gratitude of the powerful people for whom he had entered hell to quench for them it's raging fires with his blood. Yes, although black and despised, he, the slave, the hated one, had risen above his centuries of wrongs, above their bitter memories and bitterer sufferings to the love of enemies, to the forgiveness of those who had despitefully used him, ay, to those moral heights where heroes are throned and martyrs crowned. Surely, surely, he, who had been so unmindful of self in the service of country, would not be left by that country at the mercy of those who hated him then with the most terrible hatred for that very cause. He who had been mighty to save others would surely, now in his need, be saved by those whom he had saved. "Oh! Justice, thou has fled to brutish beasts, and men have lost their gratitude."

I would gladly seal forever the dark chapter of our history, which followed the close of the war. Gladly would I forget that record of national shame and selfishness. But as it is better to turn on light than to shift it off, I will, with your forbearance, turn it on for our illumination and guidance, in the lowering present.

The chapter opened with an introduction of characteristic indifference on the part of the country in respect to the fate of the Negro. With his shackles lying close beside him, he was left in the hands of his old master who, seizing the opportunity, proceeded straightway to refit them on the disenthralled limbs of the former slave. State after State did so with such promptitude and to such effect that within a few months a formidable system of Negro serfdom had actually been constructed, and cunningly substituted in place of the system of Negro slavery, which the war had destroyed. An African serf power, Phoenix like, was rising out of the ashes of the old slave power into national politics. At sight of this truly appalling apparition, the apparition of a returning slave power in thin disguise, all the old sectional fear and hatred which had existed against it in the free States before the Rebellion, awoke suddenly and hotly in the breast of the North. Thinking mainly, if not wholly of its own safety in the emergency which confronted it, and how best to avert the fresh perils which impended in consequence over its ascendancy, the North prepared to make, and did in fact make, for the time being, short shrift of this boldly retroactive scheme of the South to recover within the Union all that it had lost by its defeated attempt to land itself outside of the Union.

Having tested to its entire satisfaction the Negro's value as a soldier in its war for the preservation of the Union, the North determined at this juncture to enlist his aid as a citizen in its further conflicts with the South, for the preservation or its sectional domination in the newly restored Union. To this end the Fourteenth and the Fifteenth Amendments to the Constitution were, in the progress of events, incorporated into that instrument. By these two great acts, the North had secured itself against the danger of an immediate return of the South to anything like political equality with it in the Republic. Between its supremacy and the attacks of its old rival, it had erected a solid wall of Negro votes. But immensely important as was the ballot to its black contingent, it was not enough to meet all of his tremendous needs. Nevertheless, as the North was considering mainly its own and not the Negro's necessities at this crisis, and as the elective franchise in his hands was deemed by it adequate to satisfy its own pressing floods, it gave the peculiar wants of the Negro beyond that of the ballot but scant attention.

Homeless, landless, illiterate, just emerging from the blackness of two centuries of slavery, this simple and faithful folk had surely other sacred claims on the North and the National Government than this right to the ballot. They had in truth a strong claim to unselfish friendship and statesmanship, to unfaltering care and guardianship, during the whole of their transition from slavery to citizenship. They needed the organized hands, the wise heads, the warm hearts, the piled up wealth, the sleepless eyes, the faith, hope, and charity of a Christian people and a Christian government to teach them to walk and to save them from industrial exploitation by their old masters, as well as to vote. Did they receive from the Republic what the Republic owed them by every consideration of justice, gratitude and humanity, as of enlightened self interest? Alas? not a tithe of this immense debt has the Republic ever undertaken to pay to those who should have been, under all circumstances, its sacredly preferred creditors. On the contrary they were left to themselves by the government in the outer darkness of that social state which had been their sad lot for more than two centuries. They were left in that darkest night of moral and civil anarchy to fight not alone their own terrible battle with poverty, ignorance, and untutored appetites and passions, but also the unequal, the cruel battle for the preservation of Northern political domination in the Union. For ten awful years they fought that battle for the North, for the Republican party, in the face of persecutions and oppressions, terrors and atrocities, at the glare of which the country and the civilized world shrank aghast.

Aghast shrank the North, but not for the poor Negro, faithful unto death to it. For itself rather it shrank from the threatening shadows which such a carnival of horrors was casting athwart its vast and spreading network of trade and production. The clamor of all its million wheeled industry and prosperity was for peace. "Let us have peace," said Grant, and "let us have peace" blew forthwith and in deafening unison, all the big and little whistles of all the big and little factories and locomotives, and steamships from Maine to California. Every pen of merchant and editor scratched paper to the same mad tune. The pulpit and the platform of the land cooed their Cuckoo song in honor of those piping times of peace. The lone noise of chinking coin pouring into vaults like coal into bins, drowned the, agonized cry of the forgotten and long suffering Negro. Deserting him in 1876, the North, stretching across the bloody chasm its two greedy, commercial hands, grasped the ensanguined ones of the South, and repeated, "let us have peace." Little did the Northern people and the government reck then or now that at the bottom of that bloody chasm lay their faithful black friends. Little did they care that the blood on those Southern hands had been wrung drop by drop from tire loyal heart of the Negro. But enough.

Years of struggle and oppression follow and we come to another chapter of American history; namely, the Spanish American War. In the Spanish American War the Negro attracted the attention of the world by his clashing valor. He attracted the attention of his country also. His fighting quality was of the highest, unsurpassed, and perhaps unequalled in brilliancy by the rest of the American army that invaded Cuba. He elicited applause and grudging justice from his countrymen, clashed with envy and race prejudice. Still it seemed for a brief time that his conspicuous service had given his case against the Republic a little better standing in Court—a little better chance for a fair hearing at the Bar of Public Opinion. But our characteristic national emotionalism was too shallow and insincere to last. In fact, it died aborning. The national habit of a century and a half reasserted itself. There was no attempt made to square national profession and national practice, national promise and national performance. The Negro again had given his all to his country and had got in return at the hands of that country wrong and injustice. Southern propaganda presently renewed all of its vicious and relentless activity against the Negro. He was different, he was alien, he was unassimilable, he was inferior, and he must be kept so, and in the scheme of things he must be made forever subordinate to the white race. In this scheme of things white domination could best be preserved by the establishment of a caste system based on race and color. And so following the Spanish American War the North and the South put their heads together to complete their caste system. Everywhere throughout the Republic race prejudice, color proscription grew apace. One by one rights and privileges which the Negroes had enjoyed for a brief space were withdrawn and the wall of caste rose higher and higher. He was slowly and surely being shut out from all the things which white men enjoyed by virtue of their citizenship, and shut within narrowing limits of freedom. Everywhere within his prison house he read in large and sinister letters, "Thus far and no farther." He was trapped, and about to be caged. In spite of the Emancipation Proclamation and the three War Amendments he found that white men were becoming bolder in ignoring or violating his freedom and citizenship under them. The walls of the new bondage were closing about his right to life, liberty and the pursuit of happiness in this boasted Land of the Free and Christian Home of Democratic Hypocrisy and Cruelty.

Then Mr. Taft appeared upon the scene and became famous or infamous as a builder on the walls of the Temple of the New American Jerusalem, where profession is High Priest to the God of Broken Promises. He proved himself a master workman in following the lines of caste, in putting into place a new stone in the edifice when he announced as his policy at the beginning of his administration that he would not appoint any colored man to office in the South where the whites objected. Caste had won and the Negro's status was fixed, as far as this bourgeois apostle of American Democracy was able to fix it. His adds but another illustrious name to the long list of those architects of national dishonor who sought to build the Temple of American Liberty upon a basis of caste.

Then in the fullness of time came Woodrow Wilson, the ripe consummate fruit of all this national contradiction between profession and practice, promise and performance. He can give Messrs. Washington, Jefferson, Jackson and Company odds and beat them in the subtle art of saying sonorously, grandiosely, what in action he does not hesitate to flout and spurn. When seeking the Negro's vote in 1912, he was the most profuse and generous in eloquent profession, in iridescent promises, but when he was elected he forgot straightway those fair professions and promises and began within a week after he entered the White House to put into office men filled with colorphobia, the better to finish the work of undoing in the government the citizenship of the Negro, to whom he had promised not grudging justice but the highly sympathetic article, heaping up and running over. Mr. Taft had established the principle that no Negro was to be appointed to office in the South where the whites objected—Mr. Wilson carried the principle logically one step farther, namely, no Negro was to be put to work in any department of the government with white men and women if these white men and women objected to his presence. Segregation along the color line in Federal employment became forthwith the fixed policy of the Wilson administration.

There sprang up under the malign influence of this false prophet of the New Freedom all sorts of movements in the District of Columbia and in the Federal Government hostile to the Negro—movements to exclude him from all positions under the Civil Service above that of laborer and messenger and charwoman, to jim-crow him on the street cars, to prohibit him from intermarrying with the whites, to establish for him a residential pale in the District; in short, to fix forever his status as a permanently inferior caste in the land for which he had toiled in peace and bled and died in war. The evil influence of this false apostle of freedom spread far and wide and spurred the enemies of the Negro to unwonted activity. The movement of residential segregation and for rural segregation grew in volume and momentum in widely separated parts of the country until it was finally checked by the decision of the Supreme Court in 1917.

The condition of the Negro was at its worst and his outlook in America at its darkest when the Government declared war against Germany. Then was revived the Republic's program of false promises and hypocritical professions in order to bring this black man with his brawn and brains, and with his horny hands and lion heart, with his unquenchable loyalty and enthusiasm to its aid. No class of its citizens surpassed him in the swiftness and self-forgetfulness of his response to the call of country. What he had to give he brought to the alter [sic] and laid it there—labor and wealth, wounds and death, with unsurpassed devotion and patriotism. But what he received in return was the same old treatment, evil for his good, ingratitude and treachery for his loyalty and service. He was discriminated against everywhere—was used and abused, shut out from equal recognition and promotion with white men and women. Then when he went overseas he found American colorphobia more deadly than the gun and poison gas of the Germans. In the American army there was operated a ceaseless propaganda of meanness and malice, of jealousy and detraction against him. If our Expeditionary Force had given itself with a tithe of the zeal and industry to fighting the Germans, which a large section of it devoted to fighting the black soldier, it would have come out of the war with more honor and credit, and left behind in France a keener sense of gratitude, and regard than exists for them in that country today. But, alas, thousands of them were more interested in watching the Negro and his reception by the French, in concocting villainous plots to degrade him in the eyes of that people, in segregating him from all social contact with them, and in keeping him in his place, within the hard and fast lines of caste which they had laid for him in America.

But the Negro went and saw—saw the incredible meanness and malice of his own country by the side of the immense genius for Liberty and Brotherhood of France. There he found himself a man and brother regardless of his race and color. But if he has seen these things in France he has also conquered certain other things in himself, and has come back not as he went but a New Negro. He has come back to challenge injustice in his own land and to fight wrong with a courage that will not fail him in the bitter and perhaps bloody years to come. For he knows now as he has never known before that he is an American citizen with the title deeds of his citizenship written in a century and a half of labor and suffering and blood. From his brave black lips I hear the ringing challenge, "This is my right and by the Eternal I have come back to claim all that belongs to me of industrial and political equality and liberty." And let us answer his high resolve with a courage and will to match his own, and so help to redeem our country for its shame of a century and a half of broken promises and dishonored ideals.

But be not deceived, friends. Let us, like brave men and women, face the stern reality of our situation. We are where we are. We are in the midst of a bitter and hitherto an invincible race prejudice, which beats down into the dust of all our rights, all of our attainments, all of our aspirations after freedom and excellence. The North and the South are in substantial accord in respect to us and in respect to the position which we are to occupy in this land. We are to be forever exploited, forever treated as an alien race, allowed to live here in strict subordination and subjection to the white race. We are to hew for it wood, draw for it water, till for it the earth, drive for it coaches, wait for it at tables, black for it boots, run for it errands, receive from it crumbs and kicks, to be for it, in short, social mudsills on which shall rest the foundations of the vast fabric of its industrial democracy and civilization.

No one can save us from such a fate but God, but ourselves. You think, I know, that the North is more friendly to you than the South, that the Republican party does more for the solution of this problem than the Democratic. Friends, you are mistaken. A white man is a white man on this question, whether he lives in the North or the South. Of course, there are splendid exceptions. Scratch the skin of Republican or Democrat, of Northern white men or southern white men, and you will find close to the surface race prejudice, American colorphobia. The difference, did you but know it, is not even epidermal, is not skin-deep. The hair is Democratic Esau's, and the voice is Republican Jacob's. That is all. Make no mistake here, for a true understanding of our actual position at this point is vital.

On Boston Commons stands a masterpiece in bronze, erected to commemorate the heroism and patriotism of Col. Robert Gould Shaw and his black regiment. There day and night, through summer and winter, storm and shine, are to march forever those brave men by the side of their valiant young leader. Into the unknown they are hurrying to front and to fight their enemies and the enemies of their country. They are not afraid. A high courage looks from their faces, lives in the martial motion of their bodies, flashes from the barrels of their guns. On and yet ever on they are marching, grim bolts of war, across the Commons, through State Street, past the old State House, over ground consecrated by the martyr's blood of Crispus Attucks, and the martyr's feet of William Lloyd Garrison. Farther and father they are pressing forward into the unknown, into the

South, to Wagner and immortal deeds, to death and an immortal crown.

Friends, we too are marching through a living and lowering present into the unknown, through an enemy's land, at the summons of duty. We are to face great labors, great dangers, to fight like men our passions and American caste-prejudice and oppression, and God helping us, to conquer them.

~~~~~~

Edward Franklin Frazier

"New Currents of Thought among the Colored People of America"

Master's thesis, Clark University, 1920

[. . .]

A distinct tendency of the new philosophy among Negroes has been to make the Negro problem an international question. This tendency is represented, first, by the Universal Negro Improvement Association with its weekly paper, the Negro World; second, by the secret trip of William Monroe Trotter to the Peace Conference; and third, by the Pan-African Conference held in Paris in 1919 at the call of Dr. W. E. B. DuBois. The first movement indicates a permanent effort at uniting the forces, economic and political, of the black world to obtain justice while the latter two are endeavors to bring international opinion to bear upon the United States.

The first movement, represented by the Universal Negro Improvement Association, attempts to solidify the Negro races in all parts of the earth by economic cooperation. Its program is announced in the Negro World, whose editor is a West Indian: "We have long realized that in order to command the respect and admiration of the world the Negro must cease being an object of charity and sympathy. . . . For this reason we believed that the starting of a steamship line to carry the produce of Africa, the West Indies and Central America to the United States and the erection of factories to change the raw material into the manufactured products and to make shoes, clothing and other necessities of life would give employment to thousands of Negro men and women . . ." (48).[11]

The movement is being approved by the Negroes, and its leaders can boast that: "Seven months ago today the U.N.I.A. [Universal Negro Improvement Association] and the Black Star Line Steamship Corporation had a very small bank account. Today the U.N.I.A. publishes a newspaper with a circulation of 40,000 and owns Liberty Hall and the adjoining lot and two office buildings. . . . Today the Black Star Line owns the S.S. Yarmouth, soon to be rechristened the S. S. Frederick Douglass . . ." (48).

The business enterprises effecting this economic foundation are the West African Baking Co., Inc., The Black Star Line, Inc., and The Negro Factories Corporation of New York, and the West Indies Trading Association, Ltd. of Canada.

The hope of these leaders is to be able to wring justice from the white race by the threat of the strike of black labor who supply the raw materials and food at the base of man's resources and finally build a new African Empire.

The second attempt to internationalize the Negro question was the secret trip of William Monroe Trotter to the Peace Conference at Paris. The government refused passports to representatives of the National Equal Rights League to attend the Peace Conference. In spite of this refusal Trotter disguised himself as a cook; and after many discouraging attempts for weeks to secure employment on board a ship, he succeeded in arriving in Paris in the greasy garb of a scullion. After accoutring himself according to the manners of a delegate, Trotter presented a memorandum to Sir Eric Drummond, Secretary General of the League of Nations, setting forth the complaints of the American Negro. The petition declared that "It is notoriously indisputable that colored Americans were deprived of or denied, either in law or in fact, full liberty and democracy." Besides this petition a memorandum was presented to every member of the Peace Conference describing the position of the Negro in the United States. Then further publicity was given to American injustices. The French dailies carried on their front page vivid accounts of lynchings in Georgia. While the President of the United States announced to the world that America was the champion of democracy and righteousness, the daily propaganda of Trotter held up to the attention of the world, then fixed upon Paris, the hypocritical position of America. President Wilson had dismissed Trotter from the White House when the latter headed a committee to present the case of the Negro. Again the president had refused to receive him in Paris. This Trotter proclaimed to the world. The French press wondered. French citizens gave a suite of offices to Trotter, from which he sent out daily accounts of America's treatment of the Negro.[12] It is difficult to estimate the effort of this propaganda, but it is certain from the tone of the French press that it helped to free the world from the spell of America, while Trotter whom the president had smothered in America became his nemesis in Paris (49, 28).[13]

Another scheme to unite peoples of African descent is represented by the Pan-African Congress. This is significant of the trend of thought of American Negroes not only because they were represented in the Congress, but because the Congress was called at the instigation of an American Negro, Dr. W. E. B. DuBois. This congress met in Paris during February, 1919. Representatives, fifty-seven in all, came from the United States, French West Indies,

Haiti, France, Liberia, Spanish colonies, Portuguese colonies, Santo Domingo, England, British Africa, French Africa, Algeria, Egypt, Belgian Congo and Abyssinia (50).[14]

After these representatives of black men from all parts of the world gave the status of their people in their respective localities, resolutions were passed providing for another Congress to be held in Paris during the year 1921.

The following resolutions were unanimously adopted and presented to the Peace Conference:

I. The Negroes of the world in Pan-African Congress assembled demand in the interests of justice and humanity, for the purpose of strengthening the forces of civilization, that immediately steps be taken to develop the 200,000,000 of Negroes and Negroids; to this end, they propose:

1. That the Allied and Associated Powers establish a Code of Laws for the international protection of the Natives of Africa similar to the proposed international Code for Labor,

2. That the League of Nations establish a permanent Bureau charged with the special duty of overseeing the application of these laws to the political, social and economic welfare of the Natives.

II. The Negroes of the world demand that hereafter the Natives of Africa and the Peoples of African descent be governed according to the following principles:

1. *The Land*: The land and its natural resources shall be held in trust for the Natives and at all times they shall have effective ownership of as much land as they can profitably develop.

2. *Capital*: The investment of capital and granting of concessions shall be so regulated as to prevent the

exploitation of Natives and the exhaustion of the natural wealth of the country. Concessions shall always be limited in time and subject to State control. The growing social needs of the Natives must be regarded and the profits taxed for the social and material benefit of the Natives.

3. *Labor*: Slavery, forced labor and corporal punishment, except in punishment of crime, shall be abolished; and the general conditions of labor shall be prescribed and regulated by the State.

4. *Education*: It shall be the right of every Native child to learn to read and write his own language and the language of the trustee nation, at public expense, and to be given technical instruction in some branch of industry. The State shall also educate as large a number of Natives as possible in higher technical and cultural training and maintain a corps of Native teachers.

5. *Medicine and Hygiene*: It shall be recognized that human existence in the tropics calls for special safeguards and a scientific system of public hygiene. The State shall be responsible for medical care and sanitary conditions without discouraging collective and individual initiative. A service created by the State shall provide physicians and hospitals, and shall enforce rules. The State shall establish a native medical staff.

6. *The State*: The Natives of Africa must have the right to participate in the government as fast as their development permits in conformity with the principle that the government exists for the Native and not the Natives for the government. The Natives shall have voice in the government to the extent that their development permits, beginning at

once with local and tribal government according to ancient usage, and extending gradually as education and experience proceeds, to the higher offices of State, to the end that, in time, Africa be ruled by consent of the Africans.

7. *Culture and Religion*: No particular religion shall be imposed and no particular form of human culture. There shall be liberty of conscience. The uplift of the Natives shall take into consideration their present condition and shall allow the utmost scope to racial genius, social inheritance and individual bent, so long as these are not contrary to the best established principles of civilization.

8. *Civilized Negroes*: Wherever persons of African descent are civilized and able to meet the tests of surrounding culture, they shall be accorded the same rights as their fellow-citizens; they shall not be denied on account of race or color a voice in their own government, justice before the courts, and economic and social equality according to ability and desert.

9. *The League of Nations*: Greater security of life and property shall be guaranteed the Natives; international labor legislation shall cover Native workers as well as whites; they shall have equitable representation in all the international institutions of the League of Nations, and the participation of the blacks themselves in every domain of endeavor shall be encouraged in accordance with the declared subject of Article 19 of the League of Nations, to wit: "The well being and the development of these people constitute a sacred mission of civilization and it is proper in establishing the League of Nations to incor-

porate therein pledges for the accomplishment of this mission."

Whenever it is proven that African Natives are not receiving just treatment at the hands of any State or that any State deliberately excludes its civilized citizens or subjects of Negro descent from its body politic and cultural, it shall be the duty of the League of Nations to bring the matter to the attention of the civilized world.

Blaise Diagne, *President.*
W. E. B. Du Bois, *Secretary.* (50)

The 8th and 9th articles of these resolutions are clearly an attempt to bring international pressure to bear upon the treatment of American Negroes. They show, in addition, that the Negro is beginning to recognize that his problem is only one of the many problems of subject *races* and that racial solidarity is the only way to escape the fate of disappearing races.

Economic enterprise among Negroes has been confined largely to individual efforts. Many successful enterprises are the results of cooperation. But this has been among the few adventurous individuals. There is a movement on foot at present to organize the Negroes in cooperative guilds so that through the combination of many owners of small amounts of capital the Negro may retain his resources within the race and thereby increase his economic resistance to oppression.

"At meetings of twelve representatives from seven states in the *Crisis* office, August 26 and 27, the Negro Cooperative Guild was established. Its program is threefold: 1. To induce individuals and clubs to study modern consumers cooperation, its extent, methods and objects. 2. To hold an annual meeting for encouraging the establishment of cooperative stores. 3. To form a central committee for the guidance and insurance of such stores" (51).[15] This is offered by the editors of the Messenger as a means to prevent bankers and capitalists from fleecing the Negro farmer (15).[16]

In an article entitled: "Why every Negro should be a Co-operator," the *Messenger* furnishes economic reasons for cooperation and advantages accruing thereto (18).[17] Other issues of this magazine continue the advocacy of this movement. The campaign has been successful for cooperative stores and banks have sprung up throughout the country.

In the religious life of the Negro we see a significant change. Although it is difficult to procure written evidence of this change it is nevertheless reflected in the church attendance and the cry from the Negro pulpit. The religious ardor of the Negro has always been one of his peculiar traits. Christian teachers found in his meek and docile soul fertile soil for implanting doctrines of love and forgiveness. The first forms of religion was [sic] a mixture of Christianity and reminiscent African rites. But a more purified form of worship has succeeded the old. All classes of Negro society have found their way into the church on Sunday. During periods of unusual oppression the altar has been sought where prayers for deliverance were sent up. A new day has come. They no longer see the use of carrying their troubles "to the Lord, in prayer." A recent writer has noticed this change in attitude. "The growing indifference is especially noticeable among the Negroes of the younger generation" (52).[18] Then the causes of this growing indifference on the part of younger Negroes are given: "First, the Negro has reached the conviction that Christianity, as preached and practiced, is not the great moral force or agency for good that they are asked to believe it is. . . . [T]he Christian church has watched with vacant unconcern the burning alive of his people at the stake—men, women and children—and their persecution worse than man of the Middle Ages." The writer believes that this is a favorable sign. "But the growing agnostic tendency of the Negro is emblematic of increasing racial intelligence, for as intelligence spreads, superstition and fear will be dissipated; and in superstition and fear, Christianity is deeply rooted" (52).

There are other factors besides the intellectual awakening that have contributed to the failure of the church to attract young Negroes. These are the same agencies that operate with other races. Once the church was the center of the social life of the Negro. It was here that the social instinct was gratified. But today there are many centers of his social life. While the Negro preacher is complaining that he is unable to have a prayer meeting, the young people are congregating at the Y.M.C.A. or at the moving picture show. Just as the Negro church once afforded more of an outlet for his lively social nature than the home, so today the various social centers are more attractive than the dull church meeting.

This changed attitude on the part of the Negro has attracted the attention of Congress. Congressman Byrnes of South Carolina opened the attack on the New Negro in a speech in which he said: "It is manifest that when sanguinary conflicts take place in cities so widely separated and within so short a time, the cause is general and not local."[19] He speaks truly for the new voice of resistance to oppression is heard in every section of the country. Then representative Byrnes read excerpts from the many radical Negro publications. He sees in all this the inauguration of a new leadership. He said: "It is evident that the leadership of Moton and others, who, following in the footsteps of Booker Washington, preached conservatism to the race, is now being challenged by a crowd of radicals who are appealing to the passions of the Negroes and inciting them to deeds of violence" (53).[20] Byrnes would invoke the espionage law and prosecute these new leaders.

The Messenger editors did not hesitate to make a reply to Congressman Byrnes. They not only accepted his indictment as true but said that the new Negro was resolved to act on the "Lawful principles of self defence" and that they, the editors of the Messenger, believed in meeting violence with violence" (16).[21]

The interest of Congress did not cease here. In the letter from the Attorney General in response to a Senate Resolution of Oct. 17, 1919, for a report on the activities of the Bureau of Investigation of the Department of Justice against persons advising anarchy, sedition, and the

forcible overthrow of the Government, twenty-six pages are devoted to the activities of Negro radicals. It reports the following:

> Among the more salient points to be noted in the present attitude of the Negro leaders are, first, the ill-governed reaction toward race rioting; second, the threat of retaliatory measures in connection with lynching; third, the more openly expressed demand for social equality, in which demand the sex problem is not infrequently included; fourth, the identification of the Negro with such radical organizations as the I.W.W. [Industrial Workers of the World] and an outspoken advocacy of the Bolsheviki or Soviet doctrines; fifth, the political stand assumed toward the present Federal administration, the South in general, and incidentally, toward the peace treaty and the league of nations. Underlying these more salient viewpoints is the increasingly emphasized feeling of a race consciousness, in many of these publications always antagonistic to the white race and openly, defiantly assertive of its own equality and even superiority. When it is borne in mind that this boast finds its most frequent expression in the pages of those journals whose editors are men of education, in at least one instance, men holding degrees conferred by Harvard University, it may be seen that the boast is not to be dismissed lightly as the ignorant vaporing of untrained minds. Neither is the influence of the Negro press in general to be reckoned with lightly. The Negro World for October 18, 1919, states that "there are a dozen Negro papers with a circulation of over 20,000, and scores with a similar circulation, and there are easily over 50 writers wo can write interesting editorials and special articles, written in fine, pure English, with a background of scholarship behind them" (54).[22]

Besides special legislation which was recommended in this letter to curb this propaganda, mailing privileges have been refused the

Crisis and the Messenger at various times. Individual states have concerned themselves with this matter. In Jackson, Mississippi, a Negro, Rev. Franklin was fined $400. and sentenced fifteen months in the chain gang for selling the Crisis. The governor said in reply to a protest that the mildness of this sentence was due to the ignorance of the offender and threatened the editors of the Crisis if they should come to the state of Mississippi (57).[23]

IV.

When we come to estimate the influence of this new philosophy it is necessary to determine to what extent the literature is disseminated among the masses of Negroes and the caliber of its leaders. The total circulation of these radical publications is nearly half a million. While they are published mostly in Chicago and New York, they are to be found in all the cities of the South, dispensed at newsstands and in the churches. Some of these papers are peddled on street corners by the ubiquitous newsboy. The magazines are well put up and printed on dressed paper. The newspapers present an equally orderly and standard arrangement. The editors are mostly young men who are graduates from Harvard, Columbia and other northern colleges having had special training in history, political science, modern sociology and economics. In addition, these publications are constantly filled with articles from equally as well trained supporters. Those who can not write logical and coherent essays express their revolt against the old resignation in poems and songs. Cartoons express the rebel sentiments of the black artist. Thus we see the circulations of these publications is equal to about one twenty-fifth of the Negro population and are edited by men of training, intelligence, and talent.

What does the new philosophy mean? As we follow its leaders upon their iconoclastic career, they destroy the churches, deny the existence of God, repudiate the former leaders, vituperate the white race, scourge the workers for their indifference and ridicule the social surgeon. Convention is hypocrisy and traditions

are lies. But all their revolt is not formless and without a sound basis. They seem to see in the American race problem an inevitable struggle which, as Karl Pearson holds, is a suspended struggle (56, p. 23).[24] When two dissimilar races meet upon the same territory and assimilation does not seem probable, one generally annihilates the other. It becomes more acute as the inferior race rises in the culture to the level of the superior and the inferior race must accept a subordinate position or enter the lists against the dominant race. These new leaders accept the challenge of the race struggle. The race problem has reached this crisis in America. While these leaders unhesitatingly advocate the use of force in self defense, they must realize that in any general uprising victory lies on the side of the heaviest artillery—and the white man possesses all the artillery. One wing of this party is revolutionary. It holds the interests of the race above that of the nation. It advocates a new social order and a change in the form of government. It bids the masses of workers to rise and capture the means of production. Its leaders pledge themselves to support the Socialist Party in politics and the I.W.W.'s in labor organization. There is some ground for the new political alignment, for the traditional, blind and emotional adhesion to the Republican Party has not brought any substantial good to the Negroes in spite of the plums that have fallen to some fortunate politicians. But these leaders overlook the local advantages that have come in the form of better schools and representation, through the support of the Republican Party that has not been generally inimical, although indifferent at times. Moreover, the present impotence of the Socialist Party in national affairs should be considered. The Negro cannot afford to be martyred to future possibilities.

The strongest point of this new philosophy lies in its advice to the Negro to achieve economic independence. This was not originated by the new school. The same was advocated by Booker Washington. Self-respect is an attribute of possession. The large number of Negroes in personal service has been the basis of his servility and dependence. It has given him a superficial culture. A substantial industrial class supporting a prosperous enterprising class will give the only sure foundation to culture and independence. Therein rests the strength of the new movement.

But the method of attaining economic independence as advocated by these new leaders differs from that advocated by Washington. The latter emphasized individual enterprise and initiative while the former, recognizing the growing tendency towards cooperative enterprise, urges the establishment of collective undertaking. This advice is sound for few Negroes possess sufficient capital to undertake business careers. This is only possible by uniting small quantities of capital. Many enterprises have been the fruits of this advice. Besides the cases cited there are found in the South banks and stores run on this basis. The periodicals themselves which voice the new sentiment are supported by the cooperation of large number of Negroes who have bought the stock.

These successful efforts at cooperation and the universality of the new philosophy brings us to a new phase of the race problem. While the Negro has always been conscious of his race in America, he has not always had race consciousness. The northern Negro has heretofore felt little interest in the difficulties of his southern brother. The prosperous man of color has been inclined to be unsympathetic towards his less fortunate kinsman. But in this new philosophy the North has become one with the South and the well-to-do resents the ills done the low. This race consciousness extends beyond America. Negro leaders have heretofore concerned themselves only with the American problem and have shown indifference to Africa and the West Indies. But now this awakened race consciousness is expanding through the race wherever it is found. The West Indian Negro is conspicuous

in the radical movement in America while the Universal Negro Improvement Association is planting branches in Africa. The Pan-African Congress initiated by Du Bois illustrates the same tendency. Once the American Negro centered his attention upon his meagre achievements in America, but now he is digging up the former glories of African culture. He has become conscious of everything that affects men of color in any part of the world. The Negro has thus achieved race consciousness which now must be reckoned with.

Thus far we have considered the effect of the new philosophy upon the Negro. Now it remains to indicate the effect of the new thought upon the white man. From the north we have those who represent the abolitionist type warning the Negro that they remain loyal to him in his strivings for justice—abstract—but they can not follow him in his alliance with the radical elements that make the prosperous tremble. From the South we hear defiance. They would make no truce with these leaders who advocate Socialism. These are the reactions of the ruling classes in the two sections. But the laboring white man who has cast aside the delusion of his superiority extends his hand in sympathy. This is apparent both in the North and in the South. The reaction to the stand taken by the Negro in the riots has elicited respect from all classes. The press has sounded warning that Negroes will not be shot down as formerly and that those who incite such conflicts must pay the price. No doubt, the psychological effect produced in the white man will make him hesitate before using violence against men of color.

The new spirit which has produced the New Negro bids fair to transform the whole race. America faces a new race that has awakened, and in the realization of its strength has girt its loins to run the race with other men.

Joseph Bibb
"Radicals and Raids"

Chicago Whip, January 10, 1920

The raids upon the so-called Reds last week did not meet with the approbation of the general public. It is not so clear to many how every economic organization that is evolving along new sciences can be accused of plotting to overthrow the government by violence. There are some anarchists and loyal citizens here. Many loyal citizens are radicals, many radicals are reds, all reds are radicals but all radicals are not reds.

The New Negro does not wish to overthrow the government by violence or force[;] neither does he belong to any anarchistic order. The New Negro does wish the government to overthrow all agencies and forces that are depriving him of full American citizenship. We are dissatisfied with the treatment we are receiving. We want the existing order of social economic and political affairs changed. The Negro wants to be treated as a man and consideration on the basis of merit and citizenship. The New Negro is disgusted with lynching and mob violence. He believes in defending his life and his home and all other sacred institutions. For this reason he is radical because the old regime is satisfied with [an] "Uncle Tom" and "Aunt Liza" position. We do not approve of direct action and sabotage. We do advocate intelligent collective bargaining and race solidarity.

Let the anarchists be raided. Let public opinion be changed by constructive methods. Let not the institution of free speech and press be abrogated as long as this country aspires toward a true democracy. Let the Negro have a man's chance. Let radicalism arouse his slumbering soul. Let ignorance and political crookedness be raided. Let intelligence and hope maintain.

Herbert J. Seligmann
"The New Negro"

In *The Negro Faces America*, 1920

The American Negro, before the World War, was the despair of radicals, even of liberals. In education the mass of colored people had been living on the discarded remnants, both textbooks and methods, of white schools. Politically they had all but accepted the belief current in the Southern states that their government was not and would not be a democracy. As individuals, fiercely though their resentment might blaze at brutalities and indignities visited upon men and women of color and at the universal discrimination in industry, they had to acquiesce in the treatment meted out to them.

The avenue to power for the colored citizen apparently lay outside politics, in acquiring technical skill, possessions and the influence accompanying them. Negro leadership, especially as it was represented by Booker T. Washington, looked to their becoming indispensable to the nation as toilers—artisan or farmers. The problem of adjusting the race to the American scene was envisaged mainly as one of putting it upon its feet financially. With all except a militant, though growing, minority, emphasis was upon qualifying for the white man's civilization by meeting his economic requirements. Of this adjustment the social implication was a Negro as nearly as possible like the white man, at the expense even of trying to be like the white man. Many a Negro hoped to achieve peace by conformity; therefore conservatism became a sort of norm for colored people in the United States. Social standards are rarely flexible, and the tendency of colored people to adopt those of white persons made for a certain intellectual inflexibility in people otherwise sensitive to suggestion and to the vivid and the new. This and a lasting gratitude toward the Republican party, as representing federal protection for colored people, made what seemed to be a solid block of conservatives of colored people in the United States. Economically, the attitude had value and bore fruit. Even its bitterest critics admit the accomplishments of trade and agricultural schools. Many colored people were enabled to leave behind them the wasting hazards of casual and exploited labor. Many, having obtained business training, taught their fellows or advanced their own fortunes. The story of Tuskegee, as Booker Washington has told it, has much that should give to every generous American pride and inspiration.

But Negroes in the United States found the attempt at economic progress alone insufficient. That progress was checked by the barriers of the white man's civilization. As early as 1910 and before then, groups of colored people and their white friends realized that the white man's political power could be used to nullify the Negro's economic progress. With a dominant and aggressive white minority in control, after 1876, not only of the ballot and political machinery, but of courts, no colored man's progress became secure. Given agrarian conditions such as are illumined by the Arkansas disorders, with the impossibility of obtaining redress and the absence of adequate education, and it was obvious numbers of colored people had little or no opportunity for advancement. Add to political and civil disabilities social discrimination directed especially against the successful individual of color, and Booker Washington's avenue to freedom became perilously insecure. One of the most forceful of Washington's critics,

Dr. W. E. B. DuBois, soon came to the conclusion that if the Negro was to find existence in the United States tolerable he must boldly demand and conquer for himself full civil rights and the ballot. In the development of political consciousness of the Negro in the United States Doctor DuBois and his periodical, *The Crisis*, played an important part. Pride and assertion of the dignity of manhood and womanhood for individuals of the race came from him and found increasing response among colored people throughout the nation. Doctor DuBois took American professions at their face value, and inquired pointedly and bitterly into mob violence and lynching, into segregation, disfranchisement, and discrimination. Accompanying the spiritual revolt from what many colored people regarded as the submissiveness of Booker Washington and his followers—a willingness to acknowledge the superiority of the white man—came the rapid growth of a Negro middle class, with its professional men, its industrial leaders, and its urban standards of life and social intercourse. A Negro press grew until there were few communities so small as to be untouched by some publication edited by and for colored people. It is invidious to measure the progress of any group of people by its economic standing: philosophy, fable, and the most moving of the world's poetry and songs have come from slaves. But the Negro's economic status conditioned his political consciousness in the United States. Thus, it is significant that in the decade 1900 to 1910, whereas the number of Negroes in agricultural pursuits increased 35 per cent., the increase in trade and transportation amounted to 103 per cent, and in manufacturing and mechanical pursuits to 156 per cent. The increase of 186 per cent., represented a rise in the number of Negroes engaged in industry from 275,149 to 704,174. Mr. Monroe Work has published a statistical abstract of fifty-three years of progress of the Negro in the United States. His figures show an increase in the number of homes owned from 12,000 in 1866 to 600,000 in 1919. In the same period colored people increased the number of farms they operate by 980,000. In *The Negro Year-Book for*

1918–19 Mr. Work estimated the number of Negroes engaged in business enterprises as not less than 50,000, exclusive of more than 10,000 boarding- and lodging-house keepers. An illuminating parallel of the industrial advance of the Negro in fifty years shows him engaged in 37 sorts of business in 1867 and in 187 kinds of business in 1917. In the latter year his enterprises included automobile service and garage, contracting and building, hotelkeeping, lumber business, real estate, and banking, tailoring, stock-raising, and theaters. Insurance, according to Mr. Work, one of the most important forms of business activity of American Negroes, is conducted by their own companies, of which one had $1,944,910 insurance in force in 1915. For the bourgeoisie thus developing, a press was essential. Mr. Work listed some 450 periodicals published by or for Negroes in the United States, of which 220 were newspapers and 7 were magazines of general literature. Among the foremost of the Negro newspapers in the United States are *The Chicago Defender* with a nationwide circulation of more than 150,000, *The New York Age* and *The News*, *The Colorado Statesman*, the Atlanta (Georgia) *Independent*, *The St. Louis Argus*, *The Pittsburgh Courier*, and *The Richmond Planet*. The development of the Negro press in the United States represents in part business enterprise. But its astonishing success, the multiplicity of tiny and obscure sheets in small communities, as well as the avid reception of powerful organs like *The Chicago Defender* in the South, represent a well-founded distrust of the accounts of Negro doings in the white press. As late as December, 1919, the Associated Negro Press sent a news story to its subscribers, pointing out that in an Associated Press (white) report of a new diving apparatus which would enable salvage operations at hitherto unattempted depths, the fact had been omitted that the inventor was a Negro. Frequently accounts of racial troubles which appear in the Negro press contradict the assertions or the implications to be drawn from statements in the white press. Where a propaganda occurs in the white press such as helped bring about the disorders in Omaha, Washington, and Chi-

cago, the Negro press vigilantly runs down exaggerations and misstatements. Frequently, as has been said, the Negro is better informed of the cause and the nature of race conflict than is the white man. Exaggerations occur on both sides. The Negro press, with a few exceptions, has not the machinery or the means which make possible the largest white news services, and bitterness more often shows itself obviously in the presentation of news in the Negro press than in the white. The distinction, however, is one of subtlety rather than of standards. White newspapers have nothing to teach the Negro press of fairness in the treatment of news of race relations.

How important the Negro press has been in the process of the Negro's becoming politically articulate can be measured by the statements of white men. Magazines like *The Crisis* and *Challenge*, newspapers like *The Defender*, are cordially execrated among white men in the South. An article in *The Defender* was held responsible for the riot in Longview, Texas. Gov. Charles Brough of Arkansas said he believed *The Crisis* and *Defender* were responsible for Arkansas riots and announced his intention of asking the Postmaster-General to exclude them from the mails. Measured by the editorial utterances of their haters and detractors, Negro editors have been potent indeed, for they are credited with the power of creating the most violent conflicts that American communities have known, short of war. It will be seen that before the war the American Negro had the nucleus at least of a fully evolved bourgeois society. Representatives of his race served the government as legal officers, as consular agents with diplomatic responsibilities. Poets of the race, Paul Laurence Dunbar, James Weldon Johnson; entertainers and actors among whom Bert Williams stands out; essayists and critics of the caliber of William Stanley Braithwaite and Doctor DuBois; musicians of the rank of R. Nathaniel Dett, J. Rosamond Johnson, Harry Burleigh—have a place in American civilization independent of any condescension to their Negro blood. Whether or not the American musical comedy is an art form or merely a form of dissipation is a question subject to the vagary of individual taste. That it has been the medium through which countless Americans have experienced what passes for instrumental music, the dance, song, gaiety is indubitable. To no small degree is the development of American musical comedy, its intriguing rhythms and its popular songs, due to colored composers and librettists. In the gap between American idealism and the hard-boned soul of American practicality the American Negro has interposed his warmth and vivacity. More and more the Negro spirituals and plantation melodies, debased and all but obscured by jazz, are coming seriously into their own on the concert stage and in the works of serious composers. It is not here a question of comparative merit. The Negro has introduced human values into American civilization of a sort in which it has been found peculiarly lacking. The Negro plays, sings, dances for the love of what he is doing and experiencing. In this he is fitted to become the teacher and a vivifying force in a civilization preoccupied by ulterior motives.

It will be seen that in all but name the "new Negro" was already in existence, a far cry from the humble servitor, the "good old darky," the mythical personality compounded of servility, vice, and gratitude. If between the evolved and educated Negro citizen and the drifting roustabout of the far South yawns the interval between the primitive and the civilized, the same gap is observable among white men in New York City. It is almost needless to remind that the manner of the Aurignacian age sometimes disguises itself in the language of United States Senators. The "new Negro," then, is a name not so much for a being brought into existence during the World War as for that being's awareness of himself and his immediate problems. . . .

It will be noted that the growth of radical sentiment, the determination that race relations must be fundamentally altered in United States, was not sudden. Every Negro leader of any vitality was forced to be a radical from the point of view of the reactionary groups of white people prepared to concede nothing. But the most potent force in precipitating radicalism was the entrance of the United States into the World War. The treatment of the colored soldier by Americans in France and in their own country has been referred to, as has been the exploitation of colored people under the powers conferred by "work or fight" laws. Not many Negroes became as articulate in their disillusion as the editors of *The Messenger*. But disillusion set in that was nation-wide. The firm hold which the Republican party had held on the gratitude of the mass of colored people began to be loosened. The consequence was not the creation of any definite new political alignments, but rather of an unstable equilibrium in which colored people took stock of their resources and powers and became increasingly aware of themselves as a potential voting block. In all the disorders that took place in 1919 the Negro fought in self-protection. He no longer relied on promises or on protection even of the federal government. With a Democratic administration in power, the Negro had little to hope from federal protection during and immediately after the World War. In the National Capital Jim-Crowism had crept in. Negroes were not served in the restaurants of the capital, and they found the attitude of the South reflected everywhere in Washington. They found the Department of Justice being used, not to examine into deplorable conditions which had brought about race riots, but to trace the tenuous connections between "Reds," I. W. W. [Industrial Workers of the World], and the Negro, and to proclaim Negro insurrection and radicalism to a willing press and a credulous public. It is emancipation to distrust others and to rely upon oneself. Never, perhaps, in the history of the country was there more distrust of American white men by Negroes than after the World War. They had taken the measure of the white press and its news-distributing organizations. They had seen local government crumble and brutality rein almost unchecked except by their own bullets. They had seen the federal government, through its one department articulate on their affairs, pursue not their oppressors, but those who were voicing their heartfelt, burning sense of injustice. Something of the ethics of real politics was borne in upon the American Negro by the treatment accorded him. Nowhere, perhaps, was the American Negro's position brought to more dramatic focus than before two United States Senators in Washington in January, 1920. The Senators were conducting a hearing on a resolution introduced by one of them, providing for a Congressional investigation into mob violence and lynching in the United States. The evidence had been given. Statistics and stories of horror lay in the typewritten sheets on the table. And the question raised was one of jurisdiction. A Senator pointed out that the interpretation placed by the courts upon the Constitution and constitutional amendments prevented legislation by states infringing personal liberty, but gave the federal government no power to act in protection of that liberty. The Senators paused. A white-haired gentleman rose. His face was dark in color as if he had been deeply sunburnt. "Gentlemen," he said, in effect, "we come to you deeply aggrieved by injustice. The states have failed to protect us. The federal government professes itself powerless. I am an old man of seventy years. I have served my country abroad. I have passed through almost every phase of government service, and, like many another of my race, have given freely of myself. Yet when we come to you, in behalf of twelve million American Negroes, you tell us there is no redress for our wrongs. What are we to expect? What are we to hope for?" A Senator hastened to express interest, sympathy, his desire to remedy the conditions set down in the documents before him. But the questions: "What are we to expect? What are we to hope for?" remained unanswered.

No intelligent answer to the question put by that colored leader has yet been attempted. In a sense there is no solution of the problems of race relations, even on paper and by Northern dilettanti. It is idle to say, give the Negro his full rights, when the granting of those rights lies with an illiterate white electorate at the mercy of brutal and vituperative editors. Yet approaches to the problems have been made. It is coming to be realized that the problems of race

relations can be and must be cleft vertically into the constituent problem of democracy: a free press serving the people with news, not rumor and innuendo; real representation and control by the electorate over their elected representatives; proprietorship by the producer not only in political fictions, but in the industrial processes which depend upon him and by which he lives. To this extent the "new Negro," as he is represented in *The Messenger*, has affirmed a significant and vital fact: there is no race question independent of other problems of democracy; race relations constitute democracy's most essential problem, a problem compounded of all the other adjustments which free men are called upon to make in forming and maintaining social relations. Shameful as was the year 1919, with bloodshed, lynching, and race riot in the United States, its function was still to bring before the attention of the nation that a national problem, long unsolved, demanded serious attention. A condition which had been glossed over, the illegal disfranchisement by methods of terrorism of millions of colored Americans, was brought boldly to light. The Negro became aware of his economic power. The white South came to know that in losing Negro labor it was allowing to slip away the very foundation of its productivity and prosperity. And in a few communities the lesson had already been learned by white Americans that their colored neighbors were able and were eager to co-operate in establishing decent conditions under which white men and men of color could live in peace and security.

Halting steps were taken in 1919 and early in 1920 to attack the most obvious of race maladjustments. Two resolutions, one in the Senate and one in the House of Representatives, providing for Congressional investigation of lynching and race riots, and a number of bills which would make lynching a crime under federal jurisdiction, showed the increasing attention directed toward race relations. The steps proposed were laudable, but would leave the mainsprings of racial maladjustment untouched. The experience of Atlanta and of Chicago after their race riots might well be drawn upon by the nation. Here, joint bodies of colored and white men met to devise means for making mob violence in the streets of their city impossible. In Illinois, after the Chicago riots, and in Arkansas the governors of the states appointed commissions to investigate into the causes of the disturbances. Communities in the South have discovered the advantage in forming joint bodies of white and colored citizens to deal with matters of local concern. In the course of such conferences as have been held, both white and colored men have made interesting discoveries about one another. White men have been impressed with the administrative ability of their colored neighbors. Colored men have found, often to their astonishment, a body of white men eager to give them fair treatment and equal opportunity.

Unfortunately, the growth of local cooperation must remain slow. It depends largely upon the emancipation of the American people from their newspapers. Little is to be expected from the federal government. At the hearing in Washington called to inquire into the need for investigating lynching and race riots, one Senator took occasion to read into the record an effusion from the Department of Justice ascribing race riots to the activities of "Reds." Not even the Department of Justice, however, had the temerity to connect "Reds" with lynching. So long as the complexion of the national legislature is determined on the basis of open and flagrant disregard of amendments to the federal Constitution and violation of their provisions, little is to be hoped or expected from that source. The Republican party in its endeavor to invade the solid Democratic South finds it necessary to pander to the South's color psychosis through its "lily-white" state organizations. In the old political parties there is hope neither for the Negro nor for the man who desires a decent approach to the problems of race relations.

The future of race relations, in so far as they are not allowed to degenerate into violence and irremediable bitterness, would seem to lie with labor and with liberal political forces that represent working-class sentiment as the old parties do not and cannot. It will be largely on the

job and in the labor union that the identity of interest of the colored worker and the white will be demonstrated, probably despite all efforts to maintain the color line in industry by using unorganized colored men to break white strikes. A tolerable future for the relations between white and colored people in the United States depends for the most part upon white labor. The Negro has found a place in industry. He has discovered his strategic importance in the contest of capital and labor. He has armed himself for self-defense and is prepared to fight. Pushing the issue to sporadic and embittered clashes between white and colored people in the United States involves a sort of smoldering civil war that no American can contemplate with anything but deep concern and anxiety. If white unions have learned from the northward migration of Negroes, they will ignore the propaganda in the white press; they will attempt to break down the Negro's distrust of the American labor union by giving him the square deal.

In so far as the South is concerned, conditions improve as the Negro moves out. The migration northward continued after the war and was still in full progress early in 1920. Yet such testimony as that published by Mr. T. Arnold Hill, referred to in an earlier chapter, indicates little, if any, improvement in the treatment of colored people as a direct consequence of their services in the war. The statement of the Governor of Mississippi that "niggers," not colored men and women, were wanted in his state indicates little perception of the change of mind and attitude that is imperative. One is forced to the conclusion that in many parts of the South the Negro can expect decency only when his absence has hurt the prosperity of his white neighbors. When white planters offer to build schools as an inducement to Negroes to stay on the farms and to return from cities of the North, as they announced late in 1919, it is a sign that the beginning of a lesson has been learned. The sort of minority opinion from which much that is hopeful of better race relations emanates is represented by a group of professors in Southern universities, known as the University Commission on Race Questions. Among the institutions represented on the commission were the Universities of Alabama, Arkansas, Florida, Georgia, Louisiana, Mississippi, South Carolina, and Texas. The commission published four open letters to college men of the South in which lynching, education, the migration, and reconstruction were treated forcibly and with courage. These Southern professors pointed out that of fifty-two persons lynched in 1914, "only seven—two white and five Colored—or 13 per cent., were charged with the crime against womanhood." Lynching they termed a "contagious social disease, and as such is of deep concern to every American citizen and to every lover of civilization." They pointed out ruthlessly that "in at least four cases" of lynching in 1915, "it later was discovered that the victims of the mob were innocent of the crime of which they were accused." In the letter on education, dated September 1, 1916, the commission pointed out that "inadequate provision for the education of the Negro is more than an injustice to him; it is an injury to the white man" in that it made for inefficiency. The letter on the migration, written in 1917, made clear that humane treatment would be effective in stopping the exodus. In the final communication, entitled "A New Reconstruction," dated April 26, 1919, the commission urged "a more general appreciation of the Negro's value as a member of the community," alluded to his services in the World War, and spoke of "a splendid record of which the Negroes and their white friends may be justly proud." Despite a faint suggestion of patronizing tone, the communications of these professors represent a spirit that, if it is given expression, will make it possible for white and black to live amicably side by side. But such a point of view is too often submerged in the clamor of the press.

Little has been said thus far of the need in the United States of systematic information on matters concerning colored people and their relation to white people. Investigations conducted by men of science have been few. The political obstacle to the truth about race and race relations weighs upon the universities of the North, even. An anthropologist of international repute told me late in 1919 that he had for years been endeavoring to stimulate interest in university studies to be undertaken among American Negroes, with a view to making important racial determinations of various sorts. He had about given over his efforts because the universities feared to antagonize those of their benefactors who had preconceived notions on the subject of race and race relations. Yet the crying need for even elementary facts is evident. White people who call themselves educated are subject to the most amazing delusions and prejudices with regard to race, and especially, with regard to their own colored neighbors. If there were not this almost universal ignorance, colored by the back-stairs gossip of newspapers, there would hardly be occasion for such a volume as this. The misconceptions which are at the root of race prejudice and violence would long since have evaporated. But violence and prejudice perpetuate themselves by preventing the acquisition of any reliable body of fact. It is only from a realization on the part of Americans white and colored that the poison of color hatred affects every phase of American life, vitiates politics, is used to intrench exploiting classes, to further the plans of self-seeking politicians and editors, to foster the intolerance and parochialism which make for imperialism and wars of aggression, that any demand for right can spring. On the face of race relations now is written the word "menace." With any but the sort of appointees that are to be expected from the Republican or Democratic parties, one would be tempted to urge as an immediate step the creation of a federal department of race relations, with a Cabinet officer responsible not only for investigating maladjustments where they show themselves, but for initiating campaigns of the information and education of which the body of United States citizens are sorely in need. The one experiment in that direction undertaken by the federal government, the Bureau of Negro Economics of the Department of Labor, was permitted virtually to go out of existence for lack of appropriations of funds to carry on its valuable and useful work.

The chief problem of race relations in the United States is the education of white people to decency in their attitude toward colored citizens. The nation will never be made whole in its own conscience while overt lawlessness stalks in the United States Senate and the House of Representatives. Hypocrisy must be of the very essence of American public life while the word democracy and disfranchisement of Negroes, ideals of liberty and oppression of colored people under the guise of denying them "social equality," are juxtaposed; while white men take their freedom with colored women and torture with bestial cruelty any colored man who has committed the crime of attracting a white woman's regard. The first step in an approach to the problems of race relations will be a demand upon the part of United States citizens for information, exact information not only of the anthropologist, but with regard to the treatment of colored men and women by white men and women in the United States. When those facts are made known, as some effort has been made to suggest them in this survey, American public opinion will demand a change amounting to revolution. If such a demand is not made, antagonism between white and colored people, played upon for political and chiefly for economic and industrial purposes, bolstering inefficiency, ignorance, and Prussianism in the South, infecting the entire people with intolerance, will become one of many forces disintegrating any orderly progress of civilization. Truly the United States stands with problems of race before its people which, as Mr. Harold Stearns has observed, the Civil War did not solve, but created. It rests with informed and intelligent minorities, with class-conscious laborites, colored and white, to rescue the relations between white and colored Americans from the embitterment into which they threaten to gravitate. Meanwhile the American Negro, disillusioned, newly emancipated from reliance upon any white savior, stands ready to make his unique contribution to what may some time become American civilization.

Hubert Harrison

"The New Politics: The New Politics for the New Negro" and "Education and the Race"

In *When Africa Awakes*, 1920

Chapter IV.

The New Politics: The New Politics for the New Negro

The world of the future will look upon the world of today as an essentially new turning point in the path of human progress. All over the world the spirit of democratic striving is making itself felt. The new issues have brought forth new ideas of freedom, politics, industry and society at large. The new Negro living in this new World is just as responsive to these new impulses as other people are.

In the "good old days" it was quite easy to tell the Negro to follow the footsteps of those who had gone before. The mere mention of the name Lincoln or the Republican party was sufficient to secure his allegiance to that party which had seen him stripped of all political power and of civil rights without protest—effective or otherwise.

Things are different now. The new Negro is demanding elective representation in Baltimore, Chicago and other places. He is demanding it in New York. The pith of the present occasion is, that he is no longer begging or asking. He is demanding as a right that which he is in position to enforce.

In the presence of this new demand the old political leaders are bewildered, and afraid; for the old idea of Negro leadership by virtue of the white man's selection has collapsed. The new Negro leader must be chosen by his fellows— by those whose strivings he is supposed to represent.

Any man today who aspires to lead the Negro race must set squarely before his face the idea of "Race First." Just as the white men of these and other lands are white men before they are Christians, Anglo-Saxons or Republicans; so the Negroes of this and other lands are intent upon being Negroes before they are Christians, Englishmen, or Republicans.

Sauce for the goose is sauce for the gander. Charity begins at home, and our first duty is to ourselves. It is not what we wish but what we must, that we are concerned with. The world, as it ought to be, is still for us, as for others, the world that does not exist. The world as it is, is the real world, and it is to that real world that we address ourselves. Striving to be men, and finding no effective aid in government or in politics, the Negro of the Western world must follow the path of the Swadesha movement of India and the Sinn Fein movement of Ireland. The meaning of both these terms is "ourselves first." This is the mental background of the new politics of the New Negro, and we commend it to the consideration of all the political parties. For it is upon this background that we will predicate such policies as shall seem to us necessary and desirable.

Hubert H. Harrison teaching a class, "World Problems of Race," with Richard B. Moore and W. A. Domingo in attendance, September 9, 1926, New York City. Courtesy of the Hubert Harrison Papers, Rare Book & Manuscript Library, Butler Library, Columbia University.

In the British Parliament the Irish Home Rule party clubbed its full strength and devoted itself so exclusively to the cause of Free Ireland that it virtually dictated for a time the policies of Liberals and Conservatives alike.

> *The new Negro race in America will not achieve political self-respect until it is in a position to organize itself as a politically independent party and follow the example of the Irish Home Rulers. This is what will happen in American politics.*—September, 1917.

The Drift in Politics

The Negroes of America—those of them who think—are suspicious of everything that comes from the white people of America. They have seen that every movement for the extension of democracy here has broken down as soon as it reached the color line. Political democracy declared that "all men are created equal," meant only all white men; the Christian church found that the brotherhood of man did not include God's bastard children; the public school system proclaimed that the school house was the backbone of democracy—"for white people only," and the civil service says that Negroes must keep their place—at the bottom. So that they can hardly be blamed for looking askance at any new gospel of freedom. Freedom to them has been like one of

> those juggling fiends
>
> That palter with us in a double sense;
> That keep the word of promise to our ear,
>
> And break it to our hope.

In this connection, some explanation of the former political solidarity of those Negroes who were voters may be of service. Up to six years ago the one great obstacle to the political progress of the colored people was their sheep-like allegiance to the Republican party. They were taught to believe that God had raised up a peculiar race of men called Republicans who had loved the slaves so tenderly that they had taken guns in their hands and rushed on the ranks of the southern slaveholders to free the slaves; that

this race of men was still in existence, marching under the banner of the Republican party and showing their great love for Negroes by appointing from six to sixteen near-Negroes to soft political snaps. Today that great political superstition is falling to pieces before the advance of intelligence among Negroes. They begin to realize that they were sold out by the Republican party in 1876; that the last twenty-five years lynchings have increased, disfranchisement has spread all over the South and "Jim-crow" cars run even into the national capitol—with the continuing consent of a Republican Congress, a Republican Supreme Court and Republican President.

Ever since the Brownsville affair, but more clearly since Taft declared and put in force the policy of pushing out the few near-Negro officeholders, the rank and file have come to see that the Republican party is a great big sham. Many went over to the Democratic party because, as the *Amsterdam News* puts it, "They had nowhere else to go."[25] Twenty years ago the colored men who joined that party were ostracized as scalawags and crooks. But today, the defection to the Democrats of such men as Bishop Walters, Wood, Morton, Carr and Langston—whose uncle was a colored Republican Congressman from Virginia—has made the colored democracy respectable and given quite tone to political heterodoxy.

All this loosens the bonds of their allegiance and breaks the bigotry of the last forty years. But of this change their political viewpoint the white world knows nothing. The two leading Negro newspapers are subsidized by the same political pirates who own the title-deeds to the handful of hirelings holding office the name of the Negro race. One of these papers is an organ of Mr. Washington, the other pretends to be independent—that is, must be bought on the installment plan, and both of them are in New York. Despite this "conspiracy of silence" the Negroes are waking up, are beginning to think for themselves, to look with more favor on "new doctrines."[26]

Today the politician who wants the support of the Negro voter will have to give something more than piecrust promises. The old professional "friend to the colored people" must have something more solid than the name of Lincoln and party appointments.

We demand what the Irish and the Jewish voter get: nominations on the party's ticket in our own districts. And if we don't get this we will smash the party that refuses to give it.

For we are not Republicans, Democrats or Socialists any longer. We are Negroes first. And we are no longer begging for sops. We demand, not "recognition," but representation, and we are out to throw our votes to any party which gives us this, and withhold them from any party which refuses to give it. No longer will we follow any leader whose job the party controls. For we know that no leader so controlled can oppose such party in our interests beyond a given point.

That is why so much interest attaches to the mass-meeting to be held at Palace Casino on the 29th where the Citizens' Committee will make its report to the Negro voters of Harlem and tell them how it was "turned down" by the local representatives of the Republican party when it begged the boon of elective representation. All such rebuffs will make for manhood—if we are men—and will drive us to play in American politics the same role which the Irish party played in British politics. That is the new trend in Negro politics, and we must not let any party forget it.—1917.

A Negro for President

For many tears the Negro has been the football of American politics. Kicked from pillar to post, he goes begging, hat in hand, from a Republican convention to a Democratic one. Always is he asking some one else to do something for him. Always is he begging, pleading, demanding or threatening. In all these cases his dependence is on the good will, sense of justice or gratitude of the other fellow. And in none of these cases is the political reaction of the other fellow within the control of the Negro.

But change for the better is approaching. Four years ago, the present writer was propounding in lectures, indoors and outdoors, the thesis that the Negro people of America would never amount to anything much politically until they should see fit to imitate the Irish of Britain and to organize themselves into a political party of their own whose leaders, on the basis of this large collective vote, could "hold up" Republicans, Democrats, Socialists or any other political group of American whites. As in many other cases, we have lived to see time ripen the fruits of our own thought for some one else to pluck. Here is the editor of the *Challenge* making a campaign along these very lines. His version of the idea takes the form of advocating the nomination of a Negro for the Presidency of the United States. In this form we haven't the slightest doubt that this idea will meet with a great deal of ridicule and contempt. Nevertheless, we venture to prophesy that, whether the hands of Mr. Bridges or another, it will come to be ultimately accepted as one of the finest contributions to Negro statesmanship.

No one pretends, of course, that the votes of Negroes can elect a Negro to the high office of President of the United States. Nor would any one expect that the votes of white people will be forthcoming to assist them in such a project. The only way in which a Negro could he elected President of the United States would he by virtue of the voters not knowing that the particular candidate was of Negro ancestry. This, we believe, has already happened within the memory of living men. But, the essential intent of this new plan is to furnish a focusing-point around which the ballots of the Negro voters may be concentrated for the realization of racial demands for justice and equality of opportunity and treatment. It would be carrying "Race First" with a vengeance into the arena of domestic politics. It would take the Negro voter out of the ranks of the Republican, Democratic and Socialist parties and would enable their leaders to trade the votes of their followers, openly and above-board, for those things for which masses of men largely exchange their votes.

Mr. Bridges will find that the idea of a Negro candidate for President presupposes the creation of a purely Negro party and upon that prerequisite he will find himself compelled to concentrate. Doubtless, most of the political wise-acres of the Negro race will argue that the idea is impossible because it antagonizes the white politicians of the various parties. They will close their eyes to the fact that politics implies antagonism and a conflict of interest. They will fail to see that the only things which count with politicians are votes, and that, just as one white man will cheerfully cut another white man's throat to get the dollars which a black man has, so will one white politician or party cut another one's throat politically to get the votes which black men may cast at the polls. But these considerations will finally carry the day. Let there be no mistake. The Negro will never be accepted by the white American democracy except in so far as he can by the use of force, financial, political or other, win, seize or maintain in the teeth of opposition that position which he finds necessary to his own security and salvation. And we Negroes may as well make up our minds now that we can't depend upon the good-will of white men in anything or at any point where our interests and theirs conflict. Disguise it as we may, in business, politics, education or other departments of life, we as Negroes are compelled to fight for what we want to win from the white world.

It is easy enough for those colored men whose psychology is shaped by their white inheritance to argue the ethics of compromise and inter-racial co-operation. But we whose brains are still unbastardized must face the frank realities of this situation of racial conflict and competition. Wherefore, it is well that we marshal our forces to withstand and make head against the constant racial pressure. Action and reaction are equal and opposite. Where there is but slight pressure a slight resistance will suffice. But where, as in our case, that pressure is grinding and pitiless, the resistance that would re-establish equal conditions of freedom must of necessity be intense and radical. And it is this philosophy which must furnish the motive for such a new and radical departure as is implied in the joint idea of a Negro party in American politics and a Negro candidate for the Presidency of these United States.—June, 1920.

When the Tail Wags the Dog

Politically, these United States may be roughly divided into two sections, so far as the Negroes are concerned. In the North the Negro population has the vote. In the South it hasn't. This was not always so. There was a time when the Negro voters of the South sent in to Congress a thin but steady stream of black men who represented their political interests directly. Due to the misadventures of the reconstruction period, this stream was shut off until at the beginning of this century George White, of North Carolina, was the sole and last representative of the black man with a ballot in the South.

This result was due largely to the characteristic stupidity of the Negro voter. He was a Republican, he was. He would do anything with his ballot for Abraham Lincoln—who was dead— but not a thing for himself and his family, who were all alive and kicking. For this the Republican party loved him so much that it permitted the Democrats to disfranchise him while it controlled Congress and the courts, the army and navy, and all the machinery of law-enforcement in the United States. With its continuing consent, Jim-crowism, disfranchisement, segregation and lynching spread abroad over the land. The end of it all was the reduction of the Negro in the South to the position of a political serf, an industrial peon and a social outcast.

Recently there has been developed in the souls of black folk a new manhood dedicated to the proposition that, if all Americans are equal in the matter of baring their breasts to foreign bayonets, then all Americans must, by their own efforts, be made equal in balloting for Presidents and other officers of the government. This principle is compelling the Republican party in certain localities to consider the necessity of nominating Negroes on its local electoral tickets. Yet the old attitude of that party on the political rights of Negroes remains substantially the same. . . .

And now in this election the standards will advance and the cohorts go forward under the simple impulse of the same corrupting influence. But whether the new movement for a

Negro party comes to a head or not, the new Negro in America will never amount to anything politically until he enfranchises himself from the Grand Old Party which has made a political joke of him.—July, 1920.

Chapter VIII

Education and the Race

[With most of the present sources of power controlled by the white race it behooves my race as well as the other subject races to learn the wisdom of the weak and to develop to the fullest that organ whereby weakness has been able to overcome strength; namely, the intellect. It is not with our teeth that we will tear the white man out of our ancestral land. It isn't with our jaws that we can ring from his hard hands consideration and respect. It must be done by the upper and not by the lower parts of our heads. Therefore, I have insisted ever since my entry into the arena of racial discussion that we Negroes must take to reading, study and the development of intelligence as we have never done before. In this respect we must pattern ourselves after the Japanese who have gone to school to Europe but have never used Europe's education to make them the apes of Europe's culture. They have absorbed, adopted, transformed and utilized, and we Negroes must do the same. The three editorials in this chapter and the article which follows them were written to indicate from time to time the duty of the transplanted African in this respect.]

Reading for Knowledge

Some time ago we wrote an editorial entitled "Read, Read, Read!" We touched upon the same subject again, because in our recent trip to Washington we found thousands of people who are eager to get in touch with the stored-up knowledge which the books contain, but do not know just where to turn for it. In New York the same situation obtains, and no help is afforded by the papers of our race.

The reason is that some of our newspaper editors don't read and don't know beans themselves. James W. Johnson is one of the notable exceptions. We were cheered up a good deal by noting his recent editorial advice to our "leaders" to read Arthur Henderson's "The Aims of Labor." But that was six months after the editor of *The Voice* had been telling thousands of the "led" all about it and about the British Labor Party and the Russian Bolsheviki in his outdoor talks in Harlem.

But there is no doubt that the New Negro is producing a New Leadership and that this new leadership will be based not upon the ignorance of the masses, but upon their intelligence. The old leadership was possible partly because the masses were ignorant. Today the masses included educated laymen who have studied science, theology, history and economics, not, perhaps in college but, nevertheless, deeply and down to date. These young men and women are not going to follow fools and, indeed, are not going to follow *any one*, blindly. They want a reason for the things that they are asked to do and to respect. The others, the so-called Common People, are beginning to read and understand. As we sat in the great John Wesley A.M.E. Zion Church in Washington one Sunday night, and heard the cultured black minister speak to his people on literature, science, history and sociology, and yet so simply that even the dullest could catch the meat and inspiration of his great ideas, we could not help saying as we went out of the church: "Depend upon it, these people will demand as much from their next minister." In fact our race will demand as much from *all* its leaders. And they will demand no less for themselves.

So, with a glad heart, we reprint the following paragraphs from our earlier editorial trusting that our readers everywhere may find them helpful:

As a people our bent for books is not encouraging. We mostly read trash. And this is true not only of our rank and file but even of our leaders. When we heard Kelly Miller address the Sunrise Club of New York at a Broadway hotel two or three years ago, we were shocked at the ignorance of modern science and modern thought which his remarks displayed. His biology was of the brand of Pliny who lived about eighteen hundred years ago. For him Darwin and Spencer and Jacques Loeb had never existed nor written. His ignorance of the A. B. C.'s of astronomy and geology was pitiful.

If this is true of the leaders to whom our reading masses look, what can we expect from those reading masses? The masses must be taught to love good books. But to love them they must first know them. The handicaps placed on us in America are too great to allow us to ignore the help which we can get from that education which we get out of school for ourselves—the only one that is really worth while.

Without the New Knowledge the New Negro is no better than the old. And this new knowledge will be found in the books. Therefore, it would be well if every Negro of the new model were to make up his (or her) mind to get the essentials of modern science and modern thought as they are set down in the books which may be easily had. Don't talk about Darwin and Spencer: read them!

To help the good work along we append the following list of books that are essential. When you *master* these you will have a better "education" than is found in nine-tenths of the graduates of the average American college.

"Modern Science and Modern Thought," by Samuel Laing; "The Origin of Species" and "The Descent of Man," by Charles Darwin; "The Principles of Sociology" and "First Principles," by Herbert Spencer; "The Childhood of the World" and "The Childhood of Religion," by Edward Clodd; "Anthropology," by E. B. Tylor (very easy to read and a work of standard information on Races, Culture and the origins of Religion, Art and Science); Buckle's "History of Civilization"; Gibbon's "Decline and Fall of the Roman Empire"; "The Martyrdom of Man," by Winwood Reade; the books on Africa by Livingstone and Mungo Park, and "The Mind of Primitive Man," by Franz Boas.—Sept., 1918.

Education and the Race

In the dark days of Russia, when the iron heel of Czarist despotism was heaviest on the necks of the people, those who wished to rule decreed that the people should remain ignorant. Loyalty to interests that were opposed to theirs was the prevailing public sentiment of the masses. In vain did the pioneers of freedom for the masses perish under the knout and the rigors of Siberia. They sacrificed to move the masses, but the masses, strong in their love of liberty, lacked the head to guide the moving feet to any successful issue. It was then that Leo Tolstoi and the other intelligentsia began to carry knowledge to the masses. Not only in the province of Tula, but in every large city, young men of university experience would assemble in secret classes of instruction, teaching them to read, to write, to know, to think and to love knowledge. Most of this work was underground at first. But it took. Thousands of educated persons gave themselves to this work—without pay: their only hope of reward lay in the future effectiveness of an instructed mass movement.

What were the results? As knowledge spread, enthusiasm was backed by brains. The Russian revolution began to be sure of itself. The workingmen of the cities studied the thing that they were "up against," gauged their own weakness and strength as well as their opponents'. The despotism of the Czar could not provoke them to a mass movement before they were ready and had the means; and when at last they moved, they swept not only the Czar's regime but the whole exploiting system upon which it stood into utter oblivion.

What does this mean to the Negro of the Western world? It may mean much, or little: that depends on him. If other men's experiences have value for the New Negro Manhood Movement it will seek now to profit by them and to bottom the new fervor of faith in itself with the solid support of knowledge. The chains snap from the limbs of the young giant as he rises, stretches himself, and sits up to take notice. But let him, for his future's sake, insist on taking notice. To drop the figure of speech, we Negroes who have shown our *manhood* must back it by our *mind*. This world, at present, is a white man's world—even in Africa. We, being what we are, want to shake loose the chains of his control from our corner of it. We must either accept his domination and our inferiority, or we must contend against it. But we go up to win; and whether we carry on that contest with ballots, bullets or business, we can not win from the white man unless we know at least as much as the white man knows. For, after all, knowledge *is* power.

But that isn't all. What kind of knowledge is it that enables white men to rule black men's lands? Is it the knowledge of Hebrew and Greek, philosophy or literature? It isn't. It is the knowledge of explosives and deadly compounds: that is chemistry. It is the knowledge which can build ships, bridges, railroads and factories: that is engineering. It is the knowledge which harnesses the visible and invisible forces of the earth and air and water: that is science, modern science. And that is what the New Negro must enlist upon his side. Let us, like the Japanese, become a race of knowledge-getters, preserving our racial soul, but digesting into it all that we can glean or grasp, so that when Israel goes up out of bondage he will be "skilled in all the learning of the Egyptians" and competent to control his destiny.

Those who have knowledge must come down from their Sinais and give it to the common people. Theirs is the great duty to simplify and make clear, to light the lamps of knowledge that the eyes of their race may see; that the feet of their people may not stumble. This is the task of the Talented Tenth.

To the masses of our people we say: Read! Get the reading habit; spend your spare time not so much in training the feet to dance, as in training the head to think. And, at the very outset, draw the line between books of opinion and books of information. Saturate your minds with the latter and you will be forming your own opinions, which will be worth ten times more to you than the opinions of the greatest minds on earth. Go to school whenever you can. If you can't go in the day, go at night. But remember always that the best college is that on your bookshelf: the best education is that on the inside of your own head. For in this work-a-day world people ask first, not "Where were you educated?" but "What do you know?" and next,

"What can you do with it?" And if we of the Negro race can master modern knowledge, the kind that counts—we will be able to win for ourselves the priceless gifts of freedom and power, and we will be able to hold them against the world.

The Racial Roots of Culture

Education is the name which we give to that process by which the ripened generation brings to bear upon the rising generation the stored-up knowledge and experience of the past and present generations to fit it for the business of life. If we are not to waste money and energy, our educational systems should shape our youth for what we intend them to become. . . .

But what seems to escape attention is the fact that the Negro boy and girl, getting the same (though worse) instruction, also get from it the same notion of the Negro's place and part in life which the white children get. Is it any wonder, then, that they readily accept the status of inferiors; that they tend to disparage themselves, and think themselves worth while only to the extent to which they look and act and think like the whites? They know nothing of the stored-up knowledge and experience of the past and present generations of Negroes in their ancestral lands, and conclude there is no such store of knowledge and experience. They readily accept the assumption that Negroes have never been anything but slaves and that they never had a glorious past as other fallen peoples like the Greeks and Persians have. And this despite the mass of collected testimony in the works of Barth, Schweinfurth, Mary Kingsley, Lady Lugard, Morel, Ludolphus, Blyden, Ellis, Ratzel, Kidd, Es-Saadi, Casely Hayford and a host of others, Negro and white.

A large part of the blame for this deplorable condition must be put upon the Negro colleges like Howard, Fisk, Livingstone and Lincoln in the United States, and Codrington, Harrison and the Mico in the West Indies. These are the institutions in which our cultural ideals and educational systems are fashioned for the shaping of the minds of the future generations of Negroes. It cannot be expected that it shall begin with the common schools; for, in spite of logic, educational ideas and ideals spread from above downwards. If we are ever to enter into the confraternity of colored peoples it should seem the duty of our Negro colleges to drop their silly smatterings of "little Latin and less Greek" and establish modern courses in Hausa and Arabic, for these are the living languages of millions of our brethren in modern Africa. Courses in Negro history and the culture of West African peoples, at least, should be given in every college that claims to be an institution of learning for Negroes. Surely an institution of learning for Negroes should not fail to be also an institution of Negro learning.

The New Negro, Sept. 1919. . . .

The Knowledge We Need

Now, what is the knowledge which the New Negro needs most? He needs above all else a knowledge of the wider world and of the long past. But that is history, modern and ancient:

History as written by Herodotus and John Back McMaster; sociology not as conceived by Giddings, but as presented by Spencer and Ward, and anthropology as worked out by Boas and Thomas. The Negro needs also the knowledge of the best thought; but that is literature as conceived, not as a collection of flowers from the tree of life, but as its garnered fruit. And, finally, the Negro needs a knowledge of his own kind, concerning which we shall have something to say later. And the purposes of this knowledge? They are, to know our place in the human processes, to strengthen our minds by contact with the best and most useful thought-products evolved during the long rise of man from anthropoid to scientist; to inspire our souls and to lift our race industrially, commercially, intellectually to the level of the best that there is in the world about us. *For never until the Negro's knowledge of nitrates and engineering, of chemistry and agriculture, of history, science and business is on a level, at least, with that of the whites, will the Negro be able to measure arms successfully with them.*

Josiah Morse
"The Outlook for the Negro"
Sewanee Review 28, no. 2 (1920)[27]

The Great War, which shook the whole world and shattered Europe, upsetting institutions, governments, and customs, and in some places (*e.g.*, Russia) turning them completely upside down, has affected variously the different orders of the Great Society. The unduly privileged it has filled with grief and despair. There is no silver lining to the cloud above them. The deluge is here, and their doom is sealed. The exploited, the oppressed and disinherited—at the other extreme—it has filled with new hopes and dreams, in which, according to Freudian laws, they are seeking full compensation for their long repressed desires and denied ideas of justice and fair play.

This is true of the American Negro no less than of the Russian, the Pole, the Jugo-Slav, the Armenian, and the other peoples of Eastern and Central Europe. For the American Negro had his share also in the war, and did his bit very creditably. He furnished 250,000 men, sent an equal number into the various war industries, purchased more than $225,000,000 worth of the war bonds, and gave liberally to the Red Cross and other war organizations. The war made a new man of him, *and therein lies one of the chief causes of the recent clashes between some members of his race and some members of the white race.*

Borrowing terms from genetic psychology, we may say that the war brought the Negro's

BACHELORS OF ART

" Success is to be able to look God in the face without fear, and any man in the face without servility."

The Strength and Character Written Upon These Faces Indicate Highly Successful Futures

(1) Miss Willie Mae King, Chattanooga, Tenn. A. B. Degree in Education, Wilberforce University, '20. Magna Cum Laude.

(2) Ruth Cravath Kingsley, Talledega College. A. B. 1920. Talledega, Ala.

(3) Miss Hazel Wells, A. B. '20. Oberlin University, Oberlin, Ohio.

(4) Miss Marie La Grande Hackley, A. B. Cum Laude, 1920. Wilberforce University.

(5) Miss Mabel Lowell Harris, Talledega College. A. B. 1920. Talledega, Ala.

"Bachelors of Art," portraits of female college graduates, *Competitor*, July 1920.

long period of childhood to a close and projected him almost violently into adolescence, giving him a new sense of strength and ability, mental and physical, and a corresponding desire for larger opportunities and privileges. He has now entered upon the "storm and stress" period of his racial existence, a period which, as the descriptive phrase characterizing it indicates, is the opposite of peaceful and satisfied. The Negro is going to be, for a time, more restless, possibly more lawless and troublesome, and certainly more dissatisfied, than he has been in all his history. And it is not going to be because he will have less of anything (indeed, he already has much more of everything), but because his flood of new impulses will not be under adequate control, and his wants and ambitions will have outrun both his own capacity to satisfy them at once, and the willingness of the whites to grant them forthwith and *in toto*.

This leads us to the second factor in the race problem—the new adjustments to the changed conditions which the whites will find it necessary to make. It is always difficult for an individual, and much more so for a group, to make such adjustments. Even parents find it difficult to adjust themselves to the changes in their children which natural growth and development bring about. It means the breaking up of old habits and attitudes and the formation of new ones. Most human beings are so lazy-minded that they hate the persons or conditions that compel them to exert themselves.

This "lazy-mindedness" is a universal human trait of profound significance, and deserving of further consideration. Biologically and psychologically, it means resistance on the part of the mind to whatever threatens to disturb its comfortable adjustments and throw it into a state of unstable equilibrium, that is, of unrest, uncertainty, and uneasiness. In the lower animals this natural inertia meets with no counter force or stimulus; consequently each species long ago adjusted itself most comfortably and with the least expenditure of effort to its own environment, and has remained there contentedly ever since. The lower animals have made no progress. They feel no need of progress. They and their environments remain fixed.

In man there is much of the animal with its natural inertia and aversion to change. But there is also (and this it is which differentiates him from the rest of the animal kingdom) a "divine discontent" with things and adjustments as they are: an initiative and inventiveness that impel him to explore and experiment in the hope of improving upon former conditions. This spiritual "urge" is the secret of human advancement.

Of course, it is not present in equal degree in all human beings. In the vast majority of men the animal inertia is greater than the "divine discontent," which accounts for the survival of outworn customs and traditions, for hyper-conservatism and lack of progress. The business of education, in the broadest sense of the term, is continuously to seek to overcome the animal inertia and to make improved adjustments to the new, the different, difficult, and increasingly complex elements in our environment. The educated man is one who is tolerant of the new and the different, and who has the energy and intelligence to make and un-make adjustments. There is a new Negro in the South, the product of five years of human struggle which are easily the equivalent of any hundred earlier years of human history. We shall prove the quality of our education by our willingness and ability to adjust ourselves to him.

First cousin to the above-mentioned inertia is what is commonly known as prejudice. Prejudice is an undue and unwarranted aversion to or predilection for anything or anybody. It is blind and deaf to reason. Its roots reach down to the instincts which have to do with self-preservation and the perpetuation of the species, and to the habits and customs which in the long ago made living safe and easy. The species-prejudice of the lower animals and the race-prejudice of man find their explanations in these biological considerations. Lacking reason, the animals have used instinct and blind prejudice to protect themselves against actual and potential foes. But with the dawn of reason in man a new and better instrument of protection and aggression was given, and man became emancipated from the complete domination of instinct and prejudice. More and more he could afford to observe, get acquainted, and postpone action until judgment had matured and decision had been reached.

Our age has frequently been labelled the "age of reason," but this of course is only partly true. Prejudice is by no means dead in the world. Indeed, it seems to have taken on a new lease of life. Everywhere reason and justice are at grips with prejudice and instinct in a postbellum struggle, but happily there is little doubt of the outcome. In the new era, reason and justice will dominate instinct and prejudice.

The foregoing observations are already exemplified in the condition of the Negro in our country. Despite the increase in lynchings and mob violence during the last year and their spread over the entire country, the status of the Negro is better and higher, and his human rights more widely and readily recognized than they have ever been. Contemporary race disturbances are in reality evidences of rapid growth, not of deterioration or decay. Everywhere in the South the whites are acknowledging that not nearly enough has been spent on Negro education, and are of their own accord making substantial increases in the appropriations therefor. Likewise, they are admitting that the housing and sanitary conditions should be greatly improved, and are making beginnings in these directions. They are not only paying the Negro much larger wages, but are admitting the justice of the increase. Judges and juries are becoming more even-handed, notwithstanding the contrary evidences that get into the newspapers. The Negroes are prospering, working with less strain, and living better than ever before. Many elements in the working classes of Europe are not so well conditioned as the Southern Negro. Despite the great change that has come over him and the difficulty of making readjustments to him, the prejudice against him has considerably decreased.

A noteworthy evidence of this fact is to be seen in the work of the Committee on the After-the-War Program to bring about a better relationship between the two races in the South.[28] This Committee is composed of one or more citizens from each of the Southern states, and has a field agent and white and colored workers in each state, organizing county committees to meet from time to time with similar Negro committees and to discuss in a friendly and helpful way all matters that concern the wellbeing of both races, separately and collectively. The platform the county committees are asked to adopt is as follows: (1) Justice before the law, to include prevention of lynching and other denials of legal justice to the Negro; (2) adequate educational facilities; (3) sanitary housing and living conditions; (4) recreational facilities; (5) economic justice; (6) equality of travelling facilities; (7) welcoming returned colored soldiers; and (8) employment for colored soldiers. Some idea of the size of the work of the Committee may be gained from the fact that at the end of the first year more than $200,000 will have been spent upon it.

Race friction and conflict, as observed above, spring from instinct and prejudice, and all the misunderstandings, suspicions, and evil passions that are bred by them. In these interracial conferences dominated by reason, such suspicions and misunderstandings tend to be dispelled, and feelings of sympathy and goodwill and a spirit of coöperation are generated that will enable the two races to live side by side with more harmony and mutual helpfulness. The writer spent some six weeks last summer meeting with groups of representative citizens in thirty communities in South Carolina. Day after day he was agreeably surprised and often amazed by the advanced positions taken by one or more of the best citizens in these communities. Everywhere there was enthusiastic approval of the conference idea, and everywhere the desire was manifest to live with the Negro in peace and to be of substantial service to him. Similar reports continue to come from all the other Southern states.

Not less important is the work that the University Commission on Race Questions has been doing among college students during the past eight years. The Commission is composed of one representative from each of the Southern state universities. It has held a number of meetings in various Southern cities, and in all these and in several of the larger Negro colleges it has listened to presentations by capable Negroes of their side of the race problem. From time to time the Commission has issued open letters to the college men of the South, setting forth the results of its deliberations, and these have recently been collected and published in pamphlet form under the title, *Four Open Letters from the University Commission on Race Questions to the College Men of the South.* These letters deal with the crime of lynching, the need of better educational facilities for the Negro, the Negro migration, and the new reconstruction. Their publication has elicited widespread discussion and has stimulated the study of the Negro problem in Southern colleges.

These efforts to mitigate race prejudice and to secure justice for the Negro have not weakened in the slightest degree the determinations that there shall be no infusion of Negro blood in the white race, and that socially the two peoples shall remain apart. Happily, these determinations are in accord with the wishes of all self-respecting Negroes, and as the pride of race continues to develop in their people, the large amount of friction now due to the fear of these things on the part of the whites will cease. Both peoples need to realize that racial integrity is not incompatible with mutual respect. The brotherhood of man towards which civilization is struggling does not mean a promiscuous mingling of the races, but only a decent and wholesome regard for the personality of each race.

Less strong is the determination to deny to the Negro all political privileges. Numbers of Southerners are admitting that no obstacle to voting should be put in the way of respectable, property-owning Negroes. But the memories of the corrupt and humiliating Negro rule during the Reconstruction period continue to hang over the South like a pall. If the white South could believe that the Negro would vote for the best measures and men, and not for the worst, the opposition to his enfranchisement would be reduced to a minimum. But there is a natural reluctance to jeopardize again the white civilization by an act of impractical idealism. The Negro must clearly earn his enfranchisement and prove his fitness for it, not merely insist on it as his right. No group has a right to tear down civilization, or to lower the standard of culture

already attained. A fundamental democratic principle is that the right to govern should rest solely upon the capacity to govern, but until the Negroes generally show their capacity those who now have it will suffer more or less curtailment of their right.

Here we encounter a species of prejudice that is most unjust and unjustifiable in its operation, and which must be overcome, if the fullest measure of justice and fair play is to obtain in the relationship between the two races. It is the prejudice that makes sweeping generalizations and acts upon them as if they were true. All Negroes are lumped together, reduced to the lowest common denominator, and dealt with on that basis. As a matter of fact, there are as wide differences among Negroes as among other races. Indeed, we should speak of Negro races rather than of the Negro race. The *Encyclopedia Britannica* enumerates some four hundred different tribes in Africa, varying widely among themselves in physique and appearance, in language, customs, occupations, and in many other ways, indicating mentalities of different orders. The American Negro is also of many varieties and orders of mentality and character, the tendency to overlook which and to observe only the similarity or sameness of color among them is the cause of a large measure of the personal wrongs suffered by the better elements of the race. The whites need to learn that the Negroes now occupy several cultural levels, and that those occupying the highest level should be treated with more consideration than is now accorded those occupying the lowest. There is a group of Negroes of high school and college education, professional and business men and women, property and home-owning, moral, religious, useful members of the communities in which they live. A second and larger group is composed of Negroes of but little education, yet honest, steady-working, and ambitious to rise, or at least for their children to rise. A third group is composed of the improvident, unambitious, good-natured, playful, and, on occasion hardworking Negroes. Lastly, there are the immoral, vicious and criminal, the kind that fill the courtrooms and prisons. If each class were treated according to its merits, or, better still, if each individual were treated according to his merits, there would be less ground for complaint.

Complicating and aggravating the race prejudice is the almost equally powerful economic prejudice. One need not be a Marxian Socialist to recognize the enormous rôle played by the economic factor in all human affairs. Whether in California, or Georgia, or Pennsylvania, there will always be an implacable enmity between the members of a higher-standard-of-living group and those of a lower-standard-of-living group. When the Negro's standard of living shall have risen to the point where he will be unable and unwilling to live on less than the white man's minimum, the prejudice now existing against him will be considerably softened. But so long as his presence tends to lower the standard of living he will be considered a menace by those who are economically nearest to him. The economic "signs of the times" indicate that this source of prejudice will soon be greatly diminished.

The greatest advance has been made in the direction of public equality. The disposition is rapidly growing to give the Negro equal public facilities and service for equal pay. This is seen in improved schools, parks and playgrounds, streets and houses, street-car and railroad facilities, court-room practices and business dealings. When the state legislature of South Carolina appropriated $100,000 for a memorial to the white soldiers, it appropriated an equal amount for a memorial for the Negro soldiers.

In all things material the ideal of the white South is to be at least mathematically honest, to coöperate [*sic*] and be of assistance; in all things racial and social it is determined to remain distinct. It is not chauvinism to say that the heart of the South is warm and big, as human hearts go. No one knows, not even a Southerner, unless he has especially interested himself in this matter, how much fine thinking and feeling and doing for the Negro is going on all the time, for very little of this is recorded in the press. Only the frictions are heralded in flaming headlines. The Southern whites can justly make the same complaint as that often voiced by the Negroes: that only their faults and crimes are advertised to the world; their good deeds are hidden in small print and often not noticed at all. But it has always been so. The intelligent South does not complain: it is heartily ashamed of the misdeeds of some of its members, even though the provocations are often great. It knows that the true mark of the educated is self-control and respect for law and the institutions of civilized society. But when enemies and fanatics train their eyes and ears to see and hear only the evil in the South, and their tongues and pens to speak and write of it, it is permissible to point out that the notable progress the Negro has made since his emancipation, and the wealth he has accumulated, have been made and accumulated with the consent and encouragement and assistance of the white South. Without these he could hardly have moved a step. And it is safe to predict even greater and swifter progress for him, if only he will be guided by the sane, peace-loving leaders of his own and the white race in the South.

J. R. Ralph Casimir, ca. 1920.

J. R. R. C. [J. R. Ralph Casimir]
"Letter to the Editor"

Dominica Guardian, April 29, 1920[29]

Dear Mr. Editor,—Kindly allow me a short space in your valuable columns to state a few facts:

Conditions in Dominica are going from bad to worse. Who and what are responsible for such unrest? Are the poor Negro labourers responsible? Is the circulation of the *Negro World* due to such unrest? Or is the recently established branch of the Universal Negro Improvement Association (commonly called Black Star Line Society by the majority of the people here) responsible? No! not at all.

Unrest and bad state of affairs are due to Crown Colony Rule (one man Rule), unnecessary prohibitive laws, high rate of exchange, high costs of living, low wages, profiteering, poor educational system, lack of steamship communication, need for coastal steamer, inland communication, etc.

Much has been said in the past and is being said at present in regards to Crown Colony Rule which is unsatisfactory throughout. Everybody desires that this form of Government be done away with. This can be proved by the agitation here and elsewhere for Representative Government. Dominica, I believe, suffers the most under this (Crown Colony) form of Government. "Away with Crown Colony Rule, the time has come for the Negro to take a share in the Government of the country. He is tired of being oppressed." . . .

The poor labourers are bound to demand higher wages owing to the high costs of living. If they cannot obtain higher wages, what must they do? Are not the labourers of England and other countries demanding more wages even though their wages have sometimes already been raised? Are not there frequent labour riots in such places? Why should it be a crime if the Dominica labourer strikes? The rise in wages in various occupations in England is shown in the following list comparing rates in 1913–14 with those prevailing in 1919:—

	1913–14.	1919.
Miners	8s. 5d. per shift	18s. per shift
Porters	20s. to 26s. weekly	53s. to 59s. weekly
Carting (one horse drivers)	24s. to 27s. weekly	54s. to 57s. weekly
Bakers (table hands)	28s. to 38s. weekly	60s. to 70s. weekly

In Dominica the labourers get about 50 per cent more than in pre-war days. Articles of clothing, foodstuffs, etc., etc., were selling from 100 to 500 per cent cheaper than now. How can a poor man with wife and children live on even a wee shilling and six pence a day? Why not raise his pay by even 100 per cent?

At a recent meeting of Planters held at the Masonic Lodge here, a certain Englishman stated that miners in England work eight hours a day in the coal pits, endure all hardships without grumbling and give skilled labour comparing their industry with the indolence of the Dominica labourers. How absurd! English miners endure all hardships without grumbling! What about all the strikes and riots for more wages? What about the destruction of coal mines? Compare the pay of the English miner with the Dominica labourer. Would any white labourer, whether skilled or unskilled, work for 1s. 6r. a day (9 hours)? Compare the pay of the English porter (53s. to 59s. weekly) with that of the Dominica Negro porter. Must the Negro labourer stay in rags or naked and without food while the white labourer is well paid, well clad and well fed? Negro labourers of Dominica, strive for thy right, fear God and know no other fear!

Profiteering is carried on to a very large extent by some of the merchants and shopkeepers, who are mostly sycophants. Some of these have no sympathy for their poorer brothers and think that because they have a little money, they are white and superior to the poorer Negroes though their skin is black.

The educational system is even worse than 15 years ago. It is one of the worst, if not the worst, in the entire West Indies. Many parents cannot afford to send their children to school owing to the high costs of living and low wages. Why does not Government take more interest in this matter? Why are no better means adopted to educate the future men and women of the island in this progressive era? What shall become of the future generation in Dominica if such conditions are allowed to become worse? Are we not living in the 20th century just as the inhabitants of other places?

The lack of steamship communication is a very serious one. The steamers usually arrive late now-a-days. Negroes when travelling in the Quebec liners are not well treated. Sometimes they are refused any passage. Sometimes they have to wait as long as four months before they can get a passage to the United States. They pay their money just as anybody else and still this is not taken into consideration. All these ill treatments make the Negroes feel more anxious for the Black Star Liners and the cry everywhere is "When will a Black Stare Liner come to Dominica!" . . .

I don't know how to write or what words to use to describe the rotten state of inland communication. The island is mountainous indeed but no efforts are being made to keep the roads in proper order. More public money is being wasted than anything else. There are many roads which are entirely abandoned and these roads get ruined. All this helps to cripple the island.

The intended suppression of the *Negro World* is causing much uneasiness among the inhabitants and it would be better to exercise a wise discretion and leave it alone. The *Negro World* is Negro, by the Negro and for the Negro, why should any Government or individual (white or black) try to prevent the Dominica Negro from reading the *New World*? Does the white man think that all the Negroes in Dominica are fools? Does he know what is a New Negro? . . .

The *Negro World* must come to Dominica and will circulate in Dominica as long as there is life in the Dominica Negro. Long live the Negro World!

Some people (including Government Officials) here say that the officers and members of the Universal Negro Improvement Association in this island are responsible for every unlawful act committed in Dominica. Recently there have been petty strikes on different estates and there were rumours about that the U. N. I. A. [Universal Negro Improvement Association] is responsible. Who was responsible for the stevedores', boatmen's and porters' strike here about two years ago? Who was responsible for every unlawful act committed by individuals before the Negroes here had ever dreamt or heard of The Universal Negro Improvement Association?

The Universal Negro Improvement Association is for the betterment of the Negro Race, intellectually, educationally, financially, commercially, and otherwise. It is an Association to establish a universal confraternity among the race; to promote the spirit of race pride and love and to administer to and assist the needy; to work for better conditions among our people in Dominica; to promote industries and commerce in this island for the betterment of the Negroes. Can these cause any harm? Can these be any cause for unrest among the inhabitants or Government? What proof can any one give that such an Association is revolutionary or Bolshevik? Is it a crime for Negroes to ask for freedom and independence? If other races live in unity and better their conditions, is it a crime for Negroes to do the same?

Unless the Negro gets his due and be treated as a MAN and is given all the privileges due to MAN he will fight in every constitutional way to get his due and to be treated as a MAN. The U. N. I. A. is there to enable the Negro to get all what is due to him and it must exist as long as the Negro exists. God bless the universal negro improvement association.

Thank you Mr. Editor for space allowed.

I am, dear Sir,
Fraternally yours,
J. R. R. C.
"A New Negro."
Dominica, 21.4.20.

Dear Sir,—This is to thank you very sincerely for your editorial of recent date, concerning us and our efforts to establish a coastal Steamship Service around the island of Dominica.

We assure you that we are working hard on the project, and have touched all points in the matter. We, therefore, feel confident that if the people of Dominica will *agitate vigorously* for the service, our present negotiations with the Secretary of State for the Colonies and His Excellency the Administrator of Dominica will be successful, and the subsidy granted.

With best wishes to you,
We remain,
Yours very truly,

Intercolonial Steamship & Trading Company[30]
S. A. Roach,
Secretary.

Geroid Robinson
"The New Negro"

Freeman, June 2, 1920[31]

Before the war, the Negroes of the United States suffered more than a full measure of all the wrongs that have led to the double revolt of small nations and suppressed classes in Europe. Individually the Negro workers, who form a very large portion of the coloured population, have borne all the hardships of their economic class, and collectively the race has been subjected to special disabilities, political, economic and social, such as the limitation of the right to vote and to hold office, the denial of justice, the practices of lynching and peonage, the discrimination of white labour unions, segregation in trains and in residential districts, and the limitation of educational opportunities. Now it is perfectly obvious that every sort of discrimination against Negroes, as such, tends to unite them as a racial group, and it is equally obvious that the appearance of economic differences among the Negroes themselves has exactly the opposite effect. During recent years, the development of economic differentiations has been very marked, but there is some evidence that racial animosity is likewise on the increase; and it is precisely this complication of class and race alinements that make the Negro problem the most uncertain factor in the future of the country.

The people who are attempting to deal with this situation fall naturally into three groups, as determined by the attitude they take toward the questions of race and class. Certain politicians and an increasing number of welfare-workers and educators hold an essentially liberal position, in that they disregard racial and economic divisions and attempt to appeal to black men and white as individual citizens. The second group champions Socialism and industrial unionism, and attempts to unite all workers, irrespective of race and colour, upon the basis of common economic interest. The third group considers white Socialists almost as hateful as white Democrats; and against them all it preaches the doctrine of racial unity, Negro nationalism, and the final overthrow of Caucasian supremacy.

In so far as it may be classed as an attempt at solution, the whole "Black Republican" movement belongs to the category of non-racial, non-economic answers to the Negro problem. Tradition and sentiment have bound the coloured people so completely to the Grand Old Party, that Republican candidates have generally secured the black vote without giving either promise or performance in return. It would be hard to find better proof of this proposition than is contained in the report on a questionnaire sent by the National Association for the Advancement of Coloured [*sic*] People to seventeen Presidential candidates now before the country. In the questionnaire the candidates were asked to state, among other things, whether they would favour the enactment of Federal laws against lynching, and the enforcement of the Fourteenth Amendment by the reduction of the representation of States which disfranchise some of their citizens. In reply, Senator Harding stated that it was the business of the National Conventions to frame platforms and policies, and Senator Poindexter declared himself "in favour of maintaining the legal rights and opportunities of all citizens, regardless of colour or condition." As for the rest, Citizens Hoover and Johnson were as silent as Generals Wood and Pershing. The point is this: in the northern States, where the coloured vote counts, the Negroes will vote Republican whatever happens; whereas some of the northern white men might be frightened into Democracy by too much pro-Africanism on the part of the Republican candidate. On the other hand, the coloured vote in the south isn't worth a buffalo nickel to anybody under present conditions, and can hardly be made so, at an early date, by any means short of another Civil War.

The mess the Arkansas Republicans have gotten into will show pretty clearly how the black Republican vote is handled south of the Line. When Negro delegates were denied seats at the State Convention at Little Rock, they bolted and elected their own delegates to the National Convention, and also nominated a Negro candidate for governor. The entire delegations to the Republican National Convention from Florida, Louisiana, Mississippi, South Carolina and Virginia are being contested; of 122 places in the Convention now in dispute, 118 are from Southern Democratic States, where the fight between the so-called "Lily White" and "Black and Tan" elements is running its usual course. And the saddest part of it is, that all this fuss is being made over the business of nominating a candidate who will promise the southern Negroes nothing, and for whom most of them will not be allowed to vote.

If the Republicans disregard racial and economic lines, the educational-welfare groups go even farther toward universal brotherhood by dropping even political partisanship. Somewhat typical of this attitude are the rejoicings of Robert R. Moton, President of Tuskegee Institute, over the fact that "Although there are 15,000,000 Negroes in this country, not one of them was ever captured in the Federal dragnets which recently gathered in bolsheviks, anarchists and other 'reds.'" President Moton's conclusion is that "the loyalty of the Negro race can never be questioned."

The National Association for the Advancement of Coloured People fairly represents the co-operation of white and coloured citizens in the liberal "appeal to the conscience of America" on behalf of the civil and political rights of the Negro. The Board of Directors of the Association is half white and half coloured, and its membership of 91,000 is about ninety per cent coloured. The *Crisis*, a magazine published by this organization, has a circulation of about 100,000 copies per month, some of which go to Africa. The Association has no economic or political programme, and its appeal is quite spe-

cifically an appeal to the righteous; nevertheless, its work in general, and its agitation against lynching in particular, have unquestionably been of very considerable value.

The civil-rights programme of the N.A.A.C.P. is supplemented, on the side of industrial welfare, by the work of the National Urban League. It is the aim of this organization to open up new industrial opportunities to Negro workers, and to give attention to conditions of work and recreation in communities where Negroes are employed in considerable numbers. During 1919 the various locals of the League persuaded the managers of 135 industrial plants to employ Negroes for the first time; and during the same period twenty-two welfare workers were placed in plants where Negroes were engaged. The organization has also declared its sympathy with efforts to unionize Negro labour.

At the last National Convention of the American Federation of Labour, it became evident that trade unionism was prepared to give considerable attention to the organization of Negro workers. Forty-six or more of the hundred and thirteen Internationals included in the Federation already admit Negro members, and the Convention for 1919 voted to bring pressure to bear upon the other Internationals by organizing independent locals directly under the Federation wherever the existing unions will not accept coloured applicants. According to a statement made by President Gompers, the A. F. of L. [American Federation of Labor] now has two paid organizers and thirteen volunteers at work among the Negroes.

But respectable trade-unionism—like Republican politics, and the liberal appeal to the American conscience—is by no means satisfactory to the leaders of the second major school of thought on the Negro problem. Here, in place of a liberal disregard of class and race lines, we have the preaching of a class-war in which "the workers of the world," irrespective of race and colour, are urged to unite against their oppressors. In politics this group is Socialist; in the field of labour-organization, it inclines to favour the I. W. W. [Industrial Workers of the World] rather than the unions of the A.F. of L. The Socialist party, on its part, has recognized the potential value of the Negro vote, and has included in its national platform a declaration in favour of full political and economic rights for Negroes; this party has also made special provision for the spread of propaganda among the Negroes, and has employed three organizers for this purpose. No statistics are available as to the number of Negro Socialists in this country; but, according to the statement of an I. W. W. organizer, ten per cent of the members of the latter organization are coloured; in other words, the membership of the I. W. W. corresponds pretty closely with the population of the United States in the matter of colour-composition.

The chief organ of the Negro Socialist-syndicalists—a magazine with a circulation of some 20,000 copies a month—is characterized in the following terms by Attorney-General Palmer:

> The *Messenger* [he says] . . . is by long odds the most able and the most dangerous of all the Negro publications. It is representative of the most educated thought among the Negroes.

Referring to the Socialist party, and to the National Labour party, which has also adopted a demand in favour of Negro rights, this interesting publication says:

> We have constantly maintained that the solution of the Negro problem rests with the alliance of Negroes with radical organization. . . . Here are two organizations largely composed of white people, who have adopted fundamental methods for the solution of the problems affecting the white and Negro races in the United States. This is not because there is any special love for the Negro on the part of the groups which compose these conventions, but because it is impossible for them to attain the ends and objects at which they are aiming unless these fundamental rights of the Negro are granted to him.

In another number the editor peaks further in the same vein:

> We do not depend, upon professions of friendship or flowery promises, but only intelligent self-interest. The position of white labour is already changing rapidly in its relation to Negro labour, not because white labour likes Negro labour any better, but because it realizes that the only way white labour can raise its standard of living is to raise the standard of living of its competitors. This sound position will be taken by white labour as rapidly as it becomes more intelligent and class conscious. . . .

> Our political philosophy is Socialism, not State Socialism. For more than two years, now, it has functioned in Russia. . . . The [Negro] Left Wing group holds that the greatest power the Negro possesses is his power to combine with the Socialist present minority and assist it in becoming the majority.

It would appear then that the *Messenger* group is convinced that the solution of the Negro problem is to be found in the solidarity of all workers, white and black. And yet it is very evident that, from time to time, lynchings and race-riots put a rude strain upon the inter-racial creed of these Socialist-syndicalists. Take, for example, this quotation, also from the *Messenger:*

> We are . . . urging Negroes and other oppressed groups confronted with lynching or mob violence to act upon the recognized and accepted law of self-defence. . . . The black man has no rights which will be respected unless the black man enforces that respect. It is his business to decide that just as he went 3000 miles away to fight for alleged democracy in Europe and for others, he can lay down his life, honourably and peacefully, for himself in the United States. . . . New Negroes are determined to make their dying a costly investment for all concerned. . . . This new spirit is but a reflex of the Great War.

And it is this spirit that, in time of pressure—in the time of such riots as those of Washington and Chicago—must unite the Negro radicals with the supporters of the third and most startling answer to the race problem—"African nationalism." Perhaps this expression will always remain strange to American ears—and then again it may become quite familiar within a few years. For, after all, a rebellious hatred of the white race as a whole is the Negro's easiest reaction to wrongs, most of which certainly seem to fall upon him rather as a black man than as a workingman; this rebellious spirit needs only a common racial objective to give it unity, and that it seems now in a measure to have gotten. The "Negro-First" propaganda is largely the work of the Universal Negro Improvement Association and African Communities League of the World—an organization which claims a million adherents in the United States, the West Indies, South America and South Africa, and announces as its final object the establishment of a black empire in Africa. The following quotation from the *Negro World* will give an idea of the nature of this remarkable movement:

> Mobs of white men all over the world will continue to lynch and burn Negroes as long as we remain divided among ourselves. The very moment all the Negroes of this and other countries start to stand together, that very time will see the white man standing in fear of the Negro race even as he stands in fear of the yellow race of Japan to-day. The Negro must now organize all over the world, 400,000,000 strong, to administer to our oppressors their Waterloo. . . . Let every Negro all over the world prepare for the new emancipation. The Fatherland, Africa, has been kept by God Almighty for the Negro to redeem, and we, young men and women of the race, have pledged ourselves to plant there the flag of freedom and of empire.

Connected with the U. N. I. A. are the Black Star Steamship Line, capitalized at $10,000,000, and the Negro Factories Corporation, capital-

ized at $1,000,000. Just what these astonishing figures represent in actual cash we have no means of knowing, but this much is certain: the Black Star Line has already in operation one of the multitude of steamers which—say the prophets of the movement—will some day ply between the Negro lands of the world. To cap the climax, the U. N. I. A. will hold in New York during the month of August an "International Convention of Deputies" who will elect "His Supreme Highness, the Potentate; His Highness, the Supreme Deputy, and other high officials who will preside over the destiny of the Negro peoples of the world until the African Empire is founded."

However laughable this language may be, there is no doubt that something is happening in the Negro world—something that can not be laughed down, any more than the Germans could laugh down the Senegalese. If any further proof of this is needed, it can be found in the pages of a magazine called the *Crusader*. On the cover of this magazine is the figure of a black man bearing a spear and a shield, and inside one finds this sort of thing:

> Let us notice a combat between black boys and white boys, and we will see that the blacks exchange two or three cuffs for one. And no single white man will attack a Negro until he is first sure that he has some other help than himself, for the Negro would endeavor to greet him with such blows as only one who knows that there is no other god but God can. . . . Do not fail to teach your children the truth, for Africa is our heritage, the hope of our salvation.

And in another number, this:

> What the Negro needs to know is that in many qualities he is the superior of the white man. He needs to know these qualities and to believe in them and insist on them.

To complete the familiar paraphernalia of nationalism with historical illusion, the coloured people are urged by the *Negro World* to "restore the ancient glories of Ethiopia."

In the face of this movement, American liberalism seeks to preserve its calm unconsciousness of race; even as it has sought to keep up the appearance of moral disinterestedness in the realm of economic interests. And just as the liberals, for all their good intentions, did not succeed in forestalling class-movements among the white workers, it is pretty certain that they can not find palliatives enough to sweep back "the rising tide of colour." The Socialist-syndicalist group, on the other hand, replaces the appeal to racial unity with a frank appeal to economic interest.

The conflict between the class-movement and the race-movement is fundamental and direct. If the expansion of American unionism leaves the Negroes for the most part unorganized, the white workers may rest assured that their coloured competitors will turn to racial organization—black unions against white. If, on the other hand, the Negro workers can be absorbed into a general labour movement, the race problem may lose some of its difficulty, as, in the course of time, the labour-problem approaches a solution. Racial division may serve the interest of the old order for the present, but in the end it will profit no one but the munitions-makers.

Robert T. Kerlin
"The Negro Fourth Estate"

Reedy's Mirror 28, no. 4 (1920)[32]

Activity of the colored press of the country in these troublous times, the spirit, the boldness, and the influence of it, may well excite alarm, as it has done, even "in the seats of the mighty." There are nearly four hundred Negro newspapers published in this country, and they are prosperous as never before. Their circulation during the war period vastly increased, and new papers—all of the more outspoken and abler type—have subsequently sprung into existence. The colored people are fully informed of this, their papers make it a matter of rejoicing and pride. It is, indeed, a sign of the times.

We are informed by this press that a New Era has come, brought to birth by the World War; that with the New Era has appeared the New Negro: a man who stands erect and looks the white man in the face; a man who asks no odds, but a square deal; a man who does not cringe or fawn, "licking the hand that smites," but demands his rights under the Constitution,—equal opportunities in the common affairs of life, equal conditions, equal com-

forts, equal recognition for character and worth: in a word, Justice.

The World War and the Negro's part therein are responsible for it. Not, of course, for the origin of the principle of manhood in the Negro, but for its swift leaping into evidence, its sudden self-assertion in new tones. What we fought for the Negro fully appreciated. Why should he not have been able to? He was quick to apply that aim to himself—for the Negro is quick. President Wilson's notes and addresses, the Treaty and the League Covenant, had for the Negro the force of a new Emancipation Proclamation.

The colored press claimed—and rightly—great credit for itself in pushing the various war measures and promoting the drives. Papers of every kind, denominational, fraternal, secular, gave their columns freely to the stimulation of patriotism, appeals to race pride, exhortations to "go over the top," and instruction regarding the various requirements of the government. With all this went a strong championing of our humanitarian purposes in the war—the liberation of subject minority races, the righting of old wrongs, the making democracy prevail.

The Negroes' subscriptions to the liberty loans, to Red Cross funds, and the whole list, they quote as evidence of their patriotism and spirit in the country's time of need. It is a record of which they are justly proud. They make it the basis of democratic demands, quite naturally. Of the valor of their troops overseas they make the same argument. Those troops fought with endurance and heroism at Chateau Thierry and in the Argonne, and mingled their blood with that of the white soldiers in the dust of France. Those troops labored in the Service of Supplies at Bordeaux and Brest without counting the hours, counting only the loss to our cause of any slacking on their part. They buried the soldier dead— the most repellant task of the war—at Belleau Wood and Romaigne. This, while lynchings were being reported in their papers from home. Comparisons were inevitably made between Americans and Germans.

It is this story that has embittered the Negro. It is this story that has given a new potency to his newspaper. It will be found instructive to compare the two following poems with their dates. The first is a typical war poem, published in various weeklies during the period of the drives. This is the first of its two stanzas:

THERE'S NO ONE BUSTED YET
When I hear some folks complainin'
'Bout the burdens they must bear
Just to keep our soldiers fightin'
In the trenches "over there,"
Then I want to show a picture,
One I saw th' other day,
Of a little Belgian young 'un
An' her granny, old an' gray.
In each face was tears and terror,
Born of Teuton greed and lust,
An' I pledged my all to Freedom,
If to give my all I must.
Then a new song woke within me,
A refrain I can't forget;
"We'll all go broke if we haf' to—
But there's no one busted yet!"

WILLIAM HERSCHELL

That has the characteristic African light-heartedness. Now read these two stanzas of the second poem alluded to, of date February 1920. Its four omitted stanzas proceed climactically in biblical anathemas:

PRAY FOR YOUR ENEMIES
'Tis commanded in the scriptures
That we pray for our foes,
Even those who heap upon us
Our burdens and our woes.
I believe in this commandment
And shall take it unto me,
And for those who lynch the Negro
This my daily prayer shall be:—

May their days be "days of sorrow"
And their house the "house of death,"
And may dread and terror seize them
With the drawing of each breath.
May the pains their victims suffered—
Multiplied ten thousand fold—
Rend their very soul asunder
Till their errors they behold.

THEDORE [*SIC*] HENRY SHACKELFORD

There is no lack of evidence that the Negroes are going to their own papers in these days for their information and guidance. Those papers, in the small communities and rural districts, are coming to them from the large cities, preferably Northern cities—whose editors dwell in the "safety zone." In my own town, with a colored population of less than one thousand, I found the Chicago *Defender*, the Boston *Guardian*, the New York *Age*, the *Crisis*, the *Afro-American* (Baltimore), the *Washington Eagle*, the Richmond *Planet*, and the *Southwestern Christian Advocate* (New Orleans)—the last two being among the ablest and most outspoken papers in the country. But all these are "radical." Apparently the colored people of today will have nothing to do with any other kind.

To these papers and others of like quality the Negroes are going for the news, for trustworthy reports of "Negro uprisings," "Negro riots"—so-called by the white press—and lynchings, and for wrathful denunciations of them. The colored press is now the rival of colored pulpit influence. There are signs that it is coming into the first place. The Negro appreciates his newly discovered Fourth Estate.

Shortly after the Washington riot I decided that it would be a good thing to study the Negro's reactions to that occurrence. For there were two circumstances that gave it distinction: It was in our nation's capital, in the vicinity of the White House itself; and the Negro defended himself, did so with resolution and effectiveness. Therefore, sending to all the weeklies for sample copies, which were readily supplied me, I selected about seventy from the hundreds and subscribed for them. The generalizations and assertions contained in this article are based upon a careful reading and rereading of these stacks of weeklies, and some eight or ten monthly magazines. Eighty-five per cent of my newspapers are published south of the Mason and Dixon line. But my initial mustard seed of an idea germinated marvelously and "waxed into a great tree."

Was it not worth while to discover how the colored man was thinking on all matters pertaining to racial relations? Was it not worth while to get his point of view on racial adjustment, to learn definitely his complaints against us, to hear him state his remedies for the wrongs against which he protests? The least quantum of a sense of justice dictated an affirmative answer. Hence the application of myself to the Negro's newspapers—his one and only faithful exponent.

To convey an adequate impression of the tone and temper and effectiveness of the colored weekly press in these times is impossible in the compass of an article, which will not admit of extracts of any length. I must therefore resort to description. In a former period of racial distress the great Frederick Douglass, in the columns of his paper, *The North Star*, thus described the needs of the hour:

> At a time like this, scorching irony, not convincing argument is needed. Oh, had I the ability, and could I reach the nation's ear, I would pour out a fiery streak of biting ridicule, blasting reproach, withering sarcasm, and stern rebuke.
>
> For it is not light that is needed, but fire; it is not the gentle shower, but thunder. We need the storm, the whirlwind, and the earthquake.
>
> The feeling of this nation must be quickened; the conscience must be roused; the propriety of the nation must be startled; the hypocrisy of the nation must be exposed; and its crimes against God and man must be denounced.

These words seem to have been taken by many of the colored editors of this period as describing the forces of correction that should now be released. Their editorials fulfill the requirements.

But to make Douglass' description fit another large portion of the Afro-American press all the adjectives must be omitted or changed. The irony is not scorching, the ridicule not biting, the reproach not blasting, the sarcasm not withering, the rebuke not stern. How, then, can they be described? Their irony, ridicule, reproach, sarcasm, and rebuke are conveyed all by the method of "sweet reasonableness": mild comment, plain statement of fact, inverted exaggeration, subtle indirection, side remarks, and the gentle request to "look upon this picture, now upon that."

> YAZOO, MISS.—Because of her activity in selling colored newspapers here, Miss Pauline Willis, a young colored woman, has been ordered to leave town.
>
> VICKSBURG, MISS.—A white man raped a colored girl in Bovina, Miss., one day last week. Bovina is only four miles from Vicksburg, and in the same county. A charge was promptly made against him and he was arrested and placed in jail at Vicksburg, but not one word has been heard of the kerosene can, the rope, nor the outraged public conscience.

Effective? I think so. Scores of papers in the Black Belt are masters of the art. News items such as these sprinkle the front page.

There is usually a sting in the tail of the harmless-appearing little things—not deadly but disturbing.

Editorials one sentence long exhibit a similar self restraint:

> As long as American citizens are disfranchised, segregated, jim-crowed, lynched, brow-beaten, intimidated, held in contumely and contempt, victims of lawlessness, and mistreated generally because of their color, the riot spirit will be rampant—*Houston Informer*.

> Some one has said that our newspapers never have anything in them to make one smile. O yes, they do—read what some of the white Southerners think of a "square deal."—*Ibid*.

Even the feeblest of their papers will carry the news items of the Associated Negro Press and quote the stronger papers. The editorial columns of the *Southern Indicator* (Columbia, S.C.) on November the 1st, contain nothing racial, but on the front page, occupying the top two-thirds of a column, is a report of the most radical pronouncements of the National Race Congress, under the capitalized heading, "*National Race Congress Speaks Plainly to Nation. South Must Take Notice*." In the extended quotation of the Congress' "Address to the Country" this paragraph occurs, with others of like character:

> The migration of the Colored people now going on from the several Southern States is primarily due to the lack of safety of the home and is indicative of the fact that the Negro is sensible of the economic value of his labor. This movement clearly demonstrates to the South that all forms of prescription, Jim Crow cars, segregation, and lawlessness must cease; and better school facilities, better housing conditions, and better wages must be provided if the migration is to be checked.

Undoubtedly the Southern papers are in general milder in tone than the Northern, but not less comprehensive in their demands nor less firm in purpose. The same grievances are voiced, the same petitions and pleadings are set forth, the same rights are asserted and urged not less cogently. The Southern Negro's utterance of his protests, demands, determinations, and all that weighs upon his soul, suggests courage rather than boldness, and a sober sense of responsibility. The manifest restraint he imposes upon himself for the good of the cause, and for personal safety, only increases the force of his words, adding the pathos of entreaty to the cogency of argument.

Notwithstanding this moderation of tone—or perhaps because of it—the Southern papers get the messages delivered and make them understood.

We white people must give the colored people credit for more percipiency than we are wont to do. They have quite as good a faculty as we for reading between the lines, for taking the force of an innuendo, for perceiving the point of a bit of mild irony or gentle sarcasm. Vague and indirect pronouncements, perfectly harmless in appearance to us, are hand grenades to them. Editorial reticence they well understand to mean "safety first" for the editor, a longer career of usefulness.

But even some of the weeklies from which I take mild cracks—papers published within the bounds of the old Confederacy—can use the artillery of the skies desired by Douglass. Some of their braver neighbors in the large cities make constant use of this heavy artillery as well as of the small arms.

In almost every considerable Southern city, there are colored papers which, if not to be described as outspoken and "radical," one may well inquire how they are to be characterized and what they hold back unexpressed. Passing by Baltimore with its *Afro-American, Twice-a-Week Herald*, and Washington with its *Eagle* and *Bee*—though by all their traditions these are Southern cities; passing by St. Louis, with its *Argus* and *Independent-Clarion* and Kansas City with its *Sun* and *Call*—though these also are essentially Southern cities, come to the old capital of the Confederacy: Richmond has a weekly, the *Planet*, and a monthly, the *People's Pilot*, which vie with any Negro publications of New

York, Boston, or Chicago in radicalism. Savannah, Georgia, has its *Tribune*, of like character; Charleston, South Carolina, has its *Messenger*; Raleigh, North Carolina, its *Independent*; New Orleans, its *Southwestern Christian Advocate*; Arkansas, its Hot Springs *Echo*; Texas, its Houston *Informer* and Houston *Observer*, its Dallas *Express*, its Fort Worth *Hornet*; Arizona, its Phoenix *Tribune*; Oklahoma, its *Black Dispatch*: all of the same temper and spirit, purpose and vigor as the New York *Age*, the Boston *Chronicle*, and the Chicago *Defender*. Many more of like character might be named, but at this moment these particular ones stand out in my mind as representative of the aggressive, forceful and radical group. Do these papers represent the Southern Negro? Are they his spokesmen, his instructors, his leaders? It is unreasonable in the extreme to doubt it. They are the voice of the millions of colored folks south of the Mason and Dixon line.

The Negro's ability as a speaker in the pulpit and on the public rostrum has always been recognized. It is something new to find him mighty with the pen. But there are editorial writers not a few in the South who are quite a match for their white "contemporaries." They frequently find occasion to contest statements made in the white dailies, to challenge positions, to expose fallacies and inconsistencies, and to set argument against argument. In these polemics the Negro cannot be said to be found wanting. Seldom is there eloquence, seldom is there circumlocution, seldom any fine writing or pedantry, but there is straightforward speech, very telling in effect.

Besides, many of the papers large and small, are strengthened by the syndicated editorials of contributing editors. A half dozen able pens, the pens of university-trained men, are employed in this work regularly. Practically all the papers also report lectures, sermons, addresses, the resolutions of conferences and congresses, and other such matter that, even when the editorials are weak and inconsequential, carry to their readers the messages of the leaders.

Every paper has correspondents in all of its territory and in states beyond that might be supposed to be its territory. There are also news agencies. The most important of these by far is the Associated Negro Press. Through special correspondents in every city of the country it gathers the racial news and sends this out regularly to its large membership. About seventy-five papers receive these communications directly, but all get it sooner or later. Nothing racial escapes the Argus-eyed colored press.

> *There's a chiel amang ye takin' notes,*
> *And, faith, he'll print 'em.*

I have quoted two of the song-makers. There are a dozen whose work comes up to a high standard of expression. Their poems, pregnant with fire, are printed and reprinted throughout the entire colored press. They are not of the school of Dunbar—they are of the genus *New Negro*. No cause is greatly to be feared until it gets into song. But once the suffering heart, the wounded spirit has uttered the lyrical cry, the world pays attention, its conscience is pricked, its human feelings are rallied. The Negro poet of today has a flaming message.

The editorial writer, the reporter, and the poet are ably seconded by the picture-maker. A half-dozen very effective cartoonists are providing single papers or groups with the story of current events: riots, lynchings, travesties of justice, jim crowism, disfranchisement, and all the effects of racial prejudice and hate. Everybody can read a picture. Nor does the scene it conjures up fade out of the soul.

This press features two or three classes of items of a racial import. Equal prominence is given on the front page and in the head-lines to the wrongs and injustices inflicted upon the Negroes because of color, and to racial achievements, new activities, new business firms and enterprises, Negro benevolences, and the like. Race progress—race persecution: that is their main story. But a third species of news ranks close to these, sometimes taking precedence: news of movements on the part of the whites towards real race adjustment on the basis of justice, news of serious efforts toward racial coöperation [*sic*], news of forthright utterances in advocacy of their cause. This news they offer on their front page under conspicuous headlines.

The new-born prosperity of the Negro press signifies a corresponding neglect on the part of the colored people of the white press. They will not longer trust the whites to furnish them the news, to teach them how to think. Too often have they been beguiled. The saying now runs:—"There's a white man somewhere in the wood-pile." In the columns of the colored papers alongside of expressions of exultation in their own success run the severest arraignments of the white press for its falsification and suppression of racial news, for prejudiced comment, and for neglect of the Negro—except to report his crimes (alleged). The white papers by their false and flaring headlines and exaggerated, mainly fictitious, accounts of Negro assaults upon white women are denounced by the colored editors as responsible for practically all of the race riots of last year.

The universal radicalism of the Afro-American press—using that term in the sense of demanding a fundamental change; the almost absolute unanimity of that press in its statement of grievances and demands—many voices, but only one mind; the resoluteness of tone and manifest determination never to withdraw from the battle for "equal rights": these are the impressions that are the most outstanding with me from my much perusal of the weeklies that regularly load my study table.

The Editors
"The New Negro—What Is He?"

Messenger, August 1920

Our title was the subject of an editorial in the New York *Age* which formed the basis of an extensive symposium. Most of the replies, however, have been vague and nebulous. THE MESSENGER, therefore, undertakes to supply the New York Age and the general public with a definite and clear portrayal of the New Negro.

It is well nigh axiomatic that the most accurate test of what a man or institution or a movement is, is first, what its aims are; second, what its methods are, or how it expects to achieve its aims; and third, its general relations to current movements.

Now, what are the aims of the New Negro? The answer to this question will fall under three general heads, namely, political, economic, and social.

In politics, the New Negro, unlike the Old Negro, cannot be lulled into a false sense of security with political spoils and patronage. A job is not the price of his vote. He will not continue to accept political promissory notes from a political debtor, who has already had the power, but who has refused to satisfy his political obligations. The New Negro demands political equality. He recognizes the necessity of selective as well as elective representation. He realizes that so long as the Negro votes for the Republican or Democratic party, he will have only the right and privilege to elect but not to select his representatives. And he who selects the representatives controls the representative. The New Negro stands for universal suffrage.

A word about the economic aims of the New Negro. Here, as a worker, he demands the full product of his toil. His immediate aim is more wages, shorter hours and better working conditions. As a consumer, he seeks to buy in the market, commodities at the lowest possible price.

The social aims of the New Negro are decidedly different from those of the Old Negro. Here he stands for absolute and unequivocal "*social equality*." He realizes that there cannot be any qualified equality. He insists that a society which is based upon justice can only be a society composed of *social equals*. He insists upon identity of social treatment. With respect to intermarriage, he maintains that it is the only logical, sound and correct aim for the Negro to entertain. He realizes that the acceptance of laws against intermarriage is tantamount to the acceptance of the stigma of inferiority. Besides, laws against intermarriage expose Negro women to sexual exploitation, and deprive their offspring, by white men, of the right to inherit the property of their father. Statistics show that there are nearly four million mulattoes in America as a result of miscegenation.

So much then for the aims of the New Negro. A word now about his methods. It is with respect to methods that the essential difference between the New and the Old Negro relates.

First, the methods by which the New Negro expects to realize his political aims are radical. He would repudiate and discard both of the old parties—Republican and Democratic. His knowledge of political science enables him to see that a political organization must have an economic foundation. A party whose money comes from working people, must and will represent working people. Now, everybody concedes that the Negro is essentially a worker. There are no big capitalists among them. There are a few petit bourgeoisie, but the process of money concentration is destined to weed them out and drop them down into the ranks of the working class. In fact, the interests of all Negroes are tied up with the workers. Therefore, the Negro should support a working class political party. He is a fool or insane, who opposes his best interests by supporting his enemy. As workers, Negroes have nothing in common with their employers. The Negro wants high wages; the employer wants to pay low wages. The Negro wants to work short hours; the employer wants to work him long hours. Since this is true, it follows as a logical corollary that the Negro should not support the party of the employing class. Now, it is a question of fact that the Republican and Democratic Parties are parties of the employing or capitalist class.

On the economic field, the New Negro advocates that the Negro join the labor unions.

Wherever white unions discriminate against the Negro worker, then the only sensible thing to do is to form independent unions to fight both the white capitalists for more wages and shorter hours, on the one hand, and white labor unions for justice, on the other. It is folly for the Negro to fight labor organization because some white unions ignorantly ignore or oppose him. It is about as logical and wise as to repudiate and condemn writing on the ground that it is used by some crooks for forgery. As a consumer, he would organize cooperative societies to reduce the high cost of living.

The social methods are: education and physical action in self-defense. That education must constitute the basis of all action, is beyond the realm of question. And to fight back in self-defense, should be accepted as a matter of course. No one who will not fight to protect his life is fit to live. Self defense is recognized as a legitimate weapon in all civilized countries. Yet the Old Crowd Negroes have counseled the doctrine of non-resistance.

As to current movements, the Negro would accept, praise and support that which his enemies reject, condemn and oppose. He is tolerant. He would restore free speech, a free press and freedom of assemblage. He would release Debs. He would recognize the right of Russia to self determination. He is opposed to the Treaty and the League of Nations. Yet, he rejects Lodge's reservations. He knows that neither will help the people. As to Negro leaders, his object is to destroy them all and build up new ones.

Finally, the New Negro arrived upon the scene at the time of all other forward, progressive groups and movements—after the great world war. He is the product of the same world wide forces that have brought into being the great liberal and radical movements that are now seizing the reins of political, economic and social power in all of the civilized countries of the world.

His presence is inevitable in these times of economic chaos, political upheaval and social distress. Yes, there is a New Negro. And it is he who will pilot the Negro through this terrible hour of storm and stress.

Hodge Kirnon

"The New Negro & His Will to Manhood & Achievement"

Promoter, August 1920[33]

Every generation or every century witnesses the birth of a new spirit or a new idea which dominates and underlies the thoughts and actions of the people of that time. Their behavior in general springs from the prevailing sentiment and idea, and around which it is centered.

In our day, the prevailing idea which runs through all of our philosophy and actions is the "Will" idea. This is the idea of laying the greatest emphasis upon the power of the will, the individual and collective will and initiative to bring success in life, or in other words to secure individual, racial or national emancipation.

The writings of most of the leading thinkers of the day are pervaded with this spirit. The Christian Science and the New Thought movements are founded upon this sentiment and idea. The nucleus of their teachings is that one's relief from pain, and other forms of disagreeable sensations are to be secured through the strong and persistent direction of the Will upon things agreeable and pleasant—thus reducing all concentration upon pains to naught, by which all ills will be banished.

In common every day language, this idea manifests itself in such forms of expression as one having "get up," "grit," "nerve," "push,"—all of which mean that the "Will to Achievement," is powerful in that person. This simply means that the secret of success is in one's strong and strenuous application of will, initiative and perseverance to the affairs of life and the surrounding conditions. In other words, it means that to succeed, one must put determination and will into life, or, as a writer differently states it: "Our failure establishes only this: that our determination to succeed was not strong enough."

The Negro has been seized by this spirit. He has taken a real change of attitude and conduct. So great has been the change that he has designated himself under the name of "The New Negro."

The new terminology, "New Negro" has recently come into vogue. It is obvious that this term does not imply any new physical differences. It has a psychological interpretation, which means that the younger Negroes have taken a different outlook in life—have adopted a somewhat different behavior and attitude towards conditions which affect them in general. It remains to be seen what will be the ultimate results of these characteristics of the New Negro; but one thing is certain and that is that the Negro of today has taken an entirely different outlook and has adopted a decidedly different method towards life conditions. His party affiliation, literature, business activities, etc., are evidences enough in justification of this. It is even to be noted that the Negro Church, the most static and reactionary of Negro institutions, is beginning to show a slight change of attitude; and this is a hopeful sign.

True enough, this phrase "New Negro" is becoming somewhat overworked. It is becoming a catch-word for every Negro, without any understanding or feeling of its true meaning and significance, just as the word "democracy" became the by-word during the war, without the slightest idea or thought given its deeper meaning. Still more so is the fact that there are thousands of Negroes who are masquerading under the name of "New Negro," who are undoubtedly more conservative and servile than the oldest of the Old Negro is in spirit. Our memories are still fresh with instances of pre-war radical internationalists and socialists who, when the war broke out, exhibited more superficiality, mob-hysteria, nationalism and chauvinism than the most ardent nationalists and reactionaries.

Some of the outstanding differences between the Old Negro and the New Negro are that the Old Negro pleaded to the white man for mercy, whereas the New Negro demands jus-

Portrait of Hodge Kirnon by Alfred Stieglitz, 1917. Image © The Metropolitan Museum of Art. Image source Art Resource, NY.

tice; the Old Negro begged for help, the New Negro asks for an opportunity to help himself; the Old Negro appealed to the white man's sense of sympathy, the New Negro appeals to his sense of manhood and fairness; the Old Negro was servile and humble, the New Negro is aggressive and dignified; the Old Negro suppressed his manhood, the New Negro expresses his manhood; the Old Negro meekly asked for a chance to live, the New Negro demands the right and opportunity to live.

The Old Negro's actions and ways of thinking were more or less of a negative character, whilst the New Negro's are decidedly more positive and affirmative. Because of the long years of slavery and subjection under which the Negro was held, a broken manhood was the dominant trait with the large majority of Negroes. Any Negro who dared to manifest any degree of courage and aggressiveness in thought or action, was looked upon by the white man as a "nigger" out of his senses. Such a Negro was either openly or silently rebuked by his fellowmen of his race; hence it became the natural thing to look upon the Negro as a servile being. This servile, passive, yes-sah-boss attitude was interpreted by the white man as the natural psychology of the Negro race. He did not seem to comprehend the fact that this was nothing more than the result of several years of subjection, ill-treatment and ignorance, which the race was heavily subjected to. Even up to the present day, the white man, with but rare exceptions, seems incapable of understanding the New Negro. He is perplexed and puzzled over his radicalism in thought and action in every sphere of activity. Mental indolence and laziness, combined with age-long habitual wrong thinking and conclusions have prevented him from seeing the New Negro in the light of modern times and conditions. It is for these reasons why his attitude is hostile and unfriendly rather than sympathetic and sensible. It might also be said that a number of older Negroes share this unfriendly and hostile spirit towards the awakening of the younger Negroes. These are they who have been schooled in the slave or semi-slave atmosphere, and are there fore [*sic*] out of harmony with the

New Negro. They rightly belong to the class called the Old Negro and are to be more pitied than criticized.

Not less conspicuous is the fact that the Old Negro was a careless, happy-go-lucky, childishly optimistic sort of a creature. He never seemed to have taken his problems seriously to heart for any length of time. He never seemed to have interested himself seriously with any of the gigantic problems which confronted his race. Optimistic and hopeful as he was, his optimism was seldom, if ever, directed towards an earthly paradise, towards the day when justice would be applicable to him as to any other man. He was of the opinion, and this opinion was strengthened by blatantly ignorant clergymen, that his era and place of social justice would be after death and in heaven; and for this reason the oppression and injustice meted out to him in this world he considered providential and were therefore for his own good. He was also deeply imbued with the primitive Christian sentiment that God possessed some special benignant love for him, not necessarily for any acts of virtue on his part, but simply because he belonged to the oppressed classes, or was either too weak or ignorant to defend himself. His God was a lover of classes, not necessarily a lover of righteous conduct.

The New Negro is just the opposite in sentiment and thought. He is facing life with its realism. He is understanding that his problems are serious and must be treated seriously; and that they are to be solved in this world and must be done through perseverance and the will to conquest and achievement. . . .

The resolute and defiant spirit which is now the leading characteristic of the New Negro press is giving the white man cause for much anxiety. He views this change from a dog-like fealty to a tiger-like ferocity with awe and consternation. To him the Negro was so devoid of sense and feeling that it was deemed impossible for him to be affected by the World War and the frequent and fervid mouthings of democracy during that time. It was not thought that he would join the proletariat of the world in demanding the fulfillment of the pledges and promises made by the spokesmen of democracy.

Surpassing all of the foregoing in educational effectiveness, the New Negro press has shown a still wider contrast in its scope over the Old Negro press in its international spirit. The Old Negro press was nationalistic to the extreme, even at times manifesting antipathy and scorn for foreign born Negroes. One widely circulated paper went as far as to cast sarcasm and slur upon the dress, dialect, etc., of the West Indian Negro, and even advised their migration and deportation back to their native lands—a people who are in every way law abiding, thrifty and industrious. The new publications have eliminated all of this narrow national sentimental stupidity. They have advanced above this. They have recognized the oneness of interests and the kindredship between all Negro peoples the world over. As was said some time ago by a writer in one of our leading daily papers, "the same journal will advertise a delegation of Basuto chiefs to the British Government and the Jim-Crow car in Alabama. Between the British Empire and the United States, therefore, the Negro furnishes a new point of contact." This is nothing short of proof of the international spirit which is taking possession of the New Negro.

Another additional service which the New Negro press is rendering the Negro public is its explanation to its readers of the economic reasons for the silence and indifference of the leading white press on racial questions of vital importance. It is also bringing to light the economic reasons for the passiveness and the cringing attitude of our so-called leaders and the reactionary and conservative Negro press. Of course, everything cannot be explained in terms of economics. Other factors are to be taken into consideration; but it must be remembered that the power of the economic factor is in no way to be under-estimated.

One other notable distinguishing feature between the conservative press of the Old Negro

and the new radical publications is that the new publications consistently and regularly keep before the eyes of the Negro workmen how closely allied are their interests with white workers. They are shown as forcibly and as clearly as possible the necessity of the union with white workers for securing higher wages and better working conditions, just as the white workers are being shown by the radical white press.

The Negro is now getting more accurate, reliable and broader information upon matters of interest to the working classes through his press. Through this, his ignorant and sheepish following of the capitalist press will be greatly changed. He is not to be so easily duped nowadays. Professor Kerlin, in an article contributed to "Reedy's Mirror," said that the Negro is now disbelieving the ordinary newspapers on matters pertaining to the race question, and that he is going to his own press for trustworthy reports on any question concerning the race.

The New Negro journalism is strongly accentuating the common interests that Negroes all over the world have in common; also the identity of interests with the white workers. One of the ways in which this is done is by giving prominent publicity to news matter, editorial comments, etc., contained in the leading white press of progressive thought. Through these and other means, the Negro is now seeing and understanding that wars waged on weaker peoples which he has been instrumental in pushing to a success are really carried out in the direct interest of the big business interests of the capitalists. The Negro is now just beginning to realize what all liberal and progressive thinking white men have fully realized long ago. . . .

The New Negro has come to recognize the great truth that Life and Progress are positive forces—that nothing but the application of the principle of the Will to Manhood and Achievement will bring him into his own.

D. Hamilton Jackson
"Editorial"

Herald, September 13, 1920[34]

In one of his recent Campaign speeches, Senator Harding has come out in plain language for the Negro.

Very few presidential candidates have come out stronger. Of course, we Negroes are not yet *American Negroes*, and perhaps the Honorable Senator was not thinking of us in his speech. But as *American Nationals*, we are entitled to all the protection guaranteed AMERICAN CITIZENS by the American Flag, and by the Constitution of the United States.

In a very few months, we hope, Senator Harding, either from the Presidential Chair in the White House, or from his desk in the Senate Chamber, will have to give more than a passing glance at us down here.

The Philippines, in danger of being swallowed up commercially and otherwise by Japan, are coming to the foreground in the next opening session of Congress. These islands are rich in resources, and therefore America is not going to allow any other nation to take first place in the far East. So the Philippines situation will command attention in Congress.

But to return to Senator Harding's promise to the Negroes of America. The Senator knows the "New Negro" of America is not the type of 10 years ago. He is not going to be slapped upon one cheek and turn the other to be spat upon. No, the New Negro of America is demanding Justice. He is saying like Patrick Henry, "Give me Liberty or give me death."

David Hamilton Jackson, West Indian labor leader, ca. early 1900s. Courtesy of the Royal Danish Archive.

And from the part played by the Negro in the late World War, and from the Negro's splendid fight in self-defence in the recent race-riots in Chicago, Washington, and East St. Louis, the Washington authorities know the New Negro has now become a problem which cannot wait long for a solution.

We shall therefore take Senator Harding at his word "*Justice for the Negro*," and urge our colored friends throughout the United States to vote for Harding and a Republican Administration.

[D. H. J.]

Anonymous

"A. M. E. Church and Negro Movement"

The Black Man: A Journal Propagating the Interests of Workers throughout the African Continent, October 1, 1920[35]

We are extremely shaken by the statement published by the S.A. Delegates from the General Conference of the A.M.E. Church, which was in session during the last few months in the United States of America, of which the Rev. F. M. Gow appeared as the head of the delegates.[36] Though not wholly wedded with some of the objects of this movement, yet we must candidly confess that we are wholly wrapped up with the new Negro movement.

Nothing would bring nearer the salvation of the Black races from being continually exploited by the White race than the immediate return of our brothers and sisters from the land of banishment to the land of their progenitors, where they were taken only to be made hewers of wood and drawers of water by the authors of Christian civilization. What, in the name of Providence, will make us divert God's scheme of creation in preference to the White man's paradise, which is so abhorrent to humanity at large; to forsake members of our own family to the convenience of this big white master, whose principle of government is only to kill the Black man?

No sane leader of any nation will every allow himself to be the useful instrument of the enemies of his race like Rev. Gow and Co., only those who have made it a practice to court the favour of the White man at the expense of their poor people. We would like to know how many of the members of this denomination are in fa-vour of Africa, our only hope, being made a White man's country? If not, why then allow those divine gentlemen, who purport to represent you, and who, 35 years ago, championed the cause of severing relations with the White man's Church, to publish in the White man's paper such low and disgraceful statements to the detriment of the general welfare of our race here and abroad? We say the leadership of such men must come to an end. They are not at all fit to guide the sentiments and aspirations of the new Black man—their ranks is [*sic*] with those who are striving to make the land of our birth the ever-lasting habitation of the White race. Now that God has answered our prayers, the Black races of Africa must come together and strengthen the cause of brothers and sisters in America.

A new move to check the wishes of the Black race has been set afoot under the heading of "The 1820 Settlers."[37] The White people are contributing large sums of money to flood your country with new settlers from various European centres. In this scheme there appears to be no chance for a Black man, as the scheme is inaugurated for no other purpose than to hasten their dream of a White South Africa.

H.G., writing in L.S.D. of the 25th September (continuing) says:—"The Negros of the United States of America are discussing and passing resolutions in favour of the foundation of a Native South Africa. It behoves [*sic*] us to see that such a possibility is made impossible, and the best way to nullify such an effort is by effective white colonisation. We trust that the South African Government will immediately take the necessary steps to propagate this issue."

"The Umteleleli wa Bantu," an official organ of the Transvaal slave owners commenting on Sir Harry Johnstone's version on the Negro movements, the editor, in concluding, says:—In South Africa we have little to fear from the Afro-American activities, who—with all their numbers, opportunities, and resources—have done little to earn our respect; and that we should enter into a political alliance with them can be contemplated by none but those who suf-

fer from racial insanity. We won't be far wrong if we classify Gow and Co. with those insane subsidised agents of the White man, who say we must not claim our country from the White man. We don't ask that which does not belong to us. They can take their all, and leave us peaceful only to get back our country. The Negros in America don't ask to go to Australia, England, or France—they are coming back home to Africa, where Nature, together with us, put them. No settlers will run to Africa just to be turned out after a few years. The Negro movement is a reality, and the hand of the Almighty in it is very far from Sophistrism.

Africa for the Africans.

Anonymous
"The Negro Woman Voter"

Messenger, November 1920

AT last women have the vote, at least, the Susan B. Anthony Amendment, granting them the right of suffrage, has been ratified by the required number of states, and it has become a part of the Federal Constitution. However, from all reports from the South, Negro women, like Negro men, in that section of the country, have the right of suffrage only in name. Already, subterfuges and tricks are being employed to deprive the Negro women of their constitutional right to participate in the government which their taxes maintain.

The MESSENGER is not at all surprised at the attitude of the South toward the Negro woman voter. Could any one be so foolish as to believe that the South would enfranchise Negro women, while disfranchising Negro men? The so-called chivalry of white Southern men is a hypocritical farce. They are not even chivalrous to their own women. Why, haven't they got their women working in the fields and factories? Is this chivalry? It is reported that the worse form of child labor in America exists in the South,

and it is not black child labor either; it is white child labor.

The bourbon capitalists of the South don't want white working men to vote, to say nothing about black men.

It is reported that only 17 per cent of the white population of voting age, votes in the state of Virginia. White men are disfranchised by poll taxes.

What will Negro women in the North, East and West, who have the right to vote, do to help their Southern sisters?

Will they vote for the Republican party which has winked at the disfranchisement of Negro men in the South for the last 30 or 40 years? If they do, they are no better than ignorant Negro men. Their right to vote, is merely the right to keep themselves in economic, political and social serfdom. Negro women ought to be able to profit from the political record of Negro men. What is it? Here it is. Negro men have in every campaign voted for the Republican party, only to be rewarded with one or two political jobs for some hat-in-hand, me-too-boss Negro leader, whose stock in trade is to sell out for a mess of political pottage.

It is, indeed, pathetic to note the resignation of young intelligent Negro women to the ignorant leadership of the Old Crowd Negro women.

The MESSENGER calls upon the young, virile, aggressive, courageous, and intelligent Negro womanhood to repudiate and condemn this growing band of discredited, easily flattered, childish, well-meaning, but stupid, hand-picked Negro women political leaders.

It is an unpardonable crime against the children of this and coming generations that Negro motherhood shall be dragged down and debauched by shameless and disgraceful schemes and tricks of cunning, unscrupulous, wicked and corrupt Negro and white Republican and Democratic politicians.

Already the slavish grin and hee-haw laugh of old, decrepit Negro women, when addressed by so-called big, rich, respectable white men and women politicians, are creating disgust and shame in the hearts of the New Negro men and women.

Now, the editors of the MESSENGER are tolerant, but they are impatient of ignorance and servility. Of course, we are not surprised at the present trend of Negro women in politics. What else could be expected. They are the wives, sisters, mothers and sweethearts of credulous, ignorant, infantile Negro men who boast about voting for the grand old Republican party, while they are mobbed, burned, lynched, jim-crowed and disfranchised in the South.

The political ideals of Negro men are a back-stairs, messenger boy's lackey job as a reward for a beer and sandwich, buck and wing, crap-shooting campaign they have carried on for some weak, colorless, insipid, designing, com-promising, time-serving, criminal white capitalist Republican and Democratic politicians.

We want Negro women to stand up and fight as the political, economic and social equals of their white sisters.

The MESSENGER editors know Negro women who are the equals in intellect, courage and responsibility of any white women. They are in every state, city and hamlet of the country. They have come out of the country. They have come out of the best schools and colleges of America. They are ready, willing and able to assume the leadership of their people, but they are cowed, brow-beaten, intimidated, discouraged and elbowed aside by old, ignorant, lickspittling, sycophant, slave-psychology Negro men and women who have been bought and paid for by the money-power of the country, which profits by keeping the Negro marking time.

We appeal to the forward looking radical Negro womanhood to show their true colors, show their brains by breaking away from a leadership which gets you nowhere.

This is an age of thought, of progress. Don't be deceived by the political tommy-rot of Negro and white political hirelings who are paid to lie. Let us not mark time; let us catch up with the political vanguard of mankind.

All women, black and white, will benefit from the defeat of the Republican and Democratic parties, for these are the parties that foster and perpetuate the shameless trade of prostitution. They drive young tender girlhood upon the public highways to sell their souls for gold, by protecting the capitalists who rob the black and white working girls in the factories, on the fields, and in the mills.

In this campaign, you can strike a blow for the freedom of your class, your race and your sex by voting for Debs, and the whole Socialist ticket.

Anonymous

"A Desideratum"

Sierra Leone Weekly News, December 11, 1920[38]

United West Africa

The booklet entitled "United West Africa" bearing the imprimatur of the Hon. CASELY HAYFORD, M.B.E., a pure African and a Native of the Gold Coast and which has been advertised by this Office, is the latest literary output of the well-known Gold Coast Barrister.[39] Mr. HAYFORD whose pen is, for a Negro, both prolific and powerful, has written "Ethiopia Unbound" dedicated to the sons of Ethiopia the wide world over, and "Gold Coast: Native Institutions" which is a literary attempt to indicate the true nature of the problem which Great Britain has to face in her administration of the Gold Coast and her hinterland.

In these last days men have been mouthing phrases in Negro Africa which is the result of certain real changes that are coming to pass. The phrase "New Negro" appears to hav[e] come to stay specially among our young people; and the words "patriot" and "patriotism" stir the emotion of men and women from one extremity of West Africa to the other.

There is this pity. In mouthing phrases the average West African does not stay to find out the true meanings of the phrase he utters or the words. In consequence he speaks a lot, blusters a lot, but almost always rests there. To find out the true meanings of words is to get down to depths where power is derived and inspiration.

For instance, what a wealth of meaning lies hidden in the expression "New Negro!" To catch the meaning at the foundations is to become converted—to turn from darkness of ignorance and laissez-faire to the light of knowledge, race-consciousness and what not? We need teaching[.] We need teachers. We of the NEWS affirm that at the present a vast deal is waiting to be done and it is not Europeans that shall do it for us.

A patriot is not a man in whom the emotion is stirred when he hears the name of his country mentioned, or is told in a lecture that the well-being of his land is at stake. We do not sneer at emotion of the kind but we say that a patriotism which is mere sentiment is without foundation, and may evaporate at any time.

Patriotism, says one who knows, is more than a sentiment. It is a **conviction** based upon a comprehension of the duties of a citizen and a **determination** loyally to perform such duties. Patriotism is love of country born of familiarity with its history, reverence for its institutions and faith in its possibilities. Tried by this description Mr. CASELY HAYFORD takes his place in the very front rank of Negro patriots.

A man is not a patriot because he is a lawyer. Certainly not. But if being a lawyer he employs his energy of mind and force of intellect in expounding to men of his race the [virtues?] that he [illegible] in them and the potentialities which they could, by effort on right lines, materialize for the benefit of their country, that man is certainly a patriot and deserves the reverence, the affection, and the gratitude of all who bear the same colour and the same ground-plan of soul and spirit like himself.

We believe that there are several talented men in West Africa, men who are sons of the soil. But they are useless not being patriots. They die unheard of, unhonou[r]ed, and unsung because they did a thing for world benefit; and even if, catching a temporary inspiration they made a beginning they were held back by their selfishness. They are not idealistic. Is a true patriot born, then, and not made as some people tell us the poet is? Is the patriot born with a patriotic texture of soul? We leave this thought for others to work out. But if a patriot is born not made then men like CASELY HAYFORD are the choice gifts of GOD to their race and we bid Mr. HAYFORD hearken

Joseph Ephraim Casely Hayford. Courtesy of Bright Kojo Botwe, director, Needmet International.

and push on—burning himself for his race until he has burnt to the socket.

But a country like West Africa which is gifted by GOD with men of the calibre and soul-quality of the late Dr. BLYDEN and of Mr. CASELY HAYFORD ought to be a country that stoops to learn, *attends* to learn and seeks to learn from these great minds. The awfully slow progress of West Africa at the present is due in our opinion not so much to hindrances from without as to hindrances from within. To debar an eagle from soaring into the empyrean that has spread his wings purposefully for a flight is not an easy thing. He is stirred and he must go. And if you stop him dead you must be extraordinarily powerful. Similarly, our enemies could do very little against us if we should be stirred from the depths for a forward move. The trouble is with ourselves. We are not stirred. If stirred we are not stirred to the depths. And why? We do not listen to, do not study with interest the mind and speech of our teachers. The plague of West Africa to-day is materialism. The Negro there has been inoculated with the virus of money-getting and he has become the man with the muck-rake.

Now, even money getting is allied in a degree to real character and people gets or ought to get its character from its best teachers.

Dr. BLYDEN is dead; but where in West Africa can be found his writings beginning with the early volume "From West Africa to Palestine" and ending with Christianity, Islam, and the Negro and certain other minor writings? And even if these may be hunted out, who is studying them among Negroes of West Africa? Are the vital principles therein contained being expounded in the schools where true Negro character has got to be made? And HENRY HAROLD LARDNER, the man devoted to agricultural pursuits, who died feeling and preaching that the prosperity of West Africa lay in devotion to agricultural pursuits.[40] Where are LARDNER's books and who is studying them? Rather it is all PLATO, all THUCYDIDES—men who in their inwardness of thought and intention are aliens to the Negro?

The Negro of West Africa has got to study his own teachers and where their thoughts are true, they have to be followed; and only along this line is there hope for the future of our portion of the great Negro continent. . . .

W. E. B. Du Bois
"The Damnation of Women"

In *Darkwater: Voices from within the Veil*, 1920

I REMEMBER four women of my boyhood: my mother, cousin Inez, Emma, and Ide Fuller. They represented the problem of the widow, the wife, the maiden, and the outcast. They were, in color, brown and light-brown, yellow with brown freckles, and white. They existed not for themselves, but for men; they were named after the men to whom they were related and not after the fashion of their own souls.

They were not beings, they were relations and these relations were enfilmed with mystery and secrecy. We did not know the truth or believe it when we heard it. Motherhood! What was it? We did not know or greatly care. My mother and I were good chums. I liked her. After she was dead I loved her with a fierce sense of personal loss.

Inez was a pretty, brown cousin who married. What was marriage? We did not know, neither did she, poor thing! It came to mean for her a litter of children, poverty, a drunken, cruel companion, sickness, and death. Why?

There was no sweeter sight than Emma,— slim, straight, and dainty, darkly flushed with the passion of youth; but her life was a wild, awful struggle to crush her natural, fierce joy of love. She crushed it and became a cold, calculating mockery.

Last there was that awful outcast of the town, the white woman, Ide Fuller. What she was, we did not know. She stood to us as embodied filth and wrong,—but whose filth, whose wrong?

Grown up I see the problem of these women transfused; I hear all about me the unanswered call of youthful love, none the less glorious because of its clean, honest, physical passion. Why unanswered? Because the youth are too poor to marry or if they marry, too poor to have children. They turn aside, then, in three directions: to marry for support, to what men call shame, or to that which is more evil than nothing. It is an unendurable paradox; it must be changed or the bases of culture will totter and fall.

The world wants healthy babies and intelligent workers. Today we refuse to allow the combination and force thousands of intelligent workers to go childless at a horrible expenditure of moral force, or we damn them if they break our idiotic conventions. Only at the sacrifice of intelligence and the chance to do their best work can the majority of modern women bear children. This is the damnation of women.

All womanhood is hampered today because the world on which it is emerging is a world that tries to worship both virgins and mothers and in the end despises motherhood and despoils virgins.

The future woman must have a life work and economic independence. She must have knowledge. She must have the right of motherhood at her own discretion. The present mincing horror at free womanhood must pass if we are ever to be rid of the bestiality of free manhood; not by guarding the weak in weakness do we gain strength, but by making weakness free and strong.

The world must choose the free woman or the white wraith of the prostitute. Today it wavers between the prostitute and the nun. Civilization must show two things: the glory and beauty of creating life and the need and duty of power and intelligence. This and this only will make the perfect marriage of love and work.

> God is Love,
> Love is God;
> There is no God but Love
> And Work is His Prophet!

All this of woman,—but what of black women? . . .

The father and his worship is Asia; Europe is the precocious, self-centered, forward-striving child; but the land of the mother is and was Africa. In subtle and mysterious way, despite her curious history, her slavery, polygamy, and toil, the spell of the African mother pervades her land. Isis, the mother, is still titular goddess, in thought if not in name, of the dark continent. Nor does this all seem to be solely a survival of the historic matriarchate through which all nations pass,—it appears to be more than this,—as if the great black race in passing up the steps of human culture gave the world, not only the Iron Age, the cultivation of the soil, and the domestication of animals, but also, in peculiar emphasis, the mother-idea.

"No mother can love more tenderly and none is more tenderly loved than the Negro mother," writes Schneider. Robin tells of the slave who bought his mother's freedom instead of his own. Mungo Park writes: "Everywhere in Africa, I have noticed that no greater affront can be offered a Negro than insulting his mother. 'Strike me,' cries a Mandingo to his enemy, 'but revile not my mother!'" And the Krus and Fantis say the same. The peoples on the Zambezi and the great lakes cry in sudden fear or joy: "O, my mother!" And the Herero swears (endless oath) "By my mother's tears!" "As the mist in the swamps," cries the Angola Negro, "so lives the love of father and mother."

A student of the present Gold Coast life describes the work of the village headman, and adds: "It is a difficult task that he is set to, but in this matter he has all-powerful helpers in the female members of the family, who will be either the aunts or the sisters or the cousins or the nieces of the headman, and as their interests are identical with his in every particular, the good women spontaneously train up their children to implicit obedience to the headman, whose rule in the family thus becomes a simple and an easy matter. 'The hand that rocks the cradle rules the world.' What a power for good in the native state system would the mothers of the Gold Coast and Ashanti become by judicious training upon native lines!"

Schweinfurth declares of one tribe: "A bond between mother and child which lasts for life is the measure of affection shown among the Dyoor" and Ratzel adds:

> Agreeable to the natural relation the mother stands first among the chief influences affecting the children. From the Zulus to the Waganda, we find the mother the most influential counsellor at the court of ferocious sovereigns, like Chaka or Mtesa; sometimes sisters take her place. Thus even with chiefs who possess wives by hundreds the bonds of blood are the strongest and that the woman, though often heavily burdened, is in herself held in no small esteem among the Negroes is clear from the numerous Negro queens, from the medicine women, from the participation in public meetings permitted to women by many Negro peoples.

As I remember through memories of others, backward among my own family, it is the mother I ever recall,—the little, far-off mother of my grandmothers, who sobbed her life away in song, longing for her lost palm-trees and scented waters; the tall and bronzen grandmother, with beaked nose and shrewish eyes, who loved and scolded her black and laughing husband as he smoked lazily in his high oak chair; above all, my own mother, with all her soft brownness,—the brown velvet of her skin, the sorrowful black-brown of her eyes, and the tiny brown-capped waves of her midnight hair as it lay new parted on her forehead. All the way back in these dim distances it is mothers and mothers of mothers who seem to count, while fathers are shadowy memories.

Upon this African mother-idea, the westward slave trade and American slavery struck like doom. In the cruel exigencies of the traffic in men and in the sudden, unprepared emancipation the great pendulum of social equilibrium swung from a time, in 1800,—when America had but eight or less black women to every ten black men,—all too swiftly to a day, in 1870,—when there were nearly eleven women to ten men in our Negro population. This was but the outward numerical fact of social dislocation; within lay polygamy, polyandry, concubinage, and moral degradation. They fought against all this desperately, did these black slaves in the West Indies, especially among the half-free artisans; they set up their ancient household gods, and when Toussaint and Cristophe founded their kingdom in Haiti, it was based on old African tribal ties and beneath it was the mother-idea.

The crushing weight of slavery fell on black women. Under it there was no legal marriage, no legal family, no legal control over children. To be sure, custom and religion replaced here and there what the law denied, yet one has but to read advertisements like the following to see the hell beneath the system:

> One hundred dollars reward will be given for my two fellows, Abram and Frank. Abram has a wife at Colonel Stewart's, in Liberty County, and a mother at Thunderbolt, and a sister in Savannah.
>
> "WILLIAM ROBERTS."

> Fifty dollars reward—Ran away from the subscriber a Negro girl named Maria. She is of a copper color, between thirteen and fourteen years of age—bareheaded and barefooted. She is small for her age—very sprightly and very likely. She stated she was going to see her mother at Maysville.
>
> "SANFORD THOMSON."

> Fifty dollars reward—Ran away from the subscriber his Negro man Pauladore, commonly called Paul. I understand General

R. Y. Hayne has purchased his wife and children from H. L. Pinckney, Esq., and has them now on his plantation at Goose Creek, where, no doubt, the fellow is frequently lurking.

"T. Davis."

The Presbyterian synod of Kentucky said to the churches under its care in 1835: "Brothers and sisters, parents and children, husbands and wives, are torn asunder and permitted to see each other no more. These acts are daily occurring in the midst of us. The shrieks and agony often witnessed on such occasions proclaim, with a trumpet tongue, the iniquity of our system. There is not a neighborhood where these heartrending scenes are not displayed. There is not a village or road that does not behold the sad procession of manacled outcasts whose mournful countenances tell that they are exiled by force from all that their hearts hold dear."

A sister of a president of the United States declared: "We Southern ladies are complimented with the names of wives, but we are only the mistresses of seraglios." . . .

Alexander Crummell once said of his sister in the blood: "In her girlhood all the delicate tenderness of her sex has been rudely outraged. In the field, in the rude cabin, in the press-room, in the factory she was thrown into the companionship of coarse and ignorant men. No chance was given her for delicate reserve or tender modesty. From her childhood she was the doomed victim of the grossest passion. All the virtues of her sex were utterly ignored. If the instinct of chastity asserted itself, then she had to fight like a tiger for the ownership and possession of her own person and ofttimes had to suffer pain and lacerations for her virtuous self-assertion. When she reached maturity, all the tender instincts of her womanhood were ruthlessly violated. At the age of marriage,—always prematurely anticipated under slavery—she was mated as the stock of the plantation were mated, not to be the companion of a loved and chosen husband, but to be the breeder of human cattle for the field or the auction block."

Down in such mire has the black motherhood of this race struggled,—starving its own wailing offspring to nurse to the world their swaggering masters; welding for its children chains which affronted even the moral sense of an unmoral world. Many a man and woman in the South have lived in wedlock as holy as Adam and Eve and brought forth their brown and golden children, but because the darker woman was helpless, her chivalrous and whiter mate could cast her off at his pleasure and publicly sneer at the body he had privately blasphemed.

I shall forgive the white South much in its final judgment day: I shall forgive its slavery, for slavery is a world-old habit; I shall forgive its fighting for a well-lost cause, and for remembering that struggle with tender tears; I shall forgive its so-called "pride of race," the passion of its hot blood, and even its dear, old, laughable strutting and posing; but one thing I shall never forgive, neither in this world nor the world to come: its wanton and continued and persistent insulting of the black womanhood which it sought and seeks to prostitute to its lust. I cannot forget that it is such Southern gentlemen into whose hands smug Northern hypocrites of today are seeking to place our women's eternal destiny,—men who insist upon withholding from my mother and wife and daughter those signs and appellations of courtesy and respect which elsewhere he withholds only from bawds and courtesans.

The result of this history of insult and degradation has been both fearful and glorious. It has birthed the haunting prostitute, the brawler, and the beast of burden; but it has also given the world an efficient womanhood, whose strength lies in its freedom and whose chastity was won in the teeth of temptation and not in prison and swaddling clothes.

To no modern race does its women mean so much as to the Negro nor come so near to the fulfilment of its meaning. As one of our women writes: "Only the black woman can say 'when and where I enter, in the quiet, undisputed dignity of my womanhood, without violence and without suing or special patronage, then and there the whole Negro race enters with me.'"

They came first, in earlier days, like foam flashing on dark, silent waters,—bits of stern, dark womanhood here and there tossed almost carelessly aloft to the world's notice. First and naturally they assumed the panoply of the ancient African mother of men, strong and black, whose very nature beat back the wilderness of oppression and contempt. Such a one was that cousin of my grandmother, whom western Massachusetts remembers as "Mum Bett." Scarred for life by a blow received in defense of a sister, she ran away to Great Barrington and was the first slave, or one of the first, to be declared free under the Bill of Rights of 1780. The son of the judge who freed her, writes:

> Even in her humble station, she had, when occasion required it, an air of command which conferred a degree of dignity and gave her an ascendancy over those of her rank, which is very unusual in persons of any rank or color. Her determined and resolute character, which enabled her to limit the ravages of Shay's mob, was manifested in her conduct and deportment during her whole life. She claimed no distinction, but it was yielded to her from her superior experience, energy, skill, and sagacity. Having known this woman as familiarly as I knew either of my parents, I cannot believe in the moral or physical inferiority of the race to which she belonged. The degradation of the African must have been otherwise caused than by natural inferiority.

It was such strong women that laid the foundations of the great Negro church of today, with its five million members and ninety millions of dollars in property. One of the early mothers of the church, Mary Still, writes thus quaintly, in the forties:

> When we were as castouts and spurned from the large churches, driven from our knees, pointed at by the proud, neglected by the careless, without a place of worship, Allen, faithful to the heavenly calling, came forward and laid the foundation of this connection. The women, like the women at

the sepulcher, were early to aid in laying the foundation of the temple and in helping to carry up the noble structure and in the name of their God set up their banner; most of our aged mothers are gone from this to a better state of things. Yet some linger still on their staves, watching with intense interest the ark as it moves over the tempestuous waves of opposition and ignorance. . . .

But the labors of these women stopped not here, for they knew well that they were subject to affliction and death. For the purpose of mutual aid, they banded themselves together in society capacity, that they might be better able to administer to each others' sufferings and to soften their own pillows. So we find the females in the early history of the church abounding in good works and in acts of true benevolence.

From such spiritual ancestry came two striking figures of war-time,—Harriet Tubman and Sojourner Truth. . . .

Such strong, primitive types of Negro womanhood in America seem to some to exhaust its capabilities. They know less of a not more worthy, but a finer type of black woman wherein trembles all of that delicate sense of beauty and striving for self-realization, which is as characteristic of the Negro soul as is its quaint strength and sweet laughter. George Washington wrote in grave and gentle courtesy to a Negro woman, in 1776, that he would "be happy to see" at his headquarters at any time, a person "to whom nature has been so liberal and beneficial in her dispensations." This child, Phillis Wheatley, sang her trite and halting strain to a world that wondered and could not produce her like. Measured today her muse was slight and yet, feeling her striving spirit, we call to her still in her own words:

"Through thickest glooms look back, immortal shade."

Perhaps even higher than strength and art loom human sympathy and sacrifice as characteristic of Negro womanhood. . . .

After the war the sacrifice of Negro women for freedom and uplift is one of the finest chapters in their history. Let one life typify all: Louise De Mortie, a free-born Virginia girl, had lived most of her life in Boston. Her high forehead, swelling lips, and dark eyes marked her for a woman of feeling and intellect. She began a successful career as a public reader. Then came the War and the Call. She went to the orphaned colored children of New Orleans,—out of freedom into insult and oppression and into the teeth of the yellow fever. She toiled and dreamed. In 1887 she had raised money and built an orphan home and that same year, in the thirty-fourth year of her young life, she died, saying simply: "I belong to God."

As I look about me today in this veiled world of mine, despite the noisier and more spectacular advance of my brothers, I instinctively feel and know that it is the five million women of my race who really count. Black women (and women whose grandmothers were black) are today furnishing our teachers; they are the main pillars of those social settlements which we call churches; and they have with small doubt raised three-fourths of our church property. If we have today, as seems likely, over a billion dollars of accumulated goods, who shall say how much of it has been wrung from the hearts of servant girls and washerwomen and women toilers in the fields? As makers of two million homes these women are today seeking in marvelous ways to show forth our strength and beauty and our conception of the truth.

In the United States in 1910 there were 4,931,882 women of Negro descent; over twelve hundred thousand of these were children, another million were girls and young women under twenty, and two and a half-million were adults. As a mass these women were unlettered,—a fourth of those from fifteen to twenty-five years of age were unable to write. These women are passing through, not only a moral, but an economic revolution. Their grandmothers married at twelve and fifteen, but twenty-seven per cent of these women today who have passed fifteen are still single.

Yet these black women toil and toil hard. There were in 1910 two and a half million Negro homes in the United States. Out of these homes walked daily to work two million women and girls over ten years of age,—over half of the colored female population as against a fifth in the case of white women. These, then, are a group of workers, fighting for their daily bread like men; independent and approaching economic freedom! They furnished a million farm laborers, 80,000 farmers, 22,000 teachers, 600,000 servants and washerwomen, and 50,000 in trades and merchandizing.

The family group, however, which is the ideal of the culture with which these folk have been born, is not based on the idea of an economically independent working mother. Rather its ideal harks back to the sheltered harem with the mother emerging at first as nurse and homemaker, while the man remains the sole breadwinner. What is the inevitable result of the clash of such ideals and such facts in the colored group? Broken families.

Among native white women one in ten is separated from her husband by death, divorce, or desertion. Among Negroes the ratio is one in seven. Is the cause racial? No, it is economic, because there is the same high ratio among the white foreign-born. The breaking up of the present family is the result of modern working and sex conditions and it hits the laborers with terrible force. The Negroes are put in a peculiarly difficult position, because the wage of the male breadwinner is below the standard, while the openings for colored women in certain lines of domestic work, and now in industries, are many. Thus while toil holds the father and brother in country and town at low wages, the sisters and mothers are called to the city. As a result the Negro women outnumber the men nine or ten to eight in many cities, making what Charlotte Gilman bluntly calls "cheap women."

What shall we say to this new economic equality in a great laboring class? Some people within and without the race deplore it. "Back to the homes with the women," they cry, "and higher wage for the men." But how impossible this is has been shown by war conditions. Cessation of foreign migration has raised Negro men's wages, to be sure—but it has not only raised Negro women's wages, it has opened to them a score of new avenues of earning a living. Indeed, here, in microcosm and with differences emphasizing sex equality, is the industrial history of labor in the 19th and 20th centuries. We cannot abolish the new economic freedom of women. We cannot imprison women again in a home or require them all on pain of death to be nurses and housekeepers.

What is today the message of these black women to America and to the world? The uplift of women is, next to the problem of the color line and the peace movement, our greatest modern cause. When, now, two of these movements—woman and color—combine in one, the combination has deep meaning.

In other years women's way was clear: to be beautiful, to be petted, to bear children. Such has been their theoretic destiny and if perchance they have been ugly, hurt, and barren, that has been forgotten with studied silence. In partial compensation for this narrowed destiny the white world has lavished its politeness on its womankind,—its chivalry and bows, its uncoverings and courtesies—all the accumulated homage disused for courts and kings and craving exercise. The revolt of white women against this preordained destiny has in these latter days reached splendid proportions, but it is the revolt of an aristocracy of brains and ability,—the middle class and rank and file still plod on in the appointed path, paid by the homage, the almost mocking homage, of men.

From black women of America, however, (and from some others, too, but chiefly from black women and their daughters' daughters) this gauze has been withheld and without semblance of such apology they have been frankly trodden under the feet of men. They are and have been objected to, apparently for reasons peculiarly exasperating to reasoning human beings. When in this world a man comes forward with a thought, a deed, a vision, we ask not, how does he look,—but what is his message? It is of but passing interest whether or not the messenger is beautiful or ugly,—the *message* is the

thing. This, which is axiomatic among men, has been in past ages but partially true if the messenger was a woman. The world still wants to ask that a woman primarily be pretty and if she is not, the mob pouts and asks querulously, "What else are women for?" Beauty "is its own excuse for being," but there are other excuses, as most men know, and when the white world objects to black women because it does not consider them beautiful, the black world of right asks two questions: "What is beauty?" and, "Suppose you think them ugly, what then? If ugliness and unconventionality and eccentricity of face and deed do not hinder men from doing the world's work and reaping the world's reward, why should it hinder women?"

Other things being equal, all of us, black and white, would prefer to be beautiful in face and form and suitably clothed; but most of us are not so, and one of the mightiest revolts of the century is against the devilish decree that no woman is a woman who is not by present standards a beautiful woman. This decree the black women of America have in large measure escaped from the first. Not being expected to be merely ornamental, they have girded themselves for work, instead of adorning their bodies only for play. Their sturdier minds have concluded that if a woman be clean, healthy, and educated, she is as pleasing as God wills and far more useful than most of her sisters. If in addition to this she is pink and white and straight-haired, and some of her fellow-men prefer this, well and good; but if she is black or brown and crowned in curled mists (and this to us is the most beautiful thing on earth), this is surely the flimsiest excuse for spiritual incarceration or banishment.

The very attempt to do this in the case of Negro Americans has strangely over-reached itself. By so much as the defective eyesight of the white world rejects black women as beauties, by so much the more it needs them as human beings,—an enviable alternative, as many a white woman knows. Consequently, for black women alone, as a group, "handsome is that handsome does" and they are asked to be no more beautiful than God made them, but they are asked to be efficient, to be strong, fertile, muscled, and able to work. If they marry, they must as independent workers be able to help support their children, for their men are paid on a scale which makes sole support of the family often impossible.

On the whole, colored working women are paid as well as white working women for similar work, save in some higher grades, while colored men get from one-fourth to three-fourths less than white men. The result is curious and three-fold: the economic independence of black women is increased, the breaking up of Negro families must be more frequent, and the number of illegitimate children is decreased more slowly among them than other evidences of culture are increased, just as was once true in Scotland and Bavaria.

What does this mean? It forecasts a mighty dilemma which the whole world of civilization, despite its will, must one time frankly face: the unhusbanded mother or the childless wife. God send us a world with woman's freedom and married motherhood inextricably wed, but until He sends it, I see more of future promise in the betrayed girl-mothers of the black belt than in the childless wives of the white North, and I have more respect for the colored servant who yields to her frank longing for motherhood than for her white sister who offers up children for clothes. Out of a sex freedom that today makes us shudder will come in time a day when we will no longer pay men for work they do not do, for the sake of their harem; we will pay women what they earn and insist on their working and earning it; we will allow those persons to vote who know enough to vote, whether they be black or female, white or male; and we will ward race suicide, not by further burdening the over-burdened, but by honoring motherhood, even when the sneaking father shirks his duty.

"Wait till the lady passes," said a Nashville white boy.

"She's no lady; she's a nigger," answered another.

So some few women are born free, and some amid insult and scarlet letters achieve freedom; but our women in black had freedom thrust contemptuously upon them. With that freedom they are buying an untrammeled independence and dear as is the price they pay for it, it will in the end be worth every taunt and groan. Today the dreams of the mothers are coming true. We have still our poverty and degradation, our lewdness and our cruel toil; but we have, too, a vast group of women of Negro blood who for strength of character, cleanness of soul, and unselfish devotion of purpose, is today easily the peer of any group of women in the civilized world. And more than that, in the great rank and file of our five million women we have the up-working of new revolutionary ideals, which must in time have vast influence on the thought and action of this land.

For this, their promise, and for their hard past, I honor the women of my race. Their beauty,—their dark and mysterious beauty of midnight eyes, crumpled hair, and soft, full-featured faces—is perhaps more to me than to you, because I was born to its warm and subtle spell; but their worth is yours as well as mine. No other women on earth could have emerged from the hell of force and temptation which once engulfed and still surrounds black women in America with half the modesty and womanliness that they retain. I have always felt like bowing myself before them in all abasement, searching to bring some tribute to these long-suffering victims, these burdened sisters of mine, whom the world, the wise, white world, loves to affront and ridicule and wantonly to insult. I have known the women of many lands and nations,—I have known and seen and lived beside them, but none have I known more sweetly feminine, more unswervingly loyal, more desperately earnest, and more instinctively pure in body and in soul than the daughters of my black mothers. This, then,—a little thing—to their memory and inspiration.

[Du Bois appends his poem "Children of the Moon" here.]

Anonymous
"The New Negro"

Bulawayo Chronicle, June 4, 1921[41]

FROM America comes cable news of a conflict between Whites and Blacks which must constitute a record even for the State of Oklahoma. A local race war is recorded in which seventy motor cars and half a dozen aeroplanes have been used in a fierce attack upon the coloured quarters. White Americans armed with rifles have fired indiscriminately into the houses of the negroes, and casualties are naturally numerous. Though the affair appears to have begun in the usual way with a real or reputed Black Peril case, it bears a far uglier appearance that [*sic*] the lamentable bloodshed at Bullhoek, near Queenstown, a fortnight ago,[42] [illegible] association between the two and there is satisfaction in knowing that the relationship between the white and coloured races in South Africa is such as to render impossible a lawless and blindly homicidal outbreak such as disgraced the Oklahoma town. The Bullhoek fatalities resulted from an attack on the police by a band of coloured fanatics who had been defying the law for months, and who had received countless warnings. The deaths were due to the police defending themselves—whether they could have restrained their weapons somewhat only a careful enquiry would show—and not to any exercise of vengeance or race hatred. Equally as desirable as an enquiry into the deaths of these Eastern Province natives would be an investigation as to how far the fanaticism of the "Israelites" was caused by the queer racial propaganda now proceeding amongst the Black races. Of such influences we had samples twenty years ago in the "Ethiopian" movement, which was followed by the Natal native rebellion of 1906.[43] In that rebellion the chief sufferers were not any semi-educated and propagandist coloured men, but the more ignorant natives, and the same may be said of Bullhoek.

A serious obligation rests with the Governments and White people of South Africa to see that our native races are given legitimate opportunities and encouragement for their advancement. This is not merely a duty owing by the Whites to a backward people, but is the only safe means of preventing the latter getting into the hands of ignorant visionaries and ambitious exploiters of their own colour. America is the centre of such movements, for the reason that there more than anywhere the negro has come into close contact with European civilization and has acquire some basis of moral and mental stamina. There have been and still are a good number of educated coloured men in America well qualified to instruct their fellows in matters of religion, industry and social organization. Of late, however, there has been such a development in the racial self-consciousness of the negro that it has burst outside the old, slow methods, and is reaching forward to startling developments. Perhaps this was inevitable, but the prospect is none the less disconcerting, having behind it an enormous mass of vague impulse in a setting of extraordinary capacity for taking the wrong line.

About two years have elapsed since we began to hear of the Universal Negro Improvement Association and African Communities League of the World. Like certain associations amongst less-educated Europeans, the organization mentioned is fond of extravagant designations, and its acknowledged chief is "His Highness, Gabriel Johnson, Potentate," Mayor of Monrovia, Liberia. The founder of the U.N.I.A. is a Jamaican negro named Garvey, who is credited with having secured within two years over 3,000,000 subscription members, who are distributed all over the United States and in British and other Colonies wherever negroes are found. So far, the movement does not appear to have completely conquered the religious organizations of the coloured peoples, apparently because it has struck at the roots of their old associations by preaching a new "Black religion," of which the aforesaid Potentate is to be the "Pope." But it is on industrial and political lines that the U.N.I.A. is [chiefly] working. Over a year ago it established the Black Star Line of steamships, which aims at linking up American, West Indian and African ports purely in negro interests. It is not likely that this would seriously compete with the White enterprise; but that is not the point, the apparent object being not competition, but exclusiveness. There is a strong commercial programme and an equally strong political one, each with it own heads and the two working in a close understanding. The fact that in America all coloured men are "negroes" has inevitably thrown on to the side of colour those few educated men of mixed race whose intellect is superior even to the average European standard. They are preaching the doctrine of "The New Negro," and demanding that he shall have a new status, not among the Whites, but in the world at large. A "constitution" has been published which says: "We believe in the freedom of Africa for the Negro people of the world and by the principle of Europe for the Europeans, and Asia for the Asiatics, we also demand Africa for the Africans at home and abroad."

There appears to be nothing in the reputed intention to ship America's ten million coloured people "back" to Africa, but it would be folly to ignore the preaching, in the United States and elsewhere, of the doctrine that a whole Continent—the one in which Rhodesia stands very near the centre—is the rightful property of the Black man. The leaders of the U.N.I.A. realize that there is a certain dignity for "the New Negro" in this claim, and in teaching them to

sing a national anthem, "Ethiopia, Thou Land of Our Fathers." The association between this movement and the Bullhoek affair is made clear by the leading native newspaper of South Africa, which takes a reasonable line about the "Israelites." A few days before the tragedy near Queenstown, "Imvo" said "The Israelites of Bullhoek are a tough lot. They have withstood the blandishments of the Native Affairs Commission and the Government to obey the laws of the country. The next step is with the Government, and the Israelites have left them no other course than that of coercion. That the Israelites take themselves seriously is clear from the fact that they have sent from Bullhoek emissaries to native chiefs to urge them to adopt the damnable doctrine to rise up against the Government and every white man."[44] [Illegible portion.]

The story of Garvey's Americans coming to assist them, or even the Kaiser and his son having visited them, is told with great gusto, and American aeroplanes have come as far as Queenstown from the territories. All this drivel is being circulated among the crowd. Yet we find the South African Native Congress passing resolutions against the action of the Government, whom they accuse of not respecting the "religious conviction" of a section of the Bantu people. One speaker, while asserting the loyalty of the native peoples, foretold that "under present conditions we shall come to a clash one day." It is the duty of White and Black to prevent the possibility of such a "clash" by mutual forbearance and the cultivation of mutual sympathy, and above all by the exercise of justice, which includes the encouragement of native progress educationally and socially.

Cyril Briggs
"To New Negroes Who Really Seek Liberation"

Pamphlet, African Blood Brotherhood, August 6, 1921

To the Delegates of the Second Negro International Convention and to the Negro Race in General

The GREAT BLACK Race is waking up to its strength with new longings for freedom and a determination to win for itself its rights as a People to live and prosper and enjoy the blessings of civilization. This new will for freedom and liberty manifests itself in the desire to organize into one strong body, the Negro People, so that they may as one man fight oppression, peonage and slavery wherever found.

There are gathered at the Second Negro International Convention the leaders of our people from many organizations and many lands.[45] May everyone of those present show himself worthy of his People, may everyone go forth from this congress proud of his record in the fulfillment of his duty to his race, may they go forth preparing our people to be ready for the occasion with a stern determination to bring nearer the day of emancipation.

Negroes of the World! To be equal to the occasion there must be but one purpose, and one organization with a strong discipline, and a strong center, whose commands must be obeyed. This organization must prepare our People for the manifold struggle. It must protect their lives, their material interests; it must educate and advance the cultural life of the Race; it must develop the fighting spirit of our people and keep high their morale. To accomplish these things there must be a clear evaluation of the forces of the enemy, his strength, his weaknesses, his methods of struggle, and out of a sound understanding of the enemy's position and strategy, there must evolve a plan and a program that will unite those worthy and proud of the Race into one army with one principal purpose: the emancipation of our People from oppression, bondage and slavery, and be it said here by us once for all: WOE TO THOSE WHO SHAMELESSLY FOR THEIR OWN PERSONAL AGGRANDIZEMENT AND GLORY SHALL TREAT LIGHTLY THE HONOR AND WELFARE OF THE RACE. . . .

In order to achieve, the above outlined purpose the African Blood Brotherhood delegation and other delegates of this Congress have adopted the following manifesto to the delegates of the Second Negro International Congress meeting in New York City during the month of August, 1921, to serve for their guidance during this history-making Congress.

Manifesto

The world is in the throes of unrest and transformation. Empires crumble into dust, kingdoms are overthrown, misery, starvation, pestilence and strife are stalking in the wake of the Great World War. The slaughter of millions for the benefit and advantage of profiteering capitalists has aroused the indignation of all the exploited and oppressed, new alignments take place, new ideas sweep the world, new organizations and powers arise. It is useful and necessary for us, the Negro people, to properly understand this situation, and to make it serviceable for our emancipation to foster the divisions in the camp of the enemy and make alliances that strengthen those that are with us.

The Negro People being a great Race, inhabiting many lands and continents, cannot escape the changes and vicissitudes of the situation. More than any other people they suffer from the tyranny and degradation of Imperialism. Nearly all of their countries on the African and American continents suffer the oppression of foreign capitalists and their governments. Thus Africa is partitioned among the big white Powers, all of whom keep up a well-equipped and strong army in their respective "colonies" to keep our people in subjection and to exploit them mercilessly. On the American continent the same situation is developing. One after the other the free Negro republics are being subjugated by American marines who establish a rule of terror, brutalizing and torturing our people. To openly revolt against these conditions while Capitalism is still in power in the big white countries would be equivalent to the committing of suicide. It is a rank illusion to imagine that by moving from one "colony" to another our people can escape oppression, for the same oppressor awaits us everywhere, always ready to mercilessly subjugate and exploit us, and even those few Negro countries which have retained a measure of freedom are dependent upon the toleration of the Big Powers and will no doubt be subjugated like all the others as soon as the Capitalists' greed for profit requires it.

There is but one great exception which stands out as a beacon of hope to all the oppressed.

The old autocratic despotism in Russia was overthrown after the defeat in the World War, and the oppressed took charge of the government. The new government which represents the interests of the former oppressed class: the workers and peasants, is conducting an aggressive struggle in behalf of the oppressed in all lands. It is fighting French and British as well as American Imperialism, it is liberating the oppressed small nations from the yoke of the big oppressors, it grants full freedom and self-determination to all oppressed upon their liberation. It has entered into treaties of brotherly protection with dark-skinned Persia and Afghanistan, Yellow China and Nationalist Turkey. It has also given genuine independence to Latvia, Azerbaijan, Georgia and hapless Armenia. The Workers' Republic of Soviet Russia recognizes that the world cannot exist half slave and half free, half in capitalist bondage and half in Communist freedom. Therefore, Russia's interest and many acts in behalf of the liberation of the Darker Peoples. Soviet Russia is to-day the greatest menace to Imperialism. Her doctrine of freedom and equality for all peoples is diametrically opposed to the doctrine of exploitation, oppression and degradation of

England, France and the United States. Because of this, Soviet Russia is fanatically hated and viciously attacked by the capitalist press and pulpit of those countries. But Negroes of the World! Be not misled! Remember that the day the European workers arise in "armed insurrection" against the capitalist exploiters of black and white toilers will be the day of your opportunity to conquer power and seize control on the continent of Africa. On that day, Negroes of the World, we must see to it that Negro troops are not available as "White Guards" to crush the rising power of the workers' revolution! On that day, Negro Comrades! the cause of the white workers will be the cause of the black workers, the cause of a free Africa the cause of a Europe freed from capitalist control.

Under the lead of the new power which has arisen in Russia there are millions of determined, well-organized, well-disciplined revolutionists before whom the Capitalists and Imperialists tremble in all lands. The revolution of the oppressed and exploited of their own race threatens to shake into dust their power. The only certain way, and therefore the best way, of reducing the enemy is to besiege and destroy him in his own land. Only then will the peoples in the "colonies" be able to successfully rise and free themselves from their aggressors. To attempt to fight our enemy without allying ourselves with all those forces that are seeking his destruction would be to destroy all hope of early success. For us, of our own accord, to choose the tactics he would have us choose would be the height of folly.

The A. B. B. [African Blood Brotherhood] challenges anyone to deny the correctness of this analysis. This being so, what shall be the task of the Negro People? What shall be their stand in relation to the World Situation? Their task shall be to ally themselves with the oppressed of all lands even now forming into one mighty army to accomplish the abolition of the exploitation, oppression and tyranny of the Capitalist Powers and to effect the establishment of a Commonwealth of free Republics, where each people according to its own choosing shall enjoy the blessings and good things of Life.

Thus, this Congress shall devise means to organize and prepare our people so that they shall be ready when needed to defend themselves, that they may be ready after the downfall of Capitalism to establish their own governments.

This Congress must devise means to raise and protect the standard of living of the Negro People.

This Congress must take a stand and devise means to stop the mob-murder of our People and to protect them against sinister secret societies of cracker whites, and to fight the ever expanding peonage system.

Out of this Congress there must emerge a federation of all existent Negro organizations, molding all Negro factions into one mighty and irresistible factor, governed and directed by a Central Body made up of representatives from all the major Negro organizations.

Unless these things are accomplished our people will not be able to display their solidarity and their strength, will not be able to make effective preparation, and this Congress will have been in vain, and its every delegate disgraced! . . .

Marcus Mosiah Garvey

"Speech on Disarmament Conference Delivered at Liberty Hall" [November 6, 1921]

From Marcus Garvey, *Philosophy and Opinions of Marcus Garvey, Part 2* (Paterson, NJ: Frank Cass, 1925)

Just at this time the world is again preparing for a reorganization. Since the war of 1914 the world became disorganized. Many conferences have been held, in which statesmen of all the reputable governments have taken part, for the purpose of settling a world policy, by which humanity and the world could return to normal. Several of the conferences were held in France, others in Switzerland and England. On the 11th of this month will assemble in Washington what is to be known as an Armament Conference.

At this conference statesmen from Great Britain and her self-governing dominions, statesmen from France, Japan, China, Norway, Holland and several other countries will there assemble and partake in the discussion for regulating the armaments of the world.

Every race will be represented at that conference except the Negro race. It is a sad confession to make, nevertheless it is true. The world wants to return to normal, and the only people preventing it from returning to normal,

apparently, are the white and yellow peoples, and they only are taken into account. I suppose after they have met and discussed the issues, the world will return to normal, but I believe someone has a second thought coming. I have no faith in the disarmament plan of the nations. I am a pessimist as far as disarmament goes. I do not believe that man will disarm until there is universal justice. Any attempt at disarming when half of the world oppresses the other half is but a farce, because the oppressed half will make somebody get armed sooner or later, and I hope Negroes will pay no attention to what is said and what is done at the conference. It does not concern you one bit.

Disarmament may sound good for heaven and paradise, but not for this world that we live in, where we have so many robbers and plunderers. You keep a pistol or a gun in your home because the robber is at large, and you are afraid while you sleep he will creep through the window or get through the door and make an attempt to rob your property; and because you know he is at large, and may pay you a visit, you sleep with a gun under your pillow. When all the burglars and all the robbers are put in jail, and we know they are in jail, then we will throw away our pistols and our guns. Now everybody knows that the robber—the thief—is at large; he is not only robbing domestic homes, he is robbing continents; he is robbing countries, and how do you expect, in the name of reason, for races and peoples to disarm when the thief is at large trying to get into your country, trying to get into your continent to take away your land—your birthright. The whole thing is a farce, and I trust no sensible Negro will pay any attention to it.

Negroes Must Arm through Organization

I am not advising you to arm now with the things they have, I am asking you to arm through organization; arm through preparedness. You do not want to have guns and bombs just now; you have no immediate use for them, so they can throw away those things if they want in Washington on Armistice Day. I am saying to the Negro people of the world, get armed with organization; get armed by coming together 400,000,000 strong. That is your weapon. Their weapon in the past has been big guns and explosive shells; your weapon must be universal organization. You are a people most favorably situated today for getting what you want through organization. Why? Because universally Negroes have a common cause; universally Negroes suffer from one common disadvantage. You are not like the other people in that respect. The white people cannot organize as you are organizing. Why? Because their society is disrupted—is in chaos. Why do I say this? They are so disrupted—they are in such chaos that they have to fight against themselves—capital fighting labor, labor fighting capital. There is no common cause between capital and labor, and, therefore, they cannot get together, and will never get together until they realize the virtue of justice—the virtue of equity to all mankind. You

have no fight among yourselves as between capital and labor, because all of us are laborers, therefore we need not be Socialists; we have no fight against party, because all of us are belonging to the "Suffering Party." So when it comes to organization we occupy a unique position.

England cannot organize with France, for England will be looking to rob France, and France looking to rob England, and they will be suspicious of each other. The white races will never get together. They have done so many injustices one to the other that between here and heaven they will never get together. Do you think Germany and England will ever get together? Do you think France and Germany will ever get together? They have no cause that is in common; but 400,000,000 Negroes have a cause that is in common, and that is why I pointed out to you that your strongest armament is organization, and not so much big guns and bomb-shells. Later on we may have to use some of those things, however, because it appears that some people cannot hear a human voice unless something is exploding nearby. Some people sleep too soundly, when it comes to a question of human rights, and you have to touch them up with something more than our ordinary human voice. . . .

The Aim of European Statesmen

It does not take the vision of a seer; it does not take the vision of a prophet, to see what the future will be to us, as a race, through the ambitions of the present-day statesmen of Europe.

They feel that they have a divine right because of the strength of arms; because of their highly developed power to go into any part of the world and occupy it, and hold it; if that part of the world is occupied by weaker peoples. The statesmen of today believe that might makes right, and until they get that feeling out of them, until they destroy that spirit, the world cannot disarm. They fail to take into consideration, they fail to take into account, that there are 400,000,000 black men in the world today and that these 400,000,000 people are not going to allow anybody to infringe upon their rights without asking the question why. They have been playing all kinds of dodges; they have been practicing all kinds of schemes and adopting all kinds of tactics, since the armistice was signed, to keep the Negro in his old-time place, but they have failed; they cannot successfully do it. When they created the emergency, they called the Negro to battle; they placed in the Negro's hands the gun and the sword; they told him to go out and kill—kill so that the side for which you are fighting might be victorious. The Negro killed. The Negro fought his way to victory and returned the standard with honor. After the battle was won, after the victory was declared, the Negro became a puzzle. He became a puzzle to Great Britain; he became a puzzle to France; he became a puzzle to America. The American Negro was no longer wanted in active service by the American Government. What did they do? They disarmed him; they took away his pistol and his gun before he landed, so that he could not do any harm with them, and they sent him back South without any armament. What did the Frenchman do? The Frenchman is puzzled up to now; they cannot send them back yet.

All this noise they have been making about Negro soldiers being on the Rhineland, it is not because the French want the Negro to be on the Rhineland so much, but they do not know where to send him.

And do you know what they are keeping those Negroes there for? Those Negroes may never be returned to Senegal; they may never be returned to Africa. Those Negroes probably will be kept in France until they die. With the knowledge they have gained in the four years of war, they do not want those Senegalese to go back to Africa. That is why they are now on the Rhineland, and these French statesmen come and tell us it is because they love Negroes so much why they are kept in France. It is because they fear the Negroes so much why they have kept those black Senegalese on the Rhineland and in France. . . .

The new Negro is going to strike back or is going to die; and if David Lloyd George, Briand and the different statesmen believe they can assemble in Washington, in London, in Paris, or anywhere and dispose of black people's property without first consulting them they make a big mistake, because we have reared many Fochs between 1914 and 1918 on the battlefields of France and Flanders. It will be a question later on of Foch meeting Foch.

Now the world of oppressed peoples have got the spirit of liberty and from far-off India we hear the cry of a free and independent India; from far-off Egypt we hear the cry of a free and independent Egypt. The Negro loves peace; the Negro likes to disarm, but the Negro says to the world, "Let us have justice; let us have equity; let us have freedom; let us have democracy indeed"; and I from Liberty Hall, on behalf of 400,000,000 Negroes, send a plea to the statesmen at Washington in their assembly on the question of disarmament, give the Negro the consideration due him; give the Hindoo the consideration due him; give the Egyptian the consideration due him; give the weaker peoples of the world the consideration due them, and let us disarm. But until then, I repeat, there will be wars and rumors of wars.

PART V

THE NEW NEGRO RENAISSANCE: PART ONE, 1922–1926

Eric Walrond
"Art and Propaganda"

Negro World, December 31, 1921

Ernest Boyd in the Literary Review criticizes the judges who awarded the coveted "Prix Goncourt" to Rene Marin, the Martiniquan Negro, whose "Batouala" they adjudged the best French novel of the year. Tied to the conventions of literature, Boyd found too many African words in the book; it is replete with crotchets and quavers and demisemiquavers. Ignoring the rules of rhetoric, the author plunges along at a desperate rate, forgetful of the landmarks of style, form, clarity. With all these things Mr. Boyd finds fault. Also, he sniffs at the introduction to the work, which is a carping, merciless indictment of the brutal colonial system of France. As far as Mr. Boyd can see, what on earth has all this to do with a work of art, a penetrating study of a savage chieftain? Incidentally, Mr. James Weldon Johnson throws a ray of light on the subject. Mr. Johnson tells us there is a tendency on the part of Negro poets to be propagandic. For this reason it is going to be very difficult for the American Negro poet to create a lasting work of art. He must first purge himself of the feelings and sufferings and emotions of an outraged being, and think and write along colorless sectionless lines. Hate, rancor, vituperation—all these things he must cleanse himself of. But is this possible? The Negro, for centuries to come, will never be able to divorce himself from the feeling that he has not had a square deal from the rest of mankind. His music is a piercing, yelping cry against his cruel enslavement. What little he has accomplished in the field of literature is confined to the life he knows best—the life of the underdog in revolt. So far he has ignored the most potent form of literary expression, the form that brought Marin the Goncourt award. When he does take it up, it is not going to be in any half-hearted, wishy washy manner, but straight from the shoulder, slashing, murdering, disemboweling! In the manner of H. L. Mencken!

Madeleine R. Smith
"The Negro Woman of Today"

Kansas City Call, April 27, 1923[1]

"By their fruits ye shall know them!" These words may fittingly be applied to the courageous Negro woman of today, the Negro woman who, through difficulties and hardships, is establishing for herself the standard that women of other races possess.

How many of us realize that the Negro woman of yesterday and of today are different yet not entirely different? The Negro woman of the red kerchief, the family pride who crooned melodies to her master's children, is no more. She went with the age of our grandmothers. Occasionally she is to be found in some old family, tucked away as an heirloom, but never in full glory as in days of old. Not entirely different, I have said, is the Negro woman of today, for she still has the same bigness of heart, the same faithfulness to duties and above all, the love of justice toward her fellow people.

Who is the daughter of the Negro woman now to us only a faint memory? The quiet, dignified woman who is working socially, politically, and educationally for the upbuilding of the Negro race. She is to be found in all the thinking, serious-minded women of the race. She is helping to solve the big problems confronting all Americans.

I dare say there are many of our white friends who are not acquainted with this new Negro woman. After a conference of Southern white and colored women, held especially to discuss race relations, a white woman writes thusly: "I have studied and worked and hoped to be of some little value. I realize the wrong conditions, but to feel that they are imbedded in a system which encases you is to feel impotent***** The only course is to hold fast to ideals***** The Negro woman has great ideals and sane plans, and the conference gave me a clue and a point of contact." These statements show that white women are just finding out the true qualities of the Negro woman.

Today men are asking: "Is the Negro woman in industry?" The answer is: "Yes, and she will remain in industry as long as the deal is fair." She is to be found doing the same kind of work the white woman is doing. It is true she is handicapped in many instances, but she is still persistent. During the World War, her reputation as a worker was established. In many instances she was found to do work equally as well as, and in some instances, better than the white woman.

How many of us know who the champion mail sorter of the United States is? It is not a white man nor a white woman, but a Negro woman, Miss Lulu Cargill. She beat the record of Miss Nina Holmes, of Detroit, who distributed 20,610 letters in an eight-hour test.

What does the name of Mrs. C. J. Walker bring to the mind? It brings the picture of a Negro girl bending over a wash tub—a girl, who, while toiling for her daily bread, saw a vision, and worked to make that vision real. Later it brings a picture of a successful business woman of wealth and social position, one of the greatest philanthropists the race has ever had.

There is another Negro woman in the business world whom we should not fail to mention. Mrs. Maggie L. Walker, of Richmond, Va., holds the distinction of being the first and only Negro woman president of a bank. In spite of traditional and present day handicaps, surely the Negro woman can rightfully claim a place in the busines [sic] world.

The Negro woman is showing her ability also along musical, social, professional, educational, and literary lines. Madame Emma Azalia Hackley was one of the greatest teachers of vocal music our race has ever possessed. Besides conducting song festivals throughout the country with masses of her own people, stimulating interest in their own songs and helping to get better tone effects, she has inspired many of the most talented of our race, including Mr. Clarence Cameron White, the eminent composer and violinist, and Mr. Carl R. Diton the composer and pianist. We are indebted to her for the coming to Hampton of our own Mr. R. Nathaniel Dett.

To Madame Hackley our race owes a debt of gratitude for unselfish devotion to the development of talent in the race.

Ruth Whitehead Whaley

"Closed Doors: A Study in Segregation"

Messenger, July 1923

In proportion as men differ in race, characteristics or ideas, just so much do they distrust, dislike and abuse each other. The more unlike the more disliked. The natural tendency of two unlike groups is to fear, hate and exterminate the other. The stronger or better trained group becomes the dominant power. It cries aloud its superiority. Any indignity heaped upon the other group is justified in the name of their inferiority. Inferiority is an old misnomer for injustice. It is not the unique product of present day conditions. Centuries ago the Romans justified their world plunder by calling their victims barbarians. The nobility of Europe looks down upon the peasant who feeds them. The Norman called the Saxon inferior. Of this inferiority complex the Negro in America has been and is the chief sufferer. He is called inferior because he is of a different race, different color, as an excuse for the indignity heaped upon him, a blame for irritated consciences. When two different groups are living side by side there arise animosities and prejudices born of their ignorance each of the other. They have a mutual desire to exploit and exterminate. By the dominant group the dominated is called a problem or menace. Thus in America the Negro Problem—where to relegate this Black People, in what manner best to quell each noble impulse of theirs, how to feed each base inclination—the solution of this problem has been the chief pursuit of a vast majority of white America.

The first solution attempted was slavery. But the economic advantage of unpaid free labor in the South over hired labor in the North was too great. Thus slavery was ended and incidentally and as collateral to the main issue the Negro was free.

The second solution suggested was colonization in some possession of the United States or in Africa. It was never accomplished. The South was never willing to give up the easily exploited Negro labor. The second solution was cast aside. The third solution attempted is segregation (not the voluntary collecting of Negroes as the word might denote) rather the closed door. Thus far and no farther shalt thou come.

Segregation! Volumes might be written about it. It is the Negro's nemesis. The evil of segregation lies not alone in being excluded or relegated, it goes far deeper—the heritage of thinking black, the segregated atmosphere, the reaction upon the dominant group. If segregation consisted in nothing more than separate schools, churches, housing districts, etc., that alone, as despicable and undesirable as it would be, could not constitute the menace we now face. The most insidious weapon of segregation is the atmosphere it carries. This separating and setting apart is the most virulent expression of vaunted superiority. The dividing line is so visible until being constantly seen it nurtures a particular train of thought, a distinct psychological reaction. Segregation is the chief exponent of "divine right of race." The tendency is for the dominant group to excuse and justify the segregation with false and illogical reasoning. They finally believe it. The segregated group becomes over-race-conscious, hates bitterly and loses the value of inter-relation. The justification offered for segregation is the inferiority of the Negro. The blight of segregation is the belief in his inferiority it engenders in both groups. It colors the treatment which the dominant group gives the segregated. It has an unwholesome effect upon the oppressed.

The "Negro's place" has usually been applied to him socially, industrially or educationally. But in recent years this place means also his residence. Segregation ordinances began to flourish in 1911. He must not live in certain restricted areas. To be more exact he must not own homes or reside in certain restricted white districts. No one objects if he lives in the same house as servant with his employer. But to live in his own house next door—the proximity was too great. The real reason seemed to be fear of social equality. The mere proximity was not dreaded by the character of the proximity. If as servant—no objection. If as owner, as resident—it couldn't be. It doesn't follow that segregation of the Negro in residential quarters will in any manner solve the "race problem." The knowledge of the average white person concerning the Negro whom he dislikes is meagre and usually based on hearsay, or knowledge of the servant class only. If they are to be forever separated by iron bars he will learn little more about him than he already knows. The acquaintance of one intelligent Negro would give him a different view of them perhaps. Why relegate the Negro to certain sections if his taste and purse lead him elsewhere, so long as he conducts himself properly? Industry segregates the Negro—the reason he is shiftless. Remember that where the Negro has been given fair opportunity he has proven these charges false. Segregation in industry begins in the Labor Unions—the irony of it—certain jobs are gladly given him: "that's his place." But many jobs are closed to him: of these we speak. When segregation does not flourish, the Negro's good record is excused as being exceptional in the particular instance referred to. Educational segregation is not a myth, for even yet there is a prevalent idea that classical and professional education should be denied Negroes generally. That in spite of the record of hundreds and thousands of Negro college and professional graduates. One underlying object to higher education is the knowledge that the educated Negroes will not be so easily exploited. Having been trained in the same arts and sciences there will be a closer consciousness between educated Negroes and educated whites, and Banquo's ghost—social equality—might become a reality. For it is folly to give persons the same advantages and contact during formative periods, then ask them to forget it all and accept benighted dogmas again. But social equality does not of necessity mean wholesale inter-marriage, or race amalgamation. It does mean that each person will have the right to choose any other person for social intercourse, friendship or marriage. And why not? In some sections the Negro has been barred from any part in political affairs through various ingenious schemes. Where he has been allowed free use of the ballot he has in most places until recently segregated himself. As in all other cases of segregation it has proved detrimental to him.

In the Negro world there is one figure who is the victim of a two-fold segregation and discrimination—the New Negro Woman. Woman's emancipation is strangely parallel with the Negro's struggle. Inferiority is the reason given for her oppression. She has been considered as a mere chattel, cowed and subdued, taught that she, like children, must be seen and

not heard. Petted as an ornament of the home, a plaything for the male, producer of a line of warriors and race builders. Lacking all chance for development, she is called inferior because she hasn't developed. The Negro woman falls heir to all these prejudices, and to add injury to distress she is a Negro. If there is any one person against whom the doors have been closed it is the New Negro Woman. As a woman she was outside her sphere. As a Negro woman she was impossible. In industry, education and politics she is gradually coming into her own. But remember her closed doors are of the thickness of two—she is first a woman, then a Negro. May the fates be kind to her!

A fair and thoughtful view of segregation leads one to believe that it is a futile gesture of the white man to the Negro. An expiring death groan ere the inevitable happens. It is impossible to stop the upward striving of the Negro by segregation; their progress may be retarded. But Time, the great winnower and sifter of truth, will aid them. The great mass of "exceptional Negroes," who have attained far more than Negroes are supposed to attain, are now to be reckoned with. Closer association of the races in cities of the North and East produces both good and bad results. Seeing more Negroes, they of necessity see more "bad Negroes," also more intelligent and ambitious Negroes than ever before. Theories are slowly and reluctantly being revised. The result is sometimes more segregation, sometimes less dependent upon the innate justice and honesty of that particular group.

But segregation as terrible as it is, the curse of segregated atmosphere as blighting as it is, will not forever be. The Egyptians and Babylonians once were supreme in power. They also enslaved and segregated. They are now a memory of history only. The ancestors of Horace and Socrates have so lost in prestige until Macauley says of them: "Their people have degenerated into timid slaves and their language into a barbarous jargon." The barbarians, of whom Aristotle said: "It is impossible for them to count beyond their fingers," did subsequently produce a Shakespeare and Newton. In the cycle of the years, the evolution and revolution of ideas and civilizations, the segregated Negro will also come into his own. He will lose his "inferiority" when and as he loses its mate, injustice. Finally the shadow will be lifted. The closed door swings ajar.

Anonymous
"The New Negro Woman"

Messenger, July 1923

Yes, she has arrived. Like her white sister, she is the product of profound and vital changes in our economic mechanism, wrought mainly by the World War and its aftermath. Along the entire gamut of social, economic and political attitudes, the New Negro Woman has effected a revolutionary orientation. In politics, business and labor, in the professions, church and education, in science, art and literature, the New Negro Woman, with her head erect and spirit undaunted is resolutely marching forward, ever conscious of her historic and noble mission of doing her bit toward the liberation of her people in particular and the human race in general. Upon her shoulders rests the big task to create and keep alive, in the breast of black men, a holy and consuming passion to break with the slave traditions of the past; to spurn and overcome the fatal, insidious inferiority complex of the present, which, like Banquo's Ghost, bobs up ever and anon, to arrest the progress of the New Negro Manhood Movement; and to fight with increasing vigor, with dauntless courage, unrelenting zeal and intelligent vision for the attainment of the stature of a *full man*, a free race and a new world.

Countee P. Cullen
"The League of Youth"

Crisis, August 1923
Speech delivered at Town Hall, New York

Youth the world over is undergoing a spiritual and an intellectual awakening, is looking with new eyes at old customs and institutions, and is finding for them interpretations which its parents passed over. Youth everywhere is mapping out a programme for itself, is banding together in groups whose members have a common interest. In some places these various youth movements, such as the German Youth Movement, are assuming proportions of such extent that they are being viewed with trepidation by those who desire to see things continue in the same rut, who do not wish the "old order to change, yielding place to new."

And so it is not to be wondered at that the young American Negro is having his Youth Movement also. We in America have not yet reached the stage where we can speak of an American Youth Movement, else I had not been asked to speak this afternoon. The American Negro's Youth Movement is less ostentatious than others, perhaps, but it is no less intense.

And if there is any group which is both a problem for itself and a problem for others, and which needs a movement for the solving of both it is the American Negro. Details and specific instances of what I mean may be met with daily segregation, discrimination, and just this past week the barring by an American board of a colored girl from entering The Art School at Fontain[e]bleau, France, because her presence *might* be objectionable to certain people who would be along, this supposed objection being based not on character, but on color. Surely where such conditions obtain a movement is needed. I may say that the majority of people, even my own people, do not realize that we are having a Youth Movement at all. It is not crying itself from the house tops. It is a somewhat subsurface affair like a number of small underground currents, each working its individual way along, yet all bound at length to come together.

In the first place the young American Negro is going in strong for education; he realizes its potentialities for combating bigotry and blindness. Those colleges which cater exclusively to our own people are filled to capacity, while the number of Negro students enrolled in other colleges in the country is yearly increasing. Basically it may be that this increased respect for education is selfish in the case of each individual without any concern for the group effect, but that is neither here nor there, the main point to be considered is that it is working a powerful group effect.

Then the New Negro is changing somewhat in his attitude toward the Deity. I would not have you misconstrue this statement. I do not mean that he is becoming less reverent, but that he is becoming less dependent. There is a stereotype by which most of you measure all Negroes. You think of a healthy, hearty fellow, easily provoked to laughter, liking nothing better than to be slapped on the back, and to be called a "good fellow"—and to leave all to God. The young Negro of today, while he realizes that religious fervor is a good thing for any people, and while he realizes that it and the Negro are fairly inseparable, also realizes that where it exists in excess it breeds stagnation, and passive acquiescence, where a little active resistance would work better results. The finest of lines divides the phrase "Let God do it," from the phrase "Let George do it." And there are some things which neither George nor God can do. There is such a thing as working out one's own soul's salvation. And that is what the New Negro intends to do.

Finally, if I may consider myself to be fairly representative of the Young American Negro, he feels that the elder generations of both Caucasian and colored Americans have not come to the best mutual understanding. I mean both North and South. For the misunderstanding is not one of sections, but is one of degree. In the South it is more candid and vehement and aboveboard; in the North where it does obtain it is sly and crafty and cloaks itself in the guise of kindness and is therefore more cruel. We have not yet reached the stage where we realize that whether we side with Darwin or with Bryan we all spring from a common progenitor.

There is a story of a little girl of four or five years of age who asked her father, "Daddy, where were you born?" "Why, I was born in San Francisco," said her father. "And where was mother born?" "Why, in Chicago." "And I, where was I born?" "In New York." The little girl thought this over for a while, the said, "Father was born in San Francisco, Mother in Chicago, and baby in New York. Isn't it wonderful how we all got together?" Wouldn't it be wonderful if we could all get together? The Young Negro feels that understanding means meeting one another half way. This League has taken a splendid forward step. Will it go further?

In the words of a Negro poet, I bring you a challenge:

> How would you have us? As we are?
> Or sinking 'neath the load we bear?
> Our eyes fixed forward on a star?
> Or gazing empty at despair?
> Rising or falling? Men or things?
> With dragging pace or footsteps fleet?

Strong willing sinews in your wings?
　　Or tightening chains about your feet?

It is a challenge to be weighed mightily. For we must be one thing or the other, an asset or a liability, the sinew in your wing to help you soar, or the chain to bind you to earth. You cannot go forward unless you take us with you, you can-not push back unless you retrograde as much yourself. Mr. President, I hope this league will accept my challenge and will answer it in the new spirit which seems to be animating youth everywhere—the spirit of what is just and fair and honorable.

Kelly Miller
"Kelly Miller Says: The New Negro"

Afro-American, September 21, 1923[2]

Over against this type of the white man's Negro (the "pliant" and "docile" Negro) there is developing a type of defiant, discourteous, contentious Negro who resents and resists the white man merely because he is white. These are found among the city toughs, quick with gun or razor to avenge any offense real or fancied which the white man commits against the Negro race.

We also find the same spirit in the reckless intelligentsia who denounce and condemn the white race without the least restraint of prudence or courtesy. With chip on shoulder. They are eager to fly into the fury at the slightest affront or insinuation. These are apt to arrogate to themselves all of the courage and manhood of the race, and to brand all others as cowards and trimmers who do not adopt their extreme position. Both extremes are equally dangerous to the best welfare of the race. Neither submission or defiance is calculated to secure the desired results.

THE SALVATION OF THE RACE DEPENDS UPON THAT TYPE OF NEGRO WHO IS INTELLIGENT, COURAGEOUS AND MANLY, WHO IS COURTEOUS, CONSIDERATE AND SENSIBLE, BUT WHO WILL NOT, IN ANY MOOD, COMPROMISE THE MANHOOD RIGHTS OF HIS RACE BY SERVILE SUBMISSION, NOR SACRIFICE THEM BY RASH INTEMPERATE OUTBREAK OF PASSION WHICH WOULD CURSE THE WHITE GOD AND DIE.

John Eight Point
"Sparks from the Fiery Cross"

Fiery Cross, November 23, 1923[3]

A Place for All

Marcus Garvey, self-styled provisional president of Africa, has never been taken very seriously by either white or colored man. Nevertheless, his statement to 2,000 Washington negroes that "the day has come when the new negro wants his place in the world" and "his place is in Africa" ought to receive the attention due it. Garvey's judgment is good when he remarks: "We are satisfied to let the white man have America and the white man have Europe. We are satisfied to let the yellow man have Asia, but we will fight to the last for Africa." This is only saying that there should be a place for everybody and everybody should be in his place!

Saydee E. Parham
"The New Woman"

Negro World, February 2, 1924

In the Political World She Is the Source of All Reform Legislation and the One Power That Is Humanizing the World.

All life is but a continuous process of evolution. Nothing that embodies the vitalic principle of life is static. It is by the very inherent law of nature that in the changing order of every species of life we find a higher, nobler and greater ascent of life. In the mineral kingdom with its amazing wealth of stones, we find this principle in the ever increasing change of the vast variety of the mineral life. And as we ascend the scale of elevation until we reach the mammal or the animal kingdom, we find that even here is a distinctive change in the physical, mental and biological condition of men and animals. There was a time when rough men fought the ferocious beasts of the forests with their naked hands and a mere bludgeon. Today they can silence the wildest animal with a rifle. And so, onward and upward the majestic drama of civilization is proceeding scene by scene, act by act in its glorious unfolding of the higher and nobler changes in the progress of her principal actor—woman. From the brow-beaten, dominated cave woman, cowering in fear at the mercy of her brutal mate; from the petted toy reared for the sensual indulgences of the Roman and Greek nobility, from the safely cloistered woman reared like a clinging vine, destitute of all initiative and independence—a product of the middle-ages, we find her at last rising to a pinnacle of power and glory so great, so potential that she has actually become the central figure of all modern civilization. In the business world, she is the master of the clerical detail work; in the factories she is the dynamo of production; in the theatre she is the most magnetic form of entertainment; in the political world she is the source of all reform legislation and the one power that is humanizing the world. In all great movements for the redemption of the oppressed masses, she is always ready and responsive to the great appeal, and this power generated by this great civilizer of all future civilization is the new woman!

Helen B. Sayre
"Negro Women in Industry"

Opportunity, August 1924[4]

The Negro woman's sudden entrance into industry is a new adventure and a dramatic innovation. In the urgent quest for workers to "carry on" during the World War, she saw her longed-for opportunity, saw—as she visioned it—the end of the rainbow, and she came seeking it by thousands from her sunny, quiet southern home and plantation and placid housework and was at once swallowed up in the industrial centers in northern cities. Plucked so abruptly from the narrow spheres of such service as field hands, domestics and children's nurses, it is amazing to observe the transition and transformation of this same gentle, leisurely southern woman into the high-tension industrial worker in a large factory. Labor turnover, time clocks, piece work, output, maximum and minimum production, these words were unknown in her vocabulary a few years back. But today there are thousands of these girls and women, working tirelessly and patiently and steadily in our large industrial plants,—and *making good*.

At the close of the War and during the general depression in business which followed, many Negro girls were released and replaced with white help. It was a tragedy to the Negro girl, as she had not had time to lay aside anything for the rainy day, to gain needed experience and skill, and to overcome the impatience of the average employer and an antagonistic foreman. She was hired in a period of crisis, to fill the gap at the bottom of the scale,—the most undesirable and unskilled jobs in the factory were assigned to her. The idea seemed very general that she could not be trusted to do the skilled work in any event—usually she was not given an opportunity if white help could be secured. Wet and sloppy work, heavy and tedious, with little chance for advancement, and if she did succeed, it was by sheer grit and determination, as many have told me. She had to be able to outdo her white competitor; sometimes she failed through lack of experience, and this would cause employers to say she was not capable, when in most cases it was simply due to poor selective instinct on his part or lack of intelligence or adaptability in her particular case.

Left to the mercy of ignorant, prejudiced, intolerant foremen, what could be expected? However, the whole story is not so dark. Though her progress was retarded by the turn in events, still we know that she did retain some very

worthwhile places and she has progressed in them wherever possible to semi-skilled and skilled jobs. It is worthy of note, that wherever an employer was humane and appreciative and gave his Negro help a chance to advance and a square deal in wages and working conditions, he had steady, cheerful workers—which refutes a charge so prone to be made about their being undependable. Employers have found her amiable in disposition, intelligent and more adaptable than the unskilled foreign worker for whom white social agencies are engaged in season and out to aid them to adjust themselves, develop technique and become capable, highly skilled workers. For the Negro girl there are no such agencies outside of a small work being done by the Y.W.C.A. in the City of Chicago. In my experience with both white and Negro girls, I have found no difference between them in capacity for work.

Negro women are working today in the stockyards, nut factories, hat factories, lamp shade and mantel light industries, leather products, tobacco factories, paper box factories, mattress industry, as beaders and embroiderers, and workers in the insulated wire factories; as power machine operators of all kinds, including cap, apron, bathrobe and dress-makers. Some of the best core-makers in the great McCormick harvester plant are Negro women. But it is unquestionably in the sewing field that the Negro girl finds her greatest opportunity. She has a natural aptitude for this work and has become a factor with which the trades union will have to consider. During the Garment Makers' strike in Chicago this spring, Negro women operators were employed in the strikers' places in large numbers. Many had had but little experience, and I heard of one firm that had employed three different sets of ninety operators in less than three months. Efforts were made to induce these girls to join the Union. I have been informed by a young Negro woman who belonged to the Union and who had organized the shop in which she worked, that the Union has always had an open door for Negro women.

The Garment Makers are mostly recruited from the Jews and the Poles and as such they are designated on the books, but the Negro members are always classed as Americans. This is rather interesting, I think—however, it is hard to get Negro girls into the Union. One reason is that they cannot join unless experienced. They argue that this is their chance to gain experience; joining the Union can come later. The value of collective bargaining is a matter of education, and industrial education is what is greatly needed to help the Negro girl stabilize her position in the labor world.

The story of the Negro women employed at the Nachman Springfilled Cushion Company of Chicago, Illinois, may be of some value in understanding the whole situation. It will also show the splendid growth of a business whose enviable record for superior quality and excellence in manufactured products is the output of these same women power machine operators, who make the durable covers for the softly resilient springs.

In the beginning this company employed less than fifty persons. It was a simple matter for the heads of the firm to know each individual worker. Today there are between six and seven hundred on the pay-roll. The employment of such large numbers has tended to destroy any personal relation between employer and employees, and there is practically no contact with the workers. The making of these cushion covers was also a simple process in the beginning; they were used mostly for chair seats, and a perfectly "green" girl who had never seen a power machine before could learn in a very few days to sew them. Today this firm manufactures cushions for all kinds of upholstered furniture, daybeds, mattresses, and automobile seats. Each unit-spring is enclosed in a separate pocket and these covers are made in two operations.

When I tell you we have girls who can sew from five to seven thousand pockets in a day, you will realize that they have become "peppy" and mastered the speeding-up in industry. They are put on piece work in about three weeks and we have many girls making from twenty to thirty dollars per week. An average girl can make eighteen dollars per week. This is good pay for a year round job.

There came a time when this large group of girls, with no previous factory experience and no one to encourage and reprove them or give them any personal attention whatever, were doing about as they pleased. They were very irregular in attendance,—a very serious matter to the firm, in trying to give prompt service and keep up production.

The cushion is an unfinished product and is delivered in large quantities to factories to be upholstered. The girls would say, "If we stay out we are the only losers, being on piece work." So the week would go something like this: Monday— bad; Tuesday—a little better; Wednesday—very good, being pay day; Thursday—very poor; Friday—somewhat better; Saturday—a half-day and the worst day of the week. The company was about three months behind in delivery of orders due to the fact that girls were given a chance to learn to operate the machines with pay, and many stayed just long enough to learn. Continually employing new help, of course, was responsible for poor quality of work as well as a large labor turnover and financial loss. The girls were disposed to be late for work and quit anywhere from a half-hour to fifteen minutes before closing time. There was considerable lack of respect for authority when it came to the forelady and inspector, as there was more or less a division of authority; so the firm had almost decided to release all the colored help, which meant a terrible blow to future opportunities. It was at this juncture that the Chicago Urban League was appealed to and they advised putting a Negro woman as Personnel Director in charge to save the situation if possible for these hundreds of girls. The work of this Director has been very interesting and to some considerable degree satisfactory to the firm. It must be acknowledged to the credit of the firm that they have done everything possible for the Director to carry out her plans.

Her first task was to establish confidence and good-will in the hearts of the workers for herself. This was done by bringing about some very needed improvements for the physical welfare of the workers, such as individual towels, rest-room, installing a wholesome lunch service, ice-water coolers on each floor during the summer months, having the space between the rows of machines widened seventeen inches so that the girls could swing the large work more easily in sewing, installation of ventilators. There was a need to develop a spirit of respect for those in authority and this has been brought about gradually by the careful handling of individual cases needing adjustment. It was necessary to educate those in authority as to their duty and responsibility as well as to require respect from the girls toward them.

The girls soon realized that if they had just cause for complaint, they were upheld; if they were in the wrong, their Director gave them a warning the first time that a second offense would mean dismissal, and it did mean just that. Misfits were gradually released; careless and poor operators were discharged; certain factory rules were established, such as for punctuality, attendance, general conduct. This was done after heart to heart talks with the girls and they were made to realize the necessity for these adjustments.

We have without doubt today, we believe, the best disciplined group of factory employees to be found. We have an average of 97% on time; 95%–98% on the job! Our production has increased steadily from about 250,000 pockets to an average of 400,000 per day and on special occasions when we have needed an increased production they have easily speeded up to 500,000. This is the output of about 170 operators. If, of course, we add to this the workers on both operations we could approximately sew about 1,000,000 pockets in one day with 300 operators. This would give us about 17,000 cushions per day. Eighteen months ago we were three months behind in filling orders; today we guarantee a twenty-four hour delivery. Posting an hourly production scale on the bulletin board stimulates interest and it is great sport to watch the figures mount. We issue from time to time a printed bulletin or news sheet containing instructions and matters of general interest and information for the workers. We encourage the girls to larger earning effort by giving each girl a new dollar bill for every five dollars in-

crease in her paycheck; we also issue stars to the girls to wear on their caps, showing their ratings—one star for fifteen dollars; two stars for twenty dollars. . . .

We have frequent meetings of the staff of foreladies and inspectors, and instructions are passed to the girls about the work through them to develop respect for their positions as supervisors. Mass-meetings are held and subjects such as business methods, personal responsibility, cooperation, loyalty, punctuality, attendance, factory ethics, health and morals, conduct in the factory as well as when going to and from work are discussed.

The girls wear a neat uniform and cap of blue and white striped gingham made by the Angelica Uniform Factory in St. Louis. It makes a wonderful improvement in the general appearance and they like it. Many of our patrons come to visit the factory. These men are always surprised and agreeably impressed when they see these hundreds of neatly appareled girls working so quietly and industriously and making such a high quality product. I wish to say right here, that this work requires skill and a good average of intelligence, as we daily receive orders requiring exclusive and special particulars. There are in the employ of our factory Jews, Italians, Slavokians [sic], Poles, Bohemians and Americans, and when you realize that Negro men, women, boys and girls are employed in every department with absolutely no race friction, you must admit that it is a striking example of inter-racial industrial adjustment.

A word of appreciation now for the girls in this story. It has been wonderful to see the gratitude of these workers as well as the great response we have had to our plans. The majority of the girls appreciate just what it means for them to make good and they are anxious to cooperate, now that they do understand and the whole process of costs and values has been explained. They realize that they are pioneers and to them is entrusted the future possibilities for greater opportunities for Negro girls in industry if they make good. They feel satisfied that the Director will take care of their complaints and give them a square deal. All this has raised the morale of Negro help at Nachman Spring-filled Cushion Company and today these workers are assured of steady work and advancement when merited in this company.

It may be interesting to you to hear of the experience of a young white college girl student of sociology and economics who worked in our factory as a power machine operator last summer for seven weeks. Unknown to all but the Director, she was under the guardianship of the Y.W.C.A. Students of Industry Group. In the report of her experiences she made this statement: "I expected to find a low moral status existing among these factory girls. On the contrary, it was just the reverse and I never felt the least bit out of place. I found them cheerful and helpful to each other, and I felt no different than I would

in any other strange social group. There is absolutely no profanity or vulgarity in their conversation, as I expected to find." The Y.W.C.A. has again requested a placement for a student this summer! This speaks for itself.

Until the Negro woman in industry has had a longer factory experience, until she has acquired the modern industry complex, where they are employed in large numbers, they must be guided. In a few years they will have established themselves without question as to their ability and capacity for routine factory work. Then they may be counted upon to make their contribution and become an integral part of the great industrial systems of America. Give her time, give her guidance—most of all, give her opportunity.

The Men That Painted the Darby, a photograph of the Black contractor Charles Summer Blodgett and painters at the Hotel Darby, Los Angeles, 1909. Courtesy of the Workman and Temple Family Homestead Museum, City of Industry, California.

Anonymous
"Charles S. Blodgett"

California Eagle, July 11, 1924[5]

The California Eagle believes in the very practical decision of the New Negro. If per chance you have bouquets to pass—pass them now, for their beauty I might see, and fragrance smell, while I am yet alive. We want Charles S. Blodgett of this State, County and City, while he lives[,] to be cognizant of the fact . . . in the declaration which we are about to make and that is the fact that by his unselfish devotion for his people he has lighted the path of progress for greater things than have ever been dreamed of before.

The $10,000.00 gift of Mr. Blodgett has turned things around in this section. Where the Negro had been looked upon in the past as only a rift in the Sunlight of civilization and the act of Chas. S. Blodgett dispels the thought and has made a new setting for the Negro in the estimation of the captains of industry and wealth of our white people. They knew that he would give his moral support, eloquence and song but thought, money he would or could not give. But at this moment out-stepped our hero Mr. Blodgett and asked of the General Secretary of the Central Y. M. C. A., Mr. Secretary, have all restrictions of any sort against my people enjoying the benefits of vocational and other instructions at our Central Building been moved? The General Secretary answered, They have; and handed him the decision voted by the Board in black and white. Then Blodgett replied: This being so I pledge you here and now $10,000.00. This act by this black man set the blaze of fire a-going which would not be put out until the amount asked for had been pledged. It acted alike upon black and white. It was glorious, it was real sacrifice; it was superb and grand, and for these reasons alone, do we write of Chas. S. Blodgett. We appreciate him for his worth and the fact that he has proven himself worthy of any responsibility placed upon him and were he as rich as Solomon of old he bears the riches with honor and credit to himself and all who know him. And along with the indomitable Malones, of these later day[s] Chas. S. Blodget is the burden bearer who has so ably and magnificently held up the banner of progress for our Western country.

Anonymous
"Watchman What of the Night?"

Spokesman, March 1925[6]

Marcus Garvey, President General of the Universal Negro Improvement Association, has gone to Atlanta, in compliance with the decree of the Appellate Court of New York, to begin his five year sentence for using the United States mail to defraud.

The courts have spoken. And despite our personal opinions as to Mr. Garvey's guilt or innocence, pro or con, we must bow to the verdict. We however are among that minority, who refuse to go wild over the going away of this man. Even his bitterest foes must have a grain of pity for him in his hour of trial. We pity him, though we have never quite agreed with his methods, in fostering the U.N.I.A., in which we believe and will continue to have faith.

SCENE: "THE LAST JUMP", CABARET ON A SATURDAY NIGHT

Here is Nick Fie Rastus with his "teasin' brown", getting in a word or two (I'll say he is) between dances and sips of that red ale which is the rage of Negro cabarets. Note the lady's neutral attitude, expressed by the chaste and exquisite clasping of her hands

THAT TEASIN' YALLA GAL

Seen either on the stage of the "Lincoln", 135th Street and Lenox Avenue, or at "The Bucket of Blood", between the hours of 9 P. M. and 4 A. M. A lady of mystery. Unescorted. Unescortable. Likely to have a greyhound at home. Impossible to tell the exact color of her skin

KIND O' MELANCHOLY LIKE

He's jess natchely a quiet sort of fellow, dat boy is. Bin at dat table all night, sittin' down, waitin' for somebody, it seem. Don't nevah dance or sing or cut up. Nuthin'. Jess sits over there, kind o' melancholy, like. "You got to do bette'n dat, ole man. Ain't no time to git blue"

THE SHEIK OF DAHOMEY

Nothin'—Ah don't care whut it is—can get mah boy recited. Nothin'! And talk about havin' a way with wimmin, ain't nobody can tell him nuthin' . . . He's a dressin' up fool, dat boy is, an' he sure's got luck with de high yalla ladies

Enter, The New Negro, a Distinctive Type Recently

Exit, the Coloured Crooner of Lullabys, the Cotton-Picker, the Mammy-Singer and

Miguel Covarrubias, "Enter, the New Negro, a Distinctive Type Recently," illustrations, *Vanity Fair*, December 1924.

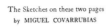

The Sketches on these two pages
by MIGUEL COVARRUBIAS

ON A SPREE
*Scene: Stage Door at the
"Chocolate Dandies"*
Looks as if dese folks is got the
blues, don't it? Well, that ain't
it, prezactly. Ah wants to tell you
that dey's gwine "out" to a party,
dat's what. That boy swings a
mean wheel-barrow; and de gal,
she ain't so bad, neither. She sure
can shake a wicked soap sud

8 A. M. ON LENOX AVENUE
"Got a job fo' you, Coolie."
"Nigger, keep still! I bin in New
York gwine on to twenty years
now and I ain't nevah had no job.
Go on 'bout yo' bizness. . . . . Az
Ah was tellin' yo', Lovey, Ah had
five to win and two for a place. . ."

2 A. M. AT "THE CAT AND THE
SAXOPHONE"
"Boy, do that thing! Tell 'em about
me! You tell 'em, sister. Be yourself,
now! 'S pretty, too. Ah mean she
ain't ugly. Oh! Kiss me, papa!
You're pretty from the ground up"

THE effortless New York public, revolving always with the fairest wind,
has recently discovered a new brand of
Negro entertainer. Not the old type, of
course. The lullaby-singer has gone. Also
the plantation darkey. And, out of the
welter of sentimentality which the old
types created, the Negro now emerges as
an individual, an individual as brisk and
as actual as your own next-door neighbour.
He no longer has to be either a Pullman
car porter, or over-fond of watermelons,
in order to be a successful type on our
stage. He is a personality, always, and
frequently an artist. A bright light has
recently been turned upon him.

The first all-coloured show, *Shuffle Along*,
written, produced and acted by Negroes,
was presented the season before last on

Broadway, and immediately became a sensation. Since then we have seen its successors, *Runnin' Wild*, *Chocolate Dandies*,
Honey, and *Dixie to Broadway*. We have
also seen a great number of Negro cabarets
which have flared up in every part of New
York, from the fashionable districts to the
Harlem black belt—all flourishing under
white, or partial white, patronage.

In the accompanying sketches, Miguel
Covarrubias, the young Mexican artist,
has miraculously caught the somewhat
exotic spirit of the new Negro, as he is
seen to be, both on the stage and in the
more characteristic moments of his life
around the cabarets. The captions for
these eight drawings were written by
Eric D. Walrond, a talented Negro poet.

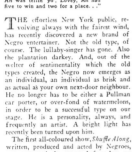

See dis Strutter! Tu'n
mo' tricks 'n a monkey,
dis boy kin. Jess like
that, jess like that. And
he don't give a doggone
if them Broadway stars

do come on uptown
where he is at, and see
him do he stuff, and den
go on back downtown
and strut his stuff as if
they jess got it natchely

Created by the Coloured Cabaret Belt in New York

the Darky Banjo-Player, for so Long Over-Exploited Figures on the American Stage

We submit that Mr. Garvey may not have made full and best use of his unusual opportunities. Nor did he use to advantage or even fairly the abilities and assistance of the many able men who had been associated with him from time to time during the past six years. Most of these men were strong and influential, mayhaps, too strong and influential. Perhaps his passing is according to the divine order of things. Who knows? Moses reached the Jordan, and passed. Joshua crossed the stream. Really Cromwell's task ended with the Civil War. The world was not yet ready for Puritanism. Washington knew when to retire. He also knew that too much Washington was dangerous. The Christ passed after contributing His bit to the world's religions. He was a few years too early.

The Day approaches! Mr. Garvey's contribution to his race is indeed noteworthy. Future generations must pass on it, to accurately estimate its real worth. Garvey made thousands think, who had never thought before; thousands who merely dreamed dreams, now see visions. Young men matured over night, and became anxious of the Morrow; old men became ambitious youths; Hope conquered Despair; Fear surrendered to Fearlessness; life was filled with new purposes and visions; those who formerly prayed for Death, no longer wanted to die, but prayed for long life instead, with the Coming of Garvey. The New Negro is Garvey's own Child, whose mother is the U.N.I.A. Garvey's monument is of the most enduring and imperishable sort of material—the hearts of men. There he will live forever. What Negro could wish a monument more splendid? Now he is gone, maybe to return, and maybe not. What of the Child? It is a vital, living and breathing force, which cannot, and will not be ignored. Its principles, though they may have been badly twisted through mismanagement, if properly nourished will become a power.

For one thing, the period of propaganda has passed. The Master propagandist is gone. He was the greatest we have seen in our day. A maker of living phrases, a moulder of burning words, a mover of men's very souls—an Idealist. He did not belong to the world of business.

No cold Materialist, no matter-of-fact business man was Garvey. This he could never be made to understand. He forgot that no one man can know and do everything. Thus his many failures in business; thus eternal friction and conflict with those around him; thus the lack of proper system and confusion which characterized his fragile and hazy plans, which resulted in the falling away from him, many able and sound men, who composed his Councils. But the public never saw *this* man. When before them, they saw and knew only Garvey, the eloquent, humble, the persecuted and sincere, and this accounts for the failure of the public to understand these men who left the association from time to time. Garvey in the *office* was a different Garvey from the Garvey on the *road*.

The future of the organization is dependent upon the ability, *bigness*, *unselfishness*, and originality of those left in charge, among whom are both *big* and *little* men, strong and weak. The big ones, and strong ones have a job on their hands. First they must convert, or overcome those weak and little souls among them. And American business methods must displace that old unbusiness-like procedure which was slowly crushing the life out of the organization, and which will destroy it, unless things are done according to Hoyle. It is dependent upon the ability of those in charge to make friends for the organization. Since even Governments cannot long endure without friends, an organization cannot hope to do so. They cannot continue to isolate themselves and dislike those who did not and do not fall on their faces before the association. In this country the people must be shown. Mere names mean nothing. It depends upon the Unselfishness of its leaders. The organization in the past has accused others of Selfishness in their attitude towards the association. It was merely a case of "pot calling the kettle black." The U.N.I.A. put Negroes to thinking and talking, and yet was first to abuse and oppose the Negro for thinking and talking, when it took the form of criticizing and advising the association. This attitude must undergo a change. This is a Free country. One may wear shoes or go bare shod.

The New leaders must be Liberalists. They must be original. Their own plans and methods, as the result of experience and knowledge of [the] needs [of] the association, must have the right of way. Again, they should urge every member in this country, who is not a citizen of these United States to set about becoming one at once. In this country Votes count, not empty names, or *voteless numbers*.

Strong *men* are needed, not a strong *man*. And again what attitude is the new leaders going to assume towards that host of men who left the organization, not because they were against it, but because like true Americans, they opposed tyranny, in every form, whether on the part of a king, group, or president? The true story of their leaving is well known to those in charge, also their ability and efficiency. Frankly they are not to be lightly ignored. They stand ready doubtless to assist the organization, together with its host of mem-

bers everywhere, who should rally to the cause, now as never before.

For the first two years West Indians loyally carried the association forward, now the greater majority of the membership consist of native Americans. Let this fact not be forgotten, nor let it not be overlooked that the latest venture was financed with American dollars. So men are needed now, who will sympathize with American ideals, as far as practicable in this new effort, and men who understand and will adopt American business methods, and who will work in harmony with the great American Government.

Finally, those in charge should clean out the old house, from bottom to top. Favoritism should go. Friendship, and social affairs will not mix with business. Oil and water will not mix. The ape and the asp should not attempt to mate. What Mr. Garvey did, is not going to count now, but by what those left behind do, will the future of the organization be determined.

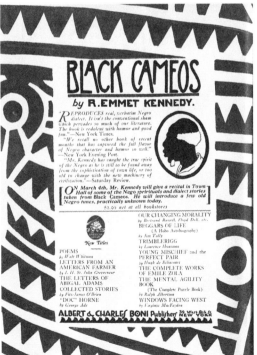

Front and back covers of *Survey Graphic* by Winold Reiss, March 1925.

It is going to take men of rugged courage to carry on. No pussyfooting will get by the man on guard now. A new program should be formulated, because there is no program. Deep in their heart those in charge know this, but have they the *courage to face the people with naked truth*, and merit their [e]verlasting, confidence, or will they continue to hide behind the veil, of make-believe until it is torn from their hands? It requires the sort of courage that does not give a damn, for anything but [the] Right to be men now.

Are those in charge big enough to measure up to the high standard now set for, and expected of them[?] MANY believe Not. Time will tell.

Alain Locke
"The New Negro"

In *The New Negro*, edited by Alain Locke, 1925

In the last decade something beyond the watch and guard of statistics has happened in the life of the American Negro and the three norms who have traditionally presided over the Negro

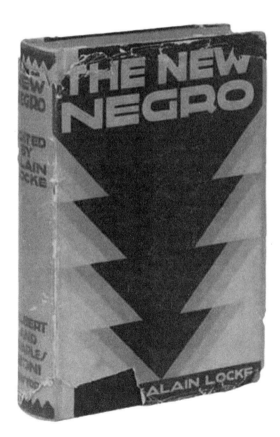

The original cover for Alain Locke, *The New Negro: An Interpretation*, 1925.

problem have a changeling in their laps. The Sociologist, The Philanthropist, the Race-leader are not unaware of the New Negro, but they are at a loss to account for him. He simply cannot be swathed in their formulae. For the younger generation is vibrant with a new psychology; the new spirit is awake in the masses, and under the very eyes of the professional observers is transforming what has been a perennial problem into the progressive phases of contemporary Negro life.

Could such a metamorphosis have taken place as suddenly as it has appeared to? The answer is no; not because the New Negro is not here, but because the Old Negro had long become more of a myth than a man. The Old Negro, we must remember, was a creature of moral debate and historical controversy. His has been a stock figure perpetuated as an historical fiction partly in innocent sentimentalism, partly in deliberate reactionism. The Negro himself has contributed his share to this through a sort of protective social mimicry forced upon him by the adverse circumstances of dependence. So for generations in the mind of America, the Negro has been more of a formula than a human being—a something to be argued about, condemned or defended, to be "kept down," or "in his place," or "helped up," to be worried with or worried over, harassed or patronized, a social bogey or a social burden. The thinking Negro even has been induced to share this same general attitude, to focus his attention on controversial issues, to see himself in the distorted perspective of a social problem. His shadow, so to speak, has been more real to him than his personality. Through having had to appeal from the unjust stereotypes of his oppressors and traducers to those of his liberators, friends and benefactors he has subscribed to the traditional positions from which his case has been viewed. Little true social or self-understanding has or could come from such a situation.

But while the minds of most of us, black and white, have thus burrowed in the trenches of the Civil War and Reconstruction, the actual march of development has simply flanked these positions, necessitating a sudden reorientation of view. We have not been watching in the right direction; set North and South on a sectional axis, we have not noticed the East till the sun has us blinking.

Recall how suddenly the Negro spirituals revealed themselves; suppressed for generations under the stereotypes of Wesleyan hymn harmony, secretive, half-ashamed, until the courage of being natural brought them out—and behold, there was folk-music. Similarly the mind of the Negro seems suddenly to have slipped from under the tyranny of social intimidation and to be shaking off the psychology of imitation and implied inferiority. By shedding the old chrysalis of the Negro problem we are achieving something like a spiritual emancipation. Until recently, lacking self-understanding, we have been almost as much of a problem to ourselves as we still are to others. But the decade that found us with a problem has left us with only a task. The multitude perhaps feels as yet only a strange relief and a new vague urge, but the thinking few know that in the reaction the vital inner grip of prejudice has been broken.

With this renewed self-respect and self-dependence, the life of the Negro community is bound to enter a new dynamic phase, the buoyancy from within compensating for whatever pressure there may be of conditions from without. The migrant masses, shifting from countryside to city, hurdle several generations of experience at a leap, but more important, the same thing happens spiritually in the life-attitudes and self-expression of the Young Negro, in his poetry, his art, his education and his new outlook, with the additional advantage, of course, of the poise and greater certainty of knowing what it is all about. From this comes the promise and warrant of a new leadership. As one of them has discerningly put it:

> We have tomorrow
> Bright before us
> Like a flame.
> Yesterday, a night-gone thing
> A sun-down name.
> And dawn today
> Broad arch above the road we came.
> We march![7]

This is what, even more than any "most creditable record of fifty years of freedom," requires that the Negro of today be seen through other than the dusty spectacles of past controversy. The day of "aunties," "uncles" and "mammies" is equally gone. Uncle Tom and Sambo have passed on, and even the "Colonel" and "George" play barnstorm roles from which they escape with relief when the public spotlight is off. The popular melodrama has about played itself out, and it is time to scrap the fictions, garret the bogeys and settle down to a realistic facing of facts.

FIRST we must observe some of the changes which since the traditional lines of opinion were drawn have rendered these quite obsolete. A main change has been, of course, that shifting of the Negro population which has made the Negro problem no longer exclusively or even predominantly Southern. Why should our minds remain sectionalized, when the problem itself no longer is? Then the trend of migration has not only been toward the North and the Central Midwest, but city-ward and to the great centers of industry—the problems of adjustment are new, practical, local and not peculiarly racial. Rather they are an integral part of the large industrial and social problems of our present-day democracy. And finally, with the Negro rapidly in process of class differentiation, if it ever was warrantable to regard and treat the Negro en masse, it is becoming with every day less possible, more unjust and more ridiculous.

In the very process of being transplanted, the Negro is becoming transformed.

The tide of Negro migration, northward and city-ward, is not to be fully explained as a blind flood started by the demands of war industry coupled with the shutting off of foreign migration, or by the pressure of poor crops coupled with increased social terrorism in certain sections of the South and Southwest. Neither labor demand, the boll-weevil, nor the Ku Klux Klan is a basic factor, however contributory any or all of them may have been. The wash and rush of this human tide on the beach line of the northern city centers is to be explained primarily in terms of a new vision of opportunity, of

social and economic freedom, of a spirit to seize, even in the face of extortionate and heavy toll, a chance for the improvement of conditions. With each successive wave of it, the movement of the Negro becomes more and more a mass movement toward the larger and the more democratic chance—in the Negro's case a deliberate flight not only from countryside to city, but from medieval America to modern.

Take Harlem as an instance of this. Here in Manhattan is not merely the largest Negro community in the world, but the first concentration in history of so many diverse elements of Negro life. It has attracted the African, the West Indian, the Negro American; has brought together the Negro of the North and the Negro of the South; the man from the city and the man from the town and village; the peasant, the student, the business man, the professional man, artist, poet, musician, adventurer and worker, preacher and criminal, exploiter and social outcast. Each group has come with its own separate motives and for its own special ends, but their greatest experience has been the finding of one another. Proscription and prejudice have thrown these dissimilar elements into a common area of contact and interaction. Within this area, race sympathy and unity have determined a further fusing of sentiment and experience. So what began in terms of segregation becomes more and more, as its elements mix and react, the laboratory of a great race-welding. Hitherto, it must be admitted that American Negroes have been a race more in name than in fact, or to be exact, more in sentiment than in experience. The chief bond between them has been that of a common condition rather than a common consciousness; a problem in common rather than a life in common. In Harlem, Negro life is seizing upon its first chances for group expression and self-determination. It is—or promises at least to be—a race capital. That is why our comparison is taken with those nascent centers of folk-expression and self-determination which are playing a creative part in the world to-day. Without pretense to their political significance, Harlem has the same rôle [*sic*] to play for the New Negro as Dublin has had for the New Ireland or Prague for the New Czechoslovakia.

Harlem, I grant you, isn't typical—but it is significant, it is prophetic. No sane observer, however sympathetic to the new trend, would contend that the great masses are articulate as yet, but they stir, they move, they are more than physically restless. The challenge of the new intellectuals among them is clear enough—the "race radicals" and realists who have broken with the old epoch of philanthropic guidance, sentimental appeal and protest. But are we after all only reading into the stirrings of a sleeping giant the dreams of an agitator? The answer is in the migrating peasant. It is the "man farthest down" who is most active in getting up. One of the most characteristic symptoms of this is the professional man, himself migrating to recapture his constituency after a vain effort to maintain in some Southern corner what for years back seemed an established living and clientele. The clergyman following his errant flock, the physician or lawyer trailing his clients, supply the true clues. In a real sense it is the rank and file who are leading, and the leaders who are following. A transformed and transforming psychology permeates the masses.

When the racial leaders of twenty years ago spoke of developing race-pride and stimulating race-consciousness, and of the desirability of race solidarity, they could not in any accurate degree have anticipated the abrupt feeling that has surged up and now pervades the awakened centers. Some of the recognized Negro leaders and a powerful section of white opinion identified with "race work" of the older order have indeed attempted to discount this feeling as a "passing phase," an attack of "race nerves" so to speak, an "aftermath of the war," and the like. It has not abated, however, if we are to gauge by the present tone and temper of the Negro press or by the shift in popular support from the officially recognized and orthodox spokesmen to those of the independent, popular, and often radical type who are unmistakable symptoms of a new order. It is a social disservice to blunt the fact that the Negro of the Northern centers has

reached a stage where tutelage, even of the most interested and well-intentioned sort, must give place to new relationships, where positive self-direction must be reckoned with in ever increasing measure. The American mind must reckon with a fundamentally changed Negro.

The Negro, too, for his part, has idols of the tribe to smash. If on the one hand the white man has erred in making the Negro appear to be that which would excuse or extenuate his treatment of him, the Negro, in turn, has too often unnecessarily excused himself because of the way he has been treated. The intelligent Negro of to-day is resolved not to make discrimination an extenuation for his shortcomings in performance, individual or collective; he is trying to hold himself at par, neither inflated by sentimental allowances nor depreciated by current social discounts. For this he must know himself and be known for precisely what he is, and for that reason he welcomes the new scientific rather than the old sentimental interest. Sentimental interest in the Negro has ebbed. We used to lament this as the falling off of our friends; now we rejoice and pray to be delivered both from self-pity and condescension. The mind of each racial group has had a bitter weaning, apathy or hatred on one side matching disillusionment or resentment on the other; but they face each other to-day with the possibility at least of entirely new mutual attitudes.

It does not follow that if the Negro were better known, he would be better liked or better treated. But mutual understanding is basic for any subsequent coöperation [*sic*] and adjustment. The effort toward this will at least have the effect of remedying in large part what has been the most unsatisfactory feature of our present state of race relationships in America, namely the fact that the more intelligent and representative elements of the two race groups have at so many points got quite out of vital touch with one another.

The fiction is that the life of the races is separate, and increasingly so. The fact is that they have touched too closely at the unfavorable and too lightly at the favorable levels.

While inter-racial councils have sprung up in the South, drawing on forward elements of both races, in the Northern cities manual laborers may brush elbows in their everyday work, but the community and business leaders have experienced no such interplay or far too little of it. These segments must achieve contact or the race situation in America becomes desperate. Fortunately this is happening. There is a growing realization that in social effort the co-operative basis must supplant long-distance philanthropy, and that the only safeguard for mass relations in the future must be provided in the carefully maintained contacts of the enlightened minorities of both race groups. In the intellectual realm a renewed and keen curiosity is replacing the recent apathy; the Negro is being carefully studied, not just talked about and discussed. In art and letters, instead of being wholly caricatured, he is being seriously portrayed and painted.

To all of this the New Negro is keenly responsive as an augury of a new democracy in American culture. He is contributing his share to the new social understanding. But the desire to be understood would never in itself have been sufficient to have opened so completely the protectively closed portals of the thinking Negro's mind. There is still too much possibility of being snubbed or patronized for that. It was rather the necessity for fuller, truer self-expression, the realization of the unwisdom of allowing social discrimination to segregate him mentally, and a counter-attitude to cramp and fetter his own living—and so the "spite-wall" that the intellectuals built over the "color-line" has happily been taken down. Much of this re-opening of intellectual contacts has centered in New York and has been richly fruitful not merely in the enlarging of personal experience, but in the definite enrichment of American art and letters and in the clarifying of our common vision of the social tasks ahead.

The particular significance in the re-establishment of contact between the more advanced and representative classes is that it promises to offset some of the unfavorable reactions of the past, or at least to re-surface race contacts somewhat for the future. Subtly the conditions that are molding a New Negro are molding a new American attitude.

However, this new phase of things is delicate; it will call for less charity but more justice; less help, but infinitely closer understanding. This is indeed a critical stage of race relationships because of the likelihood, if the new temper is not understood, of engendering sharp group antagonism and a second crop of more calculated prejudice. In some quarters, it has already done so. Having weaned the Negro, public opinion cannot continue to paternalize. The Negro to-day is inevitably moving forward under the control largely of his own objectives. What are these objectives? Those of his outer life are happily already well and finally formulated, for they are none other than the ideals of American institutions and democracy. Those of his inner life are yet in process of formation, for the new psychology at present is more of a consensus of feeling than of opinion, of attitude rather than of program. Still some points seem to have crystallized.

Up to the present one may adequately describe the Negro's "inner objectives" as an attempt to repair a damaged group psychology and reshape a warped social perspective. Their realization has required a new mentality for the American Negro. And as it matures we begin to see its effects; at first, negative, iconoclastic, and then positive and constructive. In this new group psychology we note the lapse of sentimental appeal, then the development of a more positive self-respect and self-reliance; the repudiation of social dependence, and then the gradual recovery from hyper-sensitiveness and "touchy" nerves, the repudiation of the double standard of judgment with its special philanthropic allowances and then the sturdier desire for objective and scientific appraisal; and finally the rise from social disillusionment to race pride, from the sense of social debt to the responsibilities of social contribution, and offsetting the necessary working and commonsense acceptance of restricted conditions, the belief in ultimate esteem and recognition. Therefore the Negro to-day wishes to be known for what he is, even in his faults and shortcomings, and scorns a craven and precarious survival at the price of seeming to be what he is not. He resents being spoken for as a social ward or minor, even by his own, and to being regarded a chronic patient for the sociological clinic, the sick man of American Democracy. For the same reasons, he himself is through with those social nostrums and panaceas, the so-called "solutions" of his "problem," with which he and the country have been so liberally dosed in the past. Religion, freedom, education, money—in turn, he has ardently hoped for and peculiarly trusted these things; he still believes in them, but not in blind trust that they alone will solve his life-problem.

Each generation, however, will have its creed, and that of the present is the belief in the efficacy of collective effort, in race co-operation. This deep feeling of race is at present the mainspring of Negro life. It seems to be the outcome of the reaction to proscription and prejudice; an attempt, fairly successful on the whole, to convert a defensive into an offensive position, a handicap into an incentive. It is radical in tone, but not in purpose and only the most stupid forms of opposition, misunderstanding or persecution could make it otherwise. Of course, the thinking Negro has shifted a little toward the left with the world-trend, and there is an increasing group who affiliate with radical and liberal movements. But fundamentally for the present the Negro is radical on race matters, conservative on others, in other words, a "forced radical," a social protestant rather than a genuine radical. Yet under further pressure and injustice iconoclastic thought and motives will inevitably increase. Harlem's quixotic radicalisms call for their ounce of democracy to-day lest to-morrow they be beyond cure.

The Negro mind reaches out as yet to nothing but American wants, American ideas. But this forced attempt to build his Americanism on race values is a unique social experiment, and its ultimate success is impossible except through the fullest sharing of American culture and institutions. There should be no delusion about this. American nerves in sections unstrung with race hysteria are often fed the opiate that the trend of Negro advance is wholly separatist, and that the effect of its operation will be to encyst the Negro as a benign foreign body in the body politic. This cannot be—even if it were desirable. The racialism of the Negro is no limitation or reservation with respect to American life; it is only a constructive effort to build the obstructions in the stream of his progress into an efficient dam of social energy and power. Democracy itself is obstructed and stagnated to the extent that any of its channels are closed. Indeed they cannot be selectively closed. So the choice is not between one way for the Negro and another way for the rest, but between American institutions frustrated on the one hand and American ideals progressively fulfilled and realized on the other.

There is, of course, a warrantably comfortable feeling in being on the right side of the country's professed ideals. We realize that we cannot be undone without America's undoing. It is within the gamut of this attitude that the thinking Negro faces America, but with variations of mood that are if anything more significant than the attitude itself. Sometimes we have it taken with the defiant ironic challenge of McKay:

> Mine is the future grinding down to-day
> Like a great landslip moving to the sea,
> Bearing its freight of débris [*sic*] far away
> Where the green hungry waters restlessly
> Heave mammoth pyramids, and break
>   and roar
> Their eerie challenge to the crumbling
>   shore.[8]

Sometimes, perhaps more frequently as yet, in the fervent and almost filial appeal and counsel of Weldon Johnson's:

> O Southland, dear Southland!
> Then why do you still cling
> To an idle age and a musty page,
> To a dead and useless thing.[9]

But between defiance and appeal, midway almost between cynicism and hope, the prevailing mind stands in the mood of the same author's *To America*, an attitude of sober query and stoical challenge:

> How would you have us, as we are?
>   Or sinking 'neath the load we bear,
> Our eyes fixed forward on a star,
>   Or gazing empty at despair?
> Rising or falling? Men or things?
>   With dragging pace or footsteps fleet?
> Strong, willing sinews in your wings,
>   Or tightening chains about your feet?[10]

More and more, however, an intelligent realization of the great discrepancy between the American social creed and the American social practice forces upon the Negro the taking of the moral advantage that is his. Only the steadying and sobering effect of a truly characteristic gentleness of spirit prevents the rapid rise of a definite cynicism and counter-hate and a defiant superiority feeling. Human as this reaction would be, the majority still deprecate its advent, and would gladly see it forestalled by the speedy amelioration of its causes. We wish our race pride to be a healthier, more positive achievement than a feeling based upon a realization of the shortcomings of others. But all paths toward the attainment of a sound social attitude have been difficult; only a relatively few enlightened minds have been able as the phrase puts it "to rise above" prejudice. The ordinary man has had until recently only a hard choice between the alternatives of supine and humiliating submission and stimulating but hurtful counterprejudice. Fortunately from some inner, desperate resourcefulness has recently sprung up the simple expedient of fighting prejudice by mental passive resistance, in other words by trying to ignore it. For the few, this manna may perhaps be effective, but the masses cannot thrive on it.

Fortunately there are constructive channels opening out into which the balked social feelings of the American Negro can flow freely. Without them there would be much more pressure and danger than there is. These compensating interests are racial but in a new and enlarged way. One is the consciousness of acting as the advance-guard of the African peoples in their contact with Twentieth Century civilization; the other, the sense of a mission of rehabilitating the race in world esteem from that loss of prestige for which the fate and conditions of slavery have so largely been responsible. Harlem, as we shall see, is the center of both these movements; she is the home of the Negro's "Zionism." The pulse of the Negro world has begun to beat in Harlem. A Negro newspaper carrying news material in English, French and Spanish, gathered from all quarters of America, the West Indies and Africa has maintained itself in Harlem for over five years. Two important magazines, both edited from New York, maintain their news and circulation consistently on a cosmopolitan scale. Under American auspices and backing, three pan-African congresses have been held abroad for the discussion of common interests, colonial questions and the future cooperative development of Africa. In terms of the race question as a world problem, the Negro mind has leapt, so to speak, upon the parapets of prejudice and extended its cramped horizons. In so doing it has linked up with the growing group consciousness of the dark-peoples and is gradually learning their common interests. As one of our writers has recently put it: "It is imperative that we understand the white world in its relations to the non-white world." As with the Jew, persecution is making the Negro international.

As a world phenomenon this wider race consciousness is a different thing from the much asserted rising tide of color. Its inevitable causes are not of our making. The consequences are not necessarily damaging to the best interests of civilization. Whether it actually brings into being new Armadas of conflict or argosies of cultural exchange and enlightenment can only be decided by the attitude of the dominant races in an era of critical change. With the American Negro, his new internationalism is primarily an effort to recapture contact with the scattered peoples of African derivation. Garveyism may be a transient, if spectacular, phenomenon, but the possible rôle [*sic*] of the American Negro in the future development of Africa is one of the most constructive and universally helpful missions that any modern people can lay claim to.

Constructive participation in such causes cannot help giving the Negro valuable group incentives, as well as increased prestigé at home and abroad. Our greatest rehabilitation may possibly come through such channels, but for the present, more immediate hope rests in the revaluation by white and black alike of the Negro in terms of his artistic endowments and cultural contributions, past and prospective. It must be increasingly recognized that the Negro has already made very substantial contributions, not only in his folk-art, music especially, which has always found appreciation, but in larger, though humbler and less acknowledged ways. For generations the Negro has been the peasant matrix of that section of America which has most undervalued him, and here he has contributed not only materially in labor and in social patience, but spiritually as well. The South has unconsciously absorbed the gift of his folk-temperament. In less than half a generation it will be easier to recognize this, but the fact remains that a leaven of humor, sentiment, imagination and tropic nonchalance has gone into the making of the South from a humble, unacknowledged source. A second crop of the Negro's gifts promises still more largely. He now becomes a conscious contributor and lays aside the status of a beneficiary and ward for that of a collaborator and participant in American civilization. The great social gain in this is the releasing of our talented group from the arid fields of controversy and debate to the productive fields of creative expression. The especially cultural recognition they win should in turn prove the key to that revaluation of the Negro which must precede or accompany any considerable further betterment of race relationships. But

Portrait of Alain Locke by Winold Reiss, in Alain Locke,
The New Negro: An Interpretation, 1925.

Portrait of Langston Hughes by Winold Reiss, in Alain Locke, *The New Negro: An Interpretation*, 1925.

whatever the general effect, the present generation will have added the motives of self-expression and spiritual development to the old and still unfinished task of making material headway and progress. No one who understandingly faces the situation with its substantial accomplishment or views the new scene with its still more abundant promise can be entirely without hope. And certainly, if in our lifetime the Negro should not be able to celebrate his full initiation into American democracy, he can at least, on the warrant of these things, celebrate the attainment of a significant and satisfying new phase of group development, and with it a spiritual Coming of Age.

Jean Toomer
"The Negro Emergent"

In *A Jean Toomer Reader: Selected Unpublished Writings*, edited by Frederik L. Rusch, 1993.[11]

Where life is conscious and dynamic, its processes naturally involve an extension of experience and the uncovering of new materials. Discovery, in one form or another, is provided by nature for most of us. For the larger part, however, it is reserved to childhood and is attended with no more than a child's concern. Beyond this phase the range of experience is quite limited when seen in terms of human possibilities. Even so, experience may and often does yield isolated moments of discovery. And, rarely, these moments come with such frequence and intensity as to constitute a state. It is then that the fortunate individual undergoes an inward transformation while all the world about him is revealed in fresh forms, colors, and significances. He discovers himself, and at the same time discovers the external world. One may, of course, uncover new facts by means of old modes of thought, feeling, or conduct. This is partial, often false discovery. For it means, simply, the extension of a given organism to novel ground. But real discovery means precisely this: that new facts, truths, realities, are manifest to a transformed state of being. In one sense, these new realities themselves may be nothing more than new illusions. And discovery may be seen as a process which merely substitutes a fresh appearance for an old one. But if this fresh appearance is related to a deep inward change, and the state of being approaches wonder, then one may rightly term this act discovery.

If it were possible to glance at will about the human world and accurately see it in its varied phases and conditions, it would doubtless be seen that the state or process of discovery is constant, that it is always operative in some place, individual, or a group of persons. This glance, for the present, wherever else it rested would be certain to observe the impulse at work within the Negro in America. For the Negro is discovering himself. I refer of course to individuals, and not to mass.

The Negro is emergent. From what is he emergent? To what is he emerging? An answer to these questions will define his present status and suggest his possibilities.

Generally, it may be said that the Negro is emergent from a crust, a false personality, a compound of beliefs, habits, attitudes, and emotional reactions superimposed upon him by external circumstance. The elements of this compound are numerous. I shall consider what appear to me to be the most outstanding. These fall roughly into two distinct groups. First, there are those factors which arise from the condition of being a black man in a white world. Second, there are those forms and forces which spring from the nature of our civilization, and are common to Americans. I shall treat of these [*sic*] in turn.

Because of external pressure, the Negro, unwittingly, has been divorced by attitude from his racial roots. Biologically, the Negro sprang from what he sprang from: a Negro, or a Negro and white stock. These bloods are in him. No attitude can change this fact, else it would have the power to deprive him of his physical existence. But since he himself has wished to force his slave root from his mind, and since his white root denies him, the Negro, psychologically and spiritually, has been literally uprooted, or worse, with no roots at all. From the anemia and chronic invalidism produced by this condition, the Negro is emergent.

Closely connected with his blood is the matter of his birth; not his birth in this generation, but the possible manner of birth of his great grandparents. Perhaps they were illegitimate. At any rate, he has been called a bastard. This charge has provoked feelings of shame or murder. When not openly expressed, the suspicion has been that it might exist in the white man's mind. Hence the Negro has closed himself and erected barriers, resistances, aggressions, for his own protection. But these things really enslaved the Negro, for, as the old saying goes, a wall restricts the city it surrounds. From this wall and reaction the Negro is emergent.

Then there are the factors which have to do with a century and more of slavery. The practice of using the Negro as slave laborer and concubine, and the consequent attitude of white men toward black women. The assertion that the Negro is inherently inferior, that he is a slave by nature. The Negro's child-like reliance upon the whites. The free admission of white superiority; the forced admission when the free type did not come naturally. The split within the Negro group due to difference of color and economic preferences, often stimulated by the white group. Disdain and contempt on the part of those of lighter color and better position; distrust and jealousy on the part of the others. Economic poverty. Reactions from [these?] factors.

The effects of the Civil War upon the Negro and the Negro problem are as yet to be accurately known and balanced. Certain of its influences, however, are clear. It freed the Negro nominally; it increased the Negro's bondage to white resentment and white fear (and, in a large measure added political exploitation to the already existent forms, while doing but little more than modify these forms). For the white southerner resented the Negro's forced liberation. Because of the unrest stimulated in the Negro by abolitionist propaganda and the legal paper-fact of freedom, the white man had additional cause to fear him. Nor will the South forget the sporadic dominance of Negroes during Reconstruction. From such factors as these the modern insistence on what the Negro's place is, the emphatic and sometime brutal measures taken to keep him in it, have their source. And these in turn give rise to the Negro's need for defining his own place and attempting to establish himself therein. In a word, the whole question of social equality, with its mutual bitterness. From this question the Negro is emergent.

But the Civil War and the mock-freedom which followed it, caused a more subtly unfortunate condition. Prior to the war, the Negro, though in slavery, had his roots within the soil. He had an emotional allegiance to the soil and country which he sprang from. I am aware that such a picture of the Negro lends itself to poetic exaggeration, but that it is not wholly fanciful is evident from the folk-songs. Since the war the Negro has been progressively divorced from both. For a time, he could not hear beauty even in his own spirituals; white southerners were often closer to his heritage than he was. He could not love the soil when those above him tried to force his face into it—and then allowed him no real possession. He was too well aware of the fact that he could not generously partake of America, to respond to it. He felt himself the least of aliens, though he knew himself in essence to be native. He might be patriotic. But patriotism is a lean substitute for poetry. The Negro is finding his way to them.

And, ever since emancipation, well intentioned white men, aided by Negroes, have been trying to plaster a white image on a black reality—to superimpose Boston on Georgia. This has led to an over-valuing of academic study; a prejudice against hand-training. It became a matter of shame that the men whose muscle had built the South could not read Caesar in the original. But, that the image is white is secondary. That it is an *image*, is primary. Because of it, the Negro has become a victim of education and false ideals. In terms of mastery, the results have been both ludicrous and pathetic. But this is true of most educational attempts, though it is less apparent in white examples. For Negroes had a special cause for their submission and desires: the white man claimed that the Negro was mentally inferior. Here was a chance to disprove that statement. The Negro would cram his brain with theories, dates, the Greek alphabet, and become equally civilized. He has done so; he is beginning to question the profit of his efforts. For he now seeks a balanced life, based upon capacity, wherein *all* faculties are given the necessary usage. He is beginning to discard the image for reality.

I think particularly of the illusion that the white American is free in fact, that he is actually free. Because the white man is not racially oppressed, the Negro has tended to picture him as existing in a state of perfect freedom and happiness. Economically, all sorts of avenues and opportunities are imagined to be open to him, so that, if he but wishes and works for it, the fruits of the earth will come into his possession. Every white boy has a *real* chance to become a millionaire and land in the White House. There has been a strong tendency to think of the white man as being psychologically free: he can think, feel, and do just what he pleases. It is assumed, among other things, that the white man *voluntarily* oppresses the Negro, that he freely hates him, that white mobs are acting from free will when they lynch a Negro. In brief, the white man is seen to exist above the laws of necessity and determinism. Indeed, he is believed to sit beside the throne of God, already. This attitude, more than any other, has stimulated the Negro's wish to be like the white man, to be white in fact. It is now being realized, however, that the

mass of whites, save in the single instance of racial oppression, are as bound and determined as the mass of blacks, that the fundamental limitations are common to humanity, and that their transcendence demands something more than the mere possession of a white skin, or of a white psychology.

There are, in addition to factors already considered, several other quite important ones. But for the present I will do no more than mention them. A painful self-consciousness, which makes it difficult for the Negro to meet even the well disposed of another race. A suspicion that he is being patronized. An emotionalism on the one hand, an emotional sterility on the other. The list could be continued.

Nor is it necessary that I give a detailed account of those forms and forces which arise from the nature of our civilization and are common to Americans, for these have received extended treatment: their features and effects are familiar to every one. The chaos and strain of these times, the lack of functioning religion, religious pretense and charlatanism, the reaction from these to materialism, industrialism, the ideal of material success, a devitalizing puritanism, herd psychology, the premium placed on individuality, the stupidities, lies, and superstitions that Mr. Menken [*sic*] has warred on, and so on, and so on. In general, all these elements can be grouped under the head of environmental influences as opposed to essential nature. From these, as I say, the Negro is emergent.

Precisely what, however, do I mean by emergent? Do I mean that the Negro is escaping or trying to escape from these things, that he denies their existence in him and is seeking to forget them? On the contrary, for the first time the Negro is fully recognizing that they do exist in him: this constitutes one aspect of his discovery. The Negro can no more leave them behind than a gull can leave water—but in both cases detachment is possible. The Negro is emerging to a place where he can see just what these factors are, the extent to which he has merely reacted to their stimuli, the extent to which he has been controlled by them. In a sense, he is adjusting to this feature of his reality. Further, he is discovering a self, an essence, interior to this crust-compound.

It would be premature to seek a final definition of this essence, for the act of discovery is only recently initiated, and, moreover, it is for the individual himself to reveal it in his own way and time. Nevertheless, I have already suggested certain of its features: it may be serviceable that I now bring these together and tentatively expand them.

The Negro has found his roots. He is in fruitful contact with his ancestry. He partakes of an uninterrupted stream of energy. He is moved by the vital determinants of racial heritage. And something of their spirit now lives within him. He is about to harvest whatever the past has stored, good and evil. He is about to be released from an unconscious and negative concern with it.

He is discovering his body. "For no man ever hated his own flesh; but nourisheth and cherisheth it."[12] These words are beginning to have real meaning. Save that it shares the derivation and genesis of things created, what matter who made it, the manner of its birth, the outward conditions that its parents were subject to? Here is it, this amazing instrument. It is strong and pliant, capable of work and lovely movements. In color and type it seems to include the varieties of humanity. Artists and anthropologists have been drawn to it. Now the Negro is finding it for his own experience. Let others talk about it if they have a mind to.

Beneath the reactive type, the Negro is touching emotions which have to do with the primary facts of existence. These flow with that lyricism which is so purely Negro. Sometimes they come in jerks and spurts, yet more powerful than a merely modern rhythm. Rarely, they suggest no strain or time at all, having blended with the universal. Liberated from past excess and recent throttling, love and passion may now pass in joy between man and woman. Pain is seen to be of the texture of life; not due to racial oppression, only. Likewise with fear, conflict, frustration, and tragic circumstance. Above all, the Negro finds that the poverty of

creed has not killed his religious impulse. He is on earth, so placed; somewhere is God. The need to discover himself and the desire to find God are similar. Perhaps that strange thing called soul, hardly an existence, rarely mentioned nowadays above a whisper, the Negro in his search may help uncover.

The Negro is led through himself outward to the surrounding world. He feels his own milieu to be desirable; its beauty, ugliness, passion, poverty, rhythm, and color. There is truth in the statement that Harlem differs from other communities in shade merely, but not in pattern. But it should be remembered that this shade appeals to something more than the eye of a Negro. He wishes to generously partake of it; he wishes to press beyond its boundaries, for he knows that neither his nor any similar group provides the range to satisfy a large capacity and keen appetite for experience. He is frank to recognize the advanced status of the white creative world in the matters of discovery and experiment. He wishes to learn from it. But now he does not meet it as a white world, for he recognizes there his own impulse, gone farther, more matured. He meets it as a world of similar values. While he is uncovering the life of Harlem, he is exploring New York. While he finds out things about himself, he learns what other men have found out of themselves. In short, he is emerging to the creative level of America.

But more rapidly than he emerges toward it, the white world of America takes steps towards him. The Negro is being studied in relation to the general economic problems. The problems of population. He challenges attention from those who are sincere in their democracy. His social and educational aspects are being investigated and aided. Psychoanalysis has interesting data concerning him. Articles about him are appearing with increasing frequency in the leading magazines and newspapers. Books are coming out, and publishers are receptive of Negro material. Clubs, societies, and forums wish to hear about the Negro. All this is indicative of a certain type of discovery. I had in mind particularly, however, the discovery of the Negro by creative America.

Speculations as to the Negro's genius, whether or not it was distinct, if so, what would be its contribution, how best to aid its growth—questions such as these foreshadowed direct contacts. And then they came, men who had rid themselves by search and struggle of what the Negro in his efforts toward creation is now contending with. Men who are relatively free to meet life in its own terms and respond to it, not merely through the conventions of thought, emotion, or of conduct. The influence of this discovery is mutual. It is deep-seated. It may prove to be profound. For each brings the other an essential complement: a living contact made from different levels of experience.

Thus far, the most striking evidence of discovery is the change in Negro life as expressed by attitude. To himself, the Negro says: I am. Need it be pointed out how many centuries of struggle bear their fruit inviolate within this affirmation? The Negro says: I am. *What* I am, I am searching to find out. Also, what I may become. When he faces these mysteries the Negro is humble. It is permitted that he be so; for by this act all racial factors: black, white, birth, slavery, inferior, superior, prejudice, bitterness, resentment, hatred, aggression and submission, equal, reactions, patronage, self-consciousness, false shame and false pride—gravitate to conscious placements. The crisis of race becomes a fact within a general problem. Hitherto, the Negro has been utilized by this crisis for its purposes. The question is, How may he use it for his own? And the concern is with new values.

Discovery itself is such a value. It is the first, for all higher ones depend upon it. But it may not be pursued unattended by dangers. To these, the Negro is now subject. To say, I am. To search to find out what I am and what I may become. This is the true state and temper. But it is all too easy to substitute for this, fanciful excursions and pride oneself for real achievement. Likewise can a feeling of the exotic be mistaken for won-der. One may be thought by others to be novel, and incur no risk. But if one feels himself to be exotic, then the chances are that he will never advance beyond infantilism and inflated personality. Discovery is accompanied by respect for materials. For by means of it one becomes conscious of what a thing really is. One could not touch sand in such awareness, and not respect it. . . . [13]

Discovery implies receptivity to all things: the rejection of no single one, save it be unreal. Prior to the present phase, because he was denied by others, the Negro denied them and necessarily denied himself. Forced to say nay to the white world, he was negative toward his own life. Judged by appearance, he considered appearances seriously, and had no time to find out what lay beneath the creature that America had made of him. And since he rejected this creature, he rejected everything. Something has happened. I have tried to suggest the nature of this happening. An impulse is at work within him, transforming rejections to acceptances, denials to affirmations. It is detaching the essential Negro from the social crust. One may define the impulse; it would be premature to name the substances that may be revealed by it. I think it best not to attempt it. For should there be set up an arbitrary figure of a Negro, composed of what another would have him be like, and the assertion made that he should model himself after it, this figure, though prompted by the highest interest, would nevertheless share the false and constricting nature of all superimposed images. Rather, I would be receptive of his reality as it emerges (being active only by way of aid to this emergence), assured that in proportion as he discovers what is real within him, he will create, and by that act at once create himself and contribute his value to America.

[1925?]

Earl R. Browder

"The New Negro: A Notice of Alain Locke's Book"

Daily Worker, December 12, 1925[14]

"The New Negro, An Interpretation," Edited by Alain Locke, New York, Albert and Charles Boni, 1925. Price $5.00

"This volume," begins the editor in his forward [*sic*], "aims to document the New Negro culturally and socially—to register the transformation of the inner and outer life of the Negro in America that have so significantly taken place in the last few years." And no matter how many reservations may be made, as to the adequacy of a book which almost completely ignores the economic basis of its subject, the book stands out as a ringing challenge to American society. The Negro has become conscious of himself. He feels the powers of all humanity within his own spirit. He brings these powers to expression and finds them equal to the best of the "superior races." A revolution takes place in the minds of the Negro masses!

A review of this important book, which summarizes the cultural processes that have been going on among the Negroes for some years, particularly since the war, can be written only after a careful study of it. The book is just off the press. It's [*sic*] table of contents immediately marks it as a noteworthy work, which must be brought to the attention of everyone who realizes that the awakening of the Negroes to consciousness is one of the most important and interesting facts of American life. This notice, preliminary to a later review, is intended to serve only to arouse interest in an important book, not to pass judgment upon it except as to its importance.

The book opens with essays: "The New Negro" by Alain Locke, "Negro Art and America" by Albert C. Barnes, "The Negro in American Literature" by William Stanley Braithwaite, and "Negro Youth Speaks" by Alain Locke. Then there follows the work of Negro artists, in fiction (selections from six Negro writers); poetry (from nine poets, including Claude McKay, James Weldon Johnson, and Georgia Douglas

Johnson, who are familiar to readers of the Liberator and the Workers Monthly); drama (from three Negro writers, including a play by Willis Richardson); music (four contributors). Five essays on "The Negro Digs Up His Past" complete Part I of the book which bears the general title of "The Negro Renaissance."

Part II is entitled "The New Negro in a New World." It lacks the color, the energy, the self-confidence of the first part, and shows the "New Negro" groping thru the devious paths of bourgeois culture and bourgeois institutions, quite evidently not himself, not at home, but as yet unable to sound a clear note of protest against the distortions of established middle class social forms. As one of the contributors says: "When I visit the Business Men's Association, the difference between this gathering and that of any Rotary Club is imperceptible." And Part II of "The New Negro" reeks thruout [*sic*] of the atmosphere of the Rotary Club.

This is, of course, inevitable. Only thru bitter disillusionment will the New Negro find his way out of the marshes of the middle-class "culture" of America and shake the last fetters from his mind. Only when the Negro finds his intellectual home with the revolutionary working class, abandons his dreams of a bourgeois paradise, will he reach his full stature. As yet we find but faint echoes of such development in books such as "The New Negro." To hear the real note of the future on the problems of "The New Negro in a New World" one must turn toward the American Negro Labor Congress.

The book closes its 445 pages with a rich bibliography which is of great value. And the book itself, as a product of the printer's and binder's art, is a thing of beauty of which the publishers may be proud; not the least pleasing feature being the splendid portraits and decorations by Winold Reiss. A serious review of the book must be undertaken after more prolonged study than has yet been possible—and perhaps by more competent hands.

Amy Jacques Garvey
"Woman's Function in Life"

Negro World, December 19, 1925

QUITE frequently we hear the question debated as to whether woman's place is in the home, in business, in politics or in industry. Countries differ as to woman's status; but present day events convince us that woman, lovely woman, if you please, is making her presence felt in every walk of life.

Some men are slow to admit that the woman of today has a place in nearly all phases of man's life, and when such a place is not yet properly established, her voice is heard in that regard, yet these men are the ones who more readily fall under the influence of mere woman.

The women of the East are fast being emancipated and educated to the point where they no longer consider themselves human incubators and slaves to do the bidding of their husbands, but intelligent, independent human beings to assert and maintain their rights in co-partnership with their men.

Recently Mustapha Kemal Pasha, one of the westernized leaders of the East, while addressing some students at the Girls' Training School at Smyrna, was asked the question, "What must Turkish women be?" And he replied as follows:

Turkish women must have the best cultivated minds, and must be the most virtuous and the most serious ladies in the world. The duties of Turkish women ought to be to prepare future generations who will be able to protect their country mentally, morally and physically. Women being the source of the nation and the basis of human society, they can only fulfill their duty when they are virtuous.

This splendid answer should serve as a guide for Negro women the world over. They must realize that they are indeed the basis of human society, and that the race cannot achieve nationhood and world power unless the women are prepared to wield the proper influence over the men, and exact from them service to race and love for country.

Eastern women are taking an active part in all movements for the liberation of their people. Whether they be in India, Egypt or Turkey the new woman is making her impress on the world. Who knows but because of the softening, conscientious effect of woman's entry into politics and big conferences, that the world will be better off and will in the future more readily concede to every race and nation its moral rights. Women are supposed to be tenderhearted. Well, if they can succeed in putting a little more heart in this sordid selfish world, they will be able to lessen wars and racial conflicts.

Woman's function in life is to soften the ills of this wicked old world and to draw man nearer his Creator, in the practice of his beliefs and in his mode of living. If in the carrying out of this most noble task any new departure has to be undertaken it is the duty of noble woman to rise to the exigencies of the demand and continue upon her desired course, "blessing and blessed where'er she goes."

Women of the Negro race! If you have not yet hearkened to the call to duty, do it now, and fall in line with the women of the Universal Negro Improvement Association who feel that their place is alongside of the men, in the thick

Amy Jacques Garvey, ca. 1919. Courtesy of the Schomburg Center for Research in Black Culture, The New York Public Library, Astor, Lenox and Tilden Foundations.

of the battle, if need be, but always serving the cause of their oppressed race, in the endeavor to redeem Africa, and to lift the race to the level of progress and respect enjoyed by other peoples. Think ye that this is woman's most perfect function in life? Then join our band, and make your contribution, while you are young and full of hope. Mother Africa needs the assistance of her scattered daughters, and surely she shall not call in vain.

V. F. Calverton
"The Latest Negro"

Nation, December 30, 1925[15]

The New Negro. Edited by Alain Locke. Albert and Charles Boni. $5.

This book marks an epoch in the hectic career of the American Negro. It illuminates an intellectual revolution which owes its origin and expression to a multiplying series of social changes during the past decade. In undermining and annihilating the Negro myth it functions as a clarifying and signal contribution to contemporary thought.

What is the new Negro? The old Negro, according to the common conception, was an indolent, docile creation without the spirit of resistance or the desire for independence. Like most common conceptions, this one is wildly erroneous. Before the American Revolution alone, for instance, over twenty-five rebellions of black slaves occurred. After the revolution the rebellions multiplied. The struggle in Haiti under the courageous leadership of Toussaint L'Ouveture, the aid rendered Bolivar in his vivid victories in South and Central America, the reaction of the Negro in the past war all parade in formidable contradiction to the conception. These insurrections, however, were evidences of primitive recalcitrancy and aggressiveness rather than of a provocative and intelligent rebelliousness. They were the frantic, futile struggles of a suppressed race. The new Negro represents a different reaction. He is rebellious likewise, but his passions have become subtilized, his primitivism refined. He has discovered a new weapon—the pen. A new culture is in the process of evolution. And the present volume is an expression of that culture. The great diversity among the topics it treats is a sound indication of the versatility of the Negro genius. Here is represented the effervescence of a new spirit in an ancient people.

The cultural growth of the Negro since the Civil War went through two evolutions before it reached its present culmination in the philosophy of the new Negro. The first stage was characterized by a passionate imitation of the culture of the white race. White mores, white conceptions, white ideals became for the Negro the source of both inspiration and aspiration. Negro leaders fell in line with this servile, goose-step procession. The second stage revealed a revolution in attitude. This period was marked by the literature of protest. Imitation was transformed into antagonism. Things white were denounced and things black were eulogized. In Negro fiction, for example, the heroes were black and the villains white. It was a period of melodramatic sentimentality. This stage reached its apex of extravagance and fanaticism in the Garvey movement with its "back to Africa" slogan, its Black Star Line steamship company, its black god, black madonna, and black Jesus. The third and latest stage is without the servility of the first or the exaggeration of the second. Now the aim is for firmer form and stricter substance, and there has already been attained an objectivity of description and exposition which is novel in Negro art. In the fiction of the new Negro the good characters are no longer always Negroes or the bad characters always whites; they vary with the shift of episode, the science of situation. The imitation and hostility of the first two periods have been swallowed up by the growing objectivity of the third. In Negro sociology the same vicissitudes of thought and sentiment are to be detected. Armstrong and Booker T. Washington, the founders of the schools at Hampton and Tuskegee, with their emphasis upon adaptation, their advocacy of industrial education, their denunciation of resistance, represented the first stage; Burghardt DuBois and the National Association for the Advancement of Colored People, with their defiant declaration of human rights and their sentimental exaltation of all things black, represented the second stage; while Charles Johnson (editor of *Opportunity*), Alain Locke, and Abram L. Harris, Jr., with their plea for an objective approach to the entire race problem and an equally impartial study of things Negro and white, represent the third stage.

Slavery had bred despair and a yearning for the bright vistas of another world. Without happiness or hope, it had turned the Negro from the real to the ethereal, from the earthly to the Elysian. This other-worldly religiosity, while productive of the exquisite music of the "spirituals," has handicapped the Negro in his progress in this world; and it has infused Negro art and philosophy with a sen-

timentality from which it rarely has been able to escape. It lingers yet, a vestige that scarcely has begun to wither. The fiction contained in the present volume, for instance, suffers chiefly from the defects of this sentimentality, this inability to create art without melodrama, beauty without crudity. Fisher, Matheus, Hurston, and Nugent, all earnest and sincere craftsmen, are still fettered by amateurish techniques and by styles that stumble instead of flow. The work of Eric Walrond is more advanced. Although superficial in substance, his story is redeemed by diction that glitters if not glows and by a spirit that is fresh if not spontaneous. Jean Toomer, however, is the general of the group. His work transcends in significance and beauty everything that has been produced in Negro fiction. He is the Lafcadio Hearn of Negro literature. In a style as subtle as a dream he has beautified the trivial and ensnared the elusive. And Countee Cullen has well-nigh achieved in poetry what Toomer has achieved in prose. McKay in places is brilliant, and Hughes is often persuasive, but Cullen is in a score of ways their superior. Among the essays those of Charles S. Johnson, M. J. Herskovits, Walter White, and E. Franklin Frazier are most significant.

In the next fifteen years a still newer Negro will be evolved. That Negro, in a still newer book, will leave an even greater record of the increasing genius of his race.

William H. Ferris
"The Myth of the New Negro"
Spokesman, July 1925

There has been so much talk and writing about *The New Negro* that it is well to ask, "Is the Negro of 1926 different from the Negro of 1895, 1900 and 1905?" If in the summer of 1906, when the Atlanta Riot had occurred and when Max Bar-

ber, the editor of *Voice of the Negro*, was forced to leave Atlanta, Ga., and to give up his paper, all of the issues of his brilliant magazine had been bound together and published in a single volume, I am inclined to believe that the book would have been similar in plan and scope and equally as instructive and entertaining as *The New Negro*.

And if the papers read before the American Negro Academy in March, 1897, when Dr. Alexander Crummell spoke on "Civilization, the Primal Need of the Negro Race," and "The Attitude of the American Mind Toward the Negro Intellect," Dr. Du Bois on "The Conservation of Races" and Prof. Kelly Miller on "Hoffman's 'Race Traits and Tendencies of the American Negro,'" the papers read before the same organization in December, 1897, on "The Race Problem in the Light of the Evolution Hypothesis" and "The Race Problem in the Light of Sociology," if the papers read around 1900 on "Disfranchisement," the papers read in December, 1902, on "The Negro's Religion" and the papers read in December, 1906, on "Negro Labor and Foreign Emigrant Labor" could be published in a single volume, the scholarship, philosophical analysis, sociological insight displayed would have startled the world and made as strong an impression as the essays on the New Negro.

Some may claim that the New Negro is more poetic than the Negro of 1896 and 1906, but in those days Paul Laurence Dunbar, Rev. James D. Corrothers, D. Webster Davis, Silas Floyd,

Toomey and others produced excellent poetry and Lillian Lewis, Victoria Earle Matthews and Alice Ruth Moore wrote interesting sketches.

Some may claim that the New Negro is more assertive regarding his civil and political rights than the old Negro, but at the Faneuil Hall, Mass. Meeting of the Colored National League in February, 1898, the state Sumner League convention in Savin Rock, Conn. in August, 1898, when James W. Peaker, Counsellor D. Macon Webster of New York and T. Thomas Fortune, editor of the *New York Age*, spoke, and at the Afro-American Council, called by Bishop Alexander Walters and T. Thomas Fortune in Washington, D.C., in December, 1898, speeches were delivered as bold and fearless as any heard today.

The Faneuil Hall Mass Meeting of the Colored National League caused Henry Cabot Lodge to introduce in Congress, a discussion on the floor of Congress the heralding the same through the Associated Press, the printing of the same in the Congressional Record and the appointment of a Senatorial Committee to investigate the [February 22, 1898] murder of [Black] Postmaster [Frazier B.] Baker of Lake City, S.C. The State Sumner League was so potent in the closing days of the nineteenth century that President McKinley appointed Dr. [George H.] Jackson of New Haven, Conn., consul to Cognac and LaRochelle, France. One of the statements in the resolution of the Afro-American Council in December, 1898, read, "We regret that the President saw fit to pass over in silence in his recent message to Congress the Wilmington race riot, etc." And these things occurred before Dr. Du Bois published his *Souls of Black Folk*, and organized the Niagara Movement, before even Wm. Monroe Trotter published the *Boston Guardian*, and organized the New England Suffrage League.

Some may claim that the New Negro has more interest in Literature per se than the Old Negro. But in the fall of 1898 an Omar Khayyam Club was organized by Mr. George W. Forbes in Miss Maria Baldwin's home in Cambridge, Mass., to study the *Rubaiyat* of Omar Khayyam and Dante's *Divine Comedy*. Soon after, a Book Lover's Club was organized in Washington, and a Shakespeare's Club in New Haven, Conn. In the spring of 1896, Rev. Butler, a Methodist preacher, read a paper on "The Neo-Platonic Philosophy" before the St. Mark's Lyceum. In the summer of 1909, Hon. James D. Carr, Assistant Corporation Counsel, read a paper on "Evolution" before the Philosophical Club, which met in the home of Mrs. A. C. Cowan of Brooklyn, N.Y.

Yes, the Black Man has been revealing his mind for the past thirty years; but the country did not take the revelation seriously. It is a very hopeful sign that the colored man's higher aspirations are now taken seriously.

Alice Dunbar-Nelson

"From the Woman's Point of View"

Pittsburgh Courier, January 2, 1926[16]

Far be it for women to gloat over the way the sister-hood is attaching to itself the formerly exclusive masculine prerogatives. Not to mention women governors who are in danger of impeachment, there are bandits, bank robbers, embezzlers, female Ponzis, high flyers in finance, and what not. Is it votes for women, sun spots, post-war hysteria, the restless age, or the adolescence of the sex? Short skirts and cigarettes, fancy garters or sheik bobs, and all the rest of the feminine adornment or exposement, whichever happens to be the fad; Turkish women doffing the veil, Chinese women demanding the vote, the Orient donning the habiliments of the occident, Japanese women rolling their own, and college girls demanding smoking rooms, Fur coats and chiffon hose; German women demanding the right of their own method of self expression, the youth movement, and the barefoot cult, artists and models dressed in a scant bunch of grapes, modistes threatening Victorian bustles, upheaval, unrest. Whatever is the blatant sex coming to?

So spake Isaiah twenty-six hundred years ago. Listen to his tirade: "Stretched-forth necks and wanton eyes, walking and mincing as they go, and making a tinkling with their feet; the chains and the bracelets and the mufflers; the bonnets and the ornaments of the legs, the headbands and the ear-rings; the rings and the nose jewels; the changeable suits of apparel, and the mantles and the wimples and the crisping pins, the glasses and the fine linens and the hoods and the vails. . . ."

Sic semper the female of the species.

*   *   *

She had not had time to bob her hair; the babies came too fast. She did not know much about international affairs, and the latest agony story in the howling tabloid was unread by her. Her gingham frocks were comfortable looking and she was able to hold a cooling bit of soft loveliness in the hollow of her arm, while she cut bread and butter for two others clinging to her skirts. Like Werther's Charlotte,[17] when the artists begged to be allowed to sketch her she "went on cutting bread and butter." Nothing marred the serenity of her broad brow, and when the Man came home, it was to a well ordered house and steaming dinner and the understanding smile—all the domesticities that you read about in the old-fashioned novels and see in the hokum movies, and wish that they could exist again as of yore.

Where can you find her? Or is this a picture of two generations ago?

Her name is Legion. She is all over this jazz-mad, radio-crazed hysteric nation. Black and brown and yellow and white, she is to be found in villages and hamlets, in small towns, on farms, on Main Street, in New York and Chicago and Philadelphia and Pittsburgh. North, where she puts galoshes on the children and sends them forth to school; South, where she gives them a stick of sugar cane to appease the hunger of their sweet tooth; West, where they tramp miles across the prairie to the country school house, and in the effete land of the Cod and Bean, where she helps them to scan their Emerson before they pray to the God of the Pilgrim Fathers. She exists by the million, and realizing this, we can lean back and sigh with relief that the country is not going to the dogs any more than it was in the days when the first dauntless maiden had the temerity to leave off her bustle and hoop-skirt, or than England was when the fair maids at the court of Henry the Matrimonialist essayed the awful waltz, as they stood shamelessly and allowed courtiers to place a timid hand about their tiny waists.

No, she's a pretty stable article, woman. But she is not news, because she does nothing spectacular. It is only the abnormal things that get into print—like the old wheeze about the dog and the man and the biting episode, reversed. Comforting thought that. Plenty of mothers, and babies and bread and butter and little noses carefully wiped, and placid ignorance of abnormal psychology. Those women, in the first paragraph, who persist in breaking into print—little iridescent bubbles on the surface, forced up by ephemeral disturbance in the depths. But the depths remain, cool, placid, unmoved, eternal. Basic womanhood. The backbone of the world.

*   *   *

Inhibition. Wonderful thing. When the dog was a puppy, he could not climb over a chair, that was laid length-wise across the dining room door to prevent his coming into the room. But he grew into a great dog. And still the chair was laid across the door and he would come and stand on the other side of the chair, and whine and howl most piteously to come in. He had only to lift his huge paws and step over the chair, but because he had been trained as a puppy to believe that he could not cross that chair, he stayed out in the hall and howled because he could not cross the barrier and enter the enchanted land of food and warmth and tempting smells.

So the man of color. He was told some generations ago, "Thus far shalt thou go," and he still believes it. He has only to lift his huge racial might and brush aside the frail barriers separating him from the outside of things where he has been relegated, and step into the promised land—but he does not know that the barrier that seems so huge and real is after all—nothing but a few frail lies laid on end, and he looms above them, and can step over them.

That ancient standard of beauty, for instance. How hard it died. How many battles had to be fought before that lie was brushed aside, and the true beauty of color came into its own.

The French cabinet is changed again. One needs to be a mental gymnast to keep up with the politics of Paris. If Liberia or Haiti changed governments one-fifth as often, we should have learned professors rushing into print to point out the inherent inability of the Negro to govern himself, due to his highly hysterical, volatile and unstable temperament. And so forth.

*   *   *

This poor race of ours is always getting the worst of it. Now after the stench of the Rhinelander case has died down, we will have to carry the burden of owning the Artful Alice with her oared romance and still more bared back, who married a man so dumb that he thought a girl with a brown skin father, a black brother-in-law, and a golden body was a white woman. Though she repudiated her race, it must bear her on its aching shoulders. Thank Heaven by this time next year, the whole unsavory mess will be swept away with the cross word puzzle books, and the mah jong sets that we wasted our good money upon.

*   *   *

If the custom of selecting fair maidens to represent localities and clubs at the annual football classic continues, we may expect a beauty pageant before or after the game, comparable on a small scale to the famous Atlantic City pageant of moneyed fame. Why not? Think of a huge hall with all the golden browns from all the burgs competing for a Lincoln-Howard golden cup? When this beauty pageant is a reality, and the winner of them all bows over her golden trophy—a year or two or three years hence, what fun it will be to tabulate the long list of names of those who "first thought of the idea and passed in on, you know."

Gwendolyn Bennett
"The Ebony Flute"

Opportunity, August 1926

In searching about for a heading that would make a fit label for literary chit-chat and artistic whatnot I stumbled upon "The Ebony Flute." So lovely a name it is that I should like to have made it myself, but I didn't. I say "stumbled" advisedly. Reading again William Rose Benet's poem, Harlem, in the *October Theatre Arts Magazine* I was struck by the exceeding great beauty of his use of the "ebony flute" as an instrument upon which one could "sing Harlem." An ebony flute ought to be very effective for most any sort of singing for that matter. Ebony, black and of exquisite smoothness. . . . [18] And a flute has that double quality of tone, low and sweet or high and shrill, that would make of Harlem or any other place a very human song. No better instrument then for the slim melody of what book one has read or who is writing what new play than an ebony flute . . . speaking of Benet's *Harlem,* what a lovely thing it is! It opens with:

> *I want to sing Harlem on an ebony flute*
> *While trap-drums ruffle to a crash and*
>   *blare,*
> *With a clear note*
> *From a sylvan throat*
> *Of a clarinet—of a clarinet!*
> *God and brute, black god and brute*
> *Grinning, brooding in the murk air,*
> *Moons of flame and suns of jet,*
> *Hurricane joy and dumb despair.*
>
> *Vermillion, black and peacock blue,*
> *Pink, plum-purple, zig-zag green—*
> *I want to sing Harlem with a paint-box*
>   *too,*
> *Shaking out color like a tambourine,*
> *Want a red*
> *Like a furious fire;*
> *Want a black*
> *Like midnight mire;*
> *Want a gold*
> *Like golden wire;*

> *Want a silver*
> *Like Heaven entire*
> *And God a-playing at his own front door*
> *On a slide trombone with a conical bore!*

And on through line on line of beauty that coins a Harlem as a poet would see it, lush and colorful . . . fertile like rich earth. On and on to its close which ends with the crooning of his "Mammy Earth. . . ."

> *O child of the wild, of the womb of the*
>   *night,*
> *Rest, and dream, my dark delight!*

Tropic Death, a book of short stories by Eric Walrond[,] will come out in October. Boni and Liveright are the publishers. I can scarcely wait for this book to be on the market. . . . Few of the Negro writers that are being heralded on all sides today can begin to create the color that fairly rolls itself from Mr. Walrond's facile pen. *Tropic Death* ought to have that ripe color that is usually the essence of Mr. Walrond's writing . . . and also a simple forcefulness that the author often achieves. . . . A new magazine is added to the Chicago list of Negro publications: *American Life Magazine*, Moses Jordan editing . . . the same Mr. Jordan whose book, *The Meat Man*, was published a few years back. The June issue, Volume One—Number One, carried "From Venice to Vienna" by Jessie Redmon Fauset and "Pale Lady" by Langston Hughes. I have not seen the July issue of this magazine but look forward to seeing the future copies that will come out. . . . Maude Cuney Hare has an article on *Creole Folksongs* in the July number of the *Musical Observer*. Needless to say, Mrs. Hare's article is adequate . . . certainly there are few people more authoritative in their speaking of Creole folksongs than she.

Aaron Douglas is doing the illustrations for Carl Van Vechten's *Nigger Heaven* which will appear August the twentieth. *The Publisher's*

Cover illustration by Gwendolyn B. Bennett for *Opportunity*, July 1926.

Weekly says that Mr. Douglas' advertisement for this book in the current magazines is the best for the month of June . . . but by far the most important thing about Mr. Douglas these days is his new wife. He married Miss Alta Sawyer of Kansas City, Missouri, on Friday June eighteenth. . . . The English edition of Langston Hughes' *Weary Blues* came out on July ninth . . . the second edition of *The New Negro* will be out in the fall. . . . The Negro writers must not let the first of September slip up on them without having their manuscripts ready for the Albert and Charles Boni contest. The address for sending the novels to the judges is 66 Fifth Avenue. . . . Thinking of novels makes me recall what Simeon Strunsky of the *New York Times Book Review* said not so long ago about beautifully written books . . . "The beautifully written book as

a rule is the over-written book. One sinks into beauty ankle-deep." He goes to quite some trouble to poke fun at the elegant conservatism of what is called beautiful prose today. But even in the face of Mr. Strunsky's caustic remarks on the question of beautiful writing, properly so-called, I should be ever so happy to find some of that ankle-deep beauty in the things that come out of the Boni contest . . . what of it, if some Negro should write a *Marie Chapdelaine* with its wistful but perfect simplicity or perhaps an "Ethan Frome. . . ." Mr. Strunsky rambles on to the amazing consolation that "We still have our newspapers. In them are the reservoirs of simple health upon which we can draw when the English language threatens to cave in under heavy doses of beauty between bound covers" . . . and we can do little else but wonder how any one can live in New York and see the rife yellow journalism of the daily news sheets and speak of the as the salvation of the English language . . . nor even the aridity of the *New York Times* could be set on the pinnacle that had been built for "beautiful writing."

"George Sand Reigns Again For A Day" in the *Times* for June twenty-seventh made me think of a young newspaper writer I knew in Paris who was always breaking into any conversation that chanced to be going on at the time with the information that he lived in the back part of a house the front part of which had belonged to George Sand . . . and I always think within myself that I could see in that about as much claim to fame as any. . . . F. Fraser Bond in reviewing *The Best Love Stories of* 1925: "Something has come over the American love story. . . . It seems to have grown up. No longer does it find its chief concern in the billings and cooings of tepid adolescents" . . . he goes on further to observe that "Peter Pan has put on long trousers." Can't you see some E. E. Cummings–John V. Weaver person coming forward with a "Come out of it Lovers" to scare away that something that has "come over" the love story of today. . . .

Hall Johnson's Negro operetta, *Goophered*; with the libretto by Garret is to have in it three lyrics by Langston Hughes: *Mother to Son*; *The Midnight Blues*; and *Song for a Banjo*. This operetta is for early fall or late summer production. Mr. Johnson is the winner of the third prize of the music section of the OPPORTUNITY Contest . . . and by the way, Zora Neale Hurston and Langston Hughes are collaborating on an operetta the libretto of which is to be by Miss Hurston and the lyrics by Mr. Hughes . . . they are also writing a musical comedy together. . . . Mentioning musical comedies of a dusky character reminds me of the ill-fated *My Magnolia* which ran for a single week at the Mansfield Theater.

Jean Toomer, author of *Cane*, is spending the summer at the Gurdjieff Institute in Fountainbleau [*sic*], France. . . . Countee Cullen and his father, Reverend Cullen, are traveling through Europe for the summer months . . . they will make many interesting stops chief among them a pilgrimage to the Holy Land. . . . Arthur Huff Fauset whose "Symphonesque" won first prize in the short story section of the OPPORTUNITY contest is to be a member of their party. . . . Dr. Rudolph Fisher has very endearingly nick-named his new baby "the new Negro."

Friday, July sixteenth, the annual reception for summer school students was given at the 135th Street Library. Mr. Johnson of OPPORTUNITY spoke on the OPPORTUNITY contests and what they had meant to the younger school of writers. When Mr. Johnson had finished his speech he called on several of the prize winners of the first and second OPPORTUNITY contests who chanced to be in the audience and asked them to read . . . "Golgatha Is A Mountain" was never so lovely for me until I heard Mr. Arna Bontemp [*sic*] read it himself. He reads with a voice as rich in its resonance as his prize-winning poem is in its imagery and beauty. It was good to see so many of the people who are writing and doing things together . . . Zora Neale Hurston, Bruce Nugent, John Davis . . . Langston Hughes who talked a bit about blues and spirituals and then read some of the new ones he had been doing . . . and just before he sat down he read a poem called "Brass Spittoons" . . . as lovely as are many things with much more delectable names.

Horace Liveright is busy casting his play *Black Boy* for its fall production. Paul Robeson is to play the lead which I understand is to be a prize-fighter. I heard Mr. Liveright say the other night that he was having difficulty in finding an actress for the role of Irene who plays in the lead opposite Mr. Robeson. This part is difficult to fill since the heroine is supposed all during the play to be white and is discovered at the end to be a colored girl who "passes." Remembering the harmful publicity that attended the opening of *All God's Chillun* because of a white woman's playing opposite a Negro, Mr. Liveright has been leaving no stone unturned to find a Negro girl who can take the part. There are hundreds who are fitted for the physical requirements of the piece but few whose histrionic powers would measure up to the standard of Broadway production.

Clarissa Scott of Washington dropped into the office the other day on her first trip in the interest of the new social investigation work she is to be doing in New York this summer . . . the same Clarissa Scott whose *Solace* won a prize in the OPPORTUNITY contest for last year . . . and it was good to see her again and to know that she would be in New York all the summer . . . sandwiched between talk of what was happening in Washington and at Howard the question arose as to what was the most beautiful line of poetry written by a Negro . . . her first thought was:

> *Dark Madonna of the grave she rests;*
> *Lord Death has found her sweet.*

from Countee Cullen's *A Brown Girl Dead* . . . strange how discussions of this sort get started, isn't it? I had never thought in terms of the best or most beautiful or the greatest line of Negro poetry before . . . there are several that come in

line for the distinction now that I come to think of it . . . without thinking too long my first choice is from Langston Hughes' new blues poem called *The Railroad Blues*. . . .

> *A railroad bridge is a sad song in de air*
> or
> *Where twilight is a soft bandanna*
>   *handkerchief . . .*

. . . or perhaps Lewis Alexander's

> *A body smiling with black beauty . . .*

or Jean Toomer's

> *Above the sacred whisper of the pines,*
> *Give virgin lips to cornfield concubines,*
> *Bring dreams of Christ to dusky, cane-*
>   *lipped throngs.*

We wonder what William Stanley Braithwaite would say . . . or Claude McKay . . . or Jessie Fauset. . . . But all that resolves itself into the hopelessness of deciding what the greatest of anything is . . . nothing is really greatest but greatness itself . . .

Melville J. Herskovits
"The American Negro Evolving a New Physical Type"

Current History 24, no. 6 (1926)[19]

Melville J. Herskovits
Department of Anthropology, Columbia University

FOR decades the negro has been with us, accepted as a menial, regarded as a captive savage not long out of slavery; indeed, as not far removed from the animal, doing the lowly work for the rest of us, taken as a matter of course when doing it. The negro, it has been felt, was all right in his place, and his place was not questioned by many nor even by the few until very recent times. He waited on his white masters at table, he polished their shoes or grew their corn or picked their cotton—he was the genial, obsequious Pullman porter, or the benevolently

regarded Uncle Tom type of old man, with his ever-ready, "Yas suh, massa!"

Recently, however, another view of the negro has developed. With a kind of naive astonishment, the discovery was made that this slave had produced music of fine feeling and vitality. Not only that, the words he had made to this music were of a poetic quality of no mean sort. We began to hear of his asserting his independence, of his moving North in droves from the South, where he was held in oppression; of his organizing banks and life insurance companies, of his attempting art theatres, of his writing novels and poetry, of his building a Harlem in New York City. And then the discovery was made that we had with us the new negro.

What is this new negro? That is, what may he be aside from the things he has done? What is his ancestry, and to what extent can we call him negro at all? It is amazing when we think that, with all the admitted seriousness of the negro problem before us, there has been absolutely no attempt to discover what has been happening to the negro physically and racially in all the years he has been in this country. We know, of course, that there has been a vast amount of white blood poured into the negro population during slavery times, but we have never tried to investigate how this might have affected the physical structure of the resulting generations, theorize though we may have about intellectual effect. We do not, as a matter of fact, even know the tribes of Africa from which the African ancestors of our negro population came; whether they came from the people we call "true negroes" or from the mixed peoples who live to the north of these tribes in Africa.

To be sure, we have advanced all manner of theories on this subject, and it is with them, quite unsubstantiated in the main by factual data, that we have tried to consider the problem of the negro in this country. For example, you have often heard that the negro was "breeding out" through the infusion of white blood, and that, given enough time, the negro problem will thus disappear. But there has been no attempt made to substantiate this statement and to see whether or not this was actually true. Again, you may have heard that the negro, being a cross between two racial groups, is so mixed that nothing can be done with him, and that since mixture always lowers the stamina of a people there is not much use, therefore, bothering about him.

In the light, then, of the many theories about the negro that we have heard advanced, it is interesting to try and see what has been happening to the negro since his ancestors were brought to this country from Africa, whether direct or by way of the West Indies. And about

the only way to see is actually to study the present-day negro population to the extent that we can get at it. If we take definite physical measurements, as must be done where anthropological studies of race differences, the effects of race crossings and the like are undertaken, on as large a group of male negroes as an investigator can reach, we may find some surprising results. Because, going as one is, into *terra incognita*, one does not know what to expect. Naturally, one has an idea. One expects to find the negro in America an extremely heterogeneous group, which, because of the large amount of negro-white crossing, shows little stability in physical characteristics, and which represents a combination of the extremely diverse traits which characterize the whites on the one hand and the pure African negroes on the other.

Negro Ancestry

Such an attempt at getting at the problem of how the negro has developed physically in this country has been made, and the results are of interest because of the extent to which they go counter to just what would be expected. Of course, these results are tentative and cannot be considered conclusive by any stretch of the imagination. But let us see how one goes about getting them before we discuss them. In the first place, it is essential to know the ancestral stock of the negroes who have been measured. The only way in which these data can be obtained, since there are no accurate birth records kept in the majority of the States from which the negroes have come, is to take genealogies from the individuals who have been studied. Here we encounter a grave objection, for is it not axiomatic that the genealogy of the negro is without value, that the negro does not know his ancestry? Let us allow this point to rest for the moment, since I believe that it is not a tenable one, and I think I can demonstrate why. We proceed, then, to measure those traits which are of significance in the problem that we are studying—nose width, and lip thickness, and others of the type which mark off the negro from the white. If we are going to study what has happened to the American negro, and we know that he is a cross between these two types, it is essential to see how these "key" traits have been translated in the process of mixture.

What do we find has happened to the negro? A heterogeneous type as was expected, combining the traits of the ancestral populations, which are European and African? Not at all. What we have is—the new negro actually before us in physical form. He is a homogeneous lot. He is not a cross only between negro and white, but between these two and an appreciable amount of American Indian added for good measure, and he stands, on the average, apparently midway between his ancestral populations, not having departed toward either, but, in the process of forming his own type, having merged equally the features he derived from the one and from the other.

The work on which these conclusions are based was carried on in those districts where the new negro is to be found. Working on public school children and adult males in Harlem, New York City, and at Howard University, Washington, D.C., I have been able to measure over 2,000 individuals who have come from all over the country, and not only from all over this country, but some from the West Indies as well. You may say that there has been a process of selection, which has brought these people North from where they were born, that has given them the urge to go to the university. I should not deny it, but I should merely point out that one cannot be too sure that this is the case. If you compare the averages for the series of these men measured by me with that which was measured in the army during the war—when a very large number of negroes from all over the country were measured (over 6,000)—you will find that there is no appreciable difference between those army averages and those which I obtained.

This seems to show that the sample I have measured is a representative one. Of course, you may query regarding the large infusion of negroes from the West Indies into our population in the past few years. But I do not believe that this affects our results greatly—the vast majority of the Howard University students I

measured were born in this country—nor is it likely that it would affect the findings in any case, since there is no evidence to show that the racial composition of either the African or European ancestry of the West Indian negroes is very different from that of those of this country. At any rate, it is a point which remains to be investigated, since it has not been studied thus far. And it is one which need only be mentioned in passing, since the adult sample on which I have worked is so comparatively free from the West Indian element. Let us, therefore, with this aside, see what we get.

If we take the average of the adult male group which I measured, and compare it for any physical trait such as lip thickness, or head form, or stature, or almost any other trait in which the African negro differs from the white European (the American Indian averages are usually quite near the white ones) you will find that the American negro averages are about half-way between those for the other two. Take nostril width for example—certainly a "key" trait as far as negro-white differences are concerned. For the series I measured, the average is 40.96 millimeters. American whites average 35.0, half-blood Sioux Indians 37.6; but African Ashanti have noses that are 42.5 millimeters wide on the average, and the Kajji of West Africa average 45.51. Our American negroes are about half-way between the ancestral populations.

Comparisons in Stature

Again, let us take stature, another trait. Let us see whether the group measured by me is the same as regards stature, in comparison with the European, Indian and African populations to which it is most probably related as it was with regard to nose width. On the average, these negroes are 171.1 centimeters tall. Englishmen average 174.4, old white Americans recently measured by Dr. Hrdlicka 174.3, Iroquois Indians 172.7, Creek Indians 173.5, Scotsmen 172.1. How about the Africans? The Kanuri-Bornu of West Africa (and all these tribes mentioned are West African ones) average 171.0 centimeters, the Kajji 168.3, the Ekoi 166.9, the Ashanti 164.2, the Yoruba 163.0. Here again we see that the American negro lies between the Africans, on the one hand, and the Europeans and American Indians on the other. Of course, these lists of populations are skeletal, and there are many more traits which might be cited, but they are sufficient to show what is meant when I say that the American negro—at least, such of the new negro as I have measured—averages in trait after trait midway between the figures for the peoples from which they have come.

There is another point to be considered. It was claimed that not only has the American negro blended the ancestral traits, but that he is homogeneous. Now, what is meant by this? It is not a term which is often used in the discussion of physical likenesses and differences, because our anthropologists have been so busy chasing the will-o'-the-wisp of race that they have not had time to study what has happened to actual existing populations. But it really involves what may be termed the variability of a population. If, let us say, in a given measurement, such as the height of the ear, one population ranges from 50 to 70 millimeters between the extremes and another from 40 to 80 millimeters, one would not hesitate to state the more variable to be the second of these two on this particular trait. Now, in a consideration of human populations, one trait does not have a great deal of importance, but when we find a consistent result in trait after trait (and some thirty traits have been measured on each individual in this study), then we feel that there is something of significance present.

Most students of the subject have held that low variability is an earnest of pure race. To be sure, when you find a race of people that is pure (and that really means, inbred) you will get a low variability, for all the individuals come from the same ancestry. But again, a result that is amazing when we consider the vast amount of mixture represented in these American negroes, it is found that here, too, we have this same low variability that is supposed to be an earnest of pure race. Yet obviously, there is nothing like purity of race represented in the American negro. Our common knowledge of history tells us so; the large number of the very light "ne-

groes" we see on the streets or meet in our daily existence tell us so and the genealogies tell us so. And still, if we again compare the variability of our series measured in New York and Washington with that of pure white populations, European as well as American, and with pure African negro populations, we find a result that is reasonably enough consistent to allow us to conclude that there has been developed a homogeneous type.

That is not the only reason that we conclude that the new negro is a homogeneous group. It will be remembered that work was done in this study with an unselected group of negro school children in Harlem. As is natural, there were measured numerous sets of brothers and sisters among these. Now, if we have family groups, we can, by a reasonably delicate statistical manipulation, tell the extent to which these families may be expected to be like one another. But if they are quite alike, we have homogeneity, and if they are quite different we have heterogeneity. That is, we set out to find whether the family lines of our population are alike or dissimilar when compared to the extent to which those of other populations are alike or not alike. What do we actually find? That the variability of the family lines of this American negro population is as low as that of the families of Tennessee mountaineers. On the other hand, there is much greater variation within the families, which points to what we are now beginning to suspect as true, namely, that there has been a great deal of crossing in the American negro population, but that this has been gradually diminishing, with the result of increasing homogeneity.

Misleading Census Figures

There is a point, however, of the reliability of the genealogical statements given by these new negroes.

What was obtained from the genealogical information given is vastly different from what has been accepted before as the racial background of the negro. For instance, the census of 1920 tells us that 15 per cent. of the American negroes are "mulatto," or mixed, and that the rest are pure negro. It is understood that the census figures are based on the oral statements of many different persons, and that no questions as to actual ancestry were asked. But my figures, on the other hand, show that only 20 per cent. of the men from whom I obtained information are *without* mixture, and the other 80 per cent. are mixed. It cannot be denied that here we have the effect of selection, and I am willing that my figure of 20 per cent. unmixed be raised materially when applied to the negro population of the country as a whole. I say this because of the fact that my material was gathered where it was.

There is little question in my mind that there is a strong selection within the negro community favoring those persons who look least negroid—who are the lightest in skin color, for example. This would operate to make a larger percentage of mixed individuals go to college, or perhaps to migrate to New York. This came out strikingly when comparative studies of the pigmentation of various groups was made, when I found that the Howard students were lighter than the New York school children, while these are lighter than negro pauper cadavera. So, as I say, my figure of 20 per cent. unmixed negroes may well be too low. But I am convinced that it is far nearer the truth than are the figures given by the census. In any case, I am speaking here of the new negro, primarily the type with which I have worked.

Another point which the genealogies brought out, one which is almost always overlooked, is that 33 per cent.—one-third—of the men whom I measured claimed partial American Indian ancestry. There are several ways of checking these statements. With regard to the

Indian ancestry, I tabulated the places of birth of the men who claimed to be descended from the Indian in part, and I found that by far the greatest number of them came from those States where, historically, we know there were large Indian populations. As for the amounts of negro-white mixture, the men were placed in four classes, ranging from pure negro to more white than negro ancestry, and then the average of the traits for the four classes were tabulated. The results are most striking. In every case, practically, and certainly for every important "key" trait, the group which claimed to be unmixed negro is to all intents and purposes identical with the African averages; the class that claimed to be more negro than white a bit more like the white, and so on, until the class which said it had more white than negro ancestry is not far from the averages for the European populations in the various traits.

To be specific, let us take three traits which are definite differences between whites and negroes. The negro lip is thicker than the white, the nostril is broader, and the height sitting is shorter (which means the legs of the negro are longer). If we tabulate the averages for each of the genealogical classes, remembering that each individual was placed in his class entirely on the basis of his own genealogical statement, we find the following:

Thus it seems that the validity of the genealogies is reasonably well established, to put it very conservatively, and that to say that our conclusion as to the amount of mixture represented in this population of the new Negroes is invalid because it is based on ancestral data given by the men themselves is to make a statement which must at least bear the burden of proof.

CLASS.	LIP THICKNESS. (Millimeters)	NOSE WIDTH. (Millimeters)	SITTING HEIGHT. (Centimeters)
Unmixed negro	23.9	43.4	87.3
More negro than white	22.5	41.35	88.1
About the same amount of white and negro	21.98	39.96	88.35
More white than negro	18.8	37.5	89.1

Less White-Negro Crossing

Thus, our conclusions, after all this measuring and computing, seem to show that we have, in actual physical fact, a New Negro. And how did he come to be? Certainly, if the genealogies are examined, there is a very small number of individuals who claim a White parent. But there is an appreciable number of White grandparents, and, if the record went further back, as it does in only a comparatively small number of genealogies, there would probably be even more White great-grandparents. It seems to point out that there is a lessening of the amount of crossing between the two races, a factor which would be essential to the establishment of the type which has been observed as a result of this study.

Here again, the objection might be raised that we are dealing with a selected group, that the crossing between Negroes and Whites goes on in the lower social strata of each group, and that therefore any conclusions drawn from material such as this are invalid.

A test would perhaps be to see how many White fathers there would be to a group of illegitimate Negro children. It so happens that this material, difficult as it is to obtain, is at hand. A study has been made by Dr. Ruth Reed of unmarried Negro mothers in the Harlem district, and here, too, an amazing result has been obtained. For only about two per cent. (to be exact, seven out of five hundred cases) of the fathers of the children of these Negro unmarried mothers are White men. Though these cases were studied in Harlem, I have been assured by those in a position to speak with authority on the matter that a similar percentage of crossing with Whites would obtain were the data gathered in the South. I myself have observed that there is a pressure within the Negro community against associating with Whites which parallels that in the White group with regard to Negroes.

And so I believe—for one cannot hold on the basis of the material at hand more than an opinion on the subject—that there is relatively little crossing going on between Whites and Negroes, and that it is this mechanism which has allowed of the consolidation of type which all our results seem to have shown to be in the process of being accomplished.

It is not strange, then, that we have the phenomenon of the New Negro. Along with the consolidation of physical type which has been going on, there has also been a consolidation of the American culture within this group, which now begins to express itself in the idiom of this country. I do not mean that there is to be observed any new "race," mystically endowed with peculiar qualities, which is in the process of formation, nor that there is to be coupled with this physical type any peculiar cultural ability. The Negro, after all, is the product of what he learns and the experiences to which he is exposed, plus a certain personal something which is inborn, just as are all the rest of us. And I draw no conclusions as to what may be the cultural and intellectual result of the physical mixture which he represents.

On the face of the results which have been obtained from this study—which, it must be confessed, barely scratches the surface of the field—it seems that from now on we shall have to think of the American Negro not as an African type in which there has been mixed a small amount of white blood, a mixture which is still continuing and that will continue long enough finally to achieve the absorption of the Negro into the dominant white population. We must think rather in terms of this New Negro, with his relatively homogeneous from and relatively stabilized type, who has solved the business of living in this American culture, and who, with his start fairly won, will press on in the American community as a full-fledged member of it.

Zora Neale Hurston

"'Possum or Pig?"

Forum, September 1926[20]

THE FORUM *stands four-square behind "The New Negro" in his literary as well as his economic progress. And it is a wise writer who realizes that glints of the old-time Uncle Remus "native humor" are one of the richest contributions that race has to offer:*

Before freedom there was a house slave very much in the confidence of the Master. But young pigs began to disappear, and for good reasons the faithful house slave fell under suspicion.

One night, after his duties at the "big house" were over, he was sitting before his cabin fire. From a pot was seeping the odor of young pig. There was a knock at the door.

"Who dat?" he asked cautiously.

"It's me, John," came the Master's voice. "Lawd, now, Massa, whut you want way down heah?"

"I'm cold, John. I want to come in."

"Now, Massa, ah jes' lef' a lovely hot fire at de big house. You aughter gwan up dere an' git warm."

"I want to come in, John."

"Massa, whut you wanta come in po' niggah's house an' you got dat fine big house up yander?"

"John, if you don't open this door, I'll have you whipped to-morrow."

John went to the door grumbling about rich white folks hanging around po' niggahs' cabins.

The white man sat down before the blazing fire. The pot boiled and breathed of delicious things within.

After a while he said, "I'm hungry, John. What have you got in that pot?"

"Lawd, now, Massa, whut you wanter eat mah po' vittles fuh and Mistis got roas' chicken an' ham an' chine-bone pie an' everything up to de house? White folks got de funniest ways."

"What's in that pot, John?"

"It's one lil' measly possum, Massa, ah'm bilin' tuh keep fuh a cold snack."

"I want some of it."

"Naw, Massa, you don't want none uh dat dirty lil' possum."

"Yes I do, and if you don't give me some, I'll have you whipped."

John slowly arose and got a plate, knife and fork and opened the pot.

"Well," he said resignedly before dipping in. "Ah put dis heah critter in heah a possum,—if it comes out a pig, 'tain't mah fault."

Stepped on a tin, mah story ends.

ZORA NEALE HURSTON. *Harlem, N. Y.*

William G. Nunn

"Has the Negro Church Been Weighed in the Balance and Found Wanting?"

Pittsburgh Courier, October 2, 1926

Rev. Junius C. Austin, one of the guiding lights of the National Baptist Convention, pastor of the Pilgrim Baptist Church, Chicago, and formerly associated with the Ebenezer Baptist

Church of this city, is the type of pastor who can lead the "New Negro" out of the quagmire of false satisfaction. A man whose word carries weight, and with a forceful, magnetic personality, Rev. Austin and others of his type are facing a menace we believe they can overcome.

"Hey, Hey, Charleston," Craze and Jazz Fervor of Modern Youth Presents a Serious Problem—Churches Must Realize Menace and Prepare Modern Remedy—Compilation of Figures Interesting.

Note:—This story is based on facts compiled through the Rev. Harold M. Kingsley, New York, and Lester A. Walton, feature writer for The New York World.

Is the New Negro, the Negro of 1926, turning his back on the religion of his slave-day ancestors? Is he reverting to the paganistic form of his shunted African forefathers? Has his church been weighed in the balance and found wanting?

It's the "Hey-Hey, Charleston" time and the high-priced pleasure . . . slowly but surely shove into a dull, gray background, the fervored and emotional "Amen" and "Preach it, Brother" chant of our mothers, the new situation is developing a serious angle.

Facts show that the Negro is backsliding. Visionary reactions of yesteryear have been replaced by the practicality of the pleasure-seeking mob. Estimates based on inquiries, primarily in New York, show that the Modern Negro is deserting the church. Out of a total Negro population of 12,000,000, one-half are not church members. Although these unauthoritative calculations include infants and children too young to be church members, the majority are adults.

Here are the figures compiled by Walton for your own perusal:

Place	Negro Population	No. Churched	No. Unchurched
Chicago	155,000	50,000	105,000
New York	175,000	60,000	115,000
Washington	120,000	40,000	80,000
Detroit	85,000	45,000	40,000
Cleveland	65,000	25,000	40,000
Pittsburgh	38,000	20,000	18,000
Boston	18,000	6,000	12,000
Buffalo	12,000	5,000	7,000

These figures show that although one-half of the Negro population fail to attend church, the percentage in the North is even greater. Nearly two-thirds, or over 400,000 out of 670,000 in eight Northern centers do not attend church.

That the angle is being considered seriously, is shown following a discussion of white and colored ministers of the Gospel at the eleventh biennial session of the National Convention of Congregational Workers Among Colored People at Plymouth Church, Detroit, early this month.

The Rev. Harold M. Kingsley had studied the situation thoroughly and he revealed astounding conditions. In his opinion existing conditions are practically driving the youth into the path of least resistance.

Church Becoming Negligible

He states that the Negro church, faced with new conditions arising out of unadjusted city life, is losing ground in numbers and waning in power. Rev. Kingsley goes further. He says: "As a deterrent from wrong or an inspiration for good, it is becoming negligible; that the probable explanation for this alarming condition is that the change to city and industrial life presents life to the migrant in new and complex phases."

Therefore, when The New Negro successfully readjusts himself to his new and complex environment, he has passed a test in stamina and social vitality that leaves him sophisticated, hardened, with "eyes opened." He unconsciously judges his religion in terms of usefulness and practicality.

Church "Found Wanting"

He is freed from the religious bugaboos of yesterday, from the "grave-clothes" of a dead past and conscious of the power that is his from the mastery of the hardest and highest economic environment in the world.

His church, aimless, programless, visionless, impotent, appears ineffectual and trifling. The Negro, like the Italian, is drifting from the church because it offers no solution for his new program.

The church of today is no longer the church of other years. Education has wrought a miracle. People no longer accept the ministry as the accepted standard of leadership. The church can offer no fundamental and practical solution for economic difficulties, for the poisoned barb of jim-crowism, for residential segregation, for the migrant as he faces new and difficult problems in the North, for the evils of immorality, carried on openly in many of the larger metropolitan centers where inadequate housing conditions break down clean thought and clean action.

The Negro Church has been weighed in the balance and found wanting!!!

The Goddess of Pleasure

The dull, gray, stereotyped background of the Negro Church, with its appeal purely to the emotions, has been practically obliterated by a new Goddess—reincarnated in a soft, multi-colored background of jazz and pleasure-mad youth—in short, the Goddess Of Pleasure Uncontrolled.

Carl Van Vechten, author of "Nigger Heaven," dares intimate, through one of his characters, that the Negro has always been paganistically inclined. From the days of the loin-girdled African tribesman until the present, the Negro has worshipped a God of his own imagination. As slaves on the southern plantations, the Negro inclined to unreal, fantastic religious fervor. Always emotional to the highest degree, his only salvation rested in a visionary world where "All God's Chillun" had wings. Such spirituals and other sacred songs as "Some Day, He'll Make It Plain To Me," "I Want To Be Ready," "Swing Low, Sweet Chariot," "Steal Away," and "Get On Board, Little Children" was a reactionary measure, quoted in words, of this hope.

But today, The Goddess of Pleasure has full control. No longer is the New Negro fettered and tied. His wings have been loosened, and he is flying straight into the arms of his new pagan God.

The era of the "Blues" and the "Charleston," together with the latest jazz hits, originally Negro, regardless of what the critics say to the contrary, is upon us. The Negro expresses his thoughts, his aims, his ambitions—in fact, his very soul, through his music. And now that the pendulum has swung, he has reverted to the extreme.

Suggestiveness is the keynote of his existence. Physical passion has come near carrying him back to the primitive state.

Such song titles as "Do It a Long Time, Daddy," "My Daddy Rocks Me With One Steady Roll" and "Shake That Thing," ofttimes referred to as the Negro's National Anthem, are the acme of physical suggestiveness.

From the church, where once dwelled the accepted leaders of the Negro, guiding their people from stygian darkness to the light of ultra-Americanized civilization, the "New Negro" has forsaken the teachings of his parents—"backwoodsy," he calls 'em now,—and tonight—any night—countless thousands of them may be seen following the path of least resistance.

A Discussion of the Negro's Future in America—Page 11

The Messenger

15 cents
a copy

The New
NEGRO

January, 1927

Messenger cover, January 1927.

The Path of Pleasure

And what is this new path? It is the "double standard" of youth. It is the path of pleasure,—personified in the theatres, the movie houses, the tea rooms, the cabarets.

And it is in the cabarets that the other extreme, the real contrast to the church is so highly noted. Emotion, here too, is the string upon which the harpist plays.

Soft lights, intoxicating jazz, more intoxicating anti-Volstead refreshment, the rapid swing of waiters, gliding over the floor to the latest dance craze, the suggestive songs which slip from painted lips of a female entertainer as she weaves through tables in flesh, colored tights in sensuous, undulating motions, the murky haze of cigarette smoke, used alike by the wide-trousered youth and the corsetless, bobbed haired daughter of hard-working parents—the modern girl—the close proximity of straining bodies moving in tense harmony as they sway, dip and glide in moral abandon,—the departure in the graying dawn, the swift rush of air to heated faces as a low-slung roadster swings over country roads, the halt in a secluded place, the "necking," the kissing—then, home or somewhere else—tragedy either way—that is the Code of Pleasure.

A happy medium must be struck. Negro ministers, some few of them, have looked at Religion through the eyes of modernism. In New York, Pittsburgh and other large centers, some churches are following the example set by white churches, and are luring the young people back into the fold with modern religion—in other words, talking to the New Negro in the language that the New Negro understands.

Chicago and New York lead in modernism. And if the ministers in these cities forget determination and meet on a common ground to solve a serious question, then something might be accomplished.

A. Philip Randolph
"The Brotherhood"

Speech at Manhattan Casino, December 3, 1926

The Brotherhood of Sleeping Car Porters Stands for Service Not Servitude

ON the 25th of August, 1925, in the City of New York, THE BROTHERHOOD OF SLEEPING CAR PORTERS was born. In the home of W. H. DesVerney, Roy Lancaster, A. L. Totten and the writer foregathered to plan the movement to organize the Pullman porters and maids. Joined by Brothers Frank R. Crosswaith and S. E. Grain the battle began.

It sprang out of a burning desire of the porters for the right and power to redress and correct long-existing wrongs that were naturally practiced upon them in the absence of their own organization. It was a resolute revolt against the Employee Representation Plan, an organization of, by and for the Pullman Company, which had utterly failed satisfactorily to settle their grievances. It had failed because the porter officials of the Plan were not free to speak up on the interest of their fellow-aggrieved porters because of the fear that they too, the porter officials, would be asked to turn in their keys.

It is significant that in less than a year The Brotherhood won an eight (8) percent wage in-

Cartoon depicting a dialogue among the Pullman Company, a Pullman porter, and Uncle Tom, *Messenger*, March 1927.

crease, change in the Time Sheet and better treatment generally for the porters and maids, results that have taken many unions ten and fifteen years to achieve. And this was done in the face of the bitterest and most determined opposition, backed by hundreds of millions of dollars of the Company, which bought up spineless Negro leaders and corrupt editors. And despite the importation of a few Filipinos to serve on Club Cars as a *scare* to the men, to break the morale of the organization, The Brotherhood men, with their heads erect, souls undaunted and heart throbs attuned to the hymn of solidarity, are moving steadily and victoriously forward. Out of every encounter The Brotherhood has emerged holding aloft the banner of victory.

But the struggle of the Brotherhood is far more significant than the benefits it has won and will win for porters and maids. Its influence and power have wide and deep ramifications in every phase of Negro life, developing and crystallizing a new hope, a new promise, a new courage and a new spirit of self-reliance, of independence and the *will to win* justice, economic, political and social, regardless of cost.

Brotherhood men are one hundred per cent union men. Their aim is to give one hundred per cent service as well as to demand one hundred per cent justice. Realizing that a Winner never quits and a Quitter never wins, The Brotherhood bows to the public with the slogan, Service not Servitude as the chart and compass of its struggle for simple economic justice, a struggle which will be long and determined since a practical consideration of the question leads to the conviction that the Company will fight for its Plan to the last ditch. But if we will work and not grow weary, fight and not lose the faith, we cannot fail. Long Live the Brotherhood! Long Live the New Negro! Long Live the Spirit for Economic Freedom!

Faithfully yours,

A Philip Randolph.

PART VI

THE NEW NEGRO RENAISSANCE: PART TWO, 1927–1932

Floyd J. Calvin

"'Economic Emancipation' Is Platform of 'New Negro'"

Pittsburgh Courier, January 22, 1927

A. P. Randolph, Leader of Brotherhood of Porters, Champions New Doctrine

Carries Case of Race Workers Before Government Mediation Board—First Official Recognition In History.

New York, Jan. 20.—Is there a New Negro? Some say yes and some say no. I asked A. Philip Randolph for his opinion on the matter. His answer seems to take it for granted there is a new colored man extant. He says: "The distinguishing character of the New Negro is his spirit of revolt against the old ideology and modus operandi of Negro thought and action in particular; his increasing development of a world view point, and his militant insistence upon the application of the principle of equality in the valuation of his talent, ability and genius."

As you perhaps know, Mr. Randolph is general organizer and leader of the Brotherhood of Sleeping Car Porters, the first organized economic movement in the history of the race. By the same token Randolph himself is classed as a new Negro, the most outstanding new Negro, because he has 5,000 men behind him, the greatest number of men to ever join an organization for their economic improvement. These men behind Randolph form the majority of the largest single Negro working unit in American industry.

According to a recent public statement of Samuel McCune Lindsay, economic advisor to the Harmen Foundation, and professor of social legislation at Columbia University, "The economic foundations of society are those on which all our other social structures rest." James J. Davis, Secretary of Labor, in a recent article said: "Some of the more turbulent disturbances in our history have been the result of the natural desire of man to dictate the conditions of his employment." A. Philip Randolph himself says: "Practically no economic training has been given the Negro in the past. His training has been chiefly industrial-manual or of the classical and religious type; and the chief forms of organization have been of the fraternal, religious, literary and civil rights nature. Never before has any systematic, definite, comprehensive agitation for economic labor organization as a method of solving the race problem been conducted among Negroes before the advent of the Brotherhood of Sleeping Car Porters. Thus, the movement to organize the Pullman porters and maids has been a national-school in economics for the race."

We are beginning to see, then, that the New Negro is seeking economic emancipation. He is seeking this emancipation through organized effort, by demanding that he dictate the conditions of his employment. And we have it on good authority that the matter of economic development should come before all else.

Since about 95 per cent of American Negroes are workers, any vital new movement affecting this mass would represent the New Negro. For that reason I went to A. Philip Randolph and asked him to tell me about the Brotherhood.

"The economic life of the Negro now has the center of the stage," said Mr. Randolph. "This came about in the general trend in world affairs toward economics. Internationally we hear of 'The Economic Consequences of the Peace,' 'Economic Treaties,' etc. Nationally we hear of 'mediation boards,' 'wage scales,' 'arbitration,' etc., all showing that economic subjects are of first importance in the public mind. The present machinery for dealing with the Negro problem is inadequate. Religion, civil rights and politics are but a reflex of our economic life. When dealing with these questions individually we are merely scratching the surface. Until we get down to the question of work and wages, of hours and working conditions, we will never strike at the roots of our racial ills. I believe the Negro public is gradually coming to recognize this, and when it does the race will be in a far better position to demand respect and action and get it from those in the seats of power."

The man who made this statement is the man who carried the case of the Pullman porters before the United States Mediation Board, through one of its representatives in Chicago on December 8. The Mediation Board was created by an act of Congress to adjust disputes between carriers and their employes [sic] without a strike. The appearance of the Brotherhood before the Mediation Board is considered by white labor organizers as a record-breaking feat in labor organization, since the Brotherhood is only a little over a year old, and has already enrolled half of the men in its branch of the service, thereby covering ground it has taken some white unions years to cover.

Getting the Negro workers' case before the United States Government in an official way with his own representatives is something new under the sun. It means that the powerful Pullman Company, one of the richest white corporations in America, may eventually be brought to terms by a mere porter. It means that the Negro porter, long abused and called everything but his right name, may in time sit in conference with those who have robbed him these many years and sign a contract to his own liking, stipulating how long he shall work and for how much money. All this may be forced on the Pullman Company by the United States Government, because the porters stood as one man behind their leader who has ideals and vision.

"The Brotherhood is merely the beginning of organized effort among Negroes," said Mr. Randolph. "Someday I hope to see a kind of economic organization, directing and controlling various crafts and divisions of labor among Negro workers. They will be taught how to strengthen themselves by the co-operation idea, by increasing their efficiency and getting more for their labor. Then the Negro can begin to solve some of the other problems which face him, such as are in the field of civil rights and politics. He will be able to make more headway

because he will have the economic strength to back up his demands."

Already the Brotherhood has made a daring, historical move in its fight for economic emancipation, demonstrating that it is directing its energies intelligently. In order to prove that the Pullman Company is systematically robbing the porters, it had the Labor Bureau, Inc., make an investigation of both the Pullman Company's earnings since its inception, and of the porter's standard of living. The Labor Bureau is composed of eight nationally known economists and the effort represents the first time any scientific study has ever been made of the Negro workers' economic conditions by a group of trained minds. The Labor Bureau took the history of the Pullman Company, year by years, since 1869, and showed exactly how much profit it has made, and how much surplus it has piled up at the expense of its employes. It also took the average porter's family and, according to budget statistics prepared by the U.S. Department of Labor, showed the porter cannot, on the wage paid him, live up to the minimum requirements of the American standard of living.

I asked Mr. Randolph how he came to get started in such a tremendous undertaking. "I have always been interested in labor," he said. "I was a waiter once on the Fall River line, and tried to organize the waiters to abolish the 'glory hold' [sic],[1] but was fired as soon as the bosses found out what I was trying to do. I became more deeply interested in the workers when a student at the College of the City of New York. There I was associated with a number of radical and liberal Jews, who smarted under the industrial conditions facing their own people. I began to think about the economic conditions facing my people, and from then dedicated myself to the labor movement."

Mr. Randolph was born in Crescent City, Fla., in 1889. He finished Cookman Institute at Jacksonville, and left Florida in 1911. On his arrival in New York he found a job as hall boy of an apartment house. Later he was porter and janitor for the Consolidated Gas Company. In 1913, '14, '15 and '16 he attended the College of the City of New York, taking courses in economics, history and philosophy. He was a frequent speaker at church forums, but his views were so pronounced and forceful he met considerable opposition. He founded the Hotel Messenger to fight the cause of the hotel workers, but after a time that died for lack of funds. Then he founded The Messenger Magazine, his present publication, to fight for economic freedom on a larger scale. Meantime he entered politics and was nominated by the Socialist party several times for Assembly, then State Controller, Secretary of State and for Congress. He has been fortunate in bringing to his assistance and to the assistance of the Brotherhood many white liberals and radicals of note, . . .

Devere Allen
"Building Tomorrow's World: The New White Man"

World Tomorrow 10, no. 3 (1927)

A HUSHED, rapt audience leans forward to watch in fascination the lips and gestures of an eloquent speaker. It is September 18, 1895.

He is a colored man. He raises his right hand with the fingers spread apart and utters a sentence which arouses his white hearers to intense enthusiasm. From that moment, seven months after the death of Frederick Douglass, this humble Negro becomes in the eyes of the American people the leader of his race.

That man was Booker T. Washington. And what he said was this: "In all things purely social we can be as separate as the fingers, yet one as the hand in all things essential to mutual progress."

This conception of race relations was never accepted by the leaders of the Negro race in the North, not even in Washington's lifetime. He has been dead twelve years. Those years have witnessed the greater part of the World War; our participation in it; the return of thousands of colored troops from overseas; the great post-war migration of Negroes to the North; the introduction and perpetual postponement of the Dyer Anti-Lynching Bill; the recent organization of the Brotherhood of Sleeping Car Porters—a history-making accomplishment; and, in general, a literary and artistic renaissance among our cultured Negro citizens. The emergence, in short, of the vocal, the irresistible, the "new"

Negro. The new Negro, whose soul, no less than his forerunner's, to use a phrase from Langston Hughes, "has grown deep like the rivers," but who more vigorously asserts as in Countee Cullen's line,

> We shall not always plant while others
> reap.

The new Negro, to be sure! The old Negro, emancipated though he was from chattel slavery, has lived in bondage none the less, and only now is he commencing to throw off his yoke.

But what of the white man? Despite the legend of the Civil War, he has allowed himself to be sold by his desire for dominance into a spiritual slavery. His back is bent beneath the burden of his own weighty superstitions, the load of his self-created fears. His dreams of the future are haunted by dire demons: loss of supremacy, reduction of economic gain, racial intermarriage. And exactly as the ignorant slaves of the South found their way to some famed dream interpreter, these modern bondmen have besought their scientists, so-called, to conjure Nordic strains, and cast the spell of psychological tests in order to free their dreams from goblins. But voodooism and medicine men, whether old style or new, can lure for long none but the ignorant and dull. It is because thus far we whites have not yet had *our* spiritual renaissance that we pay any heed to oracles who but bolster up our prejudices. The white man in our time is still the *old* white man, holding his hand aloft with the fingers widely spread, and mouthing still the old taboos.

The new white man will soon become articulate. Even now he is trying to find his voice. The new Negro could come first, because his burdens, though insufferable, had been laid on his back by other hands. The old white man, however, has lived these many years in thraldom to his old obsessions, and it will take much time to snap the thongs that bind him to his prejudices. Yet one by one they burst. And there will come in time the white man's renaissance, expressing itself perhaps in a new dedication to the art of living, and ushering in the new white man to lead his race from bondage.

The new white man will have to burst the bonds of *ignorance*. Last month following an address I had made at a forum, a man who had taken exception to my remarks on social equality approached me and declared that whatever came, he could never approve of social equality "because of the principle of the thing." "What principle?" I inquired. Whereupon he evaded every query I propounded, admitting that he knew nothing about Negroes personally or as a racial group, had studied the question not at all, but nevertheless was sure that social equality went counter to his "principles." The experience is so typical as to be almost banal. The new white man will not allow himself to be deterred by lazy generalities from widening the horizons of human fellowship. He will be aware of Negro achievement and cultural contributions. He will know so many Negroes personally, if he has the good fortune to deserve their friendship, that the experience of association alone will render him immune to the foolish phrases of traditionalism which often do, alas, get by as "principles."

The new white man will burst the bonds of *superstition*. "Negroes," often say uncultured whites, "are superstitious." And that, of course, is true of some, but as a fact, the superstitious Negro is excusable, since he is usually unedu-

cated. But what can be said in defense of the comparatively well educated whites who carry around in their heads superstitions about other races which are as unrelated to scientific fact as the "science" of phrenology? What of the tales to bulwark white esteem which are passed about behind hands raised to hide the lips,—the ugly jests, the myths, insinuations which are to Negroes only the vilest of lies, but to the whites who hear them, and the young whites in particular, the most insidious of poisons? The new white man will never hesitate to meet these whispers, no matter how distasteful it may be to drag them into the open. He will scotch them and the basic one on which they rest, the general faith in white supremacy.

The new white man will burst the bonds of *economic dependency*. When our country was new and cheap labor could not be had because land was free to all, slavery was the easy road for those who had to lean on the exploitation of others for their profit. Indentured labor was another contemporary escape from justice on a smaller scale. Freedom from chattel slavery brought by no means to all colored people freedom from economic exploitation. Negro labor today is "cheap" labor, and many a white-owned industry exhibits the profits that it does simply because it lives in a state of dependency on colored labor. The new white man will not fail to attack this extremely practical aspect of the race question; for without freedom to compete for his bread and butter (since we live as yet in a competitive society) what can mere physical freedom amount to? In the ranks of white labor, which for the most part refuses to admit the colored worker, will some day yet be heard the voice of the new white man, crying out the sound principle of all-inclusive labor solidarity.

The new white man will burst the bonds of *fear*. For underneath all else that stands between the races is the white man's age-long jealousy for his dominant position. The Ku Klux Klan, the post-war wave of Nordicism, were built up largely on the fear among the white "superiors" that some day if the "rising tide of color" were not checked, the pale-skinned despot would be jeopardized. It is the same fear, reflected from a different facet, which underlies the intermarriage bugaboo. You can't even mention social equality, as a rule, without being forced to discuss intermarriage in the self-same breath. It is frequently useless to point out the vast extent to which miscegenation goes on outside of wedlock, and the patent fact that social equality, by safeguarding the status of the colored woman, will tend to decrease racial mixture while slightly increasing intermarriage. The cautious may console themselves with this: that custom being what it is in the life of man, by the time when there is any wholesale intermarriage, there will be on the part of society a wholesale sanction of it. The mores can be changed; but you cannot change them fast.

It cannot be denied, of course, that economic class divisions have grown up, to some extent, within the colored race itself in the United States, and that within this minority caste group, though subject to all the psychological influences of discrimination against it, even color lines have been drawn at times between those of darker and lighter skins.

Is there any way of settling this question short of *complete* justice, *complete* equality, *complete* freedom for friendship? I know of none. It is because of this increasingly apparent fact that I am compelled to realize every now and then

afresh the audacious radicalism of Jesus' conception of human relations. Into a world regimented along racial, national, and religious divisions, he thrust the drastic concept of the Father-God and the Man-Brotherhood, all, every person, "of one blood" with all the others. It is he—not to disparage Lincoln—who was the Great Emancipator, for in his method there was nothing self-defeating, yet there were no limitations to his goal of fellowship. Equality to him was no mere sweeping away of barriers; it was a highly positive, creative, completely normal atmosphere in which could develop after the normal fashion the insatiate reach of human personalities for others.

And that is why today, anything short of his thorough-going principles is insufficient. For nothing affects the situation very much unless the new Negro and the new white man can begin to live, right now, the new life that will some day be the rule between the races. When hands are clasped as a symbol of victory over ignorance, superstition, greed, and fear, the widespread fingers,—symbols, instead, of perpetual separatism—fall very naturally together. Why not clasp hands so firmly that they stay together always?

Devere Allen [his signature]

Alice Dunbar-Nelson
"Woman's Most Serious Problem"

Messenger, March 1927

E. B. REUTER, in his latest book, "The American Race Problem," makes this comment: "During the past decade there has been a somewhat marked improvement in the economic conditions of the Negroes. This is reflected in the decline of the number of women employed, and in the shift in numbers in different occupations." This statement is followed by a table showing the shift in occupational employment.

From one elevator operator in 1910, the number jumped to 3,073 in 1920. Those engaged in lumber and furniture industries in 1910 were 1,456. In 1920, 4,066. Textile industries jumped from 2,234 to 7,257. On the other hand, chambermaids in 1910 were numbered 14,071, but in 1920 they had declined to 10,443. Untrained nurses from 17,874 to 13,888; cooks from 205,584 to 168,710; laundresses, not in public laundries, from 361,551 to 283,557. On the other hand, cigar and tobacco workers jumped from 10,746 to 21,829, and the teaching profession showed a normal increase from 22,528 to 29,244.

Just what do these figures indicate? That the Negro woman is leaving the industries of home life, cooking, domestic service generally, child nursing, laundry work and going into mills, factories, operation of elevators, clerking, stenography (for in these latter occupations there is an almost 400 per cent. increase). She is doing a higher grade of work, getting better money, commanding better respect from the community because of her higher economic value, and less menial occupation. Domestic service claims her race no longer as its inalienable right. She is earning a salary, not wages.

This sounds fine. For sixty-three years the Negro woman has been a co-worker with the Negro man. Now that she is more than ever working by his side, she feels a thrill of pride in her new economic status.

But—"the ratio of children to women has declined from census to census for both races. The decline has in general been more rapid for the Negro than for the white elements in the population." In 1850 the number of children under five years of age per 1,000 women from 15 to 44 years of age for Negro women was 741, for white women 659. In 1920 the Negro birth rate had decreased to 439, the white to 471. While the percentage of children under five years of age had decreased in the case of Negro women from 13.8 in Negro families to 10.9, and in white families from 11.9 to 10.9!

"In spite of the considerable increase in the Negro population and in the increase of the marriage rate, the actual number of Negro children under five years of age was less in 1920 than at any of the previous enumerations." In 1900 the number of Negro children under five years of age was 1,215,655; in 1910, the number was 1,263,288; in 1920 it was 1,143,699!

And this sharp decline in the face of increased knowledge of the care and feeding of infants; the work of the insurance companies in health, Negro Health Week, public health nurses, clinics, dispensaries, and all the active agencies for the conservation and preservation of health.

One startling fact is apparent. Negro women are exercising birth control in order to preserve their new economic independence. Or, because of poverty of the family, they are compelled to limit their offspring.

The same author, Dr. Reuter, tells us that a recent study showed that fifty-five Negro professors at Howard University had come from families averaging 6.5 children, while the professors themselves had an average of 0.7 children. Some were unmarried, but for each family formed, the average number of children was 1.6. "The birth rate of the cultured classes is apparently only one-third of the masses."

The race is here faced with a startling fact. Our birth rate is declining; our infant mortality is increasing; our normal rate of increase must necessarily be slowing up; our educated and intelligent classes are refusing to have children; our women are going into the kind of work that taxes both physical and mental capacities, which of itself, limits fecundity. While white women are beginning to work more away from home, at present, even with the rush of all women into the wage earners class, in New York City alone, seven times as many colored as white women work away from home.

The inevitable disruption of family life necessitated by the woman being a co-wage earner with the man has discouraged the Negro woman from child-bearing. Juvenile delinquents are recruited largely from the motherless home. That is the home that is without the constant care of the mother or head of the house. For a child to arise in the morning after both parents are gone, get itself an indifferent breakfast, go to school uncared for, lunch on a penny's worth of sweets, and return to a cold and cheerless house or apartment to await the return of a jaded and fatigued mother to get supper, is not conducive to sweetness and light in its behavior. Truancy, street walking, petty thievery and gang rowdyism are the natural results of this lack of family life. The Negro woman is awakening to the fact that the contribution she makes to the economic life of the race is too often made at the expense of the lives of the boys and girls of the race—so she is refusing to bring into the world any more potential delinquents.

This is the bald and ungarnished statement of a startling series of facts. The decline in the birth rate of the Negro. The rise in the economic life of the Negro woman. The sharpest peak of the decline—if a decline can be said to have a peak—is in the birth rate of the more cultured and more nearly leisure classes. The slow increase in the national family life, caused by the women workers not having time to make homes in the strictest sense of homemaking. The sharp rise in juvenile delinquency—in the cities, of course, and among the children of women workers. And worst of all because more subtle and insinuating in its flattering connotation of economic freedom, handsome salaries and social prestige—the growing use of married women of the child-bearing age as public school teachers, with the consequent temptation to refrain from child-bearing in order not to interfere with the independent life in the school room.

This is the situation. I would not suggest any remedy, make any criticism, raise any question, nor berate the men and women who are responsible for this crisis. For it is a serious crisis. I would only ask the young and intelligent women to give pause.

The new Negro is the topic most dwelt upon these days by the young folks, whom some call, frequently in derisive envy, the "Intelligentsia." In every race, in every nation and in every clime in every period of history there is always an eager-eyed group of youthful patriots who seriously set themselves to right the wrongs done to their race, or nation or sect or sometimes to art or self-expression. No race or nation can advance without them. Thomas Jefferson was an ardent leader of youthful patriots of his day, and Alexander Hamilton would have been dubbed a leader of the intelligentsia were he living now. They do big things, these young people.

Perhaps they may turn their attention, these race-loving slips of girls and slim ardent youths who make hot-eyed speeches about the freedom of the individual and the rights of the Negro, to the fact that at the rate we are going the Negro will become more and more negligible in the life of the nation. For we must remember that while the Negro constituted 19.3 per cent. of the population in 1790, and 18.9 in 1800, he constitutes only 9.9 per cent. today, and his percentage of increase has steadily dropped from 37.5 in 1810 to 6.3 in 1920.

No race can rise higher than its women is an aphorism that is so trite that it has ceased to be tiresome from its very monotony. If it might be phrased otherwise to catch the attention of the Negro woman, it would be worth while making the effort. No race can be said to be a growing race, whose birth rate is declining, and whose natural rate of increase is dropping sharply. No race will amount to anything economically, no matter how high the wages it collects nor how many commercial enterprises it supports, whose ownership of homes has not kept proportionate pace with its business holdings. Churches, social agencies, schools and Sunday schools cannot do the work of mothers and heads of families. Their best efforts are as cheering and comforting to the soul of a child in comparison with the welcoming smile of the mother when it comes from school as the machine-like warmth of an incubator is the a chick after the downy comfort of a clucking hen. Incubators are an essential for the mass production of chickens, but the training of human souls needs to begin at home in the old-fashioned family life, augmented later, if necessary, in the expensive schools and settlements of the great cities.

Hubert H. Harrison

"No New Literary Renaissance, Says Well Known Writer"

Pittsburgh Courier, March 12, 1927

[EDITOR'S NOTE—Dr. Harrison, who contributed an article in a recent issue on West Indians, is a staff lecturer for the New York City Board of Education. Although it publishes his article, The *Courier* does not necessarily subscribe to all of his statements. This newspaper is simply trying to arouse helpful and constructive discussion, out of which may grow a practical and sound program for our younger writers. Equal space will be given to any literary critic qualified to reply to this article.]

NEW YORK, March 10.—Doubtless you who now read these lines are "genuinely interested" in the Negro as he has been exhibited in recent or contemporary literature by white and Negro writers. Perhaps you are given one of the intelligentsia (the "g" is hard as in "get"), or one of the "new" Negroes. Of course, you know who wrote "The American Cavalryman," "The Leopard's Claw," "Veiled Aristocrats" or "The Vengeance of the Gods." No? Really? Dear me! But we will let that pass. These things are fiction and are not perhaps important. Though I did think that since you have bought and read "Nigger Heaven" you might have also read Miss Sanborn's book wherein a white author does try to hold your race up.

Well, then—But, surely, you know who is Alrutheus Ambush Taylor, and are acquainted with that fine sonnet on "The Mulatto"; have read Ferris' book, or at least know it by name? What? "Sidelights on Negro Soldiers," then? Or, "Two Colored Women, With the A. E. F.," or that immortal poem by the Baltimore poet entitled "Lenox Avenue"? No? Then, exactly what do you mean when you talk about a Negro literary renaissance?

Seriously, the matter of a Negro literary renaissance is like that of the snakes of Ireland—there isn't any. Those who think that are usually people who are blissfully ignorant of the stream of literary and artistic products which have flowed uninterruptedly from Negro writers from 1850 to the present. If you ask them about the historical works of Major Wilson, George Williams, William C. Nell, William Wells Brown, Rufus L. Perry, Atticus G. Haygood; the essays of T. Thomas Fortune, the fictional writings of Negroes from Francis [*sic*] E. Watkins to Pauline Hopkins, Dunbar and Chesnutt, they stammer and evade to cover up their confusion. And if anyone thinks that this is true only of casual colored people, I beg him to consider the following case:

In the year 1905 Professor W. E. B. DuBois of Atlanta University was hailed by black and white people as pre-eminently the "scholar" of the race. If anyone was an authority on the Negro American he was assuredly "it." In that same year the learned literateur brought forth under the auspices of Atlanta University a work which was meant to be authoritative. It was entitled "A Select Bibliography of the Negro American." Now, when this family album was assembled Charles W. Chesnutt, the greatest Negro-American novelist, had already published "The Conjure Woman," "The Wife of His Youth," "The House Behind the Cedars" and "The Marrow of Tradition." Yet you will search Dr. Du Bois' bibliography of 1905 in vain for any mention of Chesnutt. But that is nothing unusual for Dr. Du Bois. In his family magazine for February, 1927, he lists under "The Looking Glass" an unusual article by a black West Indian author in a white magazine called "The Modern Quarterly"—but he studiously refrains from mentioning the writer's name, although it was and is perfectly well known to him. He did something similar to Mr. George S. Schuyler recently. The significant thing is that this is not peculiar to Dr. Du Bois, but is a common trait of all our "guardians of the gate." No one can name a single Negro author or artist whom any one of them "discovered." They blissfully wait until some white person stumbles on him (as was the case with Dunbar, William Lonsdale Brown, Charles Gilpin and Countee Cullen) before they venture to acknowledge him; with the result that each such casual discoverer thinks that the stream of Negro literary production bubbled up at the precise point where he discovered it. And, so long as through the niggardly narrowness of the cowardly critical defect of such people the white man (who doesn't know our literary history) remains our only vendor of values in Negro writings, so long will we be cursed with Jejune Jazz artists who must have managed to hop over both Burns and Dunbar in their wild gyrations.

For, let it be said once for all, that if the hysteria of uneducated kiddies with which we are being deluged at this time is poetry, then the writings of Milton, Keats, Lowell, Dunbar, Hawkins and Claude McKay must be something else. At the moment of writing this I learn that one of these kiddies who has perpetrated two books of alleged "poems" is engaged in studying at school, for the first time, Milton's "Paradise Lost." One does insist that a violinist should have studied the violin and what has been done on it before venturing to ask people to pay for his performances. The same applies to a washerwoman with clothes—and to the entire range of art that links the two. One doesn't object to youth: Byron, Shelley, Keats and Tennyson were all youths when they mastered the technique of verse. But they mastered it first. And, after all, literature is the expression of life-values in terms of word-values. How, then, can we get literature from those who haven't lived, who haven't even read?

Over the Van Vechten matter Chicago, Pittsburgh and even Charleston have begun to sneer at this mushroom mentality, product of that enfeeblement which follows whenever the more sturdy types of mankind ape the more sophisticated and neurotic without understanding what they ape. The Negro has something to give to American literature; but that something will follow the line of "The Chipwoman's Fortune" rather than those of "Salome" or "Lulu Belle." It will root itself in the abler work of Wal-

ter White (his first novel). In scholarship it will build on Brawley, Taylor, Sinclair, Cromwell and Woodson—that is, something more solid than the mere knowing of their names! It will, see in McKay and Watkins the only capable poets of our race today—as Dunbar was, two decades ago—and will recognize in Countee Cullen (who is NOT a minister's son!) the one youngster marked out by Nature for a poet, with a fine development ahead of him rather than adequate achievement behind him. It will discover the virile short stories of William Pickens and the reasons why no white critic praises them. It will pounce on the earlier work of Kelly Miller and Du Bois (before the one began to talk twaddle in print and the other to imitate himself, like an ancient and animated dowager). But in that day the Negro writer will be going for his authority on race-values, not to Mr. Reuter (who lists Kelly Miller as a mulatto!) nor to Mr. Herskovits (who in a review of Talbot's recent work on Nigeria shows a woeful ignorance of that author's earlier studies), but to the place where he should go—to the broad bosom of his own people.

This "Negro literary renaissance" had its existence at present only in the noxious night life of Greenwich Village neurotics who invented it, not for the black brothers' profit but their own. Nor do their darker dupes stand on any safer ground. If anyone, in public, should care to pick any decade between 1850 and 1910 I will undertake to present from among the Negroes of that decade as many writers and (with Schomburg to back me) as many lines of literary and artistic endeavor as he can show for this decade. And I go further! I will also undertake to show (with perhaps three exceptions) more able Negro writers for any decade in that period than can be found today. The challenge is open to anyone—but I do suggest that they read some of the things referred to before they take up the gage.

And now, a word in closing about this Negro Harlem which the neurotics of the New Jerusalem have discovered. It has brains: I say this because I know, having lived in it for twenty years. I can walk a mile from the place where this is written and converse with the ablest economist (I used to teach economics to whites) of our race. A few blocks north I can shake hands with our best biologist (barring Ernest Just). I am acquainted with a journalist who slings niftier prose than anyone else whom I know, and a scholar whose book reveals a wider historic knowledge of racial contacts that any other scholar, white or black. Their names? Well, you would not recognize them if I gave them here. For Harlem doesn't "boost" Harlem.

Some time soon there will be a genuine literary renaissance, a release of creative energy which will face the task of expressing the life-values of our people in prose-forms redolent with the tang of great literature, with poetry that bubbles up honestly and spontaneously out of the wide experience and understanding of the Head: out of the warm intuitions of the Heart. But, depend upon it, there will be nothing in that Real Renaissance for neurotics to exploit. The men and women who create it will have to stand crucifixion upon the publishers' calvarys; they will not care to publish their writings. (For so long as the Negro plays the mountebank or the coward so long will his Boys' Brigades be worth playing with.) None of the white experts on "Negro" literature today seem to have heard of Taylor, Browne or Rogers, while they are tying ribbons on the little tabby-kittens whose reputations will be as dead as David's sow a short ten years from now. Even so, in that day to come, will they ignore all those who will be doing the good work in which neurotics find no bait for their perverted self-esteem.

Langston Hughes
"These Bad New Negroes: A Critique on Critics"

Part 1, "'Best Negroes Not Really Cultured,'" *Pittsburgh Courier*, April 9, 1927

Part 2, "Says Race Leaders, Including Preachers, Flock to Harlem Cabarets," *Pittsburgh Courier*, April 16, 1927

Young Writer, in Special Courier Article, Hits Snobbish "Nouveau Riche" Class; Defines Art

Says "Best" Negroes Think Whites Better Than Colored; "Slavishly Devoted to Nordic Standards."

(Editor's note [Part 1]: Mr. Hughes, who is a student at Lincoln University, was asked to outline his position on the "New Negro and His Art," and has done so under the title, "These Bad New Negroes: a Critique on Critics." Anyone who thinks Mr. Hughes is a literary lightweight will be surprised on reading this profound, hard-hitting, straightforward article. His article will be concluded next week, when he will discuss in detail his own works in light of the criticism that has been directed against them.)

THESE BAD NEW NEGROES: A Critique on Critics

By LANGSTON HUGHES

Tired of living penniless on bread and figs in Genoa, I found myself a job on a ship bound for New York in the fall, 1924. When, after many days of scrubbing decks on my part, the boat reached Manhattan. There was a letter waiting for me from my mother saying, "We're living in Washington now. Come home." And I went.

I'd never been in Washington before but I found it a city as beautiful as Paris and full of nice colored people, many of them nice looking and living in nice houses. For my mother and me, the city was a sort of ancestral shrine of which I had heard much. The great John M. Langston, senator, educator, and grand-uncle of mine had once lived there. Indeed, I was to stop with descendants of his and, of course, I would meet the best people. And I did.

But since this is to be an article on literature and art, I must get on into the subject. For two years, working at sea and travelling, I had been away from books. Many of my own I had thrown into the ocean because I found life more attractive than the printed word. But now I wanted to read again and talk about literature so I set out to borrow, in good Negro fashion, a copy of Jean Toomer's Cane. "What!" said the well-bred Washington folk. "Cane?" they repeated, not many having heard of it. Then I was soon given to understand by the female heads of several nice families that Cane was a vulgar book and that no one read it. "Why do you young folks write that way?" they asked. I offered no protest for I had not heard the question before and I am not much at answering questions quickly. But, amazed, I thought how a prophet is without honor in his own country, since Jean Toomer was born and had lived in Washington. Cane had received critical recognition all over America, and even in Europe, as a beautiful book, yet in the society of the author's own home-town it was almost unknown. And those who knew it thought it something low and indecent. Whenever Cane was mentioned the best Washingtonians posed this question: "Why doesn't Jean Toomer write about nice people?" and I began to think they wanted to add, "Like ourselves."

When Rudolph Fisher's City of Refuge appeared in the Atlantic Monthly (Washington is Fisher's home-town, too) the best persons again asked the same thing: "Why can't you young folks write about nice people? Rudolph Fisher knows decent folks." And then I knew the "nicer people" meant themselves.

Then Alain Locke's New Negro appeared on the scene with stories by Toomer, Fisher, Eric Walrond, Zora Hurston, Matheus and none of them were nice stories in the Washington sense of the word. "Too bad," they said. But the storm broke on the Reiss drawings. They were terrible! And anyone defending them had to answer questions like these: "Why does he make his subjects so colored?" (As though they weren't

colored.) And of the two school teachers pictured in the book: "Couldn't he find any better looking school teachers to paint than these two women?" (As though all teachers should resemble the high-yellow ladies dominating the Washington school system.) And always: "Does he call this art?" I said it was art and that the dark-skinned school teachers were beautiful. But one day a nice old grandmother, with whom I disliked to disagree, summed up everybody's aversion to Fisher, Toomer, Walrond, and the Reiss drawings in one indefinite but pregnant remark, "Lord help these bad New Negroes!"

Now that there has appeared in the colored press a definite but rather uncritical aversion to much of the work of the younger Negro writers and particularly myself; and because the Negro press reflects to a certain extent the minds of its readers, it is time to attempt to uncover the reasons for this dislike toward the "New Negro." I present these as possible solutions:

1. The best Negroes, including the newspaper critics, still think white people are better than colored people. It follows, in their minds, that since the drawings of Negroes do not look like the drawings of white people they are bad art.

2. The best Negroes believe that what white people think about Negroes is more important than what Negroes think about themselves. Then it follows that because a story by Zora Hurston does not tend to make white people think all Negroes good, then said story by Zora Hurston is a bad story.

3. Many of the so-called best Negroes are in a sort of noveau riche class, so from the snobbishness of their positions they hold the false belief that if the stories of Fisher were only about better-class people they would be better stories.

4. Again, many of the best Negroes, including the newspaper critics, are not really cultured Negroes after all and, therefore, have little appreciation of

any art and no background from which to view either their own or the white man's books or pictures.

Perhaps none of these reasons are true reasons but I offer them for consideration. Now I shall proceed to the defense.

Art is a reflection of life or an individual's comment on life. No one has labeled the work of the better known younger Negro writers as untrue to life. It may be largely about humble people, but three-fourths of the Negroes are humble people. Yet, I understand these "best" colored folks when they say that little has been written about them. I am sorry and I wish some one would put them into a nice story or a nice

novel. But I fear for them if ever a really powerful work is done about their lives. Such a story would show not only their excellencies but their pseudo-culture as well, their slavish devotion to Nordic standards, their snobbishness, their detachment from the Negro masses and their vast sense of importance to themselves. A book like that from a Negro writer, even though true and beautiful, would be more thoroughly disliked than the stories of low-class Negroes now being written. And it would be more wrathfully damned than NIGGER HEAVEN, at present vibrating throughout the land in its eleventh edition.

(Continued Next Week)

Says Race Leaders, Including Preachers, Flock to Harlem Cabarets

Langston Hughes Declares He Makes More Money as a Bell-Hop Than as a Poet-Writer

Young Author Calls Carl Van Vechten Friend of Negro; Women Put Men through Medical School, Is Claim

It seems to me too bad that the discussions of Mr. Van Vechten's novel in the colored press finally became hysterical and absurd. No book could possibly be as bad as NIGGER HEAVEN has been painted. And no book has ever been better advertised by those who wished to damn it. Because it was declared obscene everybody wanted to read it and I'll venture to say that more Negroes bought it than ever purchased a book by a Negro author. Which is all very fine because *Nigger Heaven* is not a bad book. It will do nice people good to read it and maybe it will broaden their minds a bit. Certainly the book is true to the life it pictures. There are cabarets in Harlem and both white and colored people who are nationally known and respected can be found almost any night at Smalls'. I've seen ministers there—nobody considers cabaret-going indecent any longer. And college boys, as you know, do have affairs with loose women. Some are even given allowances and put through medical school by such generous females. But nowhere in the novel does the author represent his college boy as a typical Negro college boy. And nowhere does he say he is writing about

the whole Negro race. I admit I am still at a loss to understand the yelps of the colored critics and the reason for their ill-mannered onslaught against Mr. Van Vechten. The sincere, friendly, and helpful interest in things Negro of this sophisticated author, as shown in his published reviews and magazine articles, should at least have commanded serious, rather than vulgar, reviews of his book.

That many of the Negro write-ups of my own new collection of poems, *Fine Clothes to the Jew*, were unfavorable was not surprising to me. And to be charged with painting the whole Negro race in my poems did not amaze me either. Colored critics are given to accusing all works of art touching on the Negro of portraying and representing *all* Negro life. *Porgy*, about a beggar in Charleston, is said by them to picture all Negroes as beggars, yet nowhere does DuBose Heyward imply such a thing. Newspaper critics, of course, came to the same amazing conclusion about *Nigger Heaven* picturing all Negroes as cabaret goers. And now *Fine Clothes to the Jew* "low-rates" everybody of color, in their opinion.

In analyzing their reviews of my book their main objections against my work seem to be based on the reasons I am listing below with my own comments following:

1. White people will gain a bad impression of Negroes from my poems. This then implies that a Negro artist should create largely for the benefit of and for the approval of white people. In answering this I ask these questions: Does George Bernard Shaw write his plays to show Englishmen how good the Irish are? Do any of the great Russian writers write novels for the purpose of showing the perfections of the Russians? Does any true artist anywhere work for the sake of what a limited group of people will think rather than for the sake of what he himself loves and wishes to interpret? It seems to me that there are plenty of propagandists for the Negro, but too few artists, too few poets, too few interpreters and recorders of racial life, whether choosing their material from the masses or from the best people.
2. My poems are indelicate. But so is life.
3. I write about "harlots and gin-bibers." But they are human. Solomon, Homer, Shakespeare, and Walt Whitman were not afraid or ashamed to include them.
4. "Red Silk Stockings." An ironical poem deploring the fact that in certain southern rural communities there is little work for a beautiful colored girl to do other than the selling of her body,—a fact for one to weep over rather than disdain to recognize.
5. I do not write in the conventional forms of Keats, Poe, Dunbar or McKay. But I do not write chiefly because I'm interested in forms,—in making a sonnet or a rondeau. I write because I want to say what I have to say. And I choose the form which seems to me best to express my thoughts. I fail to see why I should be expected to copy someone else's modes of expression when it amuses me to attempt to create forms of my own.

Certainly the Shakespearean sonnet would be no mould in which to express the life of Beale Street or Lenox avenue. Nor could the emotions of State Street be captured in a rondeau. I am not interested in doing tricks with rhymes. I am interested in reproducing the human soul, if I can.

6. I am prostituting my talent. But even the income from a very successful book of poems is not worth the prostitution of one's talent. I make much more money as a bell-hop than as a poet.
7. I deal with low life. But I ask this: Is life among the better classes any cleaner or any more worthy of a poet's consideration?
8. Blues are not poetry. Those who have made a more thorough study of Negro folk verse than I, and who are authorities in this field say that many Blues are excellent poetry. I refer to James Weldon Johnson, Dorothy Scarborough, Carl Van Vechten and H. O. Osgood in their published writings.
9. I am "supposed to be representative of Negro progress in the literary arts." To which I can only answer that I do not pretend, or ask anyone to suppose, that I officially represent anybody or anything other than myself. My poems are my own personal comments on life and represent me alone. I claim nothing more for them.

If the colored newspaper critics (excepting Dewey Jones and Alice Dunbar Nelson) choose to read only the words I write and not their meaning, if they choose to see only what they call the ugliness of my verse and not the protest against ugliness which my poems contain, what can I do? Such obtuse critics existed in the days of Wordsworth, Shelley, Burns, and Dunbar,— great poets with whose work I dare not compare my own. Burns was maligned because he did not write of Scottish nobles. And as Miss Nannie Burroughs says: "to come down to the nasty now," Jean Toomer is without honor in Washington. But certainly my life has been enlivened by the gentle critics who called me a "gutter-rat" and "sewer-dweller" right out in print! Variety—even in the weekly press, is the spice of criticism.

Since I am said to be the "baddest" of the bad New Negroes, I may as well express my own humble opinion on my young contemporaries, although I may vary with the race newspapers and the best Negroes. To me the stories of Rudolph Fisher are beautiful although he deals with common folks. To me it seems absurd to say that they are not elevating to the race. The stories of Sherwood Anderson deal largely with people of the same classes but white America

calls him one of the greatest of the moderns. If Rudolph Fisher can write beautifully about a poor Negro migrant from the South, more power to him. A well-written story, no matter what its subject, is a contribution to the art of the Negro and I am amazed at the educated prudes who say it isn't. Jean Toomer is an artist to be proud of. Wallace Thurman, Countee Cullen with his marvelous command of technique and his poems of passion and free love, Zora Hurston with her fine handling of Negro dialect, Edward Silvera and the newer poets, all are contributing something worthwhile to the literature of the race. To me it seems that we have much to be proud of in the work of these younger colored writers whom the old lady in Washington so disapprovingly called the "bad New Negroes."

Letter from Claude McKay to Alain Locke

18 April 1927[2]

Antibes, France

Dear Locke,

I see by Miss Gwendolyn Bennett's column, that you are again writing something about me. I don't know if it will mean anything at all to you if I say that when Louis Untermeyer was putting me in his anthology, he specially looked me up in Paris and told me just what he was going to do. I am always forced into the unpleasant position of making comparisons between white gentleman [sic] and black gentleman [sic] to the disadvantage of the black ones.

I am hoping that this time I shall not be as badly presented as I was in your "New Negro."[3] I picked up quite a number of mistakes before the volume was stolen from me at Marseille. And what you mentioned in your last letter concerning immigration and the title of my poem that you unwarrantably changed (making me appear as a ridiculous, angry person hankering after the unattainable flesh-pots of the whites) seemed so utterly irrelevant that I was dumb-struck. I could not think of any third-rate white editor and critic, who puts any value on a work of art as something worth more than a mess of American corn bread, who would deliberately violate an artist's work in the way you did. It seems to me that if you thought my poem dangerous from political motives, you should have left it out of your collection altogether and not violated it the way you did.

I write strong words because I felt strongly at the time about your action and still do. I must say frankly that from my experience, I do not think any of the American Negro intelligentzia [sic] have any real interest in art, Negro art, except as a decoration for their special social affairs. I would much prefer if you could drop me out of your contemplated book. I do not think that, as a poet, I have penetrated deeply into that racial experience that I have seen mentioned by you somewhere. There are many others to that heritage born and more deserving and humble and grateful, that you can find to put in my place.

I don't want my name nor my work to be deliberately massacred because of the exigences of false, momentary racial aspirations. We are so far apart in ideas, I don't know if I can explain this to you. But I am a man and artist first of all. The imprisoning quality of my complexion has never yet, and never will, move me to bend to flunkeyism and intellectual imprisonment with the sorry millions that are likewise tinted.

Yours Sincerely

Claude McKay
ALP TLS

Salem Tutt Whitney
"Timely Topics: Leave 'em Alone!"

Chicago Defender, June 18, 1927[4]

Men are vain, selfish egotists. They elected themselves the lords and dictators of the female of their species. They set up a standard of conduct by which women must abide or forever fall under the ban of disapproval or ostracism. It was not an equitable standard and women have been wise enough to know it. Now and then a courageous woman would come forward and make voluble protest, but the lords saw to it that she was quickly and effectively silenced. But even a worm will turn, and the female worms have turned.

They are now asserting their independence, and I glory in their spunk. They say to the lords, "If you can't make a living for me, I'll make my own, and since I am making my own living I'll do pretty much as I damn please." Now the lords are squawking louder than a farm yard full of turkey gobblers at Thinksgiving [*sic*] time.

If the women enter business the lords cry, "Masculine." If they go in for art the men say they are out of place. If they go in for a good time the lords cry, "Scandalous!" But the women seem to be deaf to their clamorings.

Even a house full of children no longer enslaves a woman. The new woman checks the kids with the next door neighbor or parks them in a day nursery and goes upon her merry way.

The average man will stand upon a street corner and look at the legs of other men's wives, sisters and sweethearts, until his eyes look like door knobs. Then he will hurry home and forbid his wife, sister or sweetheart to wear such "indecent clothing."

He'll stay out half the night and come home with an excuse that looks like a mohair suit in a thunderstorm, yet he expects his wife to go to bed as soon as she washes the supper dishes.

The new woman no longer stands for the old line of bunk. The men have their cigars and pipes and the women have their cigarets. The men have their bottles and the women have their flasks. The men have their stags and the women have their necking parties. What's good for the gander is sauce for the goose. No more double standard for them.

If men have their "chickens" the women have their "sheiks," etc., etc., ad infinitum.

"Don't preach morality to us: demonstrate it!" So saith the modern woman, and once again, as in the Garden of Eden, the man seeks to place the blame upon the woman.

Leave 'em alone: The women are all right. Nor are they a bit worse than in ancient days when they hid their charms under a white nightgown: or when they wore hoopskirts or bustles, or trains, or hobble skirts. The average woman who shows her dimpled knees in public will kick you on the chin if you speak about them in private.

The modern woman thinks as seriously of love as the old-fashioned girl that many men delight to talk about, but they are not willing to bestow their love upon a man with a heart like an apartment building. She looks forward to marriage and a home, but she insists that she be a wife and partner, not a slave or a servant girl.

Women are discarding the lords, tyrants and slave drivers as they discarded the corset and the long ground-sweeping, germ-breeding dress skirt. They bob their hair because it gives them a more youthful appearance, and since man never gets too old to fancy "chickens," who has the right to blame them?

On rainy, windy days men pick themselves choice spots on the streets and stand there in defiance of pneumonia and rheumatism, rubbering for a peek at the women's legs. The women very naturally presumed that men desired to see their legs, so they are giving them an eyeful.

The desire to please the male is the inspiration behind everything that women do. Whatever the women are the men are responsible for it. I say, play the game fair, and leave 'em alone!

W. C. Chase, "Flapperettes," cartoon, *New York Amsterdam News*, July 3, 1929.

Terence Edwards Williams

"Hard for Modern Young Man to Find Girl without Past: Writer Hits 'New Freedom' as Responsible for Girls Losing Poise and 'Finesse'"

Pittsburgh Courier, June 25, 1927

New Yorker Says Time May Come When There Won't Be Any Girls Whose Character One Can Boast About

(Known under the name of "Joe College" from contributions to the Harlem press, and Manager of the Uptown Legal Bureau.)

Just where 135th street crosses Seventh avenue is another way of terming Harlem, by which one can obtain a complete conception of New York City. It is founded on Manhattan Island, sex appeal, bootleg liquor and dough. Here is to be found the one and only Paris, Hollywood, London, Cairo, Berlin, Venice and Vienna all in one. Right here in this spot is the melting pot, it seems, of the entire world. Folks pour in here from Frisco to the rocky coast of Maine, and if you'll pardon me, I now refer to the fairer sex, and you know I love them all, love every one of them. But after all I am discussing this so-called "New Freedom," which covers a multitude of things or rather a multitude of things are covered by it. And speaking of "it," as Elinor Glynn says, one must have "it" to really appreciate this "Freedom."

I have been in many a party with many a fair one and have sipped and broken bread with the good and "bad," and it seems to me that every one has a different conception of what this "freedom" really ought to mean. Helen attends college up and around Boston and so does Herbert. Of course we all know Herbert dabbled in ginger ale or such before he went to Harvard, but somehow he fell in love with this lovely creature and—well it is a long, long story. Anyway they visited the Big City and our Harlem over the Easter holidays, but it wasn't such a fair Easter for Herbert for he saw Helen very seldom, for Henry, the former boy friend who hasn't such a bright future but holds a good job, has been "showing her the town." Herbert is somewhat in the dark. He and Helen are to be married soon and he can't quite understand her actions. But as the boys say, "don't wake him up, let him dream." We grant that Helen is the mistress of Herbert's destiny and while he came down from the East to show off his fair catch from the land of the Lowells and the Cabots, the "new freedom" kept her away from him while here, and that's that.

The "New Freedom" calls for shorter skirts, less clothes all the way through, longer hours, out nights and more Night Clubs nightly. It calls for more men or women, more cigarettes and more liquor too; it calls for more "Black Bottom" and "messing around." (You know the "Black Bottom" is quite a difficult dance for people over thirty, the "Messing Around" not quite so difficult but a bit more vulgar.) Aside from these, liquor and cash with a deal of petting thrown in make any party worthwhile.

Once upon a time—this is not a fairy tale—a man and a maid would be fair with each other, but the "new freedom" dictates the young lady must have more than six "lovers," or whatever they are—(maybe "petters"). I personally know of as many as five young ladies now who are each engaged to more than one young man at the same time. I know of cases where girls have been wearing more than one fraternity pin.

I am not so old-fashioned as some may think, but on the other hand I feel too much freedom will eventually lead to the brink of—what isn't good for the future. It is making the younger generation restless and uneasy, making it gradually lose all poise and finesse, making it put on a crude and common air.

Now you can't get away from it, gentle reader, the fair sex must eventually seek the glory and happiness that goes with marriage, a home and young ones, for which we are all aware the world was made. And somehow, to me, this new freedom detracts from the charm and tender ways of the dear creatures. Really, they haven't enough foresight, it appears, to look around and choose the better way—the straighter way. They are not able to think for themselves, and gradually they will lose "it" which is very necessary to make them desirable—to make them be in demand. To my mind this freedom has many good, sound points, yes—but they are overshadowed by evil ones, and for such reasons the lovely ones are fast slipping away from the path that spells love and joy.

Today the young man is confronted with a problem to find a girl without some dismal "past"; the plot thickens, for everywhere he turns it is something else—always someone knows something of no good whatsoever about the girl he is "rushing." After a while there won't be any girl a fellow can boast about.

I am one of those human fellows, and somehow always did favor the fair, blessed creatures of the Nth power, and will always love them—God bless them all.

Wallace H. Thurman

"Negro Life in New York's Harlem: A Lively Picture of a Popular and Interesting Section"

Haldeman-Julius Quarterly, Fall 1927[5]

I. A Lively Picture of a Popular and Interesting Section

Harlem has been called the Mecca of the New Negro, the center of black America's cultural renaissance, Nigger Heaven, Pickaninny Paradise, Capital of Black America, and various other things. It has been surveyed and interpreted, explored and exploited. It has had its day in literature, in the drama, even in the tabloid press. It is considered the most popular and interesting section of contemporary New York. Its fame is international; its personality individual and inimitable. There is no Negro settlement anywhere comparable to Harlem, just as there is no other metropolis comparable to New York. As the great south side black belt of Chicago spreads and smells with the same industrial clumsiness and stockyardish vigor of Chicago, so does the black belt of New York teem and rhyme with the cosmopolitan cross-currents of the world's greatest city. Harlem is Harlem because it is part and parcel of greater New York. Its rhythms are the lackadaisical rhythms of a transplanted minority group caught up and rendered half mad by the more speedy rhythms of the subway, Fifth Avenue and the Great White Way. . . .

IX. The New Negro

Harlem has been called the center of the American Negroes' cultural renaissance and the mecca of the New Negro. If this is so, it is so only because Harlem is a part of New York, the cultural and literary capital of America. And Harlem becomes the mecca of the so-called New Negro only because he imagines that once there he can enjoy the cultural contact and intellectual stimulation necessary for his growth.

This includes the young Negro writer who comes to Harlem in order to be near both patrons and publishers of literature, and the young

Negro artist and musician who comes to Harlem in order to be near the most reputable artistic and musical institutions in the country.

These folk, along with the librarians employed at the Harlem Branch of the New York Public Library, a few of the younger, more cultured professional men and women and the school teachers, who can be found in the grammar and high schools all over the city, constitute the Negro intelligentsia. This group is sophisticated and small and more a part of New York's life than of Harlem's. Its members are accepted as social and intellectual equals among whites downtown, and can be found at informal and formal gatherings in any of the five boroughs that compose greater New York. Harlem to most of them is just a place of residence; they are not "fixed" there as are the majority of Harlem's inhabitants.

Then there are the college youngsters and local intellectuals, whose prototypes can be found in any community. These people plan to attend lectures and concerts, given under the auspices of the Y.M.C.A., Y.W.C.A., churches, and public school civic centers. They are the people who form intercollegiate societies, who stage fraternity go-to-school campaigns, who attend the course of lectures presented by the Harlem Branch of the New York Public Library, during the winter months, and who frequent the many musical and literary entertainments given by local talent in Harlem auditoriums.

Harlem is crowded with such folk. The three great major educational institutions of New York, Columbia, New York University and the College of the City of New York, have a large Negro student attendance. Then there are many never-will-be-top-notch literary, artistic, and intellectual strivers in Harlem as there are all over New York. Since the well advertised "literary renaissance," it is almost a Negro Greenwich Village in this respect. Every other person one meets is writing a novel, a poem, or a drama. And there is seemingly no end to artists who do oils, pianists who pound out Rachmaninoff's Prelude in C Sharp Minor, and singers, with long faces and rolling eyes, who sing spirituals. . . .

X. Harlem—Mecca of the New Negro

Harlem, the so-called citadel of Negro achievement in the New World, the alleged mecca of the New Negro and the advertised center of colored America's cultural renaissance. Harlem, a thriving black city, pulsing with vivid passions, alive with colorful personalities, and packed with many types of classes of people. Harlem is a dream city pregnant with wide awake realities. It is a masterpiece of contradictory elements and surprising types. There is no end to its versatile presentation of people, personalities, and institutions. It is a mad medley.

There seems to be no end to its numerical and geographical growth. It is spreading north, east, south, and west. It is slowly pushing beyond the barriers imposed by white people. It is slowly uprooting them from their present homes in the near vicinity of Negro Harlem as it has uprooted them before. There must be expansion and Negro Harlem is too much a part of New York to remain sluggish and still while all around is activity and expansion. As New York grows, so will Harlem grow. As Negro America progresses, so will Negro Harlem progress.

New York is now most liberal. There is little racial conflict, and there have been no interracial riots since the San Juan Hill days. The question is will the relations between New York Negro and New York white man always remain as tranquil as they are today? No one knows, and once in Harlem one seldom cares, for the sight of Harlem gives any Negro a feeling of great security. It is too large and too complex to seem to be affected in any way by such a futile thing as race prejudice.

There is no typical Harlem Negro as there is no typical American Negro. There are too many different types and classes. White, yellow, brown, and black and all the intervening shades. North American, South American, African, and Asian; Northern and Southern; high and low; seer and fool—Harlem holds them all and strives to become a homogeneous community despite its motley, hodge-podge of incompatible elements and its self nurtured or outwardly imposed limitations.

I. Marie Johnson

"Women in Chicago Politics"

Light and Heebie Jeebies, November 19, 1927[6]

It has often been said, and the statement seems to have passed unchallenged, that colored women in Chicago lead the nation in politics. This is perhaps true in point of numbers, for it would be difficult to find anywhere else so large a number of women actively engaged in city, state and national politics. Among this number one finds every type of woman represented, from the social leader, who seeks stimulating diversion in contacting "gold coast" celebrities, to the humble charwoman who is doing her bit toward the payment of a debt of gratitude to the party or faction which has made it possible for her to earn a living.

Politics has not always been so popular with our women as at present, for many of them considered politics "dirty business." Gradually, however, they have awakened to a realization of the fact that if politics is dirty, our officials and institutions also must necessarily be corrupt. Politics is the machinery of our government, and if we are to have clean government, we must have clean politics.

The woman precinct worker we have always had. Long before women were granted the right of franchise, when practically all men and the majority of women were very well satisfied with this man-made and man-ruled commonwealth as they found it, there were many fine, courageous women who, in the face of popular disapproval, performed their duty as they saw it. These women could do very little more than "get out" the male vote, wear a badge on election day and stand on the street corners and remind all passers-by of their duty to vote. The reward of this service at the end of a hard day was a five-dollar bill from the precinct captain. Many a man in those days owed his position to those women who, although unable to vote themselves, were working assiduously to put into office men who, they believed, would vote to enfranchise women.

The participation of colored women in Chicago politics dates back to the beginning of the present century, which gave birth to such terms as "the new woman" and "the twentieth century woman," connoting all that is progressing and modern in feminine thought and action, and indicating that the world expected the new century to bring some change in woman's status. The strength of the colored woman as a political factor in Chicago was first felt perhaps when Miss Carrie Flowers ran for the position of trustee of the University of Illinois and made a bid for the colored vote by pledging herself to secure scholarships for colored girls and boys in case she was elected. The effect was electrical. Women's social and charity clubs were temporarily converted into political organizations which threw their full strength into the campaign. After that victory women's clubs throughout the city joined in the general agitation for unlimited suffrage and used their influence to place in office men who pledged themselves to the women's program of full franchise. It was not until 1913, however, that the first distinctly political club was organized among colored women in Chicago. Mrs. Ida B. Wells Barnett was the leading spirit in that organization, which was known as the Alpha Suffrage club. This organization is credited with a number of worthwhile achievements, and many people feel that it was through the work of this organization that Chicago had its first colored alderman.

FINALLY the Susan B. Anthony bill was enacted as an amendment to the national constitution, and though our women have since participated extensively in city, state and national politics, it must be admitted that for almost a decade they have floundered around in a pitiful effort to learn what it is all about. There has been no concerted action among them. They have never been quite sure whether their interests could best be served by allying themselves with the men or by maintaining separate organizations. This lack of any definite program has placed our women at a decided disadvantage and has resulted in an attitude on the part of man which is somewhat like—oh, well; if you insist upon meddling into this affair of mine, I must tolerate you. What woman does not remember how mother used to pinch off bits of dough for little daughter's busy fingers in order to keep them out of the pie. It is the same psychology which politicians use to keep women out of big affairs, only the little job in this case is not making "doll pies," but shaking the plums from the tree for his majesty, the male. The efforts of women on behalf of men office seekers before women were eligible to vote or hold office have led men to expect this of women, and it seems to be their present intention to have this arrangement continued indefinitely. Consequently, almost ten years after her enfranchisement, the colored women of Chicago find their political status but little better than before. It is true that they have made some progress. A few of them hold minor positions, but as a political factor, our women have not advanced beyond the stage of the ward heeler. Women all over the city are awakening to this fact and their unusual activity at this time indicates that they are going to make things quite interesting for Mr. Man.

WITHIN the past two years there have been organized in Chicago by colored women several political clubs which bid fair to play an important part in local and national affairs in the near future. We might mention first the Woman's Colored Republican National organization, not because it is the oldest, but because its membership is composed chiefly of women who have had many years of experience in politics. Mrs. Emma Stothard, who was the first colored member of the Fourth Ward Republican club, is president and founder of this organization. One of her chief supporters is Mrs. Effie Hale, who has been active in politics for thirty years. Not a few of the members are women of like experience, and it is this experience which is going to make this organization one of the

forceful groups in Chicago politics. These women have been schooled in the game of politics as men play it, and there are few tricks of the game which they have not learned. They have learned to analyze political situations and the men who direct the plays. Furthermore, they have developed leadership in their precincts and in their wards, and they are prepared to employ this priceless experience and knowledge for the purpose of achieving the end for which this club was organized—recognition of the colored woman in politics.

The second club, which was organized two years ago, is the Chicago Woman's Republican club. Mrs. Susie Myers is its founder and president. This group is composed of some of Chicago's most capable women. They are women who generally take themselves and life rather seriously and whom we somehow naturally expect to be connected with any movement for civic betterment. They are chiefly teachers, social workers, physicians, lawyers and business women—women who, in their daily work, meet with situations and problems which keep them ever-mindful of their responsibilities to their government. Many of them are nationally prominent in club life, and bring to the group a wealth of experience in organization. Such women as Mrs. Myers and Mrs. Madison C. B. Mason bring to the group much in the way of fine contacts with some of the most influential white women in the country. There is perhaps not another woman in Chicago whose contacts with men and women in high office have been as close and confidential as those enjoyed by Mrs. Myers. She directed the campaign among colored women for the late Senator McKinley, for the late Senator McCormick and for Senator Frank Smith. She also enjoys a close personal friendship with Mrs. Ruth McCormick, who is likely to be our next congressman-at-large. This club enjoys the most amicable relations with the Roosevelt Republican club and the Illinois Woman's club.

THE third group is equally as interesting as either of the other two because it approaches the subject with a freshness and openmindedness which is unique. It is known as the

The Intercollegiate's New Negro

"The Intercollegiate's New Negro," cartoon, *Survey of Negro Life in Chicago*, September 1927.

Independent Woman's Republican club. The name indicates the uniqueness of this group. It is called "Independent" not because it represents an independent party but because it is composed of women whose position makes it possible for them to take an independent stand, being women who enjoy a degree of social and financial security. The roster reads like a social register. . . . Their aim is to acquaint themselves with the political situation and to make a study of men and measures as they arise.

A fourth club is the Third Ward Political club, which was but recently organized by Mrs. Ida B. Wells Barnett. This club, like the others, is organized solely for the benefit of women.

All of this activity seems to indicate that we are soon to hear from the women of Chicago. All of the leaders of these various groups are of one mind—that the women of Chicago have not been given the recognition which has been due them. They have worked consistently and. received but little in return. It seems now that after all these years woman is determined as never before to make good her ancient threat to "clean up politics."

Carroll Binder

Excerpts from *Chicago and the New Negro*

Chicago Daily News Reprint No. 31, 1927[7]

Chicago and the New Negro: Studies in a Great Community's Changing Race Relations

How the city absorbed the huge post-war migration from the South, and what economic, social, and civic changes were wrought thereby.

I.

There can be no clearer demonstration of the new status of the Negro in Chicago and of the great change in the social, economic and political life of the south side than the metamorphosis of 47th and South Park way, as Grand boulevard is now designated. It is typical of the change taking place throughout that section and in process in several other parts of the city.

The Negro has ceased to invade Chicago from the south in the overwhelming numbers of the war and postwar years. A measure of stability is being achieved by the Negro population of Chicago which ranges somewhere between 150,000 and 200,000. Decline of the southern migration has tempered the anxiety of the white neighbors of the Negro. The colored man has shown a greater capacity for amicable citizenship than his more apprehensive white neighbors believed him capable of.

Achieves New Status.

In the final analysis, however, the new status of the Negro in metropolitan Chicago has been achieved by his own economic, political and personal power. The colored man refused to be confined within a ghetto defined by his white neighbors and he defied all the economic and social pressure applied to keep him there. He demonstrated that he had the money to invade territory once monopolized by whites and the courage to stay there in the face of bombs which wrecked his homes, churches and business places. He persisted in the face of cold shouldering from his neighbors.

Negroes are therefore to be found in almost all parts of the city. Being among the most gregarious of the races the Negro chooses to dwell in colonies but the boundaries of his colonies are so far-flung that he cannot absorb all the property which white vendors seek to thrust upon him. If anything, he is overloaded with residence, business and above all church prop-

erty and it will be years before there is a shortage of accommodations such as prevailed in the
early days of the migration. Hundreds of Negro
families live in health destroying abodes but
that is due to lack of income with which to avail
themselves of the numerous dwelling places
open to them—not to excess of home-seekers
over homes. . . .

Purchasing Power Increases.

There has been a phenomenal increase in the
number of successful Negro business and professional men in the post-war period. Negro
workers have gone far toward filling places formerly occupied by the newer immigration—a
source of labor supply sharply curtailed by federal legislation restricting immigration. This expansion has meant a great increase in the
wealth and purchasing power of the Negro
community. The educational and social level of
the race has been raised correspondingly.

Politically the race has shown no great civic
advance. It is still the prey of machine politicians of both the white and colored races and it
is subject to the same demoralization which is
manifest in the rest of a community whose politics is spoils-ridden. Negro civic leaders deplore this condition but rightly argue that until
the rest of the community progresses the Negro
group should not be condemned for its lethargy
and civic backwardness.

While the mass of Negroes still lives on a
low economic level there is evolving a Negro leisure class with social standards and practices
similar to those of the white leisure class and a
similar detachment to the problems of the less
fortunately situated of their own people. Well-
to-do Negroes patronize the arts and letters and
have country estates and country clubs like
those of white people of the same economic and
cultural status.

Erect Own Barriers.

A certain degree of segregation is voluntarily
practiced by Negroes of this class. They have no
desire to penetrate social groups which would
not be congenial and find satisfaction in their
own social groupings. In other spheres racial

barriers are transcended and Negroes and
whites mingle freely and amicably because their
interests are common.

Places of amusement and dissipation such
as cabarets and gambling houses represent one
sort of interracial intercourse, while reform and
cultural movements in which whites and Negroes co-operate represent another type. The
second variety of interracial co-operation is
happily on the increase. It leads to better understanding and enrichment of the community
life. Wisely directed it should make impossible
such social catastrophes as the race riots of 1919.

II.

Expert estimates concerning the size of Chicago's Negro population range all the way from a
low of 150,000 to a high of 250,000, with 200,000
as the figure most generally advanced. In 1920
the United States census reported 127,033 Negroes in Chicago. . . .

"Black Belt" Borders.

The so-called black belt starts at 24th street and
extends to 60th street, but [Oscar] De Priest
thinks there are 5,000 Negroes between 12th and
24th streets. Alexander L. Jackson, who has
real-estate holdings over the south side, says
that 15,000 Negroes live in the region between
63d and 69th streets and South Park way and
Drexel avenue.

There are about 5,000 colored people in
Englewood with five Negro churches to focus
their community life. Morgan Park's well-
established community of 1,200 has three
Negro churches. There are about 2,400 Negroes
in Lilydale, a settlement between 92d and
96th streets and LaSalle street and Michigan
boulevard, while the 10th ward shelters about
1,200, whose principal income comes from the
South Chicago rolling mills. . . .

III.

Negroes proudly point out that one of their
number—Jean Baptiste Ponte de Saible [sic]—
was the first property holder in Chicago. A tab-

let on a structure near the Michigan boulevard bridge commemorates the seventeen-year sojourn of the Jamaican who bought Chicago real estate 'way back in 1779.

Real estate remains the favorite form of investment of the Chicago Negro. Jesse Binga, one of the race's millionaires and a heavy investor in Chicago real estate, estimates that the realty holdings of his people in Chicago approximate $400,000,000 in value. There are heavy incumbrances, of course, on these holdings, but the ownership is significant of the new economic status of the Negro race. Negro wealth has probably increased more rapidly in Chicago than in any other community, but the Negro has been strengthening his economic foothold throughout the United States.

Desire to obtain a satisfactory place to live is the primary incentive to Negro acquisition of real estate. There is also a strong psychological urge toward property ownership. The Negro still responds to influences and ideals impressed upon him during his long sojourn in the south, where property ownership gave a desirable social status. The Chicago Negro who has saved a few thousand dollars is therefore a receptive client for a six-flat building. Unscrupulous realtors of both the white and Negro races have played upon these obvious desires to sell costly properties to Negroes whose economic resources counseled a more modest investment if one was to be made at all.

Too Many Lodgings.

All over the south side one will find postmen and stockyards laborers with annual incomes of less than $2,000 feverishly struggling to keep up the payments of a four or six-flat building. Their women and children are helping swell the family income and they take in lodgers, but there is a surplus of lodgings to be rented at the present time and the economic future of many of these purchasers is unpromising.

The south side is talking about this unwholesome real estate activity and the disservice done inexperienced people by business men who ought to know better. But that is only one side of the picture. There are hundreds of colored families who own homes free of incumbrance and who are too sophisticated to succumb to the honey-tongued salesmen proposing a mortgage on the free property to purchase an apartment building which the vendor has on his lists. There are thousands more who will soon own, free of debt, the homes which they purchased since the war.

The rapid extension of residential areas open to Negroes has created a surplus of apartments for rent. It is no longer easy to jump the rent 15 to 25 per cent when a "white building" is turned over to Negro tenants, as was the custom until recently. Nevertheless desirable residential property in the adjusted Negro neighborhoods continues to appreciate in value, experienced observers affirm.

Deny Depreciation View.

Dr. George Cleveland Hall and Alexander L. Jackson, Negro property holders with extensive knowledge of south side business and social conditions, take issue with the widely held view that Negro penetration of a district means depreciation of property values. They cite numerous instances of boulevard property appreciating in value after the Negro came into the district.

"Panic-stricken white property holders in a changing district often let alarmist realtors talk them into selling their property at a loss 'because the Negroes are coming in,'" Dr. Hall conceded. "Dealers have made fortunes by fanning these fears and then reselling the property at an outrageous profit. The property owner who exercises good judgment and sits tight will soon find a Negro purchaser who will pay him far more than he could possibly have gotten had his street remained a deteriorated white district."

In substantiation of his assertion Dr. Hall cited property in the South Park way block, in which his own well-kept, well-furnished property is situated. Houses which the frightened owners were glad to sell for $10,000 a few years ago today would not be sold for $20,000. A $3,400 house of three years ago today commands $10,000. Seven to ten-thousand-dollar properties command from $13,000 to $15,000.

"Keep cool when you see the Negroes coming and you'll get twice what you will if you mistake them for goblins," is Dr. Hall's counsel to property owners.

Old "Panic" Waning.

Oscar DePriest, a shrewd real estate man as well as a political figure in the Negro community, says that white property holders have gotten over their early panic and no longer throw their property on the market at ridiculous prices. "We used to pick up some wonderful bargains that way, but those days are gone forever," Mr. De-Priest said. He added that waning of the white man's fear of Negro invasion had immeasurably bettered the relations between the two races. . . .

Jesse Binga, banker himself, thinks his people have $60,000,000 on deposit in various city banks. Oscar DePriest thinks Negroes have $25,000,000 on deposit in loop banks and another $25,000,000 in south-side banks—a view shared by several white bankers.

Negroes carry $14,000,000 worth of insurance in seven Negro companies and a great deal more in the white industrial and old-line companies. Negro investments in stock of corporations which employ them and which conduct employe-ownership plans run into many hundreds of thousands of dollars. Blue-sky promoters still find easy plucking among Negroes, but there is an increasing tendency on the part of colored people of means to buy listed stocks and bonds through their banks. . . .

Minor Executives Negroes.

A few plants have Negro foremen in charge of crews in which there are workmen of both races. Those trade unions which admit Negroes to membership seem to have no serious interracial friction, but the Negro is not a big factor in the Chicago labor movement. Some of the more powerful labor unions exclude Negroes. There are no trade unions in several of the industries where the Negro workers are most numerous.

Generally speaking the Negroes get the same pay as whites for tasks in which both are engaged. When the Negroes first came into cer-tain industries they were utilized to reduce the wages and working conditions of their white fellow workers and friction naturally resulted. Equality of treatment reduces friction to a minimum, industrial leaders concede.

At least 30 per cent of the labor force in Chicago packing plants is colored. Negroes hold important posts in the employe [sic] representation plans or company unions at Armour's, Swift's and the other plants. The efficiency rating of the Negro employes in one of the plants is higher than that of any other racial group.

Between 12 and 20 per cent of the employes in Chicago's steel mills are colored, according to H. N. Robinson, director of industrial relations of the Chicago Urban league, which operates the largest employment bureau for Negro workers in the city and which is constantly developing new opportunities for Negroes in Chicago business and industrial establishments.

No Replacement Plan.

"The Urban League never tries to supplant any worker of any race," Mr. Robinson was quick to point out. "We merely ask that Negroes be given an opportunity to fill vacancies as they may occur and that they receive a fair trial as workmen. We are meeting with increasing success in various lines. Seldom does an employer drop Negro workmen once he has given them a trial. When slack times call for a reduction in personnel, seniority prevails and our people come back with the rest of the employes temporarily laid off."

Negro women have won a permanent place for themselves in the twine mills of the International Harvester company and have a lower labor turnover than white women, a Harvester official testified. Negro men perform many tasks in the Harvester plants.

The Corn Products company employed only one Negro eight years ago, but today employs 350, or 20 per cent of its factory personnel. The white and Negro workers at Argo may be seen working on joint tasks with manifest mutual esteem and good will.

E. C. Otis, superintendent of the Beaver Products company, 2226 West 49th street, has warm praise for Negro workers as a result of some years' experience. Three years ago 20 per cent of Mr. Otis' employes were Negro. A reduction in personnel raised the Negro percentage to 65 and production was increased 8 per cent, while the pay roll was $40,000 less. Mr. Otis plans to increase still further the percentage of Negro workers.

The American Hide and Leather company, 1320 Elston avenue, was the first tannery to use colored workmen. Satisfactory experience opened other tanneries in Chicago to Negro workmen. The foundries and laundries of the city are heavy employers of colored labor. Eleven per cent of the employes of the Pullman car shops are colored.

In Personal Service.

Negroes, of course, continue to find employment in the various forms of personal service, such as Pullman porters, waiters, porters in stores, offices and barber shops, housemen and chauffeurs. Negro women are penetrating some branches of the garment industry and now constitute about 40 per cent of the workers in lampshade factories.

Negro owned and managed business and industrial establishments provide employment for a number of high school and college trained office workers, but the problem of the educated Negro seeking employment is a serious one. A few have positions in downtown offices, plants and stores. but many well-educated Negroes must work at vocations where their training cannot be utilized.

The Urban league is canvassing the white business establishments in the Negro districts to locate opportunities for young people of promise so that they may acquire business experience as well as utilize the education they possess.

The unskilled Negro workman earns on the average from $20 to $22 weekly when he is employed the hourly rate ranging from 40 to 50 cents, depending upon the severity and congeniality of the work.

Porters in barber shops get $18 to $20 weekly, butlers $20 to $25 and chauffeurs $35. General housework without cooking commands between $10 and $12 a week, maids get $12 to $18, while the rate for day work is $4 for an eight-hour day. . . .

V.

Illiterate slaves less than 70 years ago, Negroes today conduct banks, insurance companies, brokerage houses, real-estate offices, factories employing numerous skilled workers, merchandising establishments of all sorts, publishing houses and almost every other conceivable type of business enterprise.

The Negro tends to buy where he can get the best service at the least cost. With the exception of the necessary personal services such as restaurants, barber shops, pool rooms, undertaking establishments and, in some instances, groceries, the Negro patronizes the business house which is most convenient and seldom goes out of his way to assist a race enterprise.

Phenomenal growth of Negro business in recent years must therefore be taken as indication that Negroes are attaining business proficiency to such an extent that they can compete with whites for patronage. In a race with so short an experience in business it is to be expected that there will be a certain number of failures arising out of limited capital and skill, but the percentage of Negro failures is less than might be expected.

Seventy-Three Negro Banks.

Students of Negro business say that there are seventy-three Negro banks with a total capital of $6,250,000, total surplus of $20,000,000 and an annual business of $100,000,000. This is said to be a 300 per cent increase over the banking activity of 1918. Seventy thousand Negroes are said to be in business throughout the country, and the volume of business done has been estimated at more than a billion dollars.

Chicago has become in the last decade one of the great business centers of the Negro race, surpassing New York's Negro community, which is larger in population. W. H. Bolton, postgraduate student at the University of Chicago, who is making a study of Negro business in Chicago, says that the growth has been almost entirely during the last decade and that the great majority of the new businesses have been launched by southern Negroes who came to this city during the great migration of the war and postwar period. . . .

Successes in Amusement.

Amusement might be listed as one of the important enterprises of the Negro race. Hundreds of Negroes gain their livelihood from musical or dramatic effort. There are several successful orchestras Negro managed and Negro owned and numerous Negro musical and theatrical organizations Some Negro entertainers command huge salaries.

There is a popular impression that the Negroes are making fortunes in the cabaret business. The so-called black-and-tan resorts are with one exception white owned and the Negro entertainers on duty there are employes, not proprietors. Roadhouses and other competing entertainments such as dog races have cut down the attendance at black-and-tan as well as north side cabarets, so that no one is reaping a golden harvest from these enterprises.

There are a number of small dance halls run by Negroes for Negroes in the colored districts. Supervision of these places is rather limited and colored welfare leaders look with friendly eyes upon a project of a syndicate of white men to open a large dance hall comparable to those patronized by white youth. They believe that the better supervision and superior grade of entertainment offered in the larger halls will elevate the tone of colored amusement places which is capable of improvement at the present time—an improvement difficult to realize so long as there is no centralization. . . .

VII.

Organized and protected gambling is so well intrenched in the Negro community that it is entitled to discussion as one of the industries of the race. Perhaps 2,000 men and some women earn all or part of their living from the various games of chance which flourish on the south

side regardless of the political changes in the city hall and county building. Many times that number are weekly made poorer—if not wiser—by the deflating operations of the several branches of the gambling industry.

There is a widespread belief that gambling is a peculiarly Negro dissipation. "Every Negro from the preacher to the pickaninny gambles," this school contends. One has only to visit the gambling joints outside the so-called black belt to disprove the first premise.

The white race contributes its full quota to the rank of those who believe that they are smart enough or lucky enough to beat the game. On the other hand, there are many thousands of colored people who are as cold to Lady Luck as are those whites who take no interest in gambling.

Habitual gamblers, nevertheless, abound among the colored people, and colored communities tend to maintain wealth-consuming gambling enterprises. Gambling therefore cannot be ignored in a discussion of the Chicago colored group. . . .

"Golf" Still Supreme.

"African golf" is, of course, a prime favorite.[8] Likely looking persons sauntering down the main thoroughfares of the Negro community will be flattered with an invitation to "try your wrist, sir?" "try your wrist, sir?" The games go on in the rear of the omnipresent "cigar stores," which would be hard pressed to make change if some greenhorn tried to purchase a stogie, and in the "literary clubs" and "book stores" which have sprung up in amazing numbers.

"I have never known my people to be so literary as in recent months" a leading Negro professional man observed as we passed five of these clubs in a single block.

Gambling joints of this type operate all over the south side. The residence districts of Hyde Park are no more immune than the main business districts. To assure perfect deportment among the gentlemen players a lookout relieves the visitor of any guns or bottles he may carry for protection and solace.

Visitors are admitted one at a time so that there will be no rushing the barred gate should uncouth elements presume to put in an appearance. If one calls at one of these establishments in the better residential neighborhoods—say, Drexel boulevard—toward the end of the afternoon he will note how completely chance dissolves those barriers which seem to separate races in other milieu.

Gathered about the green table where the croupier is plying his craft and repeating the time-honored incitements to hazard will be a crowd of whites and blacks altogether forgetful of race superiority or inferiority and intent only on the rolling dice. In other parts of the establishment may be seen milling crowds whose bond of interracial co-operation is mutual interest in the races or some other play of hazard.

Policy Is Big Game.

Policy, however, is the more impressive game from the standpoint of an industry. Well-posted men estimate that Chicago Negroes spend $250,000 a week on tickets for policy wheels. Two thousand men and women earn all or part of their living peddling policy tickets on a commission basis. They have customers just like milk-wagon drivers or insurance collectors, and make periodical visits to collect and report the wonderful killing made by the housewife on Federal street or South Park way—whichever district will impress the client most.

A few white men and white organizations fatten upon this enterprise. Some Negroes identified with gambling acquire extensive real estate holdings, expensive cars and costly haberdashery. For the majority of the participants gambling means going without pork chops, skimping on the clothes and living in health-destroying tenements.

VIII.

"Our people used to celebrate the fourteenth and fifteenth amendments as the great charter of the race, but honor is now due to the eighteenth amendment as a boon for Negroes," a witty colored physician remarked the other day. The doctor was commenting on the economic and social transformation effected in certain

Negroes as a result of the prohibition amendment. In his opinion trade in illicit liquor has become a greater source of wealth for lawbreaking Negroes than the old reliable standby—gambling.

This is not a discussion of the ethical or legal aspect of prohibition. The preponderance of opinion among Negro social and civic leaders seems to be that the standard of living of the colored race has been elevated by the prohibition law. Colored people spend less on drink and more on food and clothing as a result of prohibition, these observers report.

But a considerable number of colored men and women are engaged in the manufacture and sale of contraband alcoholic beverages and it is of their industry that this article treats. Observers who ought to know what they are talking about say that Negroes are close competitors with Italians for supremacy in the business of manufacturing and selling booze.

Many in Business.

A journey through the black belt will provide the investigator with tangible evidence that for a large number of Negroes Volsteadism has been beneficence itself. Bootlegging profits pay for many of the costly apartments which have recently been acquired by Negroes. Parched customers have endowed colored liquor dealers with Rolls Royces and their women folk with diamonds and costly furs and silks.

Negroes are much in demand as runners for Italian bootleggers, where they lack the enterprise to go into business for themselves. The trade concedes that the Negro has a valuable good-will asset as a peddler of white mule. His white customers have heard about the mountain dew distilled by Negroes in the legendary days when mountaineers considered it their sacred duty to make liquor in defiance of the "revenuers." Whites conjure up a picture of the fabled log cabin and the hidden still in the Kentucky hills and swallow the powerful potion, which probably was concocted in a foul south side tenement basement by a city-born sporting gentleman who never saw corn outside his wash boiler. . . .

Many Negro bootleggers have select lists of white clients and some boast of drug store clientele which requires monthly consignment of several hundred gallons. . . .

Like the gambling joints, blind pigs operate unmolested in the residence districts. It is the buffet flat, however, which causes most concern among the self-respecting Negro population. Colored people complain that they cannot isolate their families from the center of organized and occasional prostitution. White and colored women ply their craft on the residential boulevards as well as business streets. Disorderly flats invade each new community organized by colored folks and the worst elements of the two races flaunt their dissipations in the face of decent householders.

Some of the colored papers have entered vigorous protests against this laxity and a group of Negro leaders formed a committee recently to combat the more flagrant forms of vice. In deference to public opinion woman solicitors were driven off Indiana avenue between 35th and 39th streets, and from several other regions. . . .

IX.

The church continues to exercise a tremendous influence over the life and thought of the urban Negro community despite the presence of distractions and competing agencies which are absent in the simpler Negro communities of the south.

Negro pastors in the south direct the personal and social relationships of their flocks to a degree unknown in the north. Here nonsectarian religious and civic bodies perform functions which the colored church monopolizes in the south. Church members here participate in worldly affairs with a freedom undreamed of in the south. . . .

Y. M. C. A. Flourishes.

Sharing with the churches the responsibility for the moral advancement of the community are branches of the Y. M. C. A. and the Y. W. C. A. especially devoted to colored youth. The Y. M. C. A. is housed in a building valued at $400,000 and said to be the finest Negro Y. M. C. A. in the nation. Its equipment is valued at $40,000 and its activities reach into every phase of Negro life. George R. Arthur, the secretary, is a leader in civic activities, who is given credit for promoting better relations between whites and colored people, as well as for opening up new avenues of activity to his own people. Colored people raise among themselves nearly all of the association's annual budget of $108,000.

The Y. W. C. A. expects to extend its useful activities when it moves into a building in a central location. The colored community maintains other important social-service activities, such as the South Side Community Center, which is a neighborhood house available for club meetings and civic activity, and the Phyllis Wheatley home, which for years has offered shelter and comradeship to Negro girls coming to Chicago, who are without family or friends to assist them in making their adjustment to urban life.

An important feature of Negro life is the colored woman's club movement, which has far-reaching social, literary and civic influence. There are more than 3,000 women in such clubs, of which there are sixty-three in the Chicago area. One of the latest projects of these women provides for individual social service among the less-favored women of the race and the newcomers in Chicago. . . .

XII.

Chicago's Negro community includes a number of men and women of high professional and intellectual distinction. It shelters writers and artists whose work is favorably known among both whites and Negroes, but from a literary and artistic standpoint there is no group in Chicago comparable to the Harlem Negro literati. Chicago's pre-eminence lies in the business and professional attainments of its people.

If Chicago has no outstanding group of Negro artists it has a highly cultured coterie, which cherishes artistic effort of colored people. The steady output of books by Negro authors is eagerly read here. Negro musicians, such as the Johnsons and Roland Hayes, are acclaimed by their people when they give concerts here.

Appreciation of art, of course, knows no racial boundaries. There are thousands of white Chicagoans who follow with intense interest the literary and artistic development of the Negro. The latter, too, appreciate merit in art, regardless of the color or race of the artist. Local white and colored leaders are co-operating with the Chicago Woman's club to hold a "Negro in Art" week in Chicago next November, at which the work of colored people here and in other lands will be made available to Chicagoans.

The Chicago Art League of which William M. Farrow is president is one of the few organizations in the world composed exclusively of colored artists. In its membership are men and women who are successfully practicing the plastic and graphic arts.

Many Race Publications.

Moses Jordan, colored graduate of the Medill School of Journalism, publishes a monthly literary and news magazine called American Life to give expression to local authors. The Chicago Bulletin, a Negro daily, carries a weekly feature supplement. The Chicago Defender, largest and most prosperous of the weeklies of the colored race, the Chicago Bee, the Chicago Whip, Chicago Enterprise, Light and Heebie Jeebies Magazine, Half-Century Magazine, and the Broad Ax, also witness the writing and publishing activity of Chicago Negroes. The Associated Negro Press, with headquarters here, supplies Negro papers throughout the country with news and feature articles.

There are Negro physicians whose knowledge and skill is so great as to bring them numerous patients from without their own racial group. Several of these men won high academic honors while at Rush, Northwestern and other medical schools, and one, Dr. Julian H. Lewis, is assistant professor of pathology in the University of Chicago. Dr. Lewis is at present abroad on one of the Simon Guggenheim fellowships awarded to university teachers of promise for research abroad. . . .

Nowhere in the United States has the Negro attained such political recognition as in Chicago. The first Negro alderman was elected a dozen years ago. Prior to that time there had been twelve Negroes in the Illinois legislature over a forty-year period, and Negroes had served on the board of county commissioners. Today there are two Negro aldermen, one state senator and four state representatives. There is one Negro on the municipal bench, one on the state commerce commission and others in such positions as library trustee.

In politics the Negro has accepted the standards of the political organization with which he was affiliated. Negro office holders have "gone along" with their white colleagues without elevating or debasing the level of politics. In recent years the Negro electorate has shown some disposition to abandon its traditional affiliation with the republican party and vote for another candidate if such a course promised more for the race.

Republican in Politics.

The race is still overwhelmingly republican, however. It is credited with holding the balance of power in some circles but one of the foremost Negroes in the city ruefully observes that "our power doesn't do us much good when we want to get an alley cleaned up or a disorderly house closed."

Communist agitators have cultivated the Negro assiduously in recent years. An effort has been made to arouse colored people to radicalism as a cure for race disabilities, but aside from a small group of youths no progress has been made. Some of these youths were treated to a trip to Moscow for training in the propaganda college but radical doctrines seemingly have no appeal to the Negro, who prefers to try to get ahead financially. A red racing car looks better to the average Negro than a red flag. . . .

Heavy Death Rate.

When it is noted that the Negro lives in the least-favored sections of the city and often in houses which were condemned as unfit for human habitation more than a generation ago his mortality rate is better understood. Inadequate hospital resources for Negroes and the low economic level of a large section of the Negro population are also contributory factors.

Negro physicians, churches, fraternities and welfare organizations are waking up to the necessity of united effort to improve Negro health. George R. Arthur of the Y. M. C. A. thinks that the latest mortality statistics reveal the fruits of this effort. He cites the health department statistics of deaths of children under one year as proof. In 1925 the death rate for whites was 74.7 per thousand, while that for Ne-

groes was 118.6. In 1926 the white rate had come down to 64.5, but the colored had made an even greater drop to 94.6 per thousand.

Dr. Harris addresses his brochure on Negro mortality to whites as well as Negroes because "disease knows no boundary lines." Disease germs cannot be segregated and kept out of restricted neighborhoods. Chicago must realize that it spends, through loss of time in industry, through retardation in school, through decreased property values, many times the amount necessary to bring the Negro death rate down to the city's average. . . .

Charles Stokes
"The New Negro"

Kansas City Call, December 23, 1927

(An oration delivered by Charles Stokes, student at Kansas university.)

I REALIZE fully that the message I'm trying to bring to you has been discussed so many times, pro and con, that treatment of the subject now will bring to some only a feeling of disgust and repulsion; that the capacity of some for this particular topic is fast approaching satiety. Yet I feel there are extenuating circumstances which make the presentation more plausible, and further, without persistent agitation of the question no important improvement can come to the American Negro.

The United States proudly calls itself the land of the free and the home of the brave. Kansas during the Civil war was known as a free state and was referred to as "Free and Bleeding Kansas." Today these characteristics remain. It is free for some and it is bleeding for others.

At the University of Kansas, Negro students are denied the use of the swimming pool. Incidentally there is a requirement that each student be able to swim a certain distance before beging [*sic*] granted his degree. In the case of the Negro this requirement is graciously withdrawn and he is permitted to graduate without learn-

ing to swim. Why does this condition exist? Is it that the Negro does not have occasion to swim as others do? Might he never be called upon to rescue others or save himself?

Too, the Negro cannot participate in the athletic sports of the valley. It is said that the schools with whom we play object to playing opposite a Negro. Is it then that Kansas university is more eager to play these schools than are those same schools to play Kansas? And would the presence of a Negro on the team make us win or lose more consistently than we now do? As to this spirit, says Opportunity magazine, "An incident occurred this year at the beginning of the football season which has wholesome moral and meaning. A hearty team came out of West Virginia to match itself against New York university which numbers among its players a Negro. 'We object to playing against a Negro,' announced the spokesman for the West Virginia team. 'I'm sorry,' countered Coach Meehan, 'but the team will not play today without him,' and so the game went on."

The answer to these complications is found in the unalterable fact that the color of the Negro skin is black. Honestly people can tolerate black cats, black dogs, and even black sheep in the family, but never a black human being. A human being, the most perfect mechanism ever constructed, yet be it black, and it is looked upon with horror and loathing.

It is hard for us to understand this. The late Florence Mills said, "In the south, colored mammies bring up white babies and in some instances actually feed them at their own breasts. Yet when the same mammy has her own little black baby, the mother of the white child does not permit her youngster to play with the Negro. At the theatre, if a colored person is seated next to a white person, the white person objects. Yet this same white person will eat food cooked by a Negro and be waited upon by another."

I remember in our primary geography, one of the first things we studied was a short sketch of the different races. With each description appeared a picture as being a typical type of that particular group. The Caucausian [*sic*] example must have been one of the early presidents. The face peering forth from the printed pages showed self-reliance, determination, aggressiveness, will-power and almost every virtue and attribute that one could wish to possess.

And so on down through the various races. The Japanese, Chinese and what-not were shown. Finally on the last pages of the chapter came the Negro. He was black almost beyond belief, despite the fact that a large percent of Negroes are lighter. His hair was knotty. His eyes

'JIM CROW' HEARS FROM 'NEW NEGRO'

Youths Fight Rather Than Ride in Rear of Car

MEMPHIS, Tenn., Mar. 21.—Taking offense at the Jim crow tactic of the street car company here Nathan Jones, 21 years old, and Howard Eddins, 17, refused to sit in the rear of a crowded Jackson Avenue car Friday and a fight resulted.

The fight started when Herbert Haynie, newphew of a police turnkey, roughly ordered the youths to the rear of the car. The white ruffian was cut and bruised. And now Jones and Howard are being held on a charge of disorderely conduct and the white on a charge of profanity and assault with a knife.

"'Jim Crow' Hears from 'New Negro,'" *St. Louis Argus*, March 23, 1928.

bulged, fiercely expressing defiance yet somehow giving the impression that he would run at the slightest premonition of danger. He was scantily clothed and black as I am, I was repulsed at the spectacle. Why wouldn't it have been as easy to place a Frederick Douglass, a Booker T. Washington, or the now living Du Bois in the geography as representative of the Negro race rather than one of the wildest savages of barbarous Africa?

I'm trying to tell you that the New Negro of today is a more educated, more intelligent and more progressive Negro than was the one introduced into American society, albeit against his will, in the then young seventeenth century. Kansas university deserves her share of applause in helping make that statement true. The extent to which the school has gone in aiding Negroes to gain an education should not be underestimated and is coming back to

Kansas and America in general by the decreasing rate of illiteracy among Negroes. It is becoming more and more recognized that the New Negro of today is an asset rather than a liability to his community. He is more educated, his is more progressive. Conditions are better. Yet even today there are colored youths in America who after being trained as lawyers and doctors are forced to become massagers of cuspidors simply because they are black and there is no place for them.

May the time soon come when the color of a man's skin will not be used as an indication of his business ability. And can we hope for a time, not too far distant, when men will be tolerant of the views of others and when a man's a man for a' that? For countless numbers of years the Negro has been in the making. And this making—like unto life itself—has never been finished.

E. Franklin Frazier

"La Bourgeoisie Noire"

Modern Quarterly 5, no. 1 (1928–30)[9]

Radicals are constantly asking the question: Why does the Negro, the man farthest down in the economic as well as social scale, steadily refuse to ally himself with the radical groups in America? On the other hand, his failure so far to show sympathy to any extent with the class which *a priori* would appear to be his natural allies has brought praise from certain quarters. Southern white papers when inclined to indulge in sentimental encomiums about the Negro cite his immunity to radical doctrines as one of his most praiseworthy characteristics. Negro orators and, until lately, Negro publications, in pleading for the Negro's claim to equitable treatment, have never failed to boast of the Negro's undying devotion to the present economic order. Those whites who are always attempting to explain the Negro's social behavior in terms of hereditary

qualities have declared that the Negro's temperament is hostile to radical doctrines. But the answer to what is a seeming anomaly to many is to be found in the whole social background of the Negro. One need not attribute it to any peculiar virtue (according as one regards virtue) or seek an explanation in such an incalculable factor as racial temperament.

The first mistake of those who think that the Negro of all groups in America should be in revolt against the present system is that they regard the Negro group as homogeneous. As a matter of fact, the Negro group is highly differentiated, with about the same range of interests as the whites. It is very well for white and black radicals to quote statistics to show that 98 percent of the Negroes are workers and should seek release from their economic slavery; but as a matter of fact 98 percent of the Negroes do not regard themselves as in economic slavery. Class differentiation among Negroes is reflected in their church organizations, educational institutions, private clubs, and the whole range of social life. Although these class distinctions may rest upon what would seem to outsiders flimsy and inconsequential matters, they are the social realities of Negro life, and no amount of reasoning can rid his mind of them. Recently we were informed in Dr. Herskovits' book on the Negro that color is the basis of social distinctions. To an outsider or a superficial observer this would seem true; but when one probes the tissue of the Negro's social life he finds that the Negro reacts to the same illusions that feed the vanity of white men.

What are some of the marks of distinctions which make it impossible to treat the Negro group as a homogeneous mass? They are chiefly property, education, and blood or family. If those possessing these marks of distinctions are generally mulattoes, it is because the free Negro class who first acquired these things as well as a family tradition were of mixed blood. The church in Charleston, South Carolina, which was reputed not to admit blacks did not open its doors to nameless mulatto nobodies. Not only has the distinction of blood given certain Negro groups a feeling of superiority over other Negroes, but it has made them feel superior to "poor whites." The Negro's feeling of superiority to "poor whites" who do not bear in their veins "aristocratic" blood has always created a barrier to any real sympathy between the two classes. Race consciousness to be sure has constantly effaced class feeling among Negroes. Therefore we hear on every hand Negro capitalists supporting the right of the Negro worker to organize—against white capitalists, of course. Nevertheless class consciousness has never been absent.

. . . Landownership remained relatively stationery [*sic*] from 1910 to 1920; while the number of landless workers increased. If this class of black workers were to espouse doctrines which aimed to change their economic status, they would be the most revolutionary group in America. From ignorant peasants who are igno-

rant in a fundamental sense in that they have no body of traditions even, we cannot expect revolutionary doctrines. They will continue a mobile group; while the white landlords through peonage and other forms of force will continue to hold them to the land.

Another factor of consequence in the Negro's economic life is the fact of the large number of Negroes in domestic service. . . . This group is no more to be expected to embrace radical doctrines than the same class was expected to join slave insurrections, concerning which Denmark Vesey warned his followers: "Don't mention it to those waiting men who receive presents of old coats, etc., from their masters, or they'll betray us."

Even this brief consideration of the social situation which has determined the Negro's attitudes towards values in American life will afford a background for our discussion of the seeming anomaly which he presents to many spectators. We shall attempt to show that, while to most observers the Negro shows an apparent indifference to changing his status, this is in fact a very real and insistent stimulus to his struggles. The Negro can only envisage those things which have meaning for him. *The radical doctrines appeal chiefly to the industrial workers, and the Negro has only begun to enter industry.* For Negroes to enter industries which are usually in the cities and escape the confinement of the plantation, they have realized a dream that is as far beyond their former condition as the New Economic Order is beyond the present condition of the wage earner. It has often been observed that the Negro subscribes to all the canons of consumption as the owning class in the present system. Even here we find the same struggle to realize a status that he can envisage and has a meaning for him. Once the Negro struggled for a literary education because he regarded it as the earmark of freedom. The relatively segregated life which the Negro lives makes him struggle to realize the values which give status within his group. An automobile, a home, a position as a teacher, or membership in a fraternity may confer a distinction in removing the possessor from an inferior social status, that could never be appreciated by one who is a stranger to Negro life. An outsider may wonder why a downtrodden, poor, despised people seem so indifferent about entering a struggle that is aimed to give all men an equal status. But if they could enter the minds of Negroes they would find that in the world in which they live they are not downtrodden and despised, but enjoy various forms of distinction.

An interesting episode in the life of the Negro which shows to what extent he is wedded to bourgeois ideals is the present attempt of the Pullman porters to organize. Some people have very superficially regarded this movement as a gesture in the direction of economic radicalism. But anyone who is intimately acquainted with the psychology of the Negro group, especially the porters, know that this is far from true. One who is connected with the white labor movement showed a better insight through his remark to the writer that the porters showed little working class psychology and showed a disposition to use their organization to enjoy the amenities of bourgeois social life. The Pullman porters do not show any disposition to overthrow bourgeois values. In fact, for years this group was better situated economically than most Negroes and carried over into their lives as far as possible the behavior patterns which are current in the middle class. In some places they regarded themselves as a sort of aristocracy, and as a colored woman said in one of their meetings recently, "Only an educated gentleman with culture could be a Pullman porter." The advent of a large and consequential professional and business class among Negroes has relegated the Pullman porters to a lower status economically as well as otherwise. Collective bargaining will help them to continue in a role in the colored group which is more in harmony with their conception of their relative status in their group. It is far from the idea of the Pullman porters to tear down the present economic order, and hardly any of them would confess any spiritual kinship with the "poor whites." The Pullman porters are emerging, on the other hand, as an aristocratic laboring group just as the Railroad Brotherhoods have done.

The Negro's lack of sympathy with the white working class is based on more than the feeling of superiority. In the South, especially, the caste system which is based on color, determines the behavior of the white working class. If the Negro has fatuously claimed spiritual kinship with the white bourgeois, the white working class has taken over the tradition of the slaveholding aristocracy. When white labor in the South attempts to treat with black labor, the inferior status of the latter must be conceded in practice and in theory. Moreover, white labor in the South not only has used every form of trickery to drive the Negro out of the ranks of skilled labor, but it has resorted to legislation to accomplish its aims. Experience, dating from before the Civil War, with the white group, has helped to form the attitude of Negro towards white labor as well as traditional prejudices.[10]

In the February number of the *Southern Workman*, there appears an article in which the psychology of the Negro is portrayed as follows. The discovery is made by a white business in Chicago:

> The average working class Negro in Chicago earns $22 a week. His wife sends her children to the Day Nursery or leaves them with relatives or friends, and she supplements the family income by from $10 to $15 or more per week. The average white man of the same class earns $33 per week and keeps his wife at home. This colored man will rent a $65 per month apartment and buy a $50 suit of clothes while the white man will occupy a $30 per month apartment and buy a $25 suit of clothes. This average white man will come into our store to buy furniture and about $300 will be the limit of his estimated purchase, while the colored man will undertake a thousand dollar purchase without the least thought about meeting the payments from his small income.

To the writer of the article, the company's new policy in using colored salesmen is a wonderful opportunity for colored men to learn the furniture business. The furniture company is going to make Negroes better citizens, according to the author of the article, by encouraging them to have better homes. This situation represents not only the extent to which the average Negro has swallowed middle-class standards but the attitude of the upper[-]class Negro towards the same values.

There is much talk at the present time about the New Negro. He is generally thought of as the creative artist who is giving expression to all the stored-up aesthetic emotion of the race. Negro in Art Week has come to take its place beside, above, or below the other three hundred and fifty-two weeks in the American year. But the public is little aware of the Negro business man who regards himself as a new phenomenon. While the New Negro who is expressing himself in art promises in the words of one of his chief exponents not to compete with the white man either politically or economically, the Negro business man seeks the salvation of the race in economic enterprise. In the former case there is either an acceptance of the present system or an ignoring of the economic realities of life. In the case of the latter there is an acceptance of the gospel of economic success. Sometimes the New Negro of the artistic type calls the New Negro business man a Babbitt, while the latter calls the former a mystic. But the Negro business man is winning out, for he is dealing with economic realities. He can boast of the fact that he is independent of white support, while the Negro artist still seeks it. One Negro insurance company in a rather cynical acceptance of the charge of Babbittry begins a large advertisement in a Negro magazine in the words of George F. Babbitt. . . .

Many of those who criticize the Negro for selecting certain values out of American life overlook the fact that the primary struggle on his part has been to acquire a culture. In spite of the efforts of those who would have him dig up his African past, the Negro is a stranger to African culture. The manner in which he has taken over the American culture has never been studied in intimate enough detail to make it comprehensible. The educated class among Negroes has been the forerunners in this process.

Except perhaps through the church the economic basis of the civilized classes among Negroes has not been within the group. Although today the growing professional and business classes are finding support among Negroes, the upper classes are subsidized chiefly from without. To some outsiders such a situation makes the Negro intellectual appear as merely an employee of the white group. At times the emasculating effect of Negro men appearing in the role of mere entertainers for the whites has appeared in all its tragic reality. But the creation of this educated class of Negroes has made possible the civilization of the Negro. It may seem conceivable to some that the Negro could have contended on the ground of abstract right for unlimited participation in American life on the basis of individual efficiency; but the Negro had to deal with realities. It is strange that today one expects this very class which represents the most civilized group to be in revolt against the system by which it was created, rather than the group of leaders who have sprung from the soil of Negro culture.

Here we are brought face to face with a fundamental dilemma of Negro life. Dean Miller at Howard University once expressed this dilemma aphoristically, namely, that the Negro pays for what he wants and begs for what he needs. The Negro pays, on the whole, for his church, his lodges and fraternities, and his automobile, but he begs for his education. Even the radical movement which had vogue a few years back was subsidized by the white radial group. It did not spring out of any general movement among Negroes towards radical doctrines. Moreover, black radicals theorized about the small number of Negroes who had entered industry from the security of New York City; but none ever undertook to enter the South and teach the landless peasants any type of self-help. What began as the organ of the struggling working masses became the mouthpiece of Negro capitalists. The New Negro group which has shown a new orientation towards Negro life and the values which are supposed to spring from Negro life has restricted itself to the purely cultural in the narrow sense.

In this article the writer has attempted to set forth the social forces which have caused the Negro to have his present attitude towards the values in American life. From even this cursory glance at Negro life we are able to see to what extent bourgeois ideals are implanted in the Negro's mind. We are able to see that the Negro group is a highly differentiated group with various interests, and that it is far from sound to view the group as a homogeneous group of outcasts. There has come upon the stage a group which represents a nationalistic movement. This movement is divorced from any program of economic reconstruction. It is unlike the Garvey movement in that Garvey through schemes—phantastic to be sure—united his nationalistic aims with an economic program. This new movement differs from the program of Booker Washington which sought to place the culture of the Negro upon a sound basis by making him an efficient industrial worker. Nor does it openly ally itself with those leaders who condemn the organization of the Pullman porters and advise Negroes to pursue an opportunistic course with capitalism. It looks askance at the new rising class of black capitalism while it basks in the sun of white capitalism. It enjoys the congenial company of white radicals while shunning association with black radicals. The New Negro Movement functions in the third dimension of culture; but so far it knows nothing of the other two dimensions—Work and Wealth.

Jane Nardal

"Internationalisme Noir" (Black Internationalism)

La dépêche africaine, February 15, 1928[11]
Translated by T. Denean Sharpley-Whiting

There is in this postwar era a lowering or the attempt at a lowering of the barriers that exist between countries. Will the various frontiers, custom duties, prejudices, cultural mores, religion, and languages allow this project to be realized? We want to hope for this, those of us who note at the same time the birth of a movement not at all opposed to this first one. Blacks of all origins, of different nationalities, mores, and religions vaguely feel that in spite of everything they belong to one and the same race. Previously the more assimilated blacks looked down arrogantly upon their colored brethren, believing themselves surely of a different species than they; on the other hand, certain blacks who had never left African soil to be led into slavery looked down upon as so many base swine those who at the whim of whites had been enslaved, then freed, then molded into the white man's image.

Then came war, dislocation, blacks from every origin coming together in Europe, the sufferings of the war, the similar infelicities of the postwar period. Then snobs—whom we must thank here—and artists launched Negro art. They taught many blacks, who themselves were surprised, that there existed in Africa an absolutely original black literature and sculpture, that in America poetry and sublime songs, "the Spirituals," had been composed by wretched black slaves. Successively revealed to the white world as well as the black was the plasticity of black bodies in their sculptural attitudes, giving way without transition to an undulation, or to a sudden slackening, under the rule of rhythm, the sovereign master of their bodies; in this black face, so mysterious to whites, the artist would discover tones so shifting and expressions so fleeting as to make either his joy

Paulette (standing), Lucy (seated, left), and Jane Nardal (seated, right) at their apartment in Clamart, outside Paris, October 19, 1935. Nardal Collection, Collectivité Territoriale de Martinique, Archives de Martinique.

or his despair; the cinema, the theater, the music hall opened their doors to the conquering blacks.

All these reasons—from the most important to the most futile—must be taken into account to explain the birth among Negroes of a race spirit. Henceforth there would be some interest, some originality, some pride in being Negro, in turning back toward Africa, the cradle of Negroes, in remembering a common origin. The Negro would perhaps have his part to play in the concert of the races, where until now, weak and intimidated, he has kept quiet.

From these new ideas, new words, whence the creative significance of the terms: Afro-American, Afro-Latin. They confirm our thesis while casting new meaning on the nature of this Black Internationalism. If the Negro wants to know himself, assert his personality, and not be the copy of this or that type from another race (which often earns him contempt and mockery), it does not follow from that, however, that he becomes resolutely hostile to all contributions made by another race. On the contrary, he must learn to profit from others' acquired experience and intellectual wealth, but in order to know himself better and to assert his personality. To be Afro-American, to be Afro-Latin, means to be an encouragement, a consolation, an example for the blacks of Africa by showing them that certain benefits of white civilization do not necessarily lead to a rejection of one's race.

Africans, on the other hand, could profit from this example by reconciling these teachings with the millennial traditions of which they are justly proud. For it no longer comes into the head of the cultivated man to treat them en masse as savages. The work of sociologists has made known to the white world the centers of African civilization, their religious systems, their forms of government, their artistic wealth. Hence the bitterness they feel for having been despoiled is understandable and can be attenuated by that peculiar effect of the colonization: that of linking together, of unifying in a racial solidarity, and, in spite of the feuds between the conquering peoples, tribes who hadn't the slightest idea in this regard.

Along this barely trodden path, American blacks have been the pioneers, I believe. To convince oneself of this, it suffices to read *The New Negro* by Alain Locke, which is slated to appear in French translation by Payot.

The obstacles they encountered (late emancipation, economic slavery still existing in the South, humiliations, lynchings) were so many incentives. And in business and industry, as well as in the fine arts and literature, their successes are impressive, and above all—what interests us here—the prejudices of the whites who surround them have produced in them an unparalleled solidarity and race consciousness.

The Afro-Latins, in contact with a race less hostile to the man of color than the Anglo-Saxon race, have been for that reason retarded in this path. Their hesitation, what's more, is a credit to the country that understood that it should try its best to assimilate them. Even though their loyalty is reassuring, their love of the Latin country, the adoptive land, and their love of Africa, land of their ancestors, are not incompatible. The Negro spirit, so supple, so capable of assimilation, so discerning, will easily surmount this apparent difficulty. And already, helped, encouraged by black American intellectuals, the young Afro-Latins, distinguishing themselves from the preceding generation, hastening to catch the masses up with those who are evolving in that effect, will go beyond them in order the better to guide them. In tending to this task, formed in European methods, they will take advantage of these methods in order to study the spirit of their race, the past of their race with all the necessary critical verve. That black youth are already taking on the study of slavery, facing up to, with detachment, a past that is quite palpable and so painful—isn't that the greatest proof that there does finally exist a black race, a race spirit on the path of maturity? Those who know how, among black people, certain subjects have until recently been taboo can appraise the progress represented by these recent facts.

Marita Bonner

"The Young Blood Hungers"

Crisis, May 1928

The Young Blood sits—back to an Eternity—face toward an Eternity. Hands full of the things ancestry has given—thriving on the things today can give—guided vocationally—inducted spiritually—fed on vitamins—defended against diseases unthinkable—hungry.

The Young Blood hungers.

It's an old hunger. The gnawing world hunger. The hunger after righteousness.

—I speak not for myself alone.

Do not swiftly look and think you see and swiftly say, "It is not, most certainly, a hunger for righteousness this Young Blood feels!"

But it is. It is the Hunger.

Some Young Blood feels it—and then they see if they can out-strip it—if they can get rid of the gnawing—try to dance it off as a man smokes off a trouble—try to float it off on a drunken sea—try to cast a spell on it. Daze it off.

Sometimes the Old Blood perceives the hunger and offers food: "It's the World Hunger," the Old Blood says. "It's the Hunger-After-Righteousness. Take God. Take Him as we have taken Him."

That is what the Old Blood says: "Take God—Take Him as we have taken Him."

And the Young Blood sits still hungry and answers: "Not your God as you had Him."

The Young Blood sits. The Young Blood hungers yet. They cannot take God as the Old Blood takes Him.

Not God sitting at the top of a million worn orthodox steps. God in the old removed far-off Heaven. Not God showering thunder-wrath and stripping man of all Life's compensations to prove him righteous. Not God always offering a heavenly reward for an earthly Hell. Not God poured out in buttered sentences from the pulpit four or fives times a month. Not the Old Blood's God demanding incessant supplication—calling for constant fear.

Not the Old Blood's God—but the God His own Son said that He really is. His own Son, Jesus, who knew Him better than any earth-born creature knew Him. Jesus who said that He was a friendly father who wanted respectful fear and confidential chats and obedience to principle and cooperation and thanksgiving as much as He wanted supplication.—I speak not for myself alone, Lord. The Young Blood hungers.—

The Old Blood argues: "You don't seek God in too-brief garments and too-tinted cheeks—too fancy-free dance steps—too fancy-free Thoughts-about-Things."

Perhaps not—but how?

Up the million steps? Removed? Far? How? How?

The Young does not know. The Young hungers.

The Young Blood hungers and searches somehow. The Young Blood knows well that Life is built high on a crystal of tears. A crystal of tears filled with Illusory Veils of Blind Misunderstandings and Blunderings. Enough filmy veils wet with tears, stamped down hard beneath your feet to let you rise up—out—above—beyond.

Just think of the number of veils cast down! Just think of the tears to pack them down hard so you can stand on them.

Yet that is growing.

The Young Blood knows that growing means a constant tearing down of Illusory Veils that lift themselves thin—filmy—deceptive—between you and truth. Veils that flutter breath-thin across things and make you mistake the touch of Heaven for the touch of Hell.

Veils—breath-thin—so thin you feel them rather than see them.

Tearing down Illusory Veils. Jesus called it watching. Such watching that I of myself and you of yourself cannot do it alone. Veils lift themselves sometimes in the still of the night when even the soul is asleep. Eyes that kept Israel and did not slumber nor yet sleep are needed to help with the tearing down.

I speak not for myself alone, Lord. The Young Blood hungers for Eyes to watch.—

All this the Young Blood knows. All this and more.

Young Blood knows that some Truths solidified in Eternity will not rot until Eternity crumbles. Solidified in Eternity. One love perhaps is to be pure and clean or it is not love. When the mists of Half-Lies play around the face of a truth—Lord—the Young Blood hungers.

Solidified in Eternity—Rooted and tipping in Eternity. Young Blood knows this. And yet if you fumble through the mists of Half-Lies-About-Things to feel the Truth-About-Real-Things safe—sound—solid—behind you—are you a crab—a prude—out of step with your age?

Are there no regular drum-beats? Can't you mark your step to one drum that beats from the rim of Eternity up through the Dark Ages—through the Middle Ages—through Renaissances—through Wars and Remakings-of-Worlds—to the same rhythm?

Is there not a pulse-beat you can feel—beating—steady—Bloody Reigns and Terrors and Inquisitions and Torments—up to Hells-of-Republics and back?

Or is it, after all, a new gait for every new day?

A new drum?

A new rhythm?

A new pulse-beat?

A new step?

A new Heaven?

A new Hell?

Today, a Truth. Tomorrow, a Lie.

Everything new. Raw and new. No time to root before the sun sets its first rays of a new day dawning.

The Young Blood hungers for Truth for God. For the God they called Jehovah when Christ was yet to come. Where is Jehovah?—

A brief breath of a paper-weight-dress—slippers—perfumed—curled—rouged even. Can't you toss your soul out—up—beyond the mere room-full of brief breaths of dresses—perfumes—curls—rouge—and walk and talk to God?

Must you come—eyes down-cast—to an altar four or five times a month to meet God of a Sabbath morn? Can you only commune with Him when you take Christ's body and blood on an appointed day from hands not always too free from blood—before eyes that seem to lick out and eat up—lusting for Young Blood? Isn't it the call for God thrilling in the voice of Young Blood when it is lifted in song—no matter the song?

Isn't it God seeking God in the question of Young Blood when it asks: "Do you understand things? Sometimes I am afraid? Do you understand?"

If Young Blood knew how to converse with God—would so many Young feet stumble in the drunken mazes of seeking to find Self—seeking to find Truth—seeking to drown cries within—seeking enchantments to fill hollows within—seeking to catch up with something greater than yourself in a swift mad consuming fire-flash of living?

—It's the gnawing pains.—

Gnawing pains make you toss your body around. Make you toss your body now this way—now that. Young Blood hungers. Young Blood feels the gnawing pains of hunger—you do not know where your body will come—where it will go. All you wish is to toss your self away from the pain gnawing within.

—It's the gnawing pains.—

Can a mote appear to lay blindness across the vision?

Isn't there a part of Young Blood that leapt into being at Eternity and goes on through all Eternity? Isn't there something that sees beyond curls and rouge?

—I speak not for myself alone, Lord.—

Something winding and winding in the rhythmic inanities of a dance, Young Blood hears things beside the music—the feet—the talk—the chaff of laughter.

Sometimes when you teeter to a jazz-band's play voices speak within you and seem to say:

You may prance, fool, prance
You may skim, you may slide,
You may dip, you may glide,
But you've lied to yourself,
Oh you've lied—lied—lied.
—Gave a damn for the night—
—Chanced your all upon Today—
But you've lied! Yes you've lied!
—I'm the Voice that never died.

Voices and Hunger. Searchings and Seekings. Stumbling—falling—rising again.

—I speak not for myself alone, Lord! The Young Blood hungers.—Back toward an Eternity. Facing Eternity. Perhaps that is the way in which Young Blood is to sit—back toward an Eternity—face toward an Eternity—hungering.

Perhaps it must be that God must be sought in new ways—new ways—fewer steps—fewer steps—each time there comes Young Blood—each time there comes Young Blood—until they find Him.

A few less steps each time. A few less steps each time.

Soon the top.

Then—no longer Hunger.

Then no longer—Hunger.

—I speak not for myself alone, Lord! The Young Blood hungers.—

Anonymous
"Pink Teas"

Philadelphia Tribune, May 17, 1928[12]

There is a New Negro—He says so. He is the knight of the tea table. He is happy when comfortably reclining among silken cushions sipping tea. He discusses art, music and philosophy with the appearance of great learning. And the race question—he knows the answer from every angle. He is drunk with too much tea. His muscles are flabby and he never thinks of anything more substantial than layer cake. If one of his more crude brothers should make the mistake of mentioning a big juicy beef-steak, his lips curl in the direction of the smoke from his highly perfumed cigarette. The hard practical things of life mean nothing to this apostle of "pink teas." He criticizes the great mass of workers for being illiterate and unlearned. He speaks as one with authority about Negro business enterprises and political achievement. As a matter of fact he knows nothing about business and precious little about politics. While drinking his tea from beautiful pink cups he speaks a language different from that great army of Negro builders. His energies are all spent in talking pure nonsense to novel writers and those who hang on the fringe of society.

This "superior" being calls himself the "New Negro." He admits that until he came upon the scene Negroes were foolish and accomplished nothing. Of all the pure buncombe this stage lizard's attitude takes the prize. Hitting at the race problem at long range means nothing. There is work to be done. Work that calls for courage, brain and the will to put it over. Men and women with trained minds are needed, but they must get down among the people and elevate them to a higher plane. A trained mind accomplishes nothing unless it is put to more useful service than the proper manner of drinking tea. He can best prove his superiority by doing something which will contribute to the general welfare of his people. Men can not live by bread alone[;] neither will tea table discussions take the place of the substantial and fundamental things of life.

"He Had Better Go to Work"

"He Had Better Go to Work," *Philadelphia Tribune*, May 17, 1928.

Charles S. Johnson
"A Chapel Talk: To the Students of Fisk University"

October 17, 1928

I have been debating seriously with myself, for several days, the theme which I should offer you, in what might properly enough be called my maiden address. You, doubtless, have some mild curiosity about the special interest responsible for my presence here with you. And again, you may not. However, for this once I will not talk shop. There are always enough words to consume twenty minutes in refurbishing some of the familiar postulates of character building. These cannot be stressed too often; but I have decided, with your leave, to test interest in one of the occasionally neglected corners. The virtues of the conventions, even in an institution of this kind, I hope not to ignore even though I chose to begin, as you might call it, inductively, with familiar items of experience, in the effort to distil from these some satisfying and immediate philosophy. I am going to try to be exceedingly practical, and helpful on certain special problems, the existence of which, I fear, it is a part of our current dogma frequently to deny.

This experience, which is the theme of my talk this morning, will be frankly limited to the problems of racial status, which are not only intimate and real, but which, I believe, demand some re-valuation now, for the highest expression of Negro youth. . . . [13]

. . . compensations for the social disabilities of the moment, that we have in Negro life a virgin world of beauty which can yield rich satisfactions and command a new order of respect, and finally, that the freedom which these bring is a first condition of participation in world culture.

In the first place, it is well to consider what is meant by the suggestion that the implications of Negro status are escapable. I have in mind those implications which are distasteful to Negroes and present such a formidable front against their rounded development. Now it is a fact that the most depressing elements in these implications are fictitious, although they give on the surface the aspect of fundamental racial barriers. Some of these I shall mention:

The Concept Negro Is a Variable.

It never means the same biologically, geographically, historically, nor is it the same to different people of the same race, or period, or place.

The Concept Negro Is a Synthesis.

It is color and feature, but those combined with status past and present; it is isolation, inferior circumstance, social attitudes toward all of these, and reflections of the *inferior feeling* of Negroes themselves.

Isolation, it may be commented, magnifies differences of any sort; inferior circumstances induces [*sic*] scorn and pity from the outside, and indifference and hopelessness from within. The physical ugliness of certain Negro neighborhoods, for example, although explainable, contributes as much to invidious distinctions as color alone, for revulsion against sheer ugliness is as positive as revulsion against a theory of race, and when both are allowed to exist together, impressions are reinforced. Immaculateness and order can easily confound theories of race in such situations.

The difference of color between races manifests the same social features as difference between sexes of the same race.

The arguments used to establish the status of women,[—]brain weights, cranial measurements, physical structure, records of achievements,[—]have been almost precisely the same as those used to establish the status of Negroes. They have been arguments from circumstance which dispute themselves.

Economic Forces Are Stronger Than Racial Forces.

If this were not true, Negroes would not be used to break strikes, and there would have been no history of the use in the United States of black slaves by white slave owners to grind other and poorer white men pitilessly into the earth for more than a hundred years.

The Concept Negro Is a Part of the Concept "Class."

The great majority of Negroes are either peasants or laborers and share the fate of these unprotected classes. Class and race are not identical even though the angles of pressure frequently fall at the same points. Growing out of this already are a differential respect for Negroes as these classes among them become defined, and tendencies toward a crossing of racial lines when the common interests of a class are concerned.

The Concept Negro Is a Part of the Concept "Stranger."

It is human nature to look with suspicion, fear or disparagement upon outsiders. The principle of Greek and barbarian, Christian and heathen, Jew and gentile, runs uninterruptedly through the history of societies.

I have mentioned these to indicate that there are many elements in Negro status which are only incidentally racial, and are thus, escapable, both in their pressure from without and in their dangerous promptings to inner hopelessness. Now, you may ask, what of the actual social disabilities facing Negro youth in their competition with others, and how are they actually to achieve this serenity of mind and spirit in a world of struggle and in the face of ponderous disparagement? I offer two simple formulae:

> The cult of competence, and
> The cult of beauty.

Objectively, the sociologists classify Negroes with cripples, persons with recognized physical handicaps which have social consequences.[14] The cripples themselves have the choice either of resigning themselves apologetically to their handicap and selling pencils on the street; or of developing conscious compensations for their physical deficiency. In this sociological sense many persons are "cripples": the timid, the nearsighted, the too short, the too tall, the ugly, the obese, the nervous, the physically weak, the sensitive, the deaf. If they are wise, they develop healthy compensations. To employ a familiar example: Theodore Roosevelt, the apostle of the strenuous life, began life physically weak. The blindness of Milton served to sharpen sight into the vague, vast life and beauty of the universe. The Japanese, a physically small people, developed jiu-jitsu, which renders them more than the physical equal of strong men.

Negro youth, recognizing the fact of an unequal economic struggle, may either accept the status that goes with inferior economic ability, or compensate for this deficiency by actually developing a superior skill. In most parts of the country, all other things being equal, if a Negro and a white worker apply for a position the white worker will get it. This is a social disability which is unfair, of course, and should be changed. Meanwhile, however, it is uneconomical to await helplessly the slow processes of human nature. Intelligent strategy demands that the Negro applicant should assure himself of that superior competence which, in many cases, overweighs purely racial preference. It will be pardoned here, I hope, if I inject a particle of skepticism into my attitude toward many of the complaints that opportunities are denied Negroes purely on the grounds of race. These assertions assume that there is nothing objectionable in the temperament of the individual, his personal habits, his physical appearance apart from his color, his manner, and most important of all, in his peculiar abilities. The success of a Negro like, let us say, Stanley Braithwaite, suggests the weight of superior skill in a wide field of competition. There must be cultivated now a *mental set* which expects to bring an overbalance of competence, which is easily at their command to correct social disabilities which are stronger than any individual. Negro youth should be in a racial sense, precocious. The shrewdness of some cripples is forced upon them when they must substitute mental calculation for physical immobility. Here is a little poem which fits the situation completely.

> Chares of Lindus
> Was reckoned a pigmy
> Had he been Ajax,
> Or been Achilles,
> Would he have wrought the Colossus of
>   Rhodes?

However, there is a vast field of activity still open which no question of racial preference can effect. No racial theories, except those self entertained, can prevent a Negro from perfecting an invention, or tracing the behavior of bacteria in the name of science, or from painting a beautiful picture, or from projecting an idea of social value, or for that matter, from any creative exercise. "In the realm of the arts the one criterion of the right to possess is the ability to enjoy." The world's most brilliant minds of all ages live in their books. Shakespeare, Milton, Dante, Goethe, Ibsen, could not draw the color line if they would, and their companionship is open to anyone capable of appreciating them.

For Negro youth here, there is no lack of opportunity; no disparagement of success, no handicap but their own personal limitations. It is, of course, understandable why this open field is not yet crowded. One reason is the self feeling of futility; another, lack of confidence; another the low horizon of expectation; and still another, a curtailment of preparation. The ease with which one may become the greatest local Negro hastens contentment and self satisfaction, and insidiously prevents one from breaking through the boundaries of mediocrity and low expectation. There is no evidence that intelligence or high mental capacity or superiority is limited to any race, even though it is a part of the racial dogma to pretend that they are. These qualities are distributed, and one of the vast tragedies of our life is that superiority is unthinkable. Where it has developed even accidentally, it has confounded racial theories and practice.

There are frequent indications that we are still in the stage of novices of learning. Too little of it goes too far. There is not enough exposure to the rigid and exacting standards of the best in the field. The implication here is that our level of contentment in training is yet too low; that we do not read enough even to learn our shortcomings by comparison with the best that has been thought and done in the world beyond ourselves; that we have not been forced into specialization or to the intensive development of a technique; and that we are yet insensitive to the subtleties of the best.

[Professor Doyle referred last week to the fact that in the field of mathematics the circle had not been squared. Although it has been proved, I believe, that the circle cannot be squared if there is any one of you ready for these adventures in mathematics the possibility is still open, according to Dr. Haldane, that the sum of two 59th powers may turn out to be a 59th power; just as the sum of 3 squared and 4 squared is itself the square of 5. An American disproved a hypothesis about prime numbers that had held the field for 250 years. Or to be more practical one might set himself to work out tables of mathematical functions not yet tabulated, which would be of immense value to engineers and physicists. However, we would be highly pleased in the present state of affairs to have available a few good social statisticians, for whom positions are actually now open.][15]

There are 18 large Negro insurance companies and not a single Negro actuarial statistician in America; yet no racial prejudice prevents specialization in this field of social Mathematics. Tuberculosis is one of our greatest scourges; yet no Negro trained in medicine is devoting himself to this problem of science—and does anyone believe that the results of any such person could be ignored? The world obeisance to Noguchi, the scientist of the much hated Japanese race, who died recently, suggests the normal reaction to such competence.

The subject of race is a paramount one, yet there are no Negro ethnologists or anthropologists, and scarcely two psychologists, though preparation for these fields scarcely requires any equipment which is inaccessible to Negroes. Interestingly enough, the most important contributions to anthropology and ethnology in America have been made by Jews who have experienced in a much milder form the social handicaps of Negroes.

Apart from the well known professions, there are now actually opportunities for scientific and social research students, statisticians, health officers, sanitary engineers, architects and draughtsmen, designers, organization executives trained in social work, psychiatrists, social and medical clinicians, [and] physicists.

[Last summer five scholarships of $1,200 each were available for Negroes who had given positive evidences of interest in the field of social administration, and more could have been obtained if students were available. Only three such persons were located. It is not difficult to find students who are willing to take $1,200 fellowships, but it is difficult to find students who on their own initiative and before the promise of reward is offered have concerned themselves with various studies and preparations.][16]

The list of opportunities could be multiplied. But in none of these is there the least promise of distinction without training to the point of competence, and beyond.

The point, I hope is clear. And if practical hints were needed, I would offer these:

The selection of a career should not be determined primarily by the apparent limits of Negro opportunity. This reticence has tended to keep the opportunities limited. For every soundly competent Negro who is unable to engage upon the career of his choice for racial reasons, there are three who can. Too frequently our measure of competence itself is defective.

It is not often that superior talents can be concealed even in humble positions. There is a wide range of ordinary work to which intelligence alone can lend prestige and importance.

Equality for Negroes means actual superiority; superiority, however, is not an arguable thing; it is most effective when it is a subjective secret.

An unfailing self-discipline is to seek a major responsibility which has to be sustained; expose oneself at intervals beyond the familiar limits, to an unrestricted test of one's powers. "An idea cherished in secret until it becomes a passion, develops great power"; set out with secret determination to accomplish more than is expected.[17]

The impression which one gets of a man, as Mr. Cooley points out in his memoirs, comes not so much from what he is doing as from what we imagine him to be living for,—his plans, hopes, faiths and loyalties. This is true in a racial as well as in a personal sense.

From this point we may move on to the other wing of my theme, which I have referred to as the cult of beauty. When Matthew Arnold visited this country some forty years ago, he went home and wrote an essay on Civilization in the United States in which he noted the major defects of our civilization to be a want of what is elevated, of what is beautiful, and thus, of what is interesting. This was the period of great American sensitiveness to foreign criticism and of rather brutal intimations of cultural backwardness. Lowell was complaining bitterly of "a certain condescension of foreigners." A famous French critic had referred to the "hard unintelligence of the people of the United States," and to all of these cultural America had responded with irritable outbursts of indignation, boisterous and blind self-glorification, and, paradoxically enough, with a servile obeisance to European standards.

"Whenever beauty is really seen and loved" says Santayana, "it has a definite embodiment: The eye has precision, the work has style and the object has perfection." This provides a clue to the new life which should be ours, whether the expression takes the form of art, of literature, or science, or philosophy or the intimate and personal exhilaration of new spiritual concepts. It was the dull lack of some idealism here that held America in a suspended cultural animation until it sought freedom through self-criticism and its own native sources of beauty. In the same manner, American Negroes, born into a culture which they did not wholly share, have responded falsely to the dominant patterns. Their expression has been, to borrow a term which Lewis Munford employs in referring to Americans in relation to Europe, "sickly and derivative, a mere echo of old notes." There has been the same self-deception of "boasting and vain imagination[,]" the same indifference to the spiritual refinement of the beautiful, the same dull seeking of an average level, and the same mystifying sense of an imponderable shortcoming, which led inevitably to inferior feeling and apology. The form of expression merely, has been different. At bottom there has been a blindness to native values, which has kept these values concealed, not merely from themselves but from others. The cultural differences between an Englishman and an American is not so much in the germ plasm as in the accumulated stores of culture which impose for each different standards of perfection. The same condition applies in the cultural differences between Americans and American Negroes. I am convinced that the road to a new freedom for us lies in the discovery of the surrounding beauties of our lives, and in the recognition that beauty itself is a mark of the highest expression of the human spirit.[18]

Now, you may ask, what beauty is there in Negro life, and how can the appreciation of it contribute to the fullest development of Negro youth?

There was a time not so long ago when some of the rarest contributions to American art which happened to have been created by Negroes, were spurned by them as insults to their spirits. That "bloody epoch of utility" left its glamorless mark deep in the spirits of the first descendants of the slaves. The shame of it even now can never be survived so long as it is taken personally, and it is not surprising that those who uttered freedom with their lips while feeling within their souls this sting of shame accomplished little and felt their own freedom a delusion and a snare. But this period as an epoch was no more devoid of beauty to the larger spirit than the inescapable face of death itself. To Jean Toomer it "carolled softly souls of slavery." The Israelites sang of their bondage—

not apologetically or in resignation, but in a lyric note born of the pain of exile and an unquenchable spiritual fervor. There is a thrilling magnificence and grandeur in the fact of survival itself, in the tread of unconquerable life through two centuries of pain.

There is a vast unchallenged beauty in the slave music drawn up from deep flowing rivers of sorrow. Only recently have we felt the courage to admit the charm and power of this music. There is the real substance of poetry in the folklore of this period. What is most important, there is a transporting beauty which touches the buried springs of all human life in the religious expression of the slave. Religion is most real to those who most feel the need of comfort and refuge beyond the gift of man: and the deepest penetrations of divinity are experienced by philosophers and children.[19]

These, it seems to me, are no less significant than Puritanism, and the early American farm house, as spiritual and artistic antecedents of contemporary America.

But while these gifts of beauty have come into a sort of repute, and no longer stir to life consuming emotions of chagrin and defeat, there is yet the environment of the present which aesthetic appreciation has scarcely touched.

The beginning of the 20th century has been marked in America by a conscious movement "back to the concrete," which has yielded the new fascination of watching the strangeness and beauty of familiar things. It is America in revolt against the stiff conventionalism of borrowed patterns. The commentators of the present begin the new era in America with such characters as Sandburg and Robinson, apostles of freedom, who have launched the search for beauty in forgotten lives. It is the spirit of the New America. Americans are at present feverishly active in creating an art for industry. The automobile industry was revolutionized by this new urge. Macy's recent exposition revealed the quite startling fact that there can even be such a thing as a beautiful butcher shop. A profitable lesson may be taken from the wave of interest in devising an attractive hot-dog stand which would relieve this necessary nuisance of its slovenly ugliness. This compulsion exists now for the new generation of Negroes—the compulsion to find a new beauty in their own lives, ideals, and feelings.

The new generation of Negro writers and artists have led the way here. The poetry represents this liberated energy. It is beginning the embodiment of new and beautiful life conceptions. It is revising old patterns, investing Negro life with a new charm and dignity, and power. No life for them is without beauty, no beginning too low:

> I will take from the hearts
> of black men—
> Prayers their lips
> Are 'fraid to utter
> And turn their coarseness
> Into a beauty of the jungle
> Whence they came.

Color for which excuses have been found in the past, comes into its own.

> "Her skin is like dusk on the eastern
> horizon
> Oh can't you see it, oh can't you see it?
> Her skin is like dusk on the eastern
> horizon
> Before the sun goes down.

Or as in one of Cullen's conceptions—

> "That brown girl's swagger gives a twitch
> To beauty like a queen."

Or Lewis Alexander's vision of a black Medicine Man—

> "A body smiling with black beauty
> Leaping into the air."

or the tenderness of these lines of Langston Hughes:

> "Lovely, dark and lovely one
> Bare your boson to the sun
> Do not be afraid of light
> You who are a child of night."

They have found a language of beauty for their own world of color. It is a first frank affirmation of self:

> "Of Lord, not for what I saw in flesh and
> bone
> of fairer men, not raised in flesh alone;
> Lord, I will live persuaded by mine own
> I cannot play the recreant of these
> My spirit has come home, that sailed the
> doubtful seas."

For those who see no beauty in a commonplace group of Negroes working the cane fields, I commend this flash:

> "Their voices rise—the pine trees are
> guitars
> Strumming, pine needles fall like shoots
> of rain . . .
> Their voices rise . . . the chorus of the
> cane
> Is caroling a vesper to the stars."

In this mood of elevation, life takes on new meaning. Qualities of temperament become significant, old circumstance may clothe itself in bright new garments to yield new joys: [*sic*]

The rich contributions of rhythm, imagery, and the deeper stirrings of emotion are ours. Here, in this acceptance of beauty, lies the material for the hidden self to give it a quiet and serene confidence; here lies that substance which can become the matter of life itself. I have spoken of the creators of the beautiful. Those suggestions are intended have a more general application. And the observation of Millet, well carries the point of my insistence when he says: "The beautiful consists not so much in the thing represented as in the longing to represent it." In this sense we are all artists, or should be.

Now, it may be asked, in what way can these new conceptions alter Negro life. Anyone who has followed that interesting movement among the youth referred to, and, for that matter, the older ones who have paced the distance into this period, must have observed in them these new qualities:

(1)   A frank and unembarrassed
      acceptance of the fact of race.
(2)   An objectification of the facts of
      Negro life followed by analysis and
      an admission of certain weaknesses

on the philosophy—that if one is not truthful about his faults which can be seen, he need not expect to be believed about those virtues which are not always exposed.

(3) A return to sources of art in Negro Folk life, and in self-experience.

(4) A loss of much of the sensitiveness about the old racial symbols which once offended.

(5) Abandonment of apology for self and race.

(6) A note of confident self-expression in poetry and art.

(7) A gradual changing of the meaning of words and patterns and the substitution of a new content.

This is the example offered by a few of the spirits emerging from the coverts of their own fears and escapable limitations.

These are demonstrable beginnings for the spiritual emancipation which I commend to you. There is yet lacking that full flavor of an idealism that will risk discomfort for this new vision of life, but come it must.

I have offered to you the suggestion that Negro Life, and the implications of Negro status are seperable [*sic*]; that the implications of Negro status are escapable; that there are compensations for the social disabilities of the moment in the cult of competence; and that there is possible a new and exhilarating spiritual emancipation through the cultivation of a sense of beauty for the very life of which we are a part.

It is one of the most encouraging signs of our age that one no older in years or more favored in circumstance than you who sit before me now has been able thus to write:

"We build our temples for tomorrow
Strong as wo know how; and we
Stand on top of the mountain
Free within ourselves."[20]

Richard Bruce Nugent

Excerpt from Gentleman Jigger: A Novel of the Harlem Renaissance, 1928–1933

[In this roman à clef, Stuartt Brennan represents Nugent. Other characters include Raymond "Rusty" Pellman (Wallace Thurman), Howard (Aaron Douglas), and Leslie (Leland Petit), a gay political activist and organist at New York City's Grace Episcopal Church.[21]]

It always amused Stuartt to dine at De Vore's with white friends. There were many features—and many facets to each feature—of this amusement. Somehow it never seemed to Stuartt that any of it touched him, although he was immersed in it all. It was like swimming in ever-changing waters, temperatures rising and falling, running swift or slow. Only he seemed well-oiled, and the waters rolled off him—his passage through them was eased and helped. He never really got wet at all.

There was something about this walking-on-the-waters attitude of Stuartt's that annoyed Rusty exceedingly. And fascinated him just as greatly. But between them, since they were friends, they were always ready—both of them or either of them—to notice every little nuance and incidental gesture of the other diners, and they would hug it close, exchanging little looks that fenced everyone else out, and would giggle or lift an eyebrow. This secret and impolite malice would make any palefaces at their table self-conscious beneath the imagined focus of the glances of the other diners in this not-too-familiar land, and the slightly tense atmosphere so unintentionally and deliberately created at their table would tickle the senses of both Rusty and Stuartt even further, and they would titter even more. Tenseness and self-consciousness would deepen, causing their enjoyment to heighten, and it would snowball—situation growing out of nonexistent situation until Rusty and Stuartt were hilarious. It was all so impossible to explain to anyone else. That very impossibility would become a part of the almost hysterical amusement that gripped them. Rusty and Stuartt could seldom be serious dining at De Vore's. But today seemed about to be an exception.

They had finished their soup, and the conversation had turned to painting and sculpture. Rusty was holding forth on Negro art. Everyone was hanging on to Rusty's words. He had long ago convinced them that he was the logical source of all information Negroid. He was the leader of the Niggeratti, and the Niggeratti led the New Negro. But except for Rusty, they were all rather apathetic leaders. Rusty was the only one of them who had the initiative to push things to the fore—anything, everything—and shade them with black. He was the superb showman—the black Barnum, the opportunist par excellence. He was also vain and had decided that the group was to be recognized as important, and that he was to be recognized as the most important of the group. He was.

"It is a thing I think should be more greatly developed." Rusty always spoke in a manner that could be quoted and had no fear of clichés or trite expressions. "After all, we are Negroes, and as such we are entitled to draw on the culture of Africa—to borrow its forms as we have borrowed our forebears' pigmentation. Africa and the best there is in it should be inspiration in every sense of the word and every use of its meaning. Yet how many Negro artists have the courage to admit that they think African art is beautiful?"

"Or *do* think it beautiful—or for that matter, even consider it art?" Stuartt interjected in his parenthetical way.

And Rusty continued, as he almost always did when Stuartt punctuated any remark or thought he was expounding, just as though

there had been no other spoken word. "How many are proud of the fact that these things were executed by their forefathers?"

"He calls this art, 'Things!'" Stuartt was ready at that breath with further interjection. "'Executed—'"

"Only one person that I know of," Rusty continued. "Howard. Howard has taken the essence of African art and converted it into modern form. So in consequence, his drawings of Negroes, with thick lips and pointed elbows, are not liked by Negroes. Good Lord!"

Stuartt again stopped eating long enough to mildly ask, "Howard? What does Howard know about African Art?"

Sterling froze at this heresy. His reprimand stood solid and stiff in the transparency of his disapproval. "You are not going to contend that Howard's art is Nordic, are you Stuartt?"

"Don't mind Stuartt, Sterling. He just likes to needle." Rusty turned to Stuartt and continued, "What is Howard's stuff then? I suppose that with your usual destructive sort of criticism that precludes the possibility of anything constructive, you are about to contend that his stuff isn't even good."

"But he couldn't say that." Leslie's pink face was serious. "Howard's work is beautiful and—I agree with you, Rusty—essentially African."

"But 'stuff'—merely 'stuff'—as Rusty so succinctly denoted it." Stuartt was bland again, but there was a stubbornness in his attitude like a steel stay in a velvet corset. "You are all a little silly. And there is really nothing I can say at all. A fellow artist's work, workers of the world forgive me, is one thing I do not like to talk about. I don't particularly relish having the old 'professional jealousy' cliché thrown in my face. At least not at mealtime, when I am already busy digesting. Much more pleasant things to do." He took another forkful of food with all the careful precision of a dancer knowing that the next graceful step hinges upon the present graceful gesture.

"And after I said what I thought, should I be so rash, no matter how much I might belittle my own art, I would only be called insincere. No. Go on, my Philistines, believing in Howard if you like—believing in this lacquered and distorted caricature of him and his works. Listen to the great god Rusty expound on a subject about which he knows nothing at all with all the dogmatic emphasis of ignorance."

Stuartt gestured another graceful forkful into his mouth, as though to silence his lips.

"Maybe you could enlighten us, then." Rusty waited a moment and, as there was no answer from the seemingly unperturbed Stuartt, continued, "Since Mr. Brennan refuses to lift the pall of our ignorance—"

"Well, what do you know about African art?" Stuartt's voice was still soft but now more urgent. "Nothing. Or you wouldn't say so pompously and glibly, 'African Art.' One doesn't say 'German art' or 'Italian art' unless it is understood what is meant by such general classification. One might classify art into schools based on time and masters and then into locales. But in most art, the feeling that pervades and influences one country is usually felt in other countries strongly enough to produce great similarities. And—"

"Don't you be silly, Stuartt. One says 'Greek art,' 'Roman art' or 'Egyptian art' and presupposes that dates have been supplied in routine education. So—African art!" Rusty paused triumphant.

"I guess in a way that's fair enough," Stuartt admitted wryly. "But in another way you take semantic advantage. And psychological advantage. You know I can never be coherent about things that are really vital to me. I'm as much like people as people even, and I don't function on all intellectual fours when I'm emotional, either. Art is vital to me. I have not only thought about it, I feel about it as well. Silly of me, but too true. And you don't know a damned thing about African art. Emotionally, psychologically, intellectually, categorically or any god-damned way at all, except in that everlasting dilettante way that's so fashionable these days."

"Such violence!" Sterling sipped his tea with a delicacy that broadly parodied Stuartt's recent gesticular sarcasm. It seemed to spur Stuartt on, even as it brought his voice under closer control. He seemed to be directing his onslaught at Rusty, though.

"You couldn't tell a Gabun piece from an Ivory Coast or a Sudan or a Congo or a Benin. In fact, I doubt if you knew there were great enough differentiations in African art to allow for any classification."

"African art?" Rusty inserted a little maliciously.

"If," Stuartt went right on, "I were to show you a Gabun, you would probably say 'Egyptian,' if you liked it. Or 'trash' if you didn't. But you'd not appreciate its design. To explain—or I suppose what I really mean is to accent for you—the symmetry of the pattern of small repeated lines of highly conventionalized planes and masses about the nose as center would be futile. To point out the beauty of the concentric triangles of mouth, chin, eyes, ears, nose, headdress—the deft in-out-up-down swelling lines and surfaces which make the piece all one smooth perpetual rhythm—would be a waste of time."

Stuartt paused for breath. Or perhaps he paused because he felt a little silly, as one usually does when lost in explaining beauty. No one said anything for a few screamingly loud silent moments. None of them, except Rusty, had ever heard Stuartt speak really seriously before, and even Rusty was absorbed. This would come in handy someday. He recognized it for other than textbook authority. It was the actual authority of artistic and emotional appreciation.

Stuartt felt as if he were dangling in the air. He began to retrace his way back across the tightrope of speaking as he felt to the firmer platform of saying what words could say and still be dismissed.

"Or take a Gabun full figure, embodying the perfection of rhythmic concentration on individual anatomical parts, restrained only by the artist's desire to execute a living whole and his recognition that design is implicit in everything, but that each thing has its own individual design. Repetitions of soft bulbous protuberances carried out in curve of forehead, breasts, trunk, torso, legs. The intense concentration to dissociate the body into units all blending into a perfect design as a whole. I suppose you'll tell me that I couldn't differentiate either. That I, neither, could name this or that.

Well, perhaps I couldn't. Nor even vocalize about what I felt. But I do feel the differences." Stuartt wet his lips with a sip of his iced tea, then with kindly maliciousness said, "Remember these things, Rusty, if ever *The Bookman* wants an article on Negro art."

Rusty ignored the thrust for the horseplay it was. "But how does all this discourse concern anything I have been saying about Howard?"

Stuartt sighed a mock sigh, but he was rather sincerely impatient also. "After all, the discourse itself should have explained its reference. Just because Howard's figures have pointed joints and bulbous foreheads."

"But if those are the essence of African art and the essence also of Howard's, then what?" Leslie looked around the table, unable to quite finish phrasing his question.

"Yes, what then?" Sterling gave Leslie a moral boost.

"Why, are you all completely stupid or blind? Howard is his teacher. Fortunately, his teacher is an artist, so the copy isn't quite a counterfeit. And it is his *teacher* who is influenced by African art—African art and Picasso, who is likewise influenced. Howard is just a sponge. He has absorbed a technique invented, or discovered, as you will, by his teacher. He promptly adopts it, adapts it, and perfects it, and it becomes 'Howard's Art.'"

"But isn't that just what all other artists do?" Rusty's voice was so sincerely full of question as to seem timid.

"Not artists," Stuartt said quite patly. "That's my very contention. Soon Howard will have exhausted his style. Then what? If he is an artist, a creative artist, he will have derived enough to grow further. That's it—he could grow instead of reaching an end. The artist is continually evolving from what he has created in the past. He is a sieve through which all things pass, and only the finest remains to be used and then sieved again. The artist is continually advancing until, in later pieces, one cannot see the tiniest trace or similarity to his earlier work. But Howard won't. He'll reach a standstill."

"Oh, stop being highbrow and talk sense." Sue was tired of being silent.

"Right, Sue," responded Stuartt. "Say, isn't that a handsome man!" Stuartt pointed to a couple who had just come in.

"I don't think so, particularly," Bill answered.

"But you, after all, are not as aware of sex appeal in males as I am. It annoys you. It amuses me. You see, you are afraid. I am not."

"And why aren't you afraid, Stuartt?" Leslie was baiting Stuartt again. "Are you so certain of your charm—your influence with women—?"

"Yes, I am," Stuartt interrupted.

"Or," Leslie continued, "are you attracted by men?"

"Yes again." It was Stuartt's delight to play with words. Leslie was so serious.

"Then you are queer?" It was almost an assertion.

"Queer?" Stuartt thought a moment, lit a cigarette, and inhaled a puff before answering. "I don't think I'm very different from you or Rusty or Bill. But maybe I don't understand you. What do you mean by 'queer?'"

"I mean: do you like men?"

"Yes, don't you? And women, too. And I'm very fond of eats. Does that make me queer?"

Leslie was not to be shaken off. "Have you ever had a woman in love with you?"

"Yes."

"A man?"

"Yes." Stuartt was totally unperturbed.

Leslie was flushed and triumphant. At last he had cornered Stuartt. "Which did you prefer?"

Stuartt flicked his ashes into a cup. The others waited. Had Leslie really cornered the always-victorious Stuartt?

Then Stuartt answered mildly in an earnest voice. Only Rusty noticed the laughter in his eyes.

"Well you see, Leslie, I don't quite know. I enjoyed both immensely. But then, I've never been in love myself."

Leslie was silenced. During the general laughter, someone suggested that they leave. So out they went. On back up Seventh Avenue. Everyone was in excellent spirits. They stopped in a speakeasy and had a few drinks. As they were coming out, they met "Rusty's find," as Stuartt called him. He was a pickpocket. Many times, upon discovering that they were hungry, he had gone out into the subway to return an hour later with several wallets.

They all went towards 267. Stuartt and Bill left to catch a train to East Orange.

Charles S. Johnson
"The New Negro"

Typescript for a speech to be given at Fisk University, ca. 1929

No one who has paid the least attention to the Negro in America is unaware of certain definite changes that have been taking place. These changes have been wide-spread and profound. Discussion is high; at no period since that which marked the severe last struggle of opinion and economic advantage or, the question of Negro slavery, have there appeared so many books on the subject. No corner of Negro life is unaffected. Suddenly and without explanation, new figures have leaped to the horizon; new poets have appeared almost full grown; new writers have emerged from the darkness, interpreting a life which has been very real to them, but little known to the rest of the world. Nor has the fermentation limited itself to letters; art, music, and even the dance have shared in this sudden awakening.

The strange concourse of widely different interests has in it to the outside observer an element of fascination and mystery.[22] Take the field of art. For years there lay about in the curio shops of Paris great heaps of queerly grotesque brass, iron and wood pieces with strange designs. Twelve years ago, Paul Guillaume picked up a few of these, casually bought some for a song, and carried them away. The designs were more than queer. They held his interest with a subtle message, for he was discovering in these apparently crude pieces the language of an utterly new art form. The patterns were elaborations of complex geometric designs which could yield an almost infinite variety. Their utility became apparent. These fetishes and idols interpreted a sense of aesthetics with which they had never been credited. The vast diversity of these objects of art, the penetration of every institution and corner of life with these carefully perfected expressions of a real and vital skill, pointed to the existence of a thing very rare among peoples, a living folk art.

A group of young independent European artists saw them. They were searching for new molds sufficient to contain a restless creativeness unsatisfied by the conventional forms brought to perfection hundreds of years ago. They got the form of these new patterns and they adopted them. The modern art of Picasso, Modigliani, Soutine, Lipschitz began to reflect this. It spread—it became a vogue; it appealed—it still continues. Contemporary Negro intellectuals have blended these influences with others in the present "renaissance."[23]

There were a few collections of spirituals and about three recognized troupes of singers. Dvorak came and studied it. He left America saying that it was the only real American music—the basis of the country's greatest development of the future. (There must be some explanation of this sudden pausing.)[24] After fifty years, Negroes pause to collect these remnants of this poetry of slavery before it disappears forever. In the past two years there have appeared about ten books on this music, almost as many as were published in the full period before. It has not stopped with the spirituals. Interest has extended to include the common snatches of work songs, sentimental ballads, work songs and even street cries of Negro peddlers.

There (must be some explanation of) is also the strange and sudden (fascination) vogue for syncopation—jazz.[25] The mad hectic rhythm has swept both America and Europe.

Gilbert Seldes was the first to point out the irony that Paul Whiteman should become the supreme figure in this field of music.

Handy's blues created twelve years ago, sold a half million copies for the piano and a million and a half records.

It has replaced the stately waltz and mazurka; it has overridden the objection of music critics who would "beat our swords into plowshares and our jazz-bands into unconsciousness." It has become a new international word, queerly it reflects the tempo of American life.

Again, it is difficult to explain the sudden flare of new rhythmic forms in the dances that have come [from] the soil—the Charleston, Black Bottom—which with their broken rhythm strangely like the syncopation of the music has [sic] lured into its grip the smart dances here and in Europe. As an illustration of change, Jo-sephine Baker, who was an almost obscure figure in Negro musical shows, gets this ecstatic review from a Parisian Critic:

"Her lithe young body, looking like a Venetian bronze come to life, seemed to incarnate the spirit of unrestrained joy. It is a wild thing, yet graceful and harmonious—a demon unchained, yet delicate in its sleek symmetrical beauty."

These have a suddenness because we have obscured until recently the real development of Negroes with the manufactured stereotyped.

[I spoke two days ago about the evolution of attitudes which have characterized thinking on the question of the Negro. Beliefs concerning their mentality, criminality, morality, temperament and beliefs concerning racial instincts. These have all had their effect in warping the nature of Negroes and I propose to offer an explanation of the nether side of this growth—that is, the reaction through the stages of growth on the part of the Negroes.][26] [Handwritten: "Back to page on literature—." However, this section does not appear in the typescript.]

Charles Chesnutt
"The Negro in Present Day Fiction"

Speech, Oberlin, Ohio, ca. 1929

Mr. (Miss) Chairman and members of the Dunbar Forum, I regard it as a high privilege to appear before a group of students of literature in this old and historic institution of learning with its glorious tradition of human equality and equal opportunity for all. . . .

When I began to write books about life along the color line and amongst the colored people, there were not a great many such books. Mrs. Stowe had written the epoch-making *Uncle Tom's Cabin* and her other books along the same line. Judge Albion W. Tourgée had written *The Fool's Errand*—probably the first of what we call nowadays "best sellers,"—*Bricks Without Straw*, and several other novels about the freed slaves, Reconstruction and the old Ku Klux Klan.

Paul Laurence Dunbar was looming above the horizon as a poet—I think his one or two novels were written after I began to write. The Rev. Thomas Dixon was spawning his libels on the Negro in the guise of fiction. But the modern novel, depicting the different types of colored people with their emotions, their aspirations, their love affairs, in fact, all the complications and involvements of modern life, was not in evidence, and for a very good reason—

there were no modern Negroes. Most of them were absorbed in the struggle for bare existence, and the difficult effort to adjust themselves to new conditions.

The novel, even more than sculpture or painting, is the flower of culture. Poets are said to be born. The greatest of epic poets, Homer, was in a sense a primitive, at least he led the great procession of poets which has flowed down the stream of time. The *Iliad* was simple poetry. It was poetry of action. The poetic figures were not worked to death. Homer could turn a fine line without plagiarism. He did not have to scan a thesaurus or a library to ascertain whether or not some one else had used the same trope or simile in the same connection. Such a poet is born.

The sort of psychological poetry, which searches the heart for motives of action, Homer could not have written. His themes were simple, his motives direct. Love, with little sentiment, ambition, war, hate, revenge, avarice. Analytical poetry, like Browning's for instance, is, like fiction, the outgrowth of culture. So almost until our own day, there was very little worth-while literary output by American colored writers. In other countries several writers of color had distinguished themselves, but not as Negroes. The two Alexandre Dumas were Frenchmen first, last and all the time, and only incidentally colored. The same was true of Alexander Pushkin, the Russian Shakespeare. In America there had been a few feeble sprouts of genuine poetry by colored writers, but the environment was not congenial, and they faded early. A few biographies, human documents, could be found on the bookshelves, but most of the Negro output was beneath criticism. The Negro stood mute, as the legal phrase goes, before the bar of literary judgment.

But in our own day—I may well say in *your* own day—mine is mostly behind me,—the Negro has become articulate, indeed, voluble, sometimes garrulous, and now and then even strident. The criticism so plaintively voiced almost yesterday by Dr. Du Bois and James Weldon Johnson, that colored writers could not find a hearing with publishers and editors, is no longer well founded. The subjects which only yesterday were tabooed in the discussion of race contacts and relationships are open to any writer. Publishers vie with one another for books by colored writers or about Negro life. The Negro is the literary fashion of the day, and the interest in him seems to be not merely a fad but a genuine sociological development, likely to grow rather than to die away.

Southern white writers were among the first to discover the value of Negro life as literary material. The South had exploited the Negro's labor by slavery and peonage; it had exploited the Negro's uncast vote by counting it for the white congressional representation, and now they began to exploit him in literature.

To their credit, be it said, the modern Southern white novelist has not set out on purpose, generally speaking, to degrade the Negro. Indeed the present day attitude—"pose" would be perhaps an unkind word—is that of liberality—the tempered liberality of the more enlightened South—not equality, God save the mark!—but a recognition of the common humanity of darker people, of their cultural advancement, of their aspirations—mostly pathetically hopeless from the Southern viewpoint. They note their social aspirations, their improvement in dress and manners, and find them more or less amusing. Some ascribe them less to increasing self-respect than to a simian imitation of white people.

I want to comment on these present-day Negro novels—by which I mean the novels about the Negro, whether written by white or colored authors. I set out some time ago to collect them all, but they came along so fast I soon found that my restricted means would render this burdensome, so I had to fall back more or less on the public and lending libraries, and even then I haven't read them all. In fact, I got pretty well fed up on them, as the phrase goes, but I have read the outstanding ones, and enough of them to discuss them intelligently.

When Mr. Carl Van Vechten's *Nigger Heaven* appeared I criticized it—the title was the most offensive feature—but in the book he spoke of me and my writings in so friendly and complimentary a fashion that my guns were spiked. It is difficult to call a writer a liar and a horse thief who declares that you are a great man and a wonderful writer. It was in a sense the pioneer of a flood of such books. Many of them are written with great literary skill. They deal with all phases of the Race Problem—amalgamation, both legal and illegal, "passing" for white; that perversion of the Mendelian theory, the mythical black baby that is born to a seemingly pure white mother or father; the struggle for equality and the heart-breaking incidents attending it. And on the still more tragic side, lynching, burning at the stake, disfranchisement and the whole list of wrongs and outrages, as lengthy as the catalogue of Homer's ships. Subjects which once were spoken of only in whispers are not only printed in capital letters, but exhibited upon the stage.

In fact, Negro books have multiplied with that mushroom fecundity which marks the growth of every new thing in this wonderful country, in this wonderful age—witness the radio, the airplane and the talking movie, to instance the three latest. And I regret to say, the moral equality of these books has not kept pace with their growth. In fact they seem to grow baser and baser. Compared with some of the more recent output, Mr. Van Vechten's *Nigger Heaven* is a Sunday School tract.

If the term "Negro Literature" is taken in the broad sense in which it is being used nowadays, as including books by colored writers and books about the Negro, and if by the word "literature" is meant merely books and other writings, there has been for a long time a very large body of Negro literature. Any comprehensive library has many examples. Before the Civil War, and even since, there were many books by Negrophobes maintaining the hopeless inferiority of the Negro, some of them even denying him a soul—which meant more then than it does in our own day, when some advanced thinkers and writers claim there is no such thing as an immortal soul. However, those old-time writers were quite sure that white people had souls. Of course the obvious and often the declared purpose of such a line of argument was

to justify slavery. And, on the other hand books against slavery were very numerous.

Of course most of these books were written by white men. But there were occasional colored men and women who wrote. Phillis Wheatley was the first Negro poet in America. . . .

All these books can be included in the broad meaning of the word "literature," but when we come to literature in the narrower sense, that is, to *belles lettres*, "beautiful writing," imaginative writing, such as poetry or fiction, essays like Hazlitt's or Macaulay's, solid though less brilliant works of history, like those of Lecky, Prescott and Motley, nothing of this sort worth while, by any high standard, had, up to our own day emanated from colored American writers, and for the best of reasons. Literature, like the fine arts and the best music, is, as I have said, the fruit of culture. "You cannot gather grapes of thorns or figs of thistles." It is true that Aesop was a slave, and Horace the son of a freedman, but they were able and brilliant men, enslaved by conquest, but having a background of freedom and culture. The Negro in America had no such background. Some of our intellectuals are spending a lot of time trying to dig up a great and glorious past for the African Negro. They claim for him the greatness and power of the Pharaohs, and attribute to him the art and architecture of ancient Egypt. But I fear this is one of the things that people believe because they like to believe them. . . .

The term "Negro Renaissance" is a more or less inaccurate expression. "Renaissance" or "renascence" means, literally, new birth. It is applied chiefly to the revival of art and letters in Europe in the 15th and 16th centuries, after the long night of the Dark Ages. But Southern Europe had possessed, before the Dark Ages, a literature and an art even superior to that of the Renaissance. The *Iliad* and the *Aeneid* are still the greatest of epics and the art of Phidias has never been excelled. I said once to Dr. Locke that I thought a better word to describe the modern American Negro would be the "New American." In my opinion the American Negro, so called, or miscalled, is destined, if his ultimate absorption into the composite American race is long deferred, to develop a type which is very widely different from the West African type from which he has descended. There are, I will venture to say, very few Negroes whose American ancestry dates back even a hundred years, who haven't some white blood, and by the same token there are many white people who have some dark blood.

A corollary of this argument is, of course, that the very worthy achievements of the American Negro can by no means be attributed entirely to his dark blood. The white people rarely claim any credit for them, partly perhaps because to do so would be to acknowledge their blood relationship, which, though entirely obvious, they prefer to ignore, and partly because of the sense of fair play, sadly distorted at times it is true, after all a characteristic of the English people from whom the American Negro derives most of his white inheritance, which, perhaps unconsciously, inhibits the white man from claiming at one end what he disowns at the other. It is either that or a generosity we have never suspected which makes him concede to the Negro as Negro the very considerable contributions of people of mixed blood.

And now, having determined what we mean by Negro, and what we mean by literature, and put ourselves in a position to speak intelligently about Negro literature; having cleaned out the underbrush of the pre-Civil War period, and cut out the deadwood of the past generation, we can approach the very lively, the almost rank new growth of Negro books which has sprung up since the War-to-end war, which it hasn't, and to make the world safe for democracy—which it equally hasn't—and discuss the good and the bad in them.

In the first place they approach the Negro from a new viewpoint. The old Uncle Tom type seems to have disappeared entirely. He was a likable old fellow, almost too good to be true, but we cherish a pleasant memory of him, and always read with interest any item identifying the original Uncle Tom, of which there would seem to be almost as many as there are pieces of the true cross in Catholic countries. The story itself is immortal. Next to the Bible it has been the best seller in the history of book publishing. It has been translated into every tongue which has a written form and has been running on the stage steadily ever since it was dramatized. There is always a "Tom show" going somewhere, sometimes half a dozen at once, and now that the talking movie has arrived it has a new medium of expression. It might pay the new school of Negro writers to analyze the reasons for its success. It grew out of a condition which, happily, no longer exists. A modern writer cannot repeat the incidents, unless he dates his story before the Civil War. But *Uncle Tom's Cabin* registered because it dealt with deep-seated, fundamental realities, things which exist in all men, regardless of worldly station—the relations of husband and wife, parent and child, the right to the fruits of one's toil—the freedom of one's own person,—and indeed of one's own soul, for in spite of Uncle Tom's pronouncement it is exceedingly difficult for one to be the captain of his soul and control his own spiritual development, when his body all his life is under the control of some one else.

The old "mammy" type is fading, although it still survives in the novels written by Southern white authors and is still going strong in "mammy songs" along with the "mother, home and heaven" doggerel which flourishes in vaudeville. One would gather from reading Southern stories and novels of the old school and from Southern oratory of the present day, that every white child born in the South had a colored "mammy," though statistics prove that not one white Southerner in ten was a slaveholder, and therefore there couldn't have been mammies enough to go around. The Southerners not long ago proposed to erect a monument to her at Washington, but however touching the memory of the faithful slave may be to the children of the master, the relationship seems not to be one which the black mammy's own children held in especial honor, perhaps for the reason that the care and affection which she is assumed to have lavished upon her white nurslings were taken from her own children.

The self-seeking colored person who fawns on the white folks and for selfish reasons tries to prove himself the type of Negro which he assumes that they like, has also more or less disappeared from fiction, though he still survives to a degree in real life in certain preachers and teachers who

> Crook the pregnant hinges of the knee,
> That thrift may follow fawning.

The beautiful octoroon, the product of the white man's sin for several successive generations, and the victim of his passions, has given way to the modern sophisticated "near white" or "high yellow" who has been to college, and takes advantage of her complexion either by "passing" for white or at least exercising in public the privileges of the "caste of Vere de Vere." Sometimes she puts it over quite far, and marries into the old Knickerbocker or Mayflower families. It is quite within the bounds of probability that the offspring of some such ambitious and enterprising lady may yet sit in the presidential chair. A man of Indian descent who does not deny his origin, is pretty close to it, and a man said to have been of Negro descent who did deny it has occupied the throne itself.[27]

The crude and stolid field hand has almost disappeared from fiction, although Dr. Du Bois made a brave but not entirely successful attempt to idealize him in his first novel, *The Silver Fleece*. In place of him we have the migrant, the factory operative or mill hand. The squalid cabins of the plantation have given place to the sordid tenements of great cities. The overseer with his bullwhip has been replaced by the foreman with his time clock. The jolly carefree buck-and-wing dances and hoe-downs have given place to the black bottom of the hectic cabaret and night club, and the bang of the banjo, while still going strong, to some extent, to the sob of the saxophone. The black face minstrel has yielded place to the talented actor in the legitimate drama. Always excepting the perennial Uncle Tom, colored actors now star in *The Emperor Jones*, *In Abraham's Bosom* and other plays which demand a high order of histrionic talent. Topsy has been replaced by the

Florence Millses and Josephine Bakers, and the real talent of Bert Williams and Ernest Hogan by the finer artistry of Charles Gilpin and Paul Robeson.

Then we have some entirely new types which derive entirely from modern conditions. The colored doctor, for instance, unknown a generation ago, is the most outstanding representative of the race, at least in numbers and in earning power. He has been used quite freely and effectively in Negro fiction. The colored lawyer is not so popular a subject. Indeed the colored lawyer in the South is largely conspicuous by his absence. . . . The Negro preacher is almost virgin soil for the fictionist, but the black Elmer Gantrys and grafting bishops will surely come into their own, as well as the devoted men who give their lives and their talents for the uplift of their race for a meager recompense.

Colored readers have sometimes criticized the Negro characters of Mr. Octavus Roy Cohen, the Jewish writer of Alabama. I am free to say that I have found some of his stories very amusing. The imaginary best "cullud society" of "Bummingham" with its hodgepodge of lawyers, doctors, preachers, barbers, hairdressers, gamblers and shrewd swindlers, if overdrawn and therefore libelous, has some semblance of reality, though I can't imagine a lawyer being admitted to the bar even of Alabama, with as little learning, legal or otherwise, as lawyer Evans Chew. Florian Slappey is a quite convincing type of the happy-go-lucky hand-to-mouth type of social parasite who spends most of his time scheming how to get something for nothing. One fault I have to find in that connection is that our up-and-coming colored story writers have let this shrewd white man preempt this financially rich vein of Negro literature. Cohen's only real competitor is Hugh Wiley, another white man, with his vivid stories of the Negro labor battalions in the Great War, of crapshooters and "Lady Luck." One thing I cannot forgive the Cohen output is the illustrations. The artist seems to use the same tame gorilla as the model for every character, male or female— black, brown and yellow. There are perhaps some Negroes as ugly as Cohen's characters are depicted—there are homely people in all races—but we ought to be thankful to the Creator that He didn't load down the whole race with such a burden.

The grafting colored politician is another somewhat sinister development attending the progress of the colored people. Dr. Du Bois in his novel *The Dark Princess* has depicted very vividly this type in Chicago, and I suspect has done the Chicago Negro no serious injustice.

There has been much criticism among colored readers and critics about the types portrayed in the current Negro novels. With much of this criticism I concur heartily. Looking back cursorily I find no outstanding noble male character in any of the Negro novels, written by white or colored writers. The male characters are either weaklings, like the principal male character in *Nigger Heaven* and in *Birthright*, or addicted to degrading vices, such as gambling, lechery, drunkenness, the use of narcotics, or else somewhat unbalanced, like the hero of the *Dark Princess*. Porgy, with his goat and his wagon, is an interesting character, but no particular credit to his race, and the returned soldier in *Home to Harlem* is by no means an admirable character.

The Southern white writers manifest, apparently, much fairness in dealing with their Negro characters. It is to be regretted that they do not choose finer types, but they would probably reply that they use the material at hand. Catfish Alley is doubtless an interesting place, and Mr. Heyward seems very familiar with it, but I am unable—it may be snobbishness on my part or a certain Victorian hangover—to get up much enthusiasm over the characters in *Porgy*. . . .

One noteworthy thing about most of these Southern white writers is that they tell the truth about their own people—how they rob and exploit and scorn and degrade their dark neighbors. Sometimes, as in *Mamba's Daughters*, the active villain, like the black overseer in the old days, is made a colored man. A curious corollary of this is Mr. Rudolph Fisher's colored character in *The Walls of Jericho* who works the residence segregation racket for his own not at all high-minded purposes.

The heart of any romantic novel is the heroine—perhaps I should say the female protagonist in speaking of the present day Negro novel, for precious few of them are given any heroic attributes. With the exception of Mary in *Nigger Heaven*, or the heroine of Walter White's first novel, and the women of Miss Fauset's novels, they are all unchaste. When I wrote that sentence a week or two ago I had not read Miss Fauset's latest novel, in which I regret to say the heroine joins the scarlet, or at least the pink sisterhood. Of course I recognize that female virtue has gone out of fashion in fiction—I hope not so much so in real life—but I feel about the matter something like I do about the Octavus Roy Cohen illustrations. I *know* that these characters are not the best types or even average types of the womanhood of the race. Of course the female rebel is more interesting or more easy to make interesting—vice has the edge on virtue in fiction—most of the interesting women in romance have sinned for love or for profit—Beatrice Esmond, *Tess of the d'Urbervilles*, Maggie Tulliver in *The Mill on the Floss, Anna Karenina*, etc., but it remained for one of our most eminent young colored writers to have his heroine sin for no apparent reason whatsoever. She did not love her paramour, she got nothing out of it, she was not responding to any resistless sex urge, nor even to curiosity, but her lover asked, and she just consented, and did some other foolish things afterwards which contribute to the development of the story but which stamp the heroine with mental as well as moral weakness.

One of the vilest of the colored women characters in present day fiction is *Black Sadie*, who so far as I could gather, had no morals. So far as she was decent at all, it was a matter of animal instinct—many animals are decenter [*sic*] than many humans. Sadie was a constitutional thief and robbed even her benefactors with perfect sangfroid. She would take jewels or any other portable property which was not locked up or nailed down and could be easily turned into money, without blinking an eyelash. The book is brilliantly written by, I am informed, a white Baptist preacher of Richmond,

Virginia, who displays an intimate and circumstantial familiarity with the baser side of Negro life and character which suggests not only careful study but personal experience.

Claude McKay's *Home to Harlem* is very well written, but I don't recall a decent woman character in the book. Some of the male characters are steeped in baseness, some of which is so vile as to be merely hinted at. But the very nadir of vileness is reached in a novel by a colored writer, W. Thurman. It is called *The Blacker the Berry*, and by way of foreword the author quotes an alleged Negro folk saying,

The blacker the berry
The sweeter the juice.

The novel is founded on the assumed scorn of light-colored people for dark women—which in my opinion the author grossly exaggerates—and the gradual degeneration of his heroine growing out of her sensitiveness to this discrimination. I can say frankly that he hasn't helped the dark girl a particle, if she needs any help.

I read the other day an item which I cut out of a newspaper, which voices some rather pertinent reflections on the prevalent type of these books. It is a quotation from a recent number of the *Birmingham News*, based on an expression by Dana Skinner, dramatic editor of *The Commonweal*: "Those who have tried to keep tab," says the editor,

on what is being done in the way of productive literary art among Negroes cannot fail to recall the bold intermixture of animalism permeating that part of it about which most of the raving is done. It seems to be a swirling current into which much of the best talent is drawn and too much of the really proven literary talent is condoning and encouraging, either by complimentary mention or dubious silence, leaving it a right-of-way which causes it to boldly overshadow any literary art that might be really constructive.

The sad fact that it emanates from motives that appear, on the face, to be both mercenary and devoid of exalted idealism, adds a new danger to its popularity. We have

never been able to see any masterly merit in either its conception or its portrayal.

It flits from one cesspool of vice to another, holding up the worst in Negro life to public gaze as though there were nothing worthier and better to show. Certainly, it sells to a thrill-hungry, unsuspecting public curiously agape for fads.

As far as we have been able to see, it starts low, remains low, maintains a sensual note and glories in a sensual imagery suggestive of its authorship and origin. Without venturing a criticism on any particular literary effort, one can select what is styled the successes and study them according to approved standards of art to find that they exploit the worst features and explode the best theories of Negro home and social life. A literature that is truly interpretative must be in some sense moralistic; it must exalt those of low degree as well as the mighty. It may deal with the sensual for moral purposes. It must glorify the humble and degrade the haughty. It must do it—a course of events common to everyday life and everyday people. Its filth must have a moral purpose as well as an informative portrayal.

Men's vices are not to be depicted for the sake of proving them vile, only to no purpose beneficial to them or to others.

There are dark spots in Negro life—so in the life of all peoples. There is no merit in selling it to the public at the price of transient popularity or paltry coin. . . . There is heroism worthy of the pen, there is tragedy and comedy worthy of the footlights in Negro life. Also there is vice and animalism outside of New York's Black Belt and the price of its glory is a poor compensation for its bland portrayal.

But what as to the future of Negro literature? I am not concerned about the white writers about the Negro, but what about the colored writers? They have learned to write, and to write well. Their contributions to the best magazines are not only acceptable but solicited. They write with a verve and a swing like their actors and singers put into their work. Naturally a somewhat indolent people—Miss Fauset has said the Negro's capacity for rest is one of his most valuable characteristics,—it keeps the white people from working him to death and gives him time to live, with strength enough left to enjoy life— when they are doing something they enjoy doing, they develop a surprising industry. Some of you may have seen the screen picture *Hearts in Dixie*, a picture of low life, but not base life,— among the Negroes along the Mississippi River. If so, you will remember "Stepin' Fetchit" who has a "mizry" in his feet whenever he is asked to chop wood or fetch water, but who is a marvel of terpsichorean agility when the banjo or the fiddle starts a dance.

This *élan*, this verve, is reflected in the verse as well as in the prose of our colored writers. The work of our best poets glows with the divine fire. The colored writer has a great subject— the life of ten or twelve million people, becoming every day more diversified, more complicated—with the fundamental emotions and interests common to all humanity, colored or differentiated by those interests and feelings which grow out of their own peculiar position. Out of these distinguishing traits, building on the great fundamentals and imponderables, they can evolve a body of writing sufficiently distinctive to be classed as Negro literature and at the same time heartily and cordially welcomed as American literature.

Doubtless some of you have literary aspirations or have written things. In addition to the poets widely recognized whose poems appear in the leading monthlies and in the anthologies, there is a surprising quantity of promising verse and short stories that appear in the colored magazines. The colored writer has all the literary machinery. There are some excellent Negro critics. Mr. Braithwaite and Benjamin Brawley perhaps the first, Mr. George Schuyler is one, a columnist, who writes *à la* Mencken with a fine dash of wit. Eugene Gordon, a discriminating critic who wields a hammer so heavy that, when he has finished a critical article one must search the broken fragments which strew his passage to see if there is any good thing left. Mrs. Alice Dunbar-Nelson is another discriminating reviewer.

In addition to Mr. Braithwaite's Anthology there are anthologies of Negro Poetry, *Colored Who's Who*'s, and the latest development, a Negro *Bookman* magazine. So no literary gem of purest ray need remain in oblivion for lack of a medium of publicity.

I shall probably not be here to see it, although I don't know, I came of a long-lived family and events are moving very rapidly, but some day there will no doubt be a Dickens, or a Balzac, or a Dostoievski who will depict in lasting colors the real life—not merely the hectic night life, of the American colored people. May I hope that this writer may come from your ranks?

J. M. Gates, with Deacon Leon Davis, Sister Jordan, and Sister Norman

"Manish Women"

Transcript of a live recording from December 6, 1929, OKeh Records 8779, 1930[28]

I want to talk about manish women. The world is full of these kind of women. They're trying to do everything they see or hear of a man doing.

They're on the racetrack. They're in the air. In the aeroplane. Yes, sir.

[*Growls.*] They're manish women. And they're wearing pants and cutting their hair like a man. In fact, they are getting so manish, until

Advertisement for J. M. Gates's "Manish Women" from Okeh Records, *Baltimore Afro-American*, May 17, 1930. Courtesy of the AFRO Newspaper Archives.

sometimes they try to walk and talk like a man. Of course we got some men trying to walk and talk like a woman.

But I'm talking about these manish women.

So manish, until you can hardly distinguish sometimes a woman from a man.

So manish, until they stay out as late at night as any man.

So manish, until they will rob and steal like men.

So manish, until sometimes you can read about them being bank robbers and holed up at night.

So manish, until they won't raise their children. I believe sometimes the thing that makes the women manish are women because they don't raise their children.

The doctor and the nurse have to raise them, as God intended for a human child to be raised by a human, intended for the little infant child to nurse on human milk. But the doctors have to furnish the milk. Sometimes it's a [inaudible word] cow milk. Sometimes old goat milk. No wonder there are so many hardheaded men and women.

So manish. I'm talking about you manish women. Then they're getting everywhere. They're getting everywhere. They're getting in the courthouse, on the street, in the little village, out in the little towns. . . .

So manish, until they're getting in the church, getting in every auxiliary of the church. So manish, sometimes I don't know what they're going to do about them. They're getting everywhere. I'm talking about these manish women. . . .

If the women in the church, and their dress too short, may I turn them out?

[*Group sings in response.*] No, no—[If they] hem up the dress, let it down, and let the church roll on.[29]

George S. Schuyler
"An Appeal to Young Negroes," ca. 1930

Young Negroes! On you alone rests the responsibility for the future of Negroes in the United States. In you and what you accomplish lies the hopes of the generations to come.

The old Negroes have failed! On every side we see evidences of it. They have done the best they could, but the best has been pretty bad. It has been bad because it has offere little to the lovers of liberty and security among us who are willing to organize, agitate and educate to get it.

The old Negroes have failed! They have supplied no program capable of emancipating the Negro masses from subserviency, insecurity, insult, debauchery, crime, disease and death. They have meekly protested when they should have fought; been optimistic when they should have been realistic; been sentimental when they should have been scientific; religious when they should have been rational; talked Heaven while catching Hell; boasted of progress in the midst of privation; sacrificed group interests on the altar of class prejudices; mouthed freedom and accepted jim crowism; mouthed co-operation and practiced destructive individualism; mouthed race pride and aped Caucasian superficialities; questioned youth's assertiveness while sitting supine.

The Fourth Decade of the Twentieth Century is at hand. The Negro finds segregation and discrimination more widespread than ever before. He finds himself without any secure foothold in industry or business. He is constantly deviled by the ogre of insecurity. He is cursed by the damnation of disease and the miasma of moral degradation. He lives and dies in squalid alleys, dank courts and dark and dreary tenements. He has become the prey of vice, crime and undertakers. He finds the door of employment closing upon him and opportunity to rise in the industrial hierarchy cut off by color discrimination. He toils but to support others who give him no social values in exchange. After sixty-seven years of alleged freedom, his position in this complicated machine civilization is more precarious than ever before.

The Negro's past and present leadership is a failure! It is a failure because its policy has been one of constant conciliation and compromise. It is a failure because it has used white psychology and advice to solve black trials and tribulations. It has embraced the bourgeois ideology of every man for himself in economic endeavor when the times cried for intelligent, democratic, collective endeavor. It has urged the Negro to return to the farm when already there are far too many farmers. Or it has urged him to come to the city to starve and die in the no-man's-land of ruthless competition. It has pinned its faith too much on getting jobs for Negroes by begging the "good white folks" for them when the "good white folks" could not supply work for their own people. It has built churches when it should have built security; fiddled with fraternals when it should have studied finance. It has studied the past when it needed most to be concerned with the present and future. It has yelled patriotism from the well of pauperism; had faith in promises instead of performances; implicitly trusted its oppressors instead of repudiating and opposing them. It has prated of salvation in the hereafter instead of in the Here and Now. It has sentimentalized about Negro Womanhood but failed to safeguard it. It has frantically urged Negro youth to acquire education but opened no doors for it. It has sung and prayed when it should have schemed and planned. It has gabbled about Negro art and let Caucasians support it. It has pleaded for Negro artists but offered no field for them. It has cadged alms instead of creating opportunity. It has grown fearful, timorous, shaky, platitudinous, evasive and muddle headed. Yes, Negro leadership has failed and on the threshold of the Fourth Decade of the Twentieth Century, after unequalled opportunity to save the race, it stands wringing its hands helplessly while the masses flounder in dirt, disease, discrimination, degradation, disillusionment and death.

Young Negroes! It is you who must now take up the burden of leadership. You must succeed where the oldsters have failed. You can do it. You have the education, the virility and the aggressiveness of youth. Most of you wear a hat instead of a bandana handkerchief. Most of you straighten your backs instead of your hair. You look realistically at the world instead of optimistically to Heaven. You are mostly unwilling to sell your birthright of freedom for a mess of jim crow pottage. And because you are young and energetic instead of old, spiritless and world weary, you can save the Negro group from remaining the mudsill of American society.

Young Negroes! Turn your backs on the old programs and prescriptions and formulate others more in accord with the social and economic trends. Forget your petty individual interests and join in co-operative effort for the betterment of all.

Young Negroes! Without economic power and security in this country where only Gold is God, your citizenship rights can never be worth a dime. You cannot attain economic power and security when everything you consume from food to housing is owned by somebody else. You cannot get anywhere if you are always on the buying side of the counter; always banking your money with the other fellow for him to use to help his friends; always paying rent until the poorhouse or the grave claims you. You cannot hope to be free so long as your job is held at the whim of some individual who despises you for your weakness.

Young Negroes! Put your faith in individual effort and perish; put it in co-operative effort and prosper. Private ownership of the means of production and distribution and the whole philosophy of private initiative have not made the masses of white people secure after 300 years. Less than four million people in the United States have salaries that enable them to approximate an American standard of living. Only a half million earn five thousand dollars a year. Small businesses fail at the rate of 25,000 a year. The trusts meanwhile flourish and a handful of giant banks on Wall Street control the country's economic life. One child out of every ten in school is physically defective as a result of un-hygienic surroundings and under-nourishment. One out of every ten persons has either been in, is in or will soon be in, an insane asylum. If private initiative has done this to the white, can it be expected to do better for the blacks? No! Such a program can get the Negro nowhere. We may make a few millionaires but that won't help Negroes who live in the alleys.

Young Negroes! Through co-operative effort as consumers you can find your way out of the present dilemma. Collectively through democratic management of your own economic enterprises, you can supply yourselves with everything you consume, your own amusement and recreation, your own education and culture. You can make your educated Negroes serve you by controlling the institutions they head instead of leaving that to the white philanthropists who are concerned only with treating effects instead of causes. Through your economic power thus gained you can furnish employment to thousands of young Negroes now idle and drifting toward prison and the electric chair. Through this economic power you can cut down the Negro population of our jails and penitentiaries by adequately defending every arrested Negro now ruthlessly discriminated against by judge and jury everywhere. Through this economic power so gained you can wield greater political power and wipe antagonistic legislation off the books. Through the economic power so gained you can make the sort of cultural contribution to American life you want to make and not the

kind well-meaning but misinformed whites want you to make. Through this economic power so gained you can raise the prestige of the American Negro higher. You will be able to command respect because you will merit respect. The only thing the world really respects is power; when you get power you will be respected. But you cannot get this economic power except through co-operation as consumers.

Young Negroes! The time to start is now. The Young Negroes Co-Operative League offers an immediate way out of our economic and social dilemma, not ten, twenty, thirty or fifty years from now, but RIGHT NOW. If you have reached your 16th but not your 36th Birthday, you are eligible to join. We do not want those who have grown weary and disillusioned; we want those who are energetic, intelligent and believe in the power of their own organized effort.

Gordon B. Hancock
"Between the Lines: Some New Negroes Also!"

Palmetto Leader, December 20, 1930[30]

In spite of some of the so called champions and exponents of the New NEGRO this writer has some respect for the ideal in this term! Like most worthy ideals it is often abused by these who profess to love it and advance its cause. For instance, some months ago the Negro papers were carrying an account of some young Negro who claimed to be obsessed with hatred for white people. He rather boasted of the fact that his dominant passion in life was hatred for the white man and the Negro papers in some cases played up such nonsense as if its news value were really important. Some call our misguided friend a New Negro. We recently read an article, written by a supposed Christian gentleman and the said article made light and little of the idea of good will in race relations. In spite of the fact [that] the writer of the article was presum-

ably educated in a school founded by whites of good will; that the foremost instruments in our battle for manhood rights, the National Urban League and the N. A. A. C. P., were made possible by whites of good will and supported largely by these until yet; that without the good will concept the Gospel of Jesus is set at naught and the preachers thereof are impostors, the writer inveighed against good will under the pretext that he was a New Negro. The editor of a white paper called this writer in a few months ago [to] talk over a letter that a supposed New Negro had written. It was filled with abuse and the language bordered on the profane and vulgar. It was a disgrace to any person calling himself intelligent and addressing himself to the deliverance of his race from economic and social slavery. It was a case of a man having an opportunity to say something without something to say. He called himself a New Negro. I repeat, inspite [sic] of some of the so-called New Negroes and their fool-making tactics, I have a large measure of respect for the ideal connected in the term!

Some weeks ago there was in Richmond a not much heralded, but a vastly important meeting. It was called by the more than 200 workers in one of the laundries and these workers were Negroes who deeply appreciated their jobs. The meeting was very largely attended and the white employers were invited and were present. In the course of the program a very touching address was made in which the Negro workers expressed their profound appreciation of the kindliness and cooperation they had received from their employers and they appreciated most of all that there had been no lay-off[;] neither had Negroes been supplanted in any case. They pledged to their employers their cooperation and interest in the future as in the past. A white woman arose and in a most fitting way expressed a good will rec-

iprocity on the part of the employers and further the appreciation of the employees' interest in the business which has grown at the hands of the Negro workers. The manager spoke with earnestness and to the point. This writer spoke on "The Economics of Good-will." The meeting adjourned and it was apparent that those Negro men and women had sensed the challenge the adversities of this depression has brought and both whites and Negroes present were unanimous in the better that the meeting got some where! These are also New Negroes, let us not forget! The new white man is a job hunter and job taker and unless there is a job-consciousness among the New Negroes, the Negro's economic road leads up hill and into the dark. What these Richmond New Negroes did on that memorable occasion may not amount to a great deal; but the spirit manifested holds promises of a large measure of the Negro's economic salvation. It was great old Milton who said that "they also serve who only stand and wait!" Those are also new Negroes who realize that jobs are jobs these days!

Sadie T. M. Alexander
"The Emancipated Woman"

Speech, ca. 1930s

The story of the emancipation of women is or ought to be familiar to all of us present this afternoon. That great change in methods of manufacture and production, called the Industrial Revolution, was the fundamental cause of a new era, not only in industry, but also in domestic life. When Hargreaves (1764) invented [the] spinning jenny, operated by water power, by which six to twelve threads could be spun at one time, and James Watts discovered that steam would also operate a spinning jenny, the confinement of women to their homes, where every article of clothing had previously been produced, became a thing of the past. Then

came the discovery in 1765 that coal could be used to smelt iron and liquid iron could be molded into machines that would produce many more times the amount of goods than human hands. Huge iron machines were not suitable for home use; furthermore, they required many persons to operate them. So they were congregated in what became to be called factories because it was the place that factors (commercial agents) congregated. The women and children were taken from their homes to operate the factory machines.

At the end of the week's work, instead of turning over the products to the head of the family, to trade in for staples—the women workers received a wage, which they could spend themselves—without turning it over to any man. It didn't take women long to forget that habit of turning over. Thus, we developed a large group of economically independent women.

The presence of women in [the] industrial world created a number of social problems. First, the conditions, wages, and hours of labor, which are still perplexing as illustrated by efforts [of] Congress [to] fix minimum wage for women, defeated by decision—[of the] USSC [U.S. Supreme Court]—held it was interference with the liberty to contract guaranteed by the 14th Amendment. [The] Oregon statute forbade employment of women in factories for more than ten hours in one day—[as a] valid exercise of political power for health [of] women and race. Second, social freedom: [they] feared [the] morals of [the] nation [would] be lost when women were turned into [the] industrial world [of work]. The same argument was used against Woman Suffrage. A woman has as a bribe her self. It never seemed to occur to the men who advanced these objections that it was within their power to remove the problem. But thank God, the women have been able to handle the situation, whenever it arose, so perfectly that *Scarlet Letters* are truly figures of history and not of our modern-day acquaintance. [The] third problem was concerned with family life. Women engaged in labor, postponed marriage, or controlled births. Those who have families permitted them to rear themselves. Divorces increased—not because the contact with [the] world made women less faithful, but because she no longer had to put up with embarrassments, neglects, and cruelties in order to secure bread and butter—she could make that for herself.

Having gained a taste of freedom in the economic world, naturally women began to demand equality in the political world in order, if for no other reason that they might help legislate for their own protection. Like all other social reform movements, the grant of suffrage in the English-speaking countries had an impetus

in this case, the democracy cry of the Great War. So in England in 1918 and the U.S. in 1920 the vote was granted women.

What type of woman has the economic and political freedom produced? Various types. Of course we have the Reactionists, who are always with us in every field of activity. Continually wishing, hoping, praying for the return of the good "old times" but bending every effort to live on in these times. If they are genuinely sincere in their desire, I often wonder why these persons do not put on long skirts and bonnets and stay at home and operate a hand cotton jenny. The answer is obvious: they could not continue to exist under such conditions in this world of competition. The world is attractive enough for them to want to continue to live in it—so they take a half-handed part—in order to exist. When if they put their all in the game they might live and help others to live better. These persons to my mind are a drag on society. Their criticisms are destructive; not constructive lives are a nullity.

We have a second group, who also fail to contribute. They do not think enough about what is going on to lend even a destructive criticism—As Omar the old Tentmaker puts it:

Into this Universe, and why not knowing
Nor whence, like Water willy-nilly
    flowing,
And out of it, as Wind along the Waste
I know not whether, willy-nilly blowing[31]

They drift from dinner to the movies, thence to bed, thence to breakfast and to work and so on. Or if in hard luck, they struggle and wail, cursing "our day" or society. We know the pigs' object in life. It has been beautifully and permanently outlined in Carlyle's "pig catechism." The pigs' object is to get fat and keep fat—to get his [*sic*] full share of swill and as much more as he can manage to secure. And his life object is worthy. By sticking at it he develops fat hams inside his bristles, and we know, although he does not, that the production of fat hams is his destiny.

But our human destiny is not to produce fat hams. Why do so many of us live earnestly on the pig basis? Why do we struggle savagely for money to buy our kind of swill—luxury, food, autos, and cease all struggle when that money is obtained?

Is fear of poverty and dependence the only emotion that should move us?

Are we merely to stay here, eat here?

A great German scientist, very learned and about as imaginative as a warthog, declares that the human face is merely an extension and elaboration of the alimentary canal—that the beauty of expression, the marvelous qualities of a noble human face, are merely indirect results of the alimentary canal trying to satisfy its wants.

That is a hideous conception, is it not? But it is justified when we consider the average human life, women whom the industrial renaissance, which we previously outlined, placed in positions of economic ease. Their existence has much to justify German's speculations.

But we have a third type of woman, who has developed out of these social forces which we have just outlined. I call her the *Emancipated Woman*. You know, when the Emancipation Proclamation was signed and the Negro slaves received [the] right to emancipation they did not automatically become emancipated. Sixty years of emancipation—hasn't emancipated some Negroes. Mr. Charlie is still God and his word is law. So the fact that social conditions decreed the emancipation of women didn't emancipate all of them. Salvation is free—but each person has to make the step to be saved for himself. So emancipation of women is possible—but like everything else in the world, it requires some effort on the part of each woman to become emancipated.

If that is all woman does, she isn't much better off than the youngsters at dinner with the Parson and his Elders, who devoured the chicken, while the kids [sop] up the gravy. When Johnny the infant could no longer restrain his comments on the unfairness of this arrangement, he was admonished by the Parson in blind faith.

Making a living—[and] casting a vote[—] are merely the substance of things hoped for, the evidence of things not seen. You haven't tasted political freedom if all you do is cast a vote and stop there—you haven't begun to enjoy economic independence if the extent of your economic activity is a struggle to get enough money to eat, sleep and drink and go to an occasional movie. The *emancipated woman* demands

1) that her vote and those she controls show tangible evidence of making this a better world to live in. Mine is a very practical kind of religion. I believe the parable of the talents is applicable to every one of us who has a vote—if we have one vote—then we must account for its use, as much as if it were one talent and if there are ten votes in our houses—I liken them to ten talents. Women, you are not emancipated if you are not using your votes—to put women and *men* (not men and women) but women first, men second, in public offices that control our destinies. If the Italians can put a judge on the Common Pleas bench why can't the Negroes? Because neither the women nor the men are emancipated. We Negroes are truly wicked and slothful servants—to be such a religious people—we have more churches and spend more time in them yet we do not seem to have caught full import of that simple parable: Joy unto everyone that hath shall be given and he shall have abundance, but from him that hath not shall be taken away even that which he hath.

2) The emancipated woman demands (second) that her purpose in this economic struggle, of which she has become an integral part, shall be more than the securing of the necessities of life. Why do the Jews get everything they demand in this city—Municipal and C.P. [Common Pleas] judgeships, plural if you please—District Attorney, members of Council, Legislature, Congress? Because they control the money

bags—and money talks. We are the poorest group of people in this city, state, or nation. If we have a candidate for a high office, we can't raise enough money to wage an effective campaign. When other races, with adverse interests, must pay our debts—we must submit to their policies. We need money, and the women who have been recently granted political emancipation, if they would be emancipated, must learn the lesson from the better experience of our men. Yes, I say strive for money—economic independence is a concomitant of political and social freedom. You cannot have one without the other. The custom of other races will teach you the same thing. The Armenians, better known [as] Queen Mary's people—are a poverty-stricken people. Persecution, plunder, war—has been their history. We do not have to go to Armenia for examples. Common, everyday examples will suffice. Who are the women in your neighborhood, who are prominent in any line of work? I never saw a pauper [who is] president of a club—or leader of anything. Think it over for yourself and you will decide that the economically independent women and men are those who are leading in all walks of life. When all you have is a mere existence, you cannot hope to share the fruits of social or political independence. The emancipated woman is economically independent.

3) The emancipated woman uses her luxury—which affords her time and leisure—in making contacts with women of her own and other races. Wide contacts are earmarks of emancipated women. When freedom is restrained we know only those in the circles [with] which we are permitted to associate, but when we are at liberty our associations naturally increase. It is only natural that one who seeks the advantages of emancipation should form wider contacts. But if one purposefully seeks to become emancipated this is a prime necessity to accomplish her purpose. The emancipated woman is a person of wide vision, tolerant disposition and cosmopolitan nature. These qualities can only be developed by contact. Nations that are democratic in thought are those that have the greatest contact with the world. England, for example, is the pivot point for all commerce between the New and Old World. If it [is] to be wondered, with these contacts—a great democratic nation should be developed. Germany wanted to build the Baghdad Railway, so as to increase her contacts. Women who would also be democratic will build contacts—through clubs, federations—and clubhouses. There is no wonder we in Philadelphia are known to be provincial, when we haven't a single clubhouse where women of all faiths, ideals, and interests can discuss on a common informal basis their thoughts. Thoughts are things, and when a sufficient number of people think alike on a single fundamental issue—their thoughts create new mores as the sociologist term, thoughts and ideas which are sufficiently accepted to become customs. The colored women have ideas regarding our racial advancement [that are] worthy [of] acceptance; sometimes many of us have [the] same ideas but we have no contacts by which we can bring together our ideas—thrash them out and unite in thought. We accept as a consequence the ideas, thoughts, plans made for us by the white women in their more than one hundred clubhouses in the city of Philadelphia alone. While we are meeting at this house, that church, thinking to ourselves, because when we meet it is for the formal transaction of business,

they are discussing informally their ideas on our problems and formulating plans for us. The exchange of ideas brought about by wide contacts is as essential to the production of an emancipated womanhood. By these contacts a) we can unite and concentrate on our own ideas regarding racial problems. b) [W]e can break down barriers that exist between us—the woman you do not like is the woman you do not know. You like the people you know. c) [W]e can make impressive interracial contacts. We'll have a place to invite women of other races to confer with us. Being in our own home, we shall be more at ease and [in a] better position to put over the plan before us. d) If for no other reason because men have had clubs and we can match them.

To summarize, the Emancipated Woman will first get money—so that she can be independent in her thought and action. But if she wants to be more than a million other women, who had money but whose dead bodies are now mingled in the dust beneath, she will use the leisure, the power, that money gives her first to secure political emancipation that she will secure political recognition in a larger sense for herself and her race, [and] second, to build clubhouses that will afford such contacts that the broadening influences of club life will produce racial programs, made not by white women but by black women, for black people, who are democratic and united in thought, who are emancipated.

Drusilla Houston

"Writer Discusses Communism and the Negro, Finds It Undesirable"

New Journal and Guide, July 4, 1931[32]

(For the Associated Negro Press)

Real Nature of the Negro—The Red Menace Because of the widespread lack of understanding of the real nature of the Negro, just now there is a bitter contest between the "New Negro" and the "Old Guard" over what the race wants. Because I love the new and honor the old I would harmonize the differences of both. The older Negro from experience, some of it bitter, has learned more of the real nature of black folk. If you will watch them in fraternal or church organization[s] you will find them soundly democratic and conservative. It is a good thing that they are, for if it were his nature to run after every ism, he would have been exterminated long ago. Kelly Miller and his type know too that the race is not conservative from cowardice but from wisdom and commonsense. I have lived with and studied mass Negroes for many years, and I have the deepest respect for their judgment. I have not their wisdom or courage, but they have shown it to me every step of the way. It is we, intermixed with Aryan blood, who are rash and hasty.

When we are young, we are all radicals, impetuous, combative. When the Tulsa riot was in progress, I came to realize why God had never given me a son. As that airship soared over the colored district and threw bombs on black homes, anger grew hotter and hotter within me and if I had had seven sons that day I would have devoted every one of them to death. I was a few miles away in a smaller city and they should have gone out one by one to counter fire with fire. I would not have expected them to have returned except on a shield. I have always been very gentle, but that day when I went downtown, I did not stay on my side of the walk. I went recklessly down the middle. I was still angry, but sometimes that means to be a fool. Many Negroes acted that part then, for it would have done to show fear that day. The real Negro is gentle, but he does not fear death. The Negro within me was aroused.

The mood of that day was the result of my age. All of the radical things that we think that we ought to be doing are entirely unnecessary. God rules the world. In his slow infinite way he is grinding to powder the things that stand in our way. The power of our bombastic utterances is negligible as to alleviating our condition. We had nothing to do with the coming of the World War that opened the door of labor in the North to the Negro. We have had nothing to do with the "revolt" of youth by which the young white American is discarding all the "black code" opinions of his elders. The bars are almost down but radicalism, lacking faith, cannot see it. A bright, new day is ahead of us, in which we can have no part if we do not believe in it. A day in which the white and black man shall with united hands untie the knot of world problems of disaster. The mills of the gods grind slowly much better and finer than the mills of our petty ill will.

The white man came back across the water not influenced by anything we were saying but convinced by God that in the European struggle that he was paying for the exploitation and ruin of weaker peoples. He fears to heap up this debt. He sees in growing crime waves his punishment for encouragement of lynch law. He realizes, though he will not yet acknowledge it, that the Negro has grown up into the statue of a man. We do not have to join the Red Menace to secure the rights of the Negro and though the "new Negro" may rave and poke ridicule at the conservative older leader, the masses of black people are not going to stir one step into the ranks of Communism. First of all, Communism is being used as a cloak by whites out of power to get into power. So far they have been unsuccessful, therefore, they have taken the Negro into the fold, as do all whites wher-

ever shock troops are needed for an Aryan advance. At the hour of danger the Negro is ever welcome in Aryan ranks, as a kind of human breastwork.

I would not be unjust to Russia in Communism she only seeks to go back to her olden form of government. The primitive inhabitants of Russia were Hamitic. Many of the strange customs of the Scyths, such as impaling the attendants of the chief around his tomb, burying his favorite wife with him, etc., may be found in late ages on the west coast of Africa. The first ancient forms of government were communal and almost perfect in equality of opportunity. It was through communal enterprise that the pyramids were built by black Ethiopians as may be seen by the pictures on the monuments. They were not slaves as white literature would have us believe but built the pyramids as were built all the Cushite wonders of old. Once Russians lived in peaceful communal villages, like those of India. The modern Russia, more largely Aryan, cannot bring about communal equality.

In justice I want to say that there are long-headed nations in western Europe different in nature from the broad-skulled Turanian-Aryan types. They are white nations that primitively originated from Africa. In these nations is the spirit of kindness and justice toward darker peoples. In Italy we see Fascism a variation of an old Ethiopian form of government where the trade guilds dominated society. We see secret societies still strong in West Africa that once ruled. Among the nations of western Europe the long-skulled types occupy the foremost ranks in culture but we have to contend with a broader-skulled Aryan who believes in force and does not believe in equality. It is this type that today controls the Communistic movement. Bloodshed and terror is native to them, and they are not going to be followed by any intelligent son of Ham, white or black.

Already this type has overthrown the wing of their party which stood for constructive cooperative programs, that would win intelligent men. They do not want to change and improve our government, but want to throw law and order. They were a race when they first appeared on the frontiers of western Europe, who with fire and sword played the program that they outline today. They are plainly shown in the Scriptures as of the powers of hell and Satan and we are shown that they will fall. As a race we must not allow ourselves to be embittered by the sharp competitions of today. Men who believe in destruction are never creators. Out of their personal failure has grown the spirit of help and willingness to bring universal ruin, where the innocent would be more likely to suffer than the men whom they hate, where all that the spirit and intelligence of the ages up would be thrown down in moment of murderous debauchery, never to be rebuilt again in our age.

I would ever wish to see the Negro join hands will the Afra-European nations in helping to make a better world. It was because they are related to us in blood that Darwin and Huxley said: "It is more likely that our ancestors can be found on the African continent." This is why France reaches back home for her tried African auxiliaries, that to stand between her and her Teutonic foes across the Rhine. The reason why you cannot keep some of our black folk from loving white folk. We are the mother race. The root must ever rule the branch. I can see how Ethiopians could lead broad-skulled Euro-Asian types to better ideas of Communism, but I do not see how selfish individualists [who] are all east Teutonic types could lead black folk into anything that would bring real communal equality to the world. The next three articles will deal with why the Negro masses will never join the Red. We shall write with all fairness to Communists.

W. E. B. Du Bois
"What the New Negro Is Thinking"

Address, Boston Community Church, December 1931

What the New Negro Is Thinking.

It would be *effrontery* for any one person to *pretend* that he could with authority and truth state just what twelve million people were thinking. There is no such *unity* and *definiteness* in human thought which would make such knowledge possible. It is difficult enough for a single human being to be reasonably sure of his own thoughts and feelings from day to day, and while we talk glibly about a *Group Mind*, there is after all but scant reality back of such general statement.

When, therefore, I try to tell you what the *new Negro* is thinking, I must, to a large extent, be expressing my own thought. But I am *sincerely* seeking in this case to modify my own opinion by what other Americans of Negro descent have said to me and to others and have written in books and papers and have given voice to, both in private conversation and on the public platform.

My excuse for being willing to essay so large a task is the fact that I have wide personal acquaintance with this group of people. I have come in contact with them in every state of the Union during some thirty years of public life. I have not only known them in great centers of Negro population, like New York, Chicago, Philadelphia, New Orleans, St. Louis, Indianapolis, and Los Angeles, but I have also lived on the plantations of the far South and in small towns and in waste places.

Also, because it is usually difficult, even impossible, for *me* to be accommodated at public hotels or restaurants, I have been a *guest* in thousands of Negro homes of all sorts and grades. And finally, whatever community of blood and training and life-long environment make for knowledge Which we call *instinctive*—all this I have.

On this basis of fact, I am going to try to tell you what *seems* to me today to be the leading currents of thought among colored folk.

This must immediately narrow itself to those whose thinking is fairly articulate. In other words, I am talking about those who are thinking, writing, and speaking. *Not*, however, *simply* the opinions of persons of superior education, but also of *intelligent* laborers and common workers, porters, and servants, *as well as* teachers and professional men.

This stream of thought has in the last hundred years been slowly but definitely *integrating*; that is, from extreme *individualism* and discreet groups and separate cities and sections, there has gradually come so many agreements and so much of conference, so many resolutions and statements, such action, that one can with considerable approximation of truth speak today of public opinion among American Negroes.

In the 18th Century, and even in the early 19th Century, such a statement would have been *inaccurate*. There was the great division into the free Negroes and the slaves. The slaves *who were eight-ninths of all were carefully segregated into plantation groups and all communication and spread of intelligence from group to group and place to place sternly discountenanced*. Secret and casual information spread but with *difficulty* and *distortion*. The 100,000 free Negroes of the South were watched, harried, and often re-enslaved. The three hundred and more thousand Northern free Negroes in the 18th Century had little intellectual or social intercourse with each other. Small groups, like those in Boston, in Newport, and in New York and Philadelphia, seldom visited each other, had no *periodicals* that circulated between them, had few meetings. They were, however, the *thinkers* for *four and one-half* million and tended to develop a strong *individualistic* philosophy. Every man was thought to progress according to his own deserts and efforts. Two wide lines of thought, therefore, developed: *one*, that the Negro was an *American*, and eventually was going to disappear into the American nation,—not *all Negroes*, but *this particular Negro* who was doing the thinking and who was *exceptional*; and this philosophy was proven *true* in thousands of cases. *Or*, the Negro was really

an *African*. He was going to leave this country for some country in Africa or elsewhere where he could be a man. John Brown Russwurm, the first Negro college graduate, the son of a white man, with a white stepmother, came out of Bowdoin in 1826 with the idea of achieving American citizenship for himself; he faced American life two years, editing the first Negro weekly, and then he turned straight around and said, "There is no chance for me to become a man in America." He went to Liberia.

Gradually the different groups got in touch with each other. Late in the 18th Century there was written correspondence between the Negroes of Newport and Philadelphia. Intergroup travel increased. In 1830, occurred the first conference of Negroes in Philadelphia with William Lloyd Garrison as guest. From then down to the Civil War, conventions reached wider and wider circles; small monthly and weekly papers began to appear; speakers, like Frederick Douglass and others went from group to group talking not only to white people but even more effectively to colored people.

Then came the *miracle* of Emancipation. Negroes were united by one new and astonishing ideal and plan of development. For the first time among the mass of Negroes the thought that had been in the minds of only a *few* unusual and stalwart black thinkers, namely: that far from being forever slaves or members of a despised caste, there was a chance of their becoming real American citizens *appeared* as a realizable *ideal*.

There ensued those fateful years between 1863–1870 when Negroes become recognized soldiers, voters, and officeholders. They apparently had the public opinion of the United State back of them. Skin-color was but an incident, manhood and ability *only* counted, and the way to uplift was education: learning to read and write; learning to handle figures; knowing what the world *was* and *had been*! *Education!* It would not be true to say that all Negroes believed this. The thoughtful still doubted, the thoughtless had no dreams; but the great surging mass uprooted from all past experience, brought into close contact with each other for the first time and listening to the voices of orators and agitators, idealists and teachers. This *middle mass* went through a physical, spiritual and social revolution more *violent* than any that ever happened to four and one-half million people in less than a decade.

Then, from 1870–1880 came disillusion. The reassertion of power by the white master, allied with the enfranchised poor white, who feared and hated Negroes; the reappearance of race animosity in the North, which had only been disguised and lulled but not essentially changed or eradicated by War and Emancipation; the new revolution in *industry*: all this slapped the *jubilant* and *emerging* Negro in the face. The Negro group was shaken to its inmost soul. It did more thinking in those days than it had done even in the days of the war. It began to drift and swirl into centers of opposition, inquiry, despair. There were those who said: "I told you so!" You can never trust white people. There were others who said: "Our rights may be postponed, but with the ballot and even physical force, we can regain them." Still others were sure that no small minority could bring force to bear, either political or physical, against the overwhelming mass of the nation. Segregation, immigration, emigration, armed resistance, race suicide—all had their advocates.

But there was one shining and deciding *light*, and that was the influence of the white school teachers who went South to teach Negroes. Their influence from 1870–1890 was tremendous. No cynical voice could arise among Negroes, decrying whites, doubting the faith of the nation, sneering at the failure of law, but there immediately arose in opposition, the strong, quiet unswerving *knowledge* of thousands upon thousands of young men and women who knew white people as *personal friends*, knew them as teachers, advisers, leaders, companions. *Moreover*, this *young group* were the new educated *leaders* of the mass. They were the preachers, teachers, thinkers, and dreamers. Against this knowledge of a new elite *nothing* could prevail, neither despair, revolt, emigration, nor bitter recrimination; and the Negro under the leadership of these students settled down to an unswerving faith in the ultimate triumph of race equality, despite disfranchisement, "Jim Crow" laws, and lynching.

From 1890–1910 however came ominous and portentous *change*. The inner and real *economic* problem of Emancipation forced itself for the *first time* to the front. Up to then it have [*sic*] been *camouflaged* and *half-concealed* by war, politics, and sentiment. *Now* came the *real* problem of transforming four million slaves to *wage-earners* in the *new* industry. The slaves had been suddenly changed from *capital* to *labor*, with no *land* or *tools*, suddenly *enfranchised* and suddenly *disfranchised*, with little *skill*, no *labor unions*, and in bitter competition with *white labor*, *white labor* that had growing political power, strong unions and Racial prestige. When Negroes looked to white friends, the white friends, embarrassed, looked away. Funds for education decreased. Lynching increased—reaching in 1892, *two* mob murders every *three* day in the year, and this with little public protest. Matters seemed approaching an impasse when, in 1895, *Booker T. Washington* voiced his famous compromise. He proposed that Southern industry be opened to Negro workers; that Negroes no longer insist on the *ballot*; and be trained mainly to work and that Northern philanthropy furnish the funds. The South leaped at the suggestion for it meant cheap, docile *labor* and *new* industry. The North leaped just as eagerly, for it meant common ground with the *South*, and better returns for *capital*, and it evaded equality, which seemed increasingly dangerous. The *Negro eagerly* agreed to the compromise—it meant *work*, *education*, even eventual wealth, without violence or strife, and in the midst of peace, North and South. The philosophy became almost *universal*. Train the Negro to labor and thrift, and establish him as an indispensable part of the tremendous American economic organization. The thesis was clear, simply and logical, and back of it stood the most influential molders of public opinion, black and white.

Nevertheless, it eventually tore the Negro race in two; and it did so because it cut straight across the long prepared public opinion of this calm, courageous, and faithful mass of educated Negroes who were beginning to get real education. They were not agitators. They were not doctrinaires. But they knew facts because they had learned from excellent teachers.

They tried from the first quietly to speak and warn, but they had the utmost difficulty in making themselves heard. They were moving against a tremendous current of public opinion. They found themselves misrepresented as being ashamed of working with the hands, jealous of new leadership, despising all but white collar jobs, eager for Latin and Greek and the frills of education, and unwilling to buckle down to the hard tasks of achieving their own economic emancipation.

But they persisted. They had to persist or die. They hammered at the ears of public opinion and tried to say, and gradually in the early days of the 20th Century succeeded in saying, more and more clearly: the education of Negroes for entrance into the present economic organization is not enough. That organization may change and has changed. The new industry—mass production, chain distribution, concentration of capital, international trade and credit, will bring new methods, new organization, new skill, new machines. Into these new conditions the black worker must be intelligently led and guided. *Unless* he has *political* power, he cannot compete with white groups who *have* political power. As a social *outcast* he cannot protect the wealth he accumulates, no matter how much *skill* he acquires, if he has no further education, when industrial methods change, he will be helpless. The object of education and the Atlanta Conference in 1902 is not to make men *carpenters*, it is to make carpenters *men*. Thus the educated Negro minority fought for existence from 1890 to 1910.

Their words and protests grew in volume and force, and if they had *not* been listened to, if the number of educated and thinking Negroes had not in the 20th Century reached proportion of *large enough* to give the group a real thinking leadership, the American Negro would have been submerged and ruined during and since the World War.

As it was, there was sufficient thought and vision to guide him into modern industry when the World War made openings, to insist on migration from the feudal South, to make Negroes protest more and more against disfranchisement, caste legislation, and mob violence, and to organize his protest to make black folk *less* apologetic, more self-assertive and self-conscious, even in the face of increasing race separation or organized race hate.

All this brings us down to the present postwar days, and to a statement of what the Negro of average intelligence is thinking about his present situation. First of all, his earlier individualism has quite gone. He recognizes that only in inner organization and united strength is he going to defend himself or make any headway in the United States. He must more and more submit himself to inner voluntary organized control. He would like to keep these organizations inter-racial but this is at present impossible. He has lost vital connections and friendship with the whites. His organizations today are vast and intricate. Churches, of course; fraternal associations to help him in amusement and sickness; insurance organizations to escape the discrimination of white companies; even weak attempts to organize his own credit in banks; tentative entrance into retail trade to distribute goods to his own people and employ his own labor; a larger share in directing the education of his people, so that colleges and universities with white teachers have almost disappeared and all those old contacts are dying out; and *particularly* there comes an unquenchable thirst for the Negro to express for himself and in his own way the mean of this struggle in the souls of black folk.

His attitude toward this nation is, therefore, logical. He has no patriotism. He dislikes exceedingly to sing "My Country 'Tis of Thee", and he laughs, albeit secretly, at "The Star-Spangled Banner." He no longer relishes allusions and has loyalty to the flag. His patriotism is almost wholly toward his own group or mass consciousness, *even when* accompanied, as it *always is*, by bitter *self-criticism, inner bickering* and *widespread lack* of mutual faith. This is usual in hard-pressed, ignorant, poor minorities, but it leads by inevitable contradiction to sympathy with other hard-pressed and disadvantaged groups.

The American Negro is thus increasingly eager to learn about other minority groups and disadvantaged people all over the world. There is, therefore, a tendency as yet small and yet growing with rapidity toward an *international* point of view. It is handicapped by the difficulty which Negroes have in getting in direct contact with suffering minorities. It is almost impossible for Negroes to get regular and authentic news from their own kinsmen in South, East, and West Africa; with the people of India and other parts of Asia. Even intercourse with colored West Indians and South Americans is largely and artificially handicapped. An American Negro can hardly get a passport visa to visit most parts of Africa or the great black world south of us. Notwithstanding this, however, the Negro is reaching out toward these peoples with greater and greater determination and understanding.

Curiously enough, however, there is one *tremendously disadvantaged* group at his very side concerning which the Negro has little knowledge and less sympathy and that is the white American laborer, native and foreign. This is *not* because of ignorance and snobbish ideals—but it is rather because for three centuries white labor has sat on the black man's back, kicked, cuffed, and lynched him and denied him every kind of human equality. Negroes have known white teachers but never white knowledge. I can remember as a boy that the most fearsome thing in life were the yells and fists of the German and Irish factory children of my birthplace. Their squalid homes, dirt, and ignorance, were all in my child mind but part of their deep hatred and enmity toward me. It has taken some determined mental readjustments in my mature years to make me realize a common cause for their degradation and mine. No such metamorphosis has taken place today among the mass of Negroes. White labor to them is the group that steals their jobs, keeps them out of work, denies them property, hounds them out of decent living quarters, and swells the mobs.

For this reason the average Negro is the secret if not often ally of wealth and capital, *not* because he has been trained in snobbery, *not* because he is led and dominated by a black bourgeoise but because he is ignorant of the modern labor movement and its relation to him. How should he learn?

Moreover, his only recourse for defense against the political and economic attacks of white labor is white *capital*: white wealth *gives* black men *education, charity* and *jobs*, and in return gets a chance to make more wealth at the expense of *all* labor. Whose fault is this? And who shall remedy it? You might look to the Negro's leaders, but his intellectual elite in the passing generation got the old economic teaching of thrift and saving, wealth as the reward of work and sacrifice and wage as limited by inefficiency and the Wages Fund. The newer student—white and black—is getting *no* economic teaching at all, except by permission of the Power Trust and Public Utilities magnates. The best economic teaching of the present generation is coming from labor unions and radical groups and they either never think of the Negro or begin by bawling him out for not knowing instinctively, *that* which he has had no opportunity to learn.

The result is pathetic. The Negroes' great pressing problem is today economic emancipation—completing the step begun in 1863, redirected in 1895, hastened forward in the World War, and thrown into disorder by the present depression. The economic thought and planning called for by this plight is non-existent. His industrial philosophy is chaotic and the mass see no light, even in *political power*.

The political path of the Negro is strewn with difficulties which he sees all too clearly. He recognizes the social bankruptcy of the two main parties. He does *not* agree by any means with the majority of the nation as to just *where* they have failed. But he knows that so far as he is concerned, their failure has been lack of any disposition to protect him in his political or civil rights, to stop lynching, to uproot peonage, to secure him justice in the courts, and a chance to work at decent wage. *If*, even, he starts to vote independently, he is at first faced by the severe *economic* pressure brought upon him. He is liable to lose his job or his customers unless he votes the Republican ticket, or again, the bribe of *office* and even of *money* is *exaggerated* in his case because of his small *income*. If, however, he faces and ignores these considerations, the practical question is, what political allies can he find who will bid for his vote and give him consideration in return? He can expect nothing of the old-time Republican Party, except a few minor offices and small campaign largesse. He can expect little from the Democratic Party which must depend upon the South for its main support, and the political South is built upon the disfranchisement and economic slavery of the Negro. The independent Negro voter can expect little from the Northern Liberal and Reformer. He is enthusiastic for all reforms except those which mainly effect the Negro, and he is hesitant, even absolutely opposed, to giving the Negro any representation or voice. When he talks of Democracy, he not only does not think of the Negro—he definitely excludes him. The Negro can get recognition from local grafting gangs in large cities like New York and Chicago, but this involves cooperation in their political methods, for which Negroes get widely damned. From the Socialists and the Communists, he gets a determination to recognize color caste as a *problem only* insofar *as it is* a *labor* problem and to *insist* that the *solution* of the *labor* problem is going automatically to solve the *race* problem, a *dictum* which the Negro neither understands nor believes. So that the independent Negro finds himself with a ballot in his hands that nobody is really bidding for and he concludes in a large number of cases that he might just as well not go to the trouble of even casting it. Once in a while, as in the defeat of Judge Parker, he becomes part of an accidental majority and wins a startling victory. But he has no *illusions* in this case. It was accident and little more. White labor was ashamed of the alliance!

How does all this affect the Negro's attitude toward himself, his family, his friends and neighbors. The Negro *family* is not only a broken, imperfect thing, it has been systematically smashed for all the centuries that he has been American.

The magnificent and intricate organization of the African family showed determined effort to survive in the West Indies and was at the bottom of the Haitian Revolution; but it did not survive slavery in the United States. The new family on European lines simply could not adequately exist in slavery, although it made progress. It did exist among the free Northern Negroes, except that it was tremendously handicapped by poverty and ignorance which made family unity difficult and often impossible. Today the Negro family, like the white American family, is forced to be small because of its small income, and is continually broken up by migration and caste difficulties and the group *as expressed* in the church or the neighborhood tends to transplant the family in social potency. It's [*sic*] problem of the Second Generation is enormous.

The ideal of *education* still persists. No group in the United States, considering its income, is trying harder to educate its children; but there again this education is handicapped by poverty and by its tendency, even in the North, to be a closed group training with all the provincialism and group loyalties of segregated communities. Education which throws white and colored pupils and students into close [contact] . . . [33]

. . . [and understanding contact is less and less frequent, and quite contrary to the days of the past. Negro students want to go to Negro schools. They hesitate and shrink from the kind of persecution which they suffer in white schools, and they are more and more convinced that the white schools have no monopoly of knowledge or method. On the other hand, their vision of social development is clouded. They cannot at present see a way out. They are face to face with the problem of prejudice. They believe without any hesitancy that they are kept poor and ignorant by prejudice and that if they had an opportunity they could be just as effective in industry and science as any other group in the United States. Their tendency is thus naturally to exaggerate their genius, desert, and accomplishment and to attribute all failure to race discrimination.]

The resultant and growing bitterness toward white people has in this way double growth. The Negro attributes his success to his overcoming prejudice of white folks and his failure to the overwhelming difficulties of color caste. If he is weak and lazy, he excuses himself by pointing out the failures of black men who have been strong and energetic. If he is restless and ambitious, he is not willing to wait and work for success for he foresees in every obstacle *failure* because of prejudice. If he tries to overlook race discrimination, it suddenly rises and *slaps* him in the face. If he refuses to attempt to succeed because he is sure he will not be allowed to, his failure is pointed out by white and black and attributed to exactly opposite causes. The resultant conflict among Negro youth greatly handicaps its best endeavor.

It *especially* forms the key to contemporary *Negro art*. This art—this vision of life—is not natural nor spontaneous. It is involved and artificially exotic. The black man clings to his primitive enjoyment of life but it is a conscious and calculated clinging. Negro joy has today no natural spontaneity. Cynicism, bitterness among colored folk, is much more spontaneous than ebullient joy. But the motions of joy and carefree abandon must still be gone through with. *They pay.* They are almost the only things that *do* pay among Negroes, in music and vaudeville, and even in books and writings. It is, nevertheless, more and more a pose—a method of earning a living. After and when the New Negro art enjoys a real freedom with a compensating chance of livelihood, there will pour forth a flood of bitter recrimination and tragedy which will astonish the more complacent white world.

This complacency of the white world, its smug assumptions concerning Negroes, give rise to deep and twisted judgments. In the religion of white people, the American Negro has not the slightest faith, although he may still regard himself a religious person.

The inner religious attitude of the Negro race and especially of its thinking portion has undergone great change. On the naïve Calvinism of the great ignorant mass has been erected an attitude of complete indifference so far as the doctrines of Christianity are concerned. The church is still well attended, even by Negroes of intelligence, except in a few large cities, like New York. But this *church* is an effective and fairly well-equipped *social organization*. The sermon falls into two categories: an old statement of the plan of salvation without criticism and without conviction. A practical interpretation of present social affairs, particularly within the church. Between these two extremes nothing is said. There is no attempt to modernize the old religious doctrine; there is no attempt to put social organization upon an ethical or logical basis. This does not mean the persistence of religion. It means the death of it, and at the same time a persistence and growth of the church. But this growth of the church is threatened by lack of educated leadership. The only revolt against religion in the Negro race is shown by the small number of Negroes who are willing to become ministers. On the other hand, this means that Negroes are sure that nine out of ten white folks do not believe half what they profess. They say that obviously white folk do not believe in turning the other cheek, or in loving a neighbor, unless the neighbor belongs to one's own class—and even then there are exceptions. They know, of course, that white people give charity, that they support numbers of Negro institutions and efforts, but Negroes do not for a moment believe that this is because of any love for Negroes or really self-sacrificing. They think it is partly from habit, partly from fear.

Of Science among white, Negroes are equally skeptical. They realize that for years science has been misused to their disadvantage, and that many theories concerning their race which formerly had the benediction of science are proved absolutely false; and yet plenty of similar falsehoods are replacing them. With this specific knowledge and belief, Negroes' attitude toward the great moral problems of the world is naturally apathetic. Preach the cause of world peace to a colored audience and see how much enthusiasm you get. Peace, of course. They are peaceful people, and because they were peaceful, they were slaves and are still in semi-slavery. They suspect that the peace movement is mainly a movement of agreement among white people to make their domination over black, brown, and yellow people more secure.

Talk to them of the freedom and uplift of women, and they immediately assume that the real interest in this movement is white women and not colored women. They are not interested in the World Court, simply because they know that the justice of the World Court is not for colored folk. They are politely incredulous of the League of Nations because they regard it as assembling a league of white nations. This cold, cynical attitude toward the great moral movements of today thus defeats itself and reacts upon a people naturally sunny, joyful, and credulous. They are not sunny. They are not joyful. They do not believe. They disbelieve in the world and its ideals, and yet with all that, they are fighting on and pathetically searching for a cosmic ray of light.

To this *definitely* pessimistic interpretation of Negro thought there is one equally optimistic note to be added. The inclusion of the two aspects is illogical and inexplicable, and yet it is true that the Negro race in America is optimistic and has not the slightest doubt but that in the end it is going to triumph in each one of its demands. No writer, no speaker, no leader, ever suggests that the Negro is going to be submerged and held permanently in a caste position. The most pessimistic of Negro thinkers always concludes with their audience that in the end the cause of universal democracy, which includes black men, must triumph. It is hard to say whence this optimism arises. Certainly, the current facts do not support it. It is only a vague generalization to say that such thinking is the racial characteristic of an exuberant group. This may be a true statement but it is no explanation. I presume that the real cause of Negro optimism is the tremendous strides by which in their own experience or the experience of fathers and grandfathers who they have known, they have accomplished such extraordinary things. For this reason, probably no accomplishment seems too extraordinary or [illegible word], in the reasonable future. At the same time, there creeps in continually today a new element: the faint foretaste of a willingness to hopeless sacrifice; a wild call for the ordeal of blood in the very face of the impossible; all of the world-old dreams of immolation, hari-kari, and the "voice without reply." This is not yet articulate but one feels it as a groundswell. One senses flames ready to burst and burn.

Carter G. Woodson

"The New Negro Begins to Exhibit Much Pride in His Racial Identity"

New Journal and Guide, February 20, 1932

Youth Is Losing Its Former Distaste of Things Negroid

"You know we got tired of these Negro plays," said a miseducated, highly educated Negro of Washington to me the other day. "Our troupe, originally organized for this very purpose, finally reached the decision that there was not anything in it and took up plays bearing upon the life of other people."

These players, like others of old, went back to the flesh pots of Egypt rather than press forward to the promised land; but we have heard nothing of their striking achievements since that time. They occasionally present a play worked out as a poor imitation of what they see others doing; and there follow such comments as, "That was fine, for it made you think that you were at a real theatre; and that girl playing the leading role reminds you of Julia Marlowe or Maude Adams."

And this is about as far as the miseducated, highly educated Negro's mental development enables him to go. What he says and does reminds you of what someone else has said or done so much better. The Negro thus misguided does not show much originality. It is not his fault, however, for he is merely the slave of the modern tradition of keeping the Negro blindfolded. For three centuries, the Negro has been taught that the race to which he belongs does not amount to anything, and that the only thing he can do in educating himself is to imitate the traducers of the race. Having studied in this school of thought for all these years, most Negroes have learned this lesson too well.

As the result of such efforts as the celebration of Negro History Week and the scientific study of the race, however, the youth of African blood is gradually breaking away from these traditions of slavery. These younger people are beginning to see virtue in persons whose faces are black; or, as a writer said in a recent article entitled "The White God Cracks," they have found as great possibilities in themselves as in others; and they are determined to feast upon the good things of the world rather than be content with the crumbs falling from the table.

A teacher of Washington with a vision of these things to come in the development of a new race expressed this thought the other day in urging me to come to see her pupils in the pageant, "Ethiopia at the Bar of Justice." "The preparation of this play for Negro History Week," said she, "has worked a transformation of my pupils. A few years ago it was difficult to find a boy or girl willing to take the part of a Negro in anything, but now it is equally as difficult to find one who will not gladly assume such a role. Almost every girl in the school wanted to be Ethiopia; and in the assignments I had much trouble from incurring the displeasure of those who felt disappointed."

This is the rise of the new Negro; not that of the Negro who would join with the reds to destroy the present economic order. It should be changed, but the Negroes with the little common sense which most of us now have would not profit by the revolution if it came. The new Negro would dramatize the life of the race and thus inspire it to develop from within through a radicalism of its own.

In other words, this new Negro will do for the race what Horace did for the stupid Romans in teaching them not to despise the life of the lowly, the pride of the country. Instead of going to others to find something to admire, begin to appreciate yourselves. "When a man," said he, "learns how far that which he has excels that which he seeks let him return home in time to enjoy his present possessions."

What, then, in the life of the Negro should we dramatize? That will be an easy problem when the Negro learns to think. The Negro in the modern world is its most dramatic figure. This was the thought of Frederika Bremer, a foreign woman traveling in this country about 1850, when someone asked her what she thought of the future of America. She replied, "The romance of your history is the fate of the Negro." Therein lies the real American drama. As soon as we turn away from the whitewashing [of] our exploiters and oppressors, and learn to appreciate the virtues of this despised race we shall be able to see and understand life.

Paul K. Edwards

"Types of Negro Character Illustrations Most Pleasing and Most Displeasing to Negroes"

In *The Southern Urban Negro as Consumer*, 1932

Because of the significant influence in advertising copy of elements having to do with the Negro race—in particular, the Negro character illustration—either toward developing a favorable reaction to the brand of product advertised, or toward building up a barrier of hostility to it, it was believed worth while to find out, on the one hand, the types of Negro character illustrations most pleasing to Negroes and, on the other hand, the types most displeasing to them. In an effort to do this, fifteen advertisements were selected containing illustrations of about every type of Negro character used in advertising copy today. The same groups of housewives and family heads used in the preceding tests were then asked to pick from this collection those advertisements in which the Negro character illustration pleased them very much and those in which the Negro character was exceedingly displeasing.

Three advertisements used by the Cream of Wheat Company in 1914 were among the fifteen selected for this study. The illustrations of these advertisements proved to be highly displeasing to more of the 240 individuals interviewed than any of the others. One of them is reproduced here. An understanding of what there is about this illustration which gained the ill will of so many Negroes can best be obtained by reading the selected criticisms which follow:

1. White boy is driving colored man.
2. Don't like idea of white boy driving old Negro.
3. Degrades Negroes in appearance and dress.
4. Pictures wrong side of Negro.
5. White boy driving Negro and calling him "Uncle."
6. Don't like colored man pulling white child.
7. Makes colored people look foolish.
8. White boy using colored man for horse.
9. White boy driving colored man—Negro servant.
10. Don't like colored man being horse for white boy.
11. Not true to life.
12. Dislike idea of white boy making fool out of Negro.
13. Boy should not be striking Negro.
14. Makes light of Negro. General appearance disgusts me.
15. Dislike white boy striking Negro man.
16. This is burlesquing the Negro.
17. Dislike making monkey of colored folks.
18. Dislike white boy having Negro hitched up as servant.
19. Dislike "take-off" of Negro.
20. Makes fun of the Negro.
21. Takes off Negro and does not represent usual type.
22. Ignorance is exaggerated.
23. Don't like idea of colored man making fool of himself over white child.
24. Dislike advertising to public at expense of Negro.
25. Picture exaggerated.
26. Portrays old "Uncle Tom" type of Negro.
27. Portrays obsolete and objectionable type.
28. Portrays colored people burlesqued.
29. Disgusting. Shows old-time Negro instead of modern.
30. This is true, but should not be pictured publicly.

The illustration of the Gold Dust Twins . . . is another type of illustration meeting the dis-

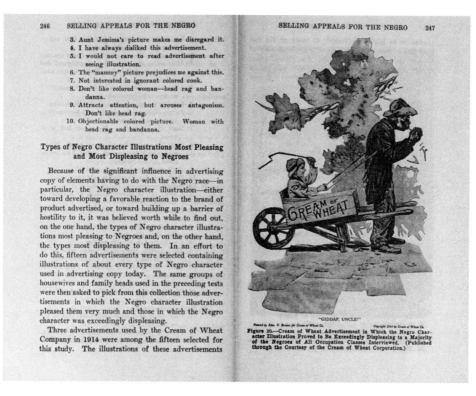

Advertisement for Cream of Wheat, in *The Southern Urban Negro as Consumer*, 1932.

approval of many Negroes. Their reaction to the utilization of this type of character in advertising copy can likewise be better appreciated after reading the following criticisms of it:

1. Dislike appearance of twins.
2. Do not see why they used colored boys to advertise Gold Dust.
3. Can't see any connection between black twins and Gold Dust.
4. Don't like advertisement with naked colored twins.
5. White twins need washing as much as black.
6. Not representative of Negro race.
7. Gold Dust twins are disgusting.
8. Negro boys pictured wrong.
9. Makes fun of colored people.
10. Not true to life.
11. Makes Negro look ridiculous.
12. Makes light of Negro. General appearance disgusting.
13. Twins too ungainly.
14. Pictures Negro in most ignorant state.
15. Dislike making fun of Negroes.
16. Portrays ignorant side of Negro life.
17. Do not like comic element in Negro advertisements.
18. Degrading picture of Negro employed, having no connection with product.
19. Not true picture of Negroes and used to get attention of whites.
20. This advertisement has no relation to washing powder except to belittle the Negro.
21. Carries idea Negro is natural-born fool.
22. I dislike a caricature of Negroes.
23. Why do whites pick out worst type of Negroes to use in illustrations?

24. Reminds of unpleasant facts of Negro race.
25. Dislike because places Negro in disrepute on general principles.

Two advertisements . . . contain illustrations of Negro characters pleasing to a large majority of the individuals interviewed. One of these advertisements concerns the products of the Madame Walker Company, a large Negro manufacturing enterprise, and was clipped from a Negro magazine. The other is for a bleaching cream and was found in a Negro weekly newspaper. The comment made by the majority who found the illustrations of these two advertisements particularly pleasing was that here were illustrations which pictured the Negro as he really is, not caricatured, degraded, or made fun of; that here the Negro was dignified and made to look as he is striving to look, and not as he looked in ante-bellum days; that here was the new Negro.

. . . Cream of White Advertisement in Which the Negro Character Illustration Proved to Be Exceedingly Displeasing to a Majority of the Negroes of All Occupation Classes Interviewed. (Published through the Courtesy of the Cream of Wheat Corporation.)

. . . Gold Dust Advertisement in Which the Negro Character Illustration Proved to Be Exceedingly Displeasing to a Majority of the Negroes of All Occupation Classes Interviewed.

. . . Advertisement of a Product of the Madame C. J. Walker Company in Which the Negro Character Illustration Proved to Be Particularly Pleasing to a Majority of the Negroes of All Occupation Classes Interviewed.

. . . Advertisement of a Product of Dr. Fred Palmer's Laboratories in Which the Negro Character Illustration Proved to Be Particularly Pleasing to a Majority of the Negroes of All Occupation Classes Interviewed.

Advertisement for Madam C. J. Walker's Superfine Face Powder, in *The Southern Urban Negro as Consumer*, 1932.

Martha Gruening

"The Negro Renaissance"

Hound and Horn 5, no. 3 (1932)[34]

"Being a Negro writer in these days is a racket and I'm going to make the most of it while it lasts. I find queer places for whites to go to in Harlem . . . out-of-the-way primitive churches, side-street speakeasies and they fall for it. About twice a year I manage to sell a story. It is acclaimed. I am a genius in the making. Thank God for this Negro Literary Renaissance! Long may it flourish!"

In these words a minor character in Wallace Thurman's *Infants of the Spring* expresses in terms of cynical self-interest what has for some time been only too apparent to some of those interested in the artistic expression of the Negro. Elsewhere in the book its hero is shown in the midst of a black and white gin party. "This," he kept repeating to himself, "is the Negro Renaissance and this is about all the whole damn thing is going to amount to. . . . It is going to be necessary, he thought, to have another emancipation to deliver the emancipated Negro from a new kind of slavery."

Yet it is only seven years ago that some of us who today find an echo of these savage words in our hearts hailed with high hopes the beautiful and colorful volume *The New Negro*, edited by Alain Locke, and accepted its premise of a younger Negro generation on the threshold of a new era of accomplishment. They were no longer bound together, Locke wrote confidently, "by a common problem, but by a common consciousness" and "shedding the chrysalis of the Negro problem they were achieving something of a spiritual emancipation."

It was inevitable that this prophecy could only be partially fulfilled. From that consciousness of which Locke wrote, and probably far more from individual impulse, unregimented by any such herd instinct, has come in the intervening years some real achievement. And much more might have come if the so-called Negro Renaissance had not been ballyhooed

and exploited commercially and socially, until it has been, to a large extent, degraded into a racket. It was always too much to hope that 12,000,000 Americans of any race or color could, in our chaotic civilization, achieve a solidarity of thought and experience which would result in genuine expression. The finest products of the Renaissance have been distinctly individual as, for instance, the extraordinary work of Jean Toomer. But Toomer has published little, if anything, since *Cane* appeared in 1923. Meanwhile the mystical and probably mythical concept of a common Negro consciousness has for some time been superseded by a very definite consciousness, common alike to white and black writers of a very definite and marketable fashion in literature and art for all things Negroid. Among Negroes this has resulted, among other things, in the kinds of writing which are the objects of Wallace Thurman's attack.

Infants of the Spring, like Thurman's earlier *The Blacker the Berry*, is in a sense a pioneering book. It is the first serious and aggressive attempt that I know of by a Negro writer to debunk the Negro Renaissance in a thoroughgoing manner. It is bitter, disillusioned, and probably unfair in its wholesale rejection of nearly everything being done by Negro artists and writers. But in spite of this and in spite of its somewhat crude and journalistic writing, there is an exhilaration to be gained from its angry honesty. It will no doubt be glibly denounced as "unconstructive," and indeed, it makes no pretense of being anything else. For it is simply the hearty individual expression of an individual disgust with life in general, and with the Negro Renaissance in particular, by a writer too keenly sincere and individualistic to find an easy escape from its sterility by such frequently suggested and ready-made panaceas as flight into communism, back to a problematical "African Inheritance" or into the ranks of the bourgeois Negro writers who "have nothing to say, and who write only because they are literate and feel they should apprise white humanity of the better classes among Negro humanity."

It is especially by their type of novel and by the uncritical acclamation with which examples of it have been received, I think, that the Negro Renaissance has been debased. One can almost establish a standard novel that will combine the worst features of all of them. Almost inevitably it will have a foreword by some professional foreworder like Carl Van Vechten or maybe Zona Gale, stating among other things how novel and unique it is. If it is in the Carl Van Vechten tradition it will probably have a glossary of Harlemese and certainly it will include a scene in which a Harlem ball or soirée is invaded by uplifting or merely curious palefaces, who are promptly knocked out by the ease, beauty, and sophistication of the rainbow-tinted members of the gathering. It is also practically obligatory for at least one member of the white group to make the very natural faux pas of mistaking some Negro light enough to "pass" for a Nordic, and to behave with a complete and pitiable lack of savoir faire when he discovers his mistake. To find this wearisome is not for a moment to deny that such incidents occur frequently in real life; a very great number of light Colored People must have experienced white uncouthness of this kind, but writing suffers as much from a stencil based on such incidents as it does from stencils of the Uncle Tom and Mammy variety to which these same writers very properly object. The real argument of these Negro novels could be summed up in almost every case as follows:

"I am writing this book because most white people still believe that all Colored People are cooks called Mandy or Pullman porters called George—but they aren't. They think we all live in cotton-field cabins or in city slums, but actually some of us live on Edgecombe Avenue or Chestnut Street. We don't all shout at Camp Meetings or even all belong to the Baptist or Methodist Church. *Some of us are Episcopalians.*

If you were privileged to visit our homes (which you aren't, for we are just as exclusive as you are) you would find bathtubs, sets of the best authors, and *etchings* on the walls! That's how refined we are. We have class distinctions, too. Our physicians' wives snub our hairdressers and our hairdressers our cooks, and so on down the line. The daughters of our upper classes are beautiful and virtuous and look like illustrations in *Vogue*. They are also far more attractive than white girls of the same class, for they come in assorted shades of bronze, tan, fawn, beige, hazel, chestnut, amber, cream, gold, lemon, orange, honey, ivory, and persimmon. You would, of course, be attracted to the heroine of this book, but as you are white, you are, in nine cases out of ten, a cad with dishonorable intentions. We'll allow the tenth case out of pure magnanimity. But in any case the heroine would scorn you because in the last chapter she will marry the dark hero and be happy ever after. She might, being human, have been tempted perhaps for a moment by the wealth and power you represent and by the immunity from insult and discrimination which 'passing' would mean for her, but even if she weren't too noble and loyal to yield to such temptation in the end the call of race would be too strong for her. Joy isn't on your side of the line, nor song, nor laughter, etc., etc." We have heard all this many times before, and we are likely to hear it many times again.

Nearly all these novels have been wholly devoid of literary merit, but they have a certain documentary value in revealing what is on the minds of a large portion of the Negro Intelligentsia, as well as of many Negroes who do not technically belong to it. Among recently published novels Jessie Fauset's *The Chinaberry Tree* is an outstanding example of this type. This, her third novel, like its predecessors is dedicated to the proposition that there are Colored ladies and gentlemen and that these constitute Colored Society. As propaganda this is no sillier than the stale counter-propaganda to which it is a retort, but the fact remains that a rather serious waste of Negro intelligence and sensitiveness is still going into the writing of such books. What is obvious from them is that the long frustrated, ambitious, struggling Negroes of the upper and middle classes still accept and jealously cherish the values of capitalistic civilization. They accept these values very much as they move into white neighborhoods as white people abandon them. And in this acceptance there has been much more than the snobbery and silliness which books like Miss Fauset's make pathetically and ludicrously evident. It represents two generations of struggle and achievement away from slavery toward a promised land, a goal which as they near it has all the unsubstantiality of a mirage. One may even concede that the struggle was noble and the achievement praiseworthy, and still feel that new day of the Negro Renaissance, if it comes, will not be made by those unable to detach their emotions from this mirage. Moreover, everything that can be said in favor of this goal was said once and for all, far better and more movingly than it has ever been said since in Du Bois's eloquent *The Souls of Black Folk*. And even *The Souls of Black Folk*, somehow, dates a little today. It is, for all its beauty, a little Victorian, moralistic, and slightly rhetorical; but it is moving as its successors are not because it is passionate and militant, where they are merely complacent, because its author was in those days the leader of a forlorn hope, rather than a Negro Babbitt.

Negro Babbitry exists and there is no reason why it should not be depicted; so do Intellectual Negro groups and Negro Smart Sets, but the Negro novels written about them have very generally been novels of neurosis. Instead of novels of Negro life they have been *prospectuses*, designed to sell to white readers the idea of Negro upper classes. But if there have been few if any good novels written about the Negro Bourgeoisie there have been at least three first rate novels about Negro Proletarian life. All three were written by Negro poets. Negro poets have very generally been spare-time poets—and proletarians. They have been cooks, dishwashers, floor-scrubbers, shoe-shiners, waiters, stevedores, Pullman porters, stokers, or have worked at any of the various forms of rough and casual menial labor open to American Negroes.

Langston Hughes is one of these poets, who having spent much of his life in the world of labor has inevitably been close to the life of the masses of his race. It was out of this experience that he wrote *Not Without Laughter*, which is not only uniquely moving and lovely among Negro novels but among books written about America. It is affirmative in a sense in which no other book by an American Negro is, for it is the story of a Negro happily identified with his own group, who because of this identification tells what is essentially, despite the handicaps of poverty and prejudice, the story of a happy childhood. The poverty was never sordid; for one thing it was country poverty in a growing small town of the Middle West, and the child had a backyard to play in, in which there was an apple tree, and flowers as well as clothes lines.

"Here the air was warm with sunlight and hundreds of purple and white morning glories laughed on the back fence. Earth and sky were fresh and clean after the heavy night rain and . . . there was the mingled scent of wet earth and golden pollen on the breeze that blew carelessly through the clear air." It was poverty, but never sodden or defeated though the child's grandmother toiled all day at her washtub washing the white folk's clothes and his mother sweated all day in the white woman's kitchen, while his handsome, vagabond father went fishing and played the guitar; even though eventually there was no place in Stanton for his pretty, fun-loving Aunt Harriet but the sinful house in the "bottoms" where on

> summer evenings little yellow and brown and black girls in pink and blue bungalow aprons laughed invitingly in door-ways and dice rattled with the staccato gaiety of jazz music on long tables in rear rooms; pimps played pool; bootleggers lounged in big, red cars; children ran in the streets until midnight with no voice of parental authority forcing them to an early sleep; young blacks fought like cocks and enjoyed it; white boys walked through the streets winking at Colored girls; men came in autos; old women ate pigs' feet and water-

melon and drank beer; whiskey flowed; gin was like water; soft indolent laughter didn't care about anything, and deep nigger-throated voices that had long ago stopped rebelling against the ways of this world rose in song.

It was poverty enlivened by singing and laughter, by strong, if casual, family affection and occasional family quarrels; by carnivals and camp meetings, by lodge meetings and regalia after the day's work was done, for: "Evening's the only time we niggers have to ourselves—Thank God for night—'cause all day you give to the white folks." Simple and touching, yet by some miracle always avoiding sentimentality, the story is told with a happy tenderness which recalls Katherine Mansfield's dictum that in fiction the beginning of art is *remembering*. It has the courage of its tenderness for Negro things, a serene and robust acceptance of the common things, the sights and smells and sounds, the folk-ways and idiosyncrasies of the people who made up one little Colored boy's background; and through this acceptance and evocation of them it communicates the very feeling and texture of life.

The only other American novel I know which seems to me comparable with *Not Without Laughter* is Willa Cather's *My Antonia*. Both books have, in common, somewhat the same quality of radiant sanity. Both communicate, in spite of relatively small canvases, a feeling of earth and sun and air, of strong life with a deep folk-roots. In both a poetic quality is due in part to the fact that the story is told reminiscently through the eyes of a child reflecting a child's curiosity and sensibility and wonder, and that the child in each case was a potential poet. In both there is ugliness and hardship and pain, but in both these incidents are dominated by a triumphant vitality, an open-eyed resilience in the face of life. And this, too, is a quality that is characteristic of Langston Hughes and which sings through his poems whether he is writing of Beale Street Love or Railroad Blues or of

The steam in hotel kitchens
And the smoke in hotel lobbies

And the slime in hotel spittoons
Part of my life

and is implicit in his high-hearted chant, "I, Too":

I, too, sing America
I am the darker brother
They send me
To eat in the kitchen
When company comes
But I laugh
And eat well
And grow strong.

Tomorrow
I'll sit at the table
When company comes
Nobody'll dare
Say to me
"Eat in the kitchen"
Then.
Besides
They'll see how beautiful I am
And be ashamed.
I, too, am America.

Claude Mackay [*sic*] is another vagabond poet who has brought a somewhat similar experience to rich fruition in his novels *Home to Harlem* and *Banjo*. Mackay, too, has worked in the white man's kitchens, and on wharves and trains and the stokeholes of steamers. He has known the life of a down-and-out beachcomber on the waterfront of Marseilles, and that of a poor farm boy in Jamaica. Older and more mature than Hughes, more complex and possibly deeper, he seems to have reached by a more difficult path an adjustment which in Hughes is instinctive. While his early associations seem to have had somewhat the same happy quality as Hughes' childhood and a far more beautiful setting—what hardships there were were due to poverty rather than to color—if one may judge by his writings he seems to have experienced the full cruelties of race and class struggle after his arrival in America in 1912. He was the first of the Negro intellectuals to be a radical in the political and economic sense as well as a militant rebel on behalf of his race. His novels *Home* to Harlem and Banjo are full of a deep and bitter wisdom, but also full of humor and zest for life. Home to Harlem specializes in those aspects of Harlem life that are not mentioned in polite Harlem society, at least if white people are present: Promiscuous and happy love making, drinking, jazzing, shooting and razor flashing; the life of the high yellow "sweet-back" and of the black women who work for him; instinctive, rhythmic life—frequently joyous, but with undertones of cruelty and savagery.

These aspects are presented convincingly through the consciousness of two very different types of Negro—Jake, a simple, uneducated, American working man who delights in most of them, and Ray, the exiled sensitive Haitian student. Ray finds in Harlem the extremes of joy and despair and finally flees from it because he was entangled with a girl and feared that some day

> the urge of the flesh and the mind's hankering after the pattern of respectable comfort might chase his high dreams out of him and deflate him to the contented animal that was a Harlem Nigger strutting his stuff. "No happy-nigger strut for me" he would mutter when the feeling for Agatha worked like a fever in his flesh. . . . And he hated Agatha and, for escape, wrapped himself darkly in self-love. . . .
>
> Going away from Harlem . . . Harlem! How terribly Ray could hate it sometimes. Its brutality, gang rowdyism, promiscuous thickness. Its hot desires. But, oh, the rich blood-red color of it! The warm accent of its composite voice, the fruitiness of its laughter, the trailing rhythm of its blues and the improvised surprise of its jazz. He had known happiness, too, in Harlem, joy that glowed gloriously upon him like the high noon sunlight of his tropic island home.

Banjo is a bitter and devastating picture of the white man's civilization as it looks to the black man at the bottom of it, and of the free and instinctive life which the irresponsible and uneducated black man can still manage to live in an ever tightening, mechanical white civilization.

> For civilization had gone out among these native, earthy people, had despoiled them of their primitive soil, had uprooted, enchained, transported and transformed them to labor under its laws, and yet lacked the spirit to tolerate them within its walls.
>
> That this primitive child, this kinky-headed, big-laughing black boy of the world did not go down and disappear under the serried rush of the trampling white feet; that he managed to remain on the scene, not worldly wise, not "getting there," yet not machine-made, nor poor-in-spirit like the regimented creatures of civilization was baffling to civilized understanding. Before the grim, pale rider-down of souls he went his careless way with a primitive hoofing and a grin. From these black boys he could learn to live . . . how to exist as a black boy in a white world and rid his conscience of the used up hussy of white morality. He could not scrap his intellectual life and be entirely like them. He did not want or feel any urge to "go back" that way. . . . Ray wanted to hold on to his intellectual acquirements without losing his instinctive gifts.
>
> But also he knew that though it was easy enough for Banjo who in all things acted instinctively it was not easy for a Negro with an intellect standing watch over his instincts to take his way through the white man's world . . . but of one thing he was resolved: civilization should not take the love of color, joy, beauty, vitality, and nobility out of his life and make him like the mass of its poor pale creatures. . . . Could he not see what Anglo-Saxon standards were doing to some of the world's most interesting people? Some Jews ashamed of being Jews. Changing their names and their religion . . . for the Jesus of the Christians! Educated Negroes ashamed of their race's intuitive love of color, wrapping themselves up in respectable gray, ashamed

of Congo sounding laughter, ashamed of their complexions . . . ashamed of their strong appetites. No being ashamed for Ray! Rather than lose his soul, let intellect go to Hell and live instinct.

Writing of this kind is, of course, very exasperating to the Negro Intelligentsia. Some of them may protest with justice that they are being *themselves* in conforming to the standards of the white civilization in which they live, since it seems to them good except in so far as it discriminates against them; that they are not merely Negroes but Americans as well, dark Americans, to be sure, but still fulfilling themselves legitimately through the usual American channels. This clash of views is not limited to Colored Americans. Every racial minority in America, with the possible exception of the Irish, is divided between those of its members who wish to sink themselves, their blood, and their differences in the majority, and the proudly or defensively race conscious who wish to take their stand on this blood and this difference. Among Colored People, particularly, the logic of facts may actually be with the first group. Owing to the extravagance of anti-Negro prejudice any person, however white, is classed as Colored if he is known to possess a single drop of colored blood. A "Negro" thus arbitrarily created is not necessarily being himself any more when he sings spirituals or jazzes, than when he follows what are usually accepted as white behavior patterns. If Negro art has struck deeper roots, as I think it has, in the soil of the race conscious attitude it is because it has been the more affirmative and liberating. Conformity to white standards, on the other hand, has very generally meant conformity to the most standardized elements in our civilization—its negations, its drabness, its gentility. But this is not, I think, inherently or eternally true and even today the best writing is by Negroes in whom this consciousness is transcended. Thus *Not Without Laughter* is not merely a chronicle of Negro family life. The story of hard working, stay-home Annjee's helpless love for her vagabond husband, of Harriet's rebellion against her

mother's puritanism, the true and sensitive picture of Sandy's boyhood and adolescence are rich and warm and full-flavored because of certain Negro qualities that Langston Hughes knows and loves, but the book's hold on our emotions is independent of these. They merely enhance the truth of what the perceptive artist in Hughes has felt about love between a man and a woman, about the clash of the generations, and the awakening consciousness of a boy. *Home to Harlem* has given us the most poignant and unforgettable picture of the substratum on which our commercial civilization is built in the half-dozen pages which describe Ray, the Negro student waiter, tossing in a half-walking nightmare in the vermin-infested bunkhouse of Pennsylvania Railroad. Here Color is an added element of torture and humiliation in the life of the underdog. It makes escape from this life difficult if not impossible, but it is only part of the picture into which Mackay has distilled the very essence of the horror and despair the cruelty at the roots of our civilization must awaken sometimes in any sensitive mind. Color again is an element, but only one element in the entrancingly comic feud between the Negro cook and the Negro waiters on the dining car which ended with the cook's discomfiture and demotion. Color again plays an important part in the sweeping epic of *Banjo*, but *Banjo* is an immensely rich book because it is far more than the story of Color. It is a story of beachcombing and vagabondage, of the clash not only between black and white, of civilization and primitive races, but of civilization at grips with itself, and of the detached and frequently humorous clarity, with which the beachcomber, black or white, who keeps clear of it except for the occasional necessity of working or panhandling sees it for the thing it is.

"A good story," Ray says at one point, "in spite of those who tell it and those who hear it is like good ore that you might find in any soil—Europe, Asia, Africa, America. The world wants the ore and gets it by a thousand men, scrambling and fighting, dying, and digging for it. The world gets its story in the same way."

PART VII

THE DEPRESSION, THE NEW DEAL, AND ETHIOPIA, 1933–1937

J. W. Rawlins
"Rawlins Writes on Segregation"

Detroit Tribune, August 12, 1933

The Tribune is in receipt of an interesting letter from J. W. Rawlins, one of Detroit's well-known business men, who makes some interesting observations regarding segregation. Mr. Rawlins' letter reads in part as follows:

> We hear a great deal today about the New Negro and his progress. As I turn back the pages to 60 years ago, and come down through this one-half century, I find that he has deteriorated in all lines of business, in which he had the whites as his competitors. His only hope for success is where he has entered into what he calls "A Gentleman's Agreement," that he will segregate between the races; in other words, he becomes an accessory to Jim Crowism.
>
> It is mostly practiced in our Y.M.C.A's [*sic*], hospitals, undertaking establishments. In fact, you will find it in public and professional business, north of the Mason and Dixon Line, and if you open a legitimate business—say, a store of good, dependable merchandise—those same Negroes, who make a living off the race, will carry their money to the white man's store.
>
> Even our preachers, who build their churches and draw their salaries from Negroes' dimes and quarters, spend in the white man's stores, regardless of the fact that the colored man's store has the same class of goods for less money.
>
> I was delighted to see the Tribune on sale down town. The Free Press on one corner, and the Tribune on another.
>
> It is well within the memory of many who are living today, when the servant in the house was colored. Colored barbers, porters, waiters, cooks in hotels and on steamboats, stewards and head-waiters at all resorts were employed; but now, there's even a transfiguration on Pullman cars.
>
> At Dayton, O., they have built for Negro children a $500,000 school; and in Detroit they are going to build modern apartment buildings, swimming pools, parks, and flower gardens in the "black belt." Beware of Greeks bearing gifts.

Letters from Dorothy West to James Weldon Johnson, 1933–1937

23 Worthington St.,
Roxbury, Mass.
October 23, 1933

Dear Mr. Johnson,

First of all I warmly greet both you and Mrs. Johnson, and realize with sadness that the years have slipped away, and where I was a girl, now I am a woman, and there is behind me much lost loveliness.

So suddenly I am serious and entirely grown-up, and I know that the promise we, the New Negroes, were so full of is enormously depleted. And now there are newer voices that are younger and sweeter. It occurred to me that I could make up for much I have wasted by some way finding space for young dark throats to sing heard songs.

I wrote to several Negro newspapers, urging them to let me edit a weekly literary page. I wrote so many to insure answers from one or two anyway. But surprisingly all of them sent interested letters, although for the most part they avoided the question of money, my stipulation, since I know nothing is more encouraging to the writer than a monetary reward. Some said that if this section caught on, then perhaps.

And now I have decided—since so many papers apparently want it—to syndicate this page. With the ensuing advertising there may be some money in it for the contributors—and myself!—because I have already promised the various people I wrote to for material that only their first contribution would be gratis. That I hope the section will be in a position to pay for all subsequent ones.

This is your part, Mr. Johnson. There is no one else—and I have written many people for this thing and that—but it is you, the dean of Negro letters, whom I very earnestly beg to write the introductory editorial.

I hope the first section will be ready the first days of next month, so I will appreciate your manuscript as soon as you can possibly send it. It is not for myself alone that I ask this. But for the New Negro that they may know a rebirth. And for the newer voices, that we may light their literary way a little.

Sincerely,

Dorothy West

Dear Mr. Johnson,

But as many words as you like! And indeed I do not limit the writer, unless he's a bad writer. So let us say something more than

fifty and less than a thousand. In all seriousness. Because I do want you to hold forth at some length on the things that are dearest to my heart, the eternal beauty of poetry and prose; that it is—if you agree with me—the life-blood of a race.

Scold us a little, I and my contemporaries who did not live up to our fine promise. Urge us to recapture. Though I am not sure I believe in such a thing. All my hopes are in the newer voices. If I can discover one of rare sweetness, it is enough. What I am doing may be a thankless task, you know. But that will make up.

So then let it be an inspirational editorial. Tell us that truth is beauty, and beauty is truth. Tell us to stare at the stars for in so doing we hold our heads high. And if you do not think it will offend my contemporaries too much, caution the younger writers that the majority of us, their literary elders, degenerated thru our vices. And thus we lost our fine vigor. And so we are without illusions while we are still young. Because I believe in the lofty spirit with all my heart.

There you have it. Add or subtract, and by all means elaborate. And know that I am deeply grateful for your interest.

Faithfully,

Dorothy West

Monday

My dear Mr. Johnson,

New Challenge finally appears, and I happy to send you a copy. As you can see, the magazine has been reorganized, and our editorial expresses its aims. We earnestly hope it will be the medium for the progressive Negro writer. This summer Marian Minus and Richard Wright came in as editors. There were several group meetings where we outlined our aims.

It so happened that Claude McKay was invited to and attended our first meeting. We asked his support, but he did not return. Today I received a form letter, signed by Claude, and find that his aims are identical with ours. That is a fine thing in itself. It bespeaks a unity of purpose. But I see no necessity for forming a separate organization if we think so similarly.

Certainly we have given our best to *New Challenge*. And we are sincere in wanting it to be the organ for the young Negro writer, and perhaps the "New Negro"—and I was one—will be revitalized—through this medium. I am only sorry there will be two banners flying, when each needs the support of the other.

I am eager to know what you think of the magazine. I remember that you were good enough to write the editorial for the old *Challenge*. Your encouragement means much. And your criticism and advice will be appreciated.

My love to Mrs. Johnson. And may I see you both sometime soon.

Sincerely,

Dorothy

Anonymous
"Alliance vs. High's Ice Cream"

New Negro Opinion, December 16, 1933[1]

The New Negro Alliance has settled itself down to a "fight to the finish" with the High Ice Cream Company in its effort to secure jobs for colored clerks in the 7th and S Street store.

To date—after two months, during which three unanswered letters were written to the management of the Ice Cream Store, and after two weeks of constant picketing—the store refuses to consider the employment of Negro clerks. The only apparent move in that direction was the placing of a Negro behind the counter for a few hours on Thanksgiving Day, no word concerning which was ever received at the Alliance headquarters.

The objective of the management of any store is the earning of money and to receive a substantial profit on its business. Stores opened in localities essentially colored derive the bulk of their revenue from the patronage of members of the Negro race. It follows then, that the only equitable and honest attitude for the owners or managers of such stores to adopt, is that of consideration, at least, to requests for colored employees. The High Ice Cream Company has shown no such consideration. The Alliance,

therefore, appeals to the entire colored population of the District of Columbia to refuse to spend money with the High Ice Cream Stores until our goal of colored clerks behind their counters has been reached.

This refers especially to the 7th and S Street store as well as the High store located at 1538 North Capitol Street.

It is interesting to note that early in the 7th and S Street picket, a clerk in the store instigated a riot call which resulted in one of our pickets, Howard Fitzhugh, being taken to Number Two Precinct. No action was taken, however, and Mr. Fitzhugh was shortly thereafter released, it having been previously determined pickets were within their rights while so doing. Incidentally, the High clerk was vehemently upbraided for his action in that regard.

The Alliance has no intention of relinquishing the activities in front of the store until Negroes are employed there as clerks. Preparations have been completed for carrying on the fight throughout the winter or as long as is necessary. All colored people with a vestige of race pride will co-operate with the New Negro Alliance in withholding our patronage from the High and other stores refusing to employ Negro clerks. These stores cannot operate without colored support. Let us make them give us a fair return for the money we spend or close their doors!

ALLIANCE PICKETS "COVERING" LOCAL CHAIN STORE
AS WE GO TO PRESS
FLASH! **** 3 Grocery Stores have employed a Negro clerk in their stores in N.W. Washington. **** There will be others.

FLASH AGAIN! * * * * Highs Ice Cream Company is being investigated by the Consumers Advisory Council of the Agricultural Adjustment Administration and the Bakers and Confectioner's Union. Highs accused of paying "Starvation Wages." **** The firm is not under the "Blue Eagle." Negroes, buy where you can work, and work at decent wages.

MORE FLASH! **** Negro white collar workers, at last being included in the C.W.A. [Civil Works Administration] **** One hundred are alleged to have gone to work in the Public Schools, the Recorder's Office and on a national and city survey. **** Negro white collar workers, sign up at 230 3rd Street, and WATCH the daily papers.

F-L-A-S-H! **** Virginia Negroes held unfit for jury service. **** What are YOU going to do about it? ****Once again—JOIN THE ALLIANCE.

Alain Locke

"Sterling Brown: The New Negro Folk-Poet"

In *Negro: An Anthology*, edited by Nancy Cunard, 1934

Many critics, writing in praise of Sterling Brown's first volume of verse, have seen fit to hail him as a significant new Negro poet. The discriminating few go further; they hail a new era in Negro poetry, for such is the deeper significance of this volume (*Southern Road*, Sterling A. Brown, Harcourt Brace, New York, 1932). Gauging the main objective of Negro poetry as the poetic portrayal of Negro folk-life true in both letter and spirit to the idiom of the folk's own way of feeling and thinking, we may say that here for the first time is that much-desired and long-awaited acme attained or brought within actual reach.

Almost since the advent of the Negro poet public opinion has expected and demanded folk-poetry of him. And Negro poets have tried hard and voluminously to cater to this popular demand. But on the whole, for very understandable reasons, folk-poetry by Negroes, with notable flash exceptions, has been very unsatisfactory and weak, and despite the intimacy of the race poet's attachments, has been representative in only a limited, superficial sense. First of all, the demand has been too insistent. "They required of us a song in a strange land." "How could we sing of thee, O Zion?" There was the canker of theatricality and exhibitionism planted at the very heart of Negro poetry, unwittingly no doubt, but just as fatally. Other captive nations have suffered the same ordeal. But with the Negro another spiritual handicap was imposed. Robbed of his own tradition, there was no internal compensation to counter the external pressure. Consequently the Negro spirit had a triple plague on its heart and mind—morbid self-consciousness, self-pity and forced exhibitionism. Small wonder that so much poetry by Negroes exhibits in one degree or another the blights of bombast, bathos and artificiality. Much genuine poetic talent has thus been blighted either by these spiritual faults or their equally vicious over-compensations. And so it is epoch-making to have developed a poet whose work, to quote a recent criticism, "has no taint of music-hall convention, is neither arrogant nor servile"—and plays up to neither side of the racial dilemma. For it is as fatal to true poetry to cater to the self-pity or racial vanity of a persecuted group as to pander to the amusement complex of the overlords and masters.

I do not mean to imply that Sterling Brown's art is perfect, or even completely mature. It is all the more promising that this volume represents the work of a young man just in his early thirties. But a Negro poet with almost complete detachment, yet with a tone of persuasive sincerity, whose muse neither clowns nor shouts, is indeed a promising and a grateful phenomenon.

By some deft touch, independent of dialect, Mr. Brown is able to compose with the freshness and naturalness of folk balladry—*Maumee Ruth, Dark O' the Moon, Sam Smiley, Slim Greer, Johnny Thomas*, and *Memphis Blues* will convince the most skeptical that modern Negro life can yield real balladry and a Negro poet achieve an authentic folk-touch. . . .

. . . [O]ther Negro poets in many ways have been too tender with their own, even though they have learned with the increasing boldness of new Negro thought not to be too gingerly and conciliatory to and about the white man. The Negro muse weaned itself of that in McKay, Fenton Johnson, Toomer, Countee Cullen and Langston Hughes. But in Sterling Brown it has learned to laugh at itself and to chide itself with the same broomstick. I have space for only two examples: *Children's Children*:

> When they hear
> These songs, born of the travail of their sires,
> Diamonds of song, deep buried beneath
>   the weight Of dark and heavy years;
> They laugh.
> They have forgotten, they have never known
> Long days beneath the torrid Dixie sun,
> . . . .
> With their paled faces, coppered lips,
> And sleek hair cajoled to Caucasian
>   straightness,

> Might drown the quiet voice of beauty
> With sensuous stridency;
> And might, on hearing these memories of
>   their sires,
> Giggle,
> And nudge each other's satin-clad
> Sleek sides.

Anent the same broomstick, it is refreshing to read *Mr. Samuel and Sam*, from which we can only quote in part:

> Mister Samuel, he belong to Rotary,
> Sam, to de Sons of Rest;
> Both wear red hats like monkey men,
> An' you cain't say which is de best . . .

> Mister Samuel die, an' de folks all
>   know,
> Sam die widout no noise;
> De Worl' go by in de same ol' way,
> And dey's both of 'em po' los' boys.

There is a world of psychological distance between this and the rhetorical defiance and the plaintive, furtive sarcasms of even some of our other contemporary poets—even as theirs, it must be said in all justice, was miles better and more representative than the sycophancies and platitudes of the older writers.

In closing it might be well to trace briefly the steps by which Negro poetry has scrambled up the sides of Parnassus from the ditches of minstrelsy and the trenches of race propaganda. In complaining against the narrow compass of dialect poetry (dialect is an organ with only two stops—pathos and humor), Weldon Johnson tried to break the Dunbar mould and shake free of the traditional stereotypes. But significant as it was, this was more a threat than an accomplishment; his own dialect poetry has all of the clichés of Dunbar without Dunbar's lilting lyric charm. Later in the *Negro Sermons* Weldon Johnson discovered a way out—in a rhapsodic form free from the verse shackles of classical minor poetry, and in the attempt to substitute an idiom of racial thought and imagery for a mere dialect of peasant speech. Claude McKay then broke with all the moods conventional in his day in Negro poetry, and presented a Negro who could challenge and hate, who knew resentment, brooded intellectual sarcasm, and felt contemplative irony. In this, so to speak, he pulled the psychological cloak off the Negro and revealed, even to the Negro himself, those facts disguised till then by his shrewd protective mimicry or pressed down under the dramatic mask of living up to what was expected of him. But though McKay sensed a truer Negro, he was at times too indignant at the older sham, and, too, lacked the requisite native touch—as of West Indian birth and training—with the local color of the American Negro. Jean Toomer went deeper still—I should say higher—and saw for the first time the glaring paradoxes and the deeper ironies of the situation, as they affected not only the Negro but the white man. He realized, too, that Negro idiom was anything but trite and derivative, and also that it was in emotional substance pagan—all of which he convincingly demonstrated, alas, all too fugitively, in *Cane*. But Toomer was not enough of a realist, or patient enough as an observer, to reproduce extensively a folk idiom.

Then Langston Hughes came with his revelation of the emotional color of Negro life, and his brilliant discovery of the flow and rhythm of the modern and especially the city Negro, substituting this jazz figure and personality for the older plantation stereotype. But it was essentially a jazz version of Negro life, and that is to say as much American, or more, as Negro; and though fascinating and true to an epoch this version was surface quality after all.

Sterling Brown, more reflective, a closer student of the folk-life, and above all a bolder and more detached observer, has gone deeper still, and has found certain basic, more sober and more persistent qualities of Negro thought and feeling; and so has reached a sort of common denominator between the old and the new Negro. Underneath the particularities of one generation are hidden universalities which only deeply penetrating genius can fathom and bring to the surface. Too many of the articulate intellects of the Negro group—including sadly enough the younger poets—themselves children of opportunity, have been unaware of these deep resources of the past. But here, if anywhere, in the ancient common wisdom of the folk, is the real treasure trove of the Negro poet; and Sterling Brown's poetic divining-rod has dipped significantly over this position. It is in this sense that I believe *Southern Road* ushers in a new era in Negro folk-expression and brings a new dimension in Negro folk-portraiture.

Alvaro de Lugo

"An Essay on the Negro"

Virgin Islands Daily News, February 20, 1934[2]

Postmaster, St. Thomas

Beyond the dim and distant centuries of antiquity, a race of men founded and developed a civilization which flourished and gave birth to many of our sciences of today. That race, besides being distinguished by its marked intelligence and high culture, was further identified by the darkness of its skin pigmentation, and by its curly black hair.

The Negro of today is the progeny of that intellectual and cultured race of antiquity. It is to that, rather should the new Negro look, than to the near yesterday of shackled physical slavery from which his master's awakening freed him.

In considering history, these questions arises [*sic*]: How did this ancient Race lose the fundamentals and glory of its civilization? How did intellectuality become a minor note in this Race? How did a nation, which by virtue of its high intelligence and developed culture became a world leader of its time, degenerate, disintegrate, and fall so low through the ages, that today its descendants, just stepped out of physical slavery must now face the problem of freeing themselves from intellectual, economic and political slavery? Must [we] fight an up hill fight against the constant vicissitudes of sanctioned ostracism and discrimination in all phases of human endeavour but the lowliest? How could the tides of time and human misfortune so ruthlessly and almost completely obliterate the glory of that Race which taught Aristotle his first principles: who were more concerned and accomplished in the trepanning of an ailing skull than in bludgeoning one on the battle field? Sargon, Darius, Alexander and before them the horde of war-loving Asiatic barbarians, who but for the silence of the grave might explain they c[o]nstantly converged their greedy f[o]rces on that Race, their sole object the spoils of victory, spoils in monetary wealth, precious stones, master pieces of art, fertile valleys and human flesh to sweat in the toils of slavery. More than all else, the new Negro should detest war.

It might have been greed for power, bringing about an internal cataclysm and shaking that civilization from its very foundation. It might have been corruption in high places arising from greed for wealth, destroying the altruism which marked their art and scientific victories. Probably religious fanaticism had something to do with it, or it might have been any or all of a thousand causes that brought about the down fall of that Nation and Race whose progeny is so sorely stepped on today. The Sphinx and the Pyramids, silent sentinels of Time, could tell us if only they would speak. These are reasonable questions answerable only by reasonable conjectures and may ever remain so.

But this we do know: That it was not with the discovery and settlement of America or even with the Roman rise to world dominance and power that Negro slavery started. History gives us the evidence of the flower of the Race, a Nation with Macedonian conquerors and the Macedonian rulers raping its civilization where the Persians and other Asiatics left off.

The history we are better acquainted with is that of yesterday. It is one of the sufferings of a people abused and maltreated and hated for being the victims of that abuse and maltreatment. That, the Negro must remember only as a bad dream. It must be pushed to the background so that the today and the tomorrow may stand out. Hatred and resentment should have no place in the mind of the Race, for that is the way back. We are seeking the way through the hidden future. It is the future with which we are concerned, and looking back on the yesterday does not go to make the tomorrow any easier except in so much as it shows us the errors of yesterday. . . .

Perhaps no greater mental degeneration can be imagined than that of Negroes despising for being Negroes. This condition altogether too prevalent, is a direct result of vicious propaganda eminating [*sic*] from a source well known to the informed. Its sole object is easily discerned as an attempt (and it has been very successful in the past) to prevent the possibility of Race solidarity by setting up grievances between the various shades of Negroes, based upon the degree of density of pigmentation. Those poor souls guilty of being injected with this particularly venemous [*sic*] propaganda, are, unknowingly to themselves, despised even by the every source of the propaganda. They should be pitied rather than railed at. Perhaps it is proper at this point to quote Maceo, the great Cuban Negro patriot who said, "The Negro will be ashamed to be a Negro until he stops being ashamed to be black."

Race solidarity and fixity of purpose, a phrase so easily glossed over and little understood, contains the certainties of a quickened process in political recognition and the fruits thereof. This makes for opportunities the Negro might tirelessly wait for and may never otherwise obtain. Racial-political solidarity is compensated by an equal amount of political recognition, and no one is more fully aware and well acquainted with the fact of it[s] significance than those Negroes who have earned a high place in the administration of our government.

Amenophis, Hannibal, Dumas, Pushkin, Douglass, etc., of past eras and Washington, Du Bois, Carter, Dett, Haines, etc., of today are the beacon lights from which the Negro will draw his inspiration. And not losing sight of the setback, and the problems of unreasoning prejudice which dogs the Negro's footsteps, and despite the encumbrance of doubt in his own ability subtely [*sic*] drilled into him, he is well on the road to his place in the sun. It must not be taken for granted that he has arrived. The untraveled road contains many pitfalls which he will have to hurdle.

New Negro Alliance
"Program of the New Negro Alliance"

New Negro Opinion, September 22, 1934

Program of the New Negro Alliance

To improve the economic and civic status of the Negro through:

1. The securing of positions which will increase the earning capacity of our group.
2. The securing of opportunities for advancement and promotion in positions secured.
3. The uniting of the purchasing power of the Colored people to be used as a lever in securing economic advantages.
4. The creation of bigger and better Negro business through increased earning power of Negroes, through a better business outlook resulting from contact and experience with successful businesses of the other group, and through the stimulation of businesses now run by Negroes to higher levels of efficiency and service.
5. The concentrated support of all businesses which employ Negroes or in which Negro capital is invested.
6. Research and investigation which will discover and thoroughly analyze the possibilities for Negro Business and Negro labor in new fields.

New Negro Opinion masthead, August 25, 1934. Anacostia Community Museum Archives, Smithsonian Institution.

Clister L. Johnson
"The New Deal, the New Year, the New Negro"

Afro-American Courier, January 1, 1936[3]

For nearly three years we have been living under a new kind of Government—The New Deal. I call it a new kind of Government for it is difficult for me to determine whether it is a Democratic, Autocratic, or Plutocratic form of Government. During the year just passed the five hundred men and women elected to make legislation for them passed a bill—one man knocked it out of existence, then nine men nullified a law that this one man has made. These things actually did happen in 1935. Congress passed the Patman Bonus Bill. The President vetoed it; then the Supreme Court declared the President's N.R.A. [National Recovery Administration] unconstitutional. Regardless of what kind of government it is we can say that we have come a long way towards national prosperity since the New Deal was put in action. Although many experts declare it is a "sham" prosperity. We who are not economists and Government scientists can only take it as it appears and as we feel it, since the beginning of the New Deal thousands of idle have been put to work, homes have been saved from mortgages, illiterates have decreased, schools have been repaired and erected and many other improvements made that I will not take time to mention. Despite the apparent success of the Roosevelt Administration, it has received more bitter attacks than did the Hoover regime and much of the criticism has come from the Democratic ranks. Headed by the late Senator Long, Governor Eugene Talmage and the former presidential candidate, Al Smith, criticism of the New Deal has been incessant. Even former N.R.A. head Gen. Hugh Johnson does not agree with some of the principles of the New Deal.

With the coming of the New Year the New Deal will get its final test. It has been tested by the Supreme Court but this year it is to be tested by the American people at the Polls. Will President Roosevelt be given a chance to carry on his New Deal policies for four more years? Or will the Government be turned over to a new administration in the midst of these new American experiments? These questions will be answered before 1936 has passed. At present it appears a certainty that President Roosevelt will be nominated as Democratic standard bearer again, but whether he will win in the November 6, election remains a question—a great question. A recent poll of the 48 states by the Literary Digest shows over sixty percent of the people are not in favor of the New Deal. These Polls made in the past by the Digest have been very dependable. As I see it there are one or two Republicans who would make a very good run in the election. Governor Landon of Kansas and Senator Borah of Idaho (Senator Borah has already made the statement that he would never sign the Wagner Anti Lynch bill). Both are bidding strong for the nomination. It is very evident in President Roosevelt's speech last night to the joint session of Congress that whoever wins, the Democratic party is going to put up a great battle.

What effect will the New Year have on the New Negro? I use the term "New Negro" for we are no longer a helpless and receptive race of people, but we have awakened to realize our place in this civilization and our duty to our race and our God. The New Deal has given this New Negro a better chance to develop than any other administration. Under the New Deal several Negroes have received high government appointments, illiteracy has decreased among us, our schools have been repaired and new ones erected and the idle have been put to work. The Negro has figured in every piece of New Deal legislation even though prejudice and tradition did come to the front in putting this legislation in action in some localities.

If the New Deal is returned to power the Negro's further progress is assured, but if the

Old regime is successful our future will be in doubt. Regardless of who wins the Senator from Idaho is least wanted by the Negro; stand by and all watch what effect the New Year will have on the New Deal and the New Negro.

~~~~~~

Frank R. Crosswaith

"The Future Is Ours"

Black Worker, August 1, 1936[4]

General Organizer, I.L.G.W.U. Chairman, Negro Labor Com.

It is with a deep and sincere sense of personal, race and class pride, that I join in the salvo of thrice-merited salutation to the officers and members of the Brotherhood of Sleeping Car Porters on the occasion of their 11th Anniversary.

The story of American labor, like the struggle of the world's workers, is replete with examples of courage, heroism and sacrifice in the face of the callous stubbornness and cruelty of the organized exploiters of labor. Albeit, the page written by the Negro Pullman Porters is one that will continue to stand out in the annals of labor like an illuminated meteor in a dark and starless night. The soldiers of labor's cause must never be permitted to forget that fateful August night eleven years ago, when enveloped by the suffocating heat of a summer's night and the stifling smoke from a hundred cigars, cigarettes and a few pipes, several hundred Pullman Porters defiantly threw down the gauntlet of battle to the nation's mightiest industrial monarch— The Pullman Company.

Demonstrating a courage hitherto unsuspected among Negroes in industrial warfare, these men at that meeting launched a crusade that has won for them the plaudits of their race the respect of their employer and the gratitude of all labor. "They fired a shot" that literally was heard "around the world." It was the Pullman Porters Union which did more than any other group of workers in America to awaken the labor movement to the serious menace of the Company Union. Until the porters turned upon this modern device of industrial tyranny the pitiless light of publicity and exposed to public scorn and ridicule the soulless carcass of "the Employee Representation Plan," American labor, by and large, was inclined to underestimate the evil. Today the Company Union in all of its disguises is known as the evil incarnate it is; a dragon to be beheaded whenever and wherever it raises its nefarious head or discloses its poisonous fangs.

That The Pullman Company would fight every inch of the way to protect and preserve its hitherto uncontested privilege of waxing wealthy at the expense of the unsuspecting Negro, was expected by the leaders of the Pullman Porters Union; also, that the Company was a foe rich, powerful, influential and a seasoned veteran in the class war was well known to these leaders. And so from the outset, the porter's fight took the turn not merely of a group of workers seeking to organize as a necessary first step to a higher standard of wages and work conditions, but a fight involving the manhood, womanhood and self respect of the Negro group. Although the Company was able to reach a few professional Negro leaders in political, religious and educational life, even these were powerless to stem the conquering spiritual tide which the campaign unleashed. No form of terror and intimidation was effective to stem this tide. The threatened lynching of Bennie Smith in Florida not only did not scare or lessen the ardor of the Union, but instead fired the souls of the members to a new heat and steeled their will to win. Attempted bribery, assault, open and covert intimidation and discharge of the more fearless porters, all failed of their desired effect upon the porters and the leaders of their Union. Thus a New Negro was fashioned in the crucible of industrial conflict. The old Negro was no more. A new day had dawned and black American labor was definitely moving out of the shadows of social and economic slavery into the lighted path that leads to power and pride regained.

Considered in the light of the modern problems predicated upon a highly mechanized industrial order, concentrated wealth and intensified class antagonisms, the organized Negro Pullman Porters have done more for their race that all the noble efforts of all the Negro rebels during the days of yesterday's slavery. But the Brotherhood must not yet rest content upon the laurels of past achievements for the fight is not yet won nor is our victory yet complete.

In ever increasing numbers, Negroes are leaving the old cotton fields and tobacco plantations of the South and finding a place in modern industry. These kinsmen of ours must not only be organized into the union of their trade, but they must have an instrumentality with which to fight for complete equality of treatment within the organized labor movement. Facing the problems of race, nationality and sex prejudice among workers, Jewish, Italian and women proletarians developed their own agency and today these groups receive more consideration than does the Negro. Given the full and sympathetic support it deserves, the Negro Labor Committee will serve the Negro worker as the United Hebrew Trades, the Italian Chamber of Labor and the Women's Trade Union League serve their respective group.

Upon every hand are potent signs indicating the march of Fascism, Hitlerism and other foes of civilized progress. In the fight against these evils, the Negro must find his place. As the economic system of private monopoly and human exploitation continues to demonstrate its unworkability, the danger to all our democratic institutions becomes more obvious. In the fight to preserve our gains and win for the working masses everywhere the full social value of the labor, the Negro worker must play an heroic part. Led and inspired by the examples of the Brotherhood and its fearless leader, Negro labor will lay upon the sepulchre of economic and social despotism a wreath woven from the fragrant roses of struggle during the years since August, 1925.

In the future as in the past, I doff my hat to the Brotherhood and hail its officers and members in the grand and glorious comradeship of the workers' world which we who work must ourselves build.

Forward Builders, the future is ours.

Gustavo E. Urrutia

"Puntos de Vista del Nuevo Negro" (Points of View of the New Negro)

Lecture, Instituto Nacional de Prevision Y Reformas Sociales, July 8, 1937[5]

Translated by Thomas Holloway

First of a series of lectures on social, scientific, and educational issues, sponsored by the National Institute for Welfare and Social Reform, at its Study Center, on July 8, 1937

Worthy audience:

The first time I gave what I thought might be a lecture was at the Universidad del Aire, of fond memory, around mid-1933. After suffering the panic the microphone imposes on most of those new to radio, and then receiving the

Portrait of Gustavo E. Urrutia, dedicated to Langston Hughes, March 7, 1930. Courtesy of the Langston Hughes Collection, Beinecke Library, Yale University.

solemn congratulations common on such occasions, a gentleman in the studio audience extended his hand, with a silent smile, and called me aside. Smiling more broadly, he said, "[Y]ou're a journalist, right? Well then, what you've just read to us is a long article. But don't be discouraged. I guarantee that someday you will write a lecture." He then left quietly without giving me a time frame for that miracle to occur.

It has been four years since that friendly piece of advice, and I don't think I've advanced at all in the art of lecturing. Quite the contrary, which is why honesty obliges me to warn you that what I'm about to read is also not a lecture, and not even a long article like that first attempt. It is a sort of weaving together of notes for a more complete report. If anyone in the audience, after kindly listening to what I have to say, feels moved to confirm that I have progressed backwards, I will be as grateful for that as for your willingness to tolerate me to the end. If that happens, I will say farewell to the lecture hall tonight. It will not be the first time I will have yielded to the impossible.

And if, ladies and gentlemen, despite knowing my limitations, I am here with my text prepared, it is for one reason: the importance of the topic, the urgent need to call attention to the points of view of the New Negro, as they bear on the complex issue of race relations in the broader Cuban context. And what better place for this than the opportunity so kindly offered by the Study Center of the National Institute for Welfare and Social Reform, and an audience such as yourselves, so accustomed to mental discipline? I might also suggest that the problem of race relations, which for far too long has been suppressed by the taboo of pseudo patriotic sentiment, enters this hall stripped of all impassioned flutter.[6] It is placed within a rigorous intellectual framework like any of the other social problems studied in the enlightened institute that has honored me with its hospitality today.

It is certainly the case that I have always dealt with the subject on that intellectual level, devoid of any trace of bitterness, whether at the lectern, in the press, or in my most intimate thoughts. I don't mean to deny that the question of race, like all social problems and most questions of human interaction, is fraught with difficult emotions. But at the same time, these racial situations, which are usually the effect rather than the cause, are subject to a series of remote and inexorable imperatives which are the result of past historical development, and of the laws of human progress in its successive development toward the future. Such imperatives definitely rule over the will of men and social groups. They modify causes and effects, adjusting them to the objective conditions of a present that is constantly evolving toward progress. In order to fruitfully analyze the effects of those overarching and superhuman imperatives, and their determinant forces, we must discard all passions, which only obscure and confuse our understanding. We must take an approach that is strictly intellectual, philosophical, and technical, using the methods of modern social science. This dispassionate and thoughtful attitude is precisely what the New Negro adopts in order to confront the problem of race relations. This gives the New Negro his calm state of mind, his firm immunity to the blows of negrophobia and the flattery of negrophilia, his self-reliance and mental toughness. Finally, it is the source of his optimistic vision of a time in the relatively near future when race might cease to be a problem because it will have lost its reason for existence; in other words, the vision of a future in which racial prejudice would be as absurd and incongruous as black slavery would be for the today's economic system.

But before going on, it would be appropriate to define this "New Negro" more specifically—this sort of "New Deal," if you will.

The New Negro is the Afro-Cuban—male or female, young or old[7]—who has reached the conclusion that our existing liberal democracy is unable on its own to overcome the subordination and socio-economic devaluation of people of color that we have inherited from our history as a slave colony. The current regime is incapable of overcoming the great disadvantages suffered by the Cuban proletariat and middle class, where the whole of the colored race is located.

The New Negro is someone who has overcome the inferiority complex imposed on him by the burden of slavery. He no longer persists in asking for social and economic equality based on his enormous historical contribution of patriotism and labor in the development of Cuba and the Republic. He has, however, developed a thorough understanding of that honorable contribution, so that he feels fully worthy of such equality in the past, in the present, and in the great work that the future holds for progressive Cubans. He is aware not only of his significance in the past and what he means for his Cuban homeland today, but also of the African Negro's place in the historical progress of the West, and since the Great War, the significance of the Negro for international equilibrium, world peace, and thus for the survival of Western civilization—as we will see in the course of this lecture.

The New Negro is not subject to the various definitions of blacks provided by his white friends and foes. Rather, he begins by defining his own self, and by having his own definition of others, as would be the case for any rational and educated person.

The New Negro of Cuba is an Afro-Cuban who studies our race problem with a clinical eye and a philosophical mind, devoid of any genuine racism, even if it were only a reflection or reaction against white racism. In this talk I hope to be able to explain, as I have explained in the press, my reasons for believing that the Negro in the Americas, and especially in Cuba, has no good reason to feel he is racist.

The New Negro, finally, is the Afro-Cuban who no longer thinks of his fellow white citizen as a big brother, and who sees the racist white Cuban as a biased and malevolent brother. He takes this attitude without rancor, but with the caution necessary to counteract the noxious effects of white racism on the good Cuban character. As for the progressive and revolutionary white Cuban, revolutionary in the most noble sense of the term, the New Negro loves him like a twin brother and as a comrade in the struggle for objectives both national and human.

This is the New Negro, who has emerged from the confusion in which his race and the rest of the Cuban lower classes were submerged, caused by the failure of our revolutionary struggles to achieve true democracy. He has again found his way, with the understanding that even genuine liberal democracy would not be able to guarantee collective economic and social justice, because it is essentially individualistic and plutocratic. He has pointed himself toward the promotion of some form of socialism—of the left for most people—compatible with our own character and our international relations.[8]

Does this make the New Negro arrogant? Instead of the New Negro, have we given birth to the New Pedant? Does he think he's the lord and master of the only truth? Was he born out of social upheaval or breakdown? Does he scorn the old Negro, his peers, the whites of the past and today? Is he stubborn, imperious, or rebellious?

No, certainly not. He is nurtured by history, and is filled with true scientific and philosophical humility. He knows that he owes his civil and political freedom to historically derived principles of western economics and politics, not from largesse or penitence. But for all that, he values the good work of the abolitionists, and the fraternal integrity of genuinely revolutionary white people in all times. (He denies that status to the pseudo revolutionaries of the past and today.) He acknowledges the legacy of white culture as well as black culture, and feels admiration for the efforts of his black ancestors, in the most adverse conditions, to raise him to the level of enlightenment and culture he now enjoys. The New Negro knows he is nothing more, after all, than the most recent version of the noble, edifying, patriotic, and brotherly spirit the Afro-Cuban has always had. He also knows that he currently finds himself in a time of mental and political transformation. That's why we are used to hearing him think out loud. That's why we commonly see him as polemical. He is trying to explain his position. He is convinced for certain that our national problems—including racial problems—cannot be solved by blacks alone or by whites alone.[9] While he develops and expounds his own ideas, he also seeks to present them to society at large for collective approval by all of Cuba, whose support he will need for the great task in which he is engaged. I owe my presence here this evening to that position, in an effort to explain the mindset of the New Negro, to substantiate his points of view. And I am prepared to answer any questions you might have at the end, as long as they are not too erudite. The Afro-Cuban has no external reasons to feel racist. He aspires to eliminate all racial discrimination. Be that as it may, the New Negro begins by identifying as black. The creation of such a specific mental autonomy, of group identity, does not constitute any lamentable lapse in either logic or tactics.

On the contrary, such a perspective is based on the reality that black people suffer economically and socially because of their race. Thus they need to reach a deep and perfect understanding of their position in Cuban society, on their own terms, in order to come up with ideas that might contribute to a solution to those problems, and specifically the problem of racial discrimination. Blacks then need to merge their own ideas with those of progressive whites, and develop a set of policies that would have a common philosophy, set of goals, and plans for achieving those objectives. More than once I have said that where discrimination exists, to achieve *racial indifferentiation* it is necessary to begin by specifying and defining the differences that exist, in order to be able to eliminate them. It is not a question of erasing biological differences, but making them innocuous.[10] This process of developing a preliminary and transitory racialized perspective, however, is one of the most difficult challenges for the very delicate mission of the New Negro, because on the one hand he is diligently seeking solutions to problems of social justice that are floating around in the world, and on the other hand because the Negro is, after all, the last person who should become addicted to racism.

When the New Negro becomes the channel for his own values and mobilizes them for the good of the community, defining for himself what the Negro means for Cuba and the world, the process of spiritual self determination will begin.[11]

*   *   *

In order to specify these ideas more concretely, we can designate the topic just mentioned as the first point of view of the New Negro: What is the significance of the black African in the global context, and what do the slavery of the past and the Afro-Cuban descendants of slaves mean for our nation? The answers will tell us why the New Negro has overcome the inferiority complex with regard to the black roots of his ancestry.

Although it may not be widely known, the fact is that the African continent and its people constitute the deep and solid foundation on which the world's economic, political, and military balance rests—and in latent form, the social problem such a balance implies. Those two factors, territories and people, were the underlying causes of the Great War. Because of them, Germany did not succeed in crushing France before the United States arrived to support the Allied Powers. Those two factors are the object of imperialistic greed, and a major shift in the distribution of colonial territories might precipitate another universal war, which is brewing precisely for control of Africa.

It seems that African territories are the only ones virtually unclaimed, where land can be taken with the least concern for violating the international code of ethics; where the people, due to their naïveté,[12] are the easiest to subjugate. This combination of weaknesses constitutes a constant temptation for those set on conquest, through diplomacy or war, and it is the weakest point in the precarious postwar situation.

After suppressing the transatlantic slave trade to suit its own interests, England made a discovery that was as important for world politics and economics as the great feat of Christopher Columbus. British merchant genius discovered that the servitude and slavery that still existed within Africa itself could be more profitable than transporting the labor force to other parts of the world. Western nations then came to colonize Africa as they had in the New World: in the name of Civilization. This dictum, of course, does not suggest any malicious intent when it is applied exclusively to the rise of civilization in Europe, although eventually the excess of civilizing zeal would stir up the sordid economic rivalries that provoked the most astounding slaughter in history—the World War.

England, France, Belgium, Germany, Italy, Portugal, Spain—all used their colonies to feed industrialization until in most of those nations it reached monstrous and heartless proportions. Market competition required that maximum advantage had to be squeezed from the human and natural resources of Africa. The European nations had to be ready for war to defend their positions and possessions, and to be vigilant for the opportunity to snatch what they could from any adversary. War industries and financial capital expanded as never before. The western plutocracies needed war on a grand scale to empty their warehouses and expand credit.

According to Burghardt Du Bois, Bismarck wanted the Congo Free State for Germany, and even after the death of the great chancellor Germany dreamed of an African empire which would include the Congo, half of the Portuguese colonial territories, and all of the French, to become the largest and strongest colonial power in Africa, which is to say the greatest world power. The eminent Afro-American sociologist states that Germany entered the war, in the course of which it was pushed out of Africa entirely, with those goals in mind.

At this perilous juncture France stopped the formidable German invasion, reinforcing their army with black troops, who were quickly recruited by all possible means—by the draft, by deception, by disguised coercion—and thrown into the horrible butchery. This new source of manpower was as surprising and effective as the German gas attacks.

Centuries ago Spain discovered a new continent where they could bring black labor to be exploited. England then invented the exploitation of that labor force in the land of the blacks itself. And more recently France introduced a new type of weapon in modern warfare: black Africans. They were novel for their military nerve, their boldness, and for their fierce heroism. They were a new factor that had never before figured in the European military balance of power. For France they meant a considerable increase in troop strength, making its armies more formidable. France put 673,000 Africans on the battlefield, in 1933 they had 1,600,000 colored troops, and today God only knows how many there are.

But these new developments have created a serious problem for those who benefit from Imperialism in Africa, and reveal an aspect of the so-called "black peril." How to counteract this unforeseen black force?

None of the other colonial powers can count on a similar source of manpower in Africa. No other European country occupies such a favorable geographical and strategic position in the Old Continent. Only France has colonies situated and prepared for such immediate and complete military and economic advantage. And now, how to head off the certain threat of an even greater influx of black French troops in the next Great War? Alliances with or against France have not managed to reduce the anxieties this gigantic innovation has provoked.

The most dramatic issue for the whites is not so much the military threat and the still irreconcilable attitude of France toward Germany. It is, rather, the threat that this introduction of African forces, initiated and now maintained by the French on a permanent basis, represents for the global hegemony of the white race. The result could be that France, pressed to guarantee the friendly cooperation of its colonies, might have to grant them a greater measure of human and political rights than they now have.

The white world had always counted on the absolute submission of the darker races, based on its own military power and industrial efficiency, and considering the lack of unity of the colored world, its babel of languages, and the immense diversity of its religions. If now a certain group of whites seeks the support of blacks, ceding to them even a minimum of prerogatives in return, the white world gets nervous, sullen, and stubborn to the core. This state of mind and attitude is similar to that of our own slaveholders, when the whites fighting for independence in 1868 and 1895 sought the cooperation of black Cubans in exchange for recognizing equal civil and political rights—which was all they could offer, since our revolutions did not imply fundamental economic or social change.

But on the other hand, it so happens that France is also a first rank industrial power engaged in a difficult battle for hegemony in the new Western Europe. How then, to deal with its African colonies? Should it be based on the merciless exploitation of the black population, as England does, in order to compete with them? By developmental policies benefiting the colonies, in exchange for military cooperation? To what point would the French investors and captains of industry put up with such economic sacrifice?

For France and the other industrialized imperialist powers, this whole matter is a problem for the whites. But there is no doubt that it is also a matter for the blacks. It follows that the black race cannot be left out of the discussion. Although the majority of black Africans live in the wild—by which I mean they are dwellers of the forest, not barbarians[13]—there are millions of native Africans and blacks born in the continental Americas and the Antilles, who are sufficiently knowledgeable to take interest in a full and fair solution.

We have a situation, then, in which, due to his decisive military contribution to the war effort, the black African has earned a reputation for military prowess, rather than for less positive qualities, in the future of western civilization—in its economic, political, social, and military aspects—not much less than the status and military prowess of the blondest of the Nordic peoples.

*   *   *

But what? Is that all the black African is good for? Can we applaud a new invasion of the barbarians? Is it great or honorable to serve as cannon fodder or attack dog?

We civilized westerners need to look at this matter carefully, so that we don't ignore its implications. In the first place, and despite more or less sophisticated ideas to the contrary, brute force, the law of strongest, so-called military prowess, continue to dominate our western world. Secondly, we have already seen that black soldiers from Africa, by their military support for the French metropole, are gaining advantages for their land and their race. But beyond that, and somewhat to the surprise of many people, the reality is that black Africa has a level of culture—literary, religious, artistic, musical, poetic, and social—which is in no way inferior to that of certain oriental peoples who have acquired prestige in those fields.

We will need to back up these assertions, and what we will see later with regard to the contribution of the black Cuban to our nation and our culture, because these elements are the essence of the mental attitude of the New Negro. His other points of view require less argumentation because they are simply the results of these basic premises, and because they deal with topics that are more familiar because they have been and continue to be part of our own lives.

What would be more important for characterizing the contribution of the black race to human progress, that a number of notable blacks have distinguished themselves within white civilization by their intellectual activities, art, holiness, and heroism; or that for more than twenty years western civilization has been nurturing its artistic essence on black art? More simply put, would it be that the Negro is a contributor to white culture, or that he participates in guiding its emotive core?

The individual achievements of blacks within white civilization of course repudiate the idea that they are inherently inferior, but that doesn't raise the status of the black race as a whole. Successful blacks are still considered to be subordinates who adapt to white culture, are a product of it, or at best are seen as evidence of the magical effect of white culture even on those who are considered to be inferior beings. In contrast, the fact that modern white civilization has voluntarily accepted inspiration from the artistic spirit of black culture, a phenomenon that is not considered to be aesthetic degeneration, is recognition and confirmation that black culture shares the first ranks of the artistic cultures of the world. So we see that the Negro is not the intelligent monkey, the domesticated and tamed new arrival from Africa, nor the mixed-race person redeemed from presumed inferiority by a few drops of someone else's blood. Instead, he is the teacher of his own race and the white race, the creator of beauty, the source of a pure art—as pure as the Greek, the Egyptian, or the Chinese.

We all recognize the prominence of jazz and the spirituals in the world.[14] Less well known is the recent renewal of European and American art, where the master works—not the eyesores—of the vanguard in sculpture, literature, and music are inspired by the sensibilities and rhythms of ancient African sculpture. Many people are repulsed by an African mask or sculpture because we want it to show us what it does not: an ideal of physical beauty or some moral, intellectual, or expressive quality. Our aesthetic attitude is therefore incapable of perceiving its *purely* artistic quality. I'm not saying "merely" artistic, but "purely" artistic. Its predominant qualities are the sculptural design, overall harmony, unexpected variations and contrasts, and the rhythmic sequences that satisfy the urge of all human beings for a sense of cadence. But to appreciate these qualities we must put aside our usual way of contemplating a sculpture—as an anatomical reproduction or expressive document—in order to perceive only its artistic message.

The sculptors of all great traditions in the past went beyond natural anatomical features, accentuating certain elements and eliminating others to turn their creations into true works of art. The distortions in African art that leave many viewers perplexed also exist in the sculpture of Ancient Greece, Egypt, and China. In black sculpture, however, the alterations are freer and go further, and are thus more amazing, richer in rhythmic variations, just as the rhythms of black music are infinitely richer than those of European music.

This richness and variety of rhythmic harmony is what has distinguished ancient African art, and places it alongside the greatest achievements of past cultures. The sculpture of ancient Africa was certainly not the work of a barbarous people, because before the invasion of Africa by the Portuguese in the sixteenth century, only a small part of the African population was in a primitive state. Their sculpture was the manifestation of a stable and organized way of life, adapted to its environment, and therefore capable of developing a natural and authentic mode of artistic expression.

All this justifies the enthusiasm of modern critics for the exotic art of Africa. More than twenty years ago, when western art was threatened with a decline into a state of orthodox formalism and eclecticism, similar to what happened to Italian art in the sixteenth century, the treasures of African art were recovered from anthropologists and antiquarians, who had reserved them for their purely scientific interest. They served as new influences on recent creations in art, music, and poetry, which have profoundly affected European and American civilization.

According to the American critic Albert C. Barnes, of the Barnes Foundation, any intelligent observer can discover black motifs in the painting and sculpture of the modern masters—Picasso, Matisse, Modigliani, Lipchitz, Soutine, and others. In the music of the famous group of French composers known as "The Six"—Satie, Auric, Honegger, Milhaud, Poulenc, and Tailleferre—the black spirit is incorporated into the representative forms of the most refined musical culture. Many of the best works of Stravinsky are in the same category. Diaghilev, director of the famous Ballets Russes, created his best dance pieces by blending the spirit of African sculpture with the essence of the music of Russian ballet.

The poetry and prose of Guillaume, Apollinaire, Jean Cocteau, Max Jacob, Blaise Cendrars, and Riverdi are also fundamentally black in their emotional content and expressive forms. The creations of the noted Parisian fashion designer Paul Poiret are influenced by his contact with black sculpture. In the 1925 Exposition of Decorative Arts in Paris, the prevalence of black motifs in the truly innovative work of the decorative artists of all nations was impressive. In Europe and America the posters that are capturing public attention are clearly inspired by primitive black sculpture. Today's creative artists openly recognize all these great and extensive influences—in painting, sculpture, music, poetry, literature, decorative arts.

Mr. Barnes also says that despite its quality, this sculpture has not been fully appreciated by the public, and even the spirituals have only recently been recognized. He adds that as black art becomes more widely known, the hope grows that the arrogance of the white race might be tamped down, and that the miserable feeling of inferiority among blacks might be put to rest—both of which are so damaging to the well-being of the two races.

For the New Negro, the highest aspiration of the modern black person should be to harmonize the essences of white culture with those of black culture, to achieve an integration that transcends them both.

* * *

As for Cuba itself, what has been the role of the African and Afro-Cuban ancestors of the New Negro? What have they taught him? What is his, and our homeland's, debt to them?

Understanding is the greatest quality that black people have contributed to our national character—intuitive, rational understanding. This explains, in sum, the intelligent attitude of the black race from our African ancestors to the people of today, an attitude of constant cooperation in the development of Cuba in all times and circumstances, however adverse they may have been; a calm spirit, self denial, sacrifice, all enlightened by a clear vision of the future; longing for a future that has not yet arrived, but which fills our pure soul and lets us look on the past without sadness nor resentment. Resentment against whom? Against the history of humankind? Isn't it better to have a simpler past one can feel satisfied with?

Of course, the black African did not come to Cuba as a tourist. But it's also clear that neither casual arrivals nor any "desirable immigration" produced more benefits for our country. Black slavery in Cuba may not have the most barbaric in the Americas, but it was hard for our ancestors, and it still affects our sensibilities as cultured people.

But both they and we understand the clearly romantic mission of black people in the New World. We are the bedrock of civilization in the Americas. We made this continent productive; from here we revived the decrepit life of Europe. We were the source of worldwide renewal. With our pain we made slavery detestable. We were the proof of the economic error of labor in chains. We spread the love of freedom through the colonies, and gave them the resources and courage to gain their independence. We have injected the negroid element into the psychological makeup of the Americas, firmly linking our spirits. And as passive educators, teaching by example, as those who suffer from it, we are showing the absurdity of race and color prejudice. This conduct is more eloquent and effective than any arguments we could bring to bear against such prejudice. All these lessons, all these notable services, were accomplished in the Americas by a minority of African slaves and their descendants with exemplary stoicism, and in the perverse conditions of which we are all aware.

Nevertheless, the Negro feels no debt to the white man for any of this. The Negro feels as though, by an order from on high, he was brought from Africa to carry out an exalted mission, like a biblical tribe torn from its homeland to teach the world a lesson. And he thanks God for choosing him, and for the fact that in the history of the Americas there is not a single page he should feel ashamed of. By being thus separated from their original tribes, the great peoples of the world were reconstituted, with no return to their former groups. But what's more, we have given soul and vitality not to one people, but to a new world, merging with it to remain forever, like a tacit and firm emotive resource. Our blood and spirit will be able to divide into infinitesimal particles through society, but every person will carry these characteristics within themselves, and we will continue to be integrated forever.

It is not strange that rational understanding should reveal these truths to us Negroes today. But it is a thing of wonder that our ancestors, both Africans and those born here, enslaved and uneducated, intuitively understood this transcendental destiny, and behaved in ways that began the journey, and make it possible for us to continue.

The Cuban slave was a hard worker. He tended the land like someone developing his own property. The lash did not cut his back except to squeeze out extortionate production. He conscientiously fulfilled his primary mission to enrich the land that should have also been his, and he was also the basis of the urban economy. Slaves worked in the skilled trades and household labor, leaving the whites largely to devote themselves to intellectual occupations, through which they acquired the skills that permitted them to conceive and develop a national identity.

In addition, despite prohibitive laws and regulations, slaves organized themselves. They established secret mutual aid societies, patterned after those in Africa, which over time became the memorable *cabildos* organized on the basis of African nationalities, which in turn became recreational and social centers for blacks. They were similar to the Regional Centers that developed during the colonial era, with the essential difference that members of the Centers had no economic or spiritual connection to their place of origin in Africa. They were organized on the basis of language, religion, and culture, but were wholly and willingly Cuban, to their last breath. They were moved by a sort of incipient nationalism that brought them together with those who felt the call of the Cuban independence movement, which had important implications.

They also tried to promote the economic and intellectual life of their race, but how could they do that, as enslaved people for whom basic education was strictly prohibited?

Many learned to read, and some also to write, contradicting the law and the will of their owners, as in a difficult conspiracy. They only did as much as they could, but they put their whole soul into the effort to educate their descendants. More than anything else, they tried to purchase freedom with cold cash. They had to raise the money by working for their own account during their scarce leisure time, on small plots of land or in urban occupations, to scrape the funds together. They formed cooperative manumission societies that pooled funds to buy the freedom of their members, one by one. And all this by their own efforts, in a hostile environment.

Those manumissions, and others obtained individually, were possible because of their commitment to an ideal. They accumulated savings through workshop production and petty retail commerce. By such activities blacks came to own nearly all the houses in the old Havana neighborhoods of El Angel, Los Sitios, and Jesús María, as well as rural and urban properties outside the capital. They were later manipulated by unscrupulous lawyers, accused of racial conspiracies, deprived of their property, harassed, and many were killed.

Nevertheless, between 1815 and 1885, thinking only of Cuba's future, that generation of slaves provided Cuban culture with an appreciable number of poets, writers, and journalists, although it was only in the last years of slavery that it was permissible to teach free blacks reading, writing, arithmetic, and religion. All others got their education by their own talent and clandestine study.

With these well established social achievements, the black race responded to the Revolution of 1868. It was not a depraved mob of slaves with no more spiritual stimulus than a primordial instinct for freedom. They brought with them the rudiments of the civilization they lived in, and the experience of structures they had built for themselves, against the current of the time. They brought economic, religious, intellectual, and patriotic understanding, and amazing ideological and political intuition, which was developed to a surprising degree in the period from the Pact of Zanjón to the War of Independence.

The Negro understood the political and economic ideals of the Revolution. He appreciated its social implications, and added the strength of his majority numbers and his heroism to the faltering liberation forces. The national unification of the Cuban people was achieved. The Revolution granted the Negro all the civil and political rights of citizenship, and all military ranks and honors. By heading for the hills to fight, all racial differences and colonial iniquities were ended in principle and in practice. The black soldier or civilian official of the Republic in arms issued or obeyed orders without regard for racial distinctions. Whites and blacks joined together in the dignity of the struggle and in responsibility for carrying it out.

The spiritual culture the Negro had developed by this time meant that no leader of color would abuse his rank, status, or authority to offend the Republic. They all served with exemplary discipline, loyalty, and intelligence.

After the Ten Years War the real political education of the Cuban people began, and the majority of the colored race became prepared and organized for the final struggle for Independence, which they were called to join. Even more than in 1868, they made up the great majority of the Liberating Army. That was the great achievement of Juan Gualberto Gómez, the patriot to whom the Cuban nation owes so much gratitude. In my opinion, neither the ideas of Martí nor the military genius of Maceo would have achieved the triumph of the Revolution without the willing and intelligent collaboration of the black masses.[15]

The reaction of the colonial government after the Ten Years War took the form of rage against blacks, who were the main force of the rebellion. With slavery abolished completely in 1886, all sorts of subtle and sordid pressures were applied in the attempt to discourage them, break their independent spirit, and frustrate their egalitarian aspirations. Such tactics turned out to be counterproductive, however, because they pushed blacks to join the independence cause, which offered them equality and real

freedoms. But for blacks, after demanding their human rights, those underhanded maneuvers were more cruel than the deep humiliations of slavery. They brought about a sort of disoriented stupor that would delay the next insurrection.

It was urgent, then, to counteract those policies. Furthermore, the future revolution created a new set of problems for all involved. It would be influenced by new internal and international factors, as well as ideological, economic, and political issues. It was necessary to promote a new philosophy, new policies, better methods of planning and propaganda. People had to be moved, and funds raised. As we well know, it was a massive undertaking, which involved a considerable part of the Cuban population.

Juan Gualberto Gómez carried out an enormous task. He taught his race to plan together. He ensured that every man, within his abilities, would be the focus of pro-independence understanding and teaching, and that every social organization would be a revolutionary center. He organized the famous Central Directorate of Societies of the Colored Race, which represented the majority of the black race, unifying it to speak on its own behalf, while at the same time working for the nation as a whole.

Parallel with their political activities, people of color put determined efforts into education. It was necessary to prepare capable citizens for the future. In place of those dear old African *cabildos*, Afrodescendant people organized numerous Societies for Mutual Aid, Instruction, and Recreation, which provided free primary education for children and adults of any race, color, or origin. These organizations were, in the three elements of their long name, both a symbol and a powerful instrument of the vast progress blacks had made prior to the Grito de Baire.[16] All the collective status of the race was incorporated into the Societies, until most of them were dissolved during 1895 to provide educated participants in the War of Independence.

And so the black race joined the last revolution for independence, in much greater numbers and with much more efficacy than had been the case in 1868. Its quota of blood, intelligence, discipline, and social skill was unmatched, and deserves universal admiration. Maceo became immortalized. The image of the people of color shone with patriotic acclaim. The black race rose to the same level as the white, to share with it the responsibilities of the independent nation.

The Republic was established at last, and so began the time of the greatest contribution of blacks to the Cuban nation, through talent, work, wealth, and social organization, as well as military acumen and discipline, blood, and sacrifice. All the qualities shown by the Negro up to that time were tangible and apparent in normal human attributes. The only unusual thing is that they would flourish in such a short time, as from a mature culture. It might have been that our African grandfathers carried latent in their spirit the strengths of a prehistoric civilization.

Our foresight prepared us to cooperate with our white compatriots in the establishment and functioning of the Republic. In the quality and significance of our participation in the political, intellectual, and artistic life of the nation, we have a record similar to whites. Although in the relative percentage of some of these activities our rate of progress is greater that the white race (as the new people that we are, avid for education and full of vitality), this is really no more of an achievement than having earned and maintained, through our own efforts, a place in the front ranks that normally takes many decades of dedication.

There is, however, one singular contribution that Cuba owes to its black citizens, something that is less common, more subtle, an indication of real originality and greater psychological refinement. It is innate in the Negro, not something blacks could have acquired from white civilization, because the latter, with its materialized culture, does not have it: stoicism and ethnic sacrifice.[17] This is the metaphysical culmination of the thorough understanding that has filled the black soul from the time the first African slaves arrived on our shores; that romantic and magisterial mission we feel invested to carry out, to serve a people

and someday disappear, leaving our indelible mark on its spirit.

The Republic has not been able to fulfill its commitment to love the black Cuban. Due to a mix of social and economic circumstances, that beautiful revolutionary program of cordial and effective equality has been unfulfilled. The letter of that program has been written into the Constitution, while in practice everything conspires to our despair and extinction, by deliberate and urgent design.

Since we understand the tragedy of the Republican regime, might we not react with racist anger, perhaps looking to build an ideological alliance with the millions of blacks that are only a short distance away all around us? But if we repudiate race prejudice in the white population, how could we allow it among blacks? Noble action brings people together. Furthermore, our greatest satisfaction comes from never causing conflict for our country, even in the moral realm. We are all aware—and history will in time confirm—that the badly named "race war" of 1912 was nothing more than the monstrous and disastrous result of the political ambition of a small group of blacks and a few white government officials.[18] It was the most sordid and lamentable episode of the Republican era, but the only effect of that disgraceful event on the Negro was the excessive and bloody repression that ensued.[19]

*   *   *

I seem to feel in the air something like an impatience to return to the question: How, then, is the New Negro different from the old Negro, or any other black these days? Well, he is different in the way that the New White is distinct from other whites. More specifically, he is different from the survivors of the struggle for freedom of 1898, because he has a less romantic and more rational interpretation of the economic and social failure of our liberal democracy. He is different for his mental synchronization with the socialist waves that vibrate today in the world's atmosphere. He differs also in directing his political confidence toward a "Cuban-style" socialist government.

I beg a little more of your attention, ladies and gentlemen, to briefly explain my position on this important point. The true revolutionaries, those still faithful to the old ideals of independence, have not convinced themselves that the current government of our republic is incapable of guaranteeing equality of economic and social opportunity without making a series of changes so drastic that they would, *ipso facto* fundamentally alter the present regime. The New Negro and the New White seek to establish a government that can only exist on the basis of those equal opportunities. Just as liberal democracy cannot survive without the vote, this new governmental system can only survive on economic and social security. It would not be a system in which those benefits would depend on the benevolence of government officials—a utopian dream. Rather, they would be guaranteed by the organization of the state itself. White and black Cubans of the old school of political thought still react today with pained and resentful pessimism against our officials, our society, and our politicians for failures for which, in the last analysis, they are not responsible, rather than recognize that the failure is in the governmental system itself. The New Negro and the New White refrain from pressuring the officials of the inept government, asking them to cross the Pacific in a pedal-powered airplane. They work toward the establishment of a state system that would rectify, complete, and surpass liberal democracy.

The New Negro and the New White, then, have the same vision for the future. So where does this leave the mental autonomy of the New Negro I spoke about earlier? It leaves it not in the future, but in a present stained by Cuban negrophobia. This Cuban negrophobia differs from the negrophobia in the United States in that over there it is explicit and violent, while here it is embarrassing, euphemistic, and passive. There blacks are insulted, segregated, and lynched; here they are cheated out of their economic and social rights, left to starve to death,

and dissolved in surrounding whiteness.[20] When the Cuban New Negro is presented with the case for the extinction of people of color through mixing with the white race, as a natural biological solution backed by science, he is sure to smile and counter with a condition that almost always stops the dialogue abruptly: I accept the proposal, the New Negro replies, as long as the white male and the black male are equally free to contribute to the mixing of the races; as long as what happened in rural huts and urban bedrooms during slave times, is over. The masculine dignity of the black race would not voluntarily agree to any other proposal.

It is true that the Afro-Cuban suffers from an inferior economic and social position like that of urban and rural laborers, and women—in other words those we call the *elements of revolution*. They are all subordinated, but the situation for blacks is aggravated by the lingering prejudice of slavery, which in Cuba today is manifested more against color than against race. The black urban laborer, the black rural worker, the black woman, the black middle class, in addition to suffering all the abuse in common with other *elements of revolution*, carry the additional burden of racial prejudice. It is what we have defined as THE SURPLUS PAIN OF THE NEGRO.[21] Today, then, Cuban blacks have specific problems to focus on, to understand their causes, to place in the context of broader national issues, and to develop their own solutions, in order to then engage in collaboration with the New White.

*   *   *

And now, ladies and gentlemen, since you have so kindly allowed me to conclude this attempt to make my case based on historical analysis, and we're coming into the home stretch, I will put before you, more or less randomly, the other points of view of the New Negro. As I have said, they are simply the consequences of what I have explained at length.

*   *   *

The Morúa Law should be modified and amended so that is no longer a political trap for the Afro-Cuban.[22] It is a good thing to prohibit political parties made up of citizens of only one race. But is unfair to exclude Negroes from executive positions in political parties and from being candidates for public office (which is how parties put their platforms into practice), and do so with impunity. The language of the law needs to be changed along the following lines: "Organizations that do not include Cubans of both the white race and the colored race will not be considered political parties for the effects of the law." And this should be added: "Candidate lists for public office, and for leadership positions in political parties, which do not include Cubans of these two races, will also be illegal."

* * *

As long as there is no change in the government that would put an end to *de facto* exclusions and privileges, it would be appropriate, if only to comply with legal technicalities, to draft the article in the Constitution along these lines: "All Cubans are equal before the Law. The Republic does not recognize individual rights or privileges based on sex, religion, race, or color. The law will impose penalties for violations of this principle, whether they be ostensible or surreptitious." Contrary to fallacious arguments that have been put forth, this of course is not to request special favors for blacks. It is to request that the exercise of privileges against blacks does not continue with impunity. What is proposed here is RACIAL INDIFFERENCE: no favors for being black, but no prejudice for not being white.

Personally, I have no faith whatsoever in a proposal to amend the Constitution that is not backed by an active mobilization of public opinion and a governmental structure that is consistent with it. Experience warns us against relying on emotions.

* * *

Another point of view: there is no black or colored race that is of one mind, whether in opinions or policies, just as there is no white race with similar characteristics. The majority of New Negroes are on the left; but there is no lack of sympathizers with fascism or Nazism. It is an insidious error to claim that all Afro-Cubans are right-wing, all leftists, all centrists, or all indifferent. The pseudo revolutionaries who opposed Machado made this mistake, or fell into this sin, when they accused the black race, or THE NEGROES of being Machadists or of being cool to the revolutionary project. Leading up to August 12, 1933, the proportion of blacks among the anti-Machado revolutionaries was commensurate with the small number of whites, and similar in that the majority were not drawn from the common people. There were more blacks among the supporters of the government than among the revolutionaries, but there were infinitely more white Machadists than rebels. The anathema the eminent Enrique José Varona proclaimed against blacks, when he was at death's door, has been shown to be neither objectively accurate nor fair with regard to Afro-Cubans, as the A B C itself has indirectly recognized, and history will prove in due time.

* * *

Another opinion of the New Negro: The secondary racial prejudice between blacks and mulattos, as it persists strongly in some regions of Cuba—and to a greater or lesser degree throughout the Republic—while it is lamentable, does not imply an inherent inferiority specific to Afro-Cubans. Such an ugly sub-prejudice will disappear on the day that being white or almost white no longer constitutes a positive advantage in our country. In order to resist the temptation to use whitening as a means of escaping the limitations that the dominant prejudice imposes on dark skinned Cubans, an exceptionally strong character is required. Our white men carefully cultivate those temptations in the Cuban Negro. This is very different from the whites in the United States, for whom anyone who has a drop of African blood in their veins, however white and blond they might look, is a Negro—and is relegated to the black world whenever they are discovered.

* * *

As for the inferiority complex of the Negro, its historical explanation stems from slavery, and continues in the economic and social devaluation of the Afro-Cuban. That defect is fading away more rapidly than one might expect. This black inferiority complex has its counterpart in the inferiority complex Cuban whites feel toward everything connected to the United States since we established the Republic, and which in colonial times they felt toward everything European: Paris . . . London! This inferiority complex of white and nearly white Cubans is most extreme in their eagerness to see blacks disappear.[23] It is extreme because even if the day might come when we would all have skin more or less the color of marble, the Cuban soul will forever be mulatto, just as the Mexican soul will always be Indian, for example. Extreme, because the Nordic man of the United States knows that Cuba is located in the negroid zone of the Caribbean, and he will not think of us as his equal until he loses his own superiority complex. History fully excuses, or at least explains, this inferiority complex of white Cubans.

* * *

Another subtle and delicate subject: There are some who disparage the Afro-Cuban a little for not defending himself by an affirmation of black racism. This school of thought claims that it would be better for Cuba if blacks were more black and whites were more white. I would prefer to let nature and the human instinct for sociability freely carry out their project of biological fusion and cultural mixture, without artificial constraints or stimuli. As plausible examples of this thesis we have the racial affirmation of blacks in the United States, the racial cohesion of the Chinese, the Jews, and so forth. This is a mistake. It's a delusion to think that African Americans advance farther because they live in isolation, turned in on themselves. One

only needs to read their newspapers and books to see how much damage they suffer from this racial isolation, and how much more progress they could make if they were not so terribly discriminated against. We in Cuba can only imagine such a situation.

But digging a little deeper, one soon discovers that blacks in the Americas, whether in the United States, Cuba, or elsewhere, have not maintained in the past nor do we now have any contact with Africa nor with blacks in Africa, that would serve as the basis of racial solidarity similar to that of the Chinese or Semites.

For blacks in the Americas, the slave trade violently and definitively tore their ancestors from their homelands and former social groups. By the nature of their situation they were automatically connected to white civilization, where they were forced to live from then on. Thus the sense of homeland and family emerging out of slavery has to be stronger than any racial or ancestral connection to Africa. Their only physical or spiritual possessions are their families, the places where they were born, the few things they have been able to acquire. They would never think of going back to Africa, where in any case they might be unwelcome. What connection do they have with those people, other than the color of their skin and a vague and distorted sense of kinship? The Semites are united by religion and the contacts they maintain around the world. We blacks in the various parts of the Americas barely know each other, and vary widely in culture, religion, education, and outlook. Even in Cuba. the Africans brought here were different from one another. This being the case, what would be the basis for a black racism? It's absurd. The solution is not racism, but in linking the common interests of blacks and whites.[24]

Finally, the New Negro feels the responsibility to provide guidance, and he wants to carry out that mission without bluster or an anachronistic autocratic style that would be inconsistent with his own project: to indoctrinate the Afro-Cuban masses, in order to prepare them for the possible change of government that he feels is coming. He modestly offers himself to carry out a program of legitimate advocacy guided by the principles I have laid out.

An Organizing Committee for a national Convention of Cuban organizations of the colored race presently exists. Note that I did not say "a convention of the colored race," because as I argued earlier, it would be a political and social impossibility to convene all the colored race or all the white race. That Committee—of which I am not a member, but whose operations I look upon favorably—wants to bring together the only social organizations the colored race has, to deliberate on the problems of Cuba and the race question, to put before the Convention ideas like those I have had the honor to present to you this evening, reach a majority agreement on a program, and proceed according to the edifying principles that might be agreed upon. The generic label "organizations of the colored race" includes those antiquated groups from the colonial era, as well as modern cultural and sport organizations, and so forth—all the civil societies that function under our Law of Association.

This Convention will probably be the most momentous and representative civic event by a substantial group of Afro-Cubans since the venerable Juan Gualberto Gómez organized that famous "Central Directorate of Societies of the Colored Race" on the eve of 1895.

The Organizing Committee has prepared a broad program covering the most fundamental issues facing our nation, and the solutions deemed appropriate. The program is not focused on the secondary question of race rela-

tions. The New Negro lays out overall solutions for Cuba's problems, with the vision of a statesman, in the spirit of justice for all, white and black. When the Convention has agreed upon a collective program, an expression of the Afro-Cuban position relative to our national problems, I believe the executive group will put it alongside the ideas of the "new whites," with those of the genuine revolutionaries of today, in order to bring those ideas together as the basis for the New Negro and the New White to carry on together, like the whites and blacks of the independence movement, in a new liberating crusade for social and economic justice for all the inhabitants of our country.

And if this Convention does not take place, or if it fails, another will be organized. It must be organized, because it is a necessity in these new times.

Dear audience:

Only the urge to explain the outlook of the New Negro has given me the audacity to ask for so much of your time. The New Negro needs to be heard, answered, and argued with, if not for the merit of his positions, at least in deference to his desire to serve the nation in the most useful way possible. He wants to have his positions confirmed, or corrected if necessary. But above all he wants to work, and to serve. I beg you to complete the gift of your presence here this evening by helping to publicize, by whatever means you have available, the essence of what you have listened to with such cordial generosity.

Thank you very much.

APPENDIX

LOOKING BACKWARD, LOOKING FORWARD, 1938–1950

Alain Locke

"The Negro: 'New' or Newer: A Retrospective Review of the Literature of the Negro for 1938"

Part 1, *Opportunity*, January 1939

Part 2, *Opportunity*, February 1939

Part I.

IT is now fifteen years, nearly a half a generation, since the literary advent of the "New Negro." In such an interval a new generation of creative talent should have come to the fore and presumably those talents who in 1924–25 were young and new should today be approaching maturity or have arrived at it. Normally too, at the rate of contemporary cultural advance, a new ideology with a changed world outlook and social orientation should have evolved. And the question back of all this needs to be raised, has it so developed or hasn't it, and do we confront today on the cultural front another Negro, either a newer Negro or a maturer "New Negro"?

A critic's business is not solely with the single file reviewing-stand view of endless squads of books in momentary dress parade but with the route and leadership of cultural advance, in short, with the march of ideas. There is no doubt in the panoramic retrospect of the years 1924 to 1938 about certain positive achievements:—a wider range of Negro self-expression in more of the arts, an increasing maturity and objectivity of approach on the part of the Negro artist to his subject-matter, a greater diversity of styles and artistic creeds, a healthier and firmer trend toward self-criticism, and perhaps most important of all, a deepening channel toward the mainstream of American literature and art as white and Negro artists share in ever-increasing collaboration the growing interest in Negro life and subject-matter. These are encouraging and praiseworthy gains, all of which were confidently predicted under the convenient but dangerous caption of "The New Negro."

But a caption's convenience is part of its danger; so is its brevity. In addition, in the case in question, there was inevitable indefiniteness as to what was meant by the "New Negro." Just that question must be answered, however, before we can judge whether today's Negro represents a matured phase of the movement of the 20's or is, as many of the youngest Negroes think and contend, a counter-movement, for which incidentally they have a feeling but no name. These "bright young people" to the contrary, it is my conviction that the former is true and that the "New Negro" movement is just coming into its own after a frothy adolescence and a first-generation course which was more like a careen than a career. Using the nautical figure to drive home the metaphor, we may say that there was at first too little ballast in the boat for the heavy head of sail that was set. Moreover, the talents of that period (and some of them still) were far from skillful mariners; artistically and sociologically they sailed many a crooked course, mistaking their directions for the lack of steadying common-sense and true group loyalty as a compass. But all that was inevitable in part; and was, as we shall later see, anticipated and predicted.

But the primary source of confusion perhaps was due to a deliberate decision not to define the "New Negro" dogmatically, but only to characterize his general traits and attitudes. And so, partly because of this indefiniteness, the phrase became a slogan for cheap race demagogues who wouldn't know a "cultural movement" if they could see one, a handy megaphone for petty exhibitionists who were only posing as "racialists" when in fact they were the rankest kind of egotists, and a gilded fetish for race idolaters who at heart were still sentimentalists seeking consolation for inferiority. But even as it was, certain greater evils were avoided—a growing race consciousness was not cramped down to a formula, and a movement with a popular ground swell and a folk significance was not tied to a partisan art creed or any one phase of culture politics.

The most deliberate aspect of the New Negro formulation—and it is to be hoped, its crowning wisdom—was just this repudiation of any and all one-formula solutions of the race question, (its own immediate emphases included), and the proposed substitution of a solidarity of group feeling for unity within a variety of artistic creeds and social programs. To quote: "The Negro today wishes to be known for what he is, even in his faults and shortcomings, and scorns a craven and precarious survival at the price of seeming to be what he is not. He thus resents being spoken of as a social ward or minor, even by his own, and to being regarded a chronic patient for the sociological clinic, the sick man of American Democracy. For the same reasons, *he himself is through with those social nostrums and panaceas, the so-called 'solutions' of his 'problem,' with which he and the country have been so liberally dosed in the past. Religion, freedom, education, money—in turn he has ardently hoped for and peculiarly trusted these things; he still believes in them, but not in blind trust that they alone will solve his life-problem.*"

How then even the *enfants terribles* of today's youth movement could see "cultural expression" as a substitute formula proposed by the "New Negro" credo I cannot understand, except on the ground that they did not read carefully what had been carefully written. Nor would a careful reading have been auspicious for their own one-formula diagnosis of "economic exploitation" and solution by "class action." Not only was there no foolish illusion that "racial prejudice would soon disappear before the altars of truth, art and intellectual achievement," as has been asserted, but a philosophy of cultural isolation from the folk ("masses") and of cultural separatism were [*sic*] expressly repudiated. It was the bright young talents of the 20's who themselves went cosmopolite when they were advised to go racial, who went exhibitionist instead of going documentarian, who got jazz-mad and cabaret-crazy instead of get-

ting folk-wise and sociologically sober. Lest this, too, seem sheer rationalizing hind-sight, let a few direct quotations from *The New Negro* testify to the contrary. Even more, the same excerpts will show that a social Reformation was called for as the sequel and proper goal of a cultural Renaissance, and that the present trends of second generation "New Negro" literature which we are now passing in review were predicted and reasonably anticipated. For reasons of space, quotations must be broken and for reasons of emphasis, some are italicized:

A transformed and transforming psychology permeates the masses. . . . In a real sense it is the rank and file who are leading, and the leaders who are following. . . . It does not follow that if the Negro were better known, he would be better liked or better treated. . . . Not all the new art is in the field of pure art values. There is poetry of sturdy social protest and fiction of calm dispassionate social analysis. But reason and realism have cured us of sentimentality: instead of the wail and appeal, there is challenge and indictment. Satire is just beneath the surface of our latest prose and tonic irony has come into our poetic wells. These are good medicines for the common mind, for us they are the necessary antidotes against social poison. Their influence means that *at least for us* the worst symptoms of the social distemper are passing. And so the social promise of our recent art is as great as the artistic. . . . Each generation, however, will have its creed, and *that of the present* is the belief in the efficacy of collective effort, in race cooperation. This deep feeling of race is *at present* the mainspring of Negro life . . . It is radical in tone, but not in purpose and only the most stupid forms of opposition, misunderstanding or persecution could make it otherwise. Of course, the thinking Negro has shifted a little toward the left with the world trend, and there is an increasing group who affiliate with radical and liberal movements. But fundamentally *for the pre-*

sent the Negro is radical on race matters, conservative on others, in other words a "forced radical," a social protestant rather than a genuine radical. Yet under further pressure and injustice iconoclastic thought and motives will inevitably increase. Harlem's quixotic radicalisms call for their ounce of democracy today lest tomorrow they be beyond cure.

It is important, finally, to sum up the social aspect of the New Negro front with clarity because today's literature and art, an art of searching social documentation and criticism, thus becomes a consistent development and matured expression of the trends that were seen and analyzed in 1925.

The Negro mind reaches out as yet to nothing but American wants, American ideas. But this forced attempt to build his Americanism on race values is a *unique social experiment*, and its ultimate success *is impossible except through the fullest sharing of American culture and institutions. There should be no delusion about this.* American nerves in sections unstrung with race hysteria are often fed the opiate that the trend of Negro advance is wholly separatist, and that the effect of its operation will be to encyst the Negro as a benign foreign body in the body politic. This cannot be—even if it were desirable. The racialism of the Negro is no limitation or reservation with respect to American life; it is only a constructive effort to build the obstructions in the stream of his progress into an efficient dam of social energy and power. Democracy itself is obstructed and stagnated to the extent that any of its channels are closed. Indeed they cannot be selectively closed. So the choice is not between one way for the Negro and another for the rest, but between American institutions frustrated on the one hand and American ideals progressively fulfilled and realized on the other."

The generation of the late 30's is nearer such a cultural course and closer to such social insight than the tangential generation of the late 20's. Artistic exploitation is just as possible from the inside as from the outside, and if our writers and artists are becoming sounder in their conception of the social role of themselves and their art, as indeed they are, it is all the more welcome after considerable delay and error. If, also, they no longer see cultural racialism as cultural separatism, which it never was or was meant to be, then, too, an illusory dilemma has lost its paralyzing spell. And so, we have only to march forward instead of to counter-march; only to broaden the phalanx and flatten out the opposition salients that threaten divided ranks. Today we pivot on a sociological front with our novelists, dramatists and social analysts in deployed formation. But for vision and morale we have to thank the spiritual surge and aesthetic inspiration of the first generation artists of the renaissance decade.

And now, to the literature of this year of reformation, stir, and strife.

In fiction, two novels by white authors remind us of the background use of Negro materials that used to be so universal. Many such have been ignored as not basically "Negro literature" at all. . . .

However, it is noteworthy how much serious social commentary there really is in this year's crop of fiction, from both the white and the Negro authors. Already we are used to the semi-doctrinal criticism of the Erskine Caldwell school, which by the way he continues with usual unsparing and unrelieved realism in his latest volume of stories, *Southways*, but there are other and as I think more effective brands of realism. Certainly one of the most convincing and moving bits of documentary fiction on the racial situation is Don Tracy's reportorial but beautifully restrained *How Sleeps the Beast*. More even than the famous movie *Fury*, this novel gives the physiology of American lynching; not just its horror and bestialities, but its moods and its social mechanisms. Vince, who starts out by saying to his girl, "I ain't goin', I got no truck with lynchin's," eventually goes under her taunts; Al Purvis, whose life poor Jim had saved, starts out to rescue him but succumbs to social cowardice and mob hysteria; the Sheriff is jostled from official indifference to sectional hate at the sign of a "Yankee meddler," and a newspaper reporter hunted by the mob for fear of exposure barely escapes the same fate by sleeping the night through in the "malodorous room marked '*Ladies,*'" after having been ordered out the back-door of the local Eastern Maryland Shore hotel while the mob pickets the entrance. In realism charged with terror, but tempered with pity and understanding, Don Tracy has written in the Steinbeckian vein the best version yet of this great American tragedy and of the social obsessions that make it happen.

More notable still, because about a more normal social subject, is Julian Meade's saga of Mary Lou Payton, the most fully characterized domestic Negro servant in all the tedious range of Negro servitors in American fiction. *The Back Door* is a book of truthful, artistically-balanced [*sic*] human documentation. Mary Lou's always precarious hold on the good things in life, on both domestic job and self-respect, on her amiable tobacco-worker lover beset by the wiles of looser women on the one hand and unemployment and occupational discase on the other, on her cherished but socially unrewarded respectability that every other week or so confronts the dreaded advances of Frank Anderson, the philandering white rent-collector, on even the job itself, are all portrayed with pity and sympathetic irony. . . .

To the fine achievements just mentioned, two Negro writers make this year a sizeable contribution. In the first, Mercedes Gilbert's *Aunt Sara's Wooden God*, the theme of the story is more important than its literary execution. Despite a too lenient introduction by Langston Hughes, this first novel is no masterpiece, not even a companion for *Ollie Miss* or *Jonah's Gourd Vine* with which it is bracketed; but it is promising and in subject matter significant. William Gordon, the illegitimate son, is the favored but profligate brother, Aunt Sara's "Wooden God." From the beginning a martyr to his mother's blind partiality, Jim, the darker brother, takes from start to finish the brunt of

the situation—the childhood taunts, the lesser chance, the lion's share of the farm work while William is in school or frittering away time in Macon, then the loss of his sweetheart, Ruth, through the machinations of William, and finally imprisonment for William's crime. Amateurish overloading, as well as the anecdotal style of developing the episodes of the story, robs the book of its full tragic possibilities. William's eventual return to a death-bed reconciliation and Aunt Sara's pious blessings is [*sic*] only relieved by his attempted confession and Jim's heroic resolve not to disillusion Aunt Sara. Our novelists must learn to master the medium before attacking the heavier themes; a smaller canvas dimensionally done is better than a thin epic or a melodramatic saga. Here is a great and typical theme only half developed, which someone—perhaps the author herself—must some day do with narrative power and character insight.

IN contrast, Richard Wright in *Uncle Tom's Children* uses the novella with the sweep and power of epic tragedy. Last year the first of these four gripping tales, *Big Boy Leaves Home*, was hailed as the most significant Negro prose since Toomer's *Cane*. Since then it has won the *Story Magazine* award for the national WPA's Writers' Project contest, and a second story, *Fire and Cloud*, has won second prize in the O. Henry awards. This is a well-merited literary launching for what must be watched as a major literary career. Mr. Wright's full-length novel is eagerly awaited; perhaps in the longer form the nemesis of race injustice which stalks the fate of every chief character in the four stories will stalk with a more natural stride. One often feels in the shorter form that the nemesis makes forced marches. This is not a nerve-wrecked reader's cry for mercy; for we grant the author the terrible truth of his situations, but merely a plea for posterity that judges finally on the note of universality and artistry. By this criterion *Big Boy* and *Long Black Song* will last longer for their poignant beauty than *Down By the Riverside*, certainly, and perhaps also, *Fire and Cloud*. Yet as social indictments, the one of white oppression and ingratitude and the other of black cowardice and gullibility, these very two have the most documentary significance. The force of Wright's versions of Negro tragedy in the South lies in the correct reading of the trivialities that in that hate-charged atmosphere precipitate these frightful climaxes of death and persecution; an innocent boy's swimming prank in *Big Boy*, a man's desperate need for a boat to rescue his pregnant wife during a Mississippi flood, a white salesman's casual infatuation while trying to sell a prosperous black farmer's wife a gramophone, a relatively tame-hearted demonstration for food relief in the other three stories. And so, by this simple but profound discovery, Richard Wright has found a key to mass interpretation through symbolic individual instances which many have been fumbling for this long while. With this, our Negro fiction of social interpretation comes of age. . . .

Returning to the adult plane, the situation of poetry must claim our attention briefly. Time was when poetry was one of the main considerations of the Negro renaissance. But obviously our verse output has shrunk, if not in quantity, certainly in quality, and for obvious reasons. Poetry of social analysis requires maturity and group contacts, while the poetry of personal lyricism finds it hard to thrive anywhere in our day. Especially so with the Negro poet whose cultural isolation is marked; to me it seems that this strain of expression is dying a natural death of spiritual suffocation, Beatrice Murphy's anthology of fledgling poets, *Negro Voices*, to the contrary. Here and there in this volume one hears a promising note; almost invariably, however, it is a poem of social analysis and reaction rather than one of personal lyricism. To the one or two veterans, like Hughes, Frank Davis, Louis Alexander, a small bevy can be added as discoveries of this meritorious but not too successful volume: Katherine Beverly, Iola Brister, Conrad Chittick, Marcus Christian, Randolph Edmonds, Leona Lyons and Helen Johnson. However it is clear that the imitation of successful poets will never give us anything but feeble echoes, whether these models be the classical masters or the outstanding poets of the Negro renaissance, Cullen, McKay and Hughes. If our

poets are to serve well this generation they must go deeper and more courageously into the heart of real Negro experience. The postponement of Sterling Brown's expected volume *No Hidin' Place* thus leaves a lean poetic year of which the best garnerings, uneven at that, are Frank Marshall Davis's *Through Sepia Eyes* and Langston Hughes's *A New Song*. Both of these writers are vehemently poets of social protest now; so much so indeed that they have twangy lyres, except for moments of clear vibrancy such as Hughes's *Ballad of Ozzie Powell* and *Song of Spain* and Davis's *Chicago Skyscrapers*, the latter seemingly the master poem of the year in a not too golden or plentiful poetic harvest. On the foreign horizon the appearance of the young Martiniquian poet, L. G. Damas, is significant; otherwise the foreign output, like the domestic, is plaintive and derivative.

Whereas poetry languishes, drama seems to flourish. The honors are about evenly divided between the experimental theatres and the Federal Theatre Project. The latter, with several successful revivals, *Run Little Chillun* among them, had as new hits Theodore Ward's *Big White Fog* and William Du Bois's moving though melodramatic *Haiti* to its credit. On the other hand, the experimental theatre has given two Negro playwrights a chance for experimentation both in form and substance that may eventually lead somewhere. Dodson's *The Divine Comedy*, the Yale Theatre's contribution, is a somewhat over-ambitious expressionistic rendition of Negro cult religion that shows promise of a new writing talent, while the Harlem Suitcase Theatre's *Don't You Want to Be Free?* has vindicated the possibilities of a new dramatic approach. Both are to be watched hopefully, but especially the latter, because a people's theatre with an intimate reaction of the audience to materials familiar to it is one of the sound new items of a cultural program that in some of the arts, drama particularly, has stalled unnecessarily. This theatre and the Richmond Peoples' Theatre, under the auspices of the Southern Youth Congress and the direction of Thomas Richardson, supply even better laboratory facilities than the drama groups of the

Negro colleges, laudable as their Intercollegiate Dramatic Association is. It is to be hoped that real folk portraiture in drama may soon issue from these experiments. In the dramatized "Blues Episodes" of *Don't You Want to Be Free?*, and in the promising satirical sketches that the same theatre has recently begun, I see potentialities such as I have previously discussed at length. I am not only anxious to see them develop but anxious for some further confirmation of the predicted role of the drama in the Negro movement of self-expression in the arts. Not that an individual critic needs to be sustained, but since the course was plotted by close comparative study of other cultural movements, some national and some racial, rather that the history of this phase of our cultural development should demonstrate the wholesome principle that the Negro is no exception to the human rule. For after all, it is the lesson of history that a cultural revival has been both the symptom and initiating cause of most people's awakenings.

Part II.

As we turn now to the biographic, historical and sociological literature of the year, we find the treatment of the Negro, almost without exception, maturing significantly. There is, on the whole, less shoddy in the material, less warping in the weaving, and even what is propaganda has at least the virtue of frank, honest labeling. The historical cloth particularly is of more expert manufacture and only here and there exhibits the frowsy irregularities of amateur homespun. General social criticism reaches a record yardage; and so far as I can see, only the patient needle-point of self-criticism has lagged in a year of unusual, perhaps forced production. Forced, because undoubtedly and obviously the pressure behind much of this prose of social interpretation is that of the serious contemporary economic and political crisis. But fortunately also, a considerable part of this literature is for that very reason, deliberately integrated with the general issues and the competing philosophies of that crisis.

Before inspecting the varied stock of the year, a brief retrospective word is needed. Committed to no one cult of aesthetics (and least of all to the creed of "art for art's sake," since it tried to focus the Negro creative writer upon the task of "folk interpretation"), *The New Negro* movement did have a rather definite set of objectives for its historical and sociological literature. These were a non-apologetic sort of biography; a boldly racial but not narrowly sectarian history; an objective, unsentimental sociology; an independent cultural anthropology that did not accept Nordic values as necessarily final; and a social critique that used the same yardstick for both external and internal criticism. A long order—which it is no marvel to see take shape gradually and by difficult stages. Again to satisfy the skeptical, let quotations from *The Negro Digs Up His Past* attest:

> The American Negro must remake his past in order to make his future. Though it is orthodox to think of America as the one country where it is unnecessary to have a past, what is a luxury for the nation as a whole becomes a prime social necessity for the Negro. For him, a group tradition must supply compensation for persecution and pride of race the antidote for prejudice. History must restore what slavery took away, for it is the social damage of slavery that the present generation must repair and offset.

But this call for a reconstructed group tradition was not necessarily pitched to the key of chauvinism, though there is some inevitable chauvinism in its train. Chauvinism is, however, the mark and brand of the tyro, the unskilled and unscientific amateur in this line, and we have had, still have and maybe always will have our brash amateurs who rush on where scientists pause and hesitate. However, this was recognized, and warned against, and was spoken of as the mark of the old, not of the newer generation. It was said:

> This sort of thing (chauvinistic biography and history) was on the whole patheti-

cally over-corrective, ridiculously over-laudatory; it was apologetics turned into biography. But today, *even if for the ultimate purpose of group justification,* history has become less a matter of argument and more a matter of record. There is the definite desire and determination to have a history, well documented, widely known at least within race circles, and administered as a stimulating and inspiring tradition for the coming generations. But gradually as the study of the Negro's past has come out of the vagaries of rhetoric and propaganda and become systematic and scientific, three outstanding conclusions have been established:

First, that the Negro has been throughout the centuries of controversy an active collaborator, and often a pioneer, in the struggle for his own freedom and advancement. This is true to a degree which makes it the more surprising that it has not been recognized earlier.

Second, that by virtue of their being regarded as something "exceptional," even by friends and well-wishers, Negroes of attainment and genius have been unfairly disassociated from the group, and group credit lost accordingly.

Third, that the remote racial origins of the Negro, far from being what the race and the world have been given to understand, offer a record of creditable group achievement when scientifically viewed, and more important still, that they are of vital *general* interest because of their bearing upon the beginnings and early development of culture.

With such crucial truths to document and establish, an ounce of fact is worth a pound of controversy. So the Negro historian today digs under the spot where his predecessor stood and argued.

THE mere re-statement of this historical credo of the New Negro (1925) shows clearly that not only has it not been superseded, but that it has yet to be fully realized. Indeed it was maintained at that time that the proper use of such materials as were available or could be unearthed by research was "not only for the first true writing of Negro history, but for *the rewriting of many important paragraphs of our common American history.*" One only needs an obvious ditto for sociology, anthropology, economics, and social criticism to get the lineaments of a point of view as progressive, as valid, and as incontestable in 1939 as fifteen years ago.

Indeed we may well and warrantably take this as a yardstick for the literature which we now have to review. Professor Brawley has excellently edited the *Best Prose of Paul Laurence Dunbar;* a service as much to social as to literary criticism. For by including with the short stories excerpts from his novels, Dunbar's pioneer attempts at the social documentation of Negro life are brought clearly to attention. Less artistic than his verse, Dunbar's prose becomes nevertheless more significant with the years; here for the most part he redeems the superficial and too stereotyped social portraiture of his poetry and shakes off the minstrel's motley for truer even if less attractive garb. Robinson's volume of stories, *Out of Bondage,* is, on the other hand, such thinly fictionalized history as to have little literary value and only to be of antiquarian interest. It is hard, no doubt, to galvanize history either in fiction or biography, but Arthur Huff Fauset's crisp and vivid *Sojourner Truth* proves that it can be done. This—beyond doubt the prize biography of the year and one of the best Negro biographies ever done—takes the fragile legend of Sojourner and reconstructs an historical portrait of illuminating value and charm. It lacks only a larger canvas giving the social background of the anti-slavery movement to be of as much historical as biographic value; and even this is from time to time hinted back of the vigorous etching of this black peasant crusader.

Just this galvanic touch is missed in the scholarly and painstaking biography, historical critique, and translation of the poems of *Juan Latino,* by Professor Valaurez Spratlin. . . .

The Life of George Washington Carver, under the slushy caption of *From Captivity to*

Fame, is a good example of what race biography once was, and today should not be. Purely anecdotal, with an incongruous mixture of petty detail and sententious moralisms, it not only does not do the subject justice, but makes Dr. Carver a "race exhibit" rather than a real human interest life and character. One is indeed impressed with the antithesis between the sentimental, philanthropic, moralistic approach and the historico-social and psychological approaches of modern-day biography. . . .

The Black Jacobins by the talented C. L. R. James is, on the other hand, individual and social analysis of high order and deep penetration. Had it been written in a tone in harmony with its careful historical research into the background of French Jacobinism, this story of the great Haitian rebel, Toussaint Louverture, and his compatriots Christophe and Dessalines, would be the definitive study in this field. However, the issues of today are pushed too passionately back to their historic parallels—which is not to discount by any means the economic interpretation of colonial slavery in the Caribbean, but only a caution to read the ideology of each age more accurately and to have historical heroes motivated by their own contemporary idiom of thought and ideas. There is more correctness in the historical materials, therefore, than in the psychological interpretation of these truly great and fascinating figures of Negro history.

UNLESS it be characterized as the breezy biography of a cult, Zora Neale Hurston's story of voodoo life in Haiti and Jamaica is more folklore and *belles lettres* than true human or social documentation. Scientific folk-lore, it surely is not, being too shot through with personal reactions and the piquant thrills of a travelogue. Recently another study has given Voodooism a more scientifically functional interpretation and defense, and Voodooism certainly merits an analysis going deeper than a playful description of it as "a harmless pagan cult that sacrifices domestic animals at its worst." Too much of [Zora Neale Hurston's] *Tell My Horse* is anthropological gossip in spite of many unforgettable word pictures; and by the way, the fine photographic

illustrations are in themselves worth the price of the book. The social and political criticism, especially of the upper-class Haitians, is thought-provoking; and caustic as it is, seems no doubt deserved in part at least. One priceless epigram just must be quoted: "Gods always behave like the people who make them."

Contrasting in thoroughness and sobriety with these excursions into *Caribbeana* are the two works of the Uruguayan race scholar, Ildefonso Pereda Valdes. Through the studies of Fernando Ortiz, the learned scholar of Afro-Cubana, and the work in Afro-Braziliana by Dr. Arthur Ramos, shortly to be published in abridged translation by the Association for the Study of Negro Life and History, the field of the Negro elements in Latin American culture is at last being opened up to the scientific world generally, and to the North American reader in particular. Not yet translated, Senor Valdes's studies are an important extension of this most important field. In *Linea de Color*, he largely interprets the contemporary culture of the American and Cuban Negro while in *El Negro Rio Platense*, he documents the Negro and African elements in the history, folklore and culture of Brazil, the Argentine and Uruguay, and traces Negro influences from Brazil right down into furthermost South America. Important studies of Negro idioms in the popular music of Brazil, of African festivals and superstitions in Uruguay and the valley of the Rio de la Plata open up a fresh vein of research in the history and influence of the Negro in the Americas. In *Linea de Color* are to be found pithy urbane essays on Nicholás Guillén, the Afro-Cuban poet, the mulatto Brazilian poet, Cruz E Souza, and on African dances in Brazil. In the other volume, more academic essays on the Negro as seen by the great Spanish writers of the Golden Age in Spain and several other cosmopolitan themes attest to the wide scholarship of Señor Valdes. It is refreshing and significant to discover in far South America an independently motivated analogue of the New Negro cultural movement. *Linea de Color* reciprocates gracefully by giving a rather detailed account of the North American Negro renaissance in terms of its chief contemporary exponents, cultural and political. It has been an unusual year for Negro biography and folk-lore, the latter capped academically by the exhaustive collation of African and Negro American proverbs in Champion's monumental *Racial Proverbs*.

As is to be expected, the documentation of Negro life in the Federal Writers' Project, *The American Guide Series*, is varied, uneven and ranges through history to folklore and from mere opinion to sociology. But on the whole the yield is sound and representative, due in considerable measure to the careful direction of these projects from the Federal editorial office. *New York Panorama*, however, in its sections on the Negro, misses its chances in spite of the collation of much new and striking material. Moderately successful in treating early New York, it fails to interpret contemporary Harlem soundly or deeply. Indeed it vacillates between superficial flippancy and hectic propagandist expose, seldom touching the golden mean of sober interpretation. In *The New Orleans City Guide* the Negro items are progressively integrated into the several topics of art, music, architecture, folk-lore and civic history in a positively refreshing way. This exceeds the usual play-up of the Creole tradition at the expense of the Negro, and for once in the Creole account the Negro element is given reasonable mention. *The Mississippi Guide* is casual, notable for its omissions in its treatment of the Negro; and savors as much of the reactionary tradition of the Old South as the New Orleans guide does of the liberal New South that we all prefer to hold with and believe in. The Old South is an undeniable part of the historical past; but as a mirror for the present it is out of place and pernicious.

Thus liberal studies like *A Southerner Discovers the South* by Jonathan Daniels and Frank Shay's *Judge Lynch: His First Hundred Years* become the really important guides to social understanding and action. They, with most of the solid literature of the New South—which someone has said is the necessary complement of the New Negro—keep accumulatively verifying these basic truths: that the history of the South itself is the history of the slave regime, that the

sociology of the South is its aftermath and retribution, and that the reconstruction of the entire South is its dilemma and only possible solution. Whatever common denominator solution can be found is the problem of the present generation. Thus for Mr. Shay, lynching is rightly not just the plight of the Negro but the disease of law and public opinion; while for Mr. Daniels the Negro is not so much a problem as a symptom. This realistic third dimension now being projected into the consideration of the race problem is the best hope of the whole situation, and should never be lost sight of by any observer, black or white, who wishes today to get credence or give enlightenment.

For this reason, Professor Stephenson's study of *Isaac Franklin: Slave Trader and Planter of the Old South* is a social history of the newer, realistic type as much a document of Negro history as it is of the socio-economic story of the plantation regime. Factual almost to a fault, it is a model of careful objective statement; no one can accuse this author of seeing history through colored spectacles of opinions. Only slightly less objective, and even more revealing is Professor Bell Wiley's study of *Southern Negroes: 1861–1865*. But a decade ago so frank and fair an account of the Negroes during the crisis of the Civil War would have been very unlikely from the pen of a Southern professor of history and certainly unthinkable as a prize award of the United Daughters of the Confederacy. Southern abolitionism, Negro unrest and military service to both sides, the dilemmas of Southern policy and strategy, are not at all glossed over in a work of most creditable historical honesty. Almost a companion volume, by chance has come Professor Wesley's penetrating study entitled *The Collapse of the Confederacy*. Here surely is a fascinating division of labor—an analysis of the policy of the Confederacy by a Negro historian and of the status and behavior of the Negro population during the same period by a white historian. Dr. Wesley carefully and incisively documents the economic breakdown of the Confederate economy, showing its military defeat as merely its sequel. He is also insistent on the too often forgotten facts of the Confederacy's last frantic dilemma about military emancipation and the proposed use of Negro soldiers to bolster its shattered man-power. Thus both the historical and the contemporary Southern scene have this year had significant, almost definitive interpretations. . . .

Turning from the regional to the national front, we find the discussion of the race problem gains by the wider angle of vision and attack. We find also one great virtue in the economic approach, apart from its specific hypotheses—an insistence on basic and common factors in the social equation. The economic interpretation of the race question is definitely gaining ground and favor among students of the situation. Both studies in the long anticipated Volume I of the *Howard University Studies in Social Science* have this emphasis, the one explicitly, the other by implication. Wilson E. Williams' dissertation on *Africa and the Rise of Capitalism* breaks pioneer ground on the importance of the slave trade in the development of European commerce and industry in the 16th, 17th and 18th centuries and establishes the thesis that it was a "very important factor in the development of the capitalist economy in England"—one might warrantably add, of Western capitalism. The second essay, by Robert E. Martin, skillfully analyzes *Negro Disfranchisement in Virginia*, not in the traditional historical way, but by documenting the shifts of political policy and the mechanisms of majority-minority interaction, thus bringing to the surface conflicts of interest and motives too often unnoticed or ignored. Apart from such clarifying information these studies, reflecting the trend of the graduate instruction of which they are products, seem to predict a new approach in this field with broad implications and deep potentialities.

IN contrast to this critical economic attack, J. W. Ford's *The Negro and the Democratic Front* hews rather dogmatically to the official Marxist line, but with frank and zealous insistence. Its frankness is a virtue to be praised; as is also the value of having a clear, simply-put statement of the Communist interpretation of major national and world issues from the angle of the Negro's position. Though largely a compendium of Mr. Ford's addresses, it does focus for the layman a unified picture of radical thought and programs of action. Quite to the opposite, John G. Van Deusen in *The Black Man in White America* has taken up the cudgels for gradualism, gratuitously and with feeble effect. To a book seven-eighths full of patiently assembled and well-organized facts about every important phase of Negro life, Professor Van Deusen adds the banalities of philanthropic platitudes and dubious advice. He counsels "patience," expects "education and understanding" and in another paragraph "that universal solvent: Time" to solve the Negro problem, yet admits that "the greatest part of the work of conciliation remains to be accomplished." . . .

But just such vital correlation with social policy and criticism of majority attitudes is boldly attempted in President Buell Gallagher's book, *American Caste and the Negro College*. Instead of just describing the Negro college, Dr. Gallagher spends seven of his fourteen chapters analyzing the social setting and frame of reference of the Negro college, namely the American system of color caste with its taboos and techniques of majority domination and minority repression. Then he illuminatingly decides that in addition to its regular function as a college, a Negro college has imposed upon it the function of transforming and transcending caste, or to quote: "the segregated college has a special set of responsibilities connected first, with the problem of transforming the caste system" and second, "with the success of the individual member of the minority group in maintaining his own personal integrity in the face of defeat, or of partial achievement." If for no other reason, such keen analysis of the social function of Negro education would make this an outstanding contribution; but in addition, the diagnosis is sound, the prescriptions liberal and suggestive, and the style charming. Indeed a noteworthy contribution!

AFRICAN life has a disproportionately voluminous literature, since any European who has been there over six weeks may write a book about it. It is safe to say that over half of this literature is false both as to fact and values, that more than half of what is true to fact is false in interpretation, and that more than half of that minimal residue is falsely generalized—for Africa is a continent of hundreds of different cultures. So, the best of all possible interpreters is the intelligent native who also knows, without having become de-racialized, the civilization of the West. Next best is the scientific interpreter who uses the native informer as the open sesame to African social values. The virtue of Rene Maran's *Livingstone* is that he himself knows by long acquaintance that same equatorial Africa which was Livingstone's country. Jose Saco speaking of slavery in Brazil, Dantes Bellegarde speaking for Haiti and, with some reservation for amateurishness, J. A. Jarvis speaking for the Virgin Islands make their respective books welcome and trustworthy as native opinion upon native materials. The same should have been true for Nnamdi Azikiwe's *Renascent Africa* but for the almost adolescent indignation distorting the outlines of a statement of native West African conditions, grievances and programs. Even so, an expression of native opinion is valuable at any price. Just as radical, in fact more so in spite of its cool reasoning, is George Padmore's *Africa and World Peace*. In addition to being one of the sharpest critiques of imperialism in a decade of increasing anti[-]imperialist attack, this book vividly expounds the close connection between fascism and imperialism, on the one hand, and fascism and African interests and issues on the other.

Turning to the less controversial, we have from Professor Herskovits a monumental and definitive two-volume study of the Dahomean culture. A careful historical and functional approach yields a sympathetic view of a much misunderstood people, and both illustrates and fortifies a growing trend toward the independent

interpretation of African life not in terms of Nordic *mores* and standards but of its own.

So conceded is this point of view becoming that even the best travel literature is now being keyed to it. *Black and Beautiful* is one such, not just by wishful thinking in its title but by virtue of twenty-five years of "going native" by the author, Marius Fortie. His natives are individuals, not types; several of them were his "wives" and sons, and he speaks passionately for and in behalf of his "adopted people," a far cry indeed from the supercilious traveler, missionary or civil servant. Even Andre Mikhelson's *Kings and Knaves in the Cameroons*, mock-heroic and ironic, is a cynical fable castigating "so-called European civilization"; while Isak Dinesen's *Out of Africa* gives a delicately sensitive and respectful account of Kenya native life and the Kikuyu, the Somali and the Masai. The approach is human rather than anthropological and we have that to thank for a general impression that these peoples have a future and not merely a tragic present and an irretrievable primitive past. An impassioned defense of pagan primitivism is the subtle theme uniting the impressionistic diary pictures of *African Mirage*, by Hoyningen Huene, by considerable odds one of the most understandingly observed and beautifully written volumes in the whole range of this literature. Even with all of our scientific revaluation, all our "New Negro" compensations, all our anti-Nordic polemics, a certain disrespect for Africa still persists widely. There is only one sure remedy—an anointing of the eyes.[1] *African Mirage* seems to me almost a miraculous cure for cultural color-blindness. Such normality of social vision is surely one of the prerequisites also for effective history, sociology and economics; no scientific lens is better except mechanically than the eye that looks through it. Let us above all else pray for clear-minded interpreters.

Alain Locke
"Frontiers of Culture"

Crescent 33 (1950)

I appreciate deeply the very kind introduction and tribute; I also appreciate the opportunity of appearing on this well-planned and inspiring cultural session of the Thirty-fifth Anniversary Conclave of the [Phi Beta Sigma] *Fraternity*. The excellent musical program has provided pure and inspiring pleasure; my own remarks cannot hope to be so unalloyed.

My assigned topic, *The Frontiers of Culture*, was doubtless supposed to tie in appropriately and harmoniously. I hope it may but I warn you that I shall have to set my own key and I am not so sure how harmonious that will be. Certainly it will not be in the traditional close harmony of "barber-shop" tonality so characteristic of old-fashioned fraternal reunions. Neither in time nor place are we assembled tonight "by the fire, by the fire; let it glow, let it glow" with its associated atmosphere of smug self-praise and sentimental satisfaction. The cup of fellowship comes on later; so there is no excuse for mawkishness at this hour. It was suggested that I discuss some of the vistas of modern art in relation to culture. I shall try in doing so to speak my own mind soberly and truthfully; yet certainly with no unusual sense of authority or finality.

What Is Culture?

First a word or so about culture itself. It was once a favorite theme-song word with me. Now I wince at its mention and frankly would like to keep silent on the subject—so great have the misconceptions and misuses been. I recall how focal the world culture was for many movements I have been interested and involved in. In fact, I may have had something to do with its appearance in this *Fraternity's* motto: "Culture for Service, Service for Humanity" (I refuse to recall how responsible.) We may have thought we knew what it all meant. God knows there

was little enough culture either locally or nationally in those distant days; there is still far too little now, as I shall try later to explain. Do not be unduly alarmed: I haven't a tub or a lantern backstage, though as I warned you, I cannot be too pleasant at the expense of the truth as I see it.

Fortunately, one can live without culture, which accounts for the survival of so much both in the past and the present. But I do believe that, though not vital, culture is nevertheless an essential. In fact, after its achievement, it always had and always will rank first; though I am commonsense enough to admit readily the basic importance of bread, with or without butter. I, too, confess that at one time of my life I may have been guilty of thinking of culture as cake contrasted with bread. Now I know better. Real, essential culture is baked into our daily bread or else it isn't truly culture. In short, I am willing to stand firmly on the side of the democratic rather than the aristocratic notion of culture and have so stood for many years, without having gotten full credit, however. I realize the inevitability of such misunderstanding; what price Harvard and Oxford and their traditional snobbisms! Culture is so precious that it is worth even this price, if we can have it only at the high cost of nurturing and conserving it on the upper levels of caste and privilege. But one should not have to pay that exorbitant price for it.

Accordingly, when the "culture clause" was incorporated in the motto of this *Fraternity*, there was the ambition to propagate the culture democratically, to help it permeate ordinary living, to root it in the soil of the group life, to profess it as a folk rather than a class inheritance. It was a daring notion—this of trying to carry culture to the people and have it leaven the lump with the yeast and richness of humane and gracious living. Behind this aim there was necessarily the hope and expectation that a title of leadership could be induced to dedicate itself to the services of the masses and that their richer insight and vision would thus be multiplied a thousand-fold throughout the land.

The New Negro Now

In the context of the life of the Negro there was also the ambitious prospect of developing in areas of lessened competition and handicap, superiorities meriting and capable of winning effective and lasting recognition both for the group and the individual exponents of culture. You will pardon passing mention of the movement that a decade or so after the founding of this *Fraternity* became known, a little too well known, as "The New Negro." Far be it from me to disclaim or disparage a brain child. But in my view, if a "New Negro" is not born and reborn every half generation or so, something is radically wrong, not only with the society in which we live but with us also. According to this calendar, we should have had at least two "New Negroes" since 1925. Be that as it may, the one of 1925 that I am both proud and ashamed of having had something to do with, failed to accomplish all that it could and should have realized. This does not mean that it accomplished nothing. It does mean, however, that because of a false conception of culture it fell short of its potentialities. This is why I bring this matter up this evening. Having signed that "New Negro's" birth certificate, I assume some right to participate in the post-mortem findings. In sum and substance, that generation of cultural effort and self-expression died of a fatal misconception of the true nature of culture.

Both the creative talent of that day and its audience were infected with sound and abortive attitudes: they made culture a marketplace commodity and out of this shallow and sordid misunderstanding did it to death prematurely. Two childish maladies of the spirit—exhibitionism and racial chauvinism—analogues one may say of St. Vitus dance and whooping cough, became epidemic and the basic health of the movement was thereby

sapped. Permit me to say that both these attitudes, fatal to any soundness in culture, were disavowed by most of the responsible leaders but to no avail. Once the movement took on public momentum and offered that irresistible American lure of a vogue of success, a ready means of quick recognition, an easy, cheap road to vicarious compensation, this dangerous infection was on. True, it was a typically American misapprehension, a characteristic American popular abuse but it brought about lamentably a Negro-American tragedy of the first magnitude. Permit me to say, further, that it need not have been. From the beginning racial chauvinism was supposed to be ruled out; five of the collaborators of *The New Negro* were whites whose readily accepted passport was competent understanding of the cultural objectives of the movement and creative participation in them. The substance of Negro life was emphasized, not its complexion. Similarly, it was not promulgated as a movement for cliques and coteries or for the parasitic elite but a movement for folk culture and folk representation, eventually even for folk participation. Ultimately, it was hoped, it would be for, by and of the people. It was democratically open to all who might be interested on the basis of collaboration and mutual understanding. Some of the most effective and welcomed spokesmen were not Negro. Negro self-expression, moreover, was expected to include the saving salt of self-criticism. It was never intended that so vital a movement should be plagued with profiteering parasites almost to the point of losing decent public presentability. And above all, it was realized that no considerable creative advance could carry the dead weight of those hangers-on whose participation was merely in terms of keeping up with the cultural Joneses.

I say these things, however, in a constructive mood, since my emphasis from now on is not to be on the somewhat wasted past but on the vital present and the promiseful future. One important characteristic of the frontiers of culture is that they are always moving (not necessarily forward but at least always moving). I welcome an opportunity to apply the principle of the criticism I have just made as constructively as I can to that present and to the future. It is no new principle, as I hope I have made clear; but it does have a new chance of test and application.

Ghetto Culture

Let us take for granted, if it hasn't been conclusively proven, that culture has no color, that although Negro life and experience should have and are having increased and increasingly effective expression, there is no monopoly, no special proprietary rights, no peculiar credit and no particular needs or benefits about culture.

(In my definition of culture I would include science as well as the arts.) On that basis, then, all we should be sanely concerned about is freer participation and fuller collaboration in the varied activities of the cultural life and that with regard both to the consumer and the producer roles of cultural creation. Democracy in culture means equally wide-scale appreciation and production of the things of the spirit.

Doubtless you will grant these cardinal principles in principle; with even, I dare say, a certain amount of ready acceptance. But follow the corollaries and wince, as well we all may, at their consistent consequences. I shall point out only a few of them. The most obvious, as well as the most important, is that there is no room for any consciously maintained racialism in matters cultural. The generation to which I belong had to do more than its normal share of defensive, promotive propaganda for the Negro but it is my greatest pride that I have never written or edited a book on a chauvinistically racialist basis. Seldom has farsighted Negro scholarship or artistry proceeded on such a basis and today racialism cannot and should not be tolerated. We can afford to be culturally patriotic but never culturally jingoistic. . . .

New Films

Now in a final page or so I come to what I presume the program chairman had in mind when he gave me the assignment: *Frontiers of Culture.*

This is the new frontier and *integration* is its best single caption. Its conquest means collaboration and fraternization, at a considerable present cost and effort but at eventual gain and enlightenment. Had I more time at my disposal I could document more specifically from personal experiences both its costs and its long-term rewards. Suffice it to point out some present-day instances and vindications of cultural integration. The National Board of Review of Motion Pictures recently announced its 1948 citations. Of nine selections on an international basis, three were films of Negro life and situation, *The Quiet One, Intruder in the Dust* and *Home of the Brave.* The first came out of an essentially Negro situation, what was once a corrective school for Negro juvenile delinquents, which fortunately had recently been broadened out to an interracial clientele. This made all the more human and significant the star role of the Negro lad who was the protagonist. *Intruder in the Dust* emerges through Hollywood from Oxford, Mississippi, where at the wise insistence of the author, William Faulkner, and the brave good sense of the director, it was filmed by a mixed cast, with local crowd and bit-part recruits. Here is a truly new horizon and a portentous conquest of a new psychological cultural frontier. And *Home of the Brave*, I hope you have noticed, was not a pro-Negro undertaking at all, despite its hero, but basically an anti-prejudice polemic. Time being short, I make a particular point of these symbolic examples of the new trends I am discussing and trying to vindicate though they are self-vindicating to any open-minded observer. Note that these are films and, therefore, in the most democratic mass medium we have, short of radio. When film and radio begin to change, we can have some realistic hope of a changed American public mind.

When the mass media begin to show signs of social enlightenment and cultural integrity, I repeat, there is a new light on the horizon. First, because they go so far with their message and their reformative influence. But close second to that, they are so accessible to all. Even in the dark zones of segregated living, if enlightened leadership will only take upon itself to praise, support and circulate them. The cultural move of prime importance today is to turn these great and almost limitless resources to the mass media of radio, films, and television to the ends of truer, more objective, mutual understanding and let that become the leaven of a people's culture. The breadth of participation which they make possible happily carries along also that high quality of art and insight which befits true culture. I am, of course, not ignoring the force or role of the more traditional arts, where, as a matter of fact, the new values and attitudes must first experimentally express themselves. *Intruder in the Dust*, for example, was an ultra-literary novel before it became a Hollywood film. However, if work of fresh insight and great artistry is to remain within such limited confines, the hope of a high democratic culture would be indefinitely below the horizon of our time.

Cultural Democracy

But I cannot end on too optimistic a note, even though I believe firmly that a people's culture of high grade will eventually come about somehow, sometime, somewhere. Under conditions that permit it, it does not necessarily follow that a culture with breadth and depth will automatically or inevitably realize itself. Where Town Hall and Senator Claghorn, Jack Armstrong and Quiz Kids, Hillbilly and the Philharmonic simultaneously crowd the ether and are to be had just for the turn of the switch and the dial,

it doesn't follow that the average selectivity will be right. But fortunately that issue is a matter of education and the general public taste rather than a mere question of racial condition or conditioning. There is, however, that special enemy, ghetto-mindedness, which may well give us more than momentary concern. So we still have two arch enemies of mass culture to fight and conquer—Philistinism and prejudice—class bias and group bias.

I know this discussion has not been altogether pleasant going but prose must be conceded its utilitarian uses and obligations. As serious-minded Americans we must all be thinking gravely and rigorously about the present state of the national culture and mindful of the special and yet unrealized demands of culture in a democratic setting. Perhaps it is [a] truism but it is worth repeating that a few present liberal trends with the radical changes of popular attitude potentially involved are projecting helpful incentives toward a more democratic American culture. So far is the emancipation of the public mind from prejudice and group stereotypes, this may be properly regarded as, in large part, a new Negro contribution to the broadening of the nation's culture. But for us as Negroes, it is even more important to realize how necessary it is to share understandingly and participate creatively in these promising enlargements of the common mind and spirit. To be democratic is as important as it is to be treated democratically; democracy is a two-way process and accomplishment.

Notes

Preface

1. Rayford Whittingham Logan, *The Negro in American Life and Thought: The Nadir, 1877–1901* (New York: Dial Press, 1954). Logan's pivotal study was later republished as *The Betrayal of the Negro: From Rutherford B. Hayes to Woodrow Wilson* (New York: Collier Books, 1965).

2. W. E. B. Du Bois and David Levering Lewis, *Black Reconstruction in America* (New York: Free Press, 1998), 30.

3. Stuart Hall, "Race, the Floating Signifier: What More Is There to Say about 'Race'?" In *Selected Writings on Race and Difference*, ed. Paul Gilroy and Ruth Wilson Gilmore (Durham, NC: Duke University Press, 2021), 359.

4. A. B. Bernd, "Reviews of New Books: Mamba's Daughters," *Macon (GA) Telegraph*, March 3, 1929. Thanks to Fred Shapiro for alerting me to this first usage.

5. Jeffrey C. Stewart, *The New Negro: The Life of Alain Locke* (New York: Oxford University Press, 2018), 436.

Introduction

1. "New-England's Great Day," *New-York Tribune*, December 23, 1886.

2. "New-England's Great Day."

3. "A National Santa Claus," *St. Louis Post-Dispatch*, December 27, 1886; "Mr. Grady and the New South," *Chicago Daily Tribune*, December 30, 1886; "New North—New South," *Cincinnati Enquirer*, December 25, 1886; "The Herald's Ticket: Grover Cleveland for President and Henry W. Grady for Vice President," *Daily American*, May 3, 1887.

4. Michael Fellman, *In the Name of God and Country: Reconsidering Terrorism in American History* (New Haven, CT: Yale University Press, 2010), 100–102. For reactions to Grady's address, see "The New South: Things Which Grady Did Not Tell—Some Unpleasant Truths," *San Francisco Chronicle*, February 8, 1887; "Cable on Grady: A Criticism in Rhyme," *Daily Inter Ocean* (Chicago), February 6,

1887; "Mr. Grady's 'New South,'" *Cleveland Gazette*, February 5, 1887; "The New South," *Cleveland Gazette*, August 20, 1887; and "'The New South' Racket," *New York Freeman*, January 22, 1887. See also "The Negro's Judgment in Voting," *New York Age*, December 3, 1887.

5. Henry Louis Gates, Jr., *Stony the Road: Reconstruction, White Supremacy, and the Rise of Jim Crow* (New York: Penguin, 2020), was the first to identify the New Negro as a likely reaction to Grady's New South.

6. Henry Louis Gates, Jr., "The Trope of a New Negro and the Reconstruction of the Image of the Black," *Representations* 24 (1988): 129–55, was the first to identify the New Negro as a trope. The trope of the New Negro continued until 1969, when *Black* became the preferred term to describe African Americans.

7. Robert L. Allen, *The Brotherhood of Sleeping Car Porters: C. L. Dellums and the Fight for Fair Treatment and Civil Rights* (Boulder, CO: Paradigm, 2014), 2. George Hutchinson, *The Cambridge Companion to the Harlem Renaissance* (New York: Cambridge University Press, 2007), for example, argues that the Harlem Renaissance ended in 1937.

8. See Marlon Bryan Ross, *Manning the Race: Reforming Black Men in the Jim Crow Era* (New York: New York University Press, 2004); Daylanne K. English, *Unnatural Selections: Eugenics in American Modernism and the Harlem Renaissance* (Chapel Hill: University of North Carolina Press, 2004); Beryl Satter, *Each Mind a Kingdom: American Women, Sexual Purity, and the New Thought Movement, 1875–1920* (Berkeley: University of California Press, 1999); Jason Chambers, *Madison Avenue and the Color Line: African Americans in the Advertising Industry* (Philadelphia: University of Pennsylvania Press, 2011); Davarian L. Baldwin and Minkah Makalani, *Escape from New York: The New Negro Renaissance beyond Harlem* (Minneapolis: University of Minnesota Press, 2013); Mark Christian Thompson, *Black Fascisms: African American Literature and Culture between the Wars* (Charlottesville: University of Virginia Press, 2007).

9. As Juan González and Joseph Torres, *News for All the People: The Epic Story of Race and the American Media* (New York: Verso Books, 2011), 138, write, the AP quickly became the nation's "gatekeeper" of national news, but "the new technology's instant speed and its monopoly pricing structure demanded shorter and simpler news items, action over reflection, screaming headlines over nuanced analysis. . . . Because of that, AP's dispatches were often filled with blatantly racist distortions." As an alternative to the AP, Claude Barnett formed in 1919 what would become the widely successful Associated Negro Press, which served well over two hundred Black newspapers in Africa and the United States; see Gerald Horne, *The Rise and Fall of the Associated Negro Press: Claude Barnett's Pan-African News and the Jim Crow Paradox* (Urbana: University of Illinois Press, 2017), 5.

10. Allissa V. Richardson, "The Platform: How Pullman Porters Used Railways to Engage in Networked Journalism." *Journalism Studies* 17, no. 4 (2016): 398–414.

11. Gerald Horne, *The Rise and Fall of the Associated Negro Press: Claude Barnett's Pan-African News and the Jim Crow Paradox* (Urbana: University of Illinois Press, 2017), 24–25.

12. Charles A. Simmons, *The African American Press: A History of News Coverage during National Crises, with Special Reference to Four Black Newspapers, 1827–1965* (Jefferson, NC: McFarland, 1997), 20–21. Some of this rise was likely due to Booker T. Washington's financial support; Betty Lou Kilbert Rathbun, "The Rise of the Modern American Negro Press: 1880 to 1914" (PhD diss., University of New York at Buffalo, 1978), 15–24. According to Rayford W. Logan, *The Betrayal of the Negro: From Rutherford B. Hayes to Woodrow Wilson* (London: Collier Books, 1965), 325, the literacy rates for Black Americans rose from 18.6 percent in 1870 to 55.5 percent in 1890.

13. Frederick G. Detweiler, *The Negro Press in the United States* (Chicago: University of Chicago Press, 1922), 10.

14. Silvio Torres-Saillant, "The Tribulations of Blackness: Stages in Dominican Racial Identity," *Latin American Perspectives* 25, no. 3 (1998): 126–46; Celso Thomas Castilho and Rafaella Valença de Andrade Galvão, "Breaking the Silence: Racial Subjectivities, Abolitionism, and Public Life in Mid-1870s Recife," in *The Boundaries of Freedom: Slavery, Abolition, and the Making of Modern Brazil*, ed. Brodwyn Fischer and Keila Grinberg (Cambridge: Cambridge University Press, 2022), 241–63.

15. Paulina L. Alberto, George Reid Andrews, and Jesse Hoffnung-Garskof, *Voices of the Race: Black Newspapers in Latin America, 1870–1960* (Cambridge: Cambridge University Press), 18, 21–23.

16. Alberto, Andrews, and Hoffnung-Garskof, *Voices of the Race*, 1–31.

17. Derek R. Peterson and Emma Hunter, "Print Culture in Colonial Africa," in *African Print Cultures: Newspapers and Their Publics in the Twentieth Century*, ed. Derek R. Peterson, Emma Hunter, and Stephanie Newell (Ann Arbor: University of Michigan Press, 2016), 1–46. According to Rosalynde Ainslie, *The Press in Africa: Communications Past and Present* (New York: Walker, 1966), 9, "Colonial policy was of its nature never designed to create a national awareness among the colonial subjects. The loyalties due to the State were focused upon a foreign metropolitan power; upon the British or the German or the Belgian sovereign, or upon 'la Patrie', which was neither 'le Senegal' nor 'l' Algérie', but 'la France.'"

18. Andrew Roberts, "African Cross-Currents," in *The Cambridge History of Africa*, vol. 7, ed. A. D. Roberts (Cambridge: Cambridge University Press, 1986), 223–66; James Brennan, "Communications and Media in African History," in *The Oxford Handbook of Modern African History*, ed. John Parker and Richard Reid, online ed., Oxford University Press, December 16, 2013, https://academic.oup.com/edited-volume/28187/chapter-abstract/213121466.

19. Evelyn Brooks Higginbotham, *Righteous Discontent: The Women's Movement in the Black Baptist Church, 1880–1920* (Cambridge, MA: Harvard University Press, 1994), 14–15, coined the phrase "politics of respectability" to describe Black Baptist women who "equated public behavior with individual self-respect and with the advancement of African Americans as a group. They felt certain that 'respectable' behavior in public would earn their people a measure of esteem from white America, and hence they strove to win the Black lower class's psychological allegiance to temperance, industriousness, thrift, refined manners, and Victorian sexual morals." Brittney C. Cooper, *Beyond Respectability: The Intellectual Thought of Race Women* (Urbana: University of Illinois Press, 2017), 9, argues that Black women intellectuals such as Anna Julia Cooper, Mary Church Terrell, and Fannie Barrier Williams emphasized "embodied and affective experiences of racism and patriarchy" over any strict allegiance to respectability.

20. Gates, "The Trope of a New Negro."

21. Karin Barber, *The Anthropology of Texts, Persons and Publics: Oral and Written Culture in Africa*

and Beyond (Cambridge: Cambridge University Press, 2007), 185.

22. In this respect, I disagree with Davarian Baldwin, *Chicago's New Negroes: Modernity, the Great Migration, and Black Urban Life* (Chapel Hill: University of North Carolina Press, 2007) and his casting of Jack Johnson as a New Negro. See also C. Weinschenk, "Ellington's Hot Music Worries Fire Chieftain: Music Heats Harlem beyond Prescribed Safety Limits," *New Journal and Guide*, January 17, 1931; "Is the 'Weary, Blues' Poetry or Just Jingle?" *Afro-American*, June 13, 1925; "Florence Mills!," *Pittsburgh Courier*, November 12, 1927, 1.

Miller, "The New Negro and the Old," *New Journal and Guide*, November 27, 1926, includes W. C. Handy and Paul Robeson as key figures in the "ministry" that will show "to the world the worth of the Negro race." My analysis herein has benefited from an online conversation with my coeditor; Henry Louis Gates, Jr., email to the author, "1933 Reference," September 6, 2024.

23. Marlon B. Ross, *Manning the Race: Reforming Black Men in the Jim Crow Era* (New York: New York University Press, 2004), 17–18.

24. Gerald Horne, *The Rise and Fall of the Associated Negro Press: Claude Barnett's Pan-African News and the Jim Crow Paradox* (Urbana: University of Illinois Press, 2017), 5; John Patrick Leary, "Havana Reads the Harlem Renaissance: Langston Hughes, Nicolás Guillén, and the Dialectics of Transnational American Literature," *Comparative Literature Studies* 47, no. 2 (2010): 133–58.

25. See Adam Ewing, *The Age of Garvey: How a Jamaican Activist Created a Mass Movement and Changed Global Black Politics* (Princeton, NJ: Princeton University Press, 2014).

26. Robert P. Smith, "Black Like That: Paulette Nardal and the Negritude Salon," *CLA Journal* 45, no. 1 (2001): 53–68; Claire Oberon Garcia, "Black Women Writers in Early Twentieth-Century Paris," in *The Routledge Companion to Black Women's Cultural Histories*, ed. Janell Hobson (Abingdon, UK: Routledge, 2021), 255–65; Jennifer Anne Boittin, "In Black and White: Gender, Race Relations, and the Nardal Sisters in Interwar Paris," *French Colonial History* 6 (2005): 119–35.

27. Arnold Rampersad, *The Life of Langston Hughes*, vol. 1, *1902–1941* (New York: Oxford University Press, 1986), 180.

28. Alexander Crummell, "The Need of New Ideas and New Aims for a New Era" (address to the graduating class of Storer College, Harper's Ferry, WV, 1885), in *Civilization and Black Progress: Selected Writings of Alexander Crummell on the South* (Charlottesville: University of Virginia Press, 1995). The speech was originally published in *AME Review* 2 (1885): 115–27.

29. Eric Foner, in Henry Louis Gates, Jr. and Eric Foner, "Penny Stamps Speaker Series," video, PBS, February 1, 2021, https://www.pbs.org/video /henry-louis-gates-jreric-foner-penny-stamps -speaker-series-w9lbc9/.

30. Douglas A. Blackmon, *Slavery by Another Name: The Re-enslavement of Black Americans from the Civil War to World War II* (New York: Doubleday, 2008), 7, 90. In response to the "The Negro on the Negro" *Independent* series, the *Hartford Daily Courant* published "The New Negro in the New South," January 8, 1887, which includes the first usage of the trope that I could find. It defined the New Negro as "the most intelligent," "ambitious" and "energetic negroes." See also Richard M. Valelly, *The Two Reconstructions: The Struggle for Black Enfranchisement* (Chicago: University of Chicago Press, 2004); Michael Pfeifer, *Rough Justice: Lynching and American Society, 1874–1947* (Urbana: University of Illinois Press, 2011); Logan, *The Betrayal of the Negro*, 85, 149–51; and Kathy Roberts Forde and Sid Bedingfield, eds., *Journalism and Jim Crow: White Supremacy and the Black Struggle for a New America* (Urbana: University of Illinois Press, 2021). For statistics on Black literacy rates, see Logan, *The Betrayal of the Negro*, 68.

31. Joel Williamson, *The Crucible of Race: Black-White Relations in the American South since Emancipation* (New York: Oxford University Press, 1984), 117.

32. The *Independent* series asked the following questions of both Black men and women: "Are the colored people fast accumulating property?" "Are there any laws in your state more oppressive to one race than another?" "What unfairness, if any, is shown to the colored people because of their color [especially in regard to churches and schools]?" "What social customs, if any, are objectionable or oppressive to the colored people?" "What is the greatest single hindrance to the race's advancement?" "Are there more children of mixed blood born now than in slavery?" "The Negro on the Negro," *Independent*, January 6, 1887; "The Negro on the Negro," *Independent*, January 13, 1887; "The Negro on the Negro," *Independent*, January 20, 1887; "The Negro on the Negro," *Independent*, January 27, 1887; "The Negro on the Negro," *Independent*, February 3, 1887; "The Negro on the Negro," *Independent*, February 17, 1887.

33. "The New Negro in the New South," *Hartford Daily Courant*, January 8, 1887.

34. "Ingalls Denounced. The Colored Press Demands Justice and Fair Play. Let Everybody Read This," *Washington Bee*, February 19, 1887. While Crummell primed the path for the first version of the New Negro in that he associated the "new" with those Black Americans who were college educated, born after slavery, and abounding with the energy of youth and race commitment, he lamented the "political ambitions" that seemed to be "the craze of very many young minds."

35. Mia Bay, *To Tell the Truth Freely: The Life of Ida B. Wells* (New York: Hill and Wang, 2009), 54; "Ingalls Denounced"; David W. Blight, *Frederick Douglass: Prophet of Freedom* (New York: Simon and Schuster, 2018), 660–61. Blight makes this assertion reflecting on a speech given by Frederick Douglass in 1884.

36. "Ingalls Denounced."

37. I am indebted to Henry Louis Gates, Jr. for identifying the New Negro as a "social media" campaign.

38. Bruce Grit [John Edward Bruce], "National Capital Topics. Discrimination in the Pension Office," *New York Age*, July 28, 1888.

39. "Pointers: Colored Voters Need Fixing" *Times-Observer* (Topeka, KS), September 4, 1891.

40. "A Journalistic Ajax of the Race," *The Freeman, An Illustrated Colored Newspaper* (Indianapolis), August 23, 1890. Beginning in the March 30, 1895, issue, the *Richmond Planet*'s masthead presented a central image of a Black man's muscular arm and raised fist with lightning bursting through the letter *o* in "Richmond."

41. John Mitchell, "'What the Negro Owes Us,'" *Richmond (VA) Planet*, December 20, 1890. For more on the 1886 lynching threat Mitchell received, see "A Journalist Ajax of the Race."

42. Mitchell's response to the lynching threat would emphasize the manliness of the New Negro. Quoting Shakespeare, he responded by declaring, "'There are no terrors, Cassius, in your threats, for I am armed so strong in honesty that they pass me by like the idle winds, which I respect not.' He then traveled by train to Charlotte County wearing Smith & Wesson revolvers." John W. Mitchell Jr., quoted in Ann Field Alexander, *Race Man: The Rise and Fall of the "Fighting Editor," John Mitchell Jr.* (Charlottesville: University of Virginia Press, 2002), 42. Although Mitchell lauded congressmen and senators as signs of "Negro progress," by 1890, only three Black congressmen remained; Ida A. Brudnick and Jennifer E. Manning, *African American Members of the United States Congress: 1870–2018*, RL30378 (Washington, DC: Congressional Research Service, December 28, 2018), 6. For a discussion of tactics used to suppress the Black vote in Richmond, including long delaying tactics, see Alexander, *Race Man*, 76–71, 102–16. For an account of the Readjuster Party's platform, see Jane Dailey, *Before Jim Crow: The Politics of Race in Postemancipation Virginia* (Chapel Hill: University of North Carolina Press, 2000), 82–83.

43. Ian R. Tyrrell, *Woman's World / Woman's Empire: The Woman's Christian Temperance Union in International Perspective, 1880–1930* (Chapel Hill: University of North Carolina Press, 1991); Anna Julia Cooper, "The Status of Woman in America," in *A Voice from the South* (New York: Oxford University Press, 1988): 127–45.

44. Cooper, "The Status of Woman in America," 131, emphasis in the original. See also Shirley Moody-Turner and James Stewart, "Gendering Africana Studies: Insights from Anna Julia Cooper," *African American Review* 43, no. 1 (2009): 35–44; and Anna Julia Cooper, *The Voice of Anna Julia Cooper: Including "A Voice from the South" and Other Important Essays, Papers, and Letters*, ed. Charles C. Lemert and Esme Bhan (Lanham, MD: Rowman and Littlefield, 1998), 60.

45. Robin D. G. Kelley and Earl Lewis, *To Make Our World Anew*, vol. 2, *A History of African Americans since 1880* (New York: Oxford University Press, 2005), 60; Fannie Barrier Williams, "The Intellectual Progress of the Colored Women of the United States since the Emancipation Proclamation," in *The World's Congress of Representative Women*, ed. May Wright Sewall (Chicago: Rand McNally, 1894), 696–711.

46. Mamie E. Locke, "Williams, Fannie Barrier," Oxford African American Studies Center, December 1, 2006, https://oxfordaasc.com/display/10.1093/acref/9780195301731.001.0001/acref-9780195301731-e-43893.

47. "A New South: Atlanta's Exposition Is Opened," *Los Angeles Times*, September 19, 1895; Booker T. Washington, "The Atlanta Exposition Address," in *Up from Slavery*, ed. William L. Andrews (New York: Norton, 1996): 99.

48. Booker T. Washington, "Negro's Jubilee Year," letter, *New York World*, September 20, 1895.

49. "The New Negro," *Daily Inter Ocean* (Chicago), October 2, 1895, 6.

50. Stewart Emory Tolnay and E. M. Beck, *A Festival of Violence: An Analysis of Southern Lynchings, 1882–1930* (Urbana: University of Illinois Press, 1995), 17, 31.

51. Mrs. Booker T. Washington, "The New Negro Woman," in *The American New Woman Revisited: A Reader, 1894–1930*, ed. Martha H. Patterson (New Brunswick, NJ: Rutgers University Press, 2008), 55.

52. See Barbara Welter, "The Cult of True Womanhood: 1820–1860," *American Quarterly* 18, no. 2, pt. 1 (1966): 151–74. For a discussion of the degendering of Black women in slavery and beyond, see Hortense Spillers, "Mama's Baby, Papa's Maybe: An American Grammar Book," *Diacritics* 17, no. 2 (1987): 65–81. For discussions of how Black writers, activists, and clubwomen used the cult of true womanhood, see Paula Giddings, *When and Where I Enter: The Impact of Black Women on Race and Sex in America* (New York: Bantam, 1988), 47–48; Hazel V. Carby, *Reconstructing Womanhood: The Emergence of the Afro-American Woman Novelist* (New York: Oxford University Press, 1987); and Claudia Tate, *Domestic Allegories of Political Desire: The Black Heroine's Text at the Turn of the Century* (New York: Oxford University Press, 1992). For the evolution of stereotypes of Black women, see Patricia Hill Collins, *Black Feminist Thought: Knowledge, Consciousness, and the Politics of Empowerment* (London: Routledge, 2000); and Melissa V. Harris-Perry, *Sister Citizen: Shame, Stereotypes, and Black Women in America* (New Haven, CT: Yale University Press, 2011).

53. Washington, "The New Negro Woman," 54, 57–58. See also Jacqueline Anne Rouse, "Out of the Shadow of Tuskegee: Margaret Murray Washington, Social Activism and Race Vindication," *Journal of Negro History* 81, nos. 1–4 (1996): 31–46; and Booker T. Washington, "Letter to Ednah Dow Littlehale Cheney," November 23, 1896, in *The Booker T. Washington Papers*, vol. 4, *1895–98*, ed. Louis R. Harlan (Urbana: University of Illinois Press, 1972), 238–39.

54. Washington, "The New Negro Woman," 54–59.

55. Florence Ledyard Cross Kitchelt, "An Excerpt from the Journal of Florence Ledyard Cross Kitchelt," April 3, 1901, in *The Booker T. Washington Papers*, vol. 6, *1901–2*, ed. Louis R. Harlan and Raymond W. Smock (Urbana: University of Illinois Press, 1977), 84–85.

56. See Martha H. Patterson, "Selling the American New Woman as Gibson Girl," in *Beyond the Gibson Girl: Reimagining the American New Woman, 1895–1915* (Urbana: University of Illinois Press, 2010), 27–49.

57. See, for example, Eleanor Tayleur, "The Negro Woman—Social and Moral Decadence," *Outlook*, January 30, 1904, 266–71; and Edward Kemble, "Ise Gwine ter Give You Gals What Straddle," *Life*, September 8, 1899, 255.

58. "A Race Problem to Solve," *Herald* (Leavenworth, KS), July 20, 1895; Pauline E. Hopkins, ed. "Women's Department," in Patterson, *The American New Woman Revisited*, 159.

59. Fannie Barrier Williams, "The Club Movement Among Colored Women of America," in *A New Negro for a New Century*, ed. Booker T. Washington, N. B. Wood, and Fannie Barrier Williams (Chicago: American Publishing House, 1900), 424–26.

60. Cooper, *Beyond Respectability*, 34–43.

61. David Levering Lewis, *W. E. B. Du Bois: A Biography* (New York: Henry Holt, 2009), 120–25. See also W. E. B. Du Bois, Letter to Booker T. Washington, September 24, 1895, in *The Correspondence of W. E. B. Du Bois*, ed. Herbert Aptheker, vol. 1, *Selections, 1877–1934* (Amherst: University of Massachusetts Press, 1973), 39. Founded in Des Moines, Iowa, in 1894, the Black-owned "fighting" *Bystander* relied on more established Black newspapers for its national coverage; Sally Steves Cotton, "The Iowa Bystander: A History of the First 25 Years" (master's thesis, Iowa State University, 1983), 1, 23. On December 3, 1895, the *Springfield (MA) Republican* also reprinted on its front-page Du Bois's creed from the *New York Age*. Before being published in the *Iowa Bystander*, Du Bois's "Creed" had first appeared in a now lost issue of *New York Age*, whose editor, T. Thomas Fortune, was well known in the early 1890s Black press for his militant campaign against lynching and for civil rights; Emma Lou Thornbrough, *T. Thomas Fortune: Militant Journalist* (Chicago: University of Chicago Press, 1972), 117–25.

62. W. E. B. Du Bois, *The Talented Tenth: Excerpt from the Negro Problem* (New York: James Pott, 1903), 15.

63. Booker T. Washington, "Booker T. Washington Delivers the 1895 Atlanta Compromise Speech," in *The Booker T. Washington Papers*, vol. 3, *1889–95*, ed. Louis R. Harlan (Urbana: University of Illinois Press, 1974), 583–87. See also Washington, "Negro's Jubilee Year." In W. E. C. Wright, "The New Negro," *Advance*, November 2, 1893, in addition to asserting the New Negro's attention to self-reliance, thrift, and education, Wright also associates the New Negro with more intellectual and less emotionally charged religious practices.

64. "Men of the Hour," *Colored American* (Washington, D.C.), July 19, 1902; David Zucchino,

Wilmington's Lie: The Murderous Coup of 1898 and the Rise of White Supremacy (New York: Atlantic Monthly Press, 2020).

65. In the frontispiece, Washington's name is printed in bold, first and larger than the other contributors, a highlighting decision that was especially misleading given that ten of *The New Negro*'s eighteen chapters were reprinted from N. B. Wood's *The White Side of a Black Subject* (1897). In the book, his name is given as MacBrady, but some other sources indicate his name as McBrady. In a letter to MacBrady, Washington protested the use of his photo on the cover, giving the impression that he had written the book, and for being underpaid by less than half of what he had been promised; Booker T. Washington, "To J. E. MacBrady" and "To Emmett J. Scott," in *Booker T. Washington Papers*, vol. 5, *1899–1900*, ed. Louis R. Harlan and Raymond W. Smock (Champaign: University of Illinois Press, 1977), 570, 591. See also Albert Nelson Marquis, ed., *The Book of Chicagoans: A Biographical Dictionary of the Leading Living Men of the City of Chicago* (Chicago: A. N. Marquis, 1911), 434. For a detailed account of T. Thomas Fortune's ghostwriting in the book, see Elizabeth McHenry, *To Make Negro Literature: Writing, Literary Practice and African American Authorship* (Durham, NC: Duke University Press, 2021), 155.

66. Robert J. Norrell, *Up from History: The Life of Booker T. Washington* (Cambridge, MA: Harvard University Press, 2009), 144. See also Kathy Peiss, *Hope in a Jar: The Making of America's Beauty Culture* (Philadelphia: University of Pennsylvania Press, 2011) 110; and Michael Bieze, *Booker T. Washington and the Art of Self-Representation* (New York: Peter Lang, 2008), 98.

67. Her chapter is advertised on the title page as "The Colored Woman and Her Part in Race Regeneration."

68. Booker T. Washington, Fannie Barrier Williams, and Norman B Wood, eds., *A New Negro for a New Century: An Accurate and Up-to-Date Record of the Upward Struggles of the Negro Race* (Chicago: American Publishing House, 1900). See also Willard B. Gatewood, "Black Americans and the Quest for Empire, 1898–1903," *Journal of Southern History* 38, no. 4 (1972): 545–66.

69. George P. Marks III, "Civil Rights, Patriotism, and the Spanish American War," *The Black Press Views American Imperialism*, ed. George P. Marks III (New York: Arno Press, 1971), 51.

70. Darlene Clark Hine, "Rape and the Inner Lives of Black Women in the Middle West— Preliminary Thoughts on the Culture of Dissemblance," in *Unequal Sisters—A Multicultural Reader in U.S. Women's History* (New York: Routledge, 1990), 292–97; Kevin Kelly Gaines, *Uplifting the Race: Black Leadership, Politics, and Culture in the Twentieth Century* (Chapel Hill: University of North Carolina Press, 1996), 5–6.

71. To claim such an ideal left the New Negro policing the Black masses and perpetually competing in a supposed racial hierarchy; Marlon B. Ross, *Manning the Race: Reforming Black Men in the Jim Crow Era* (New York: New York University Press, 2004), 15–19.

72. Gaines, *Uplifting the Race*, 9, argues that the "tragic difficulty of *racial* uplift ideology" lies in its efforts to combat an "*intellectual* dependence on dominant ideologies of whiteness and white constructions of Blackness" (emphasis in the original).

73. See John Cullen Gruesser, *A Literary Life of Sutton E. Griggs: The Man on the Firing Line* (New York: Oxford University Press, 2022), 57–82. See also John Gruesser, "Empires at Home and Abroad in Sutton E. Griggs's *Imperium in Imperio*," in *Jim Crow, Literature, and the Legacy of Sutton E. Griggs*, ed. Tess Chakkalakal and Kenneth W. Warren (Athens: University of Georgia Press, 2013), 49–68; and Caroline Levander, "Sutton Griggs and the Borderlands of Empire," in Chakkalakal and Warren, *Jim Crow, Literature, and the Legacy of Sutton E. Griggs*, 21–48.

74. For a detailed analysis of the similarities between Griggs and Piedmont, see Gruesser, *A Literary Life*, 57–82.

75. Sutton E. Griggs, *Imperium in Imperio: A Study of the Negro Race Problem; A Novel*, Project Gutenberg, July 7, 2024, www.gutenberg.org/cache /epub/15454/pg15454-images.html. I am indebted to John Gruesser's argument in "Empires at Home."

76. As Tiya Miles and Sharon P. Holland, "Introduction," in *Crossing Waters, Crossing Worlds: The African Diaspora in Indian Country*, ed. Tiya Miles and Sharon P. Holland (Durham, N.C: Duke University Press, 2006), 4, note, "By the late nineteenth century and early twentieth century, many African Americans had come to see the Western lands called Indian Territory as a refuge in America, and more, as a potential *black space* that would function metaphorically and emotionally as a substitute for the longed-for African homeland" (emphasis in the original). See also Emily Lutenski's *West of Harlem: African American Writers and the Borderlands* (Lawrence: University Press of Kansas, 2015).

77. See Painter, Nell Irvin Painter, *Exodusters: Black Migration to Kansas after Reconstruction* (Lawrence: University Press of Kansas, 1986).

78. Blanche Ketene Bruce, editorial, *Leavenworth Herald*, July 20, 1895.

79. "The Passing Throng," *Seattle Republican*, September 18, 1906.

80. Lutenski, *West of Harlem*, 28–29.

81. Emily Lutenski, email to author, "Great to meet you," November 12, 2024.

82. Douglas Flamming, *Bound for Freedom: Black Los Angeles in Jim Crow America*. 1st ed. (Berkeley: University of California Press, 2005): 1–2.

83. Editorial. "Charles S. Blodgett," *California Eagle* (Los Angeles), July 11, 1924.

84. Shawn Michelle Smith, *Photography on the Color Line: W. E. B. Du Bois, Race, and Visual Culture* (Durham, NC: Duke University Press, 2004, 2–3).

85. Booker T. Washington, "Booker T. Washington, 'Atlanta Compromise' Speech, 1895," in Mark Christian, *Booker T. Washington: A Life in American History* (Santa Barbara, CA: ABC-CLIO, 2021), 219.

86. Logan, *The Betrayal*, 62, 165.

87. S. A. Steel, "The Modern Negro," *Southwestern Christian Advocate* (New Orleans), November 28, 1895. Steel was the editor of *The Epworth Era*, the organ of the Southern branch of the Methodist Episcopal Church.

88. Thomas Nelson Page, "A New Aspect of the Negro Question," *Atlanta Constitution*, March 2, 1903. See also Glenda Elizabeth Gilmore, *Gender and Jim Crow: Women and the Politics of White Supremacy in North Carolina, 1896–1920* (Chapel Hill: University of North Carolina Press, 1996), 85.

89. Foster Morse Follett, "Life's Presidential Impossibilities: A Dark Horse from Alabama," cartoon, *Life*, April 21, 1904, 387.

90. "The Negro Problem and the New Negro Crime," *Harper's Weekly*, June 20, 1903, 1050–51.

91. "The New Negro Crime Again Considered," *Harper's Weekly*, October 3, 1903, 1577.

92. "Some Fresh Suggestions about the New Negro Crime," *Harper's Weekly*, January 23, 1904, 120–21.

93. Eleanor Tayleur, "The Negro Woman: I—Social and Moral Decadence," *Outlook*, January 30, 1904, 266–71.

94. W. E. B. Du Bois, "The Forethought" and "Of Our Spiritual Strivings" in *The Souls of Black Folk* (New York: Barnes and Noble Classics, 2003), 9. See also John Henry Adams, "Rough Sketches: William Edward Burghardt Du Bois, Ph.D," *Voice of the Negro*, March 1905, 176–81.

95. W. E. B. Du Bois, "Of Booker T. Washington and Others," in *The Souls of Black Folk*, 35–47; Adena Spingarn, *Uncle Tom: From Martyr to Traitor* (Stanford, CA: Stanford University Press, 2018), 145.

96. W. E. B. Du Bois, "The Niagara Movement: Address to the Country" (1906), in *W. E. B. Du Bois: A Reader*, ed. David Levering Lewis (New York: Henry Holt, 1995), 367–69.

97. John H. Adams Jr., "Rough Sketches: A Study of the Features of the New Negro Woman," *Voice of the Negro*, August 1904, 181.

98. Adams, "Rough Sketches," 324–26.

99. Adams, "Rough Sketches," 447, 448, 451. In the inaugural issue of *The Voice of the Negro*, J. Max Barber is listed as the managing editor and J. W. E. Bowen as the editor. "Our Monthly Review," *Voice of the Negro*, January 1904, p. 7.

100. S. Laing Williams, "The Pulpit: The New Negro," *Unity*, August 13, 1908, 375–78.

101. Zita Nunes, *Cannibal Democracy: Race and Representation in the Literature of the Americas* (Minneapolis: University of Minnesota Press, 2008): xi–xv.

102. José Clarana [James Bertram Clarke, Jaime Gil], "The Schooling of the Negro," *Crisis*, July 13, 1913, 133–36.

103. Leslie Pinckney Hill, "Negro Ideals—Their Effect and Their Embarrassments," *Journal of Race Development* 6, no. 1 (1915): 91–103.

104. "A Lesson from 'The Clansman.'" *Sedalia (MO) Weekly Conservator*, January 21, 1907.

105. Hill, "Negro Ideals"; William Pickens, "Fifty Years after Emancipation," in *The New Negro: His Political, Civil and Mental Status, and Related Essays* (New York: AMS, 1916), 58.

106. William Pickens, "The New Negro," in *The New Negro*, 232–33, 235, 239.

107. The official death toll was thirty-nine Black people and nine white, but other estimates place it much higher; Charles L. Lumpkins, *American Pogrom: The East St. Louis Race Riot and Black Politics* (Athens: Ohio University Press, 2008), 126–27, 141. See also Marcus Garvey, "Printed Address by Marcus Garvey on the East St. Louis Riots," in *The Marcus Garvey and Universal Negro Improvement Association Papers*, ed. Robert A. Hill, vol. 1, *1826–1919* (Berkeley: University of California Press, 1983), 212–13.

108. Scott Ellsworth, "Tulsa Race Massacre," in *The Encyclopedia of Oklahoma History and Culture*, online ed., Oklahoma Historical Society, n.d., https://www.okhistory.org/publications/enc/entry

.php?entry=TU013, accessed October 22, 2024; Cameron McWhirter, *Red Summer: The Summer of 1919 and the Awakening of Black America* (New York: Henry Holt, 2011), 13–17; Jan Voogd, *Race Riots and Resistance: The Red Summer of 1919* (New York: Peter Lang, 2008), 14, 21–23.

109. Hubert Harrison, "As the Currents Flow," in *A Hubert Harrison Reader*, ed. Jeffrey B. Perry (Middleton, CT: Wesleyan University Press, 2001), 98.

110. Winston James, *Holding Aloft the Banner of Ethiopia: Caribbean Radicalism in Early Twentieth-Century America* (New York: Verso Books, 1999), 109.

111. Jeffrey B. Perry, *Hubert Harrison: The Voice of Harlem Radicalism, 1883–1918* (New York: Columbia University Press, 2009), 3–11, 243, 282, 304; Jeffrey B. Perry, *Hubert Harrison: The Struggle for Equality, 1918–1927* (New York: Columbia University Press, 2021), 66–71; Hill, *The Marcus Garvey and Universal Negro Improvement Association Papers*, 1:210–11.

112. Theodore Kornweibel Jr., *No Crystal Stair: Black Life and "the Messenger," 1917–1928* (Westport, CT: Greenwood, 1975), 51.

113. "Following the Advice of the 'Old Crowd' Negroes," cartoon, *Messenger*, September 1919, 16; "The 'New Crowd Negro' Making America Safe for Himself," *Messenger*, September 1919, 17; David F. Krugler, *1919, the Year of Racial Violence: How African Americans Fought Back* (New York: Cambridge University Press, 2014), 73–77.

114. Kornweibel, *No Crystal Stair*, 53–54.

115. Kornweibel, *No Crystal Stair*, 77.

116. Theodore Kornweibel Jr., *"Seeing Red": Federal Campaigns Against Black Militancy, 1919–1925* (Bloomington: Indiana University Press, 1998), 21–25, 53. See also Jervis Anderson, *A. Philip Randolph: A Biographical Portrait* (New York: Harcourt Brace Jovanovich, 1973), 138; and Perry, *Hubert Harrison: The Voice of Harlem Radicalism*, 304.

117. William Forsythe Jr., "A. Philip Randolph Thrills Local Audience in Plea for Brotherhood: Hundreds Applaud and Subscribe to Porters' Cause Inter Club Council has Successful Program at Y.M.C.A.—Enthusiastic Speeches by Local Youths." *Pittsburgh Courier*, September 17, 1927; Eugene Gordon, "The Negro Press," *Annals of the American Academy of Political and Social Science* 140, no. 1 (1928): 248–56; see also Beth Tompkins Bates, *Pullman Porters and the Rise of Protest Politics in Black America, 1925–1945* (Chapel Hill: University of North Carolina Press, 2001), 31–33.

118. "The Negro Woman Voter," *Messenger*, November 1920, 131, 147.

119. Harry Haywood, *Black Bolshevik: Autobiography of an Afro-American Communist* (Chicago: Liberator, 1978), 126. The *Crusader* folded in 1922; see James, *Holding Aloft the Banner of Ethiopia*, 160.

120. James, *Holding Aloft the Banner of Ethiopia*, 155–77; Cyril Briggs, "Bolshevist!!!," *Crusader*, October 1919, 9; Paul M. Heideman, "Cyril V. Briggs," in *Class Struggle and the Color Line*, ed. Paul Heideman (Chicago: Haymarket, 2018), 235–37; Cyril Briggs, "The Old Negro Goes: Let Him Go in Peace," *Crusader*, October 1919, 9–10.

121. Lumpkins, *American Pogrom*; Hill, *The Marcus Garvey and Universal Negro Improvement Association Papers*, 1:lxvi.

122. Daniel Hanglberger, "Marcus Garvey and His Relation to (Black) Socialism and Communism," *American Communist History* 17, no. 2 (2018): 200–219.

123. Adam Ewing, *The Age of Garvey: How a Jamaican Activist Created a Mass Movement and Changed Global Black Politics* (Princeton, NJ: Princeton University Press, 2014), 1. See also Mary G. Rolinson, *Grassroots Garveyism: The Universal Negro Improvement Association in the Rural South, 1920–1927* (Durham, NC: University of North Carolina Press, 2007).

124. Using the digital version of the *Negro World*, former Harvard University graduate student and current British-Nigerian journalist Seun Matiluko counted 544 usages; Seun Matiluko, email to the author, "Garvey on The New Negro," September 10, 2024. McKendree University student Elizabeth Bocock counted 665 usages relying on the digitally available and legible text between 1921 and 1933. She found considerably more use of the trope in the *Negro World*'s early years before it gradually trailed off. After tallying the number of "New Negro" references in every issue, Bocock discovered that, at the trope's peak, Garvey deployed it up to nine times in one weekly issue.

125. J. R. R. C. [Joseph Raphael Ralph Casimir], letter to the editor, *Dominica Guardian*, April 29, 1920; Kathy Casimir MacLean, *Black Man Listen: The Life of JR Ralph Casimir* (London: Papillote, 2022), 43–44, Kindle.

126. "A.M.E. Church and Negro Movement," *Black Man: A Journal Propagating the Interests of Workers throughout the African Continent*, October 1, 1920, 4.

127. Jacques Garvey's series ran from February 1924 to April 1927; in 1927, the paper added the Spanish-language and French-language pages. Ac-

cording to Barbara Bair, "'Our Women and What They Think': Amy Jacques Garvey, the New Negro Woman, and the Woman's Page of the Negro World," in *Feminist Forerunners: New Womanism and Feminism in the Early Twentieth Century*, ed. Ann Heilmann (New York: Pandora, 2003), 103, "Jacques Garvey detailed her vision that the page be simultaneously grassroots, multinational, cross-class, and multicultural in its scope." Keisha N. Blain, *Set the World on Fire: Black Nationalist Women and the Global Struggle for Freedom* (Philadelphia: University of Pennsylvania Press, 2018), 16–25; Ula Y. Taylor, *The Veiled Garvey: The Life and Times of Amy Jacques Garvey* (Chapel Hill: University of North Carolina Press, 2002), 65–68, 71–72; and Amy Jacques Garvey, "Woman's Function in Life," *Negro World*, December 19, 1925.

128. Eunice Lewis, "Our Letter Box," *Negro World*, April 19, 1924; Saydee Parham, "New Woman," *Negro World*, February 2, 1924.

129. James Weldon Johnson, "Preface to the First Edition," in *The Book of American Negro Poetry*, ed. James Weldon Johnson (New York: Harcourt Brace, 1951), 9, 41–42; Johnson, "Preface to the Revised Edition," in *The Book of American Negro Poetry*, rev. ed., ed. James Weldon Johnson (New York: Harcourt Brace and World, 1958), 304; James Weldon Johnson, "Introduction to the First Edition," in *The Collected Poems of Sterling A. Brown*, edited by Michael S. Harper (Evanston, IL: TriQuarterly Books, 1996), 17.

130. Alain J. Locke, "Sterling Brown: The New Negro Folk-Poet," in *Negro: An Anthology*, ed. Nancy Cunard and Hugh D. Ford (New York: F. Ungar, 1970), 88.

131. As Nancy Cunard, "Foreword," in Cunard and Ford, *Negro*, xxxi–xxxii, writes, "the chord of oppression, struggle, and protest rings, trumpet like or muffled, but always insistent throughout. In the present day, it is not possible to write otherwise of the Negro, and to write with truth."

132. Henry Louis Gates, email to the author, "Edits!," April 8, 2024. See also Johnson, "Preface to the First Edition," *The Book of American Negro Poetry*, 9–48; James Weldon Johnson, "Introduction to *Southern Road* (1932)," in *After Winter: The Art and Life of Sterling A. Brown*, ed. John Edgar Tidwell and Steven C. Tracy (New York: Oxford University Press, 2009), 21–22.

The discussion herein is based on Gates's well-reasoned argument that the Harlem Renaissance spanned the decade 1922–32, which he makes more fully in Henry Louis Gates, Jr., *The Black Box: Writing the Race* (New York: Penguin, 2024).

133. David Levering Lewis, *When Harlem Was in Vogue* (New York: Oxford University Press, 1981), 94.

134. Jessie Fauset, quoted in Jeffrey C. Stewart, *The New Negro: The Life of Alain Locke* (New York: Oxford University Press, 2018), 408–19.

135. Lewis, *When Harlem Was in Vogue*, 122.

136. "500 Enthusiastic Porters Loudly Cheer Proposed Porters' Union," *Amsterdam News* (New York), September 2, 1925; "N.Y. Porters Launch New Labor Union," *Afro-American*, September 5, 1925; "Another New Negro," *Pittsburgh Courier*, June 11, 1927.

137. "Another New Negro," *Courier*, June 11, 1927; Cornelius L. A. Bynum, *Philip Randolph and the Struggle for Civil Rights* (Urbana: University of Illinois Press, 2010), 134, 154.

138. Alain Locke, "The New Negro," in *The New Negro: An Interpretation*, ed. Alain Locke (New York: A. and C. Boni, 1925), 3, 7, 9, 14–16.

139. Locke, "The New Negro," 11, 14, 9. For more on Garvey's commitment to "racial purity," see Tony Martin, *Race First: The Ideological and Organizational Struggles of Marcus Garvey and the Universal Negro Improvement Association* (Dover, MA: Majority Press, 1986), 22, 344–47.

140. "White-Robed Klan Cheered on March in Nation's Capital," *Washington Post*, August 9, 1925. For a discussion of Locke's *New Negro* as a liminal text, see Margo Natalie Crawford, *Black Post-Blackness: The Black Arts Movement and Twenty-First-Century Aesthetics* (Urbana: University of Illinois Press, 2017).

141. Adam McKible, *Circulating Jim Crow: The Saturday Evening Post and the War against Black Modernity* (New York: Columbia University Press, 2024).

142. Jane Nardal, "Internationalisme noir," *La dépêche africaine*, February 15, 1928, trans. T. Denean Sharpley-Whiting as "Black Internationalism," in T. Denean Sharpley-Whiting, *Negritude Women* (Minneapolis: University of Minnesota Press, 2002), 105–7. See also T. Denean Sharpley-Whiting, "Jane Nardal: A New Race Spirit and the Francophone New Negro," in *Negritude Women*, 42; and Alain Locke, "The New Negro," in Locke, *The New Negro*, 9, 11.

143. Although Nardal was not able to publish the translation, the volume was still an important source of inspiration to Négritude writers; Brent Hayes Edwards, *The Practice of Diaspora: Literature, Translation, and the Rise of Black Internationalism* (Cambridge, MA: Harvard University Press, 2003), 16–17, 20.

144. Sadie T. M. Alexander, "The Emancipated Woman," in *Democracy, Race, and Justice: The*

Speeches and Writings of Sadie T. M. Alexander, ed. Nina Banks (New Haven, CT: Yale University Press, 2021), 58–64; Alice Dunbar Nelson, "From the Woman's Point of View," *Pittsburgh Courier*, January 2, 1926; Juanita Ellsworth, "Hail, the Western Man!," *Flash*, December 1929, 14.

145. "Pink Teas," *Philadelphia Tribune*, May 17, 1928; "He Had Better Go to Work," cartoon, *Philadelphia Tribune*, May 17, 1928; Marlon Bryan Ross, *Sissy Insurgencies: A Racial Anatomy of Unfit Manliness* (Durham, NC: Duke University Press, 2022), 6; Robert Ezra Park, "Education in Its Relation to the Conflict and Fusion of Cultures," in *Race and Culture* (Glencoe, IL: Free Press, 1950), 280. On the meaning of "pink teas," see Kim E. Nielsen, *Un-American Womanhood: Antiradicalism, Antifeminism, and the First Red Scare* (Athens: Ohio State University Press, 2001), 34. Adena Spingarn argues that "the emergence of a new black masculine ideal which, following a turn-of-the-century 'crisis of masculinity,' replaced the standards of civilization and Christian virtue with self-assertion." *Uncle Tom: From Martyr to Traitor* (Stanford, CA: Stanford University Press, 2018), 143.

146. "He Had Better Go To Work"; Henry Louis Gates, Jr., "The Black Man's Burden," in *Fear of a Queer Planet: Queer Politics and Social Theory*, ed. Michael Warner (Minneapolis: University of Minnesota Press, 1993), 233.

147. Dunbar-Nelson, Alice. "Une femme dit," *Courier*, April 24, 1926, 7.

148. Devere Allen, "Building Tomorrow's World: The New White Man." *World Tomorrow* 10, no. 3 (1927): 124–25.

149. Gustavo E. Urrutia, "Puntos de vista del nuevo negro" ["Points of View of the New Negro"], Inaugural del ciclo de confer-encias de caracter social, cientifico y educacional, ofrecido por el Instituto en su centro de estudios, pronunciada el cia, 8 de Julio de 1937. Nov. 1937, Schomburg Center for Research in Black Culture, Del Caribe, N° 46, 2005, 107–19. Cuba, 1937. Trans. Thomas Holloway.

150. T. Arnold Hill, quoted in "Finds Negroes' Need Growing in Nation: Urban League Aide Says Job Discrimination Adds Heavily to Charities Burden," *New York Times*, April 5, 1931; David Levering Lewis, *When Harlem Was in Vogue* (New York: Oxford University Press, 1981); 240; Cheryl Lynn Greenberg, *To Ask for an Equal Chance: African Americans in the Great Depression* (Lanham, MD: Rowman and Littlefield, 2009), 21–41; Cheryl Lynn Greenberg, *"Or Does It Explode?" Black Harlem in the Great Depression* (New York: Oxford University Press, 1991), 42–45.

151. See George Schuyler, "An Appeal to Young Negroes," Ella Barker Papers, box 2, folder 3, Schomburg Center for Research in Black Culture, New York Public Library; Irvin J. Hunt, "Planned Failure: George Schuyler, Ella Baker, and the Young Negroes' Cooperative League," *American Quarterly* 72, no. 4 (2020): 853–79; Jessica Gordon Nembhard, *Collective Courage: A History of African American Cooperative Economic Thought and Practice* (University Park: Penn State University Press, 2015), 112–25.

152. Ella Baker and Marvel Cooke, "The Bronx Slave Market," *Crisis*, November 1935, 330–31, 340. See also Marvel Cooke, "'Modern Slaves': Domestic Jobs Are Miserable in Hours, Pay. Union Is Seeking to Relieve Their Bad Situation," *Amsterdam News* (New York), October 16, 1937.

153. "Editor Is Given Oath of Office," *Pittsburgh Courier*, July 8, 1933.

154. Nancy J. Weiss, *Farewell to the Party of Lincoln: Black Politics in the Age of FDR* (Princeton, NJ: Princeton University Press, 1983), 50–54.

155. Clister L. Johnson, "The New Deal, the New Year, the New Negro," *Afro-American Courier* (Yazoo City, MS), January 1, 1936.

156. Gilbert Ware, "The New Negro Alliance: 'Don't Buy Where You Can't Work,'" *Negro History Bulletin* 49, no. 3 (1986): 3–8; Paul D. Moreno, *From Direct Action to Affirmative Action: Fair Employment Law and Policy in America, 1933–1972* (Baton Rouge: Louisiana State University Press, 1997), 31–50. In Dutton Ferguson's "Thoughts While Picketing," he uses the phrase "Buy Where You Can Work." *New Negro Opinion*, December 16, 1933, 2.

157. Urrutia, "Puntos de vista del nuevo negro" ["Points of View of the New Negro"]; Anne Marie Guarnera, "Our Black América: Transnational Racial Identities in Twentieth-Century Cuba and Brazil" (PhD diss., University of Virginia, 2017).

158. William R. Scott, "Black Nationalism and the Italo-Ethiopian Conflict, 1934–1936," *Journal of Negro History* 63, no. 2 (1978): 118–34; Aric Putnam, "Ethiopia Is Now: J. A. Rogers and the Rhetoric of Black Anticolonialism during the Great Depression," *Rhetoric and Public Affairs* 10, no. 3 (2007): 419–44.

159. Scott, "Black Nationalism"; Putnam, "Ethiopia Is Now."

160. Andrew Buni, *Robert L. Vann of the Pittsburgh Courier: Politics and Black Journalism* (Pittsburgh: University of Pittsburgh Press, 1974), 227.

161. George Schuyler, "Views and Reviews," *Pittsburgh Courier*, August 3, 1935; Frank R. Cross-

waith, "The Future Is Ours," *Black Worker* (New York), August 1, 1936.

162. See Paul Gilroy, "Black Fascism," *Transition* 9, no. 1 (2000): 70–91; and Mark Christian Thompson, *Black Fascisms: African American Literature and Culture between the Wars* (Charlottesville: University of Virginia Press, 2007), 27–29. Although in his weekly newspaper the *Blackman*, Garvey condemned Italy's invasion of Ethiopia, in an interview with Joel A. Rogers in 1937 he insisted that the New Negro was a fascist: "We were the first Fascists. We had disciplined men, women and children in training for the liberation of Africa"; Marcus Garvey, quoted in Martin, *Race First*, 60–62.

163. Brooks E. Hefner, introduction to *Black Empire*, by George S. Schuyler (New York: Penguin, 2023).

164. Samuel L. Brooks, "The Black Internationale: Story of Black Genius against the World," *Pittsburgh Courier*, March 6, 1937; Samuel L. Brooks, "Black Empire: Martha and Her Group Shoot Their Way out of Police Trap and Arrive at Rendezvous," *Pittsburgh Courier*, January 22, 1938, 11; Samuel I. Brooks, "The Black Internationale," *Pittsburgh Courier*, January 9, 1937, 13; Brooks, Samuel I. Brooks, "Black Empire," *Pittsburgh Courier*, November 6, 1937, 11; Samuel I. Brooks, "Black Empire," *Pittsburgh Courier*, November 20, 1937, 11; Samuel I. Brooks, "The Black Internationale," *Pittsburgh Courier*, June 26, 1937, 11; Samuel I. Brooks, "Black Internationale," *Pittsburgh Courier*, November 28, 1936, 13; Samuel I. Brooks, "The Black Internationale," *Pittsburgh Courier*, December 5, 1936, 13.

165. "Questions and Answers," *Courier*, May 8, 1937; "Questions and Answers," *Courier*, December 4, 1937; George S. Schuyler, "The Rise of the Black Internationale," *Crisis*, August 1938, 277.

166. My argument is informed by Leigh Raiford's "Photography and the Practices of Critical Black Memory," *History and Theory* 48, no. 4 (2009): 112–29; and Houston A. Baker, "Critical Memory and the Black Public Sphere," *Public Culture* 7, no. 1 (1994): 3–33.

167. Ta-Nehisi Coates, *The Message* (New York: One World, an imprint of Random House, 2024), 59.

Part I. The New South and the New Negro, 1885–1894

1. With a mission to educate the formerly enslaved, Storer College (1867–1956) was a historically Black college located in Harpers Ferry, Virginia. Through-

out the 1880s, Storer "began to adopt manual labor into a formal curriculum by offering vocational and industrial courses along with its other programs." See Douglas Terry, "Reading the *Storer Record*: Negotiating Race and Industrial Education at Storer College during the Age of Jim Crow," *West Virginia History: A Journal of Regional Studies* 11, no. 2 (2017): 121.

2. Richard Chenevix Trench, *On the Study of Words: Lectures Addressed (Originally) to the Pupils at the Diocesan Training School, Winchester* (London: Macmillan, 1851), 18–19.

3. 1 Cor. 16:13.

4. Luke 1:17.

5. Founded in New York City on the principles of Congregationalism and antislavery, the white-owned *Independent* weekly newspaper (1848–1928) had a circulation of fifteen thousand in 1877. See Frank Luther Mott, "The Independent," in *A History of American Magazines, 1741–1930*, vol. 2, *1860–1865* (Cambridge, MA: Harvard University Press, 1958), 367–79, https://hdl-handle-net.ezp-prod1.hul.harvard.edu/2027/heb00678.0002.001. PDF.

6. Recognized as the longest-running American newspaper, in publication continuously since 1764, the *Hartford (CT) Courant* was at the time a leading white Republican paper. See J. Bard McNulty, *Older Than the Nation: The Story of the Hartford Courant* (Stonington, CT: Pequot, 1964).

7. Founded and edited by African American lawyer W. C. Chase, the *Washington (DC) Bee* (1882–1922) was a Black Republican weekly whose early motto was "Sting for Our Enemies—Honey for Our Friends." See "The Washington Bee (Washington, D.C.) 1884–1922," Library of Congress, n.d., https://www.loc.gov/item/sn84025891/, accessed August 22, 2023.

8. The oldest Black newspaper in Missouri, the *St. Louis Advance* (1881–1908), was founded by Philip H. Murray and was committed to the "industrial education of the Negro." See Writers' Program of the Work Projects Administration in the State of Missouri, *Missouri: The WPA Guide to the "Show Me" State* (St. Louis: Missouri Historical Society Press, 1998).

9. On December 21, 1886, President Grover Cleveland nominated James C. Matthews, who would become the first Black judge elected in New York State, to replace Frederick Douglass as Recorder of Deeds for the District of Columbia. Republican Senator John J. Ingalls led the effort to reject his candidacy. William J. Simmons, *Men of Mark: Eminent, Progressive, and Rising* (Cleveland, OH: Geo M.

Rewell, 1887), 973; "James Campbell Matthews: First African American Elected Judge in New York State," New York State Unified Court System, Third Judicial District, accessed April 2, 2025, https://www.nycourts.gov/info/Diversity_Inclusion/Newsletter/05/images/Matthews-Poster.pdf.

10. The first African American to be admitted into Philadelphia's Academy of Fine Arts, John Henry Smythe (1844–1908) graduated from Howard University Law School in 1870. In 1878 President Rutherford Hayes appointed Smythe to serve as the minister resident and consul general to Liberia, where he developed a Pan-African consciousness. Upon his return to the United States, he urged Black people to emigrate to Africa. See "John Henry Smythe (1844–1908)," Falvey Library, Villanova University, n.d., https://exhibits.library.villanova.edu/institute-colored-youth/graduates/john-henry-smyth-bio, accessed August 16, 2024.

11. Published by Fred A. Turner and edited by J. Hume Childers, the Kansas Republican *Times-Observer* (1891–92) proclaimed on its masthead, "Race Progress Financially, Industrially and Educationally." Childers, known for his pen name Fearless when writing for previous newspapers, pronounced his mission in the *Times-Observer* as considering "the Negro first, last and all the time." In 1892 he helped found the Interstate Literary Association. See Aleen J. Ratzlaff, "Black Press Pioneers in Kansas: Connecting and Extending Communities in Three Geographic Sections, 1878–1900" (PhD diss., University of Florida, 2001), https://ufdcimages.uflib.ufl.edu/AA/00/03/14/83/00001/blackpresspionee00ratz.pdf, 93–94, 108–9, 142.

12. Published by the Advance Company, a Chicago Congregationalist association, the *Advance* (1867–1917) was a white weekly paper that marketed itself as a "family newspaper of the highest excellence." "Advance," in *Newspapers and Periodicals of Illinois, 1814–1879*, ed. Frank W. Scott and Edmund J. James (Springfield: Illinois State Historical Library, 1910), 88–89.

13. Held alongside the 1893 Columbian Exposition in Chicago, the overwhelmingly white World's Congress of Representative Women celebrated the progress of women since 1492. Of the over five hundred speakers, Williams was one of six African Americans who were invited to speak. See Sara C. VanderHaagen, "'A Grand Sisterhood': Black American Women Speakers at the 1893 World's Congress of Representative Women," *Quarterly Journal of Speech* 107, no. 1 (2021): 1–25.

Part II. The Booker T. Washington Era, 1895–1903

1. When it was founded by the stalwart Republican Blanche Ketene Bruce, the first Black graduate from the University of Kansas–Lawrence, the *Leavenworth Herald* saw as its mission to provide "to all citizens the brighter, nobler and manlier side of our people, a phase not gleaned from the daily press." See Aleen J. Ratzlaff, "Black Press Pioneers in Kansas: Connecting and Extending Communities in Three Geographic Sections, 1878–1900" (PhD diss., University of Florida, 2001), https://ufdcimages.uflib.ufl.edu/AA/00/03/14/83/00001/blackpresspionee00ratz.pdf, 58.

2. In 1883, Joseph Pulitzer bought the struggling *New York World* (1860–1931) and turned it into a progressive, sensationalist powerhouse filled with tawdry stories and plenty of illustrations. By 1896 the paper boasted a circulation of six hundred thousand. See George Juergens, *Joseph Pulitzer and the New York World* (Princeton, NJ: Princeton University Press, 1966); and Frank Luther Mott, *American Journalism: A History, 1690–1960*, 3rd ed. (New York: Macmillan, 1962).

3. Founded by J. Young Scammon, Chicago's *Daily Inter Ocean* (1872–1914) ran under the motto "Republican in everything, independent in nothing." In 1875, William Penn Nixon, an Earlham College graduate and staunch Republican, became editor and gained full control of the paper in 1894 until his departure in 1897. See David Ward Wood, *History of the Republican Party and Biographies of Its Supporters: Illinois Volume* (Chicago: Lincoln Engraving and Publishing, 1895); and "Words of Wisdom," *Daily Inter Ocean* (Chicago), June 19, 1888.

4. The *Southwestern Christian Advocate* (1877–1929) was published weekly by the Episcopal Church of New Orleans and edited at this time by Rev. E. W. S. Hammond. The paper was "read by the whites more than . . . any other Afro-American journal in the Union"; see Garland Penn and Frederick Douglass, *The Afro-American Press and Its Editors* (Springfield, MA: Willey, 1891), 226. Through the first decade of the twentieth century the *Advocate* ran a "Lost Friends" column from readers hoping to find loved ones separated during slavery; see "Lost Friends: Advertisements from the Southwestern Christian Advocate," database, Historic New Orleans Collection, n.d., https://www.hnoc.org/research/lost-friends-advertisements-southwestern-christian-advocate, accessed August 24, 2023.

5. Before being published in the *Iowa State Bystander* (1894–1916), Du Bois's "Creed" first appeared in a now lost issue of the *New York Age*, whose editor, T. Thomas Fortune, was well known in the early 1890s Black press for his militant campaign against lynching and for civil rights; see Emma Lou Thornbrough, *T. Thomas Fortune; Militant Journalist* (Chicago: University of Chicago Press, 1972), 117–25. Founded in Des Moines in 1894 and edited for the majority of its run by John Lay Thompson, the Black-owned, "fighting" *Bystander* relied on more established Black newspapers for its national coverage and published under the motto of "Fear God, Tell the Truth, and Make Money"; see "About Iowa State Bystander. [volume] (Des Moines, Iowa) 1894–1916," Library of Congress, n.d., https://chroniclingamerica.loc.gov/lccn/sn83025186/, accessed August 24, 2023. At this point in his career, Du Bois, who was teaching at Wilberforce University, had not yet publicly voiced objections to Booker T. Washington's worldview; see Martha H. Patterson, introduction, in W. E. B. Du Bois, "'A Creed for the "New Negro"' and 'A Negro on Etiquet of Caste,'" *PMLA: Publications of the Modern Language Association of America* 138, no. 2 (2023): 343–45.

6. Founded by Edward Everett Hale, Boston's monthly *Lend a Hand* (1843–1982) was a journal committed to reform, philanthropy, and uplift, publishing articles on "Negroes, Indians, and immigrant groups." See Martha H. Patterson, "'The New Negro Woman,'" *The American New Woman Revisited: A Reader, 1894–1930*, ed. Martha H. Patterson (New Brunswick, NJ: Rutgers University Press, 2008), 54.

7. Organized in 1890 and restricted to avowed Republicans committed to "Civil Service reform," the Hamilton Club devoted itself to the "advancement of political science, the promotion of good government . . . and the development of patriotism and Republican principles." The club particularly celebrated its banquets, "among the great political banquets of the country," and sought to have "the South" included in each one. See *Hamilton Club of Chicago* (Chicago: Hamilton Club of Chicago, 1899): 15–18.

8. Among the first American women to own and publish a major daily newspaper, Eliza Jane Poitevent Holbrook Nicholson (pen name, Pearl Rivers) served as publisher and editor of the New Orleans *Daily Picayune* (1837–1914) from 1876 until her death in early 1896. Popular for its editorials and society pages, the *Picayune* maintained that the white race was the superior race, "[at] least by culture, and experience." In 1895, a *Picayune* editorial insisted that "the vote of the ignorant, shiftless and shifting negro . . . population" had to be eliminated to ensure honest elections. See Lamar W. Bridges, "Eliza Jane Nicholson and the *Daily Picayune*, 1876–1896," *Louisiana History* 30, no. 3 (1989): 272.

9. Some of the same phrases in this article also appear in Eleanor Tayleur's essay "The Negro Woman: I—Social and Moral Decadence" in part III of this volume.

10. Published by Louis A. Godey, edited for the majority of its run by Sarah Josepha Hale, and known for its fashion plates, literature, and endorsement of women's education, *Godey's Magazine* (1830–98)—alternatively, *Godey's Lady's Book*—had reached a peak in the 1850s but increasingly fell out of favor in the decades that followed. See Kathleen L. Endres and Therese L. Lueck, "Gody's Lady's Book," in *Women's Periodicals in the United States: Consumer Magazines* (Westport, CT: Greenwood, 1995), 113–17.

11. The character Felix Cook is a reference to the actual postmaster of Lake City, South Carolina, Frazier Blake, who, along with his young daughter, is murdered by a white mob in February of 1898; see "1898 Postmaster Lynching," National Postal Museum, Smithsonian Institution, n.d., https://postalmuseum.si.edu/exhibition/behind-the-badge-case-histories-assaults-and-murders/1898-postmaster-lynching, accessed July 25, 2024.

12. Sutton Griggs's father, Allen R. Griggs, a Texas Baptist minister, helped found the Texas Farmers' Association, whose goal was to enable Black people throughout the United States to purchase land in the Texas Panhandle to escape Jim Crow discrimination and violence. Allen Griggs is listed as one of the incorporators of the association, whose charter was filed with the Texas secretary of state in 1890; see Debra Ann Reid, *Seeking Inalienable Rights: Texans and Their Quests for Justice* (College Station: Texas A&M University Press, 2009), 7–8; "Colored Convention," *Galveston Daily News*, February 18, 1880; and "State Capitol," *Austin (TX) Weekly Statesman*, January 9, 1890. Marc Blanc, "Bleeding Heartland: Race, Region, and Radicalism in Midwest Print Culture, 1877–1939" (PhD diss., Washington University, 2024), argues that in *Imperium* Sutton Griggs essentially reimagines his father's plan. For the character Belmont as a stand-in for Griggs, see John Cullen, *A Literary Life of Sutton E. Griggs: The Man on the Firing Line* (Oxford: Oxford University Press, 2022), 78–82.

13. The official organ of the A. M. E. Zion Church, the *Star of Zion* (1876–), published in Char-

lotte, North Carolina, has historically promoted African American civil rights, educational attainment, and economic uplift; see Wiley J. Williams, "African Methodist Episcopal Zion Church," NCpedia, 2006, https://www.ncpedia.org/religion/african -methodist-episcopal-zion-church.

14. Founded by N. E. Stevens, the *Paxton Daily Record* (1865–2021) was published in Ford County, Illinois, 100 miles south of Chicago. See "Paxton Daily & Weekly Record," in *Illinois Newspaper Directory* (Champaign, IL: H. L. Williamson, 1934), 465.

15. Founded in 1833 by Thomas Meredith, the *Biblical Recorder* (Raleigh, NC) is the official journal of the North Carolina Baptist State Convention. From 1895 to 1907, the progressive Josiah Bailey served as editor. See "The History of the Biblical Recorder," *Biblical Recorder*, n.d., https://www.brnow .org/history/, accessed November 21, 2024; and "Baptists," in *Encyclopedia of North Carolina*, ed. William Stevens Powell (Chapel Hill: University of North Carolina Press, 2006), 89.

16. The Colored Co-operative Publishing Company, founded by Harper S. Fortune, Walter Alexander Johnson, Walter Wallace, and Jesse W. Watkins, launched the *Colored American Magazine* in 1900 to foreground African American literature, celebrate Black progress, and protest injustice. Pauline Hopkins edited the women's section beginning in 1901. At its peak the magazine claimed a circulation of seventeen thousand. It ceased publication in 1909. See "The Digital Colored American Magazine," n.d., https://www.coloredamerican.org/, accessed August 24, 2023.

17. Established in 1850 by the slavery advocate James Cowardin, the *Daily Dispatch*, the first penny paper south of Baltimore, maintained that slavery was essential to Virginia's economic success, decried Reconstruction, and "consistently printed racist commentary." In 1884 it changed its name to the *Richmond Dispatch*. See "About Richmond Dispatch. [volume] (Richmond, Va.) 1884–1903," Library of Congress, n.d., https://chroniclingamerica.loc.gov /lccn/sn85038614/, accessed August 24, 2023.

Part III. The W. E. B. Du Bois Era, 1903–1916

1. Founded by Fletcher Harper and made famous by its Civil War coverage, *Harper's Weekly* (1856–1916) was a popular American political magazine devoted to foreign and domestic affairs. Its circula-

tion was eighty thousand in 1904. See Frank Luther Mott, "Harper's Weekly," in *A History of American Magazines, 1741–1930*, vol. 2, *1850–1865* (Cambridge, MA: Belknap Press of Harvard University Press, 1938), 469–87; and "Harper's Weekly," in *N. W. Ayer & Son's American Newspaper Annual and Directory* (Philadelphia: N. W. Ayer and Son's, 1905), 601.

2. The *Outlook* began as the *Church Union* in 1867 in New York City. In 1893, under editor Lawrence F. Abbott, it became more secular, a family magazine devoted to the arts and news. According to Abbott, the *Outlook* believed "in the immortality of the spirit and in changes of forms, in the old religion and in a new theology, in the old patriotism and in new politics, in the old philanthropy and in new institutions, in the old brotherhood and in a new social order." From 1900 to 1902 it published Booker T. Washington's *Up from Slavery* in serial form. It boasted a circulation of one hundred thousand in 1902. See Martha H. Patterson, "'The Negro Woman—Social and Moral Decadence,'" *The American New Woman Revisited: A Reader, 1894–1930*, ed. Martha H. Patterson (New Brunswick, NJ: Rutgers University Press, 2008), 71. Since there are no other contemporaneous articles written by an "Eleanor Tayleur," nor other historical references to her, this may be a pen name.

3. Some of the same phrases in this article also appear in the anonymous essay "Domestic Evolution" in part II of this volume.

4. Founded in Boston in 1815, the *North American Review* is the oldest literary and political magazine in the United States. From 1899 to 1926 it was edited by George B. M. Harvey, who concurrently (1901–13) edited *Harper's Weekly* and also supported Theodore Roosevelt in the 1904 presidential campaign. See Frank Luther Mott, "The North American Review," in *A History of American Magazines, 1741–1930*, vol. 2, *1850–1865* (Cambridge, MA: Belknap Press of Harvard University Press, 1938), 219–61.

5. The remaining seven items in this column were still territories in 1904 and thus are not included in the table's main alphabetical listing of incorporated states.

6. * For outrages in Arkansas, see "Brooks-Baxter War." [Footnote in the original. In 1874, the supporters of two Republican contenders for Arkansas governor—Joseph Brooks, a former Radical Republican who endorsed civil rights for the formerly enslaved, and Elisha Baxter, a native Unionist— battled throughout the state until President Ul-

ysses S. Grant interceded and endorsed Baxter as the winner. The result signaled the end of Reconstruction in the South. See Ralph Hartsock, "Brooks-Baxter War (1874)," in *Revolts, Protests, Demonstrations, and Rebellions in American History: An Encyclopedia*, ed. Steven Laurence Danver (Santa Barbara, CA: ABC-CLIO), 545–48. See also Carl H. Moneyhon, "Joseph Brooks (1821–1877)," *Encyclopedia of Arkansas*, August 15, 2024, encyclopediaofarkansas.net/entries/joseph-brooks-1602/.]

7. [Footnote in the original.] It is significant that, on large plantations where the negroes, though in large numbers, are still in the position of old plantation servants, the crime of assault is unknown.

8. [Footnote in the original.] The following table is from the Chicago *Tribune*. The number of legal executions in 1900 was 118, as compared with 131 in 1899, 109 in 1898, 128 in 1897, 122 in 1896, 132 in 1895, 132 in 1894, 126 in 1893, and 107 in 1892. The executions in the several States and Territories were in 1900 as follows. . . . There were 80 hanged in the South and 39 in the North, of whom 60 were whites, 58 were blacks, and one a Chinaman. The crimes for which they were executed were: murder, 113; rape, 5; arson, 1. Thus, of the 119 hangings, about two-thirds (80) were in the South and one-third (39) in the North; about one-half (60) of the entire number were of whites, and one-half (58) were of blacks. So, the South appears to have done its part in the matter of punishing by law as well as by violence.

9. [Footnote in the original.] See "The American Negro," by William Hannibal Thomas, pp. 65, 177.

10. Terrell's "Lynching from a Negro's Point of View" was written in response to Thomas Nelson Page's "The Lynching of Negroes," which Terrell called "one of the most scurrilous attacks on colored men of this country which has ever appeared in print." Only when her friend William Dean Howells intervened with the editor on her behalf did the *North American Review* publish her response. See Martha Solomon Watson, "Mary Church Terrell vs. Thomas Nelson Page: Gender, Race, and Class in Anti-Lynching Rhetoric," *Rhetoric and Public Affairs* 12, no. 1 (2009): 65–89.

11. An Atlanta-based illustrated Black monthly devoted to race relations, education, and state and national politics, the *Voice of the Negro* (1904–7) quickly became recognized as a leading race periodical. Although managing editor Jesse Max Barber initially offered a balance between Atlanta radicals and accommodationists, he increasingly became hostile to Booker T. Washington's policy of public concili-

ation to white racism. After the Atlanta Race Riot of 1906, Barber objected to racist coverage of the massacre and was forced to flee to Chicago. At its peak, the magazine reported a circulation of fifteen thousand. See Martha H. Patterson, "Rough Sketches: A Study of the Features of the New Negro Woman," in *The American New Woman Revisited: A Reader, 1894–1930*, ed. Martha H. Patterson (New Brunswick, NJ: Rutgers University Press, 2008), 168–69.

12. Published and edited for the majority of its run by Horace Cayton Sr., with assistance from his wife Susie Revels (who, in 1900, officially became the paper's associate editor), the *Seattle Republican* (1894–1913) was the most successful of Seattle's early Black newspapers. Since Seattle's Black community in the late nineteenth century numbered only in the few hundreds and, initially, given the small numbers of Black Seattle residents, discrimination was much less than that experienced by African Americans in other parts of the United States, much of the paper's early success rose from the fact that it attracted both a Black and white readership. Even though anti-Black discrimination increased relative to the number of Black Seattle residents, Cayton repeatedly urged his Eastern readers to move west to escape the worst of Jim Crow. Readership across the state may have been as high as ten thousand. See "About the Seattle Republican. [volume] (Seattle, Wash.) 1???–1915," Library of Congress, n.d., https://chroniclingamerica.loc.gov/lccn/sn84025811/, accessed August 26, 2023; and Richard S. Hobbs, *The Cayton Legacy: An African American Family* (Pullman: Washington State University Press, 2002), 22–33.

13. Founded and edited by Harry Clay Smith until his death in 1941, the *Cleveland Gazette* (1883–1945), with the motto "In Union There Is Strength," took an uncompromising integrationist position and became one of the longest-running Republican Black newspapers begun in the nineteenth century. By the mid-1890s Smith shifted the paper's focus to stories about Black "home life, social betterment, education, and economic efficiency." By 1906 the paper had reached a circulation of five thousand. See Summer E. Stevens and Owen V. Johnson, "From Black Politics to Black Community: Harry C. Smith and the Cleveland 'Gazette.'" *Journalism Quarterly* 67, no. 4 (1990): 1090–102.

14. Published and edited by William H. Huston, the *Sedalia Weekly Conservator* (1903–9) was a four-page Black weekly newspaper printed at George R. Smith College in Sedalia, Missouri. Striving to inculcate "a higher standard of [C]hristian culture in

the home" and a "more progressive and persistent effort in the business world," the *Conservator* sought to promote racial uplift, education, and art, including the work of Scott Joplin. See "About Sedalia Weekly Conservator. (Sedalia, Mo.) 1903–1909," Library of Congress, n.d., https://chroniclingamerica .loc.gov/lccn/sn89067598/, accessed August 26, 2023.

15. In 1906, the famous muckraking monthly *McClure's Magazine* lost a number of its leading writers, including Ray Stannard Baker, when they left to purchase and edit the *American Magazine* (1906–15). Formerly *Frank Leslie's Popular Monthly* (1876–1904), the new *American Magazine* published both exposés and light content. See Frank Luther Mott, "The American Magazine," in *A History of American Magazines, 1741–1930*, vol. 3, *1865–1885* (Cambridge, MA: Belknap Press of Harvard University Press, 1938), 510–16.

16. Booker T. Washington recruited Tuskegee graduate Charles Alexander to launch the Boston monthly *Alexander's Magazine* in 1905 to counter the popularity of the civil rights militant Monroe Trotter's newspaper, the *Guardian*. Even though Washington funded the literary magazine, after the Atlanta massacre in 1906, when white mobs murdered dozens of African Americans, and the Brownsville Affair just one month later, when Washington refused to criticize President Theodore Roosevelt's railroading of Black soldiers, a disillusioned Alexander could no longer promote Washington's accommodationist stance. Openly praising W. E. B. Du Bois, Alexander strove without success to unify the Trotter, Du Bois, and Washington political factions. The magazine ceased publication in 1909. See Mark R. Schneider, "The Colored American and Alexander's: Boston's Pro-Civil Rights Bookerites," *Journal of Negro History* 80, no. 4 (1995): 157–69, https://doi.org/10.2307 /2717440; Clifford Kuhn and Gregory Mixon, "Atlanta Race Massacre of 1906," *New Georgia Encyclopedia*, last modified November 14, 2022, https://www .georgiaencyclopedia.org/articles/history -archaeology/atlanta-race-massacre-of-1906/.

17. After the white farmer James Cunningham shot the Black sharecropper Rufus Browder, Browder shot and killed Cunningham. A white mob then lynched Browder and three of his friends in Russellville, Kentucky, in early 1908. A note was pinned to one of the bodies: "Let this be a warning to you niggers to let white people alone or you will go the same way." See George C. Wright, *Racial Violence in Kentucky, 1865–1940: Lynchings, Mob Rule, and "legal Lynchings,"* (Baton Rouge: Louisiana State University Press, 1996), 124–25.

18. Burroughs is referring to herself in the third person here, and to her one-act play, *The Slabtown District Convention.*

19. Not to be confused with Samuel Taylor Coleridge, for whom he was named, Samuel Coleridge-Taylor (1875–1912) toured the United States in the early 1900s to wide acclaim. Besides his popular "Hiawatha" settings, his works include *African Romances (7 Poems of Paul Laurence Dunbar)*, op. 17. See Roanne Edwards, "Coleridge-Taylor, Samuel," Oxford African American Studies Center, December 1, 2006, https://oxfordaasc.com/display/10.1093 /acref/9780195301731.001.0001/acref-9780195301731 -e-40792.

20. The numerous mentions of "[SCORE ILLUSTRATION]" indicate examples of musical scores that were inserted as images throughout the original essay. They have not been included in this version.

21. Begun in 1903 by Black Republican and Booker T. Washington admirer Benjamin Jefferson Davis as the official organ of the fraternal organ of the Grand United Order of Odd Fellows and Knights of Pythias, the weekly *Atlanta Independent* was designed as a corrective to the Atlanta *Constitution*, which "'obscure[d] the virtues of Negroes and parade[d] their vices,' highlighting 'worthless, trifling, characterless Negroes and advertis[ing] them to the world as leaders, and pay[ing] no attention to the law-abiding, moral substantial black citizens.'" In fact, the *Constitution* was widely blamed for stoking the anti-Black racist hysteria that lit the fuse of the Atlanta massacre in 1906 when, among other atrocities, the bodies of three Black men were arranged at the base of a statue of *Constitution* editor and New South champion Henry Grady. The *Atlanta Independent* folded in 1933, during the Great Depression. See David Stephen Bennett, "Framing Atlanta: Local Newspapers' Search for a Nationally Appealing Racial Image (1920–1960)," dissertation, Michigan State University, 2020, 22–23, 95; Rebecca Burns, *Rage in the Gate City: The Story of the 1906 Atlanta Race Riot* (Athens: University of Georgia Press, 2009), 53, 123.

22. Edited for its first twenty-five years by W. E. B. Du Bois, the *Crisis* has been the official organ of the National Association for the Advancement of Colored People since 1910. See Lisa Clayton Robinson, "Crisis, The," Oxford African American Studies Center, December 1, 2006, https://oxfordaasc.com /display/10.1093/acref/9780195301731.001.0001/acref -9780195301731-e-40890.

23. Published by Clark University, the *Journal of Race Development* (1910–19) was edited by George Blakeslee and G. Stanley Hall and assembled contributions from famous intellectuals, civil servants, missionaries, diplomats, and others. Contributing editors included sociologists Franz Boas, W. E. B. Du Bois, and Thorstein Veblen. See Jessica Blatt, "'To Bring Out the Best That Is in Their Blood': Race, Reform, and Civilization in the *Journal of Race Development* (1910–1919)," *Ethnic and Racial Studies* 27, no. 5 (2004): 691–709.

24. Featuring Micheaux's alter ego, the traveling salesman Sidney Wyeth, *The Forged Note* largely takes place in the South, where Micheaux had been touring while selling his previous novels, and praises both W. E. B. Du Bois and Booker T. Washington. The novel centers on the Atlanta (Attalia in the novel) murder of the white teenage girl Mary Phagan. A Black man is the initial suspect, but later suspicions turn on the Jewish man Leo Frank, part owner of a factory, and his Black accomplice James Conley, who left a series of incriminating notes near the girl's body. In August 1915 a white mob stormed the prison and lynched Leo Frank. Micheaux's description of the Black minister Henry Hugh Hodder refers to Rev. Henry Hugh Proctor of Atlanta's First Congregational Church, and the character Mr. Herman likely refers to Alonzo Herndon, the wealthy Black barbershop owner, entrepreneur, and civil rights leader. See Patrick McGilligan, *Oscar Micheaux, the Great and Only: The Life of America's First Great Black Filmmaker* (New York: HarperCollins, 2007), 99–104; and Matthew H. Bernstein, "'At This Time in This City': Black Atlanta and the Première of *The Birth of a Nation*," in *In the Shadow of the Birth of a Nation: Racism, Reception and Resistance*, ed. Melvyn Stokes and Paul McEwan (New York: Palgrave Macmillan, 2023), 181–82.

25. Founded by Alexander Hamilton in 1801, the white-owned and edited New York *Evening Post* (1801–1922) was edited by Rollo Ogden from 1903 to 1920 and leaned Democratic in this period. See Allan Nevins, *The Evening Post: A Century of Journalism* (New York: Boni and Liveright, 1922).

Part IV. Red Summers and Black Radicalisms, 1917–1921

1. In 1916, Fenton Johnson founded *Champion Magazine* (1916–17), a monthly celebrating Black success in music, sports, and the theater, whose mission was racial reconciliation and "to impress upon the world that it is not a disgrace to be a Negro, but a privilege." After the magazine folded in 1917, Johnson launched the *Favorite Magazine* (1918–21). See Bernard W. Bell, "Johnson, Fenton," Oxford African American Studies Center, December 1, 2006, https://oxfordaasc.com/display/10.1093/acref/9780195301731.001.0001/acref-9780195301731-e-41892.

2. Published by the Workingmen's Cooperative Publishing Association, the *New York Call* (1908–23) was the second English-language Socialist daily newspaper founded in the United States. See *Ten Years of Service: A History of the New York Call* (New York: *New York Call*, 1918).

3. *Voice of the People* (191?–192?), also titled the *Weekly Voice* for part of its run, was published in Birmingham, Alabama, by Mrs. Charlotte Leslie Proctor, a Tuskegee Normal and Industrial Institute graduate who held the title Grand Protector of the Knights and Ladies of Honor of the World. It was the official organ of the Knights and Ladies of Honor of the World, the A.F. and A.M. (or Grand Lodge) of Alabama, and the Order of the Eastern Star. By 1918 it was published weekly by E. W. Howell. See Library of Congress, "The Voice of the People (Birmingham, Ala.) 191?–192?," n.d., https://www.loc.gov/item/sn88050055/, accessed November 27, 2024; and "Grand Protector Calls Honor Grand Lodge to Meet in Annual Session," *Voice of the People*, July 8, 1916.

4. The Hyde Park–Kenwood Property Owners' Association was notorious for its methods of "holding the eastern line of the Black Belt at Cottage Grove Avenue" in Chicago by employing restrictive racial covenants, intimidation, and violence against Black homeowners. In 1920, the association's *Property Owners' Journal* stated, "There is nothing in the make-up of a Negro, physically or mentally, which should induce anyone to welcome him as a neighbor." See Will Cooley, "Moving on Out: Black Pioneering in Chicago, 1915–1950," *Journal of Urban History* 36, no. 4 (2010): 497. The association's slogan was "Make Hyde Park White," and between 1917 and 1921, "unidentified assailants bombed 58 Black-owned properties, including 32 in the Hyde Park–Kenwood area." See National Park Service, U.S. Department of the Interior, National Historic Landmarks Program, *Civil Rights in America: Racial Discrimination in Housing* (Washington, DC: U.S. Department of the Interior, March 2021), https://planning.dc.gov/sites/default/files/dc/sites/op/publication/attachments/Civil_Rights_Housing_NHL_Theme_Study_final.pdf.

5. In 1916, Hygienic Manufacturing Company owner Anthony O. Overton Jr. founded *Half-Century Magazine* (1916–25), a Chicago-based general interest monthly targeted toward women to market his company's products and to promote "personal responsibility, racial pride, and black economic development." Named to commemorate fifty years since the Emancipation Proclamation, *Half-Century* reported a circulation in 1920 of forty-one thousand Black readers and six thousand white readers. See Robert E. Weems Jr., "The Half-Century Magazine," in *The Merchant Prince of Black Chicago: Anthony Overton and the Building of a Financial Empire* (Urbana: University of Illinois Press, 2020), 62.

6. Founded by A. Philip Randolph and Chandler Owen in New York in 1917, *The Messenger* proclaimed itself the "The Only Magazine of Scientific Radicalism in the World Published by Negroes." It strove "to appeal to reason, to lift our pens above the cringing demagogy of the times, and above the cheap, peanut politics of the old, reactionary Negro leaders." Taking an "uncompromising" socialist stance while urging readers toward armed self-defense, it faced government surveillance and harassment. Even as the magazine increased its attacks on Marcus Garvey, it softened its militancy in the 1920s. It reached a circulation high of twenty-six thousand in 1919. See Carolyn Wedin, "Messenger, The," Oxford African American Studies Center, December 1, 2009, https://oxfordaasc.com/display/10.1093/acref/9780195301731.001.0001/acref-9780195301731-e-45895.

7. This article appeared in "The Looking Glass" section of the *Crisis*, which Jessie Fauset edited. While W. E. B. Du Bois was in France from December 1918 through June 1919, Fauset served as acting editor of the *Crisis* and then resumed her role as literary editor. While this piece may be written by Fauset, as Teresa Zackodnik notes, Fauset regularly reprinted content in this section. Teresa Zackodnik, "Recirculation and Feminist Black Internationalism in Jessie Fauset's 'The Looking Glass' and Amy Jacques Garvey's 'Our Women and What They Think,'" *Modernism/Modernity (Baltimore)* 19, no. 3 (2012): 437–59.

8. Cyril Valentine Briggs founded and edited the *Crusader* (1918–22) in the wake of World War I and the 1917 East St. Louis riot. When, in April of 1917, President Woodrow Wilson asked Congress for a declaration of war against Germany to make the world "safe for democracy," Briggs countered in the *Crusader*'s inaugural issue that the journal's goal was

to "help make the world safe for the Negro." The *Crusader* initially promoted Black nationalism and Marcus Garvey's Universal Negro Improvement Association (UNIA), but within a year, the *Crusader* had rejected Garvey and the UNIA. From 1919 to 1921, the *Crusader* was the official publication of the Pan-African Black nationalist Hamitic League of the World, which Briggs had joined. In June 1921, the *Crusader* became the official journal of the radical African Blood Brotherhood (ABB), an organization Briggs had formed in 1919 in response to the brutal Red Summer. See Amber Moulton-Wiseman, "Briggs, Cyril Valentine," Oxford African American Studies Center, 31 May 31, 2013, https://oxfordaasc-com.ezp-prod1.hul.harvard.edu/view/10.1093/acref/9780195301731.001.0001/acref-9780195301731-e-36264; Peter Hudson, "Briggs, Cyril Valentine," Oxford African American Studies Center, December 1, 2006, https://oxfordaasc-com.ezp-prod1.hul.harvard.edu/view/10.1093/acref/9780195301731.001.0001/acref-9780195301731-e-40459; Marty Goodman, "The Crusader 1918–1922," accessed January 10, 2025, www.marxists.org/history/usa/pubs/crusader/index.htm.

9. Published and edited by civil rights leader Roscoe Dunjee (1883–1965) for the majority of its run, the *Black Dispatch* (1914–80) was Oklahoma City's only Black weekly newspaper. The masthead depicts a train pulling three cars labeled "Progress—Truth—Light," whose headlamp illuminates "Faith" toward a mountain range as a Black angel calls "Onward to the Heights." Designated as an "Organ of the Knights of Pythias," the paper urged readers to fight for civil rights and reached a circulation of twenty-four thousand. See William Bedford Clark, "The Black Dispatch: A Window on Ralph Ellison's First World." *Mississippi Quarterly* 62, no. 1 (2009): 3–18; Bob Burke, "Dunjee, Roscoe," Oxford African American Studies Center, May 31, 2013, https://oxfordaasc.com/display/10.1093/acref/9780195301731.001.0001/acref-9780195301731-e-34362; and John H. L. Thompson, "Dunjee, Roscoe," Oklahoma Historical Society, n.d., www.okhistory.org/publications/enc/entry.php?entry=DU007, accessed December 21, 2023.

10. Grimké's speech was later published as a pamphlet; see Archibald Grimké, *The Shame of America, or the Negro's Case against the Republic*, Occasional Paper No. 21 (Washington, DC: American Negro Academy, 1924).

11. [Endnote in the original.] The *Negro World*, New York, March 6, 1929. [Page numbers cited par-

enthetically in the text refer to Frazier's original sources.]

12. [Endnote in the original.] William Monroe Trotter, Lecture on Trip to Europe, Worcester, Mass. Feb. 26, 1920.

13. [Endnote in the original.] The *Crisis*, New York, September 1919.

14. [Endnote in the original.] The *Crisis*, New York, April 1919.

15. [Endnote in the original.] The *Crisis*, New York, November 1918.

16. [Endnote in the original.] The *Messenger*, New York, July 1918.

17. [Endnote in the original.] The *Messenger*, New York, August 1919.

18. [Endnote in the original.] *Evening Record*, Boston, found in the *Crisis*, N.Y., March 1919.

19. *The Messenger* published "A Reply to Congressman James F. Byrnes of South Carolina" in October 1919; the editorial includes an illustration titled "Congressman Byrnes of South Carolina Alarmed at Banquo's Ghost of the New Crowd Negro" with an image of the New Negro in a car with gun.

20. [Endnote in the original.] Congressional Record, House, August 25, 1919.

21. [Endnote in the original.] The *Messenger*, New York, October 1919.

22. [Endnote in the original.] Senate Document, No.153. Investigation of Department of Justice, pp. 161–187.

23. [Endnote in the original.] The *Afro-American*, April 30, 1920.

24. [Endnote in the original.] Pearson, Karl. *National Life from the Standpoint of Science*. Cambridge University Press. Eugenics Lecture Series II.

25. Founded by James Henry Anderson, the *New York Amsterdam News* (1909–) was a leading Black newspaper in Harlem during the 1920s and 1930s. See Frank A. Salamone, "Amsterdam News," Oxford African American Studies Center, December 1, 2009, https://oxfordaasc.com/display/10.1093/acref/9780195301731.001.0001/acref-9780195301731-e-45208.

26. [Footnote in the original.] The first part of this editorial is reprinted from an article written in 1912.

27. Founded in 1892 by William Peterfield Trent at the University of the South, the *Sewanee Review* is the oldest continuously published quarterly devoted to literary criticism in the United States. In 1920 editor George Herbert Clarke began including poetry. See Gorham Munson, "The Sewanee Review: From 1892 to 1930," *Sewanee Review* 40, no. 1 (1932): 1–4.

28. I believe that the "Committee on the After-the-War Program" is a reference to the Commission on Interracial Cooperation, which was founded in early 1919. See Charles Kirk Pilkington, "The Trials of Brotherhood: The Founding of the Commission on Interracial Cooperation," *Georgia Historical Quarterly* 69, no. 1 (1985): 55–80.

29. Founded after the La Plaine, Dominica, anti-tax uprising by mixed-race Dominican politicians William Davies, Alexander Rumsey Capoulade Lockhart, and Sholto Rawlins Pemberton, the *Dominica Guardian* (1893–1924) was a weekly "colored" paper whose motto was "Fiat Justitia" (Let Justice Be Done) and whose goal was to "guard and protect our people and our country from the tyranny of those who believe it to be their duty to add oppression to our misfortune." Edited by future Universal Negro Improvement Association backer Joseph Hilton Steber, the *Guardian* was the only newspaper on the island to be censored by Dominican authorities. See "Article in the Dominica Guardian," in *The Marcus Garvey and Universal Negro Improvement Association Papers*, ed. Robert A. Hill, vol. 11, *The Caribbean Diaspora, 1910–1920* (Durham, NC: Duke University Press, 2011), 525–26; and Kathy Casimir MacLean, *Black Man Listen: The Life of JR Ralph Casimir* (London: Papillote, 2022), 26, 40–41, Kindle.

30. Hailed by the Chicago *Defender* for offering better treatment to Afro-Caribbeans, the Intercolonial Steamship and Trading Company begun in 1920 was run by Dominicans and offered service among New York, Cuba, Santo Domingo, Haiti, Jamaica, and Panama: "They admit that they are doing business for a profit, but humanitarianism is also a feature of their trade since they hope to bring to the West Indian native produce and commodities at a price that will enable the much exploited West Indian to buy." "Intercolonial Steamship Company," Chicago *Defender*, February 14, 1920; *The American Marine Engineer*, April 1920, 14.

31. Founded and edited by Van Wyck Brooks and Albert Jay Nock in New York City, *The Freeman* (1920–24, 1930–31) was a weekly radical magazine of literary and political criticism that opposed "direct political action" but was open to "all forms of industrial organization." See Frank Luther Mott, "The Freeman," in *A History of American Magazines, 1741–1930*, vol. 5, *Sketches of 21 Magazines, 1905–1930* (Cambridge, MA: Harvard University Press, 1958), 88–99.

32. A larger-than-life, white St. Louis figure with "a genius for understanding everybody," William Reedy (1862–1920) began editing the *Mirror* in 1893. In 1913, he changed its name to *Reedy's Mirror* (1913–20) and published such notable poets as Sara Teasdale, Carl Sandburg, Edna St. Vincent Millay, Ezra Pound, and Edgar Lee Masters, whose *Spoon River Anthology* poetry first appeared in *Reedy's*. At its height, the circulation of the weekly reached roughly thirty thousand copies. See Frank Luther Mott, "Reedy's Mirror," in *A History of American Magazines, 1741–1930*, vol. 4, *1885–1905* (Cambridge, MA: Belknap Press of Harvard University Press, 1957), 652–56.

33. A West Indian scholar, historian, and elevator operator in famed photo-secessionist Alfred Stieglitz's art studio, Hodge Kirnon launched the *Promoter* in New York City in 1920. Inspired by Hubert Harrison, Marcus Garvey, and the artists who came to Stieglitz's Little Galleries, Kirnon conceived of the *Promoter* as a vehicle to promote his "ideas about radicalism as a form of social revolution—as a fight for the redistribution of cultural power and privilege." As he wrote in the *Promoter*, "'Racialism and Radicalism . . . might be considered as different varieties of the same kind . . . a bifurcation of the same stem'; they are both outcomes of unrest, of discrimination, of 'dissatisfied and discontented peoples seeking some clear solution towards alleviating their present condition.'" See Tara Kohn, "Elevated: Along the Fringes of 291 Fifth Avenue," *Panorama*, November 8, 2022.

34. Founded in 1915 by St. Croix labor leader David Hamilton Jackson, supported in part by the New York City Danish West Indian Benevolent Society, and incorporated in New York state, the *Herald* (1915–25) was a voice for the working poor in St. Croix, US Virgin Islands. According to Bolette Blaagaard, the *Herald* emphasized "a cosmopolitan citizenship and . . . a claim to civil rights specific to descendants of enslaved labourers." See Bolette Blaagaard, *Citizen Journalism as Conceptual Practice: Postcolonial Archives and Embodied Political Acts of New Media* (London: Rowman & Littlefield, 2018), 24; Angelo Capriola, "Jackson Encountered Goodwill, Challenges in Publishing First Privately-Owned Newspaper," *Virgin Islands Daily News*, November 1, 2024.

35. In 1919 in Cape Town, Clements Musa Kadalie launched the Industrial and Commercial Workers' Union, the first major South African labor union, with *The Black Man* newspaper as its organ. With Bennett Ncwana serving as its first editor, this first major South African Garveyite newspaper advanced Pan-African unionism. As the paper assailed exploitive recruiting practices, "hand-to-mouth wages," and the De Beers diamond company for relying on convict labor, it condoned some strikes while demanding improved wages and working conditions. Les Switzer and Mohamed Adhikari, "African Workers in the African Nationalist Press 1900–1960," in *South Africa's Resistance Press: Alternative Voices in the Last Generation under Apartheid* (Athens: Ohio University Center for International Studies, 2000), 97–98. According to Kadalie, his "essential object" was "to be a great African Marcus Garvey," while Garvey referred to *The Black Man* as "the *Negro World* of South Africa." See Henry Dee, "Clements Musa Kadalie and the Industrial and Commercial Workers' Union of Africa," in *Oxford Research Encyclopedia of African History*, online ed., Oxford University Press, December 22, 2021, https://oxfordre.com/africanhistory/display/10.1093/acrefore/9780190277734.001.0001/acrefore-9780190277734-e-1102; and Adam Ewing, *The Age of Garvey: How a Jamaican Activist Created a Mass Movement and Changed Global Black Politics* (Princeton, NJ: Princeton University Press, 2014), 93.

36. Born in San Francisco to Kittitian parents, Dr. Francis McDonald Gow founded the African Methodist Episcopal–affiliated Bethel Memorial Church in Cape Town, South Africa, in 1898 after hearing the visiting African American bishop Henry McNeal Turner proclaim that "'God was a Negro' and that blacks were a Godly people." See Robert Trent Vinson, "'Sea Kaffirs': 'American Negroes' and the Gospel of Garveyism in Early Twentieth-Century Cape Town," *Journal of African History* 47, no. 2 (2006): 287.

37. After the Napoleonic Wars, the British government organized the most consequential immigration movement in South African colonial history in an effort to ameliorate postwar poverty and to consolidate power against the amaXhosa farmers. Because of their enormous impact, the 1820 settlers comprise a "powerful and loaded symbol of the British contribution to the culture, tradition, and society of South Africa." See Antonia Malan, "Archaeology of Colonial Settlement at the Cape," in *Oxford Research Encyclopedia of African History*, online ed., Oxford University Press, November 22, 2019, https://oxfordre.com/africanhistory/display/10.1093

/acrefore/9780190277734.001.0001/acrefore-9780
190277734-e-447.

38. Founded in 1884 by the Sierra Leonean Joseph Claudius May and the Caribbean-born "father of Pan-Africanism," Edward W. Blyden, who had emigrated to West Africa, the *Sierra Leone Weekly News* served as the voice of the colony's coastal Krio/Creole elite, "a settler people repatriated to Africa from Great Britain and various parts of the New World"; see James Steel Thayer, "A Dissenting View of Creole Culture in Sierra Leone," *Cahiers d'études africaines* 31, nos. 121–22 (1991): 217. The *Weekly News* "sympathetically reported" Garveyite initiatives; see Adam Ewing, *The Age of Garvey: How a Jamaican Activist Created a Mass Movement and Changed Global Black Politics* (Princeton, NJ: Princeton University Press, 2014): 93. See also Musab Younis, "Third World Historical: West African Worlds," Borderlines, September 21, 2022, https://borderlines-cssaame.org/posts/2022/9/13/front-page-the-sierra-leone-weekly-news-freetown-sierra-leone-january-11-1919.

39. Lawyer, politician, writer, and Pan-African humanist J. E. Casely Hayford (1866–1930) served as a leading anticolonial activist in the Gold Coast and British West Africa and as vice president of the National Congress of British West Africa. Following in the tradition of African nationalist pioneer E. W. Blyden, Hayford embraced Blyden's racialism while developing a practical "humanist internationalism" philosophy as the basis for his Gold Coast anticolonial activism. In *Ethiopia Unbound* (1911), Hayford delivered his most significant version of "Blyden-style Ethiopianism"; see Kwaku Larbi Korang, "Casely Hayford, Joseph Ephraim," Oxford African American Studies Center, September 30, 2012, https://oxfordaasc.com/display/10.1093/acref/9780195301731.001.0001/acref-9780195301731-e-47795. Even when Garvey's *Negro World* was officially banned in British West Africa, Hayford had copies smuggled in to him; see Ewing, *The Age of Garvey*, 93.

40. An early proponent of developing African agriculture as a means of economic growth, Henry Harold Lardner published *Manual on Cultivation and Preparation for Export of Some of the Commercial Products Indigenous and Exotic in Sierra Leone, and the Reason Why Agriculture Should Be Encouraged in the Colony* (London: Messrs. Davies, Roblin, & Pearce, 1890); see also Henry Harold Lardner, *The Agricultural & Commercial Problems in Sierra Leone: With an Illustration of a Prospective Railway Train from Freetown to Timbuctoo* (pamphlet, 1893) and *Correspondence with a View to the Development of the Export Fruit Trade of the Colony of Sierra Leone* (Lagos: 1899). See Craufurd D. Goodwin, "Economic Analysis and Development in British West Africa," *Economic Development and Cultural Change* 15, no. 4 (1967): 438.

41. Founded in Bulawayo, Southern Rhodesia, in 1894, owned by the South African publisher Argus Printing and Publishing Company, and controlled by leading South African commercial and mining interests, the *Bulawayo Chronicle* pronounced on its masthead that it was the "authorized medium for government notices in Matabeleland," home to the Ndebele people; see the *Bulawayo Chronicle*, January 1, 1921, 1. The paper grew to become a popular daily that provided "telling insight into whites' perceptions of their place in evolving social, economic, and political matters"; see Julie Bonello, "The Development of Early Settler Identity in Southern Rhodesia: 1890–1914," *International Journal of African Historical Studies* 43, no. 2 (2010): 341–67. From 1890 to 1923, the British South Africa Company, chartered by Cecil B. Rhodes, governed the colony of Southern Rhodesia, including Bulawayo, and enforced segregation modeled on American Jim Crow while exploiting African laborers to extract the region's mineral wealth. See Andrew Roberts, "African Cross-Currents," in *The Cambridge History of Africa*, vol. 7, *1905–1940*, ed. A. D. Roberts (Cambridge: Cambridge University Press, 1986), 223–66; and Michael O. West, "Running against the Wind: African Social Mobility and Identity in a Settler Colonial Society," in *The Rise of an African Middle Class: Colonial Zimbabwe, 1898–1965* (Bloomington: Indiana University Press, 2002), 17.

42. In May 1921, about eight hundred white South African policemen and soldiers armed with machine guns, rifles, and cannons confronted the African prophet Enoch Mgijima and three thousand of his Black African "Israelite" followers armed with spears, swords, and knobkerries. Maintaining that Mgijima's Israelites were illegally squatting, the South Africa colonial regime demanded they leave, but the Israelites, having waited peacefully since early 1919 to witness the end of the world and to receive their redemption on land they considered their holy village of Ntabelanga, "the Mountain of the Rising Sun," refused. See Robert R. Edgar, *The Finger of God: Enoch Mgijima, the Israelites, and the Bulhoek Massacre in South Africa* (Charlottesville: University of Virginia Press, 2018),

1–6. Mgijima had been radicalized by correspondence with his Garveyite nephew, Gilbert Matshoba, who, in a 1920 letter to Mgijima, wrote, "We will not ask England, France Italy or Belgium . . . why are you . . . in this place [Africa]. We only direct them to get out. . . . The blood of all wars is about to arrive (its compensation is due). Then Europe puts her might against Asia. Then it will be time for the negroes to lift up their sword of the liberty of the Africans." On the morning of May 24, 1921, in what would be called the Bulhoek Massacre, the white South African forces in roughly twenty minutes massacred nearly two hundred Israelites; see Adam Ewing, *The Age of Garvey: How a Jamaican Activist Created a Mass Movement and Changed Global Black Politics* (Princeton, NJ: Princeton University Press, 2014), 93–94.

43. After the British colonial government of Natal in southern Africa imposed a poll tax on African men, a large contingent of Zulus led by Bambatha kaMancinza, former chief of the Zondi who lived in the Umvoti Division of the Natal Colony, took up arms against it. Over six hundred Zulu rebels of the original thousand were killed in the revolt, known chiefly as the Bambatha rebellion but also as the Natal rebellion, the Natal native rebellion, the Zulu rebellion, the poll-tax rebellion, and the "war of the heads." See Paul S. Thompson, "The Zulu Rebellion of 1906: The Collusion of Bambatha and Dinuzulu," *International Journal of African Historical Studies* 36, no. 3 (2003): 533–57; and Sean Redding, "A Blood-Stained Tax: Poll Tax and the Bambatha Rebellion in South Africa," *African Studies Review* 43, no. 2 (2000): 29–54.

44. "Imvo" revers to the newspaper *Imvo Zabantsundu*, founded by John Tengo Jabavu and published from 1884 to 1936 and again from 1962 to 1963 in Qonce (King William's Town), Eastern Cape, South Africa. It is "the oldest, continuous running newspaper founded by an African in South Africa." See National Library of South Africa, "Imvu [*sic*] Zabantsundu," n.d., https://cdm21048.contentdm .oclc.org/digital/collection/p21048coll37, accessed December 30, 2023.

45. The Second International Convention of Negroes, held at Liberty Hall, New York, during the entire month of August 1921, was called by Marcus Garvey, president general of the Universal Negro Improvement Association and the African Communities League; he was also the president of the Black Star Line, and had many other names, including "Provisional President of Africa." See

C. B. Valentine [Cyril Briggs], "The Negro Convention," *The Toiler* (New York) 4, no. 190 (1921): 13–14.

Part V. The New Negro Renaissance: Part One

1. Founded in 1919 by the Republican "race man" Chester A. Franklin, the *Kansas City (MO) Call* launched a number of successful civil rights campaigns even as it promoted "personal responsibility and black economic self-help." After Franklin's mother went door-to-door selling subscriptions, the paper achieved one of the largest Black circulation bases in the country, and by 1922, the *Call* needed to move to larger offices. In 1923, Franklin hired Roy Wilkins (who would later become editor of *The Crisis* and then executive secretary of the National Association for the Advancement of Colored People), accelerating the paper's growth. By 1940 the paper sold twenty thousand newspapers per week. See Charles E. Coulter, *"Take up the Black Man's Burden": Kansas City's African American Communities, 1865–1939* (Columbia: University of Missouri Press, 2006), 99.

2. Founded by the formerly enslaved John Henry Murphy Sr., the Baltimore *Afro-American* (1892–) is one of the longest running Black newspapers in US history. It was, by 1922, "the most widely circulated black paper along the coastal Atlantic"; following Murphy's death that year, his sons took over management and continued the paper's commitment to racial uplift and equity in employment, housing, public transportation and accommodations, and criminal justice. See "The Afro-American: Founder John Henry Murphy Sr.," PBS, n.d., https://www.pbs.org/blackpress/news _bios/afroamerican.html, accessed April 20, 2024; and Hayward Farrar, *The Baltimore Afro-American: 1892–1950* (Westport, CT: Greenwood, 1998), xi–xvii.

3. Begun in Indianapolis in late 1921 as *Fact!*, the *Fiery Cross* (1921–25) served as a crucial propaganda vehicle for the Ku Klux Klan Grand Dragon David "Curtis" Stephenson, even though he kept a low profile, had a direct hand in the periodical's tremendous growth. By January 1923, circulation had reached 50,500 in Indiana, Ohio. and other northern states. By April 1923 it claimed over three hundred thousand readers and published three editions. When Milton Elrod gained editorial control of the *Fiery Cross* in May 1923, he backed Imperial

Wizard Hiram Evan's control of the Klan. Banner headlines supported or attacked different politicians based on how the Klan perceived their degree of Americanism, and Stephenson worked diligently to enlist protestant clergy to the Klan cause. In addition to Stephenson, the *Fiery Cross*'s editorial advisory council included powerful Klansmen: George V. Coffin, who would become Republican country chairman of Indiana's Marion County; John Duvall, who later was elected mayor of Indianapolis; and Ed Jackson, who would be elected governor of Indiana. Publication ceased when Stephenson was arrested for second-degree murder. See Felix Harcourt, *Ku Klux Kulture: America and the Klan in the 1920s* (Chicago: University of Chicago Press, 2017), 31–51; and William M. Lutholtz, *Grand Dragon: D.C. Stephenson and the Ku Klux Klan in Indiana* (West Lafayette, IN: Purdue University Press, 1991).

"Sparks from the Fiery Cross," a regular column by John Eight Point (a pseudonym), began appearing in August 1923 on the editorial page, along with the "Klan's Program 1923–24," which comprised the following:

1. Militant, old-fashioned Christianity and operative patriotism.
2. Back to the Constitution.
3. Enforcement of the Eighteenth Amendment so long as it is a part of the Constitution.
4. Enforcement of present immigration laws and enactment of more stringent laws on immigration.

4. Published by the National Urban League and edited until 1933 by sociologist Charles S. Johnson, *Opportunity* (1923–49) was a monthly magazine devoted to uplift, integration, social commentary, and increasingly exceptional African American literature and illustrations. In 1928 Elmer Anderson Carter became editor. At its peak, it reached a circulation of eleven thousand, one-third of which was white. See Carolyn Wedin, "Opportunity," Oxford African American Studies Center, December 1, 2009, https://oxfordaasc.com/display/10.1093/acref/9780195301731.001.0001/acref-9780195301731-e-46023?rskey=gtcmgg&result=2.

5. Founded in Los Angeles in 1879 by John James Neimore, the *California Owl* offered Black settlers advice on adjusting to the West. When, after Neimore's death in 1912, Charlotta A. Bass gained control of the paper, she renamed the paper the *California Eagle* (1912–64). Her husband John Bass ed-

ited the paper throughout the 1920s, and together they launched a "more militant campaign against discrimination and segregation." See "The California Eagle," PBS, n.d., https://www.pbs.org/blackpress/news_bios/ca_eagle.html, accessed August 31, 2023.

Brick mason, contractor, and banker Charles Summer Blodgett (1869–1952) was a prominent Black builder of commercial buildings in Los Angeles who, with his brother Louis and other Black business leaders, organized the Liberty Building Loan Association in 1924. See Paul R. Spitzzeri, "Wo/men at Work, Labor Day Edition: A Photo of Black Contractor Charles S. Blodgett and Painters at the Hotel Darby, Los Angeles, 1909," *Homestead Blog*, September 5, 2022, https://homesteadmuseum.blog/2022/09/05/wo-men-at-work-labor-day-edition-a-photo-of-black-contractor-charles-s-blodgett-and-painters-at-the-hotel-darby-los-angeles-1909/.

6. In March 1925, both former Garveyite Thomas W. Anderson and Zora Neale Hurston served as editors of the New York City–based monthly magazine the *Spokesman* (1924–27), whose motto was Michel de Montaigne's "I speak the Truth, not so much as I would but as much as I dare." William H. Ferris served as editor from July 1925 to July 1927. Angelina Grimké, Zora Neale Hurston, Georgia Douglass Johnson, and James Weldon Johnson all published in the magazine; at its peak, its circulation was about one thousand. See Walter C. Daniel, "Spokesman, The," in *Black Journals of the United States* (Westport, CT: Greenwood, 1982), 361–63.

7. Langston Hughes, "Youth," in *African American Poetry: A Digital Anthology*, ed. Amardeep Singh, n.d., https://scalar.lehigh.edu/african-american-poetry-a-digital-anthology/langston-hughes-youth-1924, accessed December 1, 2024.

8. Claude McKay, "To the Intrenched Classes," in Singh, *African American Poetry*, https://scalar.lehigh.edu/african-american-poetry-a-digital-anthology/claude-mckay-to-the-intrenched-classes-1922, accessed December 1, 2024.

9. James Weldon Johnson, "O Southland!," in Singh, *African American Poetry*, https://scalar.lehigh.edu/african-american-poetry-a-digital-anthology/james-weldon-johnson-o-southland-1917, accessed December 1, 2024.

10. James Weldon Johnson, "To America," Academy of American Poets, n.d., https://poets.org/poem/america-5, accessed December 1, 2024.

11. Barbara Foley dates Toomer's "Negro Emergent," which we include here, to 1925, after the publication of Locke's special March 1925 *Survey*

Graphic issue. See Barbara Foley, *Jean Toomer: Race, Repression, and Revolution* (Urbana: University of Illinois Press, 2014), 71.

12. [Footnote in the original.] From the New Testament. Ephesians, 5.29.—Ed.

13. Ellipsis in the original.

14. An organ of the Communist Party USA, the *Daily Worker* (1924–58) began in 1921 as the weekly *Worker* in Chicago, and then in 1924 became the *Daily Worker* when it moved to New York City. Stalinist in perspective, the *Daily Worker* reported on collective labor organizing, government and business repression, strikes, and collective bargaining more broadly. See "The Daily Worker (Chicago, Ill.; New York, N.Y.) 1924–1958," Library of Congress, n.d., https://www.loc.gov/item/sn84020097/, accessed September 1, 2023; and Connor Monson, "The *Daily Worker*: A Communist Newspaper out of Chicago," University of Illinois Urbana Champaign, Illinois Newspaper Project, n.d., https://www.library.illinois .edu/illinoisnewspaperproject/daily-worker/, accessed September 1, 2023.

15. Founded by landscape architect Frederick Law Olmsted in 1865 as a weekly magazine committed to the goals of Reconstruction and as a defender of the freedmen, the *Nation* (originally subtitled *A Weekly Journal Devoted to Politics, Literature, Science, Drama, Music, Art, Industry*; 1865–) has always adopted a left-of-center stance. Under the editorship of Oswald Garrison Villard (1918–32) the *Nation* supported Progressive Party candidate Robert LaFollette for the presidency in 1924 and became increasingly recognized for its foreign affairs coverage. See Frank Luther Mott, "The Nation," in *A History of American Magazines, 1741–1930*, vol. 3, *1865–1885* (Cambridge, MA: Belknap Press of Harvard University Press, 1938), 331–56.

16. The *Pittsburgh Courier* (1907–) grew to become a national Black newspaper powerhouse under the leadership of Republican Robert L. Vann, who took over the paper in 1910. In 1925 Vann hired George Schuyler as a columnist, and he brought on Floyd J. Calvin a year later to write features and host radio broadcasts, "the first time in the history of Negro journalism that a Negro newspaper has brought its own program to the radio world." Julia Bumbry Jones and H. Binga Dismond meanwhile published their popular society columns. NAACP field secretary Walter White, a field secretary for the National Association for the Advancement of Colored People, launched a column in 1926, and in 1927 Vann sent Joel A. Rogers to Europe and Africa to

offer special coverage. With the circulation in 1926 at nearly fifty-five thousand, Vann began in earnest to devise plans for building his own printing plant. See Andrew Bunie, *Robert L. Vann of the "Pittsburgh Courier": Politics and Black Journalism* (Pittsburgh: University of Pittsburgh Press, 1974).

17. Charlotte is the unrequited love interest in Johann Wolfgang von Goethe's *The Sorrows of Young Werther*.

18. All ellipses are in the original.

19. Begun as a supplement to the *New York Times, Current History* (1914–) offered "news as history, to be considered and remembered." By 1922, George Washington Ochs-Oakes, who served as its editor from 1915 to 1931, increasingly relied on university professors to serve as contributors. See Frank Luther Mott, "Current History," in *A History of American Magazines, 1741–1930*, vol. 5, *Sketches of 21 Magazines, 1905–1930* (Cambridge, MA: Belknap Press of Harvard University Press, 1968), 49–58.

20. When the former Harvard University English instructor Henry Goddard Leach began editing the *Forum* (1886–1950) in 1926, he resumed the magazine's symposium format with the motto, "A non-partisan magazine of free discussion. It aims to interpret the new America that is attaining consciousness in this decade." Beginning in 1925, the *Forum* published fiction by major American writers, including Willa Cather, Rupert Hughes, and Fanny Hurst. See Frank Luther Mott, "The Forum," in *A History of American Magazines, 1741–1930*, vol. 4, *1885–1905* (Cambridge, MA: Belknap Press of Harvard University Press, 1957), 511–23.

Part VI. The New Negro Renaissance: Part Two

1. Black stewards were segregated into one overcrowded room in the bowels of the ship, known as the "glory hole." Robert L. Allen, *The Brotherhood of Sleeping Car Porters: C. L. Dellums and the Fight for Fair Treatment and Civil Rights* (Boulder, CO: Paradigm, 2014), 20–21.

2. Alain Locke Papers, Moorland-Spingarn Research Center, Howard University. See also *Claude McKay: Letters in Exile*, ed. Brooks E. Hefner and Gary Edward Holcomb (New Haven, CT: Yale University Press, 2025).

3. "McKay's relationship with Alain Locke was significantly fractured when, without McKay's permission or any prior notification, Locke changed the title of McKay's poem "The White House" to

"White Houses" for his anthology *The New Negro*. Locke was apparently anxious that the title of "The White House" was a too-direct attack on US government–sanctioned, anti-Black racism. McKay's correspondence with Locke after this editorial intervention was typically contentious." Note by Gary E. Holcomb.

4. Founded in 1905 by Robert Sengstacke Abbott (1868–1940), the *Chicago Defender* became Black America's leading newspaper in part by launching the "Great Northern Drive," encouraging African Americans to migrate north so they could "live like men." In 1923 Abbott started a column and club featuring the character Bud Billiken for African American children. He supported A. Philip Randolph's Brotherhood of Sleeping Car Porters and Maids in 1925 and in 1928 rejected Republican Herbert Hoover's campaign for the presidency, denouncing his "Lilly-White Party." See Wesley Borucki, "Chicago Defender," Oxford African American Studies Center, December 1, 2009, https://oxfordaasc.com/display/10.1093/acref/9780195301731.001.0001/acref-9780195301731-e-45375?rskey=urRzSO&result=16.

5. Published in Girard, Kansas, by the Jewish American Emanuel Haldeman-Julius, who also published the enormously popular *Little Blue Book* series, the *Haldeman-Julius Quarterly* (1926–28) was a free-thought magazine, the "most ambitious and most scholarly publication [Haldeman-Julius] would produce." See Orson Kingsley, "Freethought for the Masses: The Philosophy behind the Writings and Publications of Emanuel Haldeman-Julius" (PhD diss., Salve Regina University, April 2021).

6. Founded in Chicago by the Associated Negro Press founder Claude Barnett in 1925, the same year that A. Philip Randolph organized the Brotherhood of Sleeping Car Porters and Maids, *Heebie Jeebies: A Sign of Intelligence* (retitled the following year as *Light and Heebie Jeebies*) received financing from the Pullman Company. In return, Barnett assured the Chicago-based company that in its pages, it would avoid "spreading discontent" among Pullman porters, a key part of its target audience. Edited by influential journalist Percival Pratt and likely named after the jazz song of the same name, the magazine folded in 1928. See Beth Tompkins Bates, *Pullman Porters and the Rise of Protest Politics in Black America, 1925–1945* (Chapel Hill: University of North Carolina Press, 2001), 54–55, 203.

7. Edited throughout the 1920s by Henry Justin Smith and published by Walter A. Strong, the *Chi-cago Daily News* (1875–1978) was Chicago's first penny newspaper and was the city's most popular paper until it was surpassed by the *Chicago Tribune*. By the end of the 1920s circulation was nearly 430,000. See "Chicago Daily News Inc.," Encyclopedia of Chicago, online ed., n.d., https://www.encyclopedia.chicagohistory.org/pages/2598.html, accessed September 2, 2023.

8. "African golf" is a reference to the dice game craps.

9. Founded in 1923 by V. F. Calverton, the *Modern Quarterly* (1923–33, then 1933–40 as *Modern Monthly*) operated with the primary goal of disseminating "Socialist criticism and philosophy," though Calverton published alternative views. Committed to "comradeliness between the two races," the *Modern Quarterly* included a number of Black writers, including Charles Johnson, Abram Harris, Alain Locke, and George Schuyler. See Haim Genizi, "The Modern Quarterly, 1923–1940: An Independent Radical Magazine," *Labor History* 15, no. 2 (1974): 199–215.

10. E. Franklin Frazier, "The Negro in the Industrial South," *The Nation*, vol. 12, pp. 32–38. [Note in original.]

11. Edited by a Guadeloupean, Maurice Satineau, secretary of the Comité de Defense des Interets de la Race Noire (Committee for the Defense of Interests of the Black Race), *La dépêche africaine* (1928–32) was published in Paris with the motto, "Defendre nos colonies, c'est fortifier la France" (To defend our colonies is to fortify France). The journal included a "patchwork of militant colonial reformism, assimilationism, and cultural Pan-Africanism" and insisted that "in the assimilationist and colonial reformist fashion of the era, 'the methods of colonization by civilized nations are far from perfect; but colonization itself is a humane and necessary project.'" According to the French Ministère des Colonies (Ministry of Colonies) police prefecture, nearly ten thousand copies of *La dépêche africaine* were in circulation by late 1928. See T. Denean Sharpley-Whiting, "Femme Négritude: Jane Nardal, La Dépêche Africaine, and the Francophone New Negro," *Souls* (Boulder, CO) 2, no. 4 (2009): 8–17. The translation of Nardal's article that appears here is in T. Denean Sharpley-Whiting, *Negritude Women* (Minneapolis: University of Minnesota Press, 2002): 105–7.

12. Founded by Christopher J. Perry and edited and published in the late 1920s by lawyer Eugene Washington Rhodes, the *Philadelphia Tribune* (1884–) offered weekly coverage of the social, religious, economic, and, increasingly throughout the

1920s, political news of Black Philadelphia and surrounding Black neighborhoods. Decrying school segregation in the city and racism in the city and state's public accommodations in the 1920s, the *Tribune* helped usher an end to Philadelphia segregated schools and the enactment in 1935 of a state equal rights law. Throughout the 1920s, the *Philadelphia Tribune* claimed a weekly circulation of around twenty thousand. See V. P. Franklin, "'Voice of the Black Community': The *Philadelphia Tribune*, 1912–41," *Pennsylvania History: A Journal of Mid-Atlantic Studies* 51, no. 4 (1984): 261–84.

During the first Red Scare, "pink teas" connoted "weak" followers of Bolshevism who supposedly lacked the courage to become full "Reds." It could also suggest an attack on masculinity, a kind of "sissy Bolshevism." See Kim E. Nielsen, *Un-American Womanhood: Antiradicalism, Antifeminism, and the First Red Scare* (Athens: Ohio State University Press, 2001), 34.

13. The second page of Johnson's typescript is missing.

14. Johnson has handwritten "II" at the top of this page and placed an opening bracket before "Objectively" at the start of the first paragraph.

15. Johnson has bracketed this paragraph and written "omit" in the margin.

16. Johnson has bracketed this paragraph and written "omit" in the margin.

17. Johnson has written "End—see next note" in the margin here.

18. Johnson has crossed out "My point is" and substituted what appears to be "I am convinced," though "convinced" is not entirely legible.

19. Johnson has written "End" at the end of this paragraph and appears to indicate "Omit" for the next three paragraphs.

20. This closing passage, from Langston Hughes's "The Negro Artist and the Racial Mountain," is written in poetic lines in Johnson's typescript but not in Hughes's original.

21. See Richard Bruce Nugent, *Gay Rebel of the Harlem Renaissance: Selections from the Work of Richard Bruce Nugent*, ed. Thomas H. Wirth (Durham, NC: Duke University Press, 2002), 178–84. Nugent claimed in interviews that Wallace Thurman plagiarized his novel in *Infants of the Spring* (1932), which was why Nugent wasn't able to publish his own novel in his lifetime; see Thomas H. Wirth, "Introduction," in Richard Bruce Nugent, *Gentleman Jigger: A Novel of the Harlem Renaissance* (Philadelphia: Da Capo, 2008): x–xviii.

22. "To the outside observer" is Johnson's handwritten addition to the typed text.

23. This sentence is Johnson's handwritten addition to the typed text.

24. These are Johnson's parentheses, with the following "After" capitalized by hand, suggesting the parenthetical text was marked for deletion.

25. These are Johnson's parentheses, with substitutions of "is also" and "vogue" noted for the parenthetical text.

26. This paragraph is bracketed in the original.

27. DNA tests have debunked long-standing beliefs about Warren G. Harding's "Negro descent."

28. Launched in 1918 by German immigrant Otto K. E. Heinemann, whose initials make up the label's name, Okeh Records would become one of the leading phonograph record companies for the jazz and blues. In 1921, Okeh released Mamie Smith's "You Can't Keep a Good Man Down," which initiated the company's race record series and later Louis Armstrong's earliest recordings under his own name. In subsequent years, Duke Ellington recordings appeared on the Okeh label. See Frank Andrews, 2005. "Okeh (Label)," *Encyclopedia of Recorded Sound 2*, ed. Frank Hoffmann (New York, NY: Routledge), 1512–14.

29. "Let the Church Roll On" is a music staple with variations covered by multiple bluegrass and gospel artists. It always involves the question of what to do about the sinner in the church; solutions range from kicking the sinner out to taking a rag and wiping the paint off a woman's face.

30. Published by George Hampton and edited by Nathaniel Jerome Frederick, the *Palmetto Leader* (1925–196?) was a Black conservative weekly published in Columbia, South Carolina, that made the fight against lynching one of its primary missions. See Kerstyn M. Haram, "The *Palmetto Leader*'s Mission to End Lynching in South Carolina: Black Agency and the Black Press in Columbia, 1925–1940," *South Carolina Historical Magazine* 107, no. 4 (2006): 310–33.

31. From the *Rubaiyat* of Omar Khayyam.

32. Published by Plummer Bernard Young and run and edited by the Young family, the Norfolk, Virginia, *New Journal and Guide* (1910–) by 1935 had the largest circulation in the South with a circulation of twenty-eight thousand. Initially a Republican, Young supported Democrat Alfred E. Smith in the 1928 election and Franklin D. Roosevelt in the 1932 election. The *New Journal and Guide* campaigned for anti-lynching legislation, better housing, fair employment practices, and better Black educational oppor-

tunities. See Peter Wallenstein, "Young, Plummer Bernard," Oxford African American Studies Center, May 31, 2013, https://oxfordaasc.com/display/10.1093 /acref/9780195301731.001.0001/acref-9780195301731 -e-35025.

33. What follows in brackets is from a different version of the same speech.

34. Founded as a "Harvard Miscellany" by Lincoln Kirstein and Varian Fry, *Hound and Horn* (1927–34) moved to New York City in 1930, lost its affiliation with Harvard University, and "vacillated thereafter among humanism, Southern regionalism, Marxism and the neoclassicism of its Western editor, Yvor Winters." It published such modernists as T. S. Eliot, Ezra Pound, and Gertrude Stein. See James D. Hart and Phillip Leininger, "*Hound and Horn*," in *The Oxford Companion to American Literature*, 6th ed. (New York: Oxford University Press, 1995), 300.

Part VII. The Depression, the New Deal, and Ethiopia, 1933–1937

1. Founded in August 1933 by John Aubrey Davis, along with his friends Belford V. Lawson Jr. and M. Franklin Thorne, the Washington, DC–based New Negro Alliance was the "nation's first, and most successful, grass-roots protest organizations." After first attempting to negotiate with businesses that discriminated against African Americans, the Alliance began "Don't Buy Where You Can't Work" picketing campaigns. Late in 1933, the Alliance launched its official organ, the weekly *New Negro Opinion* (1933– 37). See Michele F. Pacifico, "'Don't Buy Where You Can't Work': The New Negro Alliance of Washington," *Washington History* 6, no. 1 (1994): 66–88.

2. Friends J. Antonio Jarvis and Ariel Melchior Sr. founded the *Virgin Islands Daily News* (1930–), printing and hand-delivering the first two hundred copies themselves. The newspaper "continues to seek to be the conscience of the community" today. See "About Us," *Virgin Islands Daily News*, n.d., https://www.virginislandsdailynews.com/about_us /, accessed April 13, 2024.

3. As the official organ of the Afro-American Sons and Daughters, the Yazoo City, Mississippi, *Afro-American Courier* (1926–57) announced that its stated purpose was "first, to keep the Lodges informed as to the progress of the Order along numerical and financial lines; second, to awaken race consciousness, along the line of mutual cooperation; third, to put ourselves on record before the civilized world, as a worth-while people." See "Our Platform,"

Afro-American Courier, October 1, 1927; and "Afro-American Courier (Yazoo City, Miss.) 1926–19??" Library of Congress, n.d., https://www.loc.gov/item /sn88067171/, accessed March 13, 2024.

4. The official organ of the Brotherhood of Sleeping Car Porters and Maids—which, in 1935 became the first African American labor union to be officially recognized by the American Federation of Labor—the *Black Worker* (1929–68) was published in New York City and edited by A. Philip Randolph. On the editorial page of this issue, Randolph urged his readers to "fight to free Tom Mooney; fight to free the Scottsboro boys; fight to drive Mussolini out of Ethiopia; fight to declare unconstitutional the Georgia slave insurrection law." See *Black Worker*, August 1, 1936; and Thomas Jessen Adams, "Brotherhood of Sleeping Car Porters," Oxford African American Studies Center, December 1, 2009, https://oxfordaasc .com/display/10.1093/acref/9780195301731.001.0001 /acref-9780195301731-e-45320.

5. The Instituto Nacional de Prevision y Reformas Sociales (National Institute for Welfare and Social Reform), founded in Havana, Cuba.

6. [Translator's note.] His audience would likely have been well aware of the famous declaration by José Martí that pro-independence forces should put race aside and unify for the struggle. That was used by the white leadership as a way to suppress any criticism of white supremacy.

7. [Translator's note.] "El negro," although gendered masculine, is one of many singular constructions in Spanish that refers to a group that might be rendered as "black people."

8. [Translator's note.] In 1937, the National Socialist Party ruled Germany, and Mussolini's Fascism, which grew out of the Italian Socialism, ruled Italy.

9. [Translator's note.] This is the first of several digs at the Partido Independiente de Color, of which more below.

10. [Translator's note.] This is one of several statements implying that Urrutia thinks that there *are* biological, and certainly cultural differences, beyond skin color. The word "innocuous" is the literal "inocuo" in Spanish, which could also be translated as "irrelevant." The invented term *racial indifferentiation* is also literal, from "indiferenciación racial," and it was bolded/italicized in the original.

11. [Translator's note.] Urrutia frequently invokes "spiritual" qualities or conditions that are difficult to render in English. It's clear he's not talking about religious concepts of spirituality—neither Christianity nor the several variants of Afro-Cuban religious

practices (Santería, Abakuá) that were thriving in his time, despite efforts to ignore or suppress them. By spiritual qualities he means something like "the human spirit," or ethos.

12. [Translator's note.] The Spanish here is "por ser ingenuos," by which he means that the tribal or non-Europeanized Africans are not sufficiently aware of or adequately prepared to fully comprehend the onslaught of European colonization, in order to resist it.

13. [Translator's note.] The Spanish is "Aunque la mayoría de los negros africanos son salvajes—selváticos quiero decir, no bárbaros—." Salvaje is literally "savage," but in English that term is so loaded with connotations of fierce aggressiveness that I have rendered it the way Urrutia explains it in his parenthetical, which is consistent with the Latin root word, "silvaticus," dwellers of the forest.

14. [Translator's note.] Both "jazz" and "spirituals" are bolded/italicized in the Spanish text, because they are English words. It's clear he is referring to the musical forms.

15. Known as the Bronze Titan, Antonio Maceo (1845–96) was a Cuban revolutionary and second-in-command in the Cuban War for Independence. Born José Antonio de la Caridad Maceo y Grajales Clayfield, Maceo is honored in Cuba for his resistance to Spanish colonizers and as a symbol of Cuban nationalism. "Maceo, Antonio," Oxford African American Studies Center, May 31, 2017, https://oxfordaasc-com.ezp-prod1.hul.harvard.edu /view/10.1093/acref/9780195301731.001.0001/acref -9780195301731-e-74411.

16. The "Grito de Baire" (Shout of Baire) marked the Cuban War of Independence from Spanish rule that commenced on February 24, 1895 in Baire, Cuba. See Paul G. Pierpaoli Jr., "Grito de Baire," in *The Encyclopedia of the Spanish-American and Philippine-American Wars: A Political, Social, and Military History*, vol. 1, ed. Spencer C. Tucker (Santa Barbara, CA: ABC-CLIO, 2009), 261–62.

17. [Translator's note.] Although this is the only time he uses the term, it's fairly apparent that Urrutia thought that the different races had innate and broadly shared qualities beyond skin color, that he referred to in such vague terms as mental outlook, spirit, etc.

18. In 1912, President José Miguel Gómez ordered the massacre of over two thousand Afro-Cubans in what became known as the Race War of 1912. Many of the victims were veterans of the wars for independence and members of the Partido Independiente de Color (Independent Party of Color). See Devyn Benson Spence, "Fears of Black Political Activism in Cuba and Beyond, 1912–2017," Black Perspectives, June 12, 2017, https://www.aaihs.org/fears -of-black-political-activism-in-cuba-and-beyond -1912-2017/.

19. [Translator's note.] This paragraph is his most explicit rejection of the "racism" and condemnation of the Partido Independiente de Color, widely recognized as the first political party in the Western Hemisphere based on racial identity. Urrutia was 31 years old in 1912 when the assault on the PIC and the ensuing massacre occurred.

20. [Translator's note.] The original language here is "disuelto en una pasta blanca," literally "dissolved in a white paste/dough/mush/slurry/pasta."

21. [Translator's note.] The phrase "surplus-pain of the Negro" involves a play on words with a term common to Marxian economic, "surplus value," which in Spanish is "plus-valor." Urrutia invents a similar term for the burden of racism, "plus-dolor," which rhymes with "plus-valor."

22. Drafted by Black civil rights activist Martín Morúa Delgado and passed by the Cuban Congress in 1910, the Morúa Law outlawed any political parties or movements based on race or color. See René De La Pedraja Tomán, *Wars of Latin America, 1899–1941* (Jefferson, NC: McFarland, 2006), 114.

23. [Translator's note.] This is another reference to the idea of eventually "whitening" the population through miscegenation, not through mass murder or expulsion.

24. [Translator's note.] African-based or -inspired religions and culinary patterns, e.g., were *widespread* among rural and less westernized Afro-Cubans—phenomena that Urrutia here denies.

Appendix. Looking Backward, Looking Forward, 1938–1950

1. This is a reference to Rev. 3:18, "Anoint thine eyes with eyesalve, that thou mayest see."

Selected Bibliography

Part I

Cooper, Anna Julia. "The Status of Woman in America." In *A Voice from the South*. Xenia, OH: Aldine, 1892.

Crummell, Alexander. "The Need of New Ideas and New Aims for a New Era." In *Civilization and Black Progress: Selected Writings of Alexander Crummell on the South*. Charlottesville: University of Virginia Press, 1995.

Fortune, T. Thomas. "The Afro-American Agitator." *New York Age*, December 21, 1889.

Grit, Bruce [John Edward Bruce]. "National Capital Topics. Discrimination in the Pension Office." *New York Age*, July 28, 1888.

Hartford (CT) Courant. "The New Negro in the New South." January 8, 1887.

Independent (New York). "The Negro on the Negro." January 6, 1887.

Mitchell, John, Jr. "What the Negroes Owe Us." *Richmond (VA) Planet*, December 20, 1890.

Times-Observer (Topeka, KS). "Pointers: Colored Voters Need Fixing." September 4, 1891.

Washington, Booker T. "Afro American Education." In *A New Negro for a New Century: An Accurate and Up-to-Date Record of the Upward Struggles of the Negro Race*. Chicago: American Publishing House, 1900.

Washington (DC) Bee. "Ingalls Denounced. The Colored Press Demands Justice and Fair Play. Let Everybody Read This." February 19, 1887.

Williams, Fannie Barrier. "The Intellectual Progress of the Colored Women of the United States since the Emancipation Proclamation." In *The World's Congress of Representative Women: A Historical Résumé for Popular Circulation of the World's Congress of Representative Women, Convened in Chicago on May 15, and Adjourned on May 22, 1893 under the Auspices of the Woman's Branch of the World's Congress Auxiliary*, edited by May Wright Sewall. Chicago: Rand, McNally, 1894.

Wright, W. E. C. "The New Negro." *Advance* (Chicago), November 2, 1893.

Part II

Abbey, John N. "Dr. Abbey on the Negro: Comparison of the New and Old Negro." *Star of Zion* (Charlotte, NC), July 26, 1900.

Bowen, J. W. E. *An Appeal to the King: The Address Delivered on Negro Day in the Atlanta Exposition*. Atlanta: Gammon Theological Seminary, October 21, 1895.

Bruce, N. C. "An Appeal from the New to the New." *Biblical Recorder, the Organ of the North Carolina Baptists* (Raleigh, NC), February 26, 1901.

Daily Picayune (New Orleans). "Domestic Evolution." May 3, 1896.

Du Bois, W. E. B. "A Creed for the 'New Negro.'" *Iowa State Bystander*, December 13, 1895.

Du Bois, W. E. B. "A Negro on Etiquet of Caste." *Iowa State Bystander*, December 13, 1895.

Griggs, Sutton E. *Imperium in Imperio: A Study of the Negro Race Problem*. Published by the author, 1899.

Herald (Leavenworth, KS). "A Race Problem to Solve." July 20, 1895.

J. J. L. "Crisis to Virginia Farmer." *Richmond (VA) Dispatch*, November 7, 1902.

L. W. B. "Is He a New Negro?" *Daily Inter Ocean* (Chicago), October 2, 1895.

MacBrady, John E. "Introduction." In *A New Negro for a New Century: An Accurate and Up-to-Date Record of the Upward Struggles of the Negro Race*. Chicago: American Publishing House, 1900.

Moore-Smith, Alberta, "Women's Development in Business." *Colored American Magazine*, March 1, 1902, 323–26.

Scanland, J. M. "Negroes as Voters." *Paxton (IL) Daily Record*, April 25, 1900.

Steel, Rev. S. A. "The Modern Negro." *Southwestern Christian Advocate* (New Orleans), November 28, 1895.

Washington, Booker T. "Our New Citizen." Address delivered to the Hamilton Club, Chicago, January 31, 1896. In *Negro Social and Political Thought, 1850–1920; Representative Texts*, edited by Howard Brotz, 359–62, 579. New York: Basic Books, 1966.

Washington, Booker T. (ghostwritten by T. Thomas Fortune). "To the Editor of the *New York World*." *New York World*, September 19, 1895.

Washington, Mrs. Booker T. "The New Negro Woman." *Lend a Hand* 15 (1895): 254–60.

White, George H. "Defense of the Negro Race— Charges Answered: Speech of Hon. George H. White, of North Carolina, in the House of Representatives, January 29, 1901." National Museum of African American History and Culture, Smithsonian Institution, https://nmaahc.si.edu/object /nmaahc_2012.160.119.1.

Williams, Fannie Barrier. "The Club Movement among Colored Women in America." In *A New Negro for a New Century: An Accurate and Up-to-Date Record of the Upward Struggles of the Negro Race*. Chicago: American Publishing House, 1900.

Williams, Fannie Barrier. "The Colored Woman of To-day." *Godey's Magazine*, July 1897, 28–32.

Part III

Adams, John Henry, Jr. "Rough Sketches: The New Negro Man." *Voice of the Negro*, October 1904, 447–52.

Adams, John Henry, Jr. "Rough Sketches: A Study of the Features of the New Woman." *Voice of the Negro*, August 1904, 323–26.

Adams, John Henry, Jr. "Rough Sketches: William Edward Burghardt Du Bois, Ph.D." *Voice of the Negro*, March 1905, 176–81.

Baker, Ray Stannard. "Following the Color Line: The Clash of the Races in a Southern City." *American Magazine*, May 1907, 3–18.

Burroughs, Nannie. "Report to the Eighth Annual Session of the Woman's Convention, Auxiliary to the National Baptist Convention." In *Journal of the Eighth Annual Assembly of the Woman's Convention Held in the First Baptist Church of Lexington, Kentucky, Sept. 16–21, 1908*. Nashville, TN: National Baptist Publishing Board, 1909.

Clarana, José. "The Schooling of the Negro." *Crisis*, July 1913, 133–36.

Cleveland (OH) Gazette. "Worm Will Turn." November 3, 1906.

Davis, Benjamin J. "Man May Evade His Duty, But He Cannot Escape the Penalty of Responsibility." *Atlanta Independent*, November 6, 1909.

Du Bois, W. E. B. "Of Mr. Booker T. Washington and Others." In *The Souls of Black Folk: Essays and Sketches*. Chicago: A. C. McClurg, 1903.

Evening Post (New York). "The Negro in Fiction." June 5, 1916.

Ferris, William. "A Historical and Psychological Account of the Genesis and Development of the Negro's Religion." *AME Church Review* 20, no. 4 (1904): 343–53.

Harper's Weekly. "Some Fresh Suggestions about the New Negro Crime." January 23, 1904, 120–21.

Hill, Leslie Pinckney. "Negro Ideals: Their Effect and Their Embarrassments." *Journal of Race Development* 6, no. 1 (1915): 91–103.

Johnson, J. Rosamond. "Why They Call American Music Ragtime." *Colored American Magazine*, January 1909, 636–39.

Micheaux, Oscar. "Chapter Eight: Henry Hugh Hodder." In *The Forged Note: A Romance of the Darker Races*, Book 1, *Which Deals with Originals*. Lincoln, NE: Western Book Supply, 1915.

Moore, W. H. A. "The New Negro Literary Movement." *AME Church Review* 21 (1904): 49–54.

Page, Thomas Nelson. "The Lynching of Negroes: Its Causes and Prevention." *North American Review* 178 (1904): 33–48.

Pickens, William. "The New Negro." In *The New Negro: His Political, Civil and Mental Status, and Related Essays*. New York: Neale, 1916.

Seattle Republican. "The Passing Throng." September 18, 1906.

Sedalia (MO) Weekly Conservator. "A Lesson from 'The Clansman.'" January 21, 1907.

Tayleur, Eleanor. "The Negro Woman: I—Social and Moral Decadence." *Outlook*, January 30, 1904, 266–71.

Terrell, Mary Church. "Lynching from a Negro's Point of View." *North American Review* 178 (1904): 853–68.

Part IV

Bibb, Joseph. "The Black Man's Barrier." *Chicago Whip*, September 27, 1919.

Bibb, Joseph. "Radicals and Raids." *Chicago Whip*, January 10, 1920.

Black Dispatch (Oklahoma City, OK). "Reconstruction: Prominent Men of Both Races Discuss a Program for the Improvement of Race Relations." October 10, 1919.

The Black Man: A Journal Propagating the Interests of Workers throughout the African Continent (Cape Town, South Africa). "A.M.E. Church and Negro Movement." October 1, 1920.

Briggs, Cyril. *To New Negroes Who Really Seek Liberation*. New York: African Blood Brotherhood, August 6, 1921.

Briggs, Cyril. "The Old Negro Goes: Let Him Go in Peace." *Crusader*, October 1919, 9–10.

Bulawayo Chronicle (Bulawayo, Southern Rhodesia). "The New Negro." June 4, 1921.

Crisis. "The Again!" March 1919, 229–31.

Crisis. "Changes in Psychology." August 1919, 196.

Domingo, W. A. "If We Must Die." *Messenger*, September 1919, 4.

Du Bois, W. E. B. "The Damnation of Women." In *Darkwater: Voices from within the Veil*. New York: Harcourt, Brace and Howe, 1920.

Du Bois, W. E. B. "Returning Soldiers." *Crisis*, May 1919, 7–14.

Frazier, Edward Franklin. "New Currents of Thought among the Colored People of America." Master's thesis, Clark University, 1920.

Garvey, Marcus. "The New Negro and the U.N.I.A." *Negro World*, November 1, 1919.

Garvey, Marcus Mosiah, Jr. "Speech on Disarmament Conference Delivered at Liberty Hall." In *Philosophy and Opinions of Marcus Garvey, Part 2*, 125–31. Paterson, NJ: Frank Cass, 1925. https://search-alexanderstreet-com.ezp-prod1.hul.harvard.edu/view/work/bibliographic_entity|bibliographic_details|4389507.

Grimké, Archibald. *The Shame of America, or the Negro's Case against the Republic*. Occasional Paper No. 21, Washington, DC: American Negro Academy, 1924.

Half-Century Magazine. "Mothers of Men and Women of Mark." May 1919, 7.

Harrison, Hubert. "As the Currents Flow." *New Negro* 3, no. 7 (1919): 3–4.

Harrison, Hubert. "Education and the Race." In *When Africa Awakes*. New York: Porro Press, 1920.

Harrison, Hubert. "The New Politics: The New Politics for the New Negro." In *When Africa Awakes*. New York: Porro Press, 1920.

Harrison, Hubert. "The White War and the Colored Races." *New Negro* 4, no. 2 (1919): 8–10.

Hyde Park–Kenwood Property Owners' Association. "The New Negro." *Property Owners' Journal*, March 1919, 590–91.

J. R. R. C. [J. R. Ralph Casimir]. "Letter to the Editor." *Dominica Guardian*, April 29, 1920.

Jackson, D. Hamilton. "Editorial." *Herald* (St. Croix, VI), September 13, 1920.

Johnson, Fenton. "The Editor's Blue Pencil." *Champion Magazine*, January 1917, 1.

Kerlin, Robert T. "The Negro Fourth Estate." *Reedy's Mirror* 28, no. 4 (1919): 468–69.

Kirnon, Hodge. "The New Negro & His Will to Manhood & Achievement." *Promoter*, August 1920, 4–8.

Messenger. "The Negro Woman Voter." November 1920, 131, 147.

Messenger. "The New Negro—What Is He?" August 1920, 73–74.

Mixon, W. H. "A Great Day for the New Negro and the New South." *Voice of the People* (Birmingham, AL), January 4, 1919.

Morse, Josiah. "The Outlook for the Negro." *Sewanee Review* 28, no. 2 (1920): 152–59.

Pippa. "The New Negro Is Here: Negro Socialists Are Helping to Solve Race Problem in New Way." *New York Call*, November 4, 1918.

Randolph, A. Philip. "Who's Who: A New Crowd—A New Negro." *Messenger*, May–June 1919, 26–27.

Robinson, Geroid. "The New Negro." *Freeman*, June 2, 1920, 278–280.

Seligmann, Herbert J. "The New Negro." In *The Negro Faces America*. New York: Harper and Brothers, 1920.

Sierra Leone Weekly News. "A Desideratum." December 11, 1920.

Part V

Bennett, Gwendolyn. "The Ebony Flute." *Opportunity*, August 1926, 260–61.

Browder, Earl R. "*The New Negro*: A Notice of Alain Locke's Book." *Daily Worker*, December 12, 1925.

California Eagle. "Charles S. Blodgett." July 11, 1924.

Calverton, V. F. "The Latest Negro." *Nation*, December 30, 1925, 761–62.

Cullen, Countee P. "The League of Youth." *Crisis*, August 1923, 167–68.

Dunbar-Nelson, Alice. "From the Woman's Point of View." *Pittsburgh Courier*, January 2, 1926.

Ferris, William H. "The Myth of the New Negro." *Spokesman* (New York), July 1925. In *Blacks at Harvard: A Documentary History of African-American Experience at Harvard and Radcliffe*, edited by Randall Kennedy, Werner Sollors, Caldwell Titcomb, and Thomas A. Underwood, 148–51. New York: New York University Press, 1993.

Garvey, Amy Jacques. "Woman's Function in Life." *Negro World*, December 19, 1925.

Herskovits, Melville J. "The American Negro Evolving a New Physical Type." *Current History* 24, no. 6 (1926): 898–903.

Hurston, Zora Neale. "'Possum or Pig?'" *Forum*, September 1926, 465.

John Eight Point [pseud.]. "Sparks from the Fiery Cross." *Fiery Cross*, November 23, 1923, 4.

Locke, Alain. "The New Negro." In *The New Negro*, edited by Alain Locke. New York: A and C Boni, 1925.

Messenger. "The New Negro Woman." July 1923, 757.

Miller, Kelly. "Kelly Miller Says: The New Negro." *Afro-American* (Baltimore), September 21, 1923, 16.

Nunn, William G. "Has the Negro Church Been Weighed in the Balance and Found Wanting?" *Pittsburgh Courier*, October 2, 1926.

Parham, Saydee E. "The New Woman." *Negro World*, February 2, 1924.

Randolph, A. Philip. "The Brotherhood." December 3, 1926, BSCP [Brotherhood of Sleeping Car Porters] Scrapbook, Vol. 1, Miscellany File, 1926–1928, Folder 001608-034-0001, January 1, 1926–December 31, 1928, Papers of A. Philip Randolph, Library of Congress, Manuscript Division.

Sayre, Helen B. "Negro Women in Industry." *Opportunity*, August 1924, 242–44.

Smith, Madeleine R. "The Negro Woman of Today." *Kansas City Call*, April 27, 1923.

Spokesman (New York). "Watchman What of the Night?" March 1925, 4–5.

Toomer, Jean. "The Negro Emergent." In *A Jean Toomer Reader: Selected Unpublished Writings*, edited by Frederik L. Rusch. New York: Oxford University Press, 1993.

Walrond, Eric. "Art and Propaganda," *Negro World*, December 31, 1921.

Whaley, Ruth Whitehead. "Closed Doors: A Study in Segregation." *Messenger*, July 1923, 771–72.

Part VI

Alexander, Sadie T. M. "The Emancipated Woman." Speech, ca. 1930s. In *Democracy, Race, and Justice: The Speeches and Writings of Sadie T. M. Alexander*, edited by Nina Banks, 58–64. New Haven, CT: Yale University Press, 2021.

Allen, Devere. "Building Tomorrow's World: The New White Man." *The World Tomorrow* 10, no. 3 (1927): 124–25.

Binder, Carroll. *Chicago and the New Negro. Chicago Daily News* Reprint No. 31. Chicago: *Chicago Daily News*, 1927.

Bonner, Marita. "The Young Blood Hungers." *Crisis*, May 1928, 151, 172.

Calvin, Floyd J. "'Economic Emancipation' Is Platform of 'New Negro.'" *Pittsburgh Courier*, January 22, 1927.

Chesnutt, Charles. "The Negro in Present Day Fiction." Speech delivered in Oberlin, Ohio, ca. 1929. In Charles W. Chesnutt, Joseph R McElrath, Robert C Leitz, and Jesse S Crisler, *Charles W. Chesnutt: Essays and Speeches*, 516–29. Stanford, CA: Stanford University Press, 1999.

Du Bois, W. E. B. "What the New Negro Is Thinking." Unpublished manuscript, W. E. B. Du Bois Papers, 1803–1999, University of Massachusetts–Amherst.

Dunbar-Nelson, Alice. "Woman's Most Serious Problem." *Messenger*, March 1927, 73, 86.

Edwards, Paul K. "Types of Negro Character Illustrations Most Pleasing and Most Displeasing to Negroes." In *The Southern Urban Negro as a Consumer*. New York: Prentice-Hall, 1932.

Frazier, E. Franklin. "La Bourgeoisie Noire." *Modern Quarterly* 5, no. 1 (1928–30): 78–84.

Gates, J. M., with Deacon Leon Davis, Sister Jordan, and Sister Norman. *Manish Women*. Recorded December 6, 1929. OKeh Records 8779, 1930, 78 rpm.

Gruening, Martha. "The Negro Renaissance." *Hound and Horn* 5, no. 3 (1932): 504–14.

Hancock, Gordon B. "Between the Lines: Some New Negroes Also!" *Palmetto Leader* (Columbia, SC), December 20, 1930.

Harrison, Hubert. "No New Literary Renaissance, Says Well Known Writer." *Pittsburgh Courier*, March 12, 1927.

Houston, Drusilla. "Writer Discusses Communism and the Negro, Finds It Undesirable." *New Journal and Guide*, July 4, 1931.

Hughes, Langston. "These Bad New Negroes: A Critique on Critics," part 1, "'Best Negroes Not Really Cultured.'" *Pittsburgh Courier*, April 9, 1927.

Hughes, Langston. "These Bad New Negroes: A Critique on Critics," part 2, "Says Race Leaders, Including Preachers, Flock to Harlem Cabarets." *Pittsburgh Courier*, April 16, 1927.

Johnson, Charles S. "A Chapel Talk to the Students of Fisk University." Typescript, October 17, 1928, Franklin Library Special Collections and Archives, Fisk University.

Johnson, Charles S. "The New Negro." Typescript, ca. 1929, Franklin Library Special Collections and Archives, Fisk University.

Johnson, I. Marie. "Women in Chicago Politics." *Light and Heebie Jeebies*, November 19, 1927.

McKay, Claude. Letter to Alain Locke, April 18, 1927. Alain Locke Papers, Moorland-Spingarn Research Center, Howard University.

Nardal, Jane. "Internationalisme noir." *La dépêche africaine*, February 15, 1928. Translated by T. Denean Sharpley-Whiting as "Black Internationalism," in T. Denean Sharpley-Whiting, "Femme Négritude, *La dépêche africaine*, and the Francophone New Negro," *Souls* 2, no. 4 (2000): 8–17.

Nugent, Richard Bruce. *Gentleman Jigger: A Novel of the Harlem Renaissance.* Philadelphia: Da Capo, 2008.

Philadelphia Tribune. "Pink Teas." May 17, 1928.

Schuyler, George S. "An Appeal to Young Negroes." Ca. 1930. Box 2, folder 3, Ella Baker Papers, Schomburg Center for Research in Black Culture, New York Public Library.

Stokes, Charles. "The New Negro." *Kansas City Call*, December 23, 1927.

Thurman, Wallace. "Negro Life in New York's Harlem: A Lively Picture of a Popular and Interesting Section." *Haldeman-Julius Quarterly*, Fall 1927, 132–45.

Whitney, Salem Tutt. "Timely Topics: Leave 'em Alone!" *Chicago Defender*, June 18, 1927.

Williams, Terence Edwards. "Hard for Modern Young Man to Find Girl without Past: Writer Hits 'New Freedom' as Responsible for Girls Losing Poise and 'Finesse.'" *Pittsburgh Courier*, June 25, 1927.

Woodson, Carter G. "The New Negro Begins to Exhibit Much Pride in His Racial Identity." *Norfolk (VA) New Journal and Guide*, February 20, 1932.

Part VII

De Lugo, Alvaro. "An Essay on the Negro." *Virgin Islands Daily News*, February 20, 1934.

Johnson, Clister L. "The New Deal, the New Year, the New Negro." *Afro-American Courier*, January 1, 1936.

Locke, Alain. "Sterling Brown: The New Negro Folk-Poet." In *Negro: An Anthology*, edited by Nancy Cunard (London: Wishart, 1934).

New Negro Alliance. "Program of the New Negro Alliance." *New Negro Opinion*, September 22, 1934.

New Negro Opinion. "Alliance vs. High's Ice Cream." December 16, 1933.

Rawlins, J. W. "Rawlins Writes on Segregation." *Detroit Tribune*, August 12, 1933.

Urrutia, Gustavo E. "Puntos de vista del Nuevo Negro" [Points of view of the New Negro]. Lecture, Instituto Nacional de Prevision y Reformas Sociales (Cuba), July 8, 1937. Trans. Thomas Holloway, The Schomburg Center for Research in Black Culture, New York Public Library.

West, Dorothy, and James Weldon Johnson. Letters from Dorothy West to James Weldon Johnson, 1933–1937, Beinecke Rare Book and Manuscript Library, Yale University.

Appendix

Locke, Alain. "Frontiers of Culture." *Crescent* 33 (1950): 37–39.

Locke, Alain. "The Negro: 'New' or Newer: A Retrospective Review of the Literature of the Negro for 1938—Part 1." *Opportunity*, January 1939, 4–10.

Locke, Alain. "The Negro: 'New' or Newer: A Retrospective Review of the Literature of the Negro for 1938—Part 2." *Opportunity*, February 1939, 36–42.

About the Authors

John N. Abbey (1857–1910), born in Tennessee, was a physician and minister who led several African Methodist Episcopal churches in Tennessee. In 1886, Abbey graduated from the historically Black Central Tennessee College in Nashville. In 1903 the Black-owned *Cleveland Gazette* castigated the "artful Dr. John N. Abbey" for "bending the knee to Baal" and asserting that the states that have disfranchised the Negro have dealt wisely, justly and have conferred a blessing upon the race." Later that month, the *Baltimore Afro-American Ledger* praised Abby (as his name is spelled in some sources) as "one of Memphis' most prominent physician[s], forceful writers and pulpit orators" for opposing the city's newly passed streetcar segregation bill. See "Catering to Southern Feeling," *Cleveland Gazette*, January 3, 1903; "Separate Street Car Bill," *Baltimore Afro American Ledger*, January 31, 1903; "Jno [*sic*] N. Abby," Twelfth Census of the United States, 1900, National Archives and Records Administration, Washington, DC, T623, Roll 1598, p. 8, Enumeration District 0073; and "Student Endowment Association," *Nashville Banner*, January 24, 1891.

John Henry Adams Jr. (1878–1948), born to a formerly enslaved father in Colquitt County, Georgia, studied art at the Drexel Institute of Art, Science, and Industry (now Drexel University) in Philadelphia before becoming one of the foremost artists of the early 1900s' version of the New Negro and New Negro Woman. In 1901 he established the Department of Art at the African Methodist Episcopal Church's Morris Brown College in Atlanta. From 1904 to 1907, Adams created over sixty illustrations for the Atlanta-based Black monthly magazine *Voice of the Negro*, including Black versions of the Gibson Girl or New Negro Woman and multiple drawings of what he saw as the era's New Negro men. See Michael Bieze, "Adams, John Henry, Jr.," Oxford African American Studies Center, May 31, 2013, https://oxfordaasc.com/display/10.1093/acref/9780195301731.001.0001/acref-9780195301731-e-36036.

Sadie Tanner Mossell Alexander (1898–1989), whose grandfather Benjamin Tucker Tanner edited the first African American scholarly magazine, the *A.M.E. Church Review*, was a trailblazing attorney and civil rights activist. Born in Philadelphia, Pennsylvania, Alexander became the first Black woman to earn a PhD in economics from the University of Pennsylvania (1921), to graduate from the University of Pennsylvania School of Law (1927), to be admitted to the Pennsylvania bar, and to practice law in the state of Pennsylvania. In 1928, she became the first African American woman to be appointed assistant city solicitor in Philadelphia, where she served until 1930 and again from 1934 to 1938. With her husband she helped draft the 1935 Pennsylvania state public accommodations law prohibiting discrimination in public places. The only female member of the John Mercer Langston Law Club, Alexander remained committed throughout her career to helping Black Americans who could not afford to hire an attorney. In 1946, President Harry S. Truman appointed Alexander as the first black woman to serve on a presidential commission, his Committee on Civil Rights. See Lia B. Epperson, "Alexander, Sadie Tanner Mossell," Oxford African American Studies Center, May 31, 2013, https://oxfordaasc.com/display/10.1093/acref/9780195301731.001.0001/acref-9780195301731-e-34199; and "Alexander, Sadie Tanner Mossell," Oxford African American Studies Center, December 1, 2006, https://oxfordaasc.com/display/10.1093/acref/9780195301731.001.0001/acref-9780195301731-e-39941.

Devere Allen (1891–1955, born Harold DeVere Allen in Providence, Rhode Island) was a prominent white pacifist, socialist, editor, and writer. As a student at Oberlin College, Allen joined the Intercollegiate Socialist Society. After World War I he joined the Oberlin branch of the Christian pacifist Fellowship of Reconciliation and published the Oberlin antiwar newspaper, the *Rational Patriot*. In the spring of 1919 Allen edited *Young Democracy*, which later merged with the Christian socialist *World Tomorrow* (1921–34), the official organ of the Fellowship of Reconciliation. In 1933, he and his wife, Marie Hollister Allen, launched the pacifist, left-leaning news service Nofrontier News (later called World-over Press), which reached at its peak over 9 million readers around the globe and continued until Allen's death. Charles Chatfield, "The Apostles of Peace: The Connected World of Devere Allen," *Peace Research* 17, no. 3 (1985): 51–59. See Charles Chatfield, "The Life of Devere Allen," in Devere Allen, *Life and Writings*, ed. Charles Chatfield (New York: Garland, 1976), 19–57.

Ray Stannard Baker (1870–1946), born in Lansing, Michigan, was one of the leading white muckraking journalists in the United States. After studying at the Michigan Agricultural College and briefly at the University of Michigan Law School, he began reporting for the *Chicago Record* and witnessed the devastating poverty, social unrest, and mass unemployment caused by the financial Panic of 1893. In 1897, he joined the staff of *McClure's Magazine*, where he published articles on lynchings and labor union corruption. In 1906 he moved to the *American Magazine*, where he interviewed Booker T. Washington and W. E. B. Du Bois during his investigation into the Atlanta Race Massacre of 1906. In 1908, he collected these articles into a volume titled *Following the Color Line*. See Wesley Borucki, "Baker, Ray Stannard," Oxford African American Studies Center, December 1, 2009, https://oxfordaasc.com/display/10.1093/acref/9780195301731.001.0001/acref -9780195301731-e-45237.

Gwendolyn Bennett (1902–81), born in Giddings, Texas, and raised for several years on the Paiute Indian Reservation where her parents worked as educators, was a leading essayist, short story writer, poet, and artist of the New Negro Renaissance. After studying art at Columbia University and the Pratt Institute, graduating from the latter in 1924, Bennett began teaching art classes at Howard University. With funding from a Delta Sigma Theta sorority fellowship, Bennett spent 1925 studying art in Paris at the Académies de la Grande Chaumière, Julian, and Colarossi and at the École du Panthéon, an experience she would describe later in her fiction as isolating and profoundly lonely. During the 1920s and early 1930s, she published her work in leading New Negro Renaissance publications, including *Opportunity*, *Crisis*, Wallace Thurman's *Fire!!* (1926), Charles Johnson's *Ebony and Topaz* (1927), Countee Cullen's *Caroling Dusk* (1927), and James Weldon Johnson's *The Book of American Negro Poetry* (1922). During the early years of the Depression, Bennett worked for the Department of Information and Education of the Welfare Council of New York, writing articles for the *Amsterdam News*, the *New York Age*, the *Baltimore Afro-American*, and *Better Times*. After her husband, Alfred Jackson, died in 1936, she lived intermittently with the prominent African American sculptor Augusta Savage and worked as a teacher and project supervisor in the Federal Art Teaching Project. In 1938, she began serving as the director of the Harlem Community Art Center before being investigated by the House Un-American Activities Committee (HUAC) and suspended in 1941. See Theresa Leininger-Miller, "Bennett, Gwendolyn," Oxford African American Studies Center, May 31, 2013, https://oxfordaasc.com/display/10.1093/acref /9780195301731.001.0001/acref-9780195301731-e-36631; Sonita Sarker, *Women Writing Race, Nation, and History: N/Native* (Oxford: Oxford University Press, 2022), 173; and Belinda Wheeler and Louis J. Parascandola, *Heroine of the Harlem Renaissance and Beyond: Gwendolyn Bennett's Selected Writings* (University Park: Pennsylvania State University Press, 2018), xx, 6.

Joseph Dandridge Bibb (1892–1966), born in Montgomery, Alabama, was a Black Chicago lawyer, civil rights' activist, government official, and journalist who edited the radical *Chicago Whip* shortly after its founding in 1919 until it folded in 1939. After studying at Atlanta University, Bibb earned a law degree from Yale University in 1919 and moved to Chicago, where he and Arthur C. MacNeal founded the *Whip*. In a 1956 interview with *Ebony*, Bibb recalled how he was known as "Red, radical, [and] revolutionary" for his writing. The Black-owned *St. Louis American* credited Bibb for launching the "Buy Where You Can Work" campaign that spread throughout the country. In 1953, Governor William Stratton named Bibb director of the Department of Public Safety. See Martha Pitts, "Bibb, Joseph Dandridge," Oxford African American Studies Center, May 31, 2013, https://oxfordaasc.com/display/10.1093/acref/9780195301731.001.0001/acref-9780195301731-e-36192; "Salute to an Early Civil Rights Commander on the Field," *St. Louis American*, December 22, 1966; and "Crusading Attorney Joseph D. Bibb Dies after Long Illness," *Chicago Daily Defender*, December 7, 1966.

Abner Carroll Binder (1896–1956), born in Mechanicsburg, Pennsylvania, was an American journalist and foreign correspondent. Educated at the University of Pennsylvania and at Harvard University, Binder, served on the American Friends Service Committee, the Quaker unit of the American Red Cross from 1914 to 1917 before becoming in 1922 a *Chicago Daily News* reporter covering industrial relations and sociological issues. In 1927 Binder joined the foreign service division of the *Daily News*, where he became an award-winning foreign correspondent. He left the paper in 1945. See "Carroll Binder Papers," Newberry Library, n.d., https://archives.newberry.org/repositories/2/resources/23, accessed September 2, 2023.

Marita Odette Bonner (1898–1971), born in Boston, Massachusetts, was an accomplished pianist, educator, and writer of the New Negro Renaissance. One of the few Black women to earn her degree in 1922 from Radcliffe College, where she founded the Radcliffe chapter of Delta Sigma Theta, Bonner won the Radcliffe song competition in both 1918 and 1922 because of her talents as a composer and piano player. Some of her best-known work focuses on the racial, sexual, and economic discrimination facing Black women. When she moved to Washington, DC, to teach in 1924, Bonner became an active member of Georgia Douglas Johnson's S Street literary salon. In "On Being Young—A Woman—and Colored," Bonner's award-winning 1925 essay for the National Association for the Advancement of Colored People's *Crisis* magazine, she writes, "That's being a woman. A woman of any color. You decide that something is wrong with a world that stifles and chokes; that cuts off and stunts; hedging in, pressing down on eyes, ears and throat." When she and her husband joined the First Church of Christ, Scientist in 1941, she ceased publishing literary works. See Althea E. Rhodes, "Bonner, Marita Odette," Oxford African American Studies Center, May 31, 2013, https://oxfordaasc.com/display/10.1093/acref/9780195301731.001.0001/acref-9780195301731-e-35196; and Marita Bonner, "On Being Young—a Woman—and Colored," in *Double-Take: A Revisionist Harlem Renaissance Anthology*, ed. Venetria K. Patton and Maureen Honey (New Brunswick, NJ: Rutgers University Press, 2001), 110.

John Wesley Edward Bowen (1855–1933), born enslaved in New Orleans, Louisiana, was a Methodist educator, theologian, and pastor, who became the second African American to earn a PhD in the United States when he graduated from Boston University in 1887. When Bowen was hired as a professor of historical theology at Gammon Theological Seminary in Atlanta in 1893, he became the first African American to hold that role. He edited the Atlanta Black monthly *The Voice of the Negro* from 1904 until its demise in 1907. Although he attended the inaugural meeting of the Niagara Movement, he became more conservative in later years under pressure from Booker T. Washington. See Ralph E. Luker, "Bowen, John Wesley Edward," Oxford African American Studies

Center, May 31, 2013, https://oxfordaasc.com/display/10.1093/acref/9780195301731.001.0001/acref
-9780195301731-e-35200; and Leroy Davis, *A Clashing of the Soul: John Hope and the Dilemma of
African American Leadership and Black Higher Education in the Early Twentieth Century* (Athens:
University of Georgia Press, 1998), 173.

Cyril Valentine Briggs (1888–1966), born out of wedlock on the Caribbean island of Nevis to a
Black mother and white Trinidadian father who worked as a plantation overseer, was a prominent
radical journalist and Communist organizer. Despite receiving a colonial education that, in Briggs'
words, "aimed to turn out Black Anglo-Saxons, glorify whites, [and] denigrate Africans," Briggs
nonetheless learned the foundation for his later radicalism, "agnosticism and free thought on one
side, and racial self- assertiveness on the other." In part because of a pronounced stutter which kept
him from public speaking, Briggs devoted his career to journalism. He immigrated to the United
States in 1905 and in 1912 began writing for the Black New York weekly the *Amsterdam News*—
where, as Briggs himself recalled, he received "my first lessons in the dreary economics of Negro
publishing"—and later the *Colored American Review*. In the fall of 1918, inspired by the 1916 Irish
Easter Rebellion and outraged by the 1917 East St. Louis massacre, Briggs founded the *Crusader*,
which emphasized militant self-defense, Pan-Africanism, socialism, and racial equality. The following year Briggs launched the African Blood Brotherhood for African Liberation and Redemption
(ABB); the *Crusader* would eventually become the ABB's organ. After the Red Summer of 1919,
Briggs became increasingly anticapitalist, anti-imperialist, and separatist, recruiting men into the
ABB ready to arm themselves in self-defense. In 1921 he joined the Communist Party USA. Until
he was expelled from the Communist Party in 1942, Briggs remained devoted to both Black nationalism and Communism. Called the "Angry Blond Negro" by the editor of the *New York Times*,
Briggs would claim the phrase as the title for his planned autobiography. See Robert A. Hill, "Racial and Radical: Cyril V. Briggs, the Crusader Magazine, and the African Blood Brotherhood,
1918–1922," in *The Essential Writings of Robert A. Hill*, ed. Adam Ewing (University Press of Florida,
2024), 294–367; Louis J. Parascandola, "Briggs, Cyril," Oxford African American Studies Center,
December 1, 2009, https://oxfordaasc.com/display/10.1093/acref/9780195301731.001.0001/acref
-9780195301731-e-45314; Radica Mahase, "Briggs, Cyril Valentine," Oxford African American
Studies Center, September 30, 2016, https://oxfordaasc.com/display/10.1093/acref/9780195301731
.001.0001/acref-9780195301731-e-50927; and Minkah Makalani, *In the Cause of Freedom: Radical
Black Internationalism from Harlem to London, 1917–1939* (Chapel Hill: University of North Carolina Press, 2011), 45–63.

Earl Russell Browder (1891–1973), born in Wichita, Kansas, began his lifelong commitment to
leftist politics when he joined the Socialist Party in 1907. Jailed for sixteen months for opposing
World War I, he rejoined the Socialist Party upon his release and began editing its pro-Communist,
Kansas-based newspaper, the *Workers World*. In 1921, he joined the Communist Party USA, and
he was a Communist Party presidential candidate in the 1936 and 1940 elections. See Christopher Riches and Jan Palmowski, "Browder, Earl Russell," in *A Dictionary of Contemporary World
History* (Oxford University Press, 2021), https://www.oxfordreference.com/view/10.1093/
acref/9780191890949.001.001/acref-9780191890949-e2825.

John Edward Bruce (1856–1924), who was born enslaved in Piscataway, Maryland, largely taught
himself the literary and research skills he would need in his fearless career as a journalist, historian, and Pan-African activist. Although he did not graduate from high school, he did attend
Howard University in 1872. After working as a correspondent for a number of Black newspapers
and adopting the pen name Rising Son, he launched the Washington, DC, *Weekly Argus* with

Charles Otley in 1879 and the *Sunday Item*, the first Black daily newspaper, in 1880. In 1882 he served as editor of the *Republican* of Norfolk, Virginia, and in 1884 he founded the *Washington (DC) Grit*, "'a campaign sheet dedicated to both the Republican party' and the advancement of African Americans." After his friend T. Thomas Fortune nicknamed him Bruce Grit, Bruce began using that as his pen name in articles for the *Cleveland Gazette* and the *New York Age*. He quickly garnered acclaim for the impassioned tone of his articles—whether denouncing mixed-race marriages, white mob violence, and imperialism or in promoting race pride, self-help, and African American history. To supplement his meager earnings as a journalist, Bruce worked throughout his career as a federal customhouse messenger in New York. When Fortune launched his uncompromising civil rights organization, the Afro-American League, in 1887, Bruce assumed a leadership role in it. While working as an associate editor of *Howard's American Magazine* in the 1890s, he wrote *The Blood Red Record*, a scathing indictment of lynching. In 1911 he and Arthur Schomburg began the Negro Society for Historical Research (NSHR), the forerunner of Carter G. Woodson's Association for the Study of African American Life and History. See Ralph L. Crowder, *John Edward Bruce: Politician, Journalist, and Self-Trained Historian of the African Diaspora* (New York: New York University Press, 2004), 5–13, 60–62; David Alvin Canton, "Bruce, John Edward," Oxford African American Studies Center, May 31, 2013, https://oxfordaasc.com/display/10.1093/acref/9780195301731.001.0001/acref-9780195301731-e-35038; and John C. Gruesser, "Bruce, John E.," Oxford African American Studies Center, December 1, 2006, https://oxfordaasc.com/display/10.1093/acref/9780195301731.001.0001/acref-9780195301731-e-47255.

Nathaniel C. Bruce (1869–1942), a onetime student of Booker T. Washington's, began his studies at Shaw University in Raleigh, North Carolina, where he worked to pay for four or five months of schooling a year. In 1889 he enrolled at Bates College in Maine and graduated with honors, becoming the first Black Bates graduate to be elected class orator. Immediately thereafter, he was hired as a professor and Dean of the College at Shaw University, a position he held until 1902. To supplement his liberal arts education, he studied at Hampton Institute in Virginia and the Tuskegee Institute in Alabama. From 1902 to 1907, he served as the principal of St. Joseph, Missouri's Colored High and Grammar School, and in 1907 he founded an agricultural school in Chariton County, Missouri, that would become the Bartlett Agricultural and Industrial School. Advertising the school as the "Tuskegee of the Midwest," Bruce and his students won the *Missouri Ruralist* first prize for best corn yield in the state in 1913. A proud Bruce declared, "Place Missouri black boys on Missouri black land, behind the world-famed Missouri mule, and nothing can beat the combination for raising corn or other crops. We have shown and are going to keep on showing that black people can make for themselves their best place and opportunity back upon black land." See "Bruce, Nathanial [*sic*] C," in *Who's Who of the Colored Race: A General Biographical Dictionary of Men and Women of African Descent*, vol. 1 (Chicago: Frank Lincoln Mather, 1915), 47; "Missouri Tuskegee," *Saint Joseph News-Press*, March 17, 1913; John F. Case, "A Black Man Champion," *Missouri Ruralist*, December 5, 1915, 18; and Lorenzo Johnston Greene, Gary R Kremer, and Antonio Frederick Holland, *Missouri's Black Heritage*, rev. ed., rev. and updated by Gary R. Kremer and Antonio F. Holland (Columbia: University of Missouri Press, 1993), 115–16.

Nannie Helen Burroughs (1879–1961), an educator, orator, and civil and women's rights activist, rose to fame in 1900 as a twenty-one-year-old after delivering the speech "How the Sisters Are Hindered from Helping" at the annual conference of the National Baptist Convention in Richmond, Virginia. Born in Orange, Virginia, to a farming father who was also a Baptist preacher and a formerly enslaved mother who was a cook, Burroughs moved with her family to Washington, DC, and in 1896 graduated with honors in business and domestic science from the rigorous M Street

High School, one of the nation's first high schools for African Americans. When Jim Crow discrimination prevented her from getting work as a public school teacher or in federal civil service, Burroughs found employment as a secretary, first for the Baptist *Christian Banner* in Philadelphia and then for the National Baptist Convention's Foreign Mission Board. In 1900, when the board's headquarters moved to Louisville, Kentucky, Burroughs relocated to that city and helped launch the Baptist Convention Woman's Auxiliary. Attracting well over a million African American women to its ranks, the Woman's Convention promoted philanthropic work at home and in missions abroad. For over six decades, Burroughs led the National Baptist Convention Woman's Auxiliary, the largest Black women's organization in the United States at the time. In 1909, Burroughs established the National Training School for Women and Girls (renamed the Nannie Helen Burroughs School in 1964, following her death), where, in 1912, she began editing *The Worker*, a missionary magazine. See Evelyn Brooks Higginbotham, "Burroughs, Nannie Helen," Oxford African American Studies Center, December 1, 2006, https://oxfordaasc.com/display/10.1093/acref/9780195301731.001.0001/acref-9780195301731-e-44056; and Marcia G. Synnott, "Burroughs, Nannie," Oxford African American Studies Center, May 31, 2013, https://oxfordaasc.com/display/10.1093/acref/9780195301731.001.0001/acref-9780195301731-e-34278.

Victor Francis Calverton (1900–1940), born George Goetz in Baltimore, Maryland, was a white socialist writer, literary critic, popular speaker and founder and editor of *Modern Quarterly*. As a student at Johns Hopkins University, Goetz met the leader of the New York Socialist Party and came to believe that only a new social order could transform an American society that was "degenerate and corrupt." After graduating in 1921, Goetz joined the Baltimore branch of the Socialist Labor Party (SLP), embraced the "new psychology" of psychoanalysis and sexual freedom, and began teaching in the Baltimore public schools. To avoid persecution during the Red Scare, Goetz adopted the pseudonym Calverton and launched *Modern Quarterly* in 1923. In 1929, he edited *The Anthology of American Negro Literature* and published, among others, W. E. B. Du Bois, George Schyler, Langston Hughes, and Alain Locke. He boasted that he had published "almost every left-wing liberal and radical who had artistic aspirations." Rejecting Stalinism and hoping to develop an American brand of socialism, he broke with the Communist Party USA in 1933. See Haim Genizi, "V. F. Calverton, a Radical Magazinist for Black Intellectuals, 1920–1940," *Journal of Negro History* 57, no. 3 (1972): 241–53; and Walter C. Daniel, "Calverton and the Black American Writers," *Negro History Bulletin* 41, no. 4 (1978): 868; Leonard Wilcox, *V. F. Calverton: Radical in the American Grain* (Philadelphia: Temple University Press, 1992), 12, 16–17, 20, 25, 28–31, 88–91, 152–56.

Floyd Joseph Calvin (1902–39), born in Washington, Arkansas, was an African American journalist, editor, groundbreaking radio broadcaster, and Black news service founder. After completing a seventh-grade education at the Rural School in Clow, Arkansas, he enrolled at the Shover State Teacher Training College from 1916 to 1920, and from 1920 to 1921, he studied at City College in New York. In 1922, A. Philip Randolph hired him as associate editor of the *Messenger*, where he published a series about the Jim Crow South titled "Eight Weeks in Dixie." In 1924 he moved to the *Pittsburgh Courier*, where he held various editorial and broadcast roles and proved a key player in the paper's national success. As part of his investigative work as a journalist, Calvin traveled more than ten thousand miles making stops in every state in the South and Southwest. On October 2, 1927, Calvin launched the first American radio show to focus on Black news events. Eight years later, in 1935, he founded Calvin's News Service, supplying copy to over 150 African American newspapers. See Robyn McGee, "Calvin, Floyd," Oxford African American Studies Center, May 31, 2013, https://oxfordaasc.com/display/10.1093/acref/9780195301731.001.0001/acref-9780195301731-e-36361.

Joseph Raphael Ralph Casimir (1898–1996), born in St Joseph, Dominica, and likely the descendant of one of the island's estates' enslaved families, was a poet, editor, journalist, legal clerk, and indefatigable organizer for Marcus Garvey's Universal Negro Improvement Association (UNIA). His only formal education appears to have been attendance at St. Joseph's Elementary School from 1903 to 1914, but he also read assiduously at the Carnegie Library in Roseau, Dominica's capital and largest city. In 1918 he became clerk to the prominent lawyer and Caribbean nationalist Cecil E. A. Rawle, who fired Casimir two years later for what he considered "offensive" articles and speeches but rehired him in 1924 after Casimir resigned from the UNIA. Reading extensively about racial discrimination worldwide, witnessing discriminatory treatment toward Afro-Dominicans on the island, and resenting the menial work West Indian soldiers were consigned to during World War I, Casimir became radicalized. Incensed by white mob attacks on African American and West Indian soldiers following World War I, Casimir formed the UNIA branch in Roseau in 1920, which quickly attracted over eight hundred members from the largely Black working class. Publishing in the National Association for the Advancement of Colored People's *Crisis*, Cyril Briggs's *Crusader*, the Black-owned *Philadelphia Courier*, the *Barbados Times*, and frequently in the *Negro World*, he also became an agent of the Black Star Line and of the *Negro World*, *Crisis*, *Promoter*, *Crusader*, and *Challenge* periodicals. When Casimir wrote in Garvey's paper about the dire living, working, and traveling conditions for Black Dominicans—including long journeys by canoes vulnerable to capsizing during storms—other West Indians applauded his candor. Despite efforts by the island's elite to repress the *Negro World*, the newspaper became the most popular newspaper on the island. Casimir, in fact, sent copies of the paper to the prominent Pan-African nationalist Joseph E. Casely Hayford because the paper was banned in the Gold Coast (now Ghana). A prolific poet and long-time correspondent with Langston Hughes, Casimir was awarded the Golden Drum Award in 1984 for his "outstanding contribution to the Cultural Development of Dominica." See "Pledge Signed by Francis Louis Gardier et al.," in Marcus Garvey, *The Marcus Garvey and Universal Negro Improvement Association Papers*, ed. Robert A. Hill, vol. 11, *The Caribbean Diaspora, 1910–1920* (Durham, NC: Duke University Press, 2011) 509–10n5; Kathy Casimir MacLean, *Black Man Listen: The Life of JR Ralph Casimir* (London: Papillote, 2022), 15, 23, 26, 28, 30, 32, 43–44, 74, 104, 122, 137, 151, Kindle; Cecil E. A. Rawle to J. R. Ralph Casimir, August 28, 1920, in Marcus Garvey, *The Marcus Garvey and Universal Negro Improvement Association Papers*, ed. Robert A. Hill, vol. 12, *The Caribbean Diaspora, 1920–1921* (Durham, NC: Duke University Press, 2014), 79.

Charles Waddell Chesnutt (1858–1932), born in Cleveland, Ohio, to free Black parents who later moved to Fayetteville, North Carolina, was the first major African American fiction writer and the first to be published by the most esteemed major American publishers. Chesnutt attended the Freedmen's Bureau Howard School in Fayetteville, North Carolina, until the age of fourteen but continued reading afterward, developing expertise to work as a teacher in both North and South Carolina. Returning to Cleveland to escape the post-Reconstruction South, Chesnutt passed the Ohio bar exam in 1887 and began a successful legal stenography business. He also started writing fiction in a number of periodicals, including *Family Fiction, Puck, Overland Monthly*, the *Crisis, Southern Workman, Century*, the *Outlook*, and *Youth's Companion*. Chesnutt is best known for the complex signifying in his fiction, including *The Conjure Woman* (1899), *The House Behind the Cedars* (1900), and *The Marrow of Tradition* (1901). Dedicating his work to exposing "the unjust spirit of caste which is so insidious as to pervade a whole nation," Chesnutt was awarded the National Association for the Advancement of Colored People's prestigious Spingarn Medal in 1928. See SallyAnn H. Ferguson, "Chesnutt, Charles W.," Oxford African American Studies Center, December 1, 2009, https://oxfordaasc.com/display/10.1093/acref/9780195301731.001.0001/acref-9780195301731-e-45372; and Julian Mason, "Chesnutt, Charles Waddell," Oxford African American

Studies Center, May 31, 2013, https://oxfordaasc.com/display/10.1093/acref/9780195301731.001.0001
/acref-9780195301731-e-34300.

José Clarana (1888–1970) was an Afro-Caribbean journalist and educator born in St. Vincent, British West Indies. He emigrated from Barbados to the United States in 1905. After graduating from Cornell University in 1912, Clarana worked as a Spanish teacher in the Brooklyn, New York, public schools before moving to Brazil in 1916. He returned to the United States in 1919. Clarana, who also wrote under the names James Bertram Clarke and Jaime Clarana Gil, "lived in the United States, Brazil, Argentina, Venezuela, Puerto Rico, Cuba, St. Vincent, St. Lucia, and Haiti under one or more of these assumed identities." During the first decades of the twentieth century Clarana, as Clarke, "wrote about the experience of racism from the diverse perspectives of these personae, forming his arguments using the language (French, Spanish, Portuguese, Italian, Hebrew—at one point, he lived as a Jew—American and British English) and the racial logic of his intended audience to advance an anti-racist agenda." See Zita Nunes, "The Multiple Selves of James Bertram Clarke: A Model for Africana Historiography," University of Maryland–Baltimore County, April 7, 2015, https://cahss.umbc.edu/events/event/31565/; and Zita Nunes, *Cannibal Democracy: Race and Representation in the Literature of the Americas* (Minneapolis: University of Minnesota Press, 2008), xi–xv.

Anna Julia Cooper (1858–1964), born Anna Julia Haywood in Raleigh, North Carolina, to an enslaved mother and, scholars speculate, either her mother's enslaver or the enslaver's brother, was a Black liberation activist, author, educator, and sociologist. In 1867 she was among the first to enroll at St. Augustine's Normal School and Collegiate Institute, an Episcopal school for the newly freed in Raleigh, North Carolina. When she graduated from Oberlin College in 1884, she, along with Mary Eliza Church (Terrell), was among the first four African American women to graduate from the institution. After earning a master's degree in mathematics, she began teaching at the Washington Colored High School and boarded with Alexander Crummell in Washington, DC. In 1892 she cofounded the Colored Women's League and published *A Voice from the South*, widely regarded as among the first Black feminist monographs. In this groundbreaking collection, Cooper criticized the racism of white feminists and endorsed Black women's rights to moral purity, education, and economic uplift. In the early 1920s, when she was in her sixties, Cooper, like New Negro Renaissance luminaries Claude McKay, Gwendolyn Bennett, Langston Hughes, and Alain Locke, traveled to Paris and participated in the new pan-African literary and political movements of the era. When she completed her dissertation, *L'Attitude de la France à L'ègard de L'esclavage pendant la Révolution* (France's Attitude toward Slavery during the Revolution), she became the first Black woman to earn a doctorate from the Université de Paris, Sorbonne. See Kimberly Springer, "Cooper, Anna Julia Haywood," Oxford African American Studies Center, May 31, 2013, https://oxfordaasc.com/display/10.1093/acref/9780195301731.001.0001/acref-9780195301731-e-34320; Elizabeth Ammons, "Voice from the South," Oxford African American Studies Center, December 1, 2006, https://oxfordaasc.com/display/10.1093/acref/9780195301731.001.0001/acref-9780195301731-e-47172; and Vivian M. May, *Anna Julia Cooper, Visionary Black Feminist: A Critical Introduction* (New York: Routledge, 2007), 17, 33, 107.

Frank Rudolph Crosswaith (1892–1965), who was born in Fredericksted, St. Croix, in the Danish West Indies, earned a scholarship to the Rand School of Social Science in New York City and quickly became a leader in socialist politics. Described as the Negro Debs (after white labor leader and Socialist Party presidential candidate Eugene V. Debs, 1855–1926), Crosswaith played a leading role in founding both the Trade Union Committee for Organizing Negro Workers (1925) and the Harlem Labor Committee (1934); the two organizations merged into the Negro

Labor Committee in 1935, with a mission to agitate for African American workers' rights while uniting Black and white workers. For more than thirty years, Crosswaith also worked on behalf of the International Ladies' Garment Workers' Union. From 1925 to 1928, Crosswaith served as an organizer for the Brotherhood of Sleeping Car Porters and Maids. In 1935 he helped organize, and spoke at, the First Negro Labor Conference. See Cleve McD. Scott, "Crosswaith, Frank Rudolph," Oxford African American Studies Center, May 31, 2017, https://oxfordaasc.com/display/10.1093/acref/9780195301731.001.0001/acref-9780195301731-e-73727.

Alexander Crummell (1819–98), an Episcopal minister, abolitionist, and Pan-Africanist, was born in New York City to a freeborn woman and Boston Crummell, a formerly enslaved African likely from what is now the nation of Sierra Leone. Ordained as an Episcopal priest in 1844, Crummell spoke tirelessly on behalf of abolitionism, the rights of free Blacks, and the American Colonization Society (ACS). With a "ruthlessness in his quest for learning," Crummell earned a degree from Cambridge University in 1853 and spent twenty years of his life as a missionary and educator in Liberia, the West African country founded by the ACS. As a Liberian professor and public intellectual, Crummell "would walk a tightrope between African nationalism and loyalty to the Episcopal church." An advocate of the assimilationist position of Liberian president Edward James Roye, Crummell encouraged educating and intermarrying with native Liberians as a means of alleviating caste barriers. Returning to the United States in 1872, Crummell was named rector of St. Mary's Episcopal Church in Washington, DC; in 1879, he formed St. Luke's Episcopal Church, where he remained for the rest of his ministerial career. The year before his death, Crummell founded the American Negro Academy. See Wilson Jeremiah Moses, *Alexander Crummell: A Study of Civilization and Discontent* (Oxford: New York: Oxford University Press, 1989), 5, 90; and Wilson J. Moses, "Crummell, Alexander," Oxford African American Studies Center, May 31, 2013, https://oxfordaasc.com/display/10.1093/acref/9780195301731.001.0001/acref-9780195301731-e-34325.

Countee Cullen (b. Countee LeRoy Porter, 1903–46), literary icon of the New Negro Renaissance, began his life under obscure origins, but after his adoption by the Reverend Frederick A. and Carolyn Belle (Mitchell) Cullen in 1918, Countee quickly earned recognition as an excellent student, publishing some of his most famous work even before completing his advanced degrees. Graduating Phi Beta Kappa from New York University in 1925 and earning a master's degree from Harvard University in 1927, Cullen wrote most of the poems for his first three collections of poetry in that time frame and published them in *Color* (1925), *Copper Sun* (1927), and *The Ballad of the Brown Girl* (1927). As Gerald Early notes, "If any event signaled the coming of the Harlem Renaissance, it was the precocious success of this rather shy black boy who, more than any other black literary figure of his generation, was being touted and bred to become a major crossover literary figure." See Gerald Early, "Cullen, Countee," Oxford African American Studies Center, December 1, 2006, https://oxfordaasc.com/display/10.1093/acref/9780195301731.001.0001/acref-9780195301731-e-46665.

Benjamin Jefferson Davis (1870–1945), born in Dawson, Georgia, to formerly enslaved parents, earned a sixth grade education before becoming a bricklayer and learning the printing trade from the white Dawson publisher and printer Tom W. Loyless. In 1903 Davis began publishing his own paper, the weekly *Independent*, which he moved to Atlanta in 1909 and continued until 1932. Within a year of its beginning, the *Independent* reported a circulation of one hundred thousand, despite being banned by whites in many towns because of its militancy, and Davis had become one of the wealthiest men in Atlanta. Although he was a supporter of Booker T. Washington, Davis seems not to have adopted Washington's accommodationist rhetoric. He wrote "scathing editorials condemning lynching, convict labor, and disenfranchisement," which made him "the idol of the backwoods poor Negro farmers" and a target of the Ku Klux Klan. W. E. B. Du Bois, in fact, called Davis a "fearless and forceful man." With his growing wealth and status, he became a leader in the Republican Party. See Gerald Horne, "Davis, Benjamin Jefferson," Oxford African American Studies Center, May 31, 2013, https://oxfordaasc.com/display/10.1093/acref/9780195301731.001.0001 /acref-9780195301731-e-34332.

Alvaro de Lugo (1906–58), a close friend of the so-called King of Policy, Harlem Renaissance benefactor and philanthropist Casper Holstein, was the first postmaster in the history of the US Virgin Islands to come from the islands. See "De Lugo's Back Home: He's Postmaster Now," *Virgin Islands Daily News*, August 17, 1933.

Wilfred Adolphus Domingo (1889–1968) , born in Kingston, Jamaica, was an author, socialist activist, and boyhood friend of Marcus Garvey. After immigrating to Boston in 1910, he enrolled in night school with the hopes of attending medical school but decided instead to move to New York in 1912, where he started what would become a successful business selling imported Caribbean food. When Garvey came to New York in 1916, Domingo introduced him to Harlem's Black political leaders. Garvey, in turn, hired him to edit the *Negro World*. During the first Red Scare in 1919, however, as Domingo found himself increasingly committed to the Socialist Party, Garvey fired Domingo as editor of the *Negro World* lest the Universal Negro Improvement Association be targeted as a leftist organization. With the Barbadian Richard B. Moore, Domingo then founded the *Emancipator* in 1920. He also served as a contributing editor for the *Messenger*, but after A. Phillip Randolph and Chandler Owen employed anti–West Indian stereotypes in their attacks on Garvey in 1923, he left the magazine. In 1925, he contributed an essay to Alain Locke's *The New Negro* on West Indians in the United States. In the 1930s and early 1940s Domingo worked tirelessly on behalf of Jamaican self-governance. In 1941, with his friend Richard B. Moore, he formed the West Indian National Committee, which, although loyal to Britain during World War II, pursued Caribbean self-rule. See Philip Howard, "Domingo, Wilfred Adolphus," Oxford African American Studies Center, May 31, 2017, https://oxfordaasc.com/display/10.1093/acref/9780195301731.001.0001/acref-9780195301731 -e-73820; Adam Ewing, *The Age of Garvey: How a Jamaican Activist Created a Mass Movement and Changed Global Black Politics* (Princeton, NJ: Princeton University Press, 2014), 80; and J. A. Zumoff, "Domingo, Wilfred Adolphus," Oxford African American Studies Center, May 31, 2013, https:// oxfordaasc.com/display/10.1093/acref/9780195301731.001.0001/acref-9780195301731-e-36716.

William Edward Burghardt Du Bois (1868–1963) was a sociologist, historian, writer, educator, civil rights leader, and internationally known Pan-Africanist organizer. Indeed, as David Levering Lewis notes, Du Bois was the "premier architect of the civil rights movement in the United States and among the first thinkers to grasp the international implications of the struggle for racial justice." Born in Great Barrington, Massachusetts, Du Bois earned bachelor of arts degrees from both Fisk University (1888) and Harvard University (1890). In 1895 he became the first African American to earn a doctorate from Harvard. In his most famous work, *The Souls of Black Folk* (1903), Du Bois criticized Booker T. Washington's accedence to segregation, trenchantly writing, "The problem of the Twentieth Century is the problem of the color-line." In 1905, he helped to organize the civil rights organization the Niagara Movement as a direct rebuttal to Washington's accommodationist approach, and in 1909 he helped to organize the National Association for the Advancement of Colored People (NAACP), founded in response to the deadly 1908 Springfield, Illinois, race riot. From 1897 to 1910 and from 1934 to 1944, Du Bois taught history and economics at Atlanta University, and from 1910 to 1934 he launched and edited the *Crisis*, the official publication of the NAACP.

Considered the "Father of Pan-Africanism," the staunchly anti-imperialist Du Bois organized a series of Pan-African Congresses in the first decades of the twentieth century devoted to achieving African independence from colonial powers. As Lewis notes, the evolution of Du Bois's thought is complicated and even contradictory: "A severe critic of racial segregation, he still enjoined other African Americans to accept, if temporarily, the segregated units and officer training facilities of the U.S. Army in 1917–18—in the hope that wartime military service would lead to full civil rights. An elitist who emphasized the leadership role of a 'talented tenth' in the liberation of black people, Du Bois moved increasingly to the Left after World War II, denouncing U.S. Cold War policies as imperialistic and espousing Communist solutions to problems of race and class." In 1961 Du Bois joined the Communist Party USA. Two years before his death, he emigrated to Ghana at the request of President Kwame Nkrumah to serve as the editor in chief of the *Encyclopedia Africana*. See David Levering Lewis, "Du Bois, W. E. B.," Oxford African American Studies Center, December 1, 2006, https://oxfordaasc.com/display/10.1093/acref/9780195301731.001.0001/acref-9780195301731-e-51111; Gerald Horne, "Du Bois, W. E. B.," Oxford African American Studies Center, September 30, 2012, https://oxfordaasc.com/display/10.1093/acref/9780195301731.001.0001/acref-9780195301731-e-48662; and W. E. B. Du Bois, *The Souls of Black Folk* (New York: Penguin, 2018), 3.

Alice Dunbar-Nelson (b. Alice Ruth Moore, 1875–1935)—born in New Orleans, Louisiana, to a seaman father and a seamstress mother who had formerly been enslaved—was a poet, fiction writer, educator, clubwoman, orator, suffragist, and civil rights activist. After graduating in 1892 from a teachers' training program at Straight College in New Orleans, Moore taught in her home city and in Brooklyn, New York. In 1898 she helped establish the White Rose Home for Girls in Harlem. After publishing her first book of poetry in 1895, she attracted the attention of the renowned African American poet Paul Laurence Dunbar, and they married in 1898. The couple separated, however, before Dunbar's death in 1906. Well known for her fiction, work on behalf of women's suffrage, the Black women's club movement, the 1922 Dyer Anti-Lynching Bill, and the education of African American girls, Dunbar-Nelson also had considerable experience in journalism before writing her column for the *Pittsburgh Courier*. Most notably, she edited the Wilmington, Delaware, *Advance* with her second husband, Robert Nelson, from 1920 to 1922. As an editor of Dunbar-Nelson's personal and professional writing, Gloria T. Hull, maintains, she "commands consideration for her many-faceted racial activism, club woman endeavors, passionate sexuality, vibrant and contradictory personality, and her achievements as a multigenre author whose work helped to maintain and extend the tradition of African American women's writing." See Alice Knox Eaton, "Dunbar-Nelson, Alice," Oxford African American Studies Center, May 31, 2013, https://oxfordaasc.com/display/10.1093/acref/9780195301731.001.0001/acref-9780195301731-e-34359; and Gloria T. Hull, "Dunbar-Nelson, Alice Ruth Moore," Oxford African American Studies Center, December 1, 2006, https://oxfordaasc.com/display/10.1093/acref/9780195301731.001.0001/acref-9780195301731-e-44123.

Paul K. Edwards (1898–1959), born in Oskaloosa, Iowa, was a white marketing and economics professor and scholar. After earning a bachelor of arts degree from Earlham College, a Quaker-founded school in Richmond, Indiana, and a master of arts degree from Harvard University. Edwards taught economics at Fisk University from 1932 to 1938. He completed his marketing analysis of Black consumers, *The Southern Urban Negro as a Consumer* (1932), under the supervision of noted African American sociologist Charles Spurgeon Johnson. Edwards was also employed as director of sales promotion in Black markets for the Rumford Company, a producer of baking soda. See "Paul K. Edwards of Rutgers Dead," *New York Times*, December 8, 1959, 45; and "Writes Book," *Chicago Defender*, March 6, 1932.

Jessie Redmon Fauset (1882–1961), born in Camden County, New Jersey, and raised in Philadelphia, was one of the key "midwives" of the New Negro Renaissance. After completing her undergraduate degree from Cornell University in 1905, where she was the first Black woman to be elected to Phi Beta Kappa, she earned a master's degree in French in 1919 from the University of Pennsylvania. In her role as literary editor of the *Crisis* from 1919 to 1926, she published some of the era's most important writers, including Arna Bontemps, Countee Cullen, Langston Hughes, Claude McKay, George Schuyler, and Jean Toomer. Fauset believed, according to Thadious M. Davis, that in "order to combat racism, white Americans had to be educated about the realities, rather than the exoticism, of black American life; and black Americans had to be represented in their home life and personal relations as similar to white Americans." As a novelist, she secured her place as one of the Harlem Renaissance's most important creative writers. She is best known for *There Is Confusion* (1924), *Plum Bun* (1929), and *The Chinaberry Tree* (1931). See Thadious M. Davis, "Fauset, Jessie Redmon," Oxford African American Studies Center, December 1, 2006, https://oxfordaasc .com/display/10.1093/acref/9780195301731.001.0001/acref-9780195301731-e-44138; and Lisa Clayton Robinson, "Fauset, Jessie Redmon," Oxford African American Studies Center, December 1, 2006, https://oxfordaasc.com/display/10.1093/acref/9780195301731.001.0001/acref-9780195301731 -e-41239.

William Henry Ferris (1874–1941), born in New Haven, Connecticut, was an educator, minister, writer, and civil rights activist. The first African American to earn degrees at both Harvard and Yale Universities, Ferris joined the American Negro Academy at its inception in 1897. From 1898 to 1903, he participated in T. Thomas Fortune's Afro-American Council, which was devoted to combatting lynching, segregation, and disenfranchisement. After years working as an educator, pastor, and entrepreneur, Ferris served as editor of the *Champion Magazine* in Chicago from 1916 to 1917, and from 1919 to 1923 he worked closely with Marcus Garvey, becoming the literary editor of the *Negro World*. From 1925 to 1927 he served as the contributing editor of *The Spokesman*. See Michele Valerie Ronnick, "Ferris, William Henry," Oxford African American Studies Center, May 31, 2018, https://oxfordaasc.com/display/10.1093/acref/9780195301731.001.0001/acref-9780195301731-e -77924; and William H Brown, "Afro-American Council," Oxford African American Studies Center, December 1, 2009, https://oxfordaasc.com/display/10.1093/acref/9780195301731.001.0001/acref -9780195301731-e-4518.

Timothy Thomas Fortune (1856–1928), born enslaved in Marianna, Florida, was a civil rights activist, publisher, orator, and the "dean of African American journalists." Although he enjoyed only a few years of formal primary education in schools run by the Freedmen's Bureau, he developed what he described as "the book learning fever." By 1887 Fortune was the nation's leading Black journalist. That same year, in an effort to defend the Black community against white violence, eradicate segregation in transportation and other public facilities, protect Black voting rights, and end convict leasing and chain gangs, Fortune formed the Afro-American League. By 1889 he was sole editor of the Republican *New York Age*, the most renowned Black newspaper in the country. In December of that year, Fortune maintained that inspired by the Afro-American League, "a new man in black . . . [who] bears no resemblance to a slave, or a coward, or an ignoramus" would "force the concession to him of absolute justice under State and Federal Constitutions." During his long career, Fortune wrote over three hundred articles—securing national recognition from 1881 to 1907 for his searing editorials on behalf of Black civil rights. Fortune's writing talents caught the attention of Booker T. Washington, who, despite disagreeing with Fortune over the importance of a public fight for civil rights, hired him as a consultant and ghostwriter, often for little or no pay. In 1923, after having been convicted of mail fraud, Marcus Garvey hired Fortune to edit the *Negro*

World. For the remainder of his life, Fortune served in this position. See T. Thomas Fortune, "The Afro-American Agitator," *Freeman*, December 1, 1889; Sholomo B. Levy, "Fortune, T. Thomas," Oxford African American Studies Center, May 31, 2013, https://oxfordaasc.com/display/10.1093 /acref/9780195301731.001.0001/acref-9780195301731-e-34392; Walter D. Greason, "Fortune, Timothy Thomas," Oxford African American Studies Center, December 1, 2009, https://oxfordaasc .com/display/10.1093/acref/9780195301731.001.0001/acref-9780195301731-e-45571#acref -9780195301731-e-45571; William Seraile, "Fortune, Timothy Thomas," Oxford African American Studies Center, December 1, 2006, https://oxfordaasc.com/display/10.1093/acref/9780195301731 .001.0001/acref-9780195301731-e-41312; Shawn Leigh Alexander, "T. Thomas Fortune the Afro-American Agitator: A Collection of Writings, 1880–1928," in T. Thomas Fortune, *T. Thomas Fortune, the Afro-American Agitator: A Collection of Writings, 1880 1928* (Gainesville: University Press of Florida, 2008), xi–xxxviii; and Emma Lou Thornbrough, *T. Thomas Fortune: Militant Journalist* (Chicago: University of Chicago Press, 1972), 78–79.

Edward Franklin Frazier (1894–1962), born in Baltimore, Maryland, to parents who emphasized the importance of education as a means of upward mobility (his father had taught himself to read and write), was a prominent African American sociologist and educator. He graduated with honors from Howard University in Washington, DC, before earning a master's degree in sociology from Clark University in 1920 and a PhD from the University of Chicago in 1931. During the 1920s, while teaching at Morehouse College, Frazier published over thirty articles on issues ranging from the Black family, Black business leaders, the evolution of the Black middle class, and—most controversially, given Jim Crow—the "pathology" of racial prejudice. When he published an essay on this last topic in 1927, he faced so much white hostility and so many threats of violence that he and his wife were forced to flee Atlanta for Chicago. In 1932 Frazier published his groundbreaking *The Negro Family in Chicago*, which examined the effects of urbanization on Black family structures. Fiercely independent and principled throughout his life, he endured jail time for protesting D. W. Griffith's *The Birth of a Nation*, attacked what he viewed as the pretentiousness of the black bourgeoisie, and publicly supported W. E. B. Du Bois and Paul Robeson during the post–World War II Red Scare. In 1948 Frazier became the first Black president of the American Sociological Society. See Eric R. Jackson, "Frazier, E. Franklin," Oxford African American Studies Center, May 31, 2013, https://oxfordaasc.com/display/10.1093/acref/9780195301731.001.0001/acref-9780195301731-e -34398; and Lawrie Balfour, "Frazier, Edward Franklin," Oxford African American Studies Center, December 1, 2006, https://oxfordaasc.com/display/10.1093/acref/9780195301731.001.0001/acref -9780195301731-e-41331.

Amy Euphemia Jacques Garvey (1896–1973), born to Black middle-class parents in Kingston, Jamaica, and educated at Kingston's elite Wolmer's Girls School, was a journalist and Pan-Africanist, the second wife of Black nationalist Marcus Garvey, and, especially during his periods of incarceration between 1923 and 1927, a Universal Negro Improvement Association (UNIA) organizer and unofficial leader. Jacques first met the charismatic Garvey after hearing him deliver a speech at Kingston's Liberty Hall in 1918 and immediately accepted his offer of employment, becoming his secretary and trusted adviser. From 1924 to 1933, she served as associate editor of the UNIA's weekly newspaper, the *Negro World*, and edited its women's page, "Our Women and What They Think." Her writing showcased her commitment to Pan-Africanism, Black nationalism, and women's activism on behalf of UNIA goals. As Ula Taylor writes, Jacques Garvey's writing in the Negro World "destabilized masculinist discourse, offering a glimpse into the range and scope of feminism possible during the 1920s and a model of women as political beings who could change the world." To offer a corrective of what she saw as misleading accounts of Garveyism in the press, Jacques Garvey edited two volumes of *The Philosophy and Opinions of Marcus Garvey* (1923–25). In 1963 she published *Garvey and Garveyism* and in 1968 *Black Power in America: Marcus Garvey's Impact on Jamaica and Africa; the Power of the Human Spirit*. See Ula Y. Taylor, "Garvey, Amy Euphemia Jacques," Oxford African American Studies Center, December 1, 2006, https://oxfordaasc.com/display/10.1093/acref /9780195301731.001.0001/acref-9780195301731-e-16823; D. A. Dunkley, "Garvey, Amy Euphemia Jacques," Oxford African American Studies Center, May 31, 2017, https://oxfordaasc.com/display/10 .1093/acref/9780195301731.001.0001/acref-9780195301731-e-74009; and Ula Y. Taylor, The Veiled Garvey: The Life and Times of Amy Jacques Garvey (Chapel Hill: University of North Carolina Press, 2002):, 1.

Marcus Mosiah Garvey (1887–1940), born in Saint Ann's Bay, Jamaica, launched in 1914 what would become the most successful grassroots Pan-African organization in the world, the Universal Negro Improvement Association (UNIA), with his first wife Amy Ashwood. By 1923 the UNIA boasted a membership of six million people, with over a thousand branches in Africa, Canada, the Caribbean, Central and South America, the United Kingdom, and the United States. Affirming race pride, self-reliance, and "Africa for the Africans," Garvey preached an ideology of "'race first' [that] connoted the unapologetic determination of Africans, whether at home or in the diaspora, to pursue their own racial self-interest." To realize his vision, Garvey founded the *Negro World* (1918–33) in New York as the UNIA's official organ and sold shares in his shipping company, the Black Star Line (1919–22). The events of 1922, however, reversed that momentum. In January of that year the federal government, which had long feared his influence, indicted Garvey for mail fraud; his Black Star Line failed; and, based on a shared commitment to racial purity, he accepted a meeting (lambasted in the Black press) with the Assistant Grand Wizard of the Ku Klux Klan, Edward Clarke. The year 1923 would not prove to be much better: Garvey was convicted of mail fraud and sentenced to five years, though he was eventually let out on bail pending an appeal. His original conviction was upheld in 1925, and Garvey returned to prison, where he remained until President Calvin Coolidge commuted his sentence and deported him to Jamaica in 1927. His second wife, Amy Jacques Garvey, played a pivotal role in defending her husband and ensuring that the UNIA remained a formidable Black international organization, in part through her editorial work for the *Negro World*. At its peak in 1925, the circulation of the paper, which in 1923 included a Spanish-language section and in 1924 a French-language section, reached over five hundred thousand readers. See D. A. Dunkley, "Garvey, Marcus Mosiah," Oxford African American Studies Center, May 31, 2017, https:// oxfordaasc.com/display/10.1093/acref/9780195301731.001.0001/acref-9780195301731-e-74010; Claudrena N. Harold, "Garvey, Marcus," Oxford African American Studies Center, December 1, 2009, https://oxfordaasc.com/display/10.1093/acref/9780195301731.001.0001/acref-9780195301731 -e-45589; Ula Y. Taylor, *The Veiled Garvey: The Life and Times of Amy Jacques Garvey* (Chapel Hill: University of North Carolina Press, 2002), 41; Frank A. Salamone, "Negro World," Oxford African American Studies Center, December 1, 2009, https://oxfordaasc.com/display/10.1093/acref /9780195301731.001.0001/acref-9780195301731-e-45988; Tony Martin, "Marcus Garvey," Oxford African American Studies Center, September 30, 2012, https://oxfordaasc.com/display/10.1093/acref /9780195301731.001.0001/acref-9780195301731-e-47871; and William F. Mugleston, "Garvey, Marcus," Oxford African American Studies Center, May 31, 2013, https://oxfordaasc.com/display/10.1093 /acref/9780195301731.001.0001/acref-9780195301731-e-34406.

James M. Gates (1884–1945), born in Hogansville, Georgia, was a nationally known Black evangelical minister. Leader of the Mount Calvary Baptist Church in the Rockdale Park neighborhood of Atlanta from 1916 to 1942, Gates quickly became one of the most popular "phonograph preachers" after the success of his sermon "Death's Black Train Is Coming." Recording folk sermons for

Black urban and rural audiences, Gates had, by 1928, "'preached his way to wealth through the phonograph!'" His Christmas sermon "'Will the Coffin Be Your Santa Claus,'" the *Pittsburgh Courier* exclaimed, "brought the big royalty checks flying in!" By 1941 Gates had recorded over two hundred of his sermons. See Lerone A. Martin, *Preaching on Wax: The Phonograph and the Shaping of Modern African American Religion* (New York: New York University Press, 2014), 94–107, 136.

Sutton E. Griggs (1872–1933), born in Chatfield, Texas, to formerly enslaved parents Allen R. Griggs and Emma Hodge, was a Baptist minister, editor, novelist, and civil rights activist. At the age of thirteen he enrolled in the Black Baptist Bishop College in Marshall, Texas, where he graduated in 1890. He then earned a bachelor of divinity degree from Richmond Theological Seminary in 1894, and from 1896 to 1899 served as a pastor in Virginia. His self-published novel, *Imperium in Imperio*, appears to have been inspired by the work of his father in 1880 to settle an all-Black community in the Texas panhandle by working with the Texas Farmers Association. Although the settlement never materialized, as Marc Blanc notes, "The Panhandle colony promised the economic self-sufficiency that the federal government had failed to deliver to formerly enslaved people when it abandoned Reconstruction in 1877." See John Cullen Gruesser, *A Literary Life of Sutton E. Griggs: The Man on the Firing Line* (Oxford: Oxford University Press, 2022), 4–7; and Marc Blanc, "Bleeding Heartland: Race, Region, and Radicalism in Midwest Print Culture, 1877–1939" (PhD diss., Washington University in St. Louis, 2024), 118–19.

Archibald Henry Grimké (1849–1930), who was born enslaved near Charleston, South Carolina, escaped enslavement and eventually graduated from Harvard Law School in 1874, becoming a Boston-based lawyer, writer, politician, and editor. In 1883 he began editing the *Hub*, a Republican "mugwump" party newspaper directed at Black readers, but later switched his allegiance to the Democratic Party and wrote well-regarded biographies of abolitionists William Lloyd Garrison and Charles Sumner. After joining the American Negro Academy in 1899, Grimké served as its president from 1903 to 1916. A member of W. E. B. Du Bois's Niagara Movement, which he promoted as editor of *Alexander's Magazine*, he later helped to found the National Association for the Advancement of Colored People (NAACP). Beginning in 1913, Grimké led the Washington, DC, chapter of the organization, and as chapter president he protested President Woodrow Wilson's order to segregate US government agencies and denounced the US entry into World War I. In 1919 the NAACP awarded Grimké the Spingarn Medal for outstanding achievement. See Dickson D. Bruce Jr., "Grimké, Archibald Henry," Oxford African American Studies Center, May 31, 2013, https://oxfordaasc.com/display/10.1093/acref/9780195301731.001.0001/acref-9780195301731-e-34424.

Martha Gruening (1889–1937), born in Philadelphia, Pennsylvania, was a Jewish American journalist, lawyer, suffragist, social activist, and educator. A graduate of Smith College and New York University's School of Law, Gruening began working for the National Association for the Advancement of Colored People shortly after its inception and collaborated with rabbis in New York City's Jewish community to promote the organization. A frequent contributor to the *Crisis*, Gruening was able as a white person to secure especially telling interviews as she investigated white mob violence, including the 1917 East St. Louis massacre. Fearless in her activism, "she picketed with striking workers, campaigned against the draft, and pushed for voting rights for women and African Americans." After returning from living in Paris in 1931, she regularly reviewed books for the *Nation*, the *New Republic*, and the *Journal of Negro History* and spoke out against the rise of fascism in Germany. See "Gruening, Martha," ProQuest Biographies, "Literature Online," Ann Arbor, 2018.

Gordon Blaine Hancock (1884–1970), born in Ninety Six, South Carolina, witnessed firsthand the 1898 Phoenix Riot in his small town, where "white men . . . rode up on horseback with rifles, [and] killed an undetermined number of blacks because they signed an affidavit to vote." The experience forged his resolve to spend his life fighting on behalf of civil rights. After earning degrees from Benedict College, Colgate, and Harvard Universities, he joined the faculty at Virginia Union University in 1921. During his career, "Hancock helped to compile a significant report on Richmond Negroes, worked in that city's branch of the National Urban League, wrote a column for the Associated Negro Press which appeared in one hundred and fourteen black weeklies, lectured at over forty black and white colleges and universities nationally and, under the auspices of the Interracial Commission, to religious and civic associations." Hancock used his nationally syndicated column in the *Norfolk Journal and Guide* to advocate for Black civil and economic rights. As he wrote in a column for the paper in 1939, "Negroes who are segregated and relegated and aggravated and exploited and subjugated and dominated and repudiated and are expected to have more crime and illegitimacy does not prove the Negro more immoral. That is turkey." See Raymond Gavins, "Hancock, Jackson, and Young: Virginia's Black Triumvirate, 1930–1945," *Virginia Magazine of History and Biography*, October 1977, 470–86; and Gordon Hancock, "Let's Start Talking Turkey," *Norfolk (VA) Journal and Guide*, June 3, 1939.

Hubert Henry Harrison (1883–1927), who was born in Concordia, St. Croix, in the Danish West Indies and immigrated to the United States in 1900, was, in the words of Jeffrey B. Perry, a "brilliant writer, orator, educator, critic, and political activist." An autodidact and mesmerizing speaker (Claude McKay reminisced that his head "resembled an African-born replica of Socrates"), Harrison would become, according to Hodge Kirnon, "the first Negro whose radicalism was comprehensive enough to include racialism, politics, theological criticism, sociology and education in a thorough-going and scientific manner." After breaking with the Socialist Party in 1914, Harrison founded the Liberty League in 1917—born out of what he maintained was a need for more "radical policy," especially in the fight against lynching, "than that of the N.A.A.C.P. [National Association for the Advancement of Colored People]"—and its publication *The Voice: A Newspaper for the New Negro*. From August through October 1919, Harrison edited *The New Negro: A Monthly Magazine of a Different Sort*, which expressed the "international consciousness of the darker races—especially of the Negro race." In 1920 he edited Marcus Garvey's *Negro World*, and the following year he was recruited by the New York City Board of Education as a public lecturer. See Jeffrey B. Perry, *Hubert Harrison: The Voice of Harlem Radicalism, 1883–1918* (New York: Columbia University Press, 2009), 1–2, 288; Jeffrey Perry, "Harrison, Hubert Henry," Oxford African American Studies Center, May 31, 2017, https://oxfordaasc.com/display/10.1093/acref/9780195301731.001.0001/acref-9780195301731-e-74120; and Jeffrey B. Perry, *Hubert Harrison: The Struggle for Equality, 1918–1927* (New York: Columbia University Press, 2021), 338.

Melville Jean Herskovits (1895–1963), born in 1895 in Bellefontaine, Ohio, to Jewish immigrant parents, was a pioneering American anthropologist. After World War I, he completed a bachelor's degree in history at the University of Chicago and a master's degree in political science at Columbia University. In 1920 he began studying under Franz Boas and embarked on a career in which he challenged dominant conceptions of race, culture, and racial hierarchies while stressing the importance of appreciating cultural diversity. Conducting fieldwork in the Caribbean, Latin America, and West Africa, Herskovits demonstrated the dynamic transmission of African cultures throughout the diaspora while foregrounding the vitality of Black cultures. In *The American Negro* (1928) Herskovits refuted racist arguments of the supposed inferiority of mixed-race individuals by contesting definitions of race rooted in supposed biological differences, arguing that most Black

Americans had both African and European ancestry and therefore constituted a mixed-race population group rather than a fixed racial category. Herskovits's study, along with that of other students of Boas (notably, Zora Neale Hurston and Margaret Mead), underscored the role of culture and environment in racial differences. See Jerry Gershenhorn, "Herskovits, Melville Jean," Oxford African American Studies Center, September 30, 2012, https://oxfordaasc.com/display/10.1093/acref /9780195301731.001.0001/acref-9780195301731-e-47892.

Leslie Pinckney Hill (1880–1960), born in Lynchburg, Virginia, and raised in Orange, New Jersey, was an educator, administrator, and author. Excelling as a student, Hill earned bachelor's and master's degrees from Harvard University, where he was also employed as a waiter. Hill began his teaching career at Booker T. Washington's Tuskegee Institute before moving to Manassas, Virginia, where he worked to reorganize and develop the Manassas Institute. In 1913 he began serving as the principal of the Institute for Colored Youth in Cheyney, Pennsylvania, where he remained for the rest of his career, retiring in 1951. In *What the Negro Wants* Hill outlined what he saw as African Americans' primary civil rights goals: "1. Protection under the law and no discrimination in the administration of the law 2. Equality of education 3. Equality of expenditure for health and hospitalization 4. Elimination of all inhibiting restrictions in voting—through taxes or otherwise 5. Equal work opportunity and equal pay 6. The right to fight in any branch of the services." See Glenda Diane Smith, "Hill, Leslie Pinckney," Oxford African American Studies Center, December 1, 2006, https://oxfordaasc.com/display/10.1093/acref/9780195301731.001.0001/acref-9780195301731-e -41662; and Rayford W. Logan, "What the Negro Wants and How to Get It: The Inward Power of the Masses," in *What the Negro Wants* (Notre Dame, IN: University of Notre Dame Press, 2020), 72, https://doi.org/10.2307/j.ctv19m62cs.9.

Drusilla Dunjee Houston (1876–1941), probably born in Harpers Ferry, West Virginia, was an educator, self-trained historian, journalist, and devout Baptist. At the age of twenty-two, Drusilla Dunjee met Price Houston, a shopkeeper and businessman; they married and moved to McAlester, Oklahoma, like thousands of other African American migrants who settled in the Oklahoma Territory. From 1898 to 1910, Drusilla ran a girls' school in McAlester, the McAlester Seminary, and later built church schools and served as an administrator to the Oklahoma Baptist College for Girls in Sapulpa from 1917 to 1923. Sometime between 1923 and 1925, she founded the private Oklahoma Vocational Institute of Fine Arts and Crafts. After her brother Roscoe Dunjee launched the *Black Dispatch* in Oklahoma City in 1915, Drusilla began her almost thirty-year tenure as a contributing editor and feature writer, offering readers social commentary and Black historical facts, especially drawn from her research on the Kushite Empire. Her most well-known work, *Wonderful Ethiopians of the Ancient Cushite Empire*, was published in 1926. See De Anna J. Reese, "Houston, Drusilla Dunjee," Oxford African American Studies Center, May 31, 2013, https://oxfordaasc.com /display/10.1093/acref/9780195301731.001.0001/acref-9780195301731-e-37118; and Peggy Brooks-Bertram, "Houston, Drusilla Dunjee," Oklahoma Historical Society, https://www.okhistory.org /publications/enc/entry?entry=HO038.

Langston Hughes (b. James Mercer Langston Hughes, 1901–67), poet, fiction writer, essayist, playwright, and journalist, stands out as one of most innovative literary artists of the New Negro Renaissance. Born in Joplin, Missouri, Hughes was raised by his maternal grandmother, Mary Langston, who instilled in Hughes a strong sense of racial pride: her first husband was a member of John Brown's doomed Harpers Ferry raid and her second husband was the famed abolitionist John Mercer Langston (Hughes's grandfather, after whom he was named), the first black person from Virginia elected to the House of Representatives and founding dean of the law school at

Howard University. After one year at Columbia University, but several in New York City, where he published poetry in the *Crisis*, Hughes left New York in 1923 and traveled to West Africa and Europe, eventually settling in Paris for a time. In 1924 he moved to Washington, DC, to live with his mother; there he worked as an assistant to Carter G. Woodson at the Association for the Study of Negro Life and History. While a busboy at the Wardman Park Hotel, he met poet Vachel Lindsay, who helped to further his career. By 1926 Hughes had enrolled in the historically Black Lincoln University, from which he graduated in 1929. He then returned to Harlem, where he spent the majority of his life. Throughout his career, Hughes published or edited forty-seven books. He was the first American poet to include jazz and blues lyrics in his writing, and his *Weary Blues* (1926) and *Fine Clothes to the Jew* (1927) characterized the innovative spirit of the New Negro Renaissance. In 1935 he was awarded a Guggenheim Fellowship and in 1960 the National Association for the Advancement of Colored People's Spingarn Medal. See Amritjit Singh, "Hughes, Langston," Oxford African American Studies Center, December 1, 2009, https://oxfordaasc.com/display/10.1093/acref/9780195301731.001.0001 /acref-9780195301731-e-45708; Arnold Rampersad, "Hughes, Langston," Oxford African American Studies Center, December 1, 2006, https://oxfordaasc.com/display/10.1093/acref/9780195301731.001 .0001/acref-9780195301731-e-46827; and Aimee Lee Cheek and William Cheek, "Langston, John Mercer," Oxford African American Studies Center, May 31, 2013, https://oxfordaasc.com/display/10 .1093/acref/9780195301731.001.0001/acref-9780195301731-e-34531.

Zora Neale Hurston (1891–1960), born in Notasulga, Alabama, and raised in Eatonville, Florida, where her father served as mayor of the all-Black incorporated town, used her expertise in Black folk culture and storytelling to become one of the most celebrated novelists, essayists, anthropologists, ethnographers, playwrights, and short story writers of the New Negro Renaissance. Throughout her literary career, Hurston became known as a master at incorporating African American folk culture and signifying as a means of wielding linguistic power in defiance of Jim Crow and patriarchal oppression. While a student at Barnard College, she met the groundbreaking anthropologist Franz Boas and later traveled to Florida, New Orleans, Jamaica, and Haiti to collect folklore and conduct field studies. Hurston's novel *Their Eyes Were Watching God* (1937) is widely regarded as a literary masterpiece. See Cherene Sherrard-Johnson, "Hurston, Zora Neale," Oxford African American Studies Center, September 30, 2012, https://oxfordaasc.com/display/10.1093 /acref/9780195301731.001.0001/acref-9780195301731-e-47901; and Nellie Y. McKay, "Hurston, Zora Neale," Oxford African American Studies Center, December 1, 2006, https://oxfordaasc.com /display/10.1093/acref/9780195301731.001.0001/acref-9780195301731-e-51024.

David Hamilton Jackson (1884–1946), born in St. Croix, Danish Virgin Islands, was known as the "Black Moses" of St. Croix for his work as an Afro-Caribbean labor leader, orator, and "crusading journalist" who fought for freedom of the press and rallied workers against the worst abuses of Danish colonial rule. Likely a classmate of Hubert Harrison's and certainly a lifelong friend, Jackson founded and edited the *Herald* (1915–25), as a voice of the working poor in St. Croix. The son of teachers, Jackson worked as an educator but was fired by Danish school teachers for criticizing the Catholic Church. After studying law at the University of Chicago, he returned to St. Croix to organize destitute farm laborers, who were earning twenty cents a day, for better wages and working conditions. He founded the St. Croix Labour Union in 1915, and the following year, when plantation owners refused their demands, organized the first general strike. He was also instrumental in establishing November 1 as a national labor holiday in the Virgin Islands. After the United States purchased the Danish West Indies in 1917, Jackson completed his law degree at Howard University and served as a politician and judge in Christiansted. See Jeffrey B. Perry, *Hubert Harrison: The Voice of Harlem Radicalism, 1883–1918* (New York: Columbia University Press,

2009), 44–46; "David Hamilton Jackson," National Park Service, n.d., www.nps.gov/articles/david
-hamilton-jackson.htm, accessed January 11, 2025; and Angelo Capriola, "Jackson Encountered
Goodwill, Challenges in Publishing First Privately-Owned Newspaper," *Virgin Islands Daily
News*, November 1, 2024, https://www.virginislandsdailynews.com/news/jackson-encountered
-goodwill-challenges-in-publishing-first-privately-owned-newspaper/article_ea563fba-979b-11ef
-9763-83065e0c984a.html.

Charles Spurgeon Johnson (1893–1956), born in Bristol, Virginia, as the eldest of six children,
was a sociologist, educator, and college president. When he volunteered with the Richmond Welfare Association as a college student, he witnessed human suffering that profoundly affected his
life. While delivering food to the needy, he observed a young Black woman moaning in labor on a
pile of rags. People repeatedly refused to help her and her child, either because she was Black or
because she had conceived out of wedlock, and "Johnson could not get the image of the young
woman out of his mind and could not 'cease pondering the anger of people at human catastrophe
while they calmly accept conditions that caused it.'" Under the pioneering sociologist Robert E.
Park, Johnson earned his PhD at the University of Chicago and shortly thereafter the National Urban
League hired him as the director of its Department of Research and Investigations and to edit
Opportunity magazine. After the Chicago race riot of 1919, he was commissioned to be the lead
author of the highly regarded *The Negro in Chicago: A Study of Race Relations and a Race Riot*
(1922). Unlike Park, Johnson argued that assimilation was the key goal for "ethnic minorities
within the race-relations cycle" and that governmental could help Black Americans achieve equality. He argued that productive racial tensions could, in fact, hasten positive social change if education encouraged whites to disavow white supremacy and prepared African Americans to assimilate completely into American society. As Yolette Trigg notes, "The solution to the Negro
problem was simple for him: nothing short of integration." In 1928 Johnson moved to Nashville,
Tennessee, to chair the Department of Sociology at Fisk University, and in 1947, he became the
first Black president of Fisk. See Marybeth Gasman, "Johnson, Charles Spurgeon," Oxford African
American Studies Center, May 31, 2013, https://oxfordaasc.com/display/10.1093/acref/9780195301731
.001.0001/acref-9780195301731-e-41890; and Yollette Trigg, "Johnson, Charles S.," Oxford African American Studies Center, December 1, 2009, https://oxfordaasc.com/display/10.1093/acref
/9780195301731.001.0001/acref-9780195301731-e-45760.

Clister Lamar Johnson (1910–60), born in Yazoo City, Mississippi, served as the Supreme Lecturer in the Afro-American Sons and Daughters, a Black fraternal organization in the Mississippi
Delta. Founded by Thomas Jefferson Huddleston Sr., the organization saw its primary mission as
building the first Black-owned and operated hospital in Mississippi. See "About Afro-American
Courier (Yazoo City, Miss.) 1926–19??," Library of Congress, n.d., https://www.loc.gov/item
/sn88067171/, accessed March 13, 2024. "Clister Lamar Johnson," US World War II Draft Cards,
Young Men 1940–1947, National Archives, St. Louis, Missouri, *Draft Cards for Mississippi Records
of the Selective Service System*; "Northeast Mississippi Afro Festival," *Afro-American Courier*
(Yazoo City, MS), September 1, 1937.

Fenton Johnson (1888–1958), born in Chicago, Illinois, was an African American dramatist,
poet, editor, and civil rights reformer whose work anticipated the artistic innovations of the Harlem
Renaissance. Having studied at the Columbia University School of Journalism, Northwestern University, and the University of Chicago, he became known for poetry that included African American dialect, what he referred to as the "language of the plantation and levee." In 1906–7 Johnson
taught in the South, returning to Chicago shortly thereafter to write plays and poetry. Between

1912 and 1917, the *Crisis* published three of Johnson's short stories. In 1920, after two short-lived magazine ventures, Johnson began the Reconciliation Movement, through which promotional materials and social settlement work would bring about interracial common purpose. See Bernard W. Bell, "Johnson, Fenton," *Oxford African American Studies Center*, December 1, 2006, https://oxfordaasc.com/display/10.1093/acref/9780195301731.001.0001/acref-9780195301731-e-41892.

John Rosamond Johnson (1873–1954), born in Jacksonville, Florida, was a successful composer, performer, and singer trained at the New England Conservatory. With his brother James Weldon Johnson, who wrote the lyrics, he composed the music for "Lift Every Voice and Sing" (1900), which the National Association for the Advancement of Colored People would herald as the official Negro national anthem in 1917. See Carolyn Wedin, "Johnson, J. Rosamond," *Oxford African American Studies Center*, December 1, 2009, https://oxfordaasc.com/display/10.1093/acref/9780195301731.001.0001/acref-9780195301731-e-45762.

Robert Thomas Kerlin (1866–1950), born in Harris County, Missouri, was a minister, professor, socialist, civil rights activist, and "reformer of the white race." From 1910 to 1921 he served as professor and chair of the English Department at the Virginia Military Institute, from which he was fired after publicly protesting the death sentences of ninety-two Black men in the aftermath of the Elaine Massacre. As Henry Louis Gates Jr. notes, "Although a white man, Kerlin was an ardent and passionate advocate of civil rights. He earned his PhD from Yale in 1906 . . . and published a brilliant anthology of African American poetry, with really wonderfully smart commentary, two years later, *Negro Poets and Their Poetry*. He had a habit of getting himself fired from more than one of the institutions of higher learning for his radical politics—fired, or forced to retire. He ended his career as a professor at Potomac State College of West Virginia University, in Keyser, West Virginia (the location of the county hospital where I was born, though we lived in Piedmont, five miles away). . . . 'Radical Hill' was the nickname that the locals gave to the neighborhood where Kerlin lived." Email from Henry Louis Gates, Jr. to Martha H. Patterson, "Your Footnotes," September 6, 2024. See Fredrick Walker, "Robert T. Kerlin Resources," Virginia Military Institute Archives, n.d., https://web.archive.org/web/20230924014902/https://www.vmi.edu/archives/genealogy-biography-alumni/featured-historical-biographies/robert-t-kerlin-resources/, accessed January 26, 2025; and "Robert Thomas Kerlin" (obituary), *Journal of Negro History* 35, no. 2 (1950): 230–32.

Hodge Kirnon (1891–1962), born in St John's, Montserrat, was a porter, a journalist, and a lecturer on issues ranging from free thought to the history of slavery in the British West Indies. After he immigrated to the United States in 1908, Kirnon settled in Harlem, and he worked as an elevator operator for Alfred Stieglitz's 291 art gallery in Midtown Manhattan. A close friend of Hubert Harrison, Kirnon became involved in the Marcus Garvey movement in 1920 and began editing the *Promoter* the same year. In an essay for the journal, he argued that racialism and radicalism both emanated from the "dissatisfied and discontented peoples seeking some clear solution towards alleviating their present condition." In 1925 Kirnon published *Montserrat and the Montserratians*. See Hodge Kirnon, "Racialism and Radicalism," *Promoter* 3, no. 1 (1920): 4; "Hodge Kirnon Analyzes Results of Anti-Garvey Campaign," *American Series Sample Documents*, vol. 5, *September 1922–August 1924*, UCLA African Studies Center, n.d., https://www.nhlrc.ucla.edu/africa/mgpp/sample05, accessed January 26, 2025, n1; Tara Kohn, "Elevated: Along the Fringes of 291 Fifth Avenue," *Panorama: Journal of the Association of Historians of American Art* 4, no. 2 (2018), https://journalpanorama.org/article/elevated/#marker-5820-15; and Jeffrey B. Perry, *Hubert Harrison: The Voice of Harlem Radicalism, 1883–1918* (New York: Columbia University Press, 2009).

Alain Leroy Locke (1885–1954), born in Philadelphia, Pennsylvania, to parents he described as "fanatically middle-class," was a philosopher, literary critic, professor, art historian, and philosophical "midwife" of the Harlem Renaissance. Locke served as "a catalyst," in the words of Jeffery C. Stewart, for "a revolution in thinking called the New Negro." The first African American Rhodes Scholar, Locke earned a PhD in philosophy from Harvard University in 1918 and spent his professional career teaching philosophy at Howard University. In March 1925 he edited a special issue of the *Survey Graphic* on the New Negro, which he then turned into his groundbreaking collection of literature, essays, illustrations, spirituals, art, and bibliographies, *The New Negro: An Interpretation of Negro Life*. A "paean to a new Black masculinity," as Stewart notes, the *Survey Graphic*'s "Harlem: Mecca of the New Negro" issue and the stunning anthology that immediately followed reflected a "new psychology" of Black self-determination, "transnational mobility," youthful "spiritual nationalism," and, given Locke's homosexuality and the number of queer Black writers he included, a sexual (albeit covert, given the prevailing homophobia in the United States at that time), social, and racial fluidity all centered in Harlem. Locke defied the pervasive stereotypical racist imagery that characterized Blackness as ugly, debased, and threatening and instead, in the words of Stewart, "demanded the right of African Americans to beauty," an aesthetic ideal he cultivated as a pioneering Black art historian. Yet by the early 1930s—as the Depression compounded economic crises for African Americans already suffering systemic Jim Crow discrimination—direct-action protest and social realism, not Locke's vision of what David Levering Lewis famously characterized as "civil rights by copyright," seemed the best strategy to meet the desperation of the era. When the period demanded anger, Locke seemed a relic of a conciliatory past. He countered by emphasizing his work on behalf of adult education, embracing the folk poet Sterling A. Brown in Nancy Cunard's bold 1934 collection *Negro: An Anthology*, celebrating the work of the consummate Black social realist Richard Wright, and casting his New Negro anthology in a different light. Rather than a sentimental tribute to Black artistic genius, Locke's New Negro had built the foundation for 1930s radicalism. For Locke, who now positioned himself foremost as a literary critic, art needed to both reflect the highest artistic standards and voice Black social protest. Email from Henry Louis Gates, Jr. to Martha H. Patterson, "Author Bios," January 12, 2025. See "Locke, Alain," in *Encyclopedia of the Harlem Renaissance*, ed. Cary D. Wintz and Paul Finkhelm, vol. 2, *K–Y* (New York: Routledge, 2004), 737–43; Jeffrey C. Stewart, *The New Negro: The Life of Alain Locke* (New York: Oxford University Press, 2018), 13, 18, 436–52, 678, 684, 721, 750, 875; and David Levering Lewis, "Dr. Johnson's Friends: Civil Rights by Copyright during Harlem's Mid-Twenties," *Massachusetts Review* 20, no. 3 (1979): 501–19.

John E. MacBrady (b. John Emmett Pickering, 1864–1951) was a white, Canadian-born entrepreneur who headed the American Publishing House of Chicago (1894–1904). Some sources indicate his surname as McBrady. See "McBrady, John Emmett," in *The Book of Chicagoans: A Biographical Dictionary of Leading Living Men of the City of Chicago*, ed. Albert Nelson Marquis (Chicago: A. N. Marquis, 1911), 434; "McBrady, John E." (obituary), *Chicago Daily Tribune*, August 30, 1951; and "John E. McBrady," Sixteenth Census of the United States, 1940, NAID 139237090, Records of the Bureau of the Census, RG 29, National Archives, Washington, DC.

Claude McKay (b. Festus Claudius McKay, 1890–1948), perhaps more than any other figure in the Harlem Renaissance, captured the spirit of the militant New Negro forged in the fires of World War I and the brutal Red Summer of 1919. According to Winston James, McKay—born to a peasant farming family in Clarendon Parish, Jamaica—cannot be understood "without an appreciation of the articulation of race and color on the island that broke his heart and drew his wrath." After immigrating to the United States in 1912, McKay enrolled at Booker T. Washington's Tuskegee

Institute before transferring to Kansas State College, where he socialized with a "small group of white students with a socialist bent." During the Red Summer of 1919, when white mobs attacked Black people across the United States, McKay published what became the anthem of the militant New Negro movement: the sonnet "If We Must Die," which appeared in Max Eastman's radical *Liberator* and was reprinted in Black periodicals around the country, calling on Black men to fight back. When McKay left for Europe in the fall of 1919, he had joined the Industrial Workers of the World. In London he wrote for Sylvia Pankhurst's procommunist newspaper *Worker's Dreadnought*. When he returned to New York in 1921, McKay became coeditor of the *Liberator* and joined Cyrus Briggs's African Blood Brotherhood for African Liberation and Redemption, which eventually merged with the Workers Party of America (later the Communist Party USA). Just five years after the Russian Revolution of 1917, McKay went to Moscow, spending eight months in what he would call a "magic pilgrimage" to what would soon become the Soviet Union. For the next twelve years, the bisexual McKay lived, worked, and wrote in Europe and North Africa, becoming part of what Gary Edward Holcomb and William J. Maxwell call the "'Lyrical Left' era of hybrid erotic and political radicalisms." As a fiction writer, McKay would become best known for the humanity of his Black folk characters, whose transatlantic migrations reflected the political, religious, and linguistic richness of the Black diaspora. See Winston James, *Claude McKay: The Making of a Black Bolshevik* (New York: Columbia University Press, 2022), 67, 207, 232, 248–49, 347; Gary Edward Holcomb and William J. Maxwell, "Introduction," in *Romance in Marseille*, by Claude McKay (New York: Penguin, 2020), xxviii; James Smethurst, "McKay, Claude," Oxford African American Studies Center, December 1, 2006, https://oxfordaasc.com/display/10.1093/acref/9780195301731 .001.0001/acref-9780195301731-e-42392; and Freda Scott Giles, "McKay, Claude," Oxford African American Studies Center, May 31, 2013, https://oxfordaasc.com/display/10.1093/acref/9780195301731 .001.0001/acref-9780195301731-e-34580.

Oscar Micheaux (1884–1951), born in Metropolis, Illinois, to formerly enslaved parents, was the first major African American professional filmmaker. He began his career working as a Pullman porter, saving his money to purchase land on the Rosebud Sioux Indian Reservation in South Dakota. While homesteading, he published articles in the Chicago *Defender* urging Black Americans to go west. When he suffered a series of land foreclosures, he began a life as a novelist, selling his books door-to-door, before forming the Western Book Supply Company, through which he published two additional semiautobiographical novels, *The Forged Note: A Romance of the Darker Races* (1915) and *The Homesteader* (1917). When the Lincoln Motion Picture Company offered to produce a film version of *The Homesteader* but refused to let Micheaux direct, he formed the Micheaux Book and Film Company and launched his filmmaking career. See Lisa E. Rivo, "Micheaux, Oscar," Oxford African American Studies Center, May 31, 2013, https://oxfordaasc.com/display/10 .1093/acref/9780195301731.001.0001/acref-9780195301731-e-34587.

Kelly Miller (1863–1939), born in Winnsboro, South Carolina, to an enslaved mother and free Black father who served in the Confederate States Army, was an educational leader, college administrator, and influential writer. After graduating from Howard University he became the first African American student to enroll at Johns Hopkins University, where he studied mathematics, physics, and astronomy. In 1890 Miller began his teaching career at Howard University, introduced sociology to the course offerings, and led the new Sociology Department from 1915 to 1925, having also served as dean of the College of Arts and Sciences from 1907 to 1919. A prolific writer, by 1915 Miller became one of the most influential Black intellectuals of his age and an enthusiastic promoter of higher education opportunities for African Americans. Seeking a midway position between the ideals of Booker T. Washington and W. E. B. Du Bois, Miller emphasized the Washington model of thrift, "racial solidarity," and self-reliance, as well as the right to protest racial injustice. After white mobs went on a rampage attacking Black people in the infamous 1917 East St. Louis massacre, Miller wrote *The Disgrace of Democracy: An Open Letter to President Woodrow Wilson*. Selling more than 250,000 copies, the pamphlet was banned on US army bases. After World War I, his views became increasingly conservative; he maintained that Black mass migration to northern cities would be destructive to the social, moral, and cultural fabric of Black communities. See Michael R. Winston, "Miller, Kelly," Oxford African American Studies Center, May 31, 2013, https://oxfordaasc .com/display/10.1093/acref/9780195301731.001.0001/acref-9780195301731-e-34589; and Sylvie Coulibaly, "Miller, Kelly," Oxford African American Studies Center, December 1, 2009, https:// oxfordaasc.com/display/10.1093/acref/9780195301731.001.0001/acref-9780195301731-e-45905.

John Mitchell Jr. (1863–1929), who was born to a coachman and seamstress who worked on the Richmond, Virginia, estate of the wealthy white secessionist James Lyons, worshipped at First African Baptist Church, attended the Navy Hill School (the only public school in Richmond to employ Black teachers), and graduated with honors from the Freedmen's Bureau–founded Richmond Normal and High School in 1881. A staunch Republican, Mitchell was bestowed the nickname the "Fighting Editor" for his work editing the weekly Black newspaper the *Richmond Planet* (1883–1938) from 1884 until his death in 1929. Mitchell served as president of the Colored Press Association from 1890 to 1894 and as a member of the Richmond City Council from the predominantly African American Jackson Ward from 1888 and 1896. As Ann Field Alexander notes, "At a time when few black southerners held elective office, he lobbied for his constituents and persuaded the city to construct new black schools and an armory for the black militia." Even when Jim Crow disenfranchisement prevented him from holding political office, Mitchell helped make the Jackson Ward the "center of black capitalism" in the early 1900s by establishing Richmond's Mechanics' Savings Bank in 1902. In 1904 he organized a boycott of Richmond's segregated streetcars, and in 1921 he campaigned to become the governor of Virginia on what whites called a "'lily-black' ticket." See Willard B. Gatewood, "Mitchell, John, Jr.," Oxford African American Studies Center, May 31, 2013, https://oxfordaasc.com/display/10.1093/acref/9780195301731.001.0001/acref-9780195301731-e -35111; and Ann Field Alexander, *Race Man: The Rise and Fall of the "Fighting Editor," John Mitchell, Jr.* (Charlottesville: University of Virginia Press, 2002), ix–x, 1–14.

Winfield Henry Mixon (1863?–1924), born near Selma, Alabama, was a prominent church leader, editor, and writer. Mixon studied at Selma University and earned a DD from Wilberforce University in Ohio. He led a number of African Methodist Episcopal churches and helped to found others, and in 1902 published *A History of the African Methodist Episcopal Church in Alabama*. Sources disagree as to the year of his birth; it may have been as early as 1859. See "Rev. Winfield Henry Mixon, D.D.," *Christian Recorder*, March 29, 1900; "Many Sided Life of Presiding Elder Mixon," *Afro-American*, November 16, 1912; and "Rev. W. H. Mixon, Leading Churchman, Dead," *Buffalo American*, November 27, 1924.

William H. A. Moore (1857–1942), born in New York City, was a prominent Chicago poet, politician, and prolific journalist. After graduating from the City College of New York and studying English at Columbia University, Moore worked as a journalist for the *Chicago Daily News* and the Associated Negro Press and became one of the first Black journalists to write for a white daily, the *Chicago Record-Herald*. A friend of Paul Lawrence Dunbar and the most celebrated Black vaudevillian of his day, Bert Williams, Moore became a leading member of Chicago's literary elite and published *Dusk Songs*, which was excerpted in James Weldon Johnson's *The Book of American Negro Poetry* (1922). Often called "Judge Moore," he also served as Cook County's deputy recorder of deeds and as an assistant secretary to President James A. Garfield. See "Death Takes Judge Moore; Rites Monday," *Chicago Defender*, May 30, 1942; and "Pioneer Dies," *Chicago Defender*, June 6, 1942.

Josiah Morse (b. Joseph Moses, 1879–1946), born in Richmond, Virginia, became the first Jewish professor at the University of South Carolina (USC) when he began teaching philosophy there in 1911; he later taught psychology. Morse offered classes on the "Southern Negro," lectured on the subject at the Young Men's Christian Association, and organized interracial events at USC. He was a charter member of the University Commission on the Southern Race Question and a member of the Commission on Interracial Cooperation. Opposed to the National Association for the Advancement of Colored People, Morse favored a more gradualist approach to improving race relations. See Amy Scully, "Josiah Morse, the First Jewish Professor at the University of South Carolina: The Role of Mixed Bias in the American University System" (master's thesis, University of South Carolina, 2011).

Jeanne "Jane" Nardal (190?–1993), born in Martinique, was, along with her sister Paulette, one of the leading figures in the Négritude movement. When in 1923 Nardal moved to Paris to study classical literature and French at the Sorbonne, becoming the first Martinican woman to do so, she found in the city the networks that enabled her to immerse herself in the era's Pan-African literary and political movements. On January 17, 1929, while back in Martinique, Nardal hosted a conference, "Le chant nègre aux États-Unis" (Black song in the United States), that featured African American spirituals and blues music. By the early 1930s she and her sister Paulette had created a salon just south of Paris in Clamart-sur-Seine, bringing together writers from the Caribbean, France, the United States, and West Africa—including Aimé Césaire, Claude McKay, Alain Locke, René Maran, and Léopold S. Senghor—with the goal of creating a Pan-African consciousness for Black liberation and cultural expression. Building on the success of their salon, the sisters launched, with author René Maran and Haitian intellectual Leo Sajous, the bilingual English-French literary magazine, *La Revue du monde noir* (The Review of the Black World). As Valerie Orlando notes, "Nardal believed that it was in the New Negro Movement that Francophone authors and intellectuals would find the race-consciousness discourse they were seeking to build their own anticolonial treatises." See Valeria Orlando, "Nardal, Jane," Oxford African American Studies Center, September 30, 2012, https://oxfordaasc.com/display/10.1093/acref/9780195301731.001.0001/acref-9780195301731-e-49572; and Emily Musil Church, "In Search of Seven Sisters: A Biography of the Nardal Sisters of Martinique," *Callaloo* 36, no. 2 (2013): 375–90.

Richard Bruce Nugent (1906–87), born in Washington, DC, to a father who worked as a Pullman porter and an elevator operator and a mother who hailed from the city's Black elite, was the most openly gay writer and artist of the Harlem Renaissance. After the death of his father, when Richard was thirteen, his mother moved the family to New York City, where Richard secured a job as a gofer and art apprentice at the catalog house of Stone, Van Dresser and Company and enrolled in courses at the New York School of Industrial Arts and at the Traphagen School of Fashion. Nugent quickly became a part of the Greenwich Village bohemian scene; his mother disapproved and sent him back to Washington, DC, where he began attending Georgia Douglass Johnson's weekly literary salons and met Alain Locke. Moving back to New York in 1925 and moving in with Wallace Thurman, Nugent quickly became known for his conspicuous gay style, witty repartee, homoerotic art deco drawings, and queer modernist fiction. In a 1927 letter to Langston Hughes, Carl Van Vechten described going to an *Opportunity* dinner where, upon leaving, William Pickens, the field secretary for the National Association for the Advancement of Colored People, "caught my arm to ask me who the 'young man in evening clothes' was. It was Bruce Nugent, of course, with his usual open chest and uncovered ankles. I suppose soon he will be going without trousers." Nugent is best known for the work he published in the periodicals *Opportunity* and *Fire!!* and in Alain Locke's famous anthology *The New Negro*. See Thomas H. Wirth, "Nugent, Richard Bruce," Oxford African American Studies Center, December 1, 2006, https://oxfordaasc.com/display/10.1093/acref/9780195301731.001.0001/acref-9780195301731-e-16880; Thomas H. Wirth, "Introduction" in Bruce Nugent, *Gay Rebel of the Harlem Renaissance: Selections from the Work of Richard Bruce Nugent*, edited by Thomas H. Wirth (Durham, NC: Duke University Press, 2002), 61; and Carl Van Vechten to Langston Hughes, May 11, 1927, in Langston Hughes and Carl Van Vechten, *Remember Me to Harlem: The Letters of Langston Hughes and Carl Van Vechten, 1925–1964*, edited by Emily Bernard (New York: Alfred A. Knopf, 2001), 52.

William Golden Nunn Sr. (1900–1969), born in Pittsburgh, Pennsylvania, was a Black American newspaper legend. From 1919 to 1963 he worked at the *Pittsburgh Courier*, first as a sports journalist, then as a managing editor, and finally as an executive editor, proving himself integral to the success of the *Courier*'s civil rights campaigns and overall circulation growth. As the newspaper noted in his obituary, Nunn "was a black man who was proud to be black and who wanted all black men to be proud, long before it became popular to shout it." President of Pittsburgh's Loendi Club, one of the oldest Black literary and social clubs in the nation, Nunn was also a leader in Republican politics, as well as African American sports: he was the first African American student to play football at Westinghouse High School in Pittsburgh, and served as secretary for the Negro National Baseball League; in 1933 he and fellow *Pittsburgh Courier* sportswriter Ira F. Lewis led the fight to integrate baseball. See "William G. Nunn, Sr., Ex-Courier Editor, Buried in Pittsburgh," *Pittsburgh Courier*, November 22, 1969; "GOP Chooses Ex-Courier Editor Nunn," *Pittsburgh Courier*, April 18, 1964; and Armistead Scott Pride and Clint C. Wilson, *A History of the Black Press* (Washington, DC: Howard University Press, 1997), 139.

Thomas Nelson Page (1853–1922) born in Oakland, Virginia, and proudly descended from Virginia's wealthy planter class, was a lawyer, diplomat, and bestselling author. His father, who enslaved approximately sixty people, served as a Confederate States Army major in the Civil War but later lost much of his wealth. The younger Page was best known for glorifying the antebellum South and the system of slavery on which it depended. Publishing stories told in dialect by a nostalgic Black narrator reminiscing about his Southern antebellum plantation life, where Negroes were cowardly, the "marse" (master) fought valiantly, and the Southern white lady was virginal and virtuous, Page gained popular success in the 1880s. In addition to producing a steady stream of romance novels in the early 1900s—including a "corrective" to Harriet Beecher Stowe's *Uncle Tom's Cabin*—Page sought, in the most respected white-owned magazines of the day, to justify systemic Jim Crow discrimination and the lynching of Black men. In 1913 President Woodrow Wilson rewarded Page with an ambassadorship to Italy for his help in Wilson's election to the presidency. See Anne E. Rowe, "Page, Thomas Nelson," in *The New Encyclopedia of Southern Culture*, vol. 9, *Literature*, ed. M. Thomas Inge (Chapel Hill: University of North Carolina Press, 2008), 382–83; and Taylor S. Hagood, "Thomas Nelson Page (1853–1922)," *Encyclopedia Virginia*, December 22, 2021, encyclopediavirginia.org/entries/page-thomas-nelson-1853-1922/.

Saydee (also Sadie, Satie) E. Parham (1891–1967), born in Jersey City, New Jersey, graduated from Jersey City High School in 1911 and shortly thereafter became a stenographer, joining the Colored Stenographers' Association. In 1915 she married Black attorney Louis A. Leavelle; she divorced him in 1920 and enrolled at Brooklyn Law School in 1922. Parham served as a secretary to Marcus Garvey until 1926, the year she married John H. James. She registered as a Democrat in

1925. See "Jersey City High School's Commencement," *Hudson Observer* (NJ), June 28, 1911; "Satie Parham: Vital, New Jersey Births and Christenings, 1660–1931," FamilySearch, n.d., https://www .familysearch.org/ark:/61903/1:1:FZC4-6DC, accessed January 27, 2025; "Sadie E Parham," Index to New York City Marriages, 1866–1937, Ancestry.com; "Sadie E. Leavelle," Bronx County, New York, U.S., Divorce and Civil Case Records, 1914–1995, Ancestry.com; "Sadie E. Leavelle," New York, New York, U.S., Extracted Marriage Index, 1866–1937, Ancestry.com; "New York City Briefs," *Chicago Defender*, October 14, 1922; and Marcus Garvey to Norton G. Thomas, March 26, 1926, in *The Marcus Garvey and Universal Negro Improvement Association Papers*, ed. Robert A. Hill, vol. 6, *September 1924–December 1927* (Berkeley: University of California Press, 1983), 406; "Sadie E. Parham," New York Municipal Archives, Manhattan Voter Registers, Year 1925, Assembly District AD 21, Electoral District ED 032.

William Pickens (1881–1954), born in Anderson County, South Carolina to formerly enslaved, itinerant sharecroppers who finally settled in Arkansas in 1887, was an indefatigable educator, educational administrator, writer, and civil rights activist. After graduating first in his class from Union High School in Little Rock, Arkansas, he earned bachelor's degrees from both Talladega College and Yale University (where he was a member of Phi Beta Kappa), a master's degree from Fisk University, and a PhD from Selma University. In 1904 Talladega College hired Pickens to teach foreign languages; he stayed there until 1914, when Wiley University recruited him to head its Greek and Sociology Departments; two years later, he accepted a position as dean at Morgan College in Baltimore. While initially a supporter of Booker T. Washington, Pickens chafed at Washington's accommodationism and preferred the uncompromising civil rights positions of W. E. B. Du Bois's Niagara Movement. In 1909 Pickens helped to launch the National Association for the Advancement of Colored People (NAACP), becoming the field secretary of the organization in 1920 under executive secretary James Weldon Johnson. A prolific author committed to integration and full Black citizenship rights, Pickens published two autobiographies, *Heir of Slaves* (1911) and *Bursting Bonds* (1923); a short story reader, *Vengeance of the Gods* (1922); an essay anthology, *The New Negro* (1916); and syndicated columns for the Associated Negro Press. In his autobiography he defined himself as a New Negro—one who, at great personal risk, stood up for his rights. Even when an Arkansas train conductor "showed his real fangs," threatening him with lynching for refusing to leave the whites-only Pullman car, Pickens—having lawfully purchased a ticket and feeling at once "desperation *and* determination"—politely but firmly refused to leave. According to William J. Cobb, Pickens was such a compelling orator, that during his twenty-year tenure at the NAACP, he "recruited more members and organized more branches than any other officer in the association". When Walter White pushed Pickens out of the organization in 1941 for his communist sympathies, Pickens took a job with the US government. See William J. Cobb, "Pickens, William," Oxford African American Studies Center, May 31, 2013, https://oxfordaasc.com/display/10.1093/acref/9780195301731.001.0001 /acref-9780195301731-e-34642; "Pickens, William, 1881–1954," ProQuest Biographies, Literature Online, Ann Arbor, MI, 2018; and William Pickens, *Bursting Bonds: The Autobiography of a "New Negro,"* ed. William L. Andrews (Notre Dame, IN: University of Notre Dame Press. 2005), 68.

Pippa, the pen name of Bella Cohen Spewack (1899–1990), was a white journalist and playwright. Born in Transylvania and raised in poverty in New York's Lower East Side, Spewack graduated from Washington Irving High School and began writing for the socialist newspaper, the *New York Call*. Bella Cohen married *New York World* correspondent Sam Spewack in 1922, and the two later became famous for writing extraordinarily popular musicals, including *Leave It to Me* (1938) and *Kiss Me Kate* (1948). See Charles Recht, "An American in Moscow on November 7," *Soviet Russia Pictorial*, March 1923, 49; and Michael Taub, "Bella Spewack," in *The Shalvi/Hyman Encyclopedia* *of Jewish Women*, ed. Jennifer Sartori, online, n.d., https://jwa.org/encyclopedia/article/spewack -bella, accessed August 8, 2023; Andrea Most, "Spewack, Bella," in *Encyclopedia Judaica*, 2nd ed., by Michael Berenbaum and Fred Skolnik, vol. 19, 99–100. Detroit, MI: Macmillan Reference USA, 2007, Gale eBooks, accessed March 10, 2025.

Asa Philip Randolph (1889–1979) was a Black socialist, editor, and labor organizer hailed by Martin Luther King Jr. as "truly the Dean of Negro Leaders." Born in Crescent City, Florida, Randolph was educated at the Cookman Institute in Jacksonville, and was profoundly influenced by the militancy of his father, who served as a minister in the African Methodist Episcopal Church and was a follower of the Black nationalist Bishop Henry McNeal Turner. Randolph took a steamboat to Harlem in 1911, where he would spend the rest of his professional career, proving himself to be one of the most important organizers in the long civil rights movement. Immediately attracted to socialism as the best means of addressing the systemic exploitation of Black workers, he joined the Socialist Party with Columbia University student Chandler Owen. Like their friend Hubert Harrison, the two started giving soapbox speeches, and founded the socialist *Messenger* magazine in 1917. In 1925, despite the formidable opposition of the Pullman Company, Randolph organized the first Black union to be officially affiliated with the American Federation of Labor, the Brotherhood of Sleeping Car Porters and Maids. In 1941 he organized what would have been the first African American march on Washington, DC, but he called it off when President Franklin Delano Roosevelt issued Executive Order 8802, which prohibited discrimination in defense industries, and created the Fair Employment Practices Commission. In 1963 Randolph realized his vision of a dramatic display of the modern civil rights movement's power when he and Bayard Rustin organized the acclaimed March on Washington. See "To A. Philip Randolph," in Martin Luther King Jr., *The Papers of Martin Luther King, Jr.*, vol. 4, *January 1957–December 1958*, ed. Susan Carson, Adrienne Clay, Virginia Shadron, and Kieran Taylor (Berkeley: University of California Press, 2000), 527; Ernest Obadele-Starks, "Randolph, A. Philip," Oxford African American Studies Center, December 1, 2009, https:// oxfordaasc.com/display/10.1093/acref/9780195301731.001.0001/acref-9780195301731-e-46126; Jervis Anderson, *A. Philip Randolph: A Biographical Portrait* (New York: Harcourt Brace Jovanovich, 1973), 30–31, 41–44, 80–81; and William J. Cobb, "Randolph, A. Philip," Oxford African American Studies Center, May 31, 2013, https://oxfordaasc.com/display/10.1093/acref/9780195301731.001 .0001/acref-9780195301731-e-34663.

James Wilson Rawlins (1862–1937), born in Mt. Sterling, Kentucky, at one time owned three women's and children's clothing shops (Rawlins' Bargain Stores) in Detroit, Michigan, but, facing stiff competition from white-owned businesses in the midst of the Great Depression, was forced to close two of them. A proud member of Detroit's Second Baptist Church, the oldest Black-owned church in Michigan, Rawlins wrote frequent letters to the editors of northern African-American newspapers in Detroit and elsewhere deploring segregation, white mob violence, attempts to repeal the Eighteenth Amendment, the Black shift to the Democratic Party, what he saw as "half-baked, half-educated and selfish" Black intellectual leaders and "dance crazy" Black youth who "make their money from colored, spend it with the whites." See "James Wilson Rawlins," Michigan, U.S., Death Records, 1867–1952 Michigan Department of Community Health, Division for Vital Records and Health Statistics, Lansing, Michigan Ancestry.com; "Second Baptist Church of Detroit (U.S. National Park Service)," National Parks Service, U.S. Department of the Interior, www.nps.gov /places/second-baptist-church-of-detroit.htm, accessed February 6, 2025; "Commends Editorial," *Pittsburgh Courier*, January 20, 1931; "On Kelly Miller," *Pittsburgh Courier*, August 13, 1932; "What We Want," *Pittsburgh Courier*, August 20, 1932; "Flays Democrats," *Pittsburgh Courier*, September 10, 1932; "Sins of Our Fathers," *Pittsburgh Courier*, November 17, 1934; "On Mitchell," *Pittsburgh*

Courier, June 1, 1935; and "J. W. Rawlins Protest[s] Discrimination," *Tribune Independent* (Detroit), August 24, 1935.

Geroid Tanquary Robinson (1892–1971), born in Chase City, Virginia, was a white editor, journalist, and administrator. When his military service in World War I interrupted his studies at Stanford University, where he had earned a reputation as a liberal writer, Robinson completed his bachelor's degree from Columbia University. In the summer of 1919, he joined the staff of the prestigious political and literary review, the *Dial*, writing primarily about labor issues and urging unions to exert more control over the production process. In the spring of 1920, he began writing for the libertarian magazine the *Freeman*, where he decried violence against African Americans. While studying Russian, Robinson graduated with a master's degree from Columbia and began teaching there shortly thereafter. He earned a PhD from Columbia in 1930. In 1946 Robinson founded the Russian Institute of Columbia University, becoming its director. See Nathaniel Knight. "Geroid Tanquary Robinson: An Architect of American Area Studies" *Slavic and East European Information Resources* 23, nos. 1–2 (2022): 73–89.

Helen (Abbott) Sayre (1872–1951), born into one of the "pioneer" Black families in Toronto, Canada, directed a kindergarten in St. Louis, Missouri, before becoming "one of the foremost social workers in Chicago." A prominent clubwoman, educator, suffragist, Republican organizer, and welfare worker, Sayre held key roles in numerous Chicago service clubs and served as secretary to the Women's Cook County Permanent Republican Club and director of employment for women at the Chicago Urban League. Sayre was employed as the personnel director for women at the Montgomery Ward mail-order house and for the Nachmann Spring-Filled Mattress Company. See "Miss Abbott's Surprise," *St. Louis Globe Democrat*, April 8, 1902; "Know Something about Club Life," *Chicago Defender*, May 4, 1929; "Mrs. Helen Sayre Gets Responsible Position," *Chicago Defender*, February 28, 1920; "Social Workers End Eight-Day Meet in Canada," *Chicago Defender*, July 12, 1924; and "Mrs. Helen Abbott Sayre" (obituary), *Chicago Daily Tribune*, March 4, 1951.

John Milton Scanland (1843–1935), born in Mississippi, was a Confederate States Army veteran and "pioneer California journalist." Scanland wrote articles throughout the South and Southwest for the majority of his life and was a long-standing contributor to the *Los Angeles Times*. See "Obituary—John Milton Scanland," *Los Angeles Times*, January 4, 1935; and Michael Taylor, "New Light on an Old Louisiana Newspaperman," Louisiana State University Libraries, April 23, 2010, https://www.lib.lsu.edu/node/22567.

George Samuel Schuyler (1895–1977), born in Syracuse, New York, and largely self-educated, became one of the most successful Black columnists of his era. Known as the "Black Mencken" for his brilliantly satiric columns in the *Messenger* and the *Pittsburgh Courier*, Schuyler, who spared virtually no one in his writing—especially not Marcus Garvey—could be counted on to spur sales. Always iconoclastic, Schuyler insisted in his most famous essay, "The Negro-Art Hokum" (1926), that African Americans had not developed a distinct artistic voice separate from American art more broadly. Langston Hughes then published his celebrated rebuttal, "The Negro Artist and the Racial Mountain." In 1928 Schuyler flouted the color line by marrying the white Texas heiress Josephine Cogdell, and in 1931 he published what is likely the first Black science fiction novel, *Black No More*. Although he joined the Socialist Party in 1921, by the 1950s he had become an archconservative sharply critical of civil rights movement leaders and going so far as to join the conspiratorial-minded, far-right John Birch Society. See Steven J. Niven, "Schuyler, George Samuel," Oxford African

American Studies Center, May 31, 2013, https://oxfordaasc.com/display/10.1093/acref/9780
195301731.001.0001/acref-9780195301731-e-34698.

Herbert Jacob Seligmann (1891–1984), born in New York City and a graduate of Harvard University, was a Jewish journalist and civil rights activist who worked on behalf of African American and Jewish causes. He served as the publicity director for the National Association for the Advancement of Colored People from 1919 to 1932. See "Herbert J. Seligmann" (obituary), *New York Times*, March 7, 1984; and Valerie Wingfield, "Biographical Note," in *Herbert J. Seligmann Papers* (New York: New York Public Library, Manuscripts and Archives Division, Humanities and Social Sciences Library, 2006), 4.

Albreta Moore Smith (1875–1957), born in Chicago, Illinois and an 1894 graduate of Chicago's Armour Institute, worked as a stenographer for the Afro-American National Republican Bureau before becoming a juvenile court probation officer. Some sources indicate her first name as Alberta. In 1900 she founded the Colored Women's Business Club in Chicago, which focused its efforts on assisting domestic workers. The same year, Booker T. Washington invited Smith to attend the first meeting of the National Negro Business League, where she was elected to serve as one its vice presidents. In 1925, she was a member of the National Association of Probation Officers, the chair of the executive board of the Associated Big Sisters, and a member of the Social Services Round Table. See Booker T. Washington, "An Article in *Gunton's Magazine*," in *The Booker T. Washington Papers*, vol. 6, *1901–1902*, ed. Louis R. Harlan and Raymond W. Smock (Urbana: University of Illinois Press, 1977), 83n2; Albreta Moore Smith, "Chicago Notes," *Colored American Magazine*, April 1901, 465–69; and Nettie George Speedy, "My Scrapbook of Doers," *Chicago Defender*, May 9, 1925, "Alberta Covington," U.S., Find a Grave Index, Ancestry.com. 1600s to Present.

Madeleine R. Smith (1901–1993), born in Southampton, New York, was a student at the Hampton Normal and Agricultural Institute, Class of 1923. She delivered the address we include in this volume at the fifty-fifth anniversary celebration of Hampton. In 1924 she began teaching at the Shinnecock Reservation in Southampton, Long Island, and in 1926, she married Ralph Graham. She is buried in the Shinnecock Indian Cemetery. "Madeleine R. Smith," Fourteenth Census of the United States, 1920, Chesapeake, Elizabeth City, Virginia, Roll T625_1887, p. 5B, Enumeration District 31, Ancestry. com; "Hampton Students Show Relation of Education to Life," *Broad Ax*, April 28, 1923; "Scans of the Book Pages—Smith Scans," email to Martha H. Patterson from Vanessa D. Thaxton-Ward, PhD Director, Hampton University Museum; "Madeleine Graham," *Find a Grave Index, 1600s–Current* [online database], 2012.

Rev. Samuel Augustus Steel (1849–1934) was a white author, orator, and prominent pastor in the Methodist Episcopal Church, South. Born on a farm near Grenada, Mississippi, he smuggled goods to the Confederate States Army as a teenager. Educated at Emory and Henry College in Virginia, he was elected to serve as the chaplain at the University of Virginia. In 1894, while a minister of West End Church in Nashville, Tennessee, he was appointed the first general secretary of the Epworth League and editor of the *Epworth Era*, a church-sponsored publication for youth. Steel delivered his speech "Home Life in Dixie during the War," devoted to the "turbulent scenes" of the Civil War and the "chaotic reconstruction period," over one thousand times across the United States. The "vivacity, spirit and aggressiveness" of his editorials apparently "put so much fire and ginger" in the paper that the church "tried him" and removed him from his position. See Will T. Hale and Dixon L. Merritt, "Rev. Samuel A. Steel," in *A History of Tennessee and Tennesseans: The Leaders and Representative Men in Commerce, Industry, and Modern Activities* (Chicago: Lewis,

1913), 1376–79; "S.A. (Samuel Augustus) Steel Papers," "Biographical Note," Emory University, archives-libraries. emory.edu/repositories/7/resources/3531.

Charles Moorehead Stokes (1903–1996), who was born in Fredonia, Kansas, and graduated from the University of Kansas Law School, broke the color barrier throughout his law career. Beginning as an attorney in Leavenworth, Stokes was elected the first Black vice chairman of the National Republican Youth Federation in 1938. He served as an assistant attorney for the Kansas State Commission of Revenue and Taxation from 1939 to 1943 and as regional director of the Legal Aid Bureau of the National Bar Association in 1941. He moved to Seattle in 1943, becoming King County's first Black state legislator in 1950 and the first Black man appointed to Seattle's District Court in 1968. See "Young Republicans Elect Negro Vice Chairman: Charles M. Stokes of Leavenworth to National Office," *Kansas City Call*, June 17, 1938; "Stokes to National Bar Post: Named Director of Free Legal Aid Bureau," *Call* (Kansas City, MO), September 26, 1941; "Stokes Resigns from Kansas Tax Office," *Call* (Kansas City, MO), August 6, 1943; and "Judge Charles Stokes, 93, Dies," *Seattle Times*, November 28, 1996, https://archive.seattletimes.com/archive/19961128/2362108/judge-charles-stokes-93-dies.

Mary Eliza Church Terrell (1863–1954), born in Memphis, Tennessee, to Robert Reed Church (who although formerly enslaved became the first Black millionaire in the South) and Louisa Ayres, the owner of a hair salon—was a famous educator, civil rights activist, suffragist, Republican activist, and writer. A graduate of Oberlin College, Terrell taught at Wilberforce College in Ohio before moving to Washington, DC, where she accepted a position at the famous M Street Colored High School (later Dunbar High School). After the 1892 lynching of her friend Thomas Moss in Memphis, Tennessee, Terrell felt so distressed that when her third child died shortly after birth, she found consolation in knowing he would be spared the threat of such racist violence. As the founder and the first president (1896–1901) of the National Association of Colored Women, she mobilized women in the fight against Jim Crow chain gangs, segregation, and lynching and in the advancement of Black women's voting rights, education, and general well-being. To help improve education standards for students, she served on the Washington, DC, Board of Education (1895–1901, 1906–11). In 1904, as the only Black delegate to the International Council of Women in Berlin, Terrell delivered a speech in German, as well as in French. In 1909 she helped found the National Association for the Advancement of Colored People (NAACP). In 1920 she accepted a position with the Republican Party, organizing Black women on the East Coast; in 1922 she marched in Washington DC's Silent Parade to protest the long Red Summer; and near the end of her life she joined a sit-in to protest segregation in Washington, DC. See Cynthia Neverdon-Morton, "Terrell, Mary Eliza Church," Oxford African American Studies Center, May 31, 2013, https://oxfordaasc.com/display/10.1093/acref/9780195301731.001.0001/acref-9780195301731-e-34738; "Mrs. M. C. Terrell Honored," *Colored American Magazine*, August 20, 1904, 5; and Mary Eliza Church Terrell, *A Colored Woman in a White World* (Salem, NH: Ayer, 1940), 105, 108.

Wallace Thurman (1902–34), born in Salt Lake City, Utah, and raised by a single mother, was an African American journalist, editor, essayist, short story writer, novelist, literary critic, dramatist, and poet, writing for Black and white publications even as he increasingly represented the vanguard of Harlem Renaissance writers. After having studied in the University of Utah's premed program for two years, he moved to Southern California, where he secured employment as a postal clerk and took journalism classes at the University of Southern California. In 1923, Thurman began writing for the *Pacific Defender*, a Black newspaper, before launching the short-lived *Outlet*. As B. Christa Schwarz notes, Thurman pursued bisexual and interracial relationships, living a life in which "transgression became . . . [his] trademark—he refused to be limited in any sense and reveled in provocation, in his professional as well as in his private life." Moving to Harlem, he helped edit the *Messenger* in 1926; helped produce the radical anthology *Fire!!* (a salvo at the conservatism of Alain Locke's 1925 collection, *The New Negro*, 1926); cowrote (with white writer William Rapp) the play *Harlem* (1929), and published *The Blacker the Berry* (a scandalous novel about intraracial colorism, 1929) and *Infants of the Spring* (his satiric account of the Harlem Renaissance's failings, 1932). In 1932 he became the editor in chief of the white publishing company Macaulay, the only black employee to hold this role. The first Black American to write Hollywood screenplays, he signed with Foy Productions in 1934. See A. B. Christa Schwarz, "Thurman, Wallace," Oxford African American Studies Center, December 1, 2009, https://oxfordaasc.com/display/10.1093/acref/9780195301731.001.0001/acref-9780195301731-e-46274.

Jean Toomer (b. Nathan Pinchback Toomer, 1894–1967), born in Washington, DC, the son of Nathan Toomer, a North Carolina planter, and Nina Pinchback, daughter of Reconstruction-era senator P.B.S. Pinchback, was a leading modernist writer in the New Negro Renaissance. After graduating from the prestigious Dunbar High School in Washington, DC, and enrolling in but never graduating from a number of colleges on the East Coast and in the Midwest, Toomer secured a job briefly as principal at the historically Black Sparta Agricultural and Industrial Institute in central Georgia, which provided the inspiration for his seminal work of experimental fiction *Cane* (1923). Phenotypically able to pass for white, Toomer rejected racial designations and considered himself American; he refused to be called "Negro," and on official forms indicated that he was white. Barbara Foley argues that Toomer was most influenced in the *Cane* years by "American socialism, the New Negro Movement, and [Waldo Frank's progressive nationalist group] Young America." After becoming an acolyte in 1924 of the Greco-Armenian philosopher George Ivanovich Gurdjieff, Toomer developed a long fascination with mysticism. Furious at Alain Locke for including parts of *Cane* in his *New Negro* anthology without his permission, Toomer was nonetheless influenced by Locke's landmark work. His later novel manuscripts, which did not include Black protagonists—"The Gallowerps" (1927), "Transatlantic" (1929), and "Caromb" (1932)—were rejected by publishers. See Barbara Foley, *Jean Toomer: Race, Repression, and Revolution* (Urbana: University of Illinois Press, 2014), 84, 70–73; Sholomo B. Levy, "Toomer, Jean," Oxford African American Studies Center, May 31, 2013, https://oxfordaasc.com/display/10.1093/acref/9780195301731.001.0001/acref-9780195301731-e-34748; and Rudolph P. Byrd, "Toomer, Jean," Oxford African American Studies Center, December 1, 2006; https://oxfordaasc.com/display/10.1093/acref/9780195301731.001.0001/acref-9780195301731-e-47149.

Gustavo E. Urrutia (1881–1958), born in Havana, Cuba, was an architect, journalist, and politician, and one of Cuba's most important intellectuals during that nation's turbulent republican period (1902–59). After earning a business degree, Urrutia returned to school in 1913 to study architecture. Beginning in 1928, he wrote a regular column, "Ideales de una raza" (Ideals of a race) for *Diario de la marina*, Cuba's main daily newspaper. Urrutia's column emphasized Black respectability, accomplishments, and, increasingly, an Afro-Cuban consciousness and transnational race consciousness. In 1930 he introduced Langston Hughes to the Afro-Cuban journalist and poet Nicolás Guillén and corresponded regularly with Arthur Schomburg in New York. In 1936 he lost his election bid for the Congress of Cuba but was named Havana's director of culture. See Andrés Pletch, "Urrutia, Gustavo," Oxford African American Studies Center, May 31, 2017, https://oxfordaasc.com/display/10.1093/acref/9780195301731.001.0001/acref-9780195301731-e-75253.

Eric Derwent Walrond (1898–1966), born in British Guiana to Barbadian parents, was a journalist, editor, and fiction writer best known for his story collection *Tropic Death* (1926). Having learned reporting skills in Panama, which was under US occupation at the time, Walrond incorporated the confluence of Afro-Caribbean cultures into his later fiction. After emigrating to the United States in 1918, he enrolled at, but did not graduate from, both the City College of New York and Columbia University. He joined Marcus Garvey's Universal Negro Improvement Association and served as associate editor of the *Negro World* before becoming disillusioned and leaving the organization in 1925. Walrond served as business manager for Charles S. Johnson's *Opportunity* and was guest editor for a Caribbean-themed special issue of the magazine in 1926. His work appeared in *Opportunity*, the *Crisis*, the *Messenger, Vanity Fair*, the *Smart Set, Current History*, and the *New Republic*. In 1928 Walrond was awarded a Guggenheim Fellowship to conduct research in the Caribbean. By the 1930s he had made his home in England, joining other Afro-Caribbean expatriates—including C. L. R. James, Una Marson, Harold Moody, and George Padmore—as part of a thriving community of anticolonial intellectuals. Checking himself into Roundway Hospital for depression in 1952, Walrond published a literary magazine featuring the work of patients and staff, the *Roundway Review*, which included scores of his own short stories, his novella set in New York about a West Indian immigrant, and over a dozen chapters of his history of Panama. See Mary Anne Boelcskevy, "Walrond, Eric," Oxford African American Studies Center, May 31, 2013, https://oxfordaasc.com/display/10.1093/acref/9780195301731.001.0001/acref-9780195301731 -e-38115; and James Davis, "Walrond, Eric Derwent," Oxford African American Studies Center, May 31, 2017, https://oxfordaasc.com/display/10.1093/acref/9780195301731.001.0001/acref-97801953 01731-e-75328.

Booker Taliaferro Washington (1856?–1915), born enslaved in Franklin County, Virginia, was an educator, prolific writer, power broker, and race leader. In 1872 Washington enrolled at the Hampton Normal and Agricultural Institute in Hampton, Virginia, where he was mentored by US Army General Samuel Chapman Armstrong, who instilled in him the belief that practical, industrial education coupled with Christian values provided the best foundation for the newly freed. In 1881 Washington founded the Tuskegee Normal School for Colored Teachers (later Tuskegee Institute and now Tuskegee University), which was devoted to the same model of character building and practical education. With the financial assistance of wealthy white benefactors and the labor of his students, he built Tuskegee from the ground up and hired Black faculty and administrators. When on September 18, 1895, at the nadir of anti-Black racism in the United States, he delivered his celebrated accommodationist address at the Cotton States and International Exposition in Atlanta, Washington became the first nationally known "New Negro." The following year, in the *Plessy v. Ferguson* decision, the US Supreme Court gave the green light to state and local governments to impose racial segregation in public facilities. Despite his public acquiescence to segregation, Washington covertly funded civil rights initiatives, strove to influence white politicians, and underwrote numerous Black publications while spying on others he considered a threat to his power. Despite his conciliatory public positions, he faced tremendous prejudice. After President Theodore Roosevelt invited Washington to dinner at the White House, Southern white journalists expressed outrage at what they saw as a fundamental affront to white supremacy. When in 1911 a white man in New York City beat Washington mercilessly, the assailant, despite overwhelming evidence, was acquitted. See William F. Mugleston, "Washington, Booker T.," Oxford African American Studies Center, May 31, 2013, https://oxfordaasc.com/view/10.1093/acref/9780195301731.001.0001/acref -9780195301731-e-34768; and Rayford Whittingham Logan, *The Betrayal of the Negro, from Rutherford B. Hayes to Woodrow Wilson* (New York: Collier Books, 1965).

Margaret Murray Washington (1865–1925), born in Macon, Mississippi, to a washerwoman and an Irish immigrant, was a leading Black women's club movement leader, organizer, educator, and writer. She was raised as a Quaker, educated at Fisk University, and employed as a teacher at the Tuskegee Normal and Industrial Institute, gaining a national platform when she married Booker T. Washington in 1891. Her passions were education and the Black women's club movement, and she served important leadership roles in both. In 1895 she helped organize the Tuskegee Women's Club and the National Federation of Afro-American Women, which became the National Association of Colored Women (NACW) the following year. Washington served as the NACW's membership coordinator, local and state club organizer, and editor of its organ, the *National Association Notes*. As Washington got older, and after the death of her husband in 1915, she began more openly to express racial protest. After W. E. B. Du Bois organized his Pan-African Congresses in 1919 and 1921, Washington and other prominent Black women's activists, including Nannie Burroughs and Mary McLeod Bethune, formed the International Council of Women of the Darker Races in 1922 to combat poverty, racism, sexism, and colonial oppression. See Bernadette Pruitt, "Washington, Margaret Murray," Oxford African American Studies Center, May 31, 2013, https://oxfordaasc.com/display/10.1093/acref/9780195301731.001.0001/acref-9780195301731-e-34771.

Dorothy West (1907–98), born in Boston, Massachusetts, to a father who had formerly been enslaved and a mother who keenly nurtured her education, was a Harlem Renaissance writer and editor. After taking creative writing classes at Columbia University, West published stories in *Opportunity* and the *Messenger*. In 1932, along with twenty-two other African Americans, including Langston Hughes, she traveled to the Soviet Union to create a film entitled *Black and White*. When the project fell apart, West returned to New York, where in 1934 she founded the magazine *Challenge*, whose first issue included a foreword by James Weldon Johnson. In 1937 West attempted to revive the magazine after Richard Wright had wrested control of it, calling it *New Challenge*, but it folded after its first issue. In 1948 she published the semiautobiographical novel *The Living Is Easy*. A longtime resident of Martha's Vineyard, she wrote a regular column for the *Vineyard Gazette* almost until her death in 1998. West was the last surviving member of the Harlem Renaissance generation; Hillary Rodham Clinton, Henry Louis Gates, Jr., and Charles Ogletree gave eulogies at her funeral at Union Chapel in Oak Bluffs, Martha's Vineyard. Email from Henry Louis Gates, Jr. to Martha H. Patterson, "Author Bios," January 12, 2025. See Regina V. Jones, "West, Dorothy," Oxford African American Studies Center, December 1, 2006, https://oxfordaasc.com/display/10.1093/acref/9780195301731.001.0001/acref-9780195301731-e-44472; and SallyAnn H. Ferguson, "West, Dorothy," Oxford African American Studies Center, May 31, 2013, https://oxfordaasc.com/display/10.1093/acref/9780195301731.001.0001/acref-9780195301731-e-34779.

Ruth Whitehead Whaley (1901–77), born in Salisbury, North Carolina, Whaley was a pioneering educator, lawyer, Democratic politician, and women's rights activist. Educated at Livingstone College, a historically Black institution in Salisbury, North Carolina, where her father was a professor, Whaley taught for a year at the State School for the Deaf and Dumb and Blind in Raleigh, North Carolina, before becoming in 1921 the first Black woman admitted into Fordham University Law School. After graduating in 1924, she became the first African American woman to practice law in New York. See "Ruth W. Whaley Lawyer, Buried," *New York Amsterdam News*, January 7, 1978; "Ruth Whitehead Whaley, First Girl in Fordham Law School," *Afro-American*, September 30, 1921; and "Colored Law Student Wins 2 Scholarships," *Colorado Statesman*, November 4, 1922.

George Henry White (1852–1918) born in Bladen County, North Carolina, was the last African American to serve in the US Congress during the nadir of Jim Crow. Working as a farm laborer to pay for his education at Howard University, White graduated in 1877, returning to North Carolina to work as a school principal while studying for the bar examination. In 1880 he ran as a Republican for the state house of representatives and won; in 1882 he won a seat to the state senate, and in 1886 he was elected district solicitor for the Second Judicial District. When he was reelected to this position in 1890, the *New York Freeman* declared that White was the only Black prosecutor in the country. After winning the Republican Party's nomination for Congress, White defeated the Democratic Party incumbent in 1896. Despite a vicious white supremacist backlash in 1898 against him and Black voting rights more broadly—which reached its apogee with the Wilmington, North Carolina, coup and massacre in November of that year—White was elected to a second term. As the only Black member of the US Congress, White introduced the first federal antilynching bill, condemned Black disenfranchisement, and countered racist assertions from fellow congressmen. After North Carolina amended its state constitution to disenfranchise Black voters in 1900, White left his home state, telling a journalist, "I cannot live in North Carolina and be a man and be treated as a man." In his farewell to Congress, he foretold that the Negro "Phoenix-like . . . will rise up some day and come again." See Eric Anderson, "White, George H(enry)," Oxford African American Studies Center, December 1, 2006, https://oxfordaasc.com/display/10.1093/acref/9780195301731.001.0001/acref-9780195301731-e-43873.

Salem Tutt Whitney (1869–1934) was a Black performer, poet, columnist, composer, playwright, and producer and one-half of the popular vaudeville duo the Tutt Brothers. Born in Logansport, Indiana, Whitney learned to read "by fathoming the words on newspapers tacked on our cabin wall to keep out the cold" and graduated from Shortridge High School in Indianapolis. After briefly studying for the ministry, he began his stage career as a bass singer with the Tennessee Warblers. Between 1910 and 1925, Whitney "wrote and produced more than 40 touring revues and musical comedies for black theatres and black audiences" including such jazz and blues sensations as Florence Mills, Bessie Smith, and Mamie Smith. For sixteen years, he wrote a "Timely Topics" column for the Chicago *Defender*, and in 1930 he became internationally famous for his portrayal of the character Noah in the stage play *The Green Pastures*. See George Tyler, "Salem Whitney," *Afro-American*, May 26, 1934; Frank Cullen, Florence Hackman, and Donald McNeilly, "Tutt Brothers," in *Vaudeville, Old and New: An Encyclopedia of Variety Performers in America* (New York: Routledge, 2007), 1136; "Salem Tutt Whitney Is Dead at 55," *St. Louis Call*, February 16, 1934; and "Salem Tutt Whitney, Noted Actor, Author, Dies," *Chicago Defender*, February 17, 1934.

Frances "Fannie" Barrier Williams (1855–1944), born in Brockport, New York, was a well-known orator, journalist, African American clubwoman, and women's rights and civil rights activist. After graduating from Brockport's State Normal School, she studied at the New England Conservatory of Music in Boston, as well as the School of Fine Arts in Washington, DC, before marrying S. Laing Williams and beginning her extraordinary career in service to the Black community. A close ally of Booker T. Washington, Williams gained national recognition in 1893 for her work on behalf of African American inclusion in Chicago's 1893 Columbian Exposition. That year she also helped establish the National League of Colored Women. In 1895 the Woman's Club of Chicago admitted Williams as their first African American female member. During her life, she was a frequent contributor to Josephine St. Pierre Ruffin's *Woman's Era*, T. Thomas Fortune's *New York Age*, and the *Chicago Record-Herald*. In the early 1900s Williams played a crucial role at the Frederick Douglass Center, also known as the "black Hull House," Chicago's first interracial organization devoted to improving the lives of African Americans. Mary Jo Deegan sees Williams as a "pioneer" of feminist pragmatism, born out of Chicago's gritty industrialization and the settlement movements' efforts to help immigrants and migrants adjust. Emphasizing education and democracy, the philosophy joined "liberal values and belief in a rational public with a cooperative, nurturing, and liberating model of the self, the other, and the community." See Mamie E. Locke, "Williams, Fannie

Barrier," Oxford African American Studies Center, May 31, 2013, https://oxfordaasc.com/display/10.1093/acref/9780195301731.001.0001/acref-9780195301731-e-35018; Mary Jo Deegan, "Introduction: Fannie Barrier Williams and Her Life as a New Woman of Color in Chicago, 1893–1918," in Fannie Barrier Williams, *The New Woman of Color: The Collected Writings of Fannie Barrier Williams, 1893–1918*, ed. Mary Jo Deegan (DeKalb: Northern Illinois University Press. 2002), xxxiii–xxxvi; and Fannie Barrier Williams, "The Need of Social Settlement Work for the Negro, in *The New Woman of Color*, 111.

Samuel Laing Williams (c. 1864–1921), born in Savannah, Georgia, and the first Black student to graduate from the Columbian University Law School (now George Washington University) in Washington, DC, was an African American author, lawyer, organizer, political activist, and close adviser to Booker T. Washington. After marrying Fannie Barrier in 1887, they worked for a number of Black social service and political organizations in Chicago, including the Equal Opportunity League, the Frederick Douglass Center, the Hyde Park Colored Voters Republican Club, the National Association for the Advancement of Colored People (NAACP), and the Taft Colored League. Despite his staunch opposition to segregation, Williams demonstrated his support for Washington by surveilling Black Chicagoans—including Ida B. Wells's husband, Ferdinand Lee Barnett—who heeded W. E. B. Du Bois's call to join the Niagara Movement and who publicly demanded civil rights justice. In 1908 Williams became the assistant United States attorney for the Northern District of Illinois and the Eastern District of Wisconsin. By 1914, near the end of Booker T. Washington's life, Williams had become a supporter of the NAACP. See Laura Crkovski, "Williams, Samuel Laing," Oxford African American Studies Center, December 1, 2009, https://oxfordaasc.com/display/10.1093/acref/9780195301731.001.0001/acref-9780195301731-e-46361; and J. Clay Smith, *Emancipation: The Making of the Black Lawyer, 1844–1944* (Philadelphia: University of Pennsylvania Press, 1993), 374–75.

Terence Edwards Williams (1902–?), who was born in Brown's Town, Jamaica, and emigrated to the United States in 1915, was a popular columnist for New York Black newspapers in the 1920s. Little information is available about him, though the byline for the article included in this volume supplies some clues: "Known under the pen name of 'Joe College' for contributions to the Harlem press, and Manager of the Uptown Legal Bureau." His first name is sometimes spelled Terrence. Williams was a member of Harlem's elite Arista Club, which was sponsored by Madame C. J. Walker. In 1972 he became a naturalized citizen of the United States. "Terence Edwards Williams," New York, U.S., Index to Petitions for Naturalization filed in New York City, 1792–1989, Ancestry.com; "Terence Edwards Williams," Jamaica, Civil Registration Birth, Marriage, and Death Records, 1878–1995, Ancestry.com; "Arista Club Entertains," *Chicago Defender*, May 24, 1924.

Carter Godwin Woodson (1875–1950), born in New Canton, Virginia, to formerly enslaved parents who worked as sharecroppers, is widely known as the "father of Black history." Raised in West Virginia, where he mined coal, Woodson attended Frederick Douglass High School in Huntington, where he also served as a teacher and principal before graduating from Kentucky's Berea College in 1903. From 1903 to 1907 he taught all grades in the Philippines, then an American colony. Believing in the power of education to improve society, build race relations, and provide upward mobility, Woodson devoted himself to teaching both at the high school and college levels while advancing the study of Black history through his scholarship and organizational initiatives. After graduating with both a bachelor's degree and a master's degree from the University of Chicago, he earned a PhD in history from Harvard University in 1912, and from 1909 to 1919 taught at the famous Armstrong and Dunbar / M Street High Schools in Washington, DC, before moving to

Howard University, where his positions included history professor, dean, and head of the graduate program. Woodson founded the Association for the Study of Negro Life and History (ASNLH) in 1915 and its *Journal of Negro History* the following year, serving as its editor until his death in 1950. In 1920 he returned to West Virginia to teach at the historically Black West Virginia Collegiate Institute (now West Virginia State University) for two years before returning to Washington, DC, to lead the ASNLH, which employed, among others, a young Langston Hughes. In 1921 Woodson founded Associated Publishers to publish texts on Black history. He inaugurated Negro History Week in February 1926, which is the origin of what is now celebrated as Black History Month in the United States and elsewhere. Using census information, slave testimonies, and oral histories, Woodson and his assistants produced scholarship that situated African Americans as major actors in American history rather than as passive victims of white racism. The National Association for the Advancement of Colored People awarded Woodson the Spingarn Medal in 1926. See Jacqueline Goggin, "Woodson, Carter Godwin," Oxford African American Studies Center, May 31, 2013, https://oxfordaasc.com/display/10.1093/acref/9780195301731.001.0001/acref-9780195301731 -e-34807; and Burnis Reginald Morris, *Carter G. Woodson: History, the Black Press, and Public Relations* (Jackson: University Press of Mississippi, 2017), xvii, 124.

Rev. Walter Eugene Colburn Wright (1843–1908), born in Whitehall, New York, a prominent white professor and minister at Berea College in Kentucky (1885–90), devoted his teaching career to the "great problem relating to the adjustment of the relations of the races." Educated at Oberlin College and at Union Theological Seminary, Wright served in the ministry in Philadelphia and Danvers, Massachusetts, for fifteen years before joining Berea as a science educator, librarian, and pastor. When Wright left Berea in 1890, he became secretary to the American Missionary Association, whose efforts were "directed toward the education of the less favored classes of our southern population and in seeking the unification of our country upon the basis of justice and equality." See "Prof. Wright's Departure," *Berea College Reporter*, February 1891; "W. E. C. Wright Dead," *Citizen* (Berea, KY), July 2, 1908; Wright, Walter Eugene Colburn, 1885–1908, Folder 16, Faculty and Staff Records (Unofficial), RG 09-9.00, Berea College Special Collections and Archives; and "Dr. Walter E. C. Wright Dead," the *Sun* (Baltimore) June 28, 1908.

Index

ABB. See African Blood Brotherhood

Abbey, John N., 101–3

Abbott, Helene, 97, 114

Abbott, Robert Sengstacke, 564n3

abolitionist propaganda, 372

Abolition movement, 137

Aborigines Protection Society, 244

Academy of Fine Arts, Philadelphia, 551n9

Accumulative Period, 50–51

Adams, John H., Jr., 13–14, 175–76, 178–79, 181–82, 183–84

Adler, Felix, 144

Advance Company, 552n11

advertisements, 485, *486*, 486–87, *487*, 498

Aeschines, 153

Afghanistan, 339

Africa, 302, 388, 521; civilization relation to, 47–48; colonization of, 323–24, 512; *Crisis* in, 308; culture in, 454, 535; development of, 368; emigration to, 77; exploitation in, 258; Fetishism in, 154; France relation to, 476, 513; Garvey, M., relation to, 351–52; imperialism in, 257; motherhood in, 329–30; Pan-African Conference relation to, 277–79; self-determination in, 259; self-government in, 118; South, 336, 337, 560n37; subjugation in, 511; UNIA relation to, 264, 266–67, 282; West, 326, 328, 475, 561nn39–40; women relation to, 379

Africa and the Rise of Capitalism (Williams, W.), 534

Africa and World Peace (Padmore), 535

African art, 455–56, 514–15

African Blood Brotherhood (ABB), 18, 338, 339–40

African Communities League, 310, 336

African Empire, 276, 310–11, 512

African Methodist Episcopal church (AME), 108, 185, 295, 323, 553n13

African Mirage (Huene), 535

African National Congress, 3

African nationalism, 310

African Shamanism, 154–56

Afro-American (newspaper), 562n2

"the Afro-American Agitator," 43–45

Afro-American Council, 381

Afro-American Courier (newspaper), 567n2

Afro-American League, 43, 45

Afro-American Sons and Daughters, 23, 567n2

Agricultural and Mechanical College, 9

agriculture, 284, 328, 561n40

"The Aims of Labor" (Henderson), 295

Alexander, Charles, 556n16

Alexander, Lewis, 452

Alexander, Sadie, T. M., 21, 470–74

Alexander's Magazine, 556n16

Alfred (King), 234

Allen, Devere, 22, 405–7

Allen, Grant, 95

All God's Chillun, 386

Alpha Suffrage Club, 422

AME. *See* African Methodist Episcopal church

American Caste and the Negro College (Gallagher), 534

American Federation of Labor, 243, 308

American Guide Series, The, 533

American Hide and Leather Company, 429

American Indians, 200–201, 391

American liberalism, 311

American Life Magazine, 384, 433

American Missionary Association, 55, 56, 106, 107, 135

American Negro, The (Thomas), 145

American Negro Academy, 381

American Negro Exhibit, Paris Exhibition, 11, 128

American Negro Labor Congress, 376

American Negro's Youth Movement, 349–50

American Peace Commission, 244–45

American Peace Society, 243

"The American Race Problem" (Reuter), 407

American Secret Service, 244

American Youth Movement, 349

A.M.E. Zion Church Quarterly (newspaper), 143

Amsterdam News (newspaper), 20, 292

anarchists, 261, 283

ancestry, 374, 388–91, 461

Anderson, James Henry, 559n25

Anderson, Sherwood, 416

Anderson, Thomas W., 563n6

Angelica Uniform Factor, 355

Anglo-Saxons, 99–101

Anthony, Susan B., 324

anthropology, 298, 388, 449–50

Anti-Lynching Bill, 405

AP. *See* Associated Press

Appeal to Young Negroes (pamphlet), 22–23

Argus Printing and Publishing Company, 561n41

Arkansas, 166, 284, 285, 308

Armistice Day, 341

Armstrong, Samuel C., 75–76, 78, 105–6, 108, 380

Arnett, Benjamin W., 143

Arnold, Matthew, 450

Arp, Bill, 57

art, 201, 413–14, 433, 453–54, 457, 525; African, 455–56, 514–15; civilization and, 513–14; culture relation to, 32, 538; exploitation of, 527; freedom in, 482; intelligentsia relation to, 416–17; propaganda and, 345

art creed, 525–26

Arthur, George R., 432, 434

Ashur, 234

aspiration, 191, 196

assault, 144–46, 159, 160–62, 165, 167–68, 172

assimilation, 137, 138

Associated Negro Press, 3, 285, 314, 315, 542n9

Associated Press (AP), 3, 43, 542n9